The Bābur-nāma

(Memoirs of Babur)

Emperor of Hindustan Babur

(Translator: Annette Susannah Beveridge)

Alpha Editions

This edition published in 2024

ISBN : 9789366385266

Design and Setting By
Alpha Editions
www.alphaedis.com
Email - info@alphaedis.com

Contents

PREFACE.

O Spring of work! O Source of power to Be!
Each line, each thought I dedicate to Thee;
Each time I fail, the failure is my own,
But each success, a jewel in Thy Throne.
JESSIE E. CADELL.

Introductory.

THIS book is a translation of Babur Padshah's Autobiography, made from the original Turki text. It was undertaken after a purely-Turki manuscript had become accessible in England, the Haidarabad Codex (1915) which, being in Babur's *ipsissima verba*, left to him the control of his translator's diction—a control that had been impracticable from the time when, under Akbar (1589), his book was translated into Persian. What has come down to us of pure text is, in its shrunken amount, what was translated in 1589. It is difficult, here and there, to interpret owing to its numerous and in some places extensive *lacunæ*, and presents more problems than one the solution of which has real importance because they have favoured suggestions of malfeasance by Babur.

My translation has been produced under considerable drawback, having been issued in four *fasciculi*, at long intervals, respectively in June 1912, May 1914, October 1917, and September 1921. I have put with it of supplementary matter what may be of service to those readers whom Babur's personality attracts and to those who study Turki as a linguistic entertainment, but owing to delays in production am unable to include the *desiderata* of maps.

CHAPTER I.
BABUR'S EXEMPLARS IN THE ARTS OF PEACE.

Babur's civilian aptitudes, whether of the author and penman, the maker of gardens, the artist, craftsman or sportsman, were nourished in a fertile soil of family tradition and example. Little about his teaching and training is now with his mutilated book, little indeed of any kind about his præ-accession years, not the date of his birth even, having escaped destruction.[4] Happily Haidar Mirza (*q.v.*) possessed a more complete Codex than has come down to us through the Timurid libraries, and from it he translated many episodes of Baburiana that help to bridge gaps and are of special service here where the personalities of Bābur's early environment are being named.

Babur's home-milieu favoured excellence in the quiet Arts and set before its children high standard and example of proficiency. Moreover, by schooling him in obedience to the Law, it planted in him some of Art's essentials, self-restraint and close attention. Amongst primal influences on him, his mother Qut-luq-nigar's ranked high; she, well-born and a scholar's daughter, would certainly be educated in Turki and Persian and in the home-accomplishments her governess possessed *(ātūn* q.v.). From her and her mother Aisan-daulat, the child would learn respect for the attainments of his wise old grandfather Yunas Khan. Aisan-daulat herself brought to her grandson much that goes to the making of a man; nomad-born and sternly-bred, she was brave to obey her opinion of right, and was practically the boy's ruling counsellor through his early struggle to hold Farghana. With these two in fine influence must be counted Khan-zada, his five-years elder sister who from his birth to his death proved her devotion to him. Her life-story tempts, but is too long to tell; her girlish promise is seen fulfilled in Gul-badan's pages. 'Umar Shaikh's own mother Shah Sultan Begim brought in a type of merit widely differing from that of Aisan-daulat Begim; as a town-lady of high Tarkhan birth, used to the amenities of life in a wealthy house of Samarkand, she was, doubtless, an accomplished and cultured woman.

'Umar Shaikh's environment was dominated for many years by two great men, the scholar and lover of town-life Yunas Khan and the saintly Ahrari (*i.e.* Khwaja 'Ubaidu'l-lah) who were frequently with him in company, came at Babur's birth and assisted at his naming. Ahrari died in 895-1491 when the child was about seven years old but his influence was life-long; in 935-1529 he was invoked as a spiritual helper by the fever-stricken Babur and his mediation believed efficacious for recovery (pp. 619, 648). For the babe or boy to be where the three friends held social session in high converse, would be thought to draw blessing on him; his hushed silence in the presence would sow the seed of reverence for wisdom and virtue, such, for example, as he felt for Jami (*q.v.*). It is worth while to tell some part at least of Yunas' attainments in the gentler Arts, because the biography from which they are quoted may well have been written on the information of his wife Aisan-daulat, and it indicates the breadth of his exemplary influence. Yunas was many things—penman, painter, singer, instrumentalist, and a past master in the crafts. He was an expert in good companionship, having even temper and perfect manners, quick perception and conversational charm. His intellectual distinction was attributed to his twelve years of wardship under the learned and highly honoured Yazdi (Sharafu'd-din 'Ali), the author of the *Zafar-nama* [Timur's Book of Victory]. That book was in hand during four years of Yunas' education; he will thus have known it and its main basis Timur's Turki *Malfūẓāt* (annals). What he learned of either book he would carry with him into 'Umar Shaikh's environment, thus magnifying the family stock of Timuriya influence. He lived to be some 74 years old, a length of days which fairly bridged the gap between Timur's death [807-1404] and Babur's birth (888-1483). It is said that no previous Khan of his (Chaghatai) line had survived his 40th year; his exceptional age earned him great respect and would deepen his influence on his restless young son-in-law 'Umar Shaikh. It appears to have been in 'Umar's 20th year (*cir.*) that Yunas Khan began the friendly association with him that lasted till Yunas' death (892-1483), a friendship which, as disparate ages would dictate, was rather that of father and son than of equal companionship. One matter mentioned in the Khan's biography would come to Babur's remembrance in the future days when he, like Yunas, broke the Law against intoxicants and, like him, repented and returned.

That two men of the calibre and high repute of Ahrari and Yunas maintained friendly guidance so long over 'Umar cannot but be held an accreditment and give fragrance of goodness to his name. Apart from the high justice and generosity his son ascribes to him, he could set other example, for he was a reader of great books, the Qoran and the *Masnawi* being amongst his favourites. This choice, it may be, led Abu'l-faẓl to say he had the darwesh-mind. Babur was old enough before 'Umar's death to profit by the sight of his father enjoying the perusal of such books. As with other parents and other children, there would follow the happy stilling to a quiet mood, the piquing of curiosity as to what was in the book, the sight of refuge taken as in a haven from self and care, and perhaps, Babur being intelligent and of inquiring mind and 'Umar a skilled reciter, the boy would marvel at the perennial miracle that a lifeless page can become eloquent—gentle hints all, pointers of the way to literary creation.

Few who are at home in Baburiana but will take Timur as Babur's great exemplar not only as a soldier but as a chronicler. Timur cannot have seemed remote from that group of people so well-informed about him and his civilian doings; his Shahrukhi grandchildren in Samarkand had carried on his author-tradition; the 74 years of Yunas Khan's life had bridged the gap between Timur's death in 807-1405 and Babur's birth in 888-1483. To Babur Timur will have been exemplary through his grandson Aulugh Beg who has two productions to his credit, the *Char-ulus* (Four Hordes) and the Kurkani Astronomical Tables. His sons, again, Babur (*qalandar*) and Ibrahim carried on the family torch of letters, the first in verse and the second by initiating and fostering Yazdi's labours on the *Zafar-nama*. Wide-radiating and potent influence for the Arts of Peace came forth from Herat during the reign of that Sultan Husain Mirza whose Court Babur describes in one of the best supplements to his autobiography. Husain was a Timurid of the elder branch of Bai-qara, an author himself but far more effective as a Macænas; one man of the shining galaxy of competence that gave him fame, set pertinent example for Babur the author, namely, the Andijani of noble Chaghatai family, 'Ali-sher *Nawa'i* who, in classic Turki verse was the master Babur was to become in its prose. That the standard of effort was high in Herat is clear from Babur's dictum (p. 233) that whatever work a man took up, he aspired to bring it to perfection. Elphinstone varies the same theme to the tune of equality of excellence apart from social status, writing to Erskine (August, 1826), that "it gives a high notion of the time to find" (in Babur's account of Husain's Court) "artists, musicians and others, described along with the learned and great of the Age".

My meagre summary of Babur's exemplars would be noticeably incomplete if it omitted mention of two of his life-long helpers in the gentler Arts, his love of Nature and his admiration for great architectural creations. The first makes joyous accompaniment throughout his book; the second is specially called forth by Timur's ennoblement of Samarkand. Timur had built magnificently and laid out stately gardens; Babur made many a fruitful pleasaunce and gladdened many an arid halting-place; he built a little, but had small chance to test his capacity for building greatly; never rich, he was poor in Kabul and several times destitute in his home-lands. But his sword won what gave wealth to his Indian Dynasty, and he passed on to it the builder's unused dower, so that Samarkand was surpassed in Hindustan and the spiritual conception Timur's creations embodied took perfect form at Sikandra where Akbar lies entombed.

CHAPTER II.
PROBLEMS OF THE MUTILATED BABUR-NAMA.

Losses from the text of Babur's book are the more disastrous because it truly embodies his career. For it has the rare distinction of being contemporary with the events it describes, is boyish in his boyhood, grows with his growth, matures as he matured. Undulled by retrospect, it is a fresh and spontaneous recital of things just seen, heard or done. It has the further rare distinction of shewing a boy who, setting a future task before him—in his case the revival of Timurid power,—began to chronicle his adventure in the book which through some 37 years was his twinned comrade, which by its special distinctions has attracted readers for nearly a half-millennium, still attracts and still is a thing apart from autobiographies which look back to recall dead years.

Much circumstance makes for the opinion that Babur left his life-record complete, perhaps repaired in places and recently supplemented, but continuous, orderly and lucid; this it is not now, nor has been since it was translated into Persian in 1589, for it is fissured by *lacunæ*, has neither Preface nor Epilogue,[5] opens in an oddly abrupt and incongruous fashion, and consists of a series of fragments so disconnected as to demand considerable preliminary explanation. Needless to say, its dwindled condition notwithstanding, it has place amongst great autobiographies, still revealing its author playing a man's part in a drama of much historic and personal interest. Its revelation is however now like a portrait out of drawing, because it has not kept the record of certain years of his manhood in which he took momentous decisions,(1) those of 1511-12 [918] in which he accepted reinforcement—at a great price—from Isma'il the Shi'a Shah of Persia, and in which, if my reading be correct, he first (1512) broke the Law against the use of wine,[6] (2) those of 1519-1525 [926-932], in which his literary occupations with orthodox Law (*see Mubin*) associated with cognate matters of 932 AH. indicate that his return to obedience had begun, in which too was taken the decision that worked out for his fifth expedition across the Indus with its sequel of the conquest of Hind.—The loss of matter so weighty cannot but destroy the balance of his record and falsify the drawing of his portrait.

a. *Problem of Titles.*

As nothing survives to decide what was Babur's chosen title for his autobiography, a modern assignment of names to distinguish it from its various descendants is desirable, particularly so since the revival of interest in it towards which the Facsimile of its Haidarabad Codex has contributed.[7]

Babur-nama (History of Babur) is a well-warranted name by which to distinguish the original Turki text, because long associated with this and rarely if ever applied to its Persian translation.[8] It is not comprehensive because not covering supplementary matter of biography and description but it has use for modern readers of classing Babur's with other Timuriya and Timurid histories such as the *Zafar-Humayun-Akbar-namas*.

Waqi'āt-i-baburi (Babur's Acts), being descriptive of the book and in common use for naming both the Turki and Persian texts, might usefully be reserved as a title for the latter alone.

Amongst European versions of the book *Memoirs of Baber* is Erskine's peculium for the Leyden and Erskine Perso-English translation—*Mémoires de Baber* is Pavet de Courteille's title for his French version of the Bukhara [Persified-Turki] compilation—*Babur-nama in English* links the translation these volumes contain with its purely-Turki source.

b. *Problems of the Constituents of the Books.*

Intact or mutilated, Babur's material falls naturally into three territorial divisions, those of the lands of his successive rule, Farghana (with Samarkand), Kabul and Hindustan. With these are distinct sub-sections of description of places and of obituaries of kinsmen.

The book might be described as consisting of annals and diary, which once met within what is now the gap of 1508-19 (914-925). Round this gap, amongst others, bristle problems of which this change of literary style is one; some are small and concern the mutilation alone, others are larger, but all are too intricate for terse statement and all might be resolved by the help of a second MS. *e.g.* one of the same strain as Haidar's.

Without fantasy another constituent might be counted in with the three territorial divisions, namely, the grouped *lacunæ* which by their engulfment of text are an untoward factor in an estimate either of Babur or of his book. They are actually the cardinal difficulty of the book as it now is; they foreshorten purview of his career and character and detract from its merits; they lose it perspective and distort its proportions. That this must be so is clear both from the value and the preponderating amount of the lost text. It is no exaggeration to say that while working on what survives, what is lost becomes like a haunting presence warning that it must be remembered always as an integral and the dominant part of the book.

The relative proportions of saved and lost text are highly significant:—Babur's commemorable years are about 47 and 10 months, *i.e.* from his birth on Feb. 14th 1483 to near his death on Dec. 26th 1530; but the aggregate of surviving text records some 18 years only, and this not continuously but broken through by numerous gaps. That these gaps result from loss of pages is frequently shewn by a broken sentence, an unfinished episode. The fragments—as they truly may be called—are divided by gaps sometimes seeming to remove a few pages only (cf. *s.a.* 935 AH.), sometimes losing the record of 6 and *cir.* 18 months, sometimes of 6 and 11 years; besides these actual clefts in the narrative there are losses of some 12 years from its beginning and some 16 months from its end. Briefly put we now have the record of *cir.* 18 years where that of over 47 could have been.[9]

c. *Causes of the gaps.*

Various causes have been surmised to explain the *lacunæ*; on the plea of long intimacy with Babur's and Haidar's writings, I venture to say that one and all appear to me the result of accident. This opinion rests on observed correlations between the surviving and the lost record, which demand complement—on the testimony of Haidar's extracts, and firmly on Babur's orderly and persistent bias of mind and on the prideful character of much of the lost record. Moreover occasions of risk to Babur's papers are known.

Of these occasions the first was the destruction of his camp near Hisar in 1512 (918; p. 357) but no information about his papers survives; they may not have been in his tent but in the fort. The second was a case of recorded damage to "book and sections" (p. 679) occurring in 1529 (935). From signs of work done to the Farghana section in Hindustan, the damage may be understood made good at the later date. To the third exposure to damage, namely, the attrition of hard travel and unsettled life during Humayun's 14 years of exile from rule in Hindustan (1441-1555) it is reasonable to attribute even the whole loss of text. For, assuming—as may well be done—that Babur left (1530) a complete autobiography, its volume would be safe so long as Humayun was in power but after the Timurid exodus (1441) his library would be exposed to the risks detailed in the admirable chronicles of Gul-badan, Jauhar and Bayazid (*q.v.*). He is known to have annotated his father's book in 1555 (p. 466 n. 1) just before marching from Kabul to attempt the re-conquest of Hindustan. His Codex would return to Dihli which he entered in July 1555, and there would be safe from risk of further mutilation. Its condition in 1555 is likely to have remained what it was found when 'Abdu'r-rahim translated it into Persian by Akbar's orders (1589) for Abu'l-faẓl's use in the *Akbar-nama.* That Persian translation with its descendant the *Memoirs of Baber*, and the purely-Turki Haidarabad Codex with its descendant the *Babur-nama in English*, contain identical contents and, so doing, carry the date of the mutilation of Babur's Turki text back through its years of safety, 1589 to 1555, to the period of Humayun's exile and its dangers for camel-borne or deserted libraries.

d. *Two misinterpretations of lacunæ.*

Not unnaturally the frequent interruptions of narrative caused by *lacunæ* have been misinterpreted occasionally, and sometimes detractory comment has followed on Babur, ranking him below the accomplished and lettered, steadfast and honest man he was. I select two examples of this comment neither of which has a casual origin.

The first is from the *B.M. Cat. of Coins of the Shahs of Persia* p. xxiv, where after identifying a certain gold coin as shewing vassalage by Babur to Isma'il *Safawi*, the compiler of the Catalogue notes, "We can now understand the omission from Babar's 'Memoirs' of the occurrences between 914 H. and 925 H." Can these words imply other than that Babur suppressed mention of minting of the coins shewing acknowledgment of Shi'a suzerainty? Leaving aside the delicate topic of the detraction the quoted words imply, much negatives the surmise that the gap is a deliberate "omission" of text:—(1) the duration of the Shi'a alliance was 19-20 months of 917-918 AH. (p. 355), why omit the peaceful or prideful and victorious record of some 9-10 years on its either verge? (2) Babur's Transoxus campaign was an episode in the struggle between Shaibaq Khan (Shaibani) *Auzbeg* and Shah Isma'il—between Sunni and Shi'a; how could "omission" from his book, always a rare one, hide what multitudes knew already? "Omission" would have proved a fiasco in another region than Central Asia, because the Babur-Haidar story of the campaign, vassal-coinage included,[10] has been brought into English literature by the English translation of the *Tarikh-i rashidi*. Babur's frank and self-judging habit of mind would, I think, lead him to write fully of the difficulties which compelled the hated alliance and certainly he would tell of his own anger at the conduct of the campaign by Isma'il's Commanders. The alliance was a tactical mistake; it would have served Babur better to narrate its failure.

The second misinterpretation, perhaps a mere surmising gloss, is Erskine's (*Memoirs* Supp. p. 289) who, in connection with 'Alam Khan's request to Babur for reinforcement in order to oust his nephew Ibrahim, observes that "Babur probably flattered 'Alam Khan with the hope of succession to the empire of Hindustan." This idea does not fit the record of either man. Elphinstone was angered by Erskine's remark which, he wrote (Aug. 26th 1826) "had a bad effect on the narrative by weakening the implicit confidence in Babur's candour and veracity which his frank way of writing is so well-calculated to command." Elphinstone's opinion of Babur is not that of a reader but of a student of his book; he was also one of Erskine's staunchest helpers in its production. From Erskine's surmise others have advanced on the detractor's path saying that Babur used and threw over 'Alam Khan (*q.v.*).

e. *Reconstruction.*

Amongst the problems mutilation has created an important one is that of the condition of the beginning of the book (p. 1 to p. 30) with its plunge into Babur's doings in his 12th year without previous mention of even his day and place of birth, the names and status of his parents, or any occurrences of his præ-accession years. Within those years should be entered the death of Yunas Khan (1487) with its sequent obituary notice, and the death of [Khwaja 'Ubaidu'l-lah] Ahrari (1491). Not only are these customary entries absent but the very introductions of the two great men are wanting, probably with the also missing account of their naming of the babe Babur. That these routine matters are a part of an autobiography planned as Babur's was, makes for assured opinion that the record of more than his first decade of life has been lost, perhaps by the attrition to which its position in the volume exposed it.

Useful reconstruction if merely in tabulated form, might be effected in a future edition. It would save at least two surprises for readers, one the oddly abrupt first sentence telling of Babur's age when he became ruler in Farghana (p. 1), which is a misfit in time and order, another that of the sudden interruption of 'Umar Shaikh's obituary by a fragment of Yunas Khan's (p. 19) which there hangs on a mere name-peg, whereas its place according to Babur's elsewhere unbroken practice is directly following the death. The record of the missing præ-accession years will have included at the least as follows:—Day of birth and its place—names and status of parents—naming and the ceremonial observances proper for Muhammadan children—visits to kinsfolk in Tashkint, and to Samarkand (æt. 5, p. 35) where he was betrothed—his initiation in school subjects, in sport, the use of arms—names of teachers—education in the rules of his Faith (p. 44), appointment to the Andijan Command *etc.*, *etc.*

There is now no fit beginning to the book; the present first sentence and its pendent description of Farghana should be removed to the position Babur's practice dictates of entering the description of a territory at once on obtaining it (cf. Samarkand, Kabul, Hindustan). It might come in on p. 30 at the end of the topic (partly omitted on p. 29 where no ground is given for the manifest anxiety about Babur's safety) of the disputed succession (Haidar, trs. p. 135) Babur's partisan begs having the better of Jahangir's (*q.v.*), and having testified obeisance, he became ruler in Farghana; his statement of age (12 years), comes in naturally and the description of his newly acquired territory follows according to rule. This removal of text to a later position has the advantage of allowing the accession to follow and not precede Babur's father's death.

By the removal there is left to consider the historical matter of pp. 12-13. The first paragraph concerns matter of much earlier date than 'Umar's death in 1494 (p. 13); it may be part of an obituary notice, perhaps that of Yunas Khan. What follows of the advance of displeased kinsmen against 'Umar Shaikh would fall into place as part of Babur's record of his boyhood, and lead on to that of his father's death.

The above is a bald sketch of what might be effected in the interests of the book and to facilitate its pleasant perusal.

CHAPTER III.
THE TURKI MSS. AND WORK CONNECTING WITH THEM.

This chapter is a literary counterpart of "Babur Padshah's Stone-heap," the roadside cairn tradition says was piled by his army, each man laying his stone when passing down from Kabul for Hindustan in the year of victory 1525 (932).[11]

For a title suiting its contents is "Babur Padshah's Book-pile," because it is fashioned of item after item of pen-work done by many men in obedience to the dictates given by his book. Unlike the cairn, however, the pile of books is not of a single occasion but of many, not of a single year but of many, irregularly spacing the 500 years through which he and his autobiography have had Earth's immortality.

Part I. The MSS. themselves.

Preliminary.—Much of the information given below was published in the Journal of the Royal Asiatic Society from 1900 onwards, as it came into my possession during a search for reliable Turki text of the *Babur-nama.* My notes were progressive; some MSS. were in distant places, some not traceable, but in the end I was able to examine in England all of whose continued existence I had become aware. It was inevitable that some of my earlier statements should be superseded later; my Notes (*see s.n.* JRAS.) need clearing of transitory matter and summarizing, in particular those on the Elphinstone Codex and Klaproth's articles. Neither they nor what is placed here makes claim to be complete. Other workers will supplement them when the World has renewed opportunity to stroll in the bye-paths of literature.

Few copies of the *Babur-nama* seem to have been made; of the few I have traced as existing, not one contains the complete autobiography, and one alone has the maximum of dwindled text shewn in the Persian translation (1589). Two books have been reputed to contain Babur's authentic text, one preserved in Hindustan by his descendants, the other issuing from Bukhara. They differ in total contents, arrangement and textual worth; moreover the Bukhara book compiles items of divers diction and origin and date, manifestly not from one pen.

The Hindustan book is a record—now mutilated—of the Acts of Babur alone; the Bukhara book as exhibited in its fullest accessible example,

Kehr's Codex, is in two parts, each having its preface, the first reciting Babur's Acts, the second Humayun's.

The Bukhara book is a compilation of oddments, mostly translated from compositions written after Babur's death. Textual and circumstantial grounds warrant the opinion that it is a distinct work mistakenly believed to be Babur's own; to these grounds was added in 1903 the authoritative verdict of collation with the Haidarabad Codex, and in 1921 of the colophon of its original MS. in which its author gives his name, with the title and date of his compilation (JRAS. 1900, p. 474). What it is and what are its contents and history are told in Part III of this chapter.

Part II. Work on the Hindustan MSS.

BABUR'S ORIGINAL CODEX.

My latest definite information about Babur's autograph MS. comes from the *Padshah-nama* (Bib. Ind. ed. ii, 4), whose author saw it in Shah-i-jahan's private library between 1628 and 1638. Inference is justified, however, that it was the archetype of the Haidarabad Codex which has been estimated from the quality of its paper as dating *cir.* 1700 (JRAS. 1906, p. 97). But two subsequent historic disasters complicate all questions of MSS. missing from Indian libraries, namely, Nadir Shah's vengeance on Dihli in 1739 and the dispersions and fires of the Mutiny. Faint hope is kept alive that the original Codex may have drifted into private hands, by what has occurred with the Rampur MS. of Babur's Hindustan verses (App. J), which also appears once to have belonged to Shah-i-jahan.

I

Amongst items of work done during Babur's life are copies of his book (or of the Hindustan section of it) he mentions sending to sons and friends.

II

The *Tabaqat-i-baburi* was written during Babur's life by his Persian secretary Shaikh Zainu'd-din of Khawaf; it paraphrases in rhetorical Persian the record of a few months of Hindustan campaigning, including the battle of Panipat.

TABLE OF THE HINDUSTAN MSS. OF THE BABUR-NAMA.[12]

Names.	Date of completi on.	Folio-standard 382.[13]	Archetype.	Scribe.	Latest known location.	Remarks.
1. Babur's Co dex.	1530.	Originally m uch over 382.	—	Babur.	Royal Libra ry between	Has disappe ared.

					1628-38.	
2. Khwaja Ka lan _Ahraris_ Codex.	1529.	Undefined 3 63(?), p. 652.	No. 1.	Unknown.	Sent to Sa markand 1529.	Possibly still in Khwaja Kalan's family.
3. Humayun's Codex = (commanded and annotate?).[14]	1531(?).	Originally = No. 1 (unmutilat ed).	No. 1.	'Ali'u-'l-katib(?).	Royal Libra ry between 1556-1567.	Seems the a rchetype of No. 5.
4. Muhamma d Haidar _Dughlat's _ Codex.	Between 1536 and 40(?).	No. 1 (unm utilated).	No. 1 or No. 2.	Haidar(?)	Kashmir 1 540-47.	Possibly no w in Kashghar.
5. Elphinston e Codex.	Between 1556 and 1567.	In 1816 and 19 07, 286 ff.	No. 3.	Unknown.	Advocates' Library (1816 to 1921).	Bought in Peshawar 1810.
6. British Mus eum MS.	1629.	97 (fragments).	Unknown.	'Ali'u'l-_kashmiri_.	British Museum.	—
7. Bib. Lindes iana MS. [now John Rylands]	Scribe liv ing in 1625.	71 (an extract).	Unknown.	Nur-muhammad (nephew o f 'Abu'l-faẓl).	John Rylands Library.	—
8. Haidarabad Codex.	Paper in dicates _cir._ 1700.	382.	(No. 1) m utilated.	No colopho n.	The late Sir Salar-jang's Library.	Centupled i n facsimile, 1905.

III

During the first decade of Humayun's reign (1530-40) at least two important codices seem to have been copied.

The earlier (*see* Table, No. 2) has varied circumstantial warrant. It meets the need of an archetype, one marginally annotated by Humayun, for the Elphinstone Codex in which a few notes are marginal and signed, others are pell-mell, interpolated in the text but attested by a scrutineer as having been marginal in its archetype and mistakenly copied into its text. This second set has been ineffectually sponged over. Thus double collation is indicated (i) with Babur's autograph MS. to clear out extra Babur matter, and (ii) with its archetype, to justify the statement that in this the interpolations were marginal.—No colophon survives with the much dwindled Elph. Codex, but one, suiting the situation, has been observed, where it is a complete misfit, appended to the Alwar Codex of the second Persian translation, (estimated as copied in 1589). Into the incongruities of that colophon it is not necessary to examine here, they are too obvious to aim at deceit; it appears fitly to be an imperfect translation from a Turki original, this especially through its odd fashion of entitling "Humayun Padshah." It can be explained as translating the colophon of the Codex (No. 2) which, as his possession, Humayun allowably annotated and which makes it known that he had ordered 'Ali'u-'l-katib to copy his father's Turki book, and that it was finished in February, 1531, some six weeks after Babur's death.[15]

The later copy made in Humayun's first decade is Haidar Mirza's (*infra*).

IV

Muhammad Haidar Mirza *Dughlat's* possession of a copy of the Autobiography is known both from his mention of it and through numerous extracts translated from it in his *Tarikh-i-rashidi*. As a good boy-penman (p. 22) he may have copied down to 1512 (918) while with Babur (p. 350), but for obtaining a transcript of it his opportunity was while with Humayun before the Timurid exodus of 1541. He died in 1551; his Codex is likely to have found its way back from Kashmir to his ancestral home in the Kashghar region and there it may still be. (*See* T.R. trs. Ney Elias' biography of him).

V

The Elphinstone Codex[16] has had an adventurous career. The enigma of its archetype is posed above; it may have been copied during Akbar's first decade (1556-67); its, perhaps first, owner was a Bai-qara rebel (d. 1567) from amongst whose possessions it passed into the Royal Library, where it was cleared of foreign matter by the expunction of Humayun's marginal notes which its scribe had interpolated into its text. At a date I do not know, it must have left the Royal Library for its fly-leaves bear entries of prices and in 1810 it was found and purchased in Peshawar by Elphinstone. It went with him to Calcutta, and there may have been seen by Leyden during the short time between its arrival and the autumn month of the same year (1810) when he sailed for Java. In 1813 Elphinstone in Poona sent it to Erskine in Bombay, saying that he had fancied it gone to Java and had been writing to 'Izzatu'l-lah to procure another MS. for Erskine in Bukhara, but that all the time it was on his own shelves. Received after

Erskine had dolefully compared his finished work with Leyden's (tentative) translation, Erskine sadly recommenced the review of his own work. The Codex had suffered much defacement down to 908 (1502) at the hands of "a Persian Turk of Ganj" who had interlined it with explanations. It came to Scotland (with Erskine?) who in 1826 sent it with a covering letter (Dec. 12th, 1826), at its owner's desire, to the Advocates' Library where it now is. In 1907 it was fully described by me in the JRAS.

VI

Of two *Waqi'at-i-baburi* (Pers. trs.) made in Akbar's reign, the earlier was begun in 1583, at private instance, by two Mughuls Payanda-hasan of Ghazni and Muhammad-quli of Hisar. The Bodleian and British Museum Libraries have copies of it, very fragmentary unfortunately, for it is careful, likeable, and helpful by its small explanatory glosses. It has the great defect of not preserving autobiographic quality in its diction.

VII

The later *Waqi'at-i-baburi* translated by 'Abdu'r-rahim Mirza is one of the most important items in Baburiana, both by its special characteristics as the work of a Turkman and not of a Persian, and by the great service it has done. Its origin is well-known; it was made at Akbar's order to help Abu'l-faẓl in the Akbar-nāma account of Babur and also to facilitate perusal of the *Babur-nama* in Hindustan. It was presented to Akbar, by its translator who had come up from Gujrat, in the last week of November, 1589, on an occasion and at a place of admirable fitness. For Akbar had gone to Kabul to visit Babur's tomb, and was halting on his return journey at Barik-ab where Babur had halted on his march down to Hindustan in the year of victory 1525, at no great distance from "Babur Padshah's Stone-heap". Abu'l-faẓl's account of the presentation will rest on 'Abdu'r-rahim's information (A.N. trs. cap. ci). The diction of this translation is noticeable; it gave much trouble to Erskine who thus writes of it (*Memoirs* Preface, lx), "Though simple and precise, a close adherence to the idioms and forms of expression of the Turki original joined to a want of distinctness in the use of the relatives, often renders the meaning extremely obscure, and makes it difficult to discover the connexion of the different members of the sentence.[17] The style is frequently not Persian.... Many of the Turki words are untranslated."

Difficult as these characteristics made Erskine's interpretation, it appears to me likely that they indirectly were useful to him by restraining his diction to some extent in their Turki fettering.—This Turki fettering has another aspect, apart from Erskine's difficulties, *viz.* it would greatly facilitate re-translation into Turki, such as has been effected, I think, in the Farghana section of the Bukhara compilation.[18]

VIII

This item of work, a harmless attempt of Salim (*i.e.* Jahangir Padshah; 1605-28) to provide the ancestral autobiography with certain stop-gaps, has caused much needless trouble and discussion without effecting any useful result. It is this:—In his own autobiography, the *Tuzuk-i-jahangiri s.a.* 1607, he writes of a Babur-nama Codex he examined, that it was all in Babur's "blessed handwriting" except four portions which were in his own and each of which he attested in Turki as so being. Unfortunately he did not specify his topics; unfortunately also no attestation has been found to passages reasonably enough attributable to his activities. His portions may consist of the "Rescue-passage" (App. D) and a length of translation from the *Akbar-nāma*, a continuous part of its Babur chapter but broken up where only I have seen it, *i.e.* the Bukhara compilation, into (1) a plain tale of Kanwa (1527), (2) episodes of Babur's latter months (1529)—both transferred to the first person—and (3) an account of Babur's death (December 26th, 1530) and Court.

Jahangir's occupation, harmless in itself, led to an imbroglio of Langlés with Erskine, for the former stating in the *Biographie Universelle* art. Babour, that Babour's Commentaries "*augmentés par Jahangir*" were translated into Persian by 'Abdu'r-rahim. Erskine made answer, "I know not on what authority the learned Langlés hazarded this assertion, which is certainly incorrect" (*Memoirs*, Preface, p. ix). Had Langlés somewhere met with Jahangir's attestations? He had authority if he had seen merely the statement of 1607, but Erskine was right also, because the Persian translation contains no more than the unaugmented Turki text. The royal stop-gaps are in Kehr's MS. and through Ilminski reached De Courteille, whence the biting and thorough analysis of the three "Fragments" by Teufel. Both episodes—the Langlés and the Teufel ones—are time-wasters but they are comprehensible in the circumstances that Jahangir could not foresee the consequences of his doubtless good intentions.

If the question arise of how writings that had had place in Jahangir's library reached Bukhara, their open road is through the Padshah's correspondence (App. Q and references), with a descendant of Ahrari in whose hands they were close to Bukhara.[19]

It groups scattered information to recall that Salim (Jahangir) was 'Abdu'r-rahim's ward, that then, as now, Babur's Autobiography was the best example of classic Turki, and that it would appeal on grounds of piety—as it did appeal on some sufficient ground—to have its broken story made good. Also that for three of the four "portions" Abu'l-fazl's concise matter was to hand.

IX

My information concerning Baburiana under Shah-i-jahan Padshah (1628-58) is very meagre. It consists of (1) his attestation of a signature of Babur (App. Q and photo), (2) his possession of Babur's autograph Codex (*Padshah-nama*, Bib. Ind. ed., ii, 4), and (3) his acceptance, and that by his literary entourage, of Mir Abu-talib *Husaini's* Persian translation of Timur's Annals, the *Malfuzat* whose preparation the *Zafar-nama* describes and whose link with Babur's writings is that of the exemplar to the emulator.[20]

X

The Haidarabad Codex may have been inscribed under Aurang-zib Padshah (1655-1707). So many particulars about it have been given already that little needs saying here.[21] It was the *grande trouvaille* of my search for Turki text wherewith to revive Babur's autobiography both in Turki and English. My husband in 1900 saw it in Haidarabad; through the kind offices of the late Sayyid Ali *Bilgrami* it was lent to me; it proved to surpass, both in volume and quality, all other Babur-nama MSS. I had traced; I made its merits known to Professor Edward Granville Browne, just when the E. J. Wilkinson Gibb Trust was in formation, with the happy and accordant result that the best prose book in classic Turki became the first item in the Memorial—*matris ad filium*—of literary work done in the name of the Turkish scholar, and Babur's very words were safeguarded in hundred-fold facsimile. An event so important for autobiography and for Turki literature may claim more than the bald mention of its occurrence, because sincere autobiography, however ancient, is human and social and undying, so that this was no mere case of multiplying copies of a book, but was one of preserving a man's life in his words. There were, therefore, joyful red-letter days in the English story of the Codex—outstanding from others being those on which its merits revealed themselves (on Surrey uplands)—the one which brought Professor Browne's acceptance of it for reproduction by the Trust—and the day of pause from work marked by the accomplished fact of the safety of the *Babur-nama.*

XI

The period from *cir.* 1700, the date of the Haidarabad Codex, and 1810, when the Elphinstone Codex was purchased by its sponsor at Peshawar, appears to have been unfruitful in work on the Hindustan MSS. Causes for this may connect with historic events, *e.g.* Nadir Shah's desolation of Dihli and the rise of the East India Company, and, in Baburiana, with the disappearance of Babur's autograph Codex (it was unknown to the Scots of 1800-26), and the transfer of the Elphinstone Codex from royal possession—this, possibly however, an accident of royal travel to and from Kabul at earlier dates.

The first quarter of the nineteenth century was, on the contrary, most fruitful in valuable work, useful impulse to which was given by Dr. John Leyden who in about 1805 began to look into Turki. Like his contemporary Julius Klaproth (*q.v.*), he was avid of tongues and attracted by Turki and by Babur's writings of which he had some knowledge through the 'Abdu'r-rahim (Persian) translation. His Turki text-book would be the MS. of the Asiatic Society of Bengal,[22] a part-copy of the Bukhara compilation, from which he had the India Office MS. copied. He took up Turki again in 1810, after his return from Malay and whilst awaiting orders in Calcutta for departure to Java. He sailed in the autumn of the year and died in August 1811. Much can be learned about him and his Turki occupations from letters (*infra* xiii) written to Erskine by him and by others of the Scottish band which now achieved such fine results for Babur's Autobiography.

It is necessary to say something of Leyden's part in producing the *Memoirs*, because Erskine, desiring to "lose nothing that might add to Leyden's reputation", has assigned to him an undue position of collaboration in it both by giving him premier place on its title-page and by attributing to him the beginning the translation. What one gleans of Leyden's character makes an impression of unassumption that would forbid his acceptance of the posthumous position given to him, and, as his translation shews the tyro in Turki, there can be no ground for supposing he would wish his competence in it over-estimated. He had, as dates show, nothing to do with the actual work of the *Memoirs* which was finished before Erskine had seen in 1813 what Leyden had set down before he died in 1811. As the *Memoirs* is now a rare book, I quote from it what Erskine says (Preface, p. ix) of Leyden's rough translation:—"This acquisition (*i.e.* of Leyden's trs.) reduced me to rather an awkward dilemma. The two translations (his own and Leyden's) differed in many important particulars; but as Dr. Leyden had the advantage of translating from the original, I resolved to adopt his translation as far as it went, changing only such expressions in it as seemed evidently to be inconsistent with the context, or with other parts of the *Memoirs*, or such as seemed evidently to originate in the oversights that are unavoidable in an unfinished work.[23] This labour I had completed with some difficulty, when Mr. Elphinstone sent me the copy of the *Memoirs of Baber* in the original Tūrkī (*i.e.* The Elphinstone Codex) which he had procured when he went to Peshawar on his embassy to Kabul. This copy, which he had supposed to have been sent with Dr. Leyden's manuscripts from Calcutta, he was now fortunate enough to recover (in his own library at Poona). "The discovery of this valuable manuscript reduced me, though heartily sick of the task, to the necessity of commencing my work once more."

Erskine's Preface (pp. x, xi) contains various other references to Leyden's work which indicate its quality as tentative and unrevised. It is now in the British Museum Library.

XII

Little need be said here about the *Memoirs of Baber.*[24] Erskine worked on a basis of considerable earlier acquaintance with his Persian original, for, as his Preface tells, he had (after Leyden's death) begun to translate this some years before he definitely accepted the counsel of Elphinstone and Malcolm to undertake the *Memoirs*. He finished his translation in 1813, and by 1816 was able to dedicate his complete volume to Elphinstone, but publication was delayed till 1826. His was difficult pioneer-work, and carried through with the drawback of working on a secondary source. It has done yeoman service, of which the crowning merit is its introduction of Babur's autobiography to the Western world.

XIII

Amongst Erskine's literary remains are several bound volumes of letters from Elphinstone, Malcolm, Leyden, and others of that distinguished group of Scots who promoted the revival of Babur's writings. Erskine's grandson, the late Mr. Lestocq Erskine, placed these, with other papers, at our disposal, and they are now located where they have been welcomed as appropriate additions:—Elphinstone's are in the Advocates' Library, where already (1826) he, through Erskine, had deposited his own Codex—and with his letters are those of Malcolm and more occasional correspondents; Leyden's letters (and various papers) are in the Memorial Cottage maintained in his birthplace Denholm (Hawick) by the Edinburgh Border Counties Association; something fitting went to the Bombay Asiatic Society and a volume of diary to the British Museum. Leyden's papers will help his fuller biography; Elphinstone's letters have special value as recording his co-operation with Erskine by much friendly criticism, remonstrance against delay, counsels and encouragement. They, moreover, shew the estimate an accomplished man of modern affairs formed of Babur Padshah's character and conduct; some have been quoted in Colebrooke's *Life of Elphinstone*, but there they suffer by detachment from the rest of his Baburiana letters; bound together as they now are, and with brief explanatory interpolations, they would make a welcome item for "Babur Padshah's Book-pile".

XIV

In May 1921 the contents of these volumes were completed, namely, the *Babur-nama in English* and its supplements, the aims of which are to make Babur known in English diction answering to his *ipsissima verba*, and to be serviceable to readers and students of his book and of classic Turki.

XV

Of writings based upon or relating to Babur's the following have appeared:—

Denkwurdigkeiten des Zahir-uddin Muhammad Babar—A. Kaiser (Leipzig, 1828). This consists of extracts translated from the Memoirs.

An abridgement of the Memoirs—R. M. Caldecott (London, 1844).

History of India—Baber and Humayun—W. Erskine (Longmans, 1854).

Babar—Rulers of India series—Stanley Lane-Poole (Oxford, 1899).

Tuzuk-i-babari or Waqi'at-i-babari (*i.e.* the Persian trs.)—Elliot and Dowson's History of India, 1872, vol. iv.

Babur Padshah *Ghazi*—H. Beveridge (Calcutta Review, 1899).

Babur's diamond, was it the Koh-i-nur?—H. Beveridge, Asiatic Quarterly Review, April, 1899.

Was 'Abdu'r-rahim the translator of Babur's Memoirs? (*i.e.* the *Babur-nama*)—H. Beveridge, AQR., July and October, 1900.

An Empire-builder of the 16th century, Babur—Laurence F. L. Williams (Allahabad, 1918).

Notes on the MSS. of the Turki text (*Babur-nāma*)—A. S. Beveridge, JRAS. 1900, 1902, 1921, 1905, and Part II 1906, 1907, 1908, p. 52 and p. 828, 1909 p. 452 (*see* Index, *s.n.* A. S. B. for topics).

[For other articles and notes by H. B. *see* Index *s.n.*]

Part III. The "Bukhara Babur-nama".

This is a singular book and has had a career as singular as its characteristics, a very comedy of (blameless) errors and mischance. For it is a compilation of items diverse in origin, diction, and age, planned to be a record of the Acts of Babur and Humayun, dependent through its Babur portion on the 'Abdu'r-rahim Persian translation for re-translation, or verbatim quotation, or dove-tailing effected on the tattered fragments of what had once been Kamran's Codex of the Babur-nama proper, the whole interspersed by stop-gaps attributable to Jahangir. These and other specialities notwithstanding, it ranked for nearly 200 years as a reproduction of Babur's authentic text, as such was sent abroad, as such was reconstructed and printed in Kasan (1857), translated in Paris (1871), catalogued for the Petrograd Oriental School (1894), and for the India Office (1903).[25]

Manifest causes for the confusion of identity are, (1) lack of the guidance in Bukhara and Petrograd of collation with the true text, (2) want of information, in the Petrograd of 1700-25, about Babur's career, coupled with the difficulties of communication with Bukhara, (3) the misleading feature in the compiled book of its author's retention of the autobiographic form of his sources, without explanation as to whether he entered surviving fragments of Kamran's Codex, patchings or extracts from 'Abdu'r-rahim's Persian translation, or quotations of Jahangir's stop-gaps. Of these three causes for error the first is dominant, entailing as it does the drawbacks besetting work on an inadequate basis.

It is necessary to enumerate the items of the Compilation here as they are arranged in Kehr's autograph Codex, because that codex (still in London) may not always be accessible,[26] and because the imprint does not obey its model, but aims at closer agreement of the Bukhara Compilation with Ilminski's gratefully acknowledged guide—*The Memoirs of Baber.* Distinction in commenting on the Bukhara and the Kasan versions is necessary; their discrepancy is a scene in the comedy of errors.

Outline of the History of the Compilation.

An impelling cause for the production of the Bukhara compilation is suggested by the date 1709 at which was finished the earliest example known to me. For in the first decade of the eighteenth century Peter the Great gave attention to Russian relations with foreign states of Central Asia and negociated with the Khan of Bukhara for the reception of a Russian mission.[31] Political aims would be forwarded if envoys were familiar with Turki; books in that tongue for use in the School of Oriental Languages would be desired; thus the Compilation may have been prompted and, as will be shown later, it appears to have been produced, and not merely copied, in 1709. The Mission's despatch was delayed till 1719;[32] it arrived in Bukhara in 1721; during its stay a member of its secretariat bought a Compilation MS. noted as finished in 1714 and on a fly-leaf of it made the following note:—

"I, Timur-pulad son of Mirza Rajab son of Pay-chin, bought this book Babur-nama after coming to Bukhara with [the] Russian Florio Beg Beneveni, envoy of the Padshah ... whose army is numerous as the stars.... May it be well received! Amen! O Lord of both Worlds!"

Timur-pulad's hope for a good reception indicates a definite recipient, perhaps a commissioned purchase. The vendor may have been asked for a history of Babur; he sold one, but "Babur-nama" is not necessarily a title, and is not suitable for the Compilation; by conversational mischance it may have seemed so to the purchaser and thus have initiated the mistake of confusing the "Bukhara Babur-nama" with the true one.

Thus endorsed, the book in 1725 reached the Foreign Office; there in 1737 it was obtained by George Jacob Kehr, a teacher of Turki, amongst other languages, in the Oriental School, who copied it with meticulous care, understanding its meaning imperfectly, in order to produce a Latin version of it. His Latin rendering was a fiasco, but his reproduction of the Arabic forms of his archetype was so obedient that on its sole basis Ilminski edited the Kasan Imprint (1857). A collateral copy of the Timur-pulad Codex was made in 1742 (as has been said).

In 1824 Klaproth (who in 1810 had made a less valuable extract perhaps from Kehr's Codex) copied from the Timur-pulad MS. its purchaser's note, the Auzbeg?(?) endorsement as to the transfer of the "Kamran-docket" and Babur's letter to Kamran (*Mémoires relatifs à l'Asie* Paris).

In 1857 Ilminski, working in Kasan, produced his imprint, which became de Courteille's source for *Les Mémoires de Baber* in 1871. No worker in the above series shews doubt about accepting the Compilation as containing Babur's authentic text. Ilminski was in the difficult position of not having entire reliance on Kehr's transcription, a natural apprehension in face of the quality of the Latin version, his doubts sum up into his words that a reliable text could not be made from his source (Kehr's MS.), but that a Turki reading-book could—and was. As has been said, he did not obey the dual plan of the Compilation Kehr's transcript reveals, this, perhaps, because of the misnomer Babur-nama under which Timur-pulad's Codex had come to Petrograd; this, certainly, because he thought a better history of Babur could be produced by following Erskine than by obeying Kehr—a series of errors following the verbal mischance of 1725. Ilminski's transformation of the items of his source had the ill result of misleading Pavet de Courteille to over-estimate his Turki source at the expense of Erskine's Persian one which, as has been said, was Ilminski's guide—another scene in the comedy. A mischance hampering the French work was its falling to be done at a time when, in Paris 1871, there can have been no opportunity available for learning the contents of Ilminski's Russian Preface or for quiet research and the examination of collateral aids from abroad.[33]

THE AUTHOR OF THE COMPILATION.

The Haidarabad Codex having destroyed acquiescence in the phantasmal view of the Bukhara book, the question may be considered, who was its author?

This question a convergence of details about the Turki MSS. reputed to contain the *Babur-nama*, now allows me to answer with some semblance of truth. Those details have thrown new light upon a colophon which I received in 1900 from Mr. C. Salemann with other particulars concerning the "*Senkovski Babur-nama*," this being an extract from the Compilation; its archetype reached Petrograd from Bukhara a century after Kehr's [*viz.* the Timur-pulad Codex]; it can be taken as a direct copy of the Mulla's original because it bears his colophon.[34] In 1900 I accepted it as merely that of a scribe who had copied Senkovski's archetype, but in 1921 reviewing the colophon for this Preface, it seems to me to be that of the original autograph MS. of the Compilation and to tell its author's name, his title for his book, and the year (1709) in which he completed it.

TABLE OF BUKHARA REPUTED-BABUR-NAMA MSS. (*Waqi'nama-i-padshahi?*).

Names.	Date of completio n.	Scribe.	Last known l ocation.	Archetype.	Remarks.
1. Waqi'nama-i-padshahi _alias_ Babur -nama.	1121-1709. Date of coloph on of earliest k nown example.	'Ābdu'l-wahhab _q.v._ Taken t o be also the author.	Bukhara.	Believed to b e the original com pilation.	_See_ Part III.
2. Nazar Bai Turki stani's MS.	Unknown.	Unknown.	In owner's ch arge in Petrograd, 1824.	No. 1, the colophon of which it repr oduces.	Senkovski's archetype who copied its (transferred) colophon.
3. F. O. Codex (Timurpulad's MS.).	1126-1714.	Unknown.	F.O. Petrograd, where copied in 1742.	Not stated, an indirect copy of No. 1.	Bought in Bukhara, brought to Petro. 1725.
4. Kehr's Autog raph	1737.	George Jacob	Pet. Or. Scho ol, 1894. London T.O. 1921.	No. 3.	_See_ Part I II.
5. Name not lea rned.	1155-1742.	Unknown.	Unknown.	No. 3.	Archetype of 9.
6. (Mysore) A.S. B. Codex.	Unknown. JRAS. 1900, Nos. vii and viii.	Unknown.	Asiatic Society of Bengal.	Unknown.	—

7. India Office Codex (Bib. Leydeniana).	Cir. 1810.	Unknown.	India Office, 1921.	No. 6.	Copied for Leyden.
"The Senkovski Babur-nama."	1824.	J. Senkovski.	Pet. Asiatic Museum, 1900.	No. 2.	Bears a copy of the colophon of No. 1.
9. Pet. Universit y Codex.	1839?	Mulla Faizkhan ov?	Pet. Univ. Library.	No. 5 (?).	—

Senkovski brought it over from his archetype; Mr. Salemann sent it to me in its original Turki form. (JRAS. 1900, p. 474). Senkovski's own colophon is as follows:—

"*J'ai achevé cette copie le 4 Mai, 1824, à St. Petersburg; elle a éte faite d'àpres un exemplaire appartenant à Nazar Bai Turkistani, négociant Boukhari, qui etait venu cette année à St. Petersburg. J. Senkovski.*"

The colophon Senkovski copied from his archetype is to the following purport:—

"*Known and entitled Waqi'nama-i-padshahi (Record of Royal Acts), [this] autograph and composition (bayad u navisht) of Mulla 'Abdu'l-wahhāb the Teacher, of Ghaj-davan in Bukhara—God pardon his mistakes and the weakness of his endeavour!—was finished on Monday, Rajab 5, 1121* (Aug. 31st, 1709).—*Thank God!*"

It will be observed that the title Waqi'nama-i-padshahi suits the plan of dual histories (of Babur and Humayun) better than does the "Babur-nama" of Timur-pulad's note, that the colophon does not claim for the Mulla to have copied the elder book (1494-1530) but to have written down and composed one under a differing title suiting its varied contents; that the Mulla's deprecation and thanks tone better with perplexing work, such as his was, than with the steadfast patience of a good scribe; and that it exonerates the Mulla from suspicion of having caused his compilation to be accepted as Babur's authentic text. Taken with its circumstanding matters, it may be the dénoument of the play.

CHAPTER IV.

THE LEYDEN AND ERSKINE MEMOIRS OF BABER.

The fame and long literary services of the *Memoirs of Baber* compel me to explain why these volumes of mine contain a verbally new English translation of the *Babur-nama* instead of a second edition of the *Memoirs.* My explanation is the simple one of textual values, of the advantage a primary source has over its derivative, Babur's original text over its Persian translation which alone was accessible to Erskine.

If the *Babur-nama* owed its perennial interest to its valuable multifarious matter, the *Memoirs* could suffice to represent it, but this it does not; what has kept interest in it alive through some four centuries is the autobiographic presentment of an arresting personality its whole manner, style and diction produce. It is characteristic throughout, from first to last making known the personal quality of its author. Obviously that quality has the better chance of surviving a transfer of Babur's words to a foreign tongue when this can be effected by imitation of them. To effect this was impracticable to Erskine who did not see any example of the Turki text during the progress of his translation work and had little acquaintance with Turki. No blame attaches to his results; they have been the one introduction of Babur's writings to English readers for almost a century; but it would be as sensible to expect a potter to shape a vessel for a specific purpose without a model as a translator of autobiography to shape the new verbal container for Babur's quality without seeing his own. Erskine was the pioneer amongst European workers on Baburiana—Leyden's fragment of unrevised attempt to translate the Bukhara Compilation being a negligible matter, notwithstanding friendship's deference to it; he had ready to his hand no such valuable collateral help as he bequeathed to his successors in the Memoirs volume. To have been able to help in the renewal of his book by preparing a second edition of it, revised under the authority of the Haidarabad Codex, would have been to me an act of literary piety to an old book-friend; I experimented and failed in the attempt; the wording of the Memoirs would not press back into the Turki mould. Being what it is, sound in its matter and partly representative of Babur himself, the all-round safer plan, one doing it the greater honour, was to leave it unshorn of its redundance and unchanged in its wording, in the place of worth and dignity it has held so long.

Brought to this point by experiment and failure, the way lay open to make bee-line over intermediaries back to the fountain-head of re-discovered

Turki text preserved in the Haidarabad Codex. Thus I have enjoyed an advantage no translator has had since 'Abdu'r-rahim in 1589.

Concerning matters of style and diction, I may mention that three distinct impressions of Babur's personality are set by his own, Erskine's and de Courteille's words and manner. These divergencies, while partly due to differing textual bases, may result mainly from the use by the two Europeans of unsifted, current English and French. Their portrayal might have been truer, there can be no doubt, if each had restricted himself to such under-lying component of his mother-tongue as approximates in linguistic stature to classic Turki. This probability Erskine could not foresee for, having no access during his work to a Turki source and no familiarity with Turki, he missed their lessoning.

Turki, as Babur writes it—terse, word-thrifty, restrained and lucid,—comes over neatly into Anglo-Saxon English, perhaps through primal affinities. Studying Babur's writings in verbal detail taught me that its structure, idiom and vocabulary dictate a certain mechanism for a translator's imitation. Such are the simple sentence, devoid of relative phrasing, copied in the form found, whether abrupt and brief or, ranging higher with the topic, gracious and dignified—the retention of Babur's use of "we" and "I" and of his frequent impersonal statement—the matching of words by their root-notion—the strict observance of Babur's limits of vocabulary, effected by allotting to one Turki word one English equivalent, thus excluding synonyms for which Turki has little use because not shrinking from the repeated word; lastly, as preserving relations of diction, the replacing of Babur's Arabic and Persian aliens by Greek and Latin ones naturalized in English. Some of these aids towards shaping a counterpart of Turki may be thought small, but they obey a model and their aggregate has power to make or mar a portrait.

(1) Of the uses of pronouns it may be said that Babur's "we" is neither regal nor self-magnifying but is co-operative, as beseems the chief whose volunteer and nomad following makes or unmakes his power, and who can lead and command only by remittent consent accorded to him. His "I" is individual. The *Memoirs* varies much from these uses.

(2) The value of reproducing impersonal statements is seen by the following example, one of many similar:—When Babur and a body of men, making a long saddle-journey, halted for rest and refreshment by the road-side; "There was drinking," he writes, but Erskine, "I drank"; what is likely being that all or all but a few shared the local *vin du pays*.

(3) The importance of observing Babur's limits of vocabulary needs no stress, since any man of few words differs from any man of many. Measured by the Babur-nama standard, the diction of the *Memoirs* is

redundant throughout, and frequently over-coloured. Of this a pertinent example is provided by a statement of which a minimum of seven occurrences forms my example, namely, that such or such a man whose life Babur sketches was vicious or a vicious person (*fisq*, *fāsiq*). Erskine once renders the word by "vicious" but elsewhere enlarges to "debauched, excess of sensual enjoyment, lascivious, libidinous, profligate, voluptuous". The instances are scattered and certainly Erskine could not feel their collective effect, but even scattered, each does its ill-part in distorting the Memoirs portraiture of the man of the one word.[35]

POSTSCRIPT OF THANKS.

I take with gratitude the long-delayed opportunity of finishing my book to express the obligation I feel to the Council of the Royal Asiatic Society for allowing me to record in the Journal my Notes on the Turki Codices of the *Babur-nama* begun in 1900 and occasionally appearing till 1921. In minor convenience of work, to be able to gather those progressive notes together and review them, has been of value to me in noticeable matters, two of which are the finding and multiplying of the Haidarabad Codex, and the definite clearance of the confusion which had made the Bukhara (reputed) *Babur-nama* be mistaken for a reproduction of Babur's true text.

Immeasurable indeed is the obligation laid on me by the happy community of interests which brought under our roof the translation of the biographies of Babur, Humayun, and Akbar. What this has meant to my own work may be surmised by those who know my husband's wide reading in many tongues of East and West, his retentive memory and his generous communism in knowledge. One signal cause for gratitude to him from those caring for Baburiana, is that it was he made known the presence of the Haidarabad Codex in its home library (1899) and thus led to its preservation in facsimile.

It would be impracticable to enumerate all whose help I keep in grateful memory and realize as the fruit of the genial camaraderie of letters.

ANNETTE S. BEVERIDGE.

PITFOLD, SHOTTERMILL, HASLEMERE.
August, 1921.

SECTION I. FARGHĀNA.

AH.—OCT. 12TH 1493 TO OCT. 2ND 1494 AD.

In the name of God, the Merciful, the Compassionate.

IN[36] the month of Ramẓān of the year 899 (June 1494) andḤaidarābād MS. fol.
1b. in the twelfth year of my age,[37] I became ruler[38] in the country of Farghāna.

(*a. Description of Farghāna.*)

Farghāna is situated in the fifth climate[39] and at the limit of settled habitation. On the east it has Kāshghar; on the west, Samarkand; on the south, the mountains of the Badakhshān border; on the north, though in former times there must have been towns such as Ālmālīgh, Ālmātū and Yāngī which in books they write Tarāz,[40] at the present time all is desolate, no settled population whatever remaining, because of the Mughūls and the Aūzbegs.[41]

Farghāna is a small country,[42] abounding in grain and fruits. It is girt round by mountains except on the west, *i.e.* towards Khujand and Samarkand, and in winter[43] an enemy can enter only on that side.

Fol. 2.The Saiḥūn River (*daryā*) commonly known as the Water of Khujand, comes into the country from the north-east, flows westward through it and after passing along the north of Khujand and the south of Fanākat,[44] now known as Shāhrukhiya, turns directly north and goes to Turkistān. It does not join any sea[45] but sinks into the sands, a considerable distance below [the town of] Turkistān.

Farghāna has seven separate townships,[46] five on the south and two on the north of the Saiḥūn.

Of those on the south, one is Andijān. It has a central position and is the capital of the Farghāna country. It produces much grain, fruits in abundance, excellent grapes and melons. In the melon season, it is not customary to sell them out at the beds.[47] Better than the Andijān *nāshpātī*,[48] there is none. After Samarkand and Kesh, the fort[49] of Andijān is the largest in Mawārā'u'n-nahr (Transoxiana). It has three gates. Its citadel (*ark*) is on its south side. Into it water goes by nine channels; out of it, it is strange that none comes at even a single place.[50] Round the outer edge of the ditch[51] runs a gravelled highway; the width of this highway divides the fort from the suburbs surrounding it.

Andijān has good hunting and fowling; its pheasants grow so surprisingly fat that rumour has it four people could not Fol. 2b.finish one they were eating with its stew.[52]

Andijānīs are all Turks, not a man in town or bāzār but knows Turkī. The speech of the people is correct for the pen; hence the writings of Mīr 'Alī-shīr *Nawā'ī*,[53] though he was bred and grew up in Hīrī (Harāt), are one with their dialect. Good looks are common amongst them. The famous musician, Khwāja Yūsuf, was an Andijānī.[54] The climate is malarious; in autumn people generally get fever.[55]

Again, there is Aūsh (Ūsh), to the south-east, inclining to east, of Andijān and distant from it four *yīghāch* by road.[56] It has a fine climate, an abundance of running waters[57] and a most beautiful spring season. Many traditions have their rise in its excellencies.[58] To the south-east of the walled town (*qūrghān*) lies a symmetrical mountain, known as the Barā Koh;[59] on the top of this, Sl. Maḥmūd Khān built a retreat (*ḥajra*) and lower down, on its shoulder, I, in 902AH. (1496AD.) built another, having a porch. Though his lies the higher, mine is the better placed, the whole of the town and the suburbs being at its foot.

The Andijān torrent[60] goes to Andijān after having traversedFol. 3. the suburbs of Aūsh. Orchards (*bāghāt*)[61] lie along both its banks; all the Aūsh gardens (*bāghlār*) overlook it; their violets are very fine; they have running waters and in spring are most beautiful with the blossoming of many tulips and roses.

On the skirt of the Barā-koh is a mosque called the Jauza Masjid (Twin Mosque).[62] Between this mosque and the town, a great main canal flows from the direction of the hill. Below the outer court of the mosque lies a shady and delightful clover-meadow where every passing traveller takes a rest. It is the joke of the ragamuffins of Aūsh to let out water from the canal[63] on anyone happening to fall asleep in the meadow. A very beautiful stone, waved red and white[64] was found in the Barā Koh in 'Umar Shaikh Mīrzā's latter days; of it are made knife handles, and clasps for belts and many other things. For climate and for pleasantness, no township in all Farghāna equals Aūsh.

Again there is Marghīnān; seven *yīghāch*[65] by road to the west of Andijān,—a fine township full of good things. Its apricots (*aūrūk*) and pomegranates are most excellent. One sort of pomegranate, they call the Great Seed (*Dāna-i-kalān*); its sweetness has a little of the pleasant flavour of the small apricot (*zard-alū*) and it may be thought better than the Semnān pomegranate. Fol. 3b.Another kind of apricot (*aūrūk*) they dry after stoning it and putting back the kernel;[66] they then call it *subḥānī*; it is very palatable. The hunting and fowling of Marghīnān are good; *āq kīyīk*[67] are had close by. Its people are Sārts,[68] boxers, noisy and turbulent. Most of the noted bullies (*jangralār*) of Samarkand and Bukhārā are Marghīnānīs. The author of the Hidāyat[69] was from Rashdān, one of the villages of Marghīnān.

Again there is Asfara, in the hill-country and nine *yīghāch*[70] by road south-west of Marghīnān. It has running waters, beautiful little gardens (*bāghcha*) and many fruit-trees but almonds for the most part in its orchards. Its people are all Persian-speaking[71] Sārts. In the hills some two miles (*bīrshar'ī*) to the south of the town, is a piece of rock, known as the Mirror Stone.[72] It is some 10 arm-lengths (*qārī*) long, as high as a man in parts, up to his waist in others. Everything is reflected by it as by a mirror. The Asfara district (*wilāyat*) is in four subdivisions (*balūk*) in the hill-country, one Asfara, one Warūkh, one Sūkh and one Hushyār. When Muḥammad *Shaibānī* Khān defeated Sl. Maḥmūd Khān and Alacha Khān and took Tāshkīnt and Shāhrukhiya,[73] I went into the Sūkh and HushyārFol. 4. hill-country and from there, after about a year spent in great misery, I set out (*'azīmat*) for Kābul.[74]

Again there is Khujand,[75] twenty-five *yīghāch* by road to the west of Andijān and twenty-five *yīghāch* east of Samarkand.[76] Khujand is one of the ancient towns; of it were Shaikh Maṣlaḥat and Khwāja Kamāl.[77] Fruit grows well there; its pomegranates are renowned for their excellence; people talk of a Khujand pomegranate as they do of a Samarkand apple; just now however, Marghīnān pomegranates are much met with.[78] The walled town (*qūrghān*) of Khujand stands on high ground; the Saiḥūn River flows past it on the north at the distance, may be, of an arrow's flight.[79] To the north of both the town and the river lies a mountain range called Munūghul;[80] people say there are turquoise and other mines in it and there are many snakes. The hunting and fowling-grounds of Khujand are first-rate; *āq kīyīk*,[81] *būghū-marāl*,[82] pheasant and hare are all had in great plenty. The climate is very malarious; in autumn there is much fever;[83] people rumour it about that the very sparrows get fever and say that the cause of the malaria is the mountain range on the north (*i.e.* Munūghul).

Kand-i-badām (Village of the Almond) is a dependency of Khujand; though it is not a township (*qaṣba*) it is rather a good approach to one (*qaṣbacha*). Its almonds are excellent, hence its name; they all go to Hormuz or to Hindūstān. It is five orFol. 4b. six *yīghāch*[84] east of Khujand.

Between Kand-i-badām and Khujand lies the waste known as Hā Darwesh. In this there is always (*hamesha*) wind; from it wind goes always (*hameshā*) to Marghīnān on its east; from it wind comes continually (*dā'im*) to Khujand on its west.[85] It has violent, whirling winds. People say that some darweshes, encountering a whirlwind in this desert,[86] lost one another and kept crying, "Hāy Darwesh! Hāy Darwesh!" till all had perished, and that the waste has been called Hā Darwesh ever since.

Of the townships on the north of the Saiḥūn River one is Akhsī. In books they write it Akhsīkīt[87] and for this reason the poet Aṣiru-d-dīn is known as *Akhsīkītī*. After Andijān no township in Farghāna is larger than Akhsī. It is nine *yīghāch*[88] by road to the west of Andijān. 'Umar Shaikh Mīrzā made it his capital.[89] The Saiḥūn River flows below its walled town (*qūrghān*). This stands above a great ravine (*buland jar*) and it has deep ravines (*'uṃiq jarlār*) in place of a moat. When 'Umar Shaikh Mīrzā made it his capital, he once or twice cut other ravines from the outer ones. In all Farghāna no fort is so strong as Akhsī. *Its suburbs extend some two miles further Fol. 5.than the walled town.* People seem to have made of Akhsī the saying (*miṣal*), "Where is the village? Where are the trees?" (*Dih kujā? Dirakhtān kujā?*) Its melons are excellent; they call one kind Mīr Tīmūrī; whether in the world there is another to equal it is not known. The melons of Bukhārā are famous; when I took Samarkand, I had some brought from there and some from Akhsī; they were cut up at an entertainment and nothing from Bukhārā compared with those from Akhsī. The fowling and hunting of Akhsī are very good indeed; *āq kīyīk* abound in the waste on the Akhsī side of the Saihūn; in the jungle on the Andijān side *būghū-marāl*,[90] pheasant and hare are had, all in very good condition.

Again there is Kāsān, rather a small township to the north of Akhsī. From Kāsān the Akhsī water comes in the same way as the Andijān water comes from Aūsh. Kāsān has excellent air and beautiful little gardens (*bāghcha*). As these gardens all lie along the bed of the torrent (*sā'ī*) people call them the "fine front of the coat."[91] Between Kāsānīs and Aūshīs there is rivalry about the beauty and climate of their townships.

In the mountains round Farghāna are excellent summer-pastures (*yīlāq*). There, and nowhere else, the *tabalghū*[92]grows, a tree (*yīghāch*) with red bark; they make staves of it; theyFol. 5b. make bird-cages of it; they scrape it into arrows;[93] it is an excellent wood (*yīghāch*) and is carried as a rarity[94] to distant places. Some books write that the mandrake[95] is found in these mountains but for this long time past nothing has been heard of it. A plant called *Āyīq aūtī*[96] and having the qualities of the mandrake (*mihr-giyāh*), is heard of in Yītī-kīnt;[97] it seems to be the mandrake (*mihr-giyāh*) the people there call by this name (*i.e. āyīq aūtī*). There are turquoise and iron mines in these mountains.

If people do justly, three or four thousand men[98] may be maintained by the revenues of Farghāna.

(b. Historical narrative resumed.)[99]

As 'Umar Shaikh Mīrzā was a ruler of high ambition and great pretension, he was always bent on conquest. On several occasions he led an army against Samarkand; sometimes he was beaten, sometimes retired against his will.[100] More than once he asked his father-in-law into the country, that is to say, my grandfather, Yūnas Khān, the then Khān of the Mughūls in the camping ground (*yūrt*) of his ancestor, Chaghatāī Khān, the second son of Chīngīz Khān. Each time the Mīrzā brought The Khān into the Farghāna country he gave him lands, but, partly owing to his misconduct, partly to the thwarting of the Fol. 6.Mughūls,[101] things did not go as he wished and Yūnas Khān, not being able to remain, went out again into Mughūlistān. When the Mīrzā last brought The Khān in, he was in possession of

Tāshkīnt, which in books they write Shash, and sometimes Chāch, whence the term, a Chāchī, bow.[102] He gave it to The Khān, and from that date (890AH.-1485AD.) down to 908AH. (1503AD.) it and the Shāhrukhiya country were held by the Chaghatāī Khāns.

At this date (*i.e.*, 899AH.-1494AD.) the Mughūl Khānship was in Sl. Maḥ=mūd Khān, Yūnas Khān's younger son and a half-brother of my mother. As he and 'Umar Shaikh Mīrzā's elder brother, the then ruler of Samarkand, Sl. Aḥmad Mīrzā were offended by the Mīrzā's behaviour, they came to an agreement together; Sl. Aḥmad Mīrzā had already given a daughter to Sl. Maḥmūd Khān;[103] both now led their armies against 'Umar Shaikh Mīrzā, the first advancing along the south of the Khujand Water, the second along its north.

Meantime a strange event occurred. It has been mentionedFol. 6b that the fort of Akhsī is situated above a deep ravine;[104] along this ravine stand the palace buildings, and from it, on Monday, Ramẓān 4, (June 8th.) 'Umar Shaikh Mīrzā flew, with his pigeons and their house, and became a falcon.[105]

He was 39 (lunar) years old, having been born in Samarkand, in 860AH. (1456AD.) He was Sl. Abū-sa'īd Mīrzā's fourth son,[106] being younger than Sl. Aḥmad M. and Sl. Muḥammad M. and Sl. Maḥmūd Mīrzā. His father, Sl. Abū-sa'īd Mīrzā, was the son of Sl. Muḥammad Mīrzā, son of Tīmūr Beg's third son, Mīrān-shāh M. and was younger than 'Umar Shaikh Mīrzā, (the elder) and Jahāngīr M. but older than Shāhrukh Mīrzā.

c. 'Umar Shaikh Mīrẓā's country.

His father first gave him Kābul and, with Bābā-i-Kābulī[107] for his guardian, had allowed him to set out, but recalled him from the Tamarisk Valley[108] to

Samarkand, on account of the Mīrzās' Circumcision Feast. When the Feast was over, he gave him Andijān with the appropriateness that Tīmūr Beg had given Farghāna (Andijān) to his son, the elder 'Umar Shaikh Mīrzā. This done, he sent him off with Khudāī-bīrdī *Tūghchī Tīmūr-tāsh*[109] for his guardian.

d. His appearance and characteristics.

He was a short and stout, round-bearded and fleshy-faced Fol. 7.person.[110] He used to wear his tunic so very tight that to fasten the strings he had to draw his belly in and, if he let himself out after tying them, they often tore away. He was not choice in dress or food. He wound his turban in a fold (*dastar-pech*); all turbans were in four folds (*chār-pech*) in those days; people wore them without twisting and let the ends hang down.[111] In the heats and except in his Court, he generally wore the Mughūl cap.

e. His qualities and habits.

He was a true believer (*Ḥanafī maẕhablīk*) and pure in the Faith, not neglecting the Five Prayers and, his life through, making up his Omissions.[112] He read the Qur'ān very frequently and was a disciple of his Highness Khwāja 'Ubaidu'l-lāh (*Aḥrārī*) who honoured him by visits and even called him son. His current readings[113] were the two Quintets and the *Maṣnawī*;[114] of histories he read chiefly the *Shāh-nāma*. He had a poetic nature, but no taste for composing verses. He was so just that when he heard of a caravan returning from Khitāī as overwhelmed by snow in the mountains of Eastern Andijān,[115] and that of its thousand heads of houses (*awīlūq*) two only had escaped, he sent his overseers to take charge of all goods and, though no heirs wereFol. 7b. near and though he was in want himself, summoned the heirs from Khurāsān and Samarkand, and in the course of a year or two had made over to them all their property safe and sound.

He was very generous; in truth, his character rose altogether to the height of generosity. He was affable, eloquent and sweet-spoken, daring and bold. Twice out-distancing all his braves,[116] he got to work with his own sword, once at the Gate of Akhsī, once at the Gate of Shāhrukhiya. A middling archer, he was strong in the fist,—not a man but fell to his blow. Through his ambition, peace was exchanged often for war, friendliness for hostility.

In his early days he was a great drinker, later on used to have a party once or twice a week. He was good company, on occasions reciting verses admirably. Towards the last he rather preferred intoxicating confects[117] and, under their sway, used to lose his head. His disposition[118] was amorous, and he bore many a lover's mark.[119] He played draughts a good deal, sometimes even threw the dice.

f. His battles and encounters.

He fought three ranged battles, the first with Yūnas Khān, Fol. 8.on the Saiḥūn, north of Andijān, at the Goat-leap,[120] a village so-called because near it the foot-hills so narrow the flow of the water that people say goats leap across.[121] There he was beaten and made prisoner. Yūnas Khān for his part did well by him and gave him leave to go to his own district (Andijān). This fight having been at that place, the Battle of the Goat-leap became a date in those parts.

His second battle was fought on the Urūs,[122] in Turkistān, with Aūzbegs returning from a raid near Samarkand. He crossed the river on the ice, gave them a good beating, separated off all their prisoners and booty and, without coveting a single thing for himself, gave everything back to its owners.

His third battle he fought with (his brother) Sl. Aḥmad Mīrzā at a place between Shāhrukhiya and Aūrā-tīpā, named Khwāṣ.[123] Here he was beaten.

g. His country.

The Farghāna country his father had given him; Tāshkīnt and Sairām, his elder brother, Sl. Aḥmad Mīrzā gave, and they were in his possession for a time; Shāhrukhiya he took by a ruse and held awhile. Later on, Tāshkīnt and Shāhrukhiya passed out of his hands; there then remained the Farghāna country and Khujand,—some do not include Khujand inFol. 8b. Farghāna,—and Aūrā-tīpā, of which the original name was Aūrūshnā and which some call Aūrūsh. In Aūrā-tīpā, at the time Sl. Aḥmad Mīrzā went to Tāshkīnt against the Mughūls, and was beaten on the Chīr[124] (893AH.-1488AD.) was Ḥafiẓ Beg *Dūldāī*; he made it over to 'Umar Shaikh M. and the Mīrzā held it from that time forth.

h. His children.

Three of his sons and five of his daughters grew up. I, Ẓahīru'd-dīn Muḥammad Bābur,[125] was his eldest son; my mother was Qūtlūq-nigār Khānīm. Jahāngīr Mīrzā was his second son, two years younger than I; his mother, Fāṭima-sulṭān by name, was of the Mughūl *tūmān*-begs.[126] Nāṣir Mīrzā was his third son; his mother was an Andijānī, a mistress,[127] named Umīd. He was four years younger than I.

'Umar Shaikh Mīrzā's eldest daughter was Khān-zāda Begīm,[128] my full sister, five years older than I. The second time I took Samarkand (905AH.-1500AD.), spite of defeat at Sar-i-pul,[129] I went back and held it through a five months' siege, but as no sort of help or reinforcement came from any beg or ruler thereabouts, I left it in despair and got away; in that throneless time (*fatrat*) Khān-zāda Begīm fell[130] to Muḥammad *Shaibānī* Khān. She had one child by him, a pleasant boy,[131] Fol. 9.named Khurram Shāh. The Balkh country was given to him; he went to God's mercy a few years after the death of his father (916AH.-1510AD.). Khān-zāda Begīm was in Merv when Shāh Ismā'īl (*Ṣafawī*) defeated the Aūzbegs near that town (916AH.-1510AD.); for my sake he treated her well, giving her a sufficient escort to Qūndūz where she rejoined me. We had been apart for some ten years; when Muḥammadī *kūkūldāsh* and I went to see her, neither she nor those about her knew us, although I spoke. They recognized us after a time.

Mihr-bānū Begīm was another daughter, Nāṣir Mīrzā's full-sister, two years younger than I. Shahr-bānū Begīm was another, also Nāṣir Mīrzā's full-sister, eight years younger than I. Yādgār-sulṭān Begīm was another, her mother was a mistress, called Āghā-sulṭān. Ruqaiya-sulṭān Begīm was another; her mother, Makhdūm-sulṭān Begīm, people used to call the Dark-eyed Begīm. The last-named two were born after the Mīrzā's death. Yādgār-sulṭān Begīm was brought up by my grandmother, Aīsān-daulat Begīm; she fell to 'Abdu'l-laṭīf Sl., a son of Ḥamza Sl. when Shaibānī Khān took Andijān and Akhsī (908AH.-1503AD.). She rejoined me when (917AH.-1511AD.) in Khutlān I defeated Ḥamza Sl. and Fol. 9b.other sulṭāns and took Ḥiṣār. Ruqaiya-sulṭān Begīm fell in that same throneless time (*fatrat*) to Jānī Beg Sl. (*Aūzbeg*). By him she had one or two children who did not live. In these days of our leisure (*furṣatlār*)[132] has come news that she has gone to God's mercy.

i. His ladies and mistresses.

Qūtlūq-nigār Khānīm was the second daughter of Yūnas Khān and the eldest (half-) sister of Sl. Maḥmūd Khān and Sl. Aḥmad Khān.

(*j. Interpolated account of Bābur's mother's family.*)

Yūnas Khān descended from Chaghatāī Khān, the second son of Chīngīz Khān (as follows,) Yūnas Khān, son of Wais Khān, son of Sher-'alī *Aūghlān*, son of Muḥammad Khān, son of Khiẓr Khwāja Khān, son of Tūghlūq-tīmūr Khān, son of Aīsān-būghā Khān, son of Dāwā Khān, son of Barāq Khān, son of Yīsūntawā Khān, son of Mūātūkān, son of Chaghatāī Khān, son of Chīngīz Khān.

Since such a chance has come, set thou down[133] now a summary of the history of the Khāns.

Yūnas Khān (d. 892 AH.-1487 AD.) and Aīsān-būghā Khān (d. 866 AH.-1462 AD.) were sons of Wais Khān (d. 832 AH.-1428 AD.).[134] Yūnas Khān's mother was either a daughter or a grand-daughter of Shaikh

Nūru'd-dīn Beg, a Turkistānī Qīpchāq favoured by Tīmūr Beg. When Wais Khān died, the Mughūl horde split in two, one portion being for Yūnas Khān, the greater for Aīsān-būghā Khān. For help in getting the upper hand in the horde, Aīrzīn (var. Aīrāzān) one of the Bārīn *tūmān*-begs and Beg Mīrik *Turkmān*, one of the Chīrās *tūmān*-begs, took Yūnas Khān (aet. 13) and with himFol. 10. three or four thousand Mughūl heads of houses (*awīlūq*), to Aūlūgh Beg Mīrzā (*Shāhrukhī*) with the fittingness that Aūlūgh Beg M. had taken Yūnas Khān's elder sister for his son, 'Abdu'l-'azīz Mīrzā. Aūlūgh Beg Mīrzā did not do well by them; some he imprisoned, some scattered over the country[135] one by one. The Dispersion of Aīrzīn became a date in the Mughūl horde.

Yūnas Khān himself was made to go towards 'Irāq; one year he spent in Tabrīz where Jahān Shāh *Baranī* of the Black Sheep Turkmāns was ruling. From Tabrīz he went to Shīrāz where was Shāhrukh Mīrzā's second son, Ibrāhīm Sulṭān Mīrzā.[136] He having died five or six months later (Shawwal 4, 838 AH.-May 3rd, 1435 AD.), his son, 'Abdu'l-lāh Mīrzā sat in his place. Of this 'Abdu'l-lāh Mīrzā Yūnas Khān became a retainer and to him used to pay his respects. The Khān was in those parts for 17 or 18 years.

In the disturbances between Aūlūgh Beg Mīrzā and his sons, Aīsān-būghā Khān found a chance to invade Farghāna; he plundered as far as Kand-i-badām, came on and, having plundered Andijān, led all its people into captivity.[137] Sl. Abū-sa'īd Mīrzā, after seizing the throne of Samarkand, led an army out to beyond Yāngī (Tarāz) to Aspara in Mughūlistān, Fol. 10b.there gave Aīsān-būghā a good beating and then, to spare himself further trouble from him and with the fittingness that he had just taken to wife[138] Yūnas Khān's elder sister, the former wife of 'Abdu'l-'azīz Mīrzā (*Shāhrukhī*), he invited Yūnas Khān from Khurāsān and 'Irāq, made a feast, became friends and proclaimed him Khān of the Mughūls. Just when he was speeding him forth, the Sāghārīchī *tūmān*-begs had all come into Mughūlistān, in anger with Aīsān-būghā Khān.[139] Yūnas Khān went amongst them and took to wife Aīsān-daulat Begīm, the daughter of their chief, 'Alī-shīr Beg. They then seated him and her on one and the same white felt and raised him to the Khānship.[140]

By this Aīsān-daulat Begīm, Yūnas Khān had three daughters. Mihr-nigār Khānīm was the eldest; Sl. Abū-sa'īd Mīrzā set her aside[141] for his eldest son, Sl. Aḥmad Mīrzā; she had no child. In a throneless time (905 AH.) she fell to Shaibānī Khān; she left Samarkand[142] with Shāh Begīm for Khurāsān (907 AH.) and both came on to me in Kābul (911 AH.). At the time Shaibānī Khān was besieging Nāṣir Mīrzā in Qandahār and I set out for Lamghān[143] (913 AH.) they went to Badakhshān with Khān Mīrzā (Wais).[144] When Mubārak Shāh invited Khān Mīrzā into Fort Victory,[145] they wereFol. 11. captured, together with the wives and families of all their people, by marauders of Ābā-bikr *Kāshgharī* and, as captives to that ill-doing miscreant, bade farewell to this transitory world (*circa* 913 AH.-1507 AD.).

Qūtlūq-nigār Khānīm, my mother, was Yūnas Khān's second daughter. She was with me in most of my guerilla expeditions and throneless times. She went to God's mercy in Muḥarram 911 AH. (June 1505 AD.) five or six months after the capture of Kābul.

Khūb-nigār Khānīm was his third daughter. Her they gave to Muḥammad Ḥusain *Kūrkān Dūghlāt* (899 AH.). She had one son and one daughter by him. 'Ubaid Khān (*Aūzbeg*) took the daughter (Ḥabība).[146] When I captured Samarkand and Bukhārā (917 AH.-1511 AD.), she stayed behind,[147] and when her paternal uncle, Sayyid Muḥammad *Dūghlāt* came as Sl. Sa'īd Khān's envoy to me in Samarkand, she joined him and with him went to Kāshghar where (her cousin), Sl. Sa'īd Khān took her. Khūb-nigār's son was Ḥaidar Mīrzā.[148] He was in my service for three or four years after the Aūzbegs slew his father, then (918 AH.-1512 AD.) asked leave to go to Kāshghar to the presence of Sl. Sa'īd Khān.

"Everything goes back to its source.

Pure gold, or silver or tin."[149]

People say he now lives lawfully (*tā'ib*) and has found the right way (*ṭarīqa*).[150] He has a hand deft in everything, penmanship and painting, and in making arrows and arrow-barbs Fol. 11b.and string-grips; moreover he is a born poet and in a petition written to me, even his style is not bad.[151]

Shāh Begīm was another of Yūnas Khān's ladies. Though he had more, she and Aīsān-daulat Begīm were the mothers of his children. She was one of the (six) daughters of Shāh Sulṭān Muḥammad, Shāh of Badakhshān.[152] His line, they say, runs back to Iskandar Fīlkūs.[153] Sl. Abū-sa'īd Mīrzā took another daughter and by her had Ābā-bikr Mīrzā.[154] By this Shāh Begīm Yūnas Khān had two sons and two daughters. Her first-born but younger than all Aīsān-daulat Begīm's daughters, was Sl. Maḥmūd Khān, called Khānika Khān[155] by many in and about Samarkand. Next younger than he was Sl. Aḥmad Khān, known as Alacha Khān. People say he was called this because he killed many Qālmāqs on the several occasions he beat them. In the Mughūl and Qālmāq tongues, one who will kill (*aūltūrgūchī*) is called *ālāchī*; Alāchī they called him therefore and this by repetition, became Alacha.[156] As occasion arises, the acts and circumstances of these two Khāns will find mention in this history (*tārīkh*).

Sulṭān-nigār Khānīm was the youngest but one of Yūnas Khān's children. Her they made go forth (*chīqārīb īdīlār*)Fol. 12. to Sl. Maḥmūd Mīrzā; by him she had one child, Sl. Wais (Khān Mīrzā), mention of whom will come into this history. When Sl. Maḥmūd Mīrzā died (900 AH.-1495 AD.), she took her son off to her brothers in Tāshkīnt without a word to any single person. They, a few years later, gave her to Adik (Aūng) Sulṭān,[157] a Qāzāq sulṭān of the line of Jūjī Khān, Chīngīz Khān's eldest son. When Shaibānī Khān defeated the Khāns (her brothers), and took Tāshkīnt and Shāhrukhiya (908 AH.), she got away with 10 or 12 of her Mughūl servants, to (her husband), Adik Sulṭān. She had two daughters by Adik Sulṭān; one she gave to a Shaibān sulṭān, the other to Rashīd Sulṭān, the son of (her cousin) Sl. Sa'īd Khān. After Adik Sulṭān's death, (his brother), Qāsim Khān, Khān of the Qāzāq horde, took her.[158] Of all the Qāzāq khāns and sulṭāns, no one, they say, ever kept the horde in such good order as he; his army was reckoned at 300,000 men. On his death the Khānīm went to Sl. Sa'īd Khān's presence in Kāshghar. Daulat-sulṭān Khānīm was Yūnas Khān's youngest child. Fol. 12b.In the Tāshkīnt disaster (908 AH.) she fell to Tīmūr Sulṭān, the son of Shaibānī Khān. By him she had one daughter; they got out of Samarkand with me (918 AH.-1512 AD.), spent three or four years in the Badakhshān country, then went (923 AH.-1420 AD.) to Sl. Sa'īd Khān's presence in Kāshghar.[159]

(*k. Account resumed of Bābur's father's family.*)

In 'Umar Shaikh Mīrzā's *ḥaram* was also Aūlūs Āghā, a daughter of Khwāja Ḥusain Beg; her one daughter died in infancy and they sent her out of the *ḥaram* a year or eighteen months later. Fāṭima-sulṭān Āghā was another; she was of the Mughūl *tūmān*-begs and the first taken of his wives. Qarāgūz (Makhdūm sulṭān) Begīm was another; the Mīrzā took her towards the end of his life; she was much beloved, so to please him, they made her out descended from (his uncle) Minūchihr Mīrzā, the elder brother of Sl. Abū-sa'īd Mīrzā. He had many mistresses and concubines; one, Umīd Āghāchā died before him. Latterly there were also Tūn-sulṭān (var. Yun) of the Mughūls and Āghā Sulṭān.

l. 'Umar Shaikh Mīrzā's Amīrs.

There was Khudāī-bīrdī *Tūghchī Tīmūr-tāsh*, a descendant of the brother of Āq-būghā Beg, the Governor of Hīrī (Herāt, for Tīmūr Beg.) When Sl. Abū-sa'īd Mīrzā, after besieging Jūkī Mīrzā (*Shāhrukhī*) in Shāhrukhiya (868AH.-1464AD.) gave the Fol. 13.Farghāna country to 'Umar Shaikh Mīrzā, he put this Khudāī-bīrdī Beg at the head of the Mīrzā's Gate.[160] Khudāī-bīrdī was then 25 but youth notwithstanding, his rules and management were very good indeed. A few years later when Ibrāhīm *Begchīk* was plundering near Aūsh, he followed him up, fought him, was beaten and became a martyr. At the time, Sl. Aḥmad Mīrzā was in the summer pastures of Āq Qāchghāī, in Aūrā-tīpā, 18 *yīghāch* east of Samarkand, and Sl. Abū-sa'īd Mīrzā was at Bābā Khākī, 12 *yīghāch* east of Hīrī. People sent the news post-haste to the Mīrzā(s),[161] having humbly represented it through 'Abdu'l-wahhāb *Shaghāwal.* In four days it was carried those 120 *yīghāch* of road.[162]

Ḥāfiẓ Muḥammad Beg *Dūldāī* was another, Sl. Malik *Kāshgharī's* son and a younger brother of Aḥmad Ḥājī Beg. After the death of Khudāī-bīrdī Beg, they sent him to control 'Umar Shaikh Mīrzā's Gate, but he did not get on well with the Andijān begs and therefore, when Sl. Abū-sa'īd Mīrzā died, went to Samarkand and took service with Sl. Aḥmad Mīrzā. At the time of the disaster on the Chīr, he was in Aūrā-tīpā and made it over to 'Umar Shaikh Mīrzā when the Mīrzā Fol. 13b.passed through on his way to Samarkand, himself taking service with him. The Mīrzā, for his part, gave him the Andijān Command. Later on he went to Sl. Maḥmūd Khān in Tāshkīnt and was there entrusted with the guardianship of Khān Mīrzā (Wais) and given Dīzak. He had started for Makka by way of Hind before I took Kābul (910AH. Oct. 1504AD.), but he went to God's mercy on the road. He was a simple person, of few words and not clever.

Khwāja Ḥusain Beg was another, a good-natured and simple person. It is said that, after the fashion of those days, he used to improvise very well at drinking parties.[163]

Shaikh Mazīd Beg was another, my first guardian, excellent in rule and method. He must have served (*khidmat qīlghān dūr*) under Bābur Mīrzā (*Shāhrukhī*). There was no greater beg in 'Umar Shaikh Mīrzā's presence. He was a vicious person and kept catamites.

'Alī-mazīd *Qūchīn* was another;[164] he rebelled twice, once at Akhsī, once at Tāshkīnt. He was disloyal, untrue to his salt, vicious and good-for-nothing.

Ḥasan (son of) Yaq'ūb was another, a small-minded, good-tempered, smart and active man. This verse is his:—

"Return, O Huma, for without the parrot-down of thy lip,

The crow will assuredly soon carry off my bones."[165]

Fol. 14.He was brave, a good archer, played polo (*chaughān*) well and leapt well at leap-frog.[166] He had the control of my Gate after 'Umar Shaikh Mīrzā's accident. He had not much sense, was narrow-minded and somewhat of a strife-stirrer.

Qāsim Beg *Qūchīn*, of the ancient army-begs of Andijān, was another. He had the control of my Gate after Ḥasan Yaq'ūb Beg. His life through, his authority and consequence waxed without decline. He was a brave man;

once he gave some Aūzbegs a good beating when he overtook them raiding near Kāsān; his sword hewed away in 'Umar Shaikh Mīrzā's presence; and in the fight at the Broad Ford (Yāsī-kījīt *circa* 904AH.-July, 1499AD.) he hewed away with the rest. In the guerilla days he went to Khusrau Shāh (907AH.) at the time I was planning to go from the Macha hill-country[167] to Sl. Maḥmūd Khān, but he came back to me in 910AH. (1504AD.) and I shewed him all my old favour and affection. When I attacked the Turkmān Hazāra raiders in Dara-i-khwush (911AH.) he made better advance, spite of his age, than the younger men; I gave him Bangash as a reward and later on, after returning to Kābul, made him Humāyūn's guardian. He went to God's mercyFol. 14b. about the time Zamīn-dāwar was taken (*circa* 928AH.-1522AD.). He was a pious, God-fearing Musalmān, an abstainer from doubtful aliments; excellent in judgment and counsel, very facetious and, though he could neither read nor write (*ummiy*), used to make entertaining jokes.

Bābā Beg's Bābā Qulī ('Alī) was another, a descendant of Shaikh 'Alī *Bahādur.*[168] They made him my guardian when Shaikh Mazīd Beg died. He went over to Sl. Aḥmad Mīrzā when the Mīrzā led his army against Andijān (899AH.), and gave him Aūrā-tīpā. After Sl. Maḥmūd Mīrzā's death, he left Samarkand and was on his way to join me (900AH.) when Sl. 'Alī Mīrzā, issuing out of Aūrā-tīpā, fought, defeated and slew him. His management and equipment were excellent and he took good care of his men. He prayed not; he kept no fasts; he was like a heathen and he was a tyrant.

'Alī-dost Ṭaghāī[169] was another, one of the Sāghārīchī *tumān*-begs and a relation of my mother's mother, Aīsān-daulat Begīm. I favoured him more than he had been favoured in 'Umar Shaikh Mīrzā's time. People said, "Work will come from his hand." But in the many years he was in my presence, no Fol. 15.work to speak of[170] came to sight. He must have served Sl. Abū-sa'īd Mīrzā. He claimed to have power to bring on rain with the jade-stone. He was the Falconer (*qūshchī*),worthless by nature and habit, a stingy, severe, strife-stirring person, false, self-pleasing, rough of tongue and cold-of-face.

Wais *Lāgharī*,[171] one of the Samarkand *Tūghchī* people, was another. Latterly he was much in 'Umar Shaikh Mīrzā's confidence; in the guerilla times he was with me. Though somewhat factious, he was a man of good judgment and counsel.

Mīr Ghiyāṡ Ṭaghāi was another, a younger brother of 'Ali-dost Ṭaghāī. No man amongst the leaders in Sl. Abū-sa'īd Mīrzā's Gate was more to the front than he; he had charge of the Mīrzā's square seal[172] and was much in his confidence latterly. He was a friend of Wais *Lāgharī*. When Kāsān had been given to Sl. Maḥmūd Khān (899AH.-1494AD.), he was continuously in The Khān's service and was in high favour. He was a laugher, a joker and fearless in vice.

'Ali-darwesh *Khurāsānī* was another. He had served in the Khurāsān Cadet Corps, one of two special corps of serviceable young men formed by Sl. Abū-sa'īd Mīrzā when he first began Fol. 15b.to arrange the government of Khurāsān and Samarkand, and, presumably, called by him the Khurāsān Corps and the Samarkand Corps. 'Alī-darwesh was a brave man; he did well in my presence at the Gate of Bīshkārān.[173] He wrote the *naskh ta'līq* hand clearly.[174] His was the flatterer's tongue and in his character avarice was supreme.

Qaṃbar-'alī *Mughūl* of the Equerries (*akhtachī*) was another. People called him The Skinner because his father, on first coming into the (Farghāna) country, worked as a skinner. Qaṃbar-'alī had been Yūnas Khān's water-bottle bearer,[175] later on he became a beg. Till he was a made man, his conduct was excellent; once arrived, he was slack. He was full of talk and of foolish talk,—a great talker is sure to be a foolish one,—his capacity was limited and his brain muddy.

(*l. Historical narrative.*)

At the time of 'Umar Shaikh Mīrzā's accident, I was in the Four Gardens (*Chār-bāgh*) of Andijān.[176] The news reached Andijān on Tuesday, Ramẓan 5 (June 9th); I mounted at once, with my followers and retainers, intending to go into the fort but, on our getting near the Mīrzā's Gate, Shīrīm Ṭaghāī[177] took hold of my bridle and moved off towards the Praying Place.[178] It had crossed his mind that if a great ruler like Sl. Aḥmad Mīrzā came in force, the Andijān begs would make over to himFol. 16. me and the country,[179] but that if he took me to Aūzkīnt and the foothills thereabouts, I, at any rate, should not be made over and could go to one of my mother's (half-) brothers, Sl. Maḥmūd Khān or Sl. Aḥmad Khān.[180] When Khwāja Maulānā-i-qāẓī[181] and the begs in the fort heard of (the intended departure), they sent after us Khwāja Muḥammad, the tailor,[184] an old servant (*bāyrī*) of my father and the foster-father of one of his daughters. He dispelled our fears and, turning back from near the Praying Fol. 16b.Place, took me with him into the citadel (*ark*) where I dismounted. Khwāja Maulānā-i-qāẓī and the begs came to my presence there and after bringing their counsels to a head,[185] busied themselves in making good the towers and ramparts of the fort.[186] A few days later, Ḥasan, son of Yaq'ūb, and Qāsim *Qūchīn*, arrived, together with other begs who had been sent to reconnoitre in Marghīnān and those parts.[187] They also, after waiting on me, set themselves with one heart and mind and with zeal and energy, to hold the fort.

(*Author's note on Khwāja Maulānā-i-qāẓī.*) He was the son of Sl. Aḥmad Qāẓī, of the line of Burhānu'd-dīn 'Alī *Qīlīch*[182] and through his mother, traced back to Sl. Aīlīk *Māẓī*.[183] By hereditary right (*yūsūnlūq*) his high family (*khānwādalār*) must have come to be the Refuge (*marji'*) and Pontiffs (*Shaikhu'l-islām*) of the (Farghāna) country.

Meantime Sl. Aḥmad Mīrzā took Aūrā-tīpā, Khujand and Marghīnān, came on to Qabā,[188] 4 *yīghāch* from Andijān and there made halt. At this crisis, Darwesh Gau, one of the Andijān notables, was put to death on account of his improper proposals; his punishment crushed the rest.

Khwāja Qāẓī and Aūzūn (Long) Ḥasan,[189] (brother) of Khwāja Ḥusain, were then sent to Sl. Aḥmad Mīrzā to say in effect that, as he himself would place one of his servants in the country and as I was myself both a servant and (as) a son, he would attain his end most readily and easily if he entrusted the service to me. He was a mild, weak man, of few words who, without his begs, decided no opinion or compact (*aun*), action or move; they paid attention to our proposal, gave it a harsh answer and moved forward.

But the Almighty God, who, of His perfect power and without mortal aid, has ever brought my affairs to their right issue, made such things happen here that they became disgusted at having advanced (*i.e.* from Qabā), repented indeed that they had ever set out on this expedition and turned back with nothing done.

One of those things was this: Qabā has a stagnant, morass-like Water,[190] passable only by the bridge. As they were many, there was crowding on the bridge and numbers of horses andFol. 17. camels were pushed off to perish in the water. This disaster recalling the one they had had three or four years earlier when they were badly beaten at the passage of the Chīr, they gave way to fear. Another thing was that such a murrain broke out amongst their horses that, massed together, they began to die off in bands.[191] Another was that they found in our soldiers and peasants a resolution and single-mindedness such as would not let them flinch from making offering of their lives[192] so long as there was breath and power in their bodies. Need being therefore, when one *yīghāch* from Andijān, they sent Darwesh Muḥammad Tarkhān[193] to us; Ḥasan of Yaq'ūb went out from those in the fort; the two had an interview near the Praying Place and a sort of peace was made. This done, Sl. Aḥmad Mīrzā's force retired.

Meantime Sl. Maḥmūd Khān had come along the north of the Khujand Water and laid siege to Akhsī.[194] In Akhsī was Jahāngīr Mīrzā (aet. 9) and of begs, 'Alī-darwesh Beg, Mīrzā Qulī *Kūkūldāsh*, Muḥ. Bāqir Beg and Shaikh 'Abdu'l-lāh, Lord of the Gate. Wais *Lāgharī* and Mīr Ghiyāṡ Ṭaghāī had been there too, but being afraid of the (Akhsī) begs had gone off to Kāsān, Wais *Lāgharī's* district, where, he being Nāṣir Mīrzā's guardian, the Mīrzā was.[195] They went over to Sl. Maḥmūd Khān when he got near Akhsī; Mīr Ghiyāṣ̤ entered his service; Fol. 17b.Wais *Lāgharī* took Nāṣir Mīrzā to Sl. Aḥmad Mīrzā, who entrusted him to Muh. Mazīd Tarkhān's charge. The Khān, though he fought several times near Akhsī, could not effect anything because the Akhsī begs and braves made such splendid offering of their lives. Falling sick, being tired of fighting too, he returned to his own country (*i.e.* Tāshkīnt).

For some years, Ābā-bikr *Kāshgharī Dūghlāt*,[196] bowing the head to none, had been supreme in Kāshgar and Khutan. He now, moved like the rest by desire for my country, came to the neighbourhood of Aūzkīnt, built a fort and began to lay the land waste. Khwāja Qāzī and several begs were appointed to drive him out. When they came near, he saw himself no match for such a force, made the Khwāja his mediator and, by a hundred wiles and tricks, got himself safely free.

Throughout these great events, 'Umar Shaikh Mīrzā's former begs and braves had held resolutely together and made daring offer of their lives. The Mīrzā's mother, Shāh Sulṭān Begīm,[197] and Jaḥāngīr Mīrzā and the *ḥaram* household and the begs came from Akhsī to Andijān; the customary mourning was fulfilled and food and victuals spread for the poor and destitute.[198]

Fol. 18.In the leisure from these important matters, attention was given to the administration of the country and the ordering of the army. The Andijān Government and control of my Gate were settled (*mukarrar*) for Ḥasan (son) of Yaq'ūb; Aūsh was decided on (*qarār*) for Qāsim *Qūchīn*; Akhsī and Marghīnān assigned (*ta'īn*) to Aūzun Ḥasan and 'Alī-dost Ṭaghāī. For the rest of 'Umar Shaikh Mīrzā's begs and braves, to each according to his circumstances, were settled and assigned district (*wilāyat*) or land (*yīr*) or office (*mauja*) or charge (*jīrga*) or stipend (*wajh*).

When Sl. Aḥmad Mīrzā had gone two or three stages on his return-march, his health changed for the worse and high fever appeared. On his reaching the Āq Sū near Aūrā-tīpā, he bade farewell to this transitory world, in the middle of Shawwāl of the date 899 (mid July 1494 AD.) being then 44 (lunar) years old.

m. Sl. Aḥmad Mīrzā's birth and descent.

He was born in 855 AH. (1451 AD.) the year in which his father took the throne (*i.e.* Samarkand). He was Sl. Abū-sa'īd Mīrzā's eldest son; his mother was a daughter of Aūrdū-būghā Tarkhān (*Arghūn*), the elder sister of

Darwesh Muḥammad Tarkhān, and the most honoured of the Mīrzā's wives.

n. His appearance and habits.

He was a tall, stout, brown-bearded and red-faced man. He had beard on his chin but none on his cheeks. He had veryFol. 18b. pleasing manners. As was the fashion in those days, he wound his turban in four folds and brought the end forward over his brows.

o. His characteristics and manners.

He was a True Believer, pure in the Faith; five times daily, without fail, he recited the Prayers, not omitting them even on drinking-days. He was a disciple of his Highness Khwāja 'Ubaidu'l-lāh (*Aḥrāri*), his instructor in religion and the strengthener of his Faith. He was very ceremonious, particularly when sitting with the Khwāja. People say he never drew one knee over the other[199] at any entertainment of the Khwāja. On one occasion contrary to his custom, he sat with his feet together. When he had risen, the Khwāja ordered the place he had sat in to be searched; there they found, it may have been, a bone.[200] He had read nothing whatever and was ignorant (*'ami*), and though town-bred, unmannered and homely. Of genius he had no share. He was just and as his Highness the Khwāja was there, accompanying him step by step,[201] most of his affairs found lawful settlement. He was true and faithful to his vow and word; nothing was ever seen to the contrary. He had courage, and though he never happened to get in his own hand to work, gave sign of it, they say, in some of his encounters. Fol. 19.He drew a good bow, generally hitting the duck[202] both with his arrows (*aūq*) and his forked-arrows (*tīr-giz*), and, as a rule, hit the gourd[203] in riding across the lists (*maidān*). Latterly, when he had grown stout, he used to take quail and pheasant with the goshawks,[204] rarely failing. A sportsman he was, hawking mostly and hawking well; since Aūlūgh Beg Mīrzā, such a sporting *pādshāh* had not been seen. He was extremely decorous; people say he used to hide his feet even in the privacy of his family and amongst his intimates. Once settled down to drink, he would drink for 20 or 30 days at a stretch; once risen, would not drink again for another 20 or 30 days. He was a good drinker;[205] on non-drinking days he ate without conviviality (*basīṭ*). Avarice was dominant in his character. He was kindly, a man of few words whose will was in the hands of his begs.

p. His battles.

He fought four battles. The first was with Ni'mat *Arghūn*, Shaikh Jamāl *Arghūn's* younger brother, at Āqār-tūzī, near Zamīn. This he won. The second was with 'Umar Shaikh Mīrzā at Khwaṣ; this also he won. The third affair was when he encountered Sl. Maḥmūd Khān on the Chīr, near Tāshkīnt Fol. 19b.(895 AH.-1469 AD.). There was no real fighting, but some Mughūl plunderers coming up, by ones and twos, in his rear and laying hands on his baggage, his great army, spite of its numbers, broke up without a blow struck, without an effort made, without a coming face to face, and its main body was drowned in the Chīr.[206] His fourth affair was with Ḥaidar *Kūkūldāsh* (*Mughūl*), near Yār-yīlāq; here he won.

q. His country.

Samarkand and Bukhārā his father gave him; Tāshkīnt and Sairām he took and held for a time but gave them to his younger brother, 'Umar Shaikh Mīrzā, after 'Abdu'l-qadūs (*Dūghlāt*) slew Shaikh Jamāl (*Arghūn*); Khujand and Aūrātīpā were also for a time in his possession.

r. His children.

His two sons did not live beyond infancy. He had five daughters, four by Qātāq Begīm.[207]

Rābi'a-sulṭān Begīm, known as the Dark-eyed Begīm, was his eldest. The Mīrzā himself made her go forth to Sl. Maḥmūd Khān;[208] she had one child, a nice little boy, called Bābā Khān. The Aūzbegs killed him and several others of age as unripe as his when they martyred (his father) The Khān, in Khujand, (914 AH.-1508 AD.). At that time she fell to Jānī Beg Sulṭān (*Aūzbeg*).Fol. 20.

Ṣāliḥa-sulṭān (Ṣalīqa) Begīm was his second daughter; people called her the Fair Begīm. Sl. Maḥmūd Mīrzā, after her father's death, took her for his eldest son, Sl. Mas'ūd Mīrzā and made the wedding feast (900 AH.). Later on she fell to the Kāshgharī with Shāh Begīm and Mihr-nigār Khānim.

'Āyisha-sulṭān Begīm was the third. When I was five and went to Samarkand, they set her aside for me; in the guerilla times[209] she came to Khujand and I took her (905 AH.); her one little daughter, born after the second taking of Samarkand, went in a few days to God's mercy and she herself left me at the instigation of an older sister.

Sulṭānīm Begīm was the fourth daughter; Sl. 'Alī Mīrzā took her; then Tīmūr Sulṭān (*Aūzbeg*) took her and after him, Mahdī Sulṭān (*Aūzbeg*).

Ma'sūma-sulṭān Begīm was the youngest of Sl. Aḥmad Mīrzā's daughters. Her mother, Ḥabība-sulṭān Begīm, was of the Arghūns, a daughter of Sl. Ḥusain *Arghūn's* brother. I saw her when I went to Khurāsān (912 AH.-1506 AD.), liked her, asked for her, had her brought to Kābul and took her (913 AH.-1507 AD.). She had one daughter and there and then, went to

God's mercy, through the pains of the birth. Her name was at once given to her child.

s. His ladies and mistresses.

Mihr-nigār Khānīm was his first wife, set aside for him by his father, Sl. Abū-sa'īd Mīrzā. She was Yūnas Khān's eldest Fol. 20b.daughter and my mother's full-sister.

Tarkhān Begīm of the Tarkhāns was another of his wives.

Qātāq Begīm was another, the foster-sister of the Tarkhān Begīm just mentioned. Sl. Aḥmad Mīrzā took her *par amours* (*'āshiqlār bīlā*): she was loved with passion and was very dominant. She drank wine. During the days of her ascendancy (*tīrīklīk*), he went to no other of his *ḥaram*; at last he took up a proper position (*aūlnūrdī*) and freed himself from his reproach.[210]

Khān-zāda Begīm, of the Tīrmīẕ Khāns, was another. He had just taken her when I went, at five years old, to Samarkand; her face was still veiled and, as is the Turkī custom, they told me to uncover it.[211]

Laṭīf Begīm was another, a daughter's child of Aḥmad Ḥājī Beg *Dūldāī* (*Barlās*). After the Mīrzā's death, Ḥamza Sl. took her and she had three sons by him. They with other sulṭāns' children, fell into my hands when I took Ḥiṣār (916 AH.-1510 AD.) after defeating Ḥamza Sulṭān and Tīmūr Sulṭān. I set all free.

Ḥabība-sulṭān Begīm was another, a daughter of the brother of Sl. Ḥusain *Arghūn*.

t. His amīrs.

Jānī Beg *Dūldāī* (*Barlās*) was a younger brother of Sl. Malik *Kāshgharī*. Sl. Abū-sa'īd Mīrzā gave him the Government of Samarkand and Sl. Aḥmad Mīrzā gave him the control of his own Gate.[212] He must have had singular habits andFol. 21. manners;[213] many strange stories are told about him. One is this:—While he was Governor in Samarkand, an envoy came to him from the Aūzbegs renowned, as it would seem, for his strength. An Aūzbeg, is said to call a strong man a bull (*būkuh*). "Are you a *būkuh*?" said Jānī Beg to the envoy, "If you are, come, let's have a friendly wrestle together (*kūrāshālīng*)." Whatever objections the envoy raised, he refused to accept. They wrestled and Jānī Beg gave the fall. He was a brave man.

Aḥmad Ḥājī (*Dūldāī Barlās*) was another, a son of Sl. Malik *Kāshgharī*. Sl. Abū-sa'īd Mīrzā gave him the Government of Hīrī (Harāt) for a time but sent him when his uncle, Jānī Beg died, to Samarkand with his uncle's appointments. He was pleasant-natured and brave. Wafā'ī was his pen-name and he put together a dīwān in verse not bad. This couplet is his:

"I am drunk, Inspector, to-day keep your hand off me,

"Inspect me on the day you catch me sober."

Mīr 'Alī-sher Nāwā'ī when he went from Hīrī to Samarkand, was with Aḥmad Ḥājī Beg but he went back to Hīrī when Sl. Ḥusain Mīrzā (Bāī-qarā) became supreme (873 AH.-1460 AD.) and he there received exceeding favour.

Fol. 21b.Aḥmad Ḥājī Beg kept and rode excellent *tīpūchāqs*,[214] mostly of his own breeding. Brave he was but his power to command did not match his courage; he was careless and what was necessary in his affairs, his retainers and followers put through. He fell into Sl. 'Alī Mīrzā's hands when the Mīrzā defeated Bāī-sunghar Mīrzā in Bukhārā (901 AH.), and was then put to a dishonourable death on the charge of the blood of Darwesh Muḥammad Tarkhān.[215]

Darwesh Muḥammad Tarkhān (*Arghūn*) was another, the son of Aūrdū-būghā Tarkhān and full-brother of the mother of Sl. Aḥmad Mīrzā and Sl. Maḥmūd Mīrzā.[216] Of all begs in Sl. Aḥmad Mīrzā's presence, he was the greatest and most honoured. He was an orthodox Believer, kindly and darwesh-like, and was a constant transcriber of the Qu'rān.[217] He played chess often and well, thoroughly understood the science of fowling and flew his birds admirably. He died in the height of his greatness, with a bad name, during the troubles between Sl. 'Alī Mīrzā and Bāī-sunghar Mīrzā.[218]

'Abdu'l-'alī Tarkhān was another, a near relation of Darwesh Muḥammad Tarkhān, possessor also of his younger sister,[219] that is to say, Bāqī Tarkhān's mother. Though both by the Mughūl rule (*tūrā*) and by his rank, Darwesh Muḥammad Tarkhān was the superior of 'Abdu'l-'alī Tarkhān, this Pharoah regarded him not at all. For some years he had the Government of Bukhārā. His retainers were reckoned atFol. 22. 3,000 and he kept them well and handsomely. His gifts (*bakhshīsh*), his visits of enquiry (*purshīsh*), his public audience (*dīwān*), his work-shops (*dast-gāh*), his open-table (*shīlān*) and his assemblies (*majlis*) were all like a king's. He was a strict disciplinarian, a tyrannical, vicious, self-infatuated person. Shaibānī Khān, though not his retainer, was with him for a time; most of the lesser (Shaibān) sulṭāns did themselves take service with him. This same 'Abdu'l-'alī Tarkhān was the cause of Shaibānī Khān's rise to such a height and of the downfall of such ancient dynasties.[220]

Sayyid Yūsuf, the Grey Wolfer[221] was another; his grandfather will have come from the Mughūl horde; his father was favoured by Aūlūgh Beg

Mīrzā (*Shāhrukhī*). His judgment and counsel were excellent; he had courage too. He played well on the guitar (*qūbuz*). He was with me when I first went to Kābul; I shewed him great favour and in truth he was worthy of favour. I left him in Kābul the first year the army rode out for Hindūstān; at that time he went to God's mercy.[222]

Darwesh Beg was another; he was of the line of Aīku-tīmūr Beg,[223] a favourite of Tīmūr Beg. He was a disciple of his Highness Khwāja 'Ubaidu'l-lāh (*Aḥrārī*), had knowledge of the science of music, played several instruments and was naturallyFol. 22b. disposed to poetry. He was drowned in the Chīr at the time of Sl. Aḥmad Mīrzā's discomfiture.

Muḥammad Mazīd Tarkhān was another, a younger full-brother of Darwesh Muḥ. Tarkhān. He was Governor in Turkistān for some years till Shaibānī Khān took it from him. His judgment and counsel were excellent; he was an unscrupulous and vicious person. The second and third times I took Samarkand, he came to my presence and each time I shewed him very great favour. He died in the fight at Kūl-i-malik (918 AH.-1512 AD.).

Bāqī Tarkhān was another, the son of 'Abdu'l-'alī Tarkhān and Sl. Aḥmad Mīrzā's aunt. When his father died, they gave him Bukhārā. He grew in greatness under Sl. 'Alī Mīrzā, his retainers numbering 5 or 6,000. He was neither obedient nor very submissive to Sl. 'Alī Mīrzā. He fought Shaibānī Khān at Dabūsī (905 AH.) and was crushed; by the help of this defeat, Shaibānī Khān went and took Bukhārā. He was very fond of hawking; they say he kept 700 birds. His manners and habits were not such as may be told;[224] he grew up with a Mīrzā's state and splendour. Because his father had shewn favour to Shaibānī Khān, he went to the Khān's presence, but that inhuman ingrate made him no sort of return in favour and kindness. Fol. 23.He left the world at Akhsī, in misery and wretchedness.

Sl. Ḥusain *Arghūn* was another. He was known as Qarā-kūlī because he had held the Qarā-kūl government for a time. His judgment and counsel were excellent; he was long in my presence also.

Qulī Muḥammad *Būghdā*[225] was another, a *qūchīn*; he must have been a brave man.

'Abdu'l-karīm *Ishrit*[226] was another; he was an Aūīghūr, Sl. Aḥmad Mīrzā's Lord of the Gate, a brave and generous man.

(*u. Historical narrative resumed.*)

After Sl. Aḥmad Mīrzā's death, his begs in agreement, sent a courier by the mountain-road to invite Sl. Maḥmūd Mīrzā.[227]

Malik-i-Muḥammad Mīrzā, the son of Minūchihr Mīrzā, Sl. Abū-sa'īd Mīrzā's eldest brother, aspired for his own part to rule. Having drawn a few adventurers and desperadoes to himself, they dribbled away[228] from (Sl. Aḥmad Mīrzā's) camp and went to Samarkand. He was not able to effect anything, but he brought about his own death and that of several innocent persons of the ruling House.

At once on hearing of his brother's death, Sl. Maḥmūd Mīrzā went off to Samarkand and there seated himself on the throne, without difficulty. Some of his doings soon disgusted and alienated high and low, soldier and peasant. The first of these was that he sent the above-named Malik-i-Muḥammad to theFol. 23b. Kūk-sarāī,[229] although he was his father's brother's son and his own son-in-law.[230] With him he sent others, four Mīrzās in all. Two of these he set aside; Malik-i-Muḥammad and one other he martyred. Some of the four were not even of ruling rank and had not the smallest aspiration to rule; though Malik-i-Muḥammad Mīrzā was a little in fault, in the rest there was no blame whatever. A second thing was that though his methods and regulations were excellent, and though he was expert in revenue matters and in the art of administration, his nature inclined to tyranny and vice. Directly he reached Samarkand, he began to make new regulations and arrangements and to rate and tax on a new basis. Moreover the dependants of his (late) Highness Khwāja 'Ubaid'l-lāh, under whose protection formerly many poor and destitute persons had lived free from the burden of dues and imposts, were now themselves treated with harshness and oppression. On what ground should hardship have touched them? Nevertheless oppressive exactions were made from them, indeed from the Khwāja's very children. Yet another thing was that just as he was vicious and tyrannical, so were his begs, small and great, and his retainers and followers. The Ḥiṣārīs and in particular the followers of Khusrau Shāh engaged themselves unceasingly with wine and fornication. Once one of them enticed and took away a certain man's wife. Fol. 24.When her husband went to Khusrau Shāh and asked for justice, he received for answer: "She has been with you for several years; let her be a few days with him." Another thing was that the young sons of the townsmen and shopkeepers, nay! even of Turks and soldiers could not go out from their houses from fear of being taken for catamites. The Samarakandīs, having passed 20 or 25 years under Sl. Aḥmad Mīrzā in ease and tranquillity, most matters carried through lawfully and with justice by his Highness the Khwāja, were wounded and troubled in heart and soul, by this oppression and this vice. Low and high, the poor, the destitute, all opened the mouth to curse, all lifted the hand for redress.

"Beware the steaming up of inward wounds,

For an inward wound at the last makes head;

Avoid while thou canst, distress to one heart,

For a single sigh will convulse a world."[231]

By reason of his infamous violence and vice Sl. Maḥmud Mīrzā did not rule in Samarkand more than five or six months.

900 AH.-OCT. 2ND. 1494 TO SEP. 21ST. 1495 AD.232

This year Sl. Maḥmūd Mīrzā sent an envoy, named 'Abdu'l-qadūs Beg,[233] to bring me a gift from the wedding he had made with splendid festivity for his eldest son, Mas'ūd Mīrzā with (Ṣāliḥa-sulṭān), the Fair Begīm, the second daughter of his elder brother, Sl. Aḥmad Mīrzā. They had sent gold and silver almonds and pistachios.

There must have been relationship between this envoy and Ḥasan-i-yaq'ūb, and on its account he will have been the man sent to make Ḥasan-i-yaq'ūb, by fair promises, look towards Sl. Maḥmūd Mīrzā. Ḥasan-i-yaq'ūb returned him a smooth answer, made indeed as though won over to his side, and gave him leave to go. Five or six months later, his manners changed entirely; he began to behave ill to those about me and to others, and he carried matters so far that he would have dismissed me in order to put Jahāngīr Mīrzā in my place. Moreover his conversation with the whole body of begs and soldiers was not what should be; every-one came to know what was in his mind. Khwāja-i-Qāzī and (Sayyid) Qāsim *Qūchīn* and 'Alī-dost Ṭaghāī met other well-wishers of mine in the presence of my grandmother, Āīsān-daulat Begīm and decided to give quietus to Ḥasan-i-yaq'ūb's disloyalty by his deposition.

Few amongst women will have been my grandmother's equals for judgment and counsel; she was very wise and far-sighted and most affairs of mine were carried through under her advice. She and my mother were (living) in the Gate-house of the outer fort;[234] Ḥasan-i-yaq'ūb was in the citadel.

When I went to the citadel, in pursuance of our decision, he had ridden out, presumably for hawking, and as soon as he had Fol. 25.our news, went off from where he was towards Samarkand. The begs and others in sympathy with him,[235] were arrested; one was Muḥammad Bāqir Beg; Sl. Maḥmud *Dūldāī*, Sl. Muḥammad *Dūldāī's* father, was another; there were several more; to some leave was given to go for Samarkand. The Andijān Government and control of my Gate were settled on (Sayyid) Qāsim *Qūchīn*.

A few days after Ḥasan-i-yaq'ūb reached Kand-i-badām on the Samarkand road, he went to near the Khūqān sub-division (*aūrchīn*) with ill-intent on Akhsī. Hearing of it, we sent several begs and braves to oppose him; they, as they went, detached a scouting party ahead; he, hearing this, moved against the detachment, surrounded it in its night-quarters[236] and poured flights of arrows (*shība*) in on it. In the darkness of the night an arrow (*aūq*), shot by one of his own men, hit him just (*aūq*) in the vent (*qāchār*) and before he could take vent (*qāchār*),[237] he became the captive of his own act.

"If you have done ill, keep not an easy mind,

For retribution is Nature's law."[238]

This year I began to abstain from all doubtful food, my obedience extended even to the knife, the spoon and the table-cloth;[239] also the after-midnight Prayer (*taḥajjud*) was Fol. 25b.less neglected.

(a. Death of Sl. Maḥmūd Mīrzā.)

In the month of the latter Rabī' (January 1495 AD.), Sl. Maḥmūd Mīrzā was confronted by violent illness and in six days, passed from the world. He was 43 (lunar) years old.

b. His birth and lineage.

He was born in 857 AH. (1453 AD.), was Sl. Abū-sa'īd Mīrzā's third son and the full-brother of Sl. Aḥmad Mīrzā.[240]

c. His appearance and characteristics.

He was a short, stout, sparse-bearded and somewhat ill-shaped person. His manners and his qualities were good, his rules and methods of business excellent; he was well-versed in accounts, not a *dinār* or a *dirhām*[241] of revenue was spent without his knowledge. The pay of his servants was never disallowed. His assemblies, his gifts, his open table, were all good. Everything of his was orderly and well-arranged;[242] no soldier or peasant could deviate in the slightest from any plan of his. Formerly he must have been hard set (*qātīrār*) on hawking but latterly he very frequently hunted driven game.[243] He carried violence and vice to frantic excess, was a constant wine-bibber and kept many catamites. If anywhere in his territory, there was a handsome boy, he used, by whatever means, to have him brought for a catamite; of his begs' sons and of his sons' begs' sons he made catamites; and laid command for this service onFol. 26. his very foster brothers and on their own brothers. So common in his day was that vile practice, that no person was without his catamite; to keep one was thought a merit, not to keep one, a defect. Through his infamous violence and vice, his sons died in the day of their strength (*tamām juwān*).

He had a taste for poetry and put a *dīwān*[244] together but his verse is flat and insipid,—not to compose is better than to compose verse such as his. He was not firm in the Faith and held his Highness Khwāja 'Ubaidu'l-lāh (*Aḥrārī*) in slight esteem. He had no heart (*yūruk*) and was somewhat scant in modesty,—several of his impudent buffoons used to do their filthy and abominable acts in his full Court, in all men's sight. He spoke badly, there was no understanding him at first.

d. His battles.

He fought two battles, both with Sl. Ḥusain Mīrzā (*Bāīqarā*). The first was in Astarābād; here he was defeated. The second was at Chīkman (Sarāī),[245] near Andikhūd; here also he was defeated. He went twice to Kāfiristān, on the Fol. 26b.south of Badakhshān, and made Holy War; for this reason they wrote him Sl. Maḥmūd *Ghāzī* in the headings of his public papers.

e. His countries.

Sl. Abū-sa'īd Mīrzā gave him Astarābād.[246] After the 'Irāq disaster (*i.e.*, his father's death,) he went into Khurāsān. At that time, Qaṃbar-'alī Beg, the governor of Ḥiṣār, by Sl. Abū-sa'īd Mīrzā's orders, had mobilized the Hindūstān[247] army and was following him into 'Irāq; he joined Sl. Maḥmūd Mīrzā in Khurāsān but the Khurāsānīs, hearing of Sl. Ḥusain Mīrzā's approach, rose suddenly and drove them out of the country. On this Sl. Maḥmūd Mīrzā went to his elder brother, Sl. Aḥmad Mīrzā in Samarkand. A few months later Sayyid Badr and Khusrau Shāh and some braves under Aḥmad

Mushtāq[248] took him and fled to Qaṃbar-'alī in Ḥiṣār. From that time forth, Sl. Maḥmūd Mīrzā possessed the countries lying south of Quhqa (Quhlugha) and the Kohtin Range as far as the Hindū-kush Mountains, such as Tīrmīẕ, Chaghānīān, Ḥiṣār, Khutlān, Qūndūz and Badakhshān. He also held Sl. Aḥmad Mīrzā's lands, after his brother's death.

f. His children.

He had five sons and eleven daughters.

Sl. Mas'ūd Mīrzā was his eldest son; his mother was Khān-zādaFol 27. Begīm, a daughter of the Great Mīr of Tīrmīẕ. Bāī-sunghar Mīrzā was another; his mother was Pasha (or Pāshā) Begīm. Sl. 'Alī Mīrzā was another; his mother was an Aūzbeg, a concubine called Zuhra Begī Āghā. Sl. Ḥusain Mīrzā was another; his mother was Khān-zāda Begīm, a grand-daughter of the Great Mīr of Tīrmīẕ; he went to God's mercy in his father's life-time, at the age of 13. Sl. Wais Mīrzā (Mīrzā Khān) was another; his mother, Sulṭān-nigār Khānīm was a daughter of Yūnas Khān and was a younger (half-)

sister of my mother. The affairs of these four Mīrzās will be written of in this history under the years of their occurrence.

Of Sl. Maḥmūd Mīrzā's daughters, three were by the same mother as Bāī-sunghar Mīrzā. One of these, Bāī-sunghar Mīrzā's senior, Sl. Maḥmūd Mīrzā made to go out to Malik-i-muḥammad Mīrzā, the son of his paternal uncle, Minūchihr Mīrzā.[249]

*　*　*　*　*
*

Five other daughters were by Khān-zāda Begīm, the grand-daughter of the Great Mīr of Tīrmīẕ. The oldest of these, (Khān-zāda Begīm)[250] was given, after her father's death, to Abā-bikr Fol. 27b.*(Dūghlāt) Kāshgharī.* The second was Bega Begīm. When Sl. Ḥusain Mīrzā besieged Ḥiṣār (901 AH.), he took her for Ḥaidar Mīrzā, his son by Pāyanda Begīm, Sl. Abū-sa'īd Mīrzā's daughter, and having done so, rose from before the place.[251] The third daughter was Āq (Fair) Begīm; the fourth[252]—,was betrothed to Jahāngīr Mīrzā *(aet.* 5, *circa* 895 AH.) at the time his father, 'Umar Shaikh Mīrzā sent him to help Sl. Maḥmūd Mīrzā with the Andijān army, against Sl. Ḥusain Mīrzā, then attacking Qūndūz.[253] In 910 AH. (1504 AD.) when Bāqī *Chaghāniānī*[254] waited on me on the bank of the Amū (Oxus), these (last-named two) Begīms were with their mothers in Tīrmīẕ and joined me then with Bāqī's family. When we reached Kahmard, Jahāngīr Mīrzā took —— Begīm; one little daughter was born; she now[255] is in the Badakhshān country with her grandmother. The fifth daughter was Zainab-sulṭān Begīm; under my mother's insistence, I took her at the time of the capture of Kābul (910 AH.-Oct. 1504 AD.). She did not become very congenial; two or three years later, she left the world, through small-pox. Another daughter was Makhdūm-sulṭān Begīm, Sl. 'Alī Mīrzā's full-sister; she is now in the Badakhshān country. Two others of his daughters, Rajab-sulṭān and Muḥibb-sulṭān, were by mistresses *(ghūnchachī).*

g. His ladies (khwātīnlār) and concubines (sarārī).

His chief wife, Khān-zāda Begīm, was a daughter of the Fol. 28.Great Mīr of Tirmīẕ; he had great affection for her and must have mourned her bitterly; she was the mother of Sl. Mas'ūd Mīrzā. Later on, he took her brother's daughter, also called Khān-zāda Begīm, a grand-daughter of the Great Mīr of Tīrmīẕ. She became the mother of five of his daughters and one of his sons. Pasha (or Pāshā) Begīm was another wife, a daughter of 'Alī-shukr Beg, a Turkmān Beg of the Black Sheep Bahārlū Aīmāq.[256] She had been the wife of Jahān-shāh *(Barānī)* of the Black Sheep Turkmāns. After Aūzūn (Long) Ḥasan Beg of the White Sheep had taken Āẕar-bāījān and 'Irāq from the sons of this Jahān-shāh Mīrzā (872 AH.-1467 AD.), 'Alī-shukr Beg's sons went with four or five thousand heads-of-houses of the Black Sheep Turkmāns to serve Sl. Abū-saʿīd Mīrzā and after the Mīrzā's defeat (873 AH. by Aūzūn Ḥasan), came down to these countries and took service with Sl. Maḥmūd Mīrzā. This happened after Sl. Maḥmūd Mīrzā came to Ḥiṣār from Samarkand, and then it was he took Pasha Begīm. She became the mother of one of his sons and three of his daughters. Sulṭān-nigār Khānīm was another of his ladies; her descent has been mentioned already in the account of the (Chaghatāī) Khāns.Fol. 28b.

He had many concubines and mistresses. His most honoured concubine (*muʿatabar ghūma*) was Zuhra Begī Āghā; she was taken in his father's life-time and became the mother of one son and one daughter. He had many mistresses and, as has been said, two of his daughters were by two of them.

h. His amirs.

Khusrau Shāh was of the Turkistānī Qīpchāqs. He had been in the intimate service of the Tarkhān begs, indeed had been a catamite. Later on he became a retainer of Mazīd Beg (Tarkhān) *Arghūn* who favoured him in all things. He was favoured by Sl. Maḥmūd Mīrzā on account of services done by him when, after the 'Irāq disaster, he joined the Mīrzā on his way to Khurāsān. He waxed very great in his latter days; his retainers, under Sl. Maḥmūd Mīrzā, were a clear five or six thousand. Not only Badakhshān but the whole country from the Amū to the Hindū-kush Mountains depended on him and he devoured its whole revenue (*darobast yīr īdi*). His open table was good, so too his open hand; though he was a rough getter,[257] what he got, he spent liberally. He waxed exceeding great after Sl. Maḥmūd Mīrzā's death, in whose sons' time his retainers approached 20,000. Although he prayed and abstained from forbidden aliments, yet was he black-souled and vicious, Fol. 29.dunder-headed and senseless, disloyal and a traitor to his salt. For the sake of this fleeting, five-days world,[258] he blinded one of his benefactor's sons and murdered another. A sinner before God, reprobate to His creatures, he has earned curse and execration till the very verge of Resurrection. For this world's sake he did his evil deeds and yet, with lands so broad and with such hosts of armed retainers, he had not pluck to stand up to a hen. An account of him will come into this history.

Pīr-i-muḥammad *Aīlchī-būghā*[259] *Qūchīn* was another. In Hazārāspī's fight[260] he got in one challenge with his fists in Sl. Abū-saʿīd Mīrzā's presence at the Gate of Balkh. He was a brave man, continuously serving the Mīrzā (Maḥmūd) and guiding him by his counsel. Out of rivalry to Khusrau Shāh, he made a night-attack when the Mīrzā was besieging Qūndūz, on Sl. Ḥusain Mīrzā, with few men, without arming[261] and without plan; he could do nothing; what was there he could do against such and so large a force? He was pursued, threw himself into the river and was drowned.

Ayūb (*Begchīk Mughūl*)[262] was another. He had served in Sl. Abū-sa'īd Mīrzā's Khurāsān Cadet Corps, a brave man, Bāīsunghar Mīrzā's guardian. He was choice in dress and food; a jester and talkative, nicknamed Impudence, perhaps because the Mīrzā called him so.Fol. 29b.

Walī was another, the younger, full-brother of Khusrau Shāh. He kept his retainers well. He it was brought about the blinding of Sl. Mas'ūd Mīrzā and the murder of Bāī-sunghar Mīrzā. He had an ill-word for every-one and was an evil-tongued, foul-mouthed, self-pleasing and dull-witted mannikin. He approved of no-one but himself. When I went from the Qūndūz country to near Dūshī (910 AH.-1503 AD.), separated Khusrau Shāh from his following and dismissed him, this person (*i.e.*, Walī) had come to Andar-āb and Sīr-āb, also in fear of the Aūzbegs. The Aīmāqs of those parts beat and robbed him[263] then, having let me know, came on to Kābul. Walī went to Shaibānī Khān who had his head struck off in the town of Samarkand.

Shaikh 'Abdu'l-lāh *Barlās*[264] was another; he had to wife one of the daughters of Shāh Sulṭān Muḥammad (*Badakhshī*) *i.e.*, the maternal aunt of Abā-bikr Mīrzā (*Mīrān-shāhī*) and of Sl. Maḥmūd Khān. He wore his tunic narrow and *pur shaqq*[265]; he was a kindly well-bred man.

Maḥmūd *Barlās* of the Barlāses of Nūndāk (Badakhshān) was another. He had been a beg also of Sl. Abū-sa'īd Mīrzā and had surrendered Karmān to him when the Mīrzā took the 'Irāq countries. When Abā-bikr Mīrzā (*Mīrān-shāhī*) cameFol. 30. against Ḥiṣār with Mazīd Beg Tarkhān and the Black Sheep Turkmāns, and Sl. Maḥmūd Mīrzā went off to his elder brother, Sl. Aḥmad Mīrzā in Samarkand, Maḥmūd *Barlās* did not surrender Ḥiṣār but held out manfully.[266] He was a poet and put a *dīwān* together.

(*i. Historical narrative resumed*).

When Sl. Maḥmūd Mīrzā died, Khusrau Shāh kept the event concealed and laid a long hand on the treasure. But how could such news be hidden? It spread through the town at once. That was a festive day for the Samarkand families; soldier and peasant, they uprose in tumult against Khusrau Shāh. Aḥmad Ḥājī Beg and the Tarkhānī begs put the rising down and turned Khusrau Shāh out of the town with an escort for Ḥiṣār.

As Sl. Maḥmūd Mīrzā himself after giving Ḥiṣār to Sl. Mas'ūd Mīrzā and Bukhārā to Bāī-sunghar Mīrzā, had dismissed both to their governments, neither was present when he died. The Ḥiṣār and Samarkand begs, after turning Khusrau Shāh out, agreed to send for Bāī-sunghar Mīrzā from Bukhārā, brought him to Samarkand and seated him on the throne. When he thus became supreme (*pādshāh*), he was 18 (lunar) years old.

At this crisis, Sl. Maḥmūd Khān (*Chaghatāi*), acting on the Fol. 30b.word of Junaid *Barlās* and of some of the notables of Samarkand, led his army out to near Kān-bāī with desire to take that town. Bāī-sunghar Mīrzā, on his side, marched out in force. They fought near Kān-bāī. Ḥaidar *Kūkūldāsh*, the main pillar of the Mughūl army, led the Mughūl van. He and all his men dismounted and were pouring in flights of arrows (*shība*) when a large body of the mailed braves of Ḥiṣār and Samarkand made an impetuous charge and straightway laid them under their horses' feet. Their leader taken, the Mughūl army was put to rout without more fighting. Masses (*qālīn*) of Mughūls were wiped out; so many were beheaded in Bāī-sunghar Mīrzā's presence that his tent was three times shifted because of the number of the dead.

At this same crisis, Ibrāhīm *Sārū* entered the fort of Asfara, there read Bāī-sunghar Mīrzā's name in the *Khuṭba* and took up a position of hostility to me.

> (*Author's note.*) Ibrāhīm *Sārū* is of the Mīnglīgh people;[267] he had served my father in various ways from his childhood but later on had been dismissed for some fault.

Fol. 31.The army rode out to crush this rebellion in the month of Sha'bān (May) and by the end of it, had dismounted round Asfara. Our braves in the wantonness of enterprise, on the very day of arrival, took the new wall[268] that was in building outside the fort. That day Sayyid Qāsim, Lord of my Gate, out-stripped the rest and got in with his sword; Sl. Aḥmad *Taṃbal* and Muḥammad-dost Ṭaghāī got theirs in also but Sayyid Qāsim won the Champion's Portion. He took it in Shāhrukhiya when I went to see my mother's brother, Sl. Maḥmūd Khān.

> (*Author's note.*) The Championship Portion[269] is an ancient usage of the Mughūl horde. Whoever outdistanced his tribe and got in with his own sword, took the portion at every feast and entertainment.

My guardian, Khudāī-bīrdī Beg died in that first day's fighting, struck by a cross-bow arrow. As the assault was made without armour, several bare braves (*yīkīt yīlāng*)[270] perished and many were wounded. One of Ibrāhīm *Sārū's* cross-bowmen was an excellent shot; his equal had never been seen; he it was hit most of those wounded. When Asfara had been taken, he entered my service.

As the siege drew on, orders were given to construct head-strikes[271] in two or three places, to run mines and to make everyFol. 31b. effort to prepare appliances for taking the fort. The siege lasted 40 days; at last Ibrāhīm *Sārū* had no resource but, through the mediation of Khwāja Moulānā-i-qāẓī, to elect to serve me. In the month of Shawwāl (June 1495 A.D.) he came out, with his sword and quiver hanging from his neck, waited on me and surrendered the fort.

Khujand for a considerable time had been dependent on 'Umar Shaikh Mīrzā's Court (*dīwān*) but of late had looked towards Sl. Aḥmad Mīrzā on account of the disturbance in the Farghāna government during the interregnum.[272] As the opportunity offered, a move against it also was now made. Mīr Mughūl's father, 'Abdu'l-wahhāb *Shaghāwal*[273] was in it; he surrendered without making any difficulty at once on our arrival.

Just then Sl. Maḥmūd Khān was in Shāhrukhiya. It has been said already that when Sl. Aḥmad Mīrzā came into Andijān (899 AH.), he also came and that he laid siege to Akhsī. It occurred to me that if since I was so close, I went and waited on him, he being, as it were, my father and my elder brother, and if bye-gone resentments were laid aside, it would be good hearing and seeing for far and near. So said, I went.

I waited on The Khān in the garden Ḥaidar *Kūkūldāsh* had made outside Shāhrukhiya. He was seated in a large four-doored Fol. 32.tent set up in the middle of it. Having entered the tent, I knelt three times,[274] he for his part, rising to do me honour. We looked one another in the eyes;[275] and he returned to his seat. After I had kneeled, he called me to his side and shewed me much affection and friendliness. Two or three days later, I set off for Akhsī and Andijān by the Kīndīrlīk Pass.[276] At Akhsī I made the circuit of my Father's tomb. I left at the hour of the Friday Prayer (*i.e.*, about midday) and reached Andijān, by the Band-i-sālār Road between the Evening and Bedtime Prayers. This road *i.e.* the Band-i-sālār, people call a nine *yīghāch* road.[277]

One of the tribes of the wilds of Andijān is the Jīgrāk[278] a numerous people of five or six thousand households, dwelling in the mountains between Kāshghar and Farghāna. They have many horses and sheep and also numbers of yāks (*qūtās*), these hill-people keeping yāks instead of common cattle. As their mountains are border-fastnesses, they have a fashion of not paying tribute. An army was now sent against them under (Sayyid) Qāsim Beg in order that out of the tribute taken from them something might reach the soldiers. He took about 20,000 of their sheep and between 1000 and 1500 of their horses and shared all out to the men.

After its return from the Jīgrāk, the army set out for Aūrā-tīpā.Fol. 34. Formerly this was held by 'Umar Shaikh Mīrzā but it had gone out of hand in the year of his death and Sl. 'Alī Mīrzā was now in it on behalf of his elder brother, Bāīsunghar Mīrzā. When Sl. 'Alī Mīrzā heard of our coming, he went off himself to the Macha hill-country, leaving his guardian, Shaikh Ẕū'n-nūn *Arghūn* behind. From half-way between Khujand and Aūrā-tīpā,

Khalīfa[279] was sent as envoy to Shaikh Ẕū'n-nūn but that senseless mannikin, instead of giving him a plain answer, laid hands on him and ordered him to death. For Khalīfa to die cannot have been the Divine will; he escaped and came to me two or three days later, stripped bare and having suffered a hundred *tūmāns* (1,000,000) of hardships and fatigues. We went almost to Aūrā-tīpā but as, winter being near, people had carried away their corn and forage, after a few days we turned back for Andijān. After our retirement, The Khān's men moved on the place when the Aūrā-tīpā person[280] unable to make a stand, surrendered and came out. The Khān then gave it to Muḥammad Ḥusain *Kūrkān Dūghlāt* and in his hands it remained till 908 AH. (1503).[281]

901 AH.—SEP. 21ST. 1495 TO SEP. 9TH. 1496 AD.[282]

(*a. Sulṭān Ḥusain Mīrzā's campaign against Khusrau Shāh*).

In the winter of this year, Sl. Ḥusain Mīrzā led his army out of Khurāsān against Ḥiṣār and went to opposite Tīrmīẕ. Sl. Mas'ūd Mīrzā, for his part, brought an army (from Ḥiṣār) and sat down over against him in Tīrmīẕ. Khusrau Shāh strengthened himself in Qūndūz and to help Sl. Mas'ūd Mīrzā sent his younger brother, Walī. They (*i.e.*, the opposed forces) spent most of that winter on the river's banks, no crossing being effected. Sl. Ḥusain Mīrzā was a shrewd and experienced commander; he marched up the river,[283] his face set for Qūndūz and by this having put Sl. Mas'ūd Mīrzā off his guard, sent 'Abdu'l-laṭīf *Bakhshī* (pay-master) with 5 or 600 serviceable men, down the river to the Kilīf ferry. These crossed and had entrenched themselves on the other bank before Sl. Mas'ūd Mīrzā had heard of their movement. When he did hear of it, whether because of pressure put upon him by Bāqī *Chaghānīānī* to spite (his half-brother) Walī, or whether from his own want of heart, he did not march against those who had crossed but disregarding Walī's urgency, at once broke up his camp and turned for Ḥiṣār.[284]

Sl. Ḥusain Mīrzā crossed the river and then sent, (1) against Khusrau Shāh, Badī'u'z-zamān Mīrzā and Ibrāhīm Ḥusain Mīrzā with Muḥammad Walī Beg and Ẕū'n-nūn *Arghūn*, andFol. 33b. (2) against Khutlān, Muẓaffar Ḥusain Mīrzā with Muḥammad *Barandūq Barlās*. He himself moved for Ḥiṣār.

When those in Ḥiṣār heard of his approach, they took their precautions; Sl. Mas'ūd Mīrzā did not judge it well to stay in the fort but went off up the Kām Rūd valley[285] and by way of Sara-tāq to his younger brother, Bāī-sunghar Mīrzā in Samarkand. Walī, for his part drew off to (his own district) Khutlān. Bāqī *Chaghānīānī*, Maḥmūd *Barlās* and Qūch Beg's father, Sl. Aḥmad strengthened the fort of Ḥiṣār. Ḥamza Sl. and Mahdī Sl. (*Aūzbeg*) who some years earlier had left Shaibānī Khān for (the late) Sl. Maḥmūd Mīrzā's service, now, in this dispersion, drew off with all their Aūzbegs, for Qarā-tīgīn. With them went Muḥammad *Dūghlāt*[286] and Sl. Ḥusain *Dūghlāt* and all the Mughūls located in the Ḥiṣār country.

Upon this Sl. Ḥusain Mīrzā sent Abū'l-muḥsin Mīrzā after Sl. Mas'ūd Mīrzā up the Kām Rūd valley. They were not strong enough for such work when they reached the defile.[287] There Mīrzā Beg *Fīringī-bāz*[288] got in his sword. In pursuit of Ḥamza Sl. into Qarā-tīgīn, Sl. Ḥusain Mīrzā sent Ibrāhīm Tarkhān and Yaq'ūb-i-ayūb. They overtook the sulṭāns and Fol. 33.fought. The Mīrzā's detachment was defeated; most of his begs were unhorsed but all were allowed to go free.

(*b. Bābur's reception of the Aūzbeg sulṭāns.*)

As a result of this exodus, Ḥamza Sl. with his son, Mamāq Sl., and Mahdī Sl. and Muḥammad *Dūghlāt*, later known as *Ḥiṣārī* and his brother, Sl. Ḥusain *Dūghlāt* with the Aūzbegs dependent on the sulṭāns and the Mughūls who had been located in Ḥiṣār as (the late) Sl. Maḥmūd Mīrzā's retainers, came, after letting me know (their intention), and waited upon me in Ramẓān (May-June) at Andijān. According to the custom of Tīmūriya sulṭāns on such occasions, I had seated myself on a raised seat (*tūshāk*); when Ḥamza Sl. and Mamāq Sl. and Mahdī Sl. entered, I rose and went down to do them honour; we looked one another in the eyes and I placed them on my right, *bāghīsh dā.*[289] A number of Mughūls also came, under Muḥammad *Ḥiṣārī*; all elected for my service.

(*c. Sl. Ḥusain Mīrzā's affairs resumed*).

Sl. Ḥusain Mīrzā, on reaching Ḥiṣār, settled down at once to besiege it. There was no rest, day nor night, from the labours of mining and attack, of working catapults and mortars. Mines were run in four or five places. When one had gone well forward towards the Gate, the townsmen, countermining, struck it and forced smoke down on the Mīrzā's men; they, in turn,Fol. 34b. closed the hole, thus sent the smoke straight back and made the townsmen flee as from the very maw of death. In the end, the townsmen drove the besiegers out by pouring jar after jar of water in on them. Another day, a party dashed out from the town and drove off the Mīrzā's men from their own mine's mouth. Once the discharges from catapults and mortars in the Mīrzā's quarters on the north cracked a tower of the fort; it fell at the Bed-time Prayer; some of the Mīrzā's braves begged to assault at once but he refused, saying, "It is night." Before the shoot of the next day's dawn, the besieged had rebuilt the whole tower. That day too there was no assault; in fact, for the two to two and a half months of the siege, no attack was made except by keeping up the blockade,[290] by mining, rearing head-strikes,[291] and discharging stones.

When Badī'u'z-zamān Mīrzā and whatever (*nī kīm*) troops had been sent with him against Khusrau Shāh, dismounted some 16 m. (3 to 4 *yīghāch*) below Qūndūz,[292] Khusrau Shāh arrayed whatever men (*nī kīm*) he had, marched out, halted one night on the way, formed up to fight and came down upon the Mīrzā and his men. The Khurāsānīs may not have been twice as many as his men but what question is there they were half Fol. 35.as many more? None the less did such Mīrzās and such Commander-begs elect for prudence and remain in their entrenchments! Good and bad, small and great, Khusrau Shāh's force may have been of 4 or 5,000 men!

This was the one exploit of his life,—of this man who for the sake of this fleeting and unstable world and for the sake of shifting and faithless followers, chose such evil and such ill-repute, practised such tyranny and injustice, seized such wide lands, kept such hosts of retainers and followers,—latterly he led out between 20 and 30,000 and his countries and his districts (*parganāt*) exceeded those of his own ruler and that ruler's sons,[293]—for an exploit such as this his name and the names of his adherents were noised abroad for generalship and for this they were counted brave, while those timorous laggards, in the trenches, won the resounding fame of cowards.

Badī'u'z-zamān Mīrzā marched out from that camp and after a few stages reached the Alghū Mountain of Tāliqān[294] and there made halt. Khusrau Shāh, in Qūndūz, sent his brother, Walī, with serviceable men, to Ishkīmīsh, Fulūl and the hill-skirts thereabouts to annoy and harass the Mīrzā from outside also. Muḥibb-'alī, the armourer, (*qūrchī*) for his part, came down Fol. 35b.(from Walī's Khutlān) to the bank of the Khutlān Water, met in with some of the Mīrzā's men there, unhorsed some, cut off a few heads and got away. In emulation of this, Sayyidīm 'Alī[295] the door-keeper, and his younger brother, Qulī Beg and Bihlūl-i-ayūb and a body of their men got to grips with the Khurāsānīs on the skirt of 'Aṃbar Koh, near Khwāja Changāl but, many Khurāsānīs coming up, Sayyidīm 'Alī and Bābā Beg's (son) Qulī Beg and others were unhorsed.

At the time these various news reached Sl. Ḥusain Mīrzā, his army was not without distress through the spring rains of Ḥiṣār; he therefore brought about a peace; Maḥmūd *Barlās* came out from those in the fort; Ḥājī Pīr the Taster went from those outside; the great commanders and what there was (*nī kīm*) of musicians and singers assembled and the Mīrzā took (Bega Begīm), the eldest[296] daughter of Sl. Maḥmūd Mīrzā by Khān-zāda Begīm, for Ḥaidar Mīrzā, his son by Pāyanda Begīm and through her the grandson of Sl. Abū-sa'īd Mīrzā. This done, he rose from before Ḥiṣār and set his face for Qūndūz.

At Qūndūz also Sl. Ḥusain Mīrzā made a few trenches and took up the besieger's position but by Badī'u'z-zamān Mīrzā's intervention peace at length was made, prisoners were exchanged and the Khurāsānīs retired. The twice-repeated[297] attacks made by Sl. Ḥusain Mīrzā on Khusrau Shāh and his unsuccessful retirements were the cause of Khusrau Shāh'sFol. 36. great rise and of action of his so much beyond his province.

When the Mīrzā reached Balkh, he, in the interests of Ṃāwarā'u'n-nahr gave it to Badī'u'z-zamān Mīrzā, gave Badī'u'z-zamān Mīrzā's district of Astarābād to (a younger son), Muẓaffar Ḥusain Mīrzā and made both kneel at the same assembly, one for Balkh, the other for Astarābād. This offended Badī'u'z-zamān Mīrzā and led to years of rebellion and disturbance.[298]

(*d. Revolt of the Tarkhānīs in Samarkand*).

In Ramẓān of this same year, the Tarkhānīs revolted in Samarkand. Here is the story:—Bāī-sunghar Mīrzā was not so friendly and familiar with the begs and soldiers of Samarkand as he was with those of Ḥiṣār.[299] His favourite beg was Shaikh 'Abdu'l-lāh *Barlās*[300] whose sons were so intimate with the Mīrzā that it made a relation as of Lover and Beloved. These things displeased the Tarkhāns and the Samarkandī begs; Darwesh Muḥammad Tarkhān went from Bukhārā to Qarshī, brought Sl. 'Alī Mīrzā to Samarkand and raised him to be supreme. People then went to the New Garden where Bāī-sunghar Fol. 36b.Mīrzā was, treated him like a prisoner, parted him from his following and took him to the citadel. There they seated both mīrzās in one place, thinking to send Bāī-sunghar Mīrzā to the Gūk Sarāī close to the Other Prayer. The Mīrzā, however, on plea of necessity, went into one of the palace-buildings on the east side of the Būstān Sarāī. Tarkhānīs stood outside the door and with him went in Muḥammad Qulī *Qūchīn* and Ḥasan, the sherbet-server. To be brief:—A gateway, leading out to the back, must have been bricked up for they broke down the obstacle at once. The Mīrzā got out of the citadel on the Kafshīr side, through the water-conduit (*āb-mūrī*), dropped himself from the rampart of the water-way (*dū-tahī*), and went to Khwājakī Khwāja's[301] house in Khwāja Kafshīr. When the Tarkhānīs, in waiting at the door, took the precaution of looking in, they found him gone. Next day the Tarkhānīs went in a large body to Khwājakī Khwāja's gate but the Khwāja said, "No!"[302] and did not give him up. Even they could not take him by force, the Khwāja's dignity was too great for them to be able to use force. A few days later, Khwāja Abu'l-makāram[303] and Aḥmad Ḥājī Beg and other begs, great and Fol. 37.small, and soldiers and townsmen rose in a mass, fetched the Mīrzā away from the Khwāja's house and besieged Sl. 'Ali Mīrzā and the Tarkhāns in the citadel. They could not hold out for even a day; Muḥ. Mazīd Tarkhān went off through the Gate of the Four Roads for Bukhārā; Sl. 'Alī Mīrzā and Darwesh Muḥ. Tarkhān were made prisoner.

Bāī-sunghar Mīrzā was in Aḥmad Ḥājī Beg's house when people brought Darwesh Muḥammad Tarkhān in. He put him a few questions but got no good answer. In truth Darwesh Muḥammad's was a deed for which good answer could not be made. He was ordered to death. In his helplessness he clung to a pillar[304] of the house; would they let him go because he clung to a pillar? They made him reach his doom (*siyāsat*) and ordered Sl. 'Alī Mīrzā to the Gūk Sarāī there to have the fire-pencil drawn across his eyes.

> (*Author's note.*) The Gūk Sarāī is one of Tīmūr Beg's great buildings in the citadel of Samarkand. It has this singular and special characteristic, if a Tīmūrid is to be seated on the throne, here he takes his seat; if one lose his head, coveting the throne, here he loses it; therefore the name Gūk Sarāī has a metaphorical sense (*kināyat*) and to say of any ruler's son, "They have taken him to the Gūk Sarāī," means, to death.[305]

To the Gūk Sarāī accordingly Sl. 'Alī Mīrzā was taken but when the fire-pencil was drawn across his eyes, whether by the surgeon's choice or by his inadvertence, no harm was done.Fol. 37b. This the Mīrzā did not reveal at once but went to Khwāja Yahya's house and a few days later, to the Tarkhāns in Bukhārā.

Through these occurrences, the sons of his Highness Khwāja 'Ubaidu'l-lāh became settled partisans, the elder (Muḥammad 'Ubaidu'l-lāh, Khwājakī Khwāja) becoming the spiritual guide of the elder prince, the younger (Yahya) of the younger. In a few days, Khwāja Yahya followed Sl. 'Alī Mīrzā to Bukhārā.

Bāī-sunghar Mīrzā led out his army against Bukhārā. On his approach, Sl. 'Alī Mīrzā came out of the town, arrayed for battle. There was little fighting; Victory being on the side of Sl. 'Alī Mīrzā, Bāī-sunghar Mīrzā sustained defeat. Aḥmad Ḥājī Beg and a number of good soldiers were taken; most of the men were put to death. Aḥmad Ḥājī Beg himself the slaves and slave-women of Darwesh Muḥammad Tarkhān, issuing out of Bukhārā, put to a dishonourable death on the charge of their master's blood.

(*e. Bābur moves against Samarkand.*)

These news reached us in Andijān in the month of Shawwāl (mid-June to mid-July) and as we (*act.* 14) coveted Samarkand, we got our men to horse. Moved by a like desire, Sl. Mas'ūd Mīrzā, his mind and Khusrau Shāh's mind set at ease by Sl. Fol. 38.Ḥusain Mīrzā's retirement, came over by way of Shahr-i-sabz.[306] To reinforce him, Khusrau Shāh laid hands (*qāptī*) on his younger brother, Walī. We (three mīrzās) beleaguered the town from three sides during three or four months; then Khwāja Yahya came to me from Sl. 'Alī Mīrzā to mediate an agreement with a common aim. The matter was left at an interview arranged (*kūrūshmak*); I moved my force from Soghd to some 8m. below the town; Sl. 'Alī Mīrzā from his side, brought his own; from one bank, he, from the other, I crossed to the middle of[307] the Kohik water, each with four or five men; we just saw one another (*kūrūshūb*), asked each the other's welfare and went, he his way, I mine.

I there saw, in Khwāja Yahya's service, Mullā *Binā'ī* and Muḥammad Ṣāliḥ;[308] the latter I saw this once, the former was long in my service later on. After the interview (*kūrūshkān*) with Sl. 'Alī Mīrzā, as winter was near and as there was no great scarcity amongst the Samarkandīs, we retired, he to Bukhārā, I to Andijān.

Sl. Mas'ūd Mīrzā had a penchant for a daughter of Shaikh 'Abdu'l-lāh *Barlās*, she indeed was his object in coming to Samarkand. He took her, laid world-gripping ambition aside Fol. 38b.and went back to Ḥiṣār.

When I was near Shīrāz and Kān-bāī, Mahdī Sl. deserted to Samarkand; Ḥamza Sl. went also from near Zamīn but with leave granted.

902 AH.—SEP. 9TH. 1496 TO AUG. 30TH. 1497 AD.[309]

(a. Bābur's second attempt on Samarkand.)

This winter, Bāī-sunghar Mīrzā's affairs were altogether in a good way. When 'Abdu'l-karīm *Ushrit* came on Sl. 'Alī Mīrzā's part to near Kūfīn, Mahdī Sl. led out a body of Bāī-sunghar Mīrzā's troops against him. The two commanders meeting exactly face to face, Mahdī Sl. pricked 'Abdu'l-karīm's horse with his Chirkas[310] sword so that it fell, and as 'Abdu'l-karīm was getting to his feet, struck off his hand at the wrist. Having taken him, they gave his men a good beating.

These (Aūzbeg) sulṭāns, seeing the affairs of Samarkand and the Gates of the (Tīmūrid) Mīrzās tottering to their fall, went off in good time (*āīrtā*) into the open country (?)[311] for Shaibānī.

Pleased[312] with their small success (over 'Abdu'l-karīm), the Samarkandīs drew an army out against Sl. 'Alī Mīrzā; Bāī-sunghar Mīrzā went to Sar-i-pul (Bridge-head), Sl. 'Alī Mīrzā to Khwāja Kārzūn. Meantime, Khwāja Abū'l-makāram, at the instigation of Khwāja Munīr of Aūsh, rode light againstFol. 39. Bukhārā with Wais *Lāgharī* and Muḥammad Bāqir of the Andijān begs, and Qāsim *Dūldāī* and some of the Mīrzā's household. As the Bukhāriots took precautions when the invaders got near the town, they could make no progress. They therefore retired.

At the time when (last year) Sl. 'Alī Mīrzā and I had our interview, it had been settled[313] that this summer he should come from Bukhārā and I from Andijān to beleaguer Samarkand. To keep this tryst, I rode out in Ramẓān (May) from Andijān. Hearing when close to Yār Yīlāq, that the (two) Mīrzās were lying front to front, we sent Tūlūn Khwāja *Mūghūl*[314] ahead, with 2 or 300 scouting braves (*qāzāq yīkītlār*). Their approach giving Bāī-sunghar Mīrzā news of our advance, he at once broke up and retired in confusion. That same night our detachment overtook his rear, shot a mass (*qālīn*) of his men and brought in masses of spoil.

Two days later we reached Shīrāz. It belonged to Qāsim Beg *Dūldāī*; his *dārogha* (Sub-governor) could not hold it and surrendered.[315] It was given into Ibrāhīm *Sārū's* charge. After making there, next day, the Prayer of the Breaking of the Fast (*'Idu'l-fiṭr*), we moved for Samarkand and dismounted in the reserve (*qūrūgh*) of Āb-i-yār (Water of Might). That day waited on me with 3 or 400 men, Qāsim *Dūldāī*, Fol. 39b.Wais *Lāgharī*, Muḥammad Sīghal's grandson, Ḥasan,[316] and Sl. Muḥammad Wais. What they said was this: 'Bāī-sunghar Mīrzā came out and has gone back; we have left him therefore and are here for the *pādshāh's* service,' but it was known later that they must have left the Mīrzā at his request to defend Shīrāz, and that the Shīrāz affair having become what it was, they had nothing for it but to come to us.

When we dismounted at Qarā-būlāq, they brought in several Mughūls arrested because of senseless conduct to humble village elders coming in to us.[317] Qāsim Beg *Qūchīn* for discipline's sake (*siyāsat*) had two or three of them cut to pieces. It was on this account he left me and went to Ḥiṣār four or five years later, in the guerilla times, (907 AH.) when I was going from the Macha country to The Khān.[318]

Marching from Qarā-būlāq, we crossed the river (*i.e.* the Zar-afshān) and dismounted near Yām.[319] On that same day, our men got to grips with Bāī-sunghar Mīrzā's at the head of the Avenue. Sl. Aḥmad *Taṃbal* was struck in the neck by a spear but not unhorsed. Khwājakī Mullā-i-ṣadr, Khwāja-i-kalān's eldest brother, was pierced in the nape of the neck[320] by an arrow and went straightway to God's mercy. An excellent soldier, my father before me had favoured him, making him Keeper of the Seal; he was a student of theology, had greatFol. 40. acquaintance with words and a good style; moreover he undertook hawking and rain-making with the jade-stone.

While we were at Yām, people, dealers and other, came out in crowds so that the camp became a bazar for buying and selling. One day, at the Other Prayer, suddenly, a general hubbub arose and all those Musalmān (traders) were plundered. Such however was the discipline of our army that an order to restore everything having been given, the first watch (*pahār*) of the next day had not passed before nothing, not a tag of cotton, not a broken needle's point, remained in the possession of any man of the force, all was back with its owners.

Marching from Yām, it was dismounted in Khān Yūrtī (The Khān's Camping Ground),[321] some 6 m. (3 *kuroh*) east of Samarkand. We lay there for 40 or 50 days. During the time, men from their side and from ours chopped at one another (*chāpqū-lāshtīlār*) several times in the Avenue. One day when Ibrāhīm *Begchīk* was chopping away there, he was cut on the face; thereafter people called him *Chāpūk* (*Balafré*). Another time, this also in the Avenue, at the Maghāk (Fosse) Bridge[322] Abū'l-qāsim (*Kohbur Chaghatāī*) got in with his mace. Once, again Fol. 40b.in the Avenue, near the Mill-sluice, when Mīr Shāh *Qūchīn* also got in with his mace, they cut his neck almost half-through; most fortunately the great artery was not severed.

While we were in Khān Yūrtī, some in the fort sent the deceiving message,[323] 'Come you to-night to the Lovers' Cave side and we will give you the fort.' Under this idea, we went that night to the Maghāk Bridge and from there sent a party of good horse and foot to the rendezvous. Four or five of the household foot-soldiers had gone forward when the matter got wind. They were very active men; one, known as Ḥājī, had served me from my childhood; another people called Maḥmūd *Kūndūr-sangak*.[324] They were all killed.

While we lay in Khān Yūrtī, so many Samarkandīs came out that the camp became a town where everything looked for in a town was to be had. Meantime all the forts, Samarkand excepted, and the Highlands and the Lowlands were coming in to us. As in Aūrgūt, however, a fort on the skirt of the Shavdār (var. Shādwār) range, a party of men held fast[325], of necessity we moved out from Khān Yūrtī against them. They could not maintain themselves, and surrendered, making Fol. 41.Khwāja-i-qāẓī their mediator. Having pardoned their offences against ourselves, we went back to beleaguer Samarkand.

(*b. Affairs of Sl. Ḥusain Mīrzā and his son, Badī'u'z-zamān Mīrzā.*)[326]

This year the mutual recriminations of Sl. Ḥusain Mīrzā and Badī'u'z-zamān Mīrzā led on to fighting; here are the particulars:—Last year, as has been mentioned, Badī'u'z-zamān Mīrzā and Muẓaffar Ḥusain Mīrzā had been made to kneel for Balkh and Astarābād. From that time till this, many envoys had come and gone, at last even 'Alī-sher Beg had gone but urge it as all did, Badī'u'z-zamān Mīrzā would not consent to give up Astarābād. 'The Mīrzā,' he said, 'assigned[327] it to my son, Muḥammad Mū'min Mīrzā at the time of his circumcision.' A conversation had one day between him and 'Alī-sher Beg testifies to his acuteness and to the sensibility of 'Alī-sher Beg's feelings. After saying many things of a private nature in the Mīrzā's ear, 'Alī-sher Beg added, 'Forget these matters.'[328] 'What matters?' rejoined the Mīrzā instantly. 'Alī-sher Beg was much affected and cried a good deal.

At length the jarring words of this fatherly and filial discussion went so far that *his* father against his father, and *his* son against his son drew armies out for Balkh and Astarābād.[329]

Up (from Harāt) to the Pul-i-chirāgh meadow, below Garzawān,[330] went Sl. Ḥusain Mīrzā; down (from Balkh) cameFol. 41b. Badī'u'z-zamān Mīrzā. On the first day of Ramẓān (May 2nd.) Abū'l-muḥsin Mīrzā advanced, leading some of his father's light troops. There was nothing to call a battle; Badī'u'z-zamān Mīrzā was routed and of his braves masses were made prisoner. Sl. Ḥusain Mīrzā ordered that all prisoners should be beheaded; this not here only but wherever he defeated a rebel son, he ordered the heads of all prisoners to be struck off. And why not? Right was with him. The (rebel) Mīrzās were so given over to vice and social pleasure that even when a general so skilful and experienced as their father was within half-a-day's journey of them, and when before the blessed month of Ramẓān, one night only remained, they busied themselves with wine and pleasure, without fear of their father, without dread of God. Certain it is that those so lost (*yūtkān*) will perish and that any hand can deal a blow at those thus going to perdition (*aūtkān*). During the several years of Badī'u'z-zamān Mīrzā's rule in Astarābād, his coterie and his following, his bare (*yālāng*) braves even, were in full splendour[331] and adornment. He had many gold and silver drinking cups Fol. 42.and utensils, much silken plenishing and countless tīpūchāq horses. He now lost everything. He hurled himself in his flight down a mountain track, leading to a precipitous fall. He himself got down the fall, with great difficulty, but many of his men perished there.[331]

After defeating Badī'u'z-zamān Mīrzā, Sl. Ḥusain Mīrzā moved on to Balkh. It was in charge of Shaikh 'Alī Ṭaghāī; he, not able to defend it, surrendered and made his submission. The Mīrzā gave Balkh to Ibrāhīm Ḥusain Mīrzā, left Muḥammad Walī Beg and Shāh Ḥusain, the page, with him and went back to Khurāsān.

Defeated and destitute, with his braves bare and his bare foot-soldiers[332], Badī'u'z-zamān Mīrzā drew off to Khusrau Shāh in Qūndūz. Khusrau Shāh, for his part, did him good service, such service indeed, such kindness with horses and camels, tents and pavilions and warlike equipment of all sorts, both for himself and those with him, that eye-witnesses said between this and his former equipment the only difference might be in the gold and silver vessels.

(*c. Dissension between Sl. Mas'ūd Mīrẓā and Khusrau Shāh.*)

Ill-feeling and squabbles had arisen between Sl. Mas'ūd Mīrzā and Khusrau Shāh because of the injustices of the one and the self-magnifyings of the other. Now therefore Khusrau Shāh joined his brothers, Walī and Bāqī to Badī'u'z-zamān Mīrzā and sent the three against Ḥiṣār. They could not evenFol. 42b. get near the fort, in the outskirts swords were crossed once or twice; one day at the Bird-house[333] on the north of Ḥiṣār, Muḥibb-'alī, the armourer (*qūrchī*), outstripped his people and struck in well; he fell from his horse but at the moment of his capture, his men attacked and freed him. A few days later a somewhat compulsory peace was made and Khusrau Shāh's army retired.

Shortly after this, Badī'u'z-zamān Mīrzā drew off by the mountain-road to Ẓū'n-nūn *Arghūn* and his son, Shujā' *Arghūn* in Qandahār and Zamīn-dāwar.

Stingy and miserly as Ẕū'n-nūn was, he served the Mīrzā well, in one single present offering 40,000 sheep.

Amongst curious happenings of the time one was this: Wednesday was the day Sl. Ḥusain Mīrzā beat Badī'u'z-zamān Mīrzā; Wednesday was the day Muẓaffar Ḥusain Mīrzā beat Muḥammad Mū'min Mīrzā; Wednesday, more curious still, was the name of the man who unhorsed and took prisoner, Muḥammad Mū'min Mīrzā.[334]

903 AH.—AUG. 30TH. 1497 TO AUG. 19TH. 1498 AD.335

(*a. Resumed account of Bābur's second attempt on Samarkand.*)

When we had dismounted in the Qulba (Plough) meadow,[336] behind the Bāgh-i-maidān (Garden of the plain), the Samarkandīs came out in great numbers to near Muḥammad Chap's Fol. 43.Bridge. Our men were unprepared; and before they were ready, Bābā 'Alī's (son) Bābā Qulī had been unhorsed and taken into the fort. A few days later we moved to the top of Qulba, at the back of Kohik.[337] That day Sayyid Yūsuf,[338] having been sent out of the town, came to our camp and did me obeisance.

The Samarkandīs, fancying that our move from the one ground to the other meant, 'He has given it up,' came out, soldiers and townsmen in alliance (through the Turquoise Gate), as far as the Mīrzā's Bridge and, through the Shaikh-zāda's Gate, as far as Muḥammad Chap's. We ordered our braves to arm and ride out; they were strongly attacked from both sides, from Muḥammad Chap's Bridge and from the Mīrzā's, but God brought it right! our foes were beaten. Begs of the best and the boldest of braves our men unhorsed and brought in. Amongst them Ḥāfiẓ *Dūldāī's* (son) Muḥammad *Mīskīn*[339] was taken, after his index-finger had been struck off; Muḥammad Qāsim *Nabīra* also was unhorsed and brought in by his own younger brother, Ḥasan *Nabīra.*[340] There were many other such soldiers and known men. Of the town-rabble, were brought in Diwāna, the tunic-weaver and *Kālqāshūq*,[341] headlong leaders both, in brawl and tumult; theyFol. 43b. were ordered to death with torture in blood-retaliation for our foot-soldiers, killed at the Lovers' Cave.[342] This was a complete reverse for the Samarkandīs; they came out no more even when our men used to go to the very edge of the ditch and bring back their slaves and slave-women.

The Sun entered the Balance and cold descended on us.[343] I therefore summoned the begs admitted to counsel and it was decided, after discussion, that although the towns-people were so enfeebled that, by God's grace, we should take Samarkand, it might be to-day, it might be to-morrow, still, rather than suffer from cold in the open, we ought to rise from near it and go for winter-quarters into some fort, and that, even if we had to leave those quarters later on, this would be done without further trouble. As Khwāja Dīdār seemed a suitable fort, we marched there and having dismounted in the meadow lying before it, went in, fixed on sites for the winter-houses and covered shelters,[344] left overseers and inspectors of the work and returned to our camp in the meadow. There we lay during the few days before the winter-houses were finished.

Meantime Bāī-sunghar Mīrzā had sent again and again to ask help from Shaibānī Khān. On the morning of the very day on which, our quarters being ready, we had moved into Khwāja Dīdār, the Khān, having ridden light from Turkistān,Fol. 44. stood over against our camping-ground. Our men were not all at hand; some, for winter-quarters, had gone to Khwāja Rabāṭī, some to Kabud, some to Shīrāz. None-the-less, we formed up those there were and rode out. Shaibānī Khān made no stand but drew off towards Samarkand. He went right up to the fort but because the affair had not gone as

Bāī-sunghar Mīrzā wished, did not get a good reception. He therefore turned back for Turkistān a few days later, in disappointment, with nothing done.

Bāī-sunghar Mīrzā had sustained a seven months' siege; his one hope had been in Shaibānī Khān; this he had lost and he now with 2 or 300 of his hungry suite, drew off from Samarkand, for Khusrau Shāh in Qūndūz.

When he was near Tīrmīẕ, at the Amū ferry, the Governor of Tīrmīẕ, Sayyid Ḥusain Akbar, kinsman and confidant both of Sl. Mas'ūd Mīrzā, heard of him and went out against him. The Mīrzā himself got across the river but Mīrīm Tarkhān was drowned and all the rest of his people were captured, together with his baggage and the camels loaded with his personal effects; even his page, Muḥammad Ṭāhir, falling into Sayyid Ḥusain Akbar's hands. Khusrau Shāh, for his part, looked kindly on the Mīrzā.

Fol. 44b.When the news of his departure reached us, we got to horse and started from Khwāja Dīdār for Samarkand. To give us honourable meeting on the road, were nobles and braves, one after another. It was on one of the last ten days of the first Rabī' (end of November 1497 AD.), that we entered the citadel and dismounted at the Bū-stān Sarāī. Thus, by God's favour, were the town and the country of Samarkand taken and occupied.

(b. Description of Samarkand.)[345]

Few towns in the whole habitable world are so pleasant as Samarkand. It is of the Fifth Climate and situated in lat. 40° 6' and long. 99°.[346] The name of the town is Samarkand; its country people used to call Mā warā'u'n-nahr (Transoxania).

They used to call it *Baldat-i-maḥfūẓa* because no foe laid hands on it with storm and sack.[347] It must have become[348] Musalmān in the time of the Commander of the Faithful, his Highness 'Usmān. Quṣam ibn 'Abbās, one of the Companions[349] must have gone there; his burial-place, known as the Tomb of Shāh-i-zinda (The Living Shāh, *i.e.*, Fāqīr) is outside the Iron Gate. Iskandar must have founded Samarkand. The Turk and Mughūl hordes call it Sīmīz-kīnt.[350] Tīmūr Beg made it his capital; no ruler so great will ever have made it a capital before (*qīlghān aīmās dūr*). I ordered people to pace round the ramparts of the walled-town; it came out at 10,000 steps.[351] Samarkandīs are all orthodox (*sunnī*), pure-in-the Faith, law-abiding and religious. The number of LeadersFol. 45. of Islām said to have arisen in Mā warā'u'n-nahr, since the days of his Highness the Prophet, are not known to have arisen in any other country.[352] From the Mātarīd suburb of Samarkand came Shaikh Abū'l-manṣūr, one of the Expositors of the Word.[353] Of the two sects of Expositors, the Mātarīdiyah and the Ash'ariyah,[354] the first is named from this Shaikh Abū'l-manṣūr. Of Mā warā'u'n-nahr also was Khwāja Ismā'īl *Khartank*, the author of the *Ṣāḥiḥ-i-bukhārī*.[355] From the Farghāna district, Marghīnān—Farghāna, though at the limit of settled habitation, is included in Mā warā'u'n-nahr,—came the author of the *Hidāyat*,[356] a book than which few on Jurisprudence are more honoured in the sect of Abū Ḥanīfa.

On the east of Samarkand are Farghāna and Kāshghar; on the west, Bukhārā and Khwārizm; on the north, Tāshkīnt and Shāhrukhiya,—in books written Shāsh and Banākat; and on the south, Balkh and Tīrmīẕ.

The Kohik Water flows along the north of Samarkand, at the distance of some 4 miles (2 *kuroh*); it is so-called because it comes out from under the upland of the Little Hill (*Kohik*)[357] lying between it and the town. The Dar-i-gham Water (canal) flows along the south, at the distance of some two miles (1 *sharī'*). This is a large and swift torrent,[358] indeed it is like a large river, cut off from the Kohik Water. All the gardens and suburbs and some of the *tūmāns* of Samarkand are cultivated by it. By the Kohik Water a stretch of from 30 to 40 *yīghāch*,[359] by road, is made habitable and cultivated, as far as Bukhārā and Qarā-kūl. Large as the river is, it is not too large for its dwellings and its culture; during three or four months of theFol. 45b. year, indeed, its waters do not reach Bukhārā.[360] Grapes, melons, apples and pomegranates, all fruits indeed, are good in Samarkand; two are famous, its apple and its *ṣāḥibī* (grape).[361] Its winter is mightily cold; snow falls but not so much as in Kābul; in the heats its climate is good but not so good as Kābul's.

In the town and suburbs of Samarkand are many fine buildings and gardens of Tīmur Beg and Aūlūgh Beg Mīrzā.[362]

In the citadel,[363] Tīmūr Beg erected a very fine building, the great four-storeyed kiosque, known as the Gūk Sarāī.[364] In the walled-town, again, near the Iron Gate, he built a Friday Mosque[365] of stone (*sangīn*); on this worked many stone-cutters, brought from Hindūstān. Round its frontal arch is inscribed in letters large enough to be read two miles away, the Qu'rān verse, *Wa az yerfa' Ibrāhīm al Qawā'id alī akhara.*[366] This also is a very fine building. Again, he laid out two gardens, on the east of the town, one, the more distant, the Bāgh-i-bulandī,[367] the other and nearer, the Bāgh-i-dilkushā.[368] From Dilkushā to the Turquoise Gate, he planted an Avenue of White Poplar,[369] and in the garden itself erected a great kiosque, painted inside Fol. 46.with pictures of his battles in Hindūstān. He made another garden, known as the Naqsh-i-jahān (World's Picture), on the skirt of Kohik, above the Qarā-sū or, as people also call it, the Āb-i-raḥmat (Water-of-mercy) of Kān-i-gil.[370] It had gone to ruin when I saw it, nothing remaining of it except its name. His also are the Bāgh-i-chanār,[371] near the walls and below the town on the south,[372] also the Bāgh-i-shamāl (North Garden) and the Bāgh-i-bihisht (Garden of Paradise). His own tomb and those of his descendants who have ruled in Samarkand, are in a College, built at the exit (*chāqār*) of the walled-town, by Muḥammad Sulṭān Mīrzā, the son of Tīmūr Beg's son, Jahāngīr Mīrzā.[373]

Amongst Aūlūgh Beg Mīrzā's buildings inside the town are a College and a monastery (*Khānqāh*). The dome of the monastery is very large, few so large are shown in the world. Near these two buildings, he constructed an excellent Hot Bath (*ḥammām*) known as the Mīrzā's Bath; he had the pavements in this made of all sorts of stone (? mosaic); such another bath is not known in Khurāsān or in Samarkand.[374] Again;—to the south of the College is his mosque, known as the Fol. 46b.Masjid-i-maqaṭa' (Carved Mosque) because its ceiling and its walls are all covered with *islīmī*[375] and Chinese pictures formed of segments of wood.[376] There is great discrepancy between the *qibla* of this mosque and that of the College; that of the mosque seems to have been fixed by astronomical observation.

Another of Aūlūgh Beg Mīrzā's fine buildings is an observatory, that is, an instrument for writing Astronomical Tables.[377] This stands three storeys high, on the skirt of the Kohik upland. By its means the Mīrzā worked out the Kūrkānī Tables, now used all over the world. Less work is done with any others. Before these were made, people used the Aīl-khānī Tables, put together at Marāgha, by Khwāja Naṣīr *Tūsī*,[378] in the time of Hulākū Khān. Hulākū Khān it is, people call *Aīl-khānī.*[379]

> (*Author's note.*) Not more than seven or eight observatories seem to have been constructed in the world. Māmūm Khalīfa[380] (Caliph) made one with which the *Mamūmī* Tables were written. Batalmūs (Ptolemy)

constructed another. Another was made, in Hindūstān, in the time of Rājā Vikramāditya *Hīndū*, in Ujjain and Dhar, that is, the Mālwa country, now known as Māndū. The Hindūs of Hindūstān use the Tables of this Observatory. They were put together 1,584 years ago.[381]Fol. 47. Compared with others, they are somewhat defective.

Aūlūgh Beg Mīrzā again, made the garden known as the Bāgh-i-maidān (Garden of the Plain), on the skirt of the Kohik upland. In the middle of it he erected a fine building they call Chihil Sitūn (Forty Pillars). On both storeys are pillars, all of stone (*tāshdīn*).[382] Four turrets, like minarets, stand on its four corner-towers, the way up into them being through the towers. Everywhere there are stone pillars, some fluted, some twisted, some many-sided. On the four sides of the upper storey are open galleries enclosing a four-doored hall (*chār-dara*); their pillars also are all of stone. The raised floor of the building is all paved with stone.

He made a smaller garden, out beyond Chihil Sitūn and towards Kohik, also having a building in it. In the open gallery of this building he placed a great stone throne, some 14 or 15 yards (*qārī*) long, some 8 yards wide and perhaps 1 yard high. They brought a stone so large by a very long road.[383] There is a crack in the middle of it which people say must have come after it was brought here. In the same Fol. 47b.garden he also built a four-doored hall, know as the Chīnī-khāna (Porcelain House) because its *īzāra*[384] are all of porcelain; he sent to China for the porcelain used in it. Inside the walls again, is an old building of his, known as the Masjid-i-laqlaqa (Mosque of the Echo). If anyone stamps on the ground under the middle of the dome of this mosque, the sound echoes back from the whole dome; it is a curious matter of which none know the secret.

In the time also of Sl. Aḥmad Mīrzā the great and lesser begs laid out many gardens, large and small.[385] For beauty, and air, and view, few will have equalled Darwesh Muḥammad Tarkhān's Chār-bāgh (Four Gardens).[386] It lies overlooking the whole of Qulba Meadow, on the slope below the Bāgh-i-maidān. Moreover it is arranged symmetrically, terrace above terrace, and is planted with beautiful *nārwān*[387] and cypresses and white poplar. A most agreeable sojourning place, its one defect is the want of a large stream.

Samarkand is a wonderfully beautified town. One of its specialities, perhaps found in few other places,[388] is that the different trades are not mixed up together in it but each has its own *bāzār*, a good sort of plan. Its bakers and its cooks are good. The best paper in the world is made there; the water for the paper-mortars[389] all comes from Kān-i-gil,[390] a meadow on the banks of the Qarā-sū (Blackwater) or Āb-i-raḥmat (WaterFol. 48. of Mercy). Another article of Samarkand trade, carried to all sides and quarters, is cramoisy velvet.

Excellent meadows lie round Samarkand. One is the famous Kān-i-gil, some 2 miles east and a little north of the town. The Qarā-sū or Āb-i-raḥmat flows through it, a stream (with driving power) for perhaps seven or eight mills. Some say the original name of the meadow must have been Kān-i-ābgīr (Mine of Quagmire) because the river is bordered by quagmire, but the histories all write Kān-i-gil (Mine of clay). It is an excellent meadow. The Samarkand sulṭāns always made it their reserve,[391] going out to camp in it each year for a month or two.

Higher up (on the river) than Kān-i-gil and to the s.e. of it is a meadow some 4 miles east of the town, known as Khān Yūrtī (Khān's Camping-ground). The Qarā-sū flows through this meadow before entering Kān-i-gil. When it comes to Khān Yūrtī it curves back so far that it encloses, with a very narrow outlet, enough ground for a camp. Having noticed these advantages, we camped there for a time during Fol. 48b.the siege of Samarkand.[392]

Another meadow is the Būdana Qūrūgh (Quail Reserve), lying between Dil-kushā and the town. Another is the Kūl-i-maghāk (Meadow of the deep pool) at some 4 miles from the town. This also is a round[393] meadow. People call it Kul-i-maghāk meadow because there is a large pool on one side of it. Sl. 'Alī Mīrzā lay here during the siege, when I was in Khān Yūrtī. Another and smaller meadow is Qulba (Plough); it has Qulba Village and the Kohik Water on the north, the Bāgh-i-maidān and Darwesh Muḥammad Tarkhān's Chār-bāgh on the south, and the Kohik upland on the west.

Samarkand has good districts and *tūmāns*. Its largest district, and one that is its equal, is Bukhārā, 25 *yīghāch*[394] to the west. Bukhārā in its turn, has several *tūmāns*; it is a fine town; its fruits are many and good, its melons excellent; none in Mā warā'u'n-nahr matching them for quality and quantity. Although the Mīr Tīmūrī melon of Akhsī[395] is sweeter and more delicate than any Bukhārā melon, still in Bukhārā many kinds of melon are good and plentiful. The Bukhārā plum is famous; no other equals it. They skin it,[396] dry it and Fol. 49.carry it from land to land with rarities (*tabarrūklār bīla*); it is an excellent laxative medicine. Fowls and geese are much looked after (*parwārī*) in Bukhārā. Bukhārā wine is the strongest made in Mā warā'u'n-nahr; it was what I drank when drinking in those countries at Samarkand.[397]

Kesh is another district of Samarkand, 9 *yīghāch*[398] by road to the south of the town. A range called the Aītmāk Pass (*Dābān*)[399] lies between Samarkand and Kesh; from this are taken all the stones for building. Kesh is called also Shahr-i-sabz (Green-town) because its barren waste (*ṣahr*) and roofs and walls become beautifully green in spring. As it was Tīmūr Beg's birth-place, he tried hard to make it his capital. He erected noble buildings in it. To seat his own Court, he built a great arched hall and in this seated his Commander-begs and his Dīwān-begs, on his right and on his left. For those attending the Court, he built two smaller halls, and to seat petitioners to his Court, built quite small recesses on the four sides of the Court-house.[400] Few arches so fine can be shown in the world. It is said to be higher than the Kisrī Arch.[401] Tīmūr Beg also built in Kesh a college and a mausoleum, in which are the tombs of Jahāngīr Mīrzā and others of his descendants.[402] As Kesh did not offer the same facilities asFol. 49b. Samarkand for becoming a town and a capital, he at last made clear choice of Samarkand.

Another district is Qarshī, known also as Nashaf and Nakhshab.[403] Qarshī is a Mughūl name. In the Mughūl tongue they call a *kūr-khāna* Qarshī.[404] The name must have come in after the rule of Chīngīz Khān. Qarshī is somewhat scantily supplied with water; in spring it is very beautiful and its grain and melons are good. It lies 18 *yīghāch*[405] by road south and a little inclined to west of Samarkand. In the district a small bird, known as the *qīl-qūyīrūgh* and resembling the *bāghrī qarā*, is found in such countless numbers that it goes by the name of the Qarshī birdie (*murghak*).[406]

Khozār is another district; Karmīna another, lying between Samarkand and Bukhārā; Qarā-kūl another, 7 *yīghāch*[407] n.w. of Bukhārā and at the furthest limit of the water.

Samarkand has good *tūmāns*. One is Soghd with its dependencies. Its head Yār-yīlāq, its foot Bukhārā, there may be not one single *yīghāch* of earth without its village and its cultivated lands. So famous is it that the saying attributed to Tīmūr Beg, 'I have a garden 30 *yīghāch* long,[408] must have been spoken of Soghd. Another *tūmān* is Shāvdār (var. Shādwār), an excellent one adjoining the town-suburbs. On one side it has the range (Aītmāk Dābān), lying between Samarkand and Fol. 50.Shahr-i-sabz, on the skirts of which are many of its villages. On the other side is the Kohik Water (*i.e.* the Dar-i-gham canal). There it lies! an excellent *tūmān*, with fine air, full of beauty, abounding in waters, its good things cheap. Observers of Egypt and Syria have not pointed out its match.

Though Samarkand has other *tūmāns*, none rank with those enumerated; with so much, enough has been said.

Tīmūr Beg gave the government of Samarkand to his eldest son, Jahāngīr Mīrzā (in 776 AH.-1375 AD.); when Jahāngīr Mīrzā died (805 AH.-1403 AD.), he gave it to the Mīrzā's eldest son, Muḥammad Sulṭān-i-jahāngīr; when Muḥammad Sulṭān Mīrzā died, it went to Shāh-rukh Mīrzā, Tīmūr Beg's youngest son. Shāh-rukh Mīrzā gave the whole of Mā warā'u'n-nahr (in 872 AH.-1467 AD.) to his eldest son, Aūlūgh Beg Mīrzā. From him his own son, 'Abdu'l-laṭīf Mīrzā took it, (853 AH.-1449 AD.), for the sake of this five days' fleeting world martyring a father so full of years and knowledge.

The following chronogram gives the date of Aūlūgh Beg Mīrzā's death:—

Aūlūgh Beg, an ocean of wisdom and science,

The pillar of realm and religion,

Sipped from the hand of 'Abbās, the mead of martyrdom,

And the date of the death is *'Abbās kasht* ('Abbās slew).[409]

Though 'Abdu'l-laṭīf Mīrzā did not rule more than five or six months, the following couplet was current about him:—

Ill does sovereignty befit the parricide;

Should he rule, be it for no more than six months.[410]

This chronogram of the death of 'Abdu'l-laṭīf Mīrzā is also well done:—

'Abdu'l-laṭīf, in glory a Khusrau and Jamshīd,Fol. 50b.

In his train a Farīdūn and Zardusht,

Bābā Ḥusain slew on the Friday Eve,

With an arrow. Write as its date, *Bābā Ḥusain kasht* (Bābā Ḥusain slew).[411]

After 'Abdu'l-laṭīf Mīrzā's death, (Jumāda I, 22, 855 AH.-June 22nd. 1450 AD.), (his cousin) 'Abdu'l-lāh Mīrzā, the grandson of Shāh-rukh Mīrzā through Ibrāhīm Mīrzā, seated himself on the throne and ruled for 18 months to two years.[412] From him Sl. Abū-sa'īd Mīrzā took it (855 AH.-1451 AD.). He in his life-time gave it to his eldest son, Sl. Aḥmad Mīrzā; Sl. Aḥmad Mīrzā continued to rule it after his father's death (873 AH.-1469 AD.). On his death (899 AH.-1494 AD.) Sl. Maḥmūd Mīrzā was seated on the throne and on his death (900 AH.-1495 AD.) Bāī-sunghar Mīrzā. Bāī-sunghar Mīrzā was made prisoner for a few days, during the Tarkhān rebellion (901 AH.-1496 AD.), and his younger brother, Sl. 'Alī Mīrzā was seated on the throne, but Bāī-sunghar Mīrzā, as has been related in this history, took it again directly. From Bāī-sunghar Mīrzā I took it (903 AH.-1497 AD.). Further details will be learned from the ensuing history.

(*c. Bābur's rule in Samarkand.*)

When I was seated on the throne, I shewed the Samarkand begs precisely the same favour and kindness they had had before. I bestowed rank and favour also on the begs with me, Fol. 51.to each according to his circumstances, the largest share falling to Sl. Aḥmad *Tamḅal*; he had been in the household begs' circle; I now raised him to that of the great begs.

We had taken the town after a seven months' hard siege. Things of one sort or other fell to our men when we got in. The whole country, with exception of Samarkand itself, had come in earlier either to me or to Sl. 'Alī Mīrzā and consequently had not been over-run. In any case however, what could have been taken from districts so long subjected to raid and rapine? The booty our men had taken, such as it was, came to an end. When we entered the town, it was in such distress that it needed seed-corn and money-advances; what place was this to take anything from? On these accounts our men suffered great privation. We ourselves could give them nothing. Moreover they yearned for their homes and, by ones and twos, set their faces for flight. The first to go was Bayān Qulī's (son) Khān Qulī; Ibrāhīm *Begchīk* was another; all the Mughūls went off and, a little later, Sl. Aḥmad *Tamḅal.*

Aūzūn Ḥasan counted himself a very sincere and faithful friend of Khwāja-i-qāẓī; we therefore, to put a stop to these desertions, sent the Khwāja to him (in Andijān) so that they,Fol. 51b. in agreement, might punish some of the deserters and send others back to us. But that very Aūzūn Ḥasan, that traitor to his salt, may have been the stirrer-up of the whole trouble and the spur-to-evil of the deserters from Samarkand. Directly Sl. Aḥmad *Tamḅal* had gone, all the rest took up a wrong position.

(*d. Andijān demanded of Bābur by The Khān, and also for Jahāngīr Mīrzā.*)

Although, during the years in which, coveting Samarkand, I had persistently led my army out, Sl. Maḥmūd Khān[413] had provided me with no help whatever, yet, now it had been taken, he wanted Andijān. Moreover, Aūzūn Ḥasan and Sl. Aḥmad *Tamḅal*, just when soldiers of ours and all the Mughūls had deserted to Andijān and Akhsī, wanted those two districts for Jahāngīr Mīrzā. For several reasons, those districts could not be given to them. One was, that though not promised to The Khān, yet he had asked for them and, as he persisted in asking, an agreement with him was necessary, if they were to be given to Jahāngīr Mīrzā. A further reason was that to ask for them just when deserters from us had fled to them, was very like a command. If the matter had been brought forward earlier, some way of tolerating a command might have been found. AtFol. 52. the moment, as the Mughūls and the Andijān army and several even of my household had gone to Andijān, I had with me in Samarkand, beg for beg, good and bad, somewhere about 1000 men.

When Aūzūn Ḥasan and Sl. Aḥmad *Taṃbal* did not get what they wanted, they invited all those timid fugitives to join them. Just such a happening, those timid people, for their own sakes, had been asking of God in their terror. Hereupon, Aūzūn Ḥasan and Sl. Aḥmad *Taṃbal*, becoming openly hostile and rebellious, led their army from Akhsī against Andijān.

Tūlūn Khwāja was a bold, dashing, eager brave of the Bārīn (Mughūls). My father had favoured him and he was still in favour, I myself having raised him to the rank of beg. In truth he deserved favour, a wonderfully bold and dashing brave! He, as being the man I favoured amongst the Mughūls, was sent (after them) when they began to desert from Samarkand, to counsel the clans and to chase fear from their hearts so that Fol. 52b.they might not turn their heads to the wind.[414] Those two traitors however, those false guides, had so wrought on the clans that nothing availed, promise or entreaty, counsel or threat. Tūlūn Khwāja's march lay through Aīkī-sū-ārāsī,[415] known also as Rabāṭik-aūrchīnī. Aūzūn Ḥasan sent a skirmishing party against him; it found him off his guard, seized and killed him. This done, they took Jahāngīr Mīrzā and went to besiege Andijān.

(*e. Bābur loses Andijān.*)

In Andijān when my army rode out for Samarkand, I had left Aūzūn Ḥasan and 'Alī-dost Ṭaghāī (Ramẓān 902 AH.-May 1497 AD.). Khwāja-i-qāẓī had gone there later on, and there too were many of my men from Samarkand. During the siege, the Khwāja, out of good-will to me, apportioned 18,000 of his own sheep to the garrison and to the families of the men still with me. While the siege was going on, letters kept coming to me from my mothers[416] and from the Khwāja, saying in effect, 'They are besieging us in this way; if at our cry of distress you do not come, things will go all to ruin. Samarkand was taken Fol. 53.by the strength of Andijān; if Andijān is in your hands, God willing, Samarkand can be had again.' One after another came letters to this purport. Just then I was recovering from illness but, not having been able to take due care in the days of convalescence, I went all to pieces again and this time, became so very ill that for four days my speech was impeded and they used to drop water into my mouth with cotton. Those with me, begs and bare braves alike, despairing of my life, began each to take thought for himself. While I was in this condition, the begs, by an error of judgment, shewed me to a servant of Aūzūn Ḥasan's, a messenger come with wild proposals, and then dismissed him. In four or five days, I became somewhat better but still could not speak, in another few days, was myself again.

Such letters! so anxious, so beseeching, coming from my mothers, that is from my own and hers, Aīsān-daulat Begīm, and from my teacher and spiritual guide, that is, Khwāja-i-maulānā-i-qāẓī, with what heart would a man not move? We left Samarkand for Andijān on a Saturday in Rajab (Feb.-March), when I had ruled 100 days in the town. It wasFol. 53b. Saturday again when we reached Khujand and on that day a person brought news from Andijān, that seven days before, that is on the very day we had left Samarkand, 'Alī-dost Ṭ̤aghāī had surrendered Andijān.

These are the particulars;—The servant of Aūzūn Ḥasan who, after seeing me, was allowed to leave, had gone to Andijān and there said, 'The *pādshāh* cannot speak and they are dropping water into his mouth with cotton.' Having gone and made these assertions in the ordinary way, he took oath in 'Alī-dost Ṭ̤aghāī's presence. 'Alī-dost Ṭ̤aghāī was in the Khākān Gate. Becoming without footing through this matter, he invited the opposite party into the fort, made covenant and treaty with them, and surrendered Andijān. Of provisions and of fighting men, there was no lack whatever; the starting point of the surrender was the cowardice of that false and faithless manikin; what was told him, he made a pretext to put himself in the right.

When the enemy, after taking possession of Andijān, heard of my arrival in Khujand, they martyred Khwāja-i-maulānā-i-qāẓī by hanging him, with dishonour, in the Gate of the citadel.Fol. 54. He had come to be known as Khwāja-maulānā-i-qāẓī but his own name was 'Abdu'l-lāh. On his father's side, his line went back to Shaikh Burhānu'd-dīn 'Alī *Qīlīch*, on his mother's to Sl. Aīlīk *Māẓī*. This family had come to be the Religious Guides (*muqtadā*) and pontiff (*Shaikhu'l-islām*) and Judge (*qāẓī*) in the Farghāna country.[417] He was a disciple of his Highness 'Ubaidu'l-lāh (*Aḥrārī*) and from him had his upbringing. I have no doubt he was a saint (*walī*); what better witnesses to his sanctity than the fact that within a short time, no sign or trace remained of those active for his death? He was a wonderful man; it was not in him to be afraid; in no other man was seen such courage as his. This quality is a further witness to his sanctity. Other men, however bold, have anxieties and tremours; he had none. When they had killed him, they seized and plundered those connected with him, retainers and servants, tribesmen and followers.

In anxiety for Andijān, we had given Samarkand out of our hands; then heard we had lost Andijān. It was like the saying, 'In ignorance, made to leave this place, shut out from that' (*Ghafil az īn jā rānda, az ān jā mānda*). It was very hard and vexing to me; for why? never since I had ruled, had I been cut Fol. 54b.off like this from my retainers and my country; never since I had known myself, had I known such annoyance and such hardship.

(*f. Bābur's action from Khujand as his base.*)

On our arrival in Khujand, certain hypocrites, not enduring to see Khalīfa in my Gate, had so wrought on Muḥammad Ḥusain Mīrzā *Dūghlāt* and others that he was dismissed towards Tāshkīnt. To Tāshkīnt also Qāsim Beg *Qūchīn* had been sent earlier, in order to ask The Khān's help for a move on Andijān. The Khān consented to give it and came himself by way of the Ahangarān Dale,[418] to the foot of the Kīndīrlīk Pass.[419] There I went also, from Khujand, and saw my Khān dādā.[420] We then crossed the pass and halted on the Akhsī side. The enemy for their part, gathered their men and went to Akhsī.

Just at that time, the people in Pāp[421] sent me word they had made fast the fort but, owing to something misleading in The Khān's advance, the enemy stormed and took it. Though The Khān had other good qualities and was in other ways businesslike, he was much without merit as a soldier and commander. Just when matters were at the point that if he made one more march, it was most probable the country would be had without fighting, at such a time! he gave ear to what the enemy said with alloy of deceit, spoke of peace and, as his messengers, sent them Khwāja Abū'l-makāram and his ownFol. 55. Lord of the Gate, Beg *Tilba* (Fool), *Taṃbal's* elder brother. To save themselves those others (*i.e.* Ḥasan and Taṃbal) mixed something true with what they fabled and agreed to give gifts and bribes either to The Khān or to his intermediaries. With this, The Khān retired.

As the families of most of my begs and household and braves were in Andijān, 7 or 800 of the great and lesser begs and bare braves, left us in despair of our taking the place. Of the begs were 'Alī-darwesh Beg, 'Alī-mazīd *Qūchīn*, Muḥammad Bāqir Beg, Shaikh 'Abdu'l-lāh, Lord of the Gate and Mīrīm *Lāgharī*. Of men choosing exile and hardship with me, there may have been, of good and bad, between 200 and 300. Of begs there were Qāsim *Qūchīn* Beg, Wais *Lāgharī* Beg, Ibrāhīm *Sārū Mīnglīgh* Beg, Shīrīm Ṭaghāī, Sayyidī Qarā Beg; and of my household, Mīr Shāh *Qūchīn*, Sayyid Qāsim *Jalāīr*, Lord of the Gate, Qāsim-'ajab, 'Alī-dost Ṭaghāī's (son) Muḥammad-dost, Muḥammad-'alī *Mubashir*,[422] Khudāī-bīrdī *Tūghchī Mughūl*, Yārīk Ṭaghāī, Bābā 'Alī's (son) Bābā Qulī, Pīr Wais, Shaikh Wais,Fol. 55b. Yār-'alī *Balāl*,[423] Qāsim *Mīr Akhwūr* (Chief Equerry) and Ḥaidar *Rikābdār* (stirrup-holder).

It came very hard on me; I could not help crying a good deal. Back I went to Khujand and thither they sent me my mother and my grandmother and the families of some of the men with me.

That Ramẓān (April-May) we spent in Khujand, then mounted for Samarkand. We had already sent to ask The Khān's help; he assigned, to act with us against Samarkand, his son, Sl. Muḥammad (Sulṭānīm) Khānika and (his son's guardian) Aḥmad Beg with 4 or 5000 men and rode himself as far as Aūrā-tīpā. There I saw him and from there went on by way of Yār-yīlāq, past the Būrka-yīlāq Fort, the head-quarters of the sub-governor (*dārogha*) of the district. Sl. Muḥammad Sulṭān and Aḥmad Beg, riding light and by another road, got to Yār-yīlāq first but on their hearing that Shaibānī Khān was raiding Shīrāz and thereabouts, turned back. There was no help for it! Back I too had to go. Again I went to Khujand!

As there was in me ambition for rule and desire of conquest, I did not sit at gaze when once or twice an affair had made no progress. Now I myself, thinking to make another move for Fol. 56.Andijān, went to ask The Khān's help. Over and above this, it was seven or eight years since I had seen Shāh Begīm[424] and other relations; they also were seen under the same pretext. After a few days, The Khān appointed Sayyid Muḥammad Ḥusain (*Dūghlāt*) and Ayūb *Begchīk* and Jān-ḥasan *Bārīn* with 7 or 8000 men to help us. With this help we started, rode light, through Khujand without a halt, left Kand-i-badām on the left and so to Nasūkh, 9 or 10 *yīghāch* of road beyond Khujand and 3 *yīghāch* (12-18 m.) from Kand-i-badām, there set our ladders up and took the fort. It was the melon season; one kind grown here, known as Ismā'īl Shaikhī, has a yellow rind, feels like shagreen leather, has seeds like an apple's and flesh four fingers thick. It is a wonderfully delicate melon; no other such grows thereabout. Next day the Mughūl begs represented to me, 'Our fighting men are few; to what would holding this one fort lead on?' In truth they were right; of what use was it to make that fort fast and stay there? Back once more to Khujand!

(*f. Affairs of Khusrau Shāh and the Tīmūrid Mīrzās.*)[425]

This year Khusrau Shāh, taking Bāī-sunghar Mīrzā with him, led his army (from Qūndūz) to Chaghānīān and with false and treacherous intent, sent this message to Ḥiṣār for Sl. Mas'ūd Mīrzā, 'Come, betake yourself to Samarkand; ifFol. 56b. Samarkand is taken, one Mīrzā may seat himself there, the other in Ḥiṣār.' Just at the time, the Mīrzā's begs and household were displeased with him, because he had shewn excessive favour to his father-in-law, Shaikh 'Abdu'l-lāh *Barlās* who from Bāī-sunghar Mīrzā had gone to him. Small district though Ḥiṣār is, the Mīrzā had made the Shaikh's allowance 1,000 *tūmāns* of *fulūs*[426] and had given him the whole of Khutlān in which were the holdings of many of the Mīrzā's begs and household. All this Shaikh 'Abdu'l-lāh had; he and his sons took also in whole and in part, the control of the Mīrzā's gate. Those angered began, one after the other, to desert to Bāī-sunghar Mīrzā.

By those words of false alloy, having put Sl. Mas'ūd Mīrzā off his guard, Khusrau Shāh and Bāī-sunghar Mīrzā moved light out of Chaghānīān, surrounded Ḥiṣār and, at beat of morning-drum, took possession of it. Sl. Mas'ūd Mīrzā was in Daulat Sarāī, a house his father had built in the suburbs. Not being able to get into the fort, he drew off towards Khutlān with Shaikh 'Abu'l-lāh *Barlās*, parted from him half-way, crossed the river at the Aūbāj ferry and betook himself to Sl. Ḥusain Mīrzā. Khusrau Shāh, having taken Ḥiṣār, set Bāī-sungharFol. 57. Mīrzā on the throne, gave Khutlān to his own younger brother, Walī and rode a few days later, to lay siege to Balkh where, with many of his father's begs, was Ibrāhīm Ḥusain Mīrzā (*Bāī-qarā*). He sent Naẕar *Bahādur*, his chief retainer, on in advance with 3 or 400 men to near Balkh, and himself taking Bāī-sunghar Mīrzā with him, followed and laid the siege.

Walī he sent off with a large force to besiege Shabarghān and raid and ravage thereabouts. Walī, for his part, not being able to lay close siege, sent his men off to plunder the clans and hordes of the Zardak Chūl, and they took him back over 100,000 sheep and some 3000 camels. He then came, plundering the Sān-chīrīk country on his way, and raiding and making captive the clans fortified in the hills, to join Khusrau Shāh before Balkh.

One day during the siege, Khusrau Shāh sent the Naẕar *Bahādur* already mentioned, to destroy the water-channels[427] of Fol. 57b.Balkh. Out on him sallied Tīngrī-bīrdī *Samānchī*,[428] Sl. Ḥusain Mīrzā's favourite beg, with 70 or 80 men, struck him down, cut off his head, carried it off, and went back into the fort. A very bold sally, and he did a striking deed.

(g. Affairs of Sl. Ḥusain Mīrzā and Badī'u'z-zamān Mīrzā.)

This same year, Sl. Ḥusain Mīrzā led his army out to Bast and there encamped,[429] for the purpose of putting down Ẕū'n-nūn *Arghūn* and his son, Shāh Shujā', because they had become Badī'u'z-zamān Mīrzā's retainers, had given him a daughter of Ẕū'n-nūn in marriage and taken up a position hostile to himself. No corn for his army coming in from any quarter, it had begun to be distressed with hunger when the sub-governor of Bast surrendered. By help of the stores of Bast, the Mīrzā got back to Khurāsān.

Since such a great ruler as Sl. Ḥusain Mīrzā had twice led a splendid and well-appointed army out and twice retired, without taking Qūndūz, or Ḥiṣār or Qandahār, his sons and his begs waxed bold in revolt and rebellion. In the spring of this year, he sent a large army under Muḥammad Walī Beg to put down (his son) Muḥammad Ḥusain Mīrzā who, supreme in Astarābād, had taken up a position hostile to himself. While Sl. Ḥusain Mīrzā was still lying in the Nīshīn meadow (near Harāt), he was surprised by Badī'u'z-zamān Mīrzā and Shāh Shujā' Beg (*Arghūn*). By unexpected good-fortune, he had beenFol. 58. joined that very day by Sl. Mas'ūd Mīrzā, a refugee after bringing about the loss of Ḥiṣār,[430] and also rejoined by a force of his own returning from Astarābād. There was no question of fighting. Badī'u'z-zamān Mīrzā and Shāh Beg, brought face to face with these armies, took to flight.

Sl. Ḥusain Mīrzā looked kindly on Sl. Mas'ūd Mīrzā, made him kneel as a son-in-law and gave him a place in his favour and affection. None-the-less Sl. Mas'ūd Mīrzā, at the instigation of Bāqī *Chaghānīānī*, who had come earlier into Sl. Ḥusain Mīrzā's service, started off on some pretext, without asking leave, and went from the presence of Sl. Ḥusain Mīrzā to that of Khusrau Shāh!

Khusrau Shāh had already invited and brought from Ḥiṣār, Bāī-sunghar Mīrzā; to him had gone Aūlūgh Beg Mīrzā's son,[431] Mīrān-shāh Mīrzā who, having gone amongst the Hazāra in rebellion against his father, had been unable to remain amongst them because of his own immoderate acts. Some short-sighted persons were themselves ready to kill these three (Tīmūrid) Mīrzās and to read Khusrau Shāh's name in the *khuṭba* but he himself did not think this combination desirable. The ungratefulFol. 58b. manikin however, for the sake of gain in this five days' fleeting world,—it was not true to him nor will it be true to any man soever,—seized that Sl. Mas'ūd Mīrzā whom he had seen grow up in his charge from childhood, whose guardian he had been, and blinded him with the lancet.

Some of the Mīrzā's foster-brethren and friends of affection and old servants took him to Kesh intending to convey him to his (half)-brother Sl. 'Alī Mīrzā in Samarkand but as that party also (*i.e.* 'Alī's) became threatening, they fled with him, crossed the river at the Aūbāj ferry and went to Sl. Ḥusain Mīrzā.

A hundred thousand curses light on him who planned and did a deed so horrible! Up to the very verge of Resurrection, let him who hears of this act of Khusrau Shāh, curse him; and may he who hearing, curses not, know cursing equally deserved!

This horrid deed done, Khusrau Shāh made Bāī-sunghar Mīrzā ruler in Ḥiṣār and dismissed him; Mīrān-shāh Mīrzā he despatched for Bāmīān with Sayyid Qāsim to help him.

904 AH.—AUG. 19TH. 1498 TO AUG. 8TH. 1499 AD.[432]

(*a. Bābur borrows Pashāghar and leaves Khujand.*)

Twice we had moved out of Khujand, once for Andijān, once for Samarkand, and twice we had gone back to it because our work was not opened out.[433] Khujand is a poor place; a man with 2 or 300 followers would have a hard time there; withFol. 59. what outlook would an ambitious man set himself down in it?

As it was our wish to return to Samarkand, we sent people to confer with Muḥammad Ḥusain *Kūrkān Dūghlāt* in Aūrā-tīpā and to ask of him the loan for the winter of Pashāghar where we might sit till it was practicable to make a move on Samarkand. He consenting, I rode out from Khujand for Pashāghar.

> (*Author's note on Pashāghar.*) Pashāghar is one of the villages of Yār-yīlāq; it had belonged to his Highness the Khwāja,[434] but during recent interregna,[435] it had become dependent on Muḥammad Ḥusain Mīrzā.

I had fever when we reached Zamīn, but spite of my fever we hurried off by the mountain road till we came over against Rabāṭ-i-khwāja, the head-quarters of the sub-governor of the Shavdār *tūmān*, where we hoped to take the garrison at unawares, set our ladders up and so get into the fort. We reached it at dawn, found its men on guard, turned back and rode without halt to Pashāghar. The pains and misery of fever notwithstanding, I had ridden 14 or 15 *yīghāch* (70 to 80 miles).

After a few days in Pashāghar, we appointed Ibrāhīm *Sārū*, Fol. 59b.Wais *Lāgharī*, Sherīm Ṭaghāī and some of the household and braves to make an expedition amongst the Yār-yīlāq forts and get them into our hands. Yār-yīlāq, at that time was Sayyid Yūsuf Beg's,[436] he having remained in Samarkand at the exodus and been much favoured by Sl. 'Ali Mīrzā. To manage the forts, Sayyid Yūsuf had sent his younger brother's son, Aḥmad-i-yūsuf, now[437] Governor of Sialkot, and Aḥmad-i-yūsuf was then in occupation. In the course of that winter, our begs and braves made the round, got possession of some of the forts peacefully, fought and took others, gained some by ruse and craft. In the whole of that district there is perhaps not a single village without its defences because of the Mughūls and the Aūzbegs. Meantime Sl. 'Alī Mīrzā became suspicious of Sayyid Yūsuf and his nephew on my account and dismissed both towards Khurāsān.

The winter passed in this sort of tug-of-war; with the oncoming heats,[438] they sent Khwāja Yaḥya to treat with me, while they, urged on by the (Samarkand) army, marched out to near Shīrāz and Kabud. I may have had 200 or 300 soldiers (*sipāhī*); powerful foes were on my every side; Fortune had Fol. 60.not favoured me when I turned to Andijān; when I put a hand out for Samarkand, no work was opened out. Of necessity, some sort of terms were made and I went back from Pashāghar.

Khujand is a poor place; one beg would have a hard time in it; there we and our families and following had been for half a year[439] and during the time the Musalmāns of the place had not been backward in bearing our charges and serving us to the best of their power. With what face could we go there again? and what, for his own part, could a man do there? 'To what home to go? For what gain to stay?'[440]

In the end and with the same anxieties and uncertainty, we went to the summer-pastures in the south of Aūrā-tīpā. There we spent some days in amazement at our position, not knowing where to go or where to stay, our heads in a whirl. On one of those days, Khwāja Abū'l-makāram came to see me, he like me, a wanderer, driven from his home.[441] He questioned us about our goings and stayings, about what had or had not been done and about our whole position. He was touched with compassion for our state and recited the *fātiḥa* for me before he left. I also was much touched; I pitied him.

(*b. Bābur recovers Marghīnān.*)

Near the Afternoon Prayer of that same day, a horseman appeared at the foot of the valley. He was a man named Yūl-chūq, presumably 'Ali-dost Ṭaghāī's own servant, and had been sent with this written message, 'Although many great misdeeds have had their rise in me, yet, if you will do me theFol. 60b. favour and kindness of coming to me, I hope to purge my offences and remove my reproach, by giving you Marghīnān and by my future submission and single-minded service.'

Such news! coming on such despair and whirl-of-mind! Off we hurried, that very hour,—it was sun-set,—without reflecting, without a moment's delay, just as if for a sudden raid, straight for Marghīnān. From where we were to Marghīnān may have been 24 or 25 *yīghāch* of road.[442] Through that night it was rushed without delaying anywhere, and on next day till at the Mid-day Prayer, halt was made at Tang-āb (Narrow-water), one of the villages of Khujand. There we cooled down our horses and gave them corn. We rode out again at beat of (twilight-) drum[443] and on through that night till shoot of dawn, and through the next day till sunset, and on through that night till, just before dawn, we were one *yīghāch* from Marghīnān. Here Wais Beg and others represented to me with some anxiety what sort of an evil-doer ‘Ali-dost was. ‘No-one,’ they said, ‘has come and gone, time and again, between him and us; no terms and compact have been made; trusting to what are we going?’ In truth their fears were just! After waiting awhile to consult, we at last agreed that Fol. 61.reasonable as anxiety was, it ought to have been earlier; that there we were after coming three nights and two days without rest or halt; in what horse or in what man was any strength left?—from where we were, how could return be made? and, if made, where were we to go?—that, having come so far, on we must, and that nothing happens without God’s will. At this we left the matter and moved on, our trust set on Him.

At the Sunnat Prayer[444] we reached Fort Marghīnān. ‘Alī-dost Ṭ̤aghāī kept himself behind (*arqa*) the closed gate and asked for terms; these granted, he opened it. He did me obeisance between the (two) gates.[445] After seeing him, we dismounted at a suitable house in the walled-town. With me, great and small, were 240 men.

As Aūzūn Ḥasan and Taṃbal had been tyrannical and oppressive, all the clans of the country were asking for me. We therefore, after two or three days spent in Marghīnān, joined to Qāsim Beg over a hundred men of the Pashāgharīs, the new retainers of Marghīnān and of ‘Alī-dost’s following, and sent them to bring over to me, by force or fair words, such hill-people of the south of Andijān as the Ashpārī, Tūrūqshār,Fol. 61b. Chīkrāk and others roundabout. Ibrāhīm Sārū and Wais *Lāgharī* and Sayyidī Qarā were also sent out, to cross the Khujand-water and, by whatever means, to induce the people on that side to turn their eyes to me.

Aūzūn Ḥasan and Taṃbal, for their parts, gathered together what soldiers and Mughūls they had and called up the men accustomed to serve in the Andijān and Akhsī armies. Then, bringing Jahāngīr Mīrzā with them, they came to Sapān, a village 2 m. east of Marghīnān, a few days after our arrival, and dismounted there with the intention of besieging Marghīnān. They advanced a day or two later, formed up to fight, as far as the suburbs. Though after the departure of the Commanders, Qāsim Beg, Ibrāhīm *Sārū* and Wais *Lāgharī*, few men were left with me, those there were formed up, sallied out and prevented the enemy from advancing beyond the suburbs. On that day, Page Khalīl, the turban-twister, went well forward and got his hand into the work. They had come; they could do nothing; on two other days they failed to get near the fort.Fol. 62.

When Qāsim Beg went into the hills on the south of Andijān, all the Ashpārī, Tūrūqshār, Chīkrāk, and the peasants and highland and lowland clans came in for us. When the Commanders, Ibrāhīm *Sārū* and Wais *Lāgharī*, crossed the river to the Akhsī side, Pāp and several other forts came in.

Aūzūn Ḥasan and Taṃbal being the heathenish and vicious tyrants they were, had inflicted great misery on the peasantry and clansmen. One of the chief men of Akhsī, Ḥasan-dīkcha by name,[446] gathered together his own following and a body of the Akhsī mob and rabble, black-bludgeoned[447] Aūzūn Ḥasan's and Taṃbal's men in the outer fort and drubbed them into the citadel. They then invited the Commanders, Ibrāhīm *Sārū*, Wais *Lāgharī* and Sayyidī Qarā and admitted them into the fort.

Sl. Maḥmūd Khān had appointed to help us, Ḥaidar *Kūkūldāsh's* (son) Banda-'alī and Ḥājī Ghāzī *Manghīt*,[448] the latter just then a fugitive from Shaibānī Khān, and also the Bārīn *tūmān* with its begs. They arrived precisely at this time.

Fol. 62b.These news were altogether upsetting to Aūzūn Ḥasan; he at once started off his most favoured retainers and most serviceable braves to help his men in the citadel of Akhsī. His force reached the brow of the river at dawn. Our Commanders and the (Tāshkīnt) Mughūls had heard of its approach and had made some of their men strip their horses and cross the river (to the Andijān side). Aūzūn Ḥasan's men, in their haste, did not draw the ferry-boat up-stream;[449] they consequently went right away from the landing-place, could not cross for the fort and went down stream.[450] Here-upon, our men and the (Tāshkīnt) Mughūls began to ride bare-back into the water from both banks. Those in the boat could make no fight at all. Qārlūghāch (var. Qārbūghāch) *Bakhshī* (Pay-master) called one of Mughūl Beg's sons to him, took him by the hand, chopped at him and killed him. Of what use was it? The affair was past that! His act was the cause why most of those in the boat went to their death. Instantly our men seized them all (*arīq*) and killed all (but a few).[451] Of Aūzūn Ḥasan's confidants escaped Qārlūghāch *Bakhshī* and Khalīl *Dīwān* and Qāẓī *Ghulām*, the last getting off by pretending to be a slave (*ghulām*); and of his trusted braves, Sayyid 'Alī, now in trust in my own service,[452] and Ḥaidar-i-qulī and Qilka *Kāshgharī* escaped. Of his 70 or 80 men, no more than this Fol. 63.same poor five or six got free.

On hearing of this affair, Aūzūn Ḥasan and Taṃbal, not being able to remain near Marghīnān, marched in haste and disorder for Andijān. There they had left Nāṣir Beg, the husband of Aūzūn Ḥasan's sister. He, if not Aūzūn Ḥasan's second, what question is there he was his third?[453] He was an experienced man, brave too; when he heard particulars, he knew their ground was lost, made Andijān fast and sent a man to me. They broke up in disaccord when they found the fort made fast against them; Aūzūn Ḥasan drew off to his wife in Akhsī, Taṃbal to his district of Aūsh. A few of Jahāngīr Mīrzā's household and braves fled with him from Aūzūn Ḥasan and joined Taṃbal before he had reached Aūsh.

(c. Bābur recovers Andijān.)

Directly we heard that Andijān had been made fast against them, I rode out, at sun-rise, from Marghīnān and by mid-day was in Andijān.[454] There I saw Nāṣir Beg and his two sons, that is to say, Dost Beg and Mīrīm Beg, questioned them and uplifted their heads with hope of favour and kindness. In this way, by God's grace, my father's country, lost to me for two years, was regained and re-possessed, in the month Ẕū'l-qa'da ofFol. 63b. the date 904 (June 1498).[455]

Sl. Aḥmad Taṃbal, after being joined by Jahāngīr Mīrzā, drew away for Aūsh. On his entering the town, the red rabble *(qīzīl ayāq)* there, as in Akhsī, black-bludgeoned *(qarā tīyāq qīlīb)* and drubbed his men out, blow upon blow, then kept the fort for me and sent me a man. Jahāngīr and Taṃbal went off confounded, with a few followers only, and entered Aūzkīnt Fort.

Of Aūzūn Ḥasan news came that after failing to get into Andijān, he had gone to Akhsī and, it was understood, had entered the citadel. He had been head and chief in the rebellion; we therefore, on getting this news, without more than four or five days' delay in Andijān, set out for Akhsī. On our arrival, there was nothing for him to do but ask for peace and terms, and surrender the fort.

We stayed in Akhsī[456] a few days in order to settle its affairs and those of Kāsān and that country-side. We gave the Mughūls who had come in to help us, leave for return (to Tāshkīnt), then went back to Andijān, taking with us Aūzūn Ḥasan and his family and dependants. In Akhsī was left, for a time, Qāsim-i-'ajab (Wonderful Qāsim), formerly one of the household circle, now arrived at beg's rank.

(d. Renewed rebellion of the Mughūls.)

As terms had been made, Aūzūn Ḥasan, without hurt to life Fol. 64.or goods, was allowed to go by the Qarā-tīgīn road for Ḥiṣār. A few of his retainers went with him, the rest parted from him and stayed behind. These were the men who in the throneless times had captured and plundered various Musalmān dependants of my own and of the Khwāja. In agreement with several begs, their affair was left at this;—'This very band have been the captors and plunderers of our faithful Musalmān dependants;[457] what loyalty have they shown to their own (Mughūl) begs that they should be loyal to us? If we had them seized and stripped bare, where would be the wrong? and this especially because they might be going about, before our very eyes, riding our horses, wearing our coats, eating our sheep. Who could put up with that? If, out of humanity, they are not imprisoned and not plundered, they certainly ought to take it as a favour if they get off with the order to give back to our companions of the hard guerilla times, whatever goods of theirs are known to be here.'

In truth this seemed reasonable; our men were ordered to take what they knew to be theirs. Reasonable and just though the order was, (I now) understand that it was a little hasty. Fol. 64b.With a worry like Jahāngīr seated at my side, there was no sense in frightening people in this way. In conquest and government, though many things may have an outside appearance of reason and justice, yet 100,000 reflections are right and necessary as to the bearings of each one of them. From this single incautious order of ours,[458] what troubles! what rebellions arose! In the end this same ill-considered order was the cause of our second exile from Andijān. Now, through it, the Mughūls gave way to anxiety and fear, marched through Rabāṯik-aūrchīnī, that is, Aīkī-sū-ārāsī, for Aūzkīnt and sent a man to Taṃbal.

In my mother's service were 1500 to 2000 Mughūls from the horde; as many more had come from Ḥiṣār with Ḥamza Sl. and Mahdī Sl. and Muḥammad *Dūghlāt Ḥiṣārī*.[459] Mischief and devastation must always be expected from the Mughūl horde. Up to now[460] they have rebelled five times against me. It must not be understood that they rebelled through not getting on with me; they have done the same thing with their own Khāns, again and again. Sl. Qulī *Chūnāq*[461] brought me the news. His late father, Khudāī-bīrdī *Būqāq*[462] I had favoured amongst the Mughūls; he was himself with the (rebel) MughūlsFol. 65. and he did well in thus leaving the horde and his own family to bring me the news. Well as he did then however, he, as will be told,[463] did a thing so shameful later on that it would hide a hundred such good deeds as this, if he had done them. His later action was the clear product of his Mughūl nature. When this news came, the begs, gathered for counsel, represented to me, 'This is a trifling matter; what need for the pādshāh to ride out? Let Qāsim Beg go with the begs and men assembled here.' So it was settled; they took it lightly; to do so must have been an error of judgment. Qāsim Beg led his force out that same day; Taṃbal meantime must have joined the Mughūls. Our men crossed the Aīlāīsh river[464] early next morning by the Yāsī-kījīt (Broad-crossing) and at once came face to face with the rebels. Well did they chop at one another (*chāpqūlāshūrlār*)! Qāsim Beg himself came face to face with Muḥammad *Arghūn* and did not desist from chopping at him in order to cut off his head.[465] Most of our braves exchanged Fol. 65b.good blows but in the end were beaten. Qāsim Beg, 'Alī-dost Ṯaghāī, Ibrāhīm *Sārū*, Wais *Lāgharī*, Sayyidī Qarā and three or four more of our begs and household got away but most of the rest fell into the hands of the rebels. Amongst them were 'Alī-darwesh Beg and Mīrīm *Lāgharī* and (Sherīm?) Ṯaghāī Beg's (son)

Tūqā[466] and 'Alī-dost's son, Muḥammad-dost and Mīr Shāh *Qūchīn* and Mīrīm Dīwān.

Two braves chopped very well at one another; on our side, Samad, Ibrāhīm *Sārū's* younger brother, and on their side, Shāh-suwār, one of the Ḥiṣārī Mughūls. Shāh-suwār struck so that his sword drove through Samad's helm and seated itself well in his head; Samad, spite of his wound, struck so that his sword cut off Shāh-suwār's head a piece of bone as large as the palm of a hand. Shāh-suwār must have worn no helm; they trepanned his head and it healed; there was no one to trepan Samad's and in a few days, he departed simply through the wound.[467]

Amazingly unseasonable was this defeat, coming as it did just in the respite from guerilla fighting and just when we had regained the country. One of our great props, Qaṃbar-'alī *Mughūl* (the Skinner) had gone to his district when Andijān Fol. 66.was occupied and therefore was not with us.

(*e. Taṃbal attempts to take Andijān.*)

Having effected so much, Taṃbal, bringing Jahāngīr Mīrzā with him, came to the east of Andijān and dismounted 2 miles off, in the meadow lying in front of the Hill of Pleasure ('Aīsh).[468]

Once or twice he advanced in battle-array, past Chihil-dukhterān[469] to the town side of the hill but, as our braves went out arrayed to fight, beyond the gardens and suburbs, he could not advance further and returned to the other side of the hill. On his first coming to those parts, he killed two of the begs he had captured, Mīrīm *Lāgharī* and Tūqā Beg. For nearly a month he lay round-about without effecting anything; after that he retired, his face set for Aūsh. Aūsh had been given to Ibrāhīm *Sārū* and his man in it now made it fast.

905 AH. AUG. 8TH. 1499 TO JULY 28TH. 1500 AD.470

(*a. Bābur's campaign against Aḥmad Taṃbal Mughūl.*)

Commissaries were sent gallopping off at once, some to call up the horse and foot of the district-armies, others to urge return on Qaṃbar-'alī and whoever else was away in his own district, while energetic people were told off to get together mantelets (*tūra*), shovels, axes and the what-not of war-material and stores for the men already with us.

As soon as the horse and foot, called up from the various districts to join the army, and the soldiers and retainers who had been scattered to this and that side on their own affairs, were gathered together, I went out, on Muḥarram 18th. (August 25th.), putting my trust in God, to Ḥāfiẓ Beg's Four-gardens Fol. 66b.and there stayed a few days in order to complete our equipment. This done, we formed up in array of right and left, centre and van, horse and foot, and started direct for Aūsh against our foe.

On approaching Aūsh, news was had that Taṃbal, unable to make stand in that neighbourhood, had drawn off to the north, to the Rabāṭ-i-sarhang sub-district, it was understood. That night we dismounted in Lāt-kīnt. Next day as we were passing through Aūsh, news came that Taṃbal was understood to have gone to Andijān. We, for our part, marched on as for Aūzkīnt, detaching raiders ahead to over-run those parts.[471] Our opponents went to Andijān and at night got into the ditch but being discovered by the garrison when they set their ladders up against the ramparts, could effect no more and retired. Our raiders retired also after over-running round about Aūzkīnt without getting into their hands anything worth their trouble.

Taṃbal had stationed his younger brother, Khalīl, with 200 or 300 men, in Māḏū,[472] one of the forts of Aūsh, renowned in that centre (*ārā*) for its strength. We turned back (on theFol. 67. Aūzkīnt road) to assault it. It is exceedingly strong. Its northern face stands very high above the bed of a torrent; arrows shot from the bed might perhaps reach the ramparts. On this side is the water-thief,[473] made like a lane, with ramparts on both sides carried from the fort to the water. Towards the rising ground, on the other sides of the fort, there is a ditch. The torrent being so near, those occupying the fort had carried stones in from it as large as those for large mortars.[474] From no fort of its class we have ever attacked, have stones been thrown so large as those taken into Māḏū. They dropped such a large one on 'Abdu'l-qāsim *Kohbur*, Kitta (Little) Beg's elder brother,[475] when he went up under the ramparts, that he spun head over heels and came rolling and rolling, without once getting to his feet, from that great height down to the foot of the glacis (*khāk-rez*). He did not trouble himself about it at all but just got on his horse and rode off. Again, a stone flung from the double water-way, hit Yār-'alī *Balāl* so hard on the head that in the end it had to be trepanned.[476] Many of our men perished by their stones. The assault began at dawn; the water-thiefFol. 67b. had been taken before breakfast-time;[477] fighting went on till evening; next morning, as they could not hold out after losing the water-thief, they asked for terms and came out. We took 60 or 70 or 80 men of Khalīl's command and sent them to Andijān for safe-keeping; as some of our begs and household were prisoners in their hands, the Māḏū affair fell out very well.[478]

From there we went to Unjū-tūpa, one of the villages of Aūsh, and there dismounted. When Taṃbal retired from Andijān and went into the Rabāṯ-i-sarhang sub-district, he dismounted in a village called Āb-i-khān. Between him and me may have been one *yīghāch* (5 m.?). At such a time as this, Qaṃbar-'alī (the Skinner) on account of some sickness, went into Aūsh.

It was lain in Unjū-tūpa a month or forty days without a battle, but day after day our foragers and theirs got to grips. All through the time our camp was mightily well watched at night; a ditch was dug; where no ditch was, branches were set close together;[479] we also made our soldiers go out in their mail Fol. 68.along the ditch. Spite of such watchfulness, a night-alarm was given every two or three days, and the cry to arms went up. One day when Sayyidī Beg Ṯaghāī had gone out with the foragers, the enemy came up suddenly in greater strength and took him prisoner right out of the middle of the fight.

(*b. Bāī-sunghar Mīrzā murdered by Khusrau Shāh.*)

Khusrau Shāh, having planned to lead an army against Balkh, in this same year invited Bāī-sunghar Mīrzā to go with him, brought him[480] to Qūndūz and rode out with him for Balkh. But when they reached the Aubāj ferry, that ungrateful infidel, Khusrau Shāh, in his aspiration to sovereignty,—and to what sort of sovereignty, pray, could such a no-body attain? a person of no merit, no birth, no lineage, no judgment, no magnanimity, no justice, no legal-mindedness,—laid hands on Bāī-sunghar Mīrzā with his begs, and bowstrung the Mīrzā. It was upon the 10th. of the month of Muḥarram (August 17th.) that he martyred that scion of sovereignty, so accomplished, so sweet-natured and so adorned by birth and lineage. He killed also a few of the Mīrzā's begs and household.

(*c. Bāī-sunghar Mīrzā's birth and descent.*)

He was born in 882 (1477 AD.), in the Ḥiṣār district. He was Sl. Maḥmūd Mīrzā's second son, younger than Sl. Mas'ud M. and older than Sl. 'Alī M. and Sl. Ḥusain M. and Sl. Wais M. known as Khān Mīrzā. His mother was Pasha Begīm.Fol. 68b.

(d. His appearance and characteristics.)

He had large eyes, a fleshy face[481] and Turkmān features, was of middle height and altogether an elegant young man (*aet.* 22).

(e. His qualities and manners.)

He was just, humane, pleasant-natured and a most accomplished scion of sovereignty. His tutor, Sayyid Maḥmūd,[482] presumably was a Shī'a; through this he himself became infected by that heresy. People said that latterly, in Samarkand, he reverted from that evil belief to the pure Faith. He was much addicted to wine but on his non-drinking days, used to go through the Prayers.[483] He was moderate in gifts and liberality. He wrote the *naskh-ta'līq* character very well; in painting also his hand was not bad. He made 'Ādilī his pen-name and composed good verses but not sufficient to form a *dīwān*. Here is the opening couplet (*maṯla'*) of one of them[484];—

Like a wavering shadow I fall here and there;

If not propped by a wall, I drop flat on the ground.

In such repute are his odes held in Samarkand, that they are to be found in most houses.

(f. His battles.)

He fought two ranged battles. One, fought when he was first seated on the throne (900 AH.-1495 AD.), was with Sl. Maḥmūd Khān[485] who, incited and stirred up by Sl. Junaid *Barlās* and others to desire Samarkand, drew an army out,Fol. 69. crossed the Āq-kutal and went to Rabāṯ-i-soghd and Kān-bāī. Bāī-sunghar Mīrzā went out from Samarkand, fought him near Kān-bāī, beat him and beheaded 3 or 4000 Mughūls. In this fight died Ḥaidar *Kūkūldāsh*, the Khān's looser and binder (*ḥall u'aqdi*). His second battle was fought near Bukhārā with Sl. 'Alī Mīrzā (901 AH.-1496 AD.); in this he was beaten.[486]

(g. His countries.)

His father, Sl. Maḥmūd Mīrzā, gave him Bukhārā; when Sl. Maḥmūd M. died, his begs assembled and in agreement made Bāī-sunghar M. ruler in Samarkand. For a time, Bukhārā was included with Samarkand in his jurisdiction but it went out of his hands after the Tarkhān rebellion (901 AH.-1496 AD.). When he left Samarkand to go to Khusrau Shāh and I got possession of it (903 AH.-1497 AD.), Khusrau Shāh took Ḥiṣār and gave it to him.

(*h. Other details concerning him.*)

He left no child. He took a daughter of his paternal uncle, Sl. Khalīl Mīrzā, when he went to Khusrau Shāh; he had no other wife or concubine.

He never ruled with authority so independent that any beg was heard of as promoted by him to be his confidant; his begs Fol. 69b.were just those of his father and his paternal uncle (Aḥmad).

(*i. Resumed account of Bābur's campaign against Taṃbal.*)

After Bāī-sunghar Mīrzā's death, Sl. Aḥmad *Qarāwal*,[487] the father of Qūch (Qūj) Beg, sent us word (of his intention) and came to us from Ḥiṣār through the Qarā-tīgīn country, together with his brethren, elder and younger, and their families and dependants. From Aūsh too came Qaṃbar-'alī, risen from his sickness. Arriving, as it did, at such a moment, we took the providential help of Sl. Aḥmad and his party for a happy omen. Next day we formed up at dawn and moved direct upon our foe. He made no stand at Āb-i-khān but marched from his ground, leaving many tents and blankets and things of the baggage for our men. We dismounted in his camp.

That evening Taṃbal, having Jahāngīr with him, turned our left and went to a village called Khūbān (var. Khūnān), some 3 *yīghāch* from us (15 m.?) and between us and Andijān. Next day we moved out against him, formed up with right and left, centre and van, our horses in their mail, our men in theirs, and with foot-soldiers, bearing mantelets, flung to the front. Our right was 'Alī-dost and his dependants, our left Ibrāhīm *Sārū*, Wais *Lāgharī*, Sayyidī Qarā, Muḥammad-'alī *Mubashir*, and Khwāja-i-kalān's elder brother, Kīchīk Beg, with several ofFol. 70. the household. In the left were inscribed[488] also Sl. Aḥmad *Qarāwal* and Qūch Beg with their brethren. With me in the centre was Qāsim Beg *Qūchīn*; in the van were Qaṃbar-'alī (the Skinner) and some of the household. When we reached Sāqā, a village two miles east of Khūbān, the enemy came out of Khūbān, arrayed to fight. We, for our part, moved on the faster. At the time of engaging, our foot-soldiers, provided how laboriously with the mantelets! were quite in the rear! By God's grace, there was no need of them; our left had got hands in with their right before they came up. Kīchīk Beg chopped away very well; next to him ranked Muḥammad 'Alī *Mubashir*. Not being able to bring equal zeal to oppose us, the enemy took to flight. The fighting did not reach the front of our van or right. Our men brought in many of their braves; we ordered the heads of all to be struck off. Favouring caution and good generalship, our begs, Qāsim Beg and, especially, 'Alī-dost did not think it advisable to send far in pursuit; forFol. 70b. this reason, many of their men did not fall into our hands. We dismounted right in Khūbān village. This was my first ranged battle; the Most High God, of His own favour and mercy, made it a day of victory and triumph. We accepted the omen.

On the next following day, my father's mother, my grandmother, Shāh Sulṭān Begīm[489] arrived from Andijān, thinking to beg off Jahāngīr Mīrzā if he had been taken.

(j. Bābur goes into winter-quarters in Between-the-two-rivers.)

As it was now almost winter and no grain or fruits[490] remained in the open country, it was not thought desirable to move against (Taṃbal in) Aūzkīnt but return was made to Andijān. A few days later, it was settled after consultation, that for us to winter in the town would in no way hurt or hamper the enemy, rather that he would wax the stronger by it through raids and guerilla fighting; moreover on our own account, it was necessary that we should winter where our men would not become enfeebled through want of grain and where we could straiten the enemy by some sort of blockade. For these desirable Fol. 71.ends we marched out of Andijān, meaning to winter near Armiyān and Nūsh-āb in the Rabāṭik-aūrchīnī, known also as Between-the-two-rivers. On arriving in the two villages above-mentioned, we prepared winter-quarters.

The hunting-grounds are good in that neighbourhood; in the jungle near the Aīlāīsh river is much *būghū-marāl*[491] and pig; the small scattered clumps of jungle are thick with hare and pheasant; and on the near rising-ground, are many foxes[492] of fine colour and swifter than those of any other place. While we were in those quarters, I used to ride hunting every two or three days; we would beat through the great jungle and hunt *būghū-marāl*, or we would wander about, making a circle round scattered clumps and flying our hawks at the pheasants. The pheasants are unlimited[493] there; pheasant-meat was abundant as long as we were in those quarters.

While we were there, Khudāī-bīrdī *Tūghchī*, then newly-favoured with beg's rank, fell on some of Taṃbal's raiders and brought in a few heads. Our braves went out also from Aūsh and Andijān and raided untiringly on the enemy, driving in his herds of horses and much enfeebling him. If the whole winter had been passed in those quarters, the more probable thing isFol. 71b. that he would have broken up simply without a fight.

(k. Qaṃbar-'alī again asks leave.)

It was at such a time, just when our foe was growing weak and helpless, that Qaṃbar-'alī asked leave to go to his district. The more he was dissuaded by reminder of the probabilities of the position, the more stupidity he shewed. An amazingly fickle and veering manikin he was! It had to be! Leave for his district was given him. That district had been Khujand formerly but when Andijān was taken this last time, Asfara and Kand-i-badām were given him in addition. Amongst our begs, he was the one with large districts and many followers; no-one's land or following equalled his. We had been 40 or 50 days in those winter-quarters. At his recommendation, leave was given also to some of the clans in the army. We, for our part, went into Andijān.

(l. Sl. Maḥmūd Khān sends Mughūls to help Taṃbal.)

Both while we were in our winter-quarters and later on in Andijān, Taṃbal's people came and went unceasingly between him and The Khān in Tāshkīnt. His paternal uncle of the full-blood, Aḥmad Beg, was guardian of The Khān's son, Sl. Muḥammad Sl. and high in favour; his elder brother of the full-blood, Beg Tīlba (Fool), was The Khān's Lord of the Gate. After all the comings and goings, these two brought The Khān to the point of reinforcing Taṃbal. Beg Tīlba, leaving his wife and domestics and family in Tāshkīnt, came on ahead of theFol. 72. reinforcement and joined his younger brother, Taṃbal,—Beg Tīlba! who from his birth up had been in Mughūlistān, had grown up amongst Mughūls, had never entered a cultivated country or served the rulers of one, but from first to last had served The Khāns!

Just then a wonderful (*'ajab*) thing happened;[494] Qāsim-i-'ajab (wonderful Qāsim) when he had been left for a time in Akhsī, went out one day after a few marauders, crossed the Khujand-water by Bachrātā, met in with a few of Taṃbal's men and was made prisoner.

When Taṃbal heard that our army was disbanded and was assured of The Khān's help by the arrival of his brother, Beg Tīlba, who had talked with The Khān, he rode from Aūzkīnt into Between-the-two-rivers. Meantime safe news had come to us from Kāsān that The Khān had appointed his son, Sl. Muḥ. Khānika, commonly known as Sulṭānīm,[495] and Aḥmad Beg, with 5 or 6000 men, to help Taṃbal, that they had crossed by the Archa-kīnt road[496] and were laying siege to Kāsān. Hereupon we, without delay, without a glance at our absent men, just with those there were, in the hard cold of winter, put our Fol. 72b.trust in God and rode off by the Band-i-sālār road to oppose them. That night we stopped no-where; on we went through the darkness till, at dawn, we dismounted in Akhsī.[497] So mightily bitter was the cold that night that it bit the hands and feet of several men and swelled up the ears of many, each ear like an apple. We made no stay in Akhsī but leaving there Yārak Ṭaghāī, temporarily also, in Qāsim-i-'ajab's place, passed on for Kāsān. Two miles from Kāsān news came that on hearing of our approach, Aḥmad Beg and Sulṭānīm had hurried off in disorder.

(*m. Bābur and Taṃbal again opposed.*)

Taṃbal must have had news of our getting to horse for he had hurried to help his elder brother.[498] Somewhere between the two Prayers of the day,[499] his blackness[500] became visible towards Nū-kīnt. Astonished and perplexed by his elder brother's light departure and by our quick arrival, he stopped short. Said we, 'It is God has brought them in this fashion! here they have come with their horses' necks at full stretch;[501] if we join hands[502] and go out, and if God bring it right, not a man of them will get off.' But Wais *Lāghari* and some others said, 'It is late in the day; even if we do not go out today, where can they go tomorrow? Wherever it is, we will meetFol. 73. them at dawn.' So they said, not thinking it well to make the joint effort there and then; so too the enemy, come so opportunely, broke up and got away without any hurt whatever. The (Turkī) proverb is, 'Who does not snatch at a chance, will worry himself about it till old age.'

(Persian) couplet. Work must be snatched at betimes,
Vain is the slacker's mistimed work.

Seizing the advantage of a respite till the morrow, the enemy slipped away in the night, and without dismounting on the road, went into Fort Archīān. When a morrow's move against a foe was made, we found no foe; after him we went and, not thinking it well to lay close siege to Archīān, dismounted two miles off (one *shar'ī*) in Ghazna-namangān.[503] We were in camp there for 30 or 40 days, Taṃbal being in Fort Archīān. Every now and then a very few would go from our side and come from theirs, fling themselves on one another midway and return. They made one night-attack, rained arrows in on us and retired. As the camp was encircled by a ditch or by branches close-set, and as watch was kept, they could effect no more.

(*n. Qaṃbar-'alī, the Skinner, again gives trouble.*)

Two or three times while we lay in that camp, Qaṃbar-'alī,Fol. 73b. in ill-temper, was for going to his district; once he even had got to horse and started in a fume, but we sent several begs after him who, with much trouble, got him to turn back.

(*o. Further action against Taṃbal and an accommodation made.*)

Meantime Sayyid Yūsuf of Macham had sent a man to Taṃbal and was looking towards him. He was the head-man of one of the two foot-hills of Andijān, Macham and Awīghūr. Latterly he had become known in my Gate, having outgrown the head-man and put on the beg, though no-one ever had made him a beg. He was a singularly hypocritical manikin, of no standing whatever. From our last taking of Andijān (June 1499) till then (Feb. 1500), he had revolted two or three times from Taṃbal and come to me, and two or three times had revolted from me and gone to Taṃbal. This was his last change of side. With him were many from the (Mughūl) horde and tribesmen and clansmen. 'Don't let him join Taṃbal,' we said and rode in between them. We got to Bīshkhārān with one night's halt. Taṃbal's men must have come earlier and entered the fort. A party of our begs, 'Alī-darwesh Beg and Qūch Beg, with his brothers, went close up to the Gate of Fol. 74.Bīshkhārān and exchanged good blows with the enemy. Qūch Beg and his brothers did very well there, their hands getting in for most of the work. We dismounted on a height some two miles from Bīshkhārān; Taṃbal, having Jahāngīr with him, dismounted with the fort behind him.

Three or four days later, begs unfriendly to us, that is to say, 'Alī-dost and Qaṃbar-'alī, the Skinner, with their followers and dependants, began to interpose with talk of peace. I and my well-wishers had no knowledge of a peace and we all[504] were utterly averse from the project. Those two manikins however were our two great begs; if we gave no ear to their words and if we did not make peace, other things from them were probable! It had to be! Peace was made in this fashion;—the districts on the Akhsī side of the Khujand-water were to depend on Jahāngīr, those on the Andijān side, on me; Aūzkīnt was to be left in my jurisdiction after they had removed their families from it; when the districts were settled and I and Jahāngīr had made our agreement, we (*bīz*) should march together against Samarkand; and when I was in possession of Samarkand, Andijān was to be given to Jahāngīr. So the affair was settled.Fol. 74b. Next day,—it was one of the last of Rajab, (end of Feb. 1500) Jahāngīr Mīrzā and Taṃbal came and did me obeisance; the terms and conditions were ratified as stated above; leave for Akhsī was given to Jahāngīr and I betook myself to Andijān.

On our arrival, Khalīl-of-Taṃbal and our whole band of prisoners were released; robes of honour were put on them and leave to go was given. They, in their turn, set free our begs and household, *viz.* the commanders[505] (Sherīm?) Ṭaghāī Beg, Muḥammad-dost, Mīr Shāh *Qūchīn*, Sayyidī Qarā Beg, Qāsim-i-'ajab, Mīr Wais, Mīrīm *Dīwān*, and those under them.

(p. The self-aggrandizement of 'Alī-dost Ṭaghāī.)

After our return to Andijān, 'Alī-dost's manners and behaviour changed entirely. He began to live ill with my companions of the guerilla days and times of hardship. First, he dismissed Khalīfa; next seized and plundered Ibrāhīm *Sārū* and Wais *Lāgharī*, and for no fault or cause deprived them of their districts and dismissed them. He entangled himself with Qāsim Beg and *he* was made to go; he openly declared, 'Khalīfa and Ibrāhīm are in sympathy about Khwāja-i-qāẓī; they will avenge him on me.'[506] His son, Muḥammad-dost set himself up on a regal footing, starting receptions and a public table and aFol. 75. Court and workshops, after the fashion of sulṭāns. Like father, like son, they set themselves up in this improper way because they had Taṃbal at their backs. No authority to restrain their unreasonable misdeeds was left to me; for why? Whatever their hearts desired, that they did because such a foe of mine as Taṃbal was their backer. The position was singularly delicate; not a word was said but many humiliations were endured from that father and that son alike.

(*q. Bābur's first marriage.*)

'Āyisha-sulṭān Begīm whom my father and hers, *i.e.* my uncle, Sl. Aḥmad Mīrzā had betrothed to me, came (this year) to Khujand[507] and I took her in the month of Sha'bān. Though I was not ill-disposed towards her, yet, this being my first marriage, out of modesty and bashfulness, I used to see her once in 10, 15 or 20 days. Later on when even my first inclination did not last, my bashfulness increased. Then my mother Khānīm used to send me, once a month or every 40 Fol. 75b.days, with driving and driving, dunnings and worryings.

(*r. A personal episode and some verses by Bābur.*)

In those leisurely days I discovered in myself a strange inclination, nay! as the verse says, 'I maddened and afflicted myself' for a boy in the camp-bazar, his very name, Bāburī, fitting in. Up till then I had had no inclination for any-one, indeed of love and desire, either by hear-say or experience, I had not heard, I had not talked. At that time I composed Persian couplets, one or two at a time; this is one of the them:—

May none be as I, humbled and wretched and love-sick;

No beloved as thou art to me, cruel and careless.

From time to time Bāburī used to come to my presence but out of modesty and bashfulness, I could never look straight at him; how then could I make conversation (*ikhtilāṭ*) and recital (*ḥikāyat*)? In my joy and agitation I could not thank him (for coming); how was it possible for me to reproach him with going away? What power had I to command the duty of service to myself?[508] One day, during that time of desire and passion when I was going with companions along a lane and suddenly met him face to face, I got into such a state of confusion that I almost went right off. To look straight at him Fol. 76.or to put words together was impossible. With a hundred torments and shames, I went on. A (Persian) couplet of Muḥammad Ṣāliḥ's[509] came into my mind:—

I am abashed with shame when I see my friend;

My companions look at me, I look the other way.

That couplet suited the case wonderfully well. In that frothing-up of desire and passion, and under that stress of youthful folly, I used to wander, bare-head, bare-foot, through street and lane, orchard and vineyard. I shewed civility neither to friend nor stranger, took no care for myself or others.

(*Turki*) Out of myself desire rushed me, unknowing
That this is so with the lover of a fairy-face.

Sometimes like the madmen, I used to wander alone over hill and plain; sometimes I betook myself to gardens and the suburbs, lane by lane. My wandering was not of my choice, not I decided whether to go or stay.

(*Turki*) Nor power to go was mine, nor power to stay;
I was just what you made me, o thief of my heart.

(*s. Sl. 'Alī Mīrzā's quarrels with the Tarkhāns.*)

In this same year, Sl. 'Alī Mīrzā fell out with Muḥammad Mazīd Tarkhān for the following reasons;—The Tarkhāns had risen to over-much predominance and honour; Bāqī had taken the whole revenue of the Bukhārā Government and gave not aFol. 76b. half-penny (*dāng*)[510] to any-one else; Muḥammad Mazīd, for his part, had control in Samarkand and took all its districts for his sons and dependants; a small sum only excepted, fixed by them, not a farthing (*fils*) from the town reached the Mīrzā by any channel. Sl. 'Alī Mīrzā was a grown man; how was he to tolerate such conduct as theirs? He and some of his household formed a design against Muḥ. Mazīd Tarkhān; the latter came to know of it and left the town with all his following and with whatever begs and other persons were in sympathy with him,[511] such as Sl. Ḥusain *Arghūn*, Pīr Aḥmad, Aūzūn Ḥasan's younger brother, Khwāja Ḥusain, Qarā *Barlās*, Ṣāliḥ Muḥammad[512] and some other begs and braves.

At the time The Khān had joined to Khān Mīrzā a number of Mughūl begs with Muḥ. Ḥusain *Dūghlāt* and Aḥmad Beg, and had appointed them to act against Samarkand.[513] Khān Mīrzā's guardians were Ḥāfiẓ Beg *Dūldāī* and his son, Ṭāhir Beg; because of relationship to them, (Muḥ. Sīghal's) grandson, Ḥasan and Hindū Beg fled with several braves from Sl. 'Alī Fol. 77.Mīrzā's presence to Khān Mīrzā's.

Muḥammad Mazīd Tarkhān invited Khān Mīrzā and the Mughūl army, moved to near Shavdār, there saw the Mīrzā and met the begs of the Mughūls. No small useful friendlinesses however, came out of the meeting between his begs and the Mughūls; the latter indeed seem to have thought of making him a prisoner. Of this he and his begs coming to know, separated themselves from the Mughūl army. As without him the Mughūls could make no stand, they retired. Here-upon, Sl. 'Alī Mīrzā hurried light out of Samarkand with a few men and caught them up where they had dismounted in Yār-yīlāq. They could not even fight but were routed and put to flight. This deed, done in his last days, was Sl. 'Alī Mīrzā's one good little affair.

Muḥ. Mazīd Tarkhān and his people, despairing both of the Mughūls and of these Mīrzās, sent Mīr Mughūl, son of 'Abdu'l-wahhāb *Shaghāwal*[514] to invite me (to Samarkand). Mīr Mughūl had already been in my service; he had risked his life in good accord with Khwāja-i-qāẓī during the siege of Andijān (903 AH.-1498 AD.).

This business hurt us also[515] and, as it was for that purpose we had made peace (with Jahāngīr), we resolved to move on Samarkand. We sent Mīr Mughūl off at once to give rendezvous[516] Fol. 77b.to Jahāngīr Mīrzā and prepared to get to horse. We rode out in the month of Ẕū'l-qa'da (June) and with two halts on the way, came to Qabā and there dismounted.[517] At the mid-afternoon Prayer of that day, news came that Taṃbal's brother, Khalīl had taken Aūsh by surprise.

The particulars are as follows;—As has been mentioned, Khalīl and those under him were set free when peace was made. Taṃbal then sent Khalīl to fetch away their wives and families from Aūzkīnt. He had gone and he went into the fort on this pretext. He kept saying untruthfully, 'We will go out today,' or 'We will go out tomorrow,' but he did not go. When we got to horse, he seized the chance of the emptiness of Aūsh to go by night and surprise it. For several reasons it was of no advantage for us to stay and entangle ourselves with him; we went straight on therefore. One reason was that as, for the purpose of making ready military equipment, all my men of name had scattered, heads of houses to their homes, we had no news of them because we had relied on the peace and were by this off our guard against the treachery and falsity of the other party. Another reason was that for some time, as has beenFol. 78. said, the misconduct of our great begs, 'Alī-dost and Qaṃbar-'alī had been such that no confidence in them was left. A further reason was that the Samarkand begs, under Muḥ. Mazīd Tarkhān had sent Mīr Mughūl to invite us and, so long as a capital such as Samarkand stood there, what would incline a man to waste his days for a place like Andijān?

From Qabā we moved on to Marghīnān (20 m.). Marghīnān had been given to Qūch Beg's father, Sl. Aḥmad *Qarāwal*, and he was then in it. As he, owing to various ties and attachments, could not attach himself to me,[518] he stayed behind while his son, Qūch Beg and one or two of his brethren, older and younger, went with me.

Taking the road for Asfara, we dismounted in one of its villages, called Mahan. That night there came and joined us in Mahan, by splendid chance, just as if to a rendezvous, Qāsim Beg *Qūchīn* with his company, 'Alī-dost with his, and Sayyid Qāsim with a large body of braves. We rode from Mahan by the Khasbān (var. Yasān) plain, crossed the Chūpān (Shepherd)-bridge and so to Aūrā-tīpā.[519]

(t. Qaṃbar-'alī punishes himself.)

Trusting to Taṃbal, Qaṃbar-'alī went from his own district (Khujand) to Akhsī in order to discuss army-matters with him. Fol. 78b.Such an event happening,[520] Taṃbal laid hands on Qaṃbar-'alī, marched against his district and carried him along. Here the (Turkī) proverb fits, 'Distrust your friend! he'll stuff your hide with straw.' While Qaṃbar-'alī was being made to go to Khujand, he escaped on foot and after a hundred difficulties reached Aūrā-tīpā.

News came to us there that Shaibānī Khān had beaten Bāqī Tarkhān in Dabūsī and was moving on Bukhārā. We went on from Aūrā-tīpā, by way of Burka-yīlāq, to Sangzār[521] which the sub-governor surrendered. There we placed Qaṃbar-'alī, as, after effecting his own capture and betrayal, he had come to us. We then passed on.

(u. Affairs of Samarkand and the end of 'Alī-dost.)

On our arrival in Khān-yūrtī, the Samarkand begs under Muḥ. Mazīd Tarkhān came and did me obeisance. Conference was held with them as to details for taking the town; they said, 'Khwāja Yaḥya also is wishing for the *pādshāh*;[522] with his consent the town may be had easily without fighting or disturbance.' The Khwāja did not say decidedly to our messengers that he had resolved to admit us to the town but at the same time, he said nothing likely to lead us to despair.

Leaving Khān-yūrtī, we moved to the bank of the Dar-i-gham (canal) and from there sent our librarian, Khwāja Muḥammad Fol. 79.'Alī to Khwāja Yaḥya. He brought word back, 'Let them come; we will give them the town.' Accordingly we rode from the Dar-i-gham straight for the town, at night-fall, but our plan came to nothing because Sl. Muḥammad *Dūldāī's* father, Sl. Maḥmūd had fled from our camp and given such information to (Sl. 'Alī's party) as put them on their guard. Back we went to the Dar-i-gham bank.

While I had been in Yār-yīlāq, one of my favoured begs, Ibrāhīm *Sārū* who had been plundered and driven off by 'Alī-dost,[523] came and did me obeisance, together with Muḥ. Yūsuf, the elder son of Sayyid Yūsuf (*Aūghlāqchī*). Coming in by ones and twos, old family servants and begs and some of the household gathered back to me there. All were enemies of 'Alī-dost; some he had driven away; others he had plundered; others again he had imprisoned. He became afraid. For why? Because with Taṃbal's backing, he had harassed and persecuted me and my well-wishers. As for me, my very nature sorted ill with the manikin's! From shame and fear, he could stay no longer with us; he asked leave; I took it as a personal favour; I gave it. On this leave, he and his son, Muḥammad-dost went to Taṃbal's presence. They became his intimates,Fol. 79b. and from father and son alike, much evil and sedition issued. 'Alī-dost died a few years later from ulceration of the hand. Muḥammad-dost went amongst the Aūzbegs; that was not altogether bad but, after some treachery to his salt, he fled from them and went into the Andijān foot-hills.[524] There he stirred up much revolt and trouble. In the end he fell into the hands of Aūzbeg people and they blinded him. The meaning of 'The salt took his eyes,' is clear in his case.[525]

After giving this pair their leave, we sent Ghūrī *Barlās* toward Bukhārā for news. He brought word that Shaibānī Khān had taken Bukhārā and was on his way to Samarkand. Here-upon, seeing no advantage in staying in that neighbourhood, we set out for Kesh where, moreover, were the families of most of the Samarkand begs.

When we had been a few weeks there, news came that Sl. 'Alī Mīrzā had given Samarkand to Shaibānī Khān. The particulars are these;—The Mīrzā's mother, Zuhra Begī Āghā

(*Aūzbeg*), in her ignorance and folly, had secretly written to Fol. 80.Shaibānī Khān that if he would take her (to wife) her son should give him Samarkand and that when Shaibānī had taken (her son's) father's country, he should give her son a country.[526] Sayyid Yūsuf *Arghūn* must have known of this plan, indeed will have been the traitor inventing it.

906 AH.—JULY 28TH. 1500 TO JULY 17TH. 1501 AD.527

(*a. Samarkand in the hands of the Aūzbegs.*)

When, acting on that woman's promise, Shaibānī Khān went to Samarkand, he dismounted in the Garden of the Plain. About mid-day Sl. 'Alī Mīrzā went out to him through the Four-roads Gate, without a word to any of his begs or unmailed braves, without taking counsel with any-one soever and accompanied only by a few men of little consideration from his own close circle. The Khān, for his part, did not receive him very favourably; when they had seen one another, he seated him on his less honourable hand.[528] Khwāja Yaḥya, on hearing of the Mīrzā's departure, became very anxious but as he could find no remedy,[529] went out also. The Khān looked at him without rising and said a few words in which blame had part, but when the Khwāja rose to leave, showed him the respect of rising.

As soon as Khwāja 'Alī[530] Bāy's[531] son, Jān-'alī heard in Rabāṭ-i-khwāja of the Mīrzā's going to Shaibānī Khān, he also went. As for that calamitous woman who, in her folly, gave her son's Fol. 80b.house and possessions to the winds in order to get herself a husband, Shaibānī Khān cared not one atom for her, indeed did not regard her as the equal of a mistress or a concubine.[532]

Confounded by his own act, Sl. 'Alī Mīrzā's repentance was extreme. Some of his close circle, after hearing particulars, planned for him to escape with them but to this he would not agree; his hour had come; he was not to be freed. He had dismounted in Tīmūr Sulṭān's quarters; three or four days later they killed him in Plough-meadow.[533] For a matter of this five-days' mortal life, he died with a bad name; having entered into a woman's affairs, he withdrew himself from the circle of men of good repute. Of such people's doings no more should be written; of acts so shameful, no more should be heard.

The Mīrzā having been killed, Shaibānī Khān sent Jān-'alī after his Mīrzā. He had apprehensions also about Khwāja Yaḥya and therefore dismissed him, with his two sons, Khwāja Muḥ. Zakarīya and Khwāja Bāqī, towards Khurāsān.[534] A few Aūzbegs followed them and near Khwāja Kārdzan martyred both the Khwāja and his two young sons. Though Shaibānī's Fol. 81.words were, 'Not through me the Khwāja's affair! Qaṃbar Bī and Kūpuk Bī did it,' this is worse than that! There is a proverb,[535] 'His excuse is worse than his fault,' for if begs, out of their own heads, start such deeds, unknown to their Khāns or Pādshāhs, what becomes of the authority of khānship and and sovereignty?

(*b. Bābur leaves Kesh and crosses the Mūra pass.*)

Since the Aūzbegs were in possession of Samarkand, we left Kesh and went in the direction of Ḥiṣār. With us started off Muḥ. Mazīd Tārkhān and the Samarkand begs under his command, together with their wives and families and people, but when we dismounted in the Chultū meadow of Chaghāniān, they parted from us, went to Khusrau Shāh and became his retainers.

Cut off from our own abiding-town and country,[536] not knowing where (else) to go or where to stay, we were obliged to traverse the very heart of Khusrau Shāh's districts, spite of what measure of misery he had inflicted on the men of our dynasty!

One of our plans had been to go to my younger Khān dādā, *i.e.* Alacha Khān, by way of Qarā-tīgīn and the Alāī,[537] but this was not managed. Next we were for going up the valley of the Kām torrent and over the Sara-tāq pass (*dābān*). When we were near Nūndāk, a servant of Khusrau Shāh brought me one set of nine horses[538] and one of nine pieces of cloth. When we dismounted at the mouth of the Kām valley, Sher-'alī.Fol. 81b. the page, deserted to Khusrau Shāh's brother, Walī and, next day, Qūch Beg parted from us and went to Ḥiṣār.[539]

We entered the valley and made our way up it. On its steep and narrow roads and at its sharp and precipitous saddles[540] many horses and camels were left. Before we reached the Sara-tāq pass we had (in 25 m.) to make three or four night-halts. A pass! and what a pass! Never was such a steep and narrow pass seen; never were traversed such ravines and precipices. Those dangerous narrows and sudden falls, those perilous heights and knife-edge saddles, we got through with much difficulty and suffering, with countless hardships and miseries. Amongst the Fān mountains is a large lake (Iskandar); it is 2 miles in circumference, a beautiful lake and not devoid of marvels.[541]

News came that Ibrāhīm Tarkhān had strengthened Fort Shīrāz and was seated in it; also that Qambar-'alī (the Skinner) and Abū'l-qāsim *Kohbur*, the latter not being able to stay in Khwāja Dīdār with the Aūzbegs in Samarkand,—had both come into Yār-yīlāq, strengthened its lower forts and occupied them.

Leaving Fān on our right, we moved on for Keshtūd. The head-man of Fān had a reputation for hospitality, generosity, Fol. 82.serviceableness and kindness. He had given tribute of 70 or 80 horses to Sl. Mas'ūd Mīrzā at the time the Mīrzā, when Sl. Ḥusain Mīrzā made attack on Ḥiṣār, went through Fān on his way to his younger brother, Bāī-sunghar Mīrzā in Samarkand. He did like service to others. To me he sent one second-rate horse; moreover he did not wait on me himself. So it was! Those renowned for liberality became misers when they had to do with me, and the politeness of the polite was forgotten. Khusrau Shāh was celebrated for liberality and kindness; what service he did Badī'u'z-zamān Mīrzā has been mentioned; to Bāqī Tarkhān and other begs he shewed great generosity also. Twice I happened to pass through his country;[542] not to speak of courtesy shewn to my peers, what he shewed to my lowest servants he did not shew to me, indeed he shewed less regard for us than for them.

(*Turkī*) Who, o my heart! has seen goodness from worldlings?
Look not for goodness from him who has none.

Under the impression that the Aūzbegs were in Keshtūd, we made an excursion to it, after passing Fān. Of itself it seemed Fol. 82b.to have gone to ruin; no-one seemed to be occupying it. We went on to the bank of the Kohik-water (Zar-afshān) and there dismounted. From that place we sent a few begs under Qāsim *Qūchīn* to surprise Rabāṯ-i-khwāja; that done, we crossed the river by a bridge from opposite Yārī, went through Yārī and over the Shunqār-khāna (Falcons'-home) range into Yār-yīlāq. Our begs went to Rabāṯ-i-khwāja and had set up ladders when the men within came to know about them and forced them to retire. As they could not take the fort, they rejoined us.

(*c. Bābur renews attack on Samarkand.*)

Qaṃbar-'alī (the Skinner) was (still) holding Sangzār; he came and saw us; Abū'l-qāsim *Kohbur* and Ibrāhīm Tarkhān showed loyalty and attachment by sending efficient men for our service. We went into Asfidik (var. Asfīndik), one of the Yār-yīlāq villages. At that time Shaibāq Khān lay near Khwāja Dīdār with 3 or 4000 Aūzbegs and as many more soldiers gathered in locally. He had given the Government of Samarkand to Jān-wafā, and Jān-wafā was then in the fort with 500 or 600 men. Ḥamza Sl. and Mahdī Sl. were lying near the fort, in the Quail-reserve. Our men, good and bad were 240.Fol. 83.

Having discussed the position with all my begs and unmailed braves, we left it at this;—that as Shaibānī Khān had taken possession of Samarkand so recently, the Samarkandīs would not be attached to him nor he to them; that if we made an effort at once, we might do the thing; that if we set ladders up and took the fort by surprise, the Samarkandīs would be for us; how should they not be? even if they gave us no help, they would not fight us for the Aūzbegs; and that Samarkand once in our hands, whatever was God's will, would happen.

Acting on this decision, we rode out of Yār-yīlāq after the Mid-day Prayer, and on through the dark till mid-night when we reached Khān-yūrtī. Here we had word that the Samarkandīs knew of our coming; for this reason we went no nearer to the town but made straight back from Khān-yūrtī. It was dawn when, after crossing the Kohik-water below Rabāṭ-i-khwāja, we were once more in Yār-yīlāq.

One day in Fort Asfīdik a household party was sitting in my presence; Dost-i-nāṣir and Nuyān[543] *Kūkūldāsh* and Khān-qulī-i-Karīm-dād and Shaikh Darwesh and Mīrīm-i-nāṣir were all there. Words were crossing from all sides when (I said), 'Come now! say when, if God bring it right, we shall takeFol. 83b. Samarkand.' Some said, 'We shall take it in the heats.' It was then late in autumn. Others said, 'In a month,' 'Forty days,' 'Twenty days.' Nuyān *Kūkūldāsh* said, 'We shall take it in 14.' God shewed him right! we did take it in exactly 14 days.

Just at that time I had a wonderful dream;—His Highness Khwāja 'Ubaid'l-lāh (*Aḥrārī*) seemed to come; I seemed to go out to give him honourable meeting; he came in and seated himself; people seemed to lay a table-cloth before him, apparently without sufficient care and, on account of this, something seemed to come into his Highness Khwāja's mind. Mullā Bābā (? *Pashāghari*) made me a sign; I signed back, 'Not through me! the table-layer is in fault!' The Khwāja understood and accepted the excuse.[544] When he rose, I escorted him out. In the hall of that house he took hold of either my right or left arm and lifted me up till one of my feet was off the ground, saying, in Turkī, 'Shaikh Maṣlaḥat has given (Samarkand).'[545] I really took Samarkand a few days later.

(*d. Bābur takes Samarkand by surprise.*)

In two or three days move was made from Fort Asfīdik to Fort Wasmand. Although by our first approach, we had let Fol. 84.our plan be known, we put our trust in God and made another expedition to Samarkand. It was after the Mid-day Prayer that we rode out of Fort Wasmand, Khwāja Abū'l-makāram accompanying us. By mid-night we reached the Deep-fosse-bridge in the Avenue. From there we sent forward a detachment of 70 or 80 good men who were to set up ladders opposite the Lovers'-cave, mount them and get inside, stand up to those in the Turquoise Gate, get possession of it and send a man to me. Those braves went, set their ladders up opposite the Lovers'-cave, got in without making anyone aware, went to the Gate, attacked Fāẓil Tarkhān, chopped at him and his few retainers, killed them, broke the lock with an axe and opened the Gate. At that moment I came up and went in.

> (*Author's note on Fāẓil Tarkhān.*) He was not one of those (Samarkand) Tarkhāns; he was a merchant-tarkhān of Turkistān. He had served Shaibānī Khān in Turkistān and had found favour with him.[546]

Abū'l-qāsim *Kohbur* himself had not come with us but had sent 30 or 40 of his retainers under his younger brother, Aḥmad-i-qāsim. No man of Ibrāhīm Tarkhān's was with us; his younger brother, Aḥmad Tarkhān came with a few retainers after I had entered the town and taken post in the Monastery.Fol. 84b.

The towns-people were still slumbering; a few traders peeped out of their shops, recognized me and put up prayers. When, a little later, the news spread through the town, there was rare delight and satisfaction for our men and the towns-folk. They killed the Aūzbegs in the lanes and gullies with clubs and stones like mad dogs; four or five hundred were killed in this fashion. Jān-wafā, the then governor, was living in Khwāja Yaḥya's house; he fled and got away to Shaibāq Khān.[547]

On entering the Turquoise Gate I went straight to the College and took post over the arch of the Monastery. There was a hubbub and shouting of 'Down! down!' till day-break. Some of the notables and traders, hearing what was happening, came joyfully to see me, bringing what food was ready and putting up prayers for me. At day-light we had news that the Aūzbegs were fighting in the Iron Gate where they had made themselves fast between the (outer and inner) doors. With 10, 15 or 20 men, I at once set off for the Gate but before I came up, the town-rabble, busy ransacking every corner of the newly-taken town for loot, had driven the Aūzbegs out through

Fol. 85.it. Shaibāq Khān, on hearing what was happening, hurried at sun-rise to the Iron Gate with 100 or 140 men. His coming was a wonderful chance but, as has been said, my men were very few. Seeing that he could do nothing, he rode off at once. From the Iron Gate I went to the citadel and there dismounted, at the Bū-stān palace. Men of rank and consequence and various head-men came to me there, saw me and invoked blessings on me.

Samarkand for nearly 140 years had been the capital of our dynasty. An alien, and of what stamp! an Aūzbeg foe, had taken possession of it! It had slipped from our hands; God gave it again! plundered and ravaged, our own returned to us.

Sl. Ḥusain Mīrzā took Harāt[548] as we took Samarkand, by surprise, but to the experienced, and discerning, and just, it will be clear that between his affair and mine there are distinctions and differences, and that his capture and mine are things apart.

Firstly there is this;—He had ruled many years, passed through much experience and seen many affairs.

Secondly;—He had for opponent, Yādgār Muḥ. Nāṣir Mīrzā, Fol. 85b.an inexperienced boy of 17 or 18.

Thirdly;—(Yādgār Mīrzā's) Head-equerry, Mīr 'Alī, a person well-acquainted with the particulars of the whole position, sent a man out from amongst Sl. Ḥusain Mīrzā's opponents to bring him to surprise them.

Fourthly;—His opponent was not in the fort but was in the Ravens'-garden. Moreover Yādgār Muḥ. Nāṣir Mīrzā and his followers are said to have been so prostrate with drink that three men only were in the Gate, they also drunk.

Fifthly;—he surprised and captured Harāt the first time he approached it.

On the other hand: firstly;—I was 19 when I took Samarkand.

Secondly;—I had as my opponent, such a man as Shaibāq Khān, of mature age and an eye-witness of many affairs.

Thirdly;—No-one came out of Samarkand to me; though the heart of its people was towards me, no-one could dream of coming, from dread of Shaibāq Khān.

Fourthly;—My foe was in the fort; not only was the fort taken but he was driven off.

Fifthly;—I had come once already; my opponent was on his guard about me. The second time we came, God brought it right! Samarkand was won.

In saying these things there is no desire to be-little the reputation of any man; the facts were as here stated. InFol. 86. writing these things, there is no desire to magnify myself; the truth is set down.

The poets composed chronograms on the victory; this one remains in my memory;—Wisdom answered, 'Know that its date is the *Victory* (*Fatḥ*) *of Bābur Bahādur*.'

Samarkand being taken, Shavdār and Soghd and the *tūmāns* and nearer forts began, one after another, to return to us. From some their Aūzbeg commandants fled in fear and escaped; from others the inhabitants drove them and came in to us; in some they made them prisoner, and held the forts for us.

Just then the wives and families of Shaibāq Khān and his Aūzbegs arrived from Turkistān;[549] he was lying near Khwāja Dīdār and 'Alī-ābād but when he saw the forts and people returning to me, marched off towards Bukhārā. By God's grace, all the forts of Soghd and Miyān-kāl returned to me within three or four months. Over and above this, Bāqī Tarkhān seized this opportunity to occupy Qarshī; Khuzār and Qarshī (? Kesh) both went out of Aūzbeg hands; Qarā-kūlFol. 86b. also was taken from them by people of Abū'l-muḥsin Mīrzā (*Bāī-qarā*), coming up from Merv. My affairs were in a very good way.

(*e. Birth of Bābur's first child.*)

After our departure (last year) from Andijān, my mothers and my wife and relations came, with a hundred difficulties and hardships, to Aūrātīpā. We now sent for them to Samarkand. Within a few days after their arrival, a daughter was born to me by 'Āyisha-sulṭān Begīm, my first wife, the daughter of Sl. Aḥmad Mīrzā. They named the child Fakhru'n-nisā' (Ornament of women); she was my first-born, I was 19. In a month or 40 days, she went to God's mercy.

(*f. Bābur in Samarkand.*)

On taking Samarkand, envoys and summoners were sent off at once, and sent again and again, with reiterated request for aid and reinforcement, to the khāns and sulṭāns and begs and marchers on every side. Some, though experienced men, made foolish refusal; others whose relations towards our family had been discourteous and unpleasant, were afraid for themselves and took no notice; others again, though they sent help, sent it insufficient. Each such case will be duly mentioned.

When Samarkand was taken the second time, 'Alī-sher Beg Fol. 87.was alive. We exchanged letters once; on the back of mine to him I wrote one of my Turkī couplets. Before his reply reached me, separations (*tafarqa*) and disturbances (*ghūghā*) had happened.[550] Mullā Binā'ī had been taken into Shaibāq Khān's service when the latter took possession of Samarkand; he stayed with him until a few days after I took the place, when he came into the town to me. Qāsim Beg had his suspicions about him and consequently dismissed him towards Shahr-i-sabz but, as he was a man of parts, and as no fault of his came to light, I had him fetched back. He constantly presented me with odes (*qaṣīda u ghazal*). He brought me a song in the Nawā mode composed to my name and at the same time the following quatrain;—[551]

No grain (*ghala*) have I by which I can be fed (*noshīd*);

No rhyme of grain (*mallah*, nankeen) wherewith I can be clad (*poshīd*);

The man who lacks both food and clothes,

In art or science where can he compete (*koshīd*)?

In those days of respite, I had written one or two couplets but had not completed an ode. As an answer to Mullā Binā'ī I made up and set this poor little Turkī quatrain;—[552]

As is the wish of your heart, so shall it be (*būlghūsīdūr*);

For gift and stipend both an order shall be made (*buyurūlghūsīdūr*);

I know the grain and its rhyme you write of;

The garments, you, your house, the corn shall fill (*tūlghūsīdūr*).

The Mullā in return wrote and presented a quatrain to me inFol. 87b. which for his refrain, he took a rhyme to (the *tūlghūsīdūr* of) my last line and chose another rhyme;—

Mīrzā-of-mine, the Lord of sea and land shall be (*yīr būlghūsīdūr*);

His art and skill, world o'er, the evening tale shall be (*samar būlghūsīdūr*);

If gifts like these reward one rhyming (*or* pointless) word;

For words of sense, what guerdon will there be (*nilār būlghūsīdūr*)?

Abū'l-barka, known as *Farāqi* (Parted), who just then had come to Samarkand from Shahr-i-sabz, said Binā'ī ought to have rhymed. He made this verse;—

Into Time's wrong to you quest shall be made (*sūrūlghūsīdūr*);

Your wish the Sulṭān's grace from Time shall ask (*qūlghūsīdūr*);

O Ganymede! our cups, ne'er filled as yet,

In this new Age, brimmed-up, filled full shall be (*tūlghūsīdūr*).

Though this winter our affairs were in a very good way and Shaibāq Khān's were on the wane, one or two occurrences were somewhat of a disservice; (1) the Merv men who had taken Qarā-kūl, could not be persuaded to stay there and it went back into the hands of the Aūzbegs; (2) Shaibāq Khān besieged Ibrāhīm Tarkhān's younger brother, Aḥmad in Dabūsī, stormed the place and made a general massacre of its inhabitants before the army we were collecting was ready to march.

With 240 proved men I had taken Samarkand; in the nextFol. 88. five or six months, things so fell out by the favour of the Most High God, that, as will be told, we fought the arrayed battle of Sar-i-pul with a man like Shaibāq Khān. The help those round-about gave us was as follows;—From The Khān had come, with 4 or 5000 Bārīns, Ayūb *Begchīk* and Qashka Maḥmūd; from Jahāngīr Mīrzā had come Khalīl, Taṃbal's younger brother, with 100 or 200 men; not a man had come from Sl. Ḥusain Mīrzā, that experienced ruler, than whom none knew better the deeds and dealings of Shaibāq Khān; none came from Badī'u'z-zamān Mīrzā; none from Khusrau Shāh because he, the author of what evil done,—as has been told,—to our dynasty! feared us more than he feared Shaibāq Khān.

(g. Bābur defeated at Sar-i-pul.)

I marched out of Samarkand, with the wish of fighting Shaibāq Khān, in the month of Shawwāl[553] and went to the New-garden where we lay four or five days for the convenience of gathering our men and completing our equipment. We took the precaution of fortifying our camp with ditch and branch. From the New-garden we advanced, march by march, to beyond Sar-i-pul (Bridge-head) and there dismounted. Fol. 88b.Shaibāq Khān came from the opposite direction and dismounted at Khwāja Kārdzan, perhaps one *yīghāch* away (? 5 m.). We lay there for four or five days. Every day our people went from our side and his came from theirs and fell on one another. One day when they were in unusual force, there was much fighting but neither side had the advantage. Out of that engagement one of our men went rather hastily back into the entrenchments; he was using a standard; some said it was Sayyidī Qarā Beg's standard who really was a man of strong words but weak sword. Shaibāq Khān made one night-attack on us but could do nothing because the camp was protected by ditch and close-set branches. His men raised their war-cry, rained in arrows from outside the ditch and then retired.

In the work for the coming battle I exerted myself greatly and took all precautions; Qaṃbar-'alī also did much. In Kesh lay Bāqī Tarkhān with 1000 to 2000 men, in a position to join us after a couple of days. In Diyūl, 4 *yīghāch* off (? 20 m.), lay Sayyid Muḥ. Mīrzā *Dūghlāt*, bringing me 1000 to 2000 men from my Khān dādā; he would have joined me atFol. 89. dawn. With matters in this position, we hurried on the fight!

Who lays with haste his hand on the sword,

Shall lift to his teeth the back-hand of regret.[554]

The reason I was so eager to engage was that on the day of battle, the Eight stars[555] were between the two armies; they would have been in the enemy's rear for 13 or 14 days if the fight had been deferred. I now understand that these considerations are worth nothing and that our haste was without reason.

As we wished to fight, we marched from our camp at dawn, we in our mail, our horses in theirs, formed up in array of right and left, centre and van. Our right was Ibrāhīm *Sārū*, Ibrāhīm Jānī, Abū'l-qāsim *Kohbur* and other begs. Our left was Muḥ. Mazīd Tarkhān, Ibrāhīm Tarkhān and other Samarkandī begs, also Sl. Ḥusain *Arghūn*, Qarā (Black) *Barlās*, Pīr Aḥmad and Khwāja Ḥusain. Qāsim Beg was (with me) in the centre and also several of my close circle and household. In the van were inscribed Qaṃbar-'alī the Skinner, Banda-'alī, Khwāja 'Alī, Mīr Shāh *Qūchīn*, Sayyid Qāsim, Lord of the Gate,—Banda-'alī's younger brother Khaldar (mole-marked) and Ḥaidar-i-qāsim's son Qūch, together with all the good braves there were, and the rest of the household.

Thus arrayed, we marched from our camp; the enemy, also in array, marched out from his. His right was Maḥmūd and Jānī and Tīmūr Sulṭāns; his left, Ḥamza and Mahdī and someFol. 89b. other sulṭāns. When our two armies approached one another, he wheeled his right towards our rear. To meet this, I turned; this left our van,—in which had been inscribed what not of our best braves and tried swordsmen!—to our right and bared our front (*i.e.* the front of the centre). None-the-less we fought those who made the front-attack on us, turned them and forced them back on their own centre. So far did we carry it that some of Shaibāq Khān's old chiefs said to him, 'We must move off! It is past a stand.' He however held fast. His right beat our left, then wheeled (again) to our rear.

(As has been said), the front of our centre was bare through our van's being left to the right. The enemy attacked us front and rear, raining in arrows on us. (Ayūb *Begchīk's*) Mughūl army, come for our help! was of no use in fighting; it set to work forthwith to unhorse and plunder our men. Not this Fol. 90.once only! This is always the way with those ill-omened Mughūls! If they win, they grab at booty; if they lose, they unhorse and pilfer their own side! We drove back the Aūzbegs who attacked our front by several vigorous assaults, but those who had wheeled to our rear came up and rained arrows on our standard. Falling on us in this way, from the front and from the rear, they made our men hurry off.

This same turning-movement is one of the great merits of Aūzbeg fighting; no battle of theirs is ever without it. Another merit of theirs is that they all, begs and retainers, from their front to their rear, ride, loose-rein at the gallop, shouting as they come and, in retiring, do not scatter but ride off, at the gallop, in a body.

Ten or fifteen men were left with me. The Kohik-water was close by,—the point of our right had rested on it. We made straight for it. It was the season when it comes down in flood. We rode right into it, man and horse in mail. It was just fordable for half-way over; after that it had to be swum. For more than an arrow's flight[556] we, man and mount in mail! made our horses swim and so got across. Once out of the water, we cut off the horse-armour and let it lie. By thus Fol. 90b.passing to the north bank of the river, we were free of our foes, but at once Mughūl wretches were the captors and pillagers of one after another of my friends. Ibrāhīm Tarkhān and some others, excellent braves all, were unhorsed and killed by Mughūls.[557] We moved along the north bank of the Kohik-river, recrossed it near Qulba, entered the town by the Shaikh-zāda's Gate and reached the citadel in the middle of the afternoon.

Begs of our greatest, braves of our best and many men perished in that fight. There died Ibrāhīm Tarkhān, Ibrāhīm *Sārū* and Ibrāhīm Jānī; oddly enough three great begs named Ibrāhīm perished. There died also Ḥaidar-i-qāsim's eldest son, Abū'l-qāsim *Kohbur*, and Khudāī-bīrdī *Tūghchī* and Khalīl, Taṃbal's younger brother, spoken of already several times. Many of our men fled in different directions; Muḥ. Mazīd Tarkhān went towards Qūndūz and Ḥiṣār for Khusrau Shāh.Fol. 91. Some of the household and of the braves, such as Karīm-dad-i-Khudāī-bīrdī *Turkmān* and Jānaka *Kūkūldāsh* and Mullā Bābā of Pashāghar got away to Aūrā-tīpā. Mullā Bābā at that time was not in my service but had gone out with me in a guest's fashion. Others again, did what Sherīm Ṭaghāī and his band did;—though he had come back with me into the town and though when consultation was had, he had agreed with the rest to make the fort fast, looking for life or death within it, yet spite of this, and although my mothers and sisters, elder and younger, stayed on in Samarkand, he sent off their wives and families to Aūrā-tīpā and remained himself with just a few men, all unencumbered. Not this once only! Whenever hard work had to be done, low and double-minded action was the thing to expect from him!

(*h. Bābur besieged in Samarkand.*)

Next day, I summoned Khwāja Abū'l-makāram, Qāsim and the other begs, the household and such of the braves as were admitted to our counsels, when after consultation, we resolved to make the fort fast and to look for life or death within it. I and Qāsim Beg with my close circle and household were the reserve. For convenience in this I took up quarters in the middle of the town, in tents pitched on the roof of Aūlūgh Beg Fol. 91b.Mīrzā's College. To other begs and braves posts were assigned in the Gates or on the ramparts of the walled-town.

Two or three days later, Shaibāq Khān dismounted at some distance from the fort. On this, the town-rabble came out of lanes and wards, in crowds, to the College gate, shouted good wishes for me and went out to fight in mob-fashion. Shaibāq Khān had got to horse but could not so much as approach the town. Several days went by in this fashion. The mob and rabble, knowing nothing of sword and arrow-wounds, never witnesses of the press and carnage of a stricken field, through these incidents, became bold and began to sally further and further out. If warned by the braves against going out so incautiously, they broke into reproach.

One day when Shaibāq Khān had directed his attack towards the Iron Gate, the mob, grown bold, went out, as usual, daringly and far. To cover their retreat, we sent several braves towards the Camel's-neck,[558] foster-brethren and some of the close household-circle, such as Nuyān *Kūkūldāsh*, Qul-naẓ̤ar (son of Sherīm?) Ṭ̤aghāī Beg, and Mazīd. An Aūzbeg or two Fol. 92.put their horses at them and with Qul-naẓ̤ar swords were crossed. The rest of the Aūzbegs dismounted and brought their strength to bear on the rabble, hustled them off and rammed them in through the Iron Gate. Qūch Beg and Mīr Shāh *Qūchīn* had dismounted at the side of Khwāja Khiẓr's Mosque and were making a stand there. While the townsmen were being moved off by those on foot, a party of mounted Aūzbegs rode towards the Mosque. Qūch Beg came out when they drew near and exchanged good blows with them. He did distinguished work; all stood to watch. Our fugitives below were occupied only with their own escape; for them the time to shoot arrows and make a stand had gone by. I was shooting with a slur-bow[559] from above the Gate and some of my circle were shooting arrows (*aūq*). Our attack from above kept the enemy from advancing beyond the Mosque; from there he retired.

During the siege, the round of the ramparts was made each night; sometimes I went, sometimes Qāsim Beg, sometimes one of the household Begs. Though from the Turquoise to the Shaikh-zāda's Gate may be ridden, the rest of the way must beFol. 92b. walked. When some men went the whole round on foot, it was dawn before they had finished.[560]

One day Shaibāq Khān attacked between the Iron Gate and the Shaikh-zāda's. I, as the reserve, went to the spot, without anxiety about the Bleaching-ground and Needle-makers' Gates. That day, (?) in a shooting wager (*aūq aūchīdā*), I made a good shot with a slur-bow, at a Centurion's horse.[561] It died at once (*aūq bārdī*) with the arrow (*aūq bīla*). They made such a vigorous attack this time that they got close under the ramparts. Busy with the fighting and the stress near the Iron Gate, we were entirely off our guard about the other side of the town. There, opposite the space between the Needle-makers' and Bleaching-ground Gates, the enemy had posted 7 or 800 good men in ambush, having with them 24 or 25 ladders so wide that two or three could mount abreast. These men came from their ambush when the attack near the Iron Gate, by occupying all our men, had left those other posts empty, and quickly set up their ladders between the two Gates,Fol. 93. just where a road leads from the ramparts to Muḥ. Mazīd Tarkhān's houses. That post was Qūch Beg's and Muḥammad-qulī *Qūchīn's*, with their detachment of braves, and they had their quarters in Muḥ. Mazīd's houses. In the Needle-makers' Gate was posted Qarā (Black) *Barlās*, in the Bleaching-ground Gate, Qūtlūq Khwāja *Kūkūldāsh* with Sherīm Ṭaghāī and his brethren, older and younger. As attack was being made on the other side of the town, the men attached to these posts were not on guard but had scattered to their quarters or to the bazar for necessary matters of service and servants' work. Only the begs were at their posts, with one or two of the populace. Qūch Beg and Mūhammad-qulī and Shāh Ṣufī and one other brave did very well and boldly. Some Aūzbegs were on the ramparts, some were coming up, when these four men arrived at a run, dealt them blow upon blow, and, by energetic drubbing, forced them all down and put them to flight. Qūch Beg did best; this was his outstanding and approved good deed; twice during this siege he got his hand into the work. Qarā *Barlās* had been left alone in the Needle-makers' Gate; he also held out well to the end. Qūtlūq Khwāja and Qul-naẓar Mīrzā were also at their posts in the Bleaching-ground Gate; they held out well too, and charged the foe in his rear.

Another time Qāsim Beg led his braves out through the Fol. 93b.Needle-makers' Gate, pursued the Aūzbegs as far as Khwāja Kafsher, unhorsed some and returned with a few heads.

It was now the time of ripening rain but no-one brought new corn into the town. The long siege caused great privation to the towns-people;[562] it went so far that the poor and destitute began to eat the flesh of dogs and asses and, as there was little grain for the horses, people fed them on leaves. Experience shewed that the leaves best suiting were those of the mulberry and elm (*qarā-yīghāch*). Some people scraped dry wood and gave the shavings, damped, to their horses.

For three or four months Shaibāq Khān did not come near the fort but had it invested at some distance and himself moved round it from post to post. Once when our men were off their guard, at mid-night, the enemy came near to the Turquoise Fol. 94.Gate, beat his drums and flung his war-cry out. I was in the College, undressed. There was great trepidation and anxiety. After that they came night after night, disturbing us by drumming and shouting their war-cry.

Although envoys and messengers had been sent repeatedly to all sides and quarters, no help and reinforcement arrived from any-one. No-one had helped or reinforced me when I was in strength and power and had suffered no sort of defeat or loss; on what score would any-one help me now? No hope in any-one whatever recommended us to prolong the siege. The old saying was that to hold a fort there must be a head, two hands and two legs, that is to say, the Commandant is the head; help and reinforcement coming from two quarters are the two arms and the food and water in the fort are the two legs. While we looked for help from those round about, their thoughts were elsewhere. That brave and experienced ruler, Sl. Ḥusain Mīrzā, gave us not even the help of an encouraging message, but none-the-less he sent Kamālu'd-dīn Ḥusain *Gāzur-gāhī*[563] as an envoy to Shaibāq Khān.

(*i. Taṃbal's proceedings in Farghāna.*)[564]

(This year) Taṃbal marched from Andijān to near Bīsh-kīnt.[565] Aḥmad Beg and his party, thereupon, made The Khān move out against him. The two armies came face to face nearFol. 94b. Lak-lakān and the Tūrāk Four-gardens but separated without engaging. Sl. Maḥmūd was not a fighting man; now when opposed to Taṃbal, he shewed want of courage in word and deed. Aḥmad Beg was unpolished[566] but brave and well-meaning. In his very rough way, he said, 'What's the measure of this person, Taṃbal? that you are so tormented with fear and fright about him. If you are afraid to look at him, bandage your eyes before you go out to face him.'

907 AH.—JULY 17TH. 1501 TO JULY 7TH. 1502 AD.567

(*a. Surrender of Samarkand to Shaibānī.*)

The siege drew on to great length; no provisions and supplies came in from any quarter, no succour and reinforcement from any side. The soldiers and peasantry became hopeless and, by ones and twos, began to let themselves down outside[568] the walls and flee. On Shaibāq Khān's hearing of the distress in the town, he came and dismounted near the Lovers'-cave. I, in turn, went to Malik-muḥammad Mīrzā's dwellings in Low-lane, over against him. On one of those days, Khwāja Ḥusain's brother, Aūzūn Ḥasan[569] came into the town with 10 or 15 of his men,—he who, as has been told, had been the cause of Jahāngīr Mīrzā's rebellion, of my exodus from Samarkand (903 AH.—March 1498 AD.) and, again! of what an amount of sedition and Fol. 95.disloyalty! That entry of his was a very bold act.[570]

The soldiery and townspeople became more and more distressed. Trusted men of my close circle began to let themselves down from the ramparts and get away; begs of known name and old family servants were amongst them, such as Pīr Wais, Shaikh Wais and Wais *Lāgharī.*[571] Of help from any side we utterly despaired; no hope was left in any quarter; our supplies and provisions were wretched, what there was was coming to an end; no more came in. Meantime Shaibāq Khān interjected talk of peace.[572] Little ear would have been given to his talk of peace, if there had been hope or food from any side. It had to be! a sort of peace was made and we took our departure from the town, by the Shaikh-zāda's Gate, somewhere about midnight.

(*b. Bābur leaves Samarkand.*)

I took my mother Khānīm out with me; two other women-folk went too, one was Bīshka (var. Peshka)-i-Khalīfa, the other, Mīnglīk *Kūkūldāsh.*[573] At this exodus, my elder sister, Khān-zāda Begīm fell into Shaibāq Khān's hands.[574] In the darkness of that night we lost our way[575] and wandered about amongst the main irrigation channels of Soghd. At shoot of dawn, after a hundred difficulties, we got past Khwāja Dīdār. At the Sunnat Prayer we scrambled up the rising-ground of Qarā-būgh.Fol. 95b. From the north slope of Qarā-būgh we hurried on past the foot of Judūk village and dropped down into Yīlān-aūtī. On the road I raced with Qāsim Beg and Qaṃbar-'alī (the Skinner); my horse was leading when I, thinking to look at theirs behind, twisted myself round; the girth may have slackened, for my saddle turned and I was thrown on my head to the ground. Although I at once got up and remounted, my brain did not steady till the evening; till then this world and what went on appeared to me like things felt and seen in a dream or fancy. Towards afternoon we dismounted in Yīlān-aūtī, there killed a horse, spitted and roasted its flesh, rested our horses awhile and rode on. Very weary, we reached Khalīla-village before the dawn and dismounted. From there it was gone on to Dīzak.

In Dīzak just then was Ḥāfiẓ Muḥ. *Dūldāī's* son, Ṭāhir. There, in Dīzak, were fat meats, loaves of fine flour, plenty of sweet melons and abundance of excellent grapes. From what privation we came to such plenty! From what stress to what repose!

From fear and hunger rest we won (*amānī tāptūq*);

A fresh world's new-born life we won (*jahānī tāptūq*).

Fol. 96.From out our minds, death's dread was chased (*rafa' būldī*);

From our men the hunger-pang kept back (*dafa' būldī*).[576]

Never in all our lives had we felt such relief! never in the whole course of them have we appreciated security and plenty so highly. Joy is best and more delightful when it follows sorrow, ease after toil. I have been transported four or five times from toil to rest and from hardship to ease.[577] This was the first. We were set free from the affliction of such a foe and from the pangs of hunger and had reached the repose of security and the relief of abundance.

(*c. Bābur in Dikh-kat.*)

After three or four days of rest in Dīzak, we set out for Aūrā-tīpā. Pashāghar is a little[578] off the road but, as we had occupied it for some time (904 AH.), we made an excursion to it in passing by. In Pashāghar we chanced on one of Khānīm's old servants, a teacher[579] who had been left behind in Samarkand from want of a mount. We saw one another and on questioning her, I found she had come there on foot.

Khūb-nigār Khānīm, my mother Khānīm's younger sister[580] already must have bidden this transitory world farewell; for they let Khānīm and me know of it in Aūrā-tīpā. My father's mother also must have died in Andijān; this too they let usFol. 96b. know in Aūrā-tīpā.[581] Since the death of my grandfather, Yūnas Khān (892 AH.), Khānīm had not seen her (step-)mother or her younger brother and sisters, that is to say, Shāh Begīm, Sl. Maḥmūd Khān, Sulṭān-nīgār Khānīm and Daulat-sulṭān Khānīm. The separation had lasted 13 or 14 years. To see these relations she now started for Tāshkīnt.

After consulting with Muḥ. Ḥusain Mīrzā, it was settled for us to winter in a place called Dikh-kat[582] one of the Aūrā-tīpā villages. There I deposited my impedimenta (*aūrūq*); then set out myself in order to visit Shāh Begīm and my Khān dādā and various relatives. I spent a few days in Tāshkīnt and waited on Shāh Begīm and my Khān dādā. My mother's elder full-sister, Mihr-nigār Khānīm[583] had come from Samarkand and was in Tāshkīnt. There my mother Khānīm fell very ill; it was a very bad illness; she passed through mighty risks.

His Highness Khwājaka Khwāja, having managed to get out of Samarkand, had settled down in Far-kat; there I visited him. I had hoped my Khān dādā would shew me affection and kindness and would give me a country or a district (*pargana*). He did promise me Aūrā-tīpā but Muḥ. Ḥusain Mīrzā. did not make it over, whether acting on his own accountFol. 97. or whether upon a hint from above, is not known. After spending a few days with him (in Aūrā-tīpā), I went on to Dikh-kat.

Dikh-kat is in the Aūrā-tīpā hill-tracts, below the range on the other side of which is the Macha[584] country. Its people, though Sārt, settled in a village, are, like Turks, herdsmen and shepherds. Their sheep are reckoned at 40,000. We dismounted at the houses of the peasants in the village; I stayed in a head-man's house. He was old, 70 or 80, but his mother was still alive. She was a woman on whom much life had been bestowed for she was 111 years old. Some relation of hers may have gone, (as was said), with Tīmūr Beg's army to Hindūstān;[585] she had this in her mind and used to tell the tale. In Dikh-kat alone were 96 of her descendants, hers and her grandchildren, great-grandchildren and grandchildren's grandchildren. Counting in the dead, 200 of her descendants were reckoned up. Her grandchild's grandson was a strong young man of 25 or 26, with full black beard. While in Dikh-kat, I constantly made excursions amongst the mountains round Fol. 97b.about. Generally I went bare-foot and, from doing this so much, my feet became so that rock and stone made no difference to them.[586] Once in one of these wanderings, a cow was seen, between the Afternoon and Evening prayers, going down by a narrow, ill-defined road. Said I, 'I wonder which way that road will be going; keep your eye on that cow; don't lose the cow till you know where the road comes out.' Khwāja Asadu'l-lāh made his joke, 'If the cow loses her way,' he said, 'what becomes of us?'

In the winter several of our soldiers asked for leave to Andijān because they could make no raids with us.[587] Qāsim Beg said, with much insistance, 'As these men are going, send something special of your own wear by them to Jahāngīr Mīrzā.' I sent my ermine cap. Again he urged, 'What harm would there be if you sent something for Taṃbal also?' Though I was very unwilling, yet as he urged it, I sent Taṃbal a large broad-sword which Nuyān *Kūkūldāsh* had had made for himself in Samarkand. This very sword it was which, as will be told with the events of next year, came down on my own head![588]

A few days later, my grandmother, Aīsān-daulat Begīm, who, when I left Samarkand, had stayed behind, arrived in Dikh-katFol. 98. with our families and baggage (*aūrūq*) and a few lean and hungry followers.

(*d. Shaibāq Khān raids in The Khān's country.*)

That winter Shaibāq Khān crossed the Khujand river on the ice and plundered near Shāhrukhiya and Bīsh-kīnt. On hearing news of this, we gallopped off, not regarding the smallness of our numbers, and made for the villages below Khujand, opposite Hasht-yak (One-eighth). The cold was mightily bitter,[589] a wind not less than the Hā-darwesh[590] raging violently the whole time. So cold it was that during the two or three days we were in those parts, several men died of it. When, needing to make ablution, I went into an irrigation-channel, frozen along both banks but because of its swift current, not ice-bound in the middle, and bathed, dipping under 16 times, the cold of the water went quite through me. Next day we crossed the river on the ice from opposite Khaṣlār and went on through the dark to Bīsh-kīnt.[591] Shaibāq Khān, however, must have gone straight back after plundering the neighbourhood of Shāhrukhiya.

(*e. Death of Nuyān Kūkūldāsh.*)

Bīsh-kīnt, at that time, was held by Mullā Ḥaidar's son, 'Abdu'l-minān. A younger son, named Mūmin, a worthless and dissipated person, had come to my presence in Samarkand and had received all kindness from me. This sodomite, Mūmin, for what sort of quarrel between them is not known, cherishedFol. 98b. rancour against Nuyān *Kūkūldāsh*. At the time when we, having heard of the retirement of the Aūzbegs, sent a man to

The Khān and marched from Bīsh-kīnt to spend two or three days amongst the villages in the Blacksmith's-dale,[592] Mullā Ḥaidar's son, Mūmin invited Nuyān *Kūkūldāsh* and Aḥmad-i-qāsim and some others in order to return them hospitality received in Samarkand. When I left Bīsh-kīnt, therefore they stayed behind. Mūmin's entertainment to this party was given on the edge of a ravine (*jar*). Next day news was brought to us in Sām-sīrak, a village in the Blacksmith's-dale, that Nuyān was dead through falling when drunk into the ravine. We sent his own mother's brother, Ḥaq-naẓar and others, who searched out where he had fallen. They committed Nuyān to the earth in Bīsh-kīnt, and came back to me. They had found the body at the bottom of the ravine an arrow's flight from the place of the entertainment. Some suspected that Mūmin, nursing his trumpery rancour, had taken Nuyān's life. None knew the truth. His death made me strangely sad; for few men have I felt such grief; I wept unceasingly for a week or Fol. 99.ten days. The chronogram of his death was found in *Nuyān is dead.*[593]

With the heats came the news that Shaibāq Khān was coming up into Aūrā-tīpā. Hereupon, as the land is level about Dikh-kat, we crossed the Āb-burdan pass into the Macha hill-country.[594] Āb-burdan is the last village of Macha; just below it a spring sends its water down (to the Zar-afshān); above the stream is included in Macha, below it depends on Palghar. There is a tomb at the spring-head. I had a rock at the side of the spring-head shaped (*qātīrib*) and these three couplets inscribed on it;—

I have heard that Jamshīd, the magnificent,

Inscribed on a rock at a fountain-head[595]

'Many men like us have taken breath at this fountain,

And have passed away in the twinkling of an eye;

We took the world by courage and might,

But we took it not with us to the tomb.'

There is a custom in that hill-country of cutting verses and things[596] on the rocks.

While we were in Macha, Mullā Hijrī,[597] the poet, came from Ḥiṣār and waited on me. At that time I composed the following opening lines;—

Let your portrait flatter you never so much, than it you are more (*āndīn artūqsīn*);

Men call you their Life (*Jān*), than Life, without doubt, you are more (*jāndīn artūqsīn*).[598]

After plundering round about in Aūrā-tīpā, Shaibāq Khān retired.[599] While he was up there, we, disregarding the fewnessFol. 99b. of our men and their lack of arms, left our impedimenta (*aūrūq*) in Macha, crossed the Āb-burdan pass and went to Dikh-kat so that, gathered together close at hand, we might miss no chance on one of the next nights. He, however, retired straightway; we went back to Macha.

It passed through my mind that to wander from mountain to mountain, homeless and houseless, without country or abiding-place, had nothing to recommend it. 'Go you right off to The Khān,' I said to myself. Qāsim Beg was not willing for this move, apparently being uneasy because, as has been told, he had put Mughūls to death at Qarā-būlāq, by way of example. However much we urged it, it was not to be! He drew off for Ḥiṣār with all his brothers and his whole following. We for our part, crossed the Āb-burdan pass and set forward for The Khān's presence in Tāshkīnt.

(*f. Bābur with The Khān.*)

In the days when Taṃbal had drawn his army out and gone into the Blacksmith's-dale,[600] men at the top of his army, such as Muḥ. *Dūghlāt*, known as *Ḥiṣārī*, and his younger brother Ḥusain, and also Qaṃbar-'alī, the Skinner, conspired to attempt his life. When he discovered this weighty matter, they, unable to remain with him, had gone to The Khān.

The Feast of Sacrifices ('Īd-i-qurbān) fell for us in Shāh-rukhiya (Ẕū'l-ḥijja 10th.-June 16th. 1502).

I had written a quatrain in an ordinary measure but was in some doubt about it, because at that time I had not studied Fol. 100.poetic idiom so much as I have now done. The Khān was good-natured and also he wrote verses, though ones somewhat deficient in the requisites for odes. I presented my quatrain and I laid my doubts before him but got no reply so clear as to remove them. His study of poetic idiom appeared to have been somewhat scant. Here is the verse;—

One hears no man recall another in trouble (*miḥnat-ta kīshī*);

None speak of a man as glad in his exile (*ghurbat-ta kīshī*);

My own heart has no joy in this exile;

Called glad is no exile, man though he be (*albatta kīshī*).

Later on I came to know that in Turkī verse, for the purpose of rhyme, *ta* and *da* are interchangeable and also *ghain*, *qāf* and *kāf*.[601]

(*g. The acclaiming of the standards.*)

When, a few days later, The Khān heard that Taṃbal had gone up into Aūrā-tīpā, he got his army to horse and rode out from Tāshkīnt. Between Bīsh-kīnt and Sām-sīrak he formed up into array of right and left and saw the count[602] of his men. This done, the standards were acclaimed in Mughūl fashion.[603] The Khān dismounted and nine standards were set up in front of him. A Mughūl tied a long strip of white cloth to the thigh-bone (*aūrta aīlīk*) of a cow and took the other end in his hand. Three other long strips of white cloth were tied to the staves of three of the (nine) standards, just below the yak-tails, and their other ends were brought for The Khān to stand on one and for me and Sl. Muḥ. Khānika to stand each on one of the two others. The Mughūl who had hold of the strip of clothFol. 100b. fastened to the cow's leg, then said something in Mughūl while he looked at the standards and made signs towards them. The Khān and those present sprinkled *qumīz*[604] in the direction of the standards; hautbois and drums were sounded towards them;[605] the army flung the war-cry out three times towards them, mounted, cried it again and rode at the gallop round them.

Precisely as Chīngīz Khān laid down his rules, so the Mughūls still observe them. Each man has his place, just where his ancestors had it; right, right,—left, left,—centre, centre. The most reliable men go to the extreme points of the right and left. The Chīrās and Begchīk clans always demand to go to the point in the right.[606] At that time the Beg of the Chīrās tūmān was a very bold brave, Qāshka (Mole-marked) Maḥmud and the beg of the renowned Begchīk tūmān was Ayūb *Begchīk*. These two, disputing which should go out to the point, drew swords on one another. At last it seems to have been settled that one should take the highest place in the hunting-circle, the other, in the battle-array.

Next day after making the circle, it was hunted near Sāmsīrak; Fol. 101.thence move was made to the Tūrāk Four-gardens. On that day and in that camp, I finished the first ode I ever finished. Its opening couplet is as follows;—

Except my soul, no friend worth trust found I (*wafādār tāpmādīm*);

Except my heart, no confidant found I (*asrār tāpmādīm*).

There were six couplets; every ode I finished later was written just on this plan.

The Khān moved, march by march, from Sām-sīrak to the bank of the Khujand-river. One day we crossed the water by way of an excursion, cooked food and made merry with the braves and pages. That day some-one stole the gold clasp of my girdle. Next day Bayān-qulī's Khān-qulī and Sl. Muḥ. Wais fled to Taṃbal. Every-one suspected them of that bad deed. Though this was not ascertained, Aḥmad-i-qāsim *Kohbur* asked leave and went away to Aūrā-tīpā. From that leave he did not return; he too went to Taṃbal.

908 AH.—JULY 7TH. 1502 TO JUNE 26TH. 1503 AD.[607]

(*a. Bābur's poverty in Tāshkīnt.*)

This move of The Khān's was rather unprofitable; to take no fort, to beat no foe, he went out and went back.

During my stay in Tāshkīnt, I endured much poverty and humiliation. No country or hope of one! Most of my retainers dispersed, those left, unable to move about with me because of their destitution! If I went to my Khān dādā's Gate,[608] I went sometimes with one man, sometimes with two. It was well he was no stranger but one of my own blood.Fol. 101b. After showing myself[609] in his presence, I used to go to Shāh Begīm's, entering her house, bareheaded and barefoot, just as if it were my own.

This uncertainty and want of house and home drove me at last to despair. Said I, 'It would be better to take my head[610] and go off than live in such misery; better to go as far as my feet can carry me than be seen of men in such poverty and humiliation.' Having settled on China to go to, I resolved to take my head and get away. From my childhood up I had wished to visit China but had not been able to manage it because of ruling and attachments. Now sovereignty itself was gone! and my mother, for her part, was re-united to her (step)-mother and her younger brother. The hindrances to my journey had been removed; my anxiety for my mother was dispelled. I represented (to Shāh Begīm and The Khān) through Khwāja Abū'l-makāram that now such a foe as Shaibāq Khān had made his appearance, Mughūl and Turk[611] alike must guard against him; that thought about him must be taken while he had not well-mastered the (Aūzbeg) horde or grown very strong, for as they have said;—[612]

To-day, while thou canst, quench the fire,

Once ablaze it will burn up the world;

Let thy foe not fix string to his bow,

While an arrow of thine can pierce him;

that it was 20 or 25 years[613] since they had seen the Younger Khān (Aḥmad *Alacha*) and that I had never seen him; should I be able, if I went to him, not only to see him myself, but to bring about the meeting between him and them?

Fol. 102.Under this pretext I proposed to get out of those surroundings;[614] once in Mughūlistān and Turfān, my reins would be in my own hands, without check or anxiety. I put no-one in possession of my scheme. Why not? Because it was impossible for me to mention such a scheme to my mother, and also because it was with other expectations that the few of all ranks who had been my companions in exile and privation, had cut themselves off with me and with me suffered change of fortune. To speak to them also of such a scheme would be no pleasure.

The Khwāja, having laid my plan before Shāh Begīm and The Khān, understood them to consent to it but, later, it occurred to them that I might be asking leave a second time,[615] because of not receiving kindness. That touching their reputation, they delayed a little to give the leave.

(*b. The Younger Khān comes to Tāshkīnt.*)

At this crisis a man came from the Younger Khān to say that he was actually on his way. This brought my scheme to naught. When a second man announced his near approach, we all went out to give him honourable meeting, Shāh Begīm and his younger sisters, Sulṭān-nigār Khānīm and Daulat-sulṭān Khānīm, and I and Sl. Muḥ. Khānika and Khān Mīrzā (Wais).

Between Tāshkīnt and Sairām is a village called Yagha (var. Yaghma), with some smaller ones, where are the tombs of Father Abraham and Father Isaac. So far we went out. Knowing nothing exact about his coming,[616] I rode out for anFol. 102b. excursion, with an easy mind. All at once, he descended on me, face to face. I went forward; when I stopped, he stopped. He was a good deal perturbed; perhaps he was thinking of dismounting in some fixed spot and there seated, of receiving me ceremoniously. There was no time for this; when we were near each other, I dismounted. He had not time even to dismount;[617] I bent the knee, went forward and saw him. Hurriedly and with agitation, he told Sl. Sa'īd Khān and Bābā Khān Sl. to dismount, bend the knee with (*bīla*) me and make my acquaintance.[618] Just these two of his sons had come with him; they may have been 13 or 14 years old. When I had seen them, we all mounted and went to Shāh Begīm's presence. After he had seen her and his sisters, and had renewed acquaintance, they all sat down and for half the night told one another particulars of their past and gone affairs.

Next day, my Younger Khān dādā bestowed on me arms of his own and one of his own special horses saddled, and a Mughūl head-to-foot dress,—a Mughūl cap,[619] a long coat of Chinese satin, with broidering of stitchery,[620] and Chinese armour; in the old fashion, they had hung, on the left side, a haversack (*chantāi*) and an outer bag,[621] and three or four things such as women usually hang on their collars, perfume-holders and various receptacles;[622] in the same way, three or four things hung on the right side also.

Fol. 103.From there we went to Tāshkīnt. My Elder Khān dādā also had come out for the meeting, some 3 or 4 *yīghāch* (12 to 15 m.) along the road. He had had an awning set up in a chosen spot and was seated there. The Younger Khān went up directly in front of him; on getting near, fetched a circle, from right to left, round him; then dismounted before him. After advancing to the place of interview (*kūrūshūr yīr*), he nine times bent the knee; that done, went close and saw (his brother). The Elder Khān, in his turn, had risen when the Younger Khān drew near. They looked long at one another (*kūrūshtīlār*) and long stood in close embrace (*qūchūshūb*). The Younger Khān again bent the knee nine times when retiring, many times also on offering his gift; after that, he went and sat down.

All his men had adorned themselves in Mughūl fashion. There they were in Mughūl caps (*būrk*); long coats of Chinese satin, broidered with stitchery, Mughūl quivers and saddles of green shagreen-leather, and Mughūl horses adorned in a unique fashion. He had brought rather few men, over 1000 and under 2000 may-be. He was a man of singular manners, a mighty master of the sword, and brave. Amongst arms he preferred to trust to the sword. He used to say that of arms there are, the *shash-par*[623] (six-flanged mace), the *piyāzī* (rugged mace), the *kīstin*,[624] the *tabar-zīn* (saddle-hatchet) and the *bāltū* (battle-axe), all, if they strike, work only with what of them first touches, but the sword, if it touch, works from point to hilt. He never parted with his keen-edged sword; it was either at his waist or to his hand. He was a little rustic and rough-of-speech,Fol. 103b. through having grown up in an out-of-the-way place.

When, adorned in the way described, I went with him to The Khān, Khwāja Abū'l-makāram asked, 'Who is this honoured sulṭān?' and till I spoke, did not recognize me.

(c. The Khāns march into Farghāna against Taṃbal.)

Soon after returning to Tāshkīnt, The Khān led out an army for Andikān (Andijān) direct against Sl. Aḥmad *Taṃbal*.[625] He took the road over the Kīndīrlīk-pass and from Blacksmiths'-dale (Āhangarān-julgasī) sent the Younger Khān and me on in advance. After the pass had been crossed, we all met again near Zarqān (var. Zabarqān) of Karnān.

One day, near Karnān, they numbered their men[626] and reckoned them up to be 30,000. From ahead news began to come that Taṃbal also was collecting a force and going to Akhsī. After having consulted together, The Khāns decided to join some of their men to me, in order that I might cross the Khujand-water, and, marching by way of Aūsh and Aūzkīnt, turn

Taṃbal's rear. Having so settled, they joined to me Ayūb *Begchīk* with his *tūmān*, Jān-ḥasan Bārīn (var. Nārīn) with his Bārīns, Muḥ. *Ḥiṣārī Dūghlāt*, Sl. Ḥusain *Dūghlāt* and Sl. Aḥmad Mīrzā *Dūghlāt*, not in command of the Dūghlāt *tūmān*,—and Qaṃbar-'alī Beg (the Skinner). The commandant (*darogha*) of their force was Sārīgh-bāsh (Yellow-head) Mīrza *Itārchī*.[627]

Leaving The Khāns in Karnān, we crossed the river on rafts near Sakan, traversed the Khūqān sub-district (*aūrchīn*), crushedFol. 104. Qabā and by way of the Alāī sub-districts[628] descended suddenly on Aūsh. We reached it at dawn, unexpected; those in it could but surrender. Naturally the country-folk were wishing much for us, but they had not been able to find their means, both through dread of Taṃbal and through our remoteness. After we entered Aūsh, the hordes and the highland and lowland tribes of southern and eastern Andijān came in to us. The Aūzkīnt people also, willing to serve us, sent me a man and came in.

> (*Author's note on Aūzkīnt.*) Aūzkīnt formerly must have been a capital of Farghāna;[629] it has an excellent fort and is situated on the boundary (of Farghāna).

The Marghīnānīs also came in after two or three days, having beaten and chased their commandant (*darogha*). Except Andijān, every fort south of the Khujand-water had now come in to us. Spite of the return in those days of so many forts, and spite of risings and revolt against him, Taṃbal did not yet come to his senses but sat down with an army of horse and foot, fortified with ditch and branch, to face The Khāns, between Karnān and Akhsī. Several times over there was a little fighting and pell-mell but without decided success to either side.

In the Andijān country (*wilāyat*), most of the tribes and Fol. 104b.hordes and the forts and all the districts had come in to me; naturally the Andijānīs also were wishing for me. They however could not find their means.

(*d. Bābur's attempt to enter Andijān frustrated by a mistake.*)

It occurred to me that if we went one night close to the town and sent a man in to discuss with the Khwāja[630] and notables, they might perhaps let us in somewhere. With this idea we rode out from Aūsh. By midnight we were opposite Forty-daughters (Chihil-dukhterān) 2 miles (one *kuroh*) from Andijān. From that place we sent Qaṃbar-'alī Beg forward, with some other begs, who were to discuss matters with the Khwāja after by some means or other getting a man into the fort. While waiting for their return, we sat on our horses, some of us patiently humped up, some wrapt away in dream, when suddenly, at about the third watch, there rose a war-cry[631] and a sound of drums. Sleepy and startled, ignorant whether the foe was many or few, my men, without looking to one another, took each his own road and turned for flight. There was no time for me to get at them; I went straight for the enemy. Only Mīr Shāh *Qūchīn* and Bābā Sher-zād (Tiger-whelp) and Nāṣir's Dost sprang forward; we four excepted, every man set his face for flight. I had gone a little way forward, when the enemy rode rapidly up, flung out his war-cry and poured arrows on us. One man, on a horse with a starred forehead,[632] came close to me; I shot at it; it rolled over and died. They made a little as if to retire. The threeFol. 105. with me said, 'In this darkness it is not certain whether they are many or few; all our men have gone off; what harm could we four do them? Fighting must be when we have overtaken our run-aways and rallied them.' Off we hurried, got up with our men and beat and horse-whipped some of them, but, do what we would, they would not make a stand. Back the four of us went to shoot arrows at the foe. They drew a little back but when, after a discharge or two, they saw we were not more than three or four, they busied themselves in chasing and unhorsing my men. I went three or four times to try to rally my men but all in vain! They were not to be brought to order. Back I went with my three and kept the foe in check with our arrows. They pursued us two or three *kuroh* (4-6 m.), as far as the rising ground opposite Kharābūk and Pashāmūn. There we met Muḥ. 'Alī *Mubashir*. Said I, 'They are only few; let us stop and put our horses at them.' So we did. When we got up to them, they stood still.[633]

Our scattered braves gathered in from this side and that, but several very serviceable men, scattering in this attack, went right away to Aūsh.

The explanation of the affair seemed to be that some of Ayūb *Begchīk's* Mughūls had slipped away from Aūsh to raid near Andijān and, hearing the noise of our troop, came somewhat stealthily towards us; then there seems to have been confusion about the pass-word. The pass-words settled on for use during this movement of ours were Tāshkīnt and Sairām. If

> Fol. 105b.(*Author's note on pass-words.*) Pass-words are of two kinds;—in each tribe there is one for use in the tribe, such as *Darwāna* or *Tūqqāī* or *Lūlū*;[634] and there is one for the use of the whole army. For a battle, two words are settled on as pass-words so that of two men meeting in the fight, one may give the one, the other give back the second, in order to distinguish friends from foes, own men from strangers.

Tāshkīnt were said, Sairām would be answered; if Sairām, Tāshkīnt. In this muddled affair, Khwāja Muḥ. 'Ali seems to have been somewhat in advance of our party and to have got bewildered,—he was a Sārt person,[635]—when the Mughūls came up saying, 'Tāshkīnt, Tāshkīnt,' for he gave them 'Tāshkīnt, Tāshkīnt,' as the counter-sign. Through this they took him for an enemy, raised their war-cry, beat their saddle-drums and poured arrows on us. It was through this we gave way, and through this false alarm were scattered! We went back to Aūsh.

(*e. Bābur again attempts Andijān.*)

Through the return to me of the forts and the highland and lowland clans, Taṃbal and his adherents lost heart and footing. His army and people in the next five or six days began to desert him and to flee to retired places and the open country.[636] Of his household some came and said, 'His affairs are nearly ruined; he will break up in three or four days, utterly ruined.' On hearing this, we rode for Andijān.

Sl. Muḥ. *Galpuk*[637] was in Andijān,—the younger of Taṃbal's cadet brothers. We took the Mulberry-road and at the Mid-day Prayer came to the Khākān (canal), south of the town. AFol. 106. foraging-party was arranged; I followed it along Khākān to the skirt of 'Aīsh-hill. When our scouts brought word that Sl. Muḥ. *Galpuk* had come out, with what men he had, beyond the suburbs and gardens to the skirt of 'Aīsh, I hurried to meet him, although our foragers were still scattered. He may have had over 500 men; we had more but many had scattered to forage. When we were face to face, his men and ours may have been in equal number. Without caring about order or array, down we rode on them, loose rein, at the gallop. When we got near, they could not stand; there was not so much fighting as the crossing of a few swords. My men followed them almost to the Khākān Gate, unhorsing one after another.

It was at the Evening Prayer that, our foe outmastered, we reached Khwāja Kitta, on the outskirts of the suburbs. My idea was to go quickly right up to the Gate but Dost Beg's father, Nāṣir Beg and Qaṃbar-'alī Beg, old and experienced begs both, represented to me, 'It is almost night; it would be ill-judged to go in a body into the fort in the dark; let us withdraw a little and dismount. What can they do to-morrow but surrender the place?' Yielding at once to the opinion of these experienced persons, we forthwith retired to the outskirts of the suburbs. If we had gone to the Gate, undoubtedly, AndijānFol. 106b. would have come into our hands.

(*f. Bābur surprised by Taṃbal.*)

After crossing the Khākān-canal, we dismounted, near the Bed-time prayer, at the side of the village of Rabāṭ-i-zauraq (var. rūzaq). Although we knew that Taṃbal had broken camp and was on his way to Andijān, yet, with the negligence of inexperience, we dismounted on level ground close to the village, instead of where the defensive canal would have protected us.[638] There we lay down carelessly, without scouts or rear-ward.

At the top (*bāsh*) of the morning, just when men are in sweet sleep, Qaṃbar-'alī Beg hurried past, shouting, 'Up with you! the enemy is here!' So much he said and went off without a moment's stay. It was my habit to lie down, even in times of peace, in my tunic; up I got instanter, put on sword and quiver and mounted. My standard-bearer had no time to adjust my standard,[639] he just mounted with it in his hand. There were ten or fifteen men with me when we started toward the enemy; after riding an arrow's flight, when we came up with his scouts, there may have been ten. Going rapidly forward, we overtook him, poured in arrows on him, over-mastered his foremost men and hurried them off. We followed them for another arrow's flight and came up with his centre where Sl. Aḥmad *Taṃbal* himself was, with as many as Fol. 107.100 men. He and another were standing in front of his array, as if keeping a Gate,[640] and were shouting, 'Strike, strike!' but his men, mostly, were sidling, as if asking themselves, 'Shall we run away? Shall we not?' By this time three were left with me; one was Nāṣir's Dost, another, Mīrzā Qulī *Kūkūldāsh*, the third, Khudāī-bīrdī *Turkmān's* Karīm-dād.[641] I shot off the arrow on my thumb,[642] aiming at Taṃbal's helm. When I put my hand into my quiver, there came out a quite new *gosha-gīr*[643] given me by my Younger Khān dādā. It would have been vexing to throw it away but before I got it back into the quiver, there had been time to shoot, maybe, two or three arrows. When once more I had an arrow on the string, I went forward, my three men even holding back. One of those two in advance, Taṃbal seemingly,[644] moved forward also. The high-road was between us; I from my side, he, from his, got upon it and came face to face, in such a way that his right hand was towards me, mine towards him. His horse's mail excepted, he was fully accoutred; but for sword and quiver, I was unprotected. I shot off the arrow in my hand, adjusting for the attachment of his shield. With matters in this position, they shot my right leg through. I had on the cap of my helm;[645] Taṃbal choppedFol. 107b. so violently at my head that it lost all feeling under the blow. A large wound was made on my head, though not a thread of the cap was cut.[646] I had not bared[647] my sword; it was in the scabbard and I had no chance to draw it. Single-handed, I was alone amongst many foes. It was not a time to stand still; I turned rein. Down came a sword again; this time on my arrows. When I had gone 7 or 8 paces, those same three men rejoined me.[648] After using his sword on me, Taṃbal seems to have used it on Nāṣir's Dost. As far as an arrrow flies to the butt, the enemy followed us.

The Khākān-canal is a great main-channel, flowing in a deep cutting, not everywhere to be crossed. God brought it right! we came exactly opposite a low place where there was a passage over. Directly we had crossed, the horse Nāṣir's Dost was on, being somewhat weakly, fell down. We stopped and remounted him, then drew off for Aūsh, over the rising-ground between Farāghīna and Khirābūk. Out on the rise, Mazīd Ṭaghāī came up and joined us. An arrow had pierced his right leg also and though it had not gone through and come out again, he got to Aūsh with difficulty. The enemy unhorsed (*tūshūrdīlār*) good men of mine; Nāṣir Beg, Muḥ. 'Alī *Mubashir*, Khwāja Muḥ. 'Alī, Khusrau *Kūkūldāsh*, Na'man the page, all fell (to them, *tūshtīlār*), and also many unmailed braves.[649]

(*g. The Khāns move from Kāsān to Andijān.*)

The Khāns, closely following on Taṃbal, dismounted near Andijān,—the Elder at the side of the Reserve (*qūrūq*) in the Fol. 108.garden, known as Birds'-mill (*Qūsh-tīgīrmān*), belonging to my grandmother, Aīsān-daulat Begīm,—the Younger, near Bābā Tawakkul's Alms-house. Two days later I went from Aūsh and saw the Elder Khān in Birds'-mill. At that interview, he simply gave over to the Younger Khān the places which had come in to me. He made some such excuse as that for our advantage, he had brought the Younger Khān, how far! because such a foe as Shaibāq Khān had taken Samarkand and was waxing greater; that the Younger Khān had there no lands whatever, his own being far away; and that the country under Andijān, on the south of the Khujand-water, must be given him to encamp in. He promised me the country under Akhsī, on the north of the Khujand-water. He said that after taking a firm grip of that country (Farghāna), they would move, take Samarkand, give it to me and then the whole of the Farghāna country was to be the Younger Khan's. These words seem to have been meant to deceive me, since there is no knowing what they would have done when they had attained their object. It had to be however! willy-nilly, I agreed.

When, leaving him, I was on my way to the Younger Khān's presence, Qaṃbar-'alī, known as the Skinner, joined me in a friendly way and said, 'Do you see? They have taken the whole of the country just become yours. There is no opening for you through them. You have in your hands Aūsh, Marghīnān,Fol. 108b. Aūzkīnt and the cultivated land and the tribes and the hordes; go you to Aūsh; make that fort fast; send a man to Taṃbal, make peace with him, then strike at the Mughūl and drive him out. After that, divide the districts into an elder and a younger brother's shares.' 'Would that be right?' said I. 'The Khāns are my blood relations; better serve them than rule for Taṃbal.' He saw that his words had made no impression, so turned back, sorry he had spoken. I went on to see my Younger Khān Dādā. At our first interview, I had come upon him without announcement and he had no time to dismount, so it was all rather unceremonious. This time I got even nearer perhaps, and he ran out as far as the end of the tent-ropes. I was walking with some difficulty because of the wound in my leg. We met and renewed acquaintance; then he said, 'You are talked about as a hero, my young brother!' took my arm and led me into his tent. The tents pitched were rather small and through his having grown up in an out-of-the-way place, he let the one he sat in be neglected; it was like a raider's, melons, grapes, saddlery, every sort of thing, in his sitting-tent. I went from his presence straight back to my own camp and there he sent his Mughūl surgeon to examine my wound. Mughūls call a surgeon also a *bakhshī*; this one was called Ātākā Bakhshī.[650]

He was a very skilful surgeon; if a man's brains had comeFol. 109. out, he would cure it, and any sort of wound in an artery he easily healed. For some wounds his remedy was in form of a plaister, for some medicines had to be taken. He ordered a bandage tied on[651] the wound in my leg and put no seton in; once he made me eat something like a fibrous root (*yīldīz*). He told me himself, 'A certain man had his leg broken in the slender part and the bone was shattered for the breadth of the hand. I cut the flesh open and took the bits of bone out. Where they had been, I put a remedy in powder-form. That remedy simply became bone where there had been bone before.' He told many strange and marvellous things such as surgeons in cultivated lands cannot match.

Three or four days later, Qaṃbar-'alī, afraid on account of what he had said to me, fled (to Taṃbal) in Andijān. A few days later, The Khāns joined to me Ayūb *Begchīk* with his *tūmān*, and Jān-ḥasan *Bārīn* with the Bārīn *tūmān* and, as their army-beg, Sārīgh-bāsh Mīrzā,—1000 to 2000 men in all, and sent us towards Akhsī.

(*h. Bābur's expedition to Akhsī.*)

Shaikh Bāyazīd, a younger brother of Taṃbal, was in Akhsī; Shahbāz *Qārlūq* was in Kāsān. At the time, Shahbāz was lying before Nū-kīnt fort; crossing the Khujand-water opposite Bīkhrātā, we hurried to fall upon him there. When, a little Fol. 109b.before dawn, we were nearing the place, the begs represented to me that as the man would have had news of us, it was advisable not to go on in broken array. We moved on therefore with less speed. Shahbāz may have been really unaware of us until we were quite close; then getting to know of it, he fled into the fort. It often happens so! Once having said, 'The enemy is on guard!' it is easily fancied true and the chance of action is lost. In short, the experience of such things is that no effort or exertion must be omitted, once the chance for action comes. After-repentance is useless. There was a little fighting round the fort at dawn but we delivered no serious attack.

For the convenience of foraging, we moved from Nū-kīnt towards the hills in the direction of Bīshkhārān. Seizing his opportunity, Shahbāz *Qārlūq* abandoned Nū-kīnt and returned to Kāsān. We went back and occupied Nū-kīnt. During those days, the army several times went out and over-ran all sides and quarters. Once they over-ran the villages of Akhsī, once those of Kāsān. Shahbāz and Long Ḥasan's adopted son, Mīrīm came out of Kāsān to fight; they fought, were beaten, and there Mīrīm died.

(*i. The affairs of Pāp.*)

Pāp is a strong fort belonging to Akhsī. The Pāpīs made it fast and sent a man to me. We accordingly sent Sayyid Qāsim with a few braves to occupy it. They crossed the riverFol. 110. (*daryā*) opposite the upper villages of Akhsī and went into Pāp.[652] A few days later, Sayyid Qāsim did an astonishing thing. There were at the time with Shaikh Bāyazīd in Akhsī, Ibrāhīm *Chāpūk* (Slash-face) Ṭaghāī,[653] Aḥmad-of-qāsim *Kohbur*, and Qāsim Khitika (?) *Arghūn*. To these Shaikh Bāyazīd joins 200 serviceable braves and one night sends them to surprise Pāp. Sayyid Qāsim must have lain down carelessly to sleep, without setting a watch. They reach the fort, set ladders up, get up on the Gate, let the drawbridge down and, when 70 or 80 good men in mail are inside, goes the news to Sayyid Qāsim! Drowsy with sleep, he gets into his vest (*kūnglāk*), goes out, with five or six of his men, charges the enemy and drives them out with blow upon blow. He cut off a few heads and sent to me. Though such a careless lying down was bad leadership, yet, with so few, just by force of drubbing, to chase off such a mass of men in mail was very brave indeed.

Meantime The Khāns were busy with the siege of Andijān but the garrison would not let them get near it. The Andijān braves used to make sallies and blows would be exchanged.

(*j. Bābur invited into Akhsī.*)

Shaikh Bāyazīd now began to send persons to us from Akhsī to testify to well-wishing and pressingly invite us to Akhsī. His object was to separate me from The Khāns, by any artifice, because without me, they had no standing-ground.Fol. 110b His invitation may have been given after agreeing with his elder brother, Taṃbal that if I were separated from The Khāns, it might be possible, in my presence, to come to some arrangement with them. We gave The Khāns a hint of the invitation. They said, 'Go! and by whatever means, lay hands on Shaikh Bāyazīd.' It was not my habit to cheat and play false; here above all places, when promises would have been made, how was I to break them? It occurred to me however, that if we could get into Akhsī, we might be able, by using all available means, to detach Shaikh Bāyazīd from Taṃbal, when he might take my side or something might turn up to favour my fortunes. We, in our turn, sent a man to him; compact was made, he invited us into Akhsī and when we went, came out to meet us, bringing my younger brother, Nāṣir Mīrzā with him. Then he took us into the town, gave us ground to camp in (*yūrt*) and to me one of my father's houses in the outer fort[654] where I dismounted.

(*k. Taṃbal asks help of Shaibāq Khān.*)

Taṃbal had sent his elder brother, Beg Tīlba, to Shaibāq Khān with proffer of service and invitation to enter Farghāna. At this very time Shaibāq Khān's answer arrived; 'I will come,' he wrote. On hearing this, The Khāns were all upset; they could sit no longer before Andijān and rose from before it.

The Younger Khān himself had a reputation for justice and orthodoxy, but his Mughūls, stationed, contrary to the expectations of the towns-people, in Aūsh, Marghīnān and other places,—places that had come in to me,—began to behave ill Fol. 111.and oppressively. When The Khāns had broken up from before Andijān, the Aūshīs and Marghīnānīs, rising in tumult, seized the Mughūls in their forts, plundered and beat them, drove them out and pursued them.

The Khāns did not cross the Khujand-water (for the Kīndīrlīk-pass) but left the country by way of Marghīnān and Kand-i-badām and crossed it at Khujand, Taṃbal pursuing them as far as Marghīnān. We had had much uncertainty; we had not had much confidence in their making any stand, yet for us to go away, without clear reason, and leave them, would not have looked well.

(*l. Bābur attempts to defend Akhsī.*)

Early one morning, when I was in the Hot-bath, Jahāngīr Mīrzā came into Akhsī, from Marghīnān, a fugitive from Taṃbal. We saw one another, Shaikh Bāyazīd also being present, agitated and afraid. The Mīrzā and Ibrāhīm Beg said, 'Shaikh Bāyazīd must be made prisoner and we must get the citadel into our hands.' In good sooth, the proposal was wise. Said I, 'Promise has been made; how can we break it?' Shaikh Bāyazīd went into the citadel. Men ought to have been posted on the bridge; not even there did we post any-one! These blunders were the fruit of inexperience. At the top of the morning came Taṃbal himself with 2 or 3000 men in mail, crossed the bridge and went into the citadel. To begin with I had had rather few men; when I first went into Akhsī some had been sent to other forts and some had been made commandants and summoners all round. Left with me in Akhsī may have been something over 100 men. WeFol. 111b.

had got to horse with these and were posting braves at the top of one lane after another and making ready for the fight, when Shaikh Bāyazīd and Qaṃbar-'alī (the Skinner), and Muḥammad-dost[655] came gallopping from Taṃbal with talk of peace.

After posting those told off for the fight, each in his appointed place, I dismounted at my father's tomb for a conference, in which I invited Jahāngīr Mīrzā to join. Muḥammad-dost went back to Taṃbal but Qaṃbar-'alī and Shaikh Bāyazīd were present. We sat in the south porch of the tomb and were in consultation when the Mīrzā, who must have settled beforehand with Ibrāhīm *Chāpūk* to lay hands on those other two, said in my ear, 'They must be made prisoner.' Said I, 'Don't hurry! matters are past making prisoners. See here! with terms made, the affair might be coaxed into something. For why? Not only are they many and we few, but they with their strength are in the citadel, we with our weakness, in the outer fort.' Shaikh Bāyazīd and Qaṃbar-'alī both being present, Jahāngīr Mīrzā looked at Ibrāhīm Beg and made him a sign to refrain. Whether he misunderstood to the contrary or whether he pretended to misunderstand, is not known; suddenly he did the ill-deed of seizing Shaikh Bāyazīd. Braves Fol. 112.closing in from all sides, flung those two to the ground. Through this the affair was taken past adjustment; we gave them into charge and got to horse for the coming fight.

One side of the town was put into Jahāngīr Mīrzā's charge; as his men were few, I told off some of mine to reinforce him. I went first to his side and posted men for the fight, then to other parts of the town. There is a somewhat level, open space in the middle of Akhsī; I had posted a party of braves there and gone on when a large body of the enemy, mounted and on foot, bore down upon them, drove them from their post and forced them into a narrow lane. Just then I came up (the lane), gallopped my horse at them, and scattered them in flight. While I was thus driving them out from the lane into the flat, and had got my sword to work, they shot my horse in the leg; it stumbled and threw me there amongst them. I got up quickly and shot one arrow off. My squire, Kahil (lazy) had a weakly pony; he got off and led it to me. Mounting this, I started for another lane-head. Sl. Muḥ. Wais noticed the weakness of my mount, dismounted and led me his own. I mounted that horse. Just then, Qāsim Beg's son, Qaṃbar-'alī came, wounded, from Jahāngīr Mīrzā and said the Mīrzā had Fol. 112b.been attacked some time before, driven off in panic, and had gone right away. We were thunderstruck! At the same moment arrived Sayyid Qāsim, the commandant of Pāp! His was a most unseasonable visit, since at such a crisis it was well to have such a strong fort in our hands. Said I to Ibrāhīm Beg, 'What's to be done now?' He was slightly wounded; whether because of this or because of stupefaction, he could give no useful answer. My idea was to get across the bridge, destroy it and make for Andijān. Bābā Sherzād did very well here. 'We will storm out at the gate and get away at once,' he said. At his word, we set off for the Gate. Khwāja Mīr Mīrān also spoke boldly at that crisis. In one of the lanes, Sayyid Qāsim and Nāṣir's Dost chopped away at Bāqī Khīz,[656] I being in front with Ibrāhīm Beg and Mīrzā Qulī *Kūkūldāsh.*

As we came opposite the Gate, we saw Shaikh Bāyazīd, wearing his pull-over shirt[657] above his vest, coming in with three or four horsemen. He must have been put into the charge of Jahāngīr's men in the morning when, against my will, he was made prisoner, and they must have carried him off when they got away. They had thought it would be well to kill him; they set him free alive. He had been released just when I chanced upon him in the Gate. I drew and shot off the arrow on my thumb; it grazed his neck, a good shot! He came confusedly in at the Gate, turned to the right and fled down a lane. We followed him instantly. Mīrzā Qulī *Kūkūldāsh* got at one man with his rugged-mace and went on. Another man tookFol. 113. aim at Ibrāhīm Beg, but when the Beg shouted 'Hāī! Hāī!' let him pass and shot me in the arm-pit, from as near as a man on guard at a Gate. Two plates of my Qālmāq mail were cut; he took to flight and I shot after him. Next I shot at a man running away along the ramparts, adjusting for his cap against the battlements; he left his cap nailed on the wall and went off, gathering his turban-sash together in his hand. Then again,—a man was in flight alongside me in the lane down which Shaikh Bāyazīd had gone. I pricked the back of his head with my sword; he bent over from his horse till he leaned against the wall of the lane, but he kept his seat and with some trouble, made good his flight. When we had driven all the enemy's men from the Gate, we took possession of it but the affair was past discussion because they, in the citadel, were 2000 or 3000, we, in the outer fort, 100 or 200. Moreover they had chased off Jahāngīr Mīrzā, as long before as it takes milk to boil, and with him had gone half my men. This notwithstanding, we sent a man, while we were in the Gate, to say to him, 'If you are near at hand, come, let us attack again.' But the matter had gone past that! Ibrāhīm Beg, either because his horse was really weak or because of his wound, said, 'My horse is done.' On this, Sulaimān, one of Muḥ. 'Alī's *Mubashir's* servants, did a plucky thing, for with mattersFol. 113b. as they were and none constraining him, while we were waiting in the Gate, he dismounted and gave his horse to Ibrāhīm Beg. Kīchīk (little) 'Alī, now the Governor of Koel,[658] also shewed courage while we were in the Gate; he was a retainer of Sl. Muḥ. Wais and twice did well, here and in Aūsh. We delayed in the Gate till those sent to Jahāngīr Mīrzā came back and said he had gone off long before. It was too late to stay there; off we flung; it was ill-judged to have stayed as long as we did. Twenty or thirty men were with me. Just as we hustled out of the Gate, a number of armed men[659] came right down upon us, reaching the town-side of the drawbridge just as we had crossed. Banda-'alī, the maternal grandfather of Qāsim Beg's son, Ḥamza, called out to Ibrāhīm Beg, 'You are always boasting of your zeal! Let's take to our swords!' 'What hinders? Come along!' said Ibrāhīm Beg, from beside me. The senseless fellows were for displaying their zeal at a time of such disaster! Ill-timed zeal! That was no time to make stand or delay! We went off quickly, the enemy following and unhorsing our men.

(*m. Bābur a fugitive before Taṃbal's men.*)

When we were passing Meadow-dome (Guṃbaz-i-chaman), two miles out of Akhsī, Ibrāhīm Beg called out to me. Looking Fol. 114.back, I saw a page of Shaikh Bāyazīd's striking at him and turned rein, but Bayān-qulī's Khān-qulī, said at my side, 'This is a bad time for going back,' seized my rein and pushed ahead. Many of our men had been unhorsed before we reached Sang, 4 miles (2 *shar'ī*) out of Akhsī.[660] Seeing no pursuers at Sang, we passed it by and turned straight up its water. In this position of our affairs there were eight men of us;—Nāṣir's Dost, Qāsim Beg's Qaṃbar-'alī, Bayān-qulī's Khān-qulī, Mīrzā Qulī *Kūkūldāsh*, Nāṣir's Shāham, Sayyidī Qarā's 'Abdu'l-qadūs, Khwāja Ḥusainī and myself, the eighth. Turning up the stream, we found, in the broad valley, a good little road, far from the beaten track. We made straight up the valley, leaving the stream on the right, reached its waterless part and, near the Afternoon Prayer, got up out of it to level land. When we looked across the plain, we saw a blackness on it, far away. I made my party take cover and myself had gone to look out from higher ground, when a number of men came at a gallop up the hill behind us. Without waiting to know whether they were many or few, we mounted and rode off. There were 20 or 25; we, as has been said, were eight. If we had known their number at first, we should have made a good stand against them but we thought they would not be pursuing us, unless they had good support behind. AFol. 114b. fleeing foe, even if he be many, cannot face a few pursuers, for as the saying is, '*Hāī* is enough for the beaten ranks.'[661]

Khān-qulī said, 'This will never do! They will take us all. From amongst the horses there are, you take two good ones and go quickly on with Mīrzā Qulī *Kūkūldāsh*, each with a led horse. May-be you will get away.' He did not speak ill; as there was no fighting to hand, there was a chance of safety in doing as he said, but it really would not have looked well to leave any man alone, without a horse, amongst his foes. In the end they all dropped off, one by one, of themselves. My horse was a little tired; Khān-qulī dismounted and gave me his; I jumped off at once and mounted his, he mine. Just then they unhorsed Sayyidī Qarā's 'Abdu'l-qadūs and Nāṣir's Shāham who had fallen behind. Khān-qulī also was left. It was no time to profer help or defence; on it was gone, at the full speed of our mounts. The horses began to flag; Dost Beg's failed and stopped. Mine began to tire; Qaṃbar-'alī got off and gave me his; I mounted his, he mine. He was left. Khwāja Ḥusainī was a lame man; he turned aside to the higher ground. I was left with Mīrzā Qulī *Kūkūldāsh*. Our Fol. 115.horses could not possibly gallop, they trotted. His began to flag. Said I, 'What will become of me, if you fall behind? Come along! let's live or die together.' Several times I looked back at him; at last he said, 'My horse is done! It can't go on. Never mind me! You go on, perhaps you will get away.' It was a miserable position for me; he remained behind, I was alone.

Two of the enemy were in sight, one Bābā of Sairām, the other Banda-'alī. They gained on me; my horse was done; the mountains were still 2 miles (1 *kuroh*) off. A pile of rock was in my path. Thought I to myself, 'My horse is worn out and the hills are still somewhat far away; which way should I go? In my quiver are at least 20 arrows; should I dismount and shoot them off from this pile of rock?' Then again, I thought I might reach the hills and once there, stick a few arrows in my belt and scramble up. I had a good deal of confidence in my feet and went on, with this plan in mind. My horse could not possibly trot; the two men came within arrow's reach. Fol. 115b.For my own sake sparing my arrows, I did not shoot; they, out of caution, came no nearer. By sunset I was near the hills. Suddenly they called out, 'Where are you going in this fashion? Jahāngīr Mīrzā has been brought in a prisoner; Nāṣir Mīrzā also is in their hands.' I made no reply and went on towards the hills. When a good distance further had been gone, they spoke again, this time more respectfully, dismounting to speak. I gave no ear to them but went on up a glen till, at the Bed-time prayer, I reached a rock as big as a house. Going behind it, I saw there were places to be jumped, where no horse could go. They dismounted again and began to speak like servants and courteously. Said they, 'Where are you going in this fashion, without a road and in the dark? Sl. Aḥmad Taṃbal will make you *pādshāh*.' They swore this. Said I, 'My mind is not easy as to that. I cannot go to him. Fol. 116.If you think to do me timely service, years may pass before you have such another chance. Guide me to a road by which I can go to The Khān's presence. If you will do this, I will shew you favour and kindness greater than your heart's-desire. If you will not do it, go back the way you came; that also would be to serve me well.' Said they, 'Would to God we had never come! But since we are here, after following you in the way we have done, how can we go back from you? If you will not go with us, we are at your service, wherever you go.' Said I, 'Swear that you speak the truth.' They, for their part, made solemn oath upon the Holy Book.

I at once confided in them and said, 'People have shewn me a road through a broad valley, somewhere near this glen; take me to it.' Spite of their oath, my trust in them was not so complete but that I gave them the lead and followed. After 2 to 4 miles (1-2 *kuroh*), we came to the bed of a torrent. 'This will not be the road for the broad valley,' I said. They drew back, saying, 'That road is a long way ahead,' but it really must have been the one we were on and they have been concealing the fact, in order to deceive me. About half through the night, we reached another stream. This time they said, 'We have been negligent; it now seems to us that the road through the broad valley is behind.' Said I, 'What is to be done?' Said they, 'The Ghawā road is certainly in front; by it people cross for Far-kat.[662] They guided me for that and we went on till inFol. 116b. the third watch of the night we reached the Karnān gully which comes down from Ghawā. Here Bābā Sairāmī said, 'Stay here a little while I look along the Ghawā road.' He came back after a time and said, 'Some men have gone along that road, led by one wearing a Mughūl cap; there is no going that way.' I took alarm at these words. There I was, at dawn, in the middle of the cultivated land, far from the road I wanted to take. Said I, 'Guide me to where I can hide today, and tonight when you will have laid hands on something for the horses, lead me to cross the Khujand-water and along its further bank.' Said they, 'Over there, on the upland, there might be hiding.'

Banda-'alī was Commandant in Karnān. 'There is no doing without food for ourselves or our horses;' he said, 'let me go into Karnān and bring what I can find.' We stopped 2 miles (1 *kuroh*) out of Karnān; he went on. He was a long time away; near dawn there was no sign of him. The day had shot when he hurried up, bringing three loaves of bread but no corn for the horses. Each of us putting a loaf into the breast of his tunic, we went quickly up the rise, tethered our horses there in the open valley and went to higher ground, each to keep watch.

Fol. 117.Near mid-day, Aḥmad the Falconer went along the Ghawā road for Akhsī. I thought of calling to him and of saying, with promise and fair word, 'You take those horses,' for they had had a day and a night's strain and struggle, without corn, and were utterly done. But then again, we were a little uneasy as we did not entirely trust him. We decided that, as the men Bābā Sairāmī had seen on the road would be in Karnān that night, the two with me should fetch one of their horses for each of us, and that then we should go each his own way.

At mid-day, a something glittering was seen on a horse, as far away as eye can reach. We were not able to make out at all what it was. It must have been Muḥ. Bāqir Beg himself; he had been with us in Akhsī and when we got out and scattered, he must have come this way and have been moving then to a hiding-place.[663]

Banda-'alī and Bābā Sairāmī said, 'The horses have had no corn for two days and two nights; let us go down into the dale and put them there to graze.' Accordingly we rode down and put them to the grass. At the Afternoon Prayer, a horseman passed along the rising-ground where we had been. We recognized him for Qādīr-bīrdī, the head-man of Ghawā. 'Call him,' I said. They called; he came. After questioning him, and speaking to him of favour and kindness, and giving him promise and fair word, I sent him to bring rope, and a grass-hook, and an axe, and material for crossing water,[664] and corn Fol. 117b.for the horses, and food and, if it were possible, other horses. We made tryst with him for that same spot at the Bed-time Prayer.

Near the Evening Prayer, a horseman passed from the direction of Karnān for Ghawā. 'Who are you?' we asked. He made some reply. He must have been Muḥ. Bāqir Beg himself, on his way from where we had seen him earlier, going at night-fall to some other hiding-place, but he so changed his voice that, though he had been years with me, I did not know it. It would have been well if I had recognized him and he had joined me. His passing caused much anxiety and alarm; tryst could not be kept with Qādīr-bīrdī of Ghawā. Banda-'alī said, 'There are retired gardens in the suburbs of Karnān where no one will suspect us of being; let us go there and send to Qādīr-bīrdī and have him brought there.' With this idea, we mounted and went to the Karnān suburbs. It was winter and very cold. They found a worn, coarse sheepskin coat and brought it to me; I put it on. They brought me a bowl of millet-porridge; I ate it and was wonderfully refreshed. 'Have you sent off the man to Qādīr-bīrdī?' said I to Banda-'alī. 'I have sent,' he said. But those luckless, clownish mannikins seem to have agreed together to send the man to Taṃbal in Akhsī!

We went into a house and for awhile my eyes closed in sleep. Those mannikins artfully said to me, 'You must not bestir yourself to leave Karnān till there is news of Qādīr-bīrdī but this house is right amongst the suburbs; on the outskirts the orchards are empty; no-one will suspect if we goFol. 118. there.' Accordingly we mounted at mid-night and went to a distant orchard. Bābā Sairāmī kept watch from the roof of a house. Near mid-day he came down and said, 'Commandant Yūsuf is coming.' Great fear fell upon me! 'Find out,' I said, 'whether he comes because he knows about me.' He went and after some exchange of words, came back and said, 'He says he met a foot-soldier in the Gate of Akhsī who said to him, "The pādshāh is in such a place," that he told no-one, put the man with Walī the Treasurer whom he had made prisoner in the fight, and then gallopped off here.' Said I, 'How does it strike you?' 'They are all your servants,' he said, 'you must go. What else can you do? They will make you their ruler.' Said I,

'After such rebellion and fighting, with what confidence could I go?' We were saying this, when Yūsuf knelt before me, saying, 'Why should it be hidden? Sl. Aḥmad Taṃbal has no news of you, but Shaikh Bāyazīd has and he sent me here.' On hearing this, my state of mind was miserable indeed, for well is it understood that nothing in the world is worse than fear for one's life. 'Tell the truth!' I said, 'if the affair is likely to go on to worse, I will make Fol. 118b.ablution.' Yūsuf swore oaths, but who would trust them? I knew the helplessness of my position. I rose and went to a corner of the garden, saying to myself, 'If a man live a hundred years or a thousand years, at the last nothing ...'[665]

TRANSLATOR'S NOTE.

Friends are likely to have rescued Bābur from his dangerous isolation. His presence in Karnān was known both in Ghawā and in Akhsī; Muḥ. Bāqir Beg was at hand (f. 117); some of those he had dropped in his flight would follow him when their horses had had rest; Jahāngīr was somewhere north of the river with the half of Bābur's former force (f. 112); The Khāns, with their long-extended line of march, may have been on the main road through or near Karnān. If Yūsuf took Bābur as a prisoner along the Akhsī road, there were these various chances of his meeting friends.

His danger was evaded; he joined his uncles and was with them, leading 1000 men (Sh. N. p. 268), when they were defeated at Archīān just before or in the season of Cancer, *i.e. circa* June (T. R. p. 164). What he was doing between the winter cold of Karnān (f. 117b) and June might have been known from his lost pages. Muḥ. Ṣāliḥ writes at length of one affair falling within the time,—Jahāngīr's occupation of Khujand, its siege and its capture by Shaibānī. This capture will have occurred considerably more than a month before the defeat of The Khāns (Sh. N. p. 230).

It is not easy to decide in what month of 908 AH. they went into Farghāna or how long their campaign lasted. Bābur chronicles a series of occurrences, previous to the march of the army, which must have filled some time. The road over the Kīndirlīk-pass was taken, one closed in Bābur's time (f. 1b) though now open through the winter. Looking at the rapidity of his own movements in Farghāna, it seems likely that the pass was crossed after and not before its closed time. If so, the campaign may have covered 4 or 5 months. Muḥ. Ṣāliḥ's account of Shaibāq's operations strengthens this view. News that Aḥmad had joined Maḥmūd in Tāshkīnt (f. 102) went to Shaibānī in Khusrau Shāh's territories; he saw his interests in Samarkand threatened by this combination of the Chaghatāī brothers to restore Bābur in Farghāna, came north therefore in order to help Taṃbal. He then waited a month in Samarkand (Sh. N. p. 230), besieged Jahāngīr, went back and stayed in Samarkand long enough to give his retainers time to equip for a year's campaigning (l. c. p. 244) then went to Akhsī and so to Archīān.

Bābur's statement (f. 110b) that The Khāns went from Andijān to the Khujand-crossing over the Sīr attracts attention because this they might have done if they had meant to leave Farghāna by Mīrzā-rabāṭ. but they are next heard of as at Akhsī. Why did they make that great détour? Why not have crossed opposite Akhsī or at Sang? Or if they had thought of retiring, what turned them east again? Did they place Jahāngīr in Khujand? Bābur's missing pages would have answered these questions no doubt. It was useful for them to encamp where they did, east of Akhsī, because they there had near them a road by which reinforcement could come from Kāshghar or retreat be made. The Akhsī people told Shaibānī that he could easily overcome The Khāns if he went without warning, and if they had not withdrawn by the Kulja road (Sh. N. p. 262). By that road the few men who went with Aḥmad to Tāshkīnt (f. 103) may have been augmented to the force, enumerated as his in the battle by Muḥ. Ṣāliḥ (Sh. N. cap. LIII.).

When The Khāns were captured, Bābur escaped and made 'for Mughūlistān,' a vague direction seeming here to mean Tāshkīnt, but, finding his road blocked, in obedience to orders from Shaibāq that he and Abū'l-makāram were to be captured, he turned back and, by unfrequented ways, went into the hill-country of Sūkh and Hushīār. There he spent about a year in great misery (f. 14 and Ḥ. S. ii, 318). Of the wretchedness of the time Ḥaidar also writes. If anything was attempted in Farghāna in the course of those months, record of it has been lost with Bābur's missing pages. He was not only homeless and poor, but shut in by enemies. Only the loyalty or kindness of the hill-tribes can have saved him and his few followers. His mother was with him; so also were the families of his men. How Qūtlūq-nigār contrived to join him from Tāshkīnt, though historically a small matter, is one he would chronicle. What had happened there after the Mughūl defeat, was that the horde had marched away for Kāshghar while Shāh Begīm remained in charge of her daughters with whom the Aūzbeg chiefs intended to contract alliance. Shaibānī's orders for her stay and for the general exodus were communicated to her by her son, The Khān, in what Muḥ. Ṣāliḥ, quoting its purport, describes as a right beautiful letter (p. 296).

By some means Qūtlūq-nigār joined Bābur, perhaps helped by the circumstance that her daughter, Khān-zāda was Shaibāq's wife. She spent at least some part of those hard months with him, when his fortunes were at their lowest ebb. A move becoming imperative, the ragged and destitute company started in mid-June 1504 (Muḥ. 910 AH.) on that perilous mountain journey to which Ḥaidar applies the Prophet's dictum, 'Travel is a foretaste of Hell,' but of which the end was the establishment of a Tīmūrid dynasty in Hindūstān. To look down the years from the destitute Bābur to Akbar, Shāh-jahān and Aurangzīb is to see a great stream of human life flow from its source in his resolve to win upward, his quenchless courage and his abounding vitality. Not yet 22, the sport of older men's intrigues, he had been tempered by failure, privation and dangers.

He left Sūkh intending to go to Sl. Ḥusain Mīrzā in Khurāsān but he changed this plan for one taking him to Kābul where a Tīmūrid might claim to dispossess the Arghūns, then holding it since the death, in 907 AH.of his uncle, Aūlūgh Beg Mīrzā *Kābulī*.

SECTION II. KĀBUL[666]

910 AH.-JUNE 14TH 1504 TO JUNE 4TH 1505 AD.667

(a. Bābur leaves Farghāna.)

In the month of Muḥarram, after leaving the Farghāna countryḤaidarābād MS. Fol. 120. intending to go to Khurāsān, I dismounted at Aīlāk-yīlāq,[668] one of the summer pastures of Ḥiṣār. In this camp I entered my 23rd year, and applied the razor to my face.[669] Those who, hoping in me, went with me into exile, were, small and great, between 2 and 300; they were almost all on foot, had walking-staves in their hands, brogues[670] on their feet, and long coats[671] on their shoulders. So destitute were we that we had but two tents *(chādar)* amongst us; my own used to be pitched for my mother, and they set an *ālāchūq* at each stage for me to sit in.[672]

Though we had started with the intention of going into Khurāsān, yet with things as they were[673] something was hoped for from the Ḥiṣār country and Khusrau Shāh's retainers. Every few days some-one would come in from the country or a tribe or the (Mughūl) horde, whose words made it probable that we had growing ground for hope. Just then Mullā Bābā of Pashāghar came back, who had been our envoy to Khusrau Shāh; from Khusrau Shāh he brought nothing likely to please, but he did from the tribes and the horde.

Fol. 120b.Three or four marches beyond Aīlāk, when halt was made at a place near Ḥiṣār called Khwāja 'Imād, Muḥibb-'alī, the Armourer, came to me from Khusrau Shāh. Through Khusrau Shāh's territories I have twice happened to pass;[674] renowned though he was for kindness and liberality, he neither time showed me the humanity he had shown to the meanest of men.

As we were hoping something from the country and the tribes, we made delay at every stage. At this critical point Sherīm Ṭaghāī, than whom no man of mine was greater, thought of leaving me because he was not keen to go into Khurāsān. He had sent all his family off and stayed himself unencumbered, when after the defeat at Sar-i-pul (906 AH.) I went back to defend Samarkand; he was a bit of a coward and he did this sort of thing several times over.

(b. Bābur joined by one of Khusrau Shāh's kinsmen.)

After we reached Qabādīān, a younger brother of Khusrau Shāh, Bāqī *Chaghānīānī*, whose holdings were Chaghānīān,[675] Shahr-i-ṣafā and Tīrmīẕ, sent the *khatīb*[676] of Qarshī to me to express his good wishes and his desire for alliance, and, after we had crossed the Amū at the Aūbāj-ferry, he came himself to wait on me. By his wish we moved down the river to opposite Tīrmīẕ, where, without fear [or, without going over himself],[677] he had their families[678] and their goods brought across to join us. This done, we set out together for Kāhmard and Bāmīān, then held by his son[679] Aḥmad-i-qāsim, the son of Khusrau Shāh's sister. Our plan was to leave the households (*awī-aīl*) safe in Fort Ajar of the Kāhmard-valley and to take action whereverFol. 121. action might seem well. At Aībak, Yār-'alī Balāl,[680] who had fled from Khusrau Shāh, joined us with several braves; he had been with me before, and had made good use of his sword several times in my presence, but was parted from me in the recent throneless times[681] and had gone to Khusrau Shāh. He represented to me that the Mughūls in Khusrau Shāh's service wished me well. Moreover, Qaṃbar-'alī Beg, known also as Qaṃbar-'alī *Silākh* (Skinner), fled to me after we reached the Zindān-valley.[682]

(*c. Occurrences in Kākmard.*)

We reached Kāhmard with three or four marches and deposited our households and families in Ajar. While we stayed there, Jahāngīr Mīrzā married (Aī Begīm) the daughter of Sl. Maḥmūd Mīrzā and Khān-zāda Begīm, who had been set aside for him during the lifetime of the Mīrzās.[683]

Meantime Bāqī Beg urged it upon me, again and again, that two rulers in one country, or two chiefs in one army are a source of faction and disorder—a foundation of dissension and ruin. "For they have said, 'Ten darwīshes can sleep under one blanket, but two kings cannot find room in one clime.'

If a man of God eat half a loaf,

He gives the other to a darwīsh;

Let a king grip the rule of a clime,

He dreams of another to grip."[684]

Bāqī Beg urged further that Khusrau Shāah's retainers and followers would be coming in that day or the next to take service with the Pādshāh (*i.e.* Bābur); that there were such Fol. 121b.sedition-mongers with them as the sons of Ayūb *Begchīk*, besides other who had been the stirrers and spurs to disloyalty amongst their Mīrzās,[685] and that if, at this point, Jahāngīr Mīrzā were dismissed, on good and friendly terms, for Khurāsān, it would remove a source of later repentance. Urge it as he would, however, I did not accept his suggestion, because it is against my nature to do an injury to my brethren, older or younger,[686] or to any kinsman soever, even when something untoward has happened. Though formerly between Jahāngīr

Mīrzā and me, resentments and recriminations had occurred about our rule and retainers, yet there was nothing whatever then to arouse anger against him; he had come out of that country (*i.e.* Farghāna) with me and was behaving like a blood-relation and a servant. But in the end it was just as Bāqī Beg predicted;—those tempters to disloyalty, that is to say, Ayūb's Yūsuf and Ayūb's Bihlūl, left me for Jahāngīr Mīrzā, took up a hostile and mutinous position, parted him from me, and conveyed him into Khurāsān.

(*d. Co-operation invited against Shaibāq Khān.*)

In those days came letters from Sl. Ḥusain Mīrzā, long and far-fetched letters which are still in my possession and in that Fol. 122.of others, written to Badī'u'z-zamān Mīrzā, myself, Khusrau Shāh and Ẕū'n-nūn Beg, all to the same purport, as follows:—"When the three brothers, Sl. Maḥmūd Mīrzā, Sl. Aḥmad Mīrzā, and Aūlūgh Beg Mīrzā, joined together and advanced against me, I defended the bank of the Murgh-āb[687] in such a way that they retired without being able to effect anything. Now if the Aūzbegs advance, I might myself guard the bank of the Murgh-āb again; let Badī'u'z-zamān Mīrzā leave men to defend the forts of Balkh, Shibarghān, and Andikhūd while he himself guards Girzawān, the Zang-valley, and the hill-country thereabouts." As he had heard of my being in those parts, he wrote to me also, "Do you make fast Kāhmard, Ajar, and that hill-tract; let Khusrau Shāh place trusty men in Ḥiṣār and Qūndūz; let his younger brother Walī make fast Badakhshān and the Khutlān hills; then the Aūzbeg will retire, able to do nothing."

These letters threw us into despair;—for why? Because at that time there was in Tīmūr Beg's territory (*yūrt*) no ruler so great as Sl. Ḥusain Mīrzā, whether by his years, armed strength, or dominions; it was to be expected, therefore, that envoys would go, treading on each other's heels, with clear and sharp orders, such as, "Arrange for so many boats at the Tīrmīz,Fol. 122b. Kilīf, and Kīrkī ferries," "Get any quantity of bridge material together," and "Well watch the ferries above Tūqūz-aūlūm,"[688] so that men whose spirit years of Aūzbeg oppression had broken, might be cheered to hope again.[689] But how could hope live in tribe or horde when a great ruler like Sl. Ḥusain Mīrzā, sitting in the place of Tīmūr Beg, spoke, not of marching forth to meet the enemy, but only of defence against his attack?

When we had deposited in Ajar what had come with us of hungry train (*aj aūrūq*) and household (*awī-aīl*), together with the families of Bāqī Beg, his son, Muḥ. Qāsim, his soldiers and his tribesmen, with all their goods, we moved out with our men.

(*e. Increase of Bābur's following.*)

One man after another came in from Khusrau Shāh's Mughūls and said, "We of the Mughūl horde, desiring the royal welfare, have drawn off from Ṭāīkhān (Ṭālīkān) towards Ishkīmīsh and Fūlūl. Let the Pādshāh advance as fast as possible, for the greater part of Khusrau Shāh's force has broken up and is ready to take service with him." Just then news arrived that Shaibāq Khān, after taking Andijān,[690] was getting to horse again against Ḥiṣār and Qūndūz. On hearing Fol. 123.this, Khusrau Shāh, unable to stay in Qūndūz, marched out with all the men he had, and took the road for Kābul. No sooner had he left than his old servant, the able and trusted Mullā Muḥammad *Turkistānī* made Qūndūz fast for Shaibāq Khān.

Three or four thousand heads-of-houses in the Mughūl horde, former dependants of Khusrau Shāh, brought their families and joined us when, going by way of Sham-tū, we were near the Qīzīl-sū.[691]

(*f. Qambar-'alī, the Skinner, dismissed.*)

Qambar-'alī Beg's foolish talk has been mentioned several times already; his manners were displeasing to Bāqī Beg; to gratify Bāqī Beg, he was dismissed. Thereafter his son, 'Abdu'l-shukūr, was in Jahāngīr Mīrzā's service.

(*g. Khusrau Shāh waits on Bābur.*)

Khusrau Shāh was much upset when he heard that the Mughūl horde had joined me; seeing nothing better to do for himself, he sent his son-in-law, Ayūb's Yaq'ūb, to make profession of well-wishing and submission to me, and respectfully to represent that he would enter my service if I would make terms and compact with him. His offer was accepted, because Bāqī *Chaghānīānī* was a man of weight, and, however steady in his favourable disposition to me, did not overlook his brother's side in this matter. Compact was made that Khusrau Shāh's life should be safe, and that whatever amount of his goods he selected, should not be refused him. After giving Yaq'ūb leave to go, we marched down the Qīzīl-sū and dismounted near to where it joins the water of Andar-āb.Fol. 123b.

Next day, one in the middle of the First Rabī' (end of August, 1504 AD.), riding light, I crossed the Andar-āb water and took my seat under a large plane-tree near Dūshī, and thither came Khusrau Shāh, in pomp and splendour, with a great company of men. According to rule and custom, he dismounted some way off and then made his approach. Three times he knelt when we saw one another, three times also on taking leave; he knelt once when asking after my welfare, once again when he offered his tribute, and he did the same with Jahāngīr Mīrzā and with Mīrzā Khān (Wais). That sluggish old mannikin who through so many years had just pleased himself, lacking of sovereignty one thing only, namely, to read the *Khuṭba* in his own name, now knelt 25 or 26 times in succession, and came and went till he was so wearied out that he tottered forward. His many years of begship and authority vanished from his view. When we had seen one another and he had offered his gift, I desired him to be seated. We stayed in that place for one or two *garīs*,[692] exchanging tale and talk. His conversation was vapid and empty, presumably because he was a coward and false to his salt. Two things he said were extraordinary for the time when, under his eyes, his trusty and trusted retainers were becoming mine, and when his affairs had reached the point that he, the sovereign-aping mannikin, had had to come, willy-nilly, abased and unhonoured, to what sortFol. 124. of an interview! One of the things he said was this:—When condoled with for the desertion of his men, he replied, "Those very servants have four times left me and returned." The other was said when I had asked him where his brother Walī would cross the Amū and when he would arrive. "If he find a ford, he will soon be here, but when waters rise, fords change; the (Persian) proverb has it, 'The waters have carried down the fords.'" These words God brought to his tongue in that hour of the flowing away of his own authority and following!

After sitting a *garī* or two, I mounted and rode back to camp, he for his part returning to his halting-place. On that day his begs, with their servants, great and small, good and bad, and tribe after tribe began to desert him and come, with their families, to me. Between the two Prayers of the next afternoon not a man remained in his presence.

"Say,—O God! who possessest the kingdom! Thou givest it to whom Thou wilt and Thou takest it from whom Thou wilt! In Thy hand is good, for Thou art almighty."[693]

Wonderful is His power! This man, once master of 20 or 30,000 retainers, once owning Sl. Maḥmūd's dominions from Qaḥlūgha,—known also as the Iron-gate,—to the range of Fol. 124b.Hindū-kush, whose old mannikin of a tax-gatherer, Ḥasan *Barlās* by name, had made us march, had made us halt, with all the tax-gatherer's roughness, from Aīlāk to Aūbāj,[694] that man He so abased and so bereft of power that, with no blow struck, no sound made, he stood, without command over servants, goods, or life, in the presence of a band of 200 or 300 men, defeated and destitute as we were.

In the evening of the day on which we had seen Khusrau Shāh and gone back to camp, Mīrzā Khān came to my presence and demanded vengeance on him for the blood of his brothers.[695] Many of us were at one with him, for truly it is right, both by Law and common justice, that such men should get their desserts, but, as terms had been made, Khusrau Shāh was let go free. An order was given that he should be allowed to take whatever of his goods he could convey; accordingly he loaded up, on three or four strings of mules and camels, all jewels, gold, silver, and precious things he had, and took them with him.[696] Sherīm Ṭaghāī was told off to escort him, who after setting Khusrau Shāh on his road for Khurāsān, by way of Ghūrī and Dahānah, was to go to Kāhmard and bring the families after us to Kābul.

(*h. Bābur marches for Kābul.*)

Marching from that camp for Kābul, we dismounted in Khwāja Zaid.

On that day, Ḥamza Bī *Mangfīt,*[697] at the head of Aūzbeg raiders, was over-running round about Dūshī. Sayyid Qāsim, the Lord of the Gate, and Aḥmad-i-qāsim *Kohbur* were sentFol. 125. with several braves against him; they got up with him, beat his Aūzbegs well, cut off and brought in a few heads.

In this camp all the armour (*jība*) of Khusrau Shāh's armoury was shared out. There may have been as many as 7 or 800 coats-of-mail (*joshan*) and horse accoutrements (*kūhah*);[698] these were the one thing he left behind; many pieces of porcelain also fell into our hands, but, these excepted, there was nothing worth looking at.

With four or five marches we reached Ghūr-bund, and there dismounted in Ushtur-shahr. We got news there that Muqīm's chief beg, Sherak (var. Sherka) *Arghūn*, was lying along the Bārān, having led an army out, not through hearing of me, but to hinder 'Abdu'r-razzāq Mīrzā from passing along the Panjhīr-road, he having fled from Kābul[699] and being then amongst the Tarkalānī Afghāns towards Lamghān. On hearing this we marched forward, starting in the afternoon and pressing on through the dark till, with the dawn, we surmounted the Hūpīān-pass.[700]

I had never seen Suhail;[701] when I came out of the pass I saw a star, bright and low. "May not that be Suhail?" said I. Said they, "It is Suhail." Bāqī *Chaghānīānī* recited this couplet;—[702]

"How far dost thou shine, O Suhail, and where dost thou rise?

A sign of good luck is thine eye to the man on whom it may light."

The Sun was a spear's-length high[703] when we reached the foot of the Sanjid (Jujube)-valley and dismounted. Our scouting Fol. 125b.braves fell in with Sherak below the Qarā-bāgh,[704] near Aīkarī-yār, and straightway got to grips with him. After a little of some sort of fighting, our men took the upper hand, hurried their adversaries off, unhorsed 70-80 serviceable braves and brought them in. We gave Sherak his life and he took service with us.

(i. Death of Walī of Khusrau.)

The various clans and tribes whom Khusrau Shāh, without troubling himself about them, had left in Qūndūz, and also the Mughūl horde, were in five or six bodies (*būlāk*). One of those belonging to Badakhshān,—it was the Rūstā-hazāra,:—came, with Sayyidīm 'Alī *darbān*,[705] across the Panjhīr-pass to this camp, did me obeisance and took service with me. Another body came under Ayūb's Yūsuf and Ayūb's Bihlūl; it also took service with me. Another came from Khutlān, under Khusrau Shāh's younger brother, Walī; another, consisting of the (Mughūl) tribesmen (*aīmāq*) who had been located in Yīlānchaq, Nikdiri (?), and the Qūndūz country, came also. The last-named two came by Andar-āb and Sar-i-āb,[706] meaning to cross by the Panjhīr-pass; at Sar-i-āb the tribesmen were ahead; Walī came up behind; they held the road, fought and beat him. He himself fled to the Aūzbegs,[707] and Shaibāq Khān had his head struck off in the Square (*Chār-sū*) of Samarkand; his followers, beaten and plundered, came on with the tribesmen, and like these, took service with me. With them came Sayyid Fol. 126.Yūsuf Beg (the Grey-wolfer).

(j. Kābul gained.)

From that camp we marched to the Āq-sarāī meadow of the Qarā-bāgh and there dismounted. Khusrau Shāh's people were well practised in oppression and violence; they tyrannized over one after another till at last I had up one of Sayyidīm 'Alī's good braves to my Gate[708] and there beaten for forcibly taking a jar of oil. There and then he just died under the blows; his example kept the rest down.

We took counsel in that camp whether or not to go at once against Kābul. Sayyid Yūsuf and some others thought that, as winter was near, our first move should be into Lamghān, from which place action could be taken as advantage offered. Bāqī Beg and some others saw it good to move on Kābul at once; this plan was adopted; we marched forward and dismounted in Ābā-qūrūq.

My mother and the belongings left behind in Kāhmard rejoined us at Ābā-qūrūq. They had been in great danger, the particulars of which are these:—Sherīm Ṭaghāī had gone to set Khusrau Shāh on his way for Khurāsān, and this done, was to fetch the families from Kāhmard. When he reached Dahānah, he found he was not his own master; Khusrau Shāh went on with him into Kāhmard, where was his sister's son, Aḥmad-i-qāsim. These two took up an altogether wrongFol. 126b. position towards the families in

Kāhmard. Hereupon a number of Bāqī Beg's Mughūls, who were with the families, arranged secretly with Sherīm Ṭaghāī to lay hands on Khusrau Shāh and Aḥmad-i-qāsim. The two heard of it, fled along the Kāhmard-valley on the Ajar side[709] and made for Khurāsān. To bring this about was really what Sherīm Ṭaghāī and the Mughūls wanted. Set free from their fear of Khusrau Shāh by his flight, those in charge of the families got them out of Ajar, but when they reached Kāhmard, the Sāqānchī (var. Asīqanchī) tribe blocked the road, like an enemy, and plundered the families of most of Bāqī Beg's men.[710] They made prisoner Qul-i-bāyazīd's little son, Tīzak; he came into Kābul three or four years later. The plundered and unhappy families crossed by the Qībchāq-pass, as we had done, and they rejoined us in Ābā-qūrūq.

Leaving that camp we went, with one night's halt, to the Chālāk-meadow, and there dismounted. After counsel taken, it was decided to lay siege to Kābul, and we marched forward. With what men of the centre there were, I dismounted between Ḥaidar *Tāqī's*[711] garden and the tomb of Qul-i-bāyazīd, the Taster (*bakāwal*);[712] Jahāngīr Mīrzā, with the men of the right, Fol. 127.dismounted in my great Four-gardens (*Chār-bāgh*), Nāṣir Mīrzā, with the left, in the meadow of Qūtlūq-qadam's tomb. People of ours went repeatedly to confer with Muqīm; they sometimes brought excuses back, sometimes words making for agreement. His tactics were the sequel of his dispatch, directly after Sherak's defeat, of a courier to his father and elder brother (in Qandahār); he made delays because he was hoping in them.

One day our centre, right, and left were ordered to put on their mail and their horses' mail, to go close to the town, and to display their equipment so as to strike terror on those within. Jahāngīr Mīrzā and the right went straight forward by the Kūcha-bāgh;[713] I, with the centre, because there was water, went along the side of Qūtlūq-qadam's tomb to a mound facing the rising-ground;[714] the van collected above Qūtlūq-qadam's bridge,—at that time, however, there was no bridge. When the braves, showing themselves off, galloped close up to the Curriers'-gate,[715] a few who had come out through it fled in again without making any stand. A crowd of Kābulīs who had come out to see the sight raised a great dust when they ran away from the high slope of the glacis of the citadel (*i.e.* Bālā-ḥiṣār). A number of pits had been dug up the rise Fol. 127b.between the bridge and the gate, and hidden under sticks and rubbish; Sl. Qulī *Chūnāq* and several others were thrown as they galloped over them. A few braves of the right exchanged sword-cuts with those who came out of the town, in amongst the lanes and gardens, but as there was no order to engage, having done so much, they retired.

Those in the fort becoming much perturbed, Muqīm made offer through the begs, to submit and surrender the town. Bāqī Beg his mediator, he came and waited on me, when all fear was chased from his mind by our entire kindness and favour. It was settled that next day he should march out with retainers and following, goods and effects, and should make the town over to us. Having in mind the good practice Khusrau Shāh's retainers had had in indiscipline and longhandedness, we appointed Jahāngīr Mīrzā and Nāṣir Mīrzā with the great and household begs, to escort Muqīm's family out of Kābul[716] and to bring out Muqīm himself with his various dependants, goods and effects. Camping-ground was assigned to him at Tīpa.[717] When the Mīrzās and the Begs went at dawn to the Gate, they saw much mobbing and tumult of the common people, so they sent me a man to say, "Unless you come yourself, there will be no holding these people in." In the end I got to horse, had two or three persons shot, two or three cut in pieces, and so stamped the rising down. Muqīm and his belongings then got out, safe and sound,Fol. 128. and they betook themselves to Tīpa.

It was in the last ten days of the Second Rabī' (Oct. 1504 AD.)[718] that without a fight, without an effort, by Almighty God's bounty and mercy, I obtained and made subject to me Kābul and Ghaznī and their dependent districts.

DESCRIPTION OF KĀBUL[719]

The Kābul country is situated in the Fourth climate and in the midst of cultivated lands.[720] On the east it has the Lamghānāt,[721] Parashāwar (Pashāwar), Hash(t)-nagar and some of the countries of Hindūstān. On the west it has the mountain region in which are Karnūd (?) and Ghūr, now the refuge and dwelling-places of the Hazāra and Nikdīrī (var. Nikudārī) tribes. On the north, separated from it by the range of Hindū-kush, it has the Qūndūz and Andar-āb countries. On the south, it has Farmūl, Naghr (var. Naghz), Bannū and Afghānistān.[722]

(*a. Town and environs of Kābul.*)

The Kābul district itself is of small extent, has its greatest length from east to west, and is girt round by mountains. Its walled-town connects with one of these, rather a low one known as Shāh-of-Kābul because at some time a (Hindū) Shāh of Kābul built a residence on its summit.[723] Shāh-of-Kābul begins at the Dūrrīn narrows and ends at those of Dih-i-yaq'ūb[724]; it may be 4 miles (2 *shar'ī*) round; its skirt is covered with gardens fertilized from a canal which was brought along the hill-slope in the time of my paternal uncle, Aūlūgh Beg Mīrzā by his guardian, Wais Atāka.[725] The water of this canal comes to an end in a retired corner, a quarter known as Kul-kīna[726] where much debauchery has gone on. About this place itFol. 128b. sometimes used to be said, in jesting parody of Khwāja Ḥāfiẓ[727],—"Ah! the happy, thoughtless time when, with our names in ill-repute, we lived days of days at Kul-kīna!"

East of Shāh-of-Kabūl and south of the walled-town lies a large pool[728] about a 2 miles [*shar'ī*] round. From the town side of the mountain three smallish springs issue, two near Kul-kīna; Khwāja Shamū's[729] tomb is at the head of one; Khwāja Khiẓr's Qadam-gāh[730] at the head of another, and the third is at a place known as Khwāja Raushānāī, over against Khwāja 'Abdu'ṣ-ṣamad. On a detached rock of a spur of Shāh-of-Kābul, known as 'Uqābain,[731] stands the citadel of Kābul with the great walled-town at its north end, lying high in excellent air, and overlooking the large pool already mentioned, and also three meadows, namely, Siyāh-sang (Black-rock), Sūng-qūrghān (Fort-back), and Chālāk (Highwayman?),—a most beautiful outlook when the meadows are green. The north-wind does not fail Kābul in the heats; people call it the Parwān-wind[732]; it makes a delightful temperature in the windowed houses on the northern part of the citadel. In praise of the citadel of Kābul, Mullā Muḥammad *Ṭ̤ālib Mu'ammāī* (the Riddler)[733]

Fol. 129.used to recite this couplet, composed on Badī'u'z-zamān Mīrzā's name:—

Drink wine in the castle of Kābul and send the cup round without pause;

For Kābul is mountain, is river, is city, is lowland in one.[734]

(*b. Kābul as a trading-town.*)

Just as 'Arabs call every place outside 'Arab (Arabia), 'Ajam, so Hindūstānīs call every place outside Hindūstān, Khurāsān. There are two trade-marts on the land-route between Hindūstān and Khurāsān; one is Kābul, the other, Qandahār. To Kābul caravans come from Kāshghar,[735] Farghāna,Turkistān, Samarkand, Bukhārā, Balkh, Ḥiṣār and Badakhshān. To Qandahār they come from Khurāsān. Kābul is an excellent trading-centre; if merchants went to Khīta or to Rūm,[736] they might make no higher profit. Down to Kābul every year come 7, 8, or 10,000 horses and up to it, from Hindūstān, come every year caravans of 10, 15 or 20,000 heads-of-houses, bringing slaves (*barda*), white cloth, sugar-candy, refined and common sugars, and aromatic roots. Many a trader is not content with a profit of 30 or 40 on 10.[737] In Kābul can be had the products of Khurāsān, Rūm, 'Irāq and Chīn (China); while it is Hindūstān's own market.

(*c. Products and climate of Kābul.*)

In the country of Kābul, there are hot and cold districts close to one another. In one day, a man may go out of the town of Kābul to where snow never falls, or he may go, in two sidereal Fol. 129b.hours, to where it never thaws, unless when the heats are such that it cannot possibly lie.

Fruits of hot and cold climates are to be had in the districts near the town. Amongst those of the cold climate, there are had in the town the grape, pomegranate, apricot, apple, quince, pear, peach, plum, *sinjid*, almond and walnut.[738] I had cuttings of the *ālū-bālū*[739] brought there and planted; they grew and have done well. Of fruits of the hot climate people bring into the town;—from the Lamghānāt, the orange, citron, *amlūk* (*diospyrus lotus*), and sugar-cane; this last I had had brought and planted there;[740]—from Nijr-au (Nijr-water), they bring the *jīl-ghūza,*[741] *and, from the hill-tracts, much honey. Bee-hives are in use; it* is only from towards Ghaznī, that no honey comes.

The rhubarb[742] of the Kābul district is good, its quinces and plums very good, so too its *badrang*;[743] it grows an excellent grape, known as the water-grape.[744] Kābul wines are heady, those of the Khwāja Khāwand Sa'īd hill-skirt being famous for their strength; at this time however I can only repeat the praise of others about them:—[745]

The flavour of the wine a drinker knows;

What chance have sober men to know it?

Kābul is not fertile in grain, a four or five-fold return is reckoned good there; nor are its melons first-rate, but they are not altogether bad when grown from Khurāsān seed.

It has a very pleasant climate; if the world has another so pleasant, it is not known. Even in the heats, one cannot sleep at night without a fur-coat.[746] Although the snow in most places lies deep in winter, the cold is not excessive; whereas in Fol. 130.Samarkand and Tabrīz, both, like Kābul, noted for their pleasant climate, the cold is extreme.

(*d. Meadows of Kābul.*)

There are good meadows on the four sides of Kābul. An excellent one, Sūng-qūrghān, is some 4 miles (2 *kuroh*) to the north-east; it has grass fit for horses and few mosquitos. To the north-west is the Chālāk meadow, some 2 miles (1 *shar'ī*) away, a large one but in it mosquitos greatly trouble the horses. On the west is the Dūrrīn, in fact there are two, Tīpa and Qūsh-nādir (var. nāwar),—if two are counted here, there would be five in all. Each of these is about 2 miles from the town; both are small, have grass good for horses, and no mosquitos; Kābul has no others so good. On the east is the Siyāh-sang meadow with Qūtlūq-qadam's tomb[747] between it and the Currier's-gate; it is not worth much because, in the heats, it swarms with mosquitos. Kamarī[748] meadow adjoins it; counting this in, the meadows of Kābul would be six, but they are always spoken of as four.

(*e. Mountain-passes into Kābul.*)

The country of Kābul is a fastness hard for a foreign foe to make his way into.

The Hindū-kush mountains, which separate Kābul from Balkh, Qūndūz and Badakhshān, are crossed by seven roads.[749] Three of these lead out of Panjhīr (Panj-sher), *viz.* Khawāk, the uppermost, Ṭ̤ūl, the next lower, and Bāzārak.[750] Of the passes on them, the one on the Ṭ̤ūl road is the best, but the road itself is ratherFol. 130b. the longest whence, seemingly, it is called Ṭ̤ūl. Bāzārak is the most direct; like Ṭ̤ūl, it leads over into Sar-i-āb; as it passes through Pārandī, local people call its main pass, the Pārandī. Another road leads up through Parwān; it has seven minor passes, known as Haft-bacha (Seven-younglings), between Parwān and its main pass (Bāj-gāh). It is joined at its main pass by two roads from Andar-āb, which go on to Parwān by it. This is a road full of difficulties. Out of Ghūr-bund, again, three roads lead over. The one next to Parwān, known as the Yāngī-yūl pass (New-road), goes through Wālīān to Khinjan; next above this is the Qīpchāq road, crossing to where the water of Andar-āb meets the Sūrkh-āb (Qīzīl-sū); this also is an excellent road; and the third leads over the Shibr-tū pass;[751] those crossing by this in the heats take their way by Bāmīān and Saighān, but those crossing by it in winter, go on by Āb-dara (Water-valley).[752] Shibr-tū excepted, all the Hindū-kush roads are closed for three or four months in winter,[753] because no road through a valley-bottom is passable when the waters are high. If any-one thinks to cross the Hindū-kush at that time, over the mountains instead of through a valley-bottom, his journey is hard indeed. The time to cross is during the three or four autumn months when the snow is less and the waters are low.Fol. 131. Whether on the mountains or in the valley-bottoms, Kāfir highwaymen are not few.

The road from Kābul into Khurāsān passes through Qandahār; it is quite level, without a pass.

Four roads lead into Kābul from the Hindūstān side; one by rather a low pass through the Khaibar mountains, another by way of Bangash, another by way of Naghr (var. Naghz),[754] and another through Farmūl;[755] the passes being low also in the three last-named. These roads are all reached from three ferries over the Sind. Those who take the Nīl-āb[756] ferry, come on through the Lamghānāt.[757] In winter, however, people ford the Sind-water (at Hāru) above its junction with the Kābul-water,[758] and ford this also. In most of my expeditions into Hindūstān, I crossed those fords, but this last time (932 AH.-1525 AD.), when I came, defeated Sl. Ibrāhīm and conquered the country, I crossed by boat at Nīl-āb. Except at the one place mentioned above, the Sind-water can be crossed only by boat. Those again, who cross at Dīn-kot[759] go on through Bangash. Those crossing at Chaupāra, if they take the Farmūl road, go on to Ghaznī, or, if they go by the Dasht, go on to Qandahār.[760]

(f. Inhabitants of Kābul.)

There are many differing tribes in the Kābul country; in its dales and plains are Turks and clansmen[761] and 'Arabs; in its town and in many villages, Sārts; out in the districts and alsoFol. 131b. in villages are the Pashāī, Parājī, Tājīk, Bīrkī and Afghān tribes. In the western mountains are the Hazāra and Nikdīrī tribes, some of whom speak the Mughūlī tongue. In the north-eastern mountains are the places of the Kāfirs, such as Kitūr (Gawār?) and Gibrik. To the south are the places of the Afghān tribes.

Eleven or twelve tongues are spoken in Kābul,—'Arabī, Persian, Turkī, Mughūlī, Hindī, Afghānī, Pashāī, Parājī, Gibrī, Bīrkī and Lamghānī. If there be another country with so many differing tribes and such a diversity of tongues, it is not known.

(e. Sub-divisions of the Kābul country.)

The [Kābul] country has fourteen *tūmāns*.[762]

Bajaur, Sawād and Hash-nagar may at one time have been dependencies of Kābul, but they now have no resemblance to cultivated countries (*wilāyāt*), some lying desolate because of the Afghāns, others being now subject to them.

In the east of the country of Kābul is the Lamghānāt, 5 *tūmāns* and 2 *bulūks* of cultivated lands.[763] The largest of these is Nīngnahār, sometimes written Nagarahār in the histories.[764] Its *dārogha's* residence is in Adīnapūr,[765] some 13 *yīghāch* east of Kābul by a very bad and tiresome road, going in three or four places over small hill-passes, and in three or four others, throughFol. 132. narrows.[766] So long as there was no cultivation along it, the Khirilchī and other Afghān thieves used to make it their beat, but it has become safe[767] since I had it peopled at Qarā-tū,[768] below Qūrūq-sāī. The hot and cold climates are separated on this road by the pass of Bādām-chashma (Almond-spring); on its Kābul side snow falls, none at Qūrūq-sāī, towards the Lamghānāt.[769] After descending this pass, another world comes into view, other trees, other plants (or grasses), other animals, and other manners and customs of men. Nīngnahār is nine torrents (*tūqūz-rūd*).[770] It grows good crops of rice and corn, excellent and abundant oranges, citrons and pomegranates. In 914 AH. (1508-9 AD.) I laid out the Four-gardens, known as the Bāgh-i-wafā (Garden-of-fidelity), on a rising-ground, facing south and having the Sūrkh-rūd between it and Fort Adīnapūr.[771] There oranges, citrons and pomegranates grow in abundance. The year I defeated Pahār Khān and took Lāhor and Dipālpūr,[772] I had plantains (bananas) brought and planted there; they did very well. The year before I had had sugar-cane planted there; it also did well; some of it was sent to Bukhārā and Badakhshān.[773] The garden lies high, has running-water close at hand, and a mild winter Fol. 132b.climate. In the middle of it, a one-mill stream flows constantly past the little hill on which are the four garden-plots. In the south-west part of it there is a reservoir, 10 by 10,[774] round which are orange-trees and a few pomegranates, the whole encircled by a trefoil-meadow. This is the best part of the garden, a most beautiful sight when the oranges take colour. Truly that garden is admirably situated!

The Safed-koh runs along the south of Nīngnahār, dividing it from Bangash; no riding-road crosses it; nine torrents (*tūqūz-rūd*) issue from it.[775] It is called Safed-koh[776] because its snow never lessens; none falls in the lower parts of its valleys, a half-day's journey from the snow-line. Many places along it have an excellent climate; its waters are cold and need no ice.

The Sūrkh-rūd flows along the south of Adīnapūr. The fort stands on a height having a straight fall to the river of some 130 ft. (40-50 *qārī*) and isolated from the mountain behind it on the north; it is very strongly placed. That mountain runs between Nīngnahār and Lamghān[777]; on its head snow falls when it snowsFol. 133. in Kābul, so Lamghānīs know when it has snowed in the town.

In going from Kābul into the Lamghānāt,[778]—if people come by Qūrūq-sāī, one road goes on through the Dīrī-pass, crosses the Bārān-water at Būlān, and so on into the Lamghānāt,—another goes through Qarā-tū, below Qūrūq-sāī, crosses the Bārān-water at Aūlūgh-nūr (Great-rock?), and goes into Lamghān by the pass of Bād-i-pīch.[779] If however people come by Nijr-aū, they traverse Badr-aū (Tag-aū), and Qarā-nakariq (?), and go on through the pass of Bād-i-pīch.

Although Nīngnahār is one of the five *tūmāns* of the Lamghān *tūmān* the name Lamghānāt applies strictly only to the three (mentioned below).

One of the three is the 'Alī-shang *tūmān*, to the north of which are fastness-mountains, connecting with Hindū-kush and inhabited by Kāfirs only. What of Kāfiristān lies nearest to 'Alī-shang, is Mīl out of which its torrent issues. The tomb of Lord Lām,[780] father of his Reverence the prophet Nuḥ

(Noah), is in this *tūmān*. In some histories he is called Lamak and Lamakān. Some people are observed often to change *kāf* for *ghain* (*k* for *gh*); it would seem to be on this account that the country is called Lamghān.

The second is Alangār. The part of Kāfiristān nearest to it is Gawār (Kawār), out of which its torrent issues (the Gau or Kau). This torrent joins that of 'Alī-shang and flows with it Fol. 133b.into the Bārān-water, below Mandrāwar, which is the third *tūmān* of the Lamghānāt.

Of the two *bulūks* of Lamghān one is the Nūr-valley.[781] This is a place (*yīr*) without a second[782]; its fort is on a beak (*tūmshūq*) of rock in the mouth of the valley, and has a torrent on each side; its rice is grown on steep terraces, and it can be traversed by one road only.[783] It has the orange, citron and other fruits of hot climates in abundance, a few dates even. Trees cover the banks of both the torrents below the fort; many are *amlūk*, the fruit of which some Turks call *qarā-yīmīsh*;[784] here they are many, but none have been seen elsewhere. The valley grows grapes also, all trained on trees.[785] Its wines are those of Lamghān that have reputation. Two sorts of grapes are grown, the *arah-tāshī* and the *sūhān-tāshī*;[786] the first are yellowish, the second, full-red of fine colour. The first make the more cheering wine, but it must be said that neither wine equals its reputation for cheer. High up in one of its glens, apes (*maimūn*) are found, none below. Those people (*i.e.* Nūrīs) used to keep swine but they have given it up in our time.[787]

Another *tūmān* of Lamghān is Kūnār-with-Nūr-gal. It lies somewhat out-of-the-way, remote from the Lamghānāt, with its borders in amongst the Kāfir lands; on these accounts its people give in tribute rather little of what they have. The Chaghān-sarāīFol. 134. water enters it from the north-east, passes on into the *bulūk* of Kāma, there joins the Bārān-water and with that flows east.

Mīr Sayyid 'Alī *Hamadānī*,[788]—God's mercy on him!—coming here as he journeyed, died 2 miles (1 *shar'ī*) above Kūnār. His disciples carried his body to Khutlān. A shrine was erected at the honoured place of his death, of which I made the circuit when I came and took Chaghān-sarāī in 920 AH.[789]

The orange, citron and coriander[790] abound in this *tūmān*. Strong wines are brought down into it from Kāfiristān.

A strange thing is told there, one seeming impossible, but one told to us again and again. All through the hill-country above Multa-kundī, *viz.* in Kūnār, Nūr-gal, Bajaur, Sawād and thereabouts, it is commonly said that when a woman dies and has been laid on a bier, she, if she has not been an ill-doer, gives the bearers such a shake when they lift the bier by its four sides, that against their will and hindrance, her corpse falls to the ground;

but, if she has done ill, no movement occurs. This was heard not only from Kūnārīs but, again and again, in Bajaur, Fol. 134b.Sawād and the whole hill-tract. Ḥaidar-'alī *Bajaurī*,—a sulṭān who governed Bajaur well,—when his mother died, did not weep, or betake himself to lamentation, or put on black, but said, "Go! lay her on the bier! if she move not, I will have her burned."[792] They laid her on the bier; the desired movement followed; when he heard that this was so, he put on black and betook himself to lamentation.

> (*Authors note to Multa-kundī.*) As Multa-kundī is known the lower part of the *tūmān* of Kūnār-with-Nūr-gal; what is below (*i.e.* on the river) belongs to the valley of Nūr and to Atar.[791]

Another *bulūk* is Chaghān-sarāī,[793] a single village with little land, in the mouth of Kāfiristān; its people, though Muṣalmān, mix with the Kāfirs and, consequently, follow their customs.[794] A great torrent (the Kūnār) comes down to it from the north-east from behind Bajaur, and a smaller one, called Pīch, comes down out of Kāfiristān. Strong yellowish wines are had there, not in any way resembling those of the Nūr-valley, however. The village has no grapes or vineyards of its own; its wines are all brought from up the Kāfiristān-water and from Pīch-i-kāfiristānī.

The Pīch Kāfirs came to help the villagers when I took the place. Wine is so commonly used there that every Kāfir has his leathern wine-bag (*khīg*) at his neck, and drinks wine instead of water.[795]

Kāma, again, though not a separate district but dependent on Nīngnahār, is also called a *bulūk*.[796]Fol. 135.

Nijr-aū[797] is another *tūmān*. It lies north of Kābul, in the Kohistān, with mountains behind it inhabited solely by Kāfirs; it is a quite sequestered place. It grows grapes and fruits in abundance. Its people make much wine but, they boil it. They fatten many fowls in winter, are wine-bibbers, do not pray, have no scruples and are Kāfir-like.[798]

In the Nijr-aū mountains is an abundance of *archa*, *jīlghūza*, *bīlūt* and *khanjak*.[799] The first-named three do not grow above Nigr-aū but they grow lower, and are amongst the trees of Hindūstān. *Jīlghūza*-wood is all the lamp the people have; it burns like a candle and is very remarkable. The flying-squirrel[800] is found in these mountains, an animal larger than a bat and having a curtain (*parda*), like a bat's wing, between its arms and legs. People often brought one in; it is said to fly, downward from one tree to another, as far as a *gīz* flies;[801] I myself have never seen one fly. Once we put one to a tree; it clambered up directly and got away, but, when people went after it, it spread its wings and came down, without hurt, as if it had flown. Another of the curiosities of the Nijr-aū mountains is the *lūkha* (var. *lūja*) bird, called also *bū-qalamūn* (chameleon) because, between head and tail, it has four or five changing colours, resplendent like a pigeon's throat.[802] It is about as large as the

kabg-i-darī and seems to be the *kabg-i-darī* of Hindūstān.[803] People tell this wonderful thing about it:—When the birds, at Fol. 135b.the on-set of winter, descend to the hill-skirts, if they come over a vineyard, they can fly no further and are taken.[804] There is a kind of rat in Nijr-aū, known as the musk-rat, which smells of musk; I however have never seen it.[805]

Panjhīr (Panj-sher) is another *tūmān*; it lies close to Kāfiristān, along the Panjhīr road, and is the thoroughfare of Kāfir highwaymen who also, being so near, take tax of it. They have gone through it, killing a mass of persons, and doing very evil deeds, since I came this last time and conquered Hindūstān (932 AH.-1526 AD.).[806]

Another is the *tūmān* of Ghūr-bund. In those countries they call a *kūtal* (*koh*?) a *bund*;[807] they go towards Ghūr by this pass (*kūtal*); apparently it is for this reason that they have called (the *tūmān*?) Ghūr-bund. The Hazāra hold the heads of its valleys.[808] It has few villages and little revenue can be raised from it. There are said to be mines of silver and lapis lazuli in its mountains.

Again, there are the villages on the skirts of the (Hindū-kush) mountains,[809] with Mīta-kacha and Parwān at their head, and Dūr-nāma[810] at their foot, 12 or 13 in all. They are fruit-bearing villages, and they grow cheering wines, those of Khwāja Khāwand Sa'īd being reputed the strongest roundabouts. The villages all lie on the foot-hills; some pay taxes but not all are taxable because they lie so far back in the mountains.

Between the foot-hills and the Bārān-water are two detached stretches of level land, one known as *Kurrat-tāziyān*,[811] the other as *Dasht-i-shaikh* (Shaikh's-plain). As the green grass of the millet[812] grows well there, they are the resort of Turks andFol. 136. (Mughūl) clans (*aīmāq*).

Tulips of many colours cover these foot-hills; I once counted them up; it came out at 32 or 33 different sorts. We named one the Rose-scented, because its perfume was a little like that of the red rose; it grows by itself on Shaikh's-plain, here and nowhere else. The Hundred-leaved tulip is another; this grows, also by itself, at the outlet of the Ghūr-bund narrows, on the hill-skirt below Parwān. A low hill known as Khwāja Reg-i-rawān (Khwāja-of-the-running-sand), divides the afore-named two pieces of level land; it has, from top to foot, a strip of sand from which people say the sound of nagarets and tambours issues in the heats.[813]

Again, there are the villages depending on Kābul itself. South-west from the town are great snow mountains[814] where snow falls on snow, and where few may be the years when, falling, it does not light on last year's snow. It is fetched, 12 miles may-be, from these mountains, to cool the drinking water when ice-houses in Kābul are empty. Like the Bāmiān mountains, these are fastnesses. Out of them issue the Harmand (Halmand), Sind, Dūghāba of Qūndūz, and Balkh-āb,[815] so that in a single day, a man might drink of the water of each of these four rivers.

It is on the skirt of one of these ranges (Pamghān) that most of the villages dependent on Kābul lie.[816] Masses of grapes ripen in their vineyards and they grow every sort of fruit in abundance. No-one of them equals Istālīf or Astarghach; these must be the Fol. 136b.two which Aūlūgh Beg Mīrzā used to call his Khurāsān and Samarkand. Pamghān is another of the best, not ranking in fruit and grapes with those two others, but beyond comparison with them in climate. The Pamghān mountains are a snowy range. Few villages match Istālīf, with vineyards and fine orchards on both sides of its great torrent, with waters needing no ice, cold and, mostly, pure. Of its Great garden Aūlūgh Beg Mīrzā had taken forcible possession; I took it over, after paying its price to the owners. There is a pleasant halting-place outside it, under great planes, green, shady and beautiful. A one-mill stream, having trees on both banks, flows constantly through the middle of the garden; formerly its course was zig-zag and irregular; I had it made straight and orderly; so the place became very beautiful. Between the village and the valley-bottom, from 4 to 6 miles down the slope, is a spring, known as Khwāja Sih-yārān (Three-friends), round which three sorts of tree grow. A group of planes gives pleasant shade above it; holm-oak Fol. 137.(*quercus bīlūt*) grows in masses on the slope at its sides,—these two oaklands (*bīlūtistān*) excepted, no holm-oak grows in the mountains of western Kābul,—and the Judas-tree (*arghwān*)[817] is much cultivated in front of it, that is towards the level ground,—cultivated there and nowhere else. People say the three different sorts of tree were a gift made by three saints,[818] whence its name. I ordered that the spring should be enclosed in mortared stone-work, 10 by 10, and that a symmetrical, right-angled platform should be built on each of its sides, so as to overlook the whole field of Judas-trees. If, the world over, there is a place to match this when the *arghwāns* are in full bloom, I do not know it. The yellow *arghwān* grows plentifully there also, the red and the yellow flowering at the same time.[819]

In order to bring water to a large round seat which I had built on the hillside and planted round with willows, I had a channel dug across the slope from a half-mill stream, constantly flowing in a valley to the south-west of Sih-yārān. The date of cutting this channel was found in *jūī-khūsh* (kindly channel).[820]

Another of the *tūmāns* of Kābul is Luhūgur (mod. Logar). Its one large village is Chīrkh from which were his Reverence Maulānā Ya'qūb and Mullā-zāda 'Uṣmān.[821] Khwāja AḥmadFol. 137b. and Khwāja Yūnas were from Sajāwand, another of its villages. Chīrkh has many gardens, but there are none in any other village of Luhūgur. Its people are Aūghān-shāl, a term common in Kābul, seeming to be a mispronouncement of Aūghān-sha'ār.[822]

Again, there is the *wilāyat*, or, as some say, *tūmān* of Ghaznī, said to have been[823] the capital of Sabuk-tīgīn, Sl. Maḥmūd and their descendants. Many write it Ghaznīn. It is said also to have been the seat of government of Shihābu'd-dīn *Ghūrī*,[824] styled Mu'izzu'd-dīn in the *Ṭabaqāt-i-nāṣirī* and also some of the histories of Hind.

Ghaznī is known also as *Zābulistān*; it belongs to the Third climate. Some hold that Qandahār is a part of it. It lies 14 *yīghāch* (south-) west of Kābul; those leaving it at dawn, may reach Kābul between the Two Prayers (*i.e.* in the afternoon); whereas the 13 *yīghāch* between Adīnapūr and Kābul can never be done in one day, because of the difficulties of the road.

Ghaznī has little cultivated land. Its torrent, a four-mill or five-mill stream may-be, makes the town habitable and fertilizes four or five villages; three or four others are cultivated from under-ground water-courses (*kārez*). Ghaznī grapes are better than those of Kābul; its melons are more abundant; its apples Fol. 138.are very good, and are carried to Hindūstān. Agriculture is very laborious in Ghaznī because, whatever the quality of the soil, it must be newly top-dressed every year; it gives a better return, however, than Kābul. Ghaznī grows madder; the entire crop goes to Hindūstān and yields excellent profit to the growers. In the open-country of Ghaznī dwell Hazāra and Afghāns. Compared with Kābul, it is always a cheap place. Its people hold to the Ḥanafī faith, are good, orthodox Muṣalmāns, many keep a three months' fast,[825] and their wives and children live modestly secluded.

One of the eminent men of Ghaznī was Mullā 'Abdu'r-raḥmān, a learned man and always a learner (*dars*), a most orthodox, pious and virtuous person; he left this world the same year as Nāṣir Mīrzā (921 AH.-1515 AD.). Sl. Maḥmūd's tomb is in the suburb called Rauẓa,[826] from which the best grapes come; there also are the tombs of his descendants, Sl. Mas'ūd and Sl. Ibrāhīm. Ghaznī has many blessed tombs. The year[827] I took Kābul and Ghaznī, over-ran Kohāt, the plain of Bannū and lands of the Afghāns, and went on to Ghaznī by way of Dūkī (Dūgī) and Āb-istāda, people told me there was a tomb, in a village of Ghaznī, which moved when a benediction on the Prophet was Fol. 138b.pronounced over it. We went to see it. In the end I discovered that the movement was a trick, presumably of the servants at the tomb, who had put a sort of platform above it which moved when pushed, so that, to those on it, the tomb seemed to move, just as the shore does to those passing in a boat. I ordered the scaffold destroyed and a dome built over the tomb; also I forbad the servants, with threats, ever to bring about the movement again.

Ghaznī is a very humble place; strange indeed it is that rulers in whose hands were Hindūstān and Khurāsānāt,[828] should have chosen it for their capital. In the Sulṯān's (Maḥmūd's) time there may have been three or four dams in the country; one he made, some three *yīghāch* (18 m.?) up the Ghaznī-water to the north; it was about 40-50 *qārī* (yards) high and some 300 long; through it the stored waters were let out as required.[829] It was destroyed by 'Alāu'u'd-dīn *Jahān-soz Ghūrī* when he conquered the country (550 AH.-1152 AD.), burned and ruined the tombs of several descendants of Sl. Maḥmūd, sacked and burned the town, in short, left undone no tittle of murder and rapine. SinceFol. 139. that time, the Sulṯān's dam has lain in ruins, but, through God's favour, there is hope that it may become of use again, by means of the money which was sent, in Khwāja Kalān's hand, in the year Hindūstān was conquered (932 AH.-1526 AD.).[830] The Sakhandam is another, 2 or 3 *yīghāch* (12-18 m.), may-be, on the east of the town; it has long been in ruins, indeed is past repair. There is a dam in working order at Sar-i-dih (Village-head).

In books it is written that there is in Ghaznī a spring such that, if dirt and foul matter be thrown into it, a tempest gets up instantly, with a blizzard of rain and wind. It has been seen said also in one of the histories that Sabuk-tīgīn, when besieged by the Rāī (Jāī-pāl) of Hind, ordered dirt and foulness to be thrown into the spring, by this aroused, in an instant, a tempest with blizzard of rain and snow, and, by this device, drove off his foe.[831] Though we made many enquiries, no intimation of the spring's existence was given us.

In these countries Ghaznī and Khwārizm are noted for cold, in the same way that Sulṯānīā and Tabrīz are in the two 'Irāqs and Azarbāījān.

Zurmut is another *tūmān*, some 12-13 *yīghāch* south of Kābul and 7-8 south-east of Ghaznī.[832] Its *dārogha's* head-quarters are Fol. 139b.in Gīrdīz; there most houses are three or four storeys high. It does not want for strength, and gave Nāṣir Mīrzā trouble when it went into hostility to him. Its people are Aūghān-shāl; they grow corn but have neither vineyards nor orchards. The tomb of Shaikh Muḥammad *Muṣalmān* is at a spring, high on the skirt of a mountain, known as Barakistān, in the south of the *tūmān*.

Farmūl is another *tūmān*,[833] a humble place, growing not bad apples which are carried into Hindūstān. Of Farmūl were the Shaikh-zādas, descendants of Shaikh Muḥammad *Muṣalmān*, who were so much in favour during the Afghān period in Hindūstān.

Bangash is another *tūmān*.[834] All round about it are Afghān highwaymen, such as the Khūgīānī, Khirilchī, Tūrī and Landar. Lying out-of-the-way, as it does, its people do not pay taxes willingly. There has been no time to bring it to obedience; greater tasks have fallen to me,—the conquests of Qandahār, Balkh, Badakhshān and Hindūstān! But, God willing! when I get the chance, I most assuredly will take order with those Bangash thieves.

One of the *bulūks* of Kābul is Ālā-sāī,[835] 4 to 6 miles (2-3 *shar'ī*) east of Nijr-aū. The direct road into it from Nijr-aū leads, at a place called Kūra, through the quite small pass which in that locality separates the hot and cold climates. Through this pass the birds migrate at the change of the seasons, and at those times many are taken by the people of Pīchghān, one of the dependencies of Nijr-aū, in the following manner:—From Fol. 140.distance to distance near the mouth of the pass, they make hiding-places for the bird-catchers. They fasten one corner of a net five or six yards away, and weight the lower side to the ground with stones. Along the other side of the net, for half its width, they fasten a stick some 3 to 4 yards long. The hidden bird-catcher holds this stick and by it, when the birds approach, lifts up the net to its full height. The birds then go into the net of themselves. Sometimes so many are taken by this contrivance that there is not time to cut their throats.[836]

Though the Ālā-sāī pomegranates are not first-rate, they have local reputation because none are better there-abouts; they are carried into Hindūstān. Grapes also do not grow badly, and the wines of Ālā-sāī are better and stronger than those of Nijr-aū.

Badr-aū (Tag-aū) is another *bulūk*; it runs with Ālā-sāī, grows no fruit, and for cultivators has corn-growing Kāfirs.[837]

(f. Tribesmen of Kābul.)

Just as Turks and (Mughūl) clans (*aīmāq*) dwell in the open country of Khurāsān and Samarkand, so in Kābul do the Hazāra and Afghāns. Of the Hazāra, the most widely-scattered are the Sulṭān-mas'ūdi Hazāra, of Afghāns, the Mahmand.

(g. Revenue of Kābul.)

The revenues of Kābul, whether from the cultivated lands or from tolls (*tamghā*) or from dwellers in the open country, amount to 8 *laks* of *shāhrukhīs*.[838]Fol. 140b.

(h. The mountain-tracts of Kābul.)

Where the mountains of Andar-āb, Khwāst,[839] and the Badakh-shānāt have conifers (*archa*), many springs and gentle slopes, those of eastern Kābul have grass (*aūt*), grass like a beautiful floor, on hill, slope and dale. For the most part it is *būta-kāh* grass (*aūt*), very suitable for horses. In the Andijān country they talk of *būta-kāh*, but why they do so was not known (to me?); in Kābul it was heard-say to be because the grass comes up in tufts (*būta, būta*).[840] The alps of these mountains are like those of Ḥiṣār, Khutlān, Farghāna, Samarkand and Mughūlistān,—all these being alike in mountain and alp, though the alps of Farghāna and Mughūlistān are beyond comparison with the rest.

From all these the mountains of Nijr-aū, the Lamghānāt and Sawād differ in having masses of cypresses,[841] holm-oak, olive and mastic (*khanjak*); their grass also is different,—it is dense, it is tall, it is good neither for horse nor sheep. Although these mountains are not so high as those already described, indeed they look to be low, none-the-less, they are strongholds; what to the eye is even slope, really is hard rock on which it is impossible to ride. Many of the beasts and birds of Hindūstān Fol. 141.are found amongst them, such as the parrot, *mīna*, peacock and *lūja* (*lūkha*), the ape, *nīl-gāu* and hog-deer (*kūta-pāī*);[842] some found there are not found even in Hindūstān.

The mountains to the west of Kābul are also all of one sort, those of the Zindān-valley, the Ṣūf-valley, Garzawān and Gharjistān (Gharchastān).[843] Their meadows are mostly in the dales; they have not the same sweep of grass on slope and top as some of those described have; nor have they masses of trees; they have, however, grass suiting horses. On their flat tops, where all the crops are grown, there is ground where a horse can gallop. They have masses of *kīyik*.[844] Their valley-bottoms are strongholds, mostly precipitous and inaccessible from above. It is remarkable that, whereas other mountains have their fastnesses in their high places, these have theirs below.

Of one sort again are the mountains of Ghūr, Karnūd (var. Kuzūd) and Hazāra; their meadows are in their dales; their trees are few, not even the *archa* being there;[845] their grass is fit for horses and for the masses of sheep they keep. They differ from those last described in this, their strong places are not below.

The mountains (south-east of Kābul) of Khwāja Ismā'īl, Dasht, Dūgī (Dūkī)[846] and Afghānistān are all alike; all low, scant of vegetation, short of water, treeless, ugly and good-for-nothing. Their people take after them, just as has been said, *Tīng būlmā-ghūncha*Fol 141b. *tūsh būlmās.*[847] Likely enough the world has few mountains so useless and disgusting.

(*h. Fire-wood of Kabul.*)

The snow-fall being so heavy in Kābul, it is fortunate that excellent fire-wood is had near by. Given one day to fetch it, wood can be had of the *khanjak* (mastic), *bīlūt* (holm-oak), *bādāmcha* (small-almond) and *qarqand.*[848] Of these *khanjak* wood is the best; it burns with flame and nice smell, makes plenty of hot ashes and does well even if sappy. Holm-oak is also first-rate fire-wood, blazing less than mastic but, like it, making a hot fire with plenty of hot ashes, and nice smell. It has the peculiarity in burning that when its leafy branches are set alight, they fire up with amazing sound, blazing and crackling from bottom to top. It is good fun to burn it. The wood of the small-almond is the most plentiful and commonly-used, but it does not make a lasting fire. The *qarqand* is quite a low shrub, thorny, and burning sappy or dry; it is the fuel of the Ghaznī people.

(*i. Fauna of Kābul.*)

The cultivated lands of Kābul lie between mountains which are like great dams[849] to the flat valley-bottoms in which most villages and peopled places are. On these mountains *kīyik* and *āhū*[850] are scarce. Across them, between its summer and winter quarters, the dun sheep,[851] the *arqārghalcha*, have their regular track,[852] to which braves go out with dogs and birds[853] to take them. Fol. 142.Towards Khūrd-kābul and the Sūrkh-rūd there is wild-ass, but there are no white *kīyik* at all; Ghaznī has both and in few other places are white *kīyik* found in such good condition.[854]

In the heats the fowling-grounds of Kābul are crowded. The birds take their way along the Bārān-water. For why? It is because the river has mountains along it, east and west, and a great Hindū-kush pass in a line with it, by which the birds must cross since there is no other near.[855] They cannot cross when the north wind blows, or if there is even a little cloud on Hindū-kush; at such times they alight on the level lands of the Bārān-water and are taken in great numbers by the local people. Towards the end of winter, dense flocks of mallards (*aūrdūq*) reach the banks of the Bārān in very good condition. Follow these the cranes and herons,[856] great birds, in large flocks and countless numbers.

(*j. Bird-catching.*)

Along the Bārān people take masses of cranes (*tūrna*) with the cord; masses of *aūqār*, *qarqara* and *qūṭān* also.[857] This method of bird-catching is unique. They twist a cord as long as the arrow's[858] flight, tie the arrow at one end and a *bīldūrga*[859] at the other, and wind it up, from the arrow-end, on a piece of wood, span-long and wrist-thick, right up to the *bīldūrga*. TheyFol. 142b. then pull out the piece of wood, leaving just the hole it was in. The *bīldūrga* being held fast in the hand, the arrow is shot off[860] towards the coming flock. If the cord twists round a neck or wing, it brings the bird down. On the Bārān everyone takes birds in this way; it is difficult; it must be done on rainy nights, because on such nights the birds do not alight, but fly continually and fly low till dawn, in fear of ravening beasts of prey. Through the night the flowing river is their road, its moving water showing through the dark; then it is, while they come and go, up and down the river, that the cord is shot. One night I shot it; it broke in drawing in; both bird and cord were brought in to me next day. By this device Bārān people catch the many herons from which they take the turban-aigrettes sent from Kābul for sale in Khurāsān.

Of bird-catchers there is also the band of slave-fowlers, two or three hundred households, whom some descendant of Tīmūr Beg made migrate from near Multān to the Bārān.[861] Bird-catchingFol. 143. is their trade; they dig tanks, set decoy-birds[862] on them, put a net over the middle, and in this way take all sorts of birds. Not fowlers only catch birds, but every dweller on the Bārān does it, whether by shooting the cord, setting the springe, or in various other ways.

(*k. Fishing.*)

The fish of the Bārān migrate at the same seasons as birds. At those times many are netted, and many are taken on wattles (*chīgh*) fixed in the water. In autumn when the plant known as *wild-ass-tail*[863] has come to maturity, flowered and seeded, people take 10-20 loads (of seed?) and 20-30 of green branches (*gūk-shībāk*) to some head of water, break it up small and cast it in. Then going into the water, they can at once pick up drugged fish. At some convenient place lower down, in a hole below a fall, they will have fixed before-hand a wattle of finger-thick willow-withes, making it firm by piling stones on its sides. The water goes rushing and dashing through the wattle, but leaves on it any fish that may have come floating down. This way of catching fish is practised in Gul-bahār, Parwān and Istālīf.

Fol. 143b.Fish are had in winter in the Lamghānāt by this curious device:—People dig a pit to the depth of a house, in the bed of a stream, below a fall, line it with stones like a cooking-place, and build up stones round it above, leaving one opening only, under water. Except by this one opening, the fish have no inlet or outlet, but the water finds its way through the stones. This makes a sort of fish-pond from which, when wanted in winter, fish can be taken, 30-40 together. Except at the opening, left where convenient, the sides of the fish-pond are made fast with rice-straw, kept in place by stones. A piece of wicker-work is pulled into the said opening by its edges, gathered together, and into this a second piece, (a tube,) is inserted, fitting it at the mouth but reaching half-way into it only.[864] The fish go through the smaller piece into the larger one, out from which they cannot get. The second narrows towards its inner mouth, its pointed ends being drawn so close that the fish, once entered, cannot Fol. 144.turn, but must go on, one by one, into the larger piece. Out of that they cannot return because of the pointed ends of the inner, narrow mouth. The wicker-work fixed and the rice-straw making the pond fast, whatever fish are inside can be taken out;[865] any also which, trying to escape may have gone into the wicker-work, are taken in it, because they have no way out. This method of catching fish we have seen nowhere else.[866]

HISTORICAL NARRATIVE RESUMED.[867]

(a. Departure of Muqīm and allotment of lands.)

A few days after the taking of Kābul, Muqīm asked leave to set off for Qandahār. As he had come out of the town on terms and conditions, he was allowed to go to his father (Ẕu'n-nūn) and his elder brother (Shāh Beg), with all his various people, his goods and his valuables, safe and sound.

Directly he had gone, the Kābul-country was shared out to the Mīrzās and the guest-begs.[868] To Jahāngīr Mīrzā was given Ghaznī with its dependencies and appurtenancies; to Nāṣir Mīrzā, the Nīngnahār *tūmān*, Mandrāwar, Nūr-valley, Kūnār, Nūr-gal (Rock-village?) and Chīghān-sarāī. To some of the begs who had been with us in the guerilla-times and had come to Kābul with us, were given villages, fief-fashion.[869] *Wilāyat*Fol. 144b. itself was not given at all.[870] It was not only then that I looked with more favour on guest-begs and stranger-begs than I did on old servants and Andijānīs; this I have always done whenever the Most High God has shown me His favour; yet it is remarkable that, spite of this, people have blamed me constantly as though I had favoured none but old servants and Andijānīs. There is a proverb, (Turkī) "What will a foe not say? what enters not into dream?" and (Persian) "A town-gate can be shut, a foe's mouth never."

(b. A levy in grain.)

Many clans and hordes had come from Samarkand, Ḥiṣār and Qūndūz into the Kābul-country. Kābul is a small country; it is also of the sword, not of the pen;[871] to take in money from it for all these tribesmen was impossible. It therefore seemed advisable to take in grain, provision for the families of these clans so that their men could ride on forays with the army. Accordingly it was decided to levy 30,000 ass-loads[872] of grain on Kābul, Ghaznī and their dependencies; we knew nothing at that time about the harvests and incomings; the impost was excessive, and under it the country suffered very grievously.

In those days I devised the Bāburī script.[873]

(*c. Foray on the Hazāra.*)

A large tribute in horses and sheep had been laid on the Sulṭān Mas'ūdī Hazāras;[874] word came a few days after collectors Fol. 145.had gone to receive it, that the Hazāras were refractory and would not give their goods. As these same tribesmen had before that come down on the Ghaznī and Gīrdīz roads, we got to horse, meaning to take them by surprise. Riding by the Maidān-road, we crossed the Nirkh-pass[875] by night and at the Morning-prayer fell upon them near Jāl-tū (var. Chā-tū). The incursion was not what was wished.[876] We came back by the Tunnel-rock (Sang-i-sūrākh); Jahāngīr Mīrzā (there?) took leave for Ghaznī. On our reaching Kābul, Yār-i-ḥusain, son of Daryā Khān, coming in from Bhīra, waited on me.[877]

(*d. Bābur's first start for Hindūstān.*)

When, a few days later, the army had been mustered, persons acquainted with the country were summoned and questioned about its every side and quarter. Some advised a march to the Plain (Dasht);[878] some approved of Bangash; some wished to go into Hindūstān. The discussion found settlement in a move on Hindūstān.

It was in the month of Sha'bān (910 AH.-Jan. 1505 AD.), the Sun being in Aquarius, that we rode out of Kābul for Hindūstān. We took the road by Bādām-chashma and Jagdālīk and reached Adīnapūr in six marches. Till that time I had never seen a hot country or the Hindūstān border-land. In Nīngnahār[879] another world came to view,—other grasses, other trees, other animals, other birds, and other manners and customs of clan and horde. We were amazed, and truly there was ground for amaze.Fol. 145b.

Nāṣir Mīrzā, who had gone earlier to his district, waited on me in Adīnapūr. We made some delay in Adīnapūr in order to let the men from behind join us, also a contingent from the clans which had come with us into Kābul and were wintering in the Lamghānāt.[880] All having joined us, we marched to below Jūī-shāhī and dismounted at Qūsh-guṃbaz.[881] There Nāṣir Mīrzā asked for leave to stay behind, saying he would follow in a few days after making some sort of provision for his dependants and followers. Marching on from Qūsh-guṃbaz, when we dismounted at Hot-spring (Garm-chashma), a head-man of the Gāgīānī was brought in, a *Fajjī*[882] presumably with his caravan. We took him with us to point out the roads. Crossing Khaibar in a march or two, we dismounted at Jām.[883]

Tales had been told us about Gūr-khattrī;[884] it was said to be a holy place of the Jogīs and Hindūs who come from long distances to shave their heads and beards there. I rode out at once from Jām to visit Bīgrām,[885] saw its great tree,[886] and all the country round, but, much as we enquired about Gūr-khattrī, our guide, one Malik Bū-sa'īd *Kamarī*,[887] would say nothing Fol. 146.about it. When we were almost back in camp, however, he told Khwāja Muḥammad-amīn that it was in Bīgrām and that he had said nothing about it because of its confined cells and narrow passages. The Khwāja, having there and then abused him, repeated to us what he had said, but we could not go back because the road was long and the day far spent.

(*e. Move against Kohāt.*)

Whether to cross the water of Sind, or where else to go, was discussed in that camp.[888] Bāqī *Chaghānīānī* represented that it seemed we might go, without crossing the river and with one night's halt, to a place called Kohāt where were many rich tribesmen; moreover he brought Kābulīs forward who represented the matter just as he had done. We had never heard of the place, but, as he, my man in great authority, saw it good to go to Kohāt and had brought forward support of his recommendation,—this being so! we broke up our plan of crossing the Sind-water into Hindūstān, marched from Jām, forded the Bāra-water, and dismounted not far from the pass (*dābān*) through the Muḥammad-mountain (*fajj*). At the time the Gāgīānī Afghāns were located in Parashawār but, in dread of our army, had drawn off to the skirt-hills. One of their headmen, coming into this camp, did me obeisance; we took him, as well as the Fajjī, with us, so that, between them, they mightFol. 146b. point out the roads. We left that camp at midnight, crossed Muḥammad-fajj at day-rise[889] and by breakfast-time descended on Kohāt. Much cattle and buffalo fell to our men; many Afghāns were taken but I had them all collected and set them free. In the Kohāt houses corn was found without limit. Our foragers raided as far as the Sind-river (*daryā*), rejoining us after one night's halt. As what Bāqī *Chaghānīānī* had led us to expect did not come to hand, he grew rather ashamed of his scheme.

When our foragers were back and after two nights in Kohāt, we took counsel together as to what would be our next good move, and we decided to over-run the Afghāns of Bangash and the Bannū neighbourhood, then to go back to Kābul, either through Naghr (Bāghzān?), or by the Farmūl-road (Tochī-valley?).

In Kohāt, Daryā Khān's son, Yār-i-ḥusain, who had waited on me in Kābul made petition, saying, "If royal orders were given me for the Dilazāk,[890] the

Yūsuf-zāī, and the Gāgīānī, these would not go far from my orders if I called up the Pādshāh's swords on the other side of the water of Sind."[891] The farmān he petitioned for being given, he was allowed to go from Kohāt.

(f. March to Thāl.)

Marching out of Kohāt, we took the Hangū-road for Bangash.Fol. 147. Between Kohāt and Hangū that road runs through a valley shut in on either hand by the mountains. When we entered this valley, the Afghāns of Kohāt and thereabouts who were gathered on both hill-skirts, raised their war-cry with great clamour. Our then guide, Malik Bū-saʿīd *Kamarī* was well-acquainted with the Afghān locations; he represented that further on there was a detached hill on our right, where, if the Afghāns came down to it from the hill-skirt, we might surround and take them. God brought it right! The Afghāns, on reaching the place, did come down. We ordered one party of braves to seize the neck of land between that hill and the mountains, others to move along its sides, so that under attack made from all sides at once, the Afghāns might be made to reach their doom. Against the allround assault, they could not even fight; a hundred or two were taken, some were brought in alive but of most, the heads only were brought. We had been told that when Afghāns are powerless to resist, they go before their foe with grass between their teeth, this being as much as to say, "I am your cow."[892] Here Fol. 147b.we saw this custom; Afghāns unable to make resistance, came before us with grass between their teeth. Those our men had brought in as prisoners were ordered to be beheaded and a pillar of their heads was set up in our camp.[893]

Next day we marched forward and dismounted at Hangū, where local Afghāns had made a *sangur* on a hill. I first heard the word *sangur* after coming to Kābul where people describe fortifying themselves on a hill as making a *sangur.* Our men went straight up, broke into it and cut off a hundred or two of insolent Afghān heads. There also a pillar of heads was set up.

From Hangū we marched, with one night's halt, to Tīl (Thāl),[894] below Bangash; there also our men went out and raided the Afghāns near-by; some of them however turned back rather lightly from a *sangur.*[895]

(g. Across country into Bannū.)

On leaving Tīl (Thāl) we went, without a road, right down a steep descent, on through out-of-the-way narrows, halted one night, and next day came down into Bannū,[896] man, horse and camel all worn out with fatigue and with most of the booty in cattle left on the way. The frequented road must have been a few miles to our right; the one we came by did not seem a riding-road at all; it was understood to be called the GosfandliyārFol. 148. (Sheep-road),—*liyār* being Afghānī for a road,—because sometimes shepherds and herdsmen take their flocks and herds by it through those narrows. Most of our men regarded our being brought down by that left-hand road as an ill-design of Malik Bū-sa'īd *Kamarī*.[897]

(*h. Bannū and the 'Īsa-khail country.*)

The Bannū lands lie, a dead level, immediately outside the Bangash and Naghr hills, these being to their north. The Bangash torrent (the Kūrām) comes down into Bannū and fertilizes its lands. South(-east) of them are Chaupāra and the water of Sind; to their east is Dīn-kot; (south-)west is the Plain (Dasht), known also as Bāzār and Tāq.[898] The Bannū lands are cultivated by the Kurānī, Kīwī, Sūr, 'Īsa-khail and Nīā-zāī of the Afghān tribesmen.

After dismounting in Bannū, we heard that the tribesmen in the Plain (Dasht) were for resisting and were entrenching themselves on a hill to the north. A force headed by Jahāngīr Mīrzā, went against what seemed to be the Kīwī *sangur*, took it at once, made general slaughter, cut off and brought in many heads. Much white cloth fell into (their) hands. In Bannū also a pillar of heads was set up. After the *sangur* had been taken, the Kīwī head-man, Shādī Khān, came to my presence, with grass between his teeth, and did me obeisance. I pardoned all the prisoners.

After we had over-run Kohāt, it had been decided that Bangash and Bannū should be over-run, and return to KābulFol. 148b. made through Naghr or through Farmūl. But when Bannū had been over-run, persons knowing the country represented that the Plain was close by, with its good roads and many people; so it was settled to over-run the Plain and to return to Kābul afterwards by way of Farmūl.[899]

Marching next day, we dismounted at an 'Īsa-khail village on that same water (the Kūrām) but, as the villagers had gone into the Chaupāra hills on hearing of us, we left it and dismounted on the skirt of Chaupāra. Our foragers went from there into the hills, destroyed the 'Īsa-khail *sangur* and came back with sheep, herds and cloth. That night the 'Īsa-khail made an attack on us but, as good watch was kept all through these operations, they could do nothing. So cautious were we that at night our right and left, centre and van were just in the way they had dismounted, each according to its place in battle, each prepared for its own post, with men on foot all round the camp, at an arrow's distance from the tents. Every night the army was posted in this way and every night three or four of my household Fol. 149.made the rounds with torches, each in his turn. I for my part made the round once each night. Those not at their posts had their noses slit and were led round through the army. Jahāngīr Mīrzā was the right wing, with Bāqī *Chaghānīānī*, Sherīm Ṭaghāī, Sayyid Ḥusain Akbar, and other begs. Mīrzā Khān was the left wing, with 'Abdu'r-razzāq Mīrzā, Qāsīm Beg and other begs. In the centre there were no great begs, all were household-begs. Sayyid Qāsim Lord-of-the-gate, was the van, with Bābā Aūghūlī, Allāh-bīrdī (var. Allāh-qulī Purān), and some other begs. The army was in six divisions, each of which had its day and night on guard.

Marching from that hill-skirt, our faces set west, we dismounted on a waterless plain (*qūl*) between Bannū and the Plain. The soldiers got water here for themselves, their herds and so on, by digging down, from one to one-and-a-half yards, into the dry water-course, when water came. Not here only did this happen for all the rivers of Hindūstān have the peculiarity that water is safe to be found by digging down from one to one-and-a-half yards in their beds. It is a wonderful provision of God that where, except for the great rivers, there are no running-waters,[900] water should be so placed within reach in dry water-courses.

We left that dry channel next morning. Some of our men, riding light, reached villages of the Plain in the afternoon, raided a few, and brought back flocks, cloth and horses bred for trade.[901] Pack-animals and camels and also the braves we had outdistanced, kept coming into camp all through that night till dawn and on till that morrow's noon. During our stay there, the foragersFol. 149b. brought in from villages in the Plain, masses of sheep and cattle, and, from Afghān traders met on the roads, white cloths, aromatic roots, sugars, *tīpūchāqs*, and horses bred for trade. Hindī (var. Mindī) *Mughūl* unhorsed Khwāja Khiẓr *Lūhānī*, a well-known and respected Afghān merchant, cutting off and bringing in his head. Once when Sherīm Ṭaghāī went in the rear of the foragers, an Afghān faced him on the road and struck off his index-finger.

(*i. Return made for Kābul.*)

Two roads were heard of as leading from where we were to Ghaznī; one was the Tunnel-rock (Sang-i-sūrākh) road, passing Birk (Barak) and going on to Farmūl; the other was one along the Gūmāl, which also comes out at Farmūl but without touching Birk (Barak).[902] As during our stay in the Plain rain had fallen incessantly, the Gūmāl was so swollen that it would have been difficult to cross at the ford we came to; moreover persons well-acquainted with the roads, represented that going by the Gūmāl road, this torrent must be crossed several times, that this was always difficult when the waters were so high and that there was always uncertainty on the Gūmāl road. Nothing was settled then as to which of these two roads to take; I expected it to be settled next day when, after the drum of departure had sounded,Fol. 150. we talked it over as we went.[903] It was the 'Īd-i-fitr (March 7th 1505 AD.); while I was engaged in the ablutions due for the breaking of the fast, Jahāngīr Mīrzā and the begs discussed the question of the roads. Some-one said that if we were to turn the bill[904] of the Mehtar Sulaimān range, this lying between the Plain and the Hill-country (*desht u dūki*),[905] we should get a level road though it might make the difference of a few marches. For this they decided and moved off; before my ablutions were finished the whole army had taken the road and most of it was across the Gūmāl. Not a man of us had ever seen the road; no-one knew whether it was long or short; we started off just on a rumoured word!

The Prayer of the 'Id was made on the bank of the Gūmāl. That year New-year's Day[906] fell close to the 'Id-i-fitr, there being only a few days between; on their approximation I composed the following (Turkī) ode:—

Glad is the Bairām-moon for him who sees both the face of the Moon and the Moon-face of his friend;

Sad is the Bairām-moon for me, far away from thy face and from thee.[907]

O Bābur! dream of your luck when your Feast is the meeting, your New-year the face;

For better than that could not be with a hundred New-years and Bairāms.

After crossing the Gūmāl torrent, we took our way along the skirt of the hills, our faces set south. A mile or two further on, Fol. 150b.some death-devoted Afghāns shewed themselves on the lower edge of the hill-slope. Loose rein, off we went for them; most of them fled but some made foolish stand on rocky-piles[908] of the foot-hills. One took post on a single rock seeming to have a precipice on the further side of it, so that he had not even a way of escape. Sl. Qulī *Chūnāq* (One-eared), all in his mail as he was, got up, slashed at, and took him. This was one of Sl. Qulī's deeds done under my own eyes, which led to his favour and promotion.[909] At another pile of rock, when Qūtlūq-qadam exchanged blows with an Afghān, they grappled and came down together, a straight fall of 10 to 12 yards; in the end Qūtlūq-qadam cut off and brought in his man's head. Kūpūk Beg got hand-on-collar with an Afghān at another hill; both rolled down to the bottom; that head also was brought in. All Afghāns taken prisoner were set free.

Marching south through the Plain, and closely skirting Mehtar Sulaimān, we came, with three nights' halt, to a small township, called Bīlah, on the Sind-water and dependent on Multān.[910] The villagers crossed the water, mostly taking to their boats, but some flung themselves in to cross. Some were seen standing on an island in front of Bīlah. Most of our men, man and horse inFol. 151. mail, plunged in and crossed to the island; some were carried down, one being Qul-i-arūk (thin slave), one of my servants, another the head tent-pitcher, another Jahāngīr Mīrzā's servant, Qāītmās *Turkmān*.[911] Cloth and things of the baggage (*partaldīk nīma*) fell to our men. The villagers all crossed by boat to the further side of the river; once there, some of them, trusting to the broad water, began to make play with their swords. Qul-i-bāyazīd, the taster, one of our men who had crossed to the island, stripped himself and his horse and, right in front of them, plunged by himself into the river. The water on that side of the island may have been twice or thrice as wide as on ours. He swum his horse straight for them till, an arrow's-flight away, he came to a shallow where his weight must have been up-borne, the water being as high as the saddle-flap. There he stayed for as long as milk takes to boil; no-one supported him from behind; he had not a chance of support. He made a dash at them; they shot a few arrows at him but, this not checking him, they took to flight. To swim such a river as the Sind, alone, bare on a bare-backed horse, no-one behind him, and to chase off a foe and occupy his ground, was a mightily bold deed! He having driven the enemy off, other soldiers went over whoFol. 151b. returned with cloth and droves of various sorts. Qul-i-bāyazīd had already his place in my favour and kindness on account of his good service, and of courage several times shewn; from the cook's office I had raised him to the royal taster's; this time, as will be told, I took up a position full of bounty, favour and promotion,—in truth he was worthy of honour and advancement.

Two other marches were made down the Sind-water. Our men, by perpetually gallopping off on raids, had knocked up their horses; usually what they took, cattle mostly, was not worth the gallop; sometimes indeed in the Plain there had been sheep, sometimes one sort of cloth or other, but, the Plain left behind, nothing was had but cattle. A mere servant would bring in 3 or 400 head during our marches along the Sind-water, but every march many more would be left on the road than they brought in.

(*j. The westward march.*)

Having made three more marches[912] close along the Sind, we left it when we came opposite Pīr Kānū's tomb.[913] Going to the tomb, we there dismounted. Some of our soldiers having injured Fol. 152.several of those in attendance on it, I had them cut to pieces. It is a tomb on the skirt of one of the Mehtar Sulaimān mountains and held in much honour in Hindūstān.

Marching on from Pīr Kānū, we dismounted in the (Pawat) pass; next again in the bed of a torrent in Dūkī.[914] After we left this camp there were brought in as many as 20 to 30 followers of a retainer of Shāh Beg, Fāẓil *Kūkūldāsh*, the dārogha of Sīwī. They had been sent to reconnoitre us but, as at that time, we were not on bad terms with Shāh Beg, we let them go, with horse and arms. After one night's halt, we reached Chūtīālī, a village of Dūkī.

Although our men had constantly gallopped off to raid, both before we reached the Sind-water and all along its bank, they had not left horses behind, because there had been plenty of green food and corn. When, however, we left the river and set our faces for Pīr Kānū, not even green food was to be had; a little land under green crop might be found every two or three marches, but of horse-corn, none. So, beyond the camps mentioned, there began the leaving of horses behind. After passing Chūtīālī, my own felt-tent[915] had to be left from want of baggage-beasts. One night at that time, it rained so much, that water stood knee-deep in my tent (*chādār*); I watched the night out till dawn, uncomfortably sitting on a pile of blankets.

(*k. Bāqī Chaghānīānī's treachery.*)

A few marches further on came Jahāngīr Mīrzā, saying, "IFol. 152b. have a private word for you." When we were in private, he said, "Bāqī *Chaghānīānī* came and said to me, 'You make the Pādshāh cross the water of Sind with 7, 8, 10 persons, then make yourself Pādshāh.'" Said I, "What others are heard of as consulting with him?" Said he, "It was but a moment ago Bāqī Beg spoke to me; I know no more." Said I, "Find out who the others are; likely enough Sayyid Ḥusain Akbar and Sl. 'Alī the page are in it, as well as Khusrau Shāh's begs and braves." Here the Mīrzā really behaved very well and like a blood-relation; what he now did was the counterpart of what I had done in Kāhmard,[916] in this same ill-fated mannikin's other scheme of treachery.[917]

On dismounting after the next march, I made Jahāngīr Mīrzā lead a body of well-mounted men to raid the Aūghāns (Afghāns) of that neighbourhood.

Many men's horses were now left behind in each camping-ground, the day coming when as many as 2 or 300 were left. Braves of the first rank went on foot; Sayyid Maḥmūd *Aūghlāqchī*, one of the best of the household-braves, left his horses behind and walked. In this state as to horses we went all the rest of the way to Ghaznī.

Three or four marches further on, Jahāngīr Mīrzā plunderedFol. 153. some Afghāns and brought in a few sheep.

(*l. The Āb-i-istāda.*)

When, with a few more marches, we reached the Standing-water (*Āb-i-istāda*) a wonderfully large sheet of water presented itself to view; the level lands on its further side could not be seen at all; its water seemed to join the sky; the higher land and the mountains of that further side looked to hang between Heaven and Earth, as in a mirage. The waters there gathered are said to be those of the spring-rain floods of the Kattawāz-plain, the Zurmut-valley, and the Qarā-bāgh meadow of the Ghaznī-torrent,—floods of the spring-rains, and the over-plus[918] of the summer-rise of streams.

When within two miles of the Āb-i-istāda, we saw a wonderful thing,—something as red as the rose of the dawn kept shewing and vanishing between the sky and the water. It kept coming and going. When we got quite close we learned that what seemed the cause were flocks of geese,[919] not 10,000, not 20,000 in a flock, but geese innumerable which, when the mass of birds flapped their wings in flight, sometimes shewed red feathers, sometimes not. Not only was this bird there in countless numbers, but birds of every sort. Eggs lay in masses on the shore. When two Afghāns, come there to collect eggs, saw us, Fol. 153b.they went into the water half a *kuroh* (a mile). Some of our men following, brought them back. As far as they went the water was of one depth, up to a horse's belly; it seemed not to lie in a hollow, the country being flat.

We dismounted at the torrent coming down to the Āb-i-istāda from the plain of Kattawāz. The several other times we have passed it, we have found a dry channel with no water whatever,[920] but this time, there was so much water, from the spring-rains, that no ford could be found. The water was not very broad but very deep. Horses and camels were made to swim it; some of the baggage was hauled over with ropes. Having got across, we went on through Old Nānī and Sar-i-dih to Ghaznī where for a few days Jahāngīr Mīrzā was our host, setting food before us and offering his tribute.

(*m. Return to Kābul.*)

That year most waters came down in flood. No ford was found through the water of Dih-i-yaq'ūb.[921] For this reason we went straight on to Kamarī, through the Sajāwand-pass. At Kamarī I had a boat fashioned in a pool, brought and set on the Dih-i-yaq'ūb-water in front of Kamarī. In this all our people were put over.

We reached Kābul in the month of Ẕū'l-ḥijja (May 1505 AD.).[922] A few days earlier Sayyid Yūsuf *Aūghlāqchī* had gone to God'sFol. 154. mercy through the pains of colic.

(*n. Misconduct of Nāṣir Mīrzā.*)

It has been mentioned that at Qūsh-guṃbaz, Nāṣir Mīrzā asked leave to stay behind, saying that he would follow in a few days after taking something from his district for his retainers and followers.[923] But having left us, he sent a force against the people of Nūr-valley, they having done something a little refractory. The difficulty of moving in that valley owing to the strong position of its fort and the rice-cultivation of its lands, has already been described.[924] The Mīrzā's commander, Faẓlī, in ground so impracticable and in that one-road tract, instead of safe-guarding his men, scattered them to forage. Out came the valesmen, drove the foragers off, made it impossible to the rest to keep their ground, killed some, captured a mass of others and of horses,—precisely what would happen to any army chancing to be under such a person as Faẓlī! Whether because of this affair, or whether from want of heart, the Mīrzā did not follow us at all; he stayed behind.

Moreover Ayūb's sons, Yūsuf and Bahlūl (Begchīk), more seditious, silly and arrogant persons than whom there may not exist,—to whom I had given, to Yūsuf Alangār, to Bahlūl 'Alī-shang, they like Nāṣir Mīrzā, were to have taken something fromFol. 154b. their districts and to have come on with him, but, he not coming, neither did they. All that winter they were the companions of his cups and social pleasures. They also over-ran the Tarkalānī Afghāns in it.[925] With the on-coming heats, the Mīrzā made march off the families of the clans, outside-tribes and hordes who had wintered in Nīngnahār and the Lamghānāt, driving them like sheep before him, with all their goods, as far as the Bārān-water.[926]

(*o. Affairs of Badakhshān.*)

While Nāṣir Mīrzā was in camp on the Bārān-water, he heard that the Badakhshīs were united against the Aūzbegs and had killed some of them.

Here are the particulars:—When Shaibāq Khān had given Qūndūz to Qaṃbar Bī and gone himself to Khwārizm[927]; Qaṃbar Bī, in order to conciliate the Badakhshīs, sent them a son of Muḥammad-i-makhdūmī, Maḥmūd by name, but Mubārak Shāh,—whose ancestors are heard of as begs of the Badakhshān Shāhs,—having uplifted his own head, and cut off Maḥmūd's and those of some Aūzbegs, made himself fast in the fort once known as Shāf-tiwār but re-named by him Qila'-i-ẓafar. Moreover, in Rustāq Muḥammad *qūrchī*, an armourer of Khusrau Shāh, then occupying Khamalangān, slew Shaibāq Khān's *ṣadr* and some Aūzbegs and made that place fast. Zubair of Rāgh, again, Fol. 155.whose forefathers also will have been begs of the Badakhshān Shāhs, uprose in Rāgh.[928] Jahāngīr *Turkmān*, again, a servant of Khusrau Shāh's Walī, collected some of the fugitive soldiers and tribesmen Walī had left behind, and with them withdrew into a fastness.[929]

Nāṣir Mīrzā, hearing these various items of news and spurred on by the instigation of a few silly, short-sighted persons to covet Badakhshān, marched along the Shibr-tū and Āb-dara road, driving like sheep before him the families of the men who had come into Kābul from the other side of the Amū.[930]

(p. Affairs of Khusrau Shāh.)

At the time Khusrau Shāh and Aḥmad-i-qāsim were in flight from Ājar for Khurāsān,[931] they meeting in with Badī'u'z-zamān Mīrzā and Ẕū'n-nūn Beg, all went on together to the presence of Sl. Ḥusain Mīrzā in Herī. All had long been foes of his; all had behaved unmannerly to him; what brands had they not set on his heart! Yet all now went to him in their distress, and all went through me. For it is not likely they would have seen him if I had not made Khusrau Shāh helpless by parting him from his following, and if I had not taken Kābul from Ẕū'n'nūn's son, Muqīm. Badī'u'z-zamān Mīrzā himself was as dough in theFol. 155b. hands of the rest; beyond their word he could not go. Sl. Ḥusain Mīrzā took up a gracious attitude towards one and all, mentioned no-one's misdeeds, even made them gifts.

Shortly after their arrival Khusrau Shāh asked for leave to go to his own country, saying, "If I go, I shall get it all into my hands." As he had reached Herī without equipment and without resources, they finessed a little about his leave. He became importunate. Muḥammad Barandūq retorted roundly on him with, "When you had 30,000 men behind you and the whole country in your hands, what did you effect against the Aūzbeg? What will you do now with your 500 men and the Aūzbegs in possession?" He added a little good advice in a few sensible words, but all was in vain because the fated hour of Khusrau Shāh's death was near. Leave was at last given because of his importunity; Khusrau Shāh with his 3 or 400 followers, went straight into the borders of Dahānah. There as Nāṣir Mīrzā had just gone across, these two met.

Now the Badakhshī chiefs had invited only the Mīrzā; they had not invited Khusrau Shāh. Try as the Mīrzā did to persuade Khusrau Shāh to go into the hill-country,[932] the latter, quite understanding the whole time, would not consent to go, his own idea being that if he marched under the Mīrzā, he would get theFol. 156. country into his own hands. In the end, unable to agree, each of them, near Ishkīmīsh, arrayed his following, put on mail, drew out to fight, and—departed. Nāṣir Mīrzā went on for Badakhshān; Khusrau Shāh after collecting a disorderly rabble, good and bad of some

1,000 persons, went, with the intention of laying siege to Qūndūz, to Khwāja Chār-tāq, one or two *yīghāch* outside it.

(*q. Death of Khusrau Shāh.*)

At the time Shaibāq Khān, after overcoming Sulṭān Aḥmad *Taṃbal* and Andijān, made a move on Ḥiṣār, his Honour Khusrau Shāh[933] flung away his country (Qūndūz and Ḥiṣār) without a blow struck, and saved himself. Thereupon Shaibāq Khān went to Ḥiṣār in which were Sherīm the page and a few good braves. *They* did not surrender Ḥiṣār, though their honourable beg had flung *his* country away and gone off; they made Ḥiṣār fast. The siege of Ḥiṣār Shaibāq Khān entrusted to Ḥamza Sl. and Mahdī Sulṭān,[934] went to Qūndūz, gave Qūndūz to his younger brother, Maḥmūd Sulṭān and betook himself without delay to Khwārizm against Chīn Ṣūfī. But as, before he reached Samarkand on his way to Khwārizm, he heard of the death in Qūndūz of his brother, Maḥmūd Sulṭān, he gave that place to Qaṃbar Bī of Marv.[935]

Qaṃbar Bī was in Qūndūz when Khusrau Shāh went against it; he at once sent off galloppers to summon Ḥamza Sl. and the Fol. 156b.others Shaibāq Khān had left behind. Ḥamza Sl. came himself as far as the *sarāī* on the Amū bank where he put his sons and begs in command of a force which went direct against Khusrau Shāh. There was neither fight nor flight for that fat, little man; Ḥamza Sulṭān's men unhorsed him, killed his sister's son, Aḥmad-i-qāsim, Sherīm the page and several good braves. Him they took into Qūndūz, there struck his head off and from there sent it to Shaibāq Khān in Khwārizm.[936]

(*r. Conduct in Kābul of Khusrau Shāh's retainers.*)

Just as Khusrau Shāh had said they would do, his former retainers and followers, no sooner than he marched against Qūndūz, changed in their demeanour to me,[937] most of them marching off to near Khwāja-i-riwāj.[938] The greater number of the men in my service had been in his. The Mughūls behaved well, taking up a position of adherence to me.[939] On all this the news of Khusrau Shāh's death fell like water on fire; it put his men out.

911 AH.—JUNE 4TH 1505 TO MAY 24TH 1506 AD.[940]

(*a. Death of Qūtlūq-nigār Khānīm.*)

In the month of Muḥarram my mother had fever. Blood was let without effect and a Khurāsānī doctor, known as Sayyid Ṭabīb, in accordance with the Khurāsān practice, gave her water-melon, but her time to die must have come, for on the Fol. 157.Saturday after six days of illness, she went to God's mercy.

On Sunday I and Qāsim Kūkūldāsh conveyed her to the New-year's Garden on the mountain-skirt[941] where Aūlūgh Beg Mīrzā had built a house, and there, with the permission of his heirs,[942] we committed her to the earth. While we were mourning for her, people let me know about (the death of) my younger Khān *dādā* Alacha Khān, and my grandmother Aīsān-daulat Begīm.[943] Close upon Khānīm's Fortieth[944] arrived from Khurāsān Shāh Begīm the mother of the Khāns, together with my maternal-aunt Mihr-nigār Khānīm, formerly of Sl. Aḥmad Mīrzā's *ḥaram*, and Muḥammad Ḥusain *Kūrkān Dūghlāt.*[945] Lament broke out afresh; the bitterness of these partings was extreme. When the mourning-rites had been observed, food and victuals set out for the poor and destitute, the Qorān recited, and prayers offered for the departed souls, we steadied ourselves and all took heart again.

(*b. A futile start for Qandahār.*)

When set free from these momentous duties, we got an army to horse for Qandahār under the strong insistance of Bāqī *Chaghānīānī.* At the start I went to Qūsh-nādir (var. nāwar) where on dismounting I got fever. It was a strange sort of illness for whenever with much trouble I had been awakened, my eyes closed again in sleep. In four or five days I got quite well.

(*c. An earthquake.*)

At that time there was a great earthquake[946] such that most of the ramparts of forts and the walls of gardens fell down; houses were levelled to the ground in towns and villages and many persons lay dead beneath them. Every house fell in Paghmān-village,Fol. 157b. and 70 to 80 strong heads-of-houses lay dead under their walls. Between Pagh-mān and Beg-tūt[947] a piece of ground, a good stone-throw[948] wide may-be, slid down as far as an arrow's-flight; where it had slid springs appeared. On the road between Istarghach and Maidān the ground was so broken up for 6 to 8 *yīghāch* (36-

48 m.) that in some places it rose as high as an elephant, in others sank as deep; here and there people were sucked in. When the Earth quaked, dust rose from the tops of the mountains. Nūru'l-lāh the *ṭambourchi*[949] had been playing before me; he had two instruments with him and at the moment of the quake had both in his hands; so out of his own control was he that the two knocked against each other. Jahāngīr Mīrzā was in the porch of an upper-room at a house built by Aūlūgh Beg Mīrzā in Tīpa; when the Earth quaked, he let himself down and was not hurt, but the roof fell on some-one with him in that upper-room, presumably one of his own circle; that this person was not hurt in the least must have been solely through God's mercy. In Tīpa most of the houses were levelled to the ground. The Earth quaked 33 times on the first day, and for a month afterwards used to quake two or three times in the 24 hours. The begs and soldiers having been ordered to repair the breaches made in the towers and ramparts Fol. 158.of the fort (Kābul), everything was made good again in 20 days or a month by their industry and energy.

(*d. Campaign against Qalāt-i-ghilzāī.*)

Owing to my illness and to the earthquake, our plan of going to Qandahār had fallen somewhat into the background. The illness left behind and the fort repaired, it was taken up again. We were undecided at the time we dismounted below Shniz[950] whether to go to Qandahār, or to over-run the hills and plains. Jahāngīr Mīrzā and the begs having assembled, counsel was taken and the matter found settlement in a move on Qalāt. On this move Jahāngīr Mīrzā and Bāqī *Chaghānīānī* insisted strongly.

At Tāzī[951] there was word that Sher-i-'alī the page with Kīchīk Bāqī *Diwāna* and others had thoughts of desertion; all were arrested; Sher-i-'alī was put to death because he had given clear signs of disloyalty and misdoing both while in my service and not in mine, in this country and in that country.[952] The others were let go with loss of horse and arms.

On arriving at Qalāt we attacked at once and from all sides, without our mail and without siege-appliances. As has been mentioned in this History, Kīchīk Khwāja, the elder brother of Khwāja Kalān, was a most daring brave; he had used his sword Fol. 158b.in my presence several times; he now clambered up the south-west tower of Qalāt, was pricked in the eye with a spear when almost up, and died of the wound two or three days after the place was taken. Here that Kīchīk Bāqī *Dīwāna* who had been arrested when about to desert with Sher-i-'alī the page, expiated his baseness by being killed with a stone when he went under the ramparts. One or two other men died also. Fighting of this sort went on till the Afternoon Prayer when, just as our men were worn-out with the struggle and labour, those in the fort asked for peace and made surrender. Qalāt had been given by

Ẕū'n-nūn *Arghūn* to Muqīm, and in it now were Muqīm's retainers, Farrukh *Arghūn* and Qarā *Bīlūt* (Afghān). When they came out with their swords and quivers hanging round their necks, we forgave their offences.[953] It was not my wish to reduce this high family[954] to great straits; for why? Because if we did so when such a foe as the Aūzbeg was at our side, what would be said by those of far and near, who saw and heard?

As the move on Qalāt had been made under the insistance of Jahāngīr Mīrzā and Bāqī *Chaghānīānī*, it was now made over to the Mīrzā's charge. He would not accept it; Bāqī also could give no good answer in the matter. So, after such a storming and assaulting of Qalāt, its capture was useless.

We went back to Kābul after over-running the Afghāns of Sawā-sang and Ālā-tāgh on the south of Qalāt.Fol. 159.

The night we dismounted at Kābul I went into the fort; my tent and stable being in the Chār-bāgh, a Khirilchī thief going into the garden, fetched out and took away a bay horse of mine with its accoutrements, and my *khachar*.[955]

(*e. Death of Bāqī Chaghānīānī.*)

From the time Bāqī *Chaghānīanī* joined me on the Amū-bank, no man of mine had had more trust and authority.[956] If a word were said, if an act were done, that word was his word, that act, his act. Spite of this, he had not done me fitting service, nor had he shewn me due civility. Quite the contrary! he had done things bad and unmannerly. Mean he was, miserly and malicious, ill-tongued, envious and cross-natured. So miserly was he that although when he left Tīrmīẕ, with his family and possessions, he may have owned 30 to 40,000 sheep, and although those masses of sheep used to pass in front of us at every camping-ground, he did not give a single one to our bare braves, tortured as they were by the pangs of hunger; at last in Kāh-mard, he gave 50!

Spite of acknowledging me for his chief (*pādshāh*), he had nagarets beaten at his own Gate. He was sincere to none, had regard for none. What revenue there is from Kābul (town) comes from the *ṭamghā*[957]; the whole of this he had, together Fol. 159b.with the *dārogha*-ship in Kābul and Panjhīr, the Gadai (var. Kidī) Hazāra, and *kūshlūk*[958] and control of the Gate.[959] With all this favour and finding, he was not in the least content; quite the reverse! What medley of mischief he planned has been told; we had taken not the smallest notice of any of it, nor had we cast it in his face. He was always asking for leave, affecting scruple at making the request. We used to acknowledge the scruple and excuse ourselves from giving the leave. This would put him down for a few days; then he would ask again. He went too far with his affected scruple and his takings of leave! Sick were we too of his conduct and his character. We gave the leave; he repented asking for it and began to agitate against it, but all in vain! He got written down and sent to me, "His Highness made compact not to call me to account till nine[960] misdeeds had issued from me." I answered with a reminder of eleven successive faults and sent this to him through Mullā Bābā of Pashāghar. He submitted and was allowed to go towards Hindūstān, taking his family and possessions. A few of his retainers escorted him through Khaibar and returned; he joined Bāqī *Gāgīānī's* caravan and crossed at Nīl-āb.

Daryā Khān's son, Yār-i-ḥusain was then in Kacha-kot,[961] having drawn into his service, on the warrant of the *farmān* taken from me in Kohāt, a few Afghāns of the Dilazāk (var. Dilah-zāk) and Yūsuf-zāī and also a few Jats and Gujūrs.[962] With these he beat the roads, taking toll with might and main. Hearing about Bāqī, he blocked the road, made the whole partyFol. 160. prisoner, killed Bāqī and took his wife.

We ourselves had let Bāqī go without injuring him, but his own misdeeds rose up against him; his own acts defeated him.

Leave thou to Fate the man who does thee wrong;

For Fate is an avenging servitor.

(f. Attack on the Turkmān Hazāras.)

That winter we just sat in the Chār-bāgh till snow had fallen once or twice.

The Turkmān Hazāras, since we came into Kābul, had done a variety of insolent things and had robbed on the roads. We thought therefore of over-running them, went into the town to Aūlūgh Beg Mīrzā's house at the Būstān-sarāī, and thence rode out in the month of Sha'bān (Feb. 1506 AD.).

We raided a few Hazāras at Janglīk, at the mouth of the Dara-i-khūsh (Happy-valley).[963] Some were in a cave near the valley-mouth, hiding perhaps. Shaikh Darwīsh Kūkūldāsh went incautiously right (*auq*) up to the cave-mouth, was shot (*aūqlāb*) in the nipple by a Hazāra inside and died there and then (*aūq*).[964]

> (*Author's note on Shaikh Darwīsh.*) He had been with me in the guerilla-times, was Master-armourer (*qūr-begī*), drew a strong bow and shot a good shaft.

As most of the Turkmān Hazāras seemed to be wintering inside the Dara-i-khūsh, we marched against them.

The valley is shut in,[965] by a mile-long gully stretching inwards from its mouth. The road engirdles the mountain, havingFol. 160b. a straight fall of some 50 to 60 yards below it and above it a precipice. Horsemen go along it in single-file. We passed the gully and went on through the day till between the Two Prayers (3 p.m.) without meeting a single person. Having spent the night somewhere, we found a fat camel[966] belonging to the Hazāras, had it killed, made part of its flesh into *kabābs*[967] and cooked part in a ewer (*aftāb*). Such good camel-flesh had never been tasted; some could not tell it from mutton.

Next day we marched on for the Hazāra winter-camp. At the first watch (9 a.m.) a man came from ahead, saying that the Hazāras had blocked a ford in front with branches, checked our men and were fighting. That winter the snow lay very deep; to move was difficult except on the road. The swampy meadows (*tuk-āb*) along the stream were all frozen; the stream could only be crossed from the road because of snow and ice. The Hazāras had cut many branches, put them at the exit from the water and were fighting in the valley-bottom with horse and foot or raining Fol. 161.arrows down from either side.

Muḥammad 'Alī *Mubashshir*[968] Beg, one of our most daring braves, newly promoted to the rank of beg and well worthy of favour, went along the branch-blocked road without his mail, was shot in the belly and instantly surrendered his life. As we had gone forward in haste, most of us were not in mail. Shaft after shaft flew by and fell; with each one Yūsuf's Aḥmad said anxiously, "Bare[969] like this you go into it! I have seen two arrows go close to your head!" Said I, "Don't fear! Many as good arrows as these have flown past my head!" So much said, Qāsim Beg, his men in full accoutrement,[970] found a ford on our right and crossed. Before their charge the Hazāras could make no stand; they fled, swiftly pursued and unhorsed one after the other by those just up with them.

In guerdon for this feat Bangash was given to Qāsim Beg. Ḥātim the armourer having been not bad in the affair, was promoted to Shaikh Darwīsh's office of *qūr-begī*. Bābā Qulī's Kīpik (*sic*) also went well forward in it, so we entrusted Muḥ. 'Alī *Mubashshir's* office to him.

Sl. Qulī *Chūnāq* (one-eared) started in pursuit of the Hazāras but there was no getting out of the hollow because of the snow. Fol. 161b.For my own part I just went with these braves.

Near the Hazāra winter-camp we found many sheep and herds of horses. I myself collected as many as 4 to 500 sheep and from 20 to 25 horses. Sl. Qulī *Chūnāq* and two or three of my personal servants were with me. I have ridden in a raid twice[971]; this was the first time; the other was when, coming in from Khurāsān (912 AH.), we raided these same Turkmān Hazāras. Our foragers brought in masses of sheep and horses. The Hazāra wives and their little children had gone off up the snowy slopes and stayed there; we were rather idle and it was getting late in the day; so we turned back and dismounted in their very dwellings. Deep indeed was the snow that winter! Off the road it was up to a horse's *qāptāl*,[972] so deep that the night-watch was in the saddle all through till shoot of dawn.

Going out of the valley, we spent the next night just inside the mouth, in the Hazāra winter-quarters. Marching from there, we dismounted at Janglīk. At Janglīk Yārak Ṭ̤aghāī and other late-comers were ordered to take the Hazāras who had killed Shaikh Darwīsh and who, luckless and death-doomed, seemed still to be in the cave. Yārak Ṭ̤aghāī and his band by sending smoke into the cave, took 70 to 80 Hazāras who mostly died by the sword.

(*g. Collection of the Nijr-aū tribute.*)

On the way back from the Hazāra expedition we went to the Āī-tūghdī neighbourhood below Bārān[973] in order to collect the revenue of Nijr-aū. Jahāngīr Mīrzā, come up from Ghaznī,Fol. 162. waited on me there. At that time, on Ramẕān 13th (Feb. 7th) such sciatic-pain attacked me that for 40 days some-one had to turn me over from one side to the other.

Of the (seven) valleys of the Nijr-water the Pīchkān-valley,—and of the villages in the Pīchkān-valley Ghain,—and of Ghain its head-man Ḥusain *Ghainī* in particular, together with his elder and younger brethren, were known and notorious for obstinacy and daring. On this account a force was sent under Jahāngīr Mīrzā, Qāsim Beg going too, which went to Sar-i-tūp (Hill-top), stormed and took a *sangur* and made a few meet their doom.

Because of the sciatic pain, people made a sort of litter for me in which they carried me along the bank of the Bārān and into the town to the Būstān-sarāī. There I stayed for a few days; before that trouble was over a boil came out on my left cheek; this was lanced and for it I also took a purge. When relieved, I went out into the Chār-bāgh.

(*h. Misconduct of Jahāngīr Mīrẕā.*)

At the time Jahāngīr Mīrzā waited on me, Ayūb's sons Yūsuf and Buhlūl, who were in his service, had taken up a strifeful and seditious attitude towards me; so the Mīrzā was not found to be what he had been earlier. In a few days he marched out of Tīpa in his mail,[974] hurried back to Ghaznī, there took Nānī, killed some of its people and plundered all. Fol. 162b.After that he marched off with whatever men he had, through the Hazāras,[975] his face set for Bāmīān. God knows that nothing had been done by me or my dependants to give him ground for anger or reproach! What was heard of later on as perhaps explaining his going off in the way he did, was this;—When Qāsim Beg went with other begs, to give him honouring meeting as he came up from Ghaznī, the Mīrzā threw a falcon off at a quail. Just as the falcon, getting close, put out its pounce to seize the quail, the quail dropped to the ground. Hereupon shouts and cries, "Taken! is it taken?" Said Qāsim Beg, "Who looses the foe in his grip?" Their misunderstanding of this was their sole reason for going off, but they backed themselves on one or two other worse and weaker old cronish matters.[976] After doing in Ghaznī what has been mentioned, they drew off through the Hazāras to the Mughūl clans.[977] These clans at that time had left Nāṣir Mīrzā but had not joined the Aūzbeg, and were in Yāī, Astar-āb and the summer-pastures thereabouts.

(i. Sl. Ḥusain Mīrzā calls up help against Shaibāq Khān.)

Sl. Ḥusain Mīrzā, having resolved to repel Shaibāq Khān, summoned all his sons; me too he summoned, sending to me Sayyid Afẓal, son of Sayyid 'Alī *Khwāb-bīn* (Seer-of-dreams). It was right on several grounds for us to start for Khurāsān. One ground was that when a great ruler, sitting, as Sl. Ḥusain Mīrzā sat, in Tīmūr Beg's place, had resolved to act againstFol. 163. such a foe as Shaibāq Khān and had called up many men and had summoned his sons and his begs, if there were some who went on foot it was for us to go if on our heads! if some took the bludgeon, we would take the stone! A second ground was that, since Jahāngīr Mīrzā had gone to such lengths and had behaved so badly,[978] we had either to dispel his resentment or to repel his attack.

(j. Chīn Ṣūfī's death.)

This year Shaibāq Khān took Khwārizm after besieging Chīn Sūfī in it for ten months. There had been a mass of fighting during the siege; many were the bold deeds done by the Khwārizmī braves; nothing soever did they leave undone. Again and again their shooting was such that their arrows pierced shield and cuirass, sometimes the two cuirasses.[979] For ten months they sustained that siege without hope in any quarter. A few bare braves then lost heart, entered into talk with the Aūzbeg and were in the act of letting him up into the fort when Chīn Ṣūfī had the news and went to the spot. Just as he was beating and forcing down the Aūzbegs, his own page, in a discharge of arrows, shot him from behind. No man was left to fight; the Aūzbegs took Khwārizm. God's mercy on Chīn Ṣūfī, who never for one moment ceased to stake his life Fol. 163b.for his chief![980]

Shaibāq Khān entrusted Khwārizm to Kūpuk (*sic*) Bī and went back to Samarkand.

(k. Death of Sultān Ḥusain Mīrzā.)

Sl. Ḥusain Mīrzā having led his army out against Shaibāq Khān as far as Bābā Ilāhī[981] went to God's mercy, in the month of Ẕū'l-ḥijja (Ẕū'l-ḥijja 11th 911 AH.-May 5th 1506 AD.).

SULṬĀN ḤUSAIN MĪRZĀ AND HIS COURT.[982]

(*a.*) *His birth and descent.*

He was born in Herī (Harāt), in (Muḥarram) 842 (AH.-June-July, 1438 AD.) in Shāhrukh Mīrzā's time[983] and was the son of Manṣūr Mīrzā, son of Bāī-qarā Mīrzā, son of 'Umar Shaikh Mīrzā, son of Amīr Tīmūr. Manṣūr Mīrzā and Bāī-qarā Mīrzā never reigned.

His mother was Fīrūza Begīm, a (great-)grandchild (*nabīra*) of Tīmūr Beg; through her he became a grandchild of Mīrān-shāh also.[984] He was of high birth on both sides, a ruler of royal lineage.[985] Of the marriage (of Manṣūr with Fīrūza) were born two sons and two daughters, namely, Bāī-qarā Mīrzā and Sl. Ḥusain Mīrzā, Ākā Begīm and another daughter, Badka Begīm whom Aḥmad Khān took.[986]

Bāī-qarā Mīrzā was older than Sl. Ḥusain Mīrzā; he was his younger brother's retainer but used not to be present as head of the Court;[987] except in Court, he used to share his brother's divan (*tūshak*). He was given Balkh by his younger brother and was its Commandant for several years. He had three sons, Sl. Muḥammad Mīrzā, Sl. Wais Mīrzā and Sl. Iskandar Mīrzā.[988]

Ākā Begīm was older than the Mīrzā; she was taken byFol. 164. Sl. Aḥmad Mīrzā,[989] a grandson (*nabīra*) of Mīrān-shāh; by him she had a son (Muḥammad Sulṭān Mīrzā), known as Kīchīk (Little) Mīrzā, who at first was in his maternal-uncle's service, but later on gave up soldiering to occupy himself with letters. He is said to have become very learned and also to have taste in verse.[990] Here is a Persian quatrain of his:—

For long on a life of devotion I plumed me,

As one of the band of the abstinent ranged me;

Where when Love came was devotion? denial?

By the mercy of God it is I have proved me!

This quatrain recalls one by the Mullā.[991] Kīchīk Mīrzā made the circuit of the *ka'ba* towards the end of his life.

Badka (Badī‘u'l-jamāl) Begīm also was older[992] than the Mīrzā. She was given in the guerilla times to Aḥmad Khān of Ḥājī-tarkhān;[993] by him she had two sons (Sl. Maḥmūd Khān and Bahādur Sl.) who went to Herī and were in the Mīrzā's service.

(*b.*) *His appearance and habits.*

He was slant-eyed (*qīyik gūzlūq*) and lion-bodied, being slender from the waist downwards. Even when old and white-bearded, he wore silken garments of fine red and green. He used to wear either the black lambskin cap (*būrk*) or the *qālpāq*,[994] but on a Feast-day would sometimes set up a little three-fold turban, wound broad and badly,[995] stick a heron's plume in it and so go to Prayers.

When he first took Herī, he thought of reciting the names of Fol. 164b.the Twelve Imāms in the *khuṭba*,[996] but ‘Alī-sher Beg and others prevented it; thereafter all his important acts were done in accordance with orthodox law. He could not perform the Prayers on account of a trouble in the joints,[997] and he kept no fasts. He was lively and pleasant, rather immoderate in temper, and with words that matched his temper. He shewed great respect for the law in several weighty matters; he once surrendered to the Avengers of blood a son of his own who had killed a man, and had him taken to the Judgment-gate (*Dāru'l-qaẓā*). He was abstinent for six or seven years after he took the throne; later on he degraded himself to drink. During the almost 40 years of his rule[998] in Khurāsān, there may not have been one single day on which he did not drink after the Mid-day prayer; earlier than that however he did not drink. What happened with his sons, the soldiers and the town was that every-one pursued vice and pleasure to excess. Bold and daring he was! Time and again he got to work with his own sword, getting his own hand in wherever he arrayed to fight; no man of Tīmūr Beg's line has been known to match him in the slashing of swords. He had a leaning to poetry and even put a *dīwān*
together, writing in Turkī with Ḥusainī for his pen-name.[999] Many couplets in his *dīwān* are not bad; it is however in one and the same metre throughout. Great ruler though he was,Fol. 165. both by the length of his reign (*yāsh*) and the breadth of his dominions, he yet, like little people kept fighting-rams, flew pigeons and fought cocks.

(*c.*) *His wars and encounters.*[1000]

He swam the Gurgān-water[1001] in his guerilla days and gave a party of Aūzbegs a good beating.

Again,—with 60 men he fell on 3000 under Pay-master Muḥammad 'Alī, sent ahead by Sl. Abū-sa'īd Mīrzā, and gave them a downright good beating (868 AH.). This was his one fine, out-standing feat-of-arms.[1002]

Again,—he fought and beat Sl. Maḥmūd Mīrzā near Astarābād (865 AH.).[1003]

Again,—this also in Astarābād, he fought and beat Sa'īdlīq Sa'īd, son of Ḥusain *Turkmān* (873 AH.?).

Again,—after taking the throne (of Herī in Ramẓān 873 AH.-March 1469 AD.), he fought and beat Yādgār-i-muḥammad Mīrzā at Chanārān (874 AH.).[1004]

Again,—coming swiftly[1005] from the Murgh-āb bridge-head (Sar-i-pul), he fell suddenly on Yādgār-i-muḥammad Mīrzā where he lay drunk in the Ravens'-garden (875 AH.), a victory which kept all Khurāsān quiet.

Again,—he fought and beat Sl. Maḥmūd Mīrzā at Chīkmān-sarāī in the neighbourhood of Andikhūd and Shibrghān (876 AH.).[1006]

Again,—he fell suddenly on Abā-bikr Mīrzā[1007] after that Mīrzā, joined by the Black-sheep Turkmāns, had come out of 'Irāq, beaten Aūlūgh Beg Mīrzā (*Kābulī*) in Takāna and Khimār (var. Ḥimār), taken Kābul, left it because of turmoil in 'Irāq, crossed Khaibar, gone on to Khūsh-āb and Multān, on again to Fol. 165b.Sīwī,[1008] thence to Karmān and, unable to stay there, had entered the Khurāsān country (884 AH.).[1009]

Again,—he defeated his son Badī'u'z-zamān Mīrzā at Pul-i-chirāgh (902 AH.); he also defeated his sons Abū'l-muḥsin Mīrzā and Kūpuk (Round-shouldered) Mīrzā at Ḥalwā-spring (904 AH.).[1010]

Again,—he went to Qūndūz, laid siege to it, could not take it, and retired; he laid siege to Ḥiṣār, could not take that either, and rose from before it (901 AH.); he went into Ẕū'n-nūn's country, was given Bast by its *dārogha*, did no more and retired (903 AH.).[1011] A ruler so great and so brave, after resolving royally on these three movements, just retired with nothing done!

Again,—he fought his son Badī'u'z-zamān Mīrzā in the Nīshīn-meadow, who had come there with Ẕū'n-nūn's son, Shāh Beg (903 AH.). In that affair were these curious coincidences:—The Mīrzā's force will have been small, most of his men being in Astarābād; on the very day of the fight, one force rejoined him coming back from Astarābād, and Sl. Mas'ūd Mīrzā arrived to join Sl. Ḥusain Mīrzā after letting Bāī-sunghar Mīrzā take Ḥiṣār, and Ḥaidar Mīrzā came back from reconnoitring Badī'u'z-zamān Mīrzā at Sabzawār.

(*d.*) *His countries.*

His country was Khurāsān, with Balkh to the east, Bistām and Damghān to the west, Khwārizm to the north, QandahārFol. 166. and Sīstān to the south. When he once had in his hands such a town as Herī, his only affair, by day and by night, was with comfort and pleasure; nor was there a man of his either who did not take his ease. It followed of course that, as he no longer tolerated the hardships and fatigue of conquest and soldiering, his retainers and his territories dwindled instead of increasing right down to the time of his departure.[1012]

(*e.*) *His children.*

Fourteen sons and eleven daughters were born to him.[1013] The oldest of all his children was Badī'u'z-zamān Mīrzā; (Bega Begīm) a daughter of Sl. Sanjar of Marv, was his mother.

Shāh-i-gharīb Mīrzā was another; he had a stoop (*būkūri*); though ill to the eye, he was of good character; though weak of body, he was powerful of pen. He even put a *dīwān* together, using Gharbatī (Lowliness) for his pen-name and writing both Turkī and Persian verse. Here is a couplet of his:—

Seeing a peri-face as I passed, I became its fool;

Not knowing what was its name, where was its home.

For a time he was his father's Governor in Herī. He died before his father, leaving no child.

Muẓaffar-i-ḥusain Mīrzā was another; he was his father's favourite son, but though this favourite, had neither accomplishments nor character. It was Sl. Ḥusain Mīrzā's over-fondness for this son that led his other sons into rebellion. The mother of Shāh-i-gharīb Mīrzā and of Muẓaffar-i-ḥusain Mīrzā was Fol. 166b.Khadīja Begīm, a former mistress of Sl. Abū-sa'īd Mīrzā by whom she had had a daughter also, known as Āq (Fair) Begīm.

Two other sons were Abū'l-ḥusain Mīrzā and Kūpuk (var. Kīpik) Mīrzā whose name was Muḥammad Muḥsin Mīrzā; their mother was Laṭīf-sulṭān Āghācha.

Abū-turāb Mīrzā was another. From his early years he had an excellent reputation. When the news of his father's increased illness[1014] reached him and other news of other kinds also, he fled with his younger brother Muḥammad-i-ḥusain Mīrzā into 'Irāq,[1015] and there abandoned soldiering to lead the darwish-life; nothing further has been heard about him.[1016] His son Sohrāb was in my service when I took Ḥiṣār after having beaten the sulṭāns led by Ḥamza Sl. and Mahdī Sl. (917 AH.-1511 AD.); he was blind of one eye and of wretchedly bad aspect; his disposition matched even his ill-looks. Owing to some immoderate act (*bī i'tidāl*), he could not stay with me, so went off. For some of his immoderate doings, Nijm Ṣānī put him to death near Astarābād.[1017]

Muḥammad-i-ḥusain Mīrzā was another. He must have been shut up (*bund*) with Shāh Ismā'īl at some place in 'Irāq and have become his disciple;[1018] he became a rank heretic later on and became this although his father and brethren, older and younger, were all orthodox. He died in Astarābād, still on the same wrong road, still with the same absurd opinions. A good deal is heard about his courage and heroism, but no deed of his stands out as worthy of record. He may have been poetically-disposed; here is a couplet of his:—

Grimed with dust, from tracking what game dost thou come?

Steeped in sweat, from whose heart of flame dost thou come?

Farīdūn-i-ḥusain Mīrzā was another. He drew a very strongFol. 167. bow and shot a first-rate shaft; people say his cross-bow (*kamān-i-guroha*) may have been 40 *bātmāns*.[1019] He himself was very brave but he had no luck in war; he was beaten wherever he fought. He and his younger brother Ibn-i-ḥusain Mīrzā were defeated at Rabāṯ-i-dūzd (var. Dudūr) by Tīmūr Sl. and 'Ubaid Sl. leading Shaibāq Khān's advance (913 AH.?), but he had done good things there.[1020] In Dāmghān he and Muḥammad-i-zamān Mīrzā[1021] fell into the hands of Shaibāq Khān who, killing neither, let both go free. Farīdūn-i-ḥusain Mīrzā went later on to Qalāt[1022] where Shāh Muḥammad *Diwāna* had made himself fast; there when the Aūzbegs took the place, he was captured and killed. The three sons last-named were by Mīnglī Bībī Āghācha, Sl. Ḥusain Mīrzā's Aūzbeg mistress.

Ḥaidar Mīrzā was another; his mother Payānda-sulṭān Begīm was a daughter of Sl. Abū-sa'īd Mīrzā. Ḥaidar Mīrzā was Governor of Balkh and Mashhad for some time during his father's life. For him his father, when besieging Ḥiṣār (901 AH.) took (Bega Begīm) a daughter of Sl. Maḥmūd Mīrzā and Khān-zāda Begīm; this done, he rose from before Ḥiṣār. One daughter only[1023] was born of that marriage; she was named Shād (Joy) Begīm and given to 'Ādil Sl.[1024] when she came to Kābul later on. Ḥaidar Mīrzā departed from the world in his father's Fol. 167b.life-time.

Muḥammad Ma'ṣūm Mīrzā was another. He had Qandahār given to him and, as was fitting with this, a daughter of Aūlūgh Beg Mīrzā, (Bega Begīm), was set aside for him; when she went to Herī (902 AH.), Sl. Ḥusain Mīrzā made a splendid feast, setting up a great *chār-ṭāq* for it.[1025] Though Qandahār was given to Muḥ. Ma'ṣūm Mīrzā, he had neither power nor influence there, since, if black were done, or if white were done, the act was Shāh Beg *Arghūn's*. On this account the Mīrzā left Qandahār and went into Khurāsān. He died before his father.

Farrukh-i-ḥusain Mīrzā was another. Brief life was granted to him; he bade farewell to the world before his younger brother Ibrāhīm-i-ḥusain Mīrzā.

Ibrāhīm-i-ḥusain Mīrzā was another. They say his disposition was not bad; he died before his father from bibbing and bibbing Herī wines.

Ibn-i-ḥusain Mīrzā and Muḥ. Qāsim Mīrzā were others;[1026] their story will follow. Pāpā Āghācha was the mother of the five sons last-named.

Of all the Mīrzā's daughters, Sulṭānīm Begīm was the oldest. She had no brother or sister of the full-blood. Her mother, known as Chūlī (Desert) Begīm, was a daughter of one of the Aẕāq begs. Sulṭānīm Begīm had great acquaintance with words (*soz bilūr aīdi*); she was never at fault for a word. Her father sent her out[1027] to Sl. Wais Mīrzā, the middle son of his own elder brother Bāī-qarā Mīrzā; she had a son and a daughter by him; the daughter was sent out to Aīsān-qulī Sl. younger brother of Yīlī-bārs of the Shabān sulṭāns;[1028] the son is that Muḥammad Sl. Mīrzā to whom I have given the Qanauj district.[1029] At that same date Sulṭānīm Begīm, when on her way with her grandsonFol. 168. from Kābul to Hindūstān, went to God's mercy at Nīl-āb. Her various people turned back, taking her bones; her grandson came on.[1030]

Four daughters were by Payānda-sulṭān Begīm. Āq Begīm, the oldest, was sent out to Muḥammad Qāsim *Arlāt*, a grandson of Bega Begīm the younger sister of Bābur Mīrzā;[1031] there was one daughter (*bīr gīna qīz*), known as Qarā-gūz (Dark-eyed) Begīm, whom Nāṣir Mīrzā (*Mīrān-shāhī*) took. Kīchīk Begīm was the second; for her Sl. Mas'ūd Mīrzā had great desire but, try as he would, Payānda-sulṭān Begīm, having an aversion for him, would not give her to him;[1032] she sent Kīchīk Begīm out afterwards to Mullā Khwāja of the line of Sayyid Ātā.[1033] Her third and fourth daughters Bega Begīm and Āghā Begīm, she gave to Bābur Mīrzā and Murād Mīrzā the sons of her younger sister, Rābī'a-sulṭān Begīm.[1034]

Two other daughters of the Mīrzā were by Mīnglī Bībī Āghācha. They gave the elder one, Bairam-sulṭān Begīm to Sayyid 'Abdu'l-lāh, one of the sayyids of Andikhūd who was a grandson of Bāī-qarā Mīrzā[1035] through a daughter. A son of this marriage, Sayyid Barka[1036] was in my service when Samarkand was taken (917 AH.-1511 AD.); he went to Aūrganj later and there made claim to rule; the Red-heads[1037] killed him in Astarābād. Mīnglī Bībī's second daughter was Fāṯima-sulṯān Begīm; her they gave to Yādgār(-i-farrukh) Mīrzā of Tīmūr Beg's line.[1038]

Three daughters[1039] were by Pāpā Āghācha. Of these the oldest, Sulṯān-nizhād Begīm was made to go out to Iskandar Mīrzā, youngest son of Sl. Ḥusain Mīrzā's elder brother Bāī-qarā Mīrzā. The second, (Sa'ādat-bakht, known as) Begīm Sulṯān, Fol. 168b.was given to Sl. Mas'ūd Mīrzā after his blinding.[1040] By Sl. Mas'ūd Mīrzā she had one daughter and one son. The daughter was brought up by Apāq Begīm of Sl. Ḥusain Mīrzā's *ḥaram*; from Herī she came to Kābul and was there given to Sayyid Mīrzā Apāq.[1041] (Sa'ādat-bakht) Begīm Sulṯān after the Aūzbeg killed her husband, set out for the *ka'ba* with her son.[1042] News has just come (*circa* 934 AH.) that they have been heard of as in Makka and that the boy is becoming a bit of a great personage.[1043] Pāpā Āghācha's third daughter was given to a sayyid of Andikhūd, generally known as Sayyid Mīrzā.[1044]

Another of the Mīrzā's daughters, 'Āyisha-sulṯān Begīm, was by a mistress, Zubaida Āghācha the grand-daughter of Ḥusain-i-Shaikh Tīmūr.[1045] They gave her to Qāsim Sl. of the Shabān sulṯāns; she had by him a son, named Qāsim-i-ḥusain Sl. who came to serve me in Hindūstān, was in the Holy Battle with Rānā Sangā, and was given Badāyūn.[1046] When Qāsim Sl. died, (his widow) 'Āyisha-sulṯān Begīm was taken by Būrān Sl. one of his relations,[1047] by whom she had a son, named 'Abdu'l-lāh Sl. now serving me and though young, not doing badly.

(f. His wives and concubines.)

The wife he first took was Bega Sulṯān Begīm, a daughter of Sl. Sanjar of Marv. She was the mother of Badī'u'z-zamān Mīrzā. She was very cross-tempered and made the Mīrzā endure much wretchedness, until driven at last to despair, he set himself Fol. 169.free by divorcing her. What was he to do? Right was with him.[1048]

A bad wife in a good man's house

Makes this world already his hell.[1049]

God preserve every Musalmān from this misfortune! Would that not a single cross or ill-tempered wife were left in the world!

Chūlī Begīm was another; she was a daughter of the Aẕāq begs and was the mother of Sulṯānīm Begīm.

Shahr-bānū Begīm was another; she was Sl. Abū-sa'īd Mīrzā's daughter, taken after Sl. Ḥusain Mīrzā took the throne (873 AH.). When the Mīrzā's other ladies got out of their litters and mounted horses, at the battle of Chīkmān, Shahr-bānū Begīm, putting her trust in her younger brother (Sl. Maḥmūd M.), did not leave her litter, did not mount a horse;[1050] people told the Mīrzā of this, so he divorced her and took her younger sister Payānda-sulṭān Begīm. When the Aūzbegs took Khurāsān (913 AH.), Payānda-sulṭān Begīm went into 'Irāq, and in 'Irāq she died in great misery.

Khadīja Begīm was another.[1051] She had been a mistress of Sl. Abū-sa'īd Mīrzā and by him had had a daughter, Āq Begīm; after his defeat (873 AH.-1468 AD.) she betook herself to Herī where Sl. Ḥusain Mīrzā took her, made her a great favourite, and promoted her to the rank of Begīm. Very dominant indeed she became later on; she it was wrought Muḥ. Mūmin Mīrzā's death;[1052] she in chief it was caused Sl. Ḥusain Mīrzā's sons to rebel against him. She took herself for a sensible woman but was a silly chatterer, may also have been a heretic. Of her were Fol. 169b.born Shāh-i-gharīb Mīrzā and Muẕaffar-i-ḥusain Mīrzā.

Apāq Begīm was another;[1053] she had no children; that Pāpā Āghācha the Mīrzā made such a favourite of was her foster-sister. Being childless, Apāq Begīm brought up as her own the children of Pāpā Āghācha. She nursed the Mīrzā admirably when he was ill; none of his other wives could nurse as she did. The year I came into Hindūstān (932 AH.)[1054] she came into Kābul from Herī and I shewed her all the honour and respect I could. While I was besieging Chandīrī (934 AH.) news came that in Kābul she had fulfilled God's will.[1055]

One of the Mīrzā's mistresses was Laṭīf-sulṭān Āghācha of the Chār-shamba people[1056]; she became the mother of Abū'l-muḥsin Mīrzā and Kūpuk (or Kīpik) Mīrzā (*i.e.* Muḥammad Muḥsin).

Another mistress was Mīnglī Bībī Āghācha,[1057] an Aūzbeg and one of Shahr-bānū Begīm's various people. She became the mother of Abū-turāb Mīrzā, Muḥammad-i-ḥusain Mīrzā, Farīdūn-i-ḥusain Mīrzā and of two daughters.

Pāpā Āghācha, the foster-sister of Apāq Begīm was another mistress. The Mīrzā saw her, looked on her with favour, took her and, as has been mentioned, she became the mother of five of his sons and four of his daughters.[1058]

Begī Sulṭān Āghācha was another mistress; she had no child. There were also many concubines and mistresses held in little respect; those enumerated were the respected wives and mistresses of Sl. Ḥusain Mīrzā.

Strange indeed it is that of the 14 sons born to a ruler so great as Sl. Ḥusain Mīrzā, one governing too in such a town as Herī, three only were born in legal marriage.[1059] In him, in his sons, and in his tribes and hordes vice and debauchery wereFol. 170. extremely prevalent. What shews this point precisely is that of the many sons born to his dynasty not a sign or trace was left in seven or eight years, excepting only Muḥammad-i-zamān Mīrzā.[1060]

(*g. His amīrs.*)

There was Muḥammad Baranduq *Barlās*, descending from Chākū *Barlās* as follows,—Muḥammad Barandūq, son of 'Alī, son of Barandūq, son of Jahān-shāh, son of Chākū *Barlās*.[1061] He had been a beg of Bābur Mīrzā's presence; later on Sl. Abū-sa'īd Mīrzā favoured him, gave him Kābul conjointly with Jahāngīr *Barlās*, and made him Aūlūgh Beg Mīrzā's guardian. After the death of Sl. Abū-sa'īd Mīrzā, Aūlūgh Beg Mīrzā formed designs against the two Barlās; they got to know this, kept tight hold of him, made the tribes and hordes march,[1062] moved as for Qūndūz, and when up on Hindū-kush, courteously compelled Aūlūgh Beg Mīrzā to start back for Kābul, they themselves going on to Sl. Ḥusain Mīrzā in Khurāsān, who, in his turn, shewed them great favour. Muḥammad Barandūq was remarkably intelligent, a very leaderlike man indeed! He was extravagantly fond of a hawk; so much so, they say, that if a hawk of his had strayed or had died, he would ask, taking the names of his sons on his lips, what it would have mattered if such or such a son had died or had broken his neck, rather than this or that bird had died or had strayed.

Muẓaffar *Barlās* was another.[1063] He had been with the Mīrzā in the guerilla fighting and, for some cause unknown, had received extreme favour. In such honour was he in those guerilla days that the compact was for the Mīrzā to take four *dāng* (sixths) Fol. 170b.of any country conquered, and for him to take two *dāng*. A strange compact indeed! How could it be right to make even a faithful servant a co-partner in rule? Not even a younger brother or a son obtains such a pact; how then should a beg?[1064] When the Mīrzā had possession of the throne, he repented the compact, but his repentance was of no avail; that muddy-minded mannikin, favoured so much already, made growing assumption to rule. The Mīrzā acted without judgment; people say Muẓaffar *Barlās* was poisoned in the end.[1065] God knows the truth!

'Alī-sher *Nawā'ī* was another, the Mīrzā's friend rather than his beg. They had been learners together in childhood and even then are said to have been close friends. It is not known for what offence Sl. Abū-sa'īd Mīrzā drove 'Alī-sher Beg from Herī; he then went to Samarkand where he was protected and supported by Aḥmad Ḥājī Beg during the several years of his stay.[1066] He was noted for refinement of manner; people fancied this due to the pride of high fortune but it may not have been so, it may have been innate, since it was equally noticeable also in Samarkand.[1067] 'Alī-sher Beg had no match. For as long as verse has been written in the Turkī tongue, no-one has written so much or so well as he. He wrote six books of poems (maṣṇawī), five of them answering to the Quintet (*Khamsah*),[1068] the sixth, entitled the *Lisānu'ṭ-ṭair* (Tongue of the birds), was in the same metre as the *Manṭiqu'ṭ-ṭair* (Speech of the birds).[1069] He put together four *dīwāns* (collections) of odes, bearing the names, *Curiosities of Childhood*, *Marvels of Youth*, *Wonders of Manhood* and *Advantages of Age*.[1070] There are good quatrains of his also. Some others of his compositions rank below thoseFol. 171. mentioned; amongst them is a collection of his letters, imitating that of Maulānā 'Abdu'r-raḥmān *Jāmī* and aiming at gathering together every letter on any topic he had ever written to any person. He wrote also the *Mīzānu'l-aūzān* (Measure of measures) on prosody; it is very worthless; he has made mistake in it about the metres of four out of twenty-four quatrains, while about other measures he has made mistake such as any-one who has given attention to prosody, will understand. He put a Persian *dīwān* together also, Fānī (transitory) being his pen-name for Persian verse.[1071] Some couplets in it are not bad but for the most part it is flat and poor. In music also he composed good things (*nīma*), some excellent airs and preludes (*nakhsh u peshrau*). No such patron and protector of men of parts and accomplishments is known, nor has one such been heard of as ever appearing. It was through his instruction and support that Master (Ustād) Qul-i-muḥammad the lutanist, Shaikhī the flautist, and Ḥusain the lutanist, famous performers all, rose to eminence and renown. It was through his effort and supervision that Master Bih-zād and Shāh Muẓaffar became so distinguished in painting. Few are heard of as having helped to lay the good foundation for future excellence he helped to lay. He had neither son nor daughter, wife or family; he let the world pass by, alone and unencumbered. At first he was Keeper of the Seal; in middle-life he became a beg and for a time was Commandant in Astarābād; later on he forsook soldiering. He took nothing from the Mīrzā, on the contrary, he each year Fol. 171b.offered considerable gifts. When the Mīrzā was returning from the Astarābād campaign, 'Alī-sher Beg went out to give him meeting; they saw one another but before 'Alī-sher Beg should have risen to leave, his condition became such that he could not rise. He was lifted up and carried away; the doctors could not tell what was wrong; he went to God's mercy next day,[1072] one of his own couplets suiting his case:—

I was felled by a stroke out of their ken and mine;

What, in such evils, can doctors avail?

Aḥmad the son of Tawakkal *Barlās* was another;[1073] for a time he held Qandahār.

Walī Beg was another; he was of Ḥājī Saifu'd-dīn Beg's line,[1074] and had been one of the Mīrzā's father's (Manṣūr's) great begs.[1075] Short life was granted to him after the Mīrzā took the throne (973 AH.); he died directly afterwards. He was orthodox and made the Prayers, was rough (*turk*) and sincere.

Ḥusain of Shaikh Tīmūr was another; he had been favoured and raised to the rank of beg[1076] by Bābur Mīrzā.

Nuyān Beg was another. He was a Sayyid of Tīrmīẕ on his father's side; on his mother's he was related both to Sl. Abū-sa'īd Mīrzā and to Sl. Ḥusain Mīrzā.[1077] Sl. Abū-sa'īd Mīrzā had favoured him; he was the beg honoured in Sl. Aḥmad Mīrzā's presence and he met with very great favour when he went to Sl. Ḥusain Mīrzā's. He was a bragging, easy-going, wine-bibbing, jolly person. Through being in his father's service,[1078] Ḥasan of Ya'qūb used to be called also Nuyān's Ḥasan.

Jahāngīr *Barlās* was another.[1079] For a time he shared the Kābul command with Muḥammad Barandūq *Barlās*, later onFol. 172. went to Sl. Ḥusain Mīrzā's presence and received very great favour. His movements and poses (*ḥarakāt u sakanāt*) were graceful and charming; he was also a man of pleasant temper. As he knew the rules of hunting and hawking, in those matters the Mīrzā gave him chief charge. He was a favourite of Badī'u'z-zamān Mīrzā and, bearing that Mīrzā's friendliness in mind, used to praise him.

Mīrzā Aḥmad of 'Alī *Farsī Barlās* was another. Though he wrote no verse, he knew what was poetry. He was a gay-hearted, elegant person, one by himself.

'Abdu'l-khalīq Beg was another. Fīrūz Shāh, Shāhrukh Mīrzā's greatly favoured beg, was his grandfather;[1080] hence people called him Fīrūz Shāh's 'Abdu'l-khalīq. He held Khwārizm for a time.

Ibrāhīm *Dūldāī* was another. He had good knowledge of revenue matters and the conduct of public business; his work was that of a second Muḥ. Barandūq.

Ẕū'n-nūn *Arghūn* was another.[1081] He was a brave man, using his sword well in Sl. Abū-sa'īd Mīrzā's presence and later on getting his hand into the work whatever the fight. As to his courage there was no question at all, but he was a bit of a fool. After he left our (*Mīrān-shāhī*) Mīrzās to go to Sl. Ḥusain Mīrzā, the Mīrzā gave him Ghūr and the Nikdīrīs. He did Fol. 172b.excellent work in those parts with 70 to 80 men, with so few beating masses and masses of Hazāras and Nikdīrīs; he had not his match for keeping those tribes in order. After a while Zamīn-dāwar was given to him. His son Shāh-i-shujā‘ *Arghūn* used to move about with him and even in childhood used to chop away with his sword. The Mīrzā favoured Shāh-i-shujā‘ and, somewhat against Ẕū'n-nūn Beg's wishes, joined him with his father in the government of Qandahār. Later on this father and son made dissension between that father and that son,[1082] and stirred up much commotion. After I had overcome Khusrau Shāh and parted his retainers from him, and after I had taken Kābul from Ẕū'n-nūn *Arghūn*'s son Muqīm, Ẕū'n-nūn Beg and Khusrau Shāh both went, in their helplessness, to see Sl. Ḥusain Mīrzā. Ẕū'n-nūn *Arghūn* grew greater after the Mīrzā's death when they gave him the districts of the Herī Koh-dāman, such as Aūba (Ubeh) and Chachcharān.[1083] He was made Lord of Badī‘u'z-zamān Mīrzā's Gate[1084] and Muḥammad Baranduq *Barlās* Lord of Muẕaffar-i-ḥusain Mīrzā's, when the two Mīrzās became joint-rulers in Herī. Brave though he was, he was a little crazed and shallow-pated; if he had not been so, would he have accepted flattery as he did? would he have made himself so contemptible? Here are the details of the matter:—While he was so dominant and so trusted in Herī, a few shaikhs and mullās went to him and said, "The Spheres are holding commerce with us; you are to be styled *Hiẕabru'l-lāh* (Lion of God); you will overcome the Aūzbeg." Fully accepting this flattery, he put his *fūṭa* (bathing-cloth) round his neck[1085] and gave thanks. Then, after Shaibāq Khān, coming against the Mīrzās, had beaten them oneFol. 173. by one near Bādghīs, Ẕū'n-nūn *Arghūn* met him face to face near Qarā-rabāṭ. and, relying on that promise, stood up against him with 100 to 150 men. A mass of Aūzbegs came up, overcame them and hustled them off; he himself was taken and put to death.[1086] He was orthodox and no neglecter of the Prayers, indeed made the extra ones. He was mad for chess; he played it according to his own fancy and, if others play with one hand, he played with both.[1087] Avarice and stinginess ruled in his character.

Darwīsh-i-‘alī Beg was another,[1088] the younger full-brother of ‘Alī-sher Beg. He had the Balkh Command for a time and there did good beg-like things, but he was a muddle-head and somewhat wanting in merit. He was dismissed from the Balkh Command because his muddle-headedness had hampered the Mīrzā in his first campaign against Qūndūz and Ḥiṣār. He came to my presence when I went to Qūndūz in 916 AH. (1510 AD.), brutalized and stupefied, far from capable begship and out-side peaceful home-life. Such favour as he had had, he appears to have had for ‘Alī-sher Beg's sake.

Mughūl Beg was another. He was Governor of Herī for a time, later on was given Astarābād, and from there fled to Ya‘qūb Beg in ‘Irāq. He was of amorous disposition[1089] and an incessant dicer.

Sayyid Badr (Full-moon) was another, a very strong man, Fol. 173b.graceful in his movements and singularly well-mannered. He danced wonderfully well, doing one dance quite unique and seeming to be his own invention.[1090] His whole service was with the Mīrzā whose comrade he was in wine and social pleasure.

Islīm *Barlās* was another, a plain (*turk*) person who understood hawking well and did some things to perfection. Drawing a bow of 30 to 40 *bātmāns* strength,[1091] he would make his shaft pass right through the target (*takhta*). In the gallop from the head of the *qabaq-maidān*,[1092] he would loosen his bow, string it again, and then hit the gourd (*qabaq*). He would tie his string-grip (*zih-gīr*) to the one end of a string from 1 to 1-1/2 yards long, fasten the other end to a tree, let his shaft fly, and shoot through the string-grip while it revolved.[1093] Many such remarkable feats he did. He served the Mīrzā continuously and was at every social gathering.

Sl. Junaid *Barlās* was another;[1094] in his latter days he went to Sl. Aḥmad Mīrzā's presence.[1095] He is the father of the Sl. Junaid *Barlās* on whom at the present time[1096] the joint-government of Jaunpūr depends.

Shaikh Abū-sa'īd Khān *Dar-miyān* (In-between) was another. It is not known whether he got the name of Dar-miyān because he took a horse to the Mīrzā *in the middle* of a fight, or whether because he put himself *in between* the Mīrzā and some-one designing on his life.[1097]

Bih-būd Beg was another. He had served in the pages' circle (*chuhra jīrgasi*) during the guerilla times and gave suchFol. 174. satisfaction by his service that the Mīrzā did him the favour of putting his name on the stamp (*tamghā*) and the coin (*sikka*).[1098]

Shaikhīm Beg was another.[1099] People used to call him Shaikhīm *Suhailī* because Suhailī was his pen-name. He wrote all sorts of verse, bringing in terrifying words and mental images. Here is a couplet of his:—

In the anguish of my nights, the whirlpool of my sighs engulphs the firmament;

Like a dragon, the torrent of my tears swallows the quarters of the world.

Well-known it is that when he once recited that couplet in Maulānā 'Abdu'r-raḥmān *Jāmī's* presence, the honoured Mullā asked him whether he was reciting verse or frightening people. He put a *dīwān* together; *maṣnawīs* of his are also in existence.

Muḥammad-i-walī Beg was another, the son of the Walī Beg already mentioned. Latterly he became one of the Mīrzā's great begs but, great beg though he was, he never neglected his service and used to recline (*yāstānīb*) day and night in the Gate. Through doing this, his free meals and open table were always set just outside the Gate. Quite certainly a man who was so constantly in waiting, *would* receive the favour he received! It is an evil noticeable today that effort must be made before the man, dubbed Beg because he has five or six of the bald and blind at his back, can be got into the Gate at all! Where this sort of service is, it must be to their own misfortune! Muḥammad-i-walī Beg's public table and free meals were good; he kept his servants neat and well-dressed and with his own hands gaveFol. 174b. ample portion to the poor and destitute, but he was foul-mouthed and evil-spoken. He and also Darwīsh-i-'alī the librarian were in my service when I took Samarkand in 917 AH. (Oct. 1511 AD.); he was palsied then; his talk lacked salt; his former claim to favour was gone. His assiduous waiting appears to have been the cause of his promotion.

Bābā 'Alī the Lord of the Gate was another. First, 'Alī-sher Beg showed him favour; next, because of his courage, the Mīrzā took him into service, made him Lord of the Gate, and promoted him to be a beg. One of his sons is serving me now (*circa* 934 AH.), that Yūnas of 'Alī who is a beg, a confidant, and of my household. He will often be mentioned.[1100]

Badru'd-dīn (Full-moon of the Faith) was another. He had been in the service of Sl. Abū-sa'īd Mīrzā's Chief Justice Mīrak 'Abdu'r-raḥīm; it is said he was very nimble and sure-footed, a man who could leap over seven horses at once. He and Bābā 'Alī were close companions.

Ḥasan of 'Alī *Jalāīr* was another. His original name was Ḥusain *Jalāīr* but he came to be called 'Alī's Ḥasan.[1101] His father 'Alī *Jalāīr* must have been favoured and made a beg by Bābur Mīrzā; no man was greater later on when Yādgār-i-muḥammad M. took Herī. Ḥasan-i-'alī was Sl. Ḥusain Mīrzā's *Qūsh-begī*.[1102] He made Ṭufailī (Uninvited-guest) his pen-name; wrote good odes and was the Master of this art in his day. He wrote odes on my name when he came to my presence at the time I took Samarkand in 917 AH. (1511 AD.). Impudent (*bī bāk*) and Fol. 175.prodigal he was, a keeper of catamites, a constant dicer and draught-player.

Khwāja 'Abdu'l-lāh *Marwārīd* (Pearl)[1103] was another; he was at first Chief Justice but later on became one of the Mīrzā's favourite household-begs. He was full of accomplishments; on the dulcimer he had no equal, and he invented the shake on the dulcimer; he wrote in several scripts, most beautifully in the *ta'līq*; he composed admirable letters, wrote good verse, with Bayānī for his pen-name, and was a pleasant companion. Compared with his other accomplishments, his verse ranks low, but he knew what was poetry. Vicious and shameless, he became the captive of a sinful disease through his vicious excesses, outlived his hands and feet, tasted the agonies of varied torture for several years, and departed from the world under that affliction.[1104]

Sayyid Muḥammad-i-aūrūs was another; he was the son of that Aūrūs (Russian?) *Arghūn* who, when Sl. Abū-sa'īd Mīrzā took the throne, was his beg in chief authority. At that time there were excellent archer-braves; one of the most distinguished was Sayyid Muḥammad-i-aūrūs. His bow strong, his shaft long, he must have been a bold (*yūrak*) shot and a good one. He was Commandant in Andikhūd for some time.

Mīr (Qaṃbar-i-)'alī the Master of the Horse was another. He it was who, by sending a man to Sl. Ḥusain Mīrzā, brought him down on the defenceless Yādgār-i-muḥammad Mīrzā.

Sayyid Ḥasan *Aūghlāqchī* was another, a son of Sayyid *Aūghlāqchī* and a younger brother of Sayyid Yūsuf Beg.[1105] He was the father of a capable and accomplished son, named Mīrzā Farrukh. He had come to my presence before I took SamarkandFol. 175b. in 917 AH. (1511 AD.). Though he had written little verse, he wrote fairly; he understood the astrolabe and astronomy well, was excellent company, his talk good too, but he was rather a bad drinker (*bad shrāb*). He died in the fight at Ghaj-dawān.[1106]

Tīngrī-bīrdī the storekeeper (*sāmānchī*) was another; he was a plain (*turk*), bold, sword-slashing brave. As has been said, he charged out of the Gate of Balkh on Khusrau Shāh's great retainer Naẕar Bahādur and overcame him (903 AH.).

There were a few Turkmān braves also who were received with great favour when they came to the Mīrzā's presence. One of the first to come was 'Alī Khān *Bāyandar*.[1107] Asad Beg and Taham-tan (Strong-bodied) Beg were others, an elder and younger brother these; Badī'u'z-zamān Mīrzā took Taham-tan Beg's daughter and by her had Muḥammad-i-zamān Mīrzā. Mīr 'Umar Beg was another; later on he was in Badī'u'z-zamān Mīrzā's service; he was a brave, plain, excellent person. His son, Abū'l-fatḥ by name, came from 'Irāq to my presence, a very soft, unsteady and feeble person; such a son from such a father!

Of those who came into Khurāsān after Shāh Ismā'īl took 'Irāq and Aẕarbāījān (*circa* 906 AH.-1500 AD.), one was 'Abdu'l-bāqī Mīrzā of Tīmūr Beg's line. He was a Mīrān-shāhī[1108] whose ancestors will have gone long before into those parts, put thought Fol. 176.of sovereignty out of their heads, served those ruling there, and from them have received favour. That

Tīmūr 'Uṣmān who was the great, trusted beg of Ya'qūb Beg (*White-sheep Turkmān*) and who had once even thought of sending against Khurāsān the mass of men he had gathered to himself, must have been this 'Abdu'l-bāqī Mīrzā's paternal-uncle. Sl. Ḥusain Mīrzā took 'Abdu'l-bāqī Mīrzā at once into favour, making him a son-in-law by giving him Sulṭānīm Begīm, the mother of Muḥammad Sl. Mīrzā.[1109] Another late-comer was Murād Beg *Bāyandarī*.

(*h. His Chief Justices* (*ṣadūr*).)

One was Mīr Sar-i-barahna (Bare-head)[1110]; he was from a village in Andijān and appears to have made claim to be a sayyid (*mutasayyid*). He was a very agreeable companion, pleasant of temper and speech. His were the judgment and rulings that carried weight amongst men of letters and poets of Khurāsān. He wasted his time by composing, in imitation of the story of Amīr Ḥamza,[1111] a work which is one long, far-fetched lie, opposed to sense and nature.

Kamālu'd-dīn Ḥusain *Gāzur-gāhī*[1112] was another. Though not a Ṣūfī, he was mystical.[1113] Such mystics as he will have gathered in 'Alī-sher Beg's presence and there have gone into their raptures and ecstacies. Kamālu'd-dīn will have been better-born than most of them; his promotion will have been due to his good birth, since he had no other merit to speak of.[1114] A production of his exists, under the name *Majālisu'l-'ushshāq* (Assemblies of lovers), the authorship of which he ascribes (in its preface) to Sl. Ḥusain Mīrzā.[1115] It is mostly a lie and a tasteless lie. He has written such irreverent things in it that someFol. 176b. of them cast doubt upon his orthodoxy; for example, he represents the Prophets,—Peace be on them,—and Saints as subject to earthly passion, and gives to each a minion and a mistress. Another and singularly absurd thing is that, although in his preface he says, "This is Sl. Ḥusain Mīrzā's own written word and literary composition," he, never-the-less, enters, in the body of the book, "All by the sub-signed author", at the head of odes and verses well-known to be his own. It was his flattery gave Ẕū'n-nūn *Arghūn* the title Lion of God.

(*i. His wazīrs.*)

One was Majdu'd-dīn Muḥammad, son of Khwāja Pīr Aḥmad of Khwāf, the one man (*yak-qalam*) of Shāhrukh Mīrzā's Finance-office.[1116] In Sl. Ḥusain Mīrzā's Finance-office there was not at first proper order or method; waste and extravagance resulted; the peasant did not prosper, and the soldier was not satisfied. Once while Majdu'd-dīn Muḥammad was still *parwānchī*[1117] and styled Mīrak (Little Mīr), it became a matter of importance to the Mīrzā to have some money; when he asked the Finance-officials for it, they said none had been collected and that there was none. Majdu'd-dīn

Muḥammad must have heard this and have smiled, for the Mīrzā asked him why he smiled; privacy was made and he told Mīrzā what was in his mind. Said he, "If the honoured Mīrzā will pledge himself to strengthen Fol. 177.my hands by not opposing my orders, it shall so be before long that the country shall prosper, the peasant be content, the soldier well-off, and the Treasury full." The Mīrzā for his part gave the pledge desired, put Majdu'd-dīn Muḥammad in authority throughout Khurāsān, and entrusted all public business to him. He in his turn by using all possible diligence and effort, before long had made soldier and peasant grateful and content, filled the Treasury to abundance, and made the districts habitable and cultivated. He did all this however in face of opposition from the begs and men high in place, all being led by 'Alī-sher Beg, all out of temper with what Majdu'd-dīn Muḥammad had effected. By their effort and evil suggestion he was arrested and dismissed.[1118] In succession to him Niẓāmu'l-mulk of Khwāf was made Dīwān but in a short time they got him arrested also, and him they got put to death.[1119] They then brought Khwāja Afẓal out of 'Irāq and made him Dīwān; he had just been made a beg when I came to Kābul (910 AH.), and he also impressed the Seal in Dīwān.

Khwāja 'Atā[1120] was another; although, unlike those already mentioned, he was not in high office or Finance-minister (*dīwān*), nothing was settled without his concurrence the whole Khura-sānāt over. He was a pious, praying, upright (*mutadaiyin*) person; he must have been diligent in business also.

(*j. Others of the Court.*)

Those enumerated were Sl. Ḥusain Mīrzā's retainers and followers.[1121] His was a wonderful Age; in it Khurāsān, andFol. 177b. Herī above all, was full of learned and matchless men. Whatever the work a man took up, he aimed and aspired at bringing that work to perfection. One such man was Maulānā 'Abdu'r-raḥmān *Jāmī*, who was unrivalled in his day for esoteric and exoteric knowledge. Famous indeed are his poems! The Mullā's dignity it is out of my power to describe; it has occurred to me merely to mention his honoured name and one atom of his excellence, as a benediction and good omen for this part of my humble book.

Shaikhu'l-islām Saifu'd-dīn Aḥmad was another. He was of the line of that Mullā Sa'du'd-dīn (Mas'ūd) *Taftazānī*[1122] whose descendants from his time downwards have given the Shaikhu'l-islām to Khurāsān. He was a very learned man, admirably versed in the Arabian sciences[1123] and the Traditions, most God-fearing and orthodox. Himself a Shafi'ī,[1124] he was tolerant of all the sects. People say he never once in 70 years omitted the

Congregational Prayer. He was martyred when Shāh Ismā'īl took Herī (916 AH.); there now remains no man of his honoured line.[1125]

Maulānā Shaikh Ḥusain was another; he is mentioned here, although his first appearance and his promotion were under Sl. Abū-sa'īd Mīrzā, because he was living still under Sl. ḤusainFol. 178. Mīrzā. Being well-versed in the sciences of philosophy, logic and rhetoric, he was able to find much meaning in a few words and to bring it out opportunely in conversation. Being very intimate and influential with Sl. Abū-sa'īd Mīrzā, he took part in all momentous affairs of the Mīrzā's dominions; there was no better *muḥtasib*[1126]; this will have been why he was so much trusted. Because he had been an intimate of that Mīrzā, the incomparable man was treated with insult in Sl. Ḥusain Mīrzā's time.

Mullā-zāda Mullā 'Uṣ̤mān was another. He was a native of Chīrkh, in the Luhūgur *tūmān* of the *tūmān* of Kābul[1127] and was called the Born Mullā (*Mullā-ẓāda*) because in Aūlūgh Beg Mīrzā's time he used to give lessons when 14 years old. He went to Herī on his way from Samarkand to make the circuit of the *ka'ba*, was there stopped, and made to remain by Sl. Ḥusain Mīrzā. He was very learned, the most so of his time. People say he was nearing the rank of Ijtihād[1128] but he did not reach it. It is said of him that he once asked, "How should a person forget a thing heard?" A strong memory he must have had!

Mīr Jamālu'd-dīn the Traditionalist[1129] was another. He had no equal in Khurāsān for knowledge of the Muḥammadan Traditions. He was advanced in years and is still alive (934 to 937 AH.).

Mīr Murtāẓ was another. He was well-versed in the sciences Fol. 178b.of philosophy and metaphysics; he was called *murtāẓ* (ascetic) because he fasted a great deal. He was madly fond of chess, so much so that if he had met two players, he would hold one by the skirt while he played his game out with the other, as much as to say, "Don't go!"

Mīr Mas'ūd of Sherwān was another.[1130]

Mīr 'Abdu'l-ghafūr of Lār was another. Disciple and pupil both of Maulānā 'Abdu'r-raḥmān *Jāmī*, he had read aloud most of the Mullā's poems (*maṣ̤nawī*) in his presence, and wrote a plain exposition of the *Nafaḥāt.*[1131] He had good acquaintance with the exoteric sciences, and in the esoteric ones also was very successful. He was a curiously casual and unceremonious person; no person styled Mullā by any-one soever was debarred from submitting a (Qorān) chapter to him for exposition; moreover whatever the place in which he heard there was a darwīsh, he had no rest till he had reached that darwīsh's presence. He was ill when I was in Khurāsān (912 AH.); I went to enquire for him where he lay in the Mullā's

College,[1132] after I had made the circuit of the Mullā's tomb. He died a few days later, of that same illness.

Mīr 'Atā'u'l-lāh of Mashhad was another.[1133] He knew the Arabian sciences well and also wrote a Persian treatise on rhyme. That treatise is well-done but it has the defect that he brings into it, as his examples, couplets of his own and, assuming themFol. 179. to be correct, prefixes to each, "As must be observed in the following couplet by your slave" (*banda*). Several rivals of his find deserved comment in this treatise. He wrote another on the curiosities of verse, entitled *Badāi'u's-sanāi*; a very well-written treatise. He may have swerved from the Faith.

Qāẓī Ikhtiyār was another. He was an excellent Qāẓī and wrote a treatise in Persian on Jurisprudence, an admirable treatise; he also, in order to give elucidation (*iqtibās*), made a collection of homonymous verses from the Qorān. He came with Muḥammad-i-yūsuf to see me at the time I met the Mīrzās on the Murgh-āb (912 AH.). Talk turning on the Bāburī script,[1134] he asked me about it, letter by letter; I wrote it out, letter by letter; he went through it, letter by letter, and having learned its plan, wrote something in it there and then.

Mīr Muḥammad-i-yūsuf was another; he was a pupil of the Shaikhu'l-islām[1135] and afterwards was advanced to his place. In some assemblies he, in others, Qāẓī Ikhtiyār took the higher place. Towards the end of his life he was so infatuated with soldiering and military command, that except of those two tasks, what could be learned from his conversation? what known from his pen? Though he failed in both, those two ambitions ended by giving to the winds his goods and his life, his house and his home. He may have been a Shī'a.

(*k. The Poets.*)

Fol. 179b.The all-surpassing head of the poet-band was Maulānā 'Abdu'r-raḥmān *Jāmī.* Others were Shaikhīm Suhailī and Ḥasan of 'Alī *Jalāīr*[1136] whose names have been mentioned already as in the circle of the Mīrzā's begs and household.

Āṣafī was another,[1137] he taking Āṣafī for his pen-name because he was a wazīr's son. His verse does not want for grace or sentiment, but has no merit through passion and ecstacy. He himself made the claim, "I have never packed up (*būlmādī*) my odes to make the oasis (*wādī*) of a collection."[1138] This was affectation, his younger brothers and his intimates having collected his odes. He wrote little else but odes. He waited on me when I went into Khurāsān (912 AH.).

Banā'i was another; he was a native of Herī and took such a pen-name (Banā'i) on account of his father Ustād Muḥammad *Sabz-banā.*[1139] His odes have grace and ecstacy. One poem (*maṣnawī*) of his on the topic of fruits, is in the *mutaqārib*measure;[1140] it is random and not worked up. Another short poem is in the *khafīf* measure, so also is a longer one finished towards the end of his life. He will have known nothing of music in his young days and 'Alī-sher Beg seems to have taunted him about it, so one winter when the Mīrzā, taking 'Alī-sher Beg with him, went to winter in Merv, Banā'i stayed behind in Herī and so applied himself to study music that before the heats he had composed several works. These he played and sang, airs with variations, when the Mīrzā came back to Herī in the heats.Fol. 180. All amazed, 'Alī-sher Beg praised him. His musical compositions are perfect; one was an air known as *Nuh-rang* (Nine modulations), and having both the theme (*tūkānash*) and the variation (*yīla*) on the note called *rāst*(?). Banā'i was 'Alī-sher Beg's rival; it will have been on this account he was so much ill-treated. When at last he could bear it no longer, he went into Aẕarbāījān and 'Irāq to the presence of Ya'qūb Beg; he did not remain however in those parts after Ya'qūb Beg's death (896 AH.-1491 AD.) but went back to Herī, just the same with his jokes and retorts. Here is one of them:—'Alī-sher at a chess-party in stretching his leg touched Banā'i on the hinder-parts and said jestingly, "It is the sad nuisance of Herī that a man can't stretch his leg without its touching a poet's backside." "Nor draw it up again," retorted Banā'i.[1141] In the end the upshot of his jesting was that he had to leave Herī again; he went then to Samarkand.[1142] A great many good new things used to be made for 'Alī-sher Beg, so whenever any-one produced a novelty, he called it 'Alī-sher's in order to give it credit and vogue.[1143] Some things were called after him in compliment *e.g.* because when he had ear-ache, he wrapped his head up in one of the blue triangular kerchiefs women tie over their heads in winter, that kerchief was called 'Alī-sher's comforter. Then again, Banā'i when he had decided to leave Herī, ordered a quite new kind of pad for his ass andFol. 180b. dubbed it 'Alī-sher's.

Maulānā Saifī of Bukhārā was another;[1144] he was a Mullā complete[1145] who in proof of his mullā-ship used to give a list of the books he had read. He put two *dīwāns* together, one being for the use of tradesmen (*ḥarfa-kar*), and he also wrote many fables. That he wrote no *maṣnawī* is shewn by the following quatrain:—

Though the *maṣnawī* be the orthodox verse,

I know the ode has Divine command;

Five couplets that charm the heart

I know to outmatch the Two Quintets.[1146]

A Persian prosody he wrote is at once brief and prolix, brief in the sense of omitting things that should be included, and prolix in the sense that plain and simple matters are detailed down to the diacritical points, down even to their Arabic points.[1147] He is said to have been a great drinker, a bad drinker, and a mightily strong-fisted man.

'Abdu'l-lāh the *maṣnawī*-writer was another.[1148] He was from Jām and was the Mullā's sister's son. Hātifī was his pen-name. He wrote poems (*maṣnawī*) in emulation of the Two Quintets,[1149] and called them *Haft-manẕar* (Seven-faces) in imitation of the *Haft-paikar* (Seven-faces). In emulation of the *Sikandar-nāma* he composed the *Tīmūr-nāma*. His most renowned *maṣnawī* is *Laila and Majnūn*, but its reputation is greater than its charm.

Mīr Ḥusain the Enigmatist[1150] was another. He seems to have had no equal in making riddles, to have given his whole time to it, and to have been a curiously humble, disconsolate (*nā-murād*) Fol. 181.and harmless (*bī-bad*) person.

Mīr Muḥammad *Badakhshī* of Ishkīmīsh was another. As Ishkīmīsh is not in Badakhshān, it is odd he should have made it his pen-name. His verse does not rank with that of the poets previously mentioned,[1151] and though he wrote a treatise on riddles, his riddles are not first-rate. He was a very pleasant companion; he waited on me in Samarkand (917 AH.).

Yūsuf the wonderful (*badī*)[1152] was another. He was from the Farghāna country; his odes are said not to be bad.

Āhī was another, a good ode-writer, latterly in Ibn-i-ḥusain Mīrzā's service, and *ṣāḥib-i-dīwān*.[1153]

Muḥammad *Ṣāliḥ* was another.[1154] His odes are tasty but better-flavoured than correct. There is Turkī verse of his also, not badly written. He went to Shaibāq Khān later on and found complete favour. He wrote a Turkī poem (*maṣnawī*), named from Shaibāq Khān, in the *raml masaddas majnūn* measure, that is to say the metre of the *Subḥat.*[1155] It is feeble and flat; Muḥammad *Ṣāliḥ*'s reader soon ceases to believe in him.[1156] Here is one of his good couplets:—

A fat man (Taṃbal) has gained the land of Farghāna,

Making Farghāna the house of the fat-man (Taṃbal-khāna).

Farghāna is known also as Taṃbal-khāna.[1157] I do not know whether the above couplet is found in the *maṣnawī* mentioned.

Muḥammad *Ṣāliḥ* was a very wicked, tyrannical and heartless person.[1158]

Maulānā Shāh Ḥusain *Kāmī*[1159] was another. There are not-bad verses of his; he wrote odes, and also seems to have put a *dīwān* together.

Hilālī (New-moon) was another; he is still alive.[1160] Correct and graceful though his odes are, they make little impression. There is a *dīwān* of his;[1161] and there is also the poem (*maṣnawī*) in the Fol. 181b.*khafīf* measure, entitled *Shāh and Darwīsh* of which, fair though many couplets are, the basis and purport are hollow and bad. Ancient poets when writing of love and the lover, have represented the lover as a man and the beloved as a woman; but Hilālī has made the lover a darwīsh, the beloved a king, with the result that the couplets containing the king's acts and words, set him forth as shameless and abominable. It is an extreme effrontery in Hilālī that for a poem's sake he should describe a young man and that young man a king, as resembling the shameless and immoral.[1162] It is heard-said that Hilālī had a very retentive memory, and that he had by heart 30 or 40,000 couplets, and the greater part of the Two Quintets,—all most useful for the minutiae of prosody and the art of verse.

Ahlī[1163] was another; he was of the common people (*'āmī*), wrote verse not bad, even produced a *dīwān*.

(*l. Artists.*)

Of fine pen-men there were many; the one standing-out in *nakhsh ta'līq* was Sl. 'Alī of Mashhad[1164] who copied many books for the Mīrzā and for 'Alī-sher Beg, writing daily 30 couplets for the first, 20 for the second.

Of the painters, one was Bih-zād.[1165] His work was very dainty but he did not draw beardless faces well; he used greatly to lengthen the double chin (*ghab-ghab*); bearded faces he drew admirably.

Shāh Muẓaffar was another; he painted dainty portraits,Fol. 182. representing the hair very daintily.[1166] Short life was granted him; he left the world when on his upward way to fame.

Of musicians, as has been said, no-one played the dulcimer so well as Khwāja 'Abdu'l-lāh *Marwārīd.*

Qul-i-muḥammad the lutanist (*'aūdī*) was another; he also played the guitar (*ghichak*) beautifully and added three strings to it. For many and good preludes (*peshrau*) he had not his equal amongst composers or performers, but this is only true of his preludes.

Shaikhī the flautist (*nāyī*) was another; it is said he played also the lute and the guitar, and that he had played the flute from his 12th or 13th year. He once produced a wonderful air on the flute, at one of Badī'u'z-zamān Mīrzā's assemblies; Qul-i-muḥammad could not reproduce it on the guitar, so declared this a worthless instrument; Shaikhī *Nāyī* at once took the guitar from Qul-i-muḥammad's hands and played the air on it, well and in perfect tune. They say he was so expert in music that having once heard an air, he was able to say, "This or that is the tune of so-and-so's or so-and-so's flute."[1167] He composed few works; one or two airs are heard of.

Shāh Qulī the guitar-player was another; he was of 'Irāq, came into Khurāsān, practised playing, and succeeded. He composed many airs, preludes and works (*nakhsh, peshrau u aīshlār*).

Ḥusain the lutanist was another; he composed and played with taste; he would twist the strings of his lute into one and play on that. His fault was affectation about playing. He Fol. 182b.made a fuss once when Shaibāq Khān ordered him to play, and not only played badly but on a worthless instrument he had brought in place of his own. The Khān saw through him at once and ordered him to be well beaten on the neck, there and then. This was the one good action Shaibāq Khān did in the world; it was well-done truly! a worse chastisement is the due of such affected mannikins!

Ghulām-i-shādī (Slave of Festivity), the son of Shādī the reciter, was another of the musicians. Though he performed, he did it less well than those of the circle just described. There are excellent themes (*ṣūt*) and beautiful airs (*nakhsh*) of his; no-one in his day composed such airs and themes. In the end Shaibāq Khān sent him to the Qāzān Khān, Muḥammad Amīn; no further news has been heard of him.

Mīr Azū was another composer, not a performer; he produced few works but those few were in good taste.

Banā'i was also a musical composer; there are excellent airs and themes of his.

An unrivalled man was the wrestler Muḥammad Bū-sa'īd; he was foremost amongst the wrestlers, wrote verse too, composed themes and airs, one excellent air of his being in *chār-gāh* (four-time),—and he was pleasant company. It is extraordinary that such accomplishments as his should be combined with wrestling.[1168]

HISTORICAL NARRATIVE RESUMED.

(a. Burial of Sl. Ḥusain Mīrzā.)

At the time Sl. Ḥusain Mīrzā took his departure from the world, there were present of the Mīrzās only Badī'u'z-zamān Mīrzā and Muẕaffar-i-ḥusain Mīrzā. The latter had been his father's favourite son; his leading beg was Muḥammad Barandūq *Barlās*; his mother Khadīja Begīm had been the Mīrzā's most influential wife; and to him the Mīrzā's people had gathered.Fol. 183. For these reasons Badī'u'z-zamān Mīrzā had anxieties and thought of not coming,[1169] but Muẕaffar-i-ḥusain Mīrzā and Muḥammad Barandūq Beg themselves rode out, dispelled his fears and brought him in.

Sl. Ḥusain Mīrzā was carried into Herī and there buried in his own College with royal rites and ceremonies.

(*b. A dual succession.*)

At this crisis Ẕū'n-nūn Beg was also present. He, Muḥ. Barandūq Beg, the late Mīrzā's begs and those of the two (young) Mīrzās having assembled, decided to make the two Mīrzās joint-rulers in Herī. Ẕū'n-nūn Beg was to have control in Badī'u'z-zamān Mīrzā's Gate, Muḥ. Barandūq Beg, in Muẕaffar-i-ḥusain Mīrzā's. Shaikh 'Alī Ṯaghāī was to be *dārogha* in Herī for the first, Yūsuf-i-'alī for the second. Theirs was a strange plan! Partnership in rule is a thing unheard of; against it stand Shaikh Sa'dī's words in the Gulistān:—"Ten darwishes sleep under a blanket (*gilīm*); two kings find no room in a clime" (*aqlīm*).[1170]

912 AH.-MAY 24TH 1506 TO MAY 13TH 1507 AD.[1171]

(*a. Bābur starts to join Sl. Ḥusain Mīrzā.*)

In the month of Muḥarram we set out by way of Ghūr-bund Fol. 183b.and Shibr-tū to oppose the Aūzbeg.

As Jahāngīr Mīrzā had gone out of the country in some sort of displeasure, we said, "There might come much mischief and trouble if he drew the clans (*aīmāq*) to himself;" and "What trouble might come of it!" and, "First let's get the clans in hand!" So said, we hurried forward, riding light and leaving the baggage (*aūrūq*) at Ushtur-shahr in charge of Walī the treasurer and Daulat-qadam of the scouts. That day we reached Fort Ẓaḥāq; from there we crossed the pass of the Little-dome (Guṃbazak-kūtal), trampled through Sāīghān, went over the Dandān-shikan pass and dismounted in the meadow of Kāhmard. From Kāhmard we sent Sayyid Afẓal the Seer-of-dreams (*Khwāb-bīn*) and Sl. Muḥammad *Dūldāī* to Sl. Ḥusain Mīrzā with a letter giving the particulars of our start from Kābul.[1172]

Jahāngīr Mīrzā must have lagged on the road, for when he got opposite Bāmīān and went with 20 or 30 persons to visit it, he saw near it the tents of our people left with the baggage. Thinking we were there, he and his party hurried back to their camp and, without an eye to anything, without regard for their own people marching in the rear, made off for Yaka-aūlāng.[1173]

(*b. Action of Shaibāq Khān.*)

When Shaibāq Khān had laid siege to Balkh, in which was Sl. Qul-i-nachāq,[1174] he sent two or three sulṭāns with 3 or 4000 men to overrun Badakhshān. At the time Mubārak Shāh and Zubair had again joined Nāṣir Mīrzā, spite of former resentments and bickerings, and they all were lying at Shakdān, below KishmFol. 184. and east of the Kishm-water. Moving through the night, one body of Aūzbegs crossed that water at the top of the morning and advanced on the Mīrzā; he at once drew off to rising-ground, mustered his force, sounded trumpets, met and overcame them. Behind the Aūzbegs was the Kishm-water in flood, many were drowned in it, a mass of them died by arrow and sword, more were made prisoner. Another body of Aūzbegs, sent against Mubārak Shāh and Zubair where they lay, higher up the water and nearer Kishm, made them retire to the rising-ground. Of this the Mīrzā heard; when he had beaten off his own assailants, he moved against theirs. So did the Kohistān begs, gathered with horse and foot, still higher up the river. Unable to make stand against this attack, the Aūzbegs fled, but of this body also a mass died by sword, arrow, and water. In all some 1000 to 1500 may have died. This was Nāṣir Mīrzā's one good success; a man of his brought us news about it while we were in the dale of Kāhmard.

(*c. Bābur moves on into Khurāsān.*)

While we were in Kāhmard, our army fetched corn from Ghūrī and Dahāna. There too we had letters from SayyidFol. 184b. Afẓal and Sl. Muḥammad *Dūldāī* whom we had sent into Khurāsān; their news was of Sl. Ḥusain Mīrzā's death.

This news notwithstanding, we set forward for Khurāsān; though there were other grounds for doing this, what decided us was anxious thought for the reputation of this (Tīmūrid) dynasty. We went up the trough (*aīchī*) of the Ājar-valley, on over Tūp and Mandaghān, crossed the Balkh-water and came out on Ṣāf-hill. Hearing there that Aūzbegs were overrunning Sān and Chār-yak,[1175] we sent a force under Qāsim Beg against them; he got up with them, beat them well, cut many heads off, and returned.

We lay a few days in the meadow of Ṣāf-hill, waiting for news of Jahāngīr Mīrzā and the clans (*aīmāq*) to whom persons had been sent. We hunted once, those hills being very full of wild sheep and goats (*kiyīk*). All the clans came in and waited on me within a few days; it was to me they came; they had not gone to Jahāngīr Mīrzā though he had sent men often enough to them, once sending even 'Imādu'd-dīn Mas'ūd. He himself was forced to come at last; he saw me at the foot of the valley when I came down off Ṣāf-hill. Being anxious about Khurāsān, we neither paid him attention nor took thought for the clans, but went right on through Gurzwān, Almār, Qaiṣār, Chīchīk-tū, and Fakhru'd-dīn's-death (*aūlūm*) into the Bām-valley, Fol. 185.one of the dependencies of Bādghīs.

The world being full of divisions,[1176] things were being taken from country and people with the long arm; we ourselves began to take something, by laying an impost on the Turks and clans of those parts, in two or three months taking perhaps 300 *tūmāns* of *kipkī*.[1177]

(*d. Coalition of the Khurāsān Mīrzās.*)

A few days before our arrival (in Bām-valley?) some of the Khurāsān light troops and of Ẕū'n-nūn Beg's men had well beaten Aūzbeg raiders in Pand-dih (Panj-dih?) and Marūchāq, killing a mass of men.[1178]

Badī'u'z-zamān Mīrzā and Muẓaffar-i-ḥusain Mīrzā with Muḥammad Barandūq *Barlās*, Ẕū'n-nūn *Arghūn* and his son Shāh Beg resolved to move on Shaibāq Khān, then besieging Sl. Qul-i-nachāq (?) in Balkh. Accordingly they summoned all Sl. Ḥusain Mīrzā's sons, and got out of Herī to effect their purpose. At Chihil-dukhtarān Abū'l-muḥsin M. joined them from Marv; Ibn-i-ḥusain M. followed, coming up from Tūn and Qāīn. Kūpuk (Kīpik) M. was in Mashhad; often though they sent to him, he behaved unmanly, spoke senseless words, and did not come. Between him and Muẕaffar Mīrzā, there was jealousy; when Muẕaffar M. was made (joint-)ruler, he said, "How should *I* go to *his* presence?" Through this disgusting jealousy he did not come now, even at this crisis when all his brethren, older and younger, were assembling in concord, resolute against such a foeFol. 185b. as Shaibāq Khān. Kūpuk M. laid his own absence to rivalry, but everybody else laid it to his cowardice. One word! In this world acts such as his outlive the man; if a man have any share of intelligence, why try to be ill-spoken of after death? if he be ambitious, why not try so to act that, he gone, men will praise him? In the honourable mention of their names, wise men find a second life!

Envoys from the Mīrzās came to me also, Mūh. Barandūq *Barlās* himself following them. As for me, what was to hinder my going? It was for that very purpose I had travelled one or two hundred *yīghāch* (500-600 miles)! I at once started with Muḥ. Barandūq Beg for Murgh-āb[1179] where the Mīrzās were lying.

(*e. Bābur meets the Mīrẕās.*)

The meeting with the Mīrzās was on Monday the 8th of the latter Jumāda (Oct. 26th 1506 AH.). Abū'l-muḥsin Mīrzā came out a mile to meet me; we approached one another; on my side, I dismounted, on his side, he; we advanced, saw one another and remounted. Near the camp Muẕaffar Mīrzā and Ibn-i-ḥusain Mīrzā met us; they, being younger than Abū'l-muḥsin Mīrzā ought to have come out further than he to meet me.[1180] Their dilatoriness may not have been due to pride, but to heavinessFol. 186. after wine; their negligence may have been no slight on me, but due to their own social pleasures. On this Muẕaffar Mīrzā laid stress;[1181] we two saw one another without dismounting, so did Ibn-i-ḥusain Mīrzā and I. We rode on together and, in an amazing crowd and press, dismounted at Badī'u'z-zamān Mīrzā's Gate. Such was the throng that some were lifted off the ground for three or four steps together, while others, wishing for some reason to get out, were carried, willy-nilly, four or five steps the other way.

We reached Badī'u'z-zamān Mīrzā's Audience-tent. It had been agreed that I, on entering, should bend the knee (*yūkūnghāī*) once, that the Mīrzā should rise and advance to the edge of the estrade,[1182] and that we should see one another there. I went in, bent the knee once, and was going right forward;

the Mīrzā rose rather languidly and advanced rather slowly; Qāsim Beg, as he was my well-wisher and held my reputation as his own, gave my girdle a tug; I understood, moved more slowly, and so the meeting was on the appointed spot.

Four divans (*tūshuk*) had been placed in the tent. Always in the Mīrzā's tents one side was like a gate-way[1183] and at the edge of this gate-way he always sat. A divan was set there now Fol. 186b.on which he and Muẓaffar Mīrzā sat together. Abū'l-muḥsin, Mīrzā and I sat on another, set in the right-hand place of honour (*tūr*). On another, to Badī'u'z-zamān Mīrzā's left, sat Ibn-i-ḥusain Mīrzā with Qāsim Sl. *Aūzbeg*, a son-in-law of the late Mīrzā and father of Qāsim-i-ḥusain Sulṭān. To my right and below my divan was one on which sat Jahāngīr Mīrzā and 'Abdu'r-razzāq Mīrzā. To the left of Qāsim Sl. and Ibn-i-ḥusain Mīrzā, but a good deal lower, were Muḥ. Barandūq Beg, Ẕū'n-nūn Beg and Qāsim Beg.

Although this was not a social gathering, cooked viands were brought in, drinkables[1184] were set with the food, and near them gold and silver cups. Our forefathers through a long space of time, had respected the Chīngīz-tūrā (ordinance), doing nothing opposed to it, whether in assembly or Court, in sittings-down or risings-up. Though it has not Divine authority so that a man obeys it of necessity, still good rules of conduct must be obeyed by whom-soever they are left; just in the same way that, if a forefather have done ill, his ill must be changed for good.

After the meal I rode from the Mīrzā's camp some 2 miles toFol. 187. our own dismounting-place.

(*f. Bābur claims due respect.*)

At my second visit Badī'u'z-zamān Mīrzā shewed me less respect than at my first. I therefore had it said to Muḥ. Barandūq Beg and to Ẕū'n-nūn Beg that, small though my age was (*aet.* 24), my place of honour was large; that I had seated myself twice on the throne of our forefathers in Samarkand by blow straight-dealt; and that to be laggard in shewing me respect was unreasonable, since it was for this (Tīmūrid) dynasty's sake I had thus fought and striven with that alien foe. This said, and as it was reasonable, they admitted their mistake at once and shewed the respect claimed.

(*g. Bābur's temperance.*)

There was a wine-party (*chāghīr-majlisi*) once when I went after the Mid-day Prayer to Badī'u'z-zamān Mīrzā's presence. At that time I drank no wine. The party was altogether elegant; every sort of relish to wine (*gazak*) was set out on the napery, with brochettes of fowl and goose, and all sorts of viands. The Mīrzā's entertainments were much renowned; truly was this one free from the pang of thirst (*bī ghall*), reposeful and tranquil. I was at two or three of his wine-parties while we were on the bank of the Murgh-āb; once it was known I did not drink, no pressure to do so was put on me.

I went to one wine-party of Muẓaffar Mīrzā's. Ḥusain of 'Alī *Jalāīr* and Mīr Badr were both there, they being in his service. When Mīr Badr had had enough (*kaifīyat*), he danced,Fol. 187b. and danced well what seemed to be his own invention.

(*h. Comments on the Mīrzās.*)

Three months it took the Mīrzās to get out of Herī, agree amongst themselves, collect troops, and reach Murgh-āb. Meantime Sl. Qul-i-nachāq (?), reduced to extremity, had surrendered Balkh to the Aūzbeg but that Aūzbeg, hearing of our alliance against him, had hurried back to Samarkand. The Mīrzās were good enough as company and in social matters, in conversation and parties, but they were strangers to war, strategy, equipment, bold fight and encounter.

(*i. Winter plans.*)

While we were on the Murgh-āb, news came that Ḥaq-naẓīr *Chapā* (var. Ḥiān) was over-running the neighbourhood of Chīchīk-tū with 4 or 500 men. All the Mīrzās there present, do what they would, could not manage to send a light troop against those raiders! It is 10 *yīghāch* (50-55 m.) from Murgh-āb to Chīchīk-tū. I asked the work; they, with a thought for their own reputation, would not give it to me.

The year being almost at an end when Shaibāq Khān retired, the Mīrzās decided to winter where it was convenient and to reassemble next summer in order to repel their foe.

They pressed me to winter in Khurāsān, but this not one of my well-wishers saw it good for me to do because, while Kābul and Ghaznī were full of a turbulent and ill-conducted medley of Fol. 188.people and hordes, Turks, Mughūls, clans and nomads (*aīmāq u aḥsham*), Afghāns and Hazāra, the roads between us and that not yet desirably subjected country of Kābul were, one, the mountain-road, a month's journey even without delay through snow or other cause,—the other, the low-country road, a journey of 40 or 50 days.

Consequently we excused ourselves to the Mīrzās, but they would accept no excuse and, for all our pleas, only urged the more. In the end Badī'u'z-zamān Mīrzā, Abū'l-muḥsin Mīrzā and Muẓaffar Mīrzā themselves rode to my tent and urged me to stay the winter. It was impossible to refuse men of such ruling position, come in person to press us to stay on. Besides this, the whole habitable world has not such a town as Herī had become under Sl.

Ḥusain Mīrzā, whose orders and efforts had increased its splendour and beauty as ten to one, rather, as twenty to one. As I greatly wished to stay, I consented to do so.

Abū'l-muḥsin M. went to Marv, his own district; Ibn-i-ḥusain M. went to his, Tūn and Qāīn; Badī'u'z-zamān M. and Muẓaffar M. set off for Herī; I followed them a few days later, taking the road by Chihil-dukhtarān and Tāsh-rabāṭ.[1185]

(j. Bābur visits the Begīms in Herī.)

All the Begīms, *i.e.* my paternal-aunt Pāyanda-sulṭān Begīm, Khadīja Begīm, Apāq Begīm, and my other paternal-aunt Begīms, daughters of Sl. Abū-sa'īd Mīrzā,[1186] were gathered together, at the time I went to see them, in Sl. Ḥusain Mīrzā's College at hisFol. 188b. Mausoleum. Having bent the knee with *(yūkūnūb bīla)* Pāyanda-sulṭān Begīm first of all, I had an interview with her; next, not bending the knee,[1187] I had an interview with Apāq Begīm; next, having bent the knee with Khadīja Begīm, I had an interview with her. After sitting there for some time during recitation of the Qorān,[1188] we went to the South College where Khadīja Begīm's tents had been set up and where food was placed before us. After partaking of this, we went to Pāyanda-sulṭān Begīm's tents and there spent the night.

The New-year's Garden was given us first for a camping-ground; there our camp was arranged; and there I spent the night of the day following my visit to the Begīms, but as I did not find it a convenient place, 'Alī-sher Beg's residence was assigned to me, where I was as long as I stayed in Herī, every few days shewing myself in Badī'u'z-zamān Mīrzā's presence in the World-adorning Garden.

(k. The Mīrzās entertain Bābur in Herī.)

A few days after Muẓaffar Mīrzā had settled down in the White-garden, he invited me to his quarters; Khadīja Begīm was also there, and with me went Jahāngīr Mīrzā. When we had eaten a meal in the Begīm's presence,[1189] Muẓaffar Mīrzā took me to where there was a wine-party, in the Ṭarab-khāna (Joy-house) built by Bābur Mīrzā, a sweet little abode, a smallish, two-storeyed house in the middle of a smallish garden. Great pains have been taken with its upper storey; this has a retreat *(ḥujra)* in each of its four corners, the space between each two retreats being like a *shāh-nīshīn*[1190]; in between these retreats and Fol. 189.*shāh-nīshīns* is one large room on all sides of which are pictures which, although Bābur Mīrzā built the house, were commanded by Abū-sa'īd Mīrzā and depict his own wars and encounters.

Two divans had been set in the north *shāh-nīshīn*, facing each other, and with their sides turned to the north. On one Muẓaffar Mīrzā and I sat, on the other Sl. Mas'ūd Mīrzā[1191] and Jahāngīr Mīrzā. We being guests, Muẓaffar Mīrzā gave me place above himself. The social cups were filled, the cup-bearers ordered to carry them to the guests; the guests drank down the mere wine as if it were water-of-life; when it mounted to their heads, the party waxed warm.

They thought to make me also drink and to draw me into their own circle. Though up till then I had not committed the sin of wine-drinking[1192] and known the cheering sensation of comfortable drunkenness, I was inclined to drink wine and my heart was drawn to cross that stream (*wāda*). I had had no inclination for wine in my childhood; I knew nothing of its cheer and pleasure. If, as sometimes, my father pressed wine on me, I excused myself; I did not commit the sin. After heFol. 189b. died, Khwāja Qāẓī's right guidance kept me guiltless; as at that time I abstained from forbidden viands, what room was there for the sin of wine? Later on when, with the young man's lusts and at the prompting of sensual passion, desire for wine arose, there was no-one to press it on me, no-one indeed aware of my leaning towards it; so that, inclined for it though my heart was, it was difficult of myself to do such a thing, one thitherto undone. It crossed my mind now, when the Mīrzās were so pressing and when too we were in a town so refined as Herī, "Where should I drink if not here? here where all the chattels and utensils of luxury and comfort are gathered and in use." So saying to myself, I resolved to drink wine; I determined to cross that stream; but it occurred to me that as I had not taken wine in Badī'u'z-zamān Mīrzā's house or from his hand, who was to me as an elder brother, things might find way into his mind if I took wine in his younger brother's house and from his hand. Having so said to myself, I mentioned my doubt and difficulty. Said they, "Both the excuse and the obstacle are reasonable," pressed me no more to drink then but settled that when I was in company with both Mīrzās, I should drink under the insistance of both.

Amongst the musicians present at this party were Ḥāfiẓ Ḥājī,Fol. 190. Jalālu'd-dīn Maḥmūd the flautist, and Ghulām *shādī*'s younger brother, Ghulām *bacha* the Jews'-harpist. Ḥāfiẓ Ḥājī sang well, as Herī people sing, quietly, delicately, and in tune. With Jahāngīr Mīrzā was a Samarkandī singer Mīr Jān whose singing was always loud, harsh and out-of-tune. The Mīrzā, having had enough, ordered him to sing; he did so, loudly, harshly and without taste. Khurāsānīs have quite refined manners; if, under this singing, one did stop his ears, the face of another put question, not one could stop the singer, out of consideration for the Mīrzā.

After the Evening Prayer we left the Ṭarab-khāna for a new house in Muẓaffar Mīrzā's winter-quarters. There Yūsuf-i-'alī danced in the drunken time, and being, as he was, a master in music, danced well. The party waxed very warm there. Muẓaffar Mīrzā gave me a sword-belt, a lambskin surtout, and a grey *tīpūchāq* (horse). Jānak recited in Turkī. Two slaves of the Mīrzā's, known as Big-moon and Little-moon, did offensive, drunken tricks in the drunken time. The party was warm till night when those assembled scattered, I, however, staying the night in that house.

Qāsim Beg getting to hear that I had been pressed to drink wine, sent some-one to Ẕū'n-nūn Beg with advice for him and for Muẓaffar Mīrzā, given in very plain words; the result was Fol. 190b.that the Mīrzās entirely ceased to press wine upon me.

Badī'u'z-zamān Mīrzā, hearing that Muẓaffar M. had entertained me, asked me to a party arranged in the Maqauwī-khāna of the World-adorning Garden. He asked also some of my close circle[1193] and some of our braves. Those about me could never drink (openly) on my own account; if they ever did drink, they did it perhaps once in 40 days, with doorstrap fast and under a hundred fears. Such as these were now invited; here too they drank with a hundred precautions, sometimes calling off my attention, sometimes making a screen of their hands, notwithstanding that I had given them permission to follow common custom, because this party was given by one standing to me as a father or elder brother. People brought in weeping-willows....[1194]

At this party they set a roast goose before me but as I was no carver or disjointer of birds, I left it alone. "Do you not like it?" inquired the Mīrzā. Said I, "I am a poor carver." On this he at once disjointed the bird and set it again before Fol. 191.me. In such matters he had no match. At the end of the party he gave me an enamelled waist-dagger, a *chār-qāb*,[1195] and a *tīpūchāq*.

(*l. Bābur sees the sights of Herī.*)

Every day of the time I was in Herī I rode out to see a new sight; my guide in these excursions was Yūsuf-i-'alī Kūkūldāsh; wherever we dismounted, he set food before me. Except Sl. Ḥusain Mīrzā's Almshouse, not one famous spot, maybe, was left unseen in those 40 days.

I saw the Gāzur-gāh,[1196] 'Alī-sher's Bāghcha (Little-garden), the Paper-mortars,[1197] Takht-astāna (Royal-residence), Pul-i-gāh, Kahad-stān,[1198] Naẓar-gāh-garden, Ni'matābād (Pleasure-place), Gāzur-gāh Avenue, Sl. Aḥmad Mīrzā's Ḥaẕirat,[1199] Takht-i-safar,[1200] Takht-i-nawā'ī, Takht-i-barkar, Takht-i-Ḥājī Beg, Takht-i-Bahā'u'd-dīn 'Umar, Takht-i-Shaikh Zainu'd-dīn, Maulānā 'Abdu'r-raḥmān *Jāmī*'s honoured shrine and tomb,[1201] Namāz-gāh-i-mukhtār,[1202] the Fish-pond,[1203] Sāq-i-sulaimān,[1204] Bulūrī (Crystal) which originally may have been Abū'l-walīd,[1205] Imām Fakhr,[1206] Avenue-garden, Mīrzā's Colleges and tomb, Guhār-shād Begīm's College, tomb,[1207] and Congregational Mosque, the Ravens'-garden,

New-garden, Zubaida-garden,[1208] Sl. Abū-sa'īd Mīrzā's White-house Fol. 191b.outside the 'Iraq-gate, Pūrān,[1209] the Archer's-seat, Chargh (hawk)-meadow, Amīr Wāḥid,[1210] Mālān-bridge,[1211] Khwāja-tāq,[1212] White-garden, Ṭarab-khāna, Bāgh-i-jahān-ārā, Kūshk,[1213] Maqauwī-khāna, Lily-house, Twelve-towers, the great tank to the north of Jahān-ārā and the four dwellings on its four sides, the five Fort-gates, *viz.* the Malik, 'Irāq, Fīrūzābād, Khūsh[1214] and Qībchāq Gates, Chārsū, Shaikhu'l-islām's College, Maliks' Congregational Mosque, Town-garden, Badī'u'z-zamān Mīrzā's College on the bank of the Anjīl-canal, 'Alī-sher Beg's dwellings where we resided and which people call Unsīya (Ease), his tomb and mosque which they call Qudsīya (Holy), his College and Almshouse which they call Khalāṣīya and Akhlāṣīya (Freedom and Sincerity), his Hot-bath and Hospital which they call Ṣafā'īya and Shafā'īya. All these I visited in that space of time.

(*m. Bābur engages Ma'ṣūma-sulṭān in marriage.*)

It must have been before those throneless times[1215] that Ḥabība-sulṭān Begīm, the mother of Sl. Aḥmad Mīrzā's youngest daughter Ma'ṣūma-sulṭān Begīm, brought her daughter into Herī. One day when I was visiting my Ākā, Ma'ṣūma-sulṭān Begīm came there with her mother and at once felt arise in her a great inclination towards me. Private messengers having been sent, my Ākā and my Yīnkā, as I used to call Pāyanda-sulṭān Begīm Fol. 192.and Habība-sulṭān Begīm, settled between them that the latter should bring her daughter after me to Kābul.[1216]

(*n. Bābur leaves Khurāsān.*)

Very pressingly had Muḥ. Barandūq Beg and Ẕū'n-nūn *Arghūn* said, "Winter here!" but they had given me no winter-quarters nor had they made any winter-arrangements for me. Winter came on; snow fell on the mountains between us and Kābul; anxiety grew about Kābul; no winter-quarters were offered, no arrangements made! As we could not speak out, of necessity we left Herī!

On the pretext of finding winter-quarters, we got out of the town on the 7th day of the month of Sha'bān (Dec. 24th 1506 AD.), and went to near

Bādghīs. Such were our slowness and our tarryings that the Ramẓān-moon was seen a few marches only beyond the Langar of Mīr Ghiyāṣ.[1217] Of our braves who were absent on various affairs, some joined us, some followed us into Kābul 20 days or a month later, some stayed in Herī and took service with the Mīrzās. One of these last was Sayyidīm 'Alī the gate-ward, who became Badī'u'z-zamān Mīrzā's retainer. To no servant of Khusrau Shāh had I shewn so much favour as to him; he had been given Ghaznī when Jahāngīr Mīrzā abandoned it, and in it when he came away with the army, had left his younger brother Dost-i-anjū (?) Shaikh. There were in truthFol. 192b. no better men amongst Khusrau Shāh's retainers than this man Sayyidīm 'Alī the gate-ward and Muḥibb-i-'alī the armourer. Sayyidīm was of excellent nature and manners, a bold swordsman, a singularly competent and methodical man. His house was never without company and assembly; he was greatly generous, had wit and charm, a variety of talk and story, and was a sweet-natured, good-humoured, ingenious, fun-loving person. His fault was that he practised vice and pederasty. He may have swerved from the Faith; may also have been a hypocrite in his dealings; some of what seemed double-dealing people attributed to his jokes, but, still, there must have been a something![1218] When Badī'u'z-zamān Mīrzā had let Shaibāq Khān take Herī and had gone to Shāh Beg (*Arghūn*), he had Sayyidīm 'Alī thrown into the Harmand because of his double-dealing words spoken between the Mīrzā and Shāh Beg. Muḥibb-i-'alī's story will come into the narrative of events hereafter to be written.

(*o. A perilous mountain-journey.*)

From the Langar of Mīr Ghiyāṣ we had ourselves guided past the border-villages of Gharjistān to Chach-charān.[1219] From the almshouse to Gharjistān was an unbroken sheet of snow; it was deeper further on; near Chach-charān itself it was above the horses' knees. Chach-charān depended on Ẕū'n-nūn *Arghūn*; his retainer Mīr Jān-aīrdī was in it now; from him we took, on payment, the whole of Ẕū'n-nūn Beg's store of provisions. A march or two further on, the snow was very deep, being above Fol. 193.the stirrup, indeed in many places the horses' feet did not touch the ground.

We had consulted at the Langar of Mīr Ghiyāṣ which road to take for return to Kābul; most of us agreed in saying, "It is winter, the mountain-road is difficult and dangerous; the Qandahār road, though a little longer, is safe and easy." Qāsim Beg said, "That road is long; you will go by this one." As he made much dispute, we took the mountain-road.

Our guide was a Pashāī named Pīr Sulṭān (Old sultan?). Whether it was through old age, whether from want of heart, whether because of the deep snow, he lost the road and could not guide us. As we were on this route under the insistance of Qāsim Beg, he and his sons, for his name's sake, dismounted, trampled the snow down, found the road again and took the lead. One day the snow was so deep and the way so uncertain that we could not go on; there being no help for it, back we turned, dismounted where there was fuel, picked out 60 or 70 good men and sent them down the valley in our tracks to fetch any one soever of the Hazāra, wintering in the valley-bottom, who might shew us the road. That place could not be left till our men returned three or four days later. They brought no Fol. 193b.guide; once more we sent Sulṭān *Pashāī* ahead and, putting our trust in God, again took the road by which we had come back from where it was lost. Much misery and hardship were endured in those few days, more than at any time of my life. In that stress I composed the following opening couplet:—

Is there one cruel turn of Fortune's wheel unseen of me?

Is there a pang, a grief my wounded heart has missed?

We went on for nearly a week, trampling down the snow and not getting forward more than two or three miles a day. I was one of the snow-stampers, with 10 or 15 of my household, Qāsim Beg, his sons Tīngrī-bīrdī and Qaṃbar-i-'alī and two or three of their retainers. These mentioned used to go forward for 7 or 8 yards, stamping the snow down and at each step sinking to the waist or the breast. After a few steps the leading man would stand still, exhausted by the labour, and another would go forward. By the time 10, 15, 20, men on foot had stamped the snow down, it became so that a horse might be led over it. A horse would be led, would sink to the stirrups, could do no more than 10 or 12 steps, and would be drawn aside to let another go on. After we, 10, 15, 20, men had stamped down the snow and had led horses forward in this fashion, very serviceableFol. 194. braves and men of renowned name would enter the beaten track, hanging their heads. It was not a time to urge or compel! the man with will and hardihood for such tasks does them by his own request! Stamping the snow down in this way, we got out of that afflicting place (*ānjūkān yīr*) in three or four days to a cave known as the Khawāl-i-qūtī (Blessed-cave), below the Zirrīn-pass.

That night the snow fell in such an amazing blizzard of cutting wind that every man feared for his life. The storm had become extremely violent by the time we reached the *khawāl*, as people in those parts call a mountain-cave (*ghar*) or hollow (*khāwāk*). We dismounted at its mouth. Deep snow! a one-man road! and even on that stamped-down and trampled road, pitfalls for horses! the days at their shortest! The first arrivals reached the cave by daylight; others kept coming in from the Evening Prayer till the Bed-time one; later than that people dismounted wherever they happened to be; dawn shot with many still in the saddle.

The cave seeming to be rather small, I took a shovel and shovelled out a place near its mouth, the size of a sitting-mat Fol. 194b.(*takiya-namad*), digging it out breast-high but even then not reaching the ground. This made me a little shelter from the wind when I sat right down in it. I did not go into the cave though people kept saying, "Come inside," because this was in my mind, "Some of my men in snow and storm, I in the comfort of a warm house! the whole horde (*aūlūs*) outside in misery and pain, I inside sleeping at ease! That would be far from a man's act, quite another matter than comradeship! Whatever hardship and wretchedness there is, I will face; what strong men stand, I will stand; for, as the Persian proverb says, to die with friends is a nuptial." Till the Bed-time Prayer I sat through that blizzard of snow and wind in the dug-out, the snow-fall being such that my head, back, and ears were overlaid four hands thick. The cold of that night affected my ears. At the Bed-time Prayer some-one, looking more carefully at the cave, shouted out, "It is a very roomy cave with place for every-body." On hearing this I shook off my roofing of snow and, asking the braves near to come also, went inside. There was room for 50 or 60! People brought out their rations, cold meat, parched grain, whatever they had. From such cold and tumult to a place so warm, cosy and quiet![1220]

Next day the snow and wind having ceased, we made an early start and we got to the pass by again stamping down Fol. 195.a road in the snow. The proper road seems to make a détour up the flank of the mountain and to go over higher up, by what is understood to be called the Zirrīn-pass. Instead of taking that road, we went straight up the valley-bottom (*qūl*).[1221] It was night before we reached the further side of the (Bakkak-)pass; we spent the night there in the mouth of the valley, a night of mighty cold, got through with great distress and suffering. Many a man had his hands and feet frost-bitten; that night's cold took both Kīpa's feet, both Sīūndūk *Turkmān*'s hands, both Āhī's feet. Early next morning we moved down the valley; putting our trust in God, we went straight down, by bad slopes and sudden falls, knowing and seeing it could not be the right way. It was the Evening Prayer when we got out of that valley. No long-memoried old man knew that any-one had been heard of as crossing that pass with the snow so deep, or indeed that it had ever entered the heart of man to cross it at that time of year. Though for a few days we had suffered greatly through the depth of the snow, yet its depth, in the end, enabled us to reach our destination. For why? How otherwise should we have traversed those pathless slopes and sudden falls?Fol. 195b.

All ill, all good in the count, is gain if looked at aright!

The Yaka-aūlāng people at once heard of our arrival and our dismounting; followed, warm houses, fat sheep, grass and horse-corn, water without stint, ample wood and dried dung for fires! To escape from such snow and cold to such a village, to such warm dwellings, was comfort those will understand who have had our trials, relief known to those who have felt our hardships. We tarried one day in Yaka-aūlāng, happy-of-heart and easy-of-mind; marched 2 *yīghāch* (10-12 m.) next day and dismounted. The day following was the Ramẓān Feast[1222]; we went on through Bāmīān, crossed by Shibr-tū and dismounted before reaching Janglīk.

(p. Second raid on the Turkmān Hazāras.)

The Turkmān Hazāras with their wives and little children must have made their winter-quarters just upon our road[1223]; they had no word about us; when we got in amongst their cattle-pens and tents (*alāchūq*) two or three groups of these went to ruin and plunder, the people themselves drawing off with their little children and abandoning houses and goods. News wasFol. 196. brought from ahead that, at a place where there were narrows, a body of Hazāras was shooting arrows, holding up part of the army, and letting no-one pass. We, hurrying on, arrived to find no narrows at all; a few Hazāras were shooting from a naze, standing in a body on the hill[1224] like very good soldiers.[1225]

They saw the blackness of the foe;

Stood idle-handed and amazed;

I arriving, went swift that way,

Pressed on with shout, "Move on! move on!"

I wanted to hurry my men on,

To make them stand up to the foe.

With a "Hurry up!" to my men,

I went on to the front.

Not a man gave ear to my words.

I had no armour nor horse-mail nor arms,

I had but my arrows and quiver.

I went, the rest, maybe all of them, stood,

Stood still as if slain by the foe!

Your servant you take that you may have use

Of his arms, of his life, the whole time;

Not that the servant stand still
While the beg makes advance to the front;
Not that the servant take rest
While his beg is making the rounds.
From no such a servant will come
Speed, or use in your Gate, or zest for your food.
At last I charged forward myself,
Fol. 196b.Herding the foe up the hill;
Seeing me go, my men also moved,
Leaving their terrors behind.
With me they swift spread over the slope,
Moving on without heed to the shaft;
Sometimes on foot, mounted sometimes,
Boldly we ever moved on,
Still from the hill poured the shafts.
Our strength seen, the foe took to flight.
We got out on the hill; we drove the Hazāras,
Drove them like deer by valley and ridge;
We shot those wretches like deer;
We shared out the booty in goods and in sheep;
The Turkmān Hazāras' kinsfolk we took;
We made captive their people of sorts (*qarā*);
We laid hands on their men of renown;
Their wives and their children we took.

I myself collected a few of the Hazāras' sheep, gave them into Yārak Ṭaghāī's charge, and went to the front. By ridge and valley, driving horses and sheep before us, we went to Tīmūr Beg's Langar and there dismounted. Fourteen or fifteen Hazāra thieves had fallen into our hands; I had thought of having them put to death when we next dismounted, with various torture, as a warning to all highwaymen and robbers, but Qāsim Beg came across them on the road and, with mistimedFol. 197. compassion, set them free.

To do good to the bad is one and the same

As the doing of ill to the good;

On brackish soil no spikenard grows,

Waste no seed of toil upon it.[1226]

Out of compassion the rest of the prisoners were released also.

(j. Disloyalty in Kābul.)

News came while we were raiding the Turkmān Hazāras, that Muḥammad Ḥusain Mīrzā *Dūghlāt* and Sl. Sanjar *Barlās* had drawn over to themselves the Mughūls left in Kābul, declared Mīrzā Khān (Wais) supreme (*pādshāh*), laid siege to the fort and spread a *report* that Badī'u'z-zamān Mīrzā and Muẓaffar Mīrzā had sent me, a prisoner, to Fort Ikhtiyāru'd-dīn, now known as Ālā-qūrghān.

In command of the Kābul-fort there had been left Mullā Bābā of Pashāghar, Khalīfa, Muḥibb-i-'alī the armourer, Aḥmad-i-yūsuf and Aḥmad-i-qāsim. They did well, made the fort fast, strengthened it, and kept watch.

(k. Bābur's advance to Kābul.)

From Tīmūr Beg's Langar we sent Qāsim Beg's servant, Muḥ. of Andijān, a *Tūqbāī*, to the Kābul begs, with written details of our arrival and of the following arrangements:—"When we are out of the Ghūr-bund narrows,[1227] we will fall on them suddenly; let our signal to you be the fire we will light directly we have passed Minār-hill; do you in reply light one in the citadel, on Fol. 197b.the old Kūshk (kiosk)," now the Treasury, "so that we may be sure you know of our coming. We will come up from our side; you come out from yours; neglect nothing your hands can find to do!" This having been put into writing, Muḥammad *Andijānī* was sent off.

Riding next dawn from the Langar, we dismounted over against Ushtur-shahr. Early next morning we passed the Ghūr-bund narrows, dismounted at Bridge-head, there watered and rested our horses, and at the Mid-day Prayer set forward again. Till we reached the *tūtqāwal*,[1228] there was no snow, beyond that, the further we went the deeper the snow. The cold between Ẕamma-yakhshī and Minār was such as we had rarely felt in our lives.

We sent on Aḥmad the messenger (*yāsāwal*) and Qarā Aḥmad *yūrūnchī*[1229] to say to the begs, "Here we are at the time promised; be ready! be bold!

"After crossing Minār-hill[1230] and dismounting on its skirt, helpless with cold, we lit fires to warm ourselves. It was not time to light the signal-fire; we just lit these because we were helpless in that mighty cold. Near shoot of dawn we rode on from Minār-hill; between it and Kābul the snow was up to the horses' knees and had hardened, so off the road to move was difficult. Riding single-file the whole way, we got to Kābul Fol. 198.in good time undiscovered.[1231] Before we were at Bībī Māh-rūī (Lady Moon-face), the blaze of fire on the citadel let us know that the begs were looking out.

(*l. Attack made on the rebels.*)

On reaching Sayyid Qāsim's bridge, Sherīm Ṭaghāī and the men of the right were sent towards Mullā Bābā's bridge, while we of the left and centre took the Bābā Lūlī road. Where Khalīfa's garden now is, there was then a smallish garden made by Aūlūgh Beg Mīrzā for a Langar (almshouse); none of its trees or shrubs were left but its enclosing wall was there. In this garden Mīrzā Khān was seated, Muḥ. Ḥusain Mīrzā being in Aūlūgh Beg Mīrzā's great Bāgh-i-bihisht. I had gone as far along the lane of Mullā Bābā's garden as the burial-ground when four men met us who had hurried forward into Mīrzā Khān's quarters, been beaten, and forced to turn back. One of the four was Sayyid Qāsim Lord of the Gate, another was Qāsim Beg's son Qaṃbar-i-'alī, another was Sher-qulī the scout, another was Sl. Aḥmad *Mughūl* one of Sher-qulī's band. These four, without a "God forbid!" (*taḥāshī*) had gone right into Mīrzā Khān's quarters; thereupon he, hearing an uproar, had mounted and got away. Abū'l-ḥasan the armourer's younger brother even, Muḥ. Ḥusain by name, had taken service with Mīrzā Khān; he had slashed at Sher-qulī,Fol. 198b. one of those four, thrown him down, and was just striking his head off, when Sher-qulī freed himself. Those four, tasters of the sword, tasters of the arrow, wounded one and all, came pelting back on us to the place mentioned.

Our horsemen, jammed in the narrow lane, were standing still, unable to move forward or back. Said I to the braves near, "Get off and force a road". Off got Nāṣir's Dost, Khwāja Muḥammad 'Alī the librarian, Bābā Sher-zād (Tiger-whelp), Shāh Maḥmūd and others, pushed forward and at once cleared the way. The enemy took to flight.

We had looked for the begs to come out from the Fort but they could not come in time for the work; they only dropped in, by ones and twos, after we had made the enemy scurry off. Aḥmad-i-yūsuf had come from them before I went into the Chār-bāgh where Mīrzā Khān had been; he went in with me, but we both turned back when we saw the Mīrzā had gone off. Coming in at the garden-gate was Dost of Sar-i-pul, a foot-soldier I had promoted for his boldness to be Kotwāl and had left in Kābul; he made straight for me, sword in hand. I had my cuirass on but had not fastened the *gharīcha*[1232] nor had I put onFol. 199. my helm. Whether he did not recognize me because of change wrought by cold and snow, or whether because of the flurry of the fight, though I shouted "Hāī Dost! hāī Dost!" and though Aḥmad-i-yūsuf also shouted, he, without a "God forbid!" brought down his sword on my unprotected arm. Only by God's grace can it have been that not a hairbreadth of harm was done to me.

If a sword shook the Earth from her place,

Not a vein would it cut till God wills.

It was through the virtue of a prayer I had repeated that the Great God averted this danger and turned this evil aside. That prayer was as follows:—

> "O my God! Thou art my Creator; except Thee there is no God. On Thee do I repose my trust; Thou art the Lord of the mighty throne. What God wills comes to pass; and what he does not will comes not to pass; and there is no power or strength but through the high and exalted God; and, of a truth, in all things God is almighty; and verily He comprehends all things by his knowledge, and has taken account of everything. O my Creator! as I sincerely trust in Thee, do Thou seize by the forelock all evil proceeding from within myself, and all evil coming from without, and all evil proceeding from every man who can be the occasion of evil, and all such evil as can proceed from any living thing, and remove them far from me; since, of a truth, Thou art the Lord of the exalted throne!"[1233]

On leaving that garden we went to Muḥ. Ḥusain Mīrzā's quarters in the Bāgh-i-bihisht, but he had fled and gone off to hide himself. Seven or eight men stood in a breach of the Fol. 199b.garden-wall; I spurred at them; they could not stand; they fled; I got up with them and cut at one with my sword; he rolled over in such a way that I fancied his head was off, passed on and went away; it seems he was Mīrzā Khān's foster-brother, Tūlik Kūkūldāsh and that my sword fell on his shoulder.

At the gate of Muḥ. Ḥusain Mīrzā's quarters, a Mughūl I recognized for one of my own servants, drew his bow and aimed at my face from a place on the roof as near me as a gate-ward stands to a Gate. People on all sides shouted, "Hāi! hāi! it is the Pādshāh." He changed his aim, shot off his arrow and ran away. The affair was beyond the shooting of arrows! His Mīrzā, his leaders, had run away or been taken; why was he shooting?

There they brought Sl. Sanjar *Barlās*, led in by a rope round his neck; he even, to whom I had given the Nīngnahār *tūmān*, had had his part in the mutiny! Greatly agitated, he kept crying out, "Hāi! what fault is in me?" Said

I, "Can there be one clearer than that you are higher than the purpose and counsels of this crew?"[1234] But as he was the sister's son of my Khān *dādā's* mother, Shāh Begīm, I gave the order, "Do not lead him with such dishonour; it is not death."

On leaving that place, I sent Aḥmad-i-qasim *Kohbur*, one of the begs of the Fort, with a few braves, in pursuit ofFol. 200. Mīrzā Khān.

(*m. Bābur's dealings with disloyal women.*)

When I left the Bāgh-i-bihisht, I went to visit Shāh Begīm and (Mihr-nigār) Khānīm who had settled themselves in tents by the side of the garden.

As townspeople and black-bludgeoners had raised a riot, and were putting hands out to pillage property and to catch persons in corners and outside places, I sent men, to beat the rabble off, and had it herded right away.[1235]

Shāh Begīm and Khānīm were seated in one tent. I dismounted at the usual distance, approached with my former deference and courtesy, and had an interview with them. They were extremely agitated, upset, and ashamed; could neither excuse themselves reasonably[1236] nor make the enquiries of affection. I had not expected this (disloyalty) of them; it was not as though that party, evil as was the position it had taken up, consisted of persons who would not give ear to the words of Shāh Begīm and Khānīm; Mīrzā Khān was the begīm's grandson, in her presence night and day; if she had not fallen in with the affair, she could have kept him with her.

Twice over when fickle Fortune and discordant Fate had parted Fol. 200b.me from throne and country, retainer and following, I, and my mother with me, had taken refuge with them and had had no kindness soever from them. At that time my younger brother (*i.e.* cousin) Mīrzā Khān and his mother Sulṭān-nigār Khānīm held valuable cultivated districts; yet my mother and I,—to leave all question of a district aside,—were not made possessors of a single village or a few yoke of plough-oxen.[1237] Was my mother not Yūnas Khān's daughter? was I not his grandson?

In my days of plenty I have given from my hand what matched the blood-relationship and the position of whatsoever member of that (Chaghatāī) dynasty chanced down upon me. For example, when the honoured Shāh Begīm came to me, I gave her Pamghān, one of the best places in Kābul, and failed in no sort of filial duty and service towards her. Again, when Sl. Sa'īd Khān, Khān in Kāshghar, came [914 *AH.*] with five or six naked followers on foot, I looked upon him as an honoured guest and gave him Mandrāwar of the Lamghān *tūmāns*. Beyond this also, when Shāh Ismā'īl had killed Shaibāq Khān in Marv and I crossed over to Qūndūz (916 *AH.*-1511 *AD.*), the Andijānīs, some driving their (Aūzbeg) *dāroghas* out, some making their places fast, turned their eyes to me and sent me a man; at that time I trusted those old family servants to that same Sl. Sa'īd Khān, gave him a force, made him Khān and sped him forth. Again, down to the present time (*circa* 934 *AH.*) I have not looked upon any member of that family who has come to me, in any other light than as a blood-relation. For example, there Fol. 201.are now in my service Chīn-tīmūr Sulṭān; Aīsān-tīmūr Sulṭān, Tūkhtā-būghā Sulṭān, and Bābā Sulṭān;[1238] on one and all of these I have looked with more favour than on blood-relations of my own.

I do not write this in order to make complaint; I have written the plain truth. I do not set these matters down in order to make known my own deserts; I have set down exactly what has happened. In this History I have held firmly to it that the truth should be reached in every matter, and that every act should be recorded precisely as it occurred. From this it follows of necessity that I have set down of good and bad whatever is known, concerning father and elder brother, kinsman and stranger; of them all I have set down carefully the known virtues and defects. Let the reader accept my excuse; let the reader pass on from the place of severity!

(*n. Letters of victory.*)

Rising from that place and going to the Chār-bāgh where Mīrzā Khān had been, we sent letters of victory to all the countries, clans, and retainers. This done, I rode to the citadel.

(*o. Arrest of rebel leaders.*)

Muḥammad Ḥusain Mīrzā in his terror having run away into Khānīm's bedding-room and got himself fastened up in a bundle of bedding, we appointed Mīrīm *Dīwān* with other begs of the fort, to take control in those dwellings, capture, and bring him in. Mīrīm *Dīwān* said some plain rough words at Khānīm'sFol. 201b. gate, by some means or other found the Mīrzā, and brought him before me in the citadel. I rose at once to receive the Mīrzā with my usual deference, not even shewing too harsh a face. If I had had that Muḥ. Ḥusain M. cut in pieces, there was the ground for it that he had had part in base and shameful action, started and spurred on mutiny and treason. Death he deserved with one after another of varied pain and torture, but because there had come to be various connexion between us, his very sons and daughters being by my own mother's sister Khūb-nigār Khānīm, I kept this just claim in mind, let him go free, and permitted him to set out towards Khurāsān. The cowardly ingrate then forgot altogether the good I did him by the gift of his life; he blamed and slandered me to

Shaibāq Khān. Little time passed, however, before the Khān gave him his deserts by death.

Leave thou to Fate the man who does thee wrong,

For Fate is an avenging servitor.[1239]

Aḥmad-i-qāsim *Kohbur* and the party of braves sent in pursuit of Mīrzā Khān, overtook him in the low hills of Qargha-yīlāq, not able even to run away, without heart or force to stir a finger! Fol. 202.They took him, and brought him to where I sat in the northeast porch of the old Court-house. Said I to him, "Come! let's have a look at one another" (*kūrūshālīng*), but twice before he could bend the knee and come forward, he fell down through agitation. When we had looked at one another, I placed him by my side to give him heart, and I drank first of the sherbet brought in, in order to remove his fears.[1240]

As those who had joined him, soldiers, peasants, Mughūls and Chaghatāīs,[1241] were in suspense, we simply ordered him to remain for a few days in his elder sister's house; but a few days later he was allowed to set out for Khurāsān[1242] because those mentioned above were somewhat uncertain and it did not seem well for him to stay in Kābul.

(*p. Excursion to Koh-dāman.*)

After letting those two go, we made an excursion to Bārān, Chāsh-tūpa, and the skirt of Gul-i-bahār.[1243] More beautiful in Spring than any part even of Kābul are the open-lands of Bārān, the plain of Chāsh-tūpa, and the skirt of Gul-i-bahār. Many sorts of tulip bloom there; when I had them counted once, it came out at 34 different kinds as [has been said].[1244] This couplet has been written in praise of these places,—

Kābul in Spring is an Eden of verdure and blossom;

Matchless in Kābul the Spring of Gul-i-bahār and Bārān.

On this excursion I finished the ode,—

My heart, like the bud of the red, red rose,

Lies fold within fold aflame;Fol. 202b.

Would the breath of even a myriad Springs

Blow my heart's bud to a rose?

In truth, few places are quite equal to these for spring-excursions, for hawking (*qūsh sālmāq*) or bird-shooting (*qūsh ātmāq*), as has been briefly mentioned in the praise and description of the Kābul and Ghaznī country.

(q. Nāṣir Mīrzā expelled from Badakhshān.)

This year the begs of Badakhshān *i.e.* Muḥammad the armourer, Mubārak Shāh, Zubair and Jahāngīr, grew angry and mutinous because of the misconduct of Nāṣir Mīrzā and some of those he cherished. Coming to an agreement together, they drew out an army of horse and foot, arrayed it on the level lands by the Kūkcha-water, and moved towards Yaftal and Rāgh, to near Khamchān, by way of the lower hills. The Mīrzā and his inexperienced begs, in their thoughtless and unobservant fashion, came out to fight them just in those lower hills. The battle-field was uneven ground; the Badakhshīs had a dense mass of men on foot who stood firm under repeated charges by the Mīrzā's horse, and returned such attack that the horsemen fled, unable to keep their ground. Having beaten the Mīrzā, the Badakhshīs plundered his dependants and connexions.

Beaten and stripped bare, he and his close circle took the road through Ishkīmīsh and Nārīn to Kīlā-gāhī, from there followed the Qīzīl-sū up, got out on the Āb-dara road, crossed at Shibr-tū, and so came to Kābul, he with 70 or 80 followers, worn-out, naked and famished.

That was a marvellous sign of the Divine might! Two or three years earlier the Mīrzā had left the Kābul country like a Fol. 203.foe, driving tribes and hordes like sheep before him, reached Badakhshān and made fast its forts and valley-strongholds. With what fancy in his mind had he marched out?[1245] Now he was back, hanging the head of shame for those earlier misdeeds, humbled and distraught about that breach with me!

My face shewed him no sort of displeasure; I made kind enquiry about himself, and brought him out of his confusion.

913 AH.-MAY 13TH 1507 TO MAY 2ND 1508 AD.[1246]

(*a. Raid on the Ghiljī Afghāns.*)

We had ridden out of Kābul with the intention of over-running the Ghiljī;[1247] when we dismounted at Sar-i-dih news was brought that a mass of Mahmands (Afghāns) was lying in Masht and Sih-kāna one *yīghāch* (*circa* 5 m.) away from us.[1248] Our begs and braves agreed in saying, "The Mahmands must be over-run", but I said, "Would it be right to turn aside and raid our own peasants instead of doing what we set out to do? It cannot be."

Riding at night from Sar-i-dih, we crossed the plain of Kattawāz in the dark, a quite black night, one level stretch of land, no mountain or rising-ground in sight, no known road or track, not a man able to lead us! In the end I took the lead. I had been in those parts several times before; drawing inferences from those times, I took the Pole-star on my right shoulder-blade[1249] and, with some anxiety, moved on. God brought it right! We went straight to the Qīāq-tū and the Aūlābā-tū torrent, that is to say, straight for Khwāja Ismā'īl *Sirītī* where the Ghiljīs were lying, the road to which crosses the torrent named. Dismounting near the torrent, we let ourselves and our horses sleep a little,Fol. 203b. took breath, and bestirred ourselves at shoot of dawn. The Sun was up before we got out of those low hills and valley-bottoms to the plain on which the Ghiljī lay with a good *yīghāch*[1250] of road between them and us; once out on the plain we could see their blackness, either their own or from the smoke of their fires.

Whether bitten by their own whim,[1251] or whether wanting to hurry, the whole army streamed off at the gallop (*chāpqūn qūīdīlār*); off galloped I after them and, by shooting an arrow now at a man, now at a horse, checked them after a *kuroh* or two (3 m.?). It is very difficult indeed to check 5 or 6000 braves galloping loose-rein! God brought it right! They were checked! When we had gone about one *shar'ī* (2 m.) further, always with the Afghān blackness in sight, the raid[1252] was allowed. Masses of sheep fell to us, more than in any other raid.

After we had dismounted and made the spoils turn back,[1253] one body of Afghāns after another came down into the plain, provoking a fight. Some of the begs and of the household went against one body and killed every man; Nāṣir Mīrzā did the same with another, and a pillar of Afghān heads was set up. An arrow pierced the foot of that foot-soldier Dost the Kotwāl who has been mentioned already;[1254] when we reached Kābul, he died.

Marching from Khwāja Ismā'īl, we dismounted once more at Aūlābā-tū. Some of the begs and of my own household were ordered to go forward and carefully separate off the Fifth (*Khums*) of the enemy's spoils. By way of favour, we did not Fol. 204.take the Fifth from Qāsim Beg and some others.[1255] From what was written down,[1256] the Fifth came out at 16,000, that is to say, this 16,000 was the fifth of 80,000 sheep; no question however but that with those lost and those not asked for, a *lak* (100,000) of sheep had been taken.

(*b. A hunting-circle.*)

Next day when we had ridden from that camp, a hunting-circle was formed on the plain of Kattawāz where deer (*kiyīk*)[1257] and wild-ass are always plentiful and always fat. Masses went into the ring; masses were killed. During the hunt I galloped after a wild-ass, on getting near shot one arrow, shot another, but did not bring it down, it only running more slowly for the two wounds. Spurring forwards and getting into position[1258] quite close to it, I chopped at the nape of its neck behind the ears, and cut through the wind-pipe; it stopped, turned over and died. My sword cut well! The wild-ass was surprisingly fat. Its rib may have been a little under one yard in length. Sherīm Ṭaghāī and other observers of *kiyīk* in Mughūlistān said with surprise, "Even in Mughūlistān we have seen few *kiyīk* so fat!" I shot another wild-ass; most of the wild-asses and deer brought down in that hunt were fat, but not one of them was so fat as the one I first killed.

Turning back from that raid, we went to Kābul and there dismounted.

(*c. Shaibāq Khān moves against Khurāsān.*)

Shaibāq Khān had got an army to horse at the end of last year, meaning to go from Samarkand against Khurāsān, hisFol. 204b. march out being somewhat hastened by the coming to him of a servant of that vile traitor to his salt, Shāh Manṣūr the Paymaster, then in Andikhūd. When the Khān was approaching Andikhūd, that vile wretch said, "I have sent a man to the Aūzbeg," relied on this, adorned himself, stuck up an aigrette on his head, and went out, bearing gift and tribute. On this the leaderless[1259] Aūzbegs poured down on him from all sides, and turned upside down (*tart-part*) the blockhead, his offering and his people of all sorts.

(*d. Irresolution of the Khurāsān Mīrzās.*)

Badī'u'z-zamān Mīrzā, Muẓaffar Mīrzā, Muḥ. Barandūq *Barlās* and Ẕū'n-nūn *Arghūn* were all lying with their army in Bābā Khākī,[1260] not decided to fight, not settled to make (Herī) fort fast, there they sat, confounded, vague, uncertain what to do. Muḥammad Barandūq *Barlās* was a knowledgeable man; he kept saying, "You let Muẓaffar Mīrzā and me make the fort fast; let

Badī'u'z-zamān Mīrzā and Ẕū'n-nūn Beg go into the mountains near Herī and gather in Sl. 'Alī *Arghūn* from Sīstān and Zamīn-dāwar, Shāh Beg and Muqīm from Qandahār with all their armies, and let them collect also what there is of Nikdīrī and Hazāra force; this done, let them make a swift and telling move. The enemy would find it difficult to go into the mountains, and could not come against the (Herī) fort because Fol. 205.he would be afraid of the army outside." He said well, his plan was practical.

Brave though Ẕū'n-nūn *Arghūn* was, he was mean, a lover-of-goods, far from businesslike or judicious, rather shallow-pated, and a bit of a fool. As has been mentioned,[1261] when that elder and that younger brother became joint-rulers in Herī, he had chief authority in Badī'u'z-zamān Mīrzā's presence. He was not willing now for Muḥ. Barandūq Beg to remain inside Herī town; being the lover-of-goods he was, he wanted to be there himself. But he could not make this seem one and the same thing![1262] Is there a better sign of his shallow-pate and craze than that he degraded himself and became contemptible by accepting the lies and flattery of rogues and sycophants? Here are the particulars[1263]:—While he was so dominant and trusted in Herī, certain Shaikhs and Mullās went to him and said, "The Spheres are holding commerce with us; you are styled *Hizabru'l-lāh* (Lion of God); you will overcome the Aūzbeg." Believing these words, he put his bathing-cloth round his neck and gave thanks. It was through this he did not accept Muḥammad Barandūq Beg's sensible counsel, did not strengthen the works (*aīsh*) of the fort, get ready fighting equipment, set scout or rearward to warn of the foe's approach, or plan out such method of array that, should the foe appear, his men would fight with ready heart.

(*e. Shaibāq Khān takes Herī.*)

Shaibāq Khān passed through Murgh-āb to near Sīr-kāī[1264] inFol. 205b. the month of Muḥarram (913 AH. May-June 1507 AD.). When the Mīrzās heard of it, they were altogether upset, could not act, collect troops, array those they had. Dreamers, they moved through a dream![1265] Ẕū'n-nūn *Arghūn*, made glorious by that flattery, went out to Qarā-rabāṭ, with 100 to 150 men, to face 40,000 to 50,000 Aūzbegs: a mass of these coming up, hustled his off, took him, killed him and cut off his head.[1266]

In Fort Ikhtiyāru'd-dīn, it is known as Ālā-qūrghān,[1267] were the Mīrzās' mothers, elder and younger sisters, wives and treasure. The Mīrzās reached the town at night, let their horses rest till midnight, slept, and at dawn flung forth again. They could not think about strengthening the fort; in the respite and crack of time there was, they just ran away,[1268] leaving mother, sister, wife and little child to Aūzbeg captivity.

What there was of Sl. Ḥusain Mīrzā's *ḥaram*, Pāyanda-sulṭān Begīm and Khadīja Begīm at the head of it, was inside Ālā-qūrghān; there too were the *ḥarams* of Badī'u'z-zamān Mīrzā[1269] and Muẓaffar Mīrzā with their little children, treasure, and households (*biyutāt*). What was desirable for making the fort fast had not been done; even braves to reinforce it had not arrived. 'Āshiq-i-muḥammad *Arghūn*, the younger brother of Mazīd Beg, had fled from the army on foot and gone into it; Fol. 206.in it was also Amīr 'Umar Beg's son 'Alī Khān (*Turkmān*); Shaikh 'Abdu'l-lāh the taster was there; Mīrzā Beg *Kāī-khusraūī* was there; and Mīrak *Gūr* (or *Kūr*) the Dīwān was there.

When Shaibāq Khān arrived two or three days later; the Shaikhu'l-islām and notables went out to him with the keys of the outer-fort. That same 'Āshiq-i-muḥammad held Ālā-qūrghān for 16 or 17 days; then a mine, run from the horse-market outside, was fired and brought a tower down; the garrison lost heart, could hold out no longer, so let the fort be taken.

(*f. Shaibāq Khān in Herī.*)

Shaibāq Khān, after taking Herī,[1270] behaved badly not only to the wives and children of its rulers but to every person soever. For the sake of this five-days' fleeting world, he earned himself a bad name. His first improper act and deed in Herī was that, for the sake of this rotten world (*chirk dunyā*), he caused Khadīja Begīm various miseries, through letting the vile wretch Pay-master Shāh Manṣūr get hold of her to loot. Then he let 'Abdu'l-wahhāb *Mughūl* take to loot a person so saintly and so revered as Shaikh Pūrān, and each one of Shaikh Pūrān's children be taken by a separate person. He let the band of poets be seized by Mullā Banā'ī, a matter about which this verse is well-known in Khurāsān:—

Except 'Abdu'l-lāh the stupid fool (*kīr-khar*),

Not a poet to-day sees the colour of gold;

From the poets' band Banā'ī would get gold,

Fol. 206b.All he will get is *kīr-khar*.[1271]

Directly he had possession of Herī, Shaibāq Khān married and took Muẓaffar Mīrzā's wife, Khān-zāda Khānīm, without regard to the running-out of the legal term.[1272] His own illiteracy not forbidding, he instructed in the exposition of the Qoran, Qāẓī Ikhtiyār and Muḥammad Mīr Yūsuf, two of the celebrated and highly-skilled mullās of Herī; he took a pen and corrected the hand-writing of Mullā Sl. 'Alī of Mashhad and the drawing of Bih-zād; and every few days, when he had composed some tasteless couplet, he would have it read from the pulpit, hung in the Chār-sū [Square], and for it accept the offerings of the towns-people![1273] Spite of his early-rising, his not neglecting the Five Prayers, and his fair knowledge of the art of reciting the Qorān, there issued from him many an act and deed as absurd, as impudent, and as heathenish as those just named.

(*g. Death of two Mīrzās.*)

Ten or fifteen days after he had possession of Herī, Shaibāq Khān came from Kahd-stān[1274] to Pul-i-sālār. From that place he sent Tīmūr Sl. and 'Ubaid Sl. with the army there present, against Abū'l-muḥsin Mīrzā and Kūpuk (Kīpik) Mīrzā then seated carelessly in Mashhad. The two Mīrzās had thought at one time of making Qalāt[1275] fast; at another, this after they had had news of the approach of the Aūzbeg, they were for moving on Shaibāq Khān himself, by forced marches and along a different road,[1276]—which might have turned out an amazingly good idea! But while they sit still there in Mashhad with nothing decided, the Sulṭāns arrive by forced marches. The Mīrzās for their part Fol. 207.array and go out; Abū'l-muḥsin Mīrzā is quickly overcome and routed; Kūpuk Mīrzā charges his brother's assailants with somewhat few men; him too they carry off; both brothers are dismounted and seated in one place; after an embrace (*qūchūsh*), they kiss farewell; Abū'l-muḥsin shews some want of courage; in Kūpuk Mirza it all makes no change at all. The heads of both are sent to Shaibāq Khān in Pul-i-sālār.

(*h. Bābur marches for Qandahār.*)

In those days Shāh Beg and his younger brother Muḥammad Muqīm, being afraid of Shaibāq Khān, sent one envoy after another to me with dutiful letters (*'arẓ-dāsht*), giving sign of amity and good-wishes. Muqīm, in a letter of his own, explicitly invited me. For us to look on at the Aūzbeg over-running the whole country, was not seemly; and as by letters and envoys, Shāh Beg and Muqīm had given me invitation, there remained little doubt they would wait upon me.[1277] When all begs and counsellors had been consulted, the matter was left at this:—We were to get an army to horse, join the Arghūn begs and decide in accord and agreement with them, whether to move into Khurāsān or elsewhere as might seem good.

(*i. In Ghasnī and Qalāt-i-ghilzāī.*)

Ḥabība-sulṭān Begīm, my aunt (*yīnkā*) as I used to call her, met us in Ghaznī, having come from Herī, according to arrangement, in order to bring her daughter Maṣ'ūma-sulṭān Begīm. Fol. 207b.With the honoured Begīm came Khusrau Kūkūldāsh, Sl. Qulī *Chūnāq* (One-eared) and Gadāī *Balāl* who had returned to me after flight from Herī, first to Ibn-i-ḥusain

Mīrzā then to Abū'l-muḥsin Mīrzā,[1278] with neither of whom they could remain.

In Qalāt the army came upon a mass of Hindūstān traders, come there to traffic and, as it seemed, unable to go on. The general opinion about them was that people who, at a time of such hostilities, are coming into an enemy's country[1279] must be plundered. With this however I did not agree; said I, "What is the traders' offence? If we, looking to God's pleasure, leave such scrapings of gain aside, the Most High God will apportion our reward. It is now just as it was a short time back when we rode out to raid the Ghiljī; many of you then were of one mind to raid the Mahmand Afghāns, their sheep and goods, their wives and families, just because they were within five miles of you! Then as now I did not agree with you. On the very next day the Most High God apportioned you more sheep belonging to Afghān enemies, than had ever before fallen to the share of the army." Something by way of *peshkash* (offering) was taken from each trader when we dismounted on the other side of Qalāt.

(*j. Further march south.*)

Beyond Qalāt two Mīrzās joined us, fleeing from Qandahār. One was Mīrzā Khān (Wais) who had been allowed to go into Khurāsān after his defeat at Kābul. The other was 'Abdu'r-razzāqFol. 208. Mīrzā who had stayed on in Khurāsān when I left. With them came and waited on me the mother of Jahāngīr Mīrzā's son Pīr-i-muḥammad, a grandson of Pahār Mīrzā.[1280]

(*k. Behaviour of the Arghūn chiefs.*)

When we sent persons and letters to Shāh Beg and Muqīm, saying, "Here we are at your word; a stranger-foe like the Aūzbeg has taken Khurāsān; come! let us settle, in concert and amity, what will be for the general good," they returned a rude and ill-mannered answer, going back from the dutiful letters they had written and from the invitations they had given. One of their incivilities was that Shāh Beg stamped his letter to me in the middle of its reverse, where begs seal if writing to begs, where indeed a great beg seals if writing to one of the lower circle.[1281] But for such ill-manners and his rude answers, his affair would never have gone so far as it did, for, as they say,—

A strife-stirring word will accomplish the downfall of an ancient line.

By these their headstrong acts they gave to the winds house, family, and the hoards of 30 to 40 years.

One day while we were near Shahr-i-ṣafā[1282] a false alarm being given in the very heart of the camp, the whole army was made to arm and mount. At the time I was occupied with a bath Fol. 208b.and purification; the begs were much flurried; I mounted when I was ready; as the alarm was false, it died away after a time.

March by march we moved on to Guzar.[1283] There we tried again to discuss with the Arghūns but, paying no attention to us, they maintained the same obstinate and perverse attitude. Certain well-wishers who knew the local land and water, represented to me, that the head of the torrents (*rūdlār*) which come down to Qandahār, being towards Bābā Ḥasan Abdāl and Khalishak,[1284] a move ought to be made in that direction, in order to cut off (*yīqmāq*) all those torrents.[1285] Leaving the matter there, we next day made our men put on their mail, arrayed in right and left, and marched for Qandahār.

(*l. Battle of Qandahār.*)

Shāh Beg and Muqīm had seated themselves under an awning which was set in front of the naze of the Qandahār-hill where I am now having a rock-residence cut out.[1286] Muqīm's men pushed forward amongst the trees to rather near us. Ṭūfān *Arghūn* had fled to us when we were near Shahr-i-ṣafā; he now betook himself alone close up to the Arghūn array to where one named 'Ashaqu'l-lāh was advancing rather fast leading 7 or 8 men. Alone, Ṭūfān *Arghūn* faced him, slashed swords with him, unhorsed him, cut off his head and brought it to me as we were passing Sang-i-lakhshak;[1287] an omen we accepted! Not thinking it well to fight where we were, amongst suburbs and trees, we went on along the skirt of the hill. Just as we had settled on ground for the camp, in a meadow on the Qandahār side of theFol. 209. torrent,[1288] opposite Khalishak, and were dismounting, Sher Qulī the scout hurried up and represented that the enemy was arrayed to fight and on the move towards us.

As on our march from Qalāt the army had suffered much from hunger and thirst, most of the soldiers on getting near Khalishak scattered up and down for sheep and cattle, grain and eatables. Without looking to collect them, we galloped off. Our force may have been 2000 in all, but perhaps not over 1000 were in the battle because those mentioned as scattering up and down could not rejoin in time to fight.

Though our men were few I had them organized and posted on a first-rate plan and method; I had never arrayed them before by such a good one. For my immediate command (*khāṣa tābīn*) I had selected braves from whose hands comes work[1289] and had inscribed them by tens and fifties, each ten and each fifty under a leader who knew the post in the right or left of the centre for his ten or his fifty, knew the work of each in the battle, and was there on the observant watch; so that, after mounting, the right and left, right and left hands, right and left sides, charged right and left without the trouble of arraying them or the need of a *tawāchī*.[1290]

> Fol. 209b.(*Author's note on his terminology.*) Although *barānghār*, *aūng qūl*, *aūng yān* and *aūng* (right wing, right hand, right side and right) all have the same meaning, I have applied them in different senses in order to vary terms and mark distinctions. As, in the battle-array, the (Ar.) *maimana* and *maisara i.e.* what people call (Turkī) *barānghār* and *jawānghār* (r. and l. wings) are not included in the (Ar.) *qalb*, *i.e.* what people call (T.) *ghūl* (centre), so it is in arraying the centre itself. Taking the array of the centre only, its (Ar.) *yamīn* and *yasār* (r. and l.) are called (by me) *aūng qūl* and *sūl qūl* (r. and l. hands). Again,—the (Ar.) *khāṣa tābīn* (royal troop) in the centre has its *yamīn* and *yasār* which are called (by me) *aūng yān* and *sūl yān* (r. and l. sides, T. *yān*). Again,—in the *khāṣa tābīn* there is the (T.) *būī* (*nīng*) *tīkīnī* (close circle); its *yamīn* and *yasār* are called *sūng* and *sūl*. In the Turkī tongue they call one single thing a *būī*,[1291] but that is not the *būī* meant here; what is meant here is close (*yāqīn*).

The right wing (*barānghār*) was Mīrzā Khān (Wais), Sherīm Ṭaghāī, Yārak Ṭaghāī with his elder and younger brethren, Chilma *Mughūl*, Ayūb Beg, Muḥammad Beg, Ibrāhīm Beg, 'Alī Sayyid *Mughūl* with his Mughūls, Sl. Qulī *chuhra*, Khudā-bakhsh and Abū'l-ḥasan with his elder and younger brethren.

The left (*jawānghār*) was 'Abdu'r-razzāq Mīrzā, Qāsim Beg, Tīngrī-bīrdī, Qambar-i-'alī, Aḥmad *Aīlchī-būghā*, Ghūrī *Barlās*, Sayyid Ḥusain Akbar, and Mīr Shāh *Qūchīn*.

The advance (*aīrāwal*) was Nāṣir Mīrzā, Sayyid Qāsim Lord of the Gate, Muḥibb-i-'alī the armourer, Pāpā Aūghulī (Pāpā's son?), Allāh-wairan *Turkmān*, Sher Qulī *Mughūl* the scout with his elder and younger brethren, and Muḥammad 'Alī.

In the centre (*ghūl*), on my right hand, were Qāsim Kūkūldāsh, Khusrau Kūkūldāsh, Sl. Muḥammad *Dūldāī*, Shāh Maḥmūd the secretary, Qūl-i-bāyazīd the taster, and Kamāl the sherbet-serverFol. 210. server; on my left were Khwāja Muḥammad 'Alī, Nāṣir's Dost, Nāṣir's Mīrīm, Bābā Sher-zād, Khān-qulī, Walī the treasurer, Qūtlūq-qadam the scout, Maqsūd the water-bearer (*sū-chī*), and Bābā Shaikh. Those in the centre were all of my household; there were no great begs; not one of those enumerated had reached the rank of beg. Those inscribed in this *būī*[1292] were Sher Beg, Ḥātim the Armoury-master, Kūpuk, Qulī Bābā, Abū'l-ḥasan the armourer;—of the Mughūls, Aūrūs (Russian) 'Alī Sayyid,[1293] Darwīsh-i-'alī Sayyid, Khūsh-kīldī, Chilma, Dost-kīldī, Chilma *Tāghchī*, Dāmāchī, Mindī;—of the Turkmāns, Manṣūr, Rustam-i-'alī with his elder and younger brother, and Shāh Nāẕir and Sīūndūk.

The enemy was in two divisions, one under Shāh Shujā' *Arghūn*, known as Shāh Beg and hereafter to be written of simply as Shāh Beg, the other under his younger brother Muqīm.

Some estimated the dark mass of Arghūns[1294] at 6 or 7000 men; no question whatever but that Shāh Beg's own men in mail were 4 or 5000. He faced our right, Muqīm with a force smaller may-be than his brother's, faced our left. Muqīm made a mightily strong attack on our left, that is on Qāsim Beg from whom two or three persons came before fighting began, to ask for reinforcement; we however could not detach a man because in front of us also the enemy was very strong. We made our onset without any delay; the enemy fell suddenly on our van,Fol. 210b. turned it back and rammed it on our centre. When we, after a discharge of arrows, advanced, they, who also had been shooting for a time, seemed likely to make a stand (*tūkhtaghāndīk*). Some-one, shouting to his men, came forward towards me, dismounted and was for adjusting his arrow, but he could do nothing because we moved on without stay. He remounted and rode off; it may have been Shāh Beg himself. During the fight Pīrī Beg *Turkmān* and 4 or 5 of his brethren turned their faces from the foe and, turban in hand,[1295] came over to us.

> (*Author's note on Pīrī Beg.*) This Pīrī Beg was one of those Turkmāns who came [into Herī] with the Turkmān Begs led by 'Abdu'l-bāqī Mīrzā and Murād Beg, after Shāh Ismā'īl vanquished the Bāyandar sulṭāns and seized the 'Irāq countries.[1296]

Our right was the first to overcome the foe; it made him hurry off. Its extreme point had gone pricking (*sānjīlīb*)[1297] as far as where I have now laid out a garden. Our left extended as far as the great tree-tangled[1298] irrigation-channels, a good way below Bābā Ḥasan Abdāl. Muqīm was opposite it, its numbers very small compared with his. God brought it right! Between it and Muqīm were three or four of the tree-tangled water-channels going on to Qandahār;[1299] it held the crossing-place and allowed no passage; small body though it was, it made splendid stand Fol. 211.and kept its ground. Ḥalwāchī Tarkhān[1300] slashed away in the water with Tīngrī-bīrdī and Qaṃbar-i-'alī. Qaṃbar-i-'alī was wounded; an arrow stuck in Qāsim Beg's forehead; another struck Ghūrī *Barlās* above the eyebrow and came out above his cheek.[1301]

We meantime, after putting our adversary to flight, had crossed those same channels towards the naze of Murghān-koh (Birds'-hill). Some-one on a grey *tīpūchāq* was going backwards and forwards irresolutely along the hill-skirt, while we were getting across; I likened him to Shāh Beg; seemingly it was he.

Our men having beaten their opponents, all went off to pursue and unhorse them. Remained with me eleven to count, 'Abdu'l-lāh the librarian being one. Muqīm was still keeping his ground and fighting. Without a glance at the fewness of our men, we had the nagarets sounded and, putting our trust in God, moved with face set for Muqīm.

(Turkī) For few or for many God is full strength;

No man has might in His Court.

(Arabic) How often, God willing it, a small force has vanquished a large one!

Learning from the nagarets that we were approaching, Muqīm forgot his fixed plan and took the road of flight. God brought it right!

After putting our foe to flight, we moved for Qandahār and dismounted in Farrukh-zād Beg's Chār-bāgh, of which at this time not a trace remains!

(*m. Bābur enters Qandahār.*)Fol. 211b.

Shāh Beg and Muqīm could not get into Qandahār when they took to flight; Shāh Beg went towards Shāl and Mastūng (Quetta), Muqīm towards Zamīn-dāwar. They left no-one able to make the fort fast. Aḥmad 'Alī Tarkhān was in it together with other elder and younger brethren of Qulī Beg *Arghūn* whose attachment and good-feeling for me were known. After parley they asked protection for the families of their elder and younger brethren; their request was granted and all mentioned were encompassed with favour. They then opened the Māshūr-gate of the town; with leaderless men in mind, no other was opened. At that gate were posted Sherīm Ṭaghāī and Yārīm Beg. I went in with a few of the household, charged the leaderless men and had two or three put to death by way of example.[1302]

(*n. The spoils of Qandahār.*)

I got to Muqīm's treasury first, that being in the outer-fort; 'Abdu'r-razzāq Mīrzā must have been quicker than I, for he was just dismounting there when I arrived; I gave him a few things from it. I put Dost-i-nāṣir Beg, Qul-i-bāyazīd the taster and, of pay-masters, Muḥammad *bakhshī* in charge of it, then passed on into the citadel and posted Khwāja Muḥammad 'Alī,

Shāh Maḥmūd and, of the pay-masters, Ṭaghāī Shāh *bakhshī* in charge of Shāh Beg's treasury.

Nāṣir's Mīrīm and Maqṣūd the sherbet-server were sent to keep the house of Ẕū'n-nūn's *Dīwān* Mīr Jān for Nāṣir Mīrzā; for Mīrzā Khān was kept Shaikh Abū-sa'īd *Tarkhānī's*; for 'Abdu'r-razzāq Mīrzā ... 's.[1303]

Fol. 212.Such masses of white money had never been seen in those countries; no-one indeed was to be heard of who had seen so much. That night, when we ourselves stayed in the citadel, Shāh Beg's slave Saṃbhal was captured and brought in. Though he was then Shāh Beg's intimate, he had not yet received his later favour.[1304] I had him given into someone's charge but as good watch was not kept, he was allowed to escape. Next day I went back to my camp in Farrukh-zād Beg's Chār-bāgh.

I gave the Qandahār country to Nāṣir Mīrzā. After the treasure had been got into order, loaded up and started off, he took the loads of white *tankas* off a string of camels (*i.e. 7* beasts) at the citadel-treasury, and kept them. I did not demand them back; I just gave them to him.

On leaving Qandahār, we dismounted in the Qūsh-khāna meadow. After setting the army forward, I had gone for an excursion, so I got into camp rather late. It was another camp! not to be recognized! Excellent *tīpūchāqs*, strings and strings of he-camels, she-camels, and mules, bearing saddle-bags (*khurzīn*) of silken stuffs and cloth,—tents of scarlet (cloth) and velvet, all sorts of awnings, every kind of work-shop, ass-load after ass-load of chests! The goods of the elder and younger (Arghūn) brethren had been kept in separate treasuries; out of each had come chest upon chest, bale upon bale of stuffs and clothes-in-wear (*artmāq artmāq*), sack upon sack of white *tankas*. In *aūtāgh* and *chādar* (lattice-tent and pole-tent) was much spoil for every man soever; many sheep also had been taken but sheep were less cared about!

I made over to Qāsim Beg Muqīm's retainers in Qalāt, underFol. 212b. Qūj *Arghūn* and Tāju'd-dīn Maḥmūd, with their goods and effects. Qāsim Beg was a knowing person; he saw it unadvisable for us to stay long near Qandahār, so, by talking and talking, worrying and worrying, he got us to march off. As has been said, I had bestowed Qandahār on Nāṣir Mīrzā; he was given leave to go there; we started for Kābul.

There had been no chance of portioning out the spoils while we were near Qandahār; it was done at Qarā-bāgh where we delayed two or three days. To count the coins being difficult, they were apportioned by weighing them in scales. Begs of all ranks, retainers and household (*tābīn*) loaded up ass-load after ass-load of sacks full of white *tankas*, and took them away for their own subsistence and the pay of their soldiers.

We went back to Kābul with masses of goods and treasure, great honour and reputation.

(*o. Bābur's marriage with Ma'ṣūma-sulṭān.*)

After this return to Kābul I concluded alliance (*'aqd qīldīm*) with Sl. Aḥmad Mīrzā's daughter Ma'ṣūma-sulṭān Begīm whom I had asked in marriage at Khurāsān, and had had brought from there.

(*p. Shaibāq Khān before Qandahār.*)

A few days later a servant of Nāṣir Mīrzā brought the news that Shaibāq Khān had come and laid siege to Qandahār. That Muqīm had fled to Zamīn-dāwar has been said already; from there he went on and saw Shaibāq Khān. From Shāh Beg also one person after another had gone to Shaibāq Khān. At the instigation and petition of these two, the Khān cameFol. 213. swiftly down on Qandahār by the mountain road,[1305] thinking to find me there. This was the very thing that experienced person

Qāsim Beg had in his mind when he worried us into marching off from near Qandahār.

(Persian) What a mirror shews to the young man,

A baked brick shews to the old one!

Shaibāq Khān arriving, besieged Nāṣir Mīrzā in Qandahār.

(*q. Alarm in Kābul.*)

When this news came, the begs were summoned for counsel. The matters for discussion were these:—Strangers and ancient foes, such as are Shaibāq Khān and the Aūzbegs, are in possession of all the countries once held by Tīmūr Beg's descendants; even where Turks and Chaghatāīs[1306] survive in corners and border-lands, they have all joined the Aūzbeg, willingly or with aversion; one remains, I myself, in Kābul, the foe mightily strong, I very weak, with no means of making terms, no strength to oppose; that, in the presence of such power and potency, we had to think of some place for ourselves and, at this crisis and in the crack of time there was, to put a wider space between us and the strong foeman; that choice lay between Badakhshān and Hindūstān and that decision must now be made.

Qāsim Beg and Sherīm Ṭaghāī were agreed for Badakhshān;

(*Author's note on Badakhshān.*) Those holding their heads up in Badakhshān at this crisis were, of Badakhshīs, Mubārak Shāh and

Zubair, Jahāngīr *Turkmān* and Muḥammad the armourer. They had driven Nāṣir Mīrzā out but had not joined the Aūzbeg.

Fol. 213b.I and several household-begs preferred going towards Hindūstān and were for making a start to Lamghān.[1307]

(*r. Movements of some Mīrzās.*)

After taking Qandahār, I had bestowed Qalāt and the Turnūk (Tarnak) country on 'Abdu'r-razzāq Mīrzā and had left him in Qalāt, but with the Aūzbeg besieging Qandahār, he could not stay in Qalāt, so left it and came to Kābul. He arriving just as we were marching out, was there left in charge.[1308]

There being in Badakhshān no ruler or ruler's son, Mīrzā Khān inclined to go in that direction, both because of his relationship to Shāh Begīm[1309] and with her approval. He was allowed to go and the honoured Begīm herself started off with him. My honoured maternal-aunt Mihr-nigār Khānīm also wished to go to Badakhshān, notwithstanding that it was more seemly for her to be with me, a blood-relation; but whatever objection was made, she was not to be dissuaded; she also betook[1310] herself to Badakhshān.

(*s. Bābur's second start for Hindūstān.*)

Under our plan of going to Hindūstān, we marched out of Kābul in the month of the first Jumāda (September 1507 AD.), taking the road through Little Kābul and going down by Sūrkh-rabāṭ to Qūrūq-sāī.

The Afghāns belonging between Kābul and Lamghān (Ningnahār) are thieves and abettors of thieves even in quiet times; for just such a happening as this they had prayed in vain. Said they, "He has abandoned Kābul", and multiplied their misdeeds by ten, changing their very merits for faults. To suchFol. 214. lengths did things go that on the morning we marched from Jagdālīk, the Afghāns located between it and Lamghān, such as the Khiẓr-khail, Shimū-khail, Khirilchī and Khūgīanī, thought of blocking the pass, arrayed on the mountain to the north, and advancing with sound of tambour and flourish of sword, began to shew themselves off. On our mounting I ordered our men to move along the mountain-side, each man from where he had dismounted;[1311] off they set at the gallop up every ridge and every valley of the saddle.[1312] The Afghāns stood awhile, but could not let even one arrow fly,[1313] and betook themselves to flight. While I was on the mountain during the pursuit, I shot one in the hand as he was running back below me. That arrow-stricken man and a few others were brought in; some were put to death by impalement, as an example.

We dismounted over against the Adīnapūr-fort in the Nīngnahār *tūmān*.

(*t. A raid for winter stores.*)

Up till then we had taken no thought where to camp, where to go, where to stay; we had just marched up and down, camping in fresh places, while waiting for news.[1314] It was late in the autumn; most lowlanders had carried in their rice. People knowing the local land and water represented that the Mīl Kāfirs up the water of the 'Alīshang *tūmān* grow great quantities of rice, so that we might be able to collect winter supplies from them for the army. Accordingly we rode out of the Nīngnahār dale (*julga*), crossed (the Bārān-water) at Sāīkal, and went swiftly as far as the Pūr-amīn (easeful) valley. Fol. 214b.There the soldiers took a mass of rice. The rice-fields were all at the bottom of the hills. The people fled but some Kāfirs went to their death. A few of our braves had been sent to a look-out (*sar-kūb*)[1315] on a naze of the Pūr-anīm valley; when they were returning to us, the Kāfirs rushed from the hill above, shooting at them. They overtook Qāsim Beg's son-in-law Pūrān, chopped at him with an axe, and were just taking him when some of the braves went back, brought strength to bear, drove them off and got Pūrān away. After one night spent in the Kāfirs' rice-fields, we returned to camp with a mass of provisions collected.

(*u. Marriage of Muqīm's daughter.*)

While we were near Mandrāwar in those days, an alliance was concluded between Muqīm's daughter Māh-chūchūk, now married to Shāh Ḥasan *Arghūn*, and Qāsim Kūkūldāsh.[1316]

(*v. Abandonment of the Hindūstān project.*)

As it was not found desirable to go on into Hindūstān, I sent Mullā Bābā of Pashāghar back to Kābul with a few braves. Meantime I marched from near Mandrāwar to Atar and Shīwa and lay there for a few days. From Atar I visited Kūnār and Nūr-gal; from Kūnār I went back to camp on a raft; it was the first time I had sat on one; it pleased me much, and the raft came into common use thereafter.

(*w. Shaibāq Khān retires from Qandahār.*)

In those same days Mullā Bābā of Farkat came from Nāṣir Mīrzā with news in detail that Shaibāq Khān, after taking the outer-fort of Qandahār, had not been able to take the citadel but had retired; also that the Mīrzā, on various accounts, had left Qandahār and gone to Ghaznī.

Shaibāq Khān's arrival before Qandahār, within a few daysFol. 215. of our own departure, had taken the garrison by surprise, and they had not been able to make fast the outer-fort. He ran mines several times round about the citadel and made several assaults. The place was about to be lost. At that anxious time Khwāja Muḥ. Amīn, Khwāja Dost Khāwand, Muḥ. 'Alī, a foot-soldier, and Shāmī (Syrian?) let themselves down from the walls and got away. Just as those in the citadel were about to surrender in despair, Shaibāq Khān interposed words of peace and uprose from before the place. Why he rose was this:—It appears that before he went there, he had sent his *ḥaram* to Nīrah-tū,[1317] and that in Nīrah-tū some-one lifted up his head and got command in the fort; the Khān therefore made a sort of peace and retired from Qandahār.

(*x. Bābur returns to Kābul.*)

Mid-winter though it was we went back to Kābul by the Bād-i-pīch road. I ordered the date of that transit and that crossing of the pass to be cut on a stone above Bād-i-pīch;[1318] Ḥāfiẓ Mīrak wrote the inscription, Ustād Shāh Muḥammad did the cutting, not well though, through haste.

I bestowed Ghaznī on Nāṣir Mīrzā and gave 'Abdu'r-razzāq Mīrzā the Nīngnahār *tūmān* with Mandrāwar, Nūr-valley, Kūnār and Nūr-gal.[1319]

(*y. Bābur styles himself Pādshāh.*)

Up to that date people had styled Tīmūr Beg's descendants *Mīrzā*, even when they were ruling; now I ordered that people should style me *Pādshāh*.[1320]

(*z. Birth of Bābur's first son.*)

At the end of this year, on Tuesday the 4th day of the month of Ẕū'l-qa'da (March 6th 1506 AD.), the Sun being in Pisces Fol. 215b.(*Ḥūt*), Humāyūn was born in the citadel of Kābul. The date of his birth was found by the poet Maulānā Masnadī in the words *Sulṭān Humāyūn Khān*,[1321] and a minor poet of Kābul found it in *Shāh-i-fīrūs-qadr* (Shāh of victorious might). A few days later he received the name Humāyūn; when he was five or six days old, I went out to the Chār-bāgh where was had the feast of his nativity. All the begs, small and great, brought gifts; such a mass of white *tankas* was heaped up as had never been seen before. It was a first-rate feast!

914 AH.—MAY 2ND 1508 TO APRIL 21ST 1509 AD.[1322]

This spring a body of Mahmand Afghāns was over-run near Muqur.[1323]

(*a. A Mughūl rebellion.*)

A few days after our return from that raid, Qūj Beg, Faqīr-i-'alī, Karīm-dād and Bābā *chuhra* were thinking about deserting, but their design becoming known, people were sent who took them below Astarghach. As good-for-nothing words of theirs had been reported to me, even during Jahāngīr M.'s life-time,[1324] I ordered that they should be put to death at the top of the *bāẓār*. They had been taken to the place; the ropes had been fixed; and they were about to be hanged when Qāsim Beg sent Khalīfa to me with an urgent entreaty that I would pardon their offences. To please him I gave them their lives, but I ordered them kept in custody.

What there was of Khusrau Shāh's retainers from Ḥiṣār and Qūndūz, together with the head-men of the Mughūls, Chilma,Fol. 216. 'Alī Sayyid,[1325] Sakma (?), Sher-qulī and Aīkū-sālam (?), and also Khusrau Shāh's favourite Chaghatāī retainers under Sl. 'Alī *chuhra* and Khudabakhsh, with also 2 or 3000 serviceable Turkmān braves led by Sīūndūk and Shāh Naẓar,[1326] the whole of these, after consultation, took up a bad position towards me. They were all seated in front of Khwāja Riwāj, from the Sūng-qūrghān meadow to the Chālāk; 'Abdu'r-razzāq Mīrzā, come in from Nīng-nahār, being in Dih-i-afghān.[1327]

Earlier on Muḥibb-i-'alī the armourer had told Khalīfa and Mullā Bābā once or twice of their assemblies, and both had given me a hint, but the thing seeming incredible, it had had no attention. One night, towards the Bed-time Prayer, when I was sitting in the Audience-hall of the Chār-bāgh, Mūsa Khwāja, coming swiftly up with another man, said in my ear, "The Mughūls are really rebelling! We do not know for certain whether they have got 'Abdu'r-razzāq M. to join them. They have not settled to rise to-night." I feigned disregard and a little later went towards the *ḥarams* which at the time were in the Yūrūnchqa-garden[1328] and the Bāgh-i-khilwat, but after page, servitor and messenger (*yasāwal*) had turned back on getting Fol. 216b.near them, I went with the chief-slave towards the town, and on along the ditch. I had gone as far as the Iron-gate when Khwāja Muḥ. 'Alī[1329] met me, he coming by the *bāẓār* road from the opposite direction. He joined me ... of the porch of the Hot-bath (*ḥammām*)....[1330]

TRANSLATOR'S NOTE ON 914 TO 925 AH.—1508 TO 1519 AD.

From several references made in the *Bābur-nāma* and from a passage in Gul-badan's *Humāyūn-nāma* (f. 15), it is inferrible that Bābur was composing the annals of 914 AH. not long before his last illness and death.[1331]

Before the diary of 925 AH. (1519 AD.) takes up the broken thread of his autobiography, there is a *lacuna* of narrative extending over nearly eleven years. The break was not intended, several references in the *Bābur-nāma* shewing Bābur's purpose to describe events of the unchronicled years.[1332] Mr. Erskine, in the Leyden and Erskine *Memoirs*, carried Bābur's biography through the major *lacunæ*, but without firsthand help from the best sources, the *Habību's-siyar* and *Tārīkh-i-rashīdī*. He had not the help of the first even in his *History of India*. M. de Courteille working as a translator only, made no attempt to fill the gaps.

Bābur's biography has yet to be completed; much time is demanded by the task, not only in order to exhaust known sources and seek others further afield, but to weigh and balance the contradictory statements of writers deep-sundered in sympathy and outlook. To strike such a balance is essential when dealing with the events of 914 to 920 AH. because in those years Bābur had part in an embittered conflict between Sunni and Shī'a. What I offer below, as a stop-gap, is a mere summary of events, mainly based on material not used by Mr. Erskine, with a few comments prompted by acquaintance with Bāburiana.

USEFUL SOURCES

Compared with what Bābur could have told of this most interesting period of his life, the yield of the sources is scant, a natural sequel from the fact that no one of them had his biography for its main theme, still less had his own action in crises of enforced ambiguity.

Of all known sources the best are Khwānd-amīr's *Ḥabību's-siyar* and Ḥaidar Mīrzā *Dūghlāt's Tārīkh-i-rashīdī.* The first was finished nominally in 930 AH. (1524-5 AD.), seven years therefore before Bābur's death, but it received much addition of matter concerning Bābur after its author went to Hindūstān in 934 AH. (f. 339). Its fourth part, a life of Shāh Ismā'īl *Ṣafawī* is especially valuable for the years of this *lacuna.* Ḥaidar's book was finished under Humāyūn in 953 AH. (1547 AD.), when its author had reigned five years in Kashmīr. It is the most valuable of all the sources for those interested in Bābur himself, both because of Ḥaidar's excellence as a biographer, and through his close acquaintance with Bābur's family. From his eleventh to his thirteenth year he lived under Bābur's protection, followed this by 19 years service under Sa'īd Khān, the cousin of both, in Kāshghar, and after that Khān's death, went to Bābur's sons Kāmrān and Humāyūn in Hindūstān.

A work issuing from a Sunnī Aūzbeg centre, Faẓl bin Ruzbahān *Isfahānī's Sūlūku'l-mulūk*, has a Preface of special value, as shewing one view of what it writes of as the spread of heresy in Māwarā'u'n-nahr through Bābur's invasions. The book itself is a Treatise on Musalmān Law, and was prepared by order of 'Ubaidu'l-lāh Khān *Aūzbeg* for his help in fulfilling a vow he had made, before attacking Bābur in 918 AH., at the shrine of Khwāja Aḥmad *Yasawī* [in Ḥaẓrat Turkistān], that, if he were victorious, he would conform exactly with the divine Law and uphold it in Māwarā'u'n-nahr (Rieu's Pers. Cat. ii, 448).

The *Tārīkh-i Ḥājī Muḥammad 'Ārif Qandahārī* appears, from the frequent use Firishta made of it, to be a useful source, both because its author was a native of Qandahār, a place much occupying Bābur's activities, and because he was a servant of Bairām Khān-i-khānān, whose assassination under Akbar he witnessed.[1333] Unfortunately, though his life of Akbar survives no copy is now known of the section of his General History which deals with Bābur's.

An early source is Yahya *Kazwīnī's Lubbu't-tawārīkh*, written in 948 AH. (1541 AD.), but brief only in the Bābur period. It issued from a Shī'a source, being commanded by Shāh Ismā'īl *Ṣafawī*'s son Bahrām.

Another work issuing also from a *Ṣafawī* centre is Mīr Sikandar's *Tārīkh-i-'ālam-arāī*, a history of Shāh 'Abbas I, with an introduction treating of his predecessors which was completed in 1025 AH. (1616 AD.). Its interest lies in its outlook on Bābur's dealings with Shāh Ismā'īl.

A later source, brief only, is Firishta's *Tārīkh-i-firishta*, finished under Jahāngīr in the first quarter of the 17th century.

Mr. Erskine makes frequent reference to Kh(w)āfī Khān's *Tārīkh*, a secondary authority however, written under Aurangzīb, mainly based on Firishta's work, and merely summarizing Bābur's period. References to detached incidents of the period are found in Shaikh 'Abdu'l-qādir's *Tārīkh-i-badāyūnī* and Mīr Ma'ṣūm's *Tārīkh-i-sind.*

EVENTS OF THE UNCHRONICLED YEARS

914 AH.-MAY 2ND 1508 TO APRIL 21ST 1509 AD.

The mutiny, of which an account begins in the text, was crushed by the victory of 500 loyalists over 3,000 rebels, one factor of success being Bābur's defeat in single combat of five champions of his adversaries.[1334] The disturbance was not of long duration; Kābul was tranquil in Sha'bān (November) when Sl. Sa'īd Khān *Chaghatāī*, then 21, arrived there seeking his cousin's protection, after defeat by his brother Manṣūr at Almātū, escape from death, commanded by Shaibānī, in Farghāna, a winter journey through Qarā-tīgīn to Mīrzā Khān in Qilā'-i-ẓafar, refusal of an offer to put him in that feeble Mīrzā's place, and so on to Kābul, where he came a destitute fugitive and enjoyed a freedom from care never known by him before (f. 200*b*; T.R. p. 226). The year was fatal to his family and to Ḥaidar's; in it Shaibānī murdered Sl. Maḥmūd Khān and his six sons, Muḥammad Ḥusain Mīrzā and other Dūghlāt sulṭāns.

915 AH.-APRIL 21ST 1509 TO APRIL 11TH 1510 AD.

In this year hostilities began between Shāh Ismā'īl *Ṣafawī* and Muḥ. Shaibānī Khān *Aūzbeg*, news of which must have excited keen interest in Kābul.

In it occurred also what was in itself a minor matter of a child's safety, but became of historical importance, namely, the beginning of personal acquaintance between Bābur and his sympathetic biographer Ḥaidar Mīrzā *Dūghlāt*. Ḥaidar, like Sa'īd, came a fugitive to the protection of a kinsman; he was then eleven, had been saved by servants from the death commanded by Shaibānī, conveyed to Mīrzā Khān in Badakhshān, thence sent for by Bābur to the greater security of Kābul (f. 11; Index *s.n.*; T.R. p. 227).

916 AH.-APRIL 11TH 1510 TO MARCH 31ST 1510 AD.

a. News of the battle of Merv.

Over half of this year passed quietly in Kābul; Ramẓān (December) brought from Mīrzā Khān (Wāis) the stirring news that Ismā'īl had defeated Shaibānī near Merv.[1335] "It is not known," wrote the Mīrzā, "whether Shāhī Beg Khān has been killed or not. All the Aūzbegs have crossed the Amū. Amīr Aūrūs, who was in Qūndūz, has fled. About 20,000 Mughūls, who left the Aūzbeg at Merv, have come to Qūndūz. I have come there." He then invited Bābur to join him and with him to try for the recovery of their ancestral territories (T.R. p. 237).

b. Bābur's campaign in Transoxiana begun.

The Mīrzā's letter was brought over passes blocked by snow; Bābur, with all possible speed, took the one winter-route through Āb-dara, kept the Ramẓān Feast in Bāmīān, and reached Qūndūz in Shawwāl (Jan. 1511 AD.). Ḥaidar's detail about the Feast seems likely to have been recorded because he had read Bābur's own remark, made in Ramẓān 933 AH. (June 1527) that up to that date, when he kept it in Sīkrī, he had not since his eleventh year kept it twice in the same place (f. 330).

c. Mughūl affairs.

Outside Qūndūz lay the Mughūls mentioned by Mīrzā Khān as come from Merv and so mentioned, presumably, as a possible reinforcement. They had been servants of Bābur's uncles Maḥmūd and Aḥmad, and when Shaibānī defeated those Khāns at Akhsī in 908 AH., had been compelled by him to migrate into Khurāsān to places remote from Mughūlistān. Many of them had served in Kāshghar; none had served a Tīmūrid Mīrzā. Set free by Shaibānī's death, they had come east, a Khān-less 20,000 of armed and fully equipped men and they were there, as Ḥaidar says, in their strength while of Chaghatāīs there were not more than 5,000. They now, and with them the Mughūls from Kābul, used the opportunity offering for return to a more congenial location and leadership, by the presence in Qūndūz of a legitimate Khāqān and the clearance in Andijān, a threshold of Mughūlistān, of its Aūzbeg governors (f. 200*b*). The chiefs of both bodies of Mughūls, Sherīm Taghāī at the head of one, Ayūb *Begchīk* of the other, proffered the Mughūl Khānship to Sa'īd with offer to set Bābur aside, perhaps to kill him. It is improbable that in making their offer they contemplated locating themselves in the confined country of Kābul; what they seem to have wished was what Bābur gave, Sa'īd for their Khāqān and permission to go north with him.

Sa'īd, in words worth reading, rejected their offer to injure Bābur, doing so on the grounds of right and gratitude, but, the two men agreeing that it was now expedient for them to part, asked to be sent to act for Bābur where their friendship could be maintained for their common welfare. The matter was settled by Bābur's sending him into Andijān in response to an urgent petition for help there just arrived from Ḥaidar's uncle. He "was made Khān" and started forth in the following year, on Ṣafar 14th 917 AH. (May 13th 1511 AD.); with him went most of the Mughūls but not all, since even of those from Merv, Ayūb *Begchīk* and others are found mentioned on several later occasions as being with Bābur.

Bābur's phrase "I made him Khān" (f. 200*b*) recalls his earlier mention of what seems to be the same appointment (f. 10*b*), made by Abū-sa'īd of Yūnas as Khān of the Mughūls; in each case the meaning seems to be that the Tīmūrid Mīrzā made the Chaghatāī Khān Khāqān of the Mughūls.

d. First attempt on Ḥiṣār.

After spending a short time in Qūndūz, Bābur moved for Ḥiṣār in which were the Aūzbeg sulṭāns Mahdī and Ḥamza. They came out into Wakhsh to meet him but, owing to an imbroglio, there was no encounter and each side retired (T.R. p. 238).

e. Intercourse between Bābur and Ismā'īl Ṣafawī.

While Bābur was now in Qūndūz his sister Khān-zāda arrived there, safe-returned under escort of the Shāh's troops, after the death in the battle of Merv of her successive husbands Shaibānī and Sayyid Hādī, and with her came an envoy from Ismā'īl proffering friendship, civilities calculated to arouse a hope of Persian help in Bābur. To acknowledge his courtesies, Bābur sent Mīrzā Khān with thanks and gifts; Ḥaidar says that the Mīrzā also conveyed protestations of good faith and a request for military assistance. He was well received and his request for help was granted; that it was granted under hard conditions then stated later occurrences shew.

917 AH.-MARCH 31ST 1511 TO MARCH 19TH 1512 AD.

a. Second attempt on Ḥiṣār.

In this year Bābur moved again on Ḥiṣār. He took post, where once his forbear Tīmūr had wrought out success against great odds, at the Pul-i-sangīn (Stone-bridge) on the Sūrkh-āb, and lay there a month awaiting reinforcement. The Aūzbeg sulṭāns faced him on the other side of the river, they too, presumably, awaiting reinforcement. They moved when they felt themselves strong enough to attack, whether by addition to their own numbers, whether by learning that Bābur had not largely increased his own. Concerning the second alternative it is open to surmise that he hoped for larger reinforcement than he obtained; he appears to have left Qūndūz before the return of Mīrzā Khān from his embassy to Ismā'īl, to have expected Persian reinforcement with the Mīrzā, and at Pul-i-sangīn, where the Mīrzā joined him in time to fight, to have been strengthened by the Mīrzā's own following, and few, if any, foreign auxiliaries. These surmises are supported by what Khwānd-amīr relates of the conditions [specified later] on which the Shāh's main contingent was despatched and by his shewing that it did not start until after the Shāh had had news of the battle at Pul-i-sangīn.

At the end of the month of waiting, the Aūzbegs one morning swam the Sūrkh-āb below the bridge; in the afternoon of the same day, Bābur retired to better ground amongst the mountain fastnesses of a local Āb-dara. In the desperate encounter which followed the Aūzbegs were utterly routed with great loss in men; they were pursued to Darband-i-ahanīn (Iron-gate) on the Ḥiṣār border, on their way to join a great force assembled at Qarshī under Kūchūm Khān, Shaibānī's successor as Aūzbeg Khāqān. The battle is admirably described by Ḥaidar, who was then a boy of 12 with keen eye watching his own first fight, and that fight with foes who had made him the last male survivor of his line. In the evening of the victory Mahdī, Ḥamza and Ḥamza's son Mamak were brought before Bābur who, says Ḥaidar, did to them what they had done to the Mughūl Khāqāns and Chaghatāī Sulṭāns, that is, he retaliated in blood for the blood of many kinsmen.

b. Persian reinforcement.

After the battle Bābur went to near Ḥiṣār, was there joined by many local tribesmen, and, some time later, by a large body of Ismā'īl's troops under Aḥmad Beg *Ṣafawī*, 'Alī Khān *Istiljū* and Shāhrukh Sl. *Afshār*, Ismā'īl's seal-keeper. The following particulars, given by Khwānd-amīr, about the despatch of this contingent help to fix the order of occurrences, and throw light on the price paid by Bābur for his auxiliaries. He announced his victory over Mahdī and Ḥamza to the Shāh, and at the same time promised that if he reconquered the rest of Transoxiana by the Shāh's help, he would read his name in the *khuṭba*, stamp it on coins together with those of the Twelve Imāms, and work to destroy the power of the Aūzbegs. These undertakings look like a response to a demand; such conditions cannot have been proffered; their acceptance must have been compelled. Khwānd-amīr says that when Ismā'īl fully understood the purport of Bābur's letter, [by which would seem to be meant, when he knew that his conditions of help were accepted,] he despatched the troops under the three Commanders named above.

The Persian chiefs advised a move direct on Bukhārā and Samarkand; and with this Bābur's councillors concurred, they saying, according to Ḥaidar, that Bukhārā was then empty of troops and full of fools. 'Ubaid Khān had thrown himself into Qarshī; it was settled not to attack him but to pass on and encamp a stage beyond the town. This was done; then scout followed scout, bringing news that he had come out of Qarshī and was hurrying to Bukhārā, his own fief. Instant and swift pursuit followed him up the 100 miles of caravan-road, into Bukhārā, and on beyond, sweeping him and his garrison, plundered as they fled, into the open land of Turkistān. Many sulṭāns had collected in Samarkand, some no doubt being, like Tīmūr its governor, fugitives escaped from Pul-i-sangīn. Dismayed by Bābur's second success, they scattered into Turkistān, thus leaving him an open road.

c. Samarkand re-occupied and relations with Ismā'īl Ṣafawī.

He must now have hoped to be able to dispense with his dangerous colleagues, for he dismissed them when he reached Bukhārā, with gifts and thanks for their services. It is Ḥaidar, himself present, who fixes Bukhārā as the place of the dismissal (T.R. p. 246).

From Bukhārā Bābur went to Samarkand. It was mid-Rajab 917 AH. (October 1511 AD.), some ten months after leaving Kābul, and after 9 years of absence, that he re-entered the town, itself gay with decoration for his welcome, amidst the acclaim of its people.[1336]

Eight months were to prove his impotence to keep it against the forces ranged against him,—Aūzbeg strength in arms compacted by Sunnī zeal, Sunnī hatred of a Shī'a's suzerainty intensified by dread lest that potent Shī'a should resolve to perpetuate his dominance. Both as a Sunnī and as one who had not owned a suzerain, the position was unpleasant for Bābur. That his alliance with Ismā'īl was dangerous he will have known, as also that his risks grew as Transoxiana was over-spread by news of Ismā'īl's fanatical barbarism to pious and learned Sunnīs, notably in Herī. He manifested desire for release both now and later,—now when he not only dismissed his Persian helpers but so behaved to the Shāh's envoy Muḥammad Jān,—he was Najm S̤ānī's Lord of the Gate,—that the envoy felt neglect and made report of Bābur as arrogant, in opposition, and unwilling to fulfil his compact,—later when he eagerly attempted success unaided against 'Ubaid Khān, and was then worsted. It illustrates the Shāh's view of his suzerain relation to Bābur that on hearing Muḥammad Jān's report, he ordered Najm S̤ānī to bring the offender to order.

Meantime the Shāh's conditions seem to have been carried out in Samarkand and Bābur's subservience clearly shewn.[1337] Of this there are the indications,—that Bābur had promised and was a man of his word; that Sunnī irritation against him waxed and did not wane as it might have done without food to nourish it; that Bābur knew himself impotent against the Aūzbegs unless he had foreign aid, expected attack, knew it was preparing; that he would hear of Muḥammad Jān's report and of Najm S̤ānī's commission against himself. Honesty, policy and necessity combined to enforce the fulfilment of his agreement. What were the precise terms of that agreement beyond the two as to the *khuṭba* and the coins, it needs close study of the wording of the sources to decide, lest metaphor be taken for fact. Great passions,—ambition, religious fervour, sectarian bigotry and fear confronted him. His problem was greater than that of Henry of

Navarre and of Napoleon in Egypt; they had but to seem what secured their acceptance; he had to put on a guise that brought him hate.

Khān-zāda was not the only member of Bābur's family who now rejoined him after marriage with an Aūzbeg. His half-sister Yādgār-sulṭān had fallen to the share of Ḥamza Sulṭān's son 'Abdu'l-laṭīf in 908 AH. when Shaibānī defeated the Khāns near Akhsī. Now that her half-brother had defeated her husband's family, she returned to her own people (f. 9).

918 AH.-MARCH 19TH 1512 TO MARCH 9TH 1513 AD.

a. Return of the Aūzbegs.

Emboldened by the departure of the Persian troops, the Aūzbegs, in the spring of the year, came out of Turkistān, their main attack being directed on Tāshkīnt, then held for Bābur.[1338] 'Ubaid Khān moved for Bukhārā. He had prefaced his march by vowing that, if successful, he would thenceforth strictly observe Musalmān Law. The vow was made in Ḥaẓrat Turkistān at the shrine of Khwāja Aḥmad *Yasawī*, a saint revered in Central Asia through many centuries; he had died about 1120 AD.; Tīmūr had made pilgrimage to his tomb, in 1397 AD., and then had founded the mosque still dominating the town, still the pilgrim's land-mark.[1339] 'Ubaid's vow, like Bābur's of 933 AH., was one of return to obedience. Both men took oath in the Ghāzī's mood, Bābur's set against the Hindū whom he saw as a heathen, 'Ubaid's set against Bābur whom he saw as a heretic.

b. Bābur's defeat at Kul-i-malik.

In Ṣafar (April-May) 'Ubaid moved swiftly down and attacked the Bukhārā neighbourhood. Bābur went from Samarkand to meet him. Several details of what followed, not given by Ḥaidar and, in one particular, contradicting him, are given by Khwānd-amīr. The statement in which the two historians contradict one another is Ḥaidar's that 'Ubaid had 3000 men only, Bābur 40,000. Several considerations give to Khwānd-amīr's opposed statement that Bābur's force was small, the semblance of being nearer the fact. Ḥaidar, it may be said, did not go out on this campaign; he was ill in Samarkand and continued ill there for some time; Khwānd-amīr's details have the well-informed air of things learned at first-hand, perhaps from some-one in Hindūstān after 934 AH.

Matters which make against Bābur's having a large effective force at Kul-i-malik, and favour Khwānd-amīr's statement about the affair are these:— 'Ubaid must have formed some estimate of what he had to meet, and he brought 3000 men. Where could Bābur have obtained 40,000 men worth reckoning in a fight? In several times of crisis his own immediate and ever-faithful troop is put at 500; as his cause was now unpopular, local accretions may have been few. Some Mughūls from Merv and from Kābul were near Samarkand (T.R. pp. 263, 265); most were with Sa'īd in Andijān; but however many Mughūls may have been in his neighbourhood, none could be counted on as resolute for his success. If too, he had had more than a small effective force, would he not have tried to hold Samarkand with the remnant of defeat until Persian help arrived? All things considered, there is ground for accepting Khwānd-amīr's statement that Bābur met 'Ubaid with a small force.

Following his account therefore:—Bābur in his excess of daring, marched to put the Aūzbeg down with a small force only, against the advice of the prudent, of whom Muḥammad Mazīd Tarkhān was one, who all said it was wrong to go out unprepared and without reinforcement. Paying them no attention, Bābur marched for Bukhārā, was rendered still more daring by news had when he neared it, that the enemy had retired some stages, and followed him up almost to his camp. 'Ubaid was in great force; many Aūzbegs perished but, in the end, they were victors and Bābur was compelled to take refuge in Bukhārā. The encounter took place near Kul-i-malik (King's-lake) in Ṣafar 918 AH. (April-May 1512 AD.).

c. Bābur leaves Samarkand.

It was not possible to maintain a footing in Samarkand; Bābur therefore collected his family and train[1340] and betook himself to Ḥiṣār. There went with him on this expedition Māhīm and her children Humāyūn, Mihr-jahān and Bārbūl,—the motherless Ma'ṣūma,—Gul-rukh with her son Kāmrān (Gulbadan f. 7). I have not found any account of his route; Ḥaidar gives no details about the journey; he did not travel with Bābur, being still invalided in Samarkand. Perhaps the absence of information is a sign that the Aūzbegs had not yet appeared on the direct road for Ḥiṣār. A local tradition however would make Bābur go round through Farghāna. He certainly might have gone into Farghāna hoping to co-operate with Sa'īd Khān; Tāshkīnt was still holding out under Aḥmad-i-qāsim *Kohbur* and it is clear that all activity in Bābur's force had not been quenched because during the Tāshkīnt siege, Dost Beg broke through the enemy's ranks and made his way into the town. Sairām held out longer than Tāshkīnt. Of any such move by Bābur into Andijān the only hint received is given by what may be a mere legend.[1341]

d. Bābur in Ḥiṣār.

After experiencing such gains and such losses, Bābur was still under 30 years of age.

The Aūzbegs, after his departure, re-occupied Bukhārā and Samarkand without harm done to the towns-people, and a few weeks later, in Jumāda I (July-August) followed him to Ḥiṣār. Meantime he with Mīrzā Khān's help, had so closed the streets of the town by massive earth-works that the sulṭāns were convinced its defenders were ready to spend the last drop of their blood in holding it, and therefore retired without attack.[1342] Some sources give as their reason for retirement that Bābur had been reinforced from Balkh; Bairām Beg, it is true, had sent a force but one of 300 men only; so few cannot have alarmed except as the harbinger of more. Greater precision as to dates would shew whether they can have heard of Najm Ṣānī's army advancing by way of Balkh.

e. Qarshī and Ghaj-davān.

Meantime Najm Ṣānī, having with him some 11,000 men, had started on his corrective mission against Bābur. When he reached the Khurāsān frontier, he heard of the defeat at Kul-i-malik and the flight to Ḥiṣār, gathered other troops from Harāt and elsewhere, and advanced to Balkh. He stayed there for 20 days with Bairām Beg, perhaps occupied, in part, by communications with the Shāh and Bābur. From the latter repeated request for help is said to have come; help was given, some sources say without the Shāh's permission. A rendezvous was fixed, Najm Ṣānī marched to Tīrmīẕ, there crossed the Amū and in Rajab (Sep.-Oct.) encamped near the Darband-i-ahanīn. On Bābur's approach through the Chak-chaq pass, he paid him the civility of going several miles out from his camp to give him honouring reception.

Advancing thence for Bukhārā, the combined armies took Khuzār and moved on to Qarshī. This town Bābur wished to pass by, as it had been passed by on his previous march for Bukhārā; each time perhaps he wished to spare its people, formerly his subjects, whom he desired to rule again, and who are reputed to have been mostly his fellow Turks. Najm Ṣānī refused to pass on; he said Qarshī must be taken because it was 'Ubaidu'l-lāh Khān's nest; in it was 'Ubaid's uncle Shaikhīm Mīrzā; it was captured; the Aūzbeg garrison was put to the sword and, spite of Bābur's earnest entreaties, all the towns-people, 15,000 persons it is said, down to the "suckling and decrepit", were massacred. Amongst the victims was Banā'ī who happened to be within it. This action roused the utmost anger against Najm Ṣānī; it disgusted Bābur, not only through its merciless slaughter but because it made clear the disregard in which he was held by his magnificent fellow-general.

From murdered Qarshī Najm Ṣānī advanced for Bukhārā. On getting within a few miles of it, he heard that an Aūzbeg force was approaching under Tīmūr and Abū-sa'īd, presumably from Samarkand therefore. He sent Bairām Beg to attack them; they drew off to the north and threw themselves into Ghaj-davān, the combined armies following them. This move placed Najm Ṣ̤ānī across the Zar-afshān, on the border of the desert with which the Aūzbegs were familiar, and with 'Ubaid on his flank in Bukhārā.

As to what followed the sources vary; they are brief; they differ less in statement of the same occurrence than in their choice of details to record; as Mr. Erskine observes their varying stories are not incompatible. Their widest difference is a statement of time but the two periods named, one a few days, the other four months, may not be meant to apply to the same event. Four months the siege is said to have lasted; this could not have been said if it had been a few days only. The siege seems to have been of some duration.

At first there were minor engagements, ending with varying success; provisions and provender became scarce; Najm Ṣ̤ānī's officers urged retirement, so too did Bābur. He would listen to none of them. At length 'Ubaid Khān rode out from Bukhārā at the head of excellent troops; he joined the Ghaj-davān garrison and the united Aūzbegs posted themselves in the suburbs where walled lanes and gardens narrowed the field and lessened Najm Ṣ̤ānī's advantage in numbers. On Tuesday Ramẓān 3rd (Nov. 12th)[1343] a battle was fought in which his army was routed and he himself slain.

f. Bābur and Yār-i-aḥmad Najm Sānī.

Some writers say that Najm Ṣ̤ānī's men did not fight well; it must be remembered that they may have been weakened by privation and that they had wished to retire. Of Bābur it is said that he, who was the reserve, did not fight at all; it is difficult to see good cause why, under all the circumstances, he should risk the loss of his men. It seems likely that Ḥaidar's strong language about this defeat would suit Bābur's temper also. "The victorious breezes of Islām overturned the banners of the schismatics.... Most of them perished on the field; the rents made by the sword at Qarshī were sewn up at Ghaj-davān by the arrow-stitches of vengeance. Najm Ṣ̤ānī and all the Turkmān amīrs were sent to hell."

The belief that Bābur had failed Najm Ṣ̤ānī persisted at the Persian Court, for his inaction was made a reproach to his son Humāyūn in 951 AH. (1544 AD.), when Humāyūn was a refugee with Ismā'īl's son Ṭahmāsp. Badāyūnī tells a story which, with great inaccuracy of name and place, represents the view taken at that time. The part of the anecdote pertinent here is that Bābur on the eve of the battle at Ghaj-davān, shot an arrow into the Aūzbeg camp which carried the following couplet, expressive of his ill-will to the Shāh and perhaps also of his rejection of the Shī'a guise he himself had worn.

I made the Shāh's Najm road-stuff for the Aūzbegs;

If fault has been mine, I have now cleansed the road.[1344]

g. The Mughūls attack Bābur.

On his second return to Ḥiṣār Bābur was subjected to great danger by a sudden attack made upon him by the Mughūls where he lay at night in his camp outside the town. Firishta says, but without particulars of their offence, that Bābur had reproached them for their misconduct; the absence of detail connecting the affair with the defeat just sustained, leads to the supposition that their misdeeds were a part of the tyranny over the country-people punished later by 'Ubaidu'l-lāh Khān. Roused from his sleep by the noise of his guards' resistance to the Mughūl attack, Bābur escaped with difficulty and without a single attendant[1345] into the fort. The conspirators plundered his camp and withdrew to Qarā-tīgīn. He was in no position to oppose them, left a few men in Ḥiṣār and went to Mīrzā Khān in Qūndūz.

After he left, Ḥiṣār endured a desolating famine, a phenomenal snowfall and the ravages of the Mughūls. 'Ubaid Khān avenged Bābur on the horde; hearing of their excesses, he encamped outside the position they had taken up in Wakhsh defended by river, hills and snow, waited till a road thawed, then fell upon them and avenged the year's misery they had inflicted on the Ḥiṣārīs. Ḥaidar says of them that it was their villainy lost Ḥiṣār to Bābur and gained it for the Aūzbeg.[1346]

These Mughūls had for chiefs men who when Sa'īd went to Andijān, elected to stay with Bābur. One of the three named by Ḥaidar was Ayūb *Begchīk*. He repented his disloyalty; when he lay dying some two years later (920 AH.) in Yāngī-ḥiṣār, he told Sa'īd Khān who visited him, that what was "lacerating his bowels and killing him with remorse", was his faithlessness to Bābur in Ḥiṣār, the oath he had broken at the instigation of those "hogs and bears", the Mughūl chiefs (T.R. p. 315).

In this year but before the Mughūl treachery to Bābur, Ḥaidar left him, starting in Rajab (Sep.-Oct.) to Sa'id in Andijān and thus making a beginning of his 19 years spell of service.

919 AH.-MARCH 9TH 1513 TO FEB. 26TH 1514 AD.

Bābur may have spent this year in Khishm (Ḥ.S. iii, 372). During two or three months of it, he had one of the Shāh's retainers in his service, Khwāja Kamālu'd-dīn Maḥmūd, who had fled from Ghaj-davān to Balkh, heard there that the Balkhīs favoured an Aūzbeg chief whose coming was announced, and therefore went to Bābur. In Jumāda 11 (August), hearing that the Aūzbeg sultan had left Balkh, he returned there but was not admitted because the Balkhīs feared reprisals for their welcome to the Aūzbeg, a fear which may indicate that he had taken some considerable reinforcement to Bābur. He went on into Khurāsān and was there killed; Balkh was recaptured for the Shāh by Deo Sulṭān, a removal from Aūzbeg possession which helps to explain how Bābur came to be there in 923 AH.

920 AH.—FEB. 26TH 1514 TO FEB. 15TH 1515 AD.

Ḥaidar writes of Bābur as though he were in Qūndūz this year (TR. p. 263), says that he suffered the greatest misery and want, bore it with his accustomed courtesy and patience but, at last, despairing of success in recovering Ḥiṣār, went back to Kābul. Now it seems to be that he made the stay in Khwāst to which he refers later (f. 241*b*) and during which his daughter Gul-rang was born, as Gul-badan's chronicle allows known.

It was at the end of the year, after the privation of winter therefore, that he reached Kābul. When he re-occupied Samarkand in 917 AH., he had given Kābul to his half-brother Nāṣir Mīrzā; the Mīrzā received him now with warm welcome and protestations of devotion and respect, spoke of having guarded Kābul for him and asked permission to return to his own old fief Ghaznī. His behaviour made a deep impression on Bābur; it would be felt as a humane touch on the sore of failure.

921 AH.—FEB. 15TH 1515 TO FEB. 5TH 1516 AD.

a. Rebellion of chiefs in Ghaznī.

Nāṣir Mīrzā died shortly after (*dar hamān ayyām*) his return to Ghaznī. Disputes then arose amongst the various commanders who were in Ghaznī; Sherīm Ṭaghāī was one of them and the main strength of the tumult was given by the Mughūls. Many others were however involved in it, even such an old servant as Bābā of Pashāghar taking part (f. 234*b*; T.R. p. 356). Ḥaidar did not know precisely the cause of the dispute, or shew why it should have turned against Bābur, since he attributes it to possession taken by Satan of the brains of the chiefs and a consequent access of vain-glory and wickedness. Possibly some question of succession to Nāṣir arose. Dost Beg distinguished himself in the regular battle which ensued; Qāsim Beg's son Qaṃbar-i-'alī hurried down from Qūndūz and also did his good part to win it for Bābur. Many of the rioters were killed, others fled to Kāshghar. Sherīm Ṭaghāī was one of the latter; as Sa'īd Khān gave him no welcome, he could not stay there; he fell back on the much injured Bābur who, says Ḥaidar, showed him his usual benevolence, turned his eyes from his offences and looked only at his past services until he died shortly afterwards (T.R. p. 357).[1347]

922 AH.—FEB. 5TH 1516 TO JAN. 24TH 1517 AD.

This year may have been spent in and near Kābul in the quiet promoted by the dispersion of the Mughūls.

In this year was born Bābur's son Muḥammad known as *'Askarī* from his being born in camp. He was the son of Gulrukh *Begchīk* and full-brother of Kāmrān.

923 AH.—JAN. 24TH 1517 TO JAN. 13TH 1518 AD.

a. Bābur visits Balkh.

Khwānd-amīr is the authority for the little that is known of Bābur's action in this year (Ḥ.S. iii, 367 *et seq.*). It is connected with the doings of Badī'u'z-zamān *Bāī-qarā's* son Muḥammad-i-zamān. This Mīrzā had had great wanderings, during a part of which Khwānd-amīr was with him. In 920 AH. he was in Shāh Ismā'īl's service and in Balkh, but was not able to keep it. Bābur invited him to Kābul,—the date of invitation will have been later therefore than Bābur's return there at the end of 920 AH. The Mīrzā was on his way but was dissuaded from going into Kābul by Mahdī Khwāja and went instead into Ghurjistān. Bābur was angered by his non-arrival and pursued him in order to punish him but did not succeed in reaching Ghurjistān and went back to Kābul by way of Fīrūz-koh and Ghūr. The Mīrzā was captured eventually and sent to Kābul. Bābur treated him with kindness, after a few months gave him his daughter Ma'ṣūma in marriage, and sent him to Balkh. He appears to have been still in Balkh when Khwānd-amīr was writing of the above occurrences in 929 AH. The marriage took place either at the end of 923 or beginning of 924 AH. The Mīrzā was then 21, Ma'ṣūma 9; she almost certainly did not then go to Balkh. At some time in 923 AH. Bābur is said by Khwānd-amīr to have visited that town.[1348]

b. Attempt on Qandahār.

In this year Bābur marched for Qandahār but the move ended peacefully, because a way was opened for gifts and terms by an illness which befell him when he was near the town.

The *Tārīkh-i-sind* gives what purports to be Shāh Beg's explanation of Bābur's repeated attempts on Qandahār. He said these had been made and would be made because Bābur had not forgiven Muqīm for taking Kābul 14 years earlier from the Tīmūrid 'Abdu'r-razzāq; that this had brought him to Qandahār in 913 AH., this had made him then take away Māhchuchak, Muqīm's daughter; that there were now (923 AH.) many unemployed Mīrzās in Kābul for whom posts could not be found in regions where the Persians and Aūzbegs were dominant; that an outlet for their ambitions and for Bābur's own would be sought against the weaker opponent he himself was.

Bābur's decision to attack in this year is said to have been taken while Shāh Beg was still a prisoner of Shāh Ismā'īl in the Harāt country; he must have been released meantime by the admirable patience of his slave Saṃbhal.

---

924 AH.—JAN. 13TH 1518 TO JAN. 3RD 1519 AD.

In this year Shāh Beg's son Shāh Ḥasan came to Bābur after quarrel with his father. He stayed some two years, and during that time was married to Khalīfa's daughter Gul-barg (Rose-leaf). His return to Qandahār will have taken place shortly before Bābur's campaign of 926 A.H. against it, a renewed effort which resulted in possession on Shawwāl 13th 928 AH. (Sep. 6th 1522 AD.).[1349]

In this year began the campaign in the north-east territories of Kābul, an account of which is carried on in the diary of 925 AH. It would seem that in the present year Chaghān-sarāī was captured, and also the fortress at the head of the valley of Bābā-qarā, belonging to Ḥaidar-i-'alī *Bajaurī* (f. 216*b*).[1350]

View from above Babur's Grave and Shah-jahan's Mosque.

925 AH.-JAN. 3RD TO DEC. 23RD 1519 AD.[1351]

(a. Bābur takes the fort of Bajaur.)

(*Jan. 3rd*) On Monday[1352] the first day of the month of Muḥarram, there was a violent earthquake in the lower part of the dale (*julga*) of Chandāwal,[1353] which lasted nearly half an astronomical hour.

(*Jan. 4th*) Marching at dawn from that camp with the intention of attacking the fort of Bajaur,[1354] we dismounted near it and sent a trusty man of the Dilazāk[1355] Afghāns to advise its sulṭān[1356] and people to take up a position of service (*qullūq*) and surrender the fort. Not accepting this counsel, that stupid and ill-fated band sent back a wild answer, where-upon the army was ordered to make ready mantelets, ladders and other appliances for taking a fort. For this purpose a day's (*Jan. 5th*) halt was made on that same ground.

(*Jan. 6th*) On Thursday the 4th of Muḥarram, orders were given that the army should put on mail, arm and get to horse;[1357] that the left wing should move swiftly to the upper side of the fort, cross the water at the water-entry,[1358] and dismount on the Fol. 217.north side of the fort; that the centre, not taking the way across the water, should dismount in the rough, up-and-down land to the north-west of the fort; and that the right should dismount to the west of the lower gate. While the begs of the left under Dost Beg were dismounting, after crossing the water, a hundred to a hundred and fifty men on foot came out of the fort, shooting arrows. The begs, shooting in their turn, advanced till they had forced those men back to the foot of the ramparts, Mullā 'Abdu'l-malūk of Khwāst, like a madman,[1359] going up right under them on his horse. There and then the fort would have been taken if the ladders and mantelets had been ready, and if it had not been so late in the day. Mullā Tirik-i-'alī[1360] and a servant of Tīngrī-bīrdī crossed swords with the enemy; each overcame his man, cut off and brought in his head; for this each was promised a reward.

As the Bajaurīs had never before seen matchlocks (*tufang*) they at first took no care about them, indeed they made fun when they heard the report and answered it by unseemly gestures. On that day[1361] Ustād 'Alī-qulī shot at and brought down five men with his matchlock; Walī the Treasurer, for his part, brought down two; other matchlockmen were also very active in firing and did well, shooting through shield, through cuirass, through *kusarū*,[1362] and bringing down one man after another. Perhaps 7, 8, or 10 Bajaurīs had fallen to the matchlock-fire (*ẓarb*) before night. After that it so became that not a head could be put out because of the fire. The orderFol. 217b. was given, "It is night; let the army retire, and at dawn, if the appliances are ready, let them swarm up into the fort."

(*Jan. 7th*) At the first dawn of light (*farẓ waqt*) on Friday the 5th of Muḥarram, orders were given that, when the battle-nagarets had sounded, the army should advance, each man from his place to his appointed post (*yīrlīk yīrdīn*) and should swarm up. The left and centre advanced from their ground with mantelets in place all along their lines, fixed their ladders, and swarmed up them. The whole left hand of the centre, under Khalīfa, Shāh Ḥasan *Arghūn* and Yūsuf's Aḥmad, was ordered to reinforce the left wing. Dost Beg's men went forward to the foot of the north-eastern tower of the fort, and busied themselves in undermining and bringing it down. Ustād 'Alī-qulī was there also; he shot very well on that day with his matchlock, and he twice fired off the *firingī*.[1363] Walī the Treasurer also brought down a man with his matchlock. Malik 'Alī *quṭnī*[1364] was first up a ladder of all the men from the left hand of the centre, and there was busy with fight and blow. At the post of the centre, Muḥ. 'Alī *Jang-jang*[1365] and his younger brother Nau-roz got up, each by a different ladder, and made lance and sword to touch. Bābā the waiting man (*yasāwal*), getting up by another ladder, occupied himself in breaking down the fort-wall with his Fol. 218.axe. Most of our braves went well forward, shooting off dense flights of arrows and not letting the enemy put out a head; others made themselves desperately busy in breaching and pulling down the fort, caring naught for the enemy's fight and blow, giving no eye to his arrows and stones. By breakfast-time Dost Beg's men had undermined and breached the north-eastern tower, got in and put the foe to flight. The men of the centre got in up the ladders by the same time, but those (*aūl*) others were first (*awwal*?) in.[1366] By the favour and pleasure of the High God, this strong and mighty fort was taken in two or three astronomical hours! Matching the fort were the utter struggle and effort of our braves; distinguish themselves they did, and won the name and fame of heroes.

As the Bajaurīs were rebels and at enmity with the people of Islām, and as, by reason of the heathenish and hostile customs prevailing in their midst, the very name of Islām was rooted out from their tribe, they were put to general massacre and their wives and children were made captive. At a guess more than 3000 men went to their death; as the fight did not reach to the eastern side of the fort, a few got away there.

The fort taken, we entered and inspected it. On the walls, in houses, streets and alleys, the dead lay, in what numbers! Comers and goers to and fro were passing over the bodies. Fol. 218b.Returning from our inspection, we sat down in the Bajaur sulṭān's residence. The country of Bajaur we bestowed on Khwāja Kalān,[1367] assigning a large number of braves to reinforce him. At the Evening Prayer we went back to camp.

(*b. Movements in Bajaur.*)

(*Jan. 8th*) Marching at dawn (Muḥ. 6th), we dismounted by the spring[1368] of Bābā Qarā in the dale of Bajaur. At Khwāja Kalān's request the prisoners remaining were pardoned their offences, reunited to their wives and children, and given leave to go, but several sulṭāns and of the most stubborn were made to reach their doom of death. Some heads of sulṭāns and of others were sent to Kābul with the news of success; some also to Badakhshān, Qūndūz and Balkh with the letters-of-victory.

Shāh Manṣūr *Yūsuf-ẓāī*,—he was with us as an envoy from his tribe,—[1369] was an eye-witness of the victory and general massacre. We allowed him to leave after putting a coat (*tūn*) on him and after writing orders with threats to the Yūsuf-zāī.

(*Jan. 11th*) With mind easy about the important affairs of the Bajaur fort, we marched, on Tuesday the 9th of Muḥarram, one *kuroh* (2 m.) down the dale of Bajaur and ordered that a tower of heads should be set up on the rising-ground.

(*Jan. 12th*) On Wednesday the 10th of Muḥarram, we rode out to visit the Bajaur fort. There was a wine-party in Khwāja Kalān's house,[1370] several goat-skins of wine having been brought down by Kāfirs neighbouring on Bajaur. All wine and fruit Fol. 219.had in Bajaur comes from adjacent parts of Kāfiristān.

(*Jan. 13th*) We spent the night there and after inspecting the towers and ramparts of the fort early in the morning (Muḥ. 11th), I mounted and went back to camp.

(*Jan. 14th*) Marching at dawn (Muḥ. 12th), we dismounted on the bank of the Khwāja Khiẓr torrent.[1371]

(*Jan. 15th*) Marching thence, we dismounted (Muḥ. 13th) on the bank of the Chandāwal torrent. Here all those inscribed in the Bajaur reinforcement, were ordered to leave.

(*Jan. 16th*) On Sunday the 14th of Muḥarram, a standard was bestowed on Khwāja Kalān and leave given him for Bajaur. A few days after I had let him go, the following little verse having come into my head, it was written down and sent to him:—[1372]

Not such the pact and bargain betwixt my friend and me,

At length the tooth of parting, unpacted grief for me!

Against caprice of Fortune, what weapons (*chāra*) arm the man?

At length by force of arms (*ba jaur*) my friend is snatched from me!

(*Jan. 19th*) On Wednesday the 17th of Muḥarram, Sl. 'Alā'u'd-dīn of Sawād, the rival (*mu'āriẓ*) of Sl. Wais of Sawād,[1373] came and waited on me.

(*Jan. 20th*) On Thursday the 18th of the month, we hunted the hill between Bajaur and Chandāwal.[1374] There the *būghū-marāl*[1375] have become quite black, except for the tail which is of another colour; lower down, in Hindūstān, they seem to become black all over.[1376] Today a *sārīq-qūsh*[1377] was taken; that was black all over, its very eyes being black! Today an eagle (*būrkūt*)[1378] took a deer (*kīyīk*).

Corn being somewhat scarce in the army, we went into the Kahrāj-valley, and took some.Fol. 219b.

(*Jan. 21st*) On Friday (Muḥ. 19th) we marched for Sawād, with the intention of attacking the Yūsuf-zāī Afghāns, and dismounted in between[1379] the water of Panj-kūra and the united waters of Chandāwal and Bajaur. Shāh Manṣūr *Yūsuf-zāī* had brought a few well-flavoured and quite intoxicating confections (*kamālī*); making one of them into three, I ate one portion, Gadāī Ṭaghāī another, 'Abdu'l-lāh the librarian another. It produced remarkable intoxication; so much so that at the Evening Prayer when the begs gathered for counsel, I was not able to go out. A strange thing it was! If in these days[1380] I ate the whole of such a confection, I doubt if it would produce half as much intoxication.

(*c. An impost laid on Kahrāj.*)

(*Jan. 22nd*) Marching from that ground, (Muḥ. 20th), we dismounted over against Kahrāj, at the mouth of the valleys of Kahrāj and Peshgrām.[1381] Snow fell ankle-deep while we were on that ground; it would seem to be rare for snow to fall thereabouts, for people were much surprised. In agreement with Sl. Wais of Sawād there was laid on the Kahrāj people an impost of 4000 ass-loads of rice for the use of the army, and he himself was sent to collect it. Never before had those rude mountaineers borne such a burden; they could not give (all) the grain and were brought to ruin.

(*cc. Raid on Panj-kūra.*)

(*Jan. 25th*) On Tuesday the 23rd of Muḥarram an army was Fol. 220.sent under Hindū Beg to raid Panj-kūra. Panj-kūra lies more than half-way up the mountain;[1382] to reach its villages a person must go for nearly a *kuroh* (2 m.) through a pass. The people had fled and got away; our men brought a few beasts of sorts, and masses of corn from their houses.

(*Jan. 26th*) Next day (Muḥ. 24th) Qūj Beg was put at the head of a force and sent out to raid.

(*Jan. 27th*) On Thursday the 25th of the month, we dismounted at the village of Māndīsh, in the trough of the Kahrāj-valley, for the purpose of getting corn for the army.

(*d. Māhīm's adoption of Dil-dār's unborn child.*)

(*Jan. 28th*) Several children born of Humāyūn's mother had not lived. Hind-āl was not yet born.[1383] While we were in those parts, came a letter from Māhīm in which she wrote, "Whether it be a boy, whether it be a girl, is my luck and chance; give it to me; I will declare it my child and will take charge of it." On Friday the 26th of the month, we being still on that ground, Yūsuf-i-'alī the stirrup-holder was sent off to Kābul with letters[1384] bestowing Hind-āl, not yet born, on Māhīm.

(*dd. Construction of a stone platform.*)

While we were still on that same ground in the Māndīsh-country, I had a platform made with stones (*tāsh bīla*) on a height in the middle of the valley, so large that it held the tents of the advance-camp. All the household and soldiers carried the stones for it, one by one like ants.

(*e. Bābur's marriage with his Afghān wife, Bībī Mubāraka.*)

In order to conciliate the Yūsuf-zāī horde, I had asked for a daughter of one of my well-wishers, Malik Sulaimān Shāh's son Malik Shāh Manṣūr, at the time he came to me as envoyFol. 220b. from the Yūsuf-zāī Afghāns.[1385]

While we were on this ground news came that his daughter[1386] was on her way with the Yūsuf-zāī tribute. At the Evening Prayer there was a wine-party to which Sl. 'Alā'u'd-dīn (of Sawād) was invited and at which he was given a seat and special dress of honour (*khilcat-i-khāṣa*).

(*Jan. 30th*) On Sunday the 28th, we marched from that valley. Shāh Manṣūr's younger brother Ṭāūs (Handsome) Khān brought the above-mentioned daughter of his brother to our ground after we had dismounted.

(*f. Repopulation of the fort of Bajaur.*)

For the convenience of having the Bī-sūt people in Bajaur-fort,[1387] Yūsuf'i-'alī the taster was sent from this camp to get them on the march and take them to that fort. Also, written orders were despatched to Kābul that the army there left should join us.

(*Feb. 4th*) On Friday the 3rd of the month of Ṣafar, we dismounted at the confluence of the waters of Bajaur and Panj-kūra.

(*Feb. 6th*) On Sunday the 5th of the month, we went from that ground to Bajaur where there was a drinking-party in Khwāja Kalān's house.

(*g. Expedition against the Afghān clans.*)

(*Feb. 8th*) On Tuesday the 7th of the month the begs and the Dilazāk Afghān headmen were summoned, and, after consultation, matters were left at this:—"The year is at its end,[1388] only a few days of the Fish are left; the plainsmen have carried in all their corn; if we went now into Sawād, the army would Fol. 221.dwindle through getting no corn. The thing to do is to march along the Aṃbahar and Pānī-mānī road, cross the Sawād-water above Hash-nagar, and surprise the Yūsuf-zāī and Muḥammadī Afghāns who are located in the plain over against the Yūsuf-zāī *sangur* of Māhūrā. Another year, coming earlier in the harvest-time, the Afghāns of this place must be our first thought." So the matter was left.

(*Feb. 9th*) Next day, Wednesday, we bestowed horses and robes on Sl. Wais and Sl. 'Alā'u'u-dīn of Sawād, gave them leave to go, marched off ourselves and dismounted over against Bajaur.

(*Feb. 10th*) We marched next day, leaving Shāh Manṣūr's daughter in Bajaur-fort until the return of the army. We dismounted after passing Khwāja Khiẓr, and from that camp leave was given to Khwāja Kalān; and the heavy baggage, the worn-out horses and superfluous effects of the army were started off into Lamghān by the Kūnār road.

(*Feb. 11th*) Next morning Khwāja Mīr-i-mīrān was put in charge of the camel baggage-train and started off by the Qūrghā-tū and Darwāza road, through the Qarā-kūpa-pass. Riding light for the raid, we ourselves crossed the Aṃbahar-pass, and yet another great pass, and dismounted at Pānī-mālī nearer[1389] the Afternoon Prayer. Aūghān-bīrdī was sent forward with a few others to learn[1390] how things were.

(*Feb. 12th*) The distance between us and the Afghāns being short, we did not make an early start. Aūghān-bīrdī came back at breakfast-time.[1391] He had got the better of an Afghān and had cut his head off, but had dropped it on the road. HeFol. 221b. brought no news so sure as the heart asks (*kūnkūl-tīladīk*). Midday come, we marched on, crossed the Sawād-water, and dismounted nearer[1392] the Afternoon Prayer. At the Bed-time Prayer, we remounted and rode swiftly on.

(*Feb. 13th*) Rustam *Turkmān* had been sent scouting; when the Sun was spear-high he brought word that the Afghāns had heard about us and were shifting about, one body of them making off by the mountain-road. On this we moved the faster, sending raiders on ahead who killed a few, cut off their heads and brought a band of prisoners, some cattle and flocks. The Dilazāk Afghāns also cut off and brought in a few heads. Turning back, we dismounted near Kātlāng and from there sent a guide to meet the baggage-train under Khwāja Mīr-i-mīrān and bring it to join us in Maqām.[1393]

(*Feb. 14th*) Marching on next day, we dismounted between Kātlāng and Maqām. A man of Shāh Manṣūr's arrived. Khusrau Kūkūldāsh and Aḥmadī the secretary were sent with a few more to meet the baggage-train.

(*Feb. 15th*) On Wednesday the 14th of the month, the baggage-train rejoined us while we were dismounting at Maqām.

It will have been within the previous 30 or 40 years that a heretic qalandar named Shahbāz perverted a body of Yūsuf-zāī and another of Dilazāk. His tomb was on a free and dominating height of the lower hill at the bill (*tūmshūq*) of theFol. 222. Maqām mountain. Thought I, "What is there to recommend the tomb of a heretic qalandar for a place in air so free?" and ordered the tomb destroyed and levelled with the ground. The place was so charming and open that we elected to sit there some time and to eat a confection (*ma'jūn*).

(*h. Bābur crosses the Indus for the first time.*)

We had turned off from Bajaur with Bhīra in our thoughts.[1394] Ever since we came into Kābul it had been in my mind to move on Hindūstān, but this had not been done for a variety of reasons. Nothing to count had fallen into the soldiers' hands during the three or four months we had been leading this army. Now that Bhīra, the borderland of Hindūstān, was so near, I thought a something might fall into our men's hands if, riding light, we went suddenly into it. To this thought I clung, but some of my well-wishers, after we had raided the Afghāns and dismounted at Maqām, set the matter in this way before me:—"If we are to go into Hindūstān, it should be on a proper basis; one part of the army stayed behind in Kābul; a body of effective braves was left behind in Bajaur; a good part of this army has gone into Lamghān because its horses were worn-out; and the horses of those who have come this far, are so poor that they have not a day's hard riding in them." Reasonable as these considerations were, yet, having made the start, we paid no Fol. 222b.attention to them but set off next day for the ford through the water of Sind.[1395] Mīr Muḥammad the raftsman and his elder and younger brethren were sent with a few braves to examine the Sind-river (*daryā*), above and below the ford.

(*Feb. 16th*) After starting off the camp for the river, I went to hunt rhinoceros on the Sawātī side which place people call also Karg-khāna (Rhino-home).[1396] A few were discovered but the jungle was dense and they did not come out of it. When one with a calf came into the open and betook itself to flight, many arrows were shot at it and it rushed into the near jungle; the jungle was fired but that same rhino was not had. Another calf was killed as it lay, scorched by the fire, writhing and palpitating. Each person took a share of the spoil. After leaving Sawātī, we wandered about a good deal; it was the Bed-time Prayer when we got to camp.

Those sent to examine the ford came back after doing it.

(*Feb. 17th*) Next day, Thursday the 16th,[1397] the horses and baggage-camels crossed through the ford and the camp-bazar and foot-soldiers were put over on rafts. Some Nīl-ābīs came and saw me at the ford-head (*guẕar-bāshī*), bringing a horse in mail and 300 *shāhrukhīs* as an offering. At the Mid-day Prayer of this same day, when every-one had crossed the river, we marched on; we went on until one watch of the night had passed (*circa* 9 p.m.) when we dismounted near the water of Kacha-kot.[1398]

(*Feb. 18th*) Marching on next day, we crossed the Kacha-kot-water; noon returning, went through the Sangdakī-pass and dismounted. While Sayyid Qāsim Lord of the Gate wasFol. 223. in charge of the rear (*chāghdāwal*) he overcame a few Gujūrs who had got up with the rear march, cut off and brought in 4 or 5 of their heads.

(*Feb. 19th*) Marching thence at dawn and crossing the Sūhān-water, we dismounted at the Mid-day Prayer. Those behind kept coming in till midnight; the march had been mightily long, and, as many horses were weak and out-of-condition, a great number were left on the road.

(*i. The Salt-range.*)

Fourteen miles (*7 kos*) north of Bhīra lies the mountain-range written of in the *Ẕafar-nāma* and other books as the Koh-i-jūd.[1399] I had not known why it was called this; I now knew. On it dwell two tribes, descendants from one parent-source, one is called Jūd, the other Janjūha. These two from of old have been the rulers and lawful commanders of the peoples and hordes (*aūlūs*) of the range and of the country between Bhīra and Nīl-āb. Their rule is friendly and brotherly however; they cannot take what their hearts might desire; the portion ancient custom has fixed is given and taken, no less and no more. The agreement is to give one *shāhrukhī*[1400] for each yoke of oxen and seven for headship in a household; there is also service in the army. The Jūd and Janjūha both are divided into several clans. The Koh-i-jūd runs for 14 miles along the Bhīra country, taking off from those Kashmīr mountains that are one with Fol. 223b.Hindū-kūsh, and it draws out to the south-west as far as the foot of Dīn-kot on the Sind-river.[1401] On one half of it are the Jūd, the Janjūha on the other. People call it Koh-i-jūd through connecting it with the Jūd tribe.[1402] The principal headman gets the title of Rāī; others, his younger brothers and sons, are styled Malik. The Janjūha headmen are maternal uncles of Langar Khan. The ruler of the people and horde near the Sūhān-water was named Malik Hast. The name originally was Asad but as Hindūstānīs sometimes drop a vowel *e.g.* they say *khabr* for *khabar* (news), they had said Asd for Asad, and this went on to Hast.

Langar Khān was sent off to Malik Hast at once when we dismounted. He galloped off, made Malik Hast hopeful of our favour and kindness, and at the Bed-time Prayer, returned with him. Malik Hast brought an offering of a horse in mail and waited on me. He may have been 22 or 23 years old.[1403]

The various flocks and herds belonging to the country-people were close round our camp. As it was always in my heart to possess Hindūstān, and as these several countries, Bhīra, Khūsh-āb, Chīn-āb and Chīnīūt[1404] had once been held by the Turk, I pictured them as my own and was resolved to get them into my hands, whether peacefully or by force. For these reasons it being imperative to treat these hillmen well, this following Fol. 224.order was given:—"Do no hurt or harm to the flocks and herds of these people, nor even to their cotton-ends and broken needles!"

(j. The Kalda-kahār lake.)

(Feb. 20th) Marching thence next day, we dismounted at the Mid-day Prayer amongst fields of densely-growing corn in Kalda-kahār.

Kalda-kahār is some 20 miles north of Bhīra, a level land shut in[1405] amongst the Jūd mountains. In the middle of it is a lake some six miles round, the in-gatherings of rain from all sides. On the north of this lake lies an excellent meadow; on the hill-skirt to the west of it there is a spring[1406] having its source in the heights overlooking the lake. The place being suitable I have made a garden there, called the Bāgh-i-ṣafā,[1407] as will be told later; it is a very charming place with good air.

(Feb. 21st) We rode from Kalda-kahār at dawn next day. When we reached the top of the Hamtātū-pass a few local people waited on me, bringing a humble gift. They were joined with 'Abdu'r-raḥīm the chief-scribe (*shaghāwal*) and sent with him to speak the Bhīra people fair and say, "The possession of this country by a Turk has come down from of old; beware not to bring ruin on its people by giving way to fear and anxiety; our eye is on this land and on this people; raid and rapine shall not be."

We dismounted near the foot of the pass at breakfast-time,Fol. 224b. and thence sent seven or eight men ahead, under Qurbān of Chīrkh and 'Abdu'l-malūk of Khwāst. Of those sent one Mīr Muḥammad (a servant ?) of Mahdī Khwāja[1408] brought in a man. A few Afghān headmen, who had come meantime with offerings and done obeisance, were joined with Langar Khān to go and speak the Bhīra people fair.

After crossing the pass and getting out of the jungle, we arrayed in right and left and centre, and moved forward for Bhīra. As we got near it there came in, of the servants of Daulat Khān *Yūsuf-khail's* son 'Alī Khān, Sīktū's son Dīwa *Hindū*; with them came several of the notables of Bhīra who brought a horse and camel as an offering and did me obeisance. At the Mid-day Prayer we dismounted on the east of Bhīra, on the bank of the Bahat (Jehlam), in a sown-field, without hurt or harm being allowed to touch the people of Bhīra.

(*k. History of Bhīra.*)

Tīmūr Beg had gone into Hindūstān; from the time he went out again these several countries *viz.* Bhīra, Khūsh-āb, Chīn-āb and Chīniūt, had been held by his descendants and the dependants and adherents of those descendants. After the death of Sl. Mas'ūd Mīrzā and his son 'Alī *Asghar* Mīrzā, the sons of Mīr 'Alī Beg Fol. 225.*viz.* Bābā-i-kābulī, Daryā Khān and Apāq Khān, known later as Ghāzī Khān, all of whom Sl. Mas'ūd M. had cherished, through their dominant position, got possession of Kābul, Zābul and the afore-named countries and *parganas* of Hindūstān. In Sl. Abū-sa'īd Mīrzā's time, Kābul and Zābul went from their hands, the Hindūstān countries remaining. In 910 AH. (1504 AD.) the year I first came into Kābul, the government of Bhīra, Khūsh-āb and Chīn-āb depended on Sayyid 'Alī Khān, son of Ghāzī Khān and grandson of Mīr 'Alī Beg, who read the *khuṭba* for Sikandar son of Buhlūl (*Lūdī Afghān*) and was subject to him. When I led that army out (910 AH.) Sayyid 'Alī Khān left Bhīra in terror, crossed the Bahat-water, and seated himself in Sher-kot, one of the villages of Bhīra. A few years later the Afghāns became suspicious about him on my account; he, giving way to his own fears and anxieties, made these countries over to the then governor Fol. 225b.in Lāhūr, Daulat Khān, son of Tātār Khān *Yūsuf-khail*, who gave them to his own eldest son 'Alī Khān, and in 'Alī Khān's possession they now were.

(*Author's note on Sl. Mas'ūd Mīrzā.*) He was the son of Sūyūrghatmīsh Mīrzā, son of Shāhrukh Mīrzā, (son of Tīmūr), and was known as Sl. Mas'ūd *Kābulī* because the government and administration of Kābul and Zābul were then dependent on him (deposed 843 AH.-1440 AD.)

(*Author's note to 910 AH.*) That year, with the wish to enter Hindūstān, Khaibar had been crossed and Parashāwūr (*sic*) had been reached, when Bāqī *Chaghānīānī* insisted on a move against Lower Bangash *i.e.* Kohāt, a mass of Afghāns were raided and scraped clean (*qīrīb*), the Bannū plain was raided and plundered, and return was made through Dūkī (Dūgī).

(*Author's note on Daulat Khān Yūsuf-khail.*) This Tātār Khān, the father of Daulat Khān, was one of six or seven *sardārs* who, sallying out and becoming dominant in Hindūstān, made Buhlūl Pādshāh. He held the country north of the Satluj (*sic*) and Sahrind,[1409] the revenues of which exceeded 3 *krūrs*.[1410] On Tātār Khān's death, Sl. Sikandar (*Lūdī*), as over-lord, took those countries from Tātār Khān's sons and gave Lāhūr only to Daulat Khān. That happened a year or two before I came into the country of Kābul (910 AH.).

(*l. Bābur's journey resumed.*)

(*Feb. 22nd*) Next morning foragers were sent to several convenient places; on the same day I visited Bhīra; and on the same day Sangur Khān *Janjūha* came, made offering of a horse, and did me obeisance.

(*Feb. 23rd*) On Wednesday the 22nd of the month, the headmen and *chauderis*[1411] of Bhīra were summoned, a sum of 400,000 *shāhrukhīs*[1412] was agreed on as the price of peace *(māl-i-amān)*, and collectors were appointed. We also made an excursion, going in a boat and there eating a confection.

(*Feb. 24th*) Ḥaidar the standard-bearer had been sent to the Bilūchīs located in Bhīra and Khūsh-āb; on Thursday morning they made an offering of an almond-coloured *tīpūchāq* [horse], and did obeisance. As it was represented to me that some of the soldiery were behaving without sense and were laying-hands on Bhīra people, persons were sent who caused some of thoseFol. 226. senseless people to meet their death-doom, of others slit the noses and so led them round the camp.

(*Feb. 25th*) On Friday came a dutiful letter from the Khūshābīs; on this Shāh Shujā' *Arghūn's* son Shāh Ḥasan was appointed to go to Khūsh-āb.

(*Feb. 26th*) On Saturday the 25th of the month,[1413] Shāh Ḥasan was started for Khūsh-āb.

(*Feb. 27th*) On Sunday so much rain fell[1414] that water covered all the plain. A small brackish stream[1415] flowing between Bhīra and the gardens in which the army lay, had become like a great river before the Mid-day Prayer; while at the ford near Bhīra there was no footing for more than an arrow's flight; people crossing had to swim. In the afternoon I rode out to watch the water coming down (*kīrkān sū*); the rain and storm were such that on the way back there was some fear about getting in to camp. I crossed that same water (*kīrkān sū*) with my horse swimming. The army-people were much alarmed; most of them abandoned tents and heavy baggage, shouldered armour, horse-mail and arms, made their horses swim and crossed bareback. Most streams flooded the plain.

(*Feb. 28th*) Next day boats were brought from the river (Jehlam), and in these most of the army brought their tents and baggage over. Towards mid-day, Qūj Beg's men went 2 miles up the water and there found a ford by which the rest crossed.

Fol. 226b.(*March 1st*) After a night spent in Bhīra-fort, Jahān-nūma they call it, we marched early on the Tuesday morning out of the worry of the rain-flood to the higher ground north of Bhīra.

As there was some delay about the moneys asked for and agreed to (*taqabbul*), the country was divided into four districts and the begs were ordered to try to make an end of the matter. Khalīfa was appointed to one district, Qūj Beg to another, Nāṣir's Dost to another, Sayyid Qāsim and Muḥibb-i-'alī to another. Picturing as our own the countries once occupied by the Turk, there was to be no over-running or plundering.

(*m. Envoys sent to the court in Dihlī.*)

(*March 3rd*) People were always saying, "It could do no harm to send an envoy, for peace' sake, to countries that once depended on the Turk." Accordingly on Thursday the 1st of Rabī'u'l-awwal, Mullā Murshid was appointed to go to Sl. Ibrāhīm who through the death of his father Sl. Iskandar had attained to rule in Hindūstān some 5 or 6 months earlier(?). I sent him a goshawk (*qārchīgha*) and asked for the countries which from of old had depended on the Turk. Mullā Murshid was given charge of writings (*khāṭṭlār*) for Daulat Khān (*Yūsuf-khail*) and writings for Sl. Ibrāhīm; matters were sent also by word-of-mouth; and he was given leave to go. Far from sense and wisdom, shut off from judgment and counsel must people in Hindūstān be, the Afghāns above all; for they could not move and make stand like a foe, nor did they know ways and rules of friendliness.Fol. 227. Daulat Khān kept my man several days in Lāhūr without seeing him himself or speeding him on to Sl. Ibrāhīm; and he came back to Kābul a few months later without bringing a reply.

(*n. Birth of Hind-āl.*)

(*March 4th*) On Friday the 2nd of the month, the foot-soldiers Shaibak and Darwesh-i-'alī,—he is now a matchlockman,—bringing dutiful letters from Kābul, brought news also of Hind-āl's birth. As the news came during the expedition into Hindūstān, I took it as an omen, and gave the name Hind-āl (Taking of Hind). Dutiful letters came also from Muḥammad-i-zamān M. in Balkh, by the hand of Qaṃbar Beg.

(*March 5th*) Next morning when the Court rose, we rode out for an excursion, entered a boat and there drank *'araq*.[1416] The people of the party were Khwāja Dost-khāwand, Khusrau, Mīrīm, Mīrzā Qulī, Muḥammadī, Aḥmadī, Gadāī, Na'man, Langar Khān, Rauh-dam,[1417] Qāsim-i-'alī the opium-eater (*tariyākī*), Yūsuf-i-'alī and Tīngrī-qulī. Towards the head of the boat there was a *tālār*[1418] on the flat top of which I sat with a few people, a few others sitting below. There was a sitting-place also at the tail of the boat; there Muḥammadī, Gadāī and Na'man sat. *'Araq* was drunk till the Other Prayer when, disgusted by its bad flavour, by consent of those at the head of the boat, *ma'jūn* was preferred. Fol. 227b.Those at the other end, knowing nothing about our *ma'jūn* drank *'araq* right through. At the Bed-time Prayer we rode from the boat and got into camp late. Thinking I had been drinking *'araq* Muḥammadī and Gadāī had said to one another, "Let's do befitting service," lifted a pitcher of *'araq* up to one another in turn on their horses, and came in saying with wonderful joviality and heartiness and speaking together, "Through this dark night have we come carrying this pitcher in turns!" Later on when they knew that the party was (now) meant to be otherwise and the hilarity to differ, that is to say, that [there would be that] of the *ma'jūn* band and that of the drinkers, they were much disturbed because never does a *ma'jūn* party go well with a drinking-party. Said I, "Don't upset the party! Let those who wish to drink *'araq*, drink *'araq*; let those who wish to eat *ma'jūn*, eat *ma'jūn*. Let no-one on either side make talk or allusion to the other." Some drank *'araq*, some ate *ma'jūn*, and for a time the party went on quite politely. Bābā Jān the *qabūz*-player had not been of our party (in the boat); we invited him when we reached the tents. He asked to drink *'araq*. We invited Tardī Muḥammad *Qībchāq* also and made him a comrade of the drinkers. A *ma'jūn* party never goes well with an *'araq* or a wine-party; the drinkers began to make wild talk and chatter from all sides, mostly in allusion to *ma'jūn* and *ma'jūnīs*. Bābā Jān even, when drunk, said many wild things. The drinkers soon made Tardī Khān mad-drunk, by giving him one full bowl after another. Try as we did Fol. 228.to keep things straight, nothing went well; there was much disgusting uproar; the party became intolerable and was broken up.

(*March 7th*) On Monday the 5th of the month, the country of Bhīra was given to Hindū Beg.

(*March 8th*) On Tuesday the Chīn-āb country was bestowed on Ḥusain *Aīkrak*(?) and leave was given to him and the Chīn-āb people to set out. At this time Sayyid 'Alī Khān's son Minūchihr Khān, having let us know (his intention), came and waited on me. He had started from Hindūstān by the upper road, had met in with Tātār Khān *Kakar*;[1419] Tātār Khān had not let him pass on, but had kept him, made him a son-in-law by giving him his own daughter, and had detained him for some time.

(*o. The Kakars.*)

In amongst the mountains of Nīl-āb and Bhīra which connect with those of Kashmīr, there are, besides the Jūd and Janjūha tribes, many Jats, Gujūrs, and others akin to them, seated in villages everywhere on every rising-ground. These are governed by headmen of the Kakar tribes, a headship like that over the Jūd and Janjūha. At this time (925 AH.) the headmen of the people of those hill-skirts were Tātār *Kakar* and Hātī *Kakar*, two descendants of one forefather; being paternal-uncles' sons.[1420] Torrent-beds and ravines are their strongholds. Tātār's place, named Parhāla,[1421] is a good deal below the snow-mountains; Hātī's country connects with the mountains and also he had made Bābū Khān's fief Kālanjar,[1422] look towards himself. TātārFol. 228b. *Kakar* had seen Daulat Khān (*Yūsuf-khail*) and looked to him with complete obedience. Hātī had not seen Daulat Khān; his attitude towards him was bad and turbulent. At the word of the Hindūstān begs and in agreement with them, Tātār had so posted himself as to blockade Hātī from a distance. Just when we were in Bhīra, Hātī moved on pretext of hunting, fell unexpectedly on Tātār, killed him, and took his country, his wives and his having (*būlghānī*).[1423]

(*p. Bābur's journey resumed.*)

Having ridden out at the Mid-day Prayer for an excursion, we got on a boat and *'araq* was drunk. The people of the party were Dost Beg, Mīrzā Qulī, Aḥmadī, Gadāī, Muḥammad 'Alī *Jang-jang*, 'Asas,[1424] and Aūghān-bīrdī *Mughūl*. The musicians were Rauḥ-dam, Bābā Jān, Qāsim-i-'alī, Yūsuf-i-'alī, Tīngrī-qulī, Abū'l-qāsim, Rāmẓān *Lūlī*. We drank in the boat till the Bed-time Prayer; then getting off it, full of drink, we mounted, took torches in our hands, and went to camp from the river's bank, leaning over from our horses on this side, leaning over from that, at one loose-rein gallop! Very drunk I must have been for, when they told me next day that we had galloped loose-rein into camp, carrying torches, I could not recall it in the very least. After reaching my quarters, I vomited a good deal.

(*March 11th*) On Friday we rode out on an excursion, crossed the water (Jehlam) by boat and went about amongst the orchards (*bāghāt*) of blossoming trees and the lands of the sugar-cultivation. We saw the wheel with buckets, had water drawn, and asked Fol. 229.particulars about getting it out; indeed we made them draw it again and again. During this excursion a confection was preferred. In returning we went on board a boat. A confection (*ma'jūn*) was given also to Minūchihr Khān, such a one that, to keep him standing, two people had to give him their arms. For a time the boat remained at anchor in mid-stream; we then went down-stream; after a while had it drawn up-stream again, slept in it that night and went back to camp near dawn.

(*March 12th*) On Saturday the 10th of the first Rabī‘, the Sun entered the Ram. Today we rode out before mid-day and got into a boat where *‘araq* was drunk. The people of the party were Khwāja Dost-khāwand, Dost Beg, Mīrīm, Mīrzā Qulī, Muḥammadī, Aḥmadī, Yūnas-i-‘alī, Muḥ. ‘Alī *Jang-jang*, Gadāī Ṭaghāī, Mīr Khurd (and ?) ‘Asas. The musicians were Rauḥdam, Bābā Jān, Qāsim, Yūsuf-i-‘alī, Tīngrī-qulī and Ramẓān. We got into a branch-water (*shakh-i-āb*), for some time went down-stream, landed a good deal below Bhīra and on its opposite bank, and went late into camp.

This same day Shāh Ḥasan returned from Khūsh-āb whither he had been sent as envoy to demand the countries which from of old had depended on the Turk; he had settled peaceably with them and had in his hands a part of the money assessed on them.

The heats were near at hand. To reinforce Hindū Beg (in Bhīra) were appointed Shāh Muḥammad Keeper of the Seal and his younger brother Dost Beg Keeper of the Seal, together with several suitable braves; an accepted (*yārāsha*) stipend Fol. 229b.was fixed and settled in accordance with each man's position. Khūsh-āb was bestowed, with a standard, on Langar Khān, the prime cause and mover of this expedition; we settled also that he was to help Hindū Beg. We appointed also to help Hindū Beg, the Turk and local soldiery of Bhīra, increasing the allowances and pay of both. Amongst them was the afore-named Minūchihr Khān whose name has been mentioned; there was also Naẓar-i-‘alī *Turk*, one of Minūchihr Khān's relations; there were also Sangar Khān *Janjūha* and Malik Hast *Janjūha.*

(*pp. Return for Kābul.*)

(*March 13th*) Having settled the country in every way making for hope of peace, we marched for Kābul from Bhīra on Sunday the 11th of the first Rabī‘. We dismounted in Kaldah-kahār. That day too it rained amazingly; people with rain-cloaks[1425] were in the same case as those who had none! The rear of the camp kept coming in till the Bed-time Prayer.

(*q. Action taken against Hātī Kakar.*)

(*March 14th*) People acquainted with the honour and glory (*āb u tāb*) of this land and government, especially the Janjūhas, old foes of these Kakars, represented, "Hātī is the bad man round-about; he it is robs on the roads; he it is brings men to ruin; he ought either to be driven out from these parts, or to be severely punished." Agreeing with this, we left Khwāja Mīr-i-mīrān and Nāṣir's Mīrīm next day with the camp, parting from them at big breakfast,[1426] and moved on Hātī *Kakar.* As has been said, he had killed Tātār a few days earlier, and having taken possession of Parhāla, was in it now. Dismounting at the OtherFol. 230. Prayer, we gave the horses corn; at the Bed-time Prayer we rode on again, our guide being a Gujūr servant of

Malik Hast, named Sar-u-pā. We rode the night through and dismounted at dawn, when Beg Muḥammad *Mughūl* was sent back to the camp, and we remounted when it was growing light. At breakfast-time (9 a.m.) we put our mail on and moved forward faster. The blackness of Parhāla shewed itself from 2 miles off; the gallop was then allowed (*chāpqūn qūiūldī*); the right went east of Parhāla, Qūj Beg, who was also of the right, following as its reserve; the men of the left and centre went straight for the fort, Dost Beg being their rear-reserve.

Parhāla stands amongst ravines. It has two roads; one, by which we came, leads to it from the south-east, goes along the top of ravines and on either hand has hollows worn out by the torrents. A mile from Parhāla this road, in four or five places before it reaches the Gate, becomes a one-man road with a ravine falling from its either side; there for more than an arrow's flight men must ride in single file. The other road comes from the north-west; it gets up to Parhāla by the trough of a valley and it also is a one-man road. There is no other road on any side. Parhāla though without breast-work or battlement, has no assailable place, its sides shooting perpendicularly Fol. 230b.down for 7, 8, 10 yards.

When the van of our left, having passed the narrow place, went in a body to the Gate, Hātī, with whom were 30 to 40 men in armour, their horses in mail, and a mass of foot-soldiers, forced his assailants to retire. Dost Beg led his reserve forward, made a strong attack, dismounted a number of Hātī's men, and beat him. All the country-round, Hātī was celebrated for his daring, but try as he did, he could effect nothing; he took to flight; he could not make a stand in those narrow places; he could not make the fort fast when he got back into it. His assailants went in just behind him and ran on through the ravine and narrows of the north-west side of the fort, but he rode light and made his flight good. Here again, Dost Beg did very well and recompense was added to renown.[1427]

Meantime I had gone into the fort and dismounted at Tātār *Kakar's* dwelling. Several men had joined in the attack for whom to stay with me had been arranged; amongst them were Amīn-i-muḥammad Tarkhān *Argkūn* and Qarācha.[1428] For this fault they were sent to meet the camp, without *sar-u-pā*, into the wilds and open country with Sar-u-pā[1429] for their guide, the Gujūr mentioned already.

(*March 16th*) Next day we went out by the north-west ravine and dismounted in a sown field. A few serviceable braves under Wālī the treasurer were sent out to meet the camp.[1430]

(*March 17th*) Marching on Thursday the 15th, we dismounted at Andarāba on the Sūhān, a fort said to have depended fromFol. 231. of old on ancestors of Malik Hast. Hātī *Kakar* had killed Malik Hast's father and destroyed the fort; there it now lay in ruins.

At the Bed-time Prayer of this same day, those left at Kalda-kahār with the camp rejoined us.

(*r. Submissions to Bābur.*)

It must have been after Hātī overcame Tātār that he started his kinsman Parbat to me with tribute and an accoutred horse. Parbat did not light upon us but, meeting in with the camp we had left behind, came on in the company of the train. With it came also Langar Khān up from Bhīra on matters of business. His affairs were put right and he, together with several local people, was allowed to leave.

(*March 18th*) Marching on and crossing the Sūhān-water, we dismounted on the rising-ground. Here Hātī's kinsman (Parbat) was robed in an honorary dress (*khil'at*), given letters of encouragement for Hātī, and despatched with a servant of Muḥammad 'Alī *Jang-jang*. Nīl-āb and the Qārlūq (Himalayan?) Hazāra had been given to Humāyūn (*aet.* 12); some of his servants under Bābā Dost and Halāhil came now for their darogha-ship.[1431]

(*March 19th*) Marching early next morning, we dismounted after riding 2 miles, went to view the camp from a height and ordered that the camp-camels should be counted; it came out at 570.Fol. 231b.

We had heard of the qualities of the saṃbhal plant[1432]; we saw it on this ground; along this hill-skirt it grows sparsely, a plant here, a plant there; it grows abundantly and to a large size further along the skirt-hills of Hindūstān. It will be described when an account is given of the animals and plants of Hindūstān.[1433]

(*March 20th*) Marching from that camp at beat of drum (*i.e.* one hour before day), we dismounted at breakfast-time (9 a.m.) below the Sangdakī-pass, at mid-day marched on, crossed the pass, crossed the torrent, and dismounted on the rising-ground.

(*March 21st*) Marching thence at midnight, we made an excursion to the ford[1434] we had crossed when on our way to Bhīra. A great raft of grain had stuck in the mud of that same ford and, do what its owners would, could not be made to move. The corn was seized and shared out to those with us. Timely indeed was that corn!

Near noon we were a little below the meeting of the waters of Kābul and Sind, rather above old Nīl-āb; we dismounted there between two waters.[1435] From Nīl-āb six boats were brought, and were apportioned to the right, left and centre, who busied themselves energetically in crossing the river (Indus). We got there on a Monday; they kept on crossing the water through the night preceding Tuesday (*March 22nd*), through Tuesday and up to Wednesday (*March 23rd*) and on Thursday (*24th*) also a few crossed.

Hātl's kinsman Parbat, he who from Andarāba was sent to Fol. 232.Hātī with a servant of Muḥ. 'Alī *Jang-jang*, came to the bank of the river with Hātī's offering of an accoutred horse. Nīlābīs also came, brought an accoutred horse and did obeisance.

(*s. Various postings.*)

Muḥammad 'Alī *Jang-jang* had wished to stay in Bhīra but Bhīra being bestowed on Hindū Beg, he was given the countries between it and the Sind-river, such as the Qārlūq Hazāra, Hātī, Ghiyāṣ-wāl and Kīb (Kitib):—

Where one is who submits like a *ra'iyat*, so treat him;

But him who submits not, strike, strip, crush and force to obey.

He also received a special head-wear in black velvet, a special Qīlmāq corselet, and a standard. When Hātī's kinsman was given leave to go he took for Hātī a sword and head-to-foot (*bāsh-ayāq*) with a royal letter of encouragement.

(*March 24th*) On Thursday at sunrise we marched from the river's bank. That day confection was eaten. While under its influence[1436] wonderful fields of flowers were enjoyed. In some places sheets of yellow flowers bloomed in plots; in others sheets of red (*arghwānī*) flowers in plots, in some red and yellow bloomed together. We sat on a mound near the camp to enjoy the sight. There were flowers on all sides of the mound, yellowFol. 232b. here, red there, as if arranged regularly to form a sextuple. On two sides there were fewer flowers but as far as the eye reached, flowers were in bloom. In spring near Parashāwar the fields of flowers are very beautiful indeed.

(*March 25th*) We marched from that ground at dawn. At one place on the road a tiger came out and roared. On hearing it, the horses, willy-nilly, flung off in terror, carrying their riders in all directions, and dashing into ravines and hollows. The tiger went again into the jungle. To bring it out, we ordered a buffalo brought and put on the edge of the jungle. The tiger again came out roaring. Arrows were shot at it from all sides[1437]; I shot with the rest. Khalwī (var. Khalwā) a foot-soldier, pricked it with a spear; it bit the spear and broke off the spearhead. After tasting of those arrows, it went into the bushes (*būta*) and stayed there. Bābā the waiting-man [*yasāwal*] went with drawn sword close up to it; it sprang; he chopped at its head; 'Alī

Sīstānī[1438] chopped at its loins; it plunged into the river and was killed right in the water. It was got out and ordered to be skinned.

(*March 26th*) Marching on next day, we reached Bīgrām and went to see Gūr-khattrī. This is a smallish abode, after the fashion of a hermitage (*ṣauma'at*), rather confined and dark. After entering at the door and going down a few steps, one must lie full length to get beyond. There is no getting in without a lamp. All round near the building there is let lie an enormous quantity of hair of the head and beard which men have shaved off there. There are a great many retreats (*ḥujra*) near Gūr-khattrī Fol. 233.like those of a rest-house or a college. In the year we came into Kābul (910 AH.) and over-ran Kohāt, Bannū and the plain, we made an excursion to Bīgrām, saw its great tree and were consumed with regret at not seeing Gūr-khattrī, but it does not seem a place to regret not-seeing.[1439]

On this same day an excellent hawk of mine went astray out of Shaikhīm the head-falconer's charge; it had taken many cranes and storks and had moulted (*tūlāb*) two or three times. So many things did it take that it made a fowler of a person so little keen as I!

At this place were bestowed 100 miṣqāls of silver, clothing (*tūnlūq*), three bullocks and one buffalo, out of the offerings of Hindūstān, on each of six persons, the chiefs of the Dilazāk Afghāns under Malik Bū Khān and Malik Mūsa; to others, in their degree, were given money, pieces of cloth, a bullock and a buffalo.

(*March 27th*) When we dismounted at 'Alī-masjid, a Dilazāk Afghān of the Yaq'ūb-khail, named Ma'rūf, brought an offering of 10 sheep, two ass-loads of rice and eight large cheeses.

(*March 28th*) Marching on from 'Alī-masjid, we dismounted at Yada-bīr; from Yada-bīr Jūī-shāhī was reached by the Midday Prayer and we there dismounted. Today Dost Beg was attacked by burning fever.

(*March 29th*) Marching from Jūī-shāhī at dawn, we ate our mid-day meal in the Bāgh-i-wafā. At the Mid-day Prayer we betook ourselves out of the garden, close to the Evening Prayer forded the Siyāh-āb at Gandamak, satisfied our horses' hunger in a field of green corn, and rode on in a *garī* or two (24-48 min.).

After crossing the Sūrkh-āb, we dismounted at Kark and tookFol. 233b. a sleep.

(*March 30th*) Riding before shoot of day from Kark, I went with 5 or 6 others by the road taking off for Qarā-tū in order to enjoy the sight of a garden there made. Khalīfa and Shāh Ḥasan Beg and the rest went by the other road to await me at Qūrūq-sāī.

When we reached Qarā-tū, Shāh Beg *Arghūn's* commissary (*tawāchī*) Qīzīl (Rufus) brought word that Shāh Beg had taken Kāhān, plundered it and retired.

An order had been given that no-one soever should take news of us ahead. We reached Kābul at the Mid-day Prayer, no person in it knowing about us till we got to Qūtlūq-qadam's bridge. As Humāyūn and Kāmrān heard about us only after that, there was not time to put them on horseback; they made their pages carry them, came, and did obeisance between the gates of the town and the citadel.[1440] At the Other Prayer there waited on me Qāsim Beg, the town Qāẓī, the retainers left in Kābul and the notables of the place.

(*April 2nd*) At the Other Prayer of Friday the 1st of the second Rabī' there was a wine-party at which a special head-to-foot (*bāsh-ayāq*) was bestowed on Shāh Ḥasan.

(*April 3rd*) At dawn on Saturday we went on board a boat and took our morning.[1441] Nūr Beg, then not obedient (*tā'ib*), played the lute at this gathering. At the Mid-day Prayer we left the boat to visit the garden made between Kul-kīna[1442] and the mountain (Shāh-i-kābul). At the Evening Prayer we went to the Violet-garden where there was drinking again. From Kul-kīna I got in by the rampart and went into the citadel.

(*u. Dost Beg's death.*)

(*April 6th*) On the night of Tuesday the 5th of the month,[1443] Dost Beg, who on the road had had fever, went to God's mercy.Fol. 234.

Sad and grieved enough we were! His bier and corpse were carried to Ghaznī where they laid him in front of the gate of the Sulṭān's garden (*rauẓa*).

Dost Beg had been a very good brave (*yīkīt*) and he was still rising in rank as a beg. Before he was made a beg, he did excellent things several times as one of the household. One time was at Rabāṭ-i-zauraq,[1444] one *yīghāch* from Andijān when Sl. Aḥmad *Tambal* attacked me at night (908 AH.). I, with 10 to 15 men, by making a stand, had forced his gallopers back; when we reached his centre, he made a stand with as many as 100 men; there were then three men with me, *i.e.* there were four counting myself. Nāṣir's Dost (*i.e.* Dost Beg) was one of the three; another was Mīrzā Qulī *Kūkūldāsh*; Karīm-dād *Turkmān* was the other. I was just in my *jība*[1445]; Taṃbal and another were standing like gate-wards in front of his array; I came face to face with Taṃbal, shot an arrow striking his helm; shot another aiming at the attachment of his shield;[1446] they shot one through my leg (*būtūm*); Taṃbal chopped at my head. It was wonderful! The (under)-cap of my helm was on my head; not a thread of it was cut, but on the head itself was a very bad wound. Of other help came none; no-one was left with me; of necessity I brought myself to gallop back. Dost Beg had been a little in my rear; (Taṃbal) on leaving me alone, chopped at him.[1447]

Fol. 234b.Again, when we were getting out of Akhsī [908 AH.],[1448] Dost Beg chopped away at Bāqī *Ḥīz*[1449] who, although people called him *Ḥīz*, was a mighty master of the sword. Dost Beg was one of the eight left with me after we were out of Akhsī; he was the third they unhorsed.

Again, after he had become a beg, when Sīūnjuk Khān (*Aūzbeg*), arriving with the (Aūzbeg) sulṯāns before Tāshkīnt, besieged Aḥmad-i-qāsim [*Kohbur*] in it [918 AH.],[1450] Dost Beg passed through them and entered the town. During the siege he risked his honoured life splendidly, but Aḥmad-i-qāsim, without a word to this honoured man,[1451] flung out of the town and got away. Dost Beg for his own part got the better of the Khān and sulṯāns and made his way well out of Tāshkīnt.

Later on when Sherīm Ṯaghāī, Mazīd and their adherents were in rebellion,[1452] he came swiftly up from Ghaznī with two or three hundred men, met three or four hundred effective braves sent out by those same Mughūls to meet him, unhorsed a mass of them near Sherūkān(?), cut off and brought in a number of heads.

Again, his men were first over the ramparts at the fort of Bajaur (925 AH.). At Parhāla, again, he advanced, beat Hātī, put him to flight, and won Parhāla.

After Dost Beg's death, I bestowed his district on his younger brother Nāṣir's Mīrīm.[1453]

(*v. Various incidents.*)

(*April 9th*) On Friday the 8th of the second Rabīʿ, the walled-town was left for the Chār-bāgh.

(*April 13th*) On Tuesday the 12th there arrived in Kābul the honoured Sulṯānīm Begīm, Sl. Ḥusain Mīrzā's eldest daughter, the mother of Muḥammad Sulṯān Mīrzā. During those throneless times,[1454] she had settled down in Khwārizm where Yīlī-pārsFol. 235. Sulṯān's younger brother

Aīsān-qulī Sl. took her daughter. The Bāgh-i-khilwat was assigned her for her seat. When she had settled down and I went to see her in that garden, out of respect and courtesy to her, she being as my honoured elder sister, I bent the knee. She also bent the knee. We both advancing, saw one another mid-way. We always observed the same ceremony afterwards.

(*April 18th*) On Sunday the 17th, that traitor to his salt, Bābā Shaikh[1455] was released from his long imprisonment, forgiven his offences and given an honorary dress.

(*w. Visit to the Koh-dāman.*)

(*April 20th*) On Tuesday the 19th of the month, we rode out at the return of noon for Khwāja Sih-yārān. This day I was fasting. All astonished, Yūnas-i-'alī and the rest said, "A Tuesday! a journey! and a fast! This is amazing!" At Bīhzādī we dismounted at the Qāẓī's house. In the evening when a stir was made for a social gathering, the Qāẓī set this before me, "In my house such things never are; it is for the honoured Pādshāh to command!" For his heart's content, drink was left out, though all the material for a party was ready.

(*April 21st*) On Wednesday we went to Khwāja Sih-yārān.

(*April 22nd*) On Thursday the 22nd of the month, we had a large round seat made in the garden under construction on the mountain-naze.[1456]

(*April 23rd*) On Friday we got on a raft from the bridge. On our coming opposite the fowlers' houses, they brought a *dang* Fol. 235b.(or *ding*)[1457] they had caught. I had never seen one before; it is an odd-looking bird. It will come into the account of the birds of Hindustan.[1458]

(*April 24th*) On Saturday the 23rd of the month cuttings were planted, partly of plane, partly of *tāl*,[1459] above the round seat. At the Mid-day Prayer there was a wine-party at the place.

(*April 25th*) At dawn we took our morning on the new seat. At noon we mounted and started for Kābul, reached Khwāja Ḥasan quite drunk and slept awhile, rode on and by midnight got to the Chār-bāgh. At Khwāja Ḥasan, 'Abdu'l-lāh, in his drunkenness, threw himself into water just as he was in his *tūn aūfrāghī*.[1460] He was frozen with cold and could not go on with us when we mounted after a little of the night had passed. He stayed on Qūtlūq Khwāja's estate that night. Next day, awakened to his past intemperance, he came on repentant. Said I, "At once! will this sort of repentance answer or not? Would to God you would repent now at once in such a way that you would drink nowhere except at my parties!" He agreed to this and kept the rule for a few months, but could not keep it longer.

(*x. Hindū Beg abandons Bhīra.*)

(*April 26th*) On Monday the 25th came Hindū Beg. There having been hope of peace, he had been left in those countries with somewhat scant support. No sooner was our back turned than a mass of Hindūstānīs and Afghāns gathered, disregarded us and, not listening to our words, moved against Hindū Beg in Bhīra. The local peoples also went over to the Afghāns. Hindū Beg could make no stand in Bhīra, came to Khūsh-āb, came through the Dīn-kot country, came to Nīl-āb, came on to Kābul.Fol. 236. Sīktū's son Dīwa *Hindū* and another Hindū had been brought prisoner from Bhīra. Each now giving a considerable ransom, they were released. Horses and head-to-foot dresses having been given them, leave to go was granted.

(*April 30th*) On Friday the 29th of the month, burning fever appeared in my body. I got myself let blood. I had fever with sometimes two, sometimes three days between the attacks. In no attack did it cease till there had been sweat after sweat. After 10 or 12 days of illness, Mullā Khwāja gave me narcissus mixed with wine; I drank it once or twice; even that did no good.

(*May 15th*) On Sunday the 15th of the first Jumāda[1461] Khwāja Muḥammad 'Alī came from Khwāst, bringing a saddled horse as an offering and also *taṣadduq* money.[1462] Muḥ. Sharīf the astrologer and the Mīr-zādas of Khwāst came with him and waited on me.

(*May 16th*) Next day, Monday, Mullā Kabīr came from Kāshghar; he had gone round by Kāshghar on his way from Andijān to Kābul.

(*May 23rd*) On Monday the 23rd of the month, Malik Shāh Manṣūr *Yūsuf-zāī* arrived from Sawād with 6 or 7 Yūsuf-zāī chiefs, and did obeisance.

(*May 31st*) On Monday the 1st of the second Jumāda, the chiefs of the Yūsuf-zāī Afghāns led by Malik Shāh Manṣūr were dressed in robes of honour (*khil'at*). To Malik Shāh Manṣūr was given a long silk coat and an under-coat (? *jība*) with its buttons; to one of the other chiefs was given a coat with silk sleeves, and to six others silk coats. To all leave to go was granted. Agreement was made with them that they were not Fol. 236b.to reckon as in the country of Sawād what was above Abuha (?), that they should make all the peasants belonging to it go out from amongst themselves, and also that the Afghān cultivators of Bajaur and Sawād should cast into the revenue 6000 ass-loads of rice.

(*June 2nd*) On Wednesday the 3rd, I drank *jul-āb.*[1463]

(*June 5th*) On Saturday the 6th, I drank a working-draught (*dārū-i-kār*).

(*June 7th*) On Monday the 8th, arrived the wedding-gift for the marriage of Qāsim Beg's youngest son Ḥamza with Khalīfa's eldest daughter. It was of 1000 *shāhrukhī*; they offered also a saddled horse.

(*June 8th*) On Tuesday Shāh Beg's Shāh Ḥasan asked for permission to go away for a wine-party. He carried off to his house Khwāja Muḥ. 'Alī and some of the household-begs. In my presence were Yūnas-i-'alī and Gadāī Ṭaghāī. I was still abstaining from wine. Said I, "Not at all in this way is it (*hech andāq būlmāī dūr*) that I will sit sober and the party drink wine, I stay sane, full of water, and that set (*būlāk*) of people get drunk; come you and drink in my presence! I will amuse myself a little by watching what intercourse between the sober and the drunk is like."[1464] The party was held in a smallish tent in which I sometimes sat, in the Plane-tree garden south-east of the Picture-hall. Later on Ghiyāṣ the house-buffoon (*kīdī*) arrived; several times for fun he was ordered kept out, but at last he made a great disturbance and his buffooneries found him a way in. We invited Tardī Muḥammad *Qībchāq* also and

Mullā *kitāb-dār* (librarian). The following quatrain, written impromptu, was sent to Shāh Ḥasan and those gathered in his Fol. 237.house:—

In your beautiful flower-bed of banquetting friends,

Our fashion it is not to be;

If there be ease (*ḥuzūr*) in that gathering of yours,

Thank God! there is here no un-ease [*bī ḥuzūr*].[1465]

It was sent by Ibrāhīm *chuhra*. Between the two Prayers (*i.e.* afternoon) the party broke up drunk.

I used to go about in a litter while I was ill. The wine-mixture was drunk on several of the earlier days, then, as it did no good I left it off, but I drank it again at the end of my convalescence, at a party had under an apple-tree on the south-west side of the Tālār-garden.

(*June 11th*) On Friday the 12th came Aḥmad Beg and Sl. Muḥammad *Dūldāī* who had been left to help in Bajaur.

(*June 16th*) On Wednesday the 17th of the month, Tīngrī-bīrdī and other braves gave a party in Ḥaidar *Tāqi's* garden; I also went and there drank. We rose from it at the Bed-time Prayer when a move was made to the great tent where again there was drinking.

(*June 23rd*) On Thursday the 25th of the month, Mullā Maḥmūd was appointed to read extracts from the Qorān[1466] in my presence.

(*June 28th*) On Tuesday the last day of the month, Abū'l-muslim Kūkūldāsh arrived as envoy from Shāh Shujā' *Arghūn* bringing a *tīpūchāq*. After bargain made about swimming the reservoir in the Plane-tree garden, Yūsuf-i-'alī the stirrup-holder swam round it today 100 times and received a gift of a head-to-foot (dress), a saddled horse and some money.

(*July 6th*) On Wednesday the 8th of Rajab, I went to Shāh Ḥasan's house and drank there; most of the household and ofFol. 237b. the begs were present.

(*July 9th*) On Saturday the 11th, there was drinking on the terrace-roof of the pigeon-house between the Afternoon and Evening Prayers. Rather late a few horsemen were observed, going from Dih-i-afghān towards the town. It was made out to be Darwīsh-i-muḥammad *Sārbān*, on his way to me as the envoy of Mīrzā Khān (Wais). We shouted to him from the roof, "Drop the envoy's forms and ceremonies! Come! come without formality!" He came and sat down in the company. He was then obedient and did not drink. Drinking went on till the end of the evening. Next day he came into the Court Session with due form and ceremony, and presented Mīrzā Khān's gifts.

(*y. Various incidents.*)

Last year[1467] with 100 efforts, much promise and threats, we had got the clans to march into Kābul from the other side (of Hindū-kush). Kābul is a confined country, not easily giving summer and winter quarters to the various flocks and herds of the Turks and (Mughūl?) clans. If the dwellers in the wilds follow their own hearts, they do not wish for Kābul! They now waited (*khidmat qīlīb*) on Qāsim Beg and made him their mediator with me for permission to re-cross to that other side. He tried very hard, so in the end, they were allowed to cross over to the Qūndūz and Bāghlān side.

Ḥāfiẓ̤ the news-writer's elder brother had come from Samarkand; when I now gave him leave to return, I sent my *Dīwān* by him to Pūlād Sulṭ̤ān.[1468] On the back of it I wrote the following Fol. 238.verse:—

O breeze! if thou enter that cypress' chamber (*ḥarīm*)

Remind her of me, my heart reft by absence;

She yearns not for Bābur; he fosters a hope

That her heart of steel God one day may melt.[1469]

(*July 15th*) On Friday the 17th of the month, Shaikh Mazīd Kūkūldāsh waited on me from Muḥammad-i-zamān Mīrzā, bringing *taṣadduq* tribute and a horse.[1470] Today Shāh Beg's envoy Abū'l-muslim Kūkūldāsh was robed in an honorary dress and given leave to go. Today also leave was given for their own districts of Khwāst and Andar-āb to Khwāja Muḥammad 'Alī and Tīngrī-bīrdī.

(July 21st) On Thursday the 23rd came Muḥ. 'Alī *Jang-jang* who had been left in charge of the countries near Kacha-kot and the Qārlūq. With him came one of Hātī's people and Mīrzā-i-malū-i-qārlūq's son Shāh Ḥasan. Today Mullā 'Alī-jān waited on me, returned from fetching his wife from Samarkand.

(z. The 'Abdu'r-raḥman Afghāns and Rustam-maidān.)

(July 27th) The 'Abdu'r-raḥman Afghāns on the Gīrdīz border were satisfactory neither in their tribute nor their behaviour; they were hurtful also to the caravans which came and went. On Wednesday the 29th of Rajab we rode out to over-run them. We dismounted and ate food near Tang-i-waghchān,[1471] and rode on again at the Mid-day Prayer. In the night we lost the road and got much bewildered in the ups and downs of the land to the south-east of Pātakh-i-āb-i-shakna.[1472] After a time we lit onFol. 238b. a road and by it crossed the Chashma-i-tūra[1473] pass.

(July 28th) At the first prayer (*farẓ-waqt*) we got out from the valley-bottom adjacent[1474] to the level land, and the raid was allowed. One detachment galloped towards the Kar-māsh[1475] mountain, south-east of Gīrdīz, the left-hand of the centre led by Khusrau, Mīrzā Qulī and Sayyid 'Alī in their rear. Most of the army galloped up the dale to the east of Gīrdīz, having in their rear men under Sayyid Qāsim Lord of the Gate, Mīr Shāh *Qūchīn*, Qayyām (Aūrdū-shāh Beg?), Hindū Beg, Qūtlūq-qadam and Ḥusain [Ḥasan?]. Most of the army having gone up the dale, I followed at some distance. The dalesmen must have been a good way up; those who went after them wore their horses out and nothing to make up for this fell into their hands.

Some Afghāns on foot, some 40 or 50 of them, having appeared on the plain, the rear-reserve went towards them. A courier was sent to me and I hastened on at once. Before I got up with them, Ḥusain Ḥāsan, all alone, foolishly and thoughtlessly, put his horse at those Afghāns, got in amongst them and began to lay on with his sword. They shot his horse, thus made him fall, slashed at him as he was getting up, flung him down, knifed him from all sides and cut him to pieces, while the other braves looked on, standing still and reaching him no helping hand! On hearing news of it, I hurried still faster forward, and sent some of the household and braves galloping loose-rein ahead Fol. 239.under Gadāī Ṭaghāī, Payānda-i-muḥammad *Qīplān*, Abū'l-ḥasan the armourer and Mūmin Ātāka. Mūmin Ātāka was the first of them to bring an Afghān down; he speared one, cut off his head and brought it in. Abū'l-ḥasan the armourer, without mail as he was, went admirably forward, stopped in front of the Afghāns, laid his horse at them, chopped at one, got him down, cut off and brought in his head. Known though both were for bravelike deeds done earlier, their action in this affair added to their fame. Every one of those 40 or 50 Afghāns, falling to the arrow, falling to the sword, was cut in pieces. After making a clean sweep of them, we dismounted in a field of growing corn and ordered a tower of their heads to be set up. As we went along the road I said, with anger and scorn, to the begs who had been with Ḥusain, "You! what men! there you stood on quite flat ground, and looked on while a few Afghāns on foot overcame such a brave in the way they did! Your rank and station must be taken from you; you must lose *pargana* and country; your beards must be shaved off and you must be exhibited in towns; for there shall be punishment assuredly for him who looks on while such a brave is beaten by such a foe Fol. 239b.on dead-level land, and reaches out no hand to help!" The troop which went to Kar-māsh brought back sheep and other spoil. One of them was Bābā Qashqa[1476] *Mughūl*; an Afghān had made at him with a sword; he had stood still to adjust an arrow, shot it off and brought his man down.

(July 29th) Next day at dawn we marched for Kābul. Pay-aster Muḥammad, 'Abdu'l-'azīz Master of the Horse, and Mīr Khūrd the taster were ordered to stop at Chashma-tūra, and get pheasants from the people there.

As I had never been along the Rustam-maidān road,[1477] I went with a few men to see it. Rustam-plain (*maidān*) lies amongst mountains and towards their head is not a very charming place. The dale spreads rather broad between its two ranges. To the south, on the skirt of the rising-ground is a smallish spring, having very large poplars near it. There are many trees also, but not so large, at the source on the way out of Rustam-maidān for Gīrdīz. This is a narrower dale, but still there is a plot of green meadow below the smaller trees mentioned, and the little dale is charming. From the summit of the range, looking south, the Karmāsh and Bangash mountains are seen at one's feet; and beyond the Karmāsh show pile upon pile of the rain-clouds of Hindūstān. Towards those other lands where no rain falls, notFol. 240. a cloud is seen.

We reached Hūnī at the Mid-day Prayer and there dismounted.

(July 30th) Dismounting next day at Muḥammad Āghā's village,[1478] we perpetrated (*irtqāb*) a *ma'jūn*. There we had a drug thrown into water for the fish; a few were taken.[1479]

(July 31st) On Sunday the 3rd of Sha'bān, we reached Kābul.

(*August 2nd*) On Tuesday the 5th of the month, Darwīsh-i-muḥammad *Fażlī* and Khusrau's servants were summoned and, after enquiry made into what short-comings of theirs there may have been when Ḥusain was overcome, they were deprived of place and rank. At the Mid-day Prayer there was a wine-party under a plane-tree, at which an honorary dress was given to Bābā Qashqa *Mughūl.*

(*August 5th*) On Friday the 8th Kīpa returned from the presence of Mīrzā Khān.

(*aa. Excursion to the Koh-dāman.*)

(*August 11th*) On Thursday at the Other Prayer, I mounted for an excursion to the Koh-dāman, Bārān and Khwāja Sih-yārān.[1480] At the Bed-time Prayer, we dismounted at Māmā Khātūn.[1481]

(*August 12th*) Next day we dismounted at Istālīf; a confection was eaten on that day.

(*August 13th*) On Saturday there was a wine-party at Istālīf.

(*August 14th*) Riding at dawn from Istālīf, we crossed the space between it and the Sinjid-valley. Near Khwāja Sih-yārān a great snake was killed as thick, it may be, as the fore-arm and as long as a *qūlāch.*[1482] From its inside came out a slenderer snake, that seemed to have been just swallowed, every part of it being Fol. 240b.whole; it may have been a little shorter than the larger one. From inside this slenderer snake came out a little mouse; it too was whole, broken nowhere.[1483]

On reaching Khwāja Sih-yārān there was a wine-party. Today orders were written and despatched by Kīch-kīna the night-watch (*tūnqṭār*) to the begs on that side (*i.e.* north of Hindū-kush), giving them a rendezvous and saying, "An army is being got to horse, take thought, and come to the rendezvous fixed."

(*August 15th*) We rode out at dawn and ate a confection. At the infall of the Parwān-water many fish were taken in the local way of casting a fish-drug into the water.[1484] Mīr Shāh Beg set food and water (*āsh u āb*) before us; we then rode on to Gul-bahār. At a wine-party held after the Evening Prayer, Darwīsh-i-muḥammad (*Sārbān*) was present. Though a young man and a soldier, he had not yet committed the sin (*irtqāb*) of wine, but was in obedience (*tā'ib*). Qūtlūq Khwāja *Kūkūldāsh* had long before abandoned soldiering to become a darwīsh; moreover he was very old, his very beard was quite white; nevertheless he took his share of wine at these parties. Said I to Darwīsh-i-muḥammad, "Qūtlūq Khwāja's beard shames you! He, a darwīsh and an old man, always drinks wine; you, a soldier, a young man, your beard quite black, never drink! What does it mean?" My custom being not to press wine on a non-drinker, with so much said, it all passed off as a joke; he was not pressed to drink.

(*August 16th*) At dawn we made our morning (*ṣubāḥī ṣubūḥī qīldūk*).

(*August 17th*) Riding on Wednesday from Gul-i-bahār, weFol. 241. dismounted in Abūn-village[1485], ate food, remounted, went to a summer-house in the orchards (*bāghāt-i-kham*) and there dismounted. There was a wine-party after the Mid-day Prayer.

(*August 18th*) Riding on next day, we made the circuit of Khwāja Khāwand Saʿīd's tomb, went to China-fort and there got on a raft. Just where the Panjhīr-water comes in, the raft struck the naze of a hill and began to sink. Rauḥ-dam, Tīngrī-qulī and Mīr Muḥammad the raftsman were thrown into the water by the shock; Rauḥ-dam and Tīngrī-qulī were got on the raft again; a China cup and a spoon and a ṭambour went into the water. Lower down, the raft struck again opposite the Sang-i-barīda (the cut-stone), either on a branch in mid-stream or on a stake stuck in as a stop-water (*qāqghān qāzūq*). Right over on his back went Shāh Beg's Shāh Ḥasan, clutching at Mīrzā Qulī Kūkūldāsh and making him fall too. Darwīsh-i-muḥammad *Sārbān* was also thrown into the water. Mīrzā Qulī went over in his own fashion! Just when he fell, he was cutting a melon which he had in his hand; as he went over, he stuck his knife into the mat of the raft. He swam in his *tūn aūfrāghī*[1486] and got out of the water without coming on the raft again. Leaving it that night, we slept at raftsmen's houses. Darwīsh-i-muḥammad *Sārbān* presented me with a seven-coloured cup exactly like the one lost in the water.

(*August 19th*) On Friday we rode away from the river's bank and dismounted below Aīndīkī on the skirt of Koh-i-bacha where, with our own hands, we gathered plenty of tooth-picks.[1487]Fol. 241b. Passing on, food was eaten at the houses of the Khwāja Khiẓr people. We rode on and at the Mid-day Prayer, dismounted in a village of Qūtlūq Khwāja's fief in Lamghān where he made ready a hasty meal (*mā ḥaẓirī*); after partaking of this, we mounted and went to Kābul.

(*bb. Various incidents.*)

(*August 22nd*) On Monday the 25th, a special honorary dress and a saddled horse were bestowed on Darwīsh-i-muḥammad *Sārbān* and he was made to kneel as a retainer (*naukar*).

(*August 24th*) For 4 or 5 months I had not had my head shaved; on Wednesday the 27th, I had it done. Today there was a wine-party.

(*August 26th*) On Friday the 29th, Mīr Khūrd was made to kneel as Hind-āl's guardian.[1488] He made an offering of 1000 *shāhrukhīs* (*circa* £50).

(*August 31st*) On Wednesday the 5th of Ramẓān, a dutiful letter was brought by Tūlik Kūkūldāsh's servant Barlās Jūkī(?). Aūzbeg raiders had gone into those parts (Badakhshān); Tūlik had gone out, fought and beaten them. Barlās Jūkī brought one live Aūzbeg and one head.

(*Sep. 2nd*) In the night of Saturday the 8th, we broke our fast[1489] in Qāsim Beg's house; he led out a saddled horse for me.

(*Sep. 3rd*) On Sunday night the fast was broken in Khalīfa's house; he offered me a saddled horse.

(*Sep. 4th*) Next day came Khwāja Muḥ. 'Alī and Jān-i-nāṣir who had been summoned from their districts for the good of the army.[1490]

(*Sep. 7th*) On Wednesday the 12th, Kāmrān's maternal uncle Fol. 242.Sl. 'Alī Mīrzā arrived.[1491] As has been mentioned,[1492] he had gone to Kāshghar in the year I came from Khwāst into Kābul.

(*cc. A Yūsuf-zāī campaign.*)

(*Sep. 8th*) We rode out on Thursday the 13th of the month of Ramẓān, resolved and determined to check and ward off the Yūsuf-zāī, and we dismounted in the meadow on the Dih-i-yaq'ūb side of Kābul. When we were mounting, the equerry Bābā Jān led forward a rather good-for-nothing horse; in my anger I struck him in the face a blow which dislocated my fist below the ring-finger.[1493] The pain was not much at the time, but was rather bad when we reached our encampment-ground. For some time I suffered a good deal and could not write. It got well at last.

To this same assembly-ground were brought letters and presents (*bīlāk*) from my maternal-aunt Daulat-sulṭān Khānīm[1494] in Kāshghar, by her foster-brother Daulat-i-muḥammad. On the same day Bū Khān and Mūsa, chiefs of the Dilazāk, came, bringing tribute, and did obeisance.

(*Sep. 11th*) On Sunday the 16th Qūj Beg came.

(*Sep. 14th*) Marching on Wednesday the 19th we passed through Būt-khāk and, as usual, dismounted on the Būt-khāk water.[1495]

As Qūj Beg's districts, Bāmīān, Kāh-mard and Ghūrī, are close to the Aūzbeg, he was excused from going with this army and given leave to return to them from this ground. I bestowed on him a turban twisted for myself, and also a head-to-foot (*bāsh-ayāq*).

(*Sep. 16th*) On Friday the 21st, we dismounted at Badām-chashma.Fol. 242b.

(*Sep. 17th*) Next day we dismounted on the Bārīk-āb, I reaching the camp after a visit to Qarā-tū. On this ground honey was obtained from a tree.

(*Sep. 20th*) We went on march by march till Wednesday the 26th, and dismounted in the Bāgh-i-wafā.

(*Sep. 21st*) Thursday we just stayed in the garden.

(*Sep. 22nd*) On Friday we marched out and dismounted beyond Sulṭānpūr. Today Shāh Mīr Ḥusain came from his country. Today came also Dilazāk chiefs under Bū Khān and Mūsa. My plan had been to put down the Yūsuf-zāī in Sawād, but these chiefs set forth to me that there was a large horde (*aūlūs*) in Hash-naghar and that much corn was to be had there. They were very urgent for us to go to Hash-naghar. After consultation the matter was left in this way:—As it is said there is much corn in Hash-naghar, the Afghāns there shall be overrun; the forts of Hash-naghar and Parashāwar shall be put into order; part of the corn shall be stored in them and they be left in charge of Shāh Mīr Ḥusain and a body of braves. To suit Shāh Mīr Ḥusain's convenience in this, he was given 15 days leave, with a rendezvous named for him to come to after going to his country and preparing his equipment.

(*Sep. 23rd*) Marching on next day, we reached Jūī-shāhī and there dismounted. On this ground Tīngrī-bīrdī and Sl. Muḥammad *Dūldāī* overtook us. Today came also Ḥamza from Qūndūz.[1496]

(*Sep. 25th*) On Sunday the last day of the month (Ramẓān), we marched from Jūī-shāhī and dismounted at Qīrīq-arīq (forty-conduits), Fol. 243.I going by raft, with a special few. The new moon of the Feast was seen at that station.[1497] People had brought a few beast-loads of wine from Nūr-valley;[1498] after the Evening Prayer there was a wine-party, those present being Muḥibb-i-'alī the armourer, Khwāja Muḥ. 'Alī the librarian, Shāh Beg's Shāh Ḥasan, Sl. Muḥ. *Dūldāī* and Darwīsh-i-muḥ. *Sārbān,* then obedient (*tā'ib*). From my childhood up it had been my rule not to press wine on a non-drinker; Darwīsh-i-muḥammad was at every party and no pressure was put on him (by me), but Khwāja Muḥ. 'Alī left him no choice; he pressed him and pressed him till he made him drink.

(*Sep. 26th*) On Monday we marched with the dawn of the Feast-day,[1499] eating a confection on the road to dispel crop-sickness. While under its composing influence (*nāklīk*), we were brought a colocynth-apple (*khunṭul*). Darwīsh-i-muḥammad had never seen one; said I, "It is a melon of Hindūstān," sliced it and gave him a piece. He bit into it at once; it was night before the bitter taste went out of his mouth. At Garm-chashma we dismounted on rising-ground where cold meat was being set out for us when Langar Khān arrived to wait on me after being for a time at his own place (Koh-i-jūd). He brought an offering of a horse and a few confections. Passing on, we dismounted at Yada-bīr, at the Other Prayer got on a raft there, went for as much as two miles on it, then left it.

(*Sep. 27th*) Riding on next morning, we dismounted below the Khaibar-pass. Today arrived Sl. Bāyazīd, come up by theFol. 243b. Bāra-road after hearing of us; he set forth that the Afrīdī Afghāns were seated in Bāra with their goods and families and that they had grown a mass of corn which was still standing (lit. on foot). Our plan being for the Yūsuf-zāī Afghāns of Hash-naghar, we paid him no attention. At the Mid-day Prayer there was a wine-party in Khwāja Muḥammad 'Alī's tent. During the party details about our coming in this direction were written and sent off by the hand of a sulṭān of Tīrah to Khwāja Kalān in Bajaur. I wrote this couplet on the margin of the letter (*farmān*):—

Say sweetly o breeze, to that beautiful fawn,

Thou hast given my head to the hills and the wild.[1500]

(*Sep. 28th*) Marching on at dawn across the pass, we got through the Khaibar-narrows and dismounted at 'Alī-masjid. At the Mid-day Prayer we rode on, leaving the baggage behind, reached the Kābul-water at the second watch (midnight) and there slept awhile.

(*Sep. 29th*) A ford[1501] was found at daylight; we had forded the water (*sū-dīn kīchīldī*), when news came from our scout that the Afghāns had heard of us and were in flight. We went on, passed through the Sawād-water and dismounted amongst the Afghān corn-fields. Not a half, not a fourth indeed of the promised corn was had. The plan of fitting-up Hash-naghar, made under the hope of getting corn here, came to nothing.Fol. 244. The Dilazāk Afghāns, who had urged it on us, were ashamed. We next dismounted after fording the water of Sawād to its Kābul side.

(*Sep. 30th*) Marching next morning from the Sawād-water, we crossed the Kābul-water and dismounted. The Begs admitted to counsel were summoned and a consultation having been had, the matter was left at this:—that the Afrīdī Afghāns spoken of by Sl. Bāyazīd should be over-run, Pūrshāwūr-fort be fitted up on the strength of their goods and corn, and some-one left there in charge.

At this station Hindū Beg *Qūchīn* and the Mīr-zādas of Khwāst overtook us. Today *ma'jūn* was eaten, the party being Darwesh-i-muḥammad *Sārbān*, Muḥammad Kūkūldāsh, Gadāī Ṭaghāī and 'Asas; later on we invited Shāh

Ḥasan also. After food had been placed before us, we went on a raft, at the Other Prayer. We called Langar Khān *Nīa-ẓāī* on also. At the Evening Prayer we got off the raft and went to camp.

(*Oct. 1st*) Marching at dawn, in accordance with the arrangement made on the Kābul-water, we passed Jām and dismounted at the outfall of the 'Alī-masjid water.[1502]

(*dd. Badakhshān affairs.*)

Sl. 'Alī (Ṭaghāī's servant ?) Abū'l-hāshim overtaking us, said, "On the night of 'Arafa,[1503] I was in Jūī-shāhī with a person from Badakhshān; he told me that Sl. Sa'īd Khān had come with designs on Badakhshān, so I came on from Jūī-shāhī along the Jām-rūd, to give the news to the Pādshāh." On this the begs were summoned and advice was taken. In consequence of this Fol. 244b.news, it seemed inadvisable to victual the fort (Pūrshāwūr), and we started back intending to go to Badakhshān.[1504] Langar Khān was appointed to help Muḥ. 'Alī *Jang-jang*; he was given an honorary dress and allowed to go.

That night a wine-party was held in Khwāja Muḥ. 'Alī's tent. We marched on next day, crossed Khaibar and dismounted below the pass.

(*ee. The Khiẓr-khail Afghāns.*)

(*Oct. 3rd*) Many improper things the Khiẓr-khail had done! When the army went to and fro, they used to shoot at the laggards and at those dismounted apart, in order to get their horses. It seemed lawful therefore and right to punish them. With this plan we marched from below the pass at daybreak, ate our mid-day meal in Dih-i-ghulāmān (Basaul),[1505] and after feeding our horses, rode on again at the Mid-day Prayer.

Muḥ. Ḥusain the armourer was made to gallop off to Kābul with orders to keep prisoner all Khiẓr-khailīs there, and to submit to me an account of their possessions; also, to write a detailed account of whatever news there was from Badakhshān and to send a man off with it quickly from Kābul to me.

That night we moved on till the second watch (midnight), got a little beyond Sulṭānpūr, there slept awhile, then rode on again. The Khiẓr-khail were understood to have their seat from Bahār (Vihāra?) and Mīch-grām to Karā-sū (*sic*). Arriving before dawn, (*Oct. 4th*) the raid was allowed. Most of the goods of the Khiẓr-khailīs and their small children fell into the army's hands; a few tribesmen, being near the mountains, drew off toFol. 245. them and were left.

(*Oct. 5th*) We dismounted next day at Qīlaghū where pheasants were taken on our ground. Today the baggage came up from the rear and was unloaded here. Owing to this punitive raid, the Wazīrī Afghāns who never had given in their tribute well, brought 300 sheep.

(*Oct. 9th*) I had written nothing since my hand was dislocated; here I wrote a little, on Sunday the 14th of the month.[1506]

(*Oct. 10th*) Next day came Afghān chiefs leading the Khirilchī [and] Samū-khail. The Dilazāk Afghāns entreated pardon for them; we gave it and set the captured free, fixed their tribute at 4000 sheep, gave coats (*tūn*) to their chiefs, appointed and sent out collectors.

(*Oct. 13th*) These matters settled, we marched on Thursday the 18th, and dismounted at Bahār (Vihāra?) and Mīch-grām.

(*Oct. 14th*) Next day I went to the Bāgh-i-wafā. Those were the days of the garden's beauty; its lawns were one sheet of trefoil; its pomegranate-trees yellowed to autumn splendour,[1507] their fruit full red; fruit on the orange-trees green and glad (*khurram*), countless oranges but not yet as yellow as our hearts desired! The pomegranates were excellent, not equal, however, to the best ones of Wilāyat.[1508] The one excellent and blessed content we have had from the Bāgh-i-wafā was had at this time. Fol. 245b.We were there three or four days; during the time the whole camp had pomegranates in abundance.

(*Oct. 17th*) We marched from the garden on Monday. I stayed in it till the first watch (9 a.m.) and gave away oranges; I bestowed the fruit of two trees on Shāh Ḥasan; to several begs I gave the fruit of one tree each; to some gave one tree for two persons. As we were thinking of visiting Lamghān in the winter, I ordered that they should reserve (*qūrūghlāīlār*) at least 20 of the trees growing round the reservoir. That day we dismounted at Gandamak.

(*Oct. 18th*) Next day we dismounted at Jagdālīk. Near the Evening Prayer there was a wine-party at which most of the household were present. After a time Qāsim Beg's sister's son Gadāī *bihjat*[1509] used very disturbing words and, being drunk, slid down on the cushion by my side, so Gadāī Ṭaghāī picked him up and carried him out from the party.

(*Oct. 19th*) Marching next day from that ground, I made an excursion up the valley-bottom of the Bārīk-āb towards Qūrūq-sāī. A few purslain trees were in the utmost autumn beauty. On dismounting, seasonable[1510] food was set out. The vintage was the cause! wine was drunk! A sheep was ordered brought from the road and made into *kabābs* (*brochettes*). We amused ourselves by setting fire to branches of holm-oak.[1511]

Mullā ʿAbdu'l-malik *dīwāna*[1512] having begged to take the news of our coming into Kābul, was sent ahead. To this place came Ḥasan Nabīra from Mīrzā Khān's presence; he must have come after letting me know [his intention of coming].[1513] There wasFol. 246. drinking till the Sun's decline; we then rode off. People in our party had become very drunk, Sayyid Qāsim so much so, that two of his servants mounted him and got him into camp with difficulty. Muḥ. Bāqir's Dost was so drunk that people, headed by Amīn-i-muḥammad Tarkhān and Mastī *chuhra*, could not get him on his horse; even when they poured water on his head, nothing was effected. At that moment a body of Afghāns appeared. Amīn-i-muḥammad, who had had enough himself, had this idea, "Rather than leave him here, as he is, to be taken, let us cut his head off and carry it with us." At last after 100 efforts, they mounted him and brought him with them. We reached Kābul at midnight.

(*ff. Incidents in Kābul.*)

In Court next morning Qulī Beg waited on me. He had been to Sl. Saʿīd Khān's presence in Kāshghar as my envoy. To him as envoy to me had been added Bīshka Mīrzā *Itārchī*[1514] who brought me gifts of the goods of that country.

(*Oct. 25th*) On Wednesday the 1st of Ẕū'l-qaʿda, I went by myself to Qābil's tomb[1515] and there took my morning. The people of the party came later by ones and twos. When the Sun waxed hot, we went to the Violet-garden and drank there, by the side of the reservoir. Mid-day coming on, we slept. At the Mid-day Prayer we drank again. At this mid-day party I gave wine to Tīngrī-qulī Beg and to Mahndī (?) to whom at any earlier party, wine had not been given. At the Bed-timeFol. 246b. Prayer, I went to the Hot-bath where I stayed the night.

(*Oct. 26th*) On Thursday honorary dresses were bestowed on the Hindūstānī traders, headed by Yaḥya *Nūḥānī*, and they were allowed to go.

(*Oct. 28th*) On Saturday the 4th, a dress and gifts were bestowed on Bīshka Mīrzā, who had come from Kāshghar, and he was given leave to go.

(*Oct. 29th*) On Sunday there was a party in the little Picture-hall over the (Chār-bāgh) gate; small retreat though it is, 16 persons were present.

(*gg. Excursion to the Koh-dāman.*)

(*Oct. 30th*) Today we went to Istālīf to see the harvest (*khizān*). Today was done the sin (? *irtikāb qīlīb aïdī*) of *maʿjūn*. Much rain fell; most of the begs and the household came into my tent, outside the Bāgh-i-kalān.

(Oct. 31st) Next day there was a wine-party in the same garden, lasting till night.

(November 1st) At dawn we took our morning (*ṣubāḥī ṣubūḥī qīldūk*) and got drunk, took a sleep, and at the Mid-day Prayer rode from Istālīf. On the road a confection was eaten. We reached Bih-zādī at the Other Prayer. The harvest-crops were very beautiful; while we were viewing them those disposed for wine began to agitate about it. The harvest-colour was extremely beautiful; wine was drunk, though *ma'jūn* had been eaten, sitting under autumnal trees. The party lasted till the Bed-time Prayer. Khalīfa's Mullā Maḥmūd arriving, we had him summoned to join the party. 'Abdu'l-lāh was very drunk Fol. 247.indeed; a word affecting Khalīfa (*ṭarfidīn*) being said, 'Abdu'l-lāh forgot Mullā Maḥmūd and recited this line:—

Regard whom thou wilt, he suffers from the same wound.[1516]

Mullā Maḥmūd was sober; he blamed 'Abdu'l-lāh for repeating that line in jest; 'Abdu'l-lāh came to his senses, was troubled in mind, and after this talked and chatted very sweetly.

Our excursion to view the harvest was over; we dismounted, close to the Evening Prayer, in the Chār-bāgh.

(Nov. 12th) On Friday the 16th, after eating a confection with a few special people in the Violet-garden, we went on a boat. Humāyūn and Kāmrān were with us later; Humāyūn made a very good shot at a duck.

(hh. A Bohemian episode.)

(Nov. 14th) On Saturday the 18th, I rode out of the Chār-bāgh at midnight, sent night-watch and groom back, crossed Mullā Bābā's bridge, got out by the Dīūrīn-narrows, round by the bāzārs and *kārez* of Qūsh-nādur (var.), along the back of the Bear-house (*khirs-khāna*), and near sunrise reached Tardī Beg *Khāk-sār's*[1517] *kārez*. He ran out quickly on hearing of me. His shortness (*qālāshlīghi*) was known; I had taken 100 *shāhrukhīs* (£5) with me; I gave him these and told him to get wine and other things ready as I had a fancy for a private and unrestrained party. He went for wine towards Bih-zādī[1518]; I sent my horse by his slave to the valley-bottom and sat down on the slope behind the *kārez*. At the first watch (9 a.m.) Tardī Beg broughtFol. 247b. a pitcher of wine which we drank by turns. After him came Muḥammad-i-qāsim *Barlās* and Shāh-zāda who had got to know of his fetching the wine, and had followed him, their minds quite empty of any thought about me. We invited them to the party. Said Tardī Beg, "Hul-hul Anīga wishes to drink wine with you." Said I, "For my part, I never saw a woman drink wine; invite her." We also invited Shāhī a qalandar, and one of the *kārez*-men who played the rebeck. There was drinking till the

Evening Prayer on the rising-ground behind the *kārez*; we then went into Tardī Beg's house and drank by lamp-light almost till the Bed-time Prayer. The party was quite free and unpretending. I lay down, the others went to another house and drank there till beat of drum (midnight). Hul-hul Anīga came in and made me much disturbance; I got rid of her at last by flinging myself down as if drunk. It was in my mind to put people off their guard, and ride off alone to Astar-ghach, but it did not come off because they got to know. In the end, I rode away at beat of drum, after letting Tardī Beg and Shāh-zāda know. We three mounted and made for Astar-ghach.

(*Nov. 15th*) We reached Khwāja Ḥasan below Istālīf by the first prayer (*farẓ waqt*); dismounted for a while, ate a confection, Fol. 248.and went to view the harvest. When the Sun was up, we dismounted at a garden in Istālīf and ate grapes. We slept at Khwāja Shahāb, a dependency of Astar-ghach. Ātā, the Master of the Horse, must have had a house somewhere near, for before we were awake he had brought food and a pitcher of wine. The vintage was very fine. After drinking a few cups, we rode on. We next dismounted in a garden beautiful with autumn; there a party was held at which Khwāja Muḥammad Amīn joined us. Drinking went on till the Bed-time Prayer. During that day and night 'Abdu'l-lāh, 'Asas, Nūr Beg and Yūsuf-i-'alī all arrived from Kābul.

(*Nov. 16th*) After food at dawn, we rode out and visited the Bāgh-i-pādshāhī below Astar-ghach. One young apple-tree in it had turned an admirable autumn-colour; on each branch were left 5 or 6 leaves in regular array; it was such that no painter trying to depict it could have equalled. After riding from Astar-ghach we ate at Khwāja Ḥasan, and reached Bih-zādī at the Evening Prayer. There we drank in the house of Khwāja Muḥ. Amīn's servant Imām-i-muḥammad.

(*Nov. 17th*) Next day, Tuesday, we went into the Chār-bāgh of Kābul.

(*Nov. 18th*) On Thursday the 23rd, having marched (*kūchūb*), the fort was entered.

(*Nov. 19th*) On Friday Muḥammad 'Alī (son of ?) Ḥaidar the stirrup-holder brought, as an offering, a *tūīgūn*[1519] he had caught.

(*Nov. 20th*) On Saturday the 25th, there was a party in the Plane-tree garden from which I rose and mounted at the Bed-time Prayer. Sayyid Qāsim being in shame at past occurrences,[1520] we dismounted at his house and drank a few cups.

Fol. 248b.(*Nov. 24th*) On Thursday the 1st of Ẕū'l-ḥijja, Tāju'd-dīn Maḥmūd, come from Qandahār, waited on me.

(*Dec. 12th*) On Monday the 19th, Muḥ. 'Alī *Jang-jang* came from Nīl-āb.

(*Dec. 13th*) On Tuesday the ... of the month, Sangar Khān *Janjūha*, come from Bhīra, waited on me.

(*Dec. 16th*) On Friday the 23rd, I finished (copying?) the odes and couplets selected according to their measure from 'Alī-sher Beg's four Dīwāns.[1521]

(*Dec. 20th*) On Tuesday the 27th there was a social-gathering in the citadel, at which it was ordered that if any-one went out from it drunk, that person should not be invited to a party again.

(*Dec. 23rd*) On Friday the 30th of Ẕū'l-ḥijja it was ridden out with the intention of making an excursion to Lamghān.

926 AH.-DEC. 23RD 1519 TO DEC. 12TH 1520 AD.[1522]

(*a. Excursion to the Koh-dāman and Kohistān.*)

(*Dec. 23rd*) On Saturday Muḥarram 1st Khwāja Sih-yārān was reached. A wine-party was had on the bank of the conduit, where this comes out on the hill.[1523]

(*Dec. 24th*) Riding on next morning (2nd), we visited the moving sands (*reg-i-rawān*). A party was held in Sayyid Qāsim's *Bulbul's* house.[1524]

(*Dec. 25th*) Riding on from there, we ate a confection (*ma'jūn*), went further and dismounted at Bilkir (?).

(*Dec. 26th*) At dawn (4th) we made our morning [*ṣubāḥī ṣubūḥī qīldūk*], although there might be drinking at night. We rode on at the Mid-day Prayer, dismounted at Dūr-nāma[1525] and there had a wine party.

(*Dec. 27th*) We took our morning early. Ḥaq-dād, the headman of Dūr-namā made me an offering (*pesh-kash*) of his garden.

(*Dec. 28th*) Riding thence on Thursday (6th), we dismounted at the villages of the Tājiks in Nijr-aū.

(*Dec. 29th*) On Friday (7th) we hunted the hill between Forty-ploughs (*Chihil-qulba*) and the water of Bārān; many deer fell. Fol. 249.I had not shot an arrow since my hand was hurt; now, with an easy[1526] bow, I shot a deer in the shoulder, the arrow going in to half up the feather. Returning from hunting, we went on at the Other Prayer in Nijr-aū.

(*Dec. 30th*) Next day (Saturday 8th) the tribute of the Nijr-aū people was fixed at 60 gold misqāls.[1527]

(*Jan. 1st*) On Monday (10th) we rode on intending to visit Lamghān.[1528] I had expected Humāyūn to go with us, but as he inclined to stay behind, leave was given him from Kūra-pass. We went on and dismounted in Badr-aū (Tag-aū).

(*b. Excursions in Lamghān.*)

(*Jan. ...*) Riding on, we dismounted at Aūlūgh-nūr.[1529] The fishermen there took fish at one draught[1530] from the water of Bārān. At the Other Prayer (afternoon) there was drinking on the raft; and there was drinking in a tent after we left the raft at the Evening Prayer.

Ḥaidar the standard-bearer had been sent from Dāwar[1531] to the Kāfirs; several Kāfir headmen came now to the foot of Bād-i-pīch (pass), brought a few goat-skins of wine, and did obeisance. In descending that pass a surprising number of ...[1532] was seen.

(*Jan. ...*) Next day getting on a raft, we ate a confection, got off below Būlān and went to camp. There were two rafts.

(*Jan. 5th*) Marching on Friday (14th), we dismounted below Mandrāwar on the hill-skirt. There was a late wine-party.

(*Jan. 6th*) On Saturday (15th), we passed through the Darūta narrows by raft, got off a little above Jahān-namā'ī (Jalālābād) and went to the Bāgh-i-wafā in front of Adīnapūr. When we were leaving the raft the governor of Nīngnahār Qayyām Aūrdū Shāh came and did obeisance. Langar Khān *Nīā-zāī*,—he hadFol. 249b. been in Nīl-āb for a time,—waited upon me on the road. We dismounted in the Bāgh-i-wafā; its oranges had yellowed beautifully; its spring-bloom was well-advanced, and it was very charming. We stayed in it five or six days.

As it was my wish and inclination (*jū dagh-dagha*)to return to obedience (*tā'ib*) in my 40th year, I was drinking to excess now that less than a year was left.

(*Jan. 7th*) On Sunday the 16th, having made my morning (*ṣubūḥī*) and became sober. Mullā Yārak played an air he had composed in five-time and in the five-line measure (*makhammas*), while I chose to eat a confection (*ma'jūn*). He had composed an excellent air. I had not occupied myself with such things for some time; a wish to compose came over me now, so I composed an air in four-time, as will be mentioned in time.[1533]

(*Jan. 10th*) On Wednesday (19th) it was said for fun, while we were making our morning (*ṣubūḥī*), "Let whoever speaks like a Sārt (*i.e.* in Persian) drink a cup." Through this many drank. At *sunnat-waqt*[1534] again, when we were sitting under the willows in the middle of the meadow, it was said, "Let whoever speaks like a Turk, drink a cup!" Through this also numbers drank. After the sun got up, we drank under the orange-trees on the reservoir-bank.

(*Jan. 11th*) Next day (20th) we got on a raft from Darūta; got off again below Jūī-shāhī and went to Atar.

(*Jan....*) We rode from there to visit Nūr-valley, went as far as Sūsān (lily)-village, then turned back and dismounted in Amla.

Fol. 250.(*Jan. 14th*) As Khwāja Kalān had brought Bajaur into good order, and as he was a friend of mine, I had sent for him and had made Bajaur over to Shāh Mīr Ḥusain's charge. On Saturday the 22nd of the month (Muḥarram), Shāh Mīr Ḥusain was given leave to go. That day in Amla we drank.

(*Jan. 15th*) It rained (*yāmghūr yāghdūrūb*) next day (23rd).

When we reached Kula-grām in Kūnār[1535] where Malik 'Alī's house is, we dismounted at his middle son's house, overlooking an orange-orchard. We did not go into the orchard because of the rain but just drank where we were. The rain was very heavy. I taught Mullā 'Alī Khān a ṭalisman I knew; he wrote it on four pieces of paper and hung them on four sides; as he did it, the rain stopped and the air began to clear.

(*Jan. 16th*) At dawn (24th) we got on a raft; on another several braves went. People in Bajaur, Sawād, Kūnār and thereabouts make a beer (*bīr būẓa*)[1536] the ferment of which is a thing they call *kīm*.[1537] This *kīm* they make of the roots of herbs and several simples, shaped like a loaf, dried and kept by them. Some sorts of beer are surprisingly exhilarating, but bitter and distasteful. We had thought of drinking beer but, because of its bitter taste, preferred a confection. 'Asas, Ḥasan *Aīkirik*,[1538] and Mastī, on the other raft, were ordered to drink some; they did so and became quite drunk. Ḥasan *Aīkirik* set up a disgusting disturbance; 'Asas, very drunk, did suchFol. 250b. unpleasant things that we were most uncomfortable (*ba tang*). I thought of having them put off on the far side of the water, but some of the others begged them off.

I had sent for Khwāja Kalān at this time and had bestowed Bajaur on Shāh Mīr Ḥusain. For why? Khwāja Kalān was a friend; his stay in Bajaur had been long; moreover the Bajaur appointment appeared an easy one.

At the ford of the Kūnār-water Shāh Mīr Ḥusain met me on his way to Bajaur. I sent for him and said a few trenchant words, gave him some special armour, and let him go.

Opposite Nūr-gal (Rock-village) an old man begged from those on the rafts; every-one gave him something, coat (*tūn*), turban, bathing-cloth and so on, so he took a good deal away.

At a bad place in mid-stream the raft struck with a great shock; there was much alarm; it did not sink but Mīr Muḥammad the raftsman was thrown into the water. We were near Atar that night.

(*Jan. 17th*) On Tuesday (25th) we reached Mandrāwar.[1539] Qūtlūq-qadam and his father had arranged a party inside the fort; though the place had no charm, a few cups were drunk there to please them. We went to camp at the Other Prayer.

(*Jan. 18th*) On Wednesday (26th) an excursion was made to Kind-kir[1540] spring. Kind-kir is a dependent village of the Mandrāwar *tūmān*, the one and only village of the Lamghānāt Fol. 251.where dates are grown. It lies rather high on the mountain-skirt, its date lands on its east side. At one edge of the date lands is the spring, in a place aside (*yān yīr*). Six or seven yards below the spring-head people have heaped up stones to make a shelter[1541] for bathing and by so-doing have raised the water in the reservoir high enough for it to pour over the heads of the bathers. The water is very soft; it is felt a little cold in wintry days but is pleasant if one stays in it.

(*Jan. 19th*) On Thursday (27th) Sher Khān *Tarkalānī* got us to dismount at his house and there gave us a feast (*ẓiyāfat*). Having ridden on at the Mid-day Prayer, fish were taken out of the fish-ponds of which particulars have been given.[1542]

(*Jan. 20th*) On Friday (28th) we dismounted near Khwāja Mīr-i-mīrān's village. A party was held there at the Evening Prayer.

(*Jan. 21st*) On Saturday (29th) we hunted the hill between 'Alī-shang and Alangār. One hunting-circle having been made on the 'Alī-shang side, another on the Alangār, the deer were driven down off the hill and many were killed. Returning from hunting, we dismounted in a garden belonging to the Maliks of Alangār and there had a party.

Half of one of my front-teeth had broken off, the other half remaining; this half broke off today while I was eating food.

(*Jan. 22nd*) At dawn (Ṣafar 1st) we rode out and had a fishing-net cast, at mid-day went into 'Alī-shang and drank in a garden.

(*Jan. 23rd*) Next day (Ṣafar 2nd) Ḥamza Khān, Malik of ‘Alī-shang was made over to the avengers-of-blood[1543] for his evil deeds in shedding innocent blood, and retaliation was made.

(*Jan. 24th*) On Tuesday, after reading a chapter of the QorānFol. 251b. (*wird*), we turned for Kābul by the Yān-būlāgh road. At the Other Prayer, we passed the [Bārān]-water from Aūlūgh-nūr (Great-rock); reached Qarā-tū by the Evening Prayer, there gave our horses corn and had a hasty meal prepared, rode on again as soon as they had finished their barley.[1544]

TRANSLATOR'S NOTE ON 926 TO 932 AH.-1520 TO 1525 AD.

Bābur's diary breaks off here for five years and ten months.[1545] His activities during the unrecorded period may well have left no time in which to keep one up, for in it he went thrice to Qandahār, thrice into India, once to Badakhshān, once to Balkh; twice at least he punished refractory tribesmen; he received embassies from Hindūstān, and must have had much to oversee in muster and equipment for his numerous expeditions. Over and above this, he produced the *Mubīn*, a Turkī poem of 2000 lines.

That the gap in his autobiography is not intentional several passages in his writings show;[1546] he meant to fill it; there is no evidence that he ever did so; the reasonable explanation of his failure is that he died before he had reached this part of his book.

The events of these unrecorded years are less interesting than those of the preceding gap, inasmuch as their drama of human passion is simpler; it is one mainly of cross-currents of ambition, nothing in it matching the maelstrom of sectarian hate, tribal antipathy, and racial struggle which engulphed Bābur's fortunes beyond the Oxus.

None-the-less the period has its distinctive mark, the biographical one set by his personality as his long-sustained effort works out towards rule in Hindūstān. He becomes felt; his surroundings bend to his purpose; his composite following accepts his goal; he gains the southern key of Kābul and Hindūstān and presses the Arghūns out from his rear; in the Panj-āb he becomes a power; the Rājpūt Rānā of Chitor proffers him alliance against Ibrāhīm; and his intervention is sought in those warrings of the Afghāns which were the matrix of his own success.

a. Dramatis personæ.

The following men played principal parts in the events of the unchronicled years:—

Bābur in Kābul, Badakhshān and Balkh,[1547] his earlier following purged of Mughūl rebellion, and augmented by the various Mīrzās-in-exile in whose need of employment Shāh Beg saw Bābur's need of wider territory.[1548]

Sulṭān Ibrāhīm *Lūdī* who had succeeded after his father Sikandar's death (Sunday Ẕū'l-qa'da 7th 923 *AH.*-Nov. 21st 1517 AD.)[1549], was now embroiled in civil war, and hated for his tyranny and cruelty.

Shāh Ismā'īl *Ṣafawī*, ruling down to Rajab 19th 930 AH. (May 24th 1524 AD.) and then succeeded by his son Ṭahmāsp *aet.* 10.

Kūchūm (Kūchkūnjī) Khān, Khāqān of the Aūzbegs, Shaibānī's successor, now in possession of Transoxiana.

Sulṭān Sa'īd Khān *Chaghatāī*, with head-quarters in Kāshghar, a ruler amongst the Mughūls but not their Khāqān, the supreme Khānship being his elder brother Manṣūr's.

Shāh Shujā' Beg *Arghūn*, who, during the period, at various times held Qandahār, Shāl, Mustang, Sīwīstān, and part of Sind. He died in 930 AH. (1524 AD.) and was succeeded by his son Ḥasan who read the *khuṭba* for Bābur.

Khān Mīrzā *Mīrānshāhī*, who held Badakhshān from Bābur, with head-quarters in Qūndūz; he died in 927 AH. (1520 AD.) and was succeeded in his appointment by Humāyūn *aet.* 13.

Muḥammad-i-zamān *Bāī-qarā* who held Balkh perhaps direct from Bābur, perhaps from Ismā'īl through Bābur.

'Alā'u'd-dīn 'Ālam Khān *Lūdī*, brother of the late Sulṭān Sikandar *Lūdī* and now desiring to supersede his nephew Ibrāhīm.

Daulat Khān *Yūsuf-khail* (as Bābur uniformly describes him), or *Lūdī* (as other writers do), holding Lāhor for Ibrāhīm *Lūdī* at the beginning of the period.

SOURCES FOR THE EVENTS OF THIS GAP

A complete history of the events the *Bābur-nāma* leaves unrecorded has yet to be written. The best existing one, whether Oriental or European, is Erskine's *History of India*, but this does not exhaust the sources—notably not using the *Ḥabību's-siyar*—and could be revised here and there with advantage.

Most of the sources enumerated as useful for filling the previous gap are so here; to them must be added, for the affairs of Qandahār, Khwānd-amīr's *Ḥabību's-siyar*. This Mīr Ma'ṣūm's *Tārīkh-i-sind* supplements usefully, but its brevity and its discrepant dates make it demand adjustment; in some details it is expanded by Sayyid Jamāl's *Tarkhān-* or *Arghūn-nāma*.

For the affairs of Hindūstān the main sources are enumerated in Elliot and Dowson's *History of India* and in Nassau Lees' *Materials for the history of India*. Doubtless all will be exhausted for the coming *Cambridge History of India*.

EVENTS OF THE UNCHRONICLED YEARS

926 AH.-DEC. 23RD 1519 TO DEC. 12TH 1520 AD.

The question of which were Bābur's "Five expeditions" into Hindūstān has been often discussed; it is useful therefore to establish the dates of those known as made. I have entered one as made in this year for the following reasons;—it broke short because Shāh Beg made incursion into Bābur's territories, and that incursion was followed by a siege of Qandahār which several matters mentioned below show to have taken place in 926 AH.

a. Expedition into Hindūstān.

The march out from Kābul may have been as soon as muster and equipment allowed after the return from Lamghān chronicled in the diary. It was made through Bajaur where refractory tribesmen were brought to order. The Indus will have been forded at the usual place where, until the last one of 932 AH. (1525 AD.), all expeditions crossed on the outward march. Bhīra was traversed in which were Bābur's own Commanders, and advance was made, beyond lands yet occupied, to Sīālkot, 72 miles north of Lāhor and in the Rechna *dū-āb*. It was occupied without resistance; and a further move made to what the MSS. call Sayyidpūr; this attempted defence, was taken by assault and put to the sword. No place named Sayyidpūr is given in the Gazetteer of India, but the *Āyīn-i-akbarī* mentions a Sidhpūr which from its neighbourhood to Sīālkot may be what Bābur took.

Nothing indicates an intention in Bābur to join battle with Ibrāhīm at this time; Lāhor may have been his objective, after he had made a demonstration in force to strengthen his footing in Bhīra. Whatever he may have planned to do beyond Sidhpūr(?) was frustrated by the news which took him back to Kābul and thence to Qandahār, that an incursion into his territory had been made by Shāh Beg.

b. Shāh Shujā' Beg's position.

Shāh Beg was now holding Qandahār, Shāl, Mustang and Sīwīstān.[1550] He knew that he held Qandahār by uncertain tenure, in face of its desirability for Bābur and his own lesser power. His ground was further weakened by its usefulness for operations on Harāt and the presence with Bābur of Bāī-qarā refugees, ready to seize a chance, if offered by Ismā'īl's waning fortunes, for recovery of their former seat. Knowing his weakness, he for several years had been pushing his way out into Sind by way of the Bolān-pass.

His relations with Bābur were ostensibly good; he had sent him envoys twice last year, the first time to announce a success at Kāhān had in the end of 924 AH. (Nov. 1519 AD.). His son Ḥasan however, with whom he was unreconciled, had been for more than a year in Bābur's company,—a matter not unlikely to stir under-currents of unfriendliness on either side.

His relations with Shāh Ismā'īl were deferential, in appearance even vassal-like, as is shewn by Khwānd-amīr's account of his appeal for intervention against Bābur to the Shāh's officers in Harāt. Whether he read the *khuṭba* for any suzerain is doubtful; his son Ḥasan, it may be said, read it later on for Bābur.

c. The impelling cause of this siege of Qandahār.

Precisely what Shāh Beg did to bring Bābur back from the Panj-āb and down upon Qandahār is not found mentioned by any source. It seems likely to have been an affair of subordinates instigated by or for him. Its immediate agents may have been the Nīkdīrī (Nūkdīrī) and Hazāra tribes Bābur punished on his way south. Their location was the western border-land; they may have descended on the Great North Road or have raided for food in that famine year. It seems certain that Shāh Beg made no serious attempt on Kābul; he was too much occupied in Sind to allow him to do so. Some unused source may throw light on the matter incidentally; the offence may have been small in itself and yet sufficient to determine Bābur to remove risk from his rear.[1551]

d. Qandahār.

The Qandahār of Bābur's sieges was difficult of capture; he had not taken it in 913 AH. (f. 208*b*) by siege or assault, but by default after one day's fight in the open. The strength of its position can be judged from the following account of its ruins as they were seen in 1879 AD., the military details of which supplement Bellew's description quoted in Appendix J.

The fortifications are of great extent with a treble line of bastioned walls and a high citadel in the centre. The place is in complete ruin and its locality now useful only as a grazing ground.... "The town is in three parts, each on a separate eminence, and capable of mutual defence. The mountain had been covered with towers united by curtains, and the one on the culminating point may be called impregnable. It commanded the citadel which stood lower down on the second eminence, and this in turn commanded the town which was on a table-land elevated above the plain. The triple walls surrounding the city were at a considerable distance from it. After exploring the citadel and ruins, we mounted by the gorge to the summit of the hill with the impregnable fort. In this gorge are the ruins of two tanks, some 80 feet square, all destroyed, with the pillars fallen; the work is *pukka* in brick and *chunām* (cement) and each tank had been domed in; they would have held about 400,000 gallons each." (Le Messurier's *Kandahar in 1879 AD.* pp. 223, 245.)

e. Bābur's sieges of Qandahār.

The term of five years is found associated with Bābur's sieges of Qandahār, sometimes suggesting a single attempt of five years' duration. This it is easy to show incorrect; its root may be Mīr Ma'ṣūm's erroneous chronology.

The day on which the keys of Qandahār were made over to Bābur is known, from the famous inscription which commemorates the event (Appendix J), as Shawwāl 13th 928 AH. Working backwards from this, it is known that in 927 AH. terms of surrender were made and that Bābur went back to Kābul; he is besieging it in 926 AH.—the year under description; his annals of 925 AH. are complete and contain no siege; the year 924 AH. appears to have had no siege, Shāh Beg was on the Indus and his son was for at least part of it with Bābur; 923 AH. was a year of intended siege, frustrated by Bābur's own illness; of any siege in 922 AH. there is as yet no record known. So that it is certain there was no unremitted beleaguerment through five years.

f. The siege of 926 AH. (1520 AD.).

When Bābur sat down to lay regular siege to Qandahār, with mining and battering of the walls,[1552] famine was desolating the country round. The garrison was reduced to great distress; "pestilence," ever an ally of Qandahār, broke out within the walls, spread to Bābur's camp, and in the month of Tīr (June) led him to return to Kābul.

In the succeeding months of respite, Shāh Beg pushed on in Sind and his former slave, now commander, Mehtar Saṃbhal revictualled the town.

927 AH.—DEC. 12TH 1520 TO DEC. 1ST 1521 AD.

a. The manuscript sources.

Two accounts of the sieges of Qandahār in this and next year are available, one in Khwānd-amīr's *Ḥabību's-siyar*, the other in Ma'ṣūm *Bhakkarī's Tārīkh-i-sind.* As they have important differences, it is necessary to consider the opportunities of their authors for information.

Khwānd-amīr finished his history in 1524-29 AD. His account of these affairs of Qandahār is contemporary; he was in close touch with several of the actors in them and may have been in Harāt through their course; one of his patrons, Amīr Ghiyāṣu'd-dīn, was put to death in this year in Harāt because of suspicion that he was an ally of Bābur; his nephew, another

Ghiyāṣu'd-dīn was in Qandahār, the bearer next year of its keys to Bābur; moreover he was with Bābur himself a few years later in Hindūstān.

Mīr Ma'ṣūm wrote in 1600 AD. 70 to 75 years after Khwānd-amīr. Of these sieges he tells what may have been traditional and mentions no manuscript authorities. Blochmann's biography of him (*Āyīn-i-akbarī* p. 514) shews his ample opportunity of learning orally what had happened in the Arghūn invasion of Sind, but does not mention the opportunity for hearing traditions about Qandahār which his term of office there allowed him. During that term it was that he added an inscription, commemorative of Akbar's dominion, to Bābur's own at Chihil-zīna, which records the date of the capture of Qandahār (928 AH.-1522 AD.).

b. The Ḥabību's-siyar account (lith. ed. iii, part 4, p. 97).

Khwānd-amīr's contemporary narrative allows Ma'ṣūm's to dovetail into it as to some matters, but contradicts it in the important ones of date, and mode of surrender by Shāh Beg to Bābur. It states that Bābur was resolved in 926 AH. (1520 AD.) to uproot Shāh Shujā' Beg from Qandahār, led an army against the place, and "opened the Gates of war". It gives no account of the siege of 926 AH. but passes on to the occurrences of 927 AH. (1521 AD.) when Shāh Beg, unable to meet Bābur in the field, shut himself up in the town and strengthened the defences. Bābur put his utmost pressure on the besieged, "often riding his piebald horse close to the moat and urging his men to fiery onset." The garrison resisted manfully, breaching the "life-fortresses" of the Kābulīs with sword, arrow, spear and death-dealing stone, but Bābur's heroes were most often victorious, and drove their assailants back through the Gates.

c. Death of Khān Mīrzā reported to Bābur.

Meantime, continues Khwānd-amīr, Khān Mīrzā had died in Badakhshān; the news was brought to Bābur and caused him great grief; he appointed Humāyūn to succeed the Mīrzā while he himself prosecuted the siege of Qandahār and the conquest of the Garm-sīr.[1553]

d. Negociations with Bābur.

The Governor of Harāt at this time was Shāh Ismā'īl's son Ṭahmāsp, between six and seven years old. His guardian Amīr Khān took chief part in the diplomatic intervention with Bābur, but associated with him was Amīr Ghiyāṣu'd-dīn—the patron of Khwānd-amīr already mentioned—until put to death as an ally of Bābur. The discussion had with Bābur reveals a complexity of motives demanding attention. Nominally undertaken though intervention was on behalf of Shāh Beg, and certainly so at his request, the

Persian officers seem to have been less anxious on his account than for their own position in Khurāsān, their master's position at the time being weakened by ill-success against the Sulṯān of Rūm. To Bābur, Shāh Beg is written of as though he were an insubordinate vassal whom Bābur was reducing to order for the Shāh, but when Amīr Khān heard that Shāh Beg was hard pressed, he was much distressed because he feared a victorious Bābur might move on Khurāsān. Nothing indicates however that Bābur had Khurāsān in his thoughts; Hindūstān was his objective, and Qandahār a help on the way; but as Amīr Khān had this fear about him, a probable ground for it is provided by the presence with Bābur of Bāī-qarā exiles whose ambition it must have been to recover their former seat. Whether for Harāt, Kābul, or Hindūstān, Qandahār was strength. Another matter not fitting the avowed purpose of the diplomatic intervention is the death of Ghiyāṣu'd-dīn because an ally of Bābur; this makes Amīr Khān seem to count Bābur as Ismā'īl's enemy.

Shāh Beg's requests for intervention began in 926 AH. (1520 AD.), as also did the remonstrance of the Persian officers with Bābur; his couriers followed one another with entreaty that the Amīrs would contrive for Bābur to retire, with promise of obeisance and of yearly tribute. The Amīrs set forth to Bābur that though Shāh Shujā' Beg had offended and had been deserving of wrath and chastisement, yet, as he was penitent and had promised loyalty and tribute, it was now proper for Bābur to raise the siege (of 926 AH.) and go back to Kābul. To this Bābur answered that Shāh Beg's promise was a vain thing, on which no reliance could be placed; please God!, said he, he himself would take Qandahār and send Shāh Beg a prisoner to Harāt; and that he should be ready then to give the keys of the town and the possession of the Garm-sīr to any-one appointed to receive them.

This correspondence suits an assumption that Bābur acted for Shāh Ismā'īl, a diplomatic assumption merely, the verbal veil, on one side, for anxiety lest Bābur or those with him should attack Harāt,—on the other, for Bābur's resolve to hold Qandahār himself.

Amīr Khān was not satisfied with Bābur's answer, but had his attention distracted by another matter, presumably 'Ubaidu'l-lāh Khān's attack on Harāt in the spring of the year (March-April 1521 AD.). Negociations appear to have been resumed later, since Khwānd-amīr claims it as their result that Bābur left Qandahār this year.

e. The Tārīkh-i-sind account.

Mīr Ma'ṣūm is very brief; he says that in this year (his 922 AH.), Bābur went down to Qandahār before the year's tribute in grain had been collected, destroyed the standing crops, encompassed the town, and reduced it to extremity; that Shāh Beg, wearied under reiterated attack and pre-occupied by operations in Sind, proposed terms, and that these were made with stipulation for the town to be his during one year more and then to be given over to Bābur. These terms settled, Bābur went to Kābul, Shāh Beg to Sīwī.

The Arghūn families were removed to Shāl and Sīwī, so that the year's delay may have been an accommodation allowed for this purpose.

f. Concerning dates.

There is much discrepancy between the dates of the two historians. Khwānd-amīr's agree with the few fixed ones of the period and with the course of events; several of Ma'ṣūm's, on the contrary, are *seriatim* five (lunar) years earlier. For instance, events Khwānd-amīr places under 927 AH. Ma'ṣūm places under 922 AH. Again, while Ma'ṣūm correctly gives 913 AH. (1507 AD.) as the year of Bābur's first capture of Qandahār, he sets up a discrepant series later, from the success Shāh Beg had at Kāhān; this he allots to 921 AH. (1515 AD.) whereas Bābur received news of it (f. 233*b*) in the beginning of 925 AH. (1519 AD.). Again, Ma'ṣūm makes Shāh Ḥasan go to Bābur in 921 AH. and stay two years; but Ḥasan spent the whole of 925 AH. with Bābur and is not mentioned as having left before the second month of 926 AH. Again, Ma'ṣūm makes Shāh Beg surrender the keys of Qandahār in 923 AH. (1517 AD.), but 928 AH. (1522 AD.) is shewn by Khwānd-amīr's dates and narrative, and is inscribed at Chihil-zīna.[1554]

928 AH.-DEC. 1ST 1521 TO NOV. 20TH 1522 AD.

a. Bābur visits Badakhshān.

Either early in this year or late in the previous one, Bābur and Māhīm went to visit Humāyūn in his government, probably to Faizābād, and stayed with him what Gul-badan calls a few days.

b. Expedition to Qandahār.

This year saw the end of the duel for possession of Qandahār. Khwānd-amīr's account of its surrender differs widely from Ma'ṣūm's. It claims that Bābur's retirement in 927 AH. was due to the remonstrances from Harāt, and that Shāh Beg, worn out by the siege, relied on the arrangement the Amīrs had made with Bābur and went to Sīwī, leaving one 'Abdu'l-bāqī in charge of the place. This man, says Khwānd-amīr, drew the line of obliteration over his duty to his master, sent to Bābur, brought him down to Qandahār, and gave him the keys of the town—by the hand of Khwānd-amīr's nephew Ghiyāṣu'd-dīn, specifies the *Tarkhān-nāma.* In this year messengers had come and gone between Bābur and Harāt; two men employed by Amīr Khān are mentioned by name; of them the last had not returned to Harāt when a courier of Bābur's, bringing a tributary gift, announced there that the town was in his master's hands. Khwānd-amīr thus fixes the year 928 AH. as that in which the town passed into Bābur's hands; this date is confirmed by the one inscribed in the monument of victory at Chihil-zīna which Bābur ordered excavated on the naze of the limestone ridge behind the town. The date there given is Shawwāl 13th 928 AH. (Sep. 6th 1522 AD.).

Ma'ṣūm's account, dated 923 AH. (1517 AD.), is of the briefest:—Shāh Beg fulfilled his promise, much to Bābur's approval, by sending him the keys of the town and royal residence.

Although Khwānd-amīr's account has good claim to be accepted, it must be admitted that several circumstances can be taken to show that Shāh Beg had abandoned Qandahār, *e.g.* the removal of the families after Bābur's retirement last year, and his own absence in a remote part of Sind this year.

c. The year of Shāh Beg's death.

Of several variant years assigned for the death of Shāh Beg in the sources, two only need consideration.[1555] There is consensus of opinion about the month and close agreement about the day, Sha'bān 22nd or 23rd. Ma'ṣūm gives a chronogram, *Shahr-Sha'bān*, (month of Sha'bān) which yields 928, but he does not mention where he obtained it, nor does anything in his narrative shew what has fixed the day of the month.

Two objections to 928 are patent: (1) the doubt engendered by Ma'ṣūm's earlier ante-dating; (2) that if 928 be right, Shāh Beg was already dead over two months when Qandahār was surrendered. This he might have been according to Khwānd-amīr's narrative, but if he died on Sha'bān 22nd 928 (July 26th 1522), there was time for the news to have reached Qandahār, and to have gone on to Harāt before the surrender. Shāh Beg's death at that time could not have failed to be associated in Khwānd-amīr's narrative with the fate of Qandahār; it might have pleaded some excuse with him for 'Abdu'l-bāqī, who might even have had orders from Shāh Ḥasan to make the town over to Bābur whose suzerainty he had acknowledged at once on succession by reading the *khuṭba* in his name. Khwānd-amīr however does not mention what would have been a salient point in the events of the siege; his silence cannot but weigh against the 928 AH.

The year 930 AH. is given by Niẓāmu'd-dīn Aḥmad's *Ṭabaqāt-i-akbarī* (lith. ed. p. 637), and this year has been adopted by Erskine, Beale, and Ney Elias, perhaps by others. Some light on the matter may be obtained incidentally as the sources are examined for a complete history of India, perhaps coming from the affairs of Multān, which was attacked by Shāh Ḥasan after communication with Bābur.

d. Bābur's literary work in 928 AH. and earlier.

1. The *Mubīn*. This year, as is known from a chronogram within the work, Bābur wrote the Turkī poem of 2000 lines to which Abū'l-faẓl and Badāyūnī give the name *Mubīn* (The Exposition), but of which the true title is said by the *Nafā'isu'l-ma'āsir* to be *Dar fiqa mubaiyan* (The Law expounded). Sprenger found it called also *Fiqa-i-bāburī* (Bābur's Law). It is a versified and highly orthodox treatise on Muḥammadan Law, written for the instruction of Kāmrān. A Commentary on it, called also *Mubīn*, was written by Shaikh Zain. Bābur quotes from it (f. 351*b*) when writing of linear measures. Berézine found and published a large portion of it as part of his *Chrestomathie Turque* (Kazan 1857); the same fragment may be what was published by Ilminsky. Teufel remarks that the MS. used by Berézine may have descended direct from one sent by Bābur to a distinguished legist of Transoxiana, because the last words of Berézine's imprint are Bābur's *Begleitschreiben* (*envoi*); he adds the expectation that the legist's name might be learned. Perhaps this recipient was the Khwāja Kalān, son of Khwāja Yaḥya, a Samarkandī to whom Bābur sent a copy of his Memoirs on March 7th 1520 (935 AH. f. 363).[1556]

2. The *Bābur-nāma* diary of 925-6 AH. (1519-20 AD.). This is almost contemporary with the *Mubīn* and is the earliest part of the *Bābur-nāma* writings now known. It was written about a decade earlier than the narrative of 899 to 914 AH. (1494 to 1507 AD.), carries later annotations, and has now the character of a draft awaiting revision.

3. A *Dīwān* (Collection of poems). By dovetailing a few fragments of information, it becomes clear that by 925 AH. (1519 AD.) Bābur had made a Collection of poetical compositions distinct from the Rāmpūr *Dīwān*; it is what he sent to Pūlād Sulṭān in 925 AH. (f. 238). Its date excludes the greater part of the Rāmpūr one. It may have contained those verses to which my husband drew attention in the Asiatic Quarterly Review of 1911, as quoted in the *Abūshqa*; and it may have contained, in agreement with its earlier date, the verses Bābur quotes as written in his earlier years. None of the quatrains found in the *Abūshqa* and there attributed to "Bābur Mīrzā", are in the Rāmpūr *Dīwān*; nor are several of those early ones of the *Bābur-nāma*. So that the Dīwān sent to Pūlād Sulṭān may be the source from which the *Abūshqa* drew its examples.

On first examining these verses, doubt arose as to whether they were really by Bābur *Mīrānshāhī*; or whether they were by "Bābur Mīrzā" *Shāhrukhī*. Fortunately my husband lighted on one of them quoted in the *Sanglakh* and there attributed to Bābur Pādshāh. The *Abūshqa* quatrains are used as examples in de Courteille's *Dictionary*, but without an author's name; they can be traced there through my husband's articles.[1557]

929 AH.—NOV. 20TH 1522 TO NOV. 10TH 1523 AD.

a. Affairs of Hindūstān.

The centre of interest in Bābur's affairs now moves from Qandahār to a Hindūstān torn by faction, of which faction one result was an appeal made at this time to Bābur by Daulat Khān *Lūdī* (*Yūsuf-khail*) and 'Alāu'd-dīn 'Ālam Khān *Lūdī* for help against Ibrāhīm.[1558]

The following details are taken mostly from Aḥmad Yādgār's *Tārīkh-i-salāṭīn-i-afāghana*[1559]:—Daulat Khān had been summoned to Ibrāhīm's presence; he had been afraid to go and had sent his son Dilāwar in his place; his disobedience angering Ibrāhīm, Dilāwar had a bad reception and was shewn a ghastly exhibit of disobedient commanders. Fearing a like fate for himself, he made escape and hastened to report matters to his father in Lāhor. His information strengthening Daulat Khān's previous apprehensions, decided the latter to proffer allegiance to Bābur and to ask his help against Ibrāhīm. Apparently 'Ālam Khān's interests were a part of this request. Accordingly Dilāwar (or Apāq) Khān went to Kābul, charged with his father's message, and with intent to make known to Bābur Ibrāhīm's evil disposition, his cruelty and tyranny, with their fruit of discontent amongst his Commanders and soldiery.

b. Reception of Dilāwar Khān in Kābul.

Wedding festivities were in progress[1560] when Dilāwar Khān reached Kābul. He presented himself, at the Chār-bāgh may be inferred, and had word taken to Bābur that an Afghān was at his Gate with a petition. When admitted, he demeaned himself as a suppliant and proceeded to set forth the distress of Hindūstān. Bābur asked why he, whose family had so long eaten the salt of the Lūdīs, had so suddenly deserted them for himself. Dilāwar answered that his family through 40 years had upheld the Lūdī throne, but that Ibrāhīm maltreated Sikandar's amīrs, had killed 25 of them without cause, some by hanging some burned alive, and that there was no hope of safety in him. Therefore, he said, he had been sent by many amīrs to Bābur whom they were ready to obey and for whose coming they were on the anxious watch.

c. Bābur asks a sign.

At the dawn of the day following the feast, Bābur prayed in the garden for a sign of victory in Hindūstān, asking that it should be a gift to himself of mango or betel, fruits of that land. It so happened that Daulat Khān had sent him, as a present, half-ripened mangoes preserved in honey; when these were set before him, he accepted them as the sign, and from that time forth, says the chronicler, made preparation for a move on Hindūstān.

d. 'Ālam Khān.

Although 'Ālam Khān seems to have had some amount of support for his attempt against his nephew, events show he had none valid for his purpose. That he had not Daulat Khān's, later occurrences make clear. Moreover he seems not to have been a man to win adherence or to be accepted as a trustworthy and sensible leader.[1561] Dates are uncertain in the absence of Bābur's narrative, but it may have been in this year that 'Ālam Khān went in person to Kābul and there was promised help against Ibrāhīm.

e. Birth of Gul-badan.

Either in this year or the next was born Dil-dār's third daughter Gul-badan, the later author of an *Humāyūn-nāma* written at her nephew Akbar's command in order to provide information for the *Akbar-nāma*.

930 AH.—NOV. 10TH 1523 TO OCT. 29TH 1524 AD.

a. Bābur's fourth expedition to Hindūstān.

This expedition differs from all earlier ones by its co-operation with Afghān malcontents against Ibrāhīm *Lūdī*, and by having for its declared purpose direct attack on him through reinforcement of 'Ālam Khān.

Exactly when the start from Kābul was made is not found stated; the route taken after fording the Indus, was by the sub-montane road through the Kakar country; the Jīhlam and Chīn-āb were crossed and a move was made to within 10 miles of Lāhor.

Lāhor was Daulat Khān's head-quarters but he was not in it now; he had fled for refuge to a colony of Bilūchīs, perhaps towards Multān, on the approach against him of an army of Ibrāhīm's under Bihār Khān *Lūdī*. A battle ensued between Bābur and Bihār Khān; the latter was defeated with great slaughter; Bābur's troops followed his fugitive men into Lāhor, plundered the town and burned some of the *bāzārs*.

Four days were spent near Lāhor, then move south was made to Dībālpūr which was stormed, plundered and put to the sword. The date of this capture is known from an incidental remark of Bābur about chronograms (f. 325), to be mid-Rabī'u'l-awwal 930 AH. (*circa* Jan. 22nd 1524 AD.).[1562]

From Dībālpūr a start was made for Sihrind but before this could be reached news arrived which dictated return to Lāhor.

b. The cause of return.

Daulat Khān's action is the obvious cause of the retirement. He and his sons had not joined Bābur until the latter was at Dībālpūr; he was not restored to his former place in charge of the important Lāhor, but was given Jalandhar and Sulṭānpūr, a town of his own foundation. This angered him extremely but he seems to have concealed his feelings for the time and to have given Bābur counsel as if he were content. His son Dilāwar, however, represented to Bābur that his father's advice was treacherous; it concerned a move to Multān, from which place Daulat Khān may have come up to Dībālpūr and connected with which at this time, something is recorded of co-operation by Bābur and Shāh Ḥasan *Arghūn*. But the incident is not yet found clearly described by a source. Dilāwar Khān told Bābur that his father's object was to divide and thus weaken the invading force, and as this would have been the result of taking Daulat Khān's advice, Bābur arrested him and Apāq on suspicion of treacherous intent. They were soon released, and Sulṭānpūr was given them, but they fled to the hills, there to await a chance to swoop on the Panj-āb. Daulat Khān's hostility and his non-fulfilment of his engagement with Bābur placing danger in the rear of an eastward advance, the Panj-āb was garrisoned by Bābur's own followers and he himself went back to Kābul.

It is evident from what followed that Daulat Khān commanded much strength in the Panj-āb; evident also that something counselled delay in the attack on Ibrāhīm, perhaps closer cohesion in favour of 'Ālam Khān, certainly removal of the menace of Daulat Khān in the rear; there may have been news already of the approach of the Aūzbegs on Balkh which took Bābur next year across Hindū-kush.

c. The Panj-āb garrison.

The expedition had extended Bābur's command considerably, notably by obtaining possession of Lāhor. He now posted in it Mīr 'Abdu'l-'azīz his Master of the Horse; in Dībālpūr he posted, with 'Ālam Khān, Bābā Qashqa *Mughūl*; in Sīālkot, Khusrau Kūkūldāsh, in Kalanūr, Muḥammad 'Alī *Tājik*.

d. Two deaths.

This year, on Rajab 19th (May 23rd) died Ismā'īl *Ṣafawī* at the age of 38, broken by defeat from Sulṭān Salīm of Rūm.[1563] He was succeeded by his son Ṭahmāsp, a child of ten.

This year may be that of the death of Shāh Shujā' *Arghūn*,[1564] on Sha'bān 22nd (July 18th), the last grief of his burden being the death of his foster-brother Fāẓil concerning which, as well as Shāh Beg's own death, Mīr Ma'ṣūm's account is worthy of full reproduction. Shāh Beg was succeeded in Sind by his son Ḥasan, who read the *khuṭba* for Bābur and drew closer links with Bābur's circle by marrying, either this year or the next, Khalīfa's daughter Gul-barg, with whom betrothal had been made during Ḥasan's visit to Bābur in Kābul. Moreover Khalīfa's son Muḥibb-i-'alī married Nāhīd the daughter of Qāsim Kūkūldāsh and Māh-chūchūk *Arghūn* (f. 214*b*). These alliances were made, says Ma'ṣūm, to strengthen Ḥasan's position at Bābur's Court.

e. A garden detail.

In this year and presumably on his return from the Panj-āb, Bābur, as he himself chronicles (f. 132), had plantains (bananas) brought from Hindūstān for the Bāgh-i-wafā at Adīnapūr.

931 AH.—OCT. 29TH 1524 TO OCT. 18TH 1525 AD.

a. Daulat Khān.

Daulat Khān's power in the Panj-āb is shewn by what he effected after dispossessed of Lāhor. On Bābur's return to Kābul, he came down from the hills with a small body of his immediate followers, seized his son Dilāwar, took Sulṭānpūr, gathered a large force and defeated 'Ālam Khān in Dībālpūr. He detached 5000 men against Sīālkot but Bābur's begs of Lāhor attacked and overcame them. Ibrāhīm sent an army to reconquer the Panj-āb; Daulat Khān, profiting by its dissensions and discontents, won over a part to himself and saw the rest break up.

b. 'Ālam Khān.

From his reverse at Dībālpūr, 'Ālam Khān fled straight to Kābul. The further help he asked was promised under the condition that while he should take Ibrāhīm's place on the throne of Dihlī, Bābur in full suzerainty should hold Lāhor and all to the west of it. This arranged, 'Ālam Khān was furnished with a body of troops, given a royal letter to the Lāhor begs ordering them to assist him, and started off, Bābur promising to follow swiftly.

'Ālam Khān's subsequent proceedings are told by Bābur in the annals of 932 AH. (1525 AD.) at the time he received details about them (f. 255*b*).

c. Bābur called to Balkh.

All we have yet found about this affair is what Bābur says in explanation of his failure to follow 'Ālam Khān as promised (f. 256), namely, that he had to go to Balkh because all the Aūzbeg Sulṭāns and Khāns had laid siege to it. Light on the affair may come from some Persian or Aūzbeg chronicle; Bābur's arrival raised the siege; and risk must have been removed, for Bābur returned to Kābul in time to set out for his fifth and last expedition to Hindūstān on the first day of the second month of next year (932 AH. 1525). A considerable body of troops was in Badakhshān with Humāyūn; their non-arrival next year delaying his father's progress, brought blame on himself.

Babur's Grave.

To face p. 445.

SECTION III. HINDŪSTĀN

932 AH.-OCT. 18TH 1525 TO OCT. 8TH 1526 AD.[1565]

(*a. Fifth expedition into Hindūstān.*)

(*Nov. 17th*) On Friday the 1st of the month of Ṣafar at theḤaidarābād MS. Fol. 251b. date 932, the Sun being in the Sign of the Archer, we set out for Hindūstān, crossed the small rise of Yak-langa, and dismounted in the meadow to the west of the water of Dih-i-ya'qūb.[1566] 'Abdu'l-malūk the armourer came into this camp; he had gone seven or eight months earlier as my envoy to Sulṭān Sa'īd Khān (in Kāshghar), and now brought one of the Khān's men, styled Yāngī Beg (new beg) Kūkūldāsh who conveyed letters, and small presents, and verbal messages[1567] from the Khānīms and the Khān.[1568]

(*Nov. 18th to 21st*) After staying two days in that camp for the convenience of the army,[1569] we marched on, halted one night,[1570] and next dismounted at Bādām-chashma. There we ate a confection (*ma'jūn*).

(*Nov. 22nd*) On Wednesday (Ṣafar 6th), when we had dismounted at Bārīk-āb, the younger brethren of Nūr Beg—he himself remaining in Hindūstān—brought gold *ashrafīs* and *tankas*[1571] to the value of 20,000 *shāhrukhīs*, sent from the Lāhor revenues by Khwāja Ḥusain. The greater part of these moneys was despatched by Mullā Aḥmad, one of the chief men of Balkh, for the benefit of Balkh.[1572]

(*Nov. 24th*) On Friday the 8th of the month (Ṣafar), after Fol. 252.dismounting at Gandamak, I had a violent discharge;[1573] by God's mercy, it passed off easily.

(*Nov. 25th*) On Saturday we dismounted in the Bāgh-i-wafā. We delayed there a few days, waiting for Humāyūn and the army from that side.[1574] More than once in this history the bounds and extent, charm and delight of that garden have been described; it is most beautifully placed; who sees it with the buyer's eye will know the sort of place it is. During the short time we were there, most people drank on drinking-days[1575] and took their morning; on non-drinking days there were parties for *ma'jūn*.

I wrote harsh letters to Humāyūn, lecturing him severely because of his long delay beyond the time fixed for him to join me.[1576]

(*Dec. 3rd*) On Sunday the 17th of Ṣafar, after the morning had been taken, Humāyūn arrived. I spoke very severely to him at once. Khwāja Kalān also arrived to-day, coming up from Ghaznī. We marched in the evening of that same Sunday, and dismounted in a new garden between Sulṭānpur and Khwāja Rustam.

(*Dec. 6th*) Marching on Wednesday (Ṣafar 20th), we got on a raft, and, drinking as we went reached Qūsh-guṃbaz,[1577] there landed and joined the camp.

(*Dec. 7th*) Starting off the camp at dawn, we ourselves went on a raft, and there ate confection (*ma'jūn*). Our encamping-ground was always Qīrīq-ārīq, but not a sign or trace of the camp could Fol. 252b.be seen when we got opposite it, nor any appearance of our horses. Thought I, "Garm-chashma (Hot-spring) is close by; they may have dismounted there." So saying, we went on from Qīrīq-ārīq. By the time we reached Garm-chashma, the very day was late;[1578] we did not stop there, but going on in its lateness (*kīchīsī*), had the raft tied up somewhere, and slept awhile.

(*Dec. 8th*) At day-break we landed at Yada-bīr where, as the day wore on, the army-folks began to come in. The camp must have been at Qīrīq-ārīq, but out of our sight.

There were several verse-makers on the raft, such as Shaikh Abū'l-wajd,[1579] Shaikh Zain, Mullā 'Alī-jān, Tardī Beg *Khāksār* and others. In this company was quoted the following couplet of Muḥammad Ṣāliḥ:—[1580]

(Persian) With thee, arch coquette, for a sweetheart, what can man do?
With another than thou where thou art, what can man do?

Said I, "Compose on these lines";[1581] whereupon those given to versifying, did so. As jokes were always being made at the expense of Mullā 'Alī-jān, this couplet came off-hand into my head:—

(Persian) With one all bewildered as thou, what can man do?
. . . . . what can man do?[1582])

(*b. Mention of the Mubīn.*[1583])

From time to time before it,[1584] whatever came into my head, of good or bad, grave or jest, used to be strung into verse and written down, however empty and harsh the verse might be, but while I was composing the *Mubīn*, this thought pierced through my dull wits and made way into my troubled heart, "A pity itFol. 253. will be if the tongue which has treasure of utterances so lofty as these are, waste itself again on low words; sad will it be if again vile imaginings find way into the mind that has made exposition of these sublime realities."[1585] Since that time I had refrained from satirical and jesting verse; I was repentant (*ta'īb*); but these matters were totally out of mind and remembrance when I made that couplet (on Mullā 'Alī-jān).[1586] A few days later in Bīgrām when I had fever and discharge, followed by cough, and I began to spit blood each time I coughed, I knew whence my reproof came; I knew what act of mine had brought this affliction on me.

"Whoever shall violate his oath, will violate it to the hurt of his own soul; but whoever shall perform that which he hath covenanted with God, to that man surely will He give great reward" (*Qorān* cap. 48 v. 10).

What is it I do with thee, ah! my tongue?

My entrails bleed as a reckoning for thee.

(*Turkī*) Good once[1587] as thy words were, has followed this verse

Jesting, empty,[1588] obscene, has followed a lie.

If thou say, "Burn will I not!" by keeping this vow

Thou turnest thy rein from this field of strife.[1589]

"O Lord! we have dealt unjustly with our own souls; if Thou forgive us not, and be not merciful unto us, we shall surely be of those that perish"[1590] (*Qorān* cap. 7 v. 22).

Taking anew the place of the penitent pleading for pardon, I gave my mind rest[1591] from such empty thinking and such unlawful occupation. I broke my pen. Made by that Court, such reproof of sinful slaves is for their felicity; happy are the highest and the slave when such reproof brings warning and its profitable fruit.

(*c. Narrative resumed.*)

(*Dec. 8th continued*) Marching on that evening, we dismounted at 'Alī-masjid. The ground here being very confined, I always Fol. 253b.used to dismount on a rise overlooking the camp in the valley-bottom.[1592] The camp-fires made a wonderful illumination there at night; assuredly it was because of this that there had always been drinking there, and was so now.

(*Dec. 9th and 10th*) To-day I rode out before dawn; I preferred a confection (*ma'jūn*)[1593] and also kept this day a fast. We dismounted near Bīgrām (Peshāwar); and next morning, the camp remaining on that same ground, rode to Karg-awī.[1594] We crossed the Siyāh-āb in front of Bīgrām, and formed our hunting-circle looking down-stream. After a little, a person brought word that there was a rhino in a bit of jungle near Bīgrām, and that people had been stationed near-about it. We betook ourselves, loose rein, to the place, formed a ring round the jungle, made a noise, and brought the rhino out, when it took its way across the plain. Humāyūn and those come with him from that side (Tramontana), who had never seen one before, were much entertained. It was pursued for two miles; many arrows were shot at it; it was brought down without having made a good set at man or horse. Two others were killed. I had often wondered how a rhino and an elephant would behave if brought face to face; this time one came out right in front of some elephants the mahauts were bringing along; it did not face themFol. 254. when the mahauts drove them towards it, but got off in another direction.

(*d. Preparations for ferrying the Indus.*[1595])

On the day we were in Bīgrām, several of the begs and household were appointed, with pay-masters and dīwāns, six or seven being put in command, to take charge of the boats at the Nīl-āb crossing, to make a list of all who were with the army, name by name, and to count them up.

That evening I had fever and discharge[1596] which led on to cough and every time I coughed, I spat blood. Anxiety was great but, by God's mercy, it passed off in two or three days.

(*Dec. 11th*) It rained when we left Bīgrām; we dismounted on the Kābul-water.

(*e. News from Lāhor.*)

News came that Daulat Khān[1597] and (Apāq) Ghāzī Khān, having collected an army of from 20 to 30,000, had taken Kilānūr, and intended to move on Lāhor. At once Mumin-i-'alī the commissary was sent galloping off to say, "We are advancing march by march;[1598] do not fight till we arrive."

(*Dec. 14th*) With two night-halts on the way, we reached the water of Sind (Indus), and there dismounted on Thursday the 28th (of Ṣafar).

(*f. Ferrying the Indus.*)

(*Dec. 16th*) On Saturday the 1st of the first Rabī', we crossed the Sind-water, crossed the water of Kacha-kot (Hārū), and dismounted on the bank of the river.[1599] The begs, pay-masters and dīwāns who had been put in charge of the boats, reported that the number of those come with the army, great and small, good and bad, retainer and non-retainer, was written down as 12,000.

(*g. The eastward march.*)

The rainfall had been somewhat scant in the plains, but Fol. 254b.seemed to have been good in the cultivated lands along the hill-skirts; for these reasons we took the road for Sīālkot along the skirt-hills. Opposite Hātī *Kakar's* country[1600] we came upon a torrent[1601] the waters of which were standing in pools. Those pools were all frozen over. The ice was not very thick, as thick as the hand may-be. Such ice is unusual in Hindūstān; not a sign or trace of any was seen in the years we were (*aīdūk*) in the country.[1602]

We had made five marches from the Sind-water; after the sixth (*Dec. 22nd*—Rabī' I. 7th) we dismounted on a torrent in the camping-ground (*yūrt*) of the Bugīāls[1603] below Balnāth Jogī's hill which connects with the Hill of Jūd.

(*Dec. 23rd*) In order to let people get provisions, we stayed the next day in that camp. *'Araq* was drunk on that day. Mullā Muḥ. *Parghari* told many stories; never had he been so talkative. Mullā Shams himself was very riotous; once he began, he did not finish till night.

The slaves and servants, good and bad, who had gone out after provisions, went further than this[1604] and heedlessly scattered over jungle and plain, hill and broken ground. Owing to this, a few were overcome; Kīchkīna *tūnqiṭār* died there.

(*Dec. 24th*) Marching on, we crossed the Bihat-water at a ford below Jīlam (Jīhlam) and there dismounted. Walī *Qīzīl* (Rufus) came there to see me. He was the Sīālkot reserve, and held the parganas of Bīmrūkī and Akrīāda. Thinking about Sīālkot,Fol. 255. I took towards him the position of censure and reproach. He excused himself, saying "I had come to my *pargana* before Khusrau Kūkūldāsh left Sīālkot; he did not even send me word." After listening to his excuse, I said, "Since thou hast paid no attention to Sīālkot, why didst thou not join the begs in Lāhor?" He was convicted, but as work was at hand, I did not trouble about his fault.

(*h. Scouts sent with orders to Lāhor.*)

(*Dec. 25th*) Sayyid Ṭūfān and Sayyid Lāchīn were sent galloping off, each with a pair-horse,[1605] to say in Lāhor, "Do not join battle; meet us at Sīālkot or Parsrūr" (mod. Pasrūr). It was in everyone's mouth that Ghāzī Khān had collected 30 to 40,000 men, that Daulat Khān, old as he was, had girt two swords to his waist, and that they were resolved to fight. Thought I, "The proverb says that ten friends are better than nine; do you not make a mistake: when the Lāhor begs have joined you, fight there and then!"

(*Dec. 26th and 27th*) After starting off the two men to the begs, we moved forward, halted one night, and next dismounted on the bank of the Chīn-āb (Chan-āb).

As Buhlūlpūr was *khalṣa*,[1606] we left the road to visit it. Its fort is situated above a deep ravine, on the bank of the Chīn-āb. It pleased us much. We thought of bringing Sīālkot to it. Please God! the chance coming, it shall be done straightway! Fol. 255b.From Buhlūlpūr we went to camp by boat.

(*i. Jats and Gujūrs.*[1607])

(*Dec. 29th*) On Friday the 14th of the first Rabī' we dismounted at Sīālkot. If one go into Hindūstān the Jats and Gujūrs always pour down in countless hordes from hill and plain for loot in bullock and buffalo. These ill-omened peoples are just senseless oppressors! Formerly their doings did not concern us much because the country was an enemy's, but they began the same senseless work after we had taken it. When we reached Sīālkot, they fell in tumult on poor and needy folks who were coming out of the town to our camp, and stripped them bare. I had the silly thieves sought for, and ordered two or three of them cut to pieces.

From Sīālkot Nūr Beg's brother Shāham also was made to gallop off to the begs in Lāhor to say, "Make sure where the enemy is; find out from some well-informed person where he may be met, and send us word."

A trader, coming into this camp, represented that 'Ālam Khān had let Sl. Ibrāhīm defeat him.

(*j. 'Ālam Khān's action and failure.*[1608])

Here are the particulars:—'Ālam Khān, after taking leave of me (in Kābul, 931 AH.), went off in that heat by double marches, regardless of those with him.[1609] As at the time I gave him leave to go, all the Aūzbeg khāns and sulṭāns had laid siege to Balkh,Fol. 256. I rode for Balkh as soon as I had given him his leave. On his reaching Lāhor, he insisted to the begs, "You reinforce me; the Pādshāh said so; march along with me; let us get (Apāq) Ghāzī Khān to join us; let us move on Dihlī and Āgra." Said they, "Trusting to what, will you join Ghāzī Khān? Moreover the royal orders to us were, 'If at any time Ghāzī Khān has sent his younger brother Ḥājī Khān with his son to Court, join him; or do so, if he has sent them, by way of pledge, to Lāhor; if he has done neither, do not join him.' You yourself only yesterday fought him and let him beat you! Trusting to what, will you join him now? Besides all this, it is not for your advantage to join him!" Having said what-not of this sort, they refused 'Ālam Khān. He did not fall in with their views, but sent his son Sher Khān to speak with Daulat Khān and with Ghāzī Khān, and afterwards all saw one another.

'Ālam Khān took with him Dilāwar Khān, who had come into Lāhor two or three months earlier after his escape from prison; he took also Maḥmūd Khān (son of) Khān-i-jahān,[1610] to whom a *pargana* in the Lāhor district had been given. They seem to have left matters at this:—Daulat Khān with Ghāzī Khān was to take all the begs posted in Hindūstān to himself, indeed he was to take everything on that side;[1611] while 'Ālam Fol. 256b.Khān was to take Dilāwar Khān and Ḥājī Khān and, reinforced by them, was to capture Dihlī and Āgra. Ismā'īl *Jilwānī* and other amīrs came and saw 'Ālam Khān; all then betook themselves, march by march, straight for Dihlī. Near Indrī came also Sulaimān Shaikh-zāda.[1612] Their total touched 30 to 40,000 men.

They laid siege to Dihlī but could neither take it by assault nor do hurt to the garrison.[1613] When Sl. Ibrāhīm heard of their assembly, he got an army to horse against them; when they heard of his approach, they rose from before the place and moved to meet him. They had left matters at this:— "If we attack by day-light, the Afghāns will not desert (to us), for the sake of their reputations with one another; but if we attack at night when one man cannot see another, each man will obey his own orders." Twice over they started at fall of day from a distance of 12 miles (6 *kurohs*), and, unable to bring matters to a point, neither advanced nor retired; but just sat on horseback for two or three watches. On a third occasion they delivered an attack when one watch of night remained—their purpose seeming to be the burning of tents and huts! They went; they set fire from every end; they made a disturbance. Jalāl Khān *Jig-hat*[1614] came with other amīrs and saw 'Ālam Khān.

Sl. Ibrāhīm did not bestir himself till shoot of dawn from where he was with a few of his own family[1615] within his own enclosure (*sarācha*). Meantime 'Ālam Khān's people were busy Fol. 257.with plunder and booty. Seeing the smallness of their number, Sl. Ibrāhīm's people moved out against them in rather small force with one elephant. 'Ālam Khān's party, not able to make stand against the elephant, ran away. He in his flight crossed over into the Mīān-dū-āb and crossed back again when he reached the Pānīpat neighbourhood. In Indrī he contrived on some pretext to get 4 *laks* from Mīān Sulaimān.[1616] He was deserted by Ismā'īl *Jilwānī*, by Biban[1617] and by his own oldest son Jalāl, who all withdrew into the Mīān-dū-āb; and he had been deserted just before the fighting, by part of his troops, namely, by Daryā Khān (*Nūḥānī*)'s son Saif Khān, by Khān-i-jahān (*Nūḥānī*)'s son Maḥmūd Khān, and by Shaikh Jamāl *Farmulī*. When he was passing through Sihrind with Dilāwar Khān, he heard of our advance and of our capture of Milwat (Malot).[1618] On this Dilāwar Khān—who always had been my well-wisher and on my account had dragged out three or four months in prison,—left ʻĀlam Khān and the rest and went to his family in Sulṭānpūr. He waited on me three or four days after we took Milwat. ʻĀlam Khān and Ḥājī Khān crossed the Shatlut (*sic*)-water and went into Gingūta,[1619] one of the strongholds in the range that lies between the valley and the plain.[1620] There our Afghān and Hazāra[1621] troops besieged them, and hadFol. 257b almost taken that strong fort when night came on. Those inside were thinking of escape but could not get out because of the press of horses in the Gate. There must have been elephants also; when these were urged forward, they trod down and killed many horses. ʻĀlam Khān, unable to escape mounted, got out on foot in the darkness. After a *lak* of difficulties, he joined Ghāzī Khān, who had not gone into Milwat but had fled into the hills. Not being received with even a little friendliness by Ghāzī Khān; needs must! he came and waited on me at the foot of the dale[1622] near Pehlūr.

(*k. Diary resumed.*)

A person came to Sīālkot from the Lāhor begs to say they would arrive early next morning to wait on me.

(*Dec. 30th*) Marching early next day (Rabīʻ I. 15th), we dismounted at Parsrūr. There Muḥ. ʻAlī *Jang-jang*, Khwāja Ḥusain and several braves waited on me. As the enemy's camp seemed to be on the Lāhor side of the Rāvī, we sent men out under Būjka for news. Near the third watch of the night they brought word that the enemy, on hearing of us, had fled, no man looking to another.

(*Dec. 31st*) Getting early to horse and leaving baggage and train in the charge of Shāh Mīr Ḥusain and Jān Beg, we bestirred ourselves. We reached Kalānūr in the afternoon, and there dismounted. Muḥammad Sl. Mīrzā and ʻĀdil Sl.[1623] came Fol. 258.to wait on me there, together with some of the begs.

(*Jan. 1st 1526 AD.*) We marched early from Kalānūr. On the road people gave us almost certain news of Ghāzī Khān and other fugitives. Accordingly we sent, flying after those fliers, the commanders Muḥammadī, Aḥmadī, Qūtlūq-qadam, Treasurer Walī and most of those begs who, in Kābul, had recently bent the knee for their begship. So far it was settled:—That it would be good indeed if they could overtake and capture the fugitives; and that, if they were not able to do this, they were to keep careful watch round Milwat (Malot), so as to prevent those inside from getting out and away. Ghāzī Khān was the object of this watch.

(*l. Capture of Milwat.*)

(Jan. 2nd and 3rd) After starting those begs ahead, we crossed the Bīāh-water (Beas) opposite Kanwāhīn[1624] and dismounted. From there we marched to the foot of the valley of Fort Milwat, making two night-halts on the way. The begs who had arrived before us, and also those of Hindūstān were ordered to dismount in such a way as to besiege the place closely.

A grandson of Daulat Khān, son of his eldest son 'Alī Khān, Ismā'īl Khān by name, came out of Milwat to see me; he took back promise mingled with threat, kindness with menace.

(Jan. 5th) On Friday (Rabī' I. 21st) I moved camp forward to within a mile of the fort, went myself to examine the place, posted right, left and centre, then returned to camp.

Daulat Khān sent to represent to me that Ghāzī Khān hadFol. 258b. fled into the hills, and that, if his own faults were pardoned, he would take service with me and surrender Milwat. Khwāja Mīr-i-mīrān was sent to chase fear from his heart and to escort him out; he came, and with him his son 'Alī Khān. I had ordered that the two swords he had girt to his waist to fight me with, should be hung from his neck. Was such a rustic blockhead possible! With things as they were, he still made pretensions! When he was brought a little forward, I ordered the swords to be removed from his neck. At the time of our seeing one another[1625] he hesitated to kneel; I ordered them to pull his leg and make him do so. I had him seated quite in front, and ordered a person well acquainted with Hindūstānī to interpret my words to him, one after another. Said I, "Thus speak:—I called thee Father. I shewed thee more honour and respect than thou couldst have asked. Thee and thy sons I saved from door-to-door life amongst the Balūchīs.[1626] Thy family and thy *ḥaram* I freed from Ibrāhīm's prison-house.[1627] Three *krors* I gave thee on Tātār Khān's lands.[1628] What ill sayest thou I have done thee, that thus thou shouldst hang a sword on thy either side,[1629] lead an army out, fall on lands of ours,[1630] and stir strife and trouble?" Dumbfounded, the old man Fol. 259.stuttered a few words, but, he gave no answer, nor indeed could answer be given to words so silencing. He was ordered to remain with Khwāja Mīr-i-mīrān.

(Jan. 6th) On Saturday the 22nd of the first Rabī', I went myself to safeguard the exit of the families and *ḥarams*[1631] from the fort, dismounting on a rise opposite the Gate. To me there came 'Alī Khān and made offering of a few *ashrafīs*. People began to bring out the families just before the Other Prayer. Though Ghāzī Khān was reported to have got away, there were some who said they had seen him in the fort. For this reason several of the household and braves[1632] were posted at the Gate, in order to prevent his escape by a ruse, for to get away was his full intention.[1633] Moreover if jewels and other valuables were being taken away by stealth,

they were to be confiscated. I spent that night in a tent pitched on the rise in front of the Gate.

(*Jan. 7th*) Early next morning, Muḥammadī, Aḥmadī, Sl. Junaid, 'Abdu'l-'azīz, Muḥammad 'Alī *Jang-jang* and Qūtlūq-qadam were ordered to enter the fort and take possession of all Fol. 259b.effects. As there was much disturbance at the Gate, I shot off a few arrows by way of chastisement. Humāyūn's story-teller (*qiṣṣa-khẉān*) was struck by the arrow of his destiny and at once surrendered his life.

(*Jan. 7th and 8th*) After spending two nights[1634] on the rise, I inspected the fort. I went into Ghāzī Khān's book-room;[1635] some of the precious things found in it, I gave to Humāyūn, some sent to Kāmrān (in Qandahār). There were many books of learned contents,[1636] but not so many valuable ones as had at first appeared. I passed that night in the fort; next morning I went back to camp.

(*Jan. 9th*) It had been in our minds that Ghāzī Khān was in the fort, but he, a man devoid of nice sense of honour, had escaped to the hills, abandoning father, brethren and sisters in Milwat.

See that man without honour who never

The face of good luck shall behold;

Bodily ease he chose for himself,

In hardship he left wife and child (*Gulistān* cap. i, story 17).

(*Jan. 10th*) Leaving that camp on Wednesday, we moved towards the hills to which Ghāzī Khān had fled. When we dismounted in the valley-bottom two miles from the camp in the mouth of Milwat,[1637] Dilāwar Khān came and waited on me. Daulat Khān, 'Alī Khān and Ismā'īl Khān, with other chiefs, were given into Kitta Beg's charge who was to convey them to the Bhīra fort of Milwat (Malot),[1638] and there keep guard overFol. 260. them. In agreement with Dilāwar Khān, blood-ransom was fixed for some who had been made over each to one man; some gave security, some were kept prisoner. Daulat Khān died when Kitta Beg reached Sulṭānpūr with the prisoners.[1639]

Milwat was given into the charge of Muḥ. 'Alī *Jang-jang* who, pledging his own life for it, left his elder brother Arghūn and a party of braves in it. A body of from 200 to 250 Afghāns were told off to reinforce him.

Khwāja Kalān had loaded several camels with Ghaznī wines. A party was held in his quarters overlooking the fort and the whole camp, some drinking *'araq*, some wine. It was a varied party.

(*m. Jaswān-valley.*)

Marching on, we crossed a low hill of the grazing-grounds (*arghā-dāl-līq*) of Milwat and went into the *dūn*, as Hindūstānīs are understood to call a dale (*julga*).[1640] In this dale is a running-water[1641] of Hindūstān; along its sides are many villages; and it is said to be the pargana of the Jaswāl, that is to say, of Dilāwar Khān's maternal uncles. It lies there shut-in, with meadows along its torrent, rice cultivated here and there, a three or four mill-stream flowing in its trough, its width from two to Fol. 260b.four miles, six even in places, villages on the skirts of its hills—hillocks they are rather—where there are no villages, peacocks, monkeys, and many fowls which, except that they are mostly of one colour, are exactly like house-fowls.

As no reliable news was had of Ghāzī Khān, we arranged for Tardīka to go with Bīrīm Deo *Malinhās* and capture him wherever he might be found.

In the hills of this dale stand thoroughly strong forts; one on the north-east, named Kūtila, has sides 70 to 80 yards (*qārī*) of straight fall, the side where the great gate is being perhaps 7 or 8 yards.[1642] The width of the place where the draw-bridge is made, may be 10 to 12 yards. Across this they have made a bridge of two tall trees[1643] by which horses and herds are taken over. This was one of the local forts Ghāzī Khān had strengthened; his man will have been in it now. Our raiders (*chāpqūnchī*) assaulted it and had almost taken it when night came on. The garrison abandoned this difficult place and went off. Near this dale is also the stronghold of Ginguta; it is girt round by precipices as Kūtila is, but is not so strong as Kūtila. As has been mentioned 'Ālam Khān went into it.[1644]Fol. 261.

(*n. Bābur advances against Ibrāhīm.*)

After despatching the light troop against Ghāzī Khān, I put my foot in the stirrup of resolution, set my hand on the rein of trust in God, and moved forward against Sulṭān Ibrāhīm, son of Sulṭān Sikandar, son of Buhlūl *Lūdī Afghān*, in possession of whose throne at that time were the Dihlī capital and the dominions of Hindūstān, whose standing-army was called a *lak* (100,000), whose elephants and whose begs' elephants were about 1,000.

At the end of our first stage, I bestowed Dībālpūr on Bāqī *shaghāwal*[1645] and sent him to help Balkh[1646]; sent also gifts, taken in the success of Milwat, for (my) younger children and various train in Kābul.

When we had made one or two marches down the (Jaswān) *dūn*, Shāh 'Imād *Shīrāzī* arrived from Araish Khān and Mullā Muḥammad *Mazhab*,[1647] bringing letters that conveyed their good wishes for the complete success of our campaign and indicated their effort and endeavour towards this. In response, we sent, by a foot-man, royal letters expressing our favour. We then marched on.

(*o. 'Ālam Khān takes refuge with Bābur.*)

The light troop we had sent out from Milwat (Malot), took Hurūr, Kahlūr and all the hill-forts of the neighbourhood—places to which because of their strength, no-one seemed to have gone for a long time—and came back to me after plundering a little. Came also 'Ālam Khān, on foot, ruined, stripped bare. We sent some of the begs to give him honourable meeting, sent horses too, and he waited (*malāẓamat qīldī*) in that Fol. 261b.neighbourhood.[1648]

Raiders of ours went into the hills and valleys round-about, but after a few nights' absence, came back without anything to count. Shāh Mīr Ḥusain, Jān Beg and a few of the braves asked leave and went off for a raid.

(*p. Incidents of the march for Pānī-pat.*)

While we were in the (Jaswān) *dūn*, dutiful letters had come more than once from Ismā'īl *Jilwānī* and Biban; we replied to them from this place by royal letters such as their hearts desired. After we got out of the dale to Rūpar, it rained very much and became so cold that a mass of starved and naked Hindūstānīs died.

When we had left Rūpar and were dismounted at Karal,[1649] opposite Sihrind, a Hindūstānī coming said, "I am Sl. Ibrāhīm's envoy," and though he had no letter or credentials, asked for an envoy from us. We responded at once by sending one or two Sawādī night-guards (*tunqiṭār*).[1650] These humble persons Ibrāhīm put in prison; they made their escape and came back to us on the very day we beat him.

After having halted one night on the way, we dismounted on the bank of the torrent[1651] of Banūr and Sanūr. Great rivers apart, one running water there is in Hindūstān, is this[1652]; they call it the water of Kakar (Ghaggar). Chitr also is on its bank. We rode up it for an excursion. The rising-place (*ẓih*) of the water of this torrent (*rūd*) is 3 or 4 *kurohs* (6-8 m.) above Chitr. Going up the (Kakar) torrent, we came to where a 4 or 5 millstream issues from a broad (side-)valley (*dara*), up which thereFol. 262. are very pleasant places, healthy and convenient. I ordered a Chār-bāgh to be made at the mouth of the broad valley of this (tributary) water, which falls into the (Kakar-) torrent after flowing for one or two *kurohs* through level ground. From its infall to the springs of the Kakar the distance may be 3 to 4 *kurohs* (6-8 m.). When it comes down in flood during the rains and joins the Kakar, they go together to Sāmāna and Sanām.[1653]

In this camp we heard that Sl. Ibrāhīm had been on our side of Dihlī and had moved on from that station, also that Ḥamīd Khān *khāṣa-khail*,[1654] the military-collector (*shiqdār*) of Ḥiṣār-fīrūza, had left that place with its army and with the army of its neighbourhood, and had advanced 10 or 15 *kurohs* (20-30 m.). Kitta Beg was sent for news to Ibrāhīm's camp, and Mumin Ātaka to the Ḥiṣār-fīrūza camp.

(*q. Humāyūn moves against Ḥamīd Khān.*)

(*Feb. 25th*) Marching from Aṃbāla, we dismounted by the side of a lake. There Mumin Ātāka and Kitta Beg rejoined us, both on the same day, Sunday the 13th of the first Jumāda.

We appointed Humāyūn to act against Ḥamīd Khān, and joined the whole of the right (wing) to him, that is to say, Khwāja Kalān, Sl. Muḥammad *Dūldāī*, Treasurer Walī, and also some of the begs whose posts were in Hindūstān, namely, Khusrau, Hindū Beg,'Abdu'l-'azīz and Muḥammad 'Alī *Jang-jang*, with also, from the household and braves of the centre, Shāh Manṣūr *Barlās*, Kitta Beg and Muḥibb-i 'alī.Fol. 262b.

Biban waited on me in this camp. These Afghāns remain very rustic and tactless! This person asked to sit although Dilāwar Khān, his superior in following and in rank, did not sit, and although the sons of 'Ālam Khān, who are of royal birth, did not sit. Little ear was lent to his unreason!

(*Feb. 26th*) At dawn on Monday the 14th Humāyūn moved out against Ḥamīd Khān. After advancing for some distance, he sent between 100 and 150 braves scouting ahead, who went close up to the enemy and at once got to grips. But when after a few encounters, the dark mass of Humāyūn's troops shewed in the rear, the enemy ran right away. Humāyūn's men unhorsed from 100 to 200, struck the heads off one half and brought the other half in, together with 7 or 8 elephants.

(*March 2nd*) On Friday the 18th of the month, Beg Mīrak *Mughūl* brought news of Humāyūn's victory to the camp. He (Humāyūn?) was there and then given a special head-to-foot and a special horse from the royal stable, besides promise of guerdon (*juldū*).

(*March 5th*) On Monday the 25th of the month, Humāyūn arrived to wait on me, bringing with him as many as 100 prisoners and 7 or 8 elephants. Ustād 'Alī-qulī and the Fol. 263.matchlockmen were ordered to shoot all the prisoners, by way of example. This had been Humāyūn's first affair, his first experience of battle; it was an excellent omen!

Our men who had gone in pursuit of the fugitives, took Ḥiṣār-fīrūza at once on arrival, plundered it, and returned to us. It was given in guerdon to

Humāyūn, with all its dependencies and appurtenances, with it also a *kror* of money.

We marched from that camp to Shāhābād. After we had despatched a news-gatherer (*tīl-tūtār kīshī*) to Sl. Ibrāhīm's camp, we stayed a few days on that ground. Raḥmat the foot-man was sent with the letters of victory to Kābul.

(*r. News of Ibrāhīm.*)

(*March 13th*) On Monday the 28th of the first Jumāda,[1655] we being in that same camp, the Sun entered the Sign of the Ram. News had come again and again from Ibrāhīm's camp, "He is coming, marching two miles" or "four miles", "stopping in each camp two days," or "three days". We for our part advanced from Shāhābād and after halting on two nights, reached the bank of the Jūn-river (Jumna) and encamped opposite Sarsāwa. From that ground Khwāja Kalān's servant Ḥaidar-qulī was sent to get news (*tīl tūtā*).

Having crossed the Jūn-river at a ford, I visited Sarsāwa. That day also we ate *ma'jūn*. Sarsāwa[1656] has a source (*chashma*) from which a smallish stream issues, not a bad place! Tardī Beg *khāksār* praising it, I said, "Let it be thine!" so justFol. 263b. because he praised it, Sarsāwa was given to him!

I had a platform fixed in a boat and used to go for excursions on the river, sometimes too made the marches down it. Two marches along its bank had been made when, of those sent to gather news, Ḥaidar-qulī brought word that Ibrāhīm had sent Daud Khān (*Lūdī*) and Ḥātīm Khān (*Lūdī*) across the river into the Mīān-dū-āb (Tween-waters) with 5 or 6000 men, and that these lay encamped some 6 or 7 miles from his own.

(*s. A successful encounter.*)

(*April 1st*) On Sunday the 18th of the second Jumāda, we sent, to ride light against this force, Chīn-tīmūr Sulṭān,[1657] Mahdī Khwāja, Muḥammad Sl. Mīrzā, 'Ādil Sulṭān, and the whole of the left, namely, Sl. Junaid, Shāh Mīr Ḥusain, Qūtlūq-qadam, and with them also sent 'Abdu'l-lāh and Kitta Beg (of the centre). They crossed from our side of the water at the Mid-day Prayer, and between the Afternoon and the Evening Prayers bestirred themselves from the other bank. Biban having crossed the water on pretext of this movement, ran away.

(*April 2nd*) At day-break they came upon the enemy;[1658] he made as if coming out in a sort of array, but our men closed with his at once, overcame them, hustled them off, pursued and unhorsed them till they were opposite Ibrāhīm's own camp. Ḥātim Khān was one of those unhorsed, who was Daud Khān (*Lūdī*)'s elder brother and one of his commanders. Our men brought him in when they waited on me. They brought also Fol. 264.60-70 prisoners and 6 or 7 elephants. Most of the prisoners, by way of warning, were made to reach their death-doom.

(*t. Preparations for battle.*)

While we were marching on in array of right, left and centre, the army was numbered;[1659] it did not count up to what had been estimated.

At our next camp it was ordered that every man in the army should collect carts, each one according to his circumstances. Seven hundred carts (*arāba*) were brought[1660] in. The order given to Ustād 'Alī-qulī was that these carts should be joined together in Ottoman[1661] fashion, but using ropes of raw hide instead of chains, and that between every two carts 5 or 6 mantelets should be fixed, behind which the matchlockmen were to stand to fire. To allow of collecting all appliances, we delayed 5 or 6 days in that camp. When everything was ready, all the begs with such braves as had had experience in military affairs were summoned to a General Council where opinion found decision at this:—Pānī-pat[1662] is there with its crowded houses and suburbs. It would be on one side of us; our other sides must be protected by carts and mantelets behind which our foot and matchlockmen would stand. With so much settled we marched forward, halted one night on the way, and reached Pānī-pat on Thursday the last day (29th) of the second Jumāda (April 12th).

(*u. The opposed forces.*)

On our right was the town of Pānī-pat with its suburbs; in front of us were the carts and mantelets we had prepared; on our left and elsewhere were ditch and branch. At distances ofFol. 264b. an arrow's flight[1663] sally-places were left for from 100 to 200 horsemen.

Some in the army were very anxious and full of fear. Nothing recommends anxiety and fear. For why? Because what God has fixed in eternity cannot be changed. But though this is so, it was no reproach to be afraid and anxious. For why? Because those thus anxious and afraid were there with a two or three months' journey between them and their homes; our affair was with a foreign tribe and people; none knew their tongue, nor did they know ours:—

A wandering band, with mind awander;

In the grip of a tribe, a tribe unfamiliar.[1664]

People estimated the army opposing us at 100,000 men; Ibrāhīm's elephants and those of his amīrs were said to be about 1000. In his hands was the treasure of two forbears.[1665] In Hindūstān, when work such as this has to be done, it is customary to pay out money to hired retainers who are known as *b:d-hindī.*[1666] If it had occurred to Ibrāhīm to do this, he might have had another *lak* or two of troops. God brought it right! Ibrāhīm could neither content his braves, nor share out his treasure. How should he content his braves when he was ruled by avarice and had a craving insatiable to pile coin on coin? He was an unproved brave[1667]; he provided nothing for his Fol. 265.military operations, he perfected nothing, nor stand, nor move, nor fight.

In the interval at Pānī-pat during which the army was preparing defence on our every side with cart, ditch and branch, Darwīsh-i-muḥammad *Sārbān* had once said to me, "With such precautions taken, how is it possible for him to come?" Said I, "Are you likening him to the Aūzbeg khāns and sulṭāns? In what of movement under arms or of planned operations is he to be compared with them?" God brought it right! Things fell out just as I said!

(*Author's note on the Aūzbeg chiefs.*) When I reached Ḥiṣār in the year I left Samarkand (918 AH.-1512 AD.), and all the Aūzbeg khāns and sulṭāns gathered and came against us, we brought the families and the goods of the Mughūls and soldiers into the Ḥiṣār suburbs and fortified these by closing the lanes. As those khāns and sulṭāns were experienced in equipment, in planned operations, and in resolute resistance, they saw from our fortification of Ḥiṣār that we were determined on life or death within it, saw they could not count on taking it by assault and, therefore, retired at once from near Nūndāk of Chaghānīān.

(*v. Preliminary encounters.*)

During the 7 or 8 days we lay in Pānī-pat, our men used to go, a few together, close up to Ibrāhīm's camp, rain arrows down on his massed troops, cut off and bring in heads. Still he madeFol. 265b. no move; nor did his troops sally out. At length, we acted on the advice of several Hindūstānī well-wishers and sent out 4 or 5000 men to deliver a night-attack on his camp, the leaders of it being Mahdī Khwāja, Muḥammad Sl. Mīrzā, 'Ādil Sulṭān, Khusrau, Shāh Mīr Ḥusain, Sl. Junaid *Barlās*, 'Abdu'l-'azīz the Master of the Horse, Muḥ. 'Alī *Jang-jang*, Qūtlūq-qadam, Treasurer Walī, Khalīfa's Muḥibb-i-'alī, Pay-master Muḥammad, Jān Beg and Qarā-qūzī. It being dark, they were not able to act together well, and, having scattered, could effect nothing on arrival. They stayed near Ibrāhīm's camp till dawn, when the nagarets sounded and troops of his came out in array with elephants. Though our men did not do their work, they got off safe and sound; not a man of them was killed, though they were in touch with such a mass of foes. One arrow pierced Muḥ. 'Alī *Jang-jang*'s leg; though the wound was not mortal, he was good-for-nothing on the day of battle.

On hearing of this affair, I sent off Humāyūn and his troops to go 2 or 3 miles to meet them, and followed him myself with the rest of the army in battle-array. The party of the night-attack joined him and came back with him. The enemy making no further advance, we returned to camp and dismounted. That night a false alarm fell on the camp; for some 20 minutes (one *garī*) there were uproar and call-to-arms; the disturbance died down after a time.Fol. 266.]

(*w. Battle of Pānī-pat.*[1668])

(*April 20th*) On Friday the 8th of Rajab,[1669] news came, when it was light enough to distinguish one thing from another (*farẓ-waqtī*) that the enemy was advancing in fighting-array. We at once put on mail,[1670] armed and mounted.[1671] Our right was Humāyūn, Khwāja Kalān, Sulṭān Muḥammad *Dūldāī*, Hindū Beg, Treasurer Walī and Pīr-qulī *Sīstānī*; our left was Muḥammad Sl. Mīrzā, Mahdī Khwāja, 'Ādil Sulṭān, Shāh Mīr Ḥusain, Sl. Junaid *Barlās*, Qūtlūq-qadam, Jān Beg, Pay-master Muḥammad, and Shāh Ḥusain (of) Yāragī *Mughūl Ghānchī*(?).[1672] The right hand of the centre[1673] was Chīn-tīmūr Sulṭān, Sulaimān Mīrzā,[1674] Muḥammadī Kūkūldāsh, Shāh Manṣūr *Barlās*, Yūnas-i-'alī, Darwīsh-i-muḥammad *Sārbān* and 'Abdu'l-lāh the librarian. The left of the centre was Khalīfa, Khwāja Mīr-i-mīrān, Secretary Aḥmadī, Tardī Beg (brother) of Qūj Beg, Khalīfa's Muḥibb-i-'alī and Mīrzā Beg Tarkhān. The advance was Khusrau Kūkūldāsh and Muḥ. 'Alī *Jang-jang*. 'Abdu'l-'azīz the Master of the Horse was posted as the reserve. For the turning-party (*tūlghuma*) at the point of the right wing,[1675] we fixed on Red Walī and Malik Qāsim (brother) of Bābā *Qashqa*, with their Mughūls; for the turning-party at the point of the left wing, we arrayed Qarā-qūzī, Abū'l-muḥammad the lance-player, Shaikh Jamāl *Bārīn's* Shaikh 'Alī, Mahndī(?) and Tīngrī-bīrdī *Bashaghī*(?) *Mughūl*; these two parties, directly the enemy got near, were to turn his rear, one from the right, the other from the left.Fol. 266b.

When the dark mass of the enemy first came in sight, he seemed to incline towards our right; 'Abdu'l-'azīz, who was the right-reserve, was sent therefore to reinforce the right. From the time that Sl. Ibrāhīm's blackness first appeared, he moved swiftly, straight for us, without a check, until he saw the dark mass of our men, when his pulled up and, observing our formation and array,[1676] made as if asking, "To stand or not? To advance or not?" They could not stand; nor could they make their former swift advance.

Our orders were for the turning-parties to wheel from right and left to the enemy's rear, to discharge arrows and to engage in the fight; and for the right and left (wings) to advance and join battle with him. The turning-parties wheeled round and began to rain arrows down. Mahdī Khwāja was the first of the left to engage; he was faced by a troop having an elephant with it; his men's flights of arrows forced it to retire. To reinforce the left I sent Secretary Aḥmadī and also Qūj Beg's Tardī Beg and Khalīfa's Muḥibb-i-'alī. On the right also there was some stubborn fighting. Orders were given for Muḥammadī Kūkūldāsh, Shāh Manṣūr *Barlās*, Yūnas-i-'alī and 'Abdu'l-lāh to engage those facing them in front of the centre. From that same position Ustād 'Alī-qulī made good discharge of *firingī* shots;[1677]

Musṭạfa the commissary for his part made excellent discharge Fol. 267.of *zarb-zan* shots from the left hand of the centre. Our right, left, centre and turning-parties having surrounded the enemy, rained arrows down on him and fought ungrudgingly. He made one or two small charges on our right and left but under our men's arrows, fell back on his own centre. His right and left hands (*qūl*) were massed in such a crowd that they could neither move forward against us nor force a way for flight.

When the incitement to battle had come, the Sun was spear-high; till mid-day fighting had been in full force; noon passed, the foe was crushed in defeat, our friends rejoicing and gay. By God's mercy and kindness, this difficult affair was made easy for us! In one half-day, that armed mass was laid upon the earth. Five or six thousand men were killed in one place close to Ibrāhīm. Our estimate of the other dead, lying all over the field, was 15 to 16,000, but it came to be known, later in Āgra from the statements of Hindūstānīs, that 40 or 50,000 may have died in that battle.[1678]

The foe defeated, pursuit and unhorsing of fugitives began. Our men brought in amīrs of all ranks and the chiefs they captured; *mahauts* made offering of herd after herd of elephants.

Ibrāhīm was thought to have fled; therefore, while pursuing Fol. 267b.the enemy, we told off Qismatāī Mīrzā, Bābā *chuhra* and Būjka of the *khaṣa-tābīn*[1679] to lead swift pursuit to Āgra and try to take him. We passed through his camp, looked into his own enclosure (*sarācha*) and quarters, and dismounted on the bank of standing-water (*qarā-sū*).

It was the Afternoon Prayer when Khalīfa's younger brother-in-law Ṭ̤āhir Tībrī[1680] who had found Ibrāhīm's body in a heap of dead, brought in his head.

(*x. Detachments sent to occupy Dihlī and Āgra.*)

On that very same day we appointed Humāyūn Mīrzā[1681] to ride fast and light to Āgra with Khwāja Kalān, Muḥammadī, Shāh Manṣūr *Barlās*, Yūnas-i-'alī, 'Abdu'l-lah and Treasurer Walī, to get the place into their hands and to mount guard over the treasure. We fixed on Mahdī Khwāja, with Muḥammad Sl. Mīrza, 'Ādil Sulṭān, Sl. Junaid *Barlās* and Qūtlūq-qadam to leave their baggage, make sudden incursion on Dihlī, and keep watch on the treasuries.[1682]

(*April 21st*) We marched on next day and when we had gone 2 miles, dismounted, for the sake of the horses, on the bank of the Jūn (Jumna).

(*April 24th*) On Tuesday (Rajab 12th), after we had halted on two nights and had made the circuit of Shaikh Niẓāmu'd-dīn *Auliyā*'s tomb[1683] we dismounted on the bank of the Jūn over against Dihlī.[1684] That same night, being Wednesday-eve, we made an excursion into the fort of Dihlī and there spent the night.

(*April 25th*) Next day (Wednesday Rajab 13th) I made the circuit of Khwāja Quṭbu'd-dīn's[1685] tomb and visited the tombs and residences of Sl. Ghiyāṣu'd-dīn *Balban*[1686] and Sl. 'Alāu'u'd-dīn

Fol. 268.*Khiljī*,[1687] his Minār, and the Ḥauẓ-shamsī, Ḥauẓ-i-khaṣ and the tombs and gardens of Sl. Buhlūl and Sl. Sikandar (*Lūdī*). Having done this, we dismounted at the camp, went on a boat, and there *'araq* was drunk.

We bestowed the Military Collectorate (*shiqdārlīghī*) of Dihlī on Red Walī, made Dost Dīwān in the Dihlī district, sealed the treasuries, and made them over to their charge.

(*April 26th*) On Thursday we dismounted on the bank of the Jūn, over against Tūghlūqābād.[1688]

(*y. The khuṭba read for Bābur in Dihlī.*)

(*April 27th*) On Friday (Rajab 15th) while we remained on the same ground, Maulānā Maḥmūd and Shaikh Zain went with a few others into Dihlī for the Congregational Prayer, read the *khuṭba* in my name, distributed a portion of money to the poor and needy,[1689] and returned to camp.

(*April 28th*) Leaving that ground on Saturday (Rajab 16th), we advanced march by march for Āgra. I made an excursion to Tūghlūqābād and rejoined the camp.

(*May 4th*) On Friday (Rajab 22nd), we dismounted at the mansion (*manzil*) of Sulaimān *Farmulī* in a suburb of Āgra, but as the place was far from the fort, moved on the following day to Jalāl Khān *Jig:hat's* house.

On Humāyūn's arrival at Āgra, ahead of us, the garrison had made excuses and false pretexts (about surrender). He and his noticing the want of discipline there was, said, "The long hand may be laid on the Treasury"! and so sat down to watch the roads out of Āgra till we should come.

(*z. The great diamond.*)

In Sultan Ibrāhīm's defeat the Rāja of Gūālīār Bikramājīt the Hindū had gone to hell.[1690]Fol. 268b.

> (*Author's note on Bikramājīt.*) The ancestors of Bikramājīt had ruled in Gūālīār for more than a hundred years.[1691] Sikandar (*Lūdī*) had sat down in Āgra for several years in order to take the fort; later on, in Ibrāhīm's time, 'Aẕim Humāyūn *Sarwānī*[1692] had completely invested it for some while; following this, it was taken on terms under which Shamsābād was given in exchange for it.[1693]

Bikramājīt's children and family were in Āgra at the time of Ibrāhīm's defeat. When Humāyūn reached Āgra, they must have been planning to flee, but his postings of men (to watch the roads) prevented this and guard was kept over them. Humāyūn himself did not let them go (*bārghālī qūīmās*). They made him a voluntary offering of a mass of jewels and valuables amongst which was the famous diamond which 'Alāu'u'd-dīn must have brought.[1694] Its reputation is that every appraiser has estimated its value at two and a half days' food for the whole world. Apparently it weighs 8 *miṣqāls*.[1695] Humāyūn offered it to me when I arrived at Āgra; I just gave it him back.

(*aa. Ibrāhīm's mother and entourage.*)

Amongst men of mark who were in the fort, there were Malik Dād *Karānī*, Millī *Sūrdūk* and Fīrūz Khān *Mīwātī*. They, being convicted of false dealing, were ordered out for capital punishment. Several persons interceded for Malik Dād *Karānī* and four or five days passed in comings and goings before the matter was arranged. We then shewed to them (all?) kindness and favour in agreement with the petition made for them, and we restored them all their goods.[1696] A *pargana* worth 7 *laks*[1697] was bestowed on Ibrāhīm's mother; *parganas* were given also to these begs of his.[1698] She was sent out of the fort with her old servants and given encamping-ground (*yūrt*) two miles below Fol. 269.Āgra.

(*May 10th*) I entered Āgra at the Afternoon Prayer of Thursday (Rajab 28th) and dismounted at the mansion (*manzil*) of Sl. Ibrāhīm.

EXPEDITIONS OF TRAMONTANE MUḤAMMADANS INTO HIND.

(*a. Bābur's five attempts on Hindūstān.*)

From the date 910 at which the country of Kābul was conquered, down to now (932 AH.) (my) desire for Hindūstān had been constant, but owing sometimes to the feeble counsels of begs, sometimes to the non-accompaniment of elder and younger brethren,[1699] a move on Hindūstān had not been practicable and its territories had remained unsubdued. At length no such obstacles were left; no beg, great or small (*beg begāt*) of lower birth,[1700] could speak an opposing word. In 925 AH. (1519 AD.) we led an army out and, after taking Bajaur by storm in 2-3 *garī* (44-66 minutes), and making a general massacre of its people, went on into Bhīra. Bhīra we neither over-ran nor plundered; we imposed a ransom on its people, taking from them in money and goods to the value of 4 *laks* of *shāhrukhīs* and having shared this out to the army and auxiliaries, returned to Kābul. From then till now we laboriously held tight[1701] to Hindūstān, five times leading an army into it.[1702] The fifth time, God the Most High, by his own mercy and favour, made such a foe as Sl. Ibrāhīm the vanquished and loser, such a realm as Hindūstān our conquest and possession.

(*b. Three invaders from Tramontana.*)

From the time of the revered Prophet down till now[1703] three men from that side[1704] have conquered and ruled Hindūstān. Sl. Maḥmūd *Ghāzī*[1705] was the first, who and whose descendants sat long on the seat of government in Hindūstān. Sl. Shihābu'd-dīnFol. 269b. of Ghūr was the second,[1706] whose slaves and dependants royally shepherded[1707] this realm for many years. I am the third.

But my task was not like the task of those other rulers. For why? Because Sl. Maḥmūd, when he conquered Hindūstān, had the throne of Khurāsān subject to his rule, vassal and obedient to him were the sulṭāns of Khwārizm and the Marches (*Dāru'l-marz*), and under his hand was the ruler of Samarkand. Though his army may not have numbered 2 *laks*, what question is there that it[1708] was one. Then again, rājas were his opponents; all Hindūstān was not under one supreme head (*pādshāh*), but each rāja ruled independently in his own country. Sl. Shihābu'd-dīn again,—though he himself had no rule in Khurāsān, his elder brother Ghiyāṣu'd-dīn had it. The *Ṭabaqāt-i-nāṣirī*[1709] brings it forward that he once led into Hindūstān an army of 120,000 men and horse in mail.[1710] His opponents also were rāīs and rājas; one man did not hold all Hindūstān.

That time we came to Bhīra, we had at most some 1500 to 2000 men. We had made no previous move on Hindūstān with an army equal to that which came the fifth time, when we beat Sl. Ibrāhīm and conquered the realm of Hindūstān, the total written down for which, taking one retainer with another, and Fol. 270.with traders and servants, was 12,000. Dependent on me were the countries of Badakhshān, Qūndūz, Kābul and Qandahār, but no reckonable profit came from them, rather it was necessary to reinforce them fully because several lie close to an enemy. Then again, all Māwarā'u'n-nahr was in the power of the Aūzbeg khāns and sulṭāns, an ancient foe whose armies counted up to 100,000. Moreover Hindūstān, from Bhīra to Bihār, was in the power of the Afghāns and in it Sl. Ibrāhīm was supreme. In proportion to his territory his army ought to have been 5 *laks*, but at that time the Eastern amīrs were in hostility to him. His army was estimated at 100,000 and people said his elephants and those of his amīrs were 1000.

Under such conditions, in this strength, and having in my rear 100,000 old enemies such as are the Aūzbegs, we put trust in God and faced the ruler of such a dense army and of domains so wide. As our trust was in Him, the most high God did not make our labour and hardships vain, but defeated that powerful foe and conquered that broad realm. Not as due to strength and effort of our own do we look upon this good fortune, but as had solely through God's pleasure and kindness. We know that this happiness was not the fruit of our own ambition and resolve, but that it was purely from His mercy and favour.

DESCRIPTION OF HINDŪSTĀN.

(*a. Hindūstān.*)

The country of Hindūstān is extensive, full of men, and full Fol. 270b.of produce. On the east, south, and even on the west, it ends at its great enclosing ocean (*muḥiṭ daryā-sī-gha*). On the north it has mountains which connect with those of Hindū-kush, Kāfiristān and Kashmīr. North-west of it lie Kābul, Ghaznī and Qandahār. Dihlī is held (*aīrīmīsh*) to be the capital of the whole of Hindūstān. From the death of Shihābu'd-dīn *Ghūrī* (d. 602 AH.-1206 AD.) to the latter part of the reign of Sl. Fīrūz Shāh (*Tūghlūq Turk* d. 790 AH.-1388 AD.), the greater part of Hindūstān must have been under the rule of the sulṭāns of Dihlī.

(*b. Rulers contemporary with Bābur's conquest.*)

At the date of my conquest of Hindūstān it was governed by five Musalmān rulers (*pādshāh*)[1711] and two Pagans (*kāfir*). These were the respected and independent rulers, but there were also, in the hills and jungles, many rāīs and rājas, held in little esteem (*kīchīk karīm*).

First, there were the Afghāns who had possession of Dihlī, the capital, and held the country from Bhīra to Bihār. Jūnpūr, before their time, had been in possession of Sl. Ḥusain *Sharqī* (Eastern)[1712] whose dynasty Hindūstānīs call Pūrabī (Eastern). His ancestors will have been cup-bearers in the presence of Sl. Fīrūz Shāh and those (Tūghlūq) sulṭāns; they became supreme in Jūnpūr after his death.[1713] At that time Dihlī was in the hands of Sl. 'Alāu'u'd-dīn ('Ālam Khān) of the Sayyid dynasty to whose ancestor Tīmūr Beg had given it when, after having captured it, he went away.[1714] Sl. Buhlūl *Lūdī* and his son (Sikandar) got possession of the capital Jūnpūr and the capital Dihlī, and brought both under one government (881 AH.-1476 AD.).

Secondly, there was Sl. Muḥammad Muẓaffer in Gujrāt; he departed from the world a few days before the defeat of Sl. Ibrāhīm. He was skilled in the Law, a ruler (*pādshāh*) seekingFol. 271. after knowledge, and a constant copyist of the Holy Book. His dynasty people call Tānk.[1715] His ancestors also will have been wine-servers to Sl. Fīrūz Shāh and those (Tūghlūq) sulṭāns; they became possessed of Gujrāt after his death.

Thirdly, there were the Bāhmanīs of the Dakkan (Deccan, *i.e.* South), but at the present time no independent authority is left them; their great begs have laid hands on the whole country, and must be asked for whatever is needed.[1716]

Fourthly, there was Sl. Maḥmūd in the country of Malwā, which people call also Mandāū.[1717] His dynasty they call Khilīj (*Turk*). Rānā Sangā had defeated Sl. Maḥmūd and taken possession of most of his country. This dynasty also has become feeble. Sl. Maḥmūd's ancestors also must have been cherished by Sl. Fīrūz Shāh; they became possessed of the Malwā country after his death.[1718]

Fifthly, there was Naṣrat Shāh[1719] in the country of Bengal. His father (Ḥusain Shāh), a sayyid styled 'Alāu'u'd-dīn, had ruled in Bengal and Naṣrat Shāh attained to rule by inheritance. A surprising custom in Bengal is that hereditary succession is rare. The royal office is permanent and there are permanent offices of amīrs, wazīrs and manṣab-dārs (officials). It is the office that Bengalis regard with respect. Attached to each office is a body of obedient, subordinate retainers and servants. If the royal heart demand that a person should be dismissed Fol. 271b.and another be appointed to sit in his place, the whole body of subordinates attached to that office become the (new) office-holder's. There is indeed this peculiarity of the royal office itself that any person who kills the ruler (*pādshāh*) and seats himself on the throne, becomes ruler himself; amīrs, wazīrs, soldiers and peasants submit to him at once, obey him, and recognize him for the rightful ruler his predecessor in office had been.[1720] Bengalis say, "We are faithful to the throne; we loyally obey whoever occupies it." As for instance, before the reign of Naṣrat Shāh's father 'Alāu'u'd-dīn, an Abyssinian (*Ḥabshī*, named Muẓaffar Shāh) had killed his sovereign (Maḥmūd Shāh *Ilyās*), mounted the throne and ruled for some time. 'Alāu'u'd-dīn killed that Abyssinian, seated himself on the throne and became ruler. When he died, his son (Naṣrat) became ruler by inheritance. Another Bengali custom is to regard it as a disgraceful fault in a new ruler if he expend and consume the treasure of his predecessors. On coming to rule he must gather treasure of his own. To amass treasure Bengalis regard as a glorious distinction. Another custom in Bengal is that from ancient times *parganas* have been assigned to meet the charges of the treasury, stables, and all royal expenditure and to defray these charges no impost is laid on other lands.

These five, mentioned above, were the great Musalmān rulers, honoured in Hindūstān, many-legioned, and broad-landed. Of the Pagans the greater both in territory and army, is the Rāja of Bījānagar.[1721]Fol. 272.

The second is Rānā Sangā who in these latter days had grown great by his own valour and sword. His original country was Chitūr; in the downfall from power of the Mandāū sulṭāns, he became possessed of many of their dependencies such as Rantanbūr, Sārangpūr, Bhīlsān and Chandīrī. Chandīrī I stormed in 934 AH. (1528 A.D.)[1722] and, by God's pleasure, took it in a few hours; in it was Rānā Sangā's great and trusted man Midnī Rāo; we made general massacre of the Pagans in it and, as will be narrated, converted what for many years had been a mansion of hostility, into a mansion of Islām.

There are very many rāīs and rājas on all sides and quarters of Hindūstān, some obedient to Islām, some, because of their remoteness or because their places are fastnesses, not subject to Musalmān rule.

(*c. Of Hindūstān.*)

Hindūstān is of the first climate, the second climate, and the third climate; of the fourth climate it has none. It is a wonderful country. Compared with our countries it is a different world; its mountains, rivers, jungles and deserts, its towns, its cultivated lands, its animals and plants, its peoples and their tongues, its rains, and its winds, are all different. In some respects the hot-country (*garm-sīl*) that depends on Kābul, is like Hindūstān, but in others, it is different. Once the water of Sind is crossed, everything is in the Hindūstān way (*ṭāriq*) Fol. 272b.land, water, tree, rock, people and horde, opinion and custom.

(*d. Of the northern mountains.*)

After crossing the Sind-river (eastwards), there are countries, in the northern mountains mentioned above, appertaining to Kashmīr and once included in it, although most of them, as for example, Paklī and Shahmang (?), do not now obey it. Beyond Kashmīr there are countless peoples and hordes, *parganas* and cultivated lands, in the mountains. As far as Bengal, as far indeed as the shore of the great ocean, the peoples are without break. About this procession of men no-one has been able to give authentic information in reply to our enquiries and investigations. So far people have been saying that they call these hill-men Kas.[1723] It has struck me that as a Hindūstānī pronounces *shīn* as *sīn* (*i.e. sh* as *s*), and as Kashmīr is the one respectable town in these mountains, no other indeed being heard of, Hindūstānīs might pronounce it Kasmīr.[1724] These people trade in musk-bags, *b:ḥrī-qūṭās*,[1725] saffron, lead and copper.

Hindīs call these mountains Sawālak-parbat. In the Hindī tongue *sawāī-lak* means one lak and a quarter, that is, 125,000, and *parbat* means a hill, which makes 125,000 hills.[1726] The snow on these mountains never lessens; it is seen white from many districts of Hind, as, for example, Lāhor, Sihrind and Saṃbal. The range, which in Kābul is known as Hindū-kush, comes from Kābul eastwards into Hindūstān, with slight inclination to the south. The Hindūstānāt[1727] are to the south of it. Tībet lies to the north of it and of that unknown horde called Kas.Fol. 273.

(*e. Of rivers.*)

Many rivers rise in these mountains and flow through Hindūstān. Six rise north of Sihrind, namely Sind, Bahat (Jīlam), Chān-āb [*sic*], Rāwī, Bīāh, and Sutluj[1728]; all meet near Multān, flow westwards under the name of Sind, pass through the Tatta country and fall into the 'Umān(-sea).

Besides these six there are others, such as Jūn (Jumna), Gang (Ganges), Rahap (Raptī?), Gūmtī, Gagar (Ghaggar), Sirū, Gandak, and many more; all unite with the Gang-daryā, flow east under its name, pass through the Bengal country, and are poured into the great ocean. They all rise in the Sawālak-parbat.

Many rivers rise in the Hindūstān hills, as, for instance, Chaṃbal, Banās, Bītwī, and Sūn (Son). There is no snow whatever on these mountains. Their waters also join the Gang-daryā.

(*f. Of the Arāvallī.*)

Another Hindūstān range runs north and south. It begins in the Dihlī country at a small rocky hill on which is Fīrūz Shāh's residence, called Jahān-nāma,[1729] and, going on from there, appears near Dihlī in detached, very low, scattered here and there, rocky Fol. 273b.little hills.[1730] Beyond Mīwāt, it enters the Bīāna country. The hills of Sīkrī, Bārī and Dūlpūr are also part of this same including (tūtā) range. The hills of Gūālīār—they write it Gālīūr—although they do not connect with it, are off-sets of this range; so are the hills of Rantanbūr, Chitūr, Chandīrī, and Mandāū. They are cut off from it in some places by 7 to 8 *kurohs* (14 to 16 m.). These hills are very low, rough, rocky and jungly. No snow whatever falls on them. They are the makers, in Hindūstān, of several rivers.

(*g. Irrigation.*)

The greater part of the Hindūstān country is situated on level land. Many though its towns and cultivated lands are, it nowhere has running waters.[1731] Rivers and, in some places, standing-waters are its "running-waters" (*āqār-sūlār*). Even where, as for some towns, it is practicable to convey water by digging channels (*ārīq*), this is not done. For not doing it there may be several reasons, one being that water is not at all a necessity in cultivating crops and orchards. Autumn crops grow by the downpour of the rains themselves; and strange it is that spring crops grow even when no rain falls. To young trees water is made to flow by means of buckets or a wheel. They are given water constantly during two or three years; after which they need no more. Some vegetables are watered constantly.

In Lāhor, Dībālpūr and those parts, people water by means of a wheel. They make two circles of ropes long enough to suit the depth of the well, fix strips of wood between them, and on these fasten pitchers. The ropes with the wood and attached Fol. 274.pitchers are put over the well-wheel. At one end of the wheel-axle a second wheel is fixed, and close (*qāsh*) to it another on an upright axle. This last wheel the bullock turns; its teeth catch in the teeth of the second, and thus the wheel with the pitchers is turned. A trough is set where the water empties from the pitchers and from this the water is conveyed everywhere.

In Āgra, Chandwār, Bīāna and those parts, again, people water with a bucket; this is a laborious and filthy way. At the well-edge they set up a fork of wood, having a roller adjusted between the forks, tie a rope to a large bucket, put the rope over the roller, and tie its other end to the bullock. One person must drive the bullock, another empty the bucket. Every time the bullock turns after having drawn the bucket out of the well, that rope lies on the bullock-track, in pollution of urine and dung, before it descends again into the well. To some crops needing water, men and women carry it by repeated efforts in pitchers.[1732]

(*h. Other particulars about Hindūstān.*)

The towns and country of Hindūstān are greatly wanting in charm. Its towns and lands are all of one sort; there are no walls to the orchards (*bāghāt*), and most places are on the dead level plain. Under the monsoon-rains the banks of some of its rivers and torrents are worn into deep channels, difficult andFol. 274b. troublesome to pass through anywhere. In many parts of the plains thorny jungle grows, behind the good defence of which the people of the *pargana* become stubbornly rebellious and pay no taxes.

Except for the rivers and here and there standing-waters, there is little "running-water". So much so is this that towns and countries subsist on the water of wells or on such as collects in tanks during the rains.

In Hindūstān hamlets and villages, towns indeed, are depopulated and set up in a moment! If the people of a large town, one inhabited for years even, flee from it, they do it in such a way that not a sign or trace of them remains in a day or a day and a half.[1733] On the other hand, if they fix their eyes on a place in which to settle, they need not dig water-courses or construct dams because their crops are all rain-grown,[1734] and as the population of Hindūstān is unlimited, it swarms in. They make a tank or dig a well; they need not build houses or set up walls—*khas*-grass (*Andropogon muricatum*) abounds, wood is unlimited, huts are made, and straightway there is a village or a town!

(*i. Fauna of Hindūstān:—Mammals.*)

The elephant, which Hindūstānīs call *hāt(h)ī*, is one of the wild animals peculiar to Hindūstān. It inhabits the (western?) borders of the Kālpī country, and becomes more numerous in its wild state the further east one goes (in Kālpī?). From this tract it is that captured elephants are brought; in Karrah and Fol. 275.Mānikpūr elephant-catching is the work of 30 or 40 villages.[1735] People answer (*jawāb bīrūrlār*) for them direct to the exchequer.[1736] The elephant is an immense animal and very sagacious. If people speak to it, it understands; if they command anything from it, it does it. Its value is according to its size; it is sold by measure (*qārīlāb*); the larger it is, the higher its price. People rumour that it is heard of in some islands as 10 *qārī*[1737] high, but in this tract it[1738] is not seen above 4 or 5. It eats and drinks entirely with its trunk; if it lose the trunk, it cannot live. It has two great teeth (tusks) in its upper jaw, one on each side of its trunk; by setting these against walls and trees, it brings them down; with these it fights and does whatever hard tasks fall to it. People call these ivory (*'āj*, var. *ghāj*); they are highly valued by Hindūstānīs. The elephant has no hair.[1739] It is much relied on by Hindūstānīs, accompanying every troop of their armies. It has some useful qualities:—it crosses great rivers with ease, carrying a mass of baggage, and three or four have gone dragging without trouble the cart of the mortar (*qazān*) it takes four or five hundred men to haul.[1740] But its stomach is large; one elephant eats the corn (*būghūz*) of two strings (*qiṭār*) of camels.[1741]

The rhinoceros is another. This also is a large animal, equalFol. 275b. in bulk to perhaps three buffaloes. The opinion current in those countries (Tramontana) that it can lift an elephant on its horn, seems mistaken. It has a single horn on its nose, more than nine inches (*qārīsh*) long; one of two *qārīsh* is not seen.[1742] Out of one large horn were made a drinking-vessel[1743] and a dice-box, leaving over [the thickness of] 3 or 4 hands.[1744] The rhinoceros' hide is very thick; an arrow shot from a stiff bow, drawn with full strength right up to the arm-pit, if it pierce at all, might penetrate 4 inches (*aīlīk*, hands). From the sides (*qāsh*) of its fore and hind legs,[1745] folds hang which from a distance look like housings thrown over it. It resembles the horse more than it does any other animal.[1746] As the horse has a small stomach (appetite?), so has the rhinoceros; as in the horse a piece of bone (pastern?) grows in place of small bones (T. *āshūq*, Fr. *osselets* (Zenker), knuckles), so one grows in the rhinoceros; as in the horse's hand (*aīlīk*, Pers. *dast*) there is *kūmūk* (or *gūmūk*, a *tibia*, or marrow), so there is in the rhinoceros.[1747] It is more ferocious than the elephant and cannot be made obedient and submissive. There are masses of it in the Parashāwar and Hashnagar jungles, so too between the Sind-river and the jungles of the Bhīra country. Masses there are also on the banks of Fol. 276.the Sārū-river in Hindūstān. Some were killed in the Parashāwar and Hashnagar jungles in our moves on Hindūstān. It strikes powerfully with its horn; men and horses enough have been horned in those hunts.[1748] In one of them the horse of a *chuhra* (brave) named Maqṣūd was tossed a spear's-length, for which reason the man was nick-named the rhino's aim (*maqṣūd-i-karg*).

The wild-buffalo[1749] is another. It is much larger than the (domestic) buffalo and its horns do not turn back in the same way.[1750] It is a mightily destructive and ferocious animal.

The *nīla-gāū* (blue-bull)[1751] is another. It may stand as high as a horse but is somewhat lighter in build. The male is bluish-gray, hence, seemingly, people call it nīla-gāū. It has two rather small horns. On its throat is a tuft of hair, nine inches long; (in this) it resembles the yak.[1752] Its hoof is cleft (*aīrī*) like the hoof of cattle. The doe is of the colour of the *būghū-marāl*[1753]; she, for her part, has no horns and is plumper than the male.

The hog-deer (*kotah-pāīcha*) is another.[1754] It may be of the size of the white deer (*āq kiyīk*). It has short legs, hence its name, little-legged. Its horns are like a *būghū*'s but smaller; like the *būghū* it casts them every year. Being rather a poor runner, it does not leave the jungle.

Another is a deer (*kiyīk*) after the fashion of the male deer (*aīrkākī hūna*) of the *jīrān*.[1755] Its back is black, its belly white, its horns longer than the *hūna's*, but more crooked. A HindūstānīFol. 276b. calls it *kalahara*,[1756] a word which may have been originally *kālā-haran*, black-buck, and which has been softened in pronunciation to *kalahara*. The doe is light-coloured. By means of this *kalahara* people catch deer; they fasten a noose (*ḥalqa*) on its horns, hang a stone as large as a ball[1757] on one of its feet, so as to keep it from getting far away after it has brought about the capture of a deer, and set it opposite wild deer when these are seen. As these (*kalahara*) deer are singularly combative, advance to fight is made at once. The two deer strike with their horns and push one another backwards and forwards, during which the wild one's horns become entangled in the net that is fast to the tame one's. If the wild one would run away, the tame one does not go; it is impeded also by the stone on its foot. People take many deer in this way; after capture they tame them and use them in their turn to take others;[1758] they also set them to fight at home; the deer fight very well.

There is a smaller deer (*kiyīk*) on the Hindūstān hill-skirts, as large may-be as the one year's lamb of the *arqārghalcha* (*Ovis poli*).

The *gīnī-cow*[1759] is another, a very small one, perhaps as large as the *qūchqār* (ram) of those countries (Tramontana). Its flesh is very tender and savoury.

The monkey (*maimūn*) is another—a Hindūstānī calls it *bandar*. Of this too there are many kinds, one being what people Fol. 277.take to those countries. The jugglers (*lūlī*) teach them tricks. This kind is in the mountains of Nūr-dara, in the skirt-hills of Safīd-koh neighbouring on Khaibar, and from there downwards all through Hindūstān. It is not found higher up. Its hair is yellow, its face white, its tail not very long.—Another kind, not found in Bajaur, Sawād and those parts, is much larger than the one taken to those countries (Tramontana). Its tail is very long, its hair whitish, its face quite black. It is in the mountains and jungles of Hindūstān.[1760]—Yet another kind is distinguished (*būlā dūr*), quite black in hair, face and limbs.[1761]

The *nawal* (*nūl*)[1762] is another. It may be somewhat smaller than the *kīsh*. It climbs trees. Some call it the *mūsh-i-khūrma* (palm-rat). It is thought lucky.

A mouse (T. *sīchqān*) people call *galāhrī* (squirrel) is another. It is just always in trees, running up and down with amazing alertness and speed.[1763]

(*j. Fauna of Hindūstān:—Birds.*)[1764]

The peacock (Ar. *ṭāūs*) is one. It is a beautifully coloured and splendid animal. Its form (*andām*) is not equal to its colouring and beauty. Its body may be as large as the crane's (*tūrna*) but it is not so tall. On the head of both cock and hen are 20 to 30 feathers rising some 2 or 3 inches high. The hen has neither colour nor beauty. The head of the cock has an iridescent collar (*ṭauq sūsanī*); its neck is of a beautiful blue;Fol. 277b. below the neck, its back is painted in yellow, parrot-green, blue and violet colours. The flowers[1765] on its back are much the smaller; below the back as far as the tail-tips are [larger] flowers painted in the same colours. The tail of some peacocks grows to the length of a man's extended arms.[1766] It has a small tail under its flowered feathers, like the tail of other birds; this ordinary tail and its primaries[1767] are red. It is in Bajaur and Sawād and below them; it is not in Kunur [Kūnūr] and the Lamghānāt or any place above them. Its flight is feebler than the pheasant's (*qīrghāwal*); it cannot do more than make one or two short flights.[1768] On account of its feeble flight, it frequents the hills or jungles, which is curious, since jackals abound in the jungles it frequents. What damage might these jackals not do to birds that trail from jungle to jungle, tails as long as a man's stretch (*qūlāch*)! Hindūstānīs call the peacock *mor*. Its flesh is lawful food, according to the doctrine of Imām Abū Ḥanīfa; it is like that of the partridge and not unsavoury, but is eaten with instinctive aversion, in the way camel-flesh is.

The parrot (H. *ṭūṭī*) is another. This also is in Bajaur and countries lower down. It comes into Nīngnahār and the Lamghānāt in the heats when mulberries ripen; it is not there at other times. It is of many, many kinds. One sort is that which people carry into those (Tramontane) countries. They Fol. 278.make it speak words.—Another sort is smaller; this also they make speak words. They call it the jungle-parrot. It is numerous in Bajaur, Sawād and that neighbourhood, so much so that 5 or 6000 fly in one flock (*khail*). Between it and the one first-named the difference is in bulk; in colouring they are just one and the same.—Another sort is still smaller than the jungle-parrot. Its head is quite red, the top of its wings (*i.e.* the primaries) is red also; the tip of its tail for two hands'-thickness is lustrous.[1769] The head of some parrots of this kind is iridescent (*sūsanī*). It does not become a talker. People call it the Kashmīr parrot.—Another sort is rather smaller than the jungle-parrot; its beak is black; round its neck is a wide black collar; its primaries are red. It is an excellent learner of words.—We used to think that whatever a parrot or a *shārak* (*mīna*) might say of words people had taught it, it could not speak of any matter out of its own head. At this juncture[1770] one of my immediate servants Abū'l-qāsim *Jalāīr*, reported a singular thing to me. A parrot of this sort whose cage must have been covered up, said, "Uncover my face; I am stifling." And another time when palkī bearers sat down to take breath, this parrot, presumably on hearing wayfarers pass by, said, "Men are going past, are you not going on?" Let credit rest with the narrator,[1771] but never-the-less, so long as a person has not heard with his own ears, he may not believe!—Another kind is of a beautiful Fol. 278b.full red; it has other colours also, but, as nothing is distinctly remembered about them, no description is made. It is a very beautiful bird, both in colour and form. People are understood to make this also speak words.[1772] Its defect is a most unpleasant, sharp voice, like the drawing of broken china on a copper plate.[1773]

The (P.) *shārak*[1774] is another. It is numerous in the Lamghānāt and abounds lower down, all over Hindūstān. Like the parrot, it is of many kinds.—The kind that is numerous in the Lamghānāt has a black head; its primaries (*qānāt*) are spotted, its body rather larger and thicker[1775] than that of the (T.) *chūghūr-chūq*.[1776] People teach it to speak words.—Another kind they call *p:ndāwalī*[1777]; they bring it from Bengal; it is black all over and of much greater bulk than the *shārak* (here, house-*mīna*). Its bill and foot are yellow and on each ear are yellow wattles which hang down and have a bad appearance.[1778] It learns to speak well and clearly.—Another kind of *shārak* is slenderer than the last and is red round the eyes. It does not learn to speak. People call it the wood-*shārak*.[1779] Again, at the time when (934 AH.) I had made a bridge over Gang (Ganges), crossed it, and put my adversaries to flight, a kind of *shārak* was seen, in the neighbourhood of Laknau and Aūd (Oude), for the first time, which had a white breast, piebald head, and black back. This kind does not learn to speak.[1780]

The *lūja*[1781] is another. This bird they call (Ar.) *bū-qalamūn* (chameleon) because, between head and tail, it has five or six changing colours, resplendent (*barrāq*) like a pigeon's throat. Fol. 279.It is about as large as the *kabg-i-darī*[1782] and seems to be the *kabg-i-darī* of Hindūstān. As the *kabg-i-darī* moves (*yūrūr*) on the heads (*kulah*) of mountains, so does this. It is in the Nijr-aū mountains of the countries of Kābul, and in the mountains lower down but it is not found higher up. People tell this wonderful thing about it:—When the birds, at the onset of winter, descend to the hill-skirts, if they come over a vineyard, they can fly no further and are taken. God knows the truth! The flesh of this bird is very savoury.

The partridge (*durrāj*)[1783] is another. This is not peculiar to Hindūstān but is also in the *Garm-sīr* countries[1784]; as however some kinds are only in Hindūstān, particulars of them are given here. The *durrāj* (*Francolinus vulgaris*) may be of the same bulk as the *kīklīk*[1785]; the cock's back is the colour of the hen-pheasant (*qīrghāwal-ning māda-sī*); its throat and breast are black, with quite white spots.[1786] A red line comes down on both sides of both eyes.[1787] It is named from its cry[1788] which is something like *Shir dāram shakrak*.[1789] It pronounces *shir* short; *dāram shakrak* it says distinctly. Astarābād partridges are said to cry *Bāt mīnī tūtīlār* (Quick! they have caught me). The partridge of Arabia and those parts is understood to cry, *Bi'l shakar tadawm al ni'am* (with sugar pleasure endures)! The hen-bird has the colour of the young pheasant. These birds are found below Nijr-aū.—Another kind is called *kanjāl.* Its bulk may be that of the one already described. Its voice is very like that of the *kīklīk* but much shriller. There is littleFol. 279b. difference in colour between the cock and hen. It is found in Parashāwar, Hashnagar and countries lower down, but not higher up.

The *p(h)ūl-paikār*[1790] is another. Its size may be that of the *kabg-i-darī*; its shape is that of the house-cock, its colour that of the hen. From forehead (*tūmāgh*) to throat it is of a beautiful colour, quite red. It is in the Hindūstān mountains.

The wild-fowl (*ṣaḥrāī-tāūgh*)[1791] is another. It flies like a pheasant, and is not of all colours as house-fowl are. It is in the mountains of Bajaur and lower down, but not higher up.

The *chīlsī* (or *jīlsī*)[1792] is another. In bulk it equals the *p(h)ūl-paikār* but the latter has the finer colouring. It is in the mountains of Bajaur.

The *shām*[1793] is another. It is about as large as a house-fowl; its colour is unique (*ghair mukarrar*).[1794] It also is in the mountains of Bajaur.

The quail (P. *būdana*) is another. It is not peculiar to Hindūstān but four or five kinds are so.—One is that which goes to our countries (Tramontana), larger and more spreading than the (Hindūstān) quail.[1795]—Another kind[1796] is smaller than the one first named. Its primaries and tail are reddish. It flies in flocks like the *chīr* (*Phasianus Wallichii*).—Another kind is smaller than that which goes to our countries and is darker on throat Fol. 280.and breast.[1797]—Another kind goes in small numbers to Kābul; it is very small, perhaps a little larger than the yellow wag-tail (*qārcha*)[1798]; they call it *qūrātū* in Kābul.

The Indian bustard (P. *kharchāl*)[1799] is another. It is about as large as the (T.) *tūghdāq* (*Otis tarda*, the great bustard), and seems to be the *tūghdāq* of Hindūstān.[1800] Its flesh is delicious; of some birds the leg is good, of others, the wing; of the bustard all the meat is delicious and excellent.

The florican (P. *charz*)[1801] is another. It is rather less than the *tūghdīrī* (*houbara*)[1802]; the cock's back is like the *tūghdīrī's*, and its breast is black. The hen is of one colour.

The Hindūstān sand-grouse (T. *bāghrī-qarā*)[1803] is another. It is smaller and slenderer than the *bāghrī-qarā* [*Pterocles arenarius*] of those countries (Tramontana). Also its cry is sharper.

Of the birds that frequent water and the banks of rivers, one is the *dīng*,[1804] an animal of great bulk, each wing measuring a *qūlāch* (fathom). It has no plumage (*tūqī*) on head or neck; a thing like a bag hangs from its neck; its back is black; its breast is white. It goes sometimes to Kābul; one year people brought one they had caught. It became very tame; if meat were thrown to it, it never failed to catch it in its bill. Once it swallowed a six-nailed shoe, another time a whole fowl, wingsFol. 280b. and feathers, all right down.

The *sāras* (*Grus antigone*) is another. Turks in Hindūstān call it *tīwa-tūrnā* (camel-crane). It may be smaller than the *dīng* but its neck is rather longer. Its head is quite red.[1805] People keep this bird at their houses; it becomes very tame.

The *mānek*[1806] is another. In stature it approaches the *sāras*, but its bulk is less. It resembles the *lag-lag* (*Ciconia alba*, the white stork) but is much larger; its bill is larger and is black. Its head is iridescent, its neck white, its wings partly-coloured; the tips and border-feathers and under parts of the wings are white, their middle black.

Another stork (*lag-lag*) has a white neck and all other parts black. It goes to those countries (Tramontana). It is rather smaller than the *lag-lag* (*Ciconia alba*). A Hindūstānī calls it *yak-rang* (one colour?).

Another stork in colour and shape is exactly like the storks that go to those countries. Its bill is blacker and its bulk much less than the *lag-lag*'s (*Ciconia alba*).[1807]

Another bird resembles the grey heron (*aūqār*) and the *lag-lag*; but its bill is longer than the heron's and its body smaller than the white stork's (*lag-lag*).

Another is the large *buzak*[1808] (black ibis). In bulk it may equal the buzzard (Turkī, *sār*). The back of its wings is white. It has a loud cry.

The white *buzak*[1809] is another. Its head and bill are black. Fol. 281.It is much larger than the one that goes to those countries,[1810] but smaller than the Hindūstān *buzak*.[1811]

The *gharm-pāī*[1812] (spotted-billed duck) is another. It is larger than the *sūna būrchīn*[1813] (mallard). The drake and duck are of one colour. It is in Hashnagar at all seasons, sometimes it goes into the Lamghānāt. Its flesh is very savoury.

The *shāh-murgh* (*Sarcidiornis melanonotus*, comb duck or *nukta*) is another. It may be a little smaller than a goose. It has a swelling on its bill; its back is black; its flesh is excellent eating.

The *zummaj* is another. It is about as large as the *būrgūt* (*Aquila chrysaetus*, the golden eagle).

The (T.) *ālā-qārgha* of Hindūstān is another (*Corvus cornix*, the pied crow). This is slenderer and smaller than the *ālā-qārgha* of those countries (Tramontana). Its neck is partly white.

Another Hindūstān bird resembles the crow (T. *qārcha*, *C. splendens*) and the magpie (Ar. *'aqqa*). In the Lamghānāt people call it the jungle-bird (P. *murgh-i-jangal*).[1814] Its head and breast are black; its wings and tail reddish; its eye quite red. Having a feeble flight, it does not come out of the jungle, whence its name.

The great bat (P. *shapara*)[1815] is another. People call it (Hindī) *chumgādur*. It is about as large as the owl (T. *yāpālāq*, *Otus brachyotus*), and has a head like a puppy's. When it is thinking of lodging for the night on a tree, it takes hold of a branch, turns head-downwards, and so remains. It has much singularity.

The magpie (Ar. *'aqqa*) is another. People call it (H.?) *matā* (*Dendrocitta rufa*, the Indian tree-pie). It may be somewhat less than the *'aqqa* (*Pica rustica*), which moreover is pied black and white, while the *matā* is pied brown and black.[1816]

Another is a small bird, perhaps of the size of the (T.) *sāndūlāch*.[1817]Fol. 281b. It is of a beautiful red with a little black on its wings.

The *karcha*[1818] is another; it is after the fashion of a swallow (T. *qārlūghāch*), but much larger and quite black.

The *kūīl*[1819] (*Eudynamys orientalis*, the koel) is another. It may be as large as the crow (P. *zāg*) but is much slenderer. It has a kind of song and is understood to be the bulbul of Hindūstān. Its honour with Hindūstānīs is as great as is the bulbul's. It always stays in closely-wooded gardens.

Another bird is after the fashion of the (Ar.) *shiqarrāk* (*Cissa chinensis*, the green-magpie). It clings to trees, is perhaps as large as the green-magpie, and is parrot-green (*Gecinus striolatus*, the little green-woodpecker?).

(*k. Fauna of Hindūstān:—Aquatic animals.*)

One is the water-tiger (P. *shīr-ābī*, *Crocodilus palustris*).[1820] This is in the standing-waters. It is like a lizard (T. *gīlās*).[1821] People say it carries off men and even buffaloes.

The (P.) *siyāh-sār* (black-head) is another. This also is like a lizard. It is in all rivers of Hindūstān. One that was taken and brought in was about 4-5 *qārī* (*cir.* 13 feet) long and as thick perhaps as a sheep. It is said to grow still larger. Its snout is over half a yard long. It has rows of small teeth in its upper and lower jaws. It comes out of the water and sinks into the mud (*bātā*).

The (Sans.) *g[h]aṛīāl* (*Gavialus gangeticus*) is another.[1822] It is said to grow large; many in the army saw it in the Sarū (Gogra) river. It is said to take people; while we were on that river's banks (934-935 A.H.), it took one or two slave-women (*dādūk*), and it took three or four camp-followers between Ghāzīpūr and Banāras. In that neighbourhood I saw one but from a distance only and not quite clearly.

The water-hog (P. *khūk-ābī*, *Platanista gangetica*, the porpoise) is another. This also is in all Hindūstān rivers. It comes up suddenly out of the water; its head appears and disappears; it Fol. 282.dives again and stays below, shewing its tail. Its snout is as long as the *siyāh-sār's* and it has the same rows of small teeth. Its head and the rest of its body are fish-like. When at play in the water, it looks like a water-carrier's bag (*mashak*). Water-hogs, playing in the Sarū, leap right out of the water; like fish, they never leave it.

Again there is the *kalah* (or *galah*)-fish [*bāligh*].[1823] Two bones each about 3 inches (*aīlīk*) long, come out in a line with its ears; these it shakes when taken, producing an extraordinary noise, whence, seemingly, people have called it *kalah* [or *galah*].

The flesh of Hindūstān fishes is very savoury; they have no odour (*aīd*) or tiresomeness.[1824] They are surprisingly active. On one occasion when people coming, had flung a net across a stream, leaving its two edges half a yard above the water, most fish passed by leaping a yard above it. In many rivers are little fish which fling themselves a yard or more out of the water if there be harshFol. 282b. noise or sound of feet.

The frogs of Hindūstān, though otherwise like those others (Tramontane), run 6 or 7 yards on the face of the water.[1825]

(*l. Vegetable products of Hindūstān: Fruits.*)

The mango (P. *anbah*) is one of the fruits peculiar to Hindūstān. Hindūstānīs pronounce the *b* in its name as though no vowel followed it (*i.e.* Sans. *anb*);[1826] this being awkward to utter, some people call the fruit [P.] *naghzak*[1827] as Khwāja Khusrau does:—

Naghzak-i mā [var. *khwash*] *naghz-kun-i būstān,*

Naghztarīn mewa [var. *na'mat*]*-i-Hindūstān.*[1828]

Mangoes when good, are very good, but, many as are eaten, few are first-rate. They are usually plucked unripe and ripened in the house. Unripe, they make excellent condiments (*qātīq*), are good also preserved in syrup.[1829] Taking it altogether, the mango is the best fruit of Hindūstān. Some so praise it as to give it preference over all fruits except the musk-melon (T. *qāwūn*), but such praise outmatches it. It resembles the *kārdī* peach.[1830] It ripens in the rains. It is eaten in two ways: one is to squeeze it to a pulp, make a hole in it, and suck out the juice,—the other, to peel and eat it like the *kārdī* peach. Its tree grows very large[1831] and has a leaf somewhat resembling the peach-tree's. The trunk is ill-looking and ill-shaped, but in Bengāl and Gujrāt is heard of as growing handsome (*khūb*).[1832]

The plantain (Sans. *kelā*, *Musa sapientum*) is another.[1833] An Fol. 283.'Arab calls it *mauz*.[1834] Its tree is not very tall, indeed is not to be called a tree, since it is something between a grass and a tree. Its leaf is a little like that of the *amān-qarā*[1835] but grows about 2 yards (*qārī*]) long and nearly one broad. Out of the middle of its leaves rises, heart-like, a bud which resembles a sheep's heart. As each leaf (petal) of this bud expands, there grows at its base a row of 6 or 7 flowers which become the plantains. These flowers become visible with the lengthening of the heart-like shoot and the opening of the petals of the bud. The tree is understood to flower once only.[1836] The fruit has two pleasant qualities, one that it peels easily, the other that it has neither stone nor fibre.[1837] It is rather longer and thinner than the egg-plant (P. *bādanjān*; *Solanum melongena*). It is not very sweet; the Bengāl plantain (*i.e. chīnī-champa*) is, however, said to be very sweet. The plantain is a very good-looking tree, its broad, broad, leaves of beautiful green having an excellent appearance.

The *anblī* (H. *imlī*, *Tamarindus indica*, the tamarind) is another. By this name (*anblī*) people call the *khurmā-i-hind* (Indian date-tree).[1838] It has finely-cut leaves (leaflets), precisely like those of the (T.) *būīā*, except that they are not so finely-cut.[1839] It is a very good-looking tree, giving dense shade. It grows wild in masses too.

The (Beng.) *mahuwā* (*Bassia latifolia*) is another.[1840] People call it also (P.) *gul-chikān* (or *chigān*, distilling-flower). This also is a very large tree. Most of the wood in the houses of HindūstānīsFol. 283b. is from it. Spirit (*'araq*) is distilled from its flowers,[1841] not only so, but they are dried and eaten like raisins, and from them thus dried, spirit is also extracted. The dried flowers taste just like *kishmish*;[1842] they have an ill-flavour. The flowers are not bad in their natural state[1843]; they are eatable. The *mahuwā* grows wild also. Its fruit is tasteless, has rather a large seed with a thin husk, and from this seed, again,[1844] oil is extracted.

The mimusops (Sans. *khirnī*, *Mimusops kauki*) is another. Its tree, though not very large, is not small. The fruit is yellow and thinner than the red jujube (T. *chīkdā*, *Elæagnus angustifolia*). It has just the grape's flavour, but a rather bad after-taste; it is not bad, however, and is eatable. The husk of its stoneæ is thin.

The (Sans.) *jāman* (*Eugenia jambolana*)[1845] is another. Its leaf, except for being thicker and greener, is quite like the willow's (T. *tāl*). The tree does not want for beauty. Its fruit is like a black grape, is sourish, and not very good.

The (H.) *kamrak* (Beng. *kamrunga*, *Averrhoa carambola*) is another. Its fruit is five-sided, about as large as the *'ain-ālū*[1846] and some 3 inches long. It ripens to yellow; gathered unripe, it is very bitter; gathered ripe, its bitterness has become sub-acid, not bad, not wanting in pleasantness.[1847]

The jack-fruit (H. *kadhil*, B. *kanthal*, *Artocarpus integrifolia*) is another.[1848] This is a fruit of singular form and flavour; it looks Fol. 284.like a sheep's stomach stuffed and made into a haggis (*gīpa*);[1849] and it is sickeningly-sweet. Inside it are filbert-like stones[1850] which, on the whole, resemble dates, but are round, not long, and have softer substance; these are eaten. The jack-fruit is very adhesive; for this reason people are said to oil mouth and hands before eating of it. It is heard of also as growing, not only on the branches of its tree, but on trunk and root too.[1851] One would say that the tree was all hung round with haggises.[1852]

The monkey-jack (H. *badhal*, B. *burhul*, *Artocarpus lacoocha*) is another. The fruit may be of the size of a quince (var. apple). Its smell is not bad.[1853] Unripe it is a singularly tasteless and empty[1854] thing; when ripe, it is not so bad. It ripens soft, can be pulled to pieces and eaten anywhere, tastes very much like a rotten quince, and has an excellent little austere flavour.

The lote-fruit (Sans. *ber*, *Zizyphus jujuba*) is another. Its Persian name is understood to be *kanār*.[1855] It is of several kinds: of one the fruit is larger than the plum (*ālūcha*)[1856]; another is shaped like the Ḥusainī grape. Most of them are not very good; we saw one in Bāndīr (Gūālīār) that was really good. The lote-tree sheds its leaves under the Signs *S̤aur* and *Jauzā* (Bull and Twins), burgeons under *Saraṭān* and *Asad* (Crab and Lion) which are the true rainy-season,—then becoming fresh and green, and it ripens its fruit under *Dalū* and *Ḥaut* (Bucket *i.e.* Aquarius, and Fish).

The (Sans.) *karaūndā* (*Carissa carandas*, the corinda) is another. It grows in bushes after the fashion of the (T.) *chīka* of our country.[1857] but the *chīka* grows on mountains, the *karaūndā* on theFol. 284b. plains. In flavour it is like the rhubarb itself,[1858] but is sweeter and less juicy.

The (Sans.) *pānīyālā* (*Flacourtia cataphracta*)[1859] is another. It is larger than the plum (*ālūcha*) and like the red-apple unripe.[1860] It is a little austere and is good. The tree is taller than the pomegranate's; its leaf is like that of the almond-tree but smaller.

The (H.) *gūlar* (*Ficus glomerata*, the clustered fig)[1861] is another. The fruit grows out of the tree-trunk, resembles the fig (P. *anjīr*), but is singularly tasteless.

The (Sans.) *āmlā* (*Phyllanthus emblica*, the myrobalan-tree) is another. This also is a five-sided fruit.[1862] It looks like the unblown cotton-pod. It is an astringent and ill-flavoured thing, but confiture made of it is not bad. It is a wholesome fruit. Its tree is of excellent form and has very minute leaves.

The (H.) *chirūnjī* (*Buchanania latifolia*)[1863] is another. This tree had been understood to grow in the hills, but I knew later about it, because there were three or four clumps of it in our gardens. It is much like the *mahuwā*. Its kernel is not bad, a thing between the walnut and the almond, not bad! rather smaller than the pistachio and round; people put it in custards (P. *pālūda*) and sweetmeats (Ar. *ḥalwa*).

The date-palm (P. *khurmā*, *Phœnix dactylifera*) is another. This is not peculiar to Hindūstān, but is here described because it is not in those countries (Tramontana). It grows in Lamghān also.[1864] Its branches (*i.e.* leaves) grow from just one place at its top; its leaves (*i.e.* leaflets) grow on both sides of the branches (midribs) from neck (*būīn*) to tip; its trunk is rough and ill-coloured; Fol. 285.its fruit is like a bunch of grapes, but much larger. People say that the date-palm amongst vegetables resembles an animal in two respects: one is that, as, if an animal's head be cut off, its life is taken, so it is with the date-palm, if its head is cut off, it dries off; the other is that, as the offspring of animals is not produced without the male, so too with the date-palm, it gives no good fruit unless a branch of the male-tree be brought into touch with the female-tree. The truth of this last matter is not known (to me). The above-mentioned head of the date-palm is called its cheese. The tree so grows that where its leaves come out is cheese-white, the leaves becoming green as they lengthen. This white part, the so-called cheese, is tolerable eating, not bad, much like the walnut. People make a wound in the cheese, and into this wound insert a leaf(let), in such a way that all liquid flowing from the wound runs down it.[1865] The tip of the leaflet is set over the mouth of a pot suspended to the tree in such a way that it collects whatever liquor is yielded by the wound. This liquor is rather pleasant if drunk at once; if drunk after two or three days, people say it is quite exhilarating (*kaifiyat*). Once when I had gone to visit Bārī,[1866] and made anFol. 285b. excursion to the villages on the bank of the Chaṃbal-river, we met in with people collecting this date-liquor in the valley-bottom. A good deal was drunk; no hilarity was felt; much must be drunk, seemingly, to produce a little cheer.

The coco-nut palm (P. *nārgīl*, *Cocos nucifera*) is another. An 'Arab gives it Arabic form[1867] and says *nārjīl*; Hindūstān people say *nālīr*, seemingly by popular error.[1868] Its fruit is the Hindī-nut from which black spoons (*qarā qāshūq*) are made and the larger ones of which serve for guitar-bodies. The coco-palm has general resemblance to the date-palm, but has more, and more glistening leaves. Like the walnut, the coco-nut has a green outer husk; but its husk is of fibre on fibre. All ropes for ships and boats and also cord for sewing boat-seams are heard of as made from these husks. The nut, when stripped of its husk, near one end shews a triangle of hollows, two of which are solid, the third a nothing (*būsh*), easily pierced. Before the kernel forms, there is fluid inside; people pierce the soft hollow and drink this; it tastes like date-palm cheese in solution, and is not bad.

The (Sans.) *tāṛ* (*Borassus flabelliformis*, the Palmyra-palm) is another. Its branches (*i.e.* leaves) also are quite at its top. Just asFol. 286. with the date-palm, people hang a pot on it, take its juice and drink it. They call this liquor *tāṛī*;[1869] it is said to be more exhilarating than date liquor. For about a yard along its branches (*i.e.* leaf-stems)[1870] there are no leaves; above this, at the tip of the branch (stem), 30 or 40 open out like the spread palm of the hand, all from one place. These leaves approach a yard in length. People often write Hindī characters on them after the fashion of account rolls (*daftar yūsūnlūq*).

The orange (Ar. *nāranj*, *Citrus aurantium*) and orange-like fruits are others of Hindūstān.[1871] Oranges grow well in the Lamghānāt, Bajaur and Sawād. The Lamghānāt one is smallish, has a navel,[1872] is very agreeable, fragile and juicy. It is not at all like the orange of Khurāsān and those parts, being so fragile that many spoil before reaching Kābul from the Lamghānāt which may be 13-14 *yīghāch* (65-70 miles), while the Astarābād orange, by reason of its thick skin and scant juice, carries with Fol. 286b.less damage from there to Samarkand, some 270-280 *yīghāch*.[1873] The Bajaur orange is about as large as a quince, very juicy and more acid than other oranges. Khwāja Kalān once said to me, "We counted the oranges gathered from a single tree of this sort in Bajaur and it mounted up to 7,000." It had been always in my mind that the word *nāranj* was an Arabic form;[1874] it would seem to be really so, since every-one in Bajaur and Sawād says (P.) *nārang*.[1875]

The lime (B. *līmū*, *C. acida*) is another. It is very plentiful, about the size of a hen's egg, and of the same shape. If a person poisoned drink the water in which its fibres have been boiled, danger is averted.[1876]

The citron (P. *turunj*,[1877] *C. medica*) is another of the fruits resembling the orange. Bajaurīs and Sawādīs call it *bālang* and hence give the name *bālang-marabbā* to its marmalade (*marabbā*) confiture. In Hindūstān people call the *turunj bajaurī*.[1878] There are two kinds of *turunj*: one is sweet, flavourless and nauseating, of no use for eating but with peel that may be good for marmalade; it has the same sickening sweetness as the Lamghānāt *turunj*; the other, that of Hindūstān and Bajaur, is acid, quite deliciously acid, and makes excellent sherbet, well-flavoured, and wholesome drinking. Its size may be that of the Khusrawī melon; it has a thick skin, wrinkled and uneven, with one end thinner and beaked. It is of a deeper yellow than the orange (*nāranj*). Its tree has no trunk, is rather low, grows in bushes, and has a largerFol. 287. leaf than the orange.

The *sangtāra*[1879] is another fruit resembling the orange (*nāranj*). It is like the citron (*turunj*) in colour and form, but has both ends of its skin level;[1880] also it is not rough and is somewhat the smaller fruit. Its tree is large, as large as the apricot (*aūrūq*), with a leaf like the orange's. It is a deliciously acid fruit, making a very pleasant and wholesome sherbet. Like the lime it is a powerful stomachic, but not weakening like the orange (*nāranj*).

The large lime which they call (H.) *gal-gal*[1881] in Hindūstān is another fruit resembling the orange. It has the shape of a goose's egg, but unlike that egg, does not taper to the ends. Its skin is smooth like the *sangtāra's*; it is remarkably juicy.

The (H.) *jānbīrī* lime[1882] is another orange-like fruit. It is orange-shaped and, though yellow, not orange-yellow. It smells like the citron (*turunj*); it too is deliciously acid.

The (Sans.) *sadā-fal* (*phal*)[1883] is another orange-like fruit. This is pear-shaped, colours like the quince, ripens sweet, but not to the sickly-sweetness of the orange (*nāranj*).

The *amrd-fal* (sic. Ḥai. MS.—Sans. *amrit-phal*)[1884] is another orange-like fruit.

The lemon (H. *karnā*, *C. limonum*) is another fruit resembling the orange (*nāranj*); it may be as large as the *gal-gal* and is also acid.

The (Sans.) *amal-bīd*[1885] is another fruit resembling the orange. After three years (in Hindūstān), it was first seen to-day.[1886] They say a needle melts away if put inside it,[1887] either from its acidityFol. 287b. or some other property. It is as acid, perhaps, as the citron and lemon (*turunj* and *līmū*).[1888]

(*m. Vegetable products of Hindūstān:—Flowers.*)

In Hindūstān there is great variety of flowers. One is the (D.) *jāsūn* (*Hibiscus rosa sinensis*), which some Hindūstānīs call (Hindī) *gaẕhal*.[1889] *It is not a grass (*giyāh*); its tree (is in stems like the bush of the red-rose; it) is rather taller than the bush of the red-rose.[1890]* The flower of the *jāsūn* is fuller in colour than that of the pomegranate, and may be of the size of the red-rose, but, the red-rose, when its bud has grown, opens simply, whereas, when the *jāsūn*-bud opens, a stem on which other petals grow, is seen like a heart amongst its expanded petals. Though the two are parts of the one flower, yet the outcome of the lengthening and thinning of that stem-like heart of the first-opened petals gives the semblance of two flowers.[1891] It is not a common matter. The beautifully coloured flowers look very well on the tree, but they do not last long; they fade in just one day. The *jāsūn* blossoms very well through the four months of the rains; it seems indeed to flower all through the year; with this profusion, however, it gives no perfume.

The (H.) *kanīr* (*Nerium odorum*, the oleander)[1892] is another. It grows both red and white. Like the peach-flower, it is five petalled. It is like the peach-bloom (in colour?), but opens 14 or 15 flowers from one place, so that seen from a distance, they look like one great flower. The oleander-bush is taller than the rose-bush. The red oleander has a sort of scent, faint and agreeable. (Like the *jāsūn*,) it also blooms well and profusely in the Fol. 288.rains, and it also is had through most of the year.

The (H.) (*kīūrā*) (*Pandanus odoratissimus*, the screw-pine) is another.[1893] It has a very agreeable perfume.[1894] Musk has the defect of being dry; this may be called moist musk—a very agreeable perfume. The tree's singular appearance notwithstanding, it has flowers perhaps 1-1/2 to 2 *qārīsh* (13-1/2 to 18 inches) long. It has long leaves having the character of the reed (P.) *gharau*[1895] and having spines. Of these leaves, while pressed together bud-like, the outer ones are the greener and more spiny; the inner ones are soft and white. In amongst these inner leaves grow things like what belongs to the middle of a flower, and from these things comes the excellent perfume. When the tree first comes up not yet shewing any trunk, it is like the bush (*būta*) of the male-reed,[1896] but with wider and more spiny leaves. What serves it for a trunk is very shapeless, its roots remaining shewn.

The (P.) *yāsman* (jasmine) is another; the white they call (B.) *champa.*[1897] It is larger and more strongly scented than our *yāsman*-flower.

(*n. Seasons of the year.*)

Again:—whereas there are four seasons in those countries,[1898] there are three in Hindūstān, namely, four months are summer; four are the rains; four are winter. The beginning of their months is from the welcome of the crescent-moons.[1899] Every three years they add a month to the year; if one had been added to the rainy season, the next is added, three years later, to the winter months, the next, in the same way, to the hot months. This is their mode of intercalation.[1900] (*Chait*, *Baisākh*, *Jeṭh* andFol. 288b. *Asāṛh*) are the hot months, corresponding with the Fish, (Ram, Bull and Twins; *Sāwan*, *Bhādoṅ*, *Kū,ār* and *Kātik*) are the rainy months, corresponding with the Crab, (Lion, Virgin and Balance; *Aghan*, *Pūs*, *Māgh* and *Phālgun*) are the cold months, corresponding with the Scorpion, (Archer, Capricorn, and Bucket or Aquarius).

The people of Hind, having thus divided the year into three seasons of four months each, divide each of those seasons by taking from each, the two months of the force of the heat, rain,[1901] and cold. Of the hot months the last two, *i.e. Jeṭh* and *Asāṛh* are the force of the heat; of the rainy months, the first two, *i.e. Sāwan* and *Bhādoṅ* are the force of the rains; of the cold season, the middle two, *i.e. Pūs* and *Māgh* are the force of the cold. By this classification there are six seasons in Hindūstān.

(*o. Days of the week.*)

To the days also they have given names:—[1902] (*Sanīchar* is Saturday; *Rabī-bār* is Sunday; *Som-wār* is Monday; *Mangal-wār* is Tuesday; *Budh-bār* is Wednesday; *Brihaspat-bār* is Thursday; *Shukr-bār* is Friday).

(*p. Divisions of time.*)

Fol. 289.(*Author's note on the daqīqa.*) The *daqīqa* is about as long as six repetitions of the *Fātiḥa* with the *Bismillāh*, so that a day-and-night is as long as 8640 repetitions of the *Fātiḥa* with the *Bismillāh.*

As in our countries what is known by the (Turkī) term *kīcha-gūndūz* (a day-and-night, nycthemeron) is divided into 24 parts, each called an hour (Ar. *sā'at*), and the hour is divided into 60 parts, each called a minute (Ar. *daqīqa*), so that a day-and-night consists of 1440 minutes,—so the people of Hind divide the night-and-day into 60 parts, each called a (S.) *g'harī.*[1903] They also divide the night into four and the day into four, calling each part a (S.) *pahr* (watch) which in Persian is a *pās*. A watch and watchman (*pās u pāsbān*) had been heard about (by us) in those countries (Transoxania), but without these particulars. Agreeing with the division into watches, a body of *g'hariālīs*[1904] is chosen and appointed in all considerable towns of Hindūstān. They cast a broad brass (plate-) thing,[1905] perhaps as large as a tray (*ṭabaq*) and about two hands'-thickness; this they call a *g'hariāl* and hang up in a high place (*bīr buland yīr-dā*). Also they have a vessel perforated at the bottom like an hour-cup[1906] and filling in one *g'harī* (*i.e.* 24 minutes). The *g'hariālīs* put this into water and wait till it fills. For example, they will put the perforatedFol. 289b. cup into water at day-birth; when it fills the first time, they strike the gong once with their mallets; when a second time, twice, and so on till the end of the watch. They announce the end of a watch by several rapid blows of their mallets. After these they pause; then strike once more, if the first day-watch has ended, twice if the second, three times if the third, and four times if the fourth. After the fourth day-watch, when the night-watches begin, these are gone through in the same way. It used to be the rule to beat the sign of a watch only when the watch ended; so that sleepers chancing to wake in the night and hear the sound of a third or fourth *g'harī*, would not know whether it was of the second or third night-watch. I therefore ordered that at night or on a cloudy day the sign of the watch should be struck after that of the *g'harī*, for example, that after striking the third *g'harī* of the first night-watch, the *g'harīālīs* were to pause and then strike the sign of the watch, in order to make it known that this third *g'harī* was of the first night-watch,—and that after striking four *g'harīs* of the third night-watch, they should pause and then strike the sign of the third watch, in order to make it known that this fourth *g'harī* was of the third night-watch. It did very well; anyone happening to wake in the night and hear the gong, would know what *g'harī* of what watch of night it was.

Again, they divide the *g'harī* into 60 parts, each part being called a *pal*;[1907] by this each night-and-day will consist of 3,500 *pals*.Fol. 290.

(*Author's note on the pal.*) They say the length of a *pal* is the shutting and opening of the eyelids 60 times, which in a night-and-day would be 216,000 shuttings and openings of the eyes. Experiment shews that a *pal* is about equal to 8 repetitions of the *Qul-huwa-allāh*[1908] and *Bismillāh*; this would be 28,000 repetitions in a night-and-day.

(*q. Measures.*)

The people of Hind have also well-arranged measures:—[1909] 8 *ratīs* = 1 *māsha*; 4 *māsha* = 1 *tānk* = 32 *ratīs*; 5 *māsha* = 1 *miṣqāl* = 40 *ratīs*; 12 *māsha* = 1 *tūla* = 96 *ratīs*; 14 *tūla* = 1 *ser*.

This is everywhere fixed:—40 *ser* = 1 *mānbān*; 12 *mānbān* = 1 *mānī*; 100 *mānī* they call a *mīnāsa*.[1910]

Pearls and jewels they weigh by the *tānk*.

(*r. Modes of reckoning.*)

The people of Hind have also an excellent mode of reckoning: 100,000 they call a *lak*; 100 *laks*, a *krūr*; 100 *krūrs*, an *arb*; 100 *arbs*, 1 *karb*; 100 *karb's*, 1 *nīl*; 100 *nīls*, 1 *padam*; 100 *padams*, 1 *sāng*. The fixing of such high reckonings as these is proof of the great amount of wealth in Hindūstān.

(*s. Hindū inhabitants of Hindūstān.*)

Most of the inhabitants of Hindūstān are pagans; they call a pagan a Hindū. Most Hindūs believe in the transmigration of souls. All artisans, wage-earners, and officials are Hindūs. In our countries dwellers in the wilds (*i.e.* nomads) get tribal names; Fol. 290b.here the settled people of the cultivated lands and villages get tribal names.[1911] Again:—every artisan there is follows the trade that has come down to him from forefather to forefather.

(*t. Defects of Hindūstān.*)

Hindūstān is a country of few charms. Its people have no good looks; of social intercourse, paying and receiving visits there is none; of genius and capacity none; of manners none; in handicraft and work there is no form or symmetry, method or quality; there are no good horses, no good dogs, no grapes, musk-melons or first-rate fruits, no ice or cold water, no good bread or cooked food in the *bāzārs*, no Hot-baths, no Colleges, no candles, torches or candlesticks.

In place of candle and torch they have a great dirty gang they call lamp-men (*diwati*), who in the left hand hold a smallish wooden tripod to one corner of which a thing like the top of a candlestick is fixed, having a wick in it about as thick as the thumb. In the right hand they hold a gourd, through a narrow slit made in which, oil is let trickle in a thin thread when the wick needs it. Great people keep a hundred or two of these lamp-men. This is the Hindūstān substitute for lamps and candlesticks! If their rulers and begs have work at night needing candles, these dirty lamp-men bring these lamps, go close up andFol. 291. there stand.

Except their large rivers and their standing-waters which flow in ravines or hollows (there are no waters). There are no running-waters in their gardens or residences (*'imāratlār*).[1912] These residences have no charm, air (*hawā*), regularity or symmetry.

Peasants and people of low standing go about naked. They tie on a thing called *lungūtā*,[1913] a decency-clout which hangs two spans below the navel. From the tie of this pendant decency-clout, another clout is passed between the thighs and made fast behind. Women also tie on a cloth (*lung*), one-half of which goes round the waist, the other is thrown over the head.

(*u. Advantages of Hindūstān.*)

Pleasant things of Hindūstān are that it is a large country and has masses of gold and silver. Its air in the Rains is very fine. Sometimes it rains 10, 15 or 20 times a day; torrents pour down all at once and rivers flow where no water had been. While it rains and through the Rains, the air is remarkably fine, not to be surpassed for healthiness and charm. The fault is that the air becomes very soft and damp. A bow of those (Transoxanian) countries after going through the Rains in Hindūstān, may not be drawn even; it is ruined; not only the bow, everything isFol. 291b. affected, armour, book, cloth, and utensils all; a house even does not last long. Not only in the Rains but also in the cold and the hot seasons, the airs are excellent; at these times, however, the north-west wind constantly gets up laden with dust and earth. It gets up in great strength every year in the heats, under the Bull and Twins when the Rains are near; so strong and carrying so much dust and earth that there is no seeing one another. People call this wind Darkener of the Sky (H. *āndhī*). The weather is hot under the Bull and Twins, but not intolerably so, not so hot as in Balkh and Qandahār and not for half so long.

Another good thing in Hindūstān is that it has unnumbered and endless workmen of every kind. There is a fixed caste (*jam'ī*) for every sort of work and for every thing, which has done that work or that thing from father to son till now. Mullā Sharaf, writing in the *Ẓafar-nāma* about the building of Tīmūr Beg's Stone Mosque, lays stress on the fact that on it 200 stone-cutters worked, from Āẕarbāījān, Fars, Hindūstān and other countries. But 680 men worked daily on my buildings in Āgra and of Āgra stone-cutters only; while 1491 stone-cutters worked daily on my buildings in Āgra, Sīkrī, Bīāna, Dūlpūr, Gūālīār and Kūīl. In Fol. 292.the same way there are numberless artisans and workmen of every sort in Hindūstān.

(*v. Revenues of Hindūstān.*)

The revenue of the countries now held by me (935 AH.-1528 AD.) from Bhīra to Bihār is 52 *krūrs*,[1914] as will be known in detail from the following summary.[1915] Eight or nine *krūrs* of this are from parganas of rāīs and rājas who, as obedient from of old, receive allowance and maintenance.

REVENUES OF HINDŪSTĀN FROM WHAT HAS SO FAR COME UNDER THE VICTORIOUS STANDARDS

Sarkārs.	Krūrs.	Laks.	Tankas.
Trans-sutluj:--Bhīra, Lāhūr, Sīālkūt, Dībālpūr, etc.	3	33	15,989
Sihrind	1	29	31,985
Ḥiṣār-fīrūza	1	30	75,174
The capital Dihlī and Mīān-dū-āb	3	69	50,254
Mīwāt, not included in Sikandar's time	1	69	81,000
Bīāna	1	44	14,930 Fol. 292b.
Āgra		29	76,919

Mīān-wilāyat (Midlands)	2	91	19
Gūālīār	2	23	57,450
Kālpī and Sehoṇda (Seondhā)	4	28	55,950
Qanauj	1	36	63,358
Saṃbhal	1	38	44,000
Laknūr and Baksar	1	39	82,433
Khairābād		12	65,000
Aūd (Oude) and Bahraj (Baraich)	1	17	1,369 Fol. 293.
Jūnpūr	4	·0	88,333
Karra and Mānikpūr	1	63	27,282
Bihār	4	5	60,000
Sāran	1	10	17,506½
Sarwār	1	55	18,373
Champāran	1	90	86,060
Kandla	1	43	30,300
Tirhut from Rāja Rup-narāīn's tribute, silver	1	43	55,000
black (i.e. copper)	1	27	50,300
Rantanbhūr from Būlī, Chātsū, and Malarna		20	00,000
Nagūr	--	--	--
Rāja Bikrāmajīt in Rantanbhūr	--	--	--
Kalanjarī	--	--	--

Rāja Bīr-sang-deo (or, Sang only)	--	--	--
Rāja Bikam-deo	--	--	--
Rāja Bikam-chand	--	--	--

[1916] So far as particulars and details about the land and people of the country of Hindūstān have become definitely known, they have been narrated and described; whatever matters worthy of record may come to view hereafter, I shall write down.

HISTORICAL NARRATIVE RESUMED.

(*a. Distribution of treasure in Āgra.*)[1917]

(*May 12th*) On Saturday the 29th[1918] of Rajab the examination and distribution of the treasure were begun. To Humāyūn were given 70 laks from the Treasury, and, over and above this, a treasure house was bestowed on him just as it was, without ascertaining and writing down its contents. To some begs 10 laks were given, 8, 7, or 6 to others.[1919] Suitable money-gifts were bestowed from the Treasury on the whole army, to every tribe there was, Afghān, Hazāra, 'Arab, Bīlūch *etc.* to each according to its position. Every trader and student, indeed every man who had come with the army, took ample portion and share of bounteous gift and largess. To those not with the army went a mass of treasure in gift and largess, as for instance, 17 laks to Kāmran, 15 laks to Muḥammad-i-zamān Mīrzā, while to 'Askarī, Hindāl and indeed to the whole various train of relations and younger children[1920] went masses of red and white (gold and silver), of plenishing, jewels and slaves.[1921] Many gifts went to the begs and soldiery on that side (Tramontana). Valuable gifts (*saughāt*) Fol. 294.were sent for the various relations in Samarkand, Khurāsān, Kāshghar and 'Irāq. To holy men belonging to Samarkand and Khurāsān went offerings vowed to God (*nuẕūr*); so too to Makka and Madīna. We gave one *shāhrukhi* for every soul in the country of Kābul and the valley-side[1922] of Varsak, man and woman, bond and free, of age or non-age.[1923]

(*b. Disaffection to Bābur.*)

On our first coming to Āgra, there was remarkable dislike and hostility between its people and mine, the peasantry and soldiers running away in fear of our men. Dilhī and Āgra excepted, not a fortified town but strengthened its defences and neither was in obedience nor submitted. Qāsim Saṃbhalī was in Saṃbhal; Niẓām Khān was in Bīāna; in Mīwāt was

Ḥasan Khān Mīwātī himself, impious mannikin! who was the sole leader of the trouble and mischief.[1924] Muḥammad *Zaitun* was in Dūlpūr; Tātār Khān *Sārang-khānī*[1925] was in Gūālīār; Ḥusain Khān *Nuḥānī* was in Rāprī; Quṭb Khān was in Itāwa (Etāwa); 'Ālam Khān (*Kālpī*) was in Kālpī. Qanauj and the other side of Gang (Ganges) was all held by Afghāns in independent hostility,[1926] such as Naṣīr Khān *Nuḥānī*, Ma'rūf *Farmūlī* and a crowd of other amīrs. These had been in rebellion for three or four years before Ibrāhīm's death and when I defeated him, were holding Qanauj and the whole country beyond it. At the present time they were lying two or three marches on our side of Qanauj and had made Bihār Khān the son of Daryā Khān *Nuḥānī* their *pādshāh*, under the style Sulṭān Muḥammad.Fol. 294b. Marghūb the slave was in Mahāwīn (*Muttra*?); he remained there, thus close, for some time but came no nearer.

(*c. Discontent in Bābur's army.*)

It was the hot-season when we came to Āgra. All the inhabitants (*khalāīq*) had run away in terror. Neither grain for ourselves nor corn for our horses was to be had. The villages, out of hostility and hatred to us had taken to thieving and highway-robbery; there was no moving on the roads. There had been no chance since the treasure was distributed to send men in strength into the parganas and elsewhere. Moreover the year was a very hot one; violent pestilential winds struck people down in heaps together; masses began to die off.

On these accounts the greater part of the begs and best braves became unwilling to stay in Hindūstān, indeed set their faces for leaving it. It is no reproach to old and experienced begs if they speak of such matters; even if they do so, this man (Bābur) has enough sense and reason to get at what is honest or what is mutinous in their representations, to distinguish between loss and gain. But as this man had seen his task whole, for himself, when he resolved on it, what taste was there in their reiterating that things should be done differently? What recommends the expression of distasteful opinions by men of little standing Fol. 295.(*kīchīk karīm*)? Here is a curious thing:—This last time of our riding out from Kābul, a few men of little standing had just been made begs; what I looked for from them was that if I went through fire and water and came out again, they would have gone in with me unhesitatingly, and with me have come out, that wherever I went, there at my side would they be,—not that they would speak against my fixed purpose, not that they would turn back from any task or great affair on which, all counselling, all consenting, we had resolved, so long as that counsel was not abandoned. Badly as these new begs behaved, Secretary Aḥmadī and Treasurer Walī behaved still worse. Khwāja Kalān had done well in the march out from Kābul, in Ibrāhīm's defeat and until Āgra was occupied; he had spoken bold words and shewn ambitious views. But a few days after the capture of Āgra, all his views changed,—the one zealous for departure at any price was Khwāja Kalān.[1927]

(*d. Bābur calls a council.*)

When I knew of this unsteadiness amongst (my) people, I summoned all the begs and took counsel. Said I, "There is no supremacy and grip on the world without means and resources; without lands and retainers sovereignty and command (*pādshāhlīq u amīrlīq*) are impossible. By the labours of several years, by encountering hardship, by long travel, by flinging myself and the army into battle, and by deadly slaughter, we, through God'sFol. 295b. grace, beat these masses of enemies in order that we might take their broad lands. And now what force compels us, what necessity has arisen that we should, without cause, abandon countries taken at such risk of life? Was it for us to remain in Kābul, the sport of harsh poverty? Henceforth, let no well-wisher of mine speak of such things! But let not those turn back from going who, weak in strong persistence, have set their faces to depart!" By these words, which recalled just and reasonable views to their minds, I made them, willy-nilly, quit their fears.

(*e. Khwāja Kalān decides to leave Hindūstān.*)

As Khwāja Kalān had no heart to stay in Hindūstān, matters were settled in this way:—As he had many retainers, he was to convoy the gifts, and, as there were few men in Kābul and Ghaznī, was to keep these places guarded and victualled. I bestowed on him Ghaznī, Girdīz and the Sulṭān Mas'ūdī Hazāra, gave also the Hindūstān *pargana* of G'hūram,[1928] worth 3 or 4 *laks*. It was settled for Khwāja Mīr-i-mīrān also to go to Kābul; the gifts were put into his immediate charge, under the custody of Mullā Ḥasan the banker (*ṣarrāf*) and Tūka[1929] *Hindū*.

Loathing Hindūstān, Khwāja Kalān, when on his way, had the following couplet inscribed on the wall of his residence Fol. 296. (*'imārati*) in Dihlī:—

If safe and sound I cross the Sind,

Blacken my face ere I wish for Hind!

It was ill-mannered in him to compose and write up this partly-jesting verse while I still stayed in Hind. If his departure caused me one vexation, such a jest doubled it.[1930] I composed the following off-hand verse, wrote it down and sent it to him:—

Give a hundred thanks, Bābur, that the generous Pardoner

Has given thee Sind and Hind and many a kingdom.

If thou (*i.e.* the Khwāja) have not the strength for their heats,

If thou say, "Let me see the cold side (*yūz*)," Ghaznī is there.[1931]

(*f. Accretions to Bābur's force.*)

At this juncture, Mullā Apāq was sent into Kūl with royal letters of favour for the soldiers and quiver-wearers (*tarkash-band*) of that neighbourhood. Shaikh Gūran (G'hūran)[1932] came trustfully and loyally to do obeisance, bringing with him from 2 to 3,000 soldiers and quiver-wearers from Between-two-waters (*Mīān-dū-āb*).

> (*Author's note on Mullā Apāq.*) Formerly he had been in a very low position indeed, but two or three years before this time, had gathered his elder and younger brethren into a compact body and had brought them in (to me), together with the Aūrūq-zāī and other Afghāns of the banks of the Sind.

Yūnas-i-'alī when on his way from Dihlī to Āgra[1933] had lost his way a little and got separated from Humāyūn; he then met in with 'Alī Khān *Farmūlī's* sons and train,[1934] had a small affair with them, took them prisoners and brought them in. Taking advantage of this, one of the sons thus captured was sent to his Fol. 296b.father in company with Daulat-qadam *Turk's* son Mīrzā *Mughūl* who conveyed royal letters of favour to 'Alī Khān. At this time of break-up, 'Alī Khān had gone to Mīwāt; he came to me when Mīrzā *Mughūl* returned, was promoted, and given valid(?) *parganas*[1935] worth 25 laks.

(*g. Action against the rebels of the East.*)

Sl. Ibrāhīm had appointed several amīrs under Muṣṭafa *Farmūlī* and Fīrūz Khān *Sārang-khānī*, to act against the rebel amīrs of the East (*Pūrab*). Muṣṭafa had fought them and thoroughly drubbed them, giving them more than one good beating. He dying before Ibrāhīm's defeat, his younger brother Shaikh Bāyazīd—Ibrāhīm being occupied with a momentous matter[1936]—had led and watched over his elder brother's men. He now came to serve me, together with Fīrūz Khān, Maḥmūd Khān *Nuḥānī* and Qāẓī Jīā. I shewed them greater kindness and favour than was their claim; giving to Fīrūz Khān 1 *krūr*, 46 *laks* and 5000 *tankas* from Jūnpūr, to Shaikh Bāyazīd 1 *krūr*, 48 *laks* and 50,000 *tankas* from Aūd (Oude), to Maḥmūd Khān 90 *laks* and 35,000 *tankas* from Ghāzīpūr, and to Qāẓī Jīā 20 *laks*.[1937]

(*h. Gifts made to various officers.*)

It was a few days after the 'Īd of Shawwāl[1938] that a large party was held in the pillared-porch of the domed building standing in the middle of Sl.

Ibrāhīm's private apartments. At this party there were bestowed on Humāyūn a *chār-qab*,[1939] a sword-belt,[1940] a *tīpūchāq* horse with saddle mounted in gold; on Chīn-tīmūr Sulṭān, Mahdī Khwāja and Muḥammad Sl. Mīrzā *chār-qabs*, sword-belts and dagger-belts; and to the begs andFol. 297. braves, to each according to his rank, were given sword-belts, dagger-belts, and dresses of honour, in all to the number specified below:—

2 items (*rā's*) of *tīpūchāq* horses with saddles.

16 items (*qabẓa*) of poinards, set with jewels, etc.

8 items (*qabẓa*) of purpet over-garments.

2 items (*tob*) of jewelled sword-belts.

— items (*qabẓa*) of broad daggers (*jamd'kar*) set with jewels.

25 items of jewelled hangers (*khanjar*).

— items of gold-hilted Hindī knives (*kārd*).

51 pieces of purpet.

On the day of this party it rained amazingly, rain falling thirteen times. As outside places had been assigned to a good many people, they were drowned out (*gharaq*).

(*i. Of various forts and postings.*)

Samāna (in Patiāla) had been given to Muḥammadī Kūkūldāsh and it had been arranged for him to make swift descent on Saṃbal (Saṃbhal), but Saṃbal was now bestowed on Humāyūn, in addition to his guerdon of Ḥiṣār-fīrūza, and in his service was Hindū Beg. To suit this, therefore, Hindū Beg was sent to make the incursion in Muḥammadī's place, and with him Kitta Beg, Bābā *Qashqa's* (brother) Malik Qāsim and his elder and younger brethren, Mullā Apāq and Shaikh Gūran (G'hūran) with the quiver-wearers from Between-two-waters (*Mīān-dū-āb*). Fol. 297b.Three or four times a person had come from Qāsim *Saṃbalī*, saying, "The renegade Bīban is besieging Saṃbal and has brought it to extremity; come quickly." Bīban, with the array and the preparation (*hayāt*) with which he had deserted us,[1941] had gone skirting the hills and gathering up Afghān and Hindūstānī deserters, until, finding Saṃbal at this juncture ill-garrisoned, he laid siege to it. Hindū Beg and Kitta Beg and the rest of those appointed to make the incursion, got to the Ahār-passage[1942] and from there sent ahead

Bābā *Qashqa's* Malik Qāsim with his elder and younger brethren, while they themselves were getting over the water. Malik Qāsim crossed, advanced swiftly with from 100 to 150 men—his own and his brethren's—and reached Saṃbal by the Mid-day Prayer. Bīban for his part came out of his camp in array. Malik Qāsim and his troop moved rapidly forward, got the fort in their rear, and came to grips. Bīban could make no stand; he fled. Malik Qāsim cut off the heads of part of his force, took many horses, a few elephants and a mass of booty. Next day when the other begs arrived, Qāsim *Saṃbalī* came out and saw them, but not liking to surrender the fort, made them false pretences. One day Shaikh Gūran (G'hūran) and Hindū Beg having talked the matter over with them, got Qāsim *Saṃbalī* out to the presence of the begs, and took men of ours into the fort. They brought Qāsim's wife and dependents safely out, and sent Qāsim (to Court).[1943]

Qalandar the foot-man was sent to Niẓ̤ām Khān in Bīāna with royal letters of promise and threat; with these was sentFol. 298. also the following little off-hand (Persian) verse:—[1944]

Strive not with the Turk, o Mīr of Bīāna!

His skill and his courage are obvious.

If thou come not soon, nor give ear to counsel,—

What need to detail (*bayān*) what is obvious?

Bīāna being one of the famous forts of Hindūstān, the senseless mannikin, relying on its strength, demanded what not even its strength could enforce. Not giving him a good answer, we ordered siege apparatus to be looked to.

Bābā Qulī Beg was sent with royal letters of promise and threat to Muḥammad *Zaitūn* (in Dūlpūr); Muḥammad *Zaitūn* also made false excuses.

While we were still in Kābul, Rānā Sangā had sent an envoy to testify to his good wishes and to propose this plan: "If the honoured Pādshāh will come to near Dihlī from that side, I from this will move on Āgra." But I beat Ibrāhīm, I took Dihlī and Āgra, and up to now that Pagan has given no sign soever of moving. After a while he went and laid siege to Kandār[1945] a fort in which was Makan's son, Ḥasan by name. This Ḥasan-of-Makan had sent a person to me several times, but had not shewn himself. We had not been able to detachFol. 298b. reinforcement for him because, as the forts round-about—Atāwa (Etāwa), Dūlpūr, and Bīāna—had not yet surrendered, and the Eastern Afghāns were seated with their army in obstinate rebellion two or three marches on the Āgra side of Qanūj, my mind was not quite free from the whirl and strain of things close at hand. Makan's Ḥasan therefore, becoming helpless, had surrendered Kandār two or three months ago.

Ḥusain Khān (*Nuḥānī*) became afraid in Rāprī, and he abandoning it, it was given to Muḥammad 'Alī *Jang-jang*.

To Quṯb Khān in Etāwa royal letters of promise and threat had been sent several times, but as he neither came and saw me, nor abandoned Etāwa and got away, it was given to Mahdī Khwāja and he was sent against it with a strong reinforcement of begs and household troops under the command of Muḥammad Sl. Mīrzā, Sl. Muḥammad *Dūldāī*, Muḥammad 'Alī *Jang-jang* and 'Abdu'l-'azīz the Master of the Horse. Qanūj was given to Sl. Muḥammad *Dūldāī*; he was also (as mentioned) appointed against Etāwa; so too were Fīrūz Khān, Maḥmūd Khān, Shaikh Bāyazīd and Qāẓī Jīā, highly favoured commanders to whom Eastern *parganas* had been given.

Fol. 299.Muḥammad *Zaitūn*, who was seated in Dūlpūr, deceived us and did not come. We gave Dūlpūr to Sl. Junaid *Barlās* and reinforced him by appointing 'Ādil Sulṭān, Muḥammadī Kūkūldāsh, Shāh Manṣūr *Barlās*, Qūtlūq-qadam, Treasurer Walī, Jān Beg, 'Abdu'l-lāh, Pīr-qulī, and Shāh Ḥasan *Yāragī* (or *Bāragī*), who were to attack Dūlpūr, take it, make it over to Sl. Junaid *Barlās* and advance on Bīāna.

(j. Plan of operations adopted.)

These armies appointed, we summoned the Turk amīrs[1946] and the Hindūstān amīrs, and tossed the following matters in amongst them:—The various rebel amīrs of the East, that is to say, those under Nāṣir Khān *Nuḥānī* and Ma'rūf *Farmūlī*, have crossed Gang (Ganges) with 40 to 50,000 men, taken Qanūj, and now lie some three miles on our side of the river. The Pagan Rānā Sangā has captured Kandār and is in a hostile and mischievous attitude. The end of the Rains is near. It seems expedient to move either against the rebels or the Pagan, since the task of the forts near-by is easy; when the great foes are got rid of, what road will remain open for the rest? Rānā Sangā is thought not to be the equal of the rebels.

To this all replied unanimously, "Rānā Sangā is the most distant, and it is not known that he will come nearer; the enemy who is closest at hand must first be got rid of. We are for riding against the rebels." Humāyūn then represented,Fol. 299b. "What need is there for the Pādshāh to ride out? This service I will do." This came as a pleasure to every-one; the Turk and Hind amīrs gladly accepted his views; he was appointed for the East. A Kābulī of Aḥmad-i-qāsim's was sent galloping off to tell the armies that had been despatched against Dūlpūr to join Humāyūn at Chandwār;[1947] also those sent against Etāwa under Mahdī Khwāja and Muḥammad Sl. M. were ordered to join him.

(*August 21st*) Humāyūn set out on Thursday the 13th of Ẕū'l-qa'da, dismounted at a little village called Jilīsīr (Jalesar) some 3 *kurohs* from Āgra, there stayed one night, then moved forward march by march.

(*k. Khwāja Kalān's departure.*)

(*August 28th*) On Thursday the 20th of this same month, Khwāja Kalān started for Kābul.

(*l. Of gardens and pleasaunces.*)

One of the great defects of Hindūstān being its lack of running-waters,[1948] it kept coming to my mind that waters should be made to flow by means of wheels erected wherever I might settle down, also that grounds should be laid out in an orderly and symmetrical way. With this object in view, we crossed the Jūn-water to look at garden-grounds a few days after entering Āgra. Those grounds were so bad and unattractive that we traversed them with a hundred disgusts and repulsions. So ugly and displeasing were they, that the idea of making aFol. 300. Chār-bāgh in them passed from my mind, but needs must! as there was no other land near Āgra, that same ground was taken in hand a few days later.

The beginning was made with the large well from which water comes for the Hot-bath, and also with the piece of ground where the tamarind-trees and the octagonal tank now are. After that came the large tank with its enclosure; after that the tank and *tālār*[1949] in front of the outer(?) residence[1950]; after that the private-house (*khilwat-khāna*) with its garden and various dwellings; after that the Hot-bath. Then in that charmless and disorderly Hind, plots of garden[1951] were seen laid out with order and symmetry, with suitable borders and parterres in every corner, and in every border rose and narcissus in perfect arrangement.

(*m. Construction of a chambered-well.*)

Three things oppressed us in Hindūstān, its heat, its violent winds, its dust. Against all three the Bath is a protection, for in it, what is known of dust and wind? and in the heats it is so chilly that one is almost cold. The bath-room in which the heated tank is, is altogether of stone, the whole, except for the *izāra* (dado?) of white stone, being, pavement and roofing, of red Biāna stone.

Khalīfa also and Shaikh Zain, Yūnas-i-'alī and whoever got Fol. 300b.land on that other bank of the river laid out regular and orderly gardens with tanks, made running-waters also by setting up wheels like those in Dīpālpūr and Lāhor. The people of Hind who had never seen grounds planned so symmetrically and thus laid out, called the side of the Jūn where (our) residences were, Kābul.

In an empty space inside the fort, which was between Ibrāhīm's residence and the ramparts, I ordered a large chambered-well (*wāīn*) to be made, measuring 10 by 10,[1952] a large well with a flight of steps, which in Hindūstān is called a *wāīn*.[1953] This well was begun before the Chār-bāgh[1954]; they were busy digging it in the true Rains (*'aīn bīshkāl*, Sāwan and Bhadon); it fell in several times and buried the hired workmen; it was finished after the Holy Battle with Rānā Sangā, as is stated in the inscription on the stone that bears the chronogram of its completion. It is a complete *wāīn*, having a three-storeyed house in it. The lowest storey consists of three rooms, each of which opens on the descending steps, at intervals of three steps from one another. When the water is at its lowest, it is one step below the bottom chamber; when it rises in the Rains, it sometimes goes into the top storey. In the middle storey an inner chamber has been excavated which connects with the domed building in which the bullock turns the well-wheel. TheFol. 301. top storey is a single room, reached from two sides by 5 or 6 steps which lead down to it from the enclosure overlooked from the well-head. Facing the right-hand way down, is the stone inscribed with the date of completion. At the side of this well is another the bottom of which may be at half the depth of the first, and into which water comes from that first one when the bullock turns the wheel in the domed building aforementioned. This second well also is fitted with a wheel, by means of which water is carried along the ramparts to the high-garden. A stone building (*tāshdīn 'imārat*) stands at the mouth of the well and there is an outer(?) mosque[1955] outside (*tāshqārī*) the enclosure in which the well is. The mosque is not well done; it is in the Hindūstānī fashion.

(*n. Humāyūn's campaign.*)

At the time Humāyūn got to horse, the rebel amīrs under Naṣīr Khān *Nuḥānī* and Ma'rūf *Farmūlī* were assembled at Jājmāū.[1956] Arrived within 20 to 30 miles of them, he sent out Mūmin Ātāka for news; it became a raid for loot; Mūmin Ātāka was not able to bring even the least useful information. The rebels heard about him however, made no stay but fled and got away. After Mūmin Ātāka, Qusm-nāī(?) was sent for news, with Bābā Chuhra[1957] and Būjka; they brought it of the breaking-up and flight of the rebels. Humāyūn advancing, took Jājmāū Fol. 301b.and passed on. Near Dilmāū[1958] Fatḥ Khān *Sarwānī* came and saw him, and was sent to me with Mahdī Khwāja and Muḥammad Sl. Mīrzā.

(*o. News of the Aūzbegs.*)

This year 'Ubaidu'l-lāh Khān (*Aūzbeg*) led an army out of Bukhārā against Marv. In the citadel of Marv were perhaps 10 to 15 peasants whom he overcame and killed; then having taken the revenues of Marv in 40 or 50 days,[1959] he went on to Sarakhs. In Sarakhs were some 30 to 40 Red-heads

(*Qīzīl-bāsh*) who did not surrender, but shut the Gate; the peasantry however scattered them and opened the Gate to the Aūzbeg who entering, killed the Red-heads. Sarakhs taken, he went against Ṭ̤ūs and Mashhad. The inhabitants of Mashhad being helpless, let him in. Ṭ̤ūs he besieged for 8 months, took possession of on terms, did not keep those terms, but killed every man of name and made their women captive.

(*p. Affairs of Gujrāt.*)

In this year Bahādur Khān,—he who now rules in Gujrāt in the place of his father Sl. Muz̤affar *Gujrātī*—having gone to Sl. Ibrāhīm after quarrel with his father, had been received without honour. He had sent dutiful letters to me while I was near Pānī-pat; I had replied by royal letters of favour and kindness summoning him to me. He had thought of coming, but changing his mind, drew off from Ibrāhīm's army towards Gujrāt. Meantime his father Sl. Muz̤affar had died (Friday Jumāda II. 2nd AH.-March 16th 1526 AD.); his elder brother Sikandar Shāh who was Sl. Muz̤affar's eldest son, had become ruler in their father's place and, owing to his evil disposition,Fol. 302. had been strangled by his slave 'Imādu'l-mulk, acting with others (Sha'ban 14th—May 25th). Bahādur Khān, while he was on his road for Gujrāt, was invited and escorted to sit in his father's place under the style Bahādur Shāh (Ramẓān 26th—July 6th). He for his part did well; he retaliated by death on 'Imādu'l-mulk for his treachery to his salt, and killed some others of his father's begs.[1960] People point at him as a dreadnaught (*bī bāk*) youth and a shedder of much blood.

933 AH.-OCT. 8TH 1526 TO SEP. 27TH 1527 AD.1961

(a. Announcement of the birth of a son.)

In Muḥarram Beg Wais brought the news of Fārūq's birth; though a footman had brought it already, he came this month for the gift to the messenger of good tidings.[1962] The birth must have been on Friday eve, Shawwāl 23rd (932 AH.-August 2nd 1526 AD.); the name given was Fārūq.

(b. Casting of a mortar.)

(October 22nd-Muḥarram 15th) Ustād 'Alī-qulī had been ordered to cast a large mortar for use against Bīāna and other forts which had not yet submitted. When all the furnaces and materials were ready, he sent a person to me and, on Monday the 15th of the month, we went to see the mortar cast. Round the mortar-mould he had had eight furnaces made in which Fol. 302b.were the molten materials. From below each furnace a channel went direct to the mould. When he opened the furnace-holes on our arrival, the molten metal poured like water through all these channels into the mould. After awhile and before the mould was full, the flow stopped from one furnace after another. Ustād 'Alī-qulī must have made some miscalculation either as to the furnaces or the materials. In his great distress, he was for throwing himself into the mould of molten metal, but we comforted him, put a robe of honour on him, and so brought him out of his shame. The mould was left a day or two to cool; when it was opened, Ustād 'Alī-qulī with great delight sent to say, "The stone-chamber (*tāsh-awī*) is without defect; to cast the powder-compartment (*dārū-khāna*) is easy." He got the stone-chamber out and told off a body of men to accoutre[1963] it, while he busied himself with casting the powder-compartment.

(c. Varia.)

Mahdī Khwāja arrived bringing Fatḥ Khān *Sarwānī* from Humāyūn's presence, they having parted from him in Dilmāū. I looked with favour on Fatḥ Khān, gave him the *parganas* that had been his father 'Aẓam-humāyūn's, and other lands also, one *pargana* given being worth a *krūr* and 60 *laks*.[1964]

In Hindūstān they give permanent titles [*muqarrarī khiṭāblār*] to highly-favoured amīrs, one such being 'Aẓam-humāyūn (*August Might*), one Khān-i-jahān (Khan-of-the-world), anotherFol. 303. Khān-i-khānān (Khān-of-khāns). Fatḥ Khān's father's title was 'Aẓam-humāyūn but I set this aside because on account of Humāyūn it was not seemly for any person to bear it, and I gave Fatḥ Khān *Sarwānī* the title of Khān-i-jahān.

(*November 14th*) On Wednesday the 8th of Ṣafar[1965] awnings were set up (in the Chār-bāgh) at the edge of the large tank beyond the tamarind-trees, and an entertainment was prepared there. We invited Fatḥ Khān *Sarwānī* to a wine-party, gave him wine, bestowed on him a turban and head-to-foot of my own wearing, uplifted his head with kindness and favour[1966] and allowed him to go to his own districts. It was arranged for his son Maḥmūd to remain always in waiting.

(*d. Various military matters.*)

(*November 30th*) On Wednesday the 24th of Muḥarram[1967] Muḥammad 'Alī (son of Mihtar) Ḥaidar the stirrup-holder was sent (to Humāyūn) with this injunction, "As—thanks be to God!—the rebels have fled, do you, as soon as this messenger arrives, appoint a few suitable begs to Jūnpūr, and come quickly to us yourself, for Rānā Sangā the Pagan is conveniently close; let us think first of him!"

After (Humāyūn's) army had gone to the East, we appointed, to make a plundering excursion into the Bīāna neighbourhood, Tardī Beg (brother) of Qūj Beg with his elder brother Sher-afgan, Muḥammad Khalīl the master-gelder (*akhta-begī*) with his brethren and the gelders (*akhtachīlār*),[1968] Rustam *Turkmān* with his brethren, and also, of the Hindūstānī people, Daud *Sarwānī*. Fol. 303b.If they, by promise and persuasion, could make the Bīāna garrison look towards us, they were to do so; if not, they were to weaken the enemy by raid and plunder.

In the fort of Tahangar[1969] was 'Ālam Khān the elder brother of that same Niẓām Khān of Bīāna. People of his had come again and again to set forth his obedience and well-wishing; he now took it on himself to say, "If the Pādshāh appoint an army, it will be my part by promise and persuasion to bring in the quiver-weavers of Bīāna and to effect the capture of that fort." This being so, the following orders were given to the braves of Tardī Beg's expedition, "As 'Ālam Khān, a local man, has taken it on himself to serve and submit in this manner, act you with him and in the way he approves in this matter of Bīāna." Swordsmen though some Hindūstānīs may be, most of them are ignorant and unskilled in military move and stand (*yūrūsh u tūrūsh*), in soldierly counsel and procedure. When our expedition joined 'Ālam Khān, he paid no attention to what any-one else said, did not consider whether his action was good or bad, but went close up to Bīāna, taking our men with him. Our expedition numbered from 250 to 300 Turks with somewhat over 2000 Hindūstānīs and local people, while Niẓām Khān of Bīāna's Afghāns and *sipāhīs*[1970] were an army of over 4000 horse and of Fol. 304.foot-men themselves again, more than 10,000. Niẓām Khān looked his opponents over, sallied suddenly out and, his massed horse charging down, put our expeditionary force to flight. His men unhorsed his elder brother 'Ālam Khān, took 5 or 6 others prisoner and contrived to capture part of the baggage. As we had already made encouraging promises to Niẓām Khān, we now, spite of this last impropriety, pardoned all earlier and this later fault, and sent him royal letters. As he heard of Rānā Sangā's rapid advance, he had no resource but to call on Sayyid Rafī'[1971] for mediation, surrender the fort to our men, and come in with Sayyid Rafī', when he was exalted to the felicity of an interview.[1972] I bestowed on him a pargana in Mīān-dū-āb worth 20 *laks*.[1973] Dost, Lord-of-the-gate was sent for a time to Bīāna, but a few days later it was bestowed on Madhī Khwāja with a fixed allowance of 70 *laks*,[1974] and he was given leave to go there.

Tātār Khān *Sārang-khānī*, who was in Gūālīār, had been sending constantly to assure us of his obedience and good-wishes. After the pagan took Kandār and was close to Bīāna, Dharmankat, one of the Gūālīār rājas, and another pagan styled Khān-i-jahān, went into the Gūālīār neighbourhood and, coveting the fort, began to stir trouble and tumult. Tātār Khān, thus placed in difficulty, was for surrendering Gūālīār (to us). Most of our begs, household and best braves being away with (Humāyūn's) army or on various raids, we joined to Raḥīm-dādFol. 304b. a few Bhīra men and Lāhorīs with Hastachī[1975] *tūnqiṭār* and his brethren. We assigned *parganas* in Gūālīār itself to all those mentioned above. Mullā Apāq and Shaikh Gurān (G'hurān) went also with them, they to return after Raḥīm-dād was established in Gūālīār. By the time they were near Gūālīār however, Tātār Khān's views had changed, and he did not invite them into the fort. Meantime Shaikh Muḥammad *Ghauṣ* (Helper), a darwīsh-like man, not only very learned but with a large following of students and disciples, sent from inside the fort to say to Raḥīm-dād, "Get yourselves into the fort somehow, for the views of this person (Tātār Khān) have changed, and he has evil in his mind." Hearing this, Raḥīm-dād sent to say to Tātār Khān, "There is danger from the Pagan to those outside; let me bring a few men into the fort and let the rest stay outside." Under insistence, Tātār Khān agreed to this, and Raḥīm-dād went in with rather few men. Said he, "Let our people stay near this Gate," posted them near the Hātī-pul (Elephant-gate) and through that Gate during that same night brought in the whole of his troop. Next day, Tātār Khān, reduced to helplessness, willy-nilly, made over the fort, and set out to come and wait on me in Āgra. A subsistence allowance of 20 *laks* was assigned to him on Bīānwān *pargana*.[1976]

Fol. 305.Muḥammad *Zaitūn* also took the only course open to him by surrendering Dūlpūr and coming to wait on me. A *pargana* worth a few *laks* was bestowed on him. Dūlpūr was made a royal domain (*khālṣa*) with Abū'l-fatḥ *Turkmān*[1977] as its military-collector (*shiqdār*).

In the Ḥiṣār-fīrūza neighbourhood Ḥamīd Khān *Sārang-khānī* with a body of his own Afghāns and of the Panī Afghāns he had collected—from 3 to 4,000 in all—was in a hostile and troublesome attitude. On Wednesday the 15th Ṣafar (Nov. 21st) we appointed against him Chīn-tīmūr Sl. (*Chaghatāī*) with the commanders Secretary Aḥmadī, Abū'l-fatḥ *Turkmān*, Malik Dād *Kararānī*[1978] and Mujāhid Khān of Multān. These going, fell suddenly on him from a distance, beat his Afghāns well, killed a mass of them and sent in many heads.

(*e. Embassy from Persia.*)

In the last days of Ṣafar, Khwājagī Asad who had been sent to Shāh-zāda Ṭahmāsp[1979] in 'Irāq, returned with a Turkmān named Sulaimān who amongst other gifts brought two Circassian girls (*qīzlār*).

(*f. Attempt to poison Bābur.*)

(*Dec. 21st*) On Friday the 16th of the first Rabī' a strange event occurred which was detailed in a letter written to Kābul. That letter is inserted here just as it was written, without addition or taking-away, and is as follows:—[1980]

"The details of the momentous event of Friday the 16th of the first Rabī' in the date 933 [Dec. 21st 1526 AD.] are as follows:—The ill-omened old woman[1981] Ibrāhim's mother heardFol. 305b. that I ate things from the hands of Hindūstānīs—the thing being that three or four months earlier, as I had not seen Hindūstānī dishes, I had ordered Ibrāhīm's cooks to be brought and out of 50 or 60 had kept four. Of this she heard, sent to Atāwa (Etāwa) for Aḥmad the *chāshnīgīr*—in Hindūstān they call a taster (*bakāwal*) a *chāshnīgīr*—and, having got him,[1982] gave a *tūla* of poison, wrapped in a square of paper,—as has been mentioned a *tūla* is rather more than 2 *misqāls*[1983]—into the hand of a slave-woman who was to give it to him. That poison Aḥmad gave to the Hindūstānī cooks in our kitchen, promising them four *parganas* if they would get it somehow into the food. Following the first slave-woman that ill-omened old woman sent a second to see if the first did or did not give the poison she had received to Aḥmad. Well was it that Aḥmad put the poison not into the cooking-pot but on a dish! He did not put it into the pot because I had strictly ordered the tasters to compel any Hindūstānīs who were present while food was cooking in the pots, to taste that food.[1984] Our graceless tasters were neglectful when the food (*āsh*) was being dished up. Thin slices of bread were put on a porcelain dish; on these less than half of the paper packet of poison was sprinkled, and over this buttered Fol. 306.fritters were laid. It would have been bad if the poison had been strewn on the fritters or thrown into the pot. In his confusion, the man threw the larger half into the fire-place."

"On Friday, late after the Afternoon Prayer, when the cooked meats were set out, I ate a good deal of a dish of hare and also much fried carrot, took a few mouthfuls of the poisoned Hindūstānī food without noticing any unpleasant flavour, took also a mouthful or two of dried-meat (*qāq*). Then I felt sick. As some dried meat eaten on the previous day had had an unpleasant taste, I thought my nausea due to the dried-meat. Again and again my heart rose; after retching two or three times I was near vomiting on the table-cloth. At last I saw it would not do, got up, went retching every moment of the way to the water-closet (*āb-khāna*) and on reaching it vomited much. Never had I vomited after food, used not to do so indeed while drinking. I became suspicious; I had the cooks put in ward and ordered some of the vomit given to a dog and the dog to be watched. It was somewhat out-of-sorts near the first watch of the next day; its belly was swollen and however much people threw stones at it and turned it over, it did not get up. In that state it remained till mid-day; it then got up; it did not die. Fol. 306b.One or two of the braves who also had eaten of that dish, vomited a good deal next day; one was in a very bad state. In the end all escaped. (*Persian*) 'An evil arrived but happily passed on!' God gave me new-birth! I am coming from that other world; I am born today of my mother; I was sick; I live; through God, I know today the worth of life!"[1985]

"I ordered Pay-master Sl. Muḥammad to watch the cook; when he was taken for torture (*qīn*), he related the above particulars one after another."

"Monday being Court-day, I ordered the grandees and notables, amīrs and wazīrs to be present and that those two men and two women should be brought and questioned. They there related the particulars of the affair. That taster I had cut in pieces, that cook skinned alive; one of those women I had thrown under an elephant, the other shot with a match-lock. The old woman (*būā*) I had kept under guard; she will meet her doom, the captive of her own act."[1986]

"On Saturday I drank a bowl of milk, on Sunday *'araq* in which stamped-clay was dissolved.[1987] On Monday I drank milk in which were dissolved stamped-clay and the best theriac,[1988] a strong purge. As on the first day, Saturday, something very dark like parched bile was voided."

"Thanks be to God! no harm has been done. Till now I had not known so well how sweet a thing life can seem! As the line has it, 'He who has been near to death knows the worth of life.' Spite of myself, I am all upset whenever the dreadfulFol. 307. occurrence comes back to my mind. It must have been God's favour gave me life anew; with what words can I thank him?"

"Although the terror of the occurrence was too great for words, I have written all that happened, with detail and circumstance, because I said to myself, 'Don't let their hearts be kept in anxiety!' Thanks be to God! there may be other days yet to see! All has passed off well and for good; have no fear or anxiety in your minds."

"This was written on Tuesday the 20th of the first Rabī', I being then in the Chār-bāgh."

When we were free from the anxiety of these occurrences, the above letter was written and sent to Kābul.

(*g. Dealings with Ibrāhīm's family.*)

As this great crime had raised its head through that ill-omened old woman (*būā-i-bad-bakht*), she was given over to Yūnas-i-'alī and Khwājagī Asad who after taking her money and goods, slaves and slave-women (*dādūk*), made her over for careful watch to 'Abdu'r-raḥīm *shaghāwal.*[1989] Her grandson, Ibrāhīm's son had been cared for with much respect and delicacy, but as the attempt on my life had been made, clearly, by that family, it did not seem advisable to keep him in Agra; he was joined therefore to Mullā Sarsān—who had come from Kāmrān on important business—and was started off with the Mullā to Kāmrān on Thursday Rabī' I. 29th (Jan. 3rd 1527 AD.).[1990]

(*h. Humāyūn's campaign.*)

Fol. 307b.Humāyūn, acting against the Eastern rebels[1991] took Jūna-pūr (*sic*), went swiftly against Naṣīr Khān (*Nūḥānī*) in Ghāzī-pūr and found that he had gone across the Gang-river, presumably on news* of Humāyūn's approach. From Ghāzī-pūr Humāyūn went against Kharīd[1992] but the Afghāns of the place had crossed the Sārū-water (Gogra) presumably on the news* of his coming. Kharīd was plundered and the army turned back.

Humāyūn, in accordance with my arrangements, left Shāh Mīr Ḥusain and Sl. Junaid with a body of effective braves in Jūna-pūr, posted Qāẓī Jīā with them, and placed Shaikh Bāyazīd [*Farmūlī*] in Aude (Oude). These important matters settled, he crossed Gang from near Karrah-Mānikpūr and took the Kālpī road. When he came opposite Kālpī, in which was Jalāl Khān *Jik-hat's* (son) 'Ālam Khān who had sent me dutiful letters but had not waited on me himself, he sent some-one to chase fear from 'Ālam Khān's heart and so brought him along (to Āgra).

Humāyūn arrived and waited on me in the Garden of Eight-paradises[1993] on Sunday the 3rd of the 2nd Rabī' (Jan. 6th 1527 AD.). On the same day Khwāja Dost-i-khāwand arrived from Kābul.

(*i. Rānā Sangā's approach.*)[1994]

Meantime Mahdī Khwāja's people began to come in, treading on one another's heels and saying, "The Rānā's advance is certain. Ḥasan Khān *Mīwātī* is heard of also as likely to join him. They must be thought about above all else. It would favour our fortune, if a troop came ahead of the army to reinforce Bīāna."Fol. 308.

Deciding to get to horse, we sent on, to ride light to Bīāna, the commanders Muḥammad Sl. Mīrzā, Yūnas-i-'alī, Shāh Manṣūr *Barlās*, Kitta Beg, Qismatī[1995] and Būjka.

In the fight with Ibrāhīm, Ḥasan Khān *Mīwātī's* son Nāhar Khān had fallen into our hands; we had kept him as an hostage and, ostensibly on his account, his father had been making comings-and-goings with us, constantly asking for him. It now occurred to several people that if Ḥasan Khān were conciliated by sending him his son, he would thereby be the more favourably disposed and his waiting on me might be the better brought about. Accordingly Nāhar Khān was dressed in a robe of honour; promises were made to him for his father, and he was given leave to go. That hypocritical mannikin [Ḥasan Khān] must have waited just till his son had leave from me to go, for on hearing of this and while his son as yet had not joined him, he came out of Alūr (Alwar) and at once joined Rānā Sangā in Toda(bhīm, Āgra District). It must have been ill-judged to let his son go just then.

Meantime much rain was falling; parties were frequent; even Humāyūn was present at them and, abhorrent though it was to him, sinned[1996] every few days.

(*j. Tramontane affairs.*)

One of the strange events in these days of respite[1997] was this:—When Humāyūn was coming from Fort Victory. (Qila'-i-ẓạfar) to join the Hindūstān army, (Muḥ. 932 AH.-Oct. 1525 AD.)Fol. 308b. Mullā Bābā of Pashāghar (*Chaghatāī*) and his younger brother Bābā Shaikh deserted on the way, and went to Kītīn-qarā Sl. (*Aūzbeg*), into whose hands Balkh had fallen through the enfeeblement of its garrison.[1998] This hollow mannikin and his younger brother having taken the labours of this side (Cis-Balkh?) on their own necks, come into the neighbourhood of Aībak, Khurram and Sār-bāgh.[1999]

Shāh Sikandar—his footing in Ghūrī lost through the surrender of Balkh—is about to make over that fort to the Aūzbeg, when Mullā Bābā and Bābā Shaikh, coming with a few Aūzbegs, take possession of it. Mīr Hamah, as his fort is close by, has no help for it; he is for submitting to the Aūzbeg, but a few days later Mullā Bābā and Bābā Shaikh come with a few Aūzbegs to Mīr Hamah's fort, purposing to make the Mīr and his troop march out and to take them towards Balkh. Mīr Hamah makes Bābā Shaikh dismount inside the fort, and gives the rest felt huts (*aūtāq*) here and there. He slashes at Bābā Shaikh, puts him and some others in bonds, and sends a man galloping off to Tīngrī-bīrdī (*Qūchīn*, in Qūndūz). Tīngrī-bīrdī sends off Yār-i-'alī and 'Abdu'l-laṭīf with a few effective braves, but before they reach Mīr Hamah's fort, Mullā Bābā has arrived there with his Aūzbegs; he had thought of a hand-to-hand fight (*aūrūsh-mūrūsh*), but he can do nothing. Mīr Hamah and his men joined Tīngrī-bīrdī's and came to Qūndūz. Bābā Shaikh's wound must have been severe; they cut his head off and Mīr Hamah brought Fol. 309.it (to Āgra) in these same days of respite. I uplifted his head with favour and kindness, distinguishing him amongst his fellows and equals. When Bāqī *shaghāwal* went [to Balkh][2000] I promised him a *ser* of gold for the head of each of the ill-conditioned old couple; one *ser* of gold was now given to Mīr Hamah for Bābā Shaikh's head, over and above the favours referred to above.[2001]

(*k. Action of part of the Bīāna reinforcement.*)

Qismatī who had ridden light for Bīāna, brought back several heads he had cut off; when he and Būjka had gone with a few braves to get news, they had beaten two of the Pagan's scouting-parties and had made 70 to 80 prisoners. Qismatī brought news that Ḥasan Khān *Mīwātī* really had joined Rānā Sangā.

(*l. Trial-test of the large mortar of f. 302.*)

(*Feb. 10th*) On Sunday the 8th of the month (Jumāda I.), I went to see Ustād 'Alī-qulī discharge stones from that large mortar of his in casting which the stone-chamber was without defect and which he had completed afterwards by casting the powder-compartment. It was discharged at the Afternoon Prayer; the throw of the stone was 1600 paces. A gift was made to the Master of a sword-belt, robe of honour, and *tīpūchāq* (horse).

(*m. Bābur leaves Āgra against Rānā Sangā.*)

(*Feb. 11th*) On Monday the 9th of the first Jumāda, we got out of the suburbs of Āgra, on our journey (*safar*) for the Holy War, and dismounted in the open country, where we remained three or four days to collect our army and be its rallying-point.[2002] As little confidence was placed in Hindūstānī people, the Hindūstān amīrs were inscribed for expeditions to this or to that side:—'Ālam Khān (*Tahangarī*) was sent hastily to Gūālīār toFol. 309b. reinforce Raḥīm-dād; Makan, Qāsim Beg *Sanbalī* (*Saṃbhalī*), Ḥamīd with his elder and younger brethren and Muḥammad *Zaitūn* were inscribed to go swiftly to Sanbal.

(*n. Defeat of the advance-force.*)

Into this same camp came the news that owing to Rānā Sangā's swift advance with all his army,[2003] our scouts were able neither to get into the fort (Bīāna) themselves nor to send news into it. The Bīāna garrison made a rather incautious sally too far out; the enemy fell on them in some force and put them to rout.[2004] There Sangur Khān *Janjūha* became a martyr. Kitta Beg had galloped into the pell-mell without his cuirass; he got one pagan afoot (*yāyāglātīb*) and was overcoming him, when the pagan snatched a sword from one of Kitta Beg's own servants and slashed the Beg across the shoulder. Kitta Beg suffered great pain; he could not come into the Holy-battle with Rānā Sangā, was long in recovering and always remained blemished.

Whether because they were themselves afraid, or whether to frighten others is not known but Qismatī, Shāh Manṣūr *Barlās* and all from Bīāna praised and lauded the fierceness and valour of the pagan army.

Qāsim Master-of-the-horse was sent from the starting-ground (*safar qīlghān yūrt*) with his spadesmen, to dig many wells where the army was next to dismount in the Madhākūr *pargana*.

(*Feb. 16th*) Marching out of Āgra on Saturday the 14th of the first Jumāda, dismount was made where the wells had been Fol. 310.dug. We marched on next day. It crossed my mind that the well-watered ground for a large camp was at Sīkrī.[2005] It being possible that the Pagan was encamped there and in possession of the water, we arrayed precisely, in right, left and centre. As Qismatī and Darwīsh-i-muḥammad *Sārbān* in their comings and goings had seen and got to know all sides of Bīāna, they were sent ahead to look for camping-ground on the bank of the Sīkrī-lake (*kūl*). When we reached the (Madhākūr) camp, persons were sent galloping off to tell Mahdī Khwāja and the Bīāna garrison to join me without delay. Humāyūn's servant Beg Mīrak *Mughūl* was sent out with a few braves to get news of the Pagan. They started that night, and next morning brought word that he was heard of as having arrived and dismounted at a place one *kuroh* (2 miles) on our side (*aīlkārāk*) of Basāwar.[2006] On this same day Mahdī Khwāja and Muḥammad Sl. Mīrzā rejoined us with the troops that had ridden light to Bīāna.

(*o. Discomfiture of a reconnoitring party.*)

The begs were appointed in turns for scouting-duty. When it was 'Abdu'l-'azīz's turn, he went out of Sīkrī, looking neither before nor behind, right out along the road to Kanwā which is 5 *kuroh* (10 m.) away. The Rānā must have been marching forward; he heard of our men's moving out in their reinless (*jalāū-sīz*) way, and made 4 or 5,000 of his own fall suddenly on them. With 'Abdu'l-'azīz and Mullā Apāq may have been 1000 to 1500 men; they took no stock of their opponents but justFol. 310b. got to grips; they were hurried off at once, many of them being made prisoner.

On news of this, we despatched Khalīfa's Muḥibb-i-'alī with Khalīfa's retainers. Mullā Ḥusain and some others *aūbrūqsūbrūq*[2007]* were sent to support them,[2008] and Muḥammad 'Alī *Jang-jang* also. Presumably it was before the arrival of this first, Muḥibb-i-'alī's, reinforcement that the Pagan had hurried off 'Abdu'l-'azīz and his men, taken his standard, martyred Mullā Ni'mat, Mullā Dāūd and the younger brother of Mullā Apāq, with several more. Directly the reinforcement arrived the pagans overcame Ṭāhir-tibrī, the maternal uncle of Khalīfa's Muḥibb-i-'alī, who had not got up with the hurrying reinforcement[?].[2009] Meantime Muḥibb-i-'alī even had been thrown down, but Bāltū getting in from the rear, brought him out. The enemy pursued for over a *kuroh* (2 m.), stopped however at the sight of the black mass of Muḥ. 'Alī *Jang-jang's* troops.

Foot upon foot news came that the foe had come near and nearer. We put on our armour and our horses' mail, took our arms and, ordering the carts to be dragged after us, rode out at the gallop. We advanced one *kuroh*. The foe must have turned aside.

(*p. Bābur fortifies his camp.*)

For the sake of water, we dismounted with a large lake (*kūl*) on one side of us. Our front was defended by carts chained together*, the space between each two, across which the chains stretched, being 7 or 8 *qārī* (*circa* yards). Musṭafa *Rūmī* had Fol. 311.had the carts made in the Rūmī way, excellent carts, very strong and suitable.[2010] As Ustād 'Alī-qulī was jealous of him, Musṭafa was posted to the right, in front of Humāyūn. Where the carts did not reach to, Khurāsānī and Hindūstānī spadesmen and miners were made to dig a ditch.

Owing to the Pagan's rapid advance, to the fighting-work in Bīāna and to the praise and laud of the pagans made by Shāh Manṣūr, Qismatī and the rest from Bīāna, people in the army shewed sign of want of heart. On the top of all this came the defeat of 'Abdu'l-'azīz. In order to hearten our men, and give a look of strength to the army, the camp was defended and shut in where there were no carts, by stretching ropes of raw hide on wooden tripods, set 7 or 8 *qārī* apart. Time had drawn out to 20 or 25 days before these appliances and materials were fully ready.[2011]

(*q. A reinforcement from Kābul.*)

Just at this time there arrived from Kābul Qāsim-i-ḥusain Sl. (*Aūzbeg Shaibān*) who is the son of a daughter of Sl. Ḥusain M. (*Bāī-qarā*), and with him Aḥmad-i-yūsuf (*Aūghlāqchī*), Qawwām-i-aūrdū Shāh and also several single friends of mine, counting up in all to 500 men. Muḥammad Sharīf, the astrologer of ill-augury, came with them too, so did Bābā Dost the water-bearer (*sūchī*) who, having gone to Kābul for wine, had thereFol. 311b. loaded three strings of camels with acceptable Ghaznī wines.

At a time such as this, when, as has been mentioned, the army was anxious and afraid by reason of past occurrences and vicissitudes, wild words and opinions, this Muḥammad Sharīf, the ill-augurer, though he had not a helpful word to say to me, kept insisting to all he met, "Mars is in the west in these days;[2012] who comes into the fight from this (east) side will be defeated." Timid people who questioned the ill-augurer, became the more shattered in heart. We gave no ear to his wild words, made no change in our operations, but got ready in earnest for the fight.

(*Feb. 24th*) On Sunday the 22nd (of Jumāda 1.) Shaikh Jamāl was sent to collect all available quiver-wearers from between the two waters (Ganges and Jumna) and from Dihlī, so that with this force he might over-run and plunder the Mīwāt villages, leaving nothing undone which could awaken the enemy's anxiety for that side. Mullā Tark-i-'alī, then on his way from Kābul, was ordered to join Shaikh Jamāl and to neglect nothing of ruin and plunder in Mīwāt; orders to the same purport were given also to Maghfūr the Dīwān. They went; they over-ran and raided a few villages in lonely corners (*būjqāq*); they took some prisoners; but their passage through did not arouse much anxiety!

(*r. Bābur renounces wine.*)

On Monday the 23rd of the first Jumāda (Feb. 25th), whenFol. 312. I went out riding, I reflected, as I rode, that the wish to cease from sin had been always in my mind, and that my forbidden acts had set lasting stain upon my heart. Said I, "Oh! my soul!"

(*Persian*)
"How long wilt thou draw savour from sin?
Repentance is not without savour, taste it!"[2013]

(*Turkī*)
Through years how many has sin defiled thee?
How much of peace has transgression given thee?
How much hast thou been thy passions' slave?
How much of thy life flung away?

With the Ghāzī's resolve since now thou hast marched,

Thou hast looked thine own death in the face!

Who resolves to hold stubbornly fast to the death,

Thou knowest what change he attains,

That far he removes him from all things forbidden,

That from all his offences he cleanses himself.

With my own gain before me, I vowed to obey,

In this my transgression,[2014] the drinking of wine.[2015]

The flagons and cups of silver and gold, the vessels of feasting,

I had them all brought;

I had them all broken up[2016] then and there.

Thus eased I my heart by renouncement of wine.

The fragments of the gold and silver vessels were shared out to deserving persons and to darwīshes. The first to agree in renouncing wine was 'Asas;[2017] he had already agreed also about leaving his beard untrimmed.[2018] That night and next day some Fol. 312b.300 begs and persons of the household, soldiers and not soldiers, renounced wine. What wine we had with us was poured on the ground; what Bābā Dost had brought was ordered salted to make vinegar. At the place where the wine was poured upon the ground, a well was ordered to be dug, built up with stone and having an almshouse beside it. It was already finished in Muḥarram 935 (AH.-Sep. 1528 AD.) at the time I went to Sīkrī from Dūlpūr on my way back from visiting Gūālīār.

(*s. Remission of a due.*)

I had vowed already that, if I gained the victory over Sangā the pagan, I would remit the *tamghā*[2019] to all Musalmāns. Of this vow Darwīsh-i-muḥammad *Sārbān* and Shaikh Zain reminded me at the time I renounced wine. Said I, "You do well to remind me."

**The tamghā* was remitted to all Musalmāns of the dominions I held.[2020] I sent for the clerks (*munshīlār*), and ordered them to write for their news-letters (*akhbar*) the *farmān* concerning the two important acts that had been done. Shaikh Zain wrote the *farmān* with his own elegance (*inshāsī bīla*) and his fine letter (*inshā*) was sent to all my dominions. It is as follows:—[2021]

FARMĀN ANNOUNCING BĀBUR'S RENUNCIATION OF WINE.[2022]

[2023] *Let us praise the Long-suffering One who loveth the penitent and who loveth the cleansers of themselves; and let thanks be rendered to the Gracious One who absolveth His debtors, and forgiveth those who seek forgiveness. Blessings be upon Muḥammad the Crown of Creatures, on the Holy family, on the pure Companions*, and on the mirrors of the glorious congregation, to wit, the Masters of Wisdom who are treasure-houses of the pearls of purity and who bear the impress of the sparkling jewels of this purport:—that the nature of man is prone to evil, and that the abandonment of sinful appetites is only feasible by Divine aidFol. 313. and the help that cometh from on high. "*Every soul is prone unto evil*,"[2024] (and again) "*This is the bounty of God*; *He will give the same unto whom He pleaseth*; *and God is endued with great bounty*."[2025]

Our motive for these remarks and for repeating these statements is that, by reason of human frailty, of the customs of kings and of the great, all of us, from the Shāh to the sipāhī, in the heyday of our youth, have transgressed and done what we ought not to have done. After some days of sorrow and repentance, we abandoned evil practices one by one, and the gates of retrogression became closed. But the renunciation of wine, the greatest and most indispensable of renunciations, remained under a veil in the chamber of deeds *pledged to appear in due season*, and did not show its countenance until the glorious hour when we had put on the garb of the holy warrior and had encamped with the army of Islām over against the infidels in order to slay them. On this occasion I received a secret inspiration and heard an infallible voice say "*Is not the time yet come unto those who believe, that their hearts should humbly submit to the admonition of God, and that truth which hath been revealed?*"[2026] Thereupon we set ourselves to extirpate the things of wickedness, and we earnestly knocked at the gates of repentance. The Guide of Help assisted us, according to the saying "*Whoever knocks and re-knocks, to him it will be opened*", and an order was given that with the Holy War there should Fol. 313b.begin the still greater war which has to be waged against sensuality. In short, we declared with sincerity that *we would subjugate our passions*, and I engraved on the tablet of my heart "*I turn unto Thee with repentance, and I am the first of true believers*".[2027] And I made public the resolution to abstain from wine, which had been hidden in the treasury of my breast. The victorious servants, in accordance with the illustrious order, dashed upon the earth of contempt and destruction the flagons and the cups, and the other utensils in gold and silver, which in their number and their brilliance were like the stars of the firmament. They dashed them in pieces, as, God willing! soon will be dashed the gods of the idolaters,—and they distributed the fragments among the poor and needy. By the blessing of this acceptable repentance, many of the courtiers, by virtue of the saying that *men follow the religion of their kings*, embraced abstinence at the same assemblage, and entirely renounced the use of wine, and up till now crowds of our subjects hourly attain this auspicious happiness. I hope that in accordance with the saying "*He who incites to good deeds has the same reward as he who does them*" the benefit of this action will react on the royal fortune and increase it day by day by victories.

After carrying out this design an universal decree was issued that in the imperial dominions—May God protect them fromFol. 314. every danger and calamity—no-one shall partake of strong drink, or engage in its manufacture, nor sell it, nor buy it or possess it, nor convey it or fetch it. "*Beware of touching it.*" "*Perchance this will give you prosperity.*"[2028]

In thanks for these great victories,[2029] and as a thank-offering for God's acceptance of repentance and sorrow, the ocean of the royal munificence became commoved, and those waves of kindness, which are the cause of the civilization of the world and of the glory of the sons of Adam, were displayed,—and throughout all the territories the tax (*tamghā*) on Musalmāns was abolished,—though its yield was more than the dreams of avarice, and though it had been established and maintained by former rulers,—for it is a practice outside of the edicts of the Prince of Apostles (Muḥammad). So a decree was passed that in no city, town, road, ferry, pass, or port, should the tax be levied or exacted. No alteration whatsoever of this order is to be permitted. "*Whoever after hearing it makes any change therein, the sin of such change will be upon him.*"[2030]

The proper course (*sabīl*) for all who shelter under the shade of the royal benevolence, whether they be Turk, Tājik, 'Arab, Hindī, or Fārsī (Persian), peasants or soldiers, of every nation or tribe of the sons of Adam, is to strengthen themselves by the tenets of religion, and to be full of hope and prayer for the dynasty which is linked with eternity, and to adhere to these ordinances, and not in any way to transgress them. It behoves all to act according to this *farmān*; they are to accept it as authentic when it comes attested by the Sign-Manual.

Written by order of the Exalted one,—May his excellence endure for ever! on the 24th of Jumāda I. 933 (February 26th 1527).

(*t. Alarm in Bābur's camp.*)

Fol. 314b.In these days, as has been mentioned, (our people) great and small, had been made very anxious and timid by past occurrences. No manly word or brave counsel was heard from any one soever. What bold speech was there from the wazīrs who are to speak out (*dīgūchī*), or from the amīrs who will devour the land (*wilāyat-yīghūchī*)?[2031] None had advice to give, none a bold plan of his own to expound. Khalīfa (however) did well in this campaign, neglecting nothing of control and supervision, painstaking and diligence.

At length after I had made enquiry concerning people's want of heart and had seen their slackness for myself, a plan occurred to me; I summoned all the begs and braves and said to them, "Begs and braves!

(*Persian*)
Who comes into the world will die;
What lasts and lives will be God.

He who hath entered the assembly of life,
Drinketh at last of the cup of death.

(*Turkī*)

He who hath come to the inn of life,
Passeth at last from Earth's house of woe.

"Better than life with a bad name, is death with a good one.

(*Persian*)
Well is it with me, if I die with good name!
A good name must I have, since the body is death's.[2032]

"God the Most High has allotted to us such happiness and has created for us such good-fortune that we die as martyrs, we kill as avengers of His cause. Therefore must each of you take oathFol. 315. upon His Holy Word that he will not think of turning his face from this foe, or withdraw from this deadly encounter so long as life is not rent from his body." All those present, beg and retainer, great and small, took the Holy Book joyfully into their hands and made vow and compact to this purport. The plan was perfect; it worked admirably for those near and afar, for seërs and hearers, for friend and foe.

(*u. Bābur's perilous position.*)

In those same days trouble and disturbance arose on every side:—Ḥusain Khān *Nuḥānī* went and took Rāprī; Quṭb Khān's man took Chandwār[2033]; a mannikin called Rustam Khān who had collected quiver-wearers from Between-the-two-waters (Ganges and Jamna), took Kūl (Koel) and made Kīchīk 'Alī prisoner; Khwāja Zāhid abandoned Saṃbal and went off; Sl. Muḥammad *Dūldāī* came from Qanūj to me; the Gūālīār pagans laid siege to that fort; 'Ālam Khān when sent to reinforce it, did not go to Gūālīār but to his own district. Every day bad news came from every side. Desertion of many Hindūstānīs set in; Haibat Khān *Karg-andāz*[2034] deserted and went to Saṃbal; Ḥasan Khān of Bārī deserted and joined the Pagan. We gave attention to none of them but went straight on with our own affair.

(*v. Bābur advances to fight.*)

The apparatus and appliances, the carts and wheeled tripods being ready, we arrayed in right, left and centre, and marched forward on New Year's Day,[2035] Tuesday, the 9th of the secondFol. 315b. Jumāda (March 13th), having the carts[2036] and wheeled tripods moving in front of us, with Ustād 'Alī-qulī and all the matchlock-men ranged behind them in order that these men, being on foot, should not be left behind the array but should advance with it.

When the various divisions, right, left and centre, had gone each to its place, I galloped from one to another to give encouragement to begs, braves, and *sipāhīs*. After each man had had assigned to him his post and usual work with his company, we advanced, marshalled on the plan determined, for as much as one *kuroh* (2 m.)[2037] and then dismounted.

The Pagan's men, for their part, were on the alert; they came from their side, one company after another.

The camp was laid out and strongly protected by ditch and carts. As we did not intend to fight that day, we sent a few unmailed braves ahead, who were to get to grips with the enemy and thus take an omen. They made a few pagans prisoner, cut off and brought in their heads. Malik Qāsim also cut off and brought in a few heads; he did well. By these successes the hearts of our men became very strong.

When we marched on next day, I had it in my mind to fight, but Khalīfa and other well-wishers represented that the camping-ground previously decided on was near and that it would favour our fortunes if we had a ditch and defences made there and went there direct. Khalīfa accordingly rode off to get Fol. 316.the ditch dug; he settled its position with the spades-men, appointed overseers of the work and returned to us. (*w. The battle of Kānwa.*)[2038]

On Saturday the 13th of the second Jumāda (March 17th, 1527 AD.) we had the carts dragged in front of us (as before), made a *kuroh* (2 m.) of road, arrayed in right, left and centre, and dismounted on the ground selected.

A few tents had been set up; a few were in setting up when news of the appearance of the enemy was brought. Mounting instantly, I ordered every man to his post and that our array should be protected with the carts.[2039]

*As the following Letter-of-victory (*Fatḥ-nāma*) which is what Shaikh Zain had indited, makes known particulars about the army of Islām, the great host of the pagans with the position of their arrayed ranks, and the encounters had between them and the army of Islām, it is inserted here without addition or deduction.[2040]

SHAIKH ZAIN'S LETTER-OF-VICTORY.

(*a. Introduction.*)

*Praise be to God the Faithful Promiser, the Helper of His servants, the Supporter of His armies, the Scatterer of hostile hosts, the One alone without whom there is nothing.*Fol. 316b.

O Thou the Exalter of the pillars of Islām, Helper of thy faithful minister, Overthrower of the pedestals of idols, Overcomer of rebellious foes, Exterminator to the uttermost of the followers of darkness!

Lauds be to God the Lord of the worlds, and may the blessing of God be upon the best of His creatures Muḥammad, Lord of ghāzīs and champions of the Faith, and upon his companions, the pointers of the way, until the Day of judgment.

The successive gifts of the Almighty are the cause of frequent praises and thanksgivings, and the number of these praises and thanksgivings is, in its turn, the cause of the constant succession of God's mercies. For every mercy a thanksgiving is due, and every thanksgiving is followed by a mercy. To render full thanks is beyond men's power; the mightiest are helpless to discharge their obligations. Above all, adequate thanks cannot be rendered for a benefit than which none is greater in the world and nothing is more blessed, in the world to come, to wit, victory over most powerful infidels and dominion over wealthiest heretics, "*these are the unbelievers, the wicked.*"[2041] In the eyes of the judicious, no blessing can be greater than this. Thanks be to God! that this great blessing and mighty boon, which from the cradle until now has been the real object of this right-thinking mind (Bābur's), has now manifested itself by the graciousness of the King of the worlds; the Opener who dispenses his treasures without awaiting solicitation, hath opened them with a master-key before our victorious Nawāb (Bābur),[2042] so that the names of our[2043] conquering heroes have been emblazoned in the records of glorious *ghāzīs*. By the help of our victorious soldiers the Fol. 317.standards of Islām have been raised to the highest pinnacles. The account of this auspicious fortune is as follows:—

(b. Rānā Sangā and his forces.)

When the flashing-swords of our Islām-guarded soldiers had illuminated the land of Hindūstān with rays of victory and conquest, as has been recorded in former letters-of-victory,[2044] the Divine favour caused our standards to be upreared in the territories of Dihlī, Āgra, Jūn-pūr, Kharīd,[2045] Bihār, *etc.*, when many chiefs, both pagans and Muḥammadans submitted to our generals and shewed sincere obedience to our fortunate Nawāb. But Rānā Sangā the pagan who in earlier times breathed submissive to the Nawāb,[2046] now *was puffed up with pride and became of the number of unbelievers*.[2047] Satan-like he threw back his head and collected an army of accursed heretics, thus gathering a rabble-rout of whom some wore the accursed torque (*ṭauq*), the *zīnār*,[2048] on the neck, some had in the skirt the calamitous thorn of apostacy.[2049] Previous to the rising in Hindūstān of the Sun of dominion and the emergence there of the light of the Shāhanshāh's Khalīfate [*i.e.* Bābur's] the authority of that execrated pagan (Sangā)—*at the Judgment Day he shall have no friend*,[2050] was such that not one of all the exalted sovereigns of this wide realm, such as the Sulṭān of Dihlī, theFol. 317b. Sulṭān of Gujrāt and the Sulṭān of Mandū, could cope with this evil-dispositioned one, without the help of other pagans; one and all they cajoled him and temporized with him; and he had this authority although the rājas and rāīs of high degree, who obeyed him in this battle, and the governors and commanders who were amongst his followers in this conflict, had not obeyed him in any earlier fight or, out of regard to their own dignity, been friendly with him. Infidel standards dominated some 200 towns in the territories of Islām; in them mosques and shrines fell into ruin; from them the wives and children of the Faithful were carried away captive. So greatly had his forces grown that, according to the Hindū calculation by which one *lak* of revenue should yield 100 horsemen, and one *krūr* of revenue, 10,000 horsemen, the territories subject to the Pagan (Sangā) yielding 10 *krūrs*, should yield him 100,000 horse. Many noted pagans who hitherto had not helped him in battle, now swelled his ranks out of hostility to the people of Islām. Ten powerful chiefs, each the leader of a pagan host, uprose in rebellion, as smoke rises, and linked themselves, as though Fol. 318.enchained, to that perverse one (Sangā); and this infidel decade who, unlike the blessed ten,[2051] uplifted misery-freighted standards which *denounce unto them excruciating punishment*,[2052] had many dependants, and troops, and wide-extended lands. As, for instance, Ṣalāḥu'd-dīn[2053] had territory yielding 30,000 horse, Rāwal Ūdai Sīngh of Bāgar had 12,000, Medinī Rāī had 12,000, Ḥasan Khān of Mīwāt had 12,000, Bār-mal of Īdr had 4,000, Narpat Hāra had 7,000, Satrvī of Kach (Cutch) had 6,000, Dharm-deo had 4,000, Bīr-sing-deo had 4,000, and Maḥmūd Khān, son of Sl. Sikandar, to whom, though he possessed neither district nor *pargana*, 10,000 horse had gathered in hope of his attaining supremacy. Thus, according to the calculation of Hind, 201,000 was the total of those sundered from salvation. In brief, that haughty pagan, inwardly blind, and hardened of heart, having joined with other pagans, dark-fated and doomed to perdition, advanced to contend with the followers of Islām and to destroy the foundations of the law of the Prince of Men (Muḥammad), on whom be God's blessing! The protagonists of the royal forces fell, like divine destiny, on that one-eyed Dajjāl[2054] who, to understanding men, shewed the truth of the saying, *When Fate arrives, the eye becomes blind*, and, setting before their eyes the scripture which saith, *Whosoever striveth to promote the true religion, striveth for the good of his own soul*,[2055]Fol. 318b. they acted on the precept to which obedience is due, *Fight against infidels and hypocrites.*

(*c. Military movements.*)

(*March 17th, 1527*) On Saturday the 13th day of the second Jumāda of the date 933, a day blessed by the words, *God hath blessed your Saturday*, the army of Islām was encamped near the village of Kānwa, a dependency of Bīāna, hard by a hill which was 2 *kurohs* (4 m.) from the enemies of the Faith. When those accursed infidel foes of Muḥammad's religion heard the reverberation of the armies of Islām, they arrayed their ill-starred forces and moved forward with one heart, relying on their mountain-like, demon-shaped elephants, as had relied the Lords of the Elephant[2056] who went to overthrow the sanctuary (*ka'ba*) of Islām.

"Having these elephants, the wretched Hindus

Became proud, like the Lords of the Elephant;

Yet were they odious and vile as is the evening of death,

Blacker[2057] than night, outnumbering the stars,

All such as fire is[2058] but their heads upraised

In hate, as rises its smoke in the azure sky,

Ant-like they come from right and from left,

Thousands and thousands of horse and foot."

They advanced towards the victorious encampment, intending Fol. 319.to give battle. The holy warriors of Islām, trees in the garden of valour, moved forward in ranks straight as serried pines and, like pines uplift their crests to heaven, uplifting their helmet-crests which shone even as shine the hearts of those *that strive in the way of the Lord*; their array was like Alexander's iron-wall,[2059] and, as is the way of the Prophet's Law, straight and firm and strong, *as though they were a well-compacted building*;[2060] and they became fortunate and successful in accordance with the saying, *They are directed by their Lord, and they shall prosper.*[2061]

In that array no rent was frayed by timid souls;

Firm was it as the Shāhanshāh's resolve, strong as the Faith;

Their standards brushed against the sky;

Verily we have granted thee certain victory.[2062]

Obeying the cautions of prudence, we imitated the *ghāzīs* of Rūm[2063] by posting matchlockmen (*tufanchīān*) and cannoneers (*ra'd-andāzān*) along the line of carts which were chained to one another in front of us; in fact, Islām's army was so arrayed and so steadfast that primal Intelligence[2064] and the firmament (*'aql-i-pīr u charkh-i-aṣīr*) applauded the marshalling thereof. To effect this arrangement and organization, Niẓāmu'd-dīn 'Alī Khalīfa, the pillar of the Imperial fortune, exerted himself strenuously; his efforts were in accord with Destiny, and were approved by his sovereign's luminous judgment.

(*d. Commanders of the centre.*)

His Majesty's post was in the centre. In the right-hand of the centre were stationed the illustrious and most uprightFol. 319b. brother, the beloved friend of Destiny, the favoured of Him whose aid is entreated (*i.e.* God), Chīn-tīmūr Sulṭān,[2065]—the illustrious son, accepted in the sight of the revered Allāh, Sulaimān Shāh,[2066]—the reservoir of sanctity, the way-shower, Khwāja Kamālu'd-dīn (Perfect-in-the Faith) Dost-i-khāwand,—the trusted of the sulṭānate, the abider near the sublime threshold, the close companion, the cream of associates, Kamālu'd-dīn Yūnas-i-'alī,—the pillar of royal retainers, the perfect in friendship, Jalālu'd-dīn (Glory-of-the-Faith) Shāh Manṣūr *Barlās*,—the pillar of royal retainers, most excellent of servants, Niẓāmu'd-dīn (Upholder-of-the-Faith) Darwīsh-i-muḥammad *Sārbān*,—the pillars of royal retainers, the sincere in fidelity, Shihābu'd-dīn (Meteor-of-the-Faith) 'Abdu'l-lāh the librarian and Nīẓāmu'd-dīn Dost Lord-of-the-Gate.

In the left-hand of the centre took each his post, the reservoir of sovereignty, ally of the Khalīfate, object of royal favour, Sulṭān 'Alā'u'd-dīn 'Ālam Khān son of Sl. Bahlūl *Lūdī*,—the intimate of illustrious Majesty, the high priest (*dastūr*) of *ṣadrs* amongst men, the refuge of all people, the pillar of Islām, Shaikh Zain of Khawāf,[2067]—the pillar of the nobility, Kamālu'd-dīn Muḥibb-i-'alī, son of the intimate counsellor named above (*i.e.* Khalīfa),—the pillar of royal retainers, Niẓāmu'd-dīn Tardī Beg brother of Qūj (son of) Aḥmad, whom God hath taken into His mercy,—ShīrafganFol. 320. son of the above-named Qūj Beg deceased,—the pillar of great ones, the mighty khān, Ārāīsh Khān,[2068]—the wazīr, greatest of wazīrs amongst men, Khwāja Kamālu'd-dīn Ḥusain,—and a number of other attendants at Court (*dīwaniān*).

(*e. Commanders of the right wing.*)

In the right wing was the exalted son, honourable and fortunate, the befriended of Destiny, the Star of the Sign of sovereignty and success, Sun of the sphere of the Khalīfate, lauded of slave and free, Muḥammad Humāyūn Bahādur. On that exalted prince's right hand there were, one whose rank approximates to royalty and who is distinguished by the favour of the royal giver of gifts, Qāsim-i-ḥusain Sulṭān,—the pillar of the nobility Niẓāmu'd-dīn Aḥmad-ī-yūsuf *Aūghlāqchī*,[2069]—the trusted of royalty, most excellent of servants, Jalālu'd-dīn Hindū Beg *qūchīn*,[2070]—the trusted of royalty, perfect in loyalty, Jalālu'd-dīn Khusrau Kūkūldāsh,—the trusted of royalty, Qawām (var. Qiyām) Beg *Aūrdū-shāh*,—the pillar of royal retainers, of perfect sincerity, Walī *Qarā-qūẓī* the treasurer,[2071]—the pillar of royal retainers, Niẓāmu'd-dīn Pīr-qulī of Sīstān,—the pillar of wazīrs, Khwāja Kamālu'd-dīn *pahlawān* (champion) of Badakhshān,—the pillar of royal retainers, 'Abdu'l-sḥakūr,—the pillar of the nobility, most excellent of servants, the envoy from 'Irāq Sulaimān Āqā,—and Ḥusain Āqā the envoy from Sīstān. On Fol. 320b.the victory-crowned left of the fortunate son already named there were, the sayyid of lofty birth, of the family of Murtiẓā ('Alī), Mīr Hama (or Hāma),—the pillar of royal retainers, the perfect in sincerity, Shamsu'd-dīn Muḥammadī Kūkūldāsh and Niẓāmu'd-dīn Khwājagī Asad *jān-dār*.[2072] In the right wing there were, of the amīrs of Hind,—the pillar of the State, the Khān-of-Khāns, Dilāwar Khān,[2073]—the pillar of the nobility, Malik Dād *Kararānī*,—and the pillar of the nobility, the Shaikh-of-shaikhs, Shaikh Gūran, each standing in his appointed place.

(*f. Commanders of the left wing.*)

In the left wing of the armies of Islām there extended their ranks,—the lord of lofty lineage, the refuge of those in authority, the ornament of the family of *Ṭa Ha* and *Ya Sin*,[2074] the model for the descendants of the prince of ambassadors (Muḥammad), Sayyid Mahdī Khwāja,—the exalted and fortunate brother, the well-regarded of his Majesty, Muḥammad Sl. Mīrzā,[2075]—the personage approximating to royalty, the descended of monarchs, 'Ādil Sulṭān son of Mahdī Sulṭān,[2076]—the trusted in the State, perfect in attachment, 'Abdu'l-'azīz Master of the Horse,—the trusted in the State, the pure in friendship, Shamsu'd-dīn Muḥammad 'Ali *Jang-jang*,[2077]—the pillar of royal retainers, Jalālu'd-dīn Qūtlūq-qadam *qarāwal* (scout),—the pillar of royal retainers, the perfect in sincerity, Jalālu'd-dīn Shāh Ḥusain *yārāgī Mughūl Ghānchī*(?),[2078]—and Niẓāmu'd-dīn Jān-i-muḥammad *Beg Ātāka*.

Of amīrs of Hind there were in this division, the scions of sulṭāns, Kamāl Khān and Jamāl Khān sons of the Sl. 'Alā'u'd-dīnFol. 321. above-mentioned,—the most excellent officer 'Alī Khān Shaikh-zāda of Farmūl,—and the pillar of the nobility, Niẓām Khān of Bīāna.

(*g. The flanking parties.*)

For the flank-movement (*tūlghāma*) of the right wing there were posted two of the most trusted of the household retainers, Tardīka[2079] and Malik Qāsim the brother of Bābā Qashqa, with a body of Mughūls; for the flank-movement of the left wing were the two trusted chiefs Mūmin Ātāka and Rustam *Turkmān*, leading a body of special troops.

(*h. The Chief of the Staff.*)

The pillar of royal retainers, the perfect in loyalty, the cream of privy-counsellors, Niẓāmu'd-dīn Sulṭān Muḥammad *Bakhshī*, after posting the *ghāzīs* of Islām, came to receive the royal commands. He despatched adjutants (*tawāchī*) and messengers (*yasāwal*) in various directions to convey imperative orders concerning the marshalling of the troops to the great sulṭāns and amīrs. And when the Commanders had taken up their positions, an imperative order was given that none should quit his post or, uncommanded, stretch forth his arm to fight.

(*i. The battle.*)

One watch[2080] of the afore-mentioned day had elapsed when the opposing forces approached each other and the battle began. As Light opposes Darkness, so did the centres of the two Fol. 321b.armies oppose one another. Fighting began on the right and left wings, such fighting as shook the Earth and filled highest Heaven with clangour.

The left wing of the ill-fated pagans advanced against the right wing of the Faith-garbed troops of Islām and charged down on Khusrau Kūkūldāsh and Bābā Qashqa's brother Malik Qāsim. The most glorious and most upright brother Chīn-tīmūr Sulṭān, obeying orders, went to reinforce them and, engaging in the conflict with bold attack, bore the pagans back almost to the rear of their centre. Guerdon was made for the brother's glorious fame.[2081] The marvel of the Age, Muṣṭafa of Rūm, had his post in the centre (of the right wing) where was the exalted son, upright and fortunate, the object of the favourable regard of

Creative Majesty (*i.e.* God), the one *distinguished by the particular grace of the mighty Sovereign who commands to do and not to do* (*i.e.* Bābur), Muḥammad Humāyūn Bahādur. This Muṣṭafa of Rūm had the carts (*arābahā*)[2082] brought forward and broke the ranks of pagans with matchlock and culverin dark like their hearts(?).[2083] In the thick of the fight, the most glorious brother Qāsim-i-ḥusain Sulṭān and the pillars of royal retainers, Niẓāmu'd-dīn Aḥmad-i-yūsuf and Qawām Beg, obeying orders, hastened to their help. And since band after band of pagan troops followed each other to help their men, so we, in our turn, sent the trusted in the State, the glory of the Faith, Hindū Beg, and, after him, the pillars of the nobility, Muhammadī Kūkūldāsh and Khwājagī Asad *jān-dār*, and, after them, the trusted inFol. 322. the State, the trustworthy in the resplendent Court, the most confided-in of nobles, the elect of confidential servants, Yūnas-i-'alī, together with the pillar of the nobility, the perfect in friendship, Shāh Manṣūr *Barlās* and the pillar of the grandees, the pure in fidelity, 'Abdu'l-lāh the librarian, and after these, the pillar of the nobles, Dost the Lord-of-the-Gate, and Muḥammad Khalīl the master-gelder (*akhta-begī*).[2084]

The pagan right wing made repeated and desperate attack on the left wing of the army of Islām, falling furiously on the holy warriors, possessors of salvation, but each time was made to turn back or, smitten with the arrows of victory, was *made to descend into Hell, the house of perdition; they shall be thrown to burn therein, and an unhappy dwelling shall it be.*[2085] Then the trusty amongst the nobles, Mūmin Ātāka and Rustam *Turkmān* betook themselves to the rear[2086] of the host of darkened pagans; and to help them were sent the Commanders Khwāja Maḥmūd and 'Alī Ātāka, servants of him who amongst the royal retainers is near the throne, the trusted of the Sulṭānate, Niẓāmu'd-din 'Alī Khalīfa.

Our high-born brother[2087] Muḥammad Sl. Mīrzā, and the representative of royal dignity, 'Ādil Sulṭān, and the trusted in the State, the strengthener of the Faith, 'Abdu'l-'azīz, the Master of the Horse, and the glory of the Faith, Qūtlūq-qadam *qarāwal*, and the meteor of the Faith, Muḥammad 'Alī *Jang-*

jang, and the pillar of royal retainers, Shāh Ḥusain *yāragī Mughūl Ghānchī*(?) stretched out the arm to fight and stood firm. To support them we sent the *Dastūr*, the highest of wazīrs, Khwāja Fol. 322b.Kamālu'd-dīn Ḥusain with a body of *dīwānīs*.[2088] Every holy warrior was eager to show his zeal, entering the fight with desperate joy as if approving the verse, *Say, Do you expect any other should befall us than one of the two most excellent things, victory or martyrdom?*[2089] and, with display of life-devotion, uplifted the standard of life-sacrifice.

As the conflict and battle lasted long, an imperative order was issued that the special royal corps (*tābīnān-i-khāṣa-i-pādshāhī*)[2090] who, heroes of one hue,[2091] were standing, like tigers enchained, behind the carts,[2092] should go out on the right and the left of the centre,[2093] leaving the matchlockmen's post in-between, and join battle on both sides. As the True Dawn emerges from its cleft in the horizon, so they emerged from behind the carts; they poured a ruddy crepuscule of the blood of those ill-fated pagans on the nadir of the Heavens, that battle-field; they made fall from the firmament of existence many heads of the headstrong, as stars fall from the firmament of heaven. The marvel of the Age, Ustād 'Alī-qulī, who with his own appurtenances stood in front of the centre, did deeds of valour, discharging against the iron-mantled forts of the infidels[2094] stones of such size that were (one) put into a scale of the Balance in which actions are weighed, that *scale shall be heavy with good works and he*

(*i.e.* its owner) *shall lead a pleasing life*[2095]; and were such stones discharged against a hill, broad of base and high of summit, it would *become like carded wool.*[2096] Such stones Ustād 'Alī-qulī discharged at the iron-clad fortress of the pagan ranks and by this discharge of stones, and abundance of culverins and matchlocks(?)[2097] destroyed many of the builded bodies of theFol. 323. pagans. The matchlockmen of the royal centre, in obedience to orders, going from behind the carts into the midst of the battle, each one of them made many a pagan taste of the poison of death. The foot-soldiers, going into a most dangerous place, made their names to be blazoned amongst those of the forest-tigers (*i.e.* heroes) of valour and the champions in the field of manly deeds. Just at this time came an order from his Majesty the Khāqān that the carts of the centre should be advanced; and the gracious royal soul (*i.e.* Bābur) moved towards the pagan soldiers, Victory and Fortune on his right, Prestige and Conquest on his left. On witnessing this event, the victorious troops followed from all sides; the whole surging ocean of the army rose in mighty waves; the courage of all the crocodiles[2098] of that ocean was manifested by the strength of their deeds; an obscuring cloud of dust o'erspread the sky(?). The dust that gathered over the battle-field was traversed by the lightning-flashes of the sword; the Sun's face was shorn of light as is a mirror's back; the striker and the struck, the victor and the vanquished were commingled, all distinction between them lost. The Wizard of Time produced such a night that its only planets were arrows,[2099] its only constellations of fixed stars were the steadfast squadrons.

Upon that day of battle sank and rose

Blood to the Fish and dust-clouds to the Moon,

While through the horse-hoofs on that spacious plain,Fol. 323b.

One Earth flew up to make another Heaven.[2100]

At the moment when the holy warriors were heedlessly flinging away their lives, they heard a secret voice say, *Be not dismayed, neither be grieved, for, if ye believe, ye shall be exalted above the unbelievers*,[2101] and from the infallible Informer heard the joyful words, *Assistance is from God, and a speedy victory! And do thou bear glad tidings to true believers.*[2102] Then they fought with such delight that the plaudits of the saints of the Holy Assembly reached them and the angels from near the Throne, fluttered round their heads like moths. Between the first and second Prayers, there was such blaze of combat that the flames thereof raised standards above the heavens, and the right and left of the army of Islām rolled back the left and right of the doomed infidels in one mass upon their centre.

When signs were manifest of the victory of the Strivers and of the up-rearing of the standards of Islām, those accursed infidels and wicked unbelievers remained for one hour confounded. At length, their hearts abandoning life, they fell upon the right and left of our centre. Their attack on the left was the more vigorous and there they approached furthest, but the holy warriors, their minds set on the reward, planted shoots (*nihāl*) of arrows in the field of the breast of each one of them, and, such being their gloomy fate, overthrew them. In this state of affairs, the breezes of victory and fortune blew over the meadow of our Fol. 324.happy Nawāb, and brought the good news, *Verily we have granted thee a manifest victory.*[2103] And Victory the beautiful woman (*shāhid*) whose world-adornment of waving tresses was embellished by *God will aid you with a mighty aid*,[2104] bestowed on us the good fortune that had been hidden behind a veil, and made it a reality. The absurd (*bāṭil*) Hindūs, knowing their position perilous, *dispersed like carded wool before the wind*, and *like moths scattered abroad.*[2105] Many fell dead on the field of battle; others, desisting from fighting, fled to the desert of exile and became the food of crows and kites. Mounds were made of the bodies of the slain, pillars of their heads.

(j. Hindū chiefs killed in the battle.)

Ḥasan Khān of Mīwāt was enrolled in the list of the dead by the force of a matchlock (*ẓarb-i-tufak*); most of those headstrong chiefs of tribes were slain likewise, and ended their days by arrow and matchlock (*tīr u tufak*). Of their number was Rāwal Ūdī Sīngh of Bāgar,[2106] ruler (*wālī*) of the Dungarpūr country, who had 12,000 horse, Rāī Chandrabān *Chūhān* who had 4,000 horse, Bhūpat Rāo son of that Ṣalāḥu'd-dīn already mentioned, who was lord of Chandīrī and had 6,000 horse, Mānik-chand *Chūhān* and Dilpat Rāo who had each 4,000 horse, Kankū (or Gangū) and Karm Sīngh and Dankūsī(?)[2107] who had each 3,000 horse, and a number of others, each one of whom was leader of a greatFol. 324b. command, a splendid and magnificent chieftain. All these trod the road to Hell, removing from this house of clay to the pit of perdition. The enemy's country (*dāru'l-ḥarb*) was full, as Hell is full, of wounded who had died on the road. The lowest pit was gorged with miscreants who had surrendered their souls to the lord of Hell. In whatever direction one from the army of Islām hastened, he found everywhere a self-willed one dead; whatever march the illustrious camp made in the wake of the fugitives, it found no foot-space without its prostrate foe.

All the Hindūs slain, abject (*khwār*, var. *ẓār*) and mean,

By matchlock-stones, like the Elephants' lords,[2108]

Many hills of their bodies were seen,

And from each hill a fount of running blood.

Dreading the arrows of (our) splendid ranks,

Passed[2109] they in flight to each waste and hill.

They turn their backs. The command of God is to be performed. Now praise be to God, All-hearing and All-wise, for victory is from God alone, the Mighty, the Wise.[2110] Written Jumāda II. 25th 933 (AH.-March 29th 1527 A.D.).[2111]

MINOR SEQUELS OF VICTORY.

(*a. Bābur assumes the title of Ghāẓī.*)

After this success *Ghāẓī* (Victor in a Holy-war) was written amongst the royal titles.

Below the titles (*ṭughrā*)[2112] entered on the *Fatḥ-nāma*, I wrote the following quatrain:—[2113]

For Islām's sake, I wandered in the wilds,

Prepared for war with pagans and Hindūs,

Resolved myself to meet the martyr's death.Fol. 325.

Thanks be to God! a *ghāzī* I became.

(*b. Chronograms of the victory.*)

Shaikh Zain had found (*tāpīb aīdī*) the words *Fatḥ-i-pādshāḥ-i-islām*[2114] (Victory of the Pādshāh of the Faith) to be a chronogram of the victory. Mīr Gesū, one of the people come from Kābul, had also found these same words to be a chronogram, had composed them in a quatrain and sent this to me. It was a coincidence that Shaikh Zain and Mīr Gesū should bring forward precisely the same words in the quatrains they composed to embellish their discoveries.[2115] Once before when Shaikh Zain found the date of the victory at Dībālpūr in the words *Wasaṭ-i-shahr Rabī'u'l-awwal*[2116] (Middle of the month Rabī' I.), Mīr Gesū had found it in the very same words.

HISTORICAL NARRATIVE RESUMED.

(*a. After the victory.*)

The foes beaten, we hurried them off, dismounting one after another. The Pagan's encirclement[2117] may have been 2 *kurohs* from our camp (*aūrdū*); when we reached his camp (*aūrdū*), we sent Muḥammadī, 'Abdu'l-'azīz, 'Alī Khān and some others in pursuit of him. There was a little slackness;[2118] I ought to have gone myself, and not have left the matter to what I expected from other people. When I had gone as much as a *kuroh* (2 m.) beyond the Pagan's camp, I turned back because it was late in the day; I came to our camp at the Bed-time Prayer.

With what ill-omened words Muḥammad Sharīf the astrologer had fretted me! Yet he came at once to congratulate me! I emptied my inwards[2119] in abuse of him, but, spite of his being heathenish, ill-omened of speech, extremely self-satisfied, and a most disagreeable person, I bestowed a *lak* upon him because there had been deserving service from him in former times, and, Fol. 325b.after saying he was not to stay in my dominions, I gave him leave to go.

(*b. Suppression of a rebellion.*)

(*March 17th*) We remained next day (*Jumāda II. 14th*) on that same ground. Muḥammad 'Alī *Jang-jang* and Shaikh Gūran and 'Abdu'l-malik[2120] the armourer were sent off with a dense (*qālīn*) army against Ilīās Khān who, having rebelled in Between-the-two-waters (Ganges and Jumna), had taken

Kūl (Koel) and made Kīchīk 'Alī prisoner.[2121] He could not fight when they came up; his force scattered in all directions; he himself was taken a few days later and brought into Āgra where I had him flayed alive.

(*c. A trophy of victory.*)

An order was given to set up a pillar of pagan heads on the infant-hill (*koh-bacha*) between which and our camp the battle had been fought.

(*d. Bīāna visited.*)

(*March 20th*) Marching on from that ground, and after halting on two nights, we reached Bīāna (*Sunday, Jumāda II. 17th*). Countless numbers of the bodies of pagans and apostates[2122] who had fallen in their flight, lay on the road as far as Bīāna, indeed as far as Alūr and Mīwāt.[2123]

(*e. Discussion of plans.*)

On our return to camp, I summoned the Turk amīrs and the amīrs of Hind to a consultation about moving into the Pagan (Sangā)'s country; the plan was given up because of the little water and much heat on the road.

(*f. Mīwāt.*)

Near Dihlī lies the Mīwāt country which yields revenue of 3 or 4 *krūrs*.[2124] Ḥasan Khān *Mīwātī*[2125] and his ancestors one after another had ruled it with absolute sway for a hundred years or two. They must have made[2126] imperfect submission to the Dihlī Sulṭāns; the Sulṭāns of Hind,[2127] whether because theirFol. 326. own dominions were wide, or because their opportunity was narrow, or because of the Mīwāt hill-country,[2128] did not turn in the Mīwāt direction, did not establish order in it, but just put up with this amount of (imperfect) submission. For our own part, we did after the fashion of earlier Sulṭāns; having conquered Hind, we shewed favour to Ḥasan Khān, but that thankless and heathenish apostate disregarded our kindness and benefits, was not grateful for favour and promotion, but became the mover of all disturbance and the cause of all misdoing.

When, as has been mentioned, we abandoned the plan (against Rānā Sangā), we moved to subdue Mīwāt. Having made 4 night-halts on the way, we dismounted on the bank of the Mānas-nī[2129] 6 *kurohs* (12 m.) from Alūr, the present seat of government in Mīwāt. Ḥasan Khān and his forefathers must have had their seat[2130] in Tijāra, but when I turned towards Hindūstan, beat Pahār (or Bihār) Khān and took Lāhor and Dībālpūr (930 AH.-1524 AD.), he bethought himself betimes and busied himself for a residence (*'imārat*) in Fort Alūr (Alwar).

His trusted man, Karm-chand by name, who had come from him to me in Āgra when his son (Nāhar *i.e.* Tiger) was with me there,[2131] came now from that son's presence in Alūr and asked Fol. 326b.for peace. 'Abdu'r-raḥīm *shaghāwal* went with him to Alūr, conveying letters of royal favour, and returned bringing Nāhar Khān who was restored to favour and received *parganas* worth several *laks* for his support.

(*g. Rewards to officers.*)

Thinking, "What good work Khusrau did in the battle!" I named him for Alūr and gave him 50 *laks* for his support, but unluckily for himself, he put on airs and did not accept this. Later on it [*khwud*, itself] came to be known that Chīn-tīmūr must have done[2132] that work; guerdon was made him for his renown(?);[2133] Tijāra-town, the seat of government in Mīwāt, was bestowed on him together with an allowance of 50 *laks* for his support.

Alūr and an allowance of 15 *laks* was bestowed on Tardīka (or, Tardī *yakka*) who in the flanking-party of the right-hand (*qūl*) had done better than the rest. The contents of the Alūr treasury were bestowed on Humāyūn.

(*h. Alwar visited.*)

(*April 13th*) Marching from that camp on Wednesday the 1st of the month of Rajab, we came to within 2 *kurohs* (4 m.) of Alūr. I went to see the fort, there spent the night, and next day went back to camp.

(*i. Leave given to various followers.*)

When the oath before-mentioned[2134] was given to great and small before the Holy-battle with Rānā Sangā, it had been mentioned[2135] that there would be nothing to hinder leave afterFol. 327. this victory, and that leave would be given to anyone wishing to go away (from Hindūstān). Most of Humāyūn's men were from Badakhshān or elsewhere on that side (of Hindū-kūsh); they had never before been of an army led out for even a month or two; there had been weakness amongst them before the fight; on these accounts and also because Kābul was empty of troops, it was now decided to give Humāyūn leave for Kābul.

(*April 11th*) Leaving the matter at this, we marched from Alūr on Thursday the 9th of Rajab, did 4 or 5 *kurohs* (8-10 m.) and dismounted on the bank of the Mānas-water.

Mahdī Khwāja also had many discomforts; he too was given leave for Kābul. The military-collectorate of Bīāna [he held] was bestowed on Dost Lord-of-the-gate, and, as previously Etāwa had been named for Mahdī Khwāja,[2136] Mahdī Khwāja's son Ja'far Khwāja was sent there in his father's place when (later) Quṭb Khān abandoned it and went off.[2137]

(j. Despatch of the Letter-of-victory.)

Because of the leave given to Humāyūn, two or three days were spent on this ground. From it Mūmin-i-'alī the messenger (*tawāchi*) was sent off for Kābul with the *Fatḥ-nāma.*

(k. Excursions and return to Āgra.)

Praise had been heard of the Fīrūzpūr-spring and of the great lake of Kūtila.[2138] Leaving the camp on that same ground, I rode out on Sunday (*Rajab 12th-April 14th*) both to visit Fol. 327b.these places and to set Humāyūn on his way. After visiting Fīrūzpūr and its spring on that same day, *ma'jūn* was eaten. In the valley where the spring rises, oleanders (*kanīr*) were in bloom; the place is not without charm but is over-praised. I ordered a reservoir of hewn stone, 10 by 10[2139] to be made where the water widened, spent the night in that valley, next day rode on and visited the Kūtila lake. It is surrounded by mountain-skirts. The Mānas-nī is heard-say to go into it.[2140] It is a very large lake, from its one side the other side is not well seen. In the middle of it is rising ground. At its sides are many small boats, by going off in which the villagers living near it are said to escape from any tumult or disturbance. Even on our arrival a few people went in them to the middle of the lake.

On our way back from the lake, we dismounted in Humāyūn's camp. There we rested and ate food, and after having put robes of honour on him and his begs, bade him farewell at the Bed-time Prayer, and rode on. We slept for a little at some place on the road, at shoot of day passed through the *pargana* of Kharī, again slept a little, and at length got to our camp which had dismounted at Toda-(bhim).[2141] After leaving Toda, we dismounted at Sūnkār; there Ḥasan Khān *Mīwātī's* sonFol. 328. Nāhar Khān escaped from 'Abdu'r-raḥīm's charge.

Going on from that place, we halted one night, then dismounted at a spring situated on the bill of a mountain between Busāwar and Chausa[2142] (or Jūsa); there awnings were set up and we committed the sin of *ma'jūn*. When the army had passed by this spring, Tardī Beg *khāksār* had praised it; he (or we) had come and seen it from on horse-back (*sar-asbgi*) and passed on. It is a perfect spring. In Hindūstān where there are never running-waters,[2143] people seek out the springs themselves. The rare springs that are found, come oozing drop by drop (*āb-zih*) out of the ground, not bubbling up like springs of those lands.[2144] From this spring comes about a half-mill-water. It bubbles up on the hill-skirt; meadows lie round it; it is very beautiful. I ordered an octagonal reservoir of hewn stone made above[2145] it. While we were at the border of the spring, under the soothing influence of *ma'jūn*,

Tardī Beg, contending for its surpassing beauty, said again and again, (*Persian*) "Since I am celebrating the beauty of the place,[2146] a name ought to be settled for it". 'Abdu'l-lāh said, "It must be called the Royal-spring approved of by Tardī Beg." This saying caused much joke and laughter.

Dost Lord-of-the-gate coming up from Bīāna, waited on me at this spring-head. Leaving this place, we visited Bīāna again,Fol. 328b. went on to Sīkrī, dismounted there at the side of a garden which had been ordered made, stayed two days supervising the garden, and on Thursday the 23rd of Rajab (*April 25th*), reached Āgra.

(*l. Chandwār and Rāprī regained.*)

During recent disturbances, the enemy, as has been mentioned,[2147] had possessed themselves of Chandwār[2148] and Rāprī. Against those places we now sent Muḥammad 'Alī *Jang-jang*, Qūj Beg's (brother) Tardī Beg, 'Abdu'l-malik the armourer, and Ḥasan Khān with his Daryā-khānīs. When they were near Chandwār, Quṭb Khān's people in it got out and away. Our men laid hands on it, and passed on to Rāprī. Here Ḥusain Khān *Nūḥānī's* people came to the lane-end[2149] thinking to fight a little, could not stand the attack of our men, and took to flight. Ḥusain Khān himself with a few followers went into the Jūn-river (Jumna) on an elephant and was drowned. Quṭb Khān, for his part, abandoned Etāwa on hearing these news, fled with a few and got away. Etāwa having been named for Mahdī Khwāja, his son Ja'far Khwāja was sent there in his place.[2150]

(*m. Apportionment of fiefs.*)

When Rānā Sangā sallied out against us, most Hindūstānīs and Afghāns, as has been mentioned,[2151] turned round against us and took possession of their *parganas* and districts.[2152]

Sl. Muḥammad *Dūldāī* who had abandoned Qanūj and come Fol. 329.to me, would not agree to go there again, whether from fear or for his reputation's sake; he therefore exchanged the 30 *laks* of Qanūj for the 15 of Sihrind, and Qanūj was bestowed with an allowance of 30 *laks* on Muḥammad Sl. Mīrzā. Badāūn[2153] was given to Qāsim-i-ḥusain Sulṭān and he was sent against Bīban who had laid siege to Luknūr[2154] during the disturbance with Rānā Sangā, together with Muḥammad Sl. Mīrzā, and, of Turk amīrs, Bābā Qashqa's Malik Qāsim with his elder and younger brethren and his Mughūls, and Abū'l-muḥammad the lance-player, and Mu'yad with his father's Daryā-khānīs and those of Ḥusain Khān *Daryā-khānī* and the retainers of Sl. Muḥammad *Dūldāī*, and again, of amīrs of Hind, 'Alī Khān *Farmūlī* and Malik Dād *Kararānī* and Shaikh Muḥammad of Shaikh *Bhakhārī*(?) and Tātār Khān Khān-i-jahān.

At the time this army was crossing the Gang-river (Ganges), Bīban, hearing about it, fled, abandoning his baggage. Our army followed him to Khairābād,[2155] stayed there a few days and then turned back.

(*n. Appointments and dispersion for the Rains.*)

After the treasure had been shared out,[2156] Rānā Sangā's great affair intervened before districts and *parganas* were apportioned. During the respite now from Holy-war against the Pagan (Sangā), this apportionment was made. As the Rains were near, it was settled for every-one to go to his *pargana*, get equipmentFol. 329b. ready, and be present when the Rains were over.

(*o. Misconduct of Humāyūn.*)

Meantime news came that Humāyūn had gone into Dihlī, there opened several treasure-houses and, without permission, taken possession of their contents. I had never looked for such a thing from him; it grieved me very much; I wrote and sent off to him very severe reproaches.[2157]

(*p. An embassy to 'Irāq.*)

Khwājagī Asad who had already gone as envoy to 'Irāq and returned with Sulaimān *Turkmān*,[2158] was again joined with him and on the 15th of Sha'bān (*May 17th*) sent with befitting gifts to Shāh-zāda Ṭ̤ahmāsp.

(*q. Tardī Beg khāksār resigns service.*)

I had brought Tardī Beg out from the darwīsh-life and made a soldier of him; for how many years had he served me! Now his desire for the darwīsh-life was overmastering and he asked for leave. It was given and he was sent as an envoy to Kāmrān conveying 3 *laks* from the Treasury for him.[2159]

(*r. Lines addressed to deserting friends.*)

A little fragment[2160] had been composed suiting the state of those who had gone away during the past year; I now addressed it to Mullā 'Alī Khān and sent it to him by Tardī Beg. It is as follows:—[2161]

Ah you who have gone from this country of Hind,

Fol. 330.Aware for yourselves of its woe and its pain,

With longing desire for Kābul's fine air,

You went hot-foot forth out of Hind.

The pleasure you looked for you will have found there

With sociable ease and charm and delight;

As for us, God be thanked! we still are alive,

In spite of much pain and unending distress;

Pleasures of sense and bodily toil

Have been passed-by by you, passed-by too by us.

(*s. Of the Ramẓān Feast.*)

Ramẓān was spent this year with ablution and *tarāwiḥ*[2162] in the Garden-of-eight-paradises. Since my 11th year I had not kept the Ramẓān Feast for two successive years in the same place; last year I had kept it in Āgra; this year, saying, "Don't break the rule!" I went on the last day of the month to keep it in Sīkrī. Tents were set up on a stone platform made on the n.e. side of the Garden-of-victory which is now being laid out at Sīkrī, and in them the Feast was held.[2163]

(*t. Playing cards.*)

The night we left Āgra Mīr 'Alī the armourer was sent to Shāh Ḥasan (*Arghūn*) in Tatta to take him playing-cards [*ganjīfa*] he much liked and had asked for.[2164]

(*u. Illness and a tour.*)

(*August 3rd*) On Sunday the 5th of Ẕū'l-qa'da I fell ill; the illness lasted 17 days.

(*August 24th*) On Friday the 24th of the same month we set out to visit Dūlpūr. That night I slept at a place half-way;Fol. 330b. reached Sikandar's dam[2165] at dawn, and dismounted there.

At the end of the hill below the dam the rock is of building-stone. I had Ustād Shāh Muḥammad the stone-cutter brought and gave him an order that if a house could be cut all in one piece in that rock, it was to be done, but that if the rock were too low for a residence (*'imārat*), it was to be levelled and have a reservoir, all in one piece, cut out of it.

From Dūlpūr we went on to visit Bārī. Next morning (*August 26th*) I rode out from Bārī through the hills between it and the Chaṃbal-river in order to view the river. This done I went back to Bārī. In these hills we saw the ebony-tree, the fruit of which people call *tindū*. It is said that there are white ebony-trees also and that most ebony-trees in these hills are of this kind.[2166]

On leaving Bārī we went to Sīkrī; we reached Āgra on the 29th of the same month (*August 28th*).

(*v. Doubts about Shaikh Bāyazīd Farmūlī.*)

As in these days people were telling wild news about Shaikh Bāyazīd, Sl. Qulī *Turk* was sent to him to give him tryst[2167] in 20 days.

(*w. Religious and metrical exercises.*)

(*August 28th*) On Friday the 2nd of Ẕū'l-ḥijja I began what one is made to read 41 times.[2168]

In these same days I cut up [*taqṭī'*] the following couplet of mine into 504 measures[2169]:—

"Shall I tell of her eye or her brow, her fire or her speech?

Shall I tell of her stature or cheek, of her hair or her waist?"

On this account a treatise[2170] was arranged.

(*x. Return of illness.*)

Fol. 331.On this day (*i.e.* 2nd Ẕū'l-ḥijja) I fell ill again; the illness lasted nine days.

(*y. Start for Saṃbal.*)

(*Sep. 24th*) On Thursday the 29th of Ẕū'l-ḥijja we rode out for an excursion to Kūl and Saṃbal.

934 AH.-SEP. 27TH 1527 TO SEP. 15TH 1528 AD.2171

(*a. Visit to Kūl (Aligarh) and Saṃbal.*)

(*Sep. 27th*) On Saturday the 1st of Muḥarram we dismounted in Kūl (Koel). Humāyūn had left Darwīsh(-i-'alī) and Yūsuf-i-'alī[2172] in Saṃbal; they crossed one river,[2173] fought Quṭ̤b *Sīrwānī*[2174] and a party of rājas, beat them well and killed a mass of men. They sent a few heads and an elephant into Kūl while we were there. After we had gone about Kūl for two days, we dismounted at Shaikh Gūran's house by his invitation, where he entertained us hospitably and laid an offering before us.

(*Sep. 30th-Muḥ. 4th*) Riding on from that place, we dismounted at Aūtrūlī (Atrauli).[2175]

(*Oct. 1st-Muḥ. 5th*) On Wednesday we crossed the river Gang (Ganges) and spent the night in villages of Saṃbal.

(*Oct. 2nd-Muḥ. 6th*) On Thursday we dismounted in Saṃbal. After going about in it for two days, we left on Saturday.

(*Oct. 5th-Muḥ. 9th*) On Sunday we dismounted in Sikandara[2176] at the house of Rāo *Sīrwānī* who set food before us and served us. When we rode out at dawn, I made some pretext to leave the rest, and galloped on alone to within a *kuroh* of Āgra where they overtook me. At the Mid-day Prayer we dismounted in Āgra.

(*b. Illness of Bābur.*)

(*Oct. 12th*) On Sunday the 16th of Muḥarram I had fever and ague. This returned again and again during the next 25 or 26 days. I drank operative medicine and at last relief came. I suffered much from thirst and want of sleep.

Fol. 331b.While I was ill, I composed a quatrain or two; here is one of them:—[2177]

Fever grows strong in my body by day,

Sleep quits my eyes as night comes on;

Like to my pain and my patience the pair,

For while that goes waxing, this wanes.

(*c. Arrival of kinswomen.*)

(*Nov. 23rd*) On Saturday the 28th of Ṣafar there arrived two of the paternal-aunt begīms, Fakhr-i-jahān Begīm and Khadīja-sulṭān Begīm.[2178] I went to above Sikandarābād to wait on them.[2179]

(*d. Concerning a mortar.*)

(*Nov. 24th-Ṣafar 29th*) On Sunday Ustād 'Alī-qulī discharged a stone from a large mortar; the stone went far but the mortar broke in pieces, one of which, knocking down a party of men, killed eight.

(*e. Visit to Sīkrī.*)

(*Dec. 1st*) On Monday the 7th of the first Rabī' I rode out to visit Sīkrī. The octagonal platform ordered made in the middle of the lake was ready; we went over by boat, had an awning set up on it and elected for *ma'jūn*.

(*f. Holy-war against Chandīrī.*)

(*Dec. 9th*) After returning from Sīkrī we started on Monday night the 14th of the first Rabī',[2180] with the intention of making Holy-war against Chandīrī, did as much as 3 *kurohs* (6 m.) and dismounted in Jalīsīr.[2181] After staying there two days for people to equip and array, we marched on Thursday (*Dec. 12th-Rabī' I. 17th*) and dismounted at Anwār. I left Anwār by boat, and disembarked beyond Chandwār.[2182]

(*Dec. 23rd*) Advancing march by march, we dismounted at the Kanār-passage[2183] on Monday the 28th.

(*Dec. 26th*) On Thursday the 2nd of the latter Rabī' I crossed the river; there was 4 or 5 days delay on one bank or the other before the army got across. On those days we went more thanFol. 332. once on board a boat and ate *ma'jūn*. The junction of the river Chaṃbal is between one and two *kurohs* (2-4 m.) above the Kanār-passage; on Friday I went into a boat on the Chaṃbal, passed the junction and so to camp.

(*g. Troops sent against Shaikh Bāyazīd Farmūlī.*)

Though there had been no clear proof of Shaikh Bāyazīd's hostility, yet his misconduct and action made it certain that he had hostile intentions. On account of this Muḥammad 'Alī *Jang-jang* was detached from the army and sent to bring together from Qanūj Muḥammad Sl. Mīrzā and the sulṭāns and amīrs of that neighbourhood, such as Qāsim-i-ḥusain Sulṭān, Bī-khūb (or, Nī-khūb) Sulṭān, Malik Qāsim, Kūkī, Abū'l-muḥammad the lancer, and Minūchihr Khān with his elder and younger brethren and Daryā-khānīs, so that they might move against the hostile Afghāns. They were to invite Shaikh Bāyazīd to go with them; if he came frankly, they were to take him along; if not, were to drive him off. Muḥammad 'Alī asking for a few elephants, ten were given him. After he had leave to set off, Bābā Chuhra (the Brave) was sent to and ordered to join him.

(*h. Incidents of the journey to Chandīrī.*)

From Kanār one *kuroh* (2 m.) was done by boat.

(*Jan. 1st 1528 AD.*) On Wednesday the 8th of the latter Rabī' we dismounted within a *kuroh* of Kālpī. Bābā Sl. came to wait on me in this camp; he is a son of Khalīl Sl. who is a younger brother of the full-blood of Sl. Sa'īd Khān. Last Fol. 332b.year he fled from his elder brother[2184] but, repenting himself, went back from the Andar-āb border; when he neared Kāshghar, The Khān (Sa'īd) sent Ḥaidar M. to meet him and take him back.

(*Jan. 2nd-Rabī' II. 9th*) Next day we dismounted at 'Ālam Khān's house in Kālpī where he set Hindūstānī food before us and made an offering.

(*Jan. 6th*) On Monday the 13th of the month we marched from Kālpī.

(*Jan. 10th-Rabī' II. 17th*) On Friday we dismounted at Īrij.[2185]

(*Jan. 11th*) On Saturday we dismounted at Bāndīr.[2186]

(*Jan. 12th*) On Sunday the 19th of the month Chīn-tīmūr Sl. was put at the head of 6 or 7000 men and sent ahead against Chandīrī. With him went the begs Bāqī *mīng-bāshī* (head of a thousand), Qūj Beg's (brother) Tardī Beg, 'Āshiq the taster, Mullā Apāq, Muḥsin[2187] *Dūldāī* and, of the Hindūstānī begs, Shaikh Gūran.

(*Jan 17th*) On Friday the 24th of the month we dismounted near Kachwa. After encouraging its people, it was bestowed on the son of Badru'd-dīn.[2188]

Kachwa[2189] is a shut-in place, having lowish hills all round it. A dam has been thrown across between hills on the south-east of it, and thus a large lake made, perhaps 5 or 6 *kurohs* (10-12 m.) round. This lake encloses Kachwa on three sides; on the north-west a space of ground is kept dry;[2190] here, therefore is its Gate. On the lake are a great many very small boats, able to hold 3 or 4 persons; in these the inhabitants go out on the lake, if they have to flee. There are two other lakes before Kachwa isFol. 333. reached, smaller than its own and, like that, made by throwing a dam across between hills.

(*Jan. 18th*) We waited a day in Kachwa in order to appoint active overseers and a mass of spadesmen to level the road and cut jungle down, so that the carts and mortar[2191] might pass along it easily. Between Kachwa and Chandīrī the country is jungly.

(*Jan. 19th-Rabī' II. 26th*) After leaving Kachwa we halted one night, passed the Burhānpūr-water (Bhurānpūr)[2192] and dismounted within 3 *kurohs* (6 m.) of Chandīrī.

(*i. Chandīrī and its capture.*)

The citadel of Chandīrī stands on a hill; below it are the town (*shahr*) and outer-fort (*tāsh-qūrghān*), and below these is the level road along which carts pass.[2193] When we left Burhānpūr (*Jan. 10th*) we marched for a *kuroh* below Chandīrī for the convenience of the carts.[2194]

(*Jan. 21st*) After one night's halt we dismounted beside Bahjat Khān's tank[2195] on the top of its dam, on Tuesday the 28th of the month.

(*Jan. 22nd-Rabī' II. 29th*) Riding out at dawn, we assigned post after post (*būljār, būljār*),[2196] round the walled town (*qūrghān*) to centre, right, and left. Ustād 'Alī-qulī chose, for his stone-discharge, ground that had no fall[2197]; overseers and spadesmen were told off to raise a place (*m:ljār*) for the mortar to rest on, and the whole army was ordered to get ready appliances for taking a fort, mantelets, ladders[2198] and ... -mantelets (*tūra*).[2199]

Formerly Chandīrī will have belonged to the Sulṭāns of Mandāū (Mandū). When Sl. Nāṣiru'd-dīn passed away,[2200] oneFol. 333b. of his sons Sl. Maḥmūd who is now holding Mandū, took possession of it and its neighbouring parts, and another son called Muḥammad Shāh laid hands on Chandīrī and put it under Sl. Sikandar *(Lūdī)'s* protection, who, in his turn, took Muḥammad Shāh's side and sent him large forces. Muḥammad Shāh survived Sl. Sikandar and died in Sl. Ibrāhīm's time, leaving a very young son called Aḥmad Shāh whom Sl. Ibrāhīm drove out and replaced by a man of his own. At the time Rānā Sangā led out an army against Sl. Ibrāhīm and Ibrāhīm's begs turned against him at Dūlpūr, Chandīrī fell into the Rānā's hands and by him was given to Medinī [Mindnī] Rāo[2201] the greatly-trusted pagan who was now in it with 4 or 5000 other pagans.

As it was understood there was friendship between Medinī Rāo and Ārāīsh Khān, the latter was sent with Shaikh Gūran to speak to Medinī Rāo with favour and kindness, and promise Shamsābād[2202] in exchange for Chandīrī. One or two of his trusted men got out(?).[2203] No adjustment of matters was reached, it is not known whether because Medinī Rāo did not trust what was said, or whether because he was buoyed up by delusion about the strength of the fort.

(*Jan. 28th*) At dawn on Tuesday the 6th of the first Jumāda we marched from Bahjat Khān's tank intending to assault Chandīrī. We dismounted at the side of the middle-tank near Fol. 334.the fort.

(*j. Bad news.*)

On this same morning after reaching that ground, Khalīfa brought a letter or two of which the purport was that the troops appointed for the East[2204] had fought without consideration, been beaten, abandoned Laknau, and gone to Qanūj. Seeing that Khalīfa was much perturbed and alarmed by these news, I said,[2205] (*Persian*) "There is no ground for perturbation or alarm; nothing comes to pass but what is predestined of God. As this task (Chandīrī) is ahead of us, not a breath must be drawn about what has been told us. Tomorrow we will assault the fort; that done, we shall see what comes."

(*k. Siege of Chandīrī, resumed.*)

The enemy must have strengthened just the citadel, and have posted men by twos and threes in the outer-fort for prudence' sake. That night our men went up from all round; those few in the outer-fort did not fight; they fled into the citadel.

(*Jan. 29th*) At dawn on Wednesday the 7th of the first Jumāda, we ordered our men to arm, go to their posts, provoke to fight, and attack each from his place when I rode out with drum and standard.

I myself, dismissing drum and standard till the fighting should grow hot, went to amuse myself by watching Ustād 'Alī-qulī's stone-discharge.[2206] Nothing was effected by it because his ground had no fall (*yāghdā*) and because the fort-walls, being entirelyFol. 334b. of stone, were extremely strong.

That the citadel of Chandīrī stands on a hill has been said already. Down one side of this hill runs a double-walled road (*dū-tahī*) to water.[2207] This is the one place for attack; it had been assigned as the post of the right and left hands and royal corps of the centre.[2208] Hurled though assault was from every side, the greatest force was here brought to bear. Our braves did not turn back, however much the pagans threw down stones and flung flaming fire upon them. At length Shāhīm the centurion[2209] got up where the *dū-tahī* wall touches the wall of the outer fort; braves swarmed up in other places; the *dū-tahī* was taken.

Not even as much as this did the pagans fight in the citadel; when a number of our men swarmed up, they fled in haste.[2210] In a little while they came out again, quite naked, and renewed the fight; they put many of our men to flight; they made them fly (*āuchūrdīlār*) over the ramparts; some they cut down and killed. Why they had gone so suddenly off the walls seems to have been that they had taken the resolve of those who give up a place as lost; they put all their ladies and beauties (*ṣūratīlār*) to death, then, looking themselves to die, came naked out to fight. Our men attacking, each one from his post, droveFol. 335. them from the walls whereupon 2 or 300 of them entered Medinī Rāo's house and there almost all killed one another in this way:—one having taken stand with a sword, the rest eagerly stretched out the neck for his blow.[2211] Thus went the greater number to hell.

By God's grace this renowned fort was captured in 2 or 3 *garīs*[2212] (*cir.* an hour), without drum and standard,[2213] with no hard fighting done. A pillar of pagan-heads was ordered set up on a hill north-west of Chandīrī. A chronogram of this victory having been found in the words *Fatḥ-i-dāru'l-ḥarb*[2214] (Conquest of a hostile seat), I thus composed them:—

Was for awhile the station Chandīrī

Pagan-full, the seat of hostile force;

By fighting, I vanquished its fort,

The date was *Fatḥ-i-dāru'l-ḥarb.*

(*l. Further description of Chandīrī.*)

Chandīrī is situated (in) rather good country,[2215] having much running-water round about it. Its citadel is on a hill and inside it has a tank cut out of the solid rock. There is another large tank[2216] at the end of the *dū-tahī* by assaulting which the fort was taken. All houses in Chandīrī, whether of high or low, are built of stone, those of chiefs being laboriously carved;[2217] those of the lower classes are also of stone but are not carved. They are covered inFol. 335b. with stone-slabs instead of with earthen tiles. In front of the fort are three large tanks made by former governors who threw dams across and made tanks round about it; their ground lies high.[2218] It has a small river (*daryācha*), Betwa[2219] by name, which may be some 3 *kurohs* (6 m.) from Chandīrī itself; its water is noted in Hindūstān as excellent and pleasant drinking. It is a perfect little river (*daryā-ghīna*). In its bed lie piece after piece of sloping rock (*qīālār*)[2220] fit for making houses.[2221] Chandīrī is 90 *kurohs* (180 m.) by road to the south of Āgra. In Chandīrī the altitude of the Pole-star (?) is 25 degrees.[2222]

(*m. Enforced change of campaign.*)

(*Jan. 30th-Jumāda I. 8th*) At dawn on Thursday we went round the fort and dismounted beside Mallū Khān's tank.[2223]

We had come to Chandīrī meaning, after taking it, to move against Rāīsīng, Bhīlsān, and Sārangpūr, pagan lands dependent on the pagan Ṣalāḥu'd-dīn, and, these taken, to move on Rānā Sangā in Chītūr. But as that bad news had come, the begs were summoned, matters were discussed, and decision made that the proper course was first to see to the rebellion of those malignants. Chandīrī was given to the Aḥmad Shāh already mentioned, a grandson of Sl. Nāṣiru'd-dīn; 50 *laks* from it were made *khalṣa*;[2224] Mullā Apāq was entrusted with its military-collectorate, and left to reinforce Aḥmad Shāh with from 2 to 3000 Turks and Hindūstānīs.

Fol. 336.(*Feb. 2nd*) This work finished, we marched from Mallū Khān's tank on Sunday the 11th of the first Jumāda, with the intention of return (north), and dismounted on the bank of the Burhānpūr-water.

(*Feb. 9th*) On Sunday again, Yakka Khwāja and Ja'far Khwāja were sent from Bāndīr to fetch boats from Kālpī to the Kanār-passage.

(*Feb. 22nd*) On Saturday the 24th of the month we dismounted at the Kanār-passage, and ordered the army to begin to cross.

(*n. News of the rebels.*)

News came in these days that the expeditionary force[2225] had abandoned Qanūj also and come to Rāprī, and that a strong body of the enemy had assaulted and taken Shamsābād although Abū'l-muḥammad the lancer must have strengthened it.[2226] There was delay of 3 or 4 days on one side or other of the river before the army got across. Once over, we moved march by march towards Qanūj, sending scouting braves (*qāzāq yīgītlār*) ahead to get news of our opponents. Two or three marches from Qanūj, news was brought that Ma'rūf's son had fled on seeing the dark mass of the news-gatherers, and got away. Bīban, Bāyazīd and Ma'rūf, on hearing news of us, crossed Gang (Ganges) and seated themselves on its eastern bank opposite Qanūj, thinking to prevent our passage.

(*o. A bridge made over the Ganges.*)

(*Feb. 27th*) On Thursday the 6th of the latter Jumāda we passed Qanūj and dismounted on the western bank of Gang. Some of the braves went up and down the river and took boatsFol. 336b. by force,[2227] bringing in 30 or 40, large or small. Mīr Muḥammad the raftsman was sent to find a place convenient for making a bridge and to collect requisites for making it. He came back approving of a place about a *kuroh* (2 m.) below the camp. Energetic overseers were told off for the work. Ustād 'Alī-qulī placed the mortar for his stone-discharge near where the bridge was to be and shewed himself active in discharging it. Muṣṭafa *Rūmī* had the culverin-carts crossed over to an island below the place for the bridge, and from that island began a culverin-discharge. Excellent matchlock fire was made from a post[2228] raised above the bridge. Malik Qāsim *Mughūl* and a very few men went across the river once or twice and fought excellently (*yakhshīlār aūrūshtīlār*). With equal boldness Bābā Sl. and Darwīsh Sl. also crossed, but went with the insufficient number of from 10 to 15 men; they went after the Evening Prayer and came back without fighting, with nothing done; they were much blamed for this crossing of theirs. At last Malik Qāsim, grown bold, attacked the enemy's camp and, by shooting arrows into it, drew him out (?);[2229] he came with a mass of men and an elephant, fell on Malik Qāsim and hurried him off. Malik Qāsim got into a boat, but before it could put off, the elephantFol. 337. came up and swamped it. In that encounter Malik Qāsim died.

In the days before the bridge was finished Ustād 'Alī-qulī did good things in stone-discharge (*yakhshīlār tāsh aīti*), on the first day discharging 8 stones, on the second 16, and going on equally well for 3 or 4 days. These stones he discharged from the Ghāzī-mortar which is so-called because it was used in the battle with Rānā Sangā the pagan. There had been another and larger mortar which burst after discharging one stone.[2230] The matchlockmen made a mass (*qālīn*) of discharges, bringing down many men and horses; they shot also slave-workmen running scared away (?) and men and horses passing-by.[2231]

(*March 11th*) On Wednesday the 19th of the latter Jumāda the bridge being almost finished, we marched to its head. The Afghāns must have ridiculed the bridge-making as being far from completion.[2232]

(*March 12th*) The bridge being ready on Thursday, a small body of foot-soldiers and Lāhorīs went over. Fighting as small followed.

(*p. Encounter with the Afghāns.*)

(*March 13th*) On Friday the royal corps, and the right and left hands of the centre crossed on foot. The whole body of Afghāns, armed, mounted, and having elephants with them, attacked us. They hurried off our men of the left hand, but our centre itself (*i.e.* the royal corps) and the right hand stood Fol. 337b.firm, fought, and forced the enemy to retire. Two men from these divisions had galloped ahead of the rest; one was dismounted and taken; the horse of the other was struck again and again, had had enough,[2233] turned round and when amongst our men, fell down. On that day 7 or 8 heads were brought in; many of the enemy had arrow or matchlock wounds. Fighting went on till the Other Prayer. That night all who had gone across were made to return; if (more) had gone over on that Saturday's eve,[2234] most of the enemy would probably have fallen into our hands, but this was in my mind:—Last year we marched out of Sīkrī to fight Rānā Sangā on Tuesday, New-year's-day, and crushed that rebel on Saturday; this year we had marched to crush these rebels on Wednesday, New-year's-day,[2235] and it would be one of singular things, if we beat them on Sunday. So thinking, we did not make the rest of the army cross. The enemy did not come to fight on Saturday, but stood arrayed a long way off.

(*Sunday March 15th-Jumāda II. 23rd*) On this day the carts were taken over, and at this same dawn the army was ordered to cross. At beat of drum news came from our scouts that the enemy had fled. Chīn-tīmūr Sl. was ordered to lead his army in pursuit and the following leaders also were made pursuers who should move with the Sulṭān and not go beyond his word:—Muḥammad ‘Alī *Jang-jang*, Ḥusamu’d-dīn ‘Alī (son) of Khalīfa, Muḥibb-i-‘alī (son) of Khalīfa, Kūkī (son) of Bābā Qashqa, Dost-i-muḥammad (son) of Bābā Qashqa, Bāqī ofFol. 338. Tāshkīnt, and Red Walī. I crossed at the Sunnat Prayer. The camels were ordered to be taken over at a passage seen lower down. That Sunday we dismounted on the bank of standing-water within a *kuroh* of Bangarmāwū.[2236] Those appointed to pursue the Afghāns were not doing it well; they had dismounted in Bangarmāwū and were scurrying off at the Mid-day Prayer of this same Sunday.

(*March 16th-Jumāda II. 24th*) At dawn we dismounted on the bank of a lake belonging to Bangarmāwū.

(*q. Arrival of a Chaghatāī cousin.*)

On this same day (*March 16th*) Tūkhtā-būghā Sl. a son of my mother’s brother (*dādā*) the Younger Khān (*Aḥmad Chaghatāī*) came and waited on me.

(*March 21st*) On Saturday the 29th of the latter Jumāda I visited Laknau, crossed the Gūī-water[2237] and dismounted. This day I bathed in the Gūī-water. Whether it was from water getting into my ear, or whether it was from the effect of the climate, is not known, but my right ear was obstructed and for a few days there was much pain.[2238]

(*r. The campaign continued.*)

One or two marches from Aūd (Oudh) some-one came from Chīn-tīmūr Sl. to say, “The enemy is seated on the far side of the river Sīrd[a?];[2239] let His Majesty send help.” We detached a reinforcement of 1000 braves under Qarācha.

(*March 28th*) On Saturday the 7th of Rajab we dismounted Fol. 338b.2 or 3 *kurohs* from Aūd above the junction of the Gagar (Gogra) and Sīrd[a]. Till today Shaikh Bāyazīd will have been on the other side of the Sīrd[a] opposite Aūd, sending letters to the Sulṭān and discussing with him, but the Sulṭān getting to know his deceitfulness, sent word to Qarācha at the Mid-day Prayer and made ready to cross the river. On Qarācha’s joining him, they crossed at once to where were some 50 horsemen with 3 or 4 elephants. These men could make no stand; they fled; a few having been dismounted, the heads cut off were sent in.

Following the Sulṭān there crossed over Bī-khūb (var. Nī-khūb) Sl. and Tardī Beg (the brother) of Qūj Beg, and Bābā Chuhra (the Brave), and Bāqī *shaghāwal.* Those who had crossed first and gone on, pursued Shaikh Bāyazīd till the Evening Prayer, but he flung himself into the jungle and escaped. Chīn-tīmūr dismounted late on the bank of standing-water, rode on at midnight after the rebel, went as much as 40 *kurohs* (80 m.), and came to where Shaikh Bāyazīd's family and relations (*nisba*?) had been; they however must have fled. He sent gallopers off in all directions from that place; Bāqī *shaghāwal* and a few braves drove the enemy like sheep before them, overtook the family and brought in some Afghān prisoners.

We stayed a few days on that ground (near Aūd) in order to settle the affairs of Aūd. People praised the land lying along the Sīrd[a] 7 or 8 *kurohs* (14-16 m.) above Aūd, saying it was hunting-ground. Mīr Muḥammad the raftsman was sent out and returned after looking at the crossings over the Gagar-water (Gogra) and the Sīrd[a]-water (Chauka?).

Fol. 339.(*April 2nd*) On Thursday the 12th of the month I rode out intending to hunt.[2240]

TRANSLATOR'S NOTE.

Here, in all known texts of the *Bābur-nāma* there is a break of the narrative between April 2nd and Sep. 18th 1528 AD.-Jumāda II. 12th 934 AH. and Muḥarram 3rd 935 AH., which, whether intentional or accidental, is unexplained by Bābur's personal circumstances. It is likely to be due to a loss of pages from Bābur's autograph manuscript, happening at some time preceding the making of either of the Persian translations of his writings and of the Elphinstone and Ḥaidarābād transcripts. Though such a loss might have occurred easily during the storm chronicled on f. 376*b*, it seems likely that Bābur would then have become aware of it and have made it good. A more probable explanation of the loss is the danger run by Humāyūn's library during his exile from rule in Hindūstān, at which same time may well have occurred the seeming loss of the record of 936 and 937 AH.

(*a. Transactions of the period of the lacuna.*)

Mr. Erskine notes (*Mems.* p. 381 n.) that he found the gap in all MSS. he saw and that historians of Hindūstān throw no light upon the transactions of the period. Much can be gleaned however as to Bābur's occupations during the 5-1/2 months of the *lacuna* from his chronicle of 935 AH. which makes several references to occurrences of "last year" and also allows several inferences to be drawn. From this source it becomes known that the

Afghān campaign the record of which is broken by the gap, was carried on and that in its course Bābur was at Jūn-pūr (f. 365), Chausa (f. 365*b*) and Baksara (f. 366-366*b*); that he swam the Ganges (f. 366*b*), bestowed Sarūn on a Farmūlī Shaikh-zāda (f. 374*b* and f. 377), negociated with Rānā Sangā's son Bikramājīt (f. 342*b*), ordered a Chār-bāgh laid out (f. 340), and was ill for 40 days (f. 346*b*). It may be inferred too that he visited Dūlpūr (f. 353*b*) recalled 'Askarī (f. 339), sent Khwāja Dost-i-khāwand on family affairs to Kābul (f. 345*b*), and was much pre-occupied by the disturbed state of Kābul (*see* his letters to Humāyūn and Khwāja Kālan written in 935 AH.).[2241]

It is not easy to follow the dates of events in 935 AH. because in many instances only the day of the week or a "next day" is entered. I am far from sure that one passage at least now found *s.a.* 935 AH. does not belong to 934 AH. It is not in the Ḥai. Codex (where its place would have been on f. 363*b*), and, so far as I can see, does not fit with the dates of 935 AH. It will be considered with least trouble with its context and my notes (*q.v.* f. 363*b* and ff. 366-366*b*).

(*b. Remarks on the lacuna.*)

One interesting biographical topic is likely to have found mention in the missing record, *viz.* the family difficulties which led to 'Askarī's supersession by Kāmrān in the government of Multān (f. 359).

Another is the light an account of the second illness of 934 AH. might have thrown on a considerable part of the Collection of verses already written in Hindūstān and now known to us as the *Rāmpūr Dīwān*. The *Bābur-nāma* allows the dates of much of its contents to be known, but there remain poems which seem prompted by the self-examination of some illness not found in the *B.N.* It contains the metrical version of Khwāja 'Ubaidu'l-lāh's *Wālidiyyah* of which Bābur writes on f. 346 and it is dated Monday Rabī' II. 15th 935 AH. (Dec. 29th 1528 AD.). I surmise that the reflective verses following the *Wālidiyyah* belong to the 40 days' illness of 934 AH. *i.e.* were composed in the period of the *lacuna*. The Collection, as it is in the "Rāmpūr Dīwān", went to a friend who was probably Khwāja Kalān; it may have been the only such collection made by Bābur. No other copy of it has so far been found. It has the character of an individual gift with verses specially addressed to its recipient. Any light upon it which may have vanished with pages of 934 AH. is an appreciable loss.

935 AH.-SEP. 15TH 1528 TO SEP. 5TH 1529 AD.[2242]

(*a. Arrivals at Court.*)

(*Sep. 18th*) On Friday the 3rd[2243] of Muḥarram, 'Askarī whom I had summoned for the good of Multān[2244] before I moved out for Chandīrī, waited on me in the private-house.[2245]

(*Sep. 19th*) Next day waited on me the historian Khwānd-amīr, Maulānā Shihāb[2246] the enigmatist, and Mīr Ibrāhīm the harper a relation of Yūnas-i-'alī, who had all come out of Herī long before, wishing to wait on me.[2247]

(*b. Bābur starts for Gūālīār.*)[2248]

(*Sep. 20th*) With the intention of visiting Gūālīār which in books they write Gālīūr,[2249] I crossed the Jūn at the Other Prayer of Sunday the 5th of the month, went into the fort of Āgra to bid farewell to Fakhr-i-jahān Begīm and Khadīja-sulṭān Begīm who were to start for Kābul in a few days, and got to horse. Muḥammad-i-zamān Mīrzā asked for leave and stayed behind in Āgra. That night we did 3 or 4 *kurohs* (6-8 m.) of the road, dismounted near a large lake (*kūl*) and there slept.

(*Sep. 21st*) We got through the Prayer somewhat before time (*Muḥ. 6th*) and rode on, nooned[2250] on the bank of the Gamb[h]īr-water[2251], and went on shortly after the Mid-day Prayer. On the way we ate[2252] powders mixed with the flour of parched Fol. 339b. grain,[2253] Mullā Rafī' having prepared them for raising the spirits. They were found very distasteful and unsavoury. Near the Other Prayer we dismounted a *kuroh* (2 m.) west of Dūlpūr, at a place where a garden and house had been ordered made.[2254]

(*c. Work in Dūlpūr (Dhūlpūr).*)

That place is at the end of a beaked hill,[2255] its beak being of solid red building-stone (*'imārat-tāsh*). I had ordered the (beak of the) hill cut down (dressed down?) to the ground-level and that if there remained a sufficient height, a house was to be cut out in it, if not, it was to be levelled and a tank (*ḥauẓ*) cut out in its top. As it was not found high enough for a house, Ūstād Shāh Muḥammad the stone-cutter was ordered to level it and cut out an octagonal, roofed tank. North of this tank the ground is thick with trees, mangoes, *jāman* (*Eugenia jambolana*), all sorts of trees; amongst them I had ordered a well made, 10 by 10; it was almost ready; its water goes to the afore-named tank. To the north of this tank Sl. Sikandar's dam is flung across (the valley); on it houses have been built, and above it the waters of the Rains gather into a great lake. On the east of this lake is a garden; I ordered a seat and four-pillared platform (*tālār*) to be cut out in the solid rock on that same side, and a mosqueFol. 340. built on the western one.

(*Sept. 22nd and 23rd—Muḥ. 7th and 8th*) On account of these various works, we stayed in Dūlpūr on Tuesday and Wednesday.

(*d. Journey to Gūālīār resumed.*)

(*Sep. 24th*) On Thursday we rode on, crossed the Chaṃbal-river and made the Mid-day Prayer on its bank, between the two Prayers (the Mid-day and the Afternoon) bestirred ourselves to leave that place, passed the Kawārī and dismounted. The Kawārī-water being high through rain, we crossed it by boat, making the horses swim over.

(*Sep. 25th*) Next day, Friday which was 'Āshūr (*Muḥ. 10th*), we rode on, took our nooning at a village on the road, and at the Bed-time Prayer dismounted a *kuroh* north of Gūālīār, in a Chār-bāgh ordered made last year.[2256]

(*Sep. 26th*) Riding on next day after the Mid-day Prayer, we visited the low hills to the north of Gūālīār, and the Praying-place, went into the fort[2257] through the Gate called Hātī-pūl which joins Mān-sing's buildings (*'imārāt*[2258]), and dismounted, close to the Other Prayer, at those (*'imāratlār*)[2259] of Rāja Bikramājīt in which Raḥīm-dād[2260] had settled himself.

To-night I elected to take opium because of ear-ache; another reason was the shining of the moon.[2261]

(*e. Visit to the Rājas' palaces.*)

(*Sep. 27th*) Opium sickness gave me much discomfort next day (*Muḥ. 12th*); I vomited a good deal. Sickness notwithstanding, I visited the buildings (*'imāratlār*) of Mān-sing and Fol. 340b.Bikramājīt thoroughly. They are wonderful buildings, entirely of hewn stone, in heavy and unsymmetrical blocks however.[2262] Of all the Rājas' buildings Mān-sing's is the best and loftiest.[2263] It is more elaborately worked on its eastern face than on the others. This face may be 40 to 50 *qārī* (yards) high,[2264] and is entirely of hewn stone, whitened with plaster.[2265] In parts it is four storeys high; the lower two are very dark; we went through them with candles.[2266] On one (or, every) side of this building are five cupolas[2267] having between each two of them a smaller one, square after the fashion of Hindūstān. On the larger ones are fastened sheets of gilded copper. On the outside of the walls is painted-tile work, the semblance of plantain-trees being shewn all round with green tiles. In a bastion of the eastern front is the Hātī-pūl,[2268] *hātī* being what these people call an elephant, *pūl*, a gate. A sculptured image of an elephant with two drivers (*fīl-bān*)[2269] stands at the out-going (*chīqīsh*) of this Gate; it is exactly like an elephant; from it the gate is called Hātī-pūl. A window in theFol. 341. lowest storey where the building has four, looks towards this elephant and gives a near view of it.[2270] The cupolas which have been mentioned above are themselves the topmost stage (*murtaba*) of the building;[2271] the sitting-rooms are on the second storey (*ṭabaqat*), in a hollow even;[2272] they are rather airless places although Hindūstānī pains have been taken with them.[2273] The buildings of Mān-sing's son Bikramājīt are in a central position (*aūrta dā*) on the north side of the fort.[2274] The son's buildings do not match the father's. He has made a great dome, very dark but growing lighter if one stays awhile in it.[2275] Under it is a smaller building into which no light comes from any side. When Raḥīm-dād settled down in Bikramājīt's buildings, he made a rather small hall [*kīchīkrāq tālārghīna*] on the top of this dome.[2276] From Bikramājīt's buildings a road has been made to his father's, a road such that nothing is seen of it from outside and nothing known of it inside, a quite enclosed road.[2277]

After visiting these buildings, we rode to a college Raḥīm-dād Fol. 341b.had made by the side of a large tank, there enjoyed a flower-garden[2278] he had laid out, and went late to where the camp was in the Chārbāgh.

(*f. Raḥīm-dād's flower-garden.*)

Raḥīm-dād has planted a great numbers of flowers in his garden (*bāghcha*), many being beautiful red oleanders. In these places the oleander-flower is peach,[2279] those of Gūālīār are beautiful, deep red. I took some of them to Āgra and had them planted in gardens there. On the south of the garden is a large lake[2280] where the waters of the Rains gather; on the west of it is a lofty idol-house,[2281] side by side with which Sl. Shihābu'd-dīn Aīltmīsh (Altamsh) made a Friday mosque; this is a very lofty building (*'imārat*), the highest in the fort; it is seen, with the fort, from the Dūlpūr-hill (*cir.* 30 m. away). People say the stone for it was cut out and brought from the large lake above-mentioned. Raḥīm-dād has made a wooden (*yīghāch*) *tālār* in his garden, and porches at the gates, which, after the Hindūstānī fashion, are somewhat low and shapeless.

(*g. The Urwāh-valley.*)

(*Sep. 28th*) Next day (*Muḥ. 13th*) at the Mid-day Prayer we rode out to visit places in Gūālīār we had not yet seen. We saw the *'imārat* called Bādalgar[2282] which is part of Mān-sing's fort (*qila'*), went through the Hātī-pūl and across the fort to a place called Urwā (Urwāh), which is a valley-bottom (*qūl*) on its western side. Though Urwā is outside the fort-wall running along the top of the hill, it has two stages (*murtaba*) of high wall at its mouth. The higher of these walls is some 30 or 40 *qārī* (yards) high; this is the longer one; at each end it joinsFol. 342. the wall of the fort. The second wall curves in and joins the middle part of the first; it is the lower and shorter of the two. This curve of wall will have been made for a water-thief;[2283] within it is a stepped well (*wā'īn*) in which water is reached by 10 or 15 steps. Above the Gate leading from the valley to this walled-well the name of Sl. Shihābu'd-dīn Aīltmīsh (Altamsh) is inscribed, with the date 630 (AH.-1233 AD.). Below this outer wall and outside the fort there is a large lake which seems to dwindle (at times) till no lake remains; from it water goes to the water-thief. There are two other lakes inside Urwā the water of which those who live in the fort prefer to all other.

Three sides of Urwā are solid rock, not the red rock of Bīāna but one paler in colour. On these sides people have cut out idol-statues, large and small, one large statue on the south side being perhaps 20 *qārī* (yds.) high.[2284] These idols are shewn quite naked without covering for the privities. Along the sides of Fol. 342b.the two Urwā lakes 20 or 30 wells have been dug, with water from which useful vegetables (*sabzī kārlīklār*), flowers and trees are grown. Urwā is not a bad place; it is shut in (T. *tūr*); the idols are its defect; I, for my part, ordered them destroyed.[2285]

Going out of Urwā into the fort again, we enjoyed the window[2286] of the Sultānī-pūl which must have been closed through the pagan time till now, went to Raḥīm-dād's flower-garden at the Evening Prayer, there dismounted and there slept.

(*h. A son of Rānā Sangā negociates with Bābur.*)

(*Sep. 29th*) On Tuesday the 14th of the month came people from Rānā Sangā's second son, Bikramājīt by name, who with his mother Padmāwatī was in the fort of Rantanbūr. Before I rode out for Gūālīār,[2287] others had come from his great and trusted Hindū, Asūk by name, to indicate Bikramājīt's submission and obeisance and ask a subsistence-allowance of 70 *laks* for him; it had been settled at that time that *parganas* to the amount he asked should be bestowed on him, his men were given leave to go, with tryst for Gūālīār which we were about to visit. They came into Gūālīār somewhat after the trysting-day. The Hindū Asūk[2288] is said to be a near relation of Bikramājīt's mother Padmāwatī; he, for his part, set these particulars forth father-like Fol. 343.and son-like;[2289] they, for theirs, concurring with him, agreed to wish me well and serve me. At the time when Sl. Maḥmūd (*Khilji*) was beaten by Rānā Sangā and fell into pagan captivity

(925 AH.-1519 AD.) he possessed a famous crown-cap (*tāj-kula*) and golden belt, accepting which Sangā let him go free. That crown-cap and golden belt must have become Bikramājīt's; his elder brother Ratan-sī, now Rānā of Chītūr in his father's place, had asked for them but Bikramājīt had not given them up,[2290] and now made the men he sent to me, speak to me about them, and ask for Bīāna in place of Rantanbūr. We led them away from the Bīāna question and promised Shamsābād in exchange for Rantanbūr. To-day (*Muḥ. 14th*) they were given a nine days' tryst for Bīāna, were dressed in robes of honour, and allowed to go.

(*i. Hindū temples visited.*)

We rode from the flower-garden to visit the idol-houses of Gūālīār. Some are two, and some are three storeys high, each storey rather low, in the ancient fashion. On their stone plinths (*izāra*) are sculptured images. Some idol-houses, College-fashion, have a portico, large high cupolas[2291] and *madrāsa*-like cells, each topped by a slender stone cupola.[2292] In the lower cells are idols carved in the rock.Fol. 343b.

After enjoying the sight of these buildings (*'imāratlār*) we left the fort by the south Gate,[2293] made an excursion to the south, and went (north) to the Chār-bāgh Raḥim-dād had made over-against the Hātī-pūl.[2294] He had prepared a feast of cooked-meat (*āsh*) for us and, after setting excellent food before us, made offering of a mass of goods and coin worth 4 *laks*. From his Chār-bāgh I rode to my own.

(*j. Excursion to a waterfall.*)

(*Sep. 30th.*) On Wednesday the 15th of the month I went to see a waterfall 6 *kurohs* (12 m.) to the south-east of Gūālīār. Less than that must have been ridden;[2295] close to the Mid-day Prayer we reached a fall where sufficient water for one mill was coming down a slope (*qīā*) an *arghamchi*[2296] high. Below the fall there is a large lake; above it the water comes flowing through solid rock; there is solid rock also below the fall. A lake forms wherever the water falls. On the banks of the water lie piece after piece of rock as if for seats, but the water is said not always to be there. We sat down above the fall and ate *ma'jūn*, went up-stream to visit its source (*badayat*), returned, got out on higher ground, and stayed while musicians played and reciters Fol. 344.repeated things (*nīma aītīlār*). The Ebony-tree which Hindīs call *tindū*, was pointed out to those who had not seen it before. We went down the hill and, between the Evening and Bed-time Prayers, rode away, slept at a place reached near the second watch (midnight), and with the on-coming of the first watch of day (6 a.m. *Muḥ. 16th-Oct. 1st*) reached the Chār-bāgh and dismounted.

(*k. Ṣalāḥu'd-dīn's birth-place.*)[2297]

(*Oct. 2nd*) On Friday the 17th of the month, I visited the garden of lemons and pumeloes (*sadā-fal*) in a valley-bottom amongst the hills above a village called Sūkhjana (?)[2298] which is Ṣalāḥu'd-dīn's birth-place. Returning to the Chār-bāgh, I dismounted there in the first watch.[2299]

(*l. Incidents of the march from Gūālīār.*)

(*Oct. 4th*) On Sunday the 19th of the month, we rode before dawn from the Chār-bāgh, crossed the Kawārī-water and took our nooning (*tūshlāndūk*). After the Mid-day Prayer we rode on, at sunset passed the Chaṃbal-water, between the Evening and Bed-time Prayers entered Dulpūr-fort, there, by lamp-light, visited a Hot-bath which Abū'l-fatḥ had made, rode on, and dismounted at the dam-head where the new Chār-bāgh is in making.

(*Oct. 5th*) Having stayed the night there, at dawn (*Monday 20th*) I visited what places had been ordered made.[2300] The face (*yūz*) of the roofed-tank, ordered cut in the solid rock, was not being got up quite straight; more stone-cutters were sent for who were to make the tank-bottom level, pour in water, and, by help of the water, to get the sides to one height. They got the face up straight just before the Other Prayer, were then ordered to fill the tank with water, by help of the water made the sidesFol. 344b. match, then busied themselves to smooth them. I ordered a water-chamber (*āb-khāna*) made at a place where it would be cut in the solid rock; inside it was to be a small tank also cut in the solid rock.

(*Here the record of 6 days is wanting.*)[2301]

(*Oct. 12th?*) To-day, Monday (*27th?*), there was a *ma'jūn* party. (*Oct. 13th*) On Tuesday I was still in that same place. (*Oct. 14th*) On the night of Wednesday,[2302] after opening the mouth and eating something[2303] we rode for Sīkrī. Near the second watch (midnight), we dismounted somewhere and slept; I myself could not sleep on account of pain in my ear, whether caused by cold, as is likely, I do not know. At the top of the dawn, we bestirred ourselves from that place, and in the first watch dismounted at the garden now in making at Sīkrī. The garden-wall and well-buildings were not getting on to my satisfaction; the overseers therefore were threatened and punished. We rode on from Sīkrī between the Other and Evening Prayers, passed through Marhākūr, dismounted somewhere and slept.

(*Oct. 15th*) Riding on (*Thursday 30th*), we got into Āgra during the first watch (6-9 a.m.). In the fort I saw the honoured Khadīja-sulṭān Begīm who had stayed behind for several reasons when Fakhr-i-jahān Begīm started for Kābul. Crossing Jūn (Jumna), I went to the Garden-of-eight paradises.[2304]

(*m. Arrival of kinswomen.*)

(*Oct. 17th*) On Saturday the 3rd of Ṣafar, between the Other and Evening Prayers, I went to see three of the great-aunt begīms,[2305] Gauhar-shād Begīm, Badī'u'l-jamāl Begīm, and Āq Begīm, with also, of lesser begīms,[2306] Sl. Maṣ'ūd Mīrzā's daughter Khān-zāda Begīm, and Sulṭān-bakht Begīm's daughter, and my *yīnkā chīcha's* grand-daughter, that is to say, Zaināb-sulṭān Begīm.[2307] They had come past Tūta and dismounted at a small Fol. 345.standing-water (*qarā sū*) on the edge of the suburbs. I came back direct by boat.

(*n. Despatch of an envoy to receive charge of Ranthaṃbhor.*)

(*Oct. 19th*) On Monday the 5th of the month of Ṣafar, Hāmūsī son of Dīwa, an old Hindū servant from Bhīra, was joined with Bikramājīt's former[2308] and later envoys in order that pact and agreement for the surrender of Ranthanbūr and for the conditions of Bikramājīt's service might be made in their own (hindū) way and custom. Before our man returned, he was to see, and learn, and make sure of matters; this done, if that person (*i.e.* Bikramājīt) stood fast to his spoken word, I, for my part, promised that, God bringing it aright, I would set him in his father's place as Rānā of Chitūr.[2309]

(*Here the record of 3 days is wanting.*)

(*o. A levy on stipendiaries.*)

(*Oct. 22nd*) By this time the treasure of Iskandar and Ibrāhīm in Dihlī and Āgra was at an end. Royal orders were given therefore, on Thursday the 8th of Ṣafar, that each stipendiary (*wajhdār*) should drop into the Dīwān, 30 in every 100 of his allowance, to be used for war-material and appliances, for equipment, for powder, and for the pay of gunners and matchlockmen.

(*p. Royal letters sent into Khurāsān.*)

(*Oct. 24th*) On Saturday the 10th of the month, Pay-master Sl. Muḥammad's foot-man Shāh Qāsim who once before had taken letters of encouragement to kinsfolk in Khurāsān,[2310] was sent to Herī with other letters to the purport that, through God's grace, our hearts were at ease in Hindūstān about the rebels andFol. 345b. pagans of east and west; and that, God bringing it aright, we should use every means and assuredly in the coming spring should touch the goal of our desire.[2311] On the margin of a royal letter sent to Ahṃad *Afshār* (*Turk*) a summons to Farīdūn the *qabūz*-player was written with my own hand.

(*Here the record of 11 days is wanting.*)

In today's forenoon (*Tuesday 20th?*) I made a beginning of eating quicksilver.[2312]

(*q. News from Kābul and Khurāsān.*)[2313]

(*Nov. 4th*) On Wednesday the 21st of the month (*Ṣafar*) a Hindūstānī foot-man (*piāda*) brought dutiful letters (*'arẓ-dāshtlār*) from Kāmrān and Khwāja Dost-i-khāwand. The Khwāja had reached Kābul on the 10th of Ẕū'l-ḥijja[2314] and will have been anxious to go on[2315] to Humāyūn's presence, but there comes to him a man from Kāmrān, saying, "Let the honoured Khwāja come (to see me); let him deliver whatever royal orders there may be; let him go on to Humāyūn when matters have been talked over."[2316] Kāmrān will have gone into Kābul on the 17th of Ẕū'l-ḥijja (*Sep. 2nd*), will have talked with the Khwāja and, on the 28th of the same month, will have let him go on for Fort Victory (*Qila'-i-ẓafar*).

There was this excellent news in the dutiful letters received:—that Shāh-zāda Ṯahmāsp, resolute to put down the Aūzbeg,[2317] had overcome and killed Rīnīsh (var. Zīnīsh) *Aūzbeg* in Dāmghān and made a general massacre of his people; that 'Ubaid Khān, getting sure news about the *Qīzīl-bāsh* (Red-head) had risen from round Herī, gone to Merv, called up to him there all the sulṯāns of Samarkand and those parts, and that all the sulṯāns of Mā warā'u'n-nahr had gone to help him.[2318]

Fol. 346.This same foot-man brought the further news that Humāyūn was said to have had a son by the daughter of Yādgār Ṯaghāī, and that Kāmrān was said to be marrying in Kābul, taking the daughter of his mother's brother Sl. 'Alī Mīrzā (*Begchīk*).[2319]

(*r. Honours for an artificer.*)[2320]

On this same day Sayyid Daknī of Shīrāz the diviner (*ghaiba-gar?*) was made to wear a dress of honour, given presents, and ordered to finish the arched(?) well (*khwāralīq-chāh*) as he best knew how.

(*s. The Wālidiyyah-risāla (Parental-tract).*)

(*Nov. 6th*) On Friday the 23rd of the month[2321] such heat[2322] appeared in my body that with difficulty I got through the Congregational Prayer in the Mosque, and with much trouble through the Mid-day Prayer, in the book-room, after due time, and little by little. Thereafter[2323] having had fever, I trembled less on Sunday (*Nov. 28th*). During the night of Tuesday[2324] the 27th of the month Ṣafar, it occurred to me to versify (*naẓm qīlmāq*) the *Wālidiyyah-risāla* of his Reverence Khwāja 'Ubaidu'l-lāh.[2325] I laid it to heart that if I, going to the soul of his Reverence[2326] for protection, were freed from this disease, it would be a sign that my poem was accepted, just as the author of the *Qaṣīdatu'l-būrda*[2327] was freed from the affliction of paralysis when his poem Fol. 346b.had been accepted. To this end I began to versify the tract, using the metre[2328] of Maulānā 'Abdu'r-raḥīm *Jāmī's Subḥatu'l-abrār* (Rosary of the Righteous). Thirteen couplets were made in that same night. I tasked myself not to make fewer than 10 a day; in the end one day had been omitted. While last year every time such illness had happened, it had persisted at least a month or 40 days,[2329] this year, by God's grace and his Reverence's favour, I was free, except for a little depression (*afsurda*), on Thursday the 29th of the month (*Nov. 12th*). The end of versifying the contents of the tract was reached on Saturday the 8th of the first Rabī' (*Nov. 20th*). One day 52 couplets had been made.[2330]

(*t. Troops warned for service.*)

(*Nov. 11th*) On Wednesday the 28th of the month royal orders were sent on all sides for the armies, saying, "God bringing it about, at an early opportunity my army will be got to horse. Let all come soon, equipped for service."

(*Here the record of 9 days is wanting.*)[2331]

(*u. Messengers from Humāyūn.*)

(*Nov. 21st*) On Sunday the 9th of the first Rabī', Beg Muḥammad *ta'alluqchī*[2332] came, who had been sent last year (934 AH.) at the end of Muḥarram to take a dress of honour and a horse to Humāyūn.[2333]

(*Nov. 22nd*) On Monday the 10th of the month there came from Humāyūn's presence Wais *Lāgharī's* (son) Beg-gīna (Little Beg) and Bīān Shaikh, one of Humāyūn's servants who had come as the messenger of the good tidings of the birth of Humāyūn's son whose name he gave as Al-amān. Shaikh Abū'l-wajd found *Shāh sa'ādatmand*[2334] to be the date of his birth.Fol. 347.

(*v. Rapid travel.*)

Bīān Shaikh set out long after Beg-gīna. He parted from Humāyūn on Friday the 9th of Ṣafar (*Oct. 23rd*) at a place below Kishm called Dū-shaṃba (Monday); he came into Āgra on Monday the 10th of the first Rabī' (*Nov. 23rd*). He came very quickly! Another time he actually came from Qila'-i-ẓafar to Qandahār in 11 days.[2335]

(*w. News of Ṭahmāsp's victory over the Aūzbegs.*)

Bīān Shaikh brought news about Shāh-zāda Ṭahmāsp's advancing out of 'Irāq and defeating the Aūzbeg.[2336] Here are his particulars:—Shāh-zāda Ṭahmāsp, having come out of 'Irāq with 40,000 men arrayed in Rūmī fashion of matchlock and cart,[2337] advances with great speed, takes Basṭām, slaughters Rīnīsh (var. Zīnīsh) *Aūzbeg* and his men in Dāmghān, and from there passes right swiftly on.[2338] Kīpīk Bī's son Qaṃbar-i-'alī Beg is beaten by one of the *Qīzīl-bāsh* (Red-head)'s men, and with his few followers goes to 'Ubaid Khān's presence. 'Ubaid Khān finds it undesirable to stay near Herī, hurriedly sends off gallopers to all the sulṭāns of Balkh, Ḥiṣār, Samarkand, and Tāshkend (Tāshkīnt) and goes himself to Merv. Sīūnjak Sl.'s younger son Bārāq Sl. from Tāshkend, Kūchūm Khān, with (his sons) Abū-sa'īd Sl. and Pūlad Sl., and Jānī Beg Sl. with his sons, from Fol. 347b.Samarkand and Mīān-kāl, Mahdī Sl.'s and Ḥamza Sl.'s sons from Ḥiṣār, Kītīn-qarā Sl. from Balkh, all these sulṭāns assemble right swiftly in Merv. To them their informers (*tīl-chī*) take news that Shāh-zāda, after saying, "'Ubaid Khān is seated near Herī with few men only," had been advancing swiftly with his 40,000 men, but that when he heard of this assembly (*i.e.* in Merv), he made a ditch in the meadow of Rādagān[2339] and seated himself there.[2340] Here-upon the Aūzbegs, with entire disregard of their opponents,[2341] left their counsels at this:—"Let all of us sulṭāns and khāns seat ourselves in Mashhad;[2342] let a few of us be told off with 20,000 men to go close to the Qīzīl-bāsh camp[2343] and not let them put head out; let us order magicians[2344] to work their magic directly Scorpio appears;[2345] by this stratagem the enemy will be enfeebled, and we shall overcome." So said, they march from Merv. Shāh-zāda gets out of Mashhad.[2346] He confronts them near Jām-and-Khirgird.[2347] There defeat befalls the Aūzbeg side.[2348] A mass of sulṭāns are overcome and slaughtered.

In one letter it (*khūd*) was written, "It is not known for certainFol. 348. that any sulṭān except Kūchūm Khān has escaped; not a man who went with the army has come back up to now." The sulṭāns who were in Ḥiṣār abandoned it. Ibrāhīm *Jānī's* son Chalma, whose real name is Ismā'īl, must be in the fort.[2349]

(*x. Letters written by Bābur.*)

(*Nov. 27th and 28th*) This same Bīān Shaikh was sent quite quickly back with letters. for Humāyūn and Kāmrān. These and other writings being ready by Friday the 14th of the month (*Nov. 27th*) were entrusted to him, his leave was given, and on Saturday the 15th he got well out of Āgra.

COPY OF A LETTER TO HUMĀYŪN.[2350]

"The first matter, after saying, 'Salutation' to Humāyūn whom I am longing to see, is this:—

Exact particulars of the state of affairs on that side and on this[2351] have been made known by the letters and dutiful representations brought on Monday the 10th of the first Rabī' by Beg-gīna and Bīān Shaikh.

(*Turki*)
Thank God! a son is born to thee!
A son to thee, to me a heart-enslaver (*dil-bandi*).

May the Most High ever allot to thee and to me tidings as joyful! So may it be, O Lord of the two worlds!"

"Thou sayest thou hast called him Al-amān; God bless and prosper this! Thou writest it so thyself (*i.e.* Al-amān), but hast over-looked that common people mostly say *alāmā* or *aïlāmān*.[2352]Fol. 348b. Besides that, this *Al* is rare in names.[2353] May God bless and prosper him in name and person; may He grant us to keep Al-amān (peace) for many years and many decades of years![2354] May He now order our affairs by His own mercy and favour; not in many decades comes such a chance as this!"[2355]

"Again:—On Tuesday the 11th of the month (*Nov. 23rd*) came the false rumour that the Balkhīs had invited and were fetching Qurbān[2356] into Balkh."

"Again:—Kāmrān and the Kābul begs have orders to join thee; this done, move on Ḥiṣār, Samarkand, Herī or to whatever side favours fortune. Mayst thou, by God's grace, crush foes and take lands to the joy of friends and the down-casting of adversaries! Thank God! now is your time to risk life and slash swords.[2357] Neglect not the work chance has brought; slothful life in retirement befits not sovereign rule:—

(*Persian*)
He grips the world who hastens;
Empire yokes not with delay;
All else, confronting marriage, stops,
Save only sovereignty.[2358]

If through God's grace, the Balkh and Ḥiṣār countries be won and held, put men of thine in Ḥiṣār, Kāmrān's men in Balkh. Should Samarkand also be won, there make thy seat. Ḥiṣār,Fol. 349. God willing, I shall make a crown-domain. Should Kāmrān regard Balkh as small, represent the matter to me; please God! I will make its defects good at once out of those other countries."

"Again:—As thou knowest, the rule has always been that when thou hadst six parts, Kāmrān had five; this having been constant, make no change."

"Again:—Live well with thy younger brother. Elders must bear the burden![2359] I have the hope that thou, for thy part, wilt keep on good terms with him; he, who has grown up an active and excellent youth, should not fail, for his part, in loyal duty to thee."[2360]

"Again:—Words from thee are somewhat few; no person has Fol. 349b.come from thee for two or three years past; the man I sent to thee (Beg Muḥammad *ta'alluqchi*) came back in something over a year; is this not so?"

"Again:—As for the "retirement", "retirement", spoken of in thy letters,—retirement is a fault for sovereignty; as the honoured (Sa'dī) says:—[2361]

(*Persian*) If thy foot be fettered, choose to be resigned;
If thou ride alone, take thou thine own head.

No bondage equals that of sovereignty; retirement matches not with rule."

"Again:—Thou hast written me a letter, as I ordered thee to do; but why not have read it over? If thou hadst thought of reading it, thou couldst not have done it, and, unable thyself to read it, wouldst certainly have made alteration in it. Though by taking trouble it can be read, it is very puzzling, and who ever saw an enigma in prose?[2362] Thy spelling, though not bad, is not quite correct; thou writest *iltafāt* with *ṭā* (*iltafāṭ*) and *qūlinj* with *yā* (*qīlinj*?).[2363] Although thy letter can be read if every sort of pains be taken, yet it cannot be quite understood because of that obscure wording of thine. Thy remissness in letter-writing seems to be due to the thing which makes thee obscure, that is to say, to elaboration. In future write without elaboration; use plain, clear words. So will thy trouble and thy reader's be less."

"Again:—Thou art now to go on a great business;[2364] take counsel with prudent and experienced begs, and act as they say. If thou seek to pleasure me, give up sitting alone and avoiding society. Summon thy younger brother and the begs twice daily to thy presence, not leaving their coming to choice; be the business what it may, take counsel and settle every word and act in agreement with those well-wishers."

"Again:—Khwāja Kalān has long had with me the house-friend's intimacy; have thou as much and even more with him.Fol. 350. If, God willing, the work becomes less in those parts, so that thou wilt not need Kāmrān, let him leave disciplined men in Balkh and come to my presence."

"Again:—Seeing that there have been such victories, and such conquests, since Kābul has been held, I take it to be well-omened; I have made it a crown-domain; let no one of you covet it."

"Again:—Thou hast done well (*yakhshī qīlīb sīn*); thou hast won the heart of Sl. Wais;[2365] get him to thy presence; act by his counsel, for he knows business."

"Until there is a good muster of the army, do not move out."

"Bīān Shaikh is well-apprized of word-of-mouth matters, and will inform thee of them. These things said, I salute thee and am longing to see thee."—

The above was written on Thursday the 13th of the first Rabi' (*Nov. 26th*). To the same purport and with my own hand, I wrote also to Kāmrān and Khwāja Kalān, and sent off the letters (by Bīān Shaikh).

(*Here the record fails from Rabī' 15th to 19th.*)

(*y. Plans of campaign.*)

(*Dec. 2nd*) On Wednesday the 19th of the month (*Rabī' I.*) the mīrzās, sulṭāns, Turk and Hind amīrs were summoned for counsel, and left the matter at this:—That this year the army must move in some direction; that 'Askarī should go in advance towards the East, be joined by the sulṭāns and amīrs from beyond Gang (Ganges), and march in whatever direction favoured fortune. These particulars having been written down, Ghīāṣu'd-dīn the Fol. 350b.armourer was given rendezvous for 16 days,[2366] and sent galloping off, on Saturday the 22nd of the month, to the amīrs of the East headed by Sl. Junaid *Barlās*. His word-of-mouth message was, that 'Askarī was being sent on before the fighting apparatus, culverin, cart and matchlock, was ready; that it was the royal order for the sulṭāns and amīrs of the far side of Gang to muster in 'Askarī's presence, and, after consultation with well-wishers on that side, to move in whatever direction, God willing! might favour fortune; that if there should be work needing me, please God! I would get to horse as soon as the person gone with the (16 days) tryst (*mī'ād*) had returned; that explicit representation should be made as to whether the Bengali (Naṣrat Shāh) were friendly and single-minded; that, if nothing needed my presence in those parts, I should not make stay, but should move elsewhere at once;[2367] and that after consulting with well-wishers, they were to take 'Askarī with them, and, God willing! settle matters on that side.

(*Here the record of 5 days is wanting.*)

(*z. 'Askarī receives the insignia and rank of a royal commander.*)

(*Dec. 12th*) On Saturday the 29th of the first Rabī', 'Askarī was made to put on a jewelled dagger and belt, and a royal dress of honour, was presented with flag, horse-tail standard, Fol. 351.drum, a set (6-8) of *tīpūchāq* (horses), 10 elephants, a string of camels, one of mules, royal plenishing, and royal utensils. Moreover he was ordered to take his seat at the head of a *Dīwān*. On his mullā and two guardians were bestowed jackets having buttons[2368]; on his other servants, three sets of nine coats.

(*aa. Bābur visits one of his officers.*)

(*Dec. 13th*) On Sunday the last day of the month (*Rabī' I. 30th*)[2369] I went to Sl. Muḥammad *Bakhshī's* house. After spreading a carpet, he brought gifts. His offering in money and goods was more than 2 *laks.*[2370] When food and offering had been set out, we went into another room where sitting, we ate *ma'jūn*. We came away at the 3rd watch (midnight?), crossed the water, and went to the private house.

(*bb. The Āgra-Kābul road measured.*)

(*Dec. 17th*) On Thursday the 4th of the latter Rabī', it was settled that Chīqmāq Beg with Shāhī *ṭamghāchī's*[2371] clerkship, should measure the road between Āgra and Kābul. At every 9th *kuroh* (*cir.* 18m.), a tower was to be erected 12 *qārīs* high[2372] and having a *chār-dara*[2373] on the top; at every 18th *kuroh* (*cir.* 36m.),[2374] 6 post-horses were to be kept fastened; and arrangement was to be made for the payment of post-masters and grooms, and for horse-corn. The order was, "If the place where the horses are fastened up,[2375] be near a crown-domain, let those there provide for the matters mentioned; if not, let the cost be charged on the beg in whose *pargana* the post-house may be." Chīqmāq Beg got out of Āgra with Shāhī on that same day.

Fol. 351b.(*Author's note on the kuroh.*) These *kurohs* were established in relation to the *mīl*, in the way mentioned in the *Mubīn*:—[2376]

Four thousand paces (*qadam*) are one *mīl*;

Know that Hind people call this a *kuroh*;

(*Turkī*) The pace (*qadam*) they say is a *qārī* and a half (36 in.);

That each *tūtām* is four fingers (*ailīk*),

Each *ailīk*, six barley-corns. Know this knowledge.[2377]

The measuring-cord (*ṭanāb*)[2378] was fixed at 40 *qārī*, each being the one-and-a-half *qārī* mentioned above, that is to say, each is 9 hand-breadths.

(*cc. A feast.*)

(*Dec. 18th*) On Saturday the 6th of the month (Rabī' II.) there was a feast[2379] at which were present Qīzīl-bāsh (Red-head), and Aūzbeg, and Hindū envoys.[2380] The Qīzīl-bāsh envoys sat under an awning placed some 70-80 *qārīs*[2381] on my right, of the begs Yūnas-i-'alī being ordered to sit with them. On my left the Aūzbeg envoys sat in the same way, of the begs 'Abdu'l-lāh being ordered to sit with them. I sat on the north side of a newly-erected octagonal pavilion (*tālār*) covered in with *khas*[2382]. Five or six *qārīs* on my right sat Tūkhtā-būgha Sl. and 'Askarī, with Khwāja 'Abdu'sh-shahīd and Khwāja Kalān, descendants of his Reverence the Khwāja,[2383] and Khwāja Chishtī (var. Ḥusainī), and Khalīfa, together with the *ḥāfizes* and *mullās* dependent on the Khwājas who had come from Samarkand. Five or six *qārīs* on my left sat Muḥammad-i-zamān M. and Tāng-ātmīsh Sl.[2384]Fol. 352. and Sayyid Rafī', Sayyid Rūmī, Shaikh Abū'l-fatḥ, Shaikh Jamālī, Shaikh Shihābu'd-dīn *'Arab* and Sayyid Daknī (var.Zaknī, Ruknī). Before food all the sulṭāns, khāns, grandees, and amīrs brought gifts[2385] of red, of white, of black,[2386] of cloth and various other goods. They poured the red and white on a carpet I had ordered spread, and side by side with the gold and silver piled plenishing, white cotton piece-cloth and purses (*badra*) of money. While the gifts were being brought and before food, fierce camels and fierce elephants[2387] were set to fight on an island opposite,[2388] so too a few rams; thereafter wrestlers grappled. After the chief of the food had been set out, Khwāja 'Abdu'sh-shahīd and Khwāja Kalān were made to put on surtouts (*jabbah*) of fine muslin,[2389] spotted with gold-embroidery, and suitable dresses of honour, and those headed by Mullā Farrūkh and *Ḥāfiz*[2390] had jackets put on them. On Kūchūm Khān's envoy[2391] and on Ḥasan *Chalabi's* younger brother[2392] were bestowed silken head-wear (*bāshlīq*) and gold-embroidered surtouts of fine muslin, with suitable dresses of honour. Gold-embroidered jackets and silk coats were presented to the envoys of Abū-sa'īd Sl. (*Aūzbeg*), of Mihr-bān Khānīm and her son Pulād Sl., and of Shāh Ḥasan Fol. 352b.(*Arghūn*). The two Khwājas and the two chief envoys, that is to say Kūchūm Khān's retainer and Ḥasan *Chalabī's* younger brother, were presented with a silver stone's weight of gold and a gold stone's weight of silver.

> (*Author's note on the Turkī stone-weight.*) The gold stone (*tāsh*) is 500 *misqāls*, that is to say, one Kābul *sīr*; the silver stone is 250 *misqāls*, that is to say, half a Kābul *sīr*.[2393]

To Khwāja Mīr Sulṭān and his sons, to Ḥāfiz of Tāshkīnt, to Mullā Farrūkh at the head of the Khwājas' servants, and also to other envoys, silver and gold were given with a quiver.[2394] Yādgār-i-nāṣir[2395] was presented with a dagger and belt. On Mīr Muḥammad the raftsman who was deserving of reward for the excellent bridge he had made over the river Gang (Ganges),[2396] a dagger was bestowed, so too on the matchlockmen Champion [*pahlawān*] Ḥājī Muḥammad and Champion Buhlūl and on Walī the cheeta-keeper (*pārschī*); one was given to Ustād 'Alī's son also. Gold and silver were presented to Sayyid Daud *Garmsīrī*. Jackets having buttons,[2397] and silk dresses of honour were presented to the servants of my daughter Ma'ṣūma[2398] and my son Hind-āl. Again:—presents of jackets and silk dresses of honour, of gold and silver, of plenishing and various goods were given to those from Andijān, and to those who had come from Sūkh and Hushīār, the places whither we had gone landless and homeless.[2399] Gifts of the same kind were given to the servants of Qurbān and Shaikhī and the peasants of Kāhmard.[2400]Fol. 353.

After food had been sent out, Hindūstānī players were ordered to come and show their tricks. Lūlīs came.[2401] Hindūstānī performers shew several feats not shewn by (Tramontane) ones. One is this:—They arrange seven rings, one on the forehead, two on the knees, two of the remaining four on fingers, two on toes, and in an instant set them turning rapidly. Another is this:—Imitating the port of the peacock, they place one hand on the ground, raise up the other and both legs, and then in an instant make rings on the uplifted hand and feet revolve rapidly. Another is this:—In those (Tramontane) countries two people grip one another and turn two somersaults, but Hindūstānī *lūlīs*, clinging together, go turning over three or four times. Another is this:—a *lūlī* sets the end of a 12 or 14 foot pole on his middle and holds it upright while another climbs up it and does hisFol. 353b. tricks up there. Another is this:—A small *lūlī* gets upon a big one's head, and stands there upright while the big one moves quickly from side to side shewing his tricks, the little one shewing his on the big one's head, quite upright and without tottering. Many dancing-girls came also and danced.

A mass of red, white, and black was scattered (*sāchīldī*) on which followed amazing noise and pushing. Between the Evening and Bed-time Prayers I made five or six special people sit in my presence for over one watch. At the second watch of the day (9 a.m., *Sunday, Rabi' II. 7th*) having sat in a boat, I went to the Eight-Paradises.

(*dd. 'Askarī starts eastwards.*)

(*Dec. 20th*) On Monday (*8th*) 'Askarī who had got (his army) out (of Āgra) for the expedition, came to the Hot-bath, took leave of me and marched for the East.

(*ee. A visit to Dhūlpūr.*)

(*Dec. 21st*) On Tuesday (*Rabī' II. 9th*) I went to see the buildings for a reservoir and well at Dūlpūr.[2402] I rode from the (Āgra) garden at one watch (*pahr*) and one *garī* (9.22 a.m.), and I entered the Dūlpūr garden when 5 *garīs* of the 1st night-watch (*pās*)[2403] had gone (7.40 p.m.).[2404]

(*Dec. 23rd*) On Thursday the 11th day of the month the stone-well (*sangīn-chāh*), the 26 rock-spouts (*tāsh-tār-nau*) and rock-pillars (*tāsh-sitūn*), and the water-courses (*ārīqlār*) cut on the solid slope (*yak pāra qīā*) were all ready.[2405] At the 3rd watch (*pahr*) of this same day preparation for drawing water from the well was made. On account of a smell (*aīd*) in the water, it was ordered, for prudence' sake, that they should turn the well-wheel without rest for 15 days-and-nights, and so draw off the water. Gifts were made to the stone-cutters, and labourers, Fol. 354.and the whole body of workmen in the way customary for master-workmen and wage-earners of Āgra.

(*Dec. 24th*) We rode from Dūlpūr while one *garī* of the 1st watch (*pahr*) of Friday remained (*cir.* 8.40 a.m.), and we crossed the river (Jumna) before the Sun had set.

(*Here the record of 3 days is wanting.*)[2406]

(*ff. A Persian account of the battle of Jām.*)

(*Dec. 28th*) On Tuesday the 16th of the month (*Rabī' II.*) came one of Dīv Sl.'s[2407] servants, a man who had been in the fight between the Qīzīl-bāsh and Aūzbeg, and who thus described it:—The battle between the Aūzbegs and Turkmāns[2408] took place on 'Āshūr-day (*Muḥ. 10th*) near Jām-and-Khirgird.[2409] They fought from the first dawn till the Mid-day Prayer. The Aūzbegs were 300,000; the Turkmāns may have been (as is said?) 40 to 50,000; he said that he himself estimated their dark mass at 100,000; on the other hand, the Aūzbegs said they themselves were 100,000. The Qīzīl-bāsh leader (*ādam*) fought after arraying cart, culverin and matchlockmen in the Rūmī fashion, and after protecting himself.[2410] Shāh-zāda[2411] and Jūha Sl. stood behind the carts with 20,000 good braves. The rest of the begs were posted right and left beyond the carts.Fol. 354b. These the Aūzbeg beat at once on coming up, dismounted and overcame many, making all scurry off. He then wheeled to the (Qīzīl-bāsh) rear and took loot in camel and baggage. At length those behind the carts loosed the chains and came out. Here also the fight was hard. Thrice they flung the Aūzbeg back; by God's grace they beat him. Nine sulṭāns, with Kūchūm Khān, 'Ubaid Khān and Abū-sa'īd Sl. at their head, were captured; one, Abū-sa'īd Sl. is said to be alive; the rest have gone to death.[2412] 'Ubaid Khān's body was found, but not his head. Of Aūzbegs 50,000, and of Turkmāns 20,000 were slain.[2413]

(*Here matter seems to have been lost.*)[2414]

(*gg. Plan of campaign.*)

(*Dec. 30th*) On this same day (Thursday *Rabī' II. 18th*) came Ghīāṣu'd-dīn the armourer[2415] who had gone to Jūna-pūr (Jūnpūr) with tryst of 16 days,[2416] but, as Sl. Junaid and the rest had led out their army for Kharīd,[2417] he (Ghīāṣu'd-dīn) was not able to be back at the time fixed.[2418] Sl. Junaid said, by word-of-mouth, "Thank God! through His grace, no work worth the Pādshāh's attention has shewn itself in these parts; if the honoured Mīrzā ('Askarī) come, and if the sulṭāns, khāns and amīrs here-abouts be ordered to move in his steps, there is hope that everything in these parts will be arranged with ease." Though such was Sl.Fol. 355. Junaid's answer,yet, as people were saying that Mullā Muḥammad Maẕhab, who had been sent as envoy to Bengal after the Holy-battle with Sangā the Pagan,[2419] would arrive today or tomorrow, his news also was awaited.

(Dec. 31st) On Friday the 19th of the month I had eaten ma'jūn and was sitting with a special few in the private house, when Mullā Maẕhab who had arrived late, that is to say, in the night of Saturday,[2420] came and waited on me. By asking one particular after another, we got to know that the attitude of the Bengalī[2421] was understood to be loyal and single-minded.

(Jan. 2nd) On Sunday *(Rabī' II. 21st)*, I summoned the Turk and Hind amīrs to the private house, when counsel was taken and the following matters were brought forward:—As the Bengalī (Naṣrat Shāh) has sent us an envoy[2422] and is said to be loyal and single-minded, to go to Bengal itself would be improper; if the move be not on Bengal, no other place on that side has treasure helpful for the army; several places to the west are both rich and near,

(Turkī)
Abounding wealth, a pagan people, a short road;
Far though the East lie, this is near.

At length the matter found settlement at this:—As our westward road is short, it will be all one if we delay a few days, so that our minds may be at ease about the East. Again Ghīāṣu'd-dīnFol. 355b. the armourer was made to gallop off, with tryst of 20 days,[2423] to convey written orders to the eastern amīrs for all the sulṭāns, khāns, and amīrs who had assembled in 'Askarī's presence, to move against those rebels.[2424] The orders delivered, he was to return by the trysted day with what ever news there might be.

(hh. Balūchī incursions.)

In these days Muḥammadī Kūkūldāsh made dutiful representation that again Balūchīs had come and overrun several places. Chīn-tīmūr Sl. was appointed for the business; he was to gather to his presence the amīrs from beyond Sihrind and Samāna and with them, equipped for 6 months, to proceed against the Balūchīs; namely, such amīrs as 'Ādil Sulṭān, Sl. Muḥ. *Dūldāī*, Khusrau Kūkūldāsh, Muḥammad 'Alī *Jang-jang*, 'Abdu'l-'azīz the Master-of-the-horse, Sayyid 'Alī, Walī Qīzil, Qarācha, Halāhil, 'Āshiq the House-steward, Shaikh 'Alī, Kitta *(Beg Kuhbur)*, Gujūr Khān, Ḥasan 'Alī *Sīwādī*. These were to present themselves at the Sulṭān's call and muster and not to transgress his word by road or in halt.[2425] The messenger[2426] appointed to carry these orders was 'Abdu'l-ghaffār; he was to deliver them first to Chīn-tīmūr Sl., Fol. 356.then to go on and shew them to the afore-named begs who were to present themselves with their troops at whatever place the Sulṭān gave rendezvous (*būljār*);[2427] 'Abdu'l-ghaffār himself was to remain with the army and was to make dutiful representation of slackness or carelessness if shewn by any person soever; this done, we should remove the offender from the circle of the approved (*muwajjah-jīrgāsi*) and from his country or *pargana*. These orders having been entrusted to 'Abdu'l-ghaffār, words-of-mouth were made known to him and he was given leave to go.

(*The last explicit date is a week back.*)

(*ii. News of the loss of Bihār reaches Dhūlpūr.*)

(*Jan. 9th*) On the eve of Sunday the 28th of the month (*Rabi' II.*) we crossed the Jūn (Jumna) at the 6th *garī* of the 3rd watch (2.15 a.m.) and started for the Lotus-garden of Dūlpūr. The 3rd watch was near[2428] (Sunday mid-day) when we reached it. Places were assigned on the border of the garden, where begs and the household might build or make camping-grounds for themselves.

(*Jan. 13th*) On Thursday the 3rd of the first Jumāda, a place was fixed in the s.e. of the garden for a Hot-bath; the ground was to be levelled; I ordered a plinth(?) (*kursi*) erected on the levelled ground, and a Bath to be arranged, in one room of which was to be a reservoir 10 X 10.

On this same day Khalīfa sent from Āgra dutiful letters of Qāẓī Jīā and Bīr-sing Deo, saying it had been heard said that Iskandar's son Maḥmūd (*Lūdī*) had taken Bihār (town). This news decided for getting the army to horse.

(*Jan. 14th*) On Friday (*Jumāda I. 4th*), we rode out from the Lotus-garden at the 6th *garī* (8.15 a.m.); at the Evening Prayer we reached Āgra. We met Muḥammad-i-zamān Mīrzā on the road who would have gone to Dūlpūr, Chīn-tīmūr also who must have been coming into Agra.[2429]

(*Jan. 15th*) On Saturday (*5th*) the counselling begs having been summoned, it was settled to ride eastwards on Thursday the 10th of the month (*Jan. 21st*).

(*jj. News of Badakhshān.*)

On this same Saturday letters came from Kābul with newsFol. 356b. that Humāyūn, having mustered the army on that side (Tramontana), and joined Sl. Wais to himself, had set out with 40,000 men for Samarkand;[2430] on this Sl. Wais' younger brother Shāh-qūlī goes and enters Ḥiṣār, Tarsūn Muḥammad leaves Tirmiẕ, takes Qabādīān and asks for help; Humāyūn sends Tūlik Kūkūldāsh and Mīr Khẉurd[2431] with many of his men and what Mughūls there were, then follows himself.[2432]

(Here 4 days record is wanting.)

(kk. Bābur starts for the East.)

(Jan. 20th) On Thursday the 10th of the first Jumāda, I set Fol. 357.out for the East after the 3rd *garī* (*cir.* 7.10 a.m.), crossed Jūn by boat a little above Jalīsīr, and went to the Gold-scattering-garden.[2433] It was ordered that the standard (*tūgh*), drum, stable and all the army-folk should remain on the other side of the water, opposite to the garden, and that persons coming for an interview[2434] should cross by boat.

(ll. Arrivals.)

(Jan. 22nd) On Saturday (*12th*) Ismā'īl Mītā, the Bengal envoy brought the Bengalī's offering (Naṣrat Shāh's), and waited on me in Hindūstān fashion, advancing to within an arrow's flight, making his reverence, and retiring. They then put on him the due dress of honour (*khi'lat*) which people call * * * *[2435], and brought him before me. He knelt thrice in our fashion, advanced, handed Naṣrat Shāh's letter, set before me the offering he had brought, and retired.

(Jan. 24th) On Monday (*14th*) the honoured Khwāja 'Abdu'l-ḥaqq having arrived, I crossed the water by boat, went to his tents and waited on him.[2436]

(Jan. 25th) On Tuesday (*15th*) Ḥasan *Chalabī* arrived and waited on me.[2437]

(mm. Incidents of the eastward march.)

On account of our aims (*chāpdūq*) for the army,[2438] some days were spent in the Chār-bāgh.

(Jan. 27th) On Thursday the 17th of the month, that ground was left after the 3rd *garī* (7.10 a.m.), I going by boat. It was dismounted 7 *kurohs* (14 m.) from Āgra, at the village of Anwār.[2439]

(Jan. 30th) On Sunday (*Jumāda I. 20th*), the Aūzbeg envoys were given their leave. To Kūchūm Khān's envoy Amīn Mīrzā were presented a dagger with belt, cloth of gold,[2440] and 70,000 *tankas*.[2441] Abū-sa'īd's servant Mullā Ṭaghāī and the servants ofFol. 357b. Mihr-bān Khānim and her son Pūlād Sl. were made to put on dresses of honour with gold-embroidered jackets, and were presented also with money in accordance with their station.

(Jan. 31st?) Next morning[2442] (*Monday 21st?*) leave was given to Khwāja 'Abdu'l-ḥaqq for stay in Āgra and to Khwāja Yaḥyā's grandson Khwāja Kalān for Samarkand, who had come by way of a mission from Aūzbeg khāns and sulṭāns.[2443]

In congratulation on the birth of Humāyūn's son and Kāmrān's marriage, Mullā Tabrīzī and Mīrzā Beg Ṭaghāī[2444] were sent with gifts (*sāchāq*) to each Mīrzā of 10,000 *shāhrukhīs*, a coat I had worn, and a belt with clasps. Through Mullā Bihishtī were sent to Hind-āl an inlaid dagger with belt, an inlaid ink-stand, a stool worked in mother-o'pearl, a tunic and a girdle,[2445] together with the alphabet of the Bāburī script and fragments (*qiṭa'lār*) written in that script. To Humāyūn were sent the translation (*tarjuma*) and verses made in Hindūstān.[2446] To Hind-āl and Khwāja Kalān also the translation and verses were sent. They were sent too to Kāmrān, through Mīrzā Beg Ṭaghāī, together with head-lines (*sar-khaṭ*) in the Bāburī script.[2447]

(*Feb. 1st*) On Tuesday, after writing letters to be taken by those going to Kābul, the buildings in hand at Āgra and Dūlpūr Fol. 358.were recalled to mind, and entrusted to the charge of Mullā Qāsim, Ustād Shāh Muḥammad the stone-cutter, Mīrak, Mīr Ghīāṣ, Mīr Sang-tarāsh (stone-cutter) and Shāh Bābā the spadesman. Their leave was then given them.

(*Feb. 2nd*) The first watch (6 a.m.) was near[2448] when we rode out from Anwār (*Wednesday, Jumāda I. 23rd*); in the end,[2449] we dismounted, at the Mid-day Prayer, in the village of Ābāpūr, one *kuroh* (2 m.) from Chandawār.[2450]

(*Feb. 3rd*) On the eve of Thursday (*24th*)[2451] 'Abdu'l-malūk the armourer[2452] was joined with Ḥasan *Chalabī* and sent as envoy to the Shāh[2453]; and Chāpūq[2454] was joined with the Aūzbeg envoys and sent to the Aūzbeg khāns and sulṭāns.

We moved from Ābāpūr while 4 *garīs* of the night remained (4.30 a.m.). After passing Chandawār at the top of the dawn, I got into a boat. I landed in front of Rāprī and at the Bed-time Prayer got to the camp which was at Fatḥpūr.[2455]

(*Feb. 4th and 5th*) Having stayed one day (*Friday*) at Fatḥpūr, we got to horse on Saturday (*26th*) after making ablution (*waẓū*) at dawn. We went through the Morning Prayer in assembly near Rāprī, Maulānā Muḥammad of Fārāb being the leader (*imām*). At sun-rise I got into a boat below the great crook[2456] of Rāprī.

Today I put together a line-marker (*misṭar*) of eleven lines[2457] in order to write the mixed hands of the translation.[2458] Today the words of the honoured man-of-God admonished my heart.[2459]

(*Feb. 6th*) Opposite Jākīn,[2460] one of the Rāprī *parganas*, we Fol. 358b.had the boats drawn to the bank and just spent the night in them. We had them moved on from that place before the dawn (*Sunday 27th*), after having gone through the Morning Prayer. When I was again on board, Pay-master Sl. Muḥammad came, bringing a servant of Khwāja Kalān, Shamsu'd-dīn Muḥammad, from whose letters and information particulars about the affairs of Kābul became known.[2461] Mahdī Khwāja also came when I was in the boat.[2462] At the Mid-day Prayer I landed in a garden opposite Etāwa, there bathed (*ghusl*) in the Jūn, and fulfilled the duty of prayer. Moving nearer towards Etāwa, we sat down in that same garden under trees on a height over-looking the river, and there set the braves to amuse us.[2463] Food ordered by Mahdī Khwāja, was set before us. At the Evening Prayer we crossed the river; at the bed-time one we reached camp.

There was a two or three days' delay on that ground both to collect the army, and to write letters in answer to those brought by Shamsu'd-dīn Muḥammad.

(*nn. Letters various.*)

(*Feb. 9th*) On Wednesday the last day (*30th*) of the 1st Jumāda, we marched from Etāwa, and after doing 8 *kurohs* (16m.), dismounted at Mūrī-and-Adūsa.[2464]

Several remaining letters for Kābul were written on this same ground. One to Humāyūn was to this purport:—If the work have not yet been done satisfactorily, stop the raiders and thieves thyself; do not let them embroil the peace now descending amongst the peoples.[2465] Again, there was this:—I have madeFol. 359. Kābul a crown-domain, let no son of mine covet it. Again:—that I had summoned Hind-āl.

Kāmrān, for his part, was written to about taking the best of care in intercourse with the Shāh-zāda,[2466] about my bestowal on himself of Multān, making Kābul a crown-domain, and the coming of my family and train.[2467]

As my letter to Khwāja Kalān makes several particulars known, it is copied in here without alteration:—[2468]

[COPY OF A LETTER TO KHWĀJA KALĀN.]

"After saying 'Salutation to Khwāja Kalān', the first matter is that Shamsu'd-dīn Muḥammad has reached Etāwa, and that the particulars about Kābul are known."

"Boundless and infinite is my desire to go to those parts.[2469] Matters are coming to some sort of settlement in Hindūstān; there is hope, through the Most High, that the work here will soon be arranged. This work brought to order, God willing! my start will be made at once."

"How should a person forget the pleasant things of those countries, especially one who has repented and vowed to sin no more? How should he banish from his mind the permitted flavours of melons and grapes? Taking this opportunity,[2470] a melon was brought to me; to cut and eat it affected me strangely; I was all tears!"

"The unsettled state[2471] of Kābul had already been written of Fol. 359b.to me. After thinking matters over, my choice fell on this:—How should a country hold together and be strong (*marbūṭ u maẓbūṭ*), if it have seven or eight Governors? Under this aspect of the affair, I have summoned my elder sister (Khān-zāda) and my wives to Hindūstān, have made Kābul and its neighbouring countries a crown-domain, and have written in this sense to both Humāyūn and Kāmrān. Let a capable person take those letters to the Mīrzās. As you may know already, I had written earlier to them with the same purport. About the safe-guarding and prosperity of the country, there will now be no excuse, and not a word to say. Henceforth, if the town-wall[2472] be not solid or subjects not thriving, if provisions be not in store or the Treasury not full, it will all be laid on the back of the inefficiency of the Pillar-of-the State."[2473]

"The things that must be done are specified below; for some of them orders have gone already, one of these being, 'Let treasure accumulate.' The things which must be done are these:—First, the repair of the fort; again:—the provision of stores; again:—the daily allowance and lodging[2474] of envoys going backwards and forwards[2475]; again:—let money, taken legally from revenue,[2476] be spent for building the Congregational Mosque; again:—the repairs of the Kārwan-sarā (Caravan-sarai) and the Hot-baths; again:—the completion of the unfinished building Fol. 360.made of burnt-brick which Ūstād Ḥasan 'Alī was constructing in the citadel. Let this work be ordered after taking counsel with Ūstād Sl. Muḥammad; if a design exist, drawn earlier by Ūstād

Ḥasan 'Alī, let Ūstād Sl. Muḥammad finish the building precisely according to it; if not, let him do so, after making a gracious and harmonious design, and in such a way that its floor shall be level with that of the Audience-hall; again:—the Khẉurd-Kābul dam which is to hold up the But-khāk-water at its exit from the Khẉurd-Kābul narrows; again:—the repair of the Ghaznī dam[2477]; again:—the Avenue-garden in which water is short and for which a one-mill stream must be diverted[2478]; again:—I had water brought from Tūtūm-dara to rising ground south-west of Khwāja Basta, there made a reservoir and planted young trees. The place got the name of Belvedere,[2479] because it faces the ford and gives a first-rate view. The best of young trees must be planted there, lawns arranged, and borders set with sweet-herbs and with flowers of beautiful colour and scent; again:—Sayyid Qāsim has been named to reinforce thee; again:—do not neglect the condition of matchlockmen and of Ūstād Muḥammad Amīn the armourer[2480]; again:—directly this letter arrives, thou must get my elder sister (Khān-zāda Begīm) and my wives right out of Kābul, and escort them to Nīl-āb. However averse they may still be, they most certainly must start within a week of the arrival ofFol. 360b. this letter. For why? Both because the armies which have gone from Hindūstān to escort them are suffering hardship in a cramped place (*tār yīrdā*), and also because they[2481] are ruining the country."

"Again:—I made it clear in a letter written to 'Abdu'l-lāh (*'asas*), that there had been very great confusion in my mind (*dúghdugha*), to counterbalance being in the oasis (*wādī*) of penitence. This quatrain was somewhat dissuading (*mānī'*):—[2482]

Through renouncement of wine bewildered am I;

How to work know I not, so distracted am I;

While others repent and make vow to abstain,

I have vowed to abstain, and repentant am I.

A witticism of Banāī's came back to my mind:—One day when he had been joking in 'Alī-sher Beg's presence, who must have been wearing a jacket with buttons,[2483] 'Alī-sher Beg said, 'Thou makest charming jokes; but for the buttons, I would give thee the jacket; they are the hindrance (*mānī'*).' Said Banāī, 'What hindrance are buttons? It is button-holes (*mādagī*) that hinder.'[2484] Let responsibility for this story lie on the teller! hold me excused for it; for God's sake do not be offended by it.[2485] Again:—that quatrain was made before last year, and in truth the longing and craving for a wine-party has been infinite and endless for two years past, so much so that sometimes the craving for wine brought me to the verge of tears. Thank God! this year that trouble has passed from my mind, perhaps by virtue of the Fol. 361.blessing and sustainment of versifying the translation.[2486] Do thou also renounce wine! If had with equal associates and boon-companions, wine and company are pleasant things; but with whom canst thou now associate? with whom drink wine? If thy boon-companions are Sher-i-aḥmad and Ḥaidar-qulī, it should not be hard for thee to forswear wine. So much said, I salute thee and long to see thee."[2487]

The above letter was written on Thursday the 1st of the latter Jumāda (*Feb. 10th*). It affected me greatly to write concerning those matters, with their mingling of counsel. The letters were entrusted to Shamsu'd-dīn

Muḥammad on Friday night,[2488] he was apprized of word-of-mouth messages and given leave to go.

(*oo. Complaints from Balkh.*)

(*Feb. 11th*) On Friday (*Jumāda II. 2nd*) we did 8 *kurohs* (16m.) and dismounted at Jumandnā.[2489] Today a servant of Kītīn-qarā Sl. arrived whom the Sulṭān had sent to his retainer and envoy Kamālu'd-din *Qīāq*,[2490] with things written concerning the behaviour of the begs of the (Balkh) border, their intercourse with himself, and complaints of theft and raid. Leave to go was given to *Qīāq*, and orders were issued to the begs of the border to put an end to raiding and thieving, to behave well and to maintain intercourse with Balkh. These orders were entrusted to Kītīn-qarā Sl.'s servant and he was dismissed from this ground.

A letter, accepting excuse for the belated arrival of Ḥasan *Chalabī*,[2491] was sent to the Shāh today by one Shāh-qulī who hadFol. 361b. come to me from Ḥasan *Chalabī* and reported the details of the battle (of Jām).[2492] Shāh-qulī was given his leave on this same day, the 2nd of the month.

(*pp. Incidents of the eastward march resumed.*)

(*Feb. 12th*) On Saturday (*3rd*) we did 8 *kurohs* (16m.) and dismounted in the Kakūra and Chachāwalī[2493] *parganas* of Kālpī.

(*Feb. 13th*) On Sunday the 4th of the month, we did 9 *kurohs* (18m.) and dismounted in Dīrapūr[2494] a *pargana* of Kālpī. Here I shaved my head,[2495] which I had not done for the past two months, and bathed in the Sīngar-water (Sengar).

(*Feb. 14th*) On Monday (*5th*) we did 14 *kurohs* (28m.), and dismounted in Chaparkada[2496] one of the *parganas* of Kālpī.

(*Feb. 15th*) At the dawn of Tuesday (*6th*), a Hindūstānī servant of Qarācha's arrived who had taken a command (*farmān*) from Māhīm to Qarācha from which it was understood that she was on the road. She had summoned escort from people in Lāhor, Bhīra and those parts in the fashion I formerly wrote orders (*parwānas*) with my own hand. Her command had been written in Kābul on the 7th of the 1st Jumāda (*Jan. 17th*).[2497]

(*Feb. 16th*) On Wednesday (*7th*) we did 7 *kurohs* (14m.), and dismounted in the Ādampūr *pargana*.[2498] Today I mounted before dawn, took the road[2499] alone, reached the Jūn (Jumna), and went on along its bank. When I came opposite to Ādampūr, I had awnings set up on an island (*ārāl*) near the camp and seated there, ate *ma'jūn*.

Today we set Ṣādiq to wrestle with Kalāl who had come to Fol. 362.Āgra with a challenge.[2500] In Āgra he had asked respite for 20 days on the plea of fatigue from his journey; as now 40-50 days had passed since the end of his respite, he was obliged to wrestle. Ṣādiq did very well, throwing him easily. Ṣādiq was given 10,000 *tankas*, a saddled horse, a head-to-foot, and a jacket with buttons; while Kalāl, to save him from despair, was given 3000 *tankas*, spite of his fall.

The carts and mortar were ordered landed from the boats, and we spent 3 or 4 days on this same ground while the road was made ready, the ground levelled and the landing effected.

(Feb. 21st) On Monday the 12th of the month *(Jumāda II.)*, we did 12 *kurohs* (24 m.) and dismounted at Kūrarah.[2501] Today I travelled by litter.

(Feb. 22nd-25th) After marching 12 *kurohs* (24 m.) from Kūrarah *(13th)*, we dismounted in Kūrīa[2502] a *pargana* of Karrah. From Kūrīa we marched 8 *kurohs* (16m.) and dismounted *(14th)* in Fatḥpūr-Aswa.[2503] After 8 *kurohs* (16m.) done from Fatḥpūr, we dismounted *(15th)* at Sarāī Munda.[2504]... Today at the Bedtime Prayer *(Friday 16th, after dark)*, Sl. Jalālu'd-dīn *(Sharqī)*[2505] came with his two young sons to wait on me.

(Feb. 26th) Next day, Saturday the 17th of the month, we did 8 *kurohs* (16m.), and dismounted at Dugdugī a Karrah *pargana* on the bank of the Gang.[2506]

(Feb. 27th) On Sunday *(18th)* came to this ground Muḥammad Sl. M., Nī-khūb (or, Bī-khūb) Sl. and Tardīka (or, Tardī *yakka*,Fol. 362b. champion).

(Feb. 28th) On Monday *(19th)* 'Askarī also waited on me. They all came from the other side of Gang (Ganges). 'Askarī and his various forces were ordered to march along the other bank of the river keeping opposite the army on this side, and wherever our camp might be, to dismount just opposite it.

(qq. News of the Afghāns.)

While we were in these parts news came again and again that Sl. Maḥmūd *(Lūdī)* had collected 10,000 Afghāns; that he had detached Shaikh Bāyazīd and Bīban with a mass of men towards Sarwār [Gorakhpūr]; that he himself with Fatḥ Khān *Sarwānī* was on his way along the river for Chunār; that Sher Khān *Sūr* whom I had favoured last year with the gift of several *parganas* and had left in charge of this neighbourhood,[2507] had joined these Afghāns who thereupon had made him and a few other amīrs cross the water; that Sl. Jalālu'd-dīn's man in Benares had not been able to hold that place, had fled, and got away; what he was understood to have said being, that he had left soldiers (*sipahīlār*) in Benares-fort and gone along the river to fight Sl. Maḥmūd.[2508]

(*rr. Incidents of the march resumed.*)

(*March 1st*) Marching from Dugdugī (*Tuesday, Jumāda II. 20th*) the army did 6 *kurohs* (12m.) and dismounted at Kusār,[2509] 3 or 4 *kurohs* from Karrah. I went by boat. We stayed here 3 or 4 Fol. 363.days because of hospitality offered by Sl. Jalālu'd-dīn.

(*March 4th*) On Friday (*23rd*), I dismounted at Sl. Jalālu'd-dīn's house inside Karrah-fort where, host-like, he served me a portion of cooked meat and other viands.[2510] After the meal, he and his sons were dressed in unlined coats (*yaktāī jāmah*) and short tunics (*nīmcha*).[2511] At his request his elder son was given the style Sl. Maḥmūd.[2512] On leaving Karrah, I rode about one *kuroh* (2m.) and dismounted on the bank of Gang.

Here letters were written and leave was given to Shahrak Beg who had come from Māhīm to our first camp on Gang (*i.e.* Dugdugī). As Khwāja Yaḥyā's grandson Khwāja Kalān had been asking for the records I was writing,[2513] I sent him by Shahrak a copy I had had made.

(*March 5th*) On Saturday move was made at dawn (*24th*), I going by boat direct, and after 4 *kurohs* done (8m.), halt was made at Koh.[2514] Our ground, being so near, was reached quite early. After awhile, we seated ourselves inside[2515] a boat where we ate *ma'jūn*. We invited the honoured Khwāja 'Abdu'sh-shahīd[2516] who was said to be in Nūr Beg's quarters (*awī*), invited also Mullā Maḥmūd (*Farābī?*), bringing him from Mullā 'Alī Khān's. After staying for some time on that spot, we crossed the river, and on the other side, set wrestlers to wrestle. In opposition to the rule of gripping the strongest first, Dost-i-yāsīn-khairFol. 363b. was told not to grapple with Champion Ṣādiq, but with others; he did so very well with eight.

(*ss. News of the Afghān enemy.*)

At the Afternoon Prayer, Sl. Muḥammad the Pay-master came by boat from the other side of the river, bringing news that the army of Sl. Iskandar's son Maḥmūd Khān whom rebels style Sl. Maḥmūd,[2517] had broken up. The same news was brought in by a spy who had gone out at the Mid-day Prayer from where we were; and a dutiful letter, agreeing with what the spy had reported, came from Tāj Khān *Sārang-khānī* between the Afternoon and Evening Prayers. Sl. Muḥammad gave the following particulars:—that the rebels on reaching Chunār seemed to have laid siege to it and to have done a little fighting, but had risen in disorderly fashion when they heard of our approach; that Afghāns who had crossed the river for Benares, had turned back in like disorder; that two of their boats had sunk in crossing and a body of their men been drowned.

(*tt. Incidents of the eastward march resumed.*)

(*March 6th*) After marching at Sunday's dawn (*25th*) and doing 6 *kurohs* (12m.), Sīr-auliya,[2518] a *pargana* of Pīāg*[2519] was reached. I went direct by boat.

Aīsan-tīmūr Sl. and Tūkhta-būghā Sl. had dismounted half-way, and were waiting to see me.[2520] I, for my part, invited them into the boat. Tūkhta-būghā Sl. must have wrought magic, for a bitter wind rose and rain began to fall. It became quite windy(?)[2521] on which account I ate *ma'jūn*, although I had done so on the previous day. Having come to the encamping-ground....[2522]

(*March 7th?*) Next day (*Monday 26th?*) we remained on the same ground.

(*March 8th?*) On Tuesday (*27th?*) we marched on.

Opposite the camp was what may be an island,[2523] large and verdant. I went over by boat to visit it, returning to the boat during the 1st watch (6-9 a.m.). While I rode carelessly along the ravine (*jar*) of the river, my horse got to where it was fissured and had begun to give way. I leapt off at once and flung myself on the bank; even the horse did not go down; probably, however, if I had stayed on its back, it and I would have gone down together.

On this same day, I swam the Gang-river (Ganges), counting every stroke;[2524] I crossed with 33, then, without resting, swam back. I had swum the other rivers, Gang had remained to do.[2525]

We reached the meeting of the waters of Gang and Jūn at the Evening Prayer, had the boat drawn to the Pīāg side, and got to camp at 1 watch, 4 *garīs* (10.30 p.m.).

(*March 9th*) On Wednesday (*Jumāda II. 28th*) from the 1st watch onwards, the army began to cross the river Jūn; there were 420 boats.[2526]

(*March 11th*) On Friday, the 1st of the month of Rajab, I crossed the river.

(*March 14th*) On Monday, the 4th of the month, the march for Bihār began along the bank of Jūn. After 5 *kurohs* (10m.) done, halt was made at Lawāīn.[2527] I went by boat. The people of the army were crossing the Jūn up to today. They were ordered to put the culverin-carts[2528] which had been landed at Ādampūr, into boats again and to bring them on by water from Pīāg.

On this ground we set wrestlers to wrestle. Dost-i-yāsīn-khair gripped the boatman Champion of Lāhor; the contest was stubborn; it was with great difficulty that Dost gave the throw. A head-to-foot was bestowed on each.

(*March 15th and 16th*) People said that ahead of us was a swampy, muddy, evil river called Tūs.[2529] In order to examine the ford*[2530] and repair the road, we waited two days (*Tuesday Ramẓān 5th and Wednesday 6th*) on this ground. For the horses and camels a ford was found higher up, but people said laden carts could not get through it because of its uneven, stony bottom. Fol. 364.They were just ordered to get them through.

(*March 17th*) On Thursday (*7th*) we marched on. I myself went by boat down to where the Tūs meets the Gang (Ganges), there landed, thence rode up the Tūs, and, at the Other Prayer, reached where the army had encamped after crossing the ford. Today 6 *kurohs* (12 m.) were done.

(*March 18th*) Next day (*Friday 8th*), we stayed on that ground.

(*March 19th*) On Saturday (*9th*), we marched 12 *kurohs* and got to the bank of Gang again at Nulibā.[2531]

(*March 20th*) Marching on (*Sunday 10th*), we did 6 *kurohs* of road, and dismounted at Kintit.[2532]

(*March 21st*) Marching on (*Monday 11th*), we dismounted at Nānāpur.[2533] Tāj Khān *Sārang-khānī* came from Chunār to this ground with his two young sons, and waited on me.

In these days a dutiful letter came from Pay-master Sl. Muḥammad, saying that my family and train were understood to be really on their way from Kābul.[2534]

(*March 23rd*) On Wednesday (*13th*) we marched from that ground. I visited the fort of Chunār, and dismounted about one *kuroh* beyond it.

During the days we were marching from Pīāg, painful boils had come out on my body. While we were on this ground, an Ottoman Turk (Rūmī) used a remedy which had been recently discovered in Rūm. He boiled pepper in a pipkin; I held the sores in the steam and, after steaming ceased, laved them with the hot water. The treatment lasted 2 sidereal hours.

While we were on this ground, a person said he had seen tiger and rhinoceros on an *ārāl*[2535] by the side of the camp.

(*March 24th?*) In the morning (*14th?*), we made the hunting-circle[2536]Fol. 364b. on that *ārāl*, elephants also being brought. Neither tiger nor rhino appeared; one wild buffalo came out at the end of the line. A bitter wind rising and the whirling dust being very troublesome, I went back to the boat and in it to the camp which was 2 *kurohs* (4m.) above Banāras.

(*uu. News of the Afghāns.*)

(*March 25th* (?) *and 26th*) Having heard there were many elephants in the Chunār jungles, I had left (Thursday's) ground thinking to hunt them, but Tāj Khān bringing the news (*Friday 15th*(?)) that Maḥmūd Khān (*Lūdī*) was near the Son-water, I summoned the begs and took counsel as to whether to fall upon him suddenly. In the end it was settled to march on continuously, fast[2537] and far.

(*March 27th*) Marching on (*Sunday 17th*), we did 9 *kurohs* (18m.), and dismounted at the Bilwah-ferry.[2538]

(*March 28th*) On Monday night[2539] the 18th of the month, Ṭ̤āhir was started for Āgra from this camp (Bilwah-ferry), taking money-drafts for the customary gifts of allowance and lodging[2540] to those on their way from Kābul.

Before dawn next morning (Monday) I went on by boat. When we came to where the Gūī-water (Gūmtī) which is the water of Jūnpūr, meets the Gang-water (Ganges), I went a little Fol. 365.way up it and back. Narrower[2541] though it is, it has no ford; the army-folk crossed it (last year) by boat, by raft, or by swimming their horses.

To look at our ground of a year ago,[2542] from which we had started for Jūnpūr,[2543] I went to about a *kuroh* lower than the mouth of the Jūnpūr-water (Gūmtī). A favourable wind getting up behind, our larger boat was tied to a smaller Bengalī one which, spreading its sail, made very quick going. Two *garīs* of day remained (5.15 p.m.) when we had reached that ground (Sayyidpur?), we went on without waiting there, and by the Bed-time Prayer had got to camp, which was a *kuroh* above Madan-Benāres,[2544] long before the boats following us. Mughūl Beg had been ordered to measure all marches from Chunār on the direct road, Luṭ̤fī Beg to measure the river's bank whenever I went by boat. The direct road today was said to be 11 *kurohs* (22m.), the distance along the river, 18 (36m.).

(*March 29th*) Next day (*Tuesday 19th*), we stayed on that ground.

(*March 30th*) On Wednesday (*20th*), we dismounted a *kuroh* (2m.) below Ghāzīpūr, I going by boat.

(*March 31st*) On Thursday (*21st*) Maḥmūd Khān *Nuḥānī*[2545] waited on me on that ground. On this same day dutiful letters[2546] came from Bihār Khān *Bihārī's* son Jalāl Khān (*Nuḥānī*),[2547] from Naṣīr Khān (*Nūḥānī*)'s son Farīd

Khān,[2548] from Sher Khān *Sūr*, from 'Alāūl Khān *Sūr* also, and from other Afghān amīrs. TodayFol. 365b. came also a dutiful letter from 'Abdu'l-'azīz *Master-of-the-horse*, which had been written in Lāhor on the 20th of the latter Jumāda (*Feb. 29th*), the very day on which Qarācha's Hindūstānī servant whom we had started off from near Kālpī,[2549] reached Lāhor. 'Abdu'l-'azīz wrote that he had gone with the others assigned to meet my family at Nīl-āb, had met them there on the 9th of the latter Jumāda (*Feb. 18th*), had accompanied them to Chīn-āb (Chan-āb), left them there, and come ahead to Lāhor where he was writing his letter.

(*April 1st*) We moved on, I going by boat, on Friday (*Rajab 22nd*). I landed opposite Chausā to look at the ground of a year ago[2550] where the Sun had been eclipsed and a fast kept.[2551] After I got back to the boat, Muḥammad-i-zamān Mīrzā, coming up behind by boat, overtook me; at his suggestion *ma'jūn* was eaten.

The army had dismounted on the bank of the Karmā-nāśā-river, about the water of which Hindūs are understood to be extremely scrupulous. They do not cross it, but go past its mouth by boat along the Gang (Ganges). They firmly believe that, if its water touch a person, the merit of his works is destroyed; with this belief its name accords.[2552] I went some way up it by Fol. 366.boat, turned back, went over to the north bank of Gang, and tied up. There the braves made a little fun, some wrestling. Muḥsin the cup-bearer challenged, saying, "I will grapple with four or five." The first he gripped, he threw; the second, who was Shādmān (Joyous), threw him, to Muḥsin's shame and vexation. The (professional) wrestlers came also and set to.

(*April 2nd*) Next morning, Saturday (*23rd*) we moved, close to the 1st watch (6 a.m.), in order to get people off to look at the ford through the Karmā-nāśā-water. I rode up it for not less than a *kuroh* (2 m.), but the ford being still far on,[2553] took boat and went to the camp below Chausā.

Today I used the pepper remedy again; it must have been somewhat hotter than before, for it blistered (*qāpārdi*) my body, giving me much pain.

(*April 3rd*) We waited a day for a road to be managed across a smallish, swampy rivulet heard to be ahead.[2554]

(*April 4th*) On the eve of Monday (*25th*),[2555] letters were written and sent off in answer to those brought by the Hindūstānī footman of 'Abdu'l-'azīz.

The boat I got into at Monday's dawn, had to be towed because of the wind. On reaching the ground opposite Baksara (Buxar) Fol. 366b.where the army had been seated many days last year,[2556] we went over to look at it. Between 40 and 50 landing-steps had been then made on the bank; of them the upper two only were left, the river having destroyed the rest. *Ma'jūn* was eaten after return to the boat. We tied up at an *ārāl*[2557] above the camp, set the champions to wrestle, and went on at the Bed-time Prayer. A year ago (*yīl-tūr*), an excursion had been made to look at the ground on which the camp now was, I passing through Gang swimming (? *dastak bīla*),[2558] some coming mounted on horses, some on camels. That day I had eaten opium.

(*vv. Incidents of the military operations.*)

(*April 5th*) At Tuesday's dawn (*26th*), we sent out for news not under 200 effective braves led by Karīm-bīrdī and Ḥaidar the stirrup-holder's son Muḥammad 'Alī and Bābā Shaikh.

While we were on this ground, the Bengal envoy was commanded to set forth these three articles:—[2559]

(*April 6th*) On Wednesday (*27th*) Yūnas-i-'alī who had been sent to gather Muḥammad-i-zamān Mīrzā's objections to Bihār, brought back rather a weak answer.

Dutiful letters from the (Farmūlī) Shaikh-zādas of Bihār gave news that the enemy had abandoned the place and gone off.

(*April 7th*) On Thursday (*28th*) as many as 2000 men of the Turk and Hind amīrs and quiver-wearers were joined to Muḥammad 'Alī *Jang-jang's* son Tardī-muḥammad, and he wasFol. 367. given leave to go, taking letters of royal encouragement to people in Bihār. He was joined also by Khwāja Murshid *'Irāqī* who had been made Dīwān of Bihār.

(*April 8th* (?)) Muḥammad-i-zamān M. who had consented to go to Bihār, made representation of several matters through

Shaikh Zain and Yūnas-i-'alī. He asked for reinforcement; for this several braves were inscribed and several others were made his own retainers.

(*April 9th*)[2560] On Saturday the 1st of the month of Sha'bān, we left that ground where we had been for 3 or 4 days. I rode to visit Bhūjpūr and Bihiya,[2561] thence went to camp.

Muḥammad 'Alī and the others, who had been sent out for news, after beating a body of pagans as they went along, reached the place where Sl. Maḥmūd (*Lūdī*) had been with perhaps 2000 men. He had heard of our reconnaissance, had broken up, killed two elephants of his, and marched off. He seemed to have left braves and an elephant[2562] scout-fashion; they made no stand when our men came up but took to flight. Ours unhorsed a few of his, cut one head off, brought in a few good men alive.

(*ww. Incidents of the eastward march resumed.*)

(*April 10th*) We moved on next day (*Sunday 2nd*), I going by boat. From our today's ground Muḥammad-i-zamān M. crossed (his army) over the river (Son), leaving none behind. We spent 2 or 3 days on this ground in order to put his work through and Fol. 367b.get him off.

(*April 13th*) On Wednesday the 4th[2563] of the month, Muḥammad-i-zamān M. was presented with a royal head-to-foot, a sword and belt, a *tīpūchāq* horse and an umbrella.[2564] He also was made to kneel (*yūkūndūrūldi*) for the Bihār country. Of the Bihār revenues one *krūr* and 25 *laks* were reserved for the Royal Treasury; its Dīwānī was entrusted to Murshid *'Irāqī.*

(*April 14th*) I left that ground by boat on Thursday (*6th*). I had already ordered the boats to wait, and on getting up with them, I had them fastened together abreast in line.[2565] Though all were not collected there, those there were greatly exceeded the breadth of the river. They could not move on, however, so-arranged, because the water was here shallow, there deep, here swift, there still. A crocodile (*gharīāl*) shewing itself, a terrified fish leaped so high as to fall into a boat; it was caught and brought to me.

When we were nearing our ground, we gave the boats names:—aFol. 368. large[2566] one, formerly the Bāburī,[2567] which had been built in Āgra before the Holy-battle with Sangā, was named Asāīsh (Repose).[2568] Another, which Arāīsh Khān had built and presented to me this year before our army got to horse, one in which I had had a platform set up on our way to this ground, was named Arāīsh (Ornament). Another, a good-sized one presented to me by Jalālu'd-dīn *Sharqī*, was named the Gunjāīsh (Capacious); in it I had ordered a second platform set up, on the top of the one already in it. To a little skiff, having a *chaukandī*,[2569] one used for every task (*har āīsh*) and duty, was given the name Farmāīsh (Commissioned).

(*April 15th*) Next day, Friday (*7th*), no move was made. Muḥammad-i-zamān M. who, his preparations for Bihār complete, had dismounted one or two *kurohs* from the camp, came today to take leave of me.[2570]

(*xx. News of the army of Bengal.*)

Two spies, returned from the Bengal army, said that Bengalīs[2571] under Makhdūm-i-'ālam were posted in 24 places on the Gandak and there raising defences; that they had hindered the Afghāns from carrying out their intention to get their families across the river (Ganges?), and had joined them to themselves.[2572] This news making fighting probable, we detained Muḥammad-i-zamān Mīrzā, and sent Shāh Iskandar to Bihār with 3 or 400 men.

(*yy. Incidents of the eastward march resumed.*)

Fol. 368b.(*April 16th*) On Saturday (*8th*) a person came in from Dūdū and her son Jalāl Khān (son) of Bihār Khān[2573] whom the Bengalī (Naṣrat Shāh) must have held as if eye-bewitched.[2574] After letting me know they were coming,[2575] they had done some straight fighting to get away from the Bengalīs, had crossed the river,[2576] reached Bihār, and were said now to be on their way to me.

This command was given today for the Bengal envoy Ismā'īl Mītā:—Concerning those three articles, about which letters have already been written and despatched, let him write that an answer is long in coming, and that if the honoured (Naṣrat Shāh) be loyal and of single-mind towards us, it ought to come soon.

(*April 17th*) In the night of Sunday (*9th*)[2577] a man came in from Tardī-muḥammad *Jang-jang* to say that when, on Wednesday the 5th of the month Sha'bān, his scouts reached Bihār from this side, the Shiqdār of the place went off by a gate on the other side.

On Sunday morning we marched on and dismounted in the *pargana* of Ārī (Ārrah).[2578]

(*zz. News and negotiations.*)

To this ground came the news that the Kharīd[2579] army, with 100-150 boats, was said to be on the far side of the Sarū near the meeting of Sarū and Gang (Ghogrā and Ganges). As a sort of peace existed between us and the Bengalī (Naṣrat Shāh *Afghān*), and as, for the sake of a benediction, peace was our first endeavour whenever such work was toward as we were now on, we kept to our rule, notwithstanding his unmannerly conduct in setting himself on our road;[2580] we associated Mullā Maẕhab with his envoy Ismā'īl Mītā, spoke once more about those three articlesFol. 369. (*faṣl soz*), and decided to let the envoy go.

(*April 18th*) On Monday (*10th*) when the Bengal envoy came to wait on me, he was let know that he had his leave, and what follows was mentioned:[2581]—"We shall be going to this side and that side, in pursuit of our foe, but no hurt or harm will be done to any dependency of yours. As one of those three articles said,[2582] when you have told the army of Kharīd to rise off our road and to go back to Kharīd, let a few Turks be joined with it to reassure these Kharīd people and to escort them to their own place.[2583] If they quit not the ferry-head, if they cease not their unbecoming words, they must regard as their own act any ill that befalls them, must count any misfortune they confront as the fruit of their own words."

(*April 20th*) On Wednesday (*12th*) the usual dress of honour was put on the Bengal envoy, gifts were bestowed on him and his leave to go was given.

(*April 21st*) On Thursday (*13th*) Shaikh Jamālī was sent with royal letters of encouragement to Dūdū and her son Jalāl Khān.

Today a servant of Māhīm's came, who will have parted from the Wālī(?)[2584] on the other side of the Bāgh-i-ṣafā.

(*April 23rd*) On Saturday (*15th*) an envoy from 'Irāq, Murād *Qajar*[2585] the life-guardsman, was seen.

(*April 24th*) On Sunday (*16th*) Mullā Maẕhab received his usual keepsakes (*yādgārlār*) and was given leave to go.

Fol. 369b.(*April 25th*) On Monday (*17th*) Khalīfa was sent, with several begs, to see where the river (Ganges) could be crossed.

(*April 27th*) On Wednesday, (*19th*) Khalīfa again was sent out, to look at the ground between the two rivers (Ganges and Ghogrā).

On this same day I rode southward in the Ārī (Ārrah) *pargana* to visit the sheets of lotus[2586] near Ārī. During the excursion Shaikh Gūran brought me fresh-set lotus-seeds, first-rate little things just like pistachios. The flower, that is to say, the *nīlūfar* (lotus), Hindūstānīs call *kuwul-kikrī* (lotus-pistachio), and its seed *dūdah* (soot).

As people said, "The Son is near," we went to refresh ourselves on it. Masses of trees could be seen down-stream; "Munīr is there," said they, "where the tomb is of Shaikh Yaḥyā the father of Shaikh Sharafu'd-dīn *Munīrī*."[2587] It being so close, I crossed the Son, went 2 or 3 *kurohs* down it, traversed the Munīr orchards, made the circuit of the tomb, returned to the Son-bank, made ablution, went through the Mid-day Prayer before time, and made for camp. Some of our horses, being fat,[2588] had fallen behind; some were worn out; a few people were left to gather them together, water them, rest them, and bring them on without pressure; but for this many would have been ruined.

When we turned back from Munīr, I ordered that some-one Fol. 370.should count a horse's steps between the Son-bank and the camp. They amounted to 23,100, which is 46,200 paces, which is 11-1/2 *kurohs* (23m.).[2589] It is about half a *kuroh* from Munīr to the Son; the return journey from Munīr to the camp was therefore 12 *kurohs* (24m.). In addition to this were some 15-16 *kurohs* done in visiting this and that place; so that the whole excursion was one of some 30 *kurohs* (60m.). Six *garīs* of the 1st night-watch had passed [8.15 p.m.] when we reached the camp.

(*April 28th*) At the dawn of Thursday (*Sha'bān 19th*) Sl. Junaid *Barlās* came in with the Jūnpūr braves from Jūnpūr. I let him know my blame and displeasure on account of his delay; I did not see him. Qāẕī Jīā I sent for and saw.

(*aaa. Plan of the approaching battle with the Bengal army.*)

On the same day the Turk and Hind amīrs were summoned for a consultation about crossing Gang (Ganges), and matters found settlement at this[2590]:—that Ūstād 'Alī-qulī should collect mortar, *firingī*,[2591] and culverin[2592] to the point of rising ground between the rivers Sarū and Gang, and, having many matchlockmen with him, should incite to battle from that place;[2593] that Muṣṭạfa, he also having many matchlockmen, should get his material and implements ready on the Bihār side of Gang, a little below the meeting of the waters and opposite to where on an island the Bengalīs had an elephant and a mass of boats tied up, and that he should engage battle from this place;[2594] that Muḥammad-i-zamān Mīrzā and the others inscribed for the work should take post behind Muṣṭạfa as his reserve; that both for Ūstād 'Alī-qulī and Muṣṭạfa shelters (*muljār*) for the culverin-firers should be raised by a mass of spadesmen and coolies (*kahār*) Fol. 370b.under appointed overseers; that as soon as these shelters were ready, 'Askarī and the sulṭạ̄ns inscribed for the work should cross quickly at the Haldī-passage[2595] and come down on the enemy; that meantime, as Sl. Junaid and Qāẕī Jīā had given information about a crossing-place[2596] 8 *kurohs* (16 m.) higher up,[2597] Zard-rūī(Pale-face?) should go with a few raftsmen and some of the people of the Sulṭạ̄n, Maḥmūd Khān *Nūḥānī* and Qāẕī Jīā to look at that crossing; and that, if crossing there were, they should go over at once, because it was rumoured that the Bengalīs were planning to post men at the Haldī-passage.

A dutiful letter from Maḥmūd Khān the Military-collector (*shiqdār*) of Sikandarpūr now came, saying that he had collected as many as 50 boats at the Haldī-passage and had given wages to the boatmen, but that these were much alarmed at the rumoured approach of the Bengalīs.

(*April 30th*) As time pressed[2598] for crossing the Sarū, I did not wait for the return of those who had gone to look at the passage, but on Saturday (*21st*) summoned the begs for consultation and said, "As it has been reported that there are (no?) crossing-places (fords?) along the whole of the ground from Chatur-mūk in Sikandarpūr to Barāīch and Aūd,[2599] let us, while seated here, assign the large force to cross at the Haldī-passage by boat and from thereFol. 371. to come down on the enemy; let Ūstād 'Alī-qulī and Muṣṭạfa engage battle with gun (*top*), matchlock, culverin and *firingī*, and by this draw the enemy out before 'Askarī comes up.[2600] Let us after crossing the river (Ganges) and assigning reinforcement to Ūstād 'Alī-qulī, take our stand ready for whatever comes; if 'Askarī's troops get near, let us fling attack from where we are, cross over and assault; let Muḥammad-i-zamān Mīrzā and those appointed to act with him, engage battle from near Muṣṭafa on the other side of Gang."

The matter having been left at this, the force for the north of the Gang was formed into four divisions to start under 'Askarī's command for the Haldī-passage. One division was of 'Askarī and his retainers; another was Sl. Jalālu'd-dīn *Sharqī*; another was of the Aūzbeg sulṭāns Qāsim-i-ḥusain Sulṭān, Bī-khūb Sulṭān and Tāng-aītmīsh Sulṭān, together with Maḥmūd Khān *Nūḥānī* of Ghāzīpūr, Bābā Qashqa's Kūkī, Tūlmīsh *Aūzbeg*, Qurbān of Chīrkh, and the Daryā-khānīs led by Ḥasan Khān; another was of Mūsā Sl. (*Farmūlī*) and Sl. Junaid with what-not of the Jūnpūr army, some 20,000 men. Officers were appointed to oversee the getting of the force to horse that very night, that is to say, theFol. 371b. night of Sunday.[2601]

(*May 1st*) The army began to cross Gang at the dawn of Sunday (*Sha'bān 22nd*); I went over by boat at the 1st watch (6a.m.). Zard-rūī and his party came in at mid-day; the ford itself they had not found but they brought news of boats and of having met on the road the army getting near them.[2602]

(*May 3rd*) On Tuesday (*Sha'bān 24th*) we marched from where the river had been crossed, went on for nearly one *kuroh* (2 m.) and dismounted on the fighting-ground at the confluence.[2603] I myself went to enjoy Ūstād 'Alī-qulī's firing of culverin and *firingī*; he hit two boats today with *firingī*-stones, broke them and sank them. Muṣṭafa did the same from his side. I had the large mortar[2604] taken to the fighting-ground, left Mullā Ghulām to superintend the making of its position, appointed a body of *yasāwals*[2605] and active braves to help him, went to an island facing the camp and there ate *ma'jūn*.

Whilst still under the influence of the confection[2606] I had the boat taken to near the tents and there slept. A strange thing happened in the night, a noise and disturbance arising about the 3rd watch (midnight) and the pages and others snatching up pieces of wood from the boat, and shouting "Strike! strike!" Fol. 372.What was said to have led to the disturbance was that a night-guard who was in the Farmāīsh along-side the Asāīsh in which I was sleeping,[2607] opening his eyes from slumber, sees a man with his hand on the Asāīsh as if meaning to climb into her. They fall on him;[2608] he dives, comes up again, cuts at the night-guard's head, wounding it a little, then runs off at once towards the river.[2609] Once before, on the night we returned from Munīr, one or two night-guards had chased several

Hindūstānīs from near the boats, and had brought in two swords and a dagger of theirs. The Most High had me in His Keeping!

(*Persian*) Were the sword of the world to leap forth,
It would cut not a vein till God will.[2610]

(*May 4th*) At the dawn of Wednesday (*25th*), I went in the boat Gunjāīsh to near the stone-firing ground (*tāsh-ātār-yīr*) and there posted each soever to his work.

(*bbb. Details of the engagement.*)

Aūghān-bīrdī *Mughūl*, leading not less than 1,000 men, had been sent to get, in some way or other, across the river (Sarū) one, two, three *kurohs* (2, 4, 6m.) higher up. A mass of foot-soldiers, crossing from opposite 'Askarī's camp,[2611] landed from 20-30 boats on his road, presumably thinking to show their superiority, but Aūghān-bīrdī and his men charged them, put them to flight, took a few and cut their heads off, shot many with arrows, and got possession of 7 or 8 boats. Today also Bengalīs crossed in a few boats to Muḥammad-i-zamān Mīrzā's side, there landed andFol. 372b. provoked to fight. When attacked they fled, and three boat-loads of them were drowned. One boat was captured and brought to me. In this affair Bābā the Brave went forward and exerted himself excellently.

Orders were given that in the darkness of night the boats Aūghān-bīrdī had captured should be drawn[2612] up-stream, and that in them there should cross Muḥammad Sl. Mīrzā, Yakka Khwāja, Yūnas-i-'alī, Aūghān-bīrdī and those previously assigned to go with them.

Today came a man from 'Askarī to say that he had crossed the [Sarū]-water, leaving none behind, and that he would come down on the enemy at next day's dawn, that is to say, on Thursday's. Here-upon those already ordered to cross over were told to join 'Askarī and to advance upon the enemy with him.

At the Mid-day Prayer a person came from Ūstā, saying "The stone is ready; what is the order?" The order was, "Fire this stone off; keep the next till I come." Going at the Other Prayer in a very small Bengalī skiff to where shelter (*muljār*) had been raised, I saw Ūstā fire off one large stone and several small *firingī* ones. Bengalīs have a reputation for fire-working;[2613] we tested it now; they do not fire counting to hit a particular spot, but fire at random.

At this same Other Prayer orders were given to draw a few boats up-stream along the enemy's front. A few were got past without a "God forbid!"[2614]

from those who, all unprotected, drew Fol. 373.them up. Aīsān-tīmūr Sl. and Tūkhta-būghā Sl. were ordered to stay at the place those boats reached, and to keep watch over them. I got back to camp in the 1st night-watch of Thursday.[2615]

Near midnight came news from (Aūghān-bīrdī's) boats which were being drawn up-stream, "The force appointed had gone somewhat ahead; we were following, drawing the boats, when the Bengalīs got to know where we were drawing them and attacked. A stone hit a boatman in the leg and broke it, we could not pass on."

(*May 5th*) At dawn on Thursday (*Sha'bān 26th*) came the news from those at the shelter, "All the boats have come from above.[2616] The enemy's horse has ridden to meet our approaching army." On this, I got our men mounted quickly and rode out to above those boats[2617] that had been drawn up in the night. A galloper was sent off with an order for Muḥammad Sl. M. and those appointed to cross with him, to do it at once and join 'Askarī. The order for Aīsān-tīmūr Sl. and Tūkhta-būghā Sl. who were above these boats,[2618] was that they should busy themselves to cross. Bābā Sl. was not at his post.[2619]

Aīsān-tīmūr Sl. at once crosses, in one boat with 30-40 of his retainers who hold their horses by the mane at the boat-side.Fol. 373b. A second boat follows. The Bengalīs see them crossing and start off a mass of foot-soldiers for them. To meet these go 7 or 8 of Aīsān-tīmūr Sl.'s retainers, keeping together, shooting off arrows, drawing those foot-soldiers towards the Sulṭān who meantime is getting his men mounted; meantime also the second boat is moving (*rawān*). When his 30-35 horsemen charge those foot-soldiers, they put them well to flight. Aīsān-tīmūr did distinguished work, first in crossing before the rest, swift, steady, and without a "God forbid!", secondly in his excellent advance, with so few men, on such a mass of foot, and by putting these to flight. Tūkhta-būghā Sl. also crossed. Then boats followed one after another. Lāhorīs and Hindūstānīs began to cross from their usual posts[2620] by swimming or on bundles of reeds.[2621] Seeing how matters were going, the Bengalīs of the boats opposite the shelter (Muṣṭafa's), set their faces for flight down-stream.

Darwīsh-i-muḥammad *Sārbān*, Dost Lord-of-the-gate, Nūr Beg and several braves also went across the river. I made a man gallop off to the Sulṭāns to say, "Gather well together those whoFol. 374. cross, go close to the opposing army, take it in the flank, and get to grips." Accordingly the Sulṭāns collected those who crossed, formed up into 3 or 4 divisions, and started for the foe. As they draw near, the enemy-commander, without breaking his array, flings his foot-soldiers to the front and so comes on. Kūkī comes up with a troop from 'Askarī's force and gets to grips on his side; the Sulṭāns get to grips on theirs; they get the upper hand, unhorse man after man, and make the enemy scurry off. Kūkī's men bring down a Pagan of repute named Basant Rāō and cut off his head; 10 or 15 of his people fall on Kūkī's, and are instantly cut to pieces. Tūkhta-būghā Sl. gallops along the enemy's front and gets his sword well in. Mughūl 'Abdu'l-wahhāb and his younger brother gets theirs in well too. Mughūl though he did not know how to swim, had crossed the river holding to his horse's mane.

I sent for my own boats which were behind;[2622] the Farmāīsh coming up first, I went over in it to visit the Bengalīs' encamping-grounds. I then went into the Gunjāīsh. "Is there a crossing-place higher up?" I asked. Mīr Muḥammad the raftsman represented that the Sarū was better to cross higher up;[2623] accordingly the army-folk[2624] were ordered to cross at the higher place he named.

While those led by Muḥammad Sl. Mīrzā were crossing the Fol. 374b.river,[2625] the boat in which Yakka Khwāja was, sank and he went to God's mercy. His retainers and lands were bestowed on his younger brother Qāsim Khwāja.

The Sulṭāns arrived while I was making ablution for the Mid-day Prayer; I praised and thanked them and led them to expect guerdon and kindness. 'Askarī also came; this was the first affair he had seen; one well-omened for him!

As the camp had not yet crossed the river, I took my rest in the boat Gunjāīsh, near an island.

(*ccc. Various incidents of the days following the battle.*)

(*May 6th*) During the day of Friday (*Sha'bān 27th*) we landed at a village named Kūndīh[2626] in the Nirhun *pargana* of Kharīd on the north side of the Sarū.[2627]

(*May 8th*) On Sunday (*29th*) Kūkī was sent to Ḥājīpūr for news.

Shāh Muḥammad (son) of Ma'rūf to whom in last year's campaign (934 AH.) I had shown great favour and had given the Sāran-country, had done well on several occasions, twice fighting and overcoming his father Ma'rūf.[2628] At the time when Sl. Maḥmūd *Lūdī* perfidiously took possession of Bihār and was opposed by Shaikh Bāyazīd and Bīban, Shāh Muḥammad had no help for it, he had to join them; but even then, when people were saying wild words about him, he had written dutifully to me. When 'Askarī crossed at the Haldī-passage, ShāhFol. 375. Muḥammad had come at once with a troop, seen him and with him gone against the Bengalīs. He now came to this ground and waited on me.

During these days news came repeatedly that Bīban and Shaikh Bāyazīd were meaning to cross the Sarū-river.

In these days of respite came the surprising news from Sanbal (Saṃbhal) where 'Alī-i-yūsuf had stayed in order to bring the place into some sort of order, that he and a physician who was by way of being a friend of his, had gone to God's mercy on one and the same day. 'Abdu'l-lāh (*kitābdār*) was ordered to go and maintain order in Sanbal.

(*May 13th*) On Friday the 5th of the month Ramẓān, 'Abdu'l-lāh was given leave for Sanbal.[2629]

(*ddd. News from the westward.*)

In these same days came a dutiful letter from Chīn-tīmūr Sl. saying that on account of the journey of the family from Kābul, several of the begs who had been appointed to reinforce him, had not been able to join him;[2630] also that he had gone out with Muḥammadī and other begs and braves, not less than 100 *kurohs* (200m.), attacked the Balūchīs and given them a good beating.[2631] Orders were sent through 'Abdu'l-lāh (*kitābdār*) for the Sulṭān that he and Sl. Muḥammad *Dūldāī*, Muḥammadī, and some of the begs and braves of that country-side should assemble in Āgra and there remain ready to move to wherever an enemy appeared.

(*eee. Settlement with the Nūḥānī Afghāns.*)

(*May 16th*) On Monday the 8th of the month, Daryā Khān's Fol. 375b.grandson Jalāl Khān to whom Shaikh Jamālī had gone, came in with his chief amīrs and waited on me.[2632] Yaḥyā *Nūḥānī* also came, who had already sent his younger brother in sign of submission and had received a royal letter accepting his service. Not to make vain the hope with which some 7 or 8,000 *Nūḥānī* Afghāns had come in to me, I bestowed 50 *laks* from Bīhār on Maḥmūd Khān *Nūḥānī*, after reserving one *krūr* for Government uses (*khalṣa*), and gave the remainder of the Bihār revenues in trust for the above-mentioned Jalāl Khān who for his part agreed to pay one *krūr* of tribute. Mullā Ghulām *yasāwal* was sent to collect this tribute.[2633] Muḥammad-i-zamān Mīrzā received the Jūnapūr-country.[2634]

(*fff. Peace made with Naṣrat Shāh.*)

(*May 19th*) On the eve of Thursday (*11th*) that retainer of Khalīfa's, Ghulām-i-'alī by name, who in company with a retainer of the Shāh-zāda of

Mungīr named Abū'l-fatḥ,[2635] had gone earlier than Ismā'īl Mītā, to convey those three articles (*faṣl soz*), now returned, again in company with Abū'l-fatḥ, bringing letters for Khalīfa written by the Shāh-zāda and by Ḥusain Khān *Laskar*(?) *Wazīr*, who, in these letters, gave assent to those three conditions, took upon themselves to act for Naṣrat Shāh and interjected a word for peace. As the object of this campaign was to put down the rebel Afghāns of whom some had taken their heads and gone off, some had come in submissive and accepting my service, and the remaining few were in the hands of the BengalīFol. 376. (Naṣrat Shāh) who had taken them in charge, and as, moreover, the Rains were near, we in our turn wrote and despatched words for peace on the conditions mentioned.

(*ggg. Submissions and guerdon.*)

(*May 21st*) On Saturday (*13th*) Ismā'īl *Jālwānī*, 'Alāūl Khān *Nūḥānī*, Auliya Khān *Ashrāqī*(?) and 5 and 6 amīrs came in and waited on me.

Today guerdon was bestowed on Aīsān-tīmūr Sl. and Tūkhta-būghā Sl., of swords and daggers with belts, cuirasses, dresses of honour, and *tīpūchāq* horses; also they were made to kneel, Aīsān-tīmūr Sl. for the grant of 36 *laks* from the Nārnūl *pargana*, Tūkhta-bughā Sl. for 30 *laks* from that of Shamsābād.

(*hhh. Pursuit of Bāyazīd and Bīban.*)

(*May 23rd*) On Monday the 15th of the month (*Ramzān*), we marched from our ground belonging to Kūndbah (or Kūndīh) on the Sarū-river, with easy mind about Bihār and Bengal, and resolute to crush the traitors Bīban and Shaikh Bāyazīd.

(*May 25th*) On Wednesday (*17th*) after making two night-halts by the way, we dismounted at a passage across the Sarū, called Chaupāra-Chaturmūk of Sikandarpūr.[2636] From today people were busy in crossing the river.

As news began to come again and again that the traitors, after crossing Sarū and Gogar,[2637] were going toward Luknū,[2638] the following leaders were appointed to bar (their) crossing[2639]:—The Turk and Hind amīrs Jalālu'd-dīn *Sharqī*, 'Alī Khān *Farmūlī*; Tardīka (or, Tardī *yakka*), Nizām Khān of Bīāna, together with Tūlmīsh *Aūzbeg*, Qurbān of Chīrk and Daryā Khān (of Bhīra's Fol. 376b.son) Ḥasan Khān. They were given leave to go on the night of Thursday.[2640]

(*iii. Damage done to the Bābur-nāma writings.*)

That same night when 1 watch (*pās*), 5 *garīs* had passed (*cir.* 10.55 p.m.) and the *tarāwīḥ*-prayers were over,[2641] such a storm burst, in the inside of a moment, from the up-piled clouds of the Rainy-season, and such a stiff gale rose, that few tents were left standing. I was in the Audience-tent, about to write (*kitābat qīlā dūr aīdīm*); before I could collect papers and sections,[2642] the tent came down, with its porch, right on my head. The *tūnglūq* went to pieces.[2643] God preserved me! no harm befell me! Sections and book[2644] were drenched under water and gathered together with much difficulty. We laid them in the folds of a woollen throne-carpet,[2645] put this on the throne and on it piled blankets. The storm quieted down in about 2 *garīs* (45m.); the bedding-tent was set up, a lamp lighted, and, after much trouble, a fire kindled. We, without sleep, were busy till shoot of day drying folios and sections.

(*jjj. Pursuit of Bīban and Bāyazīd resumed.*)

(*May 26th*) I crossed the water on Thursday morning (*Ramān 18th*).

(*May 27th*) On Friday (*19th*) I rode out to visit Sikandarpūr and Kharīd.[2646] Today came matters written by 'Abdu'l-lāh (*kitābdār*) and Bāqī about the taking of Luknūr.[2647]

(*May 28th*) On Saturday (*20th*) Kūkī was sent ahead, with a troop, to join Bāqī.[2648]

(*May 29th*) That nothing falling to be done before my arrival might be neglected, leave to join Bāqī was given on Sunday (*21st*) to Sl. Junaid *Barlās*, Khalīfa's (son) Ḥasan, Mullā Apāq'sFol. 377. retainers, and the elder and younger brethren of Mumin Ātāka.

Today at the Other Prayer a special dress of honour and a *tīpūchāq* horse were bestowed on Shāh Muḥammad (son) of Ma'rūf *Farmūlī*, and leave to go was given. As had been done last year (934 AH.), an allowance from Sāran and Kūndla[2649] was bestowed on him for the maintenance of quiver-wearers. Today too an allowance of 72 *laks*[2650] from Sarwār and a *tīpūchāq* horse were bestowed on Ismā'īl *Jalwānī*, and his leave was given.

About the boats Gunjāīsh and Arāīsh it was settled with Bengalīs that they should take them to Ghāzīpūr by way of Tīr-mūhānī.[2651] The boats Asāīsh and Farmāīsh were ordered taken up the Sarū with the camp.

(*May 30th*) On Monday (*Ramẓān 22nd*) we marched from the Chaupāra-Chaturmūk passage along the Sarū, with mind at ease about Bihār and Sarwār,[2652] and after doing as much as 10 *kurohs*

Fol. 377b.(20m.) dismounted on the Sarū in a village called Kilirah (?) dependent on Fatḥpūr.[2653]

(*kkk. A surmised survival of the record of 934. A.H.*[2654])

*After spending several days pleasantly in that place where there are gardens, running-waters, well-designed buildings, trees, particularly mango-trees, and various birds of coloured plumage, I ordered the march to be towards Ghāzīpūr.

Ismā'īl Khān *Jalwānī* and 'Alāūl Khān *Nūḥānī* had it represented to me that they would come to Āgra after seeing their native land (*watn*). On this the command was, "I will give an order in a month."*[2655]

(*lll. The westward march resumed.*)

(*May 31st*) Those who marched early (*Tuesday, Ramẓān 23rd*), having lost their way, went to the great lake of Fatḥpūr (?).[2656] People were sent galloping off to fetch back such as were near and Kīchīk Khwāja was ordered to spend the night on the lakeshore and to bring the rest on next morning to join the camp. We marched at dawn; I got into the Asāīsh half-way and had it towed to our ground higher up.

(*mmm. Details of the capture of a fort by Bīban and Bāyazīd.*)

On the way up, Khalīfa brought Shāh Muḥammad *dīwāna's* son who had come from Bāqī bringing this reliable news about Luknūr[2657]:—They (*i.e.* Bīban and Bāyazīd) hurled their assault on Saturday the 13th of the month Ramẓān (*May 21st*) but could do nothing by fighting; while the fighting was going on, a collection of wood-chips, hay, and thorns in the fort took fire, so that inside the walls it became as hot as an oven (*tanūrdīk tafsān*); the garrison could not move round the rampart; the fort was lost. When the enemy heard, two or three days later, of our return (westwards), he fled towards Dalmau.[2658]

Today after doing as much as 10 *kurohs* (20m.), we dismounted beside a village called Jalisir,[2659] on the Sarū-bank, in the Sagrī *pargāna.*

(*June 1st*) We stayed on the same ground through Wednesday (*24th*), in order to rest our cattle.

(*nnn. Dispositions against Bīban and Bāyazīd.*)

Some said they had heard that Bīban and Bāyazīd had crossed Gang, and thought of withdrawing themselves to their kinsfolkFol. 378. (*nisbahsīlār*) by way of....[2660] Here-upon the begs were summoned for a consultation and it was settled that Muḥammad-i-zamān Mīrzā and Sl. Junaid *Barlās* who in place of Jūnpūr had been given Chunār with several *parganas*, Maḥmud Khān *Nūḥānī*, Qāẓī Jīā, and Tāj Khān *Sarāng-khānī* should block the enemy's road at Chunār.[2661]

(*June 2nd*) Marching early in the morning of Thursday (*25th*), we left the Sarū-river, did 11 *kurohs* (22 m.), crossed the Parsarū (Sarjū) and dismounted on its bank.

Here the begs were summoned, discussion was had, and the leaders named below were appointed to go detached from the army, in rapid pursuit of Bīban and Bāyazīd towards Dalmūṭ. (Dalmau):—Aīsān-tīmūr Sl., Muḥammad Sl. M., Tūkhta-būghā Sl., Qāsim-i-ḥusain Sl., Bī-khūb (Nī-khūb) Sl., Muẓaffar-i-ḥusain Sl., Qāsim Khwāja, Ja'far Khwāja, Zahid Khwāja, Jānī Beg, 'Askarī's retainer Kīchīk Khwāja, and, of Hind amīrs, 'Ālam Khān of Kālpī, Malik-dād *Kararānī*, and Rāo (Rāwūī) *Sarwānī.*

(*ooo. The march continued.*)

When I went at night to make ablution in the Parsarū, people were catching a mass of fish that had gathered round a lamp on the surface of the water. I like others took fish in my hands.[2662]

(*June 3rd*) On Friday (*26th*) we dismounted on a very slender stream, the head-water of a branch of the Parsarū. In order not to be disturbed by the comings and goings of the army-folk,Fol. 378b. I had it dammed higher up and had a place, 10 by 10, made for ablution. The night of the 27th[2663] was spent on this ground.

(*June 4th*) At the dawn of the same day (*Saturday 27th*) we left that water, crossed the Tūs and dismounted on its bank.[2664]

(*June 5th*) On Sunday (*28th*) we dismounted on the bank of the same water.

(*June 6th*) On Monday the 29th of the month (*Ramẓān*), our station was on the bank of the same Tūs-water. Though tonight the sky was not quite clear, a few people saw the Moon, and so testifying to the Qāẓī, fixed the end of the month (*Ramẓān*).

(*June 7th*) On Tuesday (*Shawwāl 1st*) we made the Prayer of the Festival, at dawn rode on, did 10 *kurohs* (20 m.), and dismounted on the bank of the Gūī (Gūmtī), a *kuroh* (2 m.) from Māīng.[2665] The sin of *ma'jūn* was committed (*irtikāb qīlīldi*) near the Mid-day Prayer; I had sent this little couplet of invitation to Shaikh Zain, Mullā Shihāb and Khwānd-amīr:—

(*Turkī*) Shaikh and Mullā Shihāb and Khwānd-amir,
Come all three, or two, or on

Darwīsh-i-muḥammad (*Sārbān*), Yūnas-i-'alī and 'Abdu'l-lāh (*'asas*)[2666] were also there. At the Other Prayer the wrestlers set to.

(*June 8th*) On Wednesday (*2nd*) we stayed on the same ground. Near breakfast-time *ma'jūn* was eaten. Today Malik Sharq came in who had been to get Tāj Khān out of Chunār.[2667] When the wrestlers set to today, the Champion of Aūd who had come earlier, grappled with and threw a Hindūstānī wrestler who hadFol. 379. come in the interval.

Today Yaḥyā *Nuḥāni* was granted an allowance of 15 *laks* from Parsarūr,[2668] made to put on a dress of honour, and given his leave.

(*June 9th*) Next day (*Thursday 3rd*) we did 11 *kurohs* (22 m.), crossed the Gūī-water (Gūmtī), and dismounted on its bank.

(*ppp. Concerning the pursuit of Bīban and Bāyazīd.*)

News came in about the sulṭāns and begs of the advance that they had reached Dalmūd (Dalmau), but were said not yet to have crossed the water (Ganges). Angered by this (delay), I sent orders, "Cross the water at once; follow the track of the rebels; cross Jūn (Jumna) also; join 'Ālam Khān to yourselves; be energetic and get to grips with the adversary."

(*qqq. The march continued.*)

(*June 10th*) After leaving this water (*Gūmtī, Friday 4th*) we made two night-halts and reached Dalmūd (Dalmau), where most of the army-folk crossed Gang, there and then, by a ford. While the camp was being got over, *ma'jūn* was eaten on an island (*ārāl*) below the ford.

(*June 13th*) After crossing, we waited one day (*Monday 7th*) for all the army-folk to get across. Today Bāqī *Tāshkīndī* came in with the army of Aūd (Ajodhya) and waited on me.

(*June 14th*) Leaving the Gang-water (Ganges, *Tuesday 8th*), we made one night-halt, then dismounted (*June 15th-Shawwāl 9th*) beside Kūrarah (Kūra Khāṣ) on the Arind-water. The distance from Dalmūd (Dalmau) to Kūrarah came out at 22 *kurohs* (44 m.).[2669]

(*June 16th*) On Thursday (*10th*) we marched early from that ground and dismounted opposite the Ādampūr *pargana*.[2670]

To enable us to cross (Jūn) in pursuit of our adversaries, a few Fol. 379b.raftsmen had been sent forward to collect at Kālpī what boats were to be had; some boats arrived the night we dismounted, moreover a ford was found through the Jūn-river.

As the encamping-place was full of dust, we settled ourselves on an island and there stayed the several days we were on that ground.

(*rrr. Concerning Bīban and Bāyazīd.*)

Not getting reliable news about the enemy, we sent Bāqī *shaghāwal* with a few braves of the interior[2671] to get information about him.

(*June 17th*) Next day (*Friday 11th*) at the Other Prayer, one of Bāqī Beg's retainers came in. Bāqī had beaten scouts of Bīban and Bāyazīd, killed one of their good men, Mubārak Khān *Jalwānī*, and some others, sent in several heads, and one man alive.

(*June 18th*) At dawn (*Saturday 12th*) Paymaster Shāh Ḥusain came in, told the story of the beating of the scouts, and gave various news.

Tonight, that is to say, the night of Sunday the 13th of the month,[2672] the river Jūn came down in flood, so that by the dawn, the whole of the island on which I was settled, was under water. I moved to another an arrow's-flight down-stream, there had a tent set up and settled down.

(*June 20th*) On Monday (*14th*) Jalāl *Tāshkīndī* came from the begs and sulṭāns of the advance. Shaikh Bāyazīd and Bīban, on hearing of their expedition, had fled to the *pargana* of Mahūba.[2673]Fol. 380.

As the Rains had set in and as after 5 or 6 months of active service, horses and cattle in the army were worn out, the sulṭāns and begs of the expedition were ordered to remain where they were till they received fresh supplies from Āgra and those parts. At the Other Prayer of the same day, leave was given to Bāqī and the army of Aūd (Ajodhya). Also an allowance of 30 *lāks*[2674] from Amrohā was assigned to Mūsa (son) of Ma'rūf *Farmūlī*, who had waited on me at the time the returning army was crossing the Sarū-water,[2675] a special head-to-foot and saddled horse were bestowed on him, and he was given his leave.

(*sss. Bābur returns to Āgra.*)

(*June 21st*) With an easy mind about these parts, we set out for Āgra, raid-fashion,[2676] when 3 *pās* 1 *garī* of Tuesday night were past.[2677] In the morning (*Tuesday 15th*) we did 16 *kurohs* (32 m.), near mid-day made our nooning in the *pargana* of Balādar, one of the dependencies of Kālpī, there gave our horses barley, at the Evening Prayer rode on, did 13 *kurohs* (26 m.) in the night, at the 3rd night-watch (*mid-night, Shawwāl 15-16th*) dismounted at Bahādur Khān *Sarwānī's* tomb at Sūgandpūr, a *pargana* of Kālpī, slept a little, went through the Morning Prayer and hurried on. After doing 16 *kurohs* (32 m.), we reached Etāwa at the fall of day, where Mahdī Khwāja came out to meet us.[2678] Riding Fol. 380b.on after the 1st night-watch (9 p.m.), we slept a little on the way, did 16 *kurohs* (32 m.), took our nooning at Fatḥpūr of Rāprī, rode on soon after the Mid-day Prayer (*Thursday Shawwāl 17th*), did

17 *kurohs* (34 m.), and in the 2nd night-watch[2679] dismounted in the Garden-of-eight-paradises at Āgra.

(*June 24th*) At the dawn of Friday (*18th*) Pay-master Sl. Muḥammad came with several more to wait on me. Towards the Mid-day Prayer, having crossed Jūn, I waited on Khwāja 'Abdu'l-ḥaqq, went into the Fort and saw the begīms my paternal-aunts.

(*ttt. Indian-grown fruits.*)

A Balkhī melon-grower had been set to raise melons; he now brought a few first-rate small ones; on one or two bush-vines (*būta-tāk*) I had had planted in the Garden-of-eight-paradises very good grapes had grown; Shaikh Gūran sent me a basket of grapes which too were not bad. To have grapes and melons grown in this way in Hindūstān filled my measure of content.

(*uuu. Arrival of Māhīm Begīm.*)

(*June 26th*) Māhīm arrived while yet two watches of Sunday night (*Shawwāl 20th*)[2680] remained. By a singular agreement of things they had left Kābul on the very day, the 10th of the 1st Jumāda (*Jan. 21st 1529*) on which I rode out to the army.[2681]

(*Here the record of 11 days is wanting.*)

(*July 7th*) On Thursday the 1st of Ẕū'l-qa'da the offerings made by Humāyūn and Māhīm were set out while I sat in the large Hall of Audience.

Today also wages were given to 150 porters (*kahār*) and they were started off under a servant of Faghfūr *Dīwān* to fetch melons, grapes, and other fruits from Kābul.Fol. 381.

(*vvv. Concerning Saṃbhal.*)

(*July 9th*) On Saturday the 3rd of the month, Hindū Beg who had come as escort from Kābul and must have been sent to Saṃbhal on account of the death of 'Alī-i-yūsuf, came and waited on me.[2682] Khalīfa's (son) Ḥusāmu'd-dīn came also today from Alwār and waited on me.

(*July 10th*) On Sunday morning (*4th*) came 'Abdu'l-lāh (*kitābdār*), who from Tīr-mūhānī[2683] had been sent to Saṃbhal on account of the death of 'Alī-i-yūsuf.

(*Here the record of 7 days is wanting.*)

(*www. Sedition in Lāhor.*)

People from Kābul were saying that Shaikh Sharaf of Qarā-bāgh, either incited by 'Abdu'l-'azīz or out of liking for him, had written an attestation which attributed to me oppression I had not done, and outrage that had not happened; that he had extorted the signatures of the Prayer-leaders (*imāmlār*) of Lāhor to this accusation, and had sent copies of it to the various towns; that 'Abdu'l-'azīz himself had failed to give ear to several royal orders, had spoken unseemly words, and done acts which ought to have been left undone. On account of these matters Qaṃbar-i-'alī *Arghūn* was started off on Sunday the 11th of the month (*Ẕū'l-qa'da*), to arrest Shaikh Sharaf, the Lāhor *imāms* with their associates, and 'Abdu'l-'azīz, and to bring them all to Court.

(*xxx. Varia.*)

(*July 22nd*) On Thursday the 15th of the month Chīn-tīmūr Sl. came in from Tijāra and waited on me. Today Champion Fol. 381b.Ṣādiq and the great champion-wrestler of Aūd wrestled. Ṣādiq gave a half-throw[2684]; he was much vexed.

(*July 28th*) On Monday the 19th of the month (*Ẕū'l-qa'da*) the Qīzīl-bāsh envoy Murād the life-guardsman was made to put on an inlaid dagger with belt, and a befitting dress of honour, was presented with 2 *laks* of *tankas* and given leave to go.

(*Here the record of 15 days is wanting.*)

(*yyy. Sedition in Gūālīār.*)

(*August 11th*) Sayyid Mashhadī who had come from Gūālīār in these days, represented that Raḥīm-dād was stirring up sedition.[2685] On account of this, Khalīfa's servant Shāh Muḥammad the seal-bearer was sent to convey to Raḥīm-dād matters written with commingling of good counsel. He went; and in a few days came back bringing Raḥīm-dād's son, but, though the son came, Raḥīm-dād himself had no thought of coming. On Wednesday the 5th of *Ẕū'l-ḥijja*, Nūr Beg was sent to Gūālīār to allay Raḥīm-dād's fears, came back in a few days, and laid requests from Raḥīm-dād before us. Orders in accordance with those requests had been written and were on the point of despatch when one of Raḥīm-dād's servants arriving, represented that he had come to effect the escape of the son and that Raḥīm-dād himself had no thought of coming in. I was for riding out at once to Gūālīār, but Khalīfa set it forth to me, "Let me write one more letter commingled with good counsel; he may even yet come peacefully." On this mission Khusrau's (son?) Shihābu'd-dīn was despatched.

(*August 12th*) On Thursday the 6th of the month mentioned (*Ẕū'l-ḥijja*) Mahdī Khwāja came in from Etāwa.[2686]Fol. 382.

(*August 16th*) On the Festival-day[2687] (*Monday 10th*) Hindū Beg was presented with a special head-to-foot, an inlaid dagger with belt; also a *pargana* worth 7 *laks*[2688] was bestowed on Ḥasan-i-'alī, well-known among the Turkmāns[2689] for a Chaghatāī.[2690]

936 AH.-SEP. 5TH 1529 TO AUGUST 25TH 1530 AD.

(*a. Raḥīm-dād's affairs.*)

(*Sep. 7th*) On Wednesday the 3rd of Muḥarram, Shaikh Muḥammad *Ghauṣ*[2691] came in from Gūālīār with Khusrau's (son) Shihābu'd-dīn to plead for Raḥīm-dād. As Shaikh Muḥammad *Ghauṣ* was a pious and excellent person, Raḥīm-dād's faults were forgiven for his sake. Shaikh Gūran and Nūr Beg were sent off for Gūālīār, so that the place having been made over to their charge....[2692]

TRANSLATOR'S NOTE ON 936 TO 937 AH.-1529 TO 1530 AD.

It is difficult to find material for filling the *lacuna* of some 15 months, which occurs in Bābur's diary after the broken passage of Muḥarram 3rd 936 AH. (Sept. 7th 1529 AD.) and down to the date of his death on Jumāda 1. 6th 937 AH. (Dec. 26th 153O AD.). The known original sources are few, their historical matter scant, their contents mainly biographical. Gleanings may yet be made, however, in unexpected places, such gleanings as are provided by Aḥmad-i-yādgār's interpolation of Tīmūrid history amongst his lives of Afghān Sulṭāns.

The earliest original source which helps to fill the gap of 936 AH. is Ḥaidar Mīrzā's *Tārīkh-i-rashīdī*, finished as to its Second Part which contains Bābur's biography, in 948 AH. (1541 AD.), 12 years therefore after the year of the gap 936 AH. It gives valuable information about the affairs of Badakhshān, based on its author's personal experience at 30 years of age, and was Abū'l-faẓl's authority for the *Akbar-nāma.*

The next in date of the original sources is Gul-badan Begīm's *Humāyūn-nāma*, a chronicle of family affairs, which she wrote in obedience to her nephew Akbar's command, given in about 995 AH. (1587 AD.), some 57 years after her Father's death, that whatever any person knew of his father (Humāyūn) and grandfather (Bābur) should be written down for Abū'l-faẓl's use. It embodies family memories and traditions, and presumably gives the recollections of several ladies of the royal circle.[2693]

The *Akbar-nāma* derives much of its narrative for 936-937 AH. from Ḥaidar Mīrzā and Gul-badan Begīm, but its accounts of Bābur's self-surrender and of his dying address to his chiefs presuppose the help of information from a contemporary witness. It is noticeable that the *Akbar-nāma* records no public events as occurring in Hindūstān during 936-937 AH., nothing of the sequel of rebellion by Raḥīm-dād[2694] and 'Abdu'l-'azīz, nothing of the untiring Bīban and Bāyazīd. That something could have been told is shown by what Aḥmad-i-yādgār has preserved (*vide post*); but 50 years had passed since Bābur's death and, manifestly, interest in filling the *lacunæ* in his diary was then less keen than it is over 300 years later. What in the *Akbar-nāma* concerns Bābur is likely to have been written somewhat early in the *cir.* 15 years of its author's labours on it,[2695] but, even so, the elder women of the royal circle had had rest after the miseries Humāyūn had wrought, the forgiveness of family affection would veil his past, and certainly has provided Abū'l-faẓl with an over-mellowed estimate of him, one ill-assorting with what is justified by his Bābur-nāma record.

The contribution made towards filling the gap of 936-937 AH. in the body of Niẓāmu-'d-dīn Aḥmad's *Ṭabaqāt-i-akbarī* is limited to a curious and doubtfully acceptable anecdote about a plan for the supersession of Humāyūn as Pādshāh, and about the part played by Khwāja Muqīm *Harāwī* in its abandonment. A further contribution is made, however, in Book VII which contains the history of the Muḥammadan Kings of Kashmīr, namely, that Bābur despatched an expedition into that country. As no such expedition is recorded or referred to in surviving Bābur-nāma writings, it is likely to have been sent in 936 AH. during Bābur's tour to and from Lāhor. If it were made with the aim of extending Tīmūrid authority in the Himālayan borderlands, a hint of similar policy elsewhere may be given by the ceremonious visit of the Rāja of Kahlūr to Bābur, mentioned by Aḥmad-i-yādgār (*vide post*).[2696] The Ṭ.-i-A. was written within the term of Abū'l-faẓl's work on the *Akbar-nāma*, being begun later, and ended about 9 years earlier, in 1002 AH.-1593 AD. It appears to have been Abū'l-faẓl's authority for his account of the campaign carried on in Kashmīr by Bābur's chiefs (*Āyīn-i-akbarī* vol. ii, part i, Jarrett's trs. p. 389).

An important contribution, seeming to be authentic, is found interpolated in Aḥmad-i-yādgār's *Tārīkh-i-salāṭīn-i-afāghana*, one which outlines a journey made by Bābur to Lāhor in 936 AH. and gives circumstantial details of a punitive expedition sent by him from Sihrind at the complaint of the Qāẓī of Samāna against a certain Mundāhir Rājpūt. The whole contribution dovetails into matters found elsewhere. Its precision of detail bespeaks a closely-contemporary written source.[2697] As its fullest passage concerns the Samāna Qāẓī's affair, its basis of record may have been found in Samāna. Some considerations about the date of Aḥmad-i-yādgār's own book and what Niamatu'l-lāh says of Haibat Khān of Samāna, his own generous helper in the *Tārīkhi-Khan-i-jahān Lūdī*, point towards Haibat Khān as providing the details of the Qāẓī's wrongs and avenging. The indication is strengthened by the circumstance that what precedes and what follows the account of the punitive expedition is outlined only.[2698] Aḥmad-i-yādgār interpolates an account of Humāyūn also, which is a frank plagiarism from the *Ṭabaqāt-i-akbarī*. He tells too a story purporting to explain why Bābur "selected" Humāyūn to succeed him, one parallel with Niẓāmu'd-dīn Aḥmad's about what led Khalīfa to abandon his plan of setting the Mīrzā aside. Its sole value lies in its testimony to a belief, held by its first narrator whoever he was, that choice was exercised in the matter by Bābur. Reasons for thinking Niẓāmu'd-dīn's story, as it stands, highly improbable, will be found later in this note.

Muḥammad Qāsim Hindū Shāh *Firishta's Tārīkh-i-firishta* contains an interesting account of Bābur but contributes towards filling the gap in the events of 936-937 AH. little that is not in the earlier sources. In M. Jules Mohl's opinion it was under revision as late as 1623 AD. (1032-3 AH.).

(*a. Humāyūn and Badakhshān.*)

An occurrence which had important results, was the arrival of Humāyūn in Āgra, unsummoned by his Father, from the outpost station of Badakhshān. It will have occurred early in 936 AH. (autumn 1529 AD.), because he was in Kābul in the first ten days of the last month of 935 AH. (*vide post*). Curiously enough his half-sister Gul-badan does not mention his coming, whether through avoidance of the topic or from inadvertence; the omission may be due however to the loss of a folio from the only known MS. of her book (that now owned by the British Museum), and this is the more likely that Abū'l-faẓl writes, at some length, about the arrival and its motive, what the Begīm might have provided, this especially by his attribution of filial affection as Humāyūn's reason for coming to Āgra.

Ḥaidar Mīrzā is the authority for the Akbar-nāma account of Humāyūn's departure from Qila'-i-ẓafar and its political and military sequel. He explains the departure by saying that when Bābur had subdued Hindūstān, his sons Humāyūn and Kāmrān were grown-up; and that wishing to have one of them at hand in case of his own death, he summoned Humāyūn, leaving Kāmrān in Qandahār. No doubt these were the contemporary impressions conveyed to Ḥaidar, and strengthened by the accomplished fact before he wrote some 12 years later; nevertheless there are two clear indications that there was no royal order for Humāyūn to leave Qila'-i-ẓafar, *viz.* that no-one had been appointed to relieve him even when he reached Āgra, and that Abū'l-faẓl mentions no summons but attributes the Mīrzā's departure from his post to an overwhelming desire to see his Father. What appears probable is that Māhīm wrote to her son urging his coming to Āgra, and that this was represented as Bābur's wish. However little weight may be due to the rumour, preserved in anecdotes recorded long after 935 AH., that any-one, Bābur or Khalīfa, inclined against Humāyūn's succession, that rumour she would set herself to falsify by reconciliation.[2699]

When the Mīrzā's intention to leave Qila'-i-ẓạfar became known there, the chiefs represented that they should not be able to withstand the Aūzbeg on their frontier without him (his troops implied).[2700] With this he agreed, said that still he must go, and that he would send a Mīrzā in his place as soon as possible. He then rode, in one day, to Kābul, an item of rapid travel preserved by Abū'l-faẓl.

Humāyūn's departure caused such anxiety in Qila'-i-ẓạfar that some (if not all) of the Badakhshī chiefs hurried off an invitation to Sa'īd Khān *Chaghatāī*, the then ruler in Kāshghar in whose service Ḥaidar Mīrzā was, to come at once and occupy the fort. They said that Faqīr-i-'alī who had been left in charge, was not strong enough to cope with the Aūzbeg, begged Sa'īd to come, and strengthened their petition by reminding him of his hereditary right to Badakhshān, derived from Shāh Begīm *Badakhshī*. Their urgency convincing the Khān that risk threatened the country, he started from Kāshghar in Muḥarram 936 AH. (Sept-Oct. 1529 AD.). On reaching Sārīgh-chūpān which by the annexation of Abā-bakr Mīrzā *Dūghlāt* was now his own most western territory[2701] but which formerly was one of the upper districts of Badakhshān, he waited while Ḥaidar went on towards Qila'-i-ẓạfar only to learn on his road, that Hind-āl (*æt.* 10) had been sent from Kābul by Humāyūn and had entered the fort 12 days before.

The Kāshgharīs were thus placed in the difficulty that the fort was occupied by Bābur's representative, and that the snows would prevent their return home across the mountains till winter was past. Winter-quarters were needed and asked for by Ḥaidar, certain districts being specified in which to await the re-opening of the Pāmīr routes. He failed in his request, "They did not trust us," he writes, "indeed suspected us of deceit." His own account of Sa'īd's earlier invasion of Badakhshān (925 AH.-1519 AD.) during Khān Mīrzā's rule, serves to explain Badakhshī distrust of Kāshgharīs. Failing in his negotiations, he scoured and pillaged the country round the fort, and when a few days later the Khān arrived, his men took what Ḥaidar's had left.

Sa'īd Khān is recorded to have besieged the fort for three months, but nothing serious seems to have been attempted since no mention of fighting is made, none of assault or sally, and towards the end of the winter he was waited on by those who had invited his presence, with apology for not having admitted him into the fort, which they said they would have done but for the arrival of Hind-āl Mīrzā. To this the Khān replied that for him to oppose Bābur Pādshāh was impossible; he reminded the chiefs that he was there by request, that it would be as hurtful for the Pādshāh as for himself to have the Aūzbeg in Badakhshān and, finally, he gave it as his opinion that, as matters stood, every man should go home. His view of the general duty may include that of Badakhshī auxiliaries such as Sulṭān Wais of Kūl-āb who had reinforced the garrison. So saying, he himself set out for Kāshghar, and at the beginning of Spring reached Yārkand.

b. Humāyūn's further action.

Humāyūn will have reached Kābul before Ẕū'l-ḥijja 10th 935 AH. (Aug. 26th 1529 AD.) because it is on record that he met Kāmrān on the Kābul 'Īd-gāh, and both will have been there to keep the 'Īdu'l-kabīr, the Great Festival of Gifts, which is held on that day. Kāmrān had come from Qandahār, whether to keep the Feast, or because he had heard of Humāyūn's intended movement from Badakhshān, or because changes were foreseen and he coveted Kābul, as the *Bābur-nāma* and later records allow to be inferred. He asked Humāyūn, says Abū'l-faẓl, why he was there and was told of his brother's impending journey to Āgra under overwhelming desire to see their Father.[2702] Presumably the two Mīrzās discussed the position in which Badakhshān had been left; in the end Hind-āl was sent to Qila'-i-ẓạfar, notwithstanding that he was under orders for Hindūstān.

Humāyūn may have stayed some weeks in Kābul, how many those familiar with the seasons and the routes between Yārkand and Qila'-i-ẓạfar, might be able to surmise if the date of Hind-āl's start northward for which Humāyūn is likely to have waited, were found by dovetailing the Muḥarram of Sa'īd's start, the approximate length of his journey to Sārīgh-chūpān, and Ḥaidar's reception of news that Hind-āl had been 12 days in the fort.

Humāyūn's arrival in Āgra is said by Abū'l-faẓl to have been cheering to the royal family in their sadness for the death of Alwar (end of 935 AH.) and to have given pleasure to his Father. But the time is all too near the date of Bābur's letter (f.348) to Humāyūn, that of a dissatisfied parent, to allow the supposition that his desertion of his post would fail to displease.

That it was a desertion and not an act of obedience seems clear from the circumstance that the post had yet to be filled. Khalīfa is said to have been asked to take it and to have refused;[2703] Humāyūn to have been sounded as to return and to have expressed unwillingness. Bābur then did what was an honourable sequel to his acceptance in 926 AH. of the charge of the fatherless child Sulaimān, by sending him, now about 16, to take charge where his father Khān Mīrzā had ruled, and by still keeping him under his own protection.

Sulaimān's start from Āgra will not have been delayed, and (accepting Aḥmad-i-yādgār's record,) Bābur himself will have gone as far as Lāhor either with him or shortly after him, an expedition supporting Sulaimān, and menacing Saʿīd in his winter leaguer round Qilaʿ-i-ẓafar. Meantime Humāyūn was ordered to his fief of Saṃbhal.

After Sulaimān's appointment Bābur wrote to Saʿīd a letter of which Ḥaidar gives the gist:—It expresses surprise at Saʿīd's doings in Badakhshān, says that Hind-āl has been recalled and Sulaimān sent, that if Saʿīd regard hereditary right, he will leave "Sulaimān Shāh Mīrzā"[2704] in possession, who is as a son to them both,[2705] that this would be well, that otherwise he (Bābur) will make over responsibility to the heir (Sulaimān);[2706] and, "The rest you know."[2707]

c. Bābur visits Lāhor.

If Aḥmad-i-yādgār's account of a journey made by Bābur to Lāhor and the Panj-āb be accepted, the *lacuna* of 936 AH. is appropriately filled. He places the expedition in the 3rd year of Bābur's rule in Hindūstān, which, counting from the first reading of the *khuṭba* for Bābur in Dihlī (f. 286), began on Rajab 15th 935 AH. (March 26th 1529 AD.). But as Bābur's diary-record for 935 AH. is complete down to end of the year, (minor *lacunæ* excepted), the time of his leaving Āgra for Lāhor is relegated to 936 AH. He must have left early in the year, (1) to allow time, before the occurrence of the known events preceding his own death, for the long expedition Aḥmad-i-yādgār calls one of a year, and (2) because an early start after Humāyūn's arrival and Sulaimān's departure would suit the position of affairs and the dates mentioned or implied by Ḥaidar's and by Aḥmad-i-yādgār's narratives.

Two reasons of policy are discernible, in the known events of the time, to recommend a journey in force towards the North-west; first, the sedition of 'Abdu'l-'azīz in Lāhor (f. 381), and secondly, the invasion of Badakhshān by Saʿīd Khān with its resulting need of supporting Sulaimān by a menace of armed intervention.[2708]

In Sihrind the Rāja of Kahlūr, a place which may be one of the Simla hill-states, waited on Bābur, made offering of 7 falcons and 3 *mans*[2709] of gold, and was confirmed in his fief.[2710]

In Lāhor Kāmrān is said to have received his Father, in a garden of his own creation, and to have introduced the local chiefs as though he were the Governor of Lāhor some writers describe him as then being. The best sources, however, leave him still posted in Qandahār. He had been appointed to Multān (f. 359) when 'Askarī was summoned to Āgra (f. 339), but whether he actually went there is not assured; some months later (Ẕū'l-ḥijja 10th 935 AH.) he is described by Abū'l-faẓl as coming to Kābul from Qandahār. He took both Multān[2711] and Lāhor by force from his (half-)brother Humāyūn in 935 AH. (1531 AD.) the year after their Father's death. That he should wait upon his Father in Lāhor would be natural, Hind-āl did so, coming from Kābul. Hind-āl will have come to Lāhor after making over charge of Qila'-i-ẓafar to Sulaimān, and he went back at the end of the cold season, going perhaps just before his Father started from Lāhor on his return journey, the gifts he received before leaving being 2 elephants, 4 horses, belts and jewelled daggers.[2712]

Bābur is said to have left Lāhor on Rajab 4th (936 AH.)-(March 4th, 1530 AD.). From Aḥmad-i-yādgār's outline of Bābur's doings in Lāhor, he, or his original, must be taken as ill-informed or indifferent about them. His interest becomes greater when he writes of Samāna.

d. Punishment of the Mundāhirs.

When Bābur, on his return journey, reached Sihrind, he received a complaint from the Qāẓī of Samāna against one Mohan *Mundāhir* (or *Mundhār*)[2713] *Rājpūt* who had attacked his estates, burning and plundering, and killed his son. Here-upon 'Alī-qulī of Hamadān[2714] was sent with 3000 horse to avenge the Qāzī's wrongs, and reached Mohan's village, in the Kaithal *pargana*, early in the morning when the cold was such that the archers "could not pull their bows."[2715] A marriage had been celebrated over-night; the villagers, issuing from warm houses, shot such flights of arrows that the royal troops could make no stand; many were killed and nothing was effected; they retired into the jungle, lit fires, warmed themselves(?), renewed the attack and were again repulsed. On hearing of their failure, Bābur sent off, perhaps again from Sihrind, Tarsam Bahādur and Naurang Beg with 6000 horse and many elephants. This force reached the village at night and when marriage festivities were in progress. Towards morning it was formed into three divisions,[2716] one of which was ordered to go to the west of the village and show itself. This having been done, the villagers advanced towards it, in the pride of their recent success. The royal troops, as ordered beforehand, turned their backs and fled, the Mundāhirs pursuing them some two miles. Meantime Tarsam Bahādur had attacked and fired the village, killing many of its inhabitants. The pursuers on the west saw the flames of their burning homes, ran back and were intercepted on their way. About 1000 men, women and children were made prisoner; there was also great slaughter, and a pillar of heads was raised. Mohan was captured and later on was buried to the waist and shot to death with arrows.[2717] News of the affair was sent to the Pādshāh.[2718]

As after being in Sihrind, Bābur is said to have spent two months hunting near Dihlī, it may be that he followed up the punitive expedition sent into the Kaithal *pargana* of the Karnāl District, by hunting in Nardak, a favourite ground of the Tīmūrids, which lies in that district.

Thus the gap of 936 AH. with also perhaps a month of 937 AH. is filled by the "year's" travel west of Dihlī. The record is a mere outline and in it are periods of months without mention of where Bābur was or what affairs of government were brought before him. At some time, on his return journey presumably, he will have despatched to Kashmīr the expedition referred to in the opening section of this appendix. Something further may yet be gleaned from local chronicles, from unwritten tradition, or from the witness of place-names commemorating his visit.

e. Bābur's self-surrender to save Humāyūn.

The few months, perhaps 4 to 5, between Bābur's return to Āgra from his expedition towards the North-west, and the time of his death are filled by Gul-badan and Abū'l-faẓl with matters concerning family interests only.

The first such matter these authors mention is an illness of Humāyūn during which Bābur devoted his own life to save his son's.[2719] Of this the particulars are, briefly:—That Humāyūn, while still in Saṃbhal, had had a violent attack of fever; that he was brought by water to Āgra, his mother meeting him in Muttra; and that when the disease baffled medical skill, Bābur resolved to practise the rite believed then and now in the East to be valid, of intercession and devotion of a suppliant's most valued possession in exchange for a sick man's life. Rejecting counsel to offer the Koh-i-nūr for pious uses, he resolved to supplicate for the acceptance of his life. He made intercession through a saint his daughter names, and moved thrice round Humāyūn's bed, praying, in effect, "O God! if a life may be exchanged for a life, I, who am Bābur, give my life and my being for Humāyūn." During the rite fever surged over him, and, convinced that his prayer and offering had prevailed, he cried out, "I have borne it away! I have borne it away!"[2720] Gul-badan says that he himself fell ill on that very day, while Humāyūn poured water on his head, came out and gave audience; and that they carried her Father within on account of his illness, where he kept his bed for 2 or 3 months.

There can be no doubt as to Bābur's faith in the rite he had practised, or as to his belief that his offering of life was accepted; moreover actual facts would sustain his faith and belief. Onlookers also must have believed his prayer and offering to have prevailed, since Humāyūn went back to Saṃbhal,[2721] while Bābur fell ill at once and died in a few weeks.[2722]

f. A plan to set Bābur's sons aside from the succession.

Reading the *Akbar-nāma* alone, there would seem to be no question about whether Bābur ever intended to give Hindūstān, at any rate, to Humāyūn, but, by piecing together various contributory matters, an opposite opinion is reached, *viz.* that not Khalīfa only whom Abū'l-faẓl names perhaps on Niẓāmu'd-dīn Aḥmad's warrant, but Bābur also, with some considerable number of chiefs, wished another ruler for Hindūstān. The starting-point of this opinion is a story in the *Ṭabaqāt-i-akbarī* and, with less detail, in the *Akbar-nāma*, of which the gist is that Khalīfa planned to supersede Humāyūn and his three brothers in their Father's succession.[2723]

BĀBUR IN PRAYER, DEVOTING HIMSELF FOR HIS SON.

To face p. 702.

The story, in brief, is as follows:—At the time of Bābur's death Niẓāmu'd-dīn Aḥmad's father Khwāja Muḥammad Muqīm *Harāwī* was in the service of the Office of Works.[2724] Amīr Niẓāmu'd-dīn 'Alī Khalīfa, the Chief of the Administration, had dread and suspicion about Humāyūn and did not favour his succession as Pādshāh. Nor did he favour that of Bābur's other sons. He promised "Bābur Pādshāh's son-in-law (*dāmād*)" Mahdī Khwāja who was a generous young man, very friendly to himself, that he would make him Pādshāh. This promise becoming known, others made their *salām* to the Khwāja who put on airs and accepted the position. One day when Khalīfa, accompanied by Muqīm, went to see Mahdī Khwāja in his tent, no-one else being present, Bābur, in the pangs of his disease, sent for him[2725] when he had been seated a few minutes only. When Khalīfa had gone out, Mahdī Khwāja remained standing in such a way that Muqīm could not follow but, the Khwāja unaware, waited respectfully behind him. The Khwāja, who was noted for the wildness of youth, said, stroking his beard, "Please God! first, I will flay thee!" turned round and saw Muqīm, took him by the ear, repeated a proverb of menace, "The red tongue gives the green head to the wind," and let him go. Muqīm hurried to Khalīfa, repeated the Khwāja's threat against him, and remonstrated about the plan to set all Bābur's sons aside in favour of a stranger-house.[2726] Here-upon Khalīfa sent for Humāyūn,[2727] and despatched an officer with orders to the Khwāja to retire to his house, who found him about to dine and hurried him off without ceremony. Khalīfa also issued a proclamation forbidding intercourse with him, excluded him from Court, and when Bābur died, supported Humāyūn.

As Niẓāmu'd-dīn Aḥmad was not born till 20 years after Bābur died, the story will have been old before he could appreciate it, and it was some 60 years old when it found way into the *Ṭabaqāt-i-akbarī* and, with less detail, into the *Akbar-nāma.*

Taken as it stands, it is incredible, because it represents Khalīfa, and him alone, planning to subject the four sons of Bābur to the suzerainty of Mahdī Khwāja who was not a Tīmūrid, who, so far as well-known sources show, was not of a ruling dynasty or personally illustrious,[2728] and who had been associated, so lately as the autumn of 1529 AD., with his nephew Raḥīm-dād in seditious action which had so angered Bābur that, whatever the punishment actually ordered, rumour had it both men were to die.[2729] In two particulars the only Mahdī Khwāja then of Bābur's following, does not suit the story; he was not a young man in 1530 AD.,[2730] and was not a *dāmād* of Bābur, if that word be taken in its usual sense of son-in-law, but he was a *yazna*, husband of a Pādshāh's sister, in his case, of Khān-zāda Begīm.[2731] Some writers style him Sayyid Mahdī Khwāja, a double title which may indicate descent on both sides from religious houses; one is suggested to be that of Tirmiẕ by the circumstance that in his and Khān-zāda Begīm's mausoleum was buried a Tirmiẕ sayyid of later date, Shāh Abū'l-ma'ālī. But though he were of Tirmiẕ, it is doubtful if that religious house would be described by the word *khānwāda* which so frequently denotes a ruling dynasty.

His name may have found its way into Niẓāmu'd-dīn Aḥmad's story as a gloss mistakenly amplifying the word *dāmād*, taken in its less usual sense of brother-in-law. To Bābur's contemporaries the expression "Bābur Pādshāh's *dāmād*" (son-in-law) would be explicit, because for some 11 years before he lay on his death-bed, he had one son-in-law only, *viz.* Muḥammad-i-zamān Mīrzā *Bāī-qarā*,[2732] the husband of Ma'ṣūma Sulṭān Begīm. If that Mīrzā's name were where Mahdī Khwāja's is entered, the story of an exclusion of Bābur's sons from rule might have a core of truth.

It is incredible however that Khālīfa, with or without Bābur's concurrence, made the plan attributed to him of placing any man not a Tīmūrid in the position of Pādshāh over all Bābur's territory. I suggest that the plan concerned Hindūstān only and was one considered in connection with Bābur's intended return to Kābul, when he must have left that difficult country, hardly yet a possession, in charge of some man giving promise of power to hold it. Such a man Humāyūn was not. My suggestion rests on the following considerations:—

(1) Bābur's outlook was not that of those in Āgra in 1587 AD. who gave Abū'l-faẓl his Bāburiana material, because at that date Dihlī had become the pivot of Tīmūrid power, so that not to hold Hindūstān would imply not to be Pādshāh. Bābur's outlook on his smaller Hindūstān was different; his position in it was precarious, Kābul, not Dihlī, was his chosen centre, and from Kābul his eyes looked northwards as well as to the East. If he had lost the Hindūstān which was approximately the modern United Provinces, he might still have held what lay west of it to the Indus, as well as Qandahār.

(2) For several years before his death he had wished to return to Kābul. Ample evidence of this wish is given by his diary, his letters, and some poems in his second *Dīwān* (that found in the Rāmpūr MS.). As he told his sons more than once, he kept Kābul for himself.[2733] If, instead of dying in Āgra, he had returned to Kābul, had pushed his way on from Badakhshān, whether as far as Samarkand or less, had given Humāyūn a seat in those parts,—action foreshadowed by the records—a reasonable interpretation of the story that Humāyūn and his brothers were not to govern Hindūstān, is that he had considered with Khalīfa the apportionment of his territories according to the example of his ancestors Chīngīz Khān, Tīmūr and Abū-sa'īd; that by his plan of apportionment Humāyūn was not to have Hindūstān but something Tramontane; Kāmrān had already Qandahār;

Sulaimān, if Humāyūn had moved beyond the out-post of Badakhshān, would have replaced him there; and Hindūstān would have gone to "Bābur Pādshāh's *dāmād*".

(3) Muḥammad-i-zamān had much to recommend him for Hindūstān:—Tīmūrid-born, grandson and heir of Sl. Ḥusain Mīrzā, husband of Ma'ṣūma who was a Tīmūrid by double descent,[2734] protected by Bābur after the Bāī-qarā *débacle* in Herāt, a landless man leading such other exiles as Muḥammad Sulṭān Mīrzā,[2735] 'Ādil Sulṭān, and Qāsim-i-ḥusain Sulṭān, half-Tīmūrids all, who with their Khurāsānī following, had been Bābur's guests in Kābul, had pressed on its poor resources, and thus had helped in 932 AH. (1525 AD.) to drive him across the Indus. This Bāī-qarā group needed a location; Muḥammad-i-zamān's future had to be cared for and with his, Ma'ṣūma's.

(4) It is significant of intention to give Muḥammad-i-zamān ruling status that in April 1529 AD. (Sha'bān 935 AH.) Bābur bestowed on him royal insignia, including the umbrella-symbol of sovereignty.[2736] This was done after the Mīrzā had raised objections, unspecified now in the *Bābur-nāma* against Bihār; they were overcome, the insignia were given and, though for military reasons he was withheld from taking up that appointment, the recognition of his royal rank had been made. His next appointment was to Jūnpūr, the capital of the fallen Sharqī dynasty. No other chief is mentioned by Bābur as receiving the insignia of royalty.

(5) It appears to have been within a Pādshāh's competence to select his successor; and it may be inferred that choice was made between Humāyūn and another from the wording of more than one writer that Khalīfa "supported" Humāyūn, and from the word "selected" used in Aḥmad-i-yādgār's anecdote.[2737] Much more would there be freedom of choice in a division of territory such as there is a good deal to suggest was the basis of Niẓāmu'd-dīn Aḥmad's story. Whatever the extent of power proposed for the *dāmād*, whether, as it is difficult to believe, the Pādshāh's whole supremacy, or whether the limited sovereignty of Hindūstān, it must have been known to Bābur as well as to Khalīfa. Whatever their earlier plan however, it was changed by the sequel of Humāyūn's illness which led to his becoming Pādshāh. The *dāmād* was dropped, on grounds it is safe to believe more impressive than his threat to flay Khalīfa or than the remonstrance of that high official's subordinate Muqīm of Herāt.

Humāyūn's arrival and continued stay in Hindūstān modified earlier dispositions which included his remaining in Badakhshān. His actions may explain why Bābur, when in 936 AH. he went as far as Lāhor, did not go on to Kābul. Nothing in the sources excludes the surmise that Māhīm knew of the bestowal of royal insignia on the Bāī-qarā Mīrzā, that she summoned her son to Āgra and there kept him, that she would do this the more resolutely if the *dāmād* of the plan she must have heard of, were that Bāī-qarā, and that but for Humāyūn's presence in Āgra and its attendant difficulties, Bābur would have gone to Kābul, leaving his *dāmād* in charge of Hindūstān.

Bābur, however, turned back from Lāhor for Āgra, and there he made the self-surrender which, resulting in Humāyūn's "selection" as Pādshāh, became a turning point in history.

Humāyūn's recovery and Bābur's immediate illness will have made the son's life seem Divinely preserved, the father's as a debt to be paid. Bābur's impressive personal experience will have dignified Humāyūn as one whom God willed should live. Such distinction would dictate the bestowal on him of all that fatherly generosity had yet to give. The imminence of death defeating all plans made for life, Humāyūn was nominated to supreme power as Pādshāh.

g. Bābur's death.

Amongst other family matters mentioned by Gul-badan as occurring shortly before her Father's death, was his arrangement of marriages for Gul-rang with Aīsān-tīmūr and for Gul-chihra with Tūkhta-būghā *Chaghatāī*. She also writes of his anxiety to see Hind-āl who had been sent for from Kābul but did not arrive till the day after the death.

When no remedies availed, Humāyūn was summoned from Saṃbhal. He reached Āgra four days before the death; on the morrow Bābur gathered his chiefs together for the last of many times, addressed them, nominated Humāyūn his successor and bespoke their allegiance for him. Abū'l-faẓl thus summarizes his words, "Lofty counsels and weighty mandates were imparted. Advice was given (to Humāyūn) to be munificent and just, to acquire God's favour, to cherish and protect subjects, to accept apologies from such as had failed in duty, and to pardon transgressors. And, he (Bābur) exclaimed, the cream of my testamentary dispositions is this, 'Do naught against your brothers, even though they may deserve it.' In truth," continues the historian, "it was through obedience to this mandate that his Majesty Jannat-ashiyānī suffered so many injuries from his brothers without avenging himself." Gul-badan's account of her Father's last address is simple:—"He spoke in this wise, 'For years it has been in my heart to make over the throne to Humāyūn and to retire to the Gold-scattering Garden. By the Divine grace I have obtained in health of body everything but the fulfilment of this wish. Now that illness has laid me low, I charge you all to acknowledge Humāyūn in my stead. Fail not in loyalty towards him. Be of one heart and mind towards him. I hope to God that he, for his part, will bear himself well towards men. Moreover, Humāyūn, I commit you and your brothers and all my kinsfolk and your people and my people to God's keeping, and entrust them all to you.'"

It was on Monday Jumāda 1. 5th 937 AH. (Dec. 26th 153O AD.) that Bābur made answer to his summons with the *Adsum* of the Musalmān, "Lord! I am here for Thee."

"Black fell the day for children and kinsfolk and all," writes his daughter;

"Alas! that time and the changeful heaven should exist without thee;

Alas! and Alas! that time should remain and thou shouldst be gone;"

mourns Khwāja Kalān in the funeral ode from which Badāyūnī quoted these lines.[2738]

The body was laid in the Garden-of-rest (*Ārām-bāgh*) which is opposite to where the Tāj-i-maḥāll now stands. Khwāja Muḥammad 'Alī *'asas*[2739] was made the guardian of the tomb, and many well-voiced readers and reciters were appointed to conduct the five daily Prayers and to offer supplication for the soul of the dead. The revenues of Sīkrī and 5 *laks* from Bīāna were set aside for the endowment of the tomb, and Māhīm Begīm, during the two and a half years of her remaining life, sent twice daily from her own estate, an allowance of food towards the support of its attendants.

In accordance with the directions of his will, Bābur's body was to be conveyed to Kābul and there to be laid in the garden of his choice, in a grave open to the sky, with no building over it, no need of a door-keeper.

Precisely when it was removed from Āgra we have not found stated. It is known from Gul-badan that Kāmrān visited his Father's tomb in Āgra in 1539 AD. (946 AH.) after the battle of Chausa; and it is known from Jauhar that the body had been brought to Kābul before 1544 AD. (952 AH.), at which date Humāyūn, in Kābul, spoke with displeasure of Kāmrān's incivility to "Bega Begīm", the "Bībī" who had conveyed their Father's body to that place.[2740] That the widow who performed this duty was the Afghān Lady, Bībī Mubārika[2741] is made probable by Gul-badan's details of the movements of the royal ladies. Bābur's family left Āgra under Hind-āl's escort, after the defeat at Chausa (June 7th, 1539 AD.); whoever took charge of the body on its journey to Kābul must have returned at some later date to fetch it. It would be in harmony with Sher Shāh's generous character if he safe-guarded her in her task.

The terraced garden Bābur chose for his burial-place lies on the slope of the hill Shāh-i-Kābul, the Sher-darwāza of European writers.[2742] It has been described as perhaps the most beautiful of the Kābul gardens, and as looking towards an unsurpassable view over the Chār-dih plain towards the snows of Paghmān and the barren, rocky hills which have been the hunting-grounds of rulers in Kābul. Several of Bābur's descendants coming to Kābul from Āgra have visited and embellished his burial-garden. Shāh-i-jahān built the beautiful mosque which stands near the grave; Jahāngīr seems to have been, if not the author, at least the prompter of the well-cut inscription adorning the upright slab of white marble of Māīdān, which now stands at the grave-head. The tomb-stone itself is a low grave-covering, not less simple than those of relations and kin whose remains have been placed near Bābur's. In the thirties of the last century [the later Sir] Alexander Burnes visited and admirably described the garden and the tomb. With him was Munshī Mohan Lāl who added to his own account of the beauties of the spot, copies of the inscriptions on the monumental slab and on the portal of the Mosque.[2743] As is shown by the descriptions these two visitors give, and by Daniel's drawings of the garden and the tomb, there were in their time two upright slabs, one behind the other, near the head of the grave. Mr. H. H. Hayden who visited the garden in the first decade of the present century, shows in his photograph of the grave, one upright stone only, the place of one of the former two having been taken by a white-washed lamp holder (*chirāghdān*).

The purport of the verses inscribed on the standing-slab is as follows:—

> A ruler from whose brow shone the Light of God was that[2744] Back-bone of the Faith (*ẓahīru'd-dīn*) Muḥammad Bābur Pādshāh. Together with majesty, dominion, fortune, rectitude, the open-hand and the firm Faith, he had share in prosperity, abundance and the triumph of victorious arms. He won the material world and became a moving light; for his every conquest he looked, as for Light, towards the world of souls. When Paradise became his dwelling and Ruẓwān[2745] asked me the date, I gave him for answer, "Paradise is forever Bābur Pādshāh's abode."

h. Bābur's wives and children.[2746]

Bābur himself mentions several of his wives by name, but Gul-badan is the authority for complete lists of them and their children.

1. 'Āyisha Sulṭān Begīm, daughter of Sl. Aḥmad Mīrzā *Mīrān-shāhī* was betrothed, when Bābur was *cir.* 5 years old, in 894 AH. (1488-89 AD.), bore Fakhru'n-nisa' in 906 AH. [who died in about one month], left Bābur before 909 AH. (1503 AD.).

2. Zainab Sl. Begīm, daughter of Sl. Maḥmūd Mīrzā *Mīrān-shāhī*, was married in 910 AH. (1504-5 AD.), died childless two or three years later.

3. Māhīm Begīm, whose parentage is not found stated, was married in 912 AH. (1506 AD.), bore Bār-būd, Mihr-jān, Āīsān-daulat, Farūq [who all died in infancy], and Humāyūn.

4. Ma'ṣūma Sl. Begīm, daughter of Sl. Aḥmad Mīrzā *Mīrān-shāhī*, was married in 913 AH. (1507 AD.), bore Ma'ṣūma and died at her birth, presumably early in the *lacuna* of 914-925 AH. (1508-19 AD.).

5. Gul-rukh Begīm, whose parentage is not found stated, was perhaps a Begchīk Mughūl, was married between 914 AH. and 925 AH. (1508-19 AD.), probably early in the period, bore Shāh-rukh, Aḥmad [who both died young], Gul'iẕār [who also may have died young], Kamrān and 'Askarī.

6. Dil-dār Begīm, whose parentage is not found stated, was married in the same period as Gul-rukh, bore Gul-rang, Gul-chihra, Hind-āl, Gul-badan and Alwar, [who died in childhood].

7. The Afghān Lady (Afghānī Āghācha), Bībī Mubārika *Yūsufzāī*, was married in 925 AH. (1519 AD.), and died childless.

The two Circassian slaves Gul-nār Āghācha and Nār-gul Āghācha of whom Ṭahmāsp made gift to Bābur in 933 AH. (f. 305), became recognized ladies of the royal household. They are mentioned several times by Gul-badan as taking part in festivities and in family conferences under Humāyūn. Gul-nār is said by Abū'l-faẓl to have been one of Gul-badan's pilgrim band in 983 AH. (1575 AD.).

The above list contains the names of three wives whose parentage is not given or is vaguely given by the well-known sources,—namely, Māhīm, Gul-rukh and Dil-dār. What would sufficiently explain the absence of mention by Bābur of the parentage of Gul-rukh and Dil-dār is that his record of the years within which the two Begīms were married is not now with the *Bābur-nāma*. Presumably it has been lost, whether in diary or narrative form, in the *lacuna* of 914-25 AH. (1508-19 AD.). Gul-rukh appears to have belonged to the family of Begchīk Mughūls described by Ḥaidar Mīrzā[2747]; her brothers are styled Mīrzā; she was of good but not royal birth. Dil-dār's case is less simple. Nothing in her daughter Gul-badan's book suggests that she and her children were other than of the highest rank; numerous details and shades of expression show their ease of equality with royal personages. It is consistent with Gul-badan's method of enumerating her father's wives that she should not state her own mother's descent; she states it of none of her "mothers". There is this interest in trying to trace Dil-dār's parentage, that she may have been the third daughter of Sl. Maḥmūd Mīrzā and Pasha Begīm, and a daughter of hers may have been the mother of

Salīma Sulṭān Begīm who was given in marriage by Humāyūn to Bairām Khān, later was married by Akbar, and was a woman of charm and literary accomplishments. Later historians, Abū'l-faẓl amongst their number, say that Salīma's mother was a daughter of Bābur's wife Sālḥa Sulṭān Begīm, and vary that daughter's name as Gul-rang-rukh-barg or -'iẕār (the last form being an equivalent of *chihra*, face). As there cannot have been a wife with her daughter growing up in Bābur's household, who does not appear in some way in Gul-badan's chronicle, and as Salīma's descent from Bābur need not be questioned, the knot is most readily loosened by surmising that "Sālḥa" is the real name of Gul-badan's "Dildār". Instances of double names are frequent, *e.g.* Māhīm, Māh-chīchām, Qarā-gūz, Āq, (My Moon, My Moon sister, Black-eyed, Fair). "Heart-holding" (Dil-dār) sounds like a home-name of affection. It is the *Ma'āsir-ī-raḥīmī* which gives Sālḥa as the name of Bābur's wife, Pasha's third daughter. Its author may be wrong, writing so late as he did (1025 AH.-1616 AD.), or may have been unaware that Sālḥa was (if she were) known as Dil-dār. It would not war against seeming facts to take Pasha's third daughter to be Bābur's wife Dil-dār, and Dil-dār's daughter Gul-chihra to be Salīma's mother. Gul-chihra was born in about 1516 AD., married to Tūkhta-būghā in 1530 AD., widowed in cir. 1533 AD., might have remarried with Nūru'd-dīn *Chaqānīānī* (Sayyid Amīr), and in 945 AH. might have borne him Salīma; she was married in 1547 AD. (954 AH.) to 'Abbās Sulṭān *Aūzbeg.*[2748] Two matters, neither having much weight, make against taking Dil-dār to be a *Mīrān-shāhī*; the first being that the anonymous annotator who added to the archetype of Kehr's Codex what is entered in Appendix L.—*On Māhīm's adoption of Hind-āl,* styles her Dil-dār Āghācha; he, however, may have known no more than others knew of her descent; the second, that Māhīm forcibly took Dil-dār's child Hind-āl to rear; she was the older wife and the mother of the heir, but could she have taken the upper hand over a Mīrān-shāhī? A circumstance complicating the question of Salīma's maternal descent is, that historians searching the *Bābur-nāma* or its Persian translation the *Wāqi'āt-i-bāburī* for information about the three daughters of Maḥmūd *Mīrān-shāhī* and Pasha *Bahārlū Turkmān,* would find an incomplete record, one in which the husbands of the first and second daughters are mentioned and nothing is said about the third who was Bābur's wife and the grandmother of Salīma. Bābur himself appears to have left the record as it is, meaning to fill it in later; presumably he waited for the names of the elder two sisters to complete his details of the three. In the Ḥaidarabad Codex, which there is good ground for supposing a copy of his original manuscript, about three lines are left blank (f. 27) as if awaiting information; in most manuscripts, however, this indication of intention is destroyed by running the defective passage on to join the next sentence. Some chance remark of a less well-known writer, may clear up the obscurity and show that Sālḥa was Dil-dār.

Māhīm's case seems one having a different cause for silence about her parentage. When she was married in Herāt, shortly after the death of Sl. Ḥusain Mīrzā, Bābur had neither wife nor child. What Abū'l-faẓl tells about her is vague; her father's name is not told; she is said to have belonged to a noble Khurāsān family, to have been related (*nisbat-i-khwesh*) to Sl. Ḥusain Mīrzā and to have traced her descent to Shaikh Aḥmad of Jām. If her birth had been high, even though not royal, it is strange that it is not stated by Bābur when he records the birth of her son Humāyūn, incidentally by Gul-badan, or more precisely by Abū'l-faẓl. Her brothers belonged to Khost, and to judge from a considerable number of small records, seem to have been quiet, unwarlike Khwājas. Her marriage took place in a year of which a full record survives; it is one in the composed narrative, not in the diary. In the following year, this also being one included in the composed narrative, Bābur writes of his meeting with Ma'ṣūma *Mīrān-shāhī* in Herāt, of their mutual attraction, and of their marriage. If the marriage with Humāyūn's mother had been an equal alliance, it would agree with Bābur's custom to mention its occurrence, and to give particulars about Māhīm's descent.[2749]

i. Mr. William Erskine's estimate of Bābur.

"Ẓahīru'd-dīn Muḥammad Bābur was undoubtedly one of the most illustrious men of his age, and one of the most eminent and accomplished princes that ever adorned an Asiatic throne. He is represented as having been above the middle size, of great vigour of body, fond of all field and warlike sports, an excellent swordsman, and a skilful archer. As a proof of his bodily strength, it is mentioned, that he used to leap from one pinnacle to another of the pinnacled ramparts used in the East, in his double-soled boots; and that he even frequently took a man under each arm and went leaping along the rampart from one of the pointed pinnacles to another. Having been early trained to the conduct of business, and tutored in the school of adversity, the powers of his mind received full development. He ascended the throne at the age of twelve, and before he had attained his twentieth year, had shared every variety of fortune; he had not only been the ruler of subject provinces but had been in thraldom to his own ambitious nobles, and obliged to conceal every sentiment of his heart; he had been alternately hailed and obeyed as a conqueror and deliverer by rich and extensive kingdoms, and forced to lurk in the deserts and mountains of Farghāna as a houseless wanderer. Down to the last dregs of life, we perceive in him strong feelings of affection for his early friends and early enjoyments. * * * He had been taught betimes, by the voice of events that cannot lie, that he was a man dependent on the kindness and fidelity of other men; and, in his dangers and escapes with his followers, had learned that he was only one of an association. * * * The native benevolence and gaiety of his disposition seems ever to overflow on all around him; * * * of his companions in arms he speaks with the frank gaiety of a soldier. * * * Ambitious he was and fond of conquest and glory in all its shapes; the enterprise in which he was for a season engaged, seems to have absorbed his whole soul, and all his faculties were exerted to bring it to a fortunate issue. His elastic mind was not broken by discomfiture, and few who have achieved such glorious conquests, have suffered more numerous or more decisive defeats. His personal courage was conspicuous during his whole life. Upon the whole, if we review with impartiality the history of Asia, we find few princes entitled to rank higher than Bābur in genius and accomplishments. * * * In activity of mind, in the gay equanimity and unbroken spirit with which he bore the extremes of good and bad fortune, in the possession of the manly and social virtues, in his love of letters and his success in the cultivation of them, we shall probably find no other Asiatic prince who can justly be placed beside him."

THE END.

APPENDICES.

A.—THE SITE AND DISAPPEARANCE OF OLD AKHSĪ.

Some modern writers, amongst whom are Dr. Schuyler, General Nalivkine and Mr. Pumpelly, have inferred from the Bābur-nāma account of Akhsī, (in its translations?) that the landslip through which Bābur's father died and the disappearance of old Akhsī were brought about by erosion. Seen by the light of modern information, this erosion theory does not seem to cover the whole ground and some other cause seems necessary in explanation of both events.

For convenience of reference, the Bābur-nāma passages required, are quoted here, with their translations.

> Ḥai. MS. f. 4b. *Saiḥūn daryā-sī qūrghānī astīdīn āqār. Qūrghānī baland jar austīdā wāqi' būlūb tūr. Khandaqī-nīng aūrunīgha 'umīq jārlār dūr. 'Umar Shaikh M. kīm mūnī pāy-takht qīldī, bīr īkī martaba tāshrāq-dīn yana jarlār sāldī.*
>
> Of this the translations are as follows:—
>
> (*a*) Pers. trans. (I.O. 217, f. 3*b*): *Daryā-i Saiḥūn az pāyhā qila'-i o mīrezad u qila'-i o bar jar balandī wāqi' shuda ba jāy khandaq jarhā-i 'umīq uftāda. 'U. Sh. M. kah ānrā pāy-takht sākhta, yak du martaba az bīrūn ham bāz jarhā andākht.*
>
> (*b*) Erskine (p. 5, translating from the Persian): 'The river Saiḥūn flows under the walls of the castle. The castle is situated on a high precipice, and the steep ravines around serve instead of a moat. When U. Sh. M. made it his capital he, in one or two instances, scarped the ravines outside the fort.'
>
> (*c*) De Courteille (i, 8, translating from Ilminsky's imprint, p. 6): 'Le Seihoun coule au pied de la fortresse qui se dresse sur le sommet d'un ravin, dont les profondeurs lui tiennent lieu d'un fossé. 'U. Sh. M. à l'époque où il en avait fait son capitale, avait augmenté à une ou deux réprises, les escarpements qui la ceignent naturellement.'

Concerning 'Umar Shaikh's death, the words needed are (f. 6*b*);—

> *Mazkūr būlūb aīdī kīm Akhsī qūrghānī buland jar austīdā wāqi' būlūb tūr. 'Imāratlār jar yāqāsīdā aīrdī.... Mīrzā jardīn kabūtar u kabūtar-khāna bīla*

aüchūb shunqār būldī;—'It has been mentioned that the walled-town of Akhsī is situated above ravine(s). The royal dwellings are along a ravine. The Mīrzā, having flown with his pigeons and their house from the ravine, became a falcon (*i.e.* died).'

A few particulars about Akhsī will shew that, in the translations just quoted, certain small changes of wording are dictated by what, amongst other writers, Kostenko and von Schwarz have written about the oases of Turkistān.

The name Akhsī, as used by Ibn Haukal, Yāqūt and Bābur, describes an oasis township, *i.e.* a walled-town with its adjacent cultivated lands. In Yāqūt's time Akhsī had a second circumvallation, presumably less for defence than for the protection of crops against wild animals. The oasis was created by the Kāsān-water,[2750] upon the riverain loess of the right and higher bank of the Saiḥūn (Sīr), on level ground west of the junction of the Nārīn and the Qarā-daryā, west too of spurs from the northern hills which now abut upon the river. Yāqūt locates it in the 12th century, at one *farsākh* (*circa* 4 m.) north of the river.[2751] Depending as it did solely on the Kāsān-water, nothing dictated its location close to the Sīr, along which there is now, and there seems to have been in the 12th century, a strip of waste land. Bābur says of Akhsī what Kostenko says (i, 321) of modern Tāshkīnt, that it stood above ravines (*jarlār*). These were natural or artificial channels of the Kāsān-water.[2752]

To turn now to the translations;—Mr. Erskine imaged Akhsī as a castle, high on a precipice in process of erosion by the Sīr. But Bābur's word, *qūrghān* means the walled-town; his word for a castle is *ark*, citadel; and his *jar*, a cleft, is not rendered by 'precipice.' Again;—it is no more necessary to understand that the Sīr flowed close to the walls than it is to understand, when one says the Thames flows past below Richmond, that it washes the houses on the hill.

The key to the difficulties in the Turkī passage is provided by a special use of the word *jar* for not only natural ravines but artificial water-cuts for irrigation. This use of it makes clear that what 'Umar Shaikh did at Akhsī was not to make escarpments but to cut new water-channels. Presumably he joined those 'further out' on the deltaic fan, on the east and west of the town, so as to secure a continuous defensive cleft round the town[2753] or it may be, in order to bring it more water.

Concerning the historic pigeon-house (f. 6*b*), it can be said safely that it did not fall into the Sīr; it fell from a *jar*, and in this part of its course, the river flows in a broad bed, with a low left bank. Moreover the Mīrzā's residence was in the walled-town (f. 110*b*) and there his son stayed 9 years after the accident. The slip did not affect the safety of the residence therefore; it may have been local to the birds' house. It will have been due to some ordinary circumstance since no cause for it is mentioned by Bābur, Ḥaidar or Abū'l-faẓl. If it had marked the crisis of the Sīr's approach, Akhsī could hardly have been described, 25 years later, as a strong fort.

Something is known of Akhsī, in the 10th, the 12th, the 15th and the 19th centuries, which testifies to sæcular decadence. Ibn Haukal and Yāqūt give the township an extent of 3 *farsākh* (12 miles), which may mean from one side to an opposite one. Yāqūt's description of it mentions four gates, each opening into well-watered lands extending a whole *farsākh*, in other words it had a ring of garden-suburb four miles wide.

Two meanings have been given to Bābur's words indicating the status of the oasis in the 15th century. They are, *maḥallātī qūrghān-dīn bīr shar'ī yurāqrāq tūshūb tūr*. They have been understood as saying that the suburbs were two miles from their *urbs*. This may be right but I hesitate to accept it without pointing out that the words may mean, 'Its suburbs extend two miles farther than the walled-town.' Whichever verbal reading is correct, reveals a decayed oasis.

In the 19th century, Nalivkine and Ujfalvy describe the place then bearing the name Akhsī, as a small village, a mere winter-station, at some distance from the river's bank, that bank then protected from denudation by a sand-bank.

Three distinctly-marked stages of decadence in the oasis township are thus indicated by Yāqūt, Bābur and the two modern travellers.

It is necessary to say something further about the position of the suburbs in the 15th century. Bābur quotes as especially suitable to Akhsī, the proverbial questions, 'Where is the village?'[2754] (qy. Akhsī-kīnt.) 'Where are the trees?' and these might be asked by some-one in the suburbs unable to see Akhsī or *vice versâ*. But granting that there were no suburbs within two miles of the town, why had the whole inner circle, two miles of Yāqūt's four, gone out of cultivation? Erosion would have affected only land between the river and the town.

Again;—if the Sīr only were working in the 15th century to destroy a town standing on the Kāsān-water, how is it that this stream does not yet reach the Sīr?

Various ingatherings of information create the impression that failure of Kāsān-water has been the dominant factor in the loss of the Akhsī township. Such failure might be due to the general desiccation of Central Asia and also to increase of cultivation in the Kāsān-valley itself. There may have been erosion, and social and military change may have had its part, but for the loss of the oasis lands and for, as a sequel, the decay of the town, desiccation seems a sufficient cause.

The Kāsān-water still supports an oasis on its riverain slope, the large Aūzbeg town of Tūpa-qūrghān (Town-of-the-hill), from the modern castle of which a superb view is had up the Kāsān-valley, now thickly studded with villages.[2755]

B.—THE BIRDS, QĪL QŪYIRŪGH AND BĀGHRĪ QARĀ.

Describing a small bird (*qūsh-qīna*), abundant in the Qarshī district (f. 49*b*), Bābur names it the *qīl-qūyirūgh*, horse-tail, and says it resembles the *bāghrī qarā*.

Later on he writes (f. 280) that the *bāghrī qarā* of India is smaller and more slender than 'those' *i.e.* of Transoxiana (f. 49*b*, n. 1), the blackness of its breast less deep, and its cry less piercing.

We have had difficulty in identifying the birds but at length conclude that the *bāghrī qarā* of Transoxiana is *Pterocles arenarius*, Pallas's black-bellied sand-grouse and that the Indian one is a smaller sand-grouse, perhaps a *Syrrhaptes*. As the *qīl qūyirūgh* resembles the other two, it may be a yet smaller *Syrrhaptes*.

Muḥ. Ṣāliḥ, writing of sport Shaibāq Khān had in Qarshī (*Shaibānī-nāma*, Vambéry, p. 192) mentions the 'Little bird (*murghak*) of Qarshī,' as on all sides making lament. The Sang-lākh[2756] gives its Persian name as *khar-pala*, ass-hair, says it flies in large flocks and resembles the *bāghrī qarā*. Of the latter he writes as abundant in the open country and as making noise (*bāghīr*).

The Sang-lākh (f. 119) gives the earliest and most informing account we have found of the *bāghrī qarā*. Its says the bird is larger than a pigeon, marked with various colours, yellow especially, black-breasted and a dweller in the stony and waterless desert. These details are followed by a quotation from 'Alī-sher *Nawā'ī*, in which he likens his own heart to that of the bird of the desert, presumably referring to the gloom of the bird's plumage. Three synonyms are then given; Ar. *qiṭā*, one due to its cry (Meninsky); Pers. *sang-shikan*, stone-eating, (Steingass, *sang-khwāra*, stone-eating); and Turkī *bāghīr-tilāq* which refers, I think, to its cry.

Morier (Ḥājī Bābā) in his *Second journey through Persia* (Lond. 1818, p. 181), mentions that a bird he calls the black-breasted partridge, (*i.e. Francolinus vulgaris*) is known in Turkish as *bokara kara* and in Persian as *siyāh-sīna*, both names, (he says), meaning black-breast; that it has a horse-shoe of black feathers round the forepart of the trunk, more strongly marked in the female than in the male; that they fly in flocks of which he saw immense numbers near Tabrīz (p. 283), have a soft note, inhabit the plains, and, once settled, do not run. Cock and hen alike have a small spur,—a characteristic, it may be said, identifying rather with *Francolinus vulgaris* than with *Pterocles arenarius*. Against this identification, however, is Mr. Blandford's statement that *siyāh-sīna* (Morier's *bokara kara*) is *Pterocles arenarius* (Report of the Persian Boundary Commission, ii, 271).

In Afghānistān and Bikanir, the sand-grouse is called *tūtūrak* and *boora kurra* (Jerdon, ii, 498). Scully explains *baghītāq* as *Pterocles arenarius*.

Perhaps I may mention something making me doubt whether it is correct to translate *bāghrī qarā* by *black-liver* and *gorge-noir* or other names in which the same meaning is expressed. To translate thus, is to understand a Turkī noun and adjective in Persian construction, and to make exception to the rule, amply exemplified in lists of birds, that Turkī names of birds are commonly in Turkī construction, *e.g.* *qarā bāsh* (black-head), *āq-bāsh* (white-head), *sārīgh-sūndūk* (yellow-headed wagtail). *Bāghīr* may refer to the cry of the bird. We learn from Mr. Ogilvie Grant that the Mongol name for the sand-grouse *njūpterjūn*, is derived from its cry in flight, *truck*, *truck*, and its Arabic name *qiṭā* is said by Meninsky to be derived from its cry *kaetha*, *kaetha*. Though the dissimilarity of the two cries is against taking the *njūpterjūn* and the *qiṭā* to be of one class of sand-grouse, the significance of the derivation of the names remains, and shows that there are examples in support of thinking that when a sand-grouse is known as *bāghrī qarā*, it may be so known because of its cry (*bāghir*).

The word *qarā* finds suggestive interpretation in a B. N. phrase (f. 72*b*) *Taṃbal-nīng qarā-sī*, Taṃbal's blackness, *i.e.* the dark mass of his moving men, seen at a distance. It is used also for an indefinite number, *e.g.* 'family, servants, retainers, followers, *qarā*,' and I think it may imply a massed flock.

Bābur's words (f. 280) *bāghrī-nīng qarā-sī ham kam dūr*, [its belly (lit. liver) also is less black], do not necessarily contradict the view that the word *bāghrī* in the bird's name means crying. The root *bāgh* has many and pliable derivatives; I suspect both Bābur (here) and Muḥ. Ṣāliḥ (l. c.) of ringing changes on words.

We are indebted for kind reply to our questions to Mr. Douglas Carruthers, Mr. Ogilvie Grant and to our friend, Mr. R. S. Whiteway.

C.—ON THE GOSHA-GĪR.

I am indebted to my husband's examination of two Persian MSS. on archery for an explanation of the word *gosha-gīr*, in its technical sense in archery. The works consulted are the Cyclopædia of Archery (*Kulliyatu'r-rāmī* I. O. 2771) and the Archer's Guide (*Hidāyatu'r-rāmī* I. O. 2768).

It should be premised that in archery, the word *gosha* describes, in the arrow, the notch by which it grips and can be carried on the string, and, in the bow, both the tip (horn) and the notch near the tip in which the string catches. It is explained by Vullers as *cornu et crena arcûs cui immititur nervus.*

Two passages in the Cyclopædia of Archery (f. 9 and f. 36*b*) shew *gosha* as the bow-tip. One says that to bend the bow, two men must grasp the two *gosha*; the other reports a tradition that the Archangel Gabriel brought a bow having its two *gosha* (tips) made of ruby. The same book directs that the *gosha* be made of seasoned ivory, the Archer's Guide prescribing seasoned mulberry wood.

The C. of A. (f. 125*b*) says that a bowman should never be without two things, his arrows and his *gosha-gīr*. The *gosha-gīr* may be called an item of the repairing kit; it is an implement (f. 53) for making good a warped bow-tip and for holding the string into a displaced notch. It is known also as the *chaprās*, brooch or buckle, and the *kardāng*; and is said to bear these names because it fastens in the string. Its shape is that of the upper part of the Ar. letter *jīm*, two converging lines of which the lower curves slightly outward. It serves to make good a warped bow, without the use of fire and it should be kept upon the bow-tip till this has reverted to its original state. Until the warp has been straightened by the *gosha-gīr*, the bow must be kept from the action of fire because it, (composite of sinew and glutinous substance,) is of the nature of wax.

The same implement can be used to straighten the middle of the bow, the *kamān khāna*. It is then called *kar-dāng*. It can be used there on condition that there are not two *daur* (curves) in the bow. If there are two the bow cannot be repaired without fire. The *halāl daur* is said to be characteristic of the Turkish bow. There are three *daur*. I am indebted to Mr. Inigo Simon for the suggestions that *daur* in this connection means *warp* and that the three twists (*daur*) may be those of one horn (*gosha*), of the whole bow warped in one curve, and of the two horns warped in opposite directions.

Of repair to the *kamān-khāna* it is said further that if no *kardāng* be available, its work can be done by means of a stick and string, and if the damage be slight only, the bow and the string can be tightly tied together till the bow comes straight. 'And the cure is with God!'

Both manuscripts named contain much technical information. Some parts of this are included in my husband's article, *Oriental Crossbows* (A. Q. R. 1911, p. 1). Sir Ralph Payne-Gallwey's interesting book on the Cross-bow allows insight into the fine handicraft of Turkish bow-making.

D.—ON THE RESCUE PASSAGE.

I have omitted from my translation an account of Bābur's rescue from expected death, although it is with the Ḥaidarābād Codex, because closer acquaintance with its details has led both my husband and myself to judge it spurious. We had welcomed it because, being with the true Bābur-nāma text, it accredited the same account found in the Kehr-Ilminsky text, and also because, however inefficiently, it did something towards filling the gap found elsewhere within 908 AH.

It is in the Ḥaidarābād MS. (f. 118*b*), in Kehr's MS. (p. 385), in Ilminsky's imprint (p. 144), in *Les Mémoires de Bābour* (i, 255) and with the St. P. University Codex, which is a copy of Kehr's.

On the other hand, it is not with the Elphinstone Codex (f. 89*b*); that it was not with the archetype of that codex the scribe's note shews (f. 90); it is with neither of the *Wāqi'āt-i-bāburī* (Pers. translations) nor with Leyden and Erskine's *Memoirs* (p. 122).[2757]

Before giving our grounds for rejecting what has been offered to fill the gap of 908 AH. a few words must be said about the lacuna itself. Nothing indicates that Bābur left it and, since both in the Elphinstone Codex and its archetype, the sentence preceding it lacks the terminal verb, it seems due merely to loss of pages. That the loss, if any, was of early date is clear,—the Elph. MS. itself being copied not later than 1567 AD. (JRAS. 1907, p. 137).

Two known circumstances, both of earlier date than that of the Elphinstone Codex, might have led to the loss,—the first is the storm which in 935 AH. scattered Bābur's papers (f. 376*b*), the second, the vicissitudes to which Humāyūn's library was exposed in his exile.[2758] Of the two the first seems the more probable cause.

The rupture of a story at a point so critical as that of Bābur's danger in Karnān would tempt to its completion; so too would wish to make good the composed part of the Bābur-nāma. Humāyūn annotated the archetype of the Elphinstone Codex a good deal but he cannot have written the Rescue passage if only because he was in a position to avoid some of its inaccuracies.

CONTEXT AND TRANSLATION OF THE RESCUE PASSAGE.

To facilitate reference, I quote the last words preceding the gap purported to be filled by the Rescue passage, from several texts;—

(*a*) Elphinstone MS. f. 89*b*,—*Qūptūm. Bāgh gosha-sī-gha bārdīm. Aūzūm bīla andesha qīldīm. Dīdīm kīm kīshī agar yūz u agar mīng yāshāsā, ākhir hech....*

(*b*) The Ḥai. MS. (f. 118*b*) varies from the Elphinstone by omitting the word *hech* and adding *aūlmāk kīrāk*, he must die.

(*c*) Pāyanda-ḥasan's *Wāqi'āt-i-bāburī* (I. O. 215, f. 96*b*),—*Barkhwāstam u dar gosha-i bāgh raftam. Ba khūd andesha karda, guftam kah agar kase ṣad sāl yā hazār sāl 'umr dāshta bāshad, ākhir hech ast.* (It will be seen that this text has the *hech* of the Elph. MS.)

(*d*) 'Abdu'r-raḥīm's *Wāqi'āt-i-bāburī* (I. O. 217, f. 79),—*Barkhwāstam u ba gosha-i-bāgh raftam. Ba khūd andeshīdam u guftam kah agar kase ṣad sāl u agar hazār sāl 'umr bayābad ākhir....*

(*e*) Muḥ. *Shīrāzī's* lith. ed. (p. 75) finishes the sentence with *ākhir khūd bāyad murd*, at last one must die,—varying as it frequently does, from both of the *Wāqi'āt*.

(*f*) Kehr's MS. (p. 383-454), Ilminsky, p. 144,—*Qūpūb bāghnīng bīr būrjī-ghā bārīb, khāṭirīm-ghā kīltūrdīm kīm agar adam yūz yīl u agar mīng yīl tīrīk būlsā, ākhir aūlmāk dīn aūzkā chāra yūq tūr.* (I rose. Having gone to a tower of the garden, I brought it to my mind that if a person be alive 100 years or a thousand years, at last he has no help other than to die.)

The Rescue passage is introduced by a Persian couplet, identified by my husband as from Niẓāmī's *Khusrau u Shīrīn*, which is as follows;—

If you stay a hundred years, and if one year,

Forth you must go from this heart-delighting palace.

I steadied myself for death (*qarār bīrdīm*). In that garden a stream came flowing;[2759] I made ablution; I recited the prayer of two inclinations (*ra'kat*); having raised my head for silent prayer, I was making earnest petition when my eyes closed in sleep.[2760] I am seeing[2761] that Khwāja Yaq'ūb, the son of Khwāja Yaḥyā and grandson of His Highness Khwāja 'Ubaidu'l-lāh, came facing me, mounted on a piebald horse, with a large company of piebald horsemen (*sic*).[2762] He said: 'Lay sorrow aside! Khwāja *Aḥrār* (*i.e.* 'Ubaidu'l-lāh) has sent me to you; he said, "We, having asked help for him (*i.e.* Bābur), will seat him on the royal throne;[2763] wherever difficulty befalls him, let him look towards us (lit. bring us to sight) and call us to mind; there will we be present." Now, in this hour, victory and success are on your side; lift up your head! awake!'

At that time I awoke happy, when Yūsuf and those with him[2764] were giving one another advice. 'We will make a pretext to deceive; to seize and bind[2765] is necessary.' Hearing these words, I said, 'Your words are of this sort, but I will see which of you will come to my presence to take me.' I was saying this when outside the garden wall[2766] came the noise of approaching horsemen. Yūsuf *darogha* said, 'If we had taken you to Taṃbal our affairs would have gone forward. Now he has sent again many persons to seize you.' He was certain that this noise might be the footfall of the horses of those sent by Taṃbal. On hearing those words anxiety grew upon me; what to do I did not know. At this time those horsemen, not happening to find the garden gate, broke down the wall where it was old (and) came in. I saw (*kūrsām*, lit. might see) that Qutluq Muḥ. *Barlās* and Bābā-i *Parghari*, my life-devoted servants, having arrived [with], it may be, ten, fifteen, twenty persons, were approaching. Having flung themselves from their horses,[2767] bent the knee from afar and showed respect, they fell at my feet. In that state (*ḥal*) such ecstasy (*ḥāl*) came over me that you might say (*goyā*) God gave me life from a new source (*bāsh*). I said, 'Seize and bind that Yūsuf *darogha* and these here (*tūrghān*) hireling mannikins.' These same mannikins had taken to flight. They (*i.e.* the rescuers), having taken them, one by one, here and there, brought them bound. I said, 'Where do you come from? How did you get news?' Qutluq Muḥ. *Barlās* said: 'When, having fled from Akhsī, we were separated from you in the flight, we went to Andijān when the Khāns also came to Andijān. I saw a vision that Khwāja 'Ubaidu'l-lāh said, "Bābur *pādshāh*[2768] is in a village called Karnān; go and bring him, since the royal seat (*masnad*) has become his possession (*ta'alluq*)." I having seen this vision and become happy, represented (the matter) to the Elder Khān (and) the Younger Khān. I said to the Khāns, "I have five or six younger brothers (and) sons; do you add a few soldiers. I will go through the Karnān side and bring news." The Khāns said, "It occurs to our minds also that (he) may have gone that same road (?)." They appointed ten persons; they said, "Having gone in that direction (*sāri*) and made very sure, bring news. Would to God you might get true news!" We were saying this when Bābā-i *Parghārī* said, "I too will go and seek." He also having agreed with two young men, (his) younger brothers, we rode out. It is three days to-day that we are on the road. Thank God! we have found you.' They said (*dīdīlār*, for *dīb*). They spoke (*aītīlār*), 'Make a move! Ride off! Take these bound ones with you! To stay here is not well; Taṃbal has had news of your coming here; go, in whatever way, and join yourself to the Khāns!' At that time we having ridden out, moved towards Andijān. It was two days that we had eaten no food; the evening prayer had come when we found a sheep, went on, dismounted, killed, and roasted. Of that same roast we ate as much as a feast. After that we rode on, hurried forward, made a five days' journey in a day and two nights, came and entered Andijān. I saluted my uncle the Elder Khān (and) my uncle the Younger Khān, and made recital of past days. With the Khāns I spent four months. My servants, who had gone looking in every place, gathered themselves together; there were more than 300 persons. It came to my mind (*kīm*), 'How long must I wander, a vagabond (*sar-gardān*),[2769] in this Farghāna country? I will make search (*ṭalab*) on every side (*dīb*).' Having said, I rode out in the month of Muḥarram to seek Khurāsān, and I went out from the country of Farghāna.[2770]

REASONS AGAINST THE REJECTION OF THE RESCUE PASSAGE.

Two circumstances have weight against rejecting the passage, its presence with the Ḥaidarābād Codex and its acceptance by Dr. Ilminsky and M. de Courteille.

That it is with the Codex is a matter needing consideration and this the more that it is the only extra matter there found. Not being with the Persian translations, it cannot be of early date. It seems likely to owe its place of honour to distinguished authorship and may well be one of the four portions (*juzwe*) mentioned by Jahāngīr in the Tuzūk-i-jahāngīrī,[2771] as added by himself to his ancestor's book. If so, it may be mentioned, it will have been with Bābur's autograph MS. [now not to be found], from which the Ḥaidarābād Codex shews signs of being a direct copy.[2772]

[The incongruity of the Rescue passage with the true text has been indicated by foot-notes to the translation of it already given. What condemns it on historic and other grounds will follow.]

On linguistic grounds it is a strong argument in its favour that Dr. Ilminsky and M. de Courteille should have accepted it but the argument loses weight when some of the circumstances of their work are taken into account.

In the first place, it is not strictly accurate to regard Dr. Ilminsky as accepting it unquestioned, because it is covered by his depreciatory remarks, made in his preface, on Kehr's text. He, like M. de Courteille, worked with a single Turkī MS. and neither of the two ever saw a complete true text. When their source (the Kehr-Ilminsky) was able to be collated with the Elph. and Ḥai. MSS. much and singular divergence was discovered.

I venture to suggest what appears to me to explain M. de Courteille's acceptance of the Rescue passage. Down to its insertion, the Kehr-Ilminsky text is so continuously and so curiously corrupt that it seems necessary to regard it as being a re-translation into Turkī from one of the Persian translations of the *Bābur-nāma*. There being these textual defects in it, it would create on the mind of a reader initiated through it, only, in the book, an incorrect impression of Bābur's style and vocabulary, and such a reader would feel no transition when passing on from it to the Rescue passage.

In opposition to this explanation, it might be said that a wrong standard set up by the corrupt text, would or could be changed by the excellence of later parts of the Kehr-Ilminsky one. In words, this is sound, no doubt, and such reflex criticism is now easy, but more than the one defective MS. was wanted even to suggest the need of such reflex criticism. The *Bābur-nāma* is lengthy, ponderous to poise and grasp, and work on it is still tentative, even with the literary gains since the Seventies.

Few of the grounds which weigh with us for the rejection of the Rescue passage were known to Dr. Ilminsky or M. de Courteille;—the two good Codices bring each its own and varied help; Teufel's critique on the 'Fragments,' though made without acquaintance with those adjuncts as they stand in Kehr's own volume, is of much collateral value; several useful oriental histories seem not to have been available for M. de Courteille's use. I may add, for my own part, that I have the great advantage of my husband's companionship and the guidance of his wide acquaintance with related oriental books. In truth, looking at the drawbacks now removed, an earlier acceptance of the passage appears as natural as does today's rejection.

GROUNDS FOR REJECTING THE RESCUE PASSAGE.

The grounds for rejecting the passage need here little more than recapitulation from my husband's article in the JASB. 1910, p. 221, and are as follows;—

i. The passage is in neither of the *Wāqi'āt-i-bāburī*.

ii. The dreams detailed are too à propos and marvellous for credence.

iii. Khwāja Yaḥyā is not known to have had a son, named Ya'qūb.

iv. The *Bābur-nāma* does not contain the names assigned to the rescuers.

v. The Khāns were not in Andijān and Bābur did not go there.

vi. He did not set out for Khurāsān after spending 4 months with The Khāns but after Aḥmad's death (end of 909 AH.), while Maḥmud was still in Eastern Turkistān and after about a year's stay in Sūkh.

vii. The followers who gathered to him were not 'more than 300' but between 2 and 300.

viii. The '3 days,' and the 'day and two nights,' and the '5 days' journey was one of some 70 miles, and one recorded as made in far less time.

ix. The passage is singularly inadequate to fill a gap of 14 to 16 months, during which events of the first importance occurred to Bābur and to the Chaghatāī dynasty.

x. Khwāja *Aḥrārī's* promises did nothing to fulfil Bābur's wishes for 908 AH. while those of Ya'qūb for immediate victory were closely followed by defeat and exile. Bābur knew the facts; the passage cannot be his. It looks as though the writer saw Bābur in Karnān across Tīmūrid success in Hindūstān.

xi. The style and wording of the passage are not in harmony with those of the true text.

Other reasons for rejection are marked change in choice of the details chosen for commemoration, *e.g.* when Bābur mentions prayer, he does so simply; when he tells a dream, it seems a real one. The passage leaves the impression that the writer did not think in Turkī, composed in it with difficulty, and looked at life from another view-point than Bābur's.

On these various grounds, we have come to the conclusion that it is no part of the *Bābur-nāma.*

E.—NAGARAHĀR, AND NĪNG-NAHĀR

Those who consult books and maps about the riverain tract between the Safed-koh (Spīn-ghur) and (Anglicé) the Kābul-river find its name in several forms, the most common being Nangrahār and Nangnahār (with variant vowels). It would be useful to establish a European book-name for the district. As European opinion differs about the origin and meaning of the names now in use, and as a good deal of interesting circumstance gathers round the small problem of a correct form (there may be two), I offer about the matter what has come into the restricted field of my own work, premising that I do this merely as one who drops a casual pebble on the cairn of observation already long rising for scholarly examination.

a. The origin and meaning of the names.

I have met with three opinions about the origin and meaning of the names found now and earlier. To each one of them obvious objection can be made. They are:—

1. That all forms now in use are corruptions of the Sanscrit word Nagarahāra, the name of the Town-of-towns which in the *dū-āb* of the Bārān-sū and Sūrkh-rūd left the ruins Masson describes in Wilson's *Ariana Antigua.* But if this is so, why is the Town-of-towns multiplied into the nine of Na-nagrahār (Nangrahār)?[2773]

2. That the names found represent Sanscrit *nawā vihāra,* nine monasteries, an opinion the Gazetteer of India of 1907 has adopted from Bellew. But why precisely nine monasteries? Nine appears an understatement.

3. That Nang (Ning or Nung) -nahār verbally means nine streams, (Bābur's Tūqūz-rūd,) an interpretation of long standing (Section *b infra*). But whence *nang, ning, nung,* for nine? Such forms are not in Persian, Turkī or Pushtu dictionaries, and, as Sir G. A. Grierson assures me, do not come into the Linguistic Survey.

b. On nang, ning, nung for nine.

Spite of their absence from the natural homes of words, however, the above sounds have been heard and recorded as symbols of the number nine by careful men through a long space of time.

The following instances of the use of "Nangnahār" show this, and also show that behind the variant forms there may be not a single word but two of distinct origin and sense.

1. In Chinese annals two names appear as those of the district and town (I am not able to allocate their application with certainty). The first is Na-kie-lo-ho-lo, the second Nang-g-lo-ho-lo and these, I understand to represent Nagara-hāra and Nang-nahār, due allowance being made for Chinese idiosyncrasy.[2774]

2. Some 900 years later (1527-30 AD.) Bābur also gives two names, Nagarahār (as the book-name of his *tūmān*) and Nīng-nahār.[2775] He says the first is found in several histories (B.N. f. 131*b*); the second will have been what he heard and also presumably what appeared in revenue accounts; of it he says, "it is nine torrents" (*tūqūz-rūd*).

3. Some 300 years after Bābur, Elphinstone gives two names for the district, neither of them being Bābur's book-name, "Nangrahaur[2776] or Nungnahaur, from the nine streams which issue from the Safed-koh, *nung* in Pushtoo signifying *nine*, and *nahaura*, a stream" (*Caubul*, i, 160).

4. In 1881 Colonel H. S. Tanner had heard, in Nūr-valley on the north side of the Kābul-water, that the name of the opposite district was Nīng-nahār and its meaning Nine-streams. He did not get a list of the nine and all he heard named do not flow from Safed-koh.

5. In 1884 Colonel H. G. McGregor gives two names with their explanation, "Ningrahar and Nungnihar; the former is a corruption of the latter word[2777] which in the Afghān language signifies nine rivers or rivulets." He names nine, but of them six only issue from Safed-koh.

6. I have come across the following instances in which the number nine is represented by other words than *na* (*ni* or *nu*); *viz.* the *nenhan* of the Chitrālī Kāfir and the *noun* of the Panjābi, recorded by Leech,—the *nyon* of the Khowārī and the *huncha* of the Boorishki, recorded by Colonel Biddulph.

The above instances allow opinion that in the region concerned and through a long period of time, nine has been expressed by *nang* (*ning* or *nung*) and other nasal or high palatal sounds, side by side with *na* (*ni* or *nu*). The whole matter may be one of nasal utterance,[2778] but since a large number of tribesmen express nine by a word containing a nasal sound, should that word not find place in lists of recognized symbols of sounds?

c. Are there two names of distinct origin?

1. Certainly it makes a well-connected story of decay in the Sanscrit word Nagarahāra to suppose that tribesmen, prone by their organism to nasal utterance, pronounced that word Nangrahār, and by force of their numbers

made this corruption current,—that this was recognized as the name of the town while the Town-of-towns was great or in men's memory, and that when through the decay of the town its name became a meaningless husk, the wrong meaning of the Nine-streams should enter into possession.

But as another and better one can be put together, this fair-seeming story may be baseless. Its substitute has the advantage of explaining the double sequence of names shown in Section *b*.

The second story makes all the variant names represent one or other of two distinct originals. It leaves Nagrahār to represent Nagarahāra, the dead town; it makes the nine torrents of Safed-koh the primeval sponsors of Nīng-nahār, the name of the riverain tract. Both names, it makes contemporary in the relatively brief interlude of the life of the town. For the fertilizing streams will have been the dominant factors of settlement and of revenue from the earliest times of population and government. They arrest the eye where they and their ribbons of cultivation space the riverain waste; they are obvious units for grouping into a sub-government. Their name has a counterpart in adjacent Panj-āb; the two may have been given by one dominant power, how long ago, in what tongue matters not. The riverain tract, by virtue of its place on a highway of transit, must have been inhabited long before the town Nagarahāra was built, and must have been known by a name. What better one than Nine-streams can be thought of?

2. Bellew is quoted by the Gazetteer of India (ed. 1907) as saying, in his argument in favour of *nawā vihāra*, that no nine streams are found to stand sponsor, but modern maps shew nine outflows from Safed-koh to the Kābul-river between the Sūrkh-rūd and Daka, while if affluents to the former stream be reckoned, more than nine issue from the range.[2779]

Against Bellew's view that there are not nine streams, is the long persistence of the number nine in the popular name (Sect. *b*).

It is also against his view that he supposes there were nine monasteries, because each of the nine must have had its fertilizing water.

Bābur says there were nine; there must have been nine of significance; he knew his *tūmān* not only by frequent transit but by his revenue accounts. A supporting point in those accounts is likely to have been that the individual names of the villages on the nine streams would appear, with each its payment of revenue.

3. In this also is some weight of circumstance against taking Nagarahāra to be the parent of Nīng-nahār:—An earlier name of the town is said to be Udyānapūra, Garden town.[2780] Of this Bābur's Adīnapūr is held to be a

corruption; the same meaning of garden has survived on approximately the same ground in Bālā-bāgh and Roẓābād.

Nagarahāra is seen, therefore, to be a parenthetical name between others which are all derived from gardens. It may shew the promotion of a "Garden-town" to a "Chief-town". If it did this, there was relapse of name when the Chief-town lost status. Was it ever applied beyond the delta? If it were, would it, when dead in the delta, persist along the riverain tract? If it were not, *cadit quæstio*; the suggestion of two names distinct in origin, is upheld.

Certainly the riverain tract would fall naturally under the government of any town flourishing in the delta, the richest and most populous part of the region. But for this very reason it must have had a name older than parenthetical Nagarahāra. That inevitable name would be appropriately Nīng-nahār (or Na-nahār) Nine-streams; and for a period Nagarahāra would be the Chief-town of the district of Na-nahār (Nine-streams).[2781]

d. Bābur's statements about the name.

What the cautious Bābur says of his *tūmān* of Nīng-nahār has weight:—

1. That some histories write it Nagarahār (Ḥaidarābād Codex, f. 131*b*);

2. That Nīng-nahār is nine torrents, *i.e.* mountain streams, *tūquz-rud*;

3. That (the) nine torrents issue from Safed-koh (f. 132*b*).

Of his first statement can be said, that he will have seen the book-name in histories he read, but will have heard Nīng-nahār, probably also have seen it in current letters and accounts.

Of his second,—that it bears and may be meant to bear two senses, (*a*) that the *tūmān* consisted of nine torrents,—their lands implied; just as he says "Asfara is four *bulūks*" (sub-divisions f. 3*b*)—(*b*) that *tūqūz rūd* translates *nīng-nahār*.

Of his third,—that in English its sense varies as it is read with or without the definite article Turkī rarely writes, but that either sense helps out his first and second, to mean that verbally and by its constituent units Nīng-nahār is nine-torrents; as verbally and by its constituents Panj-āb is five-waters.

e. Last words.

Detailed work on the Kābul section of the *Bābur-nāma* has stamped two impressions so deeply on me, that they claim mention, not as novel or as special to myself, but as set by the work.

The first is of extreme risk in swift decision on any problem of words arising in North Afghānistān, because of its local concourse of tongues, the varied utterance of its unlettered tribes resident or nomad, and the frequent translation of proper names in obedience to their verbal meanings. Names lie there too in *strata*, relics of successive occupation—Greek, Turkī, Hindī, Pushtū and tribes *galore*.

The second is that the region is an exceptionally fruitful field for first-hand observation of speech, the movent ocean of the uttered word, free of the desiccated symbolism of alphabets and books.

The following books, amongst others, have prompted the above note:—

Ghoswāra Inscription, Kittoe, JASB., 1848, and Kielhorn, *Indian Antiquary*, 1888, p. 311.

H. Sastrī's *Rāmacārita*, Introduction, p. 7 (ASB. Memoirs).

Cunningham's *Ancient India*, vol. i.

Beal's *Buddhist Records*, i, xxxiv, and cii, 91.

Leech's Vocabularies, JASB., 1838.

The writings of Masson (*Travels* and *Ariana Antiqua*), Wood, Vigne, etc.

Raverty's *Ṭabaqāt-i-nāsirī.*

Jarrett's *Āyīn-i-akbarī.*

P.R.G.S. for maps, 1879; Macnair on the Kafirs, 1884; Tanner's *On the Chugānī and neighbouring tribes of Kāfiristān*, 1881.

Simpson's *Nagarahāra*, JASB., xiii.

Biddulph's *Dialects of the Hindū-kush*, JRAS.

Gazette of India, 1907, art. Jalalābād.

Bellew's *Races of Afghānistān.*

F.—ON THE NAME DARA-I-NŪR

SOME European writers have understood the name Dara-i-nūr to mean Valley of Light, but natural features and also the artificial one mentioned by Colonel H. G. Tanner (*infra*), make it better to read the component *nūr*, not as Persian *nūr*, light, but as Pushtū *nūr*, rock. Hence it translates as Valley of Rocks, or Rock-valley. The region in which the valley lies is rocky and boulder-strewn; its own waters flow to the Kābul-river east of the water of Chitrāl. It shews other names composed with *nūr*, in which *nūr* suits if it means rock, but is inexplicable if it means light, *e.g.* Nūr-lām (Nūr-fort), the master-fort in the mouth of Nūr-valley, standing high on a rock between two streams, as Bābur and Tanner have both described it from eye-witness,—Nūr-gal (village), a little to the north-west of the valley,—Aūlūgh-nūr (great rock), at a crossing mentioned by Bābur, higher up the Bārān-water,—and Koh-i-nūr (Rocky-mountains), which there is ground for taking as the correct form of the familiar "Kunar" of some European writers (Raverty's *Notes*, p. 106). The dominant feature in these places dictates reading *nūr* as rock; so too the work done in Nūr-valley with boulders, of which Colonel H. G. Tanner's interesting account is subjoined (P.R.G.S. 1881, p. 284).

"Some 10 miles from the source of the main stream of the Nur-valley the Dameneh stream enters, but the waters of the two never meet; they flow side by side about three-quarters of a mile apart for about 12 miles and empty themselves into the Kunar river by different mouths, each torrent hugging closely the foot of the hills at its own side of the valley. Now, except in countries where terracing has been practised continuously for thousands of years, such unnatural topography as exists in the valley of Nur is next to impossible. The forces which were sufficient to scoop out the valley in the first instance, would have kept a water-way at the lowest part, into which would have poured the drainage of the surrounding mountains; but in the Nur-valley long-continued terracing has gradually raised the centre of the valley high above the edges. The population has increased to its maximum limit and every available inch of ground is required for cultivation; the people, by means of terrace-walls built of ponderous boulders in the bed of the original single stream, have little by little pushed the waters out of their true course, until they run, where now found, in deep rocky cuttings at the foot of the hills on either side" (p. 280).

"I should like to go on and say a good deal more about boulders; and while I am about it I may as well mention one that lies back from a hamlet in Shulut, which is so big that a house is built in a fault or crack running across its face. Another pebble lies athwart the village and covers the whole of the houses from that side."

G.—ON THE NAMES OF TWO DARA-I-NŪR WINES.

From the two names, Arat-tāshī and Sūhān (Suhār) -tāshī, which Bābur gives as those of two wines of the Dara-i-nūr, it can be inferred that he read *nūr* to mean rock. For if in them Turkī *tāsh*, rock, be replaced by Pushtū *nūr*, rock, two place-names emerge, Arat (-nūrī) and Sūhān (-nūrī), known in the Nūr-valley.

These may be villages where the wines were grown, but it would be quite exceptional for Bābur to say that wines are called from their villages, or indeed by any name. He says here not where they grow but what they are called.

I surmise that he is repeating a joke, perhaps his own, perhaps a standing local one, made on the quality of the wines. For whether with *tāsh* or with *nūr* (rock), the names can be translated as Rock-saw and Rock-file, and may refer to the rough and acid quality of the wines, rasping and setting the teeth on edge as does iron on stone.

The villages themselves may owe their names to a serrated edge or splintered pinnacle of weathered granite, in which local people, known as good craftsmen, have seen resemblance to tools of their trade.

H.—ON THE COUNTERMARK BIH BŪD ON COINS.

As coins of Sl. Ḥusain Mīrzā *Bāī-qarā* and other rulers do actually bear the words *Bih būd*, Bābur's statement that the name of Bihbūd Beg was on the Mīrzā's coins acquires a numismatic interest which may make serviceable the following particulars concerning the passage and the beg.[2782]

a. The Turkī passage (Elph. MS. f. 135*b*; Ḥaidarābād Codex f. 173*b*; Ilminsky p. 217).

For ease of reference the Turkī, Persian and English version are subjoined:—

(1) *Yana Bihbūd Beg aīdī. Būrūnlār chuhra-jīrga-sī-dā khidmat qīlūr aīdī. Mīrzā-nīng qāzāqlīqlārīdā khidmatī bāqīb Bihbūd Beg-kā bū 'ināyatnī qīlīb aīdī kīm tamghā u sikka-dā ānīng ātī aīdī.*

(2) The Persian translation of 'Abdu'r-raḥīm (Muḥ. Shīrāzī's lith. ed. p. 110):—

Dīgar Bihbūd Beg būd. Auwalhā dar jīrga-i-chuhrahā khidmat mikard. Chūn dar qāzāqīhā Mīrzārā khidmat karda būd u ānrā mulāḥaza namūda, aīnrā 'ināyat karda būd kah dar tamghānāt sikka[2783] *nām-i-au būd.*

(3) A literal English translation of the Turkī:—

Another was Bihbūd Beg. He served formerly in the *chuhra-jīrga-sī* (corps of braves). Looking to his service in the Mīrzā's guerilla-times, the favour had been done to Bihbūd Beg that his name was on the stamp and coin.[2784]

b. Of Bihbūd Beg.

We have found little so far to add to what Bābur tells of Bihbūd Beg and what he tells we have not found elsewhere. The likely sources of his information are Daulat Shāh and Khwānd-amīr who have written at length of Ḥusain *Bāī-qarā.* Considerable search in the books of both men has failed to discover mention of signal service or public honour connected with the beg. Bābur may have heard what he tells in Harāt in 912 AH. (1506 AD.) when he would see Ḥusain's coins presumably; but later opportunity to see them must have been frequent during his campaigns and visits north of Hindū-kush, notably in Balkh.

The sole mention we have found of Bihbūd Beg in the *Ḥabību's-siyar* is that he was one of Ḥusain's commanders at the battle of Chīkmān-sarāī which was fought with Sl. Maḥmūd Mīrzā *Mīrānshāhī* in Muḥarram 876 AH. (June-July 1471 AD.).[2785] His place in the list shews him to have had importance. "Amīr Niẓāmu'd-dīn 'Alī-sher's brother Darwesh-i-'alī the librarian (*q.v.* Ḥai. Codex Index), and Amīr Bihbūd, and Muḥ. 'Alī *ātāka*, and Bakhshīka and Shāh Walī *Qīpchāq*, and Dost-i-muḥammad *chuhra*, and Amīr Qul-i-'alī, and" (another).

The total of our information about the man is therefore:—

(1) That when Ḥusain[2786] from 861 to 873 AH. (1457 to 1469 AD.) was fighting his way up to the throne of Harāt, Bihbūd served him well in the corps of braves, (as many others will have done).

(2) That he was a beg and one of Ḥusain's commanders in 876 AH. (1471 AD.).

(3) That Bābur includes him amongst Ḥusain's begs and says of him what has been quoted, doing this *circa* 934 AH. (1528 AD.), some 56 years after Khwānd-amīr's mention of him *s.a.* 876 AH. (1471 AD.).

c. Of the term chuhra-jīrga-sī used by Bābur.

Of this term Bābur supplies an explicit explanation which I have not found in European writings. His own book amply exemplifies his explanation, as do also Khwānd-amīr's and Ḥaidar's.

He gives the explanation (f. 15*b*) when describing a retainer of his father's who afterwards became one of his own begs. It is as follows:—

"'Alī-darwesh of Khurāsān served in the Khurāsān *chuhra-jīrga-sī*, one of two special corps (*khāṣa tābīn*) of serviceable braves (*yārār yīgītlār*) formed by Sl. Abū-sa'īd Mīrzā when he first began to arrange the government of Khurāsān and Samarkand and, presumably, called by him the Khurāsān corps and the Samarkand corps."

This shews the circle to have consisted of fighting-men, such serviceable braves as are frequently mentioned by Bābur; and his words "*yārār yīgīt*" make it safe to say that if instead of using a Persian phrase, he had used a Turkī one, *yīgīt*, brave would have replaced *chuhra*, "young soldier" (Erskine). A considerable number of men on active service are styled *chuhra*, one at least is styled *yīgīt*, in the same way as others are styled *beg*.[2787]

Three military circles are mentioned in the *Bābur-nāma*, consisting respectively of braves, household begs (under Bābur's own command), and great begs. Some men are mentioned who never rose from the rank of brave (*yīgīt*), some who became household-begs, some who went through the three grades.

Of the corps of braves Bābur conveys the information that Abū-saʿīd founded it at a date which will have lain between 1451 and 1457 AD.; that ʿUmar Shaikh's man 'Alī-darwesh belonged to it; and that Ḥusain's man Bihbūd did so also. Both men, 'Ali-darwesh and Bihbūd, when in its circle, would appropriately be styled *chuhra* as men of the beg-circle were styled beg; the Dost-i-muḥammad *chuhra* who was a commander, (he will have had a brave's command,) at Chīkmān-sarāī (*see* list *supra*) will also have been of this circle. Instances of the use by Bābur of the name *khaṣa-tābīn* and its equivalent *būītīkīnī* are shewn on f. 209 and f. 210*b*. A considerable number of Bābur's fighting men, the braves he so frequently mentions as sent on service, are styled *chuhra* and inferentially belong to the same circle.[2788]

d. Of Bih būd on Ḥusain Bāī-qarā's coins.

So far it does not seem safe to accept Bābur's statement literally. He may tell a half-truth and obscure the rest by his brevity.

Nothing in the sources shows ground for signal and public honour to Bihbūd Beg, but a good deal would allow surmise that jesting allusion to his name might decide for *Bih būd* as a coin mark when choice had to be made of one, in the flush of success, in an assembly of the begs, and, amongst those begs, lovers of word-play and enigma.

The personal name is found written Bihbūd, as one word and with medial *h*; the mark is *Bih būd* with the terminal *h* in the *Bih*. There have been discussions moreover as to whether to read on the coins *Bih būd*, it was good, or *Bih buvad*, let it be, or become, good (valid for currency?).

The question presents itself; would the beg's name have appeared on the coins, if it had not coincided in form with a suitable coin-mark?

Against literal acceptance of Bābur's statement there is also doubt of a thing at once so *ben trovato* and so unsupported by evidence.

Another doubt arises from finding *Bih būd* on coins of other rulers, one of Iskandar Khān's being of a later date,[2789] others, of Tīmūr, Shāhrukh and Abū-saʿīd, with nothing to shew who counterstruck it on them.

On some of Ḥusain's coins the sentence *Bih būd* appears as part of the legend and not as a counterstrike. This is a good basis for finding a half-truth in Bābur's statement. It does not allow of a whole-truth in his statement because, as it is written, it is a coin-mark, not a name.

An interesting matter as bearing on Ḥusain's use of *Bih būd* is that in 865 AH. (1461 AD.) he had an incomparable horse named Bihbūd, one he gave in return for a falcon on making peace with Mustapha Khān.[2790]

e. Of Bābur's vassal-coinage.

The following historical details narrow the field of numismatic observation on coins believed struck by Bābur as a vassal of Ismā'īl *Ṣafawī*. They are offered because not readily accessible.

The length of Bābur's second term of rule in Transoxiana was not the three solar years of the B.M. Coin Catalogues but did not exceed eight months. He entered Samarkand in the middle of Rajab 917 AH. (*c.* Oct. 1st, 1511 AD.). He returned to it defeated and fled at once, after the battle of Kūl-i-malik which was fought in Ṣafar 918 AH. (mid-April to mid-May 1512 AD.). Previous to the entry he was in the field, without a fixed base; after his flight he was landless till at the end both of 920 AH. and of 1514 AD. he had returned to Kābul.

He would not find a full Treasury in Samarkand because the Aūzbegs evacuated the fort at their own time; eight months would not give him large tribute in kind. He failed in Transoxiana because he was the ally of a Shī'a; would coins bearing the Shī'a legend have passed current from a Samarkand mint? These various circumstances suggest that he could not have struck many coins of any kind in Samarkand.

The coins classed in the B.M. Catalogues as of Bābur's vassalage, offer a point of difficulty to readers of his own writings, inasmuch as neither the "Sulṭān Muḥammad" of No. 652 (gold), nor the "Sulṭān Bābur Bahādur" of the silver coins enables confident acceptance of them as names he himself would use.

I.—ON THE WEEPING-WILLOWS OF F. 190*B*.

THE passage omitted from f. 190*b*, which seems to describe something decorative done with weeping willows, (*bed-i-mawallah*) has been difficult to all translators. This may be due to inaccurate pointing in Bābur's original MS. or may be what a traveller seeing other willows at another feast could explain.

The first Persian translation omits the passage (I.O. 215 f. 154*b*); the second varies from the Turkī, notably by changing *sāch* and *sāj* to *shākh* throughout (I.O. 217 f. 150*b*). The English and French translations differ much (*Memoirs* p. 206, *Mémoires* i, 414), the latter taking the *mawallah* to be *mūla*, a hut, against which much is clear in the various MSS.

Three Turkī sources[2791] agree in reading as follows:—

Mawallahlār-nī (or *muwallah* Ḥai. MS.) *kīltūrdīlār. Bīlmān sāchlārī-nīng yā 'amlī sāchlārī-nīng ārālārīgha k:msān-nī* (Ilminsky, *kamān*) *shākh-nīng* (Ḥai. MS. *ṣākh*) *aūzūnlūghī bīla aīnjīga aīnjīga kīsīb, qūiūb tūrlār.*

The English and French translations differ from the Turkī and from one another:—

(*Memoirs*, p. 206) They brought in branching willow-trees. I do not know if they were in the natural state of the tree, or if the branches were formed artificially, but they had small twigs cut the length of the ears of a bow and inserted between them.

(*Mémoires* i, 434) On façonna des huttes (*mouleh*). Ils les établissent en taillant des baguettes minces, de la longeur du bout recourbé de l'arc, qu'on place entre des branches naturelles ou façonnées artificiellement, je l'ignore.

The construction of the sentence appears to be thus:—*Mawal-lahlār-nī kīltūrdīlār*, they brought weeping-willows; *k:msān-nī qūiūbtūrlār*, they had put *k:msān-nī*; *aīnjīga aīnjīga kīsīb*, cut very fine (or slender); *shākh* (or *ṣākh*)*-nīng aūzūnlūghī*, of the length of a *shākh*, bow, or *ṣākh* ...; *bīlmān sāchlārī-nīng yā 'amlī sāchlārī-nīng ārālārīgha*, to (or at) the spaces of the *sāchlār* whether their (*i.e.* the willows') own or artificial *sāchlār.*

These translations clearly indicate felt difficulty. Mr. Erskine does not seem to have understood that the trees were *Salix babylonica.* The crux of the passage is the word *k:msān-nī*, which tells what was placed in the spaces. It has been read as *kamān*, bow, by all but the scribes of the two good Turkī MSS. and as in a phrase *horn of a bow*. This however is not allowed by the Turkī, for the reason that *k:msān-nī* is not in the genitive but in the accusative case. (I may say that Bābur does not use *nī* for *nīng*; he keeps strictly to the prime uses of each enclitic,

nī accusative, *nīng* genitive.) Moreover, if *k:msān-nī* be taken as a genitive, the verbs *qūīūb-tūrlār* and *kīsīb* have no object, no other accusative appearing in the sentence than *k:msān-nī*.

A weighty reason against changing *sāch* into *shākh* is that Dr. Ilminsky has not done so. He must have attached meaning to *sāch* since he uses it throughout the passage. He was nearer the region wherein the original willows were seen at a feast. Unfortunately nothing shows how he interpreted the word.

Sāchmāq is a tassel; is it also a catkin and were there decorations, *kimsān-nī* (things *kimsa*, or flowers Ar. *kim*, or something shining, *kimcha*, gold brocade) hung in between the catkins?

Ilminsky writes *mu'lah* (with *ḥamza*) and this de Courteille translates by hut. The Ḥai. MS. writes *muwallah* (marking the *ẓamma*).

In favour of reading *mawallah* (*mulah*) as a tree and that tree *Salix babylonica* the weeping-willow, there are annotations in the Second Persian translation and, perhaps following it, in the Elphinstone MS. of *nām-i-dirakht*, name of a tree, *dīdān-i-bed*, sight of the willow, *bed-i-mawallah*, mournful-willow. Standing alone *mawallah* means weeping-willow, in this use answering to *majnūn* the name Panj-ābīs give the tree, from Leila's lover the distracted *i.e.* Majnūn (Brandis).

The whole question may be solved by a chance remark from a traveller witnessing similar festive decoration at another feast in that conservative region.

J.—ON BĀBUR'S EXCAVATED CHAMBER AT QANDAHĀR (F. 208*B*).

SINCE making my note (f. 208*b*) on the wording of the passage in which Bābur mentions excavation done by him at Qandahār, I have learned that he must be speaking of the vaulted chamber containing the celebrated inscriptions about which much has been written.[2792]

The primary inscription, the one commemorating Bābur's final possession of Qandahār, gives the chamber the character of a Temple of Victory and speaks of it as *Rawāq-i-jahān namāī*, World-shewing-portal,[2793] doubtless because of its conspicuous position and its extensive view, probably also in allusion to its declaration of victory. Mīr Ma'ṣūm writes of it as a Pesh-ṭāq, frontal arch, which, coupled with Mohan Lall's word arch (*ṭāq*) suggests that the chamber was entered through an arch pierced in a parallelogram smoothed on the rock and having resemblance to the *pesh-tāq* of buildings, a suggestion seeming the more probable that some inscriptions are on the "wings" of the arch. But by neither of the above-mentioned names do Mohan Lall and later travellers call the chamber or write of the place; all describe it by its approach of forty steps, Chihil-zīna.[2794]

The excavation has been chipped out of the white-veined limestone of the bare ridge on and below which stood Old Qandahār.[2794] It does not appear from the descriptions to have been on the summit of the ridge; Bellew says that the forty steps start half-way up the height. I have found no estimate of the height of the ridge, or statement that the steps end at the chamber. The ridge however seems to have been of noticeably dominating height. It rises steeply to the north and there ends in the naze of which Bābur writes. The foot of the steps is guarded by two towers. Mohan Lall, unaccustomed to mountains, found their ascent steep and dizzy. The excavated chamber of the inscriptions, which Bellew describes as "bow-shaped and dome-roofed", he estimated as 12 feet at the highest point,

12 feet deep and 8 feet wide. Two sculptured beasts guard the entrance; Bellew calls them leopards but tigers would better symbolize the watch and ward of the Tiger Bābur. In truth the whole work, weary steps of approach, tiger guardians, commemorative chamber, laboriously incised words, are admirably symbolic of his long-sustained resolve and action, taken always with Hindūstān as the goal.

There are several inscriptions of varying date, within and without the chamber. Mohan Lall saw and copied them; Darmesteter worked on a copy; the two English observers Lumsden and Bellew made no attempt at correct interpretation. In the versions all give there are inaccuracies, arising from obvious causes, especially from want of historical *data.* The last word has not been said; revision awaits photography and the leisured expert. A part of the needed revision has been done by Beames, who deals with the geography of what Mīr Ma'ṣūm himself added under Akbar after he had gone as Governor to Qandahār in 1007 AH. (1598 AD.). This commemorates not Bābur's but Akbar's century of cities.

It is the primary inscription only which concerns this Appendix. This is one in relief in the dome of the chamber, recording in florid Persian that Abū'l-ghāzī Bābur took possession of Qandahār on Shawwāl 13th 928 AH. (Sep. 1st 1522 AD.), that in the same year he commanded the construction of this *Rawāq-i-jahān-namāī*, and that the work had been completed by his son Kāmrān at the time he made over charge of Qandahār to his brother 'Askarī in 9 ... (mutilated). After this the gravure changes in character.

In the above, Bābur's title Abū'l-ghāzī fixes the date of the inscription as later than the battle of Kanwāha (f. 324*b*), because it was assumed in consequence of this victory over a Hindū, in March 1527 (Jumāda II 933 AH.).

The mutilated date 9 ... is given by Mohan Lall as 952 AH. but this does not suit several circumstances, *e.g.* it puts completion too far beyond the time mentioned as consumed by the work, nine years,—and it was not that at which Kāmrān made over charge to 'Askarī, but followed the expulsion of both full-brothers from Qandahār by their half-brother Humāyūn.

The mutilated date 9 ... is given by Darmesteter as 933 AH. but this again does not fit the historical circumstance that Kāmrān was in Qandahār after that date and till 937 AH. This date (937 AH.) we suggest as fitting to replace the lost figures, (1) because in that year and after his father's death, Kāmrān gave the town to 'Askarī and went himself to Hindūstān, and (2) because work begun in 928 AH. and recorded as occupying 70-80 men for nine years would be complete in 937 AH.[2795] The inscription would be one of the last items of the work.

The following matters are added here because indirectly connected with what has been said and because not readily accessible.

a. Birth of Kāmrān.

Kāmrān's birth falling in a year of one of the *Bābur-nāma* gaps, is nowhere mentioned. It can be closely inferred as 914 or 915 AH. from the circumstances that he was younger than Humāyūn born late in 913 AH., that it is not mentioned in the fragment of the annals of 914 AH., and that he was one of the children enumerated by Gul-badan as going with her father to Samarkand in 916 AH. (Probably the children did not start with their father in the depth of winter across the mountains.) Possibly the joyful name Kāmrān is linked to the happy issue of the Mughūl rebellion of 914 AH. Kāmrān would thus be about 18 when left in charge of Kābul and Qandahār by Bābur in 932 AH. before the start for the fifth expedition to Hindūstān.

A letter from Bābur to Kāmrān in Qandahār is with Kehr's Latin version of the *Bābur-nāma*, in Latin and entered on the lining of the cover. It is shewn by its main topic *viz.* the despatch of Ibrāhīm *Lūdī*'s son to Kāmrān's charge, to date somewhere close to Jan. 3rd 1527 (Rabī'u'l-awwal 29th 933 AH.) because on that day Bābur writes of the despatch (Ḥai. Codex f. 306*b* foot).

Presumably the letter was with Kāmrān's own copy of the *Bābur-nāma*. That copy may have reached Humāyūn's hands

(JRAS 1908 p. 828 *et seq.*). The next known indication of the letter is given in St. Petersburg by Dr. Kehr. He will have seen it or a copy of it with the B.N. Codex he copied (one of unequaled correctness), and he, no doubt, copied it in its place on the fly-leaf or board of his own transcript, but if so, it has disappeared.

Fuller particulars of it and of other items accompanying it are given in JRAS 1908 p. 828 *et seq.*

K.—AN AFGHĀN LEGEND.

My husband's article in the Asiatic Quarterly Review of April 1901 begins with an account of the two MSS. from which it is drawn, *viz.* I.O. 581 in Pushtū, I.O. 582 in Persian. Both are mainly occupied with an account of the Yūsuf-zāī. The second opens by telling of the power of the tribe in Afghānistān and of the kindness of Malik Shāh Sulaimān, one of their chiefs, to Aūlūgh Beg Mīrzā *Kābulī*, (Bābur's paternal uncle,) when he was young and in trouble, presumably as a boy ruler.

It relates that one day a wise man of the tribe, Shaikh 'Uṣmān saw Sulaimān sitting with the young Mīrzā on his knee and warned him that the boy had the eyes of Yazīd and would destroy him and his family as Yazīd had destroyed that of the Prophet. Sulaimān paid him no attention and gave the Mīrzā his daughter in marriage. Subsequently the Mīrzā having invited the Yūsuf-zāī to Kābul, treacherously killed Sulaimān and 700 of his followers. They were killed at the place called Siyāh-sang near Kābul; it is still known, writes the chronicler in about 1770 AD. (1184 AH.), as the Grave of the Martyrs. Their tombs are revered and that of Shaikh 'Uṣmān in particular.

Shāh Sulaimān was the eldest of the seven sons of Malik Tāju'd-dīn; the second was Sulṭān Shāh, the father of Malik Aḥmad. Before Sulaimān was killed he made three requests of Aūlūgh Beg; one of them was that his nephew Aḥmad's life might be spared. This was granted.

Aūlūgh Beg died (after ruling from 865 to 907 AH.), and Bābur defeated his son-in-law and successor M. Muqīm (*Arghūn*, 910 AH.). Meantime the Yūsuf-zāī had migrated to Pashāwar but later on took Sawād from Sl. Wais (Ḥai. Codex ff. 219, 220*b*, 221).

When Bābur came to rule in Kābul, he at first professed friendship for the Yūsuf-zāī but became prejudiced against them through their enemies the Dilazāk[2796] who gave force to their charges by a promised subsidy of 70,000 *shāhrukhī*. Bābur therefore determined, says the Yūsuf-zāī chronicler, to kill Malik[2797] Aḥmad and so wrote him a friendly invitation to Kābul. Aḥmad agreed to go, and set out with four brothers who were famous musicians. Meanwhile the Dilazāk had persuaded Bābur to put Aḥmad to death at once, for they said Aḥmad was so clever and eloquent that if allowed to speak, he would induce the Pādshāh to pardon him.

On Aḥmad's arrival in Kābul, he is said to have learned that Bābur's real object was his death. His companions wanted to tie their turbans together and let him down over the wall of the fort, but he rejected their proposal as too dangerous for him and them, and resolved to await his fate. He told his companions however, except one of the musicians, to go into hiding in the town.

Next morning there was a great assembly and Bābur sat on the daïs-throne. Aḥmad made his reverence on entering but Bābur's only acknowledgment was to make bow and arrow ready to shoot him. When Aḥmad saw that Bābur's intention was to shoot him down without allowing him to speak, he unbuttoned his jerkin and stood still before the Pādshāh. Bābur, astonished, relaxed the tension of his bow and asked Aḥmad what he meant. Aḥmad's only reply was to tell the Pādshāh not to question him but to do what he intended. Bābur again asked his meaning and again got the same reply.

Bābur put the same question a third time, adding that he could not dispose of the matter without knowing more. Then Aḥmad opened the mouth of praise, expatiated on Bābur's excellencies and said that in this great assemblage many of his subjects were looking on to see the shooting; that his jerkin being very thick, the arrow might not pierce it; the shot might fail and the spectators blame the Pādshāh for missing his mark; for these reasons he had thought it best to bare his breast. Bābur was so pleased by this reply that he resolved to pardon Aḥmad at once, and laid down his bow.

Said he to Aḥmad, "What sort of man is Buhlūl *Lūdī*?" "A giver of horses," said Aḥmad.

"And of what sort his son Sikandar?" "A giver of robes."

"And of what sort is Bābur?" "He," said Aḥmad, "is a giver of heads."

"Then," rejoined Bābur, "I give you yours."

The Pādshāh now became quite friendly with Aḥmad, came down from his throne, took him by the hand and led him into another room where they drank together. Three times did Bābur have his cup filled, and after drinking a portion, give the rest to Aḥmad. At length the wine mounted to Bābur's head; he grew merry and began to dance. Meantime Aḥmad's musician played and Aḥmad who knew Persian well, poured out an eloquent harangue. When Bābur had danced for some time, he held out his hands to Aḥmad for a reward (*bakhshīsh*), saying, "I am your performer." Three times did he open his hands, and thrice did Aḥmad, with a profound reverence, drop a gold coin into them. Bābur took the coins, each time placing his hand on his head. He then took off his robe and gave it to

Aḥmad; Aḥmad took off his own coat, gave it to Adu the musician, and put on what the Pādshāh had given.

Aḥmad returned safe to his tribe. He declined a second invitation to Kābul, and sent in his stead his brother Shāh Manṣūr. Manṣūr received speedy dismissal as Bābur was displeased at Aḥmad's not coming. On his return to his tribe Manṣūr advised them to retire to the mountains and make a strong *sangur*. This they did; as foretold, Bābur came into their country with a large army. He devastated their lands but could make no impression on their fort. In order the better to judge of its character, he, as was his wont, disguised himself as a Qalandar, and went with friends one dark night to the Mahūra hill where the stronghold was, a day's journey from the Pādshāh's camp at Dīārūn.

It was the 'Īd-i-qurbān and there was a great assembly and feasting at Shāh Manṣūr's house, at the back of the Mahūra-mountain, still known as Shāh Manṣūr's throne. Bābur went in his disguise to the back of the house and stood among the crowd in the courtyard. He asked servants as they went to and fro about Shāh Manṣūr's family and whether he had a daughter. They gave him straightforward answers.

At the time Musammat Bībī Mubāraka, Shāh Manṣur's daughter was sitting with other women in a tent. Her eye fell on the qalandars and she sent a servant to Bābur with some cooked meat folded between two loaves. Bābur asked who had sent it; the servant said it was Shāh Manṣūr's daughter Bībī Mubāraka. "Where is she?" "That is she, sitting in front of you in the tent." Bābur Pādshāh became entranced with her beauty and asked the woman-servant, what was her disposition and her age and whether she was betrothed. The servant replied by extolling her mistress, saying that her virtue equalled her beauty, that she was pious and brimful of rectitude and placidity; also that she was not betrothed. Bābur then left with his friends, and behind the house hid between two stones the food that had been sent to him.

He returned to camp in perplexity as to what to do; he saw he could not take the fort; he was ashamed to return to Kābul with nothing effected; moreover he was in the fetters of love. He therefore wrote in friendly fashion to Malik Aḥmad and asked for the daughter of Shāh Manṣūr, son of Shāh Sulaimān. Great objection was made and earlier misfortunes accruing to Yūsuf-zāī chiefs who had given daughters to Aūlūgh Beg and Sl. Wais (Khān Mīrzā?) were quoted. They even said they had no daughter to give. Bābur replied with a "beautiful" royal letter, told of his visit disguised to Shāh Manṣūr's house, of his seeing Bībī Mubāraka and as token of the truth of his story, asked them to search for the food he had hidden. They searched and found. Aḥmad and Manṣūr were still averse, but the tribesmen urged that as before they had always made sacrifice for the tribe so should they do now, for by giving the daughter in marriage, they would save the tribe from Bābur's anger. The Maliks then said that it should be done "for the good of the tribe".

When their consent was made known to Bābur, the drums of joy were beaten and preparations were made for the marriage; presents were sent to the bride, a sword of his also, and the two Maliks started out to escort her. They are said to have come from Thana by M'amūra (?), crossed the river at Chakdara, taken a narrow road between two hills and past Talāsh-village to the back of Tīrī (?) where the Pādshāh's escort met them. The Maliks returned, spent one night at Chakdara and next morning reached their homes at the Mahūra *sangur*.

Meanwhile Runa the nurse who had control of Malik Manṣūr's household, with two other nurses and many male and female servants, went on with Bībī Mubāraka to the royal camp. The bride was set down with all honour at a large tent in the middle of the camp.

That night and on the following day the wives of the officers came to visit her but she paid them no attention. So, they said to one another as they were returning to their tents, "Her beauty is beyond question, but she has shewn us no kindness, and has not spoken to us; we do not know what mystery there is about her."

Now Bībī Mubāraka had charged her servants to let her know when the Pādshāh was approaching in order that she might receive him according to Malik Aḥmad's instructions. They said to her, "That was the pomp just now of the Pādshāh's going to prayers at the general mosque." That same day after the Mid-day Prayer, the Pādshāh went towards her tent. Her servants informed her, she immediately left her divan and advancing, lighted up the carpet by her presence, and stood respectfully with folded hands. When the Pādshāh entered, she bowed herself before him. But her face remained entirely covered. At length the Pādshāh seated himself on the divan and said to her, "Come Afghāniya, be seated." Again she bowed before him, and stood as before. A second time he said, "Afghāniya, be seated." Again she prostrated herself before him and came a little nearer, but still stood. Then the Pādshāh pulled the veil from her face and beheld incomparable beauty. He was entranced, he said again, "O, Afghāniya, sit down." Then she bowed herself again, and said, "I have a petition to make. If an order be given, I will make it." The Pādshāh said kindly, "Speak." Whereupon she with both hands took up her dress and said, "Think that the whole Yūsuf-zāī tribe is enfolded in my skirt, and pardon their offences for my sake." Said the Pādshāh, "I forgive the Yūsuf-zāī all their offences in thy presence, and cast them all into thy skirt. Hereafter I shall have no ill-feeling to the Yūsuf-zāī." Again she bowed before him; the Pādshāh took her hand and led her to the divan.

When the Afternoon Prayer time came and the Pādshāh rose from the divan to go to prayers, Bībī Mubāraka jumped up and fetched him his shoes.[2798] He put them on and said very pleasantly, "I am extremely pleased with you and your tribe and I have pardoned them all for your sake." Then he said with a smile, "We know it was Malik Aḥmad taught you all these ways." He then went to prayers and the Bībī remained to say hers in the tent.

After some days the camp moved from Dīārūn and proceeded by Bajaur and Tankī to Kābul.[2799]...

Bībī Mubāraka, the Blessed Lady, is often mentioned by Gul-badan; she had no children; and lived an honoured life, as her chronicler says, until the beginning of Akbar's reign, when she died. Her brother Mīr Jamāl rose to honour under Bābur, Humāyūn and Akbar.

L.—ON MĀHĪM'S ADOPTION OF HIND-ĀL.

The passage quoted below about Māhīm's adoption of the unborn Hind-āl we have found so far only in Kehr's transcript of the *Bābur-nāma* (*i.e.* the St. Petersburg Foreign Office Codex). Ilminsky reproduced it (Kāsān imprint p. 281) and de Courteille translated it (ii, 45), both with endeavour at emendation. It is interpolated in Kehr's MS. at the wrong place, thus indicating that it was once marginal or apart from the text.

I incline to suppose the whole a note made by Humāyūn, although part of it might be an explanation made by Bābur, at a later date, of an over-brief passage in his diary. Of such passages there are several instances. What is strongly against its being Bābur's where otherwise it might be his, is that Māhīm, as he always calls her simply, is there written of as Ḥaẓrat Wālida, Royal Mother and with the honorific plural. That plural Bābur uses for his own mother (dead 14 years before 925 AH.) and never for Māhīm. The note is as follows:—

"The explanation is this:—As up to that time those of one birth (*tūqqān*, womb) with him (Humāyūn), that is to say a son Bār-būl, who was younger than he but older than the rest, and three daughters, Mihr-jān and two others, died in childhood, he had a great wish for one of the same birth with him.[2800] I had said 'What it would have been if there had been one of the same birth with him!' (Humāyūn). Said the Royal Mother, 'If Dil-dār Āghācha bear a son, how is it if I take him and rear him?' 'It is very good' said I."

So far doubtfully *might* be Bābur's but it may be Humāyūn's written as a note for Bābur. What follows appears to be by some-one who knew the details of Māhīm's household talk and was in Kābul when Dil-dār's child was taken from her.

"Seemingly women have the custom of taking omens in the following way:—When they have said, 'Is it to be a boy? is it to be a girl?' they write 'Alī or Ḥasan on one of two pieces of paper and Fāṭima on the other, put each paper into a ball of clay and throw both into a bowl of water. Whichever opens first is taken as an omen; if the man's, they say a man-child will be born; if the woman's, a girl will be born. They took the omen; it came out a man."

"On this glad tidings we at once sent letters off.[2801] A few days later God's mercy bestowed a son. Three days before the news[2802] and three days after the birth, they[2803] took the child from its mother, (she) willy-nilly, brought it to our house[2804] and took it in their charge. When we sent the news of the birth, Bhīra was being taken. They named him Hind-āl for a good omen and benediction."[2805]

The whole may be Humāyūn's, and prompted by a wish to remove an obscurity his father had left and by sentiment stirred through reminiscence of a cherished childhood.

Whether Humāyūn wrote the whole or not, how is it that the passage appears only in the Russian group of Bāburiana?

An apparent answer to this lies in the following little mosaic of circumstances:—The St. Petersburg group of Bāburiana[2806] is linked to Kāmrān's own copy of the *Bābur-nāma* by having with it a letter of Bābur to Kāmrān and also what *may be* a note indicating its passage into Humāyūn's hands (JRAS 1908 p. 830). If it did so pass, a note by Humāyūn may have become associated with it, in one of several obvious ways. This would be at a date earlier than that of the Elphinstone MS. and would explain why it is found in Russia and not in Indian MSS.[2807]

M.—ON THE TERM *BAḤRĪ QŪṬĀS.*

That the term *baḥrī qūṭās* is interpreted by Meninski, Erskine, and de Courteille in senses so widely differing as *equus maritimus*, mountain-cow, and *bœuf vert de mer* is due, no doubt, to their writing when the *qūṭās*, the yāk, was less well known than it now is.

The word *qūṭās* represents both the yāk itself and its neck-tassel and tail. Hence Meninski explains it by *nodus fimbriatus ex cauda seu crinibus equi maritimi.* His "sea-horse" appears to render *baḥrī qūṭās*, and is explicable by the circumstance that the same purposes are served by horse-tails and by yāk-tails and tassels, namely, with both, standards are fashioned, horse-equipage is ornamented or perhaps furnished with fly-flappers, and the ordinary hand-fly-flappers are made, *i.e.* the *chowries* of Anglo-India.

Erskine's "mountain-cow" (*Memoirs* p. 317) may well be due to his *munshī's* giving the yāk an alternative name, *viz.* *Kosh-gau* (Vigne) or *Khāsh-gau* (Ney Elias), which appears to mean mountain-cow (cattle, oxen).[2808]

De Courteille's *Dictionary* p. 422, explains *qūtās* (*qūṭās*) as *bœuf marin* (*baḥrī qūṭās*) and his *Mémoires* ii, 191, renders Bābur's *baḥrī qūṭās* by *bœuf vert de mer* (f. 276, p. 490 and n. 8).

The term *baḥrī qūṭās* could be interpreted with more confidence if one knew where the seemingly Arabic-Turkī compound originated.[2809] Bābur uses it in Hindūstān where the neck-tassel and the tail of the domestic yāk are articles of commerce, and where, as also probably in Kābul, he will have known of the same class of yāk as a saddle-animal and as a beast of burden into Kashmīr and other border-lands of sufficient altitude to allow its survival. A part of its wide Central Asian habitat abutting on Kashmīr is Little Tibet, through which flows the upper Indus and in which tame yāk are largely bred, Skardo being a place specially mentioned by travellers as having them plentifully. This suggests that the term *baḥrī qūṭās* is due to the great river (*baḥr*) and that those of which Bābur wrote in Hindūstān were from Little Tibet and its great river. But *baḥrī* may apply to another region where also the domestic yāk abounds, that of the great lakes, inland seas such as Pangong, whence the yāk comes and goes between *e.g.* Yārkand and the Hindūstān border.

The second suggestion, *viz.* that "*baḥrī qūṭās*" refers to the habitat of the domestic yāk in lake and marsh lands of high altitude (the wild yāk also but, as Tibetan, it is less likely to be concerned here) has support in Dozy's account of the *baḥrī* falcon, a bird mentioned also by Abū'l-faẓl amongst sporting birds (*Āyīn-i-akbarī*, Blochmann's trs. p. 295):—"*Baḥrī, espèce de faucon le meilleur pour les oiseaux de marais. Ce renseignment explique peut-être l'origine du mot. Marguerite en donne la même etymologie que Tashmend et le Père*

Guagix. Selon lui ce faucon aurait été appelé ainsi parce qu'il vient de l'autre côté de la mer, mais peut-être dériva-t-il de baḥrī dans le sens de marais, flaque, étang."

Dr. E. Denison Ross' *Polyglot List of Birds* (*Memoirs of the Asiatic Society of Bengal* ii, 289) gives to the *Qarā Qīrghāwal* (Black pheasant) the synonym "Sea-pheasant", this being the literal translation of its Chinese name, and quotes from the Manchū-Chinese "Mirror" the remark that this is a black pheasant but called "sea-pheasant" to distinguish it from other black ones.

It may be observed that Bābur writes of the yāk once only and then of the *baḥrī qūṭās* so that there is no warrant from him for taking the term to apply to the wild yāk. His cousin and contemporary Ḥaidar Mīrzā, however, mentions the wild yāk twice and simply as the wild *qūṭās*.

The following are random gleanings about "*baḥrī*" and the yāk:—

(1) An instance of the use of the Persian equivalent *daryā'ī* of *baḥrī*, sea-borne or over-sea, is found in the *Akbar-nāma* (Bib. Ind. ed. ii, 216) where the African elephant is described as *fīl-i-daryā'ī.*

(2) In Egypt the word *baḥrī* has acquired the sense of northern, presumably referring to what lies or is borne across its northern sea, the Mediterranean.

(3) Vigne (*Travels in Kashmīr* ii, 277-8) warns against confounding the *qūch-qār i.e.* the gigantic *moufflon*, Pallas' *Ovis ammon*, with the *Kosh-gau*, the cow of the Kaucasus, *i.e.* the yāk. He says, "Kaucasus (*hodie* Hindū-kush) was originally from Kosh, and Kosh is applied occasionally as a prefix, *e.g. Kosh-gau*, the yāk or ox of the mountain or Kaucasus." He wrote from Skardo in Little Tibet and on the upper Indus. He gives the name of the female yāk as *yāk-mo* and of the half-breeds with common cows as *bẕch*, which class he says is common and of "all colours".

(4) Mr. Ney Elias' notes (*Tārīkh-i-rashīdī* trs. pp. 302 and 466) on the *qūṭās* are of great interest. He gives the following synonymous names for the wild yāk, *Bos Poëphagus*, *Khāsh-gau*, the Tibetan yāk or Dong.

(5) Hume and Henderson (*Lāhor to Yārkand* p. 59) write of the numerous black yāk-hair tents seen round the Pangong Lake, of fine saddle yāks, and of the tame ones as being some white or brown but mostly black.

(6) Olufsen's *Through the Unknown Pamirs* (p. 118) speaks of the large numbers of *Bos grunniens* (yāk) domesticated by the Kirghiz in the Pamirs.

(7) Cf. Gazetteer of India *s.n.* yāk.

(8) Shaikh Zain applies the word *baḥrī* to the porpoise, when paraphrasing the *Bābur-nāma* f. 281*b*.

N.—NOTES ON A FEW BIRDS.

In attempting to identify some of the birds of Bābur's lists difficulty arises from the variety of names provided by the different tongues of the region concerned, and also in some cases by the application of one name to differing birds. The following random gleanings enlarge and, in part, revise some earlier notes and translations of Mr. Erskine's and my own. They are offered as material for the use of those better acquainted with bird-lore and with Himālayan dialects.

a. Concerning the lūkha, lūja, lūcha, kūja (f.135 and f.278*b*).

The nearest word I have found to *lūkha* and its similars is *likkh*, a florican (Jerdon, ii, 615), but the florican has not the chameleon colours of the *lūkha* (var.). As Bābur when writing in Hindūstān, uses such "book-words" as Ar. *baḥrī* (*qūṭās*) and Ar. *bū-qalamūn* (chameleon), it would not be strange if his name for the "*lūkha*" bird represented Ar. *awja*, very beautiful, or connected with Ar. *loḥ*, shining splendour.

The form *kūja* is found in Ilminsky's imprint p.361 (*Mémoires* ii, 198, *koudjeh*).

What is confusing to translators is that (as it now seems to me) Bābur appears to use the name *kabg-i-darī* in both passages (f.135 and f.278*b*) to represent two birds; (1) he compares the *lūkha* as to size with the *kabg-i-darī* of the Kābul region, and (2) for size and colour with that of Hindūstān. But the bird, of the Western Himālayas known by the name *kabg-i-darī* is the Himālayan snow-cock, *Tetraogallus himālayensis*, Turkī, *aūlār* and in the Kābul region, *chūūrtika* (f.249, Jerdon, ii, 549-50); while the *kabg-i-darī* (syn. *chikor*) of Hindūstān, whether of hill or plain, is one or more of much smaller birds.

The snow-cock being 28 inches in length, the *lūkha* bird must be of this size. Such birds as to size and plumage of changing colour are the *Lophophori* and *Trapagons*, varieties of which are found in places suiting Bābur's account of the *lūkha*.

It may be noted that the Himālayan snow-cock is still called *kabg-i-darī* in Afghānistān (Jerdon, ii, 550) and in Kashmīr (Vigne's *Travels in Kashmīr* ii, 18). As its range is up to 18,000 feet, its Persian name describes it correctly whether read as "of the mountains" (*darī*), or as "royal" (*darī*) through its splendour.

I add here the following notes of Mr. Erskine's, which I have not quoted already where they occur (cf. f. 135 and f. 278*b*):—

On f. 135, "*lokheh*" is said to mean *hill-chikor.*

On f. 278*b*, to "*lūjeh*", "The Persian has *lūkheh.*"

” to "*kepki durri*", "The *kepkī deri*, or *durri* is much larger than the common *kepk* of Persia and is peculiar to Khorāsān. It is said to be a beautiful bird. The common *kepk* of Persia and Khorāsān is the *hill-chikor* of India."

” to "higher up", "The *lujeh* may be the *chikor* of the plains which Hunter calls bartavelle or Greek partridge."

The following corrections are needed about my own notes:—(1) on f. 135 (p. 213) n. 7 is wrongly referred; it belongs to the first word, *viz. kabg-i-darī*, of p. 214; (2) on f. 279 (p. 496) n. 2 should refer to the second *kabg-i-darī.*

b. Birds called mūnāl (var. monāl and moonaul).

Yule writing in *Hobson Jobson* (p. 580) of the "*moonaul*" which he identifies as *Lophophorus Impeyanus*, queries whether, on grounds he gives, the word *moonaul* is connected etymologically with Sanscrit *muni*, an "eremite". In continuation of his topic, I give here the names of other birds called *mūnāl*, which I have noticed in various ornithological works while turning their pages for other information.

Besides *L. Impeyanus* and *Trapagon Ceriornis satyra* which Yule mentions as called "*moonaul*", there are *L. refulgens*, *mūnāl* and *Ghūr* (mountain)-*mūnāl*; *Trapagon Ceriornis satyra*, called *mūnāl* in Nipāl; *T. C. melanocephalus*, called *sing* (horned)-*mūnāl* in the N.W. Himālayas; *T. himālayensis*, the *jer-* or *cher-mūnāl* of the same region, known also as *chikor*, and *Lerwa nevicola*, the snow-partridge known in Garhwal as *Quoir-* or *Qūr-mūnāl.* Do all these birds behave in such a way as to suggest that *mūnāl* may imply the individual isolation related by Jerdon of *L. Impeyanus*, "In the autumnal and winter months numbers are generally collected in the same quarter of the forest, though often so widely scattered that each bird appears to be alone?" My own search amongst vocabularies of hill-dialects for the meaning of the word has been unsuccessful, spite of the long range *mūnāls* in the Himālayas.

c. Concerning the word chūrtika, chourtka.

Jerdon's entry (ii, 549, 554) of the name *chourtka* as a synonym of *Tetraogallus himālayensis* enables me to fill a gap I have left on f. 249 (p. 491 and n. 6),[2810] with the name Himālayan snow-cock, and to allow Bābur's statement to be that he, in January 1520 AD. when coming down from the

Bād-i-pīch pass, saw many snow-cocks. The *Memoirs* (p.282) has "*chikors*", which in India is a synonym for *kabg-i-darī*; the *Mémoires* (ii, 122) has *sauterelles*, but this meaning of *chūrtika* does not suit wintry January. That month would suit for the descent from higher altitudes of snow-cocks. Griffith, a botanist who travelled in Afghānistān *cir.* 1838 AD., saw myriads of *cicadæ* between Qilat-i-ghilzai and Ghazni, but the month was July.

d. On the qūṭān (f. 142, p. 224; *Memoirs*, p. 153; *Mémoires* ii, 313).

Mr. Erskine for *qūṭān* enters *khawāṣil* [gold-finch] which he will have seen interlined in the Elphinstone Codex (f. 109*b*) in explanation of *qūṭān*.

Shaikh Effendi (Kunos' ed., p. 139) explains *qūṭān* to be the gold-finch, *Steiglitz*.

Ilminsky's *qūtān* (p. 175) is translated by M. de Courteille as *pélicane* and certainly some copies of the 2nd Persian translation [Muḥ. *Shīrāzī's* p. 90] have *ḥawāṣil*, pelican.

The pelican would class better than the small finch with the herons and egrets of Bābur's trio; it also would appear a more likely bird to be caught "with the cord".

That Bābur's *qūṭān* (*ḥawāṣil*) migrated in great numbers is however against supposing it to be *Pelicanus onocrotatus* which is seen in India during the winter, because it appears there in moderate numbers only, and Blanford with other ornithologists states that no western pelican migrates largely into India.

Perhaps the *qūṭān* was Linnæus' *Pelicanus carbo* of which one synonym is *Carbo comoranus*, the cormorant, a bird seen in India in large numbers of both the large and small varieties. As cormorants are not known to breed in that country, they will have migrated in the masses Bābur mentions.

A translation matter falls to mention here:—After saying that the *aūqār* (grey heron), *qarqara* (egret), and *qūtān* (cormorant) are taken with the cord, Bābur says that this method of bird-catching is unique (*bū nūḥ qūsh tūtmāq ghair muqarrar dūr*) and describes it. The Persian text omits to translate the *tūtmāq* (by *P. giriftan*); hence Erskine (*Mems.* p. 153) writes, "The last mentioned fowl" (*i.e.* the *qūṭān*) "is rare," notwithstanding Bābur's statement that all three of the birds he names are caught in masses. De Courteille (p. 313) writes, as though only of the *qūtān*, "*ces derniers toutefois ne se prennent qu'accidentelment*," perhaps led to do so by knowledge of the circumstance that *Pelicanus onocrotatus* is rare in India.

O.—NOTES BY HUMĀYŪN ON SOME HINDŪSTĀN FRUITS.

The following notes, which may be accepted as made by Humāyūn and in the margin of the archetype of the Elphinstone Codex, are composed in Turkī which differs in diction from his father's but is far closer to that classic model than is that of the producer [Jahāngīr?] of the "Fragments" (Index *s.n.*). Various circumstances make the notes difficult to decipher *verbatim* and, unfortunately, when writing in Jan. 1917, I am unable to collate with its original in the Advocates Library, the copy I made of them in 1910.

> *a. On the kadhil, jack-fruit, Artocarpus integrifolia* (f. 283*b*, p. 506; Elphinstone MS. f. 235*b*).[2811]

The contents of the note are that the strange-looking pumpkin (*qar'*, which is also Ibn Batuta's word for the fruit), yields excellent white juice, that the best fruit grows from the roots of the tree,[2812] that many such grow in Bengal, and that in Bengal and Dihli there grows a *kadhil*-tree covered with hairs (*Artocarpus hirsuta*?).

> *b. On the amrit-phal, mandarin-orange, Citrus aurantium* (f. 287, p. 512; Elphinstone Codex, f. 238*b*, l. 12).

The interest of this note lies in its reference to Bābur.

A Persian version of it is entered, without indication of what it is or of who was its translator, in one of the volumes of Mr. Erskine's manuscript remains, now in the British Museum (Add. 26,605, p. 88). Presumably it was made by his Turkish *munshi* for his note in the Memoirs (p. 329).

Various difficulties oppose the translation of the Turkī note; it is written into the text of the Elphinstone Codex in two instalments, neither of them in place, the first being interpolated in the account of the *amil-bīd* fruit, the second in that of the *jāsūn* flower; and there are verbal difficulties also. The Persian translation is not literal and in some particulars Mr. Erskine's rendering of this differs from what the Turkī appears to state.

The note is, tentatively, as follows:[2813]—"His honoured Majesty Firdaus-makān[2814]—may God make his proof clear!—did not favour the *amrit-phal*;[2815] as he considered it insipid,[2816] he likened it to the mild-flavoured[2817] orange and did not make choice of it. So much was the mild-flavoured orange despised that if any person had disgusted (him) by insipid flattery(?) he used to say, 'He is like orange-juice.'"[2818]

"The *amrit-phal* is one of the very good fruits. Though its juice is not relishing (? *chūchūq*), it is extremely pleasant-drinking. Later on, in my own time, its real merit became known. Its tartness may be that of the orange (*nāranj*)and *lemu*."[2819]

The above passage is followed, in the text of the Elphinstone Codex, by Bābur's account of the *jāsūn* flower, and into this a further instalment of Humāyūn's notes is interpolated, having opposite its first line the marginal remark, "This extra note, seemingly made by Humāyūn Pādshāh, the scribe has mistakenly written into the text." Whether its first sentence refer to the *amrit-phal* or to the *amil-bīd* must be left for decision to those well acquainted with the orange-tribe. It is obscure in my copy and abbreviated in its Persian translation; summarized it may state that when the fruit is unripe, its acidity is harmful to the digestion, but that it is very good when ripe.—The note then continues as below:—

c. The kāmila, H. kaunlā, the orange.[2820]

"There are in Bengal two other fruits of the acid kind. Though the *amrit-phal* be not agreeable, they have resemblance to it (?)."

"One is the *kāmila* which may be as large as an orange (*nāranj*); some took it to be a large *nārangī* (orange) but it is much pleasanter eating than the *nārangī* and is understood not to have the skin of that (fruit)."

d. The samṭara.[2821]

"The other is the *samṭara* which is larger than the orange (*nāranj*) but is not tart; unlike the *amrit-phal* it is not of poor flavour (*kam maza*) or little relish (*chūchūk*). In short a better fruit is not seen. It is good to see, good to eat, good to digest. One does not forget it. If it be there, no other fruit is chosen. Its peel may be taken off by the hand. However much of the fruit be eaten, the heart craves for it again. Its juice does not soil the hand at all. Its skin separates easily from its flesh. It may be taken during and after food. In Bengal the *samṭara* is rare (*ghārib*) (or excellent, *'asīz*). It is understood to grow in one village Sanārgām (Sonargaon) and even therein a special quarter. There seems to be no fruit so entirely good as the *samṭara* amongst fruits of its class or, rather, amongst fruits of all kinds."

Corrigendum:—In my note on the *turunj bajāurī* (p. 511, n. 3) for *bijaurā* read *bījaurā*; and on p. 510, l. 2, for *palm* read *fingers*.

Addendum:—p. 510, l. 5. After *yūsūnlūk* add:—"The natives of Hindūstān when not wearing their ear-rings, put into the large ear-ring holes, slips of the palm-leaf bought in the bāzārs, ready for the purpose. The trunk of this tree is handsomer and more stately than that of the date."

P.—REMARKS ON BĀBUR'S REVENUE LIST (FOL. 292).

a. Concerning the date of the List.

The Revenue List is the last item of Bābur's account of Hindūstān and, with that account, is found *s.a.* 932 AH., manifestly too early, (1) because it includes districts and their revenues which did not come under Bābur's authority until subdued in his Eastern campaigns of 934 and 935 AH., (2) because Bābur's statement is that the "countries" of the List "are *now* in my possession" (*in loco* p. 520).

The List appears to be one of revenues realized in 936 or 937 AH. and not one of assessment or estimated revenue, (1) because Bābur's wording states as a fact that the revenue was 52 *krūrs*; (2) because the Persian heading of the (Persian) List is translatable as "Revenue (*jama'*)[2822] of Hindūstān from what has so far come under the victorious standards".

b. The entry of the List into European Literature.

Readers of the L. and E. *Memoirs of Bābur* are aware that it does not contain the Revenue List (p. 334). The omission is due to the absence of the List from the Elphinstone Codex and from the 'Abdu'r-raḥīm Persian translation. Since the *Memoirs of Bābur* was published in 1826 AD., the List has come from the *Bābur-nāma* into European literature by three channels.

Of the three the one used earliest is Shaikh Zain's *Ṭabaqāt-i-bāburī* which is a Persian paraphrase of part of Bābur's Hindūstān section. This work provided Mr. Erskine with what he placed in his *History of India* (London 1854, i, 540, Appendix D), but his manuscript, now B.M. Add. 26,202, is not the best copy of Shaikh Zain's book, being of far less importance than B.M. Or. 1999, [as to which more will be said.][2823]

The second channel is Dr. Ilminsky's imprint of the Turkī text (Kāsān 1857, p. 379), which is translated by the *Mémoires de Bāber* (Paris 1871, ii, 230).

The third channel is the Ḥaidarābād Codex, in the English translation of which [*in loco*] the List is on p. 521.

Shaikh Zain may have used Bābur's autograph manuscript for his paraphrase and with it the Revenue List. His own autograph manuscript was copied in 998 AH. (1589-90 AD.) by Khwānd-amīr's grandson 'Abdu'l-lāh who may be the scribe "Mīr 'Abdu'l-lāh" of the *Āyīn-i-akbarī* (Blochmann's trs. p. 109). 'Abdu'l-lāh's transcript (from which a portion is now absent,) after having been in Sir Henry Elliot's possession, has become B.M. Or. 1999. It is noticed briefly by Professor Dowson (*l.c.* iv, 288), but he cannot have observed that the "old, worm-eaten" little volume contains Bābur's Revenue List, since he does not refer to it.

c. Agreement and variation in copies of the List.

The figures in the two copies (Or. 1999 and Add. 26,202) of the *Ṭabaqāt-i-bāburī* are in close agreement. They differ, however, from those in the Ḥaidarābād Codex, not only in a negligible unit and a ten of *tankas* but in having 20,000 more *tankas* from Oudh and Baraich and 30 *laks* of *tankas* more from Trans-sutlej.

The figures in the two copies of the *Bābur-nāma*, *viz.* the Ḥaidarābād Codex and the Kehr-Ilminsky imprint are not in agreement throughout, but are identical in opposition to the variants (20,000 *t.* and 30 *l.*) mentioned above. As the two are independent, being collateral descendants of Bābur's original papers, the authority of the Ḥaidarābād Codex in the matter of the List is still further enhanced.

d. Varia.

(1) The place-names of the List are all traceable, whatever their varied forms. About the entry L:knū [or L:knūr] and B:ks:r [or M:ks:r] a difficulty has been created by its variation in manuscripts, not only in the List but where the first name occurs *s.a.* 934 and 935 AH. In the Ḥaidarābād List and in that of Or. 1999 L:knūr is clearly written and may represent (approximately) modern Shahābād in Rāmpūr. Erskine and de Courteille, however, have taken it to be Lakhnau in Oudh. [The distinction of Lakhnaur from Lakhnau in the historical narrative is discussed in Appendix T.]

(2) It may be noted, as of interest, that the name Sarwār is an abbreviation of Sarjūpār which means "other side of Sarjū" (Sarū, Goghrā; E. and D.'s H. of I. i, 56, n.4).

(3) Rūp-narā[:i]n (Deo or Dev) is mentioned in Ajodhya Prasad's short history of Tirhut and Darbhanga, the *Gulzār-i-Bihār* (Calcutta 1869, Cap. v, 88) as the 9th of the Brahman rulers of Tirhut and as having reigned for 25 years, from 917 to 942 *Faslī*(?). If the years were Ḥijrī, 917-42 AH. would be 1511-1535.[2824]

(4) Concerning the *tanka* the following modern description is quoted from Mr. R. Shaw's *High Tartary* (London 1871, p. 464) "The *tanga*" (or *tanka*) "is a nominal coin, being composed of 25 little copper cash, with holes pierced in them and called *dahcheen.* These are strung together and the quantity of them required to make up the value of one of these silver ingots" ("*kooroos*

or *yamboo*, value nearly £17") "weighs a considerable amount. I once sent to get change for a *kooroos*, and my servants were obliged to charter a donkey to bring it home."

(5) The following interesting feature of Shaikh Zain's *Ṭabaqāt-i-bāburī* has been mentioned to me by my husband:—Its author occasionally reproduces Bābur's Turkī words instead of paraphrasing them in Persian, and does this for the noticeable passage in which Bābur records his dissatisfied view of Hindūstān (f. 290*b*, *in loco* p. 518), prefacing his quotation with the remark that it is best and will be nearest to accuracy not to attempt translation but to reproduce the Pādshāh's own words. The main interest of the matter lies in the motive for reproducing the *ipsissima verba*. Was that motive deferential? Did the revelation of feeling and opinion made in the quoted passage clothe it with privacy so that Shaikh Zain reserved its perusal from the larger public of Hindūstān who might read Persian but not Turkī? Some such motive would explain the insertion untranslated of Bābur's letters to Humāyūn and to Khwāja Kalān which are left in Turkī by 'Abdu'r-raḥīm Mīrzā.[2825]

Q.—CONCERNING THE "RĀMPŪR DĪWĀN".

Pending the wide research work necessary to interpret Bābur's Hindūstān poems which the Rāmpūr manuscript preserves, the following comments, some tentative and open to correction, may carry further in making the poems publicly known, what Dr. E. Denison Ross has effected by publishing his Facsimile of the manuscript.[2826] It is legitimate to associate comment on the poems with the *Bābur-nāma* because many of them are in it with their context of narrative; most, if not all, connect with it; some without it, would be dull and vapid.

a. An authorized English title.

The contents of the Rāmpūr MS. are precisely what Bābur describes sending to four persons some three weeks after the date attached to the manuscript,[2827] *viz.* "the Translation and whatnot of poems made on coming to Hindūstān";[2828] and a similar description may be meant in the curiously phrased first clause of the colophon, but without mention of the Translation (of the *Wālidiyyah-risāla*).[2829] Hence, if the poems, including the Translation, became known as the *Hindūstān Poems* or *Poems made in Hindūstān*, such title would be justified by their author's words. Bābur does not call the Hindūstān poems a *dīwān* even when, as in the above quotation, he speaks of them apart from his versified translation of the Tract. In what has come down to us of his autobiography, he applies the name *Dīwān* to poems of his own once only, this in 925 AH. (f. 237*b*) when he records sending "my *dīwān*" to Pūlād Sl. *Aūzbeg.*

b. The contents of the Rāmpūr MS.

There are three separate items of composition in the manuscript, marked as distinct from one another by having each its ornamented frontispiece, each its scribe's sign (*mīm*) of Finis, each its division from its neighbour by a space without entry. The first and second sections bear also the official sign [*ṣaḥḥ*] that the copy has been inspected and found correct.

(1) The first section consists of Bābur's metrical translation of Khwāja 'Ubaidu'l-lāh *Aḥrārī's Parental Tract* (*Wālidiyyah-risāla*), his prologue in which are his reasons for versifying the Tract and his epilogue which gives thanks for accomplishing the task. It ends with the date 935 (Ḥai. MS. f. 346). Below this are *mīm* and *ṣaḥḥ*, the latter twice; they are in the scribe's handwriting, and thus make against supposing that Bābur wrote down this copy of the Tract or its archetype from which the official *ṣaḥḥ* will have

been copied. Moreover, spite of bearing two vouchers of being a correct copy, the Translation is emended, in a larger script which may be that of the writer of the marginal quatrain on the last page of the [Rāmpūr] MS. and there attested by Shāh-i-jahān as Bābur's autograph entry. His also may have been the now expunged writing on the half-page left empty of text at the end of the Tract. Expunged though it be, fragments of words are visible.[2830]

(2) The second section has in its frontispiece an inscription illegible (to me) in the Facsimile. It opens with a *masnawī* of 41 couplets which is followed by a *ghazel* and numerous poems in several measures, down to a triad of rhymed couplets (*matla*?), the whole answering to descriptions of a *Dīwān* without formal arrangement. After the last couplet are *mīm* and *ṣaḥḥ* in the scribe's hand-writing, and a blank quarter-page. Mistakes in this section have been left uncorrected, which supports the view that its *ṣaḥḥ* avouches the accuracy of its archetype and not its own.[2831]

(3) The third section shows no inscription on its frontispiece. It opens with the *masnawī* of eight couplets, found also in the *Bābur-nāma* (f. 312), one of earlier date than many of the poems in the second section. It is followed by three *rubā'ī* which complete the collection of poems made in Hindūstān. A prose passage comes next, describing the composition and transposition-in-metre of a couplet of 16 feet, with examples in three measures, the last of which ends in l. 4 of the photograph.—While fixing the date of this metrical game, Bābur incidentally allows that of his *Treatise on Prosody* to be inferred from the following allusive words:—"When going to Saṃbhal (f. 330*b*) in the year (933 AH.) after the conquest of Hindūstān (932 AH.), two years after writing the *'Arūẓ*, I composed a couplet of 16 feet."—From this the date of the Treatise is seen to be 931 AH., some two years later than that of the *Mubīn*. The above metrical exercise was done about the same time as another concerning which a Treatise was written, viz. that mentioned on f. 330*b*, when a couplet was transposed into 504 measures (Section *f*, p. lxv).—The Facsimile, it will be noticed, shows something unusual in the last line of the prose passage on Plate XVIII B, where the scattering of the words suggests that the scribe was trying to copy page *per* page.

The colophon (which begins on l. 5 of the photograph) is curiously worded, as though the frequent fate of last pages had befallen its archetype, that of being mutilated and difficult for a scribe to make good; it suggests too that the archetype was verse.[2832] Its first clause, even if read as *Hind-stān jānibī 'aẓīmat qīlghānī* (i.e. not *qīlghālī*, as it can be read), has an indirectness unlike Bābur's corresponding "after coming to Hindūstān" (f. 357*b*), and is not definite; (2) *bū aīrdī* (these were) is not the complement suiting *aūl dūrūr* (those are); (3) Bābur does not use the form *dūrūr* in prose; (4) the undue space after *dūrūr* suggests connection with verse; (5) there is no final verb such as prose needs. The meaning, however, may be as follows:—The poems made after resolving on (the) Hindūstān parts (*jānibī?*) were these I have written down (*taḥrīr qīldīm*), and past events are those I have narrated (*taqrīr*) in the way that (*nī-chūk kīm*) (has been) written in these folios (*aūrāq*) and recorded in those sections (*ajzā'*).—From this it would appear that sections of the *Bābur-nāma* (f. 376*b*, p. 678) accompanied the Hindūstān poems to the recipient of the message conveyed by the colophon.

Close under the colophon stands *Ḥarara-hu Bābur* and the date Monday, Rabī' II. 15th 935 (Monday, December 27th 1528 AD.), the whole presumably brought over from the archetype. To the question whether a signature in the above form would be copied by a scribe, the Elphinstone Codex gives an affirmative answer by providing several examples of notes, made by Humāyūn in its archetype, so-signed and brought over either into its margin or interpolated in its text. Some others of Humāyūn's notes are not so-signed, the scribe merely saying they are Humāyūn Pādshāh's.—It makes against taking the above entry of Bābur's name to be an autograph signature, (1) that it is enclosed in an ornamented border, as indeed is the case wherever it occurs throughout the manuscript; (2) that it is followed by the scribe's *mīm*. [See end of following section.]

c. The marginal entries shown in the photograph.

The marginal note written length-wise by the side of the text is signed by Shāh-i-jahān and attests that the *rubā'ī* and the signature to which it makes reference are in Bābur's autograph hand-writing. His note translates as follows:—This quatrain and blessed name are in the actual hand-writing of that Majesty (*ān ḥaẓrat*) *Firdaus-makānī* Bābur Pādshāh *Ghāẓī*—May God make his proof clear!—Signed (*Ḥararā-hu*), Shāh-i-jahān son of Jahāngīr Pādshāh son of Akbar Pādshāh son of Humāyūn Pādshāh son of Bābur Pādshāh.[2833]

The second marginal entry is the curiously placed *rubā'ī*, which is now the only one on the page, and now has no signature attaching to it. It has the character of a personal message to the recipient of one of more books having identical contents. That these two entries are there while the text seems so clearly to be written by a scribe, is open to the explanation that when (as said about the colophon, p. lx) the rectangle of text was made good from a mutilated archetype, the original margin was placed round the *rifacimento*? This superposition would explain the entries and seal-like circles, discernible against a strong light, on the reverse of the margin only, through the *rifacimento* page. The upper edge of the rectangle shows sign that the margin has been adjusted to it [so far as one can judge from a photograph]. Nothing on the face of the margin hints that the text itself is autograph; the words of the colophon, *taḥrīr qīldīm* (*i.e.* I have written down) cannot hold good against the cumulative testimony that a scribe copied the whole manuscript.—The position of the last syllable [*nī*] of the *rubā'ī* shows that the signature below the colophon was on the margin before the diagonal couplet of the *rubā'ī* was written,—therefore when the margin was fitted, as it looks to have been fitted, to the *rifacimento*. If this be the order of the two entries [*i.e.* the small-hand signature and the diagonal couplet], Shāh-i-jahān's "blessed name" may represent the small-hand signature which certainly shows minute differences from the writing of the text of the MS. in the name Bābur (*q.v. passim* in the Rāmpūr MS.).

d. The Bāburī-khaṭṭ (Bābūr's script).

So early as 910 AH. the year of his conquest of Kābul, Bābur devised what was probably a variety of *nakhsh*, and called it the *Bāburī-khaṭṭ* (f. 144*b*), a name used later by Ḥaidar Mīrzā, Niẓāmu'd-dīn Aḥmad and 'Abdu'l-qādir *Badāyūnī*. He writes of it again (f. 179) *s.a.* 911 AH. when describing an interview had in 912 AH. with one of the Harāt Qāẓīs, at which the script was discussed, its specialities (*mufradāt*) exhibited to, and read by the Qāẓī who there and then wrote in it.[2834] In what remains to us of the *Bābur-nāma* it is not mentioned again till 935 AH. (fol. 357*b*) but at some intermediate date Bābur made in it a copy of the Qorān which he sent to Makka.[2835] In 935 AH. (f. 357*b*) it is mentioned in significant association with the despatch to each of four persons of a copy of the Translation (of the *Wālidiyyah-risāla*) and the Hindūstān poems, the significance of the association being that the simultaneous despatch with these copies of specimens of the *Bāburī-khaṯṯ* points to its use in the manuscripts, and at least in Hind-āl's case, to help given for reading novel forms in their text. The above are the only instances now found in the *Bābur-nāma* of mention of the script.

The little we have met with—we have made no search—about the character of the script comes from the *Abūshqa*, *s.n. sīghnāq*, in the following entry:—

Sīghnāq ber nū'ah khaṯṯ der Chaghatāīda khaṯṯ Bāburī u ghairī kibī ki Bābur Mīrzā ash'ār'nda kīlūr bait

Khūblār khaṯṯī naṣīb'ng būlmāsā Bābur nī tāng?

Bāburī khaṯṯī aīmās dūr khaṯṯ sīghnāqī mū dūr?[2836]

The old Osmanli-Turkish prose part of this appears to mean:—"*Sīghnāq* is a sort of hand-writing, in Chaghatāī the *Bāburī-khaṯṯ* and others resembling it, as appears in Bābur Mīrzā's poems. Couplet":—

Without knowing the context of the couplet I make no attempt to translate it because its words *khaṯṯ* or *khaṭ* and

sīghnāq lend themselves to the kind of pun (*īhām*) "which consists in the employment of a word or phrase having more than one appropriate meaning, whereby the reader is often left in doubt as to the real significance of the passage."[2837] The rest of the *rubā'ī* may be given [together with the six other quotations of Bābur's verse now known only through the *Abūshqa*], in early *Tazkirātu 'sh-shu'āra* of date earlier than 967 AH.

The root of the word *sīghnāq* will be *sīq*, pressed together, crowded, included, *etc.*; taking with this notion of compression, the explanations *feine Schrift* of Shaikh Effendi (Kunos) and Vambéry's *pétite écriture*, the Sīghnāqī and Bāburī Scripts are allowed to have been what that of the Rāmpūr MS. is, a small, compact, elegant hand-writing.—A town in the Caucasus named Sīghnākh, "*située à peu près à 800 mètres d'altitude, commença par être une forteresse et un lieu de refuge, car telle est la signification de son nom tartare.*"[2838] *Sīghnāqī* is given by de Courteille (Dict. p. 368) as meaning a place of refuge or shelter.

The *Bāburī-khaṯṯ* will be only one of the several hands Bābur is reputed to have practised; its description matches it with other niceties he took pleasure in, fine distinctions of eye and ear in measure and music.

e. Is the Rāmpūr MS. an example of the Bāburī-khaṯṯ?

Though only those well-acquainted with Oriental manuscripts dating before 910 AH. (1504 AD.) can judge whether novelties appear in the script of the Rāmpūr MS. and this particularly in its head-lines, there are certain grounds for thinking that though the manuscript be not Bābur's autograph, it may be in his script and the work of a specially trained scribe.

I set these grounds down because although the signs of a scribe's work on the manuscript seem clear, it is "locally" held to be Bābur's autograph. Has a tradition of its being in the *Bāburī-khaṯṯ* glided into its being in the *khaṯṯ-i-Bābur*? Several circumstances suggest that it may be written in the *Bāburī-khaṯṯ*:—(1) the script is specially associated with the four transcripts of the Hindūstān poems (f. 357*b*), for though many letters must have gone to his sons, some indeed are mentioned in the *Bābur-nāma*, it is only with the poems that specimens of it are recorded as sent; (2) another matter shows his personal interest in the arrangement of manuscripts, namely, that as he himself about a month after the four books had gone off, made a new ruler, particularly on account of the head-lines of the Translation, it may be inferred that he had made or had adopted the one he superseded, and that his plan of arranging the poems was the model for copyists; the Rāmpūr MS. bearing, in the Translation section, corrections which may be his own, bears also a date earlier than that at which the four gifts started; it has its headlines ill-arranged and has throughout 13 lines to the page; his new ruler had 11; (3) perhaps the words *taḥrīr qīldīm* used in the colophon of the Rāmpūr MS. should be read with their full connotation of careful and elegant writing, or, put modestly, as saying, "I wrote down in my best manner," which for poems is likely to be in the *Bāburī-khaṯṯ*.[2839]

Perhaps an example of Bābur's script exists in the colophon, if not in the whole of the *Mubīn* manuscript once owned by Berézine, by him used for his *Chréstomathie Turque*, and described by him as "unique". If this be the actual manuscript Bābur sent into Mā warā'u'n-nahr (presumably to Khwāja Aḥrārī's family), its colophon which is a personal message addressed to the recipients, is likely to be autograph.

f. Metrical amusements.

(1) Of two instances of metrical amusements belonging to the end of 933 AH. and seeming to have been the distractions of illness, one is a simple transposition "in the fashion of the circles" (*dawā'ir*) into three measures (Rāmpūr MS. Facsimile, Plate XVIII and p. 22); the other is difficult

because of the high number of 504 into which Bābur says (f. 330*b*) he cut up the following couplet:—

Gūz u qāsh u soz u tilīnī mū dī?

Qad u khadd u saj u bīlīnī mū dī?

All manuscripts agree in having 504, and Bābur wrote a tract (*risāla*) upon the transpositions.[2840] None of the modern treatises on Oriental Prosody allow a number so high to be practicable, but Maulānā Saifī of Bukhārā, of Bābur's own time (f. 180*b*) makes 504 seem even moderate, since after giving much detail about *rubā'ī* measures, he observes, "Some say there are 10,000" (*Arūẓ-i-Saifī*, Ranking's trs. p. 122). Presumably similar possibilities were open for the couplet in question. It looks like one made for the game, asks two foolish questions and gives no reply, lends itself to poetic license, and, if permutation of words have part in such a game, allows much without change of sense. Was Bābur's cessation of effort at 504 capricious or enforced by the exhaustion of possible changes? Is the arithmetical statement $9 \times 8 \times 7 = 504$ the formula of the practicable permutations?

(2) To improvise verse having a given rhyme and topic must have demanded quick wits and much practice. Bābur gives at least one example of it (f. 252*b*) but Jahāngīr gives a fuller and more interesting one, not only because a *rubā'ī* of Bābur's was the model but from the circumstances of the game:[2841]—It was in 1024 AH. (1615 AD.) that a letter reached him from Māwarā'u'n-nahr written by Khwāja Hāshim *Naqsh-bandī* [who by the story is shown to have been of Aḥrārī's line], and recounting the long devotion of his family to Jahāngīr's ancestors. He sent gifts and enclosed in his letter a copy of one of Bābur's quatrains which he said Ḥaẓrat Firdaus-makānī had written for Ḥaẓrat Khwājagī (Aḥrārī's eldest son; f. 36*b*, p. 62 n. 2). Jahāngīr quotes a final hemistich only, "*Khwājagīra mānda'īm, Khwājagīrā banda'īm*" and thereafter made an impromptu verse upon the one sent to him.

A curious thing is that the line he quotes is not part of the quatrain he answered, but belongs to another not appropriate for a message between *darwesh* and *pādshāh*, though likely to have been sent by Bābur to Khwājagī. I will quote both because the matter will come up again for who works on the Hindūstān poems.[2842]

(1) The quatrain from the *Hindūstān Poems* is:—

Dar hawā'ī nafs gumrah 'umr ẓāi' karda'īm [*kanda'īm*?];

Pesh ahl-i-allāh az af'āl-i-khūd sharmanda'īm;

Yak naẓr bā mukhlaṣān-i-khasta-dil farmā ki mā

Khwājagīrā mānda'īm u Khwājagīrā banda'īm.

(2) That from the *Akbar-nāma* is:—

Darweshānrā agarcha nah as khweshānīm,

Lek az dil u jān mu'taqid eshānīm;

Dūr ast magū'ī shāhī az darweshī,

Shāhīm walī banda-i-darweshānīm.

The greater suitability of the second is seen from Jahāngīr's answering impromptu for which by sense and rhyme it sets the model; the meaning, however, of the fourth line in each may be identical, namely, "I remain the ruler but am the servant of the *darwesh.*" Jahāngīr's impromptu is as follows:—

Āī ānki marā mihr-i-tū besh az besh ast,

Az daulat yād-i-būdat āī darwesh ast;

Chandānki'z muzh dahāt dilam shād shavad

Shadīm az ānki laṭif az ḥadd besh ast.

He then called on those who had a turn for verse to "speak one" *i.e.* to improvise on his own; it was done as follows:—

Dārīm agarcha shaghal-i-shāhī dar pesh,

Har laḥza kunīm yād-i-darweshān besh;

Gar shād shavad'z mā dil-i-yak darwesh,

Ānra shumarīm ḥaṣil-i-shāhī khwesh.

R.—CHANDĪRĪ AND GŪĀLĪĀR.

The courtesy of the Government of India enables me to reproduce from the *Archæological Survey Reports* of 1871, Sir Alexander Cunningham's plans of Chandīrī and Gūālīār, which illustrate Bābur's narrative on f. 333, p. 592, and f. 340, p. 607.

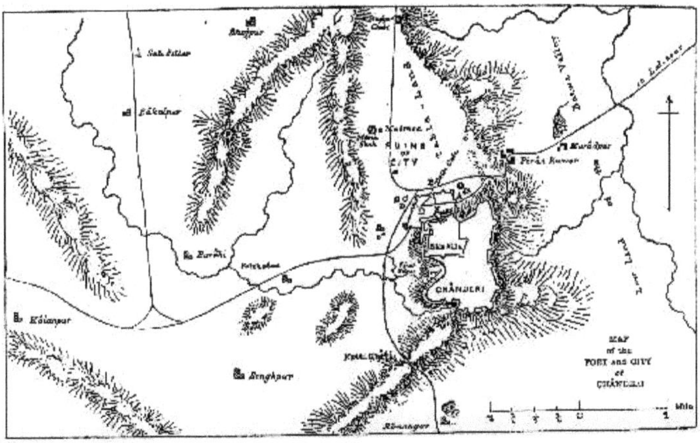

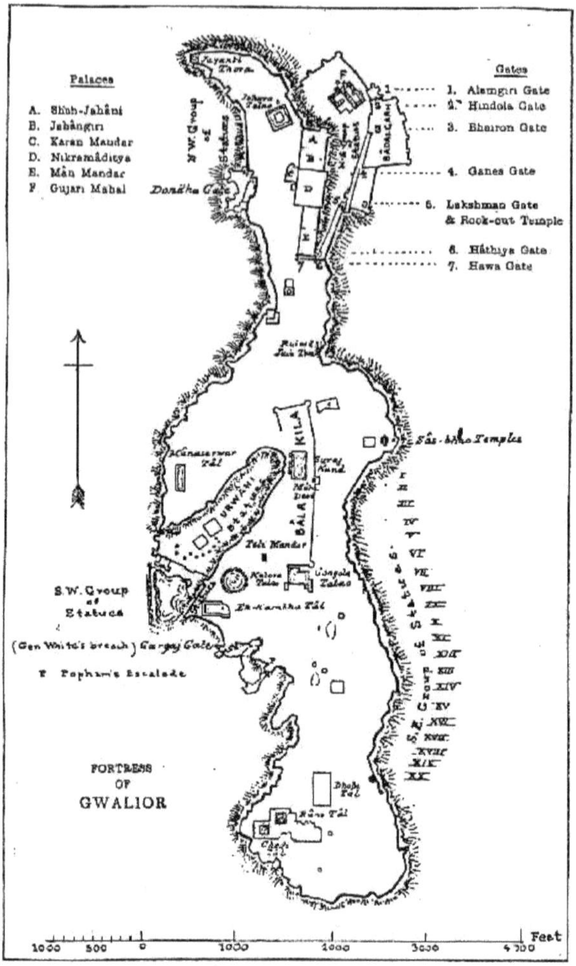

A. Cunningham del.

S.—CONCERNING THE BĀBUR-NĀMA DATING OF 935 AH.

The dating of the diary of 935 AH. (f. 339 *et seq.*) is several times in opposition to what may be distinguished as the "book-rule" that the 12 lunar months of the Ḥijra year alternate in length between 30 and 29 days (intercalary years excepted), and that Muḥarram starts the alternation with 30 days. An early book stating the rule is Gladwin's *Bengal Revenue Accounts*; a recent one, Ranking's ed. of Platts' *Persian Grammar.*

As to what day of the week was the initial day of some of the months in 935 AH. Bābur's days differ from Wüstenfeld's who gives the full list of twelve, and from Cunningham's single one of Muḥarram 1st.

It seems worth while to draw attention to the flexibility, within limits, of Bābur's dating, [not with the object of adversely criticizing a rigid and convenient rule for common use, but as supplementary to that rule from a somewhat special source], because he was careful and observant, his dating was contemporary, his record, as being *de die in diem*, provides a check of consecutive narrative on his dates, which, moreover, are all held together by the external fixtures of Feasts and by the marked recurrence of Fridays observed. Few such writings as the Bābur-nāma diaries appear to be available for showing variation within a year's limit.

In 935 AH. Bābur enters few full dates, *i.e.* days of the week and month. Often he gives only the day of the week, the safest, however, in a diary. He is precise in saying at what time of the night or the day an action was done; this is useful not only as helping to get over difficulties caused by minor losses of text, but in the more general matter of the transference of a Ḥijra night-and-day which begins after sunset, to its Julian equivalent, of a day-and-night which begins at 12 a.m. This sometimes difficult transference affords a probable explanation of a good number of the discrepant dates found in Oriental-Occidental books.

Two matters of difference between the Bābur-nāma dating and that of some European calendars are as follows:—

a. Discrepancy as to the day of the week on which Muḥ. 935 AH. *began.*

This discrepancy is not a trivial matter when a year's diary is concerned. The record of Muḥ. 1st and 2nd is missing from the *Bābur-nāma*; Friday the 3rd day of Muḥarram is the first day specified; the 1st was a Wednesday therefore. Erskine accepted this day; Cunningham and Wüstenfeld give

Tuesday. On three grounds Wednesday seems right—at any rate at that period and place:—(1) The second Friday in Muḥarram was 'Āshūr, the 10th (f. 240); (2) Wednesday is in serial order if reckoning be made from the last surviving date of 934 AH. with due allowance of an intercalary day to Ẕū'l-ḥijja (Gladwin), *i.e.* from Thursday Rajab 12th (April 2nd 1528 AD. f. 339, p. 602); (3) Wednesday is supported by the daily record of far into the year.

b. Variation in the length of the months of 935 AH.

There is singular variation between the *Bābur-nāma* and Wüstenfeld's *Tables*, both as to the day of the week on which months began, and as to the length of some months. This variation is shown in the following table, where asterisks mark agreement as to the days of the week, and the capital letters, quoted from W.'s *Tables*, denote A, Sunday; B, Tuesday, *etc.* (the bracketed names being of my entry).

	Bābur-nāma.	_Wüstenfeld_
	Days.	Days.
Muḥarram	29 Wednesday	30 C (Tuesday)
Ṣafar	30 Thursday	29 E (Thursday)*
Rabī' I.	30 Saturday	30 F (Friday)
Ra"bīiII.	29 Monday	29 A (Sunday)
Jumadā I.	30 Tuesday	30 B (Monday)
Jum"adāII.	29 Thursday	29 D (Wednesday)
Rajab	29 Friday	30 E (Thursday)
Sha'bān	30 Saturday*	29 G (Saturday)*
Ramẓān	29 Monday	30 A (Sunday)
Shawwal	30 Tuesday*	29 C (Tuesday)*
Ẕū'l-qa'da	29 Thursday	30 D (Wednesday)
Ẕū'l-ḥijja	30 Friday*	29 T (Friday)*

The table shows that notwithstanding the discrepancy discussed in section *a*, of Bābur's making 935 AH. begin on a Wednesday, and Wüstenfeld on a Tuesday, the two authorities agree as to the initial week-day of four months out of twelve, *viz.* Ṣafar, Sha'bān, Shawwal and Ẕū'l-ḥijja.

Again:—In eight of the months the *Bābur-nāma* reverses the "book-rule" of alternative Muḥarram 30 days, Ṣafar 29 days *et seq.* by giving Muḥarram 29, Ṣafar 30. (This is seen readily by following the initial days of the week.) Again:—these eight months are in pairs having respectively 29 and 30 days, and the year's total is 364.—Four months follow the fixed rule, *i.e.* as though the year had begun Muḥ. 30 days, Ṣafar 29 days—namely, the two months of Rabī' and the two of Jumāda.—Ramẓān to which under "book-rule" 30 days are due, had 29 days, because, as Bābur records, the Moon was seen on the 29th.—In the other three instances of the reversed 30 and 29, one thing is common, *viz.* Muḥarram, Rajab, Ẕū'l-qa'da (as also Ẕū'l-ḥijja) are "honoured" months.—It would be interesting if some expert in this Musalmān matter would give the reasons dictating the changes from rule noted above as occurring in 935 AH.

c. Varia.

(1) On f. 367 Saturday is entered as the 1st day of Sha'bān and Wednesday as the 4th, but on f. 368*b* stands Wednesday 5th, as suits the serial dating. If the mistake be not a mere slip, it may be due to confusion of hours, the ceremony chronicled being accomplished on the eve of the 5th, Anglicé, after sunset on the 4th.

(2) A fragment only survives of the record of Ẕū'l-ḥijja 935 AH. It contains a date, Thursday 7th, and mentions a Feast which will be that of the *'Īdu'l-kabīr* on the 10th (Sunday). Working on from this to the first-mentioned day of 936 AH. *viz.* Tuesday, Muḥarram 3rd, the month (which is the second of a pair having 29 and 30 days) is seen to have 30 days and so to fit on to 936 AH. The series is Sunday 10th, 17th, 24th (Sat. 30th) Sunday 1st, Tuesday 3rd.

Two clerical errors of mine in dates connecting with this Appendix are corrected here:—(1) On p. 614 n. 5, for Oct. 2nd read Oct. 3rd; (2) on p. 619 penultimate line of the text, for Nov. 28th read Nov. 8th.

T.—ON L:KNŪ (LAKHNAU) AND L:KNŪR (LAKHNŪR, NOW SHĀHĀBĀD IN RĀMPŪR).

One or other of the above-mentioned names occurs eight times in the *Bābur-nāma* (*s.a.* 932, 934, 935 AH.), some instances being shown by their context to represent Lakhnau in Oudh, others inferentially and by the verbal agreement of the Ḥaidarābād Codex and Kehr's Codex to stand for Lakhnūr (now Shāhābād in Rāmpūr). It is necessary to reconsider the identification of those not decided by their context, both because there is so much variation in the copies of the 'Abdu'r-raḥīm Persian translation that they give no verbal help, and because Mr. Erskine and M. de Courteille are in agreement about them and took the whole eight to represent Lakhnau. This they did on different grounds, but in each case their agreement has behind it a defective textual basis.—Mr. Erskine, as is well known, translated the 'Abdu'r-raḥīm Persian text without access to the original Turkī but, if he had had the Elphinstone Codex when translating, it would have given him no help because all the eight instances occur on folios not preserved by that codex. His only sources were not-first-rate Persian MSS. in which he found casual variation from terminal *nū* to *nūr*, which latter form may have been read by him as *nūū* (whence perhaps the old Anglo-Indian transliteration he uses, Luknow).[2843]—M. de Courteille's position is different; his uniform *Lakhnau* obeyed the same uniformity in his source the Kāsān Imprint, and would appear to him the more assured for the concurrence of the *Memoirs*. His textual basis, however, for these words is Dr. Ilminsky's and not Kehr's. No doubt the uniform *Lakhnū* of the Kāsān Imprint is the result of Dr. Ilminsky's uncertainty as to the accuracy of his single Turkī archetype [Kehr's MS.], and also of his acceptance of Mr. Erskine's uniform *Luknow*.[2844]—Since the Ḥaidarābād Codex became available and its collation with Kehr's Codex has been made, a better basis for distinguishing between the L:knū and L:knūr of the Persian MSS. has been obtained.[2845] The results of the collation are entered in the following table, together with what is found in the Kāsān Imprint and the *Memoirs*. [N.B. The two sets of bracketed instances refer each to one place; the asterisks show where Ilminsky varies from Kehr.]

	Ḥai. MS.	*Kehr's MS.*	*Kāsān Imprint.*	*Memoirs.*
1. {	f. 278*b* L:knūr	L:knū	L:knū, p. 361	Luknow.
2. {	f. 338 L:knū	"	" p. 437	"

3.	f. 292*b* L:knūr	L:knūr	”	p. 379* not entered.	
4.	f. 329 L:knūr	L:knūr	”	p. 362* Luknow.	
5.	f. 334 L:knū	L:knū	”	p. 432*	"
6.	f. 376 L:knū	L:knūr	”	p. 486*	"
7.	f. 376*b* L:knūr	"	”	p. 487*	"
8.	f. 377*b* L:knū	"	”	p. 488*	"

The following notes give some grounds for accepting the names as the two Turkī codices agree in giving them:—

The first and second instances of the above table, those of the Ḥai. Codex f. 278*b* and f. 338, are shown by their context to represent Lakhnau.

The third (f. 292*b*) is an item of Bābur's Revenue List. The Turkī codices are supported by B.M. Or. 1999, which is a direct copy of Shaikh Zain's autograph *Ṭ̤ābaqāt-i-bāburī*, all three having L:knūr. Kehr's MS. and Or. 1999 are descendants of the second degree from the original List; that the Ḥai. Codex is a direct copy is suggested by its pseudo-tabular arrangement of the various items.—An important consideration supporting *L:knūr*, is that the List is in Persian and may reasonably be accepted as the one furnished officially for the Pādshāh's information when he was writing his account of Hindūstān (cf. Appendix P, p. liv). This official character disassociates it from any such doubtful spelling by the foreign Pādshāh as cannot but suggest itself when the variants of *e.g.* Dalmau and Bangarmau are considered. L:knūr is what three persons copying independently read in the official List, and so set down that careful scribes *i.e.* Kehr and 'Abdu'l-lāh (App. P) again wrote L:knūr.[2846]—Another circumstance favouring L:knūr (Lakhnūr) is that the place assigned to it in the List is its geographical one between Saṃbhal and Khairābād.—Something for [or perhaps against] accepting Lakhnūr as the *sarkār* of the List may be known in local records or traditions. It had been an important place, and later on it paid a large revenue to Akbar [as part of Saṃbhal].—It appears to have been worth the attention of Bīban *Jalwānī* (f. 329).—Another place is associated with L:knūr in the Revenue List, the forms of which are open to a considerable number of interpretations besides that of Baksar shown *in loco* on p. 521. Only those well acquainted with the United Provinces or their bye-gone history can offer useful suggestion about it. Maps show a "Madkar" 6 m. south of old Lakhnūr; there are in the United Provinces two Baksars and as many other Lakhnūrs (none however being so suitable as what is now Shāhābād). Perhaps in the archives of some old families there may be help found to interpret the entry *L:knūr u B:ks:r* (var.), a conjecture the less improbable that the *Gazetteer of the Province of Oude* (ii, 58) mentions a *farmān* of Bābur Pādshāh's dated 1527 AD. and upholding a grant to Shaikh Qāẓī of Bīlgrām.

The fourth instance (f. 329) is fairly confirmed as Lakhnūr by its context, *viz.* an officer received the district of Badāyūn from the Pādshāh and was sent against Bīban who had laid siege to L:knūr on which Badāyūn bordered.—At the time Lakhnau may have been held from Bābur by Shaikh Bāyazīd

Farmūlī in conjunction with Aūd. Its estates are recorded as still in Farmūlī possession, that of the widow of "Kala Pahār" *Farmūlī*.—(*See infra.*)

The fifth instance (f. 334) connects with Aūd (Oudh) because royal troops abandoning the place L:knū were those who had been sent against Shaikh Bāyazīd in Aūd.

The remaining three instances (f. 376, f. 376*b*, f. 377*b*) appear to concern one place, to which Bīban and Bāyazīd were rumoured to intend going, which they captured and abandoned. As the table of variants shows, Kehr's MS. reads Lakhnūr in all three places, the Ḥai. MS. once only, varying from itself as it does in Nos. 1 and 2.—A circumstance supporting *Lakhnūr* is that one of the messengers sent to Bābur with details of the capture was the son of Shāh Muḥ. *Dīwāna* whose record associates him rather with Badakhshān, and with Humāyūn and Saṃbhal [perhaps with Lakhnūr itself] than with Bābur's own army.—Supplementing my notes on these three instances, much could be said in favour of reading Lakhnūr, about time and distance done by the messengers and by 'Abdu'l-lah *kitābdār*, on his way to Saṃbhal and passing near Lakhnūr; much too about the various rumours and Bābur's immediate counter-action. But to go into it fully would need lengthy treatment which the historical unimportance of the little problem appears not to demand.—Against taking the place to be Lakhnau there are the considerations (*a*) that Lakhnūr was the safer harbourage for the Rains and less near the westward march of the royal troops returning from the battle of the Goghrā; (*b*) that the fort of Lakhnau was the renowned old Machchi-bawan (cf. *Gazetteer of the Province of Oude*, 3 vols., 1877, ii, 366).—So far as I have been able to fit dates and transactions together, there seems no reason why the two Afghāns should not have gone to Lakhnūr, have crossed the Ganges near it, dropped down south [perhaps even intending to recross at Dalmau] with the intention of getting back to the Farmūlīs and Jalwānīs perhaps in Sārwār, perhaps elsewhere to Bāyazīd's brother Ma'rūf.

U.—THE INSCRIPTIONS ON BĀBUR'S MOSQUE IN AJODHYA (OUDH).

Thanks to the kind response made by the Deputy-Commissioner of Fyzābād to my husband's enquiry about two inscriptions mentioned by several Gazetteers as still existing on "Bābur's Mosque" in Oudh, I am able to quote copies of both.[2847]

a. The inscription inside the Mosque is as follows:—

۱. بفرموده شاه بابر که عدلش * بنایست تا کاخ گردون ملاقی

۲. بنا کرد این مهبط قدسیان * امیر سعادت نشان میر باقی

۳. بود خیر باقی چو سال بنایش * عیان شد که گفتم بود خیر باقی

1. *Ba farmūda-i-Shāh Bābur ki 'ādilash*

Banā'īst tā kākh-i-gardūn mulāqī,

2. *Banā kard īn muhbiṭ-i-qudsiyān*

Amīr-i-sa'ādat-nishān Mīr Bāqī

3. *Bavad khair bāqī! chū sāl-i-banā'īsh*

'Iyān shud ki guftam,—Buvad khair bāqī (935).

The translation and explanation of the above, manifestly made by a Musalmān and as such having special value, are as follows:—[2848]

1. By the command of the Emperor Bābur whose justice is an edifice reaching up to the very height of the heavens,

2. The good-hearted Mīr Bāqī built this alighting-place of angels;[2849]

3. *Bavad khāir bāqī!* (May this goodness last for ever!)[2850]

The year of building it was made clear likewise when I said, *Buvad khair bāqī* (= 935).[2851]

The explanation of this is:—

1st couplet:—The poet begins by praising the Emperor Bābur under whose orders the mosque was erected. As justice is the (chief) virtue of kings, he naturally compares his (Bābur's) justice to a palace reaching up to the very heavens, signifying thereby that the fame of that justice had not only spread in the wide world but had gone up to the heavens.

2nd couplet:—In the second couplet, the poet tells who was entrusted with the work of construction. M[i]r Bāqī was evidently some nobleman of distinction at Bābur's Court.—The noble height, the pure religious atmosphere, and the scrupulous cleanliness and neatness of the mosque are beautifully suggested by saying that it was to be the abode of angels.

3rd couplet:—The third couplet begins and ends with the expression *Buvad khair bāqī*. The letters forming it by their numerical values represent the number 935, thus:—

B = 2, *v* = 6, *d* = 4	total 12
Kh = 600, *ai* = 10, *r* = 200	" 810
B = 2, *ā* = 1, *q* = 100, *r* = 10	" 113
	——
	Total 935

The poet indirectly refers to a religious commandment (*dictum*?) of the Qorān that a man's good deeds live after his death, and signifies that this noble mosque is verily such a one.

b. The inscription outside the Mosque is as follows:—

۱. بنام انکه دانا هست اکبر * که خالق جمله عالم لامکانی

۲. درود مصطفیٰ بعد از ستایش * که سرور انبیائی دو جهانی

۳. فسانه در جهان بابر قلندر * که شد در دور گیتی کامرانی

1. *Ba nām-i-anki dānā hast akbar*

Ki khāliq-i-jamla 'ālam lā-makānī

2. *Durūd Muṣṭafá ba'd az sitāyish*

Ki sarwar-i-amٜbiyā' dū jahānī

3. *Fasāna dar jahān Bābur qalandar*

Ki shud dar daur gītī kāmrānī.[2852]

The explanation of the above is as follows:—

In the first couplet the poet praises God, in the second Muḥammad, in the third Bābur.—There is a peculiar literary beauty in the use of the word *lā-makānī* in the 1st couplet. The author hints that the mosque is meant to be the abode of God, although He has no fixed abiding-place.—In the first hemistich of the 3rd couplet the poet gives Bābur the appellation of *qalandar*, which means a perfect devotee, indifferent to all worldly pleasures. In the second hemistich he gives as the reason for his being so, that Bābur became and was known all the world over as a *qalandar*, because having become Emperor of India and having thus reached the summit of worldly success, he had nothing to wish for on this earth.[2853]

The inscription is incomplete and the above is the plain interpretation which can be given to the couplets that are to hand. Attempts may be made to read further meaning into them but the language would not warrant it.

V.—BĀBUR'S GARDENS IN AND NEAR KĀBUL.

The following particulars about gardens made by Bābur in or near Kābul, are given in Muḥammad Amīr of Kazwīn's *Pādshāh-nāma* (Bib. Ind. ed. p. 585, p. 588).

Ten gardens are mentioned as made:—the Shahr-ārā (Town-adorning) which when Shāh-i-jahān first visited Kābul in the 12th year of his reign (1048 AH.-1638 AD.) contained very fine plane-trees Bābur had planted, beautiful trees having magnificent trunks,[2854]—the Chār-bāgh,—the Bāgh-i-jalau-khāna,[2855]—the Aūrta-bāgh (Middle-garden),—the Ṣaurat-bāgh,—the Bāgh-i-mahtāb (Moonlight-garden),—the Bāgh-i-āhū-khāna (Garden-of-the-deer-house),—and three smaller ones. Round these gardens rough-cast walls were made (renewed?) by Jahāngīr (1016 AH.).

The above list does not specify the garden Bābur made and selected for his burial; this is described apart (*l.c.* p. 588) with details of its restoration and embellishment by Shāh-i-jahān the master-builder of his time, as follows:—

The burial-garden was 500 yards (*gaz*) long; its ground was in 15 terraces, 30 yards apart(?). On the 15th terrace is the tomb of Ruqaiya Sulṭān Begam[2856]; as a small marble platform (*chabūṭra*) had been made near it by Jahāngīr's command, Shāh-i-jahān ordered (both) to be enclosed by a marble screen three yards high.—Bābur's tomb is on the 14th terrace. In accordance with his will, no building was erected over it, but Shāh-i-jahān built a small marble mosque on the terrace below.[2857] It was begun in the 17th year (of Shāh-i-jahān's reign) and was finished in the 19th, after the conquest of Balkh and Badakhshān, at a cost of 30,000 *rūpīs*. It is admirably constructed.—From the 12th terrace running-water flows along the line (*rasta*) of the avenue;[2858] but its 12 water-falls, because not constructed with cemented stone, had crumbled away and their charm was lost; orders were given therefore to renew them entirely and lastingly, to make a small reservoir below each fall, and to finish with Kābul marble the edges of the channel and the waterfalls, and the borders of the reservoirs.—And on the 9th terrace there was to be a reservoir 11 x 11 yards, bordered with Kābul marble, and on the 10th terrace one 15 x 15, and at the entrance to the garden another 15 x 15, also with a marble border.—And there was to be a gateway adorned with gilded cupolas befitting that place, and beyond (*pesh*) the gateway a square station,[2859] one side of which should be the garden-wall and the other three filled with cells; that running-water should pass through the middle of it, so that the destitute and poor people who might gather there should eat their food in those cells, sheltered from the hardship of snow and rain.[2860]

FOOTNOTES

[1] From Atkinson's *Sketches in Afghanistan* (I.O. Lib. & B.M.).

[2] *See* p. 710 (where for "Daniels" read Atkinson).

[3] *See* Gul-badan Begim's *Humayun-nama* Index III, *in loco.*

[4] Cf. Cap. II, PROBLEMS OF THE MUTILATED BABUR-NAMA and *Tarīkh-i-rashīdi*, trs. p. 174.

[5] The suggestion, implied by my use of this word, that Babur may have definitely closed his autobiography (as Timur did under other circumstances) is due to the existence of a compelling cause *viz.* that he would be expectant of death as the price of Humayun's restored life (p. 701).

[6] Cf. p. 83 and n. and Add. Note, P. 83 for further emendation of a contradiction effected by some malign influence in the note (p. 83) between parts of that note, and between it and Babur's account of his not-drinking in Herat.

[7] Teufel held its title to be *waqi'* (this I adopted in 1908), but it has no definite support and in numerous instances of its occurrence to describe the acts or doings of Babur, it could be read as a common noun.

[8] It stands on the reverse of the frontal page of the Haidarabad Codex; it is Timur-pulad's name for the Codex he purchased in Bukhara, and it is thence brought on by Kehr (with Ilminski), and Klaproth (Cap. III); it is used by Khwafi Khan (d. *cir.* 1732), *etc.*

[9] That Babur left a complete record much indicates beyond his own persistence and literary bias, *e.g.* cross-reference with and needed complements from what is lost; mention by other writers of Babur's information, notably by Haidar.

[10] App. H, xxx.

[11] p. 446, n. 6. Babur's order for the cairn would fit into the lost record of the first month of the year (p. 445).

[12] Parts of the Babur-nama sent to Babur's sons are not included here.

[13] The standard of comparison is the 382 fols. of the Haidarabad Codex.

[14] This MS. is not to be confused with one Erskine misunderstood Humayun to have copied (*Memoirs*, p. 303 and JRAS. 1900, p. 443).

[15] For precise limits of the original annotation *see* p. 446 n.—For details about the E. Codex *see* JRAS. 1907, art. *The Elph. Codex*, and for the colophon AQR. 1900, July, Oct. and JRAS. 1905, pp. 752, 761.

[16] *See* Index *s.n.* and III *ante* and JRAS. 1900-3-5-6-7.

[17] Here speaks the man reared in touch with European classics; (pure) Turki though it uses no relatives (Radloff) is lucid. Cf. Cap. IV The Memoirs of Babur.

[18] For analysis of a retranslated passage *see* JRAS. 1908, p. 85.

[19] *Tuzuk-i-jahangiri*, Rogers & Beveridge's trs. i, 110; JRAS. 1900, p. 756, for the Persian passage, 1908, p. 76 for the "Fragments", 1900, p. 476 for Ilminski's Preface (a second translation is accessible at the B.M. and I.O. Library and R.A.S.), *Memoirs* Preface, p. ix, Index *s.nn.* de Courteille, Teufel, Bukhara MSS. and Part iii *eo cap.*

[20] For Shah-i-jahan's interest in Timur *see* sign given in a copy of his note published in my translation volume of Gul-badan Begim's *Humayun-nama*, p. xiii.

[21] JRAS. 1900 p. 466, 1902 p. 655, 1905 art. *s.n.*, 1908 pp. 78, 98; Index *in loco s.n.*

[22] Cf. JRAS. 1900, Nos. VI, VII, VIII.

[23] Ilminski's difficulties are foreshadowed here by the same confusion of identity between the *Babur-nama* proper and the Bukhara compilation (Preface, Part iii, p. li).

[24] Cf. Erskine's Preface *passim*, and *in loco* item XI, cap. iv. *The Memoirs of Baber*, and Index *s.n.*

[25] The last blow was given to the phantasmal reputation of the book by the authoritative Haidarabad Codex which now can be seen in facsimile in many Libraries.

[26] But for present difficulties of intercourse with Petrograd, I would have re-examined with Kehr's the collateral Codex of 1742 (copied in 1839 and now owned by the Petrograd University). It might be useful; as Kehr's volume has lost pages and may be disarranged here and there.

The list of Kehr's items is as follows:—

> 1 (*not in the Imprint*). A letter from Babur to Kamran the date of which is fixed as 1527 by its committing Ibrahim *Ludi's* son to Kamran's charge (p. 544). It is heard of again in the Bukhara Compilation, is lost from Kehr's Codex, and preserved from his archetype by Klaproth who translated it. Being thus found in Bukhara in the first

decade of the eighteenth century (our earliest knowledge of the Compilation is 1709), the inference is allowed that it went to Bukhara as loot from the defeated Kamran's camp and that an endorsement its companion Babur-nama (proper) bears was made by the Auzbeg of two victors over Kamran, both of 1550, both in Tramontana.[27]

2 (*not in Imp.*). Timur-pulad's memo. about the purchase of his Codex in cir. 1521 (*eo cap. post*).

3 (*Imp. 1*). Compiler's Preface of Praise (JRAS. 1900, p. 474).

4 (*Imp. 2*). Babur's Acts in Farghana, in diction such as to seem a re-translation of the Persian translation of 1589. How much of Kamran's MS. was serviceable is not easy to decide, because the Turki fettering of 'Abdu'r-rahim's Persian lends itself admirably to re-translation.[28]

5 (*Imp. 3*). The "Rescue-passage" (App. D) attributable to Jahangir.

6 (*Imp. 4*). Babur's Acts in Kabul, seeming (like No. 4) a re-translation or patching of tattered pages. There are also passages taken verbatim from the Persian.

7 (*Imp. omits*). A short length of Babur's Hindustan Section, carefully shewn damaged by dots and dashes.

8 (*Imp. 5*). Within 7, the spurious passage of App. L and also scattered passages about a feast, perhaps part of 7.

9 (*Imp. separates off at end of vol.*). Translated passage from the *Akbar-nāma*, attributable to Jahangir, briefly telling of Kanwa (1527), Babur's latter years (both changed to first person), death and court.[29]

[Babur's history has been thus brought to an end, incomplete in the balance needed of 7. In Kehr's volume a few pages are left blank except for what shews a Russian librarian's opinion of the plan of the book, "Here end the writings of Shah Babur."]

10 (*Imp. omits*). Preface to the history of Humayun, beginning at the Creation and descending by giant strides through notices of Khans and Sultans to "Babur Mirza who was the father of Humayun Padshah". Of Babur what further is said connects with the battle of Ghaj-davan (918-1512 *q.v.*). It is ill-informed, laying blame on him as if he and not Najm Sani had commanded—speaks of his preference for the counsel of young men and of the numbers of combatants. It is noticeable for more than its inadequacy however; its selection of the Ghaj-davan episode from all others in Babur's career supports

circumstantially what is dealt with later, the Ghaj-davani authorship of the Compilation.

11 (*Imp. omits*). Under a heading "Humayun Padshah" is a fragment about (his? Accession) Feast, whether broken off by loss of his pages or of those of his archetype examination of the P. Univ. Codex may show.

12 (*Imp. 6*). An excellent copy of Babur's Hindustan Section, perhaps obtained from the Ahrari house. [This Ilminski places (I think) where Kehr has No. 7.] From its position and from its bearing a scribe's date of completion (which Kehr brings over), *viz. Tamt shud 1126* (Finished 1714), the compiler may have taken it for Humayun's, perhaps for the account of his reconquest of Hind in 1555.

[The remaining entries in Kehr's volume are a quatrain which may make jesting reference to his finished task, a librarian's Russian entry of the number of pages (831), and the words *Etablissement Orientale, Fr. v. Adelung*, 1825 (the Director of the School from 1793).[30]

[27] That Babur-nama of the "Kamran-docket" is the mutilated and tattered basis, allowed by circumstance, of the compiled history of Babur, filled out and mended by the help of the Persian translation of 1589. Cf. Kehr's Latin Trs. fly-leaf entry; Klaproth *s.n.*; A.N. trs. H.B., p. 260; JRAS. 1908, 1909, on the "Kamran-docket" where are defects needing Klaproth's second article (1824).)

[28] For an analysis of an illustrative passage *see* JRAS. 1906; for facilities of re-translation *see eo cap.* p. xviii, where Erskine is quoted.)

[29] *See* A.N. trans., p. 260; Prefaces of Ilminski and de Courteille; ZDMG. xxxvii, Teufel's art.; JRAS. 1906.)

[30] For particulars about Kehr's Codex see Smirnov's Catalogue of the School Library and JRAS. 1900, 1906. Like others who have made statements resting on the mistaken identity of the Bukhara Compilation, many of mine are now given to the winds.)

[31] *See* Gregorief's "Russian policy regarding Central Asia", quoted in Schuyler's Turkistan, App. IV.

[32] The Mission was well received, started to return to Petrograd, was attacked by Turkmans, went back to Bukhara, and there stayed until it could attempt the devious route which brought it to the capital in 1725.

[33] One might say jestingly that the spirit in the book had rebelled since 1725 against enforced and changing masquerade as a phantasm of two other books!

[34] Neither Ilminski nor Smirnov mentions another "Babur-nama" Codex than Kehr's.

[35] A Correspondent combatting my objection to publishing a second edition of the *Memoirs*, backed his favouring opinion by reference to 'Umar Khayyam and Fitzgerald. Obviously no analogy exists; Erskine's redundance is not the flower of a deft alchemy, but is the prosaic consequence of a secondary source.

[36] The manuscripts relied on for revising the first section of the Memoirs, (*i.e.* 899 to 908 AH.-1494 to 1502 AD.) are the Elphinstone and the Ḥaidarābād Codices. To variants from them occurring in Dr. Kehr's own transcript no authority can be allowed because throughout this section, his text appears to be a compilation and in parts a retranslation from one or other of the two Persian translations (*Wāqi'āt-i-bāburī*) of the *Bābur-nāma.* Moreover Dr. Ilminsky's imprint of Kehr's text has the further defect in authority that it was helped out from the Memoirs, itself not a direct issue from the Turkī original.

Information about the manuscripts of the *Bābur-nāma* can be found in the JRAS for 1900, 1902, 1905, 1906, 1907 and 1908.

The foliation marked in the margin of this book is that of the Ḥaidarābād Codex and of its facsimile, published in 1905 by the Gibb Memorial Trust.

[37] Bābur, born on Friday, Feb. 14th. 1483 (Muḥarram 6, 888 AH.), succeeded his father, 'Umar Shaikh who died on June 8th. 1494 (Ramẓān 4, 899 AH.).

[38] *pād-shāh*, protecting lord, supreme. It would be an anachronism to translate *pādshāh* by King or Emperor, previous to 913 AH. (1507 AD.) because until that date it was not part of the style of any Tīmūrid, even ruling members of the house being styled Mīrzā. Up to 1507 therefore Bābur's correct style is Bābur Mīrzā. (*Cf.* f. 215 and note.)

[39] See *Āyīn-i-akbarī*, Jarrett, p. 44.

[40] The Ḥai. MS. and a good many of the W.-i-B. MSS. here write Aūtrār. [Aūtrār like Tarāz was at some time of its existence known as Yāngī (New).] Tarāz seems to have stood near the modern Auliya-ātā; Ālmālīgh,—a Metropolitan see of the Nestorian Church in the 14th. century,—to have been the old capital of Kuldja, and Ālmātū (var. Ālmātī) to have been where Vernoe (Vierny) now is. Ālmālīgh and Ālmātū owed their names to the apple (*ālmā*). *Cf.* Bretschneider's Mediæval Geography p. 140 and T.R. (Elias and Ross) *s.nn.*

[41] *Mughūl u Aūzbeg jihatdīn.* I take this, the first offered opportunity of mentioning (1) that in transliterating Turkī words I follow Turkī lettering because I am not competent to choose amongst systems which *e.g.* here, reproduce Aūzbeg as Ūzbeg, Özbeg and Euzbeg; and (2) that style being part of an autobiography, I am compelled, in pressing back the Memoirs on Bābur's Turkī mould, to retract from the wording of the western scholars, Erskine and de Courteille. Of this compulsion Bābur's bald phrase *Mughūl u Aūzbeg jihatdīn* provides an illustration. Each earlier translator has expressed his meaning with more finish than he himself; 'Abdu'r-raḥīm, by *az jihat 'ubūr-i* (*Mughūl u*) *Aūzbeg*, improves on Bābur, since the three towns lay in the tideway of nomad passage (*'ubūr*) east and west; Erskine writes "in consequence of the incursions" etc. and de C. "*grace aux ravages commis*" etc.

[42] Schuyler (ii, 54) gives the extreme length of the valley as about 160 miles and its width, at its widest, as 65 miles.

[43] Following a manifestly clerical error in the Second W.-i-B. the *Akbar-nāma* and the Mems. are without the seasonal limitation, "in winter." Bābur here excludes from winter routes one he knew well, the Kīndīrlīk Pass; on the other hand Kostenko says that this is open all the year round. Does this contradiction indicate climatic change? (*Cf.* f. 54b and note; A.N. Bib. Ind. ed. i, 85 (H. Beveridge i, 221) and, for an account of the passes round Farghāna, Kostenko's *Turkistān Region*, Tables of Contents.)

[44] Var. Banākat, Banākaṣ, Fīākat, Fanākand. Of this place Dr. Rieu writes (Pers. cat. i, 79) that it was also called Shāsh and, in modern times, Tāshkīnt. Bābur does not identify Fanākat with the Tāshkīnt of his day but he identifies it with Shāhrukhiya (*cf.* Index *s.nn.*) and distinguishes between Tāshkīnt-Shāsh and Fanākat-Shāhrukhiya. It may be therefore that Dr. Rieu's Tāshkīnt-Fanākat was Old Tāshkīnt,—(Does Fanā-kīnt mean Old Village?) some 14 miles nearer to the Saiḥūn than the Tāshkīnt of Bābur's day or our own.

[45] *hech daryā qātīlmās.* A gloss of *dīgar* (other) in the Second W.-i-B. has led Mr. Erskine to understand "meeting with no other river in its course." I understand Bābur to contrast the destination of the Saiḥūn which he [erroneously] says sinks into the sands, with the outfall of *e.g.* the Amū into the Sea of Aral.

Cf. First W.-i-B. I.O. MS. 215 f. 2; Second W.-i-B. I.O. MS. 217 f. 1b and Ouseley's Ibn Haukal p. 232-244; also Schuyler and Kostenko *l.c.*

[46] Bābur's geographical unit in Central Asia is the township or, with more verbal accuracy, the village *i.e.* the fortified, inhabited and cultivated oasis. Of frontiers he says nothing.

[47] *i.e.* they are given away or taken. Bābur's interest in fruits was not a matter of taste or amusement but of food. Melons, for instance, fresh or stored, form during some months the staple food of Turkistānīs. *Cf.* T.R. p. 303 and (in Kāshmīr) 425; Timkowski's *Travels of the Russian Mission* i, 419 and Th. Radloff's *Réceuils d'Itinéraires* p. 343.

N.B. At this point two folios of the Elphinstone Codex are missing.

[48] Either a kind of melon or the pear. For local abundance of pears *see* *Āyīn-i-akbarī*, Blochmann p. 6; Kostenko and Von Schwarz.

[49] *qūrghān*, *i.e.* the walled town within which was the citadel (*ark*).

[50] *Tūqūz tarnau sū kīrār, bū 'ajab tūr kīm bīr yīrdīn ham chīqmās.* Second W.-i-B. I.O. 217 f. 2, *nuh jū'ī āb dar qila' dar mī āyid u īn 'ajab ast kah hama az yak jā ham na mī bar āyid.* (*Cf.* Mems. p. 2 and *Méms.* i, 2.) I understand Bābur to mean that all the water entering was consumed in the town. The supply of Andijān, in the present day, is taken both from the Āq Būrā (*i.e.* the Aūsh Water) and, by canal, from the Qarā Daryā.

[51] *khandaqnīng tāsh yānī.* Second W.-i-B. I.O. 217 f. 2 *dar kīnār sang bast khandaq.* Here as in several other places, this Persian translation has rendered Turkī *tāsh*, outside, as if it were Turkī *tāsh*, stone. Bābur's adjective *stone* is *sangīn* (f. 45b l. 8). His point here is the unusual circumstance of a high-road running round the outer edge of the ditch. Moreover Andijān is built on and of loess. Here, obeying his Persian source, Mr. Erskine writes "stone-faced ditch"; M. de C. obeying his Turkī one, "*bord extérieur.*"

[52] *qīrghāwal āsh-kīnasī bīla. Āsh-kīna*, a diminutive of *āsh*, food, is the rice and vegetables commonly served with the bird. Kostenko i, 287 gives a recipe for what seems *āsh-kīna.*

[53] b. 1440; d. 1500 AD.

[54] Yūsuf was in the service of Bāī-sunghar Mīrzā *Shāhrukhī* (d. 837 AH.-1434 AD.). *Cf.* Daulat Shāh's *Memoirs of the Poets* (Browne) pp. 340 and 350-1. (H.B.)

[55] *gūzlār aīl bīzkāk kūb būlūr.* Second W.-i-B. (I.O. 217 f. 2) here and on f. 4 has read Turkī *gūz*, eye, for Turkī *gūz* or *goz*, autumn. It has here a gloss not in the Ḥaidarābād or Kehr's MSS. (*Cf.* Mems. p. 4 note.) This gloss may be one of Humāyūn's numerous notes and may have been preserved in the Elphinstone Codex, but the fact cannot now be known because of the loss of the two folios already noted. (*See* Von Schwarz and Kostenko concerning the autumn fever of Transoxiana.)

[56] The Pers. trss. render *yīghāch* by *farsang*; Ujfalvy also takes the *yīghāch* and the *farsang* as having a common equivalent of about 6 *kilomètres*. Bābur's

statements in *yīghāch* however, when tested by ascertained distances, do not work out into the *farsang* of four miles or the *kilomètre* of 8 *kil.* to 5 miles. The *yīghāch* appears to be a variable estimate of distance, sometimes indicating the time occupied on a given journey, at others the distance to which a man's voice will carry. (*Cf.* Ujfalvy *Expédition scientifique* ii, 179; Von Schwarz p. 124 and de C.'s Dict. *s.n. yīghāch.* In the present instance, if Bābur's 4 y. equalled 4 f. the distance from Aūsh to Andijān should be about 16 m.; but it is 33 m. 1-3/4 fur. *i.e.* 50 *versts.* Kostenko ii, 33.) I find Bābur's *yīghāch* to vary from about 4 m. to nearly 8 m.

[57] *āqār sū*, the irrigation channels on which in Turkistān all cultivation depends. Major-General Gérard writes, (Report of the Pamir Boundary Commission, p. 6,) "Osh is a charming little town, resembling Islāmābād in Kāshmīr,—everywhere the same mass of running water, in small canals, bordered with willow, poplar and mulberry." He saw the Āq Būrā, the *White wolf*, mother of all these running waters, as a "bright, stony, trout-stream;" Dr. Stein saw it as a "broad, tossing river." (Buried Cities of Khotan, p. 45.) *Cf.* Réclus vi, cap. Farghāna; Kostenko i, 104; Von Schwarz *s.nn.*

[58] *Aūshnīng fażīlatīdā khailī aḥādiṣ wārid dūr.* Second W.-i-B. (I.O. 217 f. 2) *Fażīlat-i-Aūsh aḥadiṣ wārid ast.* Mems. (p. 3) "The excellencies of Ush are celebrated even in the sacred traditions." *Méms.* (i, 2) "*On cite beaucoup de traditions qui célèbrent l'excellence de ce climat.*" Aūsh may be mentioned in the traditions on account of places of pilgrimage near it; Bābur's meaning may be merely that its excellencies are traditional. *Cf.* Ujfalvy ii, 172.

[59] Most travellers into Farghāna comment on Bābur's account of it. One much discussed point is the position of the Barā Koh. The personal observations of Ujfalvy and Schuyler led them to accept its identification with the rocky ridge known as the Takht-i-sulaimān. I venture to supplement this by the suggestion that Bābur, by Barā Koh, did not mean the whole of the rocky ridge, the name of which, Takht-i-sulaimān, an ancient name, must have been known to him, but one only of its four marked summits. Writing of the ridge Madame Ujfalvy says, "*Il y a quatre sommets dont le plus élevé est le troisième comptant par le nord.*" Which summit in her sketch (p. 327) is the third and highest is not certain, but one is so shewn that it may be the third, may be the highest and, as being a peak, can be described as symmetrical *i.e.* Bābur's *mauzūn.* For this peak an appropriate name would be Barā Koh.

If the name Barā Koh could be restricted to a single peak of the Takht-i-sulaimān ridge, a good deal of earlier confusion would be cleared away, concerning which have written, amongst others, Ritter (v, 432 and 732); Réclus (vi. 54); Schuyler (ii, 43) and those to whom these three refer. For an excellent account, graphic with pen and pencil, of Farghāna and of Aūsh *see* Madame Ujfalvy's *De Paris à Samarcande* cap. v.

[60] *rūd.* This is a precise word since the Āq Būrā (the White Wolf), in a relatively short distance, falls from the Kūrdūn Pass, 13,400 ft. to Aūsh, 3040 ft. and thence to Andijān, 1380 ft. *Cf.* Kostenko i, 104; Huntingdon in Pumpelly's *Explorations in Turkistān* p. 179 and the French military map of 1904.

[61] Whether Bābur's words, *bāghāt*, *bāghlār* and *bāghcha* had separate significations, such as orchard, vineyard and ordinary garden *i.e.* garden-plots of small size, I am not able to say but what appears fairly clear is that when he writes *bāghāt u bāghlār* he means *all sorts of gardens*, just as when he writes *begāt u beglār*, he means *begs of all ranks.*

[62] Madame Ujfalvy has sketched a possible successor. Schuyler found two mosques at the foot of Takht-i-sulaimān, perhaps Bābur's Jauza Masjid.

[63] *aūl shāh-jū'īdīn sū qūyārlār.*

[64] Ribbon Jasper, presumably.

[65] Kostenko (ii, 30), 71-3/4 versts *i.e.* 47 m. 4-1/2 fur. by the Postal Road.

[66] Instead of their own kernels, the Second W.-i-B. stuffs the apricots, in a fashion well known in India by *khūbānī*, with almonds (*maghz-i badām*). The Turkī wording however allows the return to the apricots of their own kernels and Mr. Rickmers tells me that apricots so stuffed were often seen by him in the Zar-afshān Valley. My husband has shewn me that Niẓāmī in his Haft Paikar appears to refer to the other fashion, that of inserting almonds:—

"I gave thee fruits from the garden of my heart,

Plump and sweet as honey in milk;

Their substance gave the lusciousness of figs,

In their hearts were the kernels of almonds."

[67] What this name represents is one of a considerable number of points in the *Bābur-nāma* I am unable to decide. *Kīyīk* is a comprehensive name (*cf.* Shaw's Vocabulary); *āq kīyīk* might mean *white sheep* or *white deer.* It is rendered in the Second W.-i-B., here, by *ahū-i-wāriq* and on f. 4, by *ahū-i-safed.* Both these names Mr. Erskine has translated by "white deer," but he mentions that the first is said to mean *argālī i.e. ovis poli*, and refers to *Voyages de Pallas* iv, 325.

[68] Concerning this much discussed word, Bābur's testimony is of service. It seems to me that he uses it merely of those settled in towns (villages) and without any reference to tribe or nationality. I am not sure that he uses it always as a noun; he writes of a *Sārt kīshī*, a Sārt person. His Asfara Sārts may have been Turkī-speaking settled Turks and his Marghīnānī ones Persian-speaking Tājiks. *Cf.* Shaw's Vocabulary; *s.n.* Sārt; Schuyler i, 104 and note; Nalivkine's *Histoire du Khanat de Khokand* p. 45 n. Von Schwarz *s.n.*; Kostenko i, 287; Petzbold's *Turkistan* p. 32.

[69] Shaikh Burhānu'd-dīn 'Alī *Qilīch*: b. *circa* 530 AH. (1135 AD.) d. 593 AH. (1197 AD.). *See* Hamilton's *Hidāyat.*

[70] The direct distance, measured on the map, appears to be about 65 m. but the road makes *détour* round mountain spurs. Mr. Erskine appended here, to the "*farsang*" of his Persian source, a note concerning the reduction of Tatar and Indian measures to English ones. It is rendered the less applicable by the variability of the *yīghāch*, the equivalent for a *farsang* presumed by the Persian translator.

[71] Ḥai. MS. *Farsī-gū'ī.* The Elph. MS. and all those examined of the W.-i-B. omit the word *Farsī*; some writing *kohī* (mountaineer) for *gū'ī.* I judge that Bābur at first omitted the word *Farsī*, since it is entered in the Ḥai. MS. above the word *gū'ī.* It would have been useful to Ritter (vii, 733) and to Ujfalvy (ii, 176). *Cf.* Kostenko i, 287 on the variety of languages spoken by Sārts.

[72] Of the Mirror Stone neither Fedtschenko nor Ujfalvy could get news.

[73] Bābur distinguishes here between Tāshkīnt and Shāhrukhiya. *Cf.* f. 2 and note to Fanākat.

[74] He left the hill-country above Sūkh in Muḥarram 910 AH. (mid-June 1504 AD.).

[75] For a good account of Khujand *see* Kostenko i, 346.

[76] Khujand to Andijān 187 m. 2 fur. (Kostenko ii, 29-31) and, helped out by the time-table of the Transcaspian Railway, from Khujand to Samarkand appears to be some 154 m. 5-1/4 fur.

[77] Both men are still honoured in Khujand (Kostenko i, 348). For Khwāja Kamāl's Life and *Dīwān*, *see* Rieu ii, 632 and Ouseley's Persian Poets p. 192. *Cf.* f. 83b and note.

[78] *kūb artūq dūr*, perhaps brought to Hindūstān where Bābur wrote the statement.

[79] Turkish arrow-flight, London, 1791, 482 yards.

[80] I have found the following forms of this name,—Ḥai. MS., M:nūgh:l; Pers. trans. and Mems., Myoghil; Ilminsky, M:tugh:l; *Méms.* Mtoughuil; Réclus, Schuyler and Kostenko, Mogul Tau; Nalivkine, "d'apres Fedtschenko," Mont Mogol; Fr. Map of 1904, M. Muzbek. It is the western end of the Kurāma Range (Kīndīr Tau), which comes out to the bed of the Sīr, is 26-2/3 miles long and rises to 4000 ft. (Kostenko, i, 101). Von Schwarz describes it as being quite bare; various writers ascribe climatic evil to it.

[81] Pers. trans. *ahū-i-safed*. *Cf.* f. 3b note.

[82] These words translate into *Cervus marāl*, the Asiatic Wapiti, and to this Bābur may apply them. Dictionaries explain *marāl* as meaning *hind* or *doe* but numerous books of travel and Natural History show that it has wider application as a generic name, *i.e.* deer. The two words *būghū* and *marāl* appear to me to be used as *e.g.* drake and duck are used. *Marāl* and duck can both imply the female sex, but also both are generic, perhaps primarily so. *Cf.* for further mention of *būghū-marāl* f. 219 and f. 276. For uses of the word *marāl*, *see* the writings *e.g.* of Atkinson, Kostenko (iii, 69), Lyddeker, Littledale, Selous, Ronaldshay, Church (Chinese Turkistan), Biddulph (Forsyth's Mission).

[83] *Cf.* f. 2 and note.

[84] Schuyler (ii, 3), 18 m.

[85] Ḥai. MS. *Hamesha bū deshttā yīl bār dūr. Marghīnānghā kīm sharqī dūr, hamesha mūndīn yīl bārūr; Khujandghā kīm gharībī dūr, dā'im mūndīn yīl kīlūr.*

This is a puzzling passage. It seems to say that wind always goes east and west from the steppe as from a generating centre. E. and de C. have given it alternative directions, east or west, but there is little point in saying this of wind in a valley hemmed in on the north and the south. Bābur limits his statement to the steppe lying in the contracted mouth of the Farghāna valley (*pace* Schuyler ii, 51) where special climatic conditions exist such as (*a*) difference in temperature on the two sides of the Khujand narrows and currents resulting from this difference,—(*b*) the heating of the narrows by sun-heat reflected from the Mogol-tau,—and (*c*) the inrush of westerly wind over Mīrzā Rabāṭ. Local knowledge only can guide a translator safely but Bābur's directness of speech compels belief in the significance of his words and this particularly when what he says is unexpected. He calls the Hā Darwesh a whirling wind and this it still is. Thinkable at least it is that a strong westerly current (the prevailing wind of Farghāna) entering over Mīrzā Rabāṭ and becoming, as it does become, the whirlwind of Hā Darwesh on the hemmed-in steppe,—becoming so perhaps by conflict with the hotter indraught through the Gates of Khujand—might force that indraught back into the Khujand Narrows (in the way *e.g.* that one Nile in flood forces back the other), and at Khujand create an easterly current. All the manuscripts agree in writing to (*ghā*) Marghīnān and to (*ghā*) Khujand. It may be observed that, looking at the map, it appears somewhat strange that Bābur should take, for his wind objective, a place so distant from his (defined) Hā Darwesh and seemingly so screened by its near hills as is Marghīnān. But that westerly winds are prevalent in Marghīnān is seen *e.g.* in Middendorff's *Einblikke in den Farghāna Thal* (p. 112). *Cf.* Réclus vi, 547; Schuyler ii, 51; Cahun's *Histoire du Khanat de Khokand* p. 28 and Sven Hedin's *Durch Asien's Wüsten s.n. būrān.*

[86] *bādiya*; a word perhaps selected as punning on *bād*, wind.

[87] *i.e.* Akhsī Village. This word is sometimes spelled Akhsīkīs̤ but as the old name of the place was Akhsī-kīnt, it may be conjectured at least that the *s̤ā'ī mas̤allas̤a* of Akhsīkīs̤ represents the three points due for the *nūn* and *tā* of *kīnt.* Of those writing Akhsīkīt may be mentioned the Ḥai. and Kehr's MSS. (the Elph. MS. here has a lacuna) the *Z̤afar-nāma* (Bib. Ind. i, 44) and Ibn Haukal (Ouseley p. 270); and of those writing the word with the *s̤ā'ī muṣallas̤a* (*i.e.* as Akhsīkīs̤), Yāqūt's Dict, i, 162, Reinaud's Abū'l-feda I. ii, 225-6, Ilminsky (p. 5) departing from his source, and I.O. Cat. (Ethé) No. 1029. It may be observed that Ibn Haukal (Ouseley p. 280) writes Banākaṣ for Banākat. For As̤īru'd-dīn *Akhsīkītī, see* Rieu ii, 563; Daulat Shāh (Browne) p. 121 and Ethé I.O. Cat. No. 1029.

[88] Measured on the French military map of 1904, this may be 80 kil. *i.e.* 50 miles.

[89] Concerning several difficult passages in the rest of Bābur's account of Akhsī, *see* Appendix A.

[90] The W.-i-B. here translates *būghū-marāl* by *gazawn* and the same word is entered, under-line, in the Ḥai. MS. *Cf.* f. 3b and note and f. 4 and note.

[91] *postīn pesh b:r:h.* This obscure Persian phrase has been taken in the following ways:—

(*a*) W.-i-B. I.O. 215 and 217 (*i.e.* both versions) reproduce the phrase.
(*b*) W.-i-B. MS., quoted by Erskine, p. 6 note, (*postīn-i mīsh burra*).
(*c*) Leyden's MS. Trs., a sheepskin mantle of five lambskins.
(*d*) Mems., Erskine, p. 6, a mantle of five lambskins.
(*e*) The Persian annotator of the Elph. MS., underlining *pesh*, writes, *panj*, five.
(*f*) Klaproth (Archives, p. 109), *pustini pisch breh, d.h. gieb den vorderen Pelz.*
(*g*) Kehr, p. 12 (Ilminsky p. 6) *postin bīsh b:r:h.*
(*h*) De. C, i, 9, *fourrure d'agneau de la première qualité.*

The "lambskins" of L. and E. carry on a notion of comfort started by their having read *sayāh*, shelter, for Turkī *sā'ī*, torrent-bed; de C. also lays stress on fur and warmth, but would not the flowery border of a mountain stream prompt rather a phrase bespeaking ornament and beauty than one expressing warmth and textile softness? If the phrase might be read as *postīn pesh perā*, what adorns the front of a coat, or as *postīn pesh bar rah*, the fine front of the coat, the phrase would recall the gay embroidered front of some leathern postins.

[92] Var. *tabarkhūn*. The explanation best suiting its uses, enumerated here, is Redhouse's second, the Red Willow. My husband thinks it may be the Hyrcanian Willow.

[93] Steingass describes this as "an arrow without wing or point" (barb?) and tapering at both ends; it may be the practising arrow, *t'alīm aūqī*, often headless.

[94] *tabarraklūq*. Cf. f. 48b foot, for the same use of the word.

[95] *yabrūju'ṣ-ṣannam*. The books referred to by Bābur may well be the *Rauẓatu'ṣ-ṣafā* and the *Ḥabību's-siyār*, as both mention the plant.

[96] The Turkī word *āyīq* is explained by Redhouse as *awake* and *alert*; and by Meninski and de Meynard as *sobered* and as *a return to right senses*. It may be used here as a equivalent of *mihr* in *mihr-giyāh*, the plant of love.

[97] Mr. Ney Elias has discussed the position of this group of seven villages. (*Cf.* T. R. p. 180 n.) Arrowsmith's map places it (as Iti-kint) approximately where Mr. Th. Radloff describes seeing it *i.e.* on the Farghāna slope of the Kurāma range. (*Cf. Réceuil d'Itinéraires* p. 188.) Mr. Th. Radloff came into Yītī-kīnt after crossing the Kīndīrlīk Pass from Tāshkīnt and he enumerates the seven villages as traversed by him before reaching the Sīr. It is hardly necessary to say that the actual villages he names may not be those of Bābur's Yītī-kint. Wherever the word is used in the *Bābur-nāma* and the *Tārīkh-i-rashīdī*, it appears from the context allowable to accept Mr. Radloff's location but it should be borne in mind that the name Yītī-kīnt (Seven villages or towns) might be found as an occasional name of Altī-shahr (Six towns). *See* T.R. *s.n.* Altī-shahr.

[98] *kīshī*, person, here manifestly fighting men.

[99] Elph. MS. f. 2b; First W.-i-B. I.O. 215 f. 4b; Second W.-i-B. I.O. 217 f. 4; Mems. p. 6; Ilminsky p. 7; *Méms.* i. 10.

The rulers whose affairs are chronicled at length in the Farghāna Section of the B.N. are, (I) of Tīmūrid Turks, (always styled Mīrzā), (*a*) the three Mīrān-shāhī brothers, Aḥmad, Maḥmūd and 'Umar Shaikh with their successors, Bāī-sunghar, 'Alī and Bābur; (*b*) the Bāī-qarā, Ḥusain of Harāt:

(II) of Chīngīz Khānīds, (always styled Khān,) (*a*) the two Chaghatāī Mughūl brothers, Maḥmūd and Aḥmad; (*b*) the Shaibānid Aūzbeg, Muḥammad Shaibānī (Shāh-i-bakht or Shaibāq or Shāhī Beg).

In electing to use the name *Shaibānī*, I follow not only the Ḥai. Codex but also Shaibānī's Boswell, Muḥammad Ṣāliḥ Mīrzā. The Elph. MS. frequently uses *Shaibāq* but its authority down to f. 198 (Ḥai. MS. f. 243b) is not so great as it is after that folio, because not till f. 198 is it a direct copy of Bābur's own. It may be more correct to write "the Shaibānī Khān" and perhaps even "the Shaibānī."

[100] *bī murād*, so translated because retirement was caused once by the overruling of Khwāja 'Ubaidu'l-lāh *Aḥrārī*. (T.R. p. 113.)

[101] Once the Mīrzā did not wish Yūnas to winter in Akhsī; once did not expect him to yield to the demand of his Mughūls to be led out of the cultivated country (*wilāyat*). His own misconduct included his attack in Yūnas on account of Akhsī and much falling-out with kinsmen. (T.R. *s.nn.*)

[102] *i.e.* one made of non-warping wood (Steingass), perhaps that of the White Poplar. The *Shāh-nāma* (Turner, Maçon ed. i, 71) writes of a Chāchī bow and arrows of *khadang*, *i.e.* white poplar. (H.B.)

[103] *i.e.* Rābī'a-sulṭān, married *circa* 893 AH.-1488 AD. For particulars about her and all women mentioned in the B.N. and the T.R. see Gulbadan Begīm's *Humāyūn-nāma*, Or. Trs. Series.

[104] *jar*, either that of the Kāsān Water or of a deeply-excavated canal. The palace buildings are mentioned again on f. 110b. *Cf.* Appendix A.

[105] *i.e.* soared from earth, died. For some details of the accident *see* A.N. (H. Beveridge, i, 220.)

[106] Ḥ.S. ii,-192, Firishta, lith. ed. p. 191 and D'Herbélot, sixth.

It would have accorded with Bābur's custom if here he had mentioned the parentage of his father's mother. Three times (fs. 17b, 70b, 96b) he writes of "Shāh Sulṭan Begīm" in a way allowing her to be taken as 'Umar Shaikh's own mother. Nowhere, however, does he mention her parentage. One even cognate statement only have we discovered, *viz.* Khwānd-amīr's (Ḥ.S. ii, 192) that 'Umar Shaikh was the own younger brother (*barādar khurdtar khūd*) of Aḥmad and Maḥmūd. If his words mean that the three were full-brothers, 'Umar Shaikh's own mother was Ābū-sa'īd's Tarkhān wife. Bābur's omission (f. 21b) to mention his father with A. and M. as a nephew of Darwesh Muḥammad Tarkhān would be negative testimony against taking Khwānd-amīr's statement to mean "full-brother," if clerical slips were not easy and if Khwānd-amir's means of information were less good. He however both was the son of Maḥmūd's wāzir (Ḥ.S. ii, 194) and supplemented his book in Bābur's presence.

To a statement made by the writer of the biographies included in Kehr's B.N. volume, that 'U.S.'s family (*aūmāgh*) is not known, no weight can be attached, spite of the co-incidence that the Mongol form of *aūmāgh*, *i.e.* *aūmāk* means *Mutter-leib*. The biographies contain too many known mistakes for their compiler to outweigh Khwānd-amīr in authority.

[107] *Cf. Rauẓatu'ṣ-ṣafā* vi, 266. (H.B.)

[108] Dara-i-gaz, south of Balkh. This historic feast took place at Merv in 870 AH. (1465 AD.). As 'Umar Shaikh was then under ten, he may have been one of the Mīrzās concerned.

[109] Khudāī-bīrdī is a Pers.-Turkī hybrid equivalent of Theodore; *tūghchī* implies the right to use or (as hereditary standard-bearer,) to guard the *tūgh*; Tīmūr-tāsh may mean *i.a.* Friend of Tīmūr (a title not excluded here as borne by inheritance. *Cf.* f. 12b and note), Sword-friend (*i.e.* Companion-in-arms), and Iron-friend (*i.e.* stanch). *Cf.* Dict. *s.n.* Tīmūr-bāsh, a sobriquet of Charles XII.

[110] Elph. and Ḥai. MSS. *qūbā yūẓlūq*; this is under-lined in the Elph. MS. by *ya'nī pur ghosht*. *Cf.* f. 68b for the same phrase. The four earlier trss. *viẓ.* the two W.-i-B., the English and the French, have variants in this passage.

[111] The apposition may be between placing the turban-sash round the turban-cap in a single flat fold and winding it four times round after twisting it on itself. *Cf.* f. 18 and Hughes *Dict. of Islām s.n.* turban.

[112] *qaẓālār*, the prayers and fasts omitted when due, through war, travel sickness, etc.

[113] *rawān sawādī bār īdī*; perhaps, wrote a running hand. De C. i, 13, *ses lectures courantes étaient....*

[114] The dates of 'Umar Shaikh's limits of perusal allow the Quintets (*Khamsatīn*) here referred to to be those of Niẓāmī and Amīr Khusrau of Dihlī. The *Maṣnawī* must be that of Jalālu'd-dīn *Rūmī*. (H.B.)

[115] Probably below the Tīrāk (Poplar) Pass, the caravan route much exposed to avalanches.

Mr. Erskine notes that this anecdote is erroneously told as of Bābur by Firishta and others. Perhaps it has been confused with the episode on f. 207b. Firishta makes another mistaken attribution to Bābur, that of Ḥasan of Yaq'ūb's couplet. (H.B.) *Cf.* f. 13b and Dow's *Hindustan* ii, 218.

[116] *yigītlār*, young men, the modern *jighit*. Bābur uses the word for men on the effective fighting strength. It answers to the "brave" of North. American Indian story; here de C. translates it by *braves*.

[117] *ma'jūn*. *Cf.* Von Schwarz p. 286 for a recipe.

[118] *mutaiyam*. This word, not clearly written in all MSS., has been mistaken for *yītīm*. *Cf.* JRAS 1910 p. 882 for a note upon it by my husband to whom I owe the emendation.

[119] *na'l u dāghī bisyār īdī*, that is, he had inflicted on himself many of the brands made by lovers and enthusiasts. *Cf.* Chardin's *Voyages* ii, 253 and Lady M. Montague's *Letters* p. 200.

[120] *tīka sīkrītkū*, lit. likely to make goats leap, from *sīkrīmāk* to jump close-footed (Shaw).

[121] *sīkrīkān dūr*. Both *sīkrītkū* and *sīkrīkān dūr*, appear to dictate translation in general terms and not by reference to a single traditional leap by one goat.

[122] *i.e.* Russian; it is the Arys tributary of the Sīr.

[123] The Fr. map of 1904 shows Kas, in the elbow of the Sīr, which seems to represent Khwāṣ.

[124] *i.e.* the Chīr-chīk tributary of the Sīr.

[125] Concerning his name, *see* T.R. p. 173.

[126] *i.e.* he was a head-man of a horde sub-division, nominally numbering 10,000, and paying their dues direct to the supreme Khān. (T.R. p. 301.)

[127] *ghūnchachī i.e.* one ranking next to the four legal wives, in Turkī *aūdālīq*, whence odalisque. Bābur and Gul-badan mention the promotion of several to Begīm's rank by virtue of their motherhood.

[128] One of Bābur's quatrains, quoted in the *Abūshqa*, is almost certainly addressed to Khān-zāda. *Cf.* A.Q. Review, Jan. 1911, p. 4; H. Beveridge's *Some verses of Bābur.* For an account of her marriage *see Shaibānī-nāma* (Vambéry) cap. xxxix.

[129] Kehr's MS. has a passage here not found elsewhere and seeming to be an adaptation of what is at the top of Ḥai. MS. f. 88. (Ilminsky, p. 10, *ba wujūd ... tāpīb.*)

[130] *tūshtī*, which here seems to mean that she fell to his share on division of captives. Muḥ. Ṣāliḥ makes it a love-match and places the marriage before Bābur's departure. *Cf.* f. 95 and notes.

[131] *aūgāhlān.* Khurram would be about five when given Balkh in *circa* 911 AH. (1505 AD.). He died when about 12. *Cf.* Ḥ.S. ii, 364.

[132] This *fatrat* (interregnum) was between Bābur's loss of Farghāna and his gain of Kābul; the *furṣatlār* were his days of ease following success in Hindūstān and allowing his book to be written.

[133] *qīlālīng,* lit. do thou be (setting down), a verbal form recurring on f. 227b l. 2. With the same form (*aīt*)*ālīng,* lit. do thou be saying, the compiler of the *Abūshqa* introduces his quotations. Shaw's paradigm, *qīlīng* only. *Cf.* A.Q.R. Jan. 1911, p. 2.

[134] Kehr's MS. (Ilminsky p. 12) and its derivatives here interpolate the erroneous statement that the sons of Yūnas were Afāq and Bābā Khāns.

[135] *i.e.* broke up the horde. *Cf.* T.R. p. 74.

[136] *See* f. 50b for his descent.

[137] Descendants of these captives were in Kāshghar when Ḥaidar was writing the T.R. It was completed in 953 AH. (1547 AD.). *Cf.* T.R. pp. 81 and 149.

[138] An omission from his Persian source misled Mr. Erskine here into making Abū-sa'īd celebrate the Khānīm's marriage, not with himself but with his defeated foe, 'Abdu'l-'azīz who had married her 28 years earlier.

[139] Aīsān-būghā was at Āq Sū in Eastern Turkistān; Yūnas Khān's head-quarters were in Yītī-kīnt. The Sāghārīchī *tūmān* was a subdivision of the Kūnchī Mughūls.

[140] *Khān kūtārdīlār.* The primitive custom was to lift the Khān-designate off the ground; the phrase became metaphorical and would seem to be so here, since there were two upon the felt. *Cf.*, however, Th. Radloff's *Récueil d'Itinéraires* p. 326.

[141] *qūyūb īdī,* probably in childhood.

[142] She was divorced by Shaibānī Khān in 907 AH. in order to allow him to make lawful marriage with her niece, Khān-zāda.

[143] This was a prudential retreat before Shaibānī Khān. *Cf.* f. 213.

[144] The "Khān" of his title bespeaks his Chaghatāī-Mughūl descent through his mother, the "Mīrzā," his Tīmūrid-Turkī, through his father. The capture of the women was facilitated by the weakening of their travelling escort through his departure. *Cf.* T.R. p. 203.

[145] Qila'-i-ẓạfar. Its ruins are still to be seen on the left bank of the Kukcha. *Cf.* T.R. p. 220 and Kostenko i, 140. For Mubārak Shāh *Muẓaffarī* *see* f. 213 and T.R. *s.n.*

[146] Ḥabība, a child when captured, was reared by Shaibānī and by him given in marriage to his nephew. *Cf.* T.R. p. 207 for an account of this marriage as saving Ḥaidar's life.

[147] *i.e.* she did not take to flight with her husband's defeated force, but, relying on the victor, her cousin Bābur, remained in the town. *Cf.* T.R. p. 268. Her case receives light from Shahr-bānū's (f. 169).

[148] Muḥammad Ḥaidar Mīrzā *Kūrkān Dūghlāt Chaghatāī Mūghūl*, the author of the *Tārīkh-i-rashīdī*; b. 905 AH. d. 958 AH. (b. 1499 d. 1551 AD.). Of his clan, the "Oghlāt" (Dūghlāt) Muḥ. ṣāliḥ says that it was called "Oghlāt" by Mughūls but Qūngūr-āt (Brown Horse) by Aūzbegs.

[149]

Baz garadad ba aṣl-i-khūd hama chīz,

Zar-i-ṣāfī u naqra u airzīn.

These lines are in Arabic in the introduction to the *Anwār-i-suhailī.* (H.B.) The first is quoted by Ḥaidar (T.R. p. 354) and in Field's *Dict. of Oriental Quotations* (p. 160). I understand them to refer here to Ḥaidar's return to his ancestral home and nearest kin as being a natural act.

[150] *tā'ib* and *ṭarīqā* suggest that Ḥaidar had become an orthodox Musalmān in or about 933 AH. (1527 AD.).

[151] Abū'l-faẓl adds music to Ḥaidar's accomplishments and Ḥaidar's own Prologue mentions yet others.

[152] *Cf.* T.R. *s.n.* and Gul-badan's H.N. *s.n.* Ḥaram Begīm.

[153] *i.e.* Alexander of Macedon. For modern mention of Central Asian claims to Greek descent *see i.a.* Kostenko, Von Schwarz, Holdich and A. Durand. *Cf.* Burnes' *Kābul* p. 203 for an illustration of a silver *patera* (now in the V. and A. Museum), once owned by ancestors of this Shāh Sulṭān Muḥammad.

[154] *Cf.* f. 6b note.

[155] *i.e.* Khān's child.

[156] The careful pointing of the Ḥai. MS. clears up earlier confusion by showing the narrowing of the vowels from *ālāchī* to *alacha.*

[157] The Elph. MS. (f. 7) writes *Aūng*, Khān's son, Prester John's title, where other MSS. have Adik. Bābur's brevity has confused his account of Sulṭān-nigār. Widowed of Maḥmūd in 900 AH. she married Adik; Adik, later, joined Shaibānī Khān but left him in 908 AH. perhaps secretly, to join his own Qāzāq horde. He was followed by his wife, apparently also making a private departure. As Adik died shortly after 908 AH. his daughters were born before that date and not after it as has been understood. *Cf.* T.R. and G.B.'s H.N. *s.nn.*; also Mems. p. 14 and *Mêms.* i, 24.

[158] Presumably by tribal custom, *yīnkālīk*, marriage with a brother's widow. Such marriages seem to have been made frequently for the protection of women left defenceless.

[159] Saʿīd's power to protect made him the refuge of several kinswomen mentioned in the B.N. and the T.R. This mother and child reached Kāshghar in 932 AH. (1526 AD.).

Here Bābur ends his [interpolated] account of his mother's family and resumes that of his father's.

[160] Bābur uses a variety of phrases to express Lordship in the Gate. Here he writes *aīshīknī bāshlātīb*; elsewhere, *aīshīk ikhtiyārī qīlmāq* and *mīnīng aīshīkīmdā ṣāḥib ikhtiyārī qīlmāq*. Von Schwarz (p. 159) throws light on the duties of the Lord of the Gate (*Aīshīk Āghāsī*). "Das Thür ... führt in eine grosse, vier-eckige, höhe Halle, deren Boden etwa 2 m. über den Weg erhoben ist. In dieser Halle, welche alle passieren muss, der durch das Thor eingeht, reitet oder fahrt, ist die Thorwache placiert. Tagsüber sind die Thore beständig öffen, nach Eintritt der Dunkelheit aber werden dieselben geschlossen und die Schlüssel dem zuständigen Polizeichef abgeliefert.... In den erwähnten Thorhallen nehmen in den hoch unabhängigen Gebieten an Bazar-tagen haufig die Richter Platz, um jedem der irgend ein Anliegen hat, so fort Recht zu sprechen. Die zudiktierten Strafen werden auch gleich in diesem selben locale vollzogen und eventuell die zum Hangen verurteilten Verbrecher an den Deckbalken aufgehängt, so dass die Besucher des Bazars unter den gehenkten durchpassieren müssen."

[161] *bu khabarnī 'Abdu'l-wahhāb shaghāwaldīn 'arẓa-dāsht qīlīb Mīrzāghā chāptūrdīlār.* This passage has been taken to mean that the *shaghāwal*, *i.e.* chief scribe, was the courier, but I think Bābur's words shew that the *shaghāwal's* act preceded the despatch of the news. Moreover the only accusative of the participle and of the verb is *khabarnī*. 'Abdu'l-wahhāb had been 'Umar Shaikh's and was now Aḥmad's officer in Khujand, on the main road for Aūrā-tīpā whence the courier started on the rapid ride. The news may have gone verbally to 'Abdu'l-wahhāb and he have written it on to Aḥmad and Abū-saʿīd.

[162] Measured from point to point even, the distance appears to be over 500 miles. Concerning Bābā Khākī *see* Ḥ.S. ii. 224; for rapid riding *i.a.* Kostenko iii, cap. Studs.

[163] *qūshūqlārnī yakhshī aïtūrā īkān dūr.* Elph. MS. for *qūshūq*, *tūyūk*. *Qūshūq* is allowed, both by its root and by usage, to describe improvisations of combined dance and song. I understand from Bābur's tense, that his information was hearsay only.

[164] *i.e.* of the military class. *Cf.* Vullers *s.n.* and T.R. p. 301.

[165] The Hūma is a fabulous bird, overshadowing by whose wings brings good-fortune. The couplet appears to be addressed to some man, under the name Hūma, from whom Ḥasan of Yaq'ūb hoped for benefit.

[166] *khāk-bīla*; the *Sanglākh*, (quoting this passage) gives *khāk-p:l:k* as the correct form of the word.

[167] *Cf.* f. 99b.

[168] One of Tīmūr's begs.

[169] *i.e.* uncle on the mother's side, of any degree, here a grandmother's brother. The title appears to have been given for life to men related to the ruling House. Parallel with it are Madame Mère, Royal Uncle, Sulṭān Wālida.

[170] *kīm dīsā būlghāī*, perhaps meaning, "Nothing of service to me."

[171] Wais the Thin.

[172] *Cf.* Chardin ed. Langlès v, 461 and ed. 1723 AD. v, 183.

[173] n.e. of Kāsān. *Cf.* f. 74. Ḥai MS., erroneously, Samarkand.

[174] An occasional doubt arises as to whether a *ṭaurī* of the text is Arabic and dispraises or Turkī and laudatory. *Cf.* Mems. p. 17 and *Méms.* i, 3.

[175] Elph. and Ḥai. MSS. *aftābachī*, water-bottle bearer on journeys; Kehr (p. 82) *aftābchī*, ewer-bearer; Ilminsky (p. 19) *akhtachi*, squire or groom. Circumstances support *aftābachī.* Yūnas was town-bred, his ewer-bearer would hardly be the rough Mughūl, Qaṃbar-'alī, useful as an *aftābachī.*

[176] Bābur was Governor of Andijān and the month being June, would be living out-of-doors. *Cf.* Ḥ.S. ii. 272 and Schuyler ii, 37.

[177] To the word Sherīm applies Abū'l-ghāzī's explanation of Nurūm and Ḥājīm, namely, that they are abbreviations of Nūr and Ḥājī Muḥammad. It explains Sulṭānīm also when used (f. 72) of Sl. Muḥammad Khānika but of Sulṭānīm as the name is common with Bābur, Ḥaidar and Gul-badan, *i.e.* as

a woman's, Busbecq's explanation is the better, namely, that it means My Sulṭān and is applied to a person of rank and means. This explains other women's titles *e.g.* Khānīm, my Khān and Ākām (Ākīm), My Lady. A third group of names formed like the last by enclitic *'m* (my), may be called names of affection, *e.g.* Māhīm, My Moon, Jānīm, My Life. (*Cf.* Persian equivalents.) Cf. Abū'l-ghāzī's *Shajarat-i-Turkī* (Désmaisons p. 272); and Ogier Ghiselin de Busbecq's *Life and Letters* (Forster and Daniel i, 38.)

[178] *Namāz-gāh*; generally an open terrace, with a wall towards the Qibla and outside the town, whither on festival days the people go out in crowds to pray. (Erskine.)

[179] *Bēglār (nīng) mīnī u wilāyatnī tāpshūrghūlārī dūr*; a noticeably idiomatic sentence. *Cf.* f. 16b 1. 6 and 1. 7 for a repetition.

[180] Maḥmūd was in Tāshkīnt, Aḥmad in Kāshghār or on the Āq-sū.

[181] The B.N. contains a considerable number of what are virtually footnotes. They are sometimes, as here, entered in the middle of a sentence and confuse the narrative; they are introduced by *kīm*, a mere sign of parenthetical matter to follow, and some certainly, known not to be Bābur's own, must have stood first on the margin of his text. It seems best to enter them as Author's notes.

[182] *i.e.* the author of the Hidāyat. *Cf.* f. 3b and note; Blochmann *Āyīn-i-akbarī s.n. qulij* and note; Bellew's *Afghan Tribes* p. 100, *Khilich.*

[183] Ar. dead, gone. The precision of Bābur's words *khānwādalār* and *yūsūnlūq* is illustrated by the existence in the days of Tīmūr, in Marghīnān, (Burhānu'd-dīn's township) of a ruler named Āīlīk Khān, apparently a descendant of Sātūq-būghrā Khān (b. 384 AH.-994 AD.) so that in Khwāja Qāẓī were united two dynasties, (*khānwādalār*), one priestly, perhaps also regal, the other of bye-gone ruling Khāns. Cf. D'Herbélot p. 433; *Yarkand Mission*, Bellew p. 121; *Tazkirat-i Sulṭān Sātūq-būghrā Khān Ghāzī Pādshāh* and *Tārīkh-i-nāṣirī* (Raverty *s.n.*)

[184] *darzī*; Ḥ.S. *khaiyāṭ*.

[185] *bīr yīrgā* (*qūyūb*), lit. to one place.

[186] *i.e.* reconstructed the earthern defences. *Cf.* Von Schwarz *s.n.* loess.

[187] They had been sent, presumably, before 'Umar Shaikh's death, to observe Sl. Aḥmad M.'s advance. *Cf.* f. 6.

[188] The time-table of the Andijān Railway has a station, Kouwa (Qabā).

[189] Bābur, always I think, calls this man Long Ḥasan; Khwānd-amīr styles him Khwāja Ḥasan; he seems to be the brother of one of 'Umar Shaikh's fathers-in-law, Khwāja Ḥusain.

[190] *bātqāq*. This word is underlined in the Elph. MS. by *dil-dil* and in the Ḥai. MS. by *jam-jama*. It is translated in the W.-i-B. by *āb pur hīla*, water full of deceit; it is our Slough of Despond. It may be remarked that neither Zenker nor Steingass gives to *dil-dil* or *jam-jama* the meaning of morass; the *Akbar-nāma* does so. (H.B. ii, 112.)

[191] *ṭawīla ṭawīla ātlār yīghīlīb aūlā kīrīshtī*. I understand the word *yīghīlīb* to convey that the massing led to the spread of the murrain.

[192] *jān tārātmāqlār i.e.* as a gift to their over-lord.

[193] Perhaps, Bābur's maternal great-uncle. It would suit the privileges bestowed on Tarkhāns if their title meant *Khān of the Gifts* (Turkī *tar*, gift). In the *Bāburnāma*, it excludes all others. Most of Aḥmad's begs were Tarkhāns, Arghūns and Chīngīz Khānids, some of them ancestors of later rulers in Tatta and Sind. Concerning the Tarkhāns *see* T.R. p. 55 and note; A.N. (H.B. *s.n.*) Elliot and Dowson's *History of India*, 498.

[194] *Cf.* f. 6.

[195] *beg ātākā*, lit. beg for father.

[196] T.R. *s.n.* Ābā-bikr.

[197] *Cf.* f. 6b and note.

[198] *faqra u masākin*, *i.e.* those who have food for one day and those who have none in hand. (Steingass.)

[199] For fashions of sitting, *see Tawārīkh-i-guzīda Naṣrat-nāma* B.M. Or. 3222. Aḥmad would appear to have maintained the deferential attitude by kneeling and sitting back upon his heels.

[200] *bīr sūnkāk bār īkān dūr*. I understand that something defiling must have been there, perhaps a bone.

[201] *Khwājanīng ham āyāghlārī ārādā īdī.*

[202] *īlbāsūn*, a kind of mallard (*Abūshqa*), here perhaps a popinjay. *Cf.* Ḥ.S. ii, 193 for Aḥmad's skill as an archer, and Payne-Gallwey's *Cross-bow* p. 225.

[203] *qabāq*, an archer's mark. Abū'l-ghāzī (Kāsān ed. p. 181. 5) mentions a hen (*tūqūq*) as a mark. *Cf.* Payne-Gallwey *l.c.* p. 231.

[204] *qīrghīcha, astar palumbarius*. (Shaw's Voc. Scully.)

[205] Perhaps, not quarrelsome.

[206] The T.R. (p. 116) attributes the rout to Shaibānī's defection. The Ḥ.S. (ii, 192) has a varied and confused account. An error in the T.R. trs. making Shaibānī plunder the Mughūls, is manifestly clerical.

[207] *i.e.* condiment, *ce qu'on ajoute au pain.*

[208] *Cf.* f. 6.

[209] *qāzāqlār*, here, if Bābur's, meaning his conflicts with Taṃbal, but as the Begīm may have been some time in Khujand, the *qāzāqlār* may be of Samarkand.

[210] All the (Turkī) Bābur-nāma MSS. and those examined of the W.-i-B. by writing *aūltūrdī* (killed) where I suggest to read *aūlnūrdī* (*devenir comme il faut*) state that Aḥmad killed Qātāq. I hesitate to accept this (1) because the only evidence of the murder is one diacritical point, the removal of which lifts Aḥmad's reproach from him by his return to the accepted rules of a polygamous household; (2) because no murder of Qātāq is chronicled by Khwānd-amīr or other writers; and (3) because it is incredible that a mild, weak man living in a family atmosphere such as Bābur, Ḥaidar and Gul-badan reproduce for us, should, while possessing facility for divorce, kill the mother of four out of his five children.

Reprieve must wait however until the word *tīrīklīk* is considered. This Erskine and de C. have read, with consistency, to mean *life-time*, but if *aūlnūrdī* be read in place of *aūltūrdī* (killed), *tīrīklīk* may be read, especially in conjunction with Bābur's *'āshīqlīklār*, as meaning *living power* or *ascendancy*. Again, if read as from *tīrik*, a small arrow and a consuming pain, *tīrīklīk* may represent Cupid's darts and wounds. Again it might be taken as from *tīrāmāk*, to hinder, or forbid.

Under these considerations, it is legitimate to reserve judgment on Aḥmad.

[211] It is customary amongst Turks for a bride, even amongst her own family, to remain veiled for some time after marriage; a child is then told to pluck off the veil and run away, this tending, it is fancied, to the child's own success in marriage. (Erskine.)

[212] Bābur's anecdote about Jānī Beg well illustrates his caution as a narrator. He appears to tell it as one who knowing the point of a story, leads up to it. He does not affirm that Jānī Beg's habits were strange or that the envoy was an athlete but that both things must have been (*īkān dūr*) from what he had heard or to suit the point of the anecdote. Nor does he affirm as of his own knowledge that Aūzbegs calls a strong man (his *zor kīshī*) a *būkuh* (bull) but says it is so understood (*dīr īmīsh*).

[213] *Cf.* f. 170.

[214] The points of a *tīpūchāq* are variously stated. If the root notion of the name be movement (*tīp*), Erskine's observation, that these horses are taught special paces, is to the point. To the verb *tīprāmāq* dictionaries assign the meaning of *movement with agitation of mind*, an explanation fully illustrated in the B.N. The verb describes fittingly the dainty, nervous action of some trained horses. Other meanings assigned to *tūpūchāq* are roadster, round-bodied and swift.

[215] *Cf.* f. 37b.

[216] *Cf.* f. 6b and note.

[217] *mashaf kitābat qīlūr īdī.*

[218] *Cf.* f. 36 and Ḥ.S. ii. 271.

[219] *sīnkīlīsī ham mūndā īdī.*

[220] *khāna-wādalār*, *viz.* the Chaghatāī, the Tīmūrid in two Mīrān-shāhī branches, 'Alī's and Bābur's and the Bāī-qarā in Harāt.

[221] *aūghlāqchī i.e.* player at *kūk-būrā.* Concerning the game, *see* Shaw's Vocabulary; Schuyler i, 268; Kostenko iii, 82; Von Schwarz *s.n. baiga.*

[222] Ẕū'l-ḥijja 910 AH.-May 1505 AD. *Cf.* f. 154. This statement helps to define what Bābur reckoned his expeditions into Hindūstān.

[223] Aīkū (Ayāgū)-tīmūr *Tarkhān Arghūn* d. *circa* 793 AH.-1391 AD. He was a friend of Tīmūr. *See* Z̤.N. i, 525 etc.

[224] *āndāq ikhlāq u aṭawārī yūq īdī kīm dīsā būlghāī.* The *Shāh-nāma* cap. xviii, describes him as a spoiled child and man of pleasure, caring only for eating, drinking and hunting. The *Shaibānī-nāma* narrates his various affairs.

[225] *i.e.*, *cutlass*, a parallel sobriquet to *qīlīch*, sword. If it be correct to translate by "cutlass," the nickname may have prompted Bābur's brief following comment, *mardāna īkān dūr*, *i.e.* Qulī Muḥ. must have been brave because known as the Cutlass. A common variant in MSS. from *Būghdā* is Bāghdād; Bāghdād was first written in the Ḥai. MS. but is corrected by the scribe to *būghdā.*

[226] So pointed in the Ḥai. MS. I surmise it a clan-name.

[227] *i.e.* to offer him the succession. The mountain road taken from Aūrā-tīpā would be by Āb-burdan, Sara-tāq and the Kām Rūd defile.

[228] *īrīldī.* The departure can hardly have been open because Aḥmad's begs favoured Maḥmūd; Malik-i-Muḥammad's party would be likely to slip away in small companies.

[229] This well-known Green, Grey or Blue palace or halting-place was within the citadel of Samarkand. *Cf.* f. 37. It served as a prison from which return was not expected.

[230] *Cf.* f. 27. He married a full-sister of Bāī-sunghar.

[231] *Gulistān* Part I. Story 27. For "steaming up," *see* Tennyson's Lotus-eaters Choric song, canto 8 (H.B.).

[232] Elph. MS. f. 16b; First W.-i-B. I.O. 215 f. 19; Second W.-i-B. I.O. 217 f. 15b; Memoirs p. 27.

[233] He was a *Dūghlāt*, uncle by marriage of Ḥaidar Mīrzā and now holding Khost for Maḥmūd. *See* T.R. s.n. for his claim on Aīsān-daulat's gratitude.

[234] *tāsh qūrghān dā chīqār dā.* Here (as *e.g.* f. 110b l. 9) the Second W.-i-B. translates *tāsh* as though it meant *stone* instead of outer. *Cf.* f. 47 for an adjectival use of *tāsh*, stone, with the preposition (*tāsh*) *din.* The places contrasted here are the citadel (*ark*) and the walled-town (*qūrghān*). The *chīqār* (exit) is the fortified Gate-house of the mud circumvallation. *Cf.* f. 46 for another example of *chīqār.*

[235] Elph. Ḥai. Kehr's MSS., *ānīng bīla bār kīshi bār beglārnī tūtūrūldī.* This idiom recurs on f. 76b l. 8. A palimpsest entry in the Elph. MS. produces the statement that when Ḥasan fled, his begs returned to Andijān.

[236] Ḥai. MS. *awī mūnkūzī*, underlined by *sāgh-i-gāū*, cows' thatched house. [*T. mūnkūz*, lit. horn, means also cattle.] Elph. MS., *awī mūnkūsh*, underlined by *dar jā'ī khwāb alfakhta*, sleeping place. [T. *mūnkūsh*, retired.]

[237] The first *qāchār* of this pun has been explained as *gurez-gāh*, *sharm-gāh*, hinder parts, *fuite* and *vertèbre inférieur.* The Ḥ.S. (ii, 273 l. 3 fr. ft.) says the wound was in a vital (*maqattal*) part.

[238] From Niẓāmī's *Khusrau u Shirīn*, Lahore lith. ed. p. 137 l. 8. It is quoted also in the A.N. Bib. Ind. ed. ii, 207 (H.B. ii, 321). (H.B.).

[239] *See* Hughes *Dictionary of Islām s.nn.* Eating and Food.

[240] *Cf.* f. 6b and note. If 'Umar Shaikh were Maḥmūd's full-brother, his name might well appear here.

[241] *i.e.* "Not a farthing, not a half-penny."

[242] Here the Mems. enters a statement, not found in the Turkī text, that Maḥmūd's dress was elegant and fashionable.

[243] *n:h:l:m.* My husband has cleared up a mistake (Mems. p. 28 and *Méms.* i, 54) of supposing this to be the name of an animal. It is explained in the A.N. (i, 255. H.B. i, 496) as a Badakhshī equivalent of *tasqāwal*; *tasqāwal* var.

tāshqāwal, is explained by the *Farhang-i-azfarī*, a Turkī-Persian Dict. seen in the Mullā Fīroz Library of Bombay, to mean *rāh band kunanda*, the stopping of the road. *Cf.* J.R.A.S. 1900 p. 137.

[244] *i.e.* "a collection of poems in the alphabetical order of the various end rhymes." (Steingass.)

[245] At this battle Daulat-shāh was present. *Cf.* Browne's D.S. for Astarābād p. 523 and for Andikhūd p. 532. For this and all other references to D.S. and Ḥ.S. I am indebted to my husband.

[246] The following dates will help out Bābur's brief narrative. Maḥmūd *æt.* 7, was given Astarābād in 864 AH. (1459-60 AD.); it was lost to Ḥusain at Jauz-wilāyat and Maḥmūd went into Khurāsān in 865 AH.; he was restored by his father in 866 AH.; on his father's death (873 AH.-1469 AD.) he fled to Harāt, thence to Samarkand and from there was taken to Ḥiṣār *æt.* 16. *Cf.* D'Herbélot *s.n.* Abū-sa'ad; Ḥ.S. i, 209; Browne's D.S. p. 522.

[247] Presumably the "Hindūstān the Less" of Clavijo (Markham p. 3 and p. 113), approx. Qaṃbar-'alī's districts. Clavijo includes Tīrmīẕ under the name.

[248] Perhaps a Ṣufī term,—longing for the absent friend. For particulars about this man *see* Ḥ.S. ii, 235 and Browne's D.S. p. 533.

[249] Here in the Ḥai. MS. is one of several blank spaces, waiting for information presumably not known to Bābur when writing. The space will have been in the archetype of the Ḥai. MS. and it makes for the opinion that the Ḥai. MS. is a direct copy of Bābur's own. This space is not left in the Elph. MS. but that MS. is known from its scribe's note (f. 198) down to f. 198 (Ḥai. MS. f. 243b) to have been copied from "other writings" and only subsequent to its f. 198 from Bābur's own. *Cf.* JRAS 1906 p. 88 and 1907 p. 143.

[250] The T.R. (p. 330) supplies this name.

[251] *Cf.* f. 35b. This was a betrothal only, the marriage being made in 903 AH. *Cf.* Ḥ.S. ii, 260 and Gul-badan's H.N. f. 24b.

[252] Kehr's MS. supplies Aī (Moon) as her name but it has no authority. The Elph. MS. has what may be *lā nām*, no name, on its margin and over *tūrūtūnchī* (4th.) its usual sign of what is problematical.

[253] *See* Ḥ.S. ii, 250. Here Pīr-i-Muḥammad *Aīlchī-būghā* was drowned. *Cf.* f. 29.

[254] Chaghānīān is marked in Erskine's (Mems.) map as somewhere about the head of (Fr. map 1904) the Ilyak Water, a tributary of the Kāfir-nighān.

[255] *i.e.* when Bābur was writing in Hindūstān.

[256] For his family *see* f. 55b note to Yār-'alī *Balāl.*

[257] *bā wujūd turklūk muhkam paidā kunanda īdī.*

[258] Roebuck's *Oriental Proverbs* (p. 232) explains the *five* of this phrase where *seven* might be expected, by saying that of this Seven days' world (qy. days of Creation) one is for birth, another for death, and that thus five only are left for man's brief life.

[259] The cognomen *Aīlchī-būghā*, taken with the bearer's recorded strength of fist, may mean Strong man of Aīlchī (the capital of Khutan). One of Tīmūr's commanders bore the name. *Cf.* f. 21b for *būghū* as *athlete.*

[260] Hazārāspī seems to be Mīr Pīr Darwesh Hazārāspī. With his brother, Mīr 'Alī, he had charge of Balkh. *See Rauẓatu'ṣ-ṣafā* B.M. Add. 23506, f. 242b; Browne's D.S. p. 432. It may be right to understand a hand-to-hand fight between Hazārāspī and Aīlchī-būghā. The affair was in 857 AH. (1453 AD.).

[261] *yārāq sīẓ*, perhaps trusting to fisticuffs, perhaps without mail. Bābur's summary has confused the facts. Muḥ. Aīlchī-būghā was sent by Sl. Maḥmūd Mīrzā from Ḥiṣār with 1,000 men and did not issue out of Qūndūz. (Ḥ.S. ii, 251.) His death occurred not before 895 AH.

[262] *See* T.R. *s.nn.* Mīr Ayūb and Ayūb.

[263] This passage is made more clear by f. 120b and f. 125b.

[264] He is mentioned in *'Alī-sher Nawā'ī's Majālis-i-nafā'is*; *see* B.M. Add. 7875, f. 278 and Rieu's Turkish Catalogue.

[265] ? full of splits or full handsome.

[266] This may have occurred after Abū-sa'īd Mīrzā's death whose son Abā-bikr was. *Cf.* f. 28. If so, over-brevity has obscured the statement.

[267] *mīnglīgh aīldīn dūr*, perhaps of those whose hereditary Command was a Thousand, the head of a Mīng (Pers. Hazāra), *i.e.* of the tenth of a *tūmān.*

[268] *qūrghān-nīng tāshīdā yāngī tām qūpārīb sālā dūr.* I understand, that what was taken was a new circumvallation in whole or in part. Such double walls are on record. *Cf.* Appendix A.

[269] *bahādurlūq aūlūsh*, an actual portion of food.

[270] *i.e.* either unmailed or actually naked.

[271] The old English noun *strike* expresses the purpose of the *sar-kob.* It is "an instrument for scraping off what rises above the top" (Webster, whose

example is grain in a measure). The *sar-kob* is an erection of earth or wood, as high as the attacked walls, and it enabled besiegers to strike off heads appearing above the ramparts.

[272] *i.e.* the dislocation due to 'Umar Shaikh's death.

[273] *Cf.* f. 13. The Ḥ.S. (ii, 274) places his son, Mīr Mughūl, in charge, but otherwise agrees with the B.N.

[274] *Cf.* Clavijo, Markham p. 132. Sir Charles Grandison bent the knee on occasions but illustrated MSS. *e.g.* the B.M. *Tawārīkh-i-guzīda Naṣrat-nāma* show that Bābur would kneel down on both knees. *Cf.* f. 123b for the fatigue of the genuflection.

[275] I have translated *kūrūshūb* thus because it appears to me that here and in other places, stress is laid by Bābur upon the mutual gaze as an episode of a ceremonious interview. The verb *kūrūshmak* is often rendered by the Persian translators as *daryāftan* and by the L. and E. Memoirs as *to embrace*. I have not found in the B.N. warrant for translating it as *to embrace*; *qūchūshmāq* is Bābur's word for this (f. 103). *Daryāftan*, taken as to grasp or see with the mind, to understand, well expresses mutual gaze and its sequel of mutual understanding. Sometimes of course, *kūrūsh*, the interview does not imply *kūrūsh*, the silent looking in the eyes with mutual understanding; it simply means *se voyer e.g.* f. 17. The point is thus dwelt upon because the frequent mention of an embrace gives a different impression of manners from that made by "interview" or words expressing mutual gaze.

[276] *dābān*. This word Réclus (vi, 171) quoting from Fedschenko, explains as a difficult rocky defile; *art*, again, as a dangerous gap at a high elevation; *bel*, as an easy low pass; and *kūtal*, as a broad opening between low hills. The explanation of *kūtal* does not hold good for Bābur's application of the word (f. 81b) to the Sara-tāq.

[277] *Cf.* f. 4b and note. From Bābur's special mention of it, it would seem not to be the usual road.

[278] The spelling of this name is uncertain. Variants are many. Concerning the tribe *see* T.R. p. 165 n.

[279] Niẕāmu'd-dīn 'Alī *Barlās*: *see* Gul-badan's H.N. *s.n.* He served Bābur till the latter's death.

[280] *i.e.* Ẕū'n-nūn or perhaps the garrison.

[281] *i.e.* down to Shaibānī's destruction of Chaghatāī rule in Tāshkīnt in 1503 AD.

[282] Elph. MS. f. 23; W.-i-B. I.O. 215 f. 26 and 217 f. 21; Mems. p. 35.

Bābur's own affairs form a small part of this year's record; the rest is drawn from the Ḥ.S. which in its turn, uses Bābur's f. 34 and f. 37b. Each author words the shared material in his own style; one adding magniloquence, the other retracting to plain statement, indeed summarizing at times to obscurity. Each passes his own judgment on events, *e.g.* here Khwānd-amīr's is more favourable to Ḥusain Bāī-qarā's conduct of the Ḥiṣār campaign than Bābur's. *Cf.* Ḥ.S. ii, 256-60 and 274.

[283] This feint would take him from the Oxus.

[284] Tīrmīẕ to Ḥiṣār, 96m. (Réclus vi, 255).

[285] Ḥ.S. Wazr-āb valley. The usual route is up the Kām Rūd and over the Mūra pass to Sara-tāq. *Cf.* f. 81b.

[286] *i.e.* the Ḥiṣārī mentioned a few lines lower and on f. 99b. Nothing on f. 99b explains his cognomen.

[287] The road is difficult. *Cf.* f. 81b.

[288] Khwānd-amīr also singles out one man for praise, Sl. Maḥmūd *Mīr-i-ākhwur*; the two names probably represent one person. The sobriquet may refer to skill with a matchlock, to top-spinning (*firnagī-bāz*) or to some lost joke. (Ḥ.S. ii, 257.)

[289] This pregnant phrase has been found difficult. It may express that Bābur assigned the sulṭāns places in their due precedence; that he seated them in a row; and that they sat cross-legged, as men of rank, and were not made, as inferiors, to kneel and sit back on their heels. Out of this last meaning, I infer comes the one given by dictionaries, "to sit at ease," since the cross-legged posture is less irksome than the genuflection, not to speak of the ease of mind produced by honour received. *Cf.* f. 18b and note on Aḥmad's posture; Redhouse *s.nn. bāghīsh* and *bāghdāsh*; and B.M. Tawārīkh-i-guzīda naṣrat-nāma, in the illustrations of which the chief personage, only, sits cross-legged.

[290] *siyāsat.* My translation is conjectural only.

[291] *sar-kob.* The old English noun *strike*, "an instrument for scraping off what appears above the top," expresses the purpose of the wall-high erections of wood or earth (*L. agger*) raised to reach what shewed above ramparts. *Cf.* Webster.

[292] Presumably lower down the Qūndūz Water.

[293] *aūz pādshāhī u mīrzālārīdīn artīb.*

[294] *sic.* Ḥai. MS.; Elph. MS. "near Tāliqān"; some W.-i-B. MSS. "Great Garden." Gul-badan mentions a Tāliqān Garden. Perhaps the Mīrzā went

so far east because, Ẕū'n-nūn being with him, he had Qandahār in mind. *Cf.* f. 42b.

[295] *i.e.* Sayyid Muḥammad 'Alī. *See* f. 15 n. to Sherīm. Khwāja Changāl lies 14 m. below Tāliqān on the Tāliqān Water. (Erskine.)

[296] f. 27b, second.

[297] The first was *circa* 895 AH.-1490 AD. *Cf.* f. 27b.

[298] Bābur's wording suggests that their common homage was the cause of Badī'u'z-zamān's displeasure but *see* f. 41.

[299] The Mīrzā had grown up with Ḥiṣārīs. *Cf.* Ḥ.S. ii, 270.

[300] As the husband of one of the six Badakhshī Begīms, he was closely connected with local ruling houses. *See* T.R. p. 107.

[301] *i.e.* Muḥammad 'Ubaidu'l-lāh the elder of *Aḥrārī's* two sons. d. 911 AH. *See Rashaḥāt-i-'ain-alḥayāt* (I.O. 633) f. 269-75; and *Khizīnatu'l-aṣfiya* lith. ed. i, 597.

[302] *Bū yūq tūr*, *i.e.* This is not to be.

[303] d. 908 AH. He was not, it would seem, of the *Aḥrārī* family. His own had provided Pontiffs (*Shaikhu'l-islām*) for Samarkand through 400 years. *Cf. Shaibānī-nāma*, Vambéry, p. 106; also, for his character, p. 96.

[304] *i.e.* he claimed sanctuary.

[305] *Cf.* f. 45b and Pétis de la Croix's *Histoire de Chingiz Khān* pp. 171 and 227. What Tīmūr's work on the Gūk Sarāī was is a question for archæologists.

[306] *i.e.* over the Aītmak Pass. *Cf.* f. 49.

[307] Ḥai. MS. *ārālighīgha*. Elph. MS. *ārāl*, island.

[308] *See* f. 179b for *Binā'ī*. Muḥammad Ṣāliḥ Mīrzā *Khwārizmī* is the author of the *Shaibānī-nāma*.

[309] Elph. MS. f. 27; W.-i-B. I.O. 215 f. 30b and 217 f. 25; Mems. p. 42.

[310] *i.e.* Circassian. Muḥammad Ṣāliḥ (Sh.N. Vambéry p. 276 l. 58) speaks of other Aūzbegs using Chirkas swords.

[311] *aīrtā yāzīghā*. My translation is conjectural. *Aīrtā* implies *i.a.* foresight. *Yāzīghā* allows a pun at the expense of the sulṭāns; since it can be read both as *to the open country* and as *for their* (*next*, *aīrtā*) *misdeeds*. My impression is that they took the opportunity of being outside Samarkand with their men, to leave Bāī-sunghar and make for Shaibānī, then in Turkistān. Muḥammad

Ṣāliḥ also marking the tottering Gate of Sl. 'Alī Mīrzā, left him now, also for Shaibānī. (Vambéry cap. xv.)

[312] *aūmāq*, to amuse a child in order to keep it from crying.

[313] *i.e.* with Khwāja Yahya presumably. *See* f. 38.

[314] This man is mentioned also in the *Tawārikh-i-guzīda Naṣratnāma* B.M. Or. 3222 f. 124b.

[315] Ḥ.S., on the last day of Ramẓān (June 28th. 1497 AD.).

[316] Muḥammad *Sīghal* appears to have been a marked man. I quote from the T.G.N.N. (*see supra*), f. 123b foot, the information that he was the grandson of Ya'qūb Beg. Zenker explains *Sīghalī* as the name of a Chaghatāī family. An *Ayūb-i-Ya'qūb Begchīk Mughūl* may be an uncle. See f. 43 for another grandson.

[317] *baẓ'ī kīrkān-kīnt-kīsākkā bāsh-sīz-qīlghān Mughūllārnī tūtūb.* I take the word *kīsāk* in this highly idiomatic sentence to be a diminutive of *kīs*, old person, on the analogy of *mīr*, *mīrāk*, *mard*, *mardak*. [The Ḥ.S. uses *Kīsāk* (ii, 261) as a proper noun.] The alliteration in *kāf* and the mighty adjective here are noticeable.

[318] Qāsim feared to go amongst the Mughūls lest he should meet retaliatory death. *Cf.* f. 99b.

[319] This appears from the context to be Yām (Jām) -bāī and not the Djouma (Jām) of the Fr. map of 1904, lying farther south. The Avenue named seems likely to be Tīmūr's of f. 45b and to be on the direct road for Khujand. *See* Schuyler i, 232.

[320] *būghān buyīnī.* W.-i-B. 215, *yān*, thigh, and 217 *gardan*, throat. I am in doubt as to the meaning of *būghān*; perhaps the two words stand for joint at the nape of the neck. Khwāja-i-kalān was one of seven brothers, six died in Bābur's service, he himself served till Bābur's death.

[321] *Cf.* f. 48.

[322] Khorochkine (Radlov's *Réceuil d'Itinéraires* p. 241) mentions Pul-i-mougak, a great stone bridge thrown across a deep ravine, east of Samarkand. *For* Kūl-i-maghāk, deep pool, or pool of the fosse, *see* f. 48b.

[323] From Khwānd-amīr's differing account of this affair, it may be surmised that those sending the message were not treacherous; but the message itself was deceiving inasmuch as it did not lead Bābur to expect opposition. *Cf.* f. 43 and note.

[324] Of this nick-name several interpretations are allowed by the dictionaries.

[325] *See* Schuyler i, 268 for an account of this beautiful Highland village.

[326] Here Bābur takes up the thread, dropped on f. 36, of the affairs of the Khurāsānī mīrzās. He draws on other sources than the Ḥ.S.; perhaps on his own memory, perhaps on information given by Khurāsānīs with him in Hindūstān *e.g.* Ḥusain's grandson. *See* f. 167b. *Cf.* Ḥ.S. ii, 261.

[327] *bāghīshlāb tūr. Cf.* f. 34 note to *bāghīsh dā.*

[328] *Bū sozlār aūnūlūng.* Some W.-i-B. MSS., *Farāmosh bakunīd* for *nakunīd,* thus making the Mīrzā not acute but rude, and destroying the point of the story *i.e.* that the Mīrzā pretended so to have forgotten as to have an empty mind. Khwānd-amīr states that 'Alī-sher prevailed at first; his tears therefore may have been of joy at the success of his pacifying mission.

[329] *i.e.* B.Z.'s father, Ḥusain, against Mū'min's father, B.Z. and Ḥusain's son, Muẕaffar Ḥusain against B.Z.'s son Mū'min;—a veritable conundrum.

[330] Garzawān lies west of Balkh. Concerning Pul-i-chirāgh Col. Grodekoff's *Ride to Harāt* (Marvin p. 103 ff.) gives pertinent information. It has also a map showing the Pul-i-chirāgh meadow. The place stands at the mouth of a triply-bridged defile, but the name appears to mean Gate of the Lamp (*cf.* Gate of Tīmūr), and not Bridge of the Lamp, because the Ḥ.S. and also modern maps write *bīl* (*bel*), pass, where the Turkī text writes *pul,* bridge, narrows, pass.

The lamp of the name is one at the shrine of a saint, just at the mouth of the defile. It was alight when Col. Grodekoff passed in 1879 and to it, he says, the name is due now—as it presumably was 400 years ago and earlier.

[331] Khwānd-amīr heard from the Mīrzā on the spot, when later in his service, that he was let down the precipice by help of turban-sashes tied together.

[332] *yīkīt yīlāng u yāyāq yālīng;* a jingle made by due phonetic change of vowels; a play too on *yālāng,* which first means stripped *i.e.* robbed and next unmailed, perhaps sometimes bare-bodied in fight.

[333] *qūsh-khāna.* As the place was outside the walls, it may be a good hawking ground and not a falconry.

[334] The Ḥ.S. mentions (ii, 222) a Sl. Aḥmad of Chār-shaṃba, a town mentioned *e.g.* by Grodekoff p. 123. It also spoils Bābur's coincidence by fixing Tuesday, Shab'ān 29th. for the battle. Perhaps the commencement of the Muḥammadan day at sunset, allows of both statements.

[335] Elph. MS. f. 30b; W.-i-B. I.O. 215 f. 34 and 217 f. 26b; Mems. p. 46.

The abruptness of this opening is due to the interposition of Sl. Ḥusain M.'s affairs between Bābur's statement on f. 41 that he returned from Aūrgūt and this first of 903 AH. that on return he encamped in Qulba.

[336] *See* f. 48b.

[337] *i.e.* Chūpān-ātā; *see* f. 45 and note.

[338] *Aūghlāqchī*, the Grey Wolfer of f. 22.

[339] A sobriquet, the *suppliant* or perhaps something having connection with musk. Ḥ.S. ii, 278, son of Ḥ.D.

[340] *i.e.* grandson (of Muḥammad Sīghal). *Cf.* f. 39.

[341] This seeming sobriquet may show the man's trade. *Kāl* is a sort of biscuit; *qāshūq* may mean a spoon.

[342] The Ḥ.S. does not ascribe treachery to those inviting Bābur into Samarkand but attributes the murder of his men to others who fell on them when the plan of his admission became known. The choice here of "town-rabble" for retaliatory death supports the account of Ḥ.S. ii.

[343] "It was the end of September or beginning of October" (Erskine).

[344] *awī u kīpa yīrlār. Awī* is likely to represent *kibitkas*. For *kīpa yīr*, *see* Zenker p. 782.

[345] Interesting reference may be made, amongst the many books on Samarkand, to Sharafu'd-dīn 'Alī *Yazdī's Ẓafar-nāma* Bib. Ind. ed. i, 300, 781, 799, 800 and ii, 6, 194, 596 etc.; to Ruy Gonzalves di Clavijo's *Embassy to Tīmūr* (Markham) cap. vi and vii; to Ujfalvy's *Turkistan* ii, 79 and Madame Ujfalvy's *De Paris à Samarcande* p. 161,—these two containing a plan of the town; to Schuyler's *Turkistan*; to Kostenko's *Turkistan Gazetteer* i, 345; to Réclus, vi, 270 and plan; and to a beautiful work of the St. Petersburg Archæological Society, *Les Mosquées de Samarcande*, of which the B.M. has a copy.

[346] This statement is confused in the Elp. and Ḥai. MSS. The second appears to give, by abjad, lat. 40° 6" and long. 99'. Mr. Erskine (p. 48) gives lat. 39' 57" and long. 99' 16", noting that this is according to Ūlūgh Beg's Tables and that the long. is calculated from Ferro. The Ency. Br. of 1910-11 gives lat. 39' 39" and long. 66' 45".

[347] The enigmatical cognomen, Protected Town, is of early date; it is used *i.a.* by Ibn Batūta in the 14th. century. Bābur's tense refers it to the past. The town had frequently changed hands in historic times before he

wrote. The name may be due to immunity from damage to the buildings in the town. Even Chīngīz Khān's capture (1222 AD.) left the place well-preserved and its lands cultivated, but it inflicted great loss of men. *Cf.* Schuyler i, 236 and his authorities, especially Bretschneider.

[348] Here is a good example of Bābur's caution in narrative. He does not affirm that Samarkand became Musalmān, or (*infra*) that Quṣam ibn 'Abbās went, or that Alexander founded but in each case uses the presumptive past tense, resp. *būlghān dūr*, *bārghān dūr*, *bīnā qīlghān dūr*, thus showing that he repeats what may be inferred or presumed and not what he himself asserts.

[349] *i.e.* of Muḥammad. See Z̤.N. ii, 193.

[350] *i.e.* Fat Village. His text misleading him, Mr. Erskine makes here the useful irrelevant note that Persians and Arabs call the place Samar-qand and Turks, Samar-kand, the former using *qaf* (q), the latter *kaf* (k). Both the Elph. and the Ḥai. MSS. write Samarqand.

For use of the name Fat Village, *see* Clavijo (Markham p. 170), Simesquinte, and Bretschneider's *Mediæval Geography* pp. 61, 64, 66 and 163.

[351] *qadam.* Kostenko (i, 344) gives 9 m. as the circumference of the old walls and 1-2/3m. as that of the citadel. *See* Mde. Ujfalvy p. 175 for a picture of the walls.

[352] *Ma'lūm aīmās kīm mūncha paidā būlmīsh būlghāī*; an idiomatic phrase.

[353] d. 333 AH. (944 AD.). *See* D'Herbélot art. Mātridī p. 572.

[354] *See* D'Herbélot art. Aschair p. 124.

[355] Abū 'Abdu'l-lāh bin Ismā'īlu'l-jausī b. 194 AH. d. 256 AH. (810-870 AD.). *See* D'Herbélot art. Bokhārī p. 191, art. Giorag p. 373, and art. Ṣāḥiḥu'l-bokhārī p. 722. He passed a short period, only, of his life in Khartank, a suburb of Samarkand.

[356] *Cf.* f. 3b and n. 1.

[357] This though 2475 ft. above the sea is only some 300 ft. above Samarkand. It is the Chūpān-ātā (Father of Shepherds) of maps and on it Tīmūr built a shrine to the local patron of shepherds. The Zar-afshān, or rather, its Qarā-sū arm, flows from the east of the Little Hill and turns round it to flow west. Bābur uses the name *Kohik Water* loosely; *e.g.* for the whole Zar-afshān when he speaks (*infra*) of cutting off the Dar-i-gham canal but for its southern arm only, the Qarā-sū in several places, and once, for the Dar-i-gham canal. *See* f. 49b and Kostenko i. 192.

[358] *rūd.* The Zar-afshān has a very rapid current. *See* Kostenko i, 196, and for the canal, i, 174. The name Dar-i-gham is used also for a musical note having charm to witch away grief; and also for a town noted for its wines.

[359] What this represents can only be guessed; perhaps 150 to 200 miles. Abū'l-fidā (Reinaud ii, 213) quotes Ibn Haukal as saying that from Bukhārā up to "Bottam" (this seems to be where the Zar-afshān emerges into the open land) is eight days' journey through an unbroken tangle of verdure and gardens.

[360] *See* Schuyler i, 286 on the apportionment of water to Samarkand and Bukhārā.

[361] It is still grown in the Samarkand region, and in Mr. Erskine's time a grape of the same name was cultivated in Aurangābād of the Deccan.

[362] *i.e. Shāhrukhī*, Tīmūr's grandson, through Shāhrukh. It may be noted here that Bābur never gives Tīmūr any other title than Beg and that he styles all Tīmūrids, Mīrzā (Mīr-born).

[363] Mr. Erskine here points out the contradiction between the statements (i) of Ibn Haukal, writing, in 367 AH. (977 AD.), of Samarkand as having a citadel (*ark*), an outer-fort (*qūrghān*) and Gates in both circumvallations; and (2) of Sharafu'd-dīn *Yazdī* (Z.N.) who mentions that when, in Tīmūr's day, the Getes besieged Samarkand, it had neither walls nor gates. *See* Ouseley's Ibn Haukal p. 253; Z.N. Bib. Ind. ed. i, 109 and Pétis de la Croix's Z.N. (*Histoire de Tīmūr Beg*) i, 91.

[364] Here still lies the Ascension Stone, the *Gūk-tāsh*, a block of greyish white marble. Concerning the date of the erection of the building and meaning of its name, *see e.g.* Pétis de la Croix's *Histoire de Chīngīz Khān* p. 171; Mems. p. 40 note; and Schuyler *s.n.*

[365] This seems to be the Bībī Khānīm Mosque. The author of *Les Mosquées de Samarcande* states that Tīmūr built Bībī Khānīm and the Gūr-i-amīr (Amīr's tomb); decorated Shāh-i-zinda and set up the Chūpān-ātā shrine. *Cf.* f. 46 and note to Jahāngīr Mīrzā, as to the Gūr-i-amīr.

[366] Cap. II. Quoting from Sale's *Qur'ān* (i, 24) the verse is, "And Ibrāhīm and Ismā'īl raised the foundations of the house, saying, 'Lord! accept it from us, for Thou art he who hearest and knowest; Lord! make us also resigned to Thee, and show us Thy holy ceremonies, and be turned to us, for Thou art easy to be reconciled, and merciful.'"

[367] or, *buland*, Garden of the Height or High Garden. The Turkī texts have what can be read as *buldī* but the Z.N. both when describing it (ii, 194) and elsewhere (*e.g.* ii, 596) writes *buland*. *Buldī* may be a clerical error for *bulandī*, the height, a name agreeing with the position of the garden.

[368] In the Heart-expanding Garden, the Spanish Ambassadors had their first interview with Tīmūr. *See* Clavijo (Markham p. 130). Also the Z̤.N. ii, 6 for an account of its construction.

[369] Judging from the location of the gardens and of Bābur's camps, this appears to be the Avenue mentioned on f. 39b and f. 40.

[370] *See infra* f. 48 and note.

[371] The Plane-tree Garden. This seems to be Clavijo's *Bayginar*, laid out shortly before he saw it (Markham p. 136).

[372] The citadel of Samarkand stands high; from it the ground slopes west and south; on these sides therefore gardens outside the walls would lie markedly below the outer-fort (*tāsh-qūrghān*). Here as elsewhere the second W.-i-B. reads *stone* for *outer* (*Cf.* index *s.n. tāsh*). For the making of the North garden *see* Z̤.N. i, 799.

[373] Tīmūr's eldest son, d. 805 AH. (1402 AD.), before his father, therefore. Bābur's wording suggests that in his day, the Gūr-i-amīr was known as the Madrāsa. *See* as to the buildings Z̤.N. i, 713 and ii, 492, 595, 597, 705; Clavijo (Markham p. 164 and p. 166); and *Les Mosquées de Samarcande.*

[374] Hindūstān would make a better climax here than Samarkand does.

[375] These appear to be pictures or ornamentations of carved wood. Redhouse describes *islīmī* as a special kind of ornamentation in curved lines, similar to Chinese methods.

[376] *i.e.* the Black Stone (*ka'ba*) at Makkah to which Musalmāns turn in prayer.

[377] As ancient observatories were themselves the instruments of astronomical observation, Bābur's wording is correct. Aūlūgh Beg's great quadrant was 180 ft. high; Abū-muḥammad *Khujandī's* sextant had a radius of 58 ft. Jā'ī Singh made similar great instruments in Jā'īpūr, Dihlī has others. *Cf.* Greaves Misc. Works i, 50; Mems. p. 51 note; *Āiyīn-i-akbarī* (Jarrett) ii, 5 and note; Murray's Hand-book to Bengal p. 331; Indian Gazetteer xiii, 400.

[378] b. 597 AH. d. 672 AH. (1201-1274 AD.). *See* D'Herbélot's art. Naṣīr-i-dīn p. 662; Abū'l-fidā (Reinaud, Introduction i, cxxxviii) and Beale's Biographical Dict. *s.n.*

[379] a grandson of Chīngīz Khān, d. 663 AH. (1265 AD.). The cognomen *Aīl-khānī* (*Īl-khānī*) may mean Khān of the Tribe.

[380] Ḥarūnu'r-rashīd's second son; d. 218 AH. (833 AD.).

[381] Mr. Erskine notes that this remark would seem to fix the date at which Bābur wrote it as 934 AH. (1527 AD.), that being the 1584th. year of the era of Vikramāditya, and therefore at three years before Bābur's death. (The Vikramāditya era began 57 BC.)

[382] *Cf.* index *s.n. tāsh.*

[383] This remark may refer to the 34 miles between the town and the quarries of its building stone. *See* f. 49 and note to Aītmāk Pass.

[384] Steingass, any support for the back in sitting, a low wall in front of a house. *See* Vullers p. 148 and *Burhān-i-qāṭi'*; p. 119. Perhaps a *dado.*

[385] *beg u begāt, bāgh u bāghcha.*

[386] Four Gardens, a quadrilateral garden, laid out in four plots. The use of the name has now been extended for any well-arranged, large garden, especially one belonging to a ruler (Erskine).

[387] As two of the trees mentioned here are large, it may be right to translate *nārwān*, not by pomegranate, but as the hard-wood elm, Madame Ujfalvy's '*karagatche*' (p. 168 and p. 222). The name *qarā-yīghāch* (*karagatch*), dark tree, is given to trees other than this elm on account of their deep shadow.

[388] Now a common plan indeed! *See* Schuyler i, 173.

[389] *juwāz-i-kaghazlār* (*nīng*) *sū'ī*, *i.e.* the water of the paper-(pulping)-mortars. Owing to the omission from some MSS. of the word *sū*, water, *juwāz* has been mistaken for a kind of paper. *See* Mems. p. 52 and *Méms.* i, 102; A.Q.R. July 1910, p. 2, art. Paper-mills of Samarkand (H.B.); and Madame Ujfalvy p. 188. Kostenko, it is to be noted, does not include paper in his list (i, 346) of modern manufactures of Samarkand.

[390] Mine of mud or clay. My husband has given me support for reading *gil*, and not *gul*, rose;—(1) In two good MSS. of the W.-i-B. the word is pointed with *kasra*, *i.e.* as for *gil*, clay; and (2) when describing a feast held in the garden by Tīmūr, the Z.N. says the mud-mine became a rose-mine, *shuda Kān-i-gil Kān-i-gul.* [Mr. Erskine refers here to Pétis de la Croix's *Histoire de Tīmūr Beg* (*i.e.* Z.N.) i, 96 and ii, 133 and 421.]

[391] *qūrūgh.* Vullers, classing the word as Arabic, Zenker, classing it as Eastern Turkī, and Erskine (p. 42 n.) explain this as land reserved for the summer encampment of princes. Shaw (Voc. p. 155), deriving it from *qūrūmāq*, to frighten, explains it as a fenced field of growing grain.

[392] *Cf.* f. 40. There it is located at one *yīghāch* and here at 3 *kurohs* from the town.

[393] *ṭaur*. *Cf.* Zenker *s.n.* I understand it to lie, as Khān Yūrtī did, in a curve of the river.

[394] 162 m. by rail.

[395] *Cf.* f. 3.

[396] *tīrīsīnī sūīūb*. The verb *sūīmāk*, to despoil, seems to exclude the common plan of stoning the fruit. *Cf.* f. 3b, *dānasīnī alīp*, taking out the stones.

[397] *Mīn Samarkandtā aūl (or auwal) aīchkāndā Bukhārā chāghīrlār nī aīchār aīdīm*. These words have been understood to refer to Bābur's initial drinking of wine but this reading is negatived by his statement (f. 189) that he first drank wine in Harāt in 912 AH. I understand his meaning to be that the wine he drank in Samarkand was Bukhārā wine. The time cannot have been earlier than 917 AH. The two words *aūl aīchkāndā*, I read as parallel to *aūl* (*bāghrī qarā*) (f. 280) 'that drinking,' 'that bird,' *i.e.* of those other countries, not of Hindūstān where he wrote.

It may be noted that Bābur's word for wine, *chāghīr*, may not always represent wine of the grape but may include wine of the apple and pear (cider and perry), and other fruits. Cider, its name seeming to be a descendant of *chāghīr*, was introduced into England by Crusaders, its manufacture having been learned from Turks in Palestine.

[398] 48 m. 3 fur. by way of the Aītmāk Pass (mod. Takhta Qarachi), and, Réclus (vi, 256) Buz-gala-khāna, Goat-house.

[399] The name Aītmāk, to build, appears to be due to the stone quarries on the range. The pass-head is 34 m. from Samarkand and 3000 ft. above it. *See* Kostenko ii, 115 and Schuyler ii, 61 for details of the route.

[400] The description of this hall is difficult to translate. Clavijo (Markham 124) throws light on the small recesses. *Cf.* Z.N. i, 781 and 300 and Schuyler ii, 68.

[401] The Tāq-i-kisrī, below Bāghdād, is 105 ft. high, 84 ft. span and 150 ft. in depth (Erskine).

[402] *Cf.* f. 46. Bābur does not mention that Tīmūr's father was buried at Kesh. Clavijo (Markham p. 123) says it was Tīmūr's first intention to be buried near his father, in Kesh.

[403] Abū'l-fidā (Reinaud II, ii, 21) says that Nasaf is the Arabic and Nakhshab the local name for Qarshī. Ibn Haukal (Ouseley p. 260) writes Nakhshab.

[404] This word has been translated *burial-place* and *cimetière* but Qarshī means castle, or royal-residence. The Z.N. (i, 111) says that Qarshī is an equivalent for Ar. *qaṣr*, palace, and was so called, from one built there by Qublāī Khān (d. 1294 AD.). Perhaps Bābur's word is connected with Gūrkhān, the title of sovereigns in Khutan, and means great or royal-house, *i.e.* palace.

[405] 94 m. 6-1/2 fur. via Jām (Kostenko i, 115.)

[406] See Appendix B.

[407] some 34 m. (Kostenko i, 196). Schuyler mentions that he heard in Qarā-kūl a tradition that the district, in bye-gone days, was fertilized from the Sīr.

[408] *Cf.* f. 45.

[409] By *abjad* the words *'Abbās kasht* yield 853. The date of the murder was Ramẓān 9, 853 AH. (Oct. 27th. 1449 AD.).

[410] This couplet is quoted in the *Rauẓatu'ṣ-ṣafā* (lith. ed. vi, f. 234 foot) and in the Ḥ.S. ii, 44. It is said, in the R.Ṣ. to be by Niẓāmī and to refer to the killing by Shīrūya of his father, Khusrau Parwīz in 7 AH. (628 AD.). The Ḥ.S. says that 'Abdu'l-laṭīf constantly repeated the couplet, after he had murdered his father. [See also Daulat Shāh (Browne p. 356 and p. 366.) H.B.]

[411] By *abjad*, *Bābā Ḥusain kasht* yields 854. The death was on Rabi' I, 26, 854 AH. (May 9th. 1450 AD.). See R.Ṣ. vi, 235 for an account of this death.

[412] This overstates the time; dates shew 1 yr. 1 mth. and a few days.

[413] *i.e.* The Khān of the Mughūls, Bābur's uncle.

[414] Elph. MS. *aūrmaghāīlār*, might not turn; Ḥai. and Kehr's MSS. (*sar bā bād*) *bīrmāghāīlār*, might not give. Both metaphors seem drawn from the protective habit of man and beast of turning the back to a storm-wind.

[415] *i.e.* betwixt two waters, the Miyān-i-dū-āb of India. Here, it is the most fertile triangle of land in Turkistān (Réclus, vi, 199), enclosed by the eastern mountains, the Nārīn and the Qarā-sū; Rabāṭik-aūrchīnī, its alternative name, means Small Station sub-district. From the uses of *aūrchīn* I infer that it describes a district in which there is no considerable head-quarters fort.

[416] *i.e.* his own, Qūtlūq-nigār Khānīm and hers, Aīsān-daulat Begīm, with perhaps other widows of his father, probably Shāh Sulṭān Begīm.

[417] *Cf.* f. 16 for almost verbatim statements.

[418] Blacksmith's Dale. *Ahangarān* appears corrupted in modern maps to *Angren*. *See* Ḥ.S. ii, 293 for Khwānd-amīr's wording of this episode.

[419] *Cf.* f. 1b and Kostenko i, 101.

[420] *i.e.* Khān Uncle (Mother's brother).

[421] n.w. of the Sang ferry over the Sīr.

[422] perhaps, messenger of good tidings.

[423] This man's family connections are interesting. He was 'Alī-shukr Beg *Bahārlū's* grandson, nephew therefore of Pāshā Begīm; through his son, Saif-'alī Beg, he was the grandfather of Bairām Khān-i-khānān and thus the g.g.f. of 'Abdu'r-raḥīm Mīrzā, the translator of the Second *Wāqi'āt-i-bāburī*. *See* Firishta lith. ed. p. 250.

[424] Bābur's (step-)grandmother, co-widow with Aīsān-daulat of Yūnas Khān and mother of Aḥmad and Maḥmud *Chaghatāī*.

[425] Here the narrative picks up the thread of Khusrau Shāh's affairs, dropped on f. 44.

[426] *mīng tūmān fulūs*, *i.e.* a thousand sets-of-ten-thousand small copper coins. Mr. Erskine (Mems. p. 61) here has a note on coins. As here the *tūmān* does not seem to be a coin but a number, I do not reproduce it, valuable as it is *per se*.

[427] *āriqlār*; this the annotator of the Elph. MS. has changed to *āshlīq*, provisions, corn.

[428] *Samān-chī* may mean Keeper of the Goods. Tīngrī-bīrdī, Theodore, is the purely Turkī form of the Khudāī-bīrdī, already met with several times in the B.N.

[429] Bast (Bost) is on the left bank of the Halmand.

[430] *Cf.* f. 56b.

[431] known as *Kābulī*. He was a son of Abū-sa'īd and thus an uncle of Bābur. He ruled Kābul and Ghaznī from a date previous to his father's death in 873 AH. (perhaps from the time 'Umar Shaikh was *not* sent there, in 870 AH. *See* f. 6b) to his death in 907 AH. Bābur was his virtual successor in Kābul, in 910 AH.

[432] Elph. MS. f. 42; W.-i-B. I.O. 215 f. 47b and 217 f. 38; Mems. p. 63. Bābur here resumes his own story, interrupted on f. 56.

[433] *aīsh achīlmādī*, a phrase recurring on f. 59b foot. It appears to imply, of trust in Providence, what the English "The way was not opened," does. *Cf.*

f. 60b for another example of trust, there clinching discussion whether to go or not to go to Marghīnān.

[434] *i.e. Aḥrārī.* He had been dead some 10 years. The despoilment of his family is mentioned on f. 23b.

[435] *fatratlār*, here those due to the deaths of Aḥmad and Maḥmūd with their sequel of unstable government in Samarkand.

[436] *Aūghlāqchī*, the player of the kid-game, the gray-wolfer. Yār-yīlāq will have gone with the rest of Samarkand into ‘Alī’s hands in Rajab 903 AH. (March 1498). Contingent terms between him and Bābur will have been made; Yūsuf may have recognized some show of right under them, for allowing Bābur to occupy Yār-yīlāq.

[437] *i.e.* after 933 AH. *Cf.* f. 46b and note concerning the Bikramāditya era. See index *s.n.* Aḥmad-i-yūsuf and Ḥ.S. ii, 293.

[438] This plural, unless ironical, cannot be read as honouring ‘Alī; Bābur uses the honorific plural most rarely and specially, *e.g.* for saintly persons, for The Khān and for elder women-kinsfolk.

[439] *bīr yārīm yīl.* Dates shew this to mean six months. It appears a parallel expression to Pers. *hasht-yak*, one-eighth.

[440] Ḥ.S. ii, 293, in place of these two quotations, has a *misra‘*,—*Na rāy ṣafar kardan u na rūy iqāmat*, (Nor resolve to march, nor face to stay).

[441] *i.e.* in Samarkand.

[442] Point to point, some 145 m. but much further by the road. Tang-āb seems likely to be one of the head-waters of Khwāja Bikargān-water. Thence the route would be by unfrequented hill-tracks, each man leading his second horse.

[443] *tūn yārīmī naqāra waqtīdā. Tūn yārīmī* seems to mean half-dark, twilight. Here it cannot mean mid-night since this would imply a halt of twelve hours and Bābur says no halt was made. The drum next following mid-day is the one beaten at sunset.

[444] The voluntary prayer, offered when the sun has well risen, fits the context.

[445] I understand that the obeisance was made in the Gate-house, between the inner and outer doors.

[446] This seeming sobriquet may be due to eloquence or to good looks.

[447] *qarā tīyāq. Cf.* f. 63 where black bludgeons are used by a red rabble.

[448] He was head-man of his clan and again with Shaibānī in 909 AH. (Sh. N. Vambéry, p. 272). Erskine (p. 67) notes that the Manghīts are the modern Nogais.

[449] *i.e.* in order to allow for the here very swift current. The Ḥ.S. varying a good deal in details from the B.N. gives the useful information that Aūzūn Ḥasan's men knew nothing of the coming of the Tāshkīnt Mughūls.

[450] *Cf.* f. 4b and App. A. as to the position of Akhsī.

[451] *bārīnī qīrdīlār.* After this statement the five exceptions are unexpected; Bābur's wording is somewhat confused here.

[452] *i.e.* in Hindūstān.

[453] Taṃbal would be the competitor for the second place.

[454] 47 m. 4-1/2 fur.

[455] Bābur had been about two lunar years absent from Andijān but his loss of rule was of under 16 months.

[456] A scribe's note entered here on the margin of the Ḥai. MS. is to the effect that certain words are not in the noble archetype (*nashka sharīf*); this supports other circumstances which make for the opinion that this Codex is a direct copy of Bābur's own MS. *See* Index s.n. Ḥai. MS. and JRAS 1906, p. 87.

[457] *Musalmān* here seems to indicate mental contrast with Pagan practices or neglect of Musalmān observances amongst Mughūls.

[458] *i.e.* of his advisors and himself.

[459] *Cf.* f. 34.

[460] *circa* 933 AH. All the revolts chronicled by Bābur as made against himself were under Mughūl leadership. Long Ḥasan, Taṃbal and 'Alī-dost were all Mughūls. The worst was that of 914 AH. (1518 AD.) in which Qulī *Chūnāq* disgraced himself (T.R. p. 357).

[461] *Chūnāq* may indicate the loss of one ear.

[462] *Būqāq*, amongst other meanings, has that of *one who lies in ambush.*

[463] This remark has interest because it shews that (as Bābur planned to write more than is now with the B.N. MSS.) the first gap in the book (914 AH. to 925 AH.) is accidental. His own last illness is the probable cause of this gap. *Cf.* JRAS 1905, p. 744. Two other passages referring to unchronicled matters are one about the Bāgh-i-ṣafā (f. 224), and one about Sl. 'Alī Ṭaghāī (f. 242).

[464] I surmise Aīlāīsh to be a local name of the Qarā-daryā affluent of the Sīr.

[465] *aīkī aūch naubat chāpqūlāb bāsh chīqārghalī qūīmās.* I cannot feel so sure as Mr. E. and M. de C. were that the man's head held fast, especially as for it to fall would make the better story.

[466] Tūqā appears to have been the son of a Ṭaghāī, perhaps of Sherīm; his name may imply blood-relationship.

[467] For the verb *awīmāq*, to trepan, *see* f. 67 note 5.

[468] The Fr. map of 1904 shews a hill suiting Bābur's location of this Hill of Pleasure.

[469] A place near Kābul bears the same name; in both the name is explained by a legend that there Earth opened a refuge for forty menaced daughters.

[470] Elph. MS. f. 47b; W.-i-B. I.O. 215 f. 53 and 217 f. 43; Mems. p. 70.

[471] From Andijān to Aūsh is a little over 33 miles. Taṃbal's road was east of Bābur's and placed him between Andijān and Aūzkīnt where was the force protecting his family.

[472] mod. Mazy, on the main Aūsh-Kāshghar road.

[473] *āb-duzd*; de C. i, 144, *prise d'eau.*

[474] This simile seems the fruit of experience in Hindūstān. *See* f. 333, concerning Chānderi.

[475] These two Mughūls rebelled in 914 AH. with Sl. Qulī *Chūnāq* (T.R. *s.n.*).

[476] *awīdī.* The head of Captain Dow, fractured at Chunār by a stone flung at it, was trepanned (*Saiyār-i-muta'akhirīn*, p. 577 and Irvine l .c. p. 283). Yār-'alī was alive in 910 AH. He seems to be the father of the great Bairām Khān-i-khānān of Akbar's reign.

[477] *chasht-gāh*; midway between sunrise and noon.

[478] *ṭaurī*; because providing prisoners for exchange.

[479] *shakh tūtūlūr īdī*, perhaps a palisade.

[480] *i.e.* from Ḥiṣār where he had placed him in 903 AH.

[481] *qūba yūzlūq* (f. 6b and note 4). The Turkmān features would be a maternal inheritance.

[482] He is "Saifī Maulānā 'Arūzī" of Rieu's Pers. Cat. p. 525. *Cf.* Ḥ.S. ii, 341. His book, *'Arūẓ-i-saifī* has been translated by Blochmann and by Ranking.

[483] *namāẓ aūtār īdī.* I understand some irony from this (de Meynard's Dict. *s.n. aūtmāq*).

[484] The *maṭla'* of poems serve as an index of first lines.

[485] *Cf.* f. 30.

[486] *Cf.* f. 37b.

[487] *i.e.* scout and in times of peace, huntsman. On the margin of the Elph. Codex here stands a note, mutilated in rebinding;—*Sl. Aḥmad pidr-i-Qūch Beg ast * * * pidr-i-Sher-afgan u Sher-afgan * * * u Sl. Ḥusain Khān * * * Qūch Beg ast. Hamesha * * * dar khāna Shaham Khān * * **.

[488] *pītīldī*; W.-i-B. *navishta shud*, words indicating the use by Bābur of a written record.

[489] *Cf.* f. 6b and note and f. 17 and note.

[490] *tūlūk*; *i.e.* other food than grain. Fruit, fresh or preserved, being a principal constituent of food in Central Asia, *tūlūk* will include several, but chiefly melons. "Les melons constituent presque seuls vers le fin d'été, la nourriture des classes pauvres (Th. Radloff. l.c. p. 343).

[491] *Cf.* f. 6b and note.

[492] *tūlkī* var. *tūlkū*, the yellow fox. Following this word the Ḥai. MS. has *u dar kamīn dūr* instead of *u rangīn dūr.*

[493] *bī ḥadd*; with which I.O. 215 agrees but I.O. 217 adds *farbih*, fat, which is right in fact (f. 2b) but less pertinent here than an unlimited quantity.

[494] Here a pun on *'ajab* may be read.

[495] *Cf.* f. 15, note to Ṭaghāī.

[496] Apparently not the usual Kīndīr-līk pass but one n.w. of Kāsān.

[497] A ride of at least 40 miles, followed by one of 20 to Kāsān.

[498] *Cf.* f. 72 and f. 72b. Tīlba would seem to have left Taṃbal.

[499] *Taṃbalnīng qarāsī.*

[500] *i.e.* the Other (Mid-afternoon) Prayer.

[501] *ātīnīng būīnīnī qātīb. Qātmāq* has also the here-appropriate meaning of *to stiffen.*

[502] *aīlīk qūshmāq*, *i.e.* Bābur's men with the Kāsān garrison. But the two W.-i-B. write merely *dast burd* and *dast kardan.*

[503] The meaning of *Ghazna* here is uncertain. The Second W.-i-B. renders it by ar. *qaryat* but up to this point Bābur has not used *qaryat* for *village.* Ghazna-namangān cannot be modern Namangān. It was 2 m. from Archīān where Taṃbal was, and Bābur went to Bīshkhārān to be between Taṃbal and Machamī, coming from the south. Archīān and Ghazna-namangān seem both to have been n. or n.w. of Bīshkārān (see maps).

It may be mentioned that at Archīān, in 909 AH. the two Chaghatāī Khāns and Bābur were defeated by Shaibānī.

[504] *bīzlār.* The double plural is rare with Bābur; he writes *bīz*, we, when action is taken in common; he rarely uses *mīn*, I, with autocratic force; his phrasing is largely impersonal, *e.g.* with rare exceptions, he writes the impersonal passive verb.

[505] *bāshlīghlār.* Teufel was of opinion that this word is not used as a noun in the B.N. In this he is mistaken; it is so used frequently, as here, in apposition. *See* ZDMG, xxxvii, art. Bābur und Abū'l-faẓl.

[506] *Cf.* f. 54 foot.

[507] *Cf.* f. 20. She may have come from Samarkand and 'Alī's household or from Kesh and the Tarkhān households.

[508] *Cf.* f. 26 l. 2 for the same phrase.

[509] He is the author of the *Shaibānī-nāma.*

[510] *dāng* and *fils* (*infra*) are small copper coins.

[511] *Cf.* f. 25 l. 1 and note 1.

[512] Probably the poet again; he had left Harāt and was in Samarkand (Sh. N. Vambéry, p. 34 l. 14).

[513] From what follows, this Mughūl advance seems a sequel to a Tarkhān invitation.

[514] By omitting the word *Mīr* the Turkī text has caused confusion between this father and son (Index *s.nn.*).

[515] *bīz khūd kharāb bū mu'āmla aīdūk.* These words have been understood earlier, as referring to the abnormal state of Bābur's mind described under Sec. *r.* They better suit the affairs of Samarkand because Bābur is able to resolve on action and also because he here writes *bīz*, we, and not *mīn*, I, as in Sec. *r.*

[516] For *būlghār*, rendezvous, *see* also f. 78 l. 2 fr. ft.

[517] 25 m. only; the halts were due probably to belated arrivals.

[518] Some of his ties would be those of old acquaintance in Ḥiṣār with 'Alī's father's begs, now with him in Samarkand.

[519] Point to point, some 90 m. but further by road.

[520] *Bū waqi' būlghāch*, manifestly ironical.

[521] Sangzār to Aūrā-tīpā, by way of the hills, some 50 miles.

[522] The Sh. N. Vambéry, p. 60, confirms this.

[523] *Cf.* f. 74b.

[524] Macham and Awīghūr, presumably.

[525] *gūzlār tūz tūtī*, *i.e.* he was blinded for some treachery to his hosts.

[526] Muḥ. Ṣāliḥ's well-informed account of this episode has much interest, filling out and, as by Shaibānī's Boswell, balancing Bābur's. Bābur is obscure about what country was to be given to 'Alī. Pāyanda-ḥasan paraphrases his brief words;—Shaibānī was to be as a father to 'Alī and when he had taken 'Alī's father's *wilāyāt*, he was to give a country to 'Alī. It has been thought that the gift to 'Alī was to follow Shaibānī's recovery of his own ancestral camping-ground (*yūrt*) but this is negatived, I think, by the word, *wilāyāt*, cultivated land.

[527] Elp. MS. f. 57b; W.-i-B. I.O. 215 f. 63b and I.O. 217 f. 52; Mems. p. 82.

Two contemporary works here supplement the B.N.; (1) the (*Tawārikh-i-guzīda*) *Naṣrat-nāma*, dated 908 AH. (B.M. Turkī Or. 3222) of which Berezin's *Shaibānī-nāma* is an abridgment; (2) Muḥ. Ṣāliḥ Mīrzā's *Shaibānī-nāma* (Vambéry trs. cap. xix *et seq.*). The Ḥ.S. (Bomb. ed. p. 302, and Tehran ed. p. 384) is also useful.

[528] *i.e.* on his right. The Ḥ.S. ii, 302 represents that 'Alī was well-received. After Shaibāq had had Zuhra's overtures, he sent an envoy to 'Alī and Yaḥya; the first was not won over but the second fell in with his mother's scheme. This difference of view explains why 'Alī slipped away while Yaḥya was engaged in the Friday Mosque. It seems likely that mother and son alike expected their Aūzbeg blood to stand them in good stead with Shaibāq.

[529] He tried vainly to get the town defended. "Would to God Bābur Mīrzā were here!" he is reported as saying, by Muḥ. Ṣāliḥ.

[530] Perhaps it is for the play of words on 'Alī and 'Alī's life (*jān*) that this man makes his sole appearance here.

[531] *i.e.* rich man or merchant, but *Bī* (*infra*) is an equivalent of Beg.

[532] Muḥ. Ṣāliḥ, invoking curses on such a mother, mentions that Zuhra was given to a person of her own sort.

[533] The Sh. N. and *Naṣrat-nāma* attempt to lift the blame of 'Alī's death from Shaibāq; the second saying that he fell into the Kohik-water when drunk.

[534] Harāt might be his destination but the Ḥ.S. names Makka. Some dismissals towards Khurāsān may imply pilgrimage to Meshhed.

[535] Used also by Bābur's daughter, Gul-badan (l.c. f. 31).

[536] Cut off by alien lands and weary travel.

[537] The Pers. annotator of the Elph. Codex has changed Alāī to *wilāyat*, and *dābān* (pass) to *yān*, side. For the difficult route *see* Schuyler, i, 275, Kostenko, i, 129 and Rickmers, JRGS. 1907, art. Fan Valley.

[538] Amongst Turks and Mughūls, gifts were made by nines.

[539] Ḥiṣār was his earlier home.

[540] Many of these will have been climbed in order to get over places impassable at the river's level.

[541] Schuyler quotes a legend of the lake. He and Kostenko make it larger.

[542] The second occasion was when he crossed from Sūkh for Kābul in 910 AH. (fol. 120).

[543] This name appears to indicate a Command of 10,000 (Bretschneider's *Mediæval Researches*, i, 112).

[544] It seems likely that the cloth was soiled. *Cf.* f. 25 and Hughes Dict. of Islām *s.n.* Eating.

[545] As, of the quoted speech, one word only, of three, is Turkī, others may have been dreamed. Shaikh Maṣlaḥat's tomb is in Khujand where Bābur had found refuge in 903 AH.; it had been circumambulated by Tīmūr in 790 AH. (1390 AD.) and is still honoured.

This account of a dream compares well for naturalness with that in the seemingly-spurious passage, entered with the Ḥai. MS. on f. 118. For examination of the passage *see* JRAS, Jan. 1911, and App. D.

[546] He was made a Tarkhān by diploma of Shaibānī (Ḥ.S. ii, 306, l. 2).

[547] Here the Ḥai. MS. begins to use the word *Shaibāq* in place of its previously uniform *Shaibānī*. As has been noted (f. 5b n. 2), the Elph. MS.

writes *Shaibāq*. It may be therefore that a scribe has changed the earlier part of the Ḥai. MS. and that Bābur wrote *Shaibāq*. From this point my text will follow the double authority of the Elph. and Ḥai. MSS.

[548] In 875 AH. (1470 AD.). Ḥusain was then 32 years old. Bābur might have compared his taking of Samarkand with Tīmūr's capture of Qarshī, also with 240 followers (Ẓ.N. i, 127). Firishta (lith. ed. p. 196) ascribes his omission to do so to reluctance to rank himself with his great ancestor.

[549] This arrival shews that Shaibānī expected to stay in Samarkand. He had been occupying Turkistān under The Chaghatāī Khān.

[550] 'Alī-sher died Jan. 3rd. 1501. It is not clear to what disturbances Bābur refers. He himself was at ease till after April 20th. 1502 and his defeat at Sar-i-pul. Possibly the reference is to the quarrels between Binā'ī and 'Alī-sher. *Cf.* Sām Mīrzā's Anthology, trs. S. de Saçy, *Notices et Extraits* iv, 287 *et seq.*

[551] I surmise a double play-of-words in this verse. One is on two rhyming words, *ghala* and *mallah* and is illustrated by rendering them as *oat* and *coat*. The other is on pointed and unpointed letters, *i.e. ghala* and *'ala*. We cannot find however a Persian word *'ala*, meaning garment.

[552] Bābur's refrain is *ghūsīdūr*, his rhymes *būl*, *(buyur)ūl* and *tūl*. Binā'ī makes *būlghūsīdūr* his refrain but his rhymes are not true *viz. yīr*, *(sa)mar* and *lār*.

[553] Shawwāl 906 AH. began April 20th. 1501.

[554] From the *Bū-stān*, Graf ed. p. 55, l. 246.

[555] Sīkīz Yīldūz. *See* Chardin's *Voyages*, v, 136 and Table; also Stanley Lane Poole's *Bābur*, p. 56.

[556] In 1791 AD. Muḥ. Effendi shot 482 yards from a Turkish bow, before the R. Tox. S.; not a good shot, he declared. Longer ones are on record. *See* Payne-Gallwey's *Cross-bow* and AQR. 1911, H. Beveridge's *Oriental Cross-bows.*

[557] In the margin of the Elph. Codex, here, stands a Persian verse which appears more likely to be Humāyūn's than Bābur's. It is as follows:

Were the Mughūl race angels, they would be bad;

Written in gold, the name Mughūl would be bad;

Pluck not an ear from the Mughūl's corn-land,

What is sown with Mughūl seed will be bad.

This verse is written into the text of the First W.-i-B. (I.O. 215 f. 72) and is introduced by a scribe's statement that it is by *ān Ḥaẓrat*, much as notes known to be Humāyūn's are elsewhere attested in the Elph. Codex. It is not in the Ḥai. and Kehr's MSS. nor with, at least many, good copies of the Second W.-i-B.

[558] This subterranean water-course, issuing in a flowing well (Erskine) gave its name to a bastion (Ḥ.S. ii, 300).

[559] *nāwak*, a diminutive of *nāo*, a tube. It is described, in a MS. of Bābur's time, by Muḥ. Budhā'ī, and, in a second of later date, by Amīnu'd-dīn (AQR 1911, H.B.'s *Oriental Cross-bows*).

[560] Kostenko, i, 344, would make the rounds 9 m.

[561] *bīr yūz ātliqnīng ātinī nāwak aūqī bīla yakhshī atīm.* This has been read by Erskine as though *būz āt*, pale horse, and not *yūz ātlīq*, Centurion, were written. De. C. translates by Centurion and a marginal note of the Elph. Codex explains *yūz ātlīq* by *ṣad aspagī.*

[562] The Sh. N. gives the reverse side of the picture, the plenty enjoyed by the besiegers.

[563] He may have been attached to the tomb of Khwāja 'Abdu'l-lāh *Anṣārī* in Harāt.

[564] The brusque entry here and elsewhere of *e.g.* Taṃbal's affairs, allows the inference that Bābur was quoting from perhaps a news-writer's, contemporary records. For a different view of Taṃbal, the Sh. N. cap. xxxiii should be read.

[565] Five-villages, on the main Khujand-Tāshkīnt road.

[566] *turk*, as on f. 28 of Khusrau Shāh.

[567] Elph. MS. f. 68b; W.-i-B. I.O. 215 f. 78 and 217 f. 61b; Mems. p. 97.

The Kehr-Ilminsky text shews, in this year, a good example of its Persification and of Dr. Ilminsky's dealings with his difficult archetype by the help of the Memoirs.

[568] *tāshlāb.* The Sh. N. places these desertions as after four months of siege.

[569] It strikes one as strange to find Long Ḥasan described, as here, in terms of his younger brother. The singularity may be due to the fact that Ḥusain was with Bābur and may have invited Ḥasan. It may be noted here that Ḥusain seems likely to be that father-in-law of 'Umar Shaikh mentioned on f. 12b and 13b.

[570] This laudatory comment I find nowhere but in the Ḥai. Codex.

[571] There is some uncertainty about the names of those who left.

[572] The Sh. N. is interesting here as giving an eye-witness' account of the surrender of the town and of the part played in the surrender by Khān-zāda's marriage (cap. xxxix).

[573] The first seems likely to be a relation of Niẓāmu'd-dīn 'Alī Khalīfa; the second was Mole-marked, a foster-sister. The party numbered some 100 persons of whom Abū'l-makāram was one (Ḥ.S. ii, 310).

[574] Bābur's brevity is misleading; his sister was not captured but married with her own and her mother's consent before attempt to leave the town was made. *Cf.* Gul-badan's H.N. f. 3b and Sh. N. Vambéry, p. 145.

[575] The route taken avoided the main road for Dīzak; it can be traced by the physical features, mentioned by Bābur, on the Fr. map of 1904. The Sh. N. says the night was extraordinarily dark. Departure in blinding darkness and by unusual ways shews distrust of Shaibāq's safe-conduct suggesting that Yaḥyā's fate was in the minds of the fugitives.

[576] The texts differ as to whether the last two lines are prose or verse. All four are in Turkī, but I surmise a clerical error in the refrain of the third, where *būlūb* is written for *būldī.*

[577] The second was in 908 AH. (f. 18*b*); the third in 914 AH. (f. 216 *b*); the fourth is not described in the B.N.; it followed Bābur's defeat at Ghaj-diwān in 918 AH. (Erskine's *History of India*, i, 325). He had a fifth, but of a different kind, when he survived poison in 933 AH. (f. 305).

[578] Ḥai. MS. *qāqāsrāq*; Elph. MS. *yānasrāq*.

[579] *ātūn*, one who instructs in reading, writing and embroidery. *Cf.* Gulbadan's H.N. f. 26. The distance walked may have been 70 or 80 m.

[580] She was the wife of the then Governor of Aūrā-tīpā, Muḥ. Ḥusain *Dūghlāt.*

[581] It may be noted here that in speaking of these elder women Bābur uses the honorific plural, a form of rare occurrence except for such women, for saintly persons and exceptionally for The supreme Khān. For his father he has never used it.

[582] This name has several variants. The village lies, in a valley-bottom, on the Aq-sū and on a road. *See* Kostenko, i, 119.

[583] She had been divorced from Shaibānī in order to allow him to make legal marriage with her niece, Khān-zāda.

[584] Amongst the variants of this name, I select the modern one. Macha is the upper valley of the Zar-afshān.

[585] Tīmūr took Dihlī in 801 AH. (Dec. 1398), *i.e.* 103 solar and 106 lunar years earlier. The ancient dame would then have been under 5 years old. It is not surprising therefore that in repeating her story Bābur should use a tense betokening hear-say matter (*bārib īkān dūr*).

[586] The anecdote here following, has been analysed in JRAS 1908, p. 87, in order to show warrant for the opinion that parts of the Kehr-Ilminsky text are retranslations from the Persian W.-i-B.

[587] Amongst those thus leaving seem to have been Qaṃbar-'alī (f. 99b).

[588] *Cf.* f. 107 foot.

[589] The Sh. N. speaks of the cold in that winter (Vambéry, p. 160). It was unusual for the Sīr to freeze in this part of its course (Sh. N. p. 172) where it is extremely rapid (Kostenko, i, 213).

[590] *Cf.* f. 4b.

[591] Point to point, some 50 miles.

[592] *Āhangarān-julgasī*, a name narrowed on maps to Angren (valley).

[593] *Faut shūd Nuyān.* The numerical value of these words is 907. Bābur when writing, looks back 26 years to the death of this friend.

[594] Āb-burdan village is on the Zar-afshān; the pass is 11,200 ft. above the sea. Bābur's boundaries still hold good and the spring still flows. *See* Ujfalvy *l.c.* i. 14; Kostenko, i, 119 and 193; Rickmers, JRGS 1907, p. 358.

[595] From the *Bū-stān* (Graf's ed. Vienna 1858, p. 561). The last couplet is also in the *Gulistān* (Platts' ed. p. 72). The Bombay lith. ed. of the *Bū-stān* explains (p. 39) that the "We" of the third couplet means Jamshīd and his predecessors who have rested by his fountain.

[596] *nīma.* The First W.-i-B. (I.O. 215 f. 81 l. 8) writes *tawārīkh*, annals.

[597] This may be the Khwāja Hijrī of the A.N. (index *s.n.*); and Badāyūnī's Ḥasan *Hijrī*, Bib. Ind. iii, 385; and Ethé's Pers. Cat. No. 793; and Bod. Cat. No. 189.

[598] The Ḥai. MS. points in the last line as though punning on Khān and Jān, but appears to be wrong.

[599] For an account of the waste of crops, the Sh. N. should be seen (p. 162 and 180).

[600] I think this refers to last year's move (f. 94 foot).

[601] In other words, the T. preposition, meaning E. in, at, *etc.* may be written with t or d, as *ta(tā)* or as *da(dā)*. Also the one meaning E. towards, may be *gha*, *qa*, or *ka* (with long or short vowel).

[602] *dīm*, a word found difficult. It may be a derivative of root *de*, tell, and a noun with the meaning of English tale (number). The First W.-i-B. renders it by *san*, and by *san*, Abū'l-ghāzī expresses what Bābur's *dīm* expresses, the numbering of troops. It occurs thrice in the B.N. (here, on f. 183b and on f. 264b). In the Elphinstone Codex it has been written-over into *Ivīm*, once resembles *vīm* more than *dīm* and once is omitted. The L. and E. *Memoirs* (p. 303) inserts what seems a gloss, saying that a whip or bow is used in the count, presumably held by the teller to 'keep his place' in the march past. The *Siyāsat-nāma* (Schefer, trs. p. 22) names the whip as used in numbering an army.

[603] The acclamation of the standards is depicted in B.M. W.-i-B. Or. 3714 f. 128b. One cloth is shewn tied to the off fore-leg of a live cow, above the knee, Bābur's word being *aūrtā aīlīk* (middle-hand).

[604] The libation was of fermented mares'-milk.

[605] *lit.* their one way.

[606] *Cf.* T.R. p. 308.

[607] Elph. MS. f. 74; W.-i-B. I.O. 215 f. 83 and 217 f. 66; Mems. p. 104.

[608] It may be noted that Bābur calls his mother's brothers, not *ṭaghāī* but *dādā* father. I have not met with an instance of his saying 'My ṭaghāī' as he says 'My dādā.' *Cf.* index *s.n. taghāī.*

[609] *kūrūnūsh qīlīb*, reflective from *kūrmak*, to see.

[610] A rider's metaphor.

[611] As touching the misnomer, 'Mughūl dynasty' for the Tīmūrid rulers in Hindūstān, it may be noted that here, as Bābur is speaking to a Chaghatāī Mughūl, his 'Turk' is left to apply to himself.

[612] Gulistān, cap. viii, Maxim 12 (Platts' ed. p. 147).

[613] This backward count is to 890 AH. when Aḥmad fled from cultivated lands (T.R. p. 113).

[614] It becomes clear that Aḥmad had already been asked to come to Tāshkīnt.

[615] *Cf.* f. 96b for his first departure without help.

[616] Yagha (Yaghma) is not on the Fr. map of 1904, but suitably located is Turbat (Tomb) to which roads converge.

[617] Elph. MS. *tūshkūcha*; Ḥai. MS. *yūkūnchā*. The importance Aḥmad attached to ceremony can be inferred by the details given (f. 103) of his meeting with Maḥmūd.

[618] *kūrūshkāīlār*. *Cf.* Redhouse who gives no support for reading the verb *kūrmak* as meaning *to embrace*.

[619] *būrk*, a tall felt cap (Redhouse). In the adjective applied to the cap there are several variants. The Ḥai. MS. writes *muftūl*, solid or twisted. The Elph. MS. has *muftūn-lūq* which has been understood by Mr. Erskine to mean, gold-embroidered.

[620] The wording suggests that the decoration is in chain-stitch, pricked up and down through the stuff.

[621] *tāsh chantāī*. These words have been taken to mean whet-stone (*bilgū-tāsh*). I have found no authority for reading *tāsh* as whet-stone. Moreover to allow 'bag of the stone' to be read would require *tāsh (nīng) chantāī-sī* in the text.

[622] lit. bag-like things. Some will have held spare bow-strings and archers' rings, and other articles of 'repairing kit.' With the gifts, it seems probable that the *gosha-gīr* (f. 107) was given.

[623] Vullers, *clava sex foliis*.

[624] Zenker, *casse-tête*. *Kīstin* would seem to be formed from the root, *kīs*, cutting, but M. de C. describes it as a ball attached by a strap or chain to a handle. *Sanglākh*, a sort of mace (*gurz*).

[625] The *Rauẓatu'ṣ-ṣafā* states that The Khāns left Tāshkīnt on Muḥarram 15th (July 21st. 1502), in order to restore Bābur and expel Taṃbal (Erskine).

[626] lit. saw the count (*dīm*). *Cf.* f. 100 and note concerning the count. Using a Persian substitute, the Kehr-Ilminsky text writes *san* (*kūrdīlār*).

[627] Elph. MS. *aṃbārchī*, steward, for Itārchī, a tribal-name. The 'Mīrzā' and the rank of the army-begs are against supposing a steward in command. Here and just above, the texts write Mīrzā-i-Itārchī and Mīrzā-i-Dūghlāt, thus suggesting that in names not ending with a vowel, the *iẓāfat* is required for exact transliteration, *e.g.* Muḥammad-i-dūghlāt.

[628] *Alāī-līq aūrchīnī*. I understand the march to have been along the northern slope of the Little Alāī, south of Aūsh.

[629] As of Ālmālīgh and Ālmātū (fol. 2b) Bābur reports a tradition with caution. The name Aūz-kīnt may be read to mean 'Own village,' independent, as *Aūz-beg*, Own-beg.

[630] He would be one of the hereditary Khwājas of Andijān (f. 16).

[631] For several battle-cries *see* Th. Radloff's *Réceuils* etc. p. 322.

[632] *qāshqa ātlīq kīshī.* For a parallel phrase *see* f. 92b.

[633] Bābur does not explain how the imbroglio was cleared up; there must have been a dramatic moment when this happened.

[634] *Darwāna* (a trap-door in a roof) has the variant *dur-dāna*, a single pearl; *tūqqāī* perhaps implies relationship; *lūlū* is a pearl, a wild cow etc.

[635] Ḥai. MS. *sāīrt kīshī.* Muḥ. 'Alī is likely to be the librarian (*cf.* index *s.n.*).

[636] Elph. MS. *ramāqgha u tūr-gā*; Ḥai. MS. *tārtātgha u tūr-gā.* Ilminsky gives no help, varying much here from the true text. The archetype of both MSS. must have been difficult to read.

[637] The Ḥai. MS.'s pointing allows the sobriquet to mean 'Butterfly.' His family lent itself to nick-names; in it three brothers were known respectively as Fat or Lubberly, Fool and, perhaps, Butterfly.

[638] *bīrk ārīgh*, doubly strong by its trench and its current.

[639] I understand that time failed to set the standard in its usual rest. E. and de C. have understood that the yak-tail (*qūtās tūghī* f. 100) was apart from the staff and that time failed to adjust the two parts. The *tūgh* however is the whole standard; moreover if the tail were ever taken off at night from the staff, it would hardly be so treated in a mere bivouac.

[640] *aīshīklīk tūrlūq*, as on f. 113. I understand this to mean that the two men were as far from their followers as sentries at a Gate are posted outside the Gate.

[641] So too 'Piero of Cosimo' and 'Lorenzo of Piero of the Medici.' *Cf.* the names of five men on f. 114.

[642] *shashtīm.* The *shasht* (thumb) in archery is the thumb-shield used on the left hand, as the *zih-gīr* (string-grip), the archer's ring, is on the right-hand thumb.

It is useful to remember, when reading accounts of shooting with the Turkī (Turkish) bow, that the arrows (*aūq*) had notches so gripping the string that they kept in place until released with the string.

[643] *sar-i-sabz gosha gīr.* The *gosha-gīr* is an implement for remedying the warp of a bow-tip and string-notch. For further particulars *see* Appendix C.

The term *sar-i-sabz*, lit. green-head, occurs in the sense of 'quite young' or 'new,' in the proverb, 'The red tongue loses the green head,' quoted in the

Ṭabaqāt-i-akbarī account of Bābur's death. Applied here, it points to the *gosha-gīr* as part of the recent gift made by Aḥmad to Bābur.

[644] *Taṃbal aīkāndūr.* By this tense I understand that Bābur was not at first sure of the identity of the pseudo-sentries, partly because of their distance, partly, it may be presumed, because of concealment of identity by armour.

[645] *dūwulgha būrkī*; *i.e.* the soft cap worn under the iron helm.

[646] Nūyān's sword dealt the blow (f. 97b). Gul-badan also tells the story (f. 77) à propos of a similar incident in Humāyūn's career. Bābur repeats the story on f. 234.

[647] *yāldāghlāmāī dūr aīdīm.* The Second W.-i-B. has taken this as from *yāltūrmāq*, to cause to glisten, and adds the gloss that the sword was rusty (I.O. 217 f. 70b).

[648] The text here seems to say that the three men were on foot, but this is negatived by the context.

[649] Amongst the various uses of the verb *tūshmak*, to descend in any way, the B.N. does not allow of 'falling (death) in battle.' When I made the index of the Ḥai. MS. facsimile, this was not known to me; I therefore erroneously entered the men enumerated here as killed at this time.

[650] Elph. MS. *yakhshī.* Zenker explains *bakhshī* (pay-master) as meaning also a Court-physician.

[651] The Ḥai. Elph. and Kehr's MS. all have *pūchqāq tāqmāq* or it may be *pūḥqāq tāqmāq*. T. *būkhāq* means bandage, *pūchāq*, rind of fruit, but the word clear in the three Turkī MSS. means, skin of a fox's leg.

[652] The *daryā* here mentioned seems to be the Kāsān-water; the route taken from Bīshkhārān to Pāp is shewn on the Fr. map to lead past modern Tūpa-qūrghān. Pāp is not marked, but was, I think, at the cross-roads east of Touss (Karnān).

[653] Presumably Jahāngīr's.

[654] Here his father was killed (f. 6b). *Cf.* App. A.

[655] 'Alī-dost's son (f. 79b).

[656] The sobriquet *Khīẕ* may mean Leaper, or Impetuous.

[657] *kūīlāk*, syn. *kūnglāk*, a shirt not opening at the breast. It will have been a short garment since the under-vest was visible.

[658] *i.e.* when Bābur was writing in Hindūstān. Exactly at what date he made this entry is not sure. 'Alī was in Koel in 933 AH. (f. 315) and then

taken prisoner, but Bābur does not say he was killed,—as he well might say of a marked man, and, as the captor was himself taken shortly after, 'Alī may have been released, and may have been in Koel again. So that the statement 'now in Koel' may refer to a time later than his capture. The interest of the point is in its relation to the date of composition of the *Bābur-nāma.*

No record of 'Alī's bravery in Aūsh has been preserved. The reference here made to it may indicate something attempted in 908 AH. after Bābur's adventure in Karnān (f. 118b) or in 909 AH. from Sūkh. *Cf.* Translator's note f. 118b.

[659] *aūpchīnlīk.* Vambéry, *gepanzert*; Shaw, four horse-shoes and their nails; Steingass, *aūpcha-khāna*, a guard-house.

[660] Sang is a ferry-station (Kostenko, i, 213). Pāp may well have been regretted (f. 109b and f. 112b)! The well-marked features of the French map of 1904 allows Bābur's flight to be followed.

[661] In the Turkī text this saying is in Persian; in the Kehr-Ilminsky, in Turkī, as though it had gone over with its Persian context of the W.-i-B. from which the K.-I. text here is believed to be a translation.

[662] *Cf.* f. 96b and Fr. Map for route over the Kīndīr-tau.

[663] This account of Muḥ. Bāqir reads like one given later to Bābur; he may have had some part in Bābur's rescue (*cf.* Translator's Note to f. 118b).

[664] Perhaps reeds for a raft. Sh. N. p. 258, *Sāl aūchūn bār qāmīsh*, reeds are there also for rafts.

[665] Here the Turkī text breaks off, as it might through loss of pages, causing a blank of narrative extending over some 16 months. *Cf.* App. D. for a passage, supposedly spurious, found with the Ḥaidarābād Codex and the Kehr-Ilminsky text, purporting to tell how Bābur was rescued from the risk in which the lacuna here leaves him.

[666] As in the Farghāna Section, so here, reliance is on the Elphinstone and Ḥaidarābād MSS. The Kehr-Ilminsky text still appears to be a retranslation from the *Wāqi'āt-i-bāburī* and verbally departs much from the true text; moreover, in this Section it has been helped out, where its archetype was illegible or has lost fragmentary passages, from the Leyden and Erskine *Memoirs.* It may be mentioned, as between the First and the Second *Wāqi'āt-i-bāburī*, that several obscure passages in this Section are more explicit in the First (Pāyanda-ḥasan's) than in its successor ('Abdu-r-raḥīm's).

[667] Elph. MS. f. 90b; W.-i-B. I.O. 215, f. 96b and 217, f. 79; Mems. p. 127. "In 1504 AD. Ferdinand the Catholic drove the French out of Naples" (Erskine). In England, Henry VII was pushing forward a commercial treaty, the *Intercursus malus*, with the Flemings and growing in wealth by the exactions of Empson and Dudley.

[668] presumably the pastures of the "Ilak" Valley. The route from Sūkh would be over the 'Alā'u'd-dīn-pass, into the Qīzīl-sū valley, down to Āb-i-garm and on to the Aīlāq-valley, Khwāja 'Imād, the Kāfirnigān, Qabādīān, and Aūbāj on the Amū. See T.R. p. 175 and Farghāna Section, p. 184, as to the character of the journey.

[669] Amongst the Turkī tribes, the time of first applying the razor to the face is celebrated by a great entertainment. Bābur's miserable circumstances would not admit of this (Erskine).

The text is ambiguous here, reading either that Sūkh was left or that Aīlāq-yīlāq was reached in Muḥarram. As the birthday was on the 8th, the journey very arduous and, for a party mostly on foot, slow, it seems safest to suppose that the start was made from Sūkh at the end of 909 AH. and not in Muḥarram, 910 AH.

[670] *chārūq*, rough boots of untanned leather, formed like a moccasin with the lower leather drawn up round the foot; they are worn by Khīrghīz mountaineers and caravan-men on journeys (Shaw).

[671] *chāpān*, the ordinary garment of Central Asia (Shaw).

[672] The *ālāchūq*, a tent of flexible poles, covered with felt, may be the *khargāh* (kibitka); Persian *chādar* seems to represent Turkī *āq awī*, white house.

[673] *i.e.* with Khusrau's power shaken by Aūzbeg attack, made in the winter of 909 AH. (*Shaibānī-nāma* cap. lviii).

[674] Cf. ff. 81 and 81b. The armourer's station was low for an envoy to Bābur, the superior in birth of the armourer's master.

[675] var. Chaqānīān and Saghānīān. The name formerly described the whole of the Ḥiṣār territory (Erskine).

[676] the preacher by whom the *Khuṭba* is read (Erskine).

[677] *bī bāqī* or *bī Bāqī*; perhaps a play of words with the double meaning expressed in the above translation.

[678] Amongst these were widows and children of Bābur's uncle, Maḥmūd (f. 27b).

[679] *aūghūl.* As being the son of Khusrau's sister, Aḥmad was nephew to Bāqī; there may be in the text a scribe's slip from one *aūghūl* to another, and the real statement be that Aḥmad was the son of Bāqī's son, Muḥ. Qāsim, which would account for his name Aḥmad-i-qāsim.

[680] Cf. f. 67.

[681] Bābur's loss of rule in Farghāna and Samarkand.

[682] about 7 miles south of Aībak, on the road to Sar-i-tāgh (mountain-head, Erskine).

[683] *viz.* the respective fathers, Maḥmūd and 'Umar Shaikh. The arrangement was made in 895 AH. (1490 AD.).

[684] *Gulistān* cap. i, story 3. Part of this quotation is used again on f. 183.

[685] Maḥmūd's sons under whom Bāqī had served.

[686] Uncles of all degrees are included as elder brethren, cousins of all degrees, as younger ones.

[687] Presumably the ferries; perhaps the one on the main road from the north-east which crosses the river at Fort Murgh-āb.

[688] Nine deaths, perhaps where the Amū is split into nine channels at the place where Mīrzā Khān's son Sulaimān later met his rebel grandson Shāh-rukh (*Ṭabaqāt-i-akbarī*, Elliot & Dowson, v, 392, and A.N. Bib. Ind., 3rd ed., 441). Tūqūz-aūlūm is too far up the river to be Arnold's "shorn and parcelled Oxus".

[689] Shaibāq himself had gone down from Samarkand in 908 AH. and in 909 AH. and so permanently located his troops as to have sent their families to them. In 909 AH. he drove Khusrau into the mountains of Badakhshān, but did not occupy Qūndūz; thither Khusrau returned and there stayed till now, when Shaibāq again came south (fol. 123). See Sh. N. cap. lviii *et seq.*

[690] From Taṃbal, to put down whom he had quitted his army near Balkh (Sh. N. cap. lix).

[691] This, one of the many Red-rivers, flows from near Kāhmard and joins the Andar-āb water near Dūshī.

[692] A *garī* is twenty-four minutes.

[693] Qorān, *Surat* iii, verse 25; Sale's Qorān, ed. 1825, i, 56.

[694] Cf. f. 82.

[695] *viz.* Bāī-sanghar, bowstrung, and Mas'ūd, blinded.

[696] Muḥ. Ṣāliḥ is florid over the rubies of Badakhshān he says Bābur took from Khusrau, but Ḥaidar says Bābur not only had Khusrau's property, treasure, and horses returned to him, but refused all gifts Khusrau offered. "This is one trait out of a thousand in the Emperor's character." Ḥaidar mentions, too, the then lack of necessaries under which Bābur suffered (Sh. N., cap. lxiii, and T.R. p. 176).

[697] Cf. T. R. p. 134 n. and 374 n.

[698] *Jība*, so often used to describe the quilted corselet, seems to have here a wider meaning, since the *jība-khāna* contained both *joshan* and *kūhah*, *i.e.* coats-of-mail and horse-mail with accoutrements. It can have been only from this source that Bābur's men obtained the horse-mail of f. 127.

[699] He succeeded his father, Aūlūgh Beg *Kābulī*, in 907 AH.; his youth led to the usurpation of his authority by Sherīm Ẕikr, one of his begs; but the other begs put Sherīm to death. During the subsequent confusions Muḥ. Muqīm *Arghūn*, in 908 AH., got possession of Kābul and married a sister of 'Abdu'r-razzāq. Things were in this state when Bābur entered the country in 910 AH. (Erskine).

[700] var. Ūpīān, a few miles north of Chārikār.

[701] Suhail (Canopus) is a most conspicuous star in Afghānistān; it gives its name to the south, which is never called Janūb but Suhail; the rising of Suhail marks one of their seasons (Erskine). The honour attaching to this star is due to its seeming to rise out of Arabia Felix.

[702] The lines are in the Preface to the *Anwār-i-suhailī* (Lights of Canopus).

[703] "Die Kirghis-qazzāq drücken die Sonnen-höhe in Pikenaus" (von Schwarz, p. 124).

[704] Presumably, dark with shade, as in *qarā-yīghāch*, the hard-wood elm (f. 47b and note to *narwān*).

[705] *i.e.* Sayyid Muḥammad 'Alī, the door-ward. These *būlāks* seem likely to have been groups of 1,000 fighting-men (Turki *Mīng*).

[706] In-the-water and Water-head.

[707] Walī went from his defeat to Khwāst; wrote to Maḥmūd *Aūzbeg* in Qūndūz to ask protection; was fetched to Qūndūz by Muḥ. Ṣāliḥ, the author of the *Shaibānī-nāma*, and forwarded from Qūndūz to Samarkand (Sh. N. cap. lxiii). Cf. f. 29b.

[708] *i.e.* where justice was administered, at this time, outside Bābur's tent.

[709] They would pass Ajar and make for the main road over the Dandān-shikan Pass.

[710] The clansmen may have obeyed Aḥmad's orders in thus holding up the families.

[711] The name may be from Turkī *tāq*, a horse-shoe, but I.O. 215 f. 102 writes Persian *naqīb*, the servant who announces arriving guests.

[712] Here, as immediately below, when mentioning the Chār-bāgh and the tomb of Qūtlūq-qadam, Bābur uses names acquired by the places at a subsequent date. In 910 AH. the Taster was alive; the Chār-bāgh was bought by Bābur in 911 AH., and Qūtlūq-qadam fought at Kānwāha in 933 AH.

[713] The Kūcha-bāgh is still a garden about 4 miles from Kābul on the north-west and divided from it by a low hill-pass. There is still a bridge on the way (Erskine).

[714] Presumably that on which the Bālā-ḥiṣār stood, the glacis of a few lines further.

[715] Cf. f. 130.

[716] One of Muqīm's wives was a Tīmūrid, Bābur's first-cousin, the daughter of Aūlūgh Beg *Kābulī*; another was Bībī Zarīf Khātūn, the mother of that Māh-chūchūq, whose anger at her marriage to Bābur's faithful Qāsim Kūkūldāsh has filled some pages of history (Gulbadan's H.N. *s.n.* Māh-chūchūq and Erskine's B. and H. i, 348).

[717] Some 9 m. north of Kābul on the road to Āq-sarāī.

[718] The Ḥai. MS. (only) writes First Rabī but the Second better suits the near approach of winter.

[719] Elph. MS. fol. 97; W.-i-B. I.O. 215 f. 102b and 217 f. 85; Mems. p. 136. Useful books of the early 19th century, many of them referring to the *Bābur-nāma*, are Conolly's *Travels*, Wood's *Journey*, Elphinstone's *Caubul*, Burnes' *Cabool*, Masson's *Narrative*, Lord's and Leech's articles in JASB 1838 and in Burnes' *Reports* (India Office Library), Broadfoot's *Report* in RGS Supp. Papers vol. I.

[720] f. 1b where Farghāna is said to be on the limit of cultivation.

[721] f. 131b. To find these *tūmāns* here classed with what was not part of Kābul suggest a clerical omission of "beyond" or "east of" (Lamghānāt). It may be more correct to write Lāmghānāt, since the first syllable may be *lām*, fort. The modern form Laghmān is not used in the *Bābur-nāma*, nor, it may be added is Paghmān for Pamghān.

[722] It will be observed that Bābur limits the name Afghānistān to the countries inhabited by Afghān tribesmen; they are chiefly those south of the road from Kābul to Pashāwar (Erskine). See Vigne, p. 102, for a boundary between the Afghāns and Khurāsān.

[723] Al-birūnī's *Indika* writes of both Turk and Hindū-shāhī Kings of Kābul. See Raverty's *Notes* p. 62 and Stein's *Shāhī Kings of Kābul.* The mountain is 7592 ft. above the sea, some 1800 ft. therefore above the town.

[724] The Kābul-river enters the Chār-dih plain by the Dih-i-yaq'ūb narrows, and leaves it by those of Dūrrīn. Cf. *S.A. War*, Plan p. 288 and Plan of action at Chār-āsiyā (Four-mills), the second shewing an off-take which may be Wais Ātāka's canal. See Vigne, p. 163 and Raverty's *Notes* pp. 69 and 689.

[725] This, the Bālā-jūī (upper-canal) was a four-mill stream and in Masson's time, as now, supplied water to the gardens round Bābur's tomb. Masson found in Kābul honoured descendants of Wais Ātāka (ii, 240).

[726] But for a, perhaps negligible, shortening of its first vowel, this form of the name would describe the normal end of an irrigation canal, a little pool, but other forms with other meanings are open to choice, *e.g.* small hamlet (Pers. *kul*), or some compound containing Pers. *gul*, a rose, in its plain or metaphorical senses. Jarrett's *Āyīn-i-akbarī* writes Gul-kīnah, little rose (?). Masson (ii, 236) mentions a similar pleasure-resort, Sanjī-tāq.

[727] The original ode, with which the parody agrees in rhyme and refrain, is in the *Dīwān, s.l. Dāl* (Brockhaus ed. 1854, i, 62 and lith. ed. p. 96). See Wilberforce Clarke's literal translation i, 286 (H. B.). A marginal note to the Ḥaidarābād Codex gives what appears to be a variant of one of the rhymes of the parody.

[728] *aūlūgh kūl*; some 3 m. round in Erskine's time; mapped as a swamp in *S.A. War* p. 288.

[729] A marginal note to the Ḥai. Codex explains this name to be an abbreviation of Khwāja Shamsū'd-dīn *Jān-bāz* (or *Jahān-bāz*; Masson, ii, 279 and iii, 93).

[730] *i.e.* the place made holy by an impress of saintly foot-steps.

[731] Two eagles or, Two poles, used for punishment. Vigne's illustration (p. 161) clearly shows the spur and the detached rock. Erskine (p. 137 n.) says that 'Uqābain seems to be the hill, known in his day as 'Āshiqān-i-'ārifān, which connects with Bābur Bādshāh. See Raverty's *Notes* p. 68.

[732] During most of the year this wind rushes through the Hindū-kush (Parwān)-pass; it checks the migration of the birds (f. 142), and it may be

the cause of the deposit of the Running-sands (Burnes, p. 158). Cf. Wood, p. 124.

[733] He was Badī'u'z-zamān's *Ṣadr* before serving Bābur; he died in 918 AH. (1512 AD.), in the battle of Kūl-i-malik where 'Ubaidu'l-lāh *Aūzbeg* defeated Bābur. He may be identical with Mīr Ḥusain the Riddler of f. 181, but seems not to be Mullā Muḥ. *Badakhshī*, also a Riddler, because the *Ḥabību's-siyār* (ii, 343 and 344) gives this man a separate notice. Those interested in enigmas can find one made by Ṭālib on the name Yaḥya (Ḥ.S. ii, 344). Sharafu'd-dīn 'Alī *Yazdī*, the author of the *Ẓafar-nāma*, wrote a book about a novel kind of these puzzles (T.R. p. 84).

[734] The original couplet is as follows:—

Bakhūr dar arg-i Kābul mai, bagardān kāsa pāy dar pāy,

Kah ham koh ast, u ham daryā, u ham shahr ast, u ham ṣaḥrā'.

What Ṭālib's words may be inferred to conceal is the opinion that like Badī'u'z-zamān and like the meaning of his name, Kābul is the Wonder-of-the-world. (Cf. M. Garçin de Tassy's *Rhétorique* [p. 165], for *ces combinaisons énigmatiques.*)

[735] All MSS. do not mention Kāshghar.

[736] Khīta (Cathay) is Northern China; Chīn (*infra*) is China; Rūm is Turkey and particularly the provinces near Trebizond (Erskine).

[737] 300% to 400% (Erskine).

[738] Persian *sinjid*, Brandis, *elæagnus hortensis*; Erskine (Mems. p. 138) jujube, presumably the *zizyphus jujuba* of Speede, Supplement p. 86. Turkī *yāngāq*, walnut, has several variants, of which the most marked is *yānghkāq*. For a good account of Kābul fruits *see* Masson, ii, 230.

[739] a kind of plum (?). It seems unlikely to be a cherry since Bābur does not mention cherries as good in his old dominions, and Firminger (p. 244) makes against it as introduced from India. Steingass explains *alū-bālū* by "sour-cherry, an armarylla"; if sour, is it the Morello cherry?

[740] The sugar-cane was seen in abundance in Lan-po (Lamghān) by a Chinese pilgrim (Beale, p. 90); Bābur's introduction of it may have been into his own garden only in Nīngnahār (f. 132b).

[741] *i.e.* the seeds of *pinus Gerardiana.*

[742] *rawāshlār*. The green leaf-stalks (*chūkri*) of *ribes rheum* are taken into Kābul in mid-April from the Pamghān-hills; a week later they are followed

by the blanched and tended *rawāsh* (Masson, ii, 7). *See* Gul-badan's H.N. trs. p. 188, Vigne, p. 100 and 107, Masson, ii, 230, Conolly, i, 213.

[743] a large green fruit, shaped something like a citron; also a large sort of cucumber (Erskine).

[744] The *ṣāḥibī*, a grape praised by Bābur amongst Samarkandī fruits, grows in Koh-dāman; another well-known grape of Kābul is the long stoneless *ḥusainī*, brought by Afghān traders into Hindūstān in round, flat boxes of poplar wood (Vigne, p. 172).

[745] An allusion, presumably, to the renouncement of wine made by Bābur and some of his followers in 933 AH. (1527 AD. f. 312). He may have had 'Umar *Khayyām's* quatrain in mind, "Wine's power is known to wine-bibbers alone" (Whinfield's 2nd ed. 1901, No. 164).

[746] *pūstīn*, usually of sheep-skin. For the wide range of temperature at Kābul in 24 hours, *see* Ency. Brtt. art. Afghānistān. The winters also vary much in severity (Burnes, p. 273).

[747] Index *s.n.* As he fought at Kānwāha, he will have been buried after March 1527 AD.; this entry therefore will have been made later. The Curriers'-gate is the later Lahor-gate (Masson, ii, 259).

[748] Index *s.n.*

[749] For lists of the Hindū-kush passes *see* Leech's Report VII; Yule's *Introductory Essay* to Wood's *Journey* 2nd ed.; PRGS 1879, Markham's art. p. 121.

The highest *cols* on the passes here enumerated by Bābur are,—Khawāk 11,640 ft.—Ṭ̤ūl, height not known,—Pārandī 15,984 ft.—Bāj-gāh (Toll-place) 12,000 ft.—Walīān (Saints) 15,100 ft.—Chahār-dār (Four-doors) 18,900 ft. and Shibr-tū 9800 ft. In considering the labour of their ascent and descent, the general high level, north and south of them, should be borne in mind; *e.g.* Chārikār (Chār-yak-kār) stands 5200 ft. and Kābul itself at 5780 ft. above the sea.

[750] *i.e.* the hollow, long, and small-bāzār roads respectively. Panjhīr is explained by Hindūs to be Panj-sher, the five lion-sons of Pandu (Masson, iii, 168).

[751] Shibr is a Hazāra district between the head of the Ghūr-bund valley and Bāmīān. It does not seem to be correct to omit the *tū* from the name of the pass. Persian *tū*, turn, twist (syn. *pīch*) occurs in other names of local passes; to read it here as a *turn* agrees with what is said of Shibr-tū pass as not crossing but turning the Hindū-kush (Cunningham). Lord uses the same wording about the Ḥājī-ghāt (var. -kāk etc.) traverse of the same spur,

which "turns the extremity of the Hindū-kush". *See* Cunningham's *Ancient Geography*, i, 25; Lord's *Ghūr-bund* (JASB 1838 p. 528), Masson, iii, 169 and Leech's *Report* VII.

[752] Perhaps through Jālmīsh into Saighān.

[753] *i.e.* they are closed.

[754] It was unknown in Mr. Erskine's day (Mems. p. 140). Several of the routes in Raverty's *Notes* (p. 92 etc.) allow it to be located as on the Īrī-āb, near to or identical with Bāghzān, 35 *kurohs* (70 m.) s.s.e. of Kābul.

[755] Farmūl, about the situation of which Mr. Erskine was in doubt, is now marked in maps, Ūrghūn being its principal village.

[756] 15 miles below Atak (Erskine). Mr. Erskine notes that he found no warrant, previous to Abū'l-faẓl's, for calling the Indus the Nīl-āb, and that to find one would solve an ancient geographical difficulty. This difficulty, my husband suggests, was Alexander's supposition that the Indus was the Nile. In books grouping round the *Bābur-nāma*, the name Nīl-āb is not applied to the Indus, but to the ferry-station on that river, said to owe its name to a spring of azure water on its eastern side. (Cf. Afẓal Khān *Khattak*, R.'s *Notes* p. 447.)

I find the name Nīl-āb applied to the Kābul-river:—1. to its Arghandī affluent (Cunningham, p. 17, Map); 2. through its boatman class, the Nīl-ābīs of Lālpūra, Jalālābād and Kūnār (G. of I. 1907, art. Kābul); 3. inferentially to it as a tributary of the Indus (D'Herbélot); 4. to it near its confluence with the grey, silt-laden Indus, as blue by contrast (Sayyid Ghulām-i-muḥammad, R.'s *Notes* p. 34). (For Nīl-āb (Naulibis?) in Ghūr-bund *see* Cunningham, p. 32 and Masson, iii, 169.)

[757] By one of two routes perhaps,—either by the Khaibar-Nīngnahār-Jagdālīk road, or along the north bank of the Kābul-river, through Goshṭa to the crossing where, in 1879, the 10th Hussars met with disaster. *See S.A. War*, Map 2 and p. 63; Leech's *Reports* II and IV (Fords of the Indus); and R.'s *Notes* p. 44.

[758] Hāru, Leech's Harroon, apparently, 10 m. above Atak. The text might be read to mean that both rivers were forded near their confluence, but, finding no warrant for supposing the Kābul-river fordable below Jalālābād, I have guided the translation accordingly; this may be wrong and may conceal a change in the river.

[759] Known also as Dhān-kot and as Mu'aẓẓam-nagar (*Ma'āṣiru'l-'umrā* i, 249 and A.N. trs. H.B. index *s.n.* Dhān-kot). It was on the east bank of the

Indus, probably near modern Kālā-bāgh, and was washed away not before 956 AH. (1549 AD. H. Beveridge).

[760] Chaupāra seems, from f. 148b, to be the Chapari of Survey Map 1889. Bābur's *Dasht* is modern Dāman.

[761] *aīmāq*, used usually of Mughūls, I think. It may be noted that Lieutenant Leech compiled a vocabulary of the tongue of the Mughūl Aīmāq in Qandahār and Harāt (JASB 1838, p. 785).

[762] The *Āyīn-i-akbarī* account of Kābul both uses and supplements the *Bābur-nāma.*

[763] *viz.* 'Alī-shang, Alangār and Mandrāwar (the Lamghānāt proper), Nīngnahār (with its *bulūk*, Kāma), Kūnār-with-Nūr-gal, (and the two *bulūks* of Nūr-valley and Chaghān-sarāī).

[764] *See* Appendix E, *On Nagarahāra.*

[765] The name Adīnapūr is held to be descended from ancient Udyānapūra (Garden-town); its ancestral form however was applied to Nagarahāra, apparently, in the Bārān-Sūrkh-rūd *dū-āb*, and not to Bābur's *dārogha's* seat. The Sūrkh-rūd's deltaic mouth was a land of gardens; when Masson visited Adīnapūr he went from Bālā-bāgh (High-garden); this appears to stand where Bābur locates his Bāgh-i-wafā, but he was shown a garden he took to be this one of Bābur's, a mile higher up the Sūrkh-rūd. A later ruler made the Chār-bāgh of maps. It may be mentioned that Bālā-bāgh has become in some maps Rozābād (Garden-town). *See* Masson, i, 182 and iii, 186; R.'s *Notes*; and Wilson's *Ariana Antiqua*, Masson's art.

[766] One of these *tangī* is now a literary asset in Mr. Kipling's *My Lord the Elephant.* Bābur's 13 y. represent some 82 miles; on f. 137b the Kābul-Ghaznī road of 14 y. represents some 85; in each case the *yīghāch* works out at over six miles (Index *s.n. yīghāch* and Vigne, p. 454). Sayyid Ghulām-i-muḥammad traces this route minutely (R.'s *Notes* pp. 57, 59).

[767] Masson was shewn "Chaghatai castles", attributed to Bābur (iii, 174).

[768] Dark-turn, perhaps, as in Shibr-tū, Jāl-tū, *etc.* (f. 130b and note to Shibr-tū).

[769] f. 145 where the change is described in identical words, as seen south of the Jagdālīk-pass. The Bādām-chashma pass appears to be a traverse of the eastern rampart of the Tīzīn-valley.

[770] Appendix E, *On Nagarahāra.*

[771] No record exists of the actual laying-out of the garden; the work may have been put in hand during the Mahmand expedition of 914 AH. (f. 216);

the name given to it suggests a gathering there of loyalists when the stress was over of the bad Mughūl rebellion of that year (f. 216b where the narrative breaks off abruptly in 914 AH. and is followed by a gap down to 925 AH.-1519 AD.).

[772] No annals of 930 AH. are known to exist; from Ṣafar 926 AH. to 932 AH. (Jan. 1520-Nov. 1525 AD.) there is a lacuna. Accounts of the expedition are given by Khāfī Khān, i, 47 and Firishta, lith. ed. p. 202.

[773] Presumably to his son, Humāyūn, then governor in Badakhshān; Bukhārā also was under Bābur's rule.

[774] Here, *qārī*, yards. The dimensions 10 by 10, are those enjoined for places of ablution.

[775] Presumably those of the *tūqūz-rūd*, *supra*. Cf. Appendix E, *On Nagarahāra.*

[776] White-mountain; Pushtū, Spīn-ghur (or ghar).

[777] *i.e.* the Lamghānāt proper. The range is variously named; in (Persian) Siyāh-koh (Black-mountain), which like Turkī Qarā-tāgh may mean non-snowy; by Tājīks, Bāgh-i-ātāka (Foster-father's garden); by Afghāns, Kanda-ghur, and by Lamghānīs Koh-i-būlān,—Kanda and Būlān both being ferry-stations below it (Masson, iii, 189; also the Times Nov. 20th 1912 for a cognate illustration of diverse naming).

[778] A comment made here by Mr. Erskine on changes of name is still appropriate, but some seeming changes may well be due to varied selection of land-marks. Of the three routes next described in the text, one crosses as for Mandrāwar; the second, as for 'Alī-shang, a little below the outfall of the Tīzīn-water; the third may take off from the route, between Kābul and Tag-aū, marked in Col. Tanner's map (PRGS 1881 p. 180). Cf. R's Route 11; and for Aūlūgh-nūr, Appendix F, *On the name Nūr.*

[779] The name of this pass has several variants. Its second component, whatever its form, is usually taken to mean *pass*, but to read it here as pass would be redundant, since Bābur writes "pass (*kūtal*) of Bād-i-pīch". Pich occurs as a place name both east (Pīch) and west (Pīchghān) of the *kūtal*, but what would suit the bitter and even fatal winds of the pass would be to read the name as Whirling-wind (*bād-i-pīch*). Another explanation suggests itself from finding a considerable number of pass-names such as Shibr-tū, Jāi-tū, Qarā-tū, in which *tū* is a synonym of *pīch*, turn, twist; thus Bād-i-pīch may be the local form of Bād-tū, Windy-turn.

[780] *See* Masson, iii, 197 and 289. Both in Pashāī and Lamghānī, *lām* means fort.

[781] *See* Appendix F, *On the name Dara-i-nūr.*

[782] *ghair mukarrar*. Bābur may allude to the remarkable change men have wrought in the valley-bottom (Appendix F, for Col. Tanner's account of the valley).

[783] f. 154.

[784] *diospyrus lotus*, the European date-plum, supposed to be one of the fruits eaten by the Lotophagi. It is purple, has bloom and is of the size of a pigeon's egg or a cherry. See Watts' *Economic Products of India*; Brandis' *Forest Trees*, Illustrations; and Speede's *Indian Hand-book*.

[785] As in Lombardy, perhaps; in Luhūgur vines are clipped into standards; in most other places in Afghānistān they are planted in deep trenches and allowed to run over the intervening ridges or over wooden framework. In the narrow Khūlm-valley they are trained up poplars so as to secure them the maximum of sun. *See* Wood's *Report* VI p. 27; Bellew's *Afghānistān* p. I75 and *Mems*. p. 142 note.

[786] Appendix G, *On the names of two Nūrī wines.*

[787] This practice Bābur viewed with disgust, the hog being an impure animal according to Muḥammadan Law (Erskine).

[788] The *Khazīnatu'l-asfiyā* (ii, 293) explains how it came about that this saint, one honoured in Kashmīr, was buried in Khutlān. He died in Hazāra (Paklī) and there the Paklī Sulṭān wished to have him buried, but his disciples, for some unspecified reason, wished to bury him in Khutlān. In order to decide the matter they invited the Sultān to remove the bier with the corpse upon it. It could not be stirred from its place. When, however, a single one of the disciples tried to move it, he alone was able to lift it, and to bear it away on his head. Hence the burial in Khutlān. The death occurred in 786 AH. (1384 AD.). A point of interest in this legend is that, like the one to follow, concerning dead women, it shews belief in the living activities of the dead.

[789] The MSS. vary between 920 and 925 AH.—neither date seems correct. As the annals of 925 AH. begin in Muḥarram, with Bābur to the east of Bājaur, we surmise that the Chaghān-sarāī affair may have occurred on his way thither, and at the end of 924 AH.

[790] *karanj, coriandrum sativum.*

[791] Some 20-24 m. north of Jalālābād. The name Multa-kundī may refer to the Rām-kundī range, or mean Lower district, or mean Below Kundī. *See* Biddulph's *Khowārī Dialect s.n* under; R.'s *Notes* p. 108 and *Dict. s.n. kund*; Masson, i, 209.

[792] *i.e.* treat her corpse as that of an infidel (Erskine).

[793] It would suit the position of this village if its name were found to link to the Turkī verb *chaqmāq*, to go out, because it lies in the mouth of a defile (Dahānah-i-koh, Mountain-mouth) through which the road for Kāfiristān goes out past the village. A not-infrequent explanation of the name to mean White-house, Āq-sarāī, may well be questioned. *Chaghān*, white, is Mughūlī and it would be less probable for a Mughūlī than for a Turkī name to establish itself. Another explanation may lie in the tribe name Chugānī. The two forms *chaghān* and *chaghār* may well be due to the common local interchange in speech of *n* with *r*. (For Dahānah-i-koh *see* [some] maps and Raverty's Bājaur routes.)

[794] Nīmchas, presumably,—half-bred in custom, perhaps in blood—; and not improbably, converted Kāfirs. It is useful to remember that Kāfiristān was once bounded, west and south, by the Bārān-water.

[795] Kāfir wine is mostly poor, thin and, even so, usually diluted with water. When kept two or three years, however, it becomes clear and sometimes strong. Sir G. S. Robertson never saw a Kāfir drunk (*Kāfirs of the Hindū-kush*, p. 591).

[796] Kāma might have classed better under Nīngnahār of which it was a dependency.

[797] *i.e.* water-of-Nijr; so too, Badr-aū and Tag-aū. Nijr-aū has seven-valleys (JASB 1838 p. 329 and Burnes' *Report X*). Sayyid Ghulām-i-muḥammad mentions that Bābur established a frontier-post between Nijr-aū and Kāfiristān which in his own day was still maintained. He was an envoy of Warren Hastings to Tīmūr Shāh *Sadozī* (R.'s *Notes* p. 36 and p. 142).

[798] *Kāfirwash*; they were Kāfirs converted to Muḥammadanism.

[799] *Archa*, if not inclusive, meaning conifer, may represent *juniperus excelsa*, this being the common local conifer. The other trees of the list are *pinus Gerardiana* (Brandis, p. 690), *quercus bīlūt*, the holm-oak, and *pistacia mutica* or *khanjak*, a tree yielding mastic.

[800] *rūba-i-parwān*, *pteromys inornatus*, the large, red flying-squirrel (Blandford's *Fauna of British India*, *Mammalia*, p. 363).

[801] The *giz* is a short-flight arrow used for shooting small birds *etc.* Descending flights of squirrels have been ascertained as 60 yards, one, a record, of 80 (Blandford).

[802] Apparently *tetrogallus himalayensis*, the Himalayan snow-cock (Blandford, iv, 143).Burnes (*Cabool* p. 163) describes the *kabg-i-darī* as the

rara avis of the Kābul Kohistān, somewhat less than a turkey, and of the *chikor* (partridge) species. It was procured for him first in Ghūr-bund, but, when snow has fallen, it could be had nearer Kābul. Bābur's *bū-qalamūn* may have come into his vocabulary, either as a survival direct from Greek occupation of Kābul and Panj-āb, or through Arabic writings. PRGS 1879 p. 251, Kaye's art. and JASB 1838 p. 863, Hodgson's art.

[803] Bartavelle's *Greek-partridge*, *tetrao-* or *perdrix-rufus* [f. 279 and Mems. p. 320 n.].

[804] A similar story is told of some fields near Whitby:—"These wild geese, which in winter fly in great flocks to the lakes and rivers unfrozen in the southern parts, to the great amazement of every-one, fall suddenly down upon the ground when they are in flight over certain neighbouring fields thereabouts; a relation I should not have made, if I had not received it from several credible men." See *Notes to Marmion* p. xlvi (Erskine); Scott's *Poems*, Black's ed. 1880, vii, 104.

[805] Are we to infer from this that the musk-rat (*Crocidura cærulea*, Lydekker, p. 626) was not so common in Hindūstān in the age of Bābur as it has now become? He was not a careless observer (Erskine).

[806] Index *s.n. Bābur-nāma*, date of composition; also f. 131.

[807] In the absence of examples of *bund* to mean *kūtal*, and the presence "in those countries" of many in which *bund* means *koh*, it looks as though a clerical error had here written *kūtal* for *koh*. But on the other hand, the wording of the next passage shows just the confusion an author's unrevised draft might shew if a place were, as this is, both a *tūmān* and a *kūtal* (*i.e.* a steady rise to a traverse). My impression is that the name Ghūr-bund applies to the embanking spur at the head of the valley-*tūmān*, across which roads lead to Ghūrī and Ghūr (PRGS 1879, Maps; Leech's Report VII; and Wood's VI).

[808] So too when, because of them, Leech and Lord turned back, *re infectâ*.

[809] It will be noticed that these villages are not classed in any *tūmān*; they include places "rich without parallel" in agricultural products, and level lands on which towns have risen and fallen, one being Alexandria ad Caucasum. They cannot have been part of the unremunerative Ghūr-bund *tūmān*; from their place of mention in Bābur's list of *tūmāns*, they may have been part of the Kābul *tūmān* (f. 178), as was Koh-dāman (Burnes' *Cabool* p. 154; Haughton's *Charikar* p. 73; and Cunningham's *Ancient History*, i, 18).

[810] Dūr-namāī, seen from afar (Masson, iii, 152) is not marked on the Survey Maps; Masson, Vigne and Haughton locate it. Bābur's "head" and "foot" here indicate status and not location.

[811] Mems. p. 146 and *Méms*, i, 297, Arabs' encampment and *Cellule des Arabes*. Perhaps the name may refer to uses of the level land and good pasture by horse *qāfilas*, since *Kurra* is written with *tashdīd* in the Ḥaidarābād Codex, as in *kurra-tāz*, a horse-breaker. Or the *tāziyān* may be the fruit of a legend, commonly told, that the saint of the neighbouring Running-sands was an Arabian.

[812] Presumably this is the grass of the millet, the growth before the ear, on which grazing is allowed (Elphinstone, i, 400; Burnes, p. 237).

[813] Wood, p. 115; Masson, iii, 167; Burnes, p. 157 and JASB 1838 p. 324 with illustration; Vigne, pp. 219, 223; Lord, JASB 1838 p. 537; *Cathay and the way thither*, Hakluyt Society vol. I. p. xx, para. 49; *History of Musical Sands*, C. Carus-Wilson.

[814] *West* might be more exact, since some of the group are a little north, others a little south of the latitude of Kābul.

[815] Affluents and not true sources in some cases (Col. Holdich's *Gates of India*, *s.n.* Koh-i-bābā; and PRGS 1879, maps pp. 80 and 160).

[816] The Pamghān range. These are the villages every traveller celebrates. Masson's and Vigne's illustrations depict them well.

[817] *Cercis siliquastrum*, the Judas-tree. Even in 1842 it was sparingly found near Kābul, adorning a few tombs, one Bābur's own. It had been brought from Sih-yārān where, as also at Chārikār, (Chār-yak-kār) it was still abundant and still a gorgeous sight. It is there a tree, as at Kew, and not a bush, as in most English gardens (Masson, ii, 9; Elphinstone, i, 194; and for the tree near Harāt, f. 191 n. to Ṣafar).

[818] Khwāja Maudūd of Chisht, Khwāja Khāwand Sa'īd and the Khwāja of the Running-sands (Elph. MS. f. 104b, marginal note).

[819] The yellow-flowered plant is not *cercis siliquastrum* but one called *mahaka*(?) in Persian, a shrubby plant with pea-like blossoms, common in the plains of Persia, Bilūchistān and Kābul (Masson, iii, 9 and Vigne, p. 216).

[820] The numerical value of these words gives 925 (Erskine). F. 246b *et seq*. for the expedition.

[821] f. 178. I.O. MS. No. 724, *Haft-iqlīm* f. 135 (Ethé, p. 402); Rieu, pp. 21*a*, 1058*b*.

[822] of Afghan habit. The same term is applied (f. 139b) to the Zurmutīs; it may be explained in both places by Bābur's statement that Zurmutīs grow corn, but do not cultivate gardens or orchards.

[823] *aīkān dūr.* Sabuk-tīgīn, d. 387 AH.-997 AD., was the father of Sl. Maḥmūd *Ghaznawī*, d. 421 AH.-1030 AD.

[824] d. 602 AH.-1206 AD.

[825] Some Musalmāns fast through the months of Rajab, Sha'bān and Ramẓān; Muḥammadans fast only by day; the night is often given to feasting (Erskine).

[826] The Garden; the tombs of more eminent Muṣalmāns are generally in gardens (Erskine). See Vigne's illustrations, pp. 133, 266.

[827] *i.e.* the year now in writing. The account of the expedition, Bābur's first into Hindūstān, begins on f. 145.

[828] *i.e.* the countries groupable as Khurāsān.

[829] For picture and account of the dam, *see* Vigne, pp. 138, 202.

[830] f. 295b.

[831] The legend is told in numerous books with varying location of the spring. One narrator, Zakarīyā *Qazwīnī*, reverses the parts, making Jāī-pāl employ the ruse; hence Leyden's note (Mems. p. 150; E. and D.'s *History of India* ii, 20, 182 and iv, 162; for historical information, R.'s *Notes* p. 320). The date of the events is shortly after 378 AH.-988 AD.

[832] R.'s *Notes s.n.* Zurmut.

[833] The question of the origin of the Farmūlī has been written of by several writers; perhaps they were Turks of Persia, Turks and Tājīks.

[834] This completes the list of the 14 *tūmāns* of Kābul, *viz.* Nīngnahār, 'Alī-shang, Alangār, Mandrāwar, Kūnār-with-Nūr-gal, Nijr-aū, Panjhīr, Ghūr-bund, Koh-dāman (with Kohistān?), Luhūgur (of the Kābul *tūmān*), Ghaznī, Zurmut, Farmūl and Bangash.

[835] Between Nijr-aū and Tag-aū (Masson, iii, 165). Mr. Erskine notes that Bābur reckoned it in the hot climate but that the change of climate takes place further east, between 'Alī-shang and Aūzbīn (*i.e.* the valley next eastwards from Tag-aū).

[836] *būghūzlārīghā furṣat būlmās*; *i.e.* to kill them in the lawful manner, while pronouncing the *Bi'smi'llāh*.

[837] This completes the *bulūks* of Kābul *viz.* Badr-aū (Tag-aū), Nūr-valley, Chaghān-sarāī, Kāma and Ālā-sāī.

[838] The *rūpī* being equal to 2-1/2 *shāhrukhīs*, the *shāhrukhī* may be taken at 10*d.* thus making the total revenue only £33,333 6*s.* 8*d.* See *Āyīn-i-akbarī* ii, 169 (Erskine).

[839] *sic* in all B. N. MSS. Most maps print Khost. Muḥ. Ṣāliḥ says of Khwāst, "Who sees it, would call it a Hell" (Vambéry, p. 361).

[840] Bābur's statement about this fodder is not easy to translate; he must have seen grass grow in tufts, and must have known the Persian word *būta* (bush). Perhaps *kāh* should be read to mean plant, not grass. Would Wood's *bootr* fit in, a small furze bush, very plentiful near Bāmiān? (Wood's Report VI, p. 23; and for regional grasses, Aitchison's *Botany of the Afghān Delimitation Commission*, p. 122.)

[841] *nāzū*, perhaps *cupressus torulosa* (Brandis, p.693).

[842] f. 276.

[843] A laborious geographical note of Mr. Erskine's is here regretfully left behind, as now needless (Mems. p. 152).

[844] Here, mainly wild-sheep and wild-goats, including *mār-khẉār.*

[845] Perhaps, no conifers; perhaps none of those of the contrasted hill-tract.

[846] While here *dasht* (plain) represents the eastern skirt of the Mehtar Sulaimān range, *dūkī* or *dūgī* (desert) seems to stand for the hill tracts on the west of it, and not, as on f. 152, for the place there specified.

[847] Mems. p. 152, "A narrow place is large to the narrow-minded"; *Méms.* i, 311, "Ce qui n'est pas trop large, ne reste pas vide." Literally, "So long as heights are not equal, there is no vis-a-vis," or, if *tāng* be read for *tīng*, "No dawn, no noon," *i.e.* no effect without a cause.

[848] I have not lighted on this name in botanical books or explained by dictionaries. Perhaps it is a Cis-oxanian name for the *sax-aol* of Transoxania. As its uses are enumerated by some travellers, it might be *Haloxylon ammodendron*, *ta-ghas etc.* and *sax-aol* (Aitchison, p. 102).

[849] f. 135b note to Ghūr-bund.

[850] I understand that wild-goats, wild-sheep and deer (*āhū*) were not localized, but that the dun-sheep migrated through. Antelope (*āhū*) was scarce in Elphinstone's time.

[851] *qīzīl kīyik* which, taken with its alternative name, *arqārghalcha*, allows it to be the dun-sheep of Wood's *Journey* p. 241. From its second name it may be *Ovis amnon* (*Raos*), or *O. argalī.*

[852] *tusqāwal*, var. *tutqāwal*, *tus̱aqāwal* and *tūshqāwal*, a word which has given trouble to scribes and translators. As a sporting-term it is equivalent to *shikār-i-nihilam*; in one or other of its forms I find it explained as *Weg-hüter*, *Fahnen-hüter*, *Zahl-meister*, *Schlucht*, *Gefahrlicher-weg* and *Schmaler-weg*. It recurs

in the B.N. on f. 197b l. 5 and l. 6 and there might mean either a narrow road or a *Weg-hüter.* If its Turkī root be *tūs*, the act of stopping, all the above meanings can follow, but there may be two separate roots, the second, *tūsh*, the act of descent (JRAS 1900 p. 137, H. Beveridge's art. *On the word nihilam*).

[853] *qūshlīk, aītlīk.* Elphinstone writes (i, 191) of the excellent greyhounds and hawking birds of the region; here the bird may be the *charkh*, which works with the dogs, fastening on the head of the game (Von Schwarz, p. 117, for the same use of eagles).

[854] An antelope resembling the usual one of Hindūstān is common south of Ghaznī (Vigne, p. 110); what is not found may be some classes of wild-sheep, frequent further north, at higher elevation, and in places more familiar to Bābur.

[855] The Parwān or Hindū-kush pass, concerning the winds of which *see* f. 128.

[856] *tūrnā u qarqara*; the second of which is the Hindī *būglā*, heron, *egret ardea gazetta*, the furnisher of the aigrette of commerce.

[857] The *aūqār* is *ardea cinerea*, the grey heron; the *qarqara* is *ardea gazetta*, the egret. *Qūṭān* is explained in the Elph. Codex (f. 110) by *khawāsil*, goldfinch, but the context concerns large birds; Scully (Shaw's Voc.) has *qodan*, water-hen, which suits better.

[858] *giz*, the short-flight arrow.

[859] a small, round-headed nail with which a whip-handle is decorated (Vambéry). Such a stud would keep the cord from slipping through the fingers and would not check the arrow-release.

[860] It has been understood (Mems. p. 158 and *Méms.* i, 313) that the arrow was flung by hand but if this were so, something heavier than the *giz* would carry the cord better, since it certainly would be difficult to direct a missile so light as an arrow without the added energy of the bow. The arrow itself will often have found its billet in the closely-flying flock; the cord would retrieve the bird. The verb used in the text is *aītmāq*, the one common to express the discharge of arrows *etc.*

[861] For Tīmūrids who may have immigrated the fowlers *see* Raverty's *Notes* p. 579 and his Appendix p. 22.

[862] *milwāh*; this has been read by all earlier translators, and also by the Persian annotator of the Elph. Codex, to mean *shākh*, bough. For decoy-ducks *see* Bellew's *Notes on Afghānistān* p. 404.

[863] *qūlān qūyirūghī*. Amongst the many plants used to drug fish I have not found this one mentioned. *Khār-zāhra* and *khār-fāq* approach it in verbal meaning; the first describes colocynth, the second, wild rue. See Watts' *Economic Products of India* iii, 366 and Bellew's *Notes* pp. 182, 471 and 478.

[864] Much trouble would have been spared to himself and his translators, if Bābur had known a lobster-pot.

[865] The fish, it is to be inferred, came down the fall into the pond.

[866] Burnes and Vigne describe a fall 20 miles from Kābul, at "Tangī Gharoi", [below where the Tag-aū joins the Bārān-water,] to which in their day, Kābulīs went out for the amusement of catching fish as they try to leap up the fall. Were these migrants seeking upper waters or were they captives in a fish-pond?

[867] Elph. MS. f. 111; W.-i-B. I.O. 215 f. 116b and 217 f. 97b; Mems. p. 155; *Mém.* i, 318.

[868] *mihmān-beglār*, an expression first used by Bābur here, and due, presumably, to accessions from Khusrau Shāh's following. A parallel case is given in Max Müller's *Science of Language* i, 348 ed. 1871, "Turkmān tribes ... call themselves, not subjects, but guests of the Uzbeg Khāns."

[869] *tiyūl-dīk* in all the Turkī MSS. Ilminsky, de Courteille and Zenker, *yitūl-dīk*, Turkī, a fief.

[870] *Wilāyat khūd hech bīrīlmādī*; W.-i-B. 215 f. 116b, *Wilāyat dāda na shuda* and 217 f. 97b, *Wilāyat khūd hech dāda na shud*. By this I understand that he kept the lands of Kābul itself in his own hands. He mentions (f. 350) and Gul-badan mentions (H.N. f. 40b) his resolve so to keep Kābul. I think he kept not only the fort but all lands constituting the Kābul *tūmān* (f. 135b and note).

[871] *Saifī dūr, qalamī aīmās*, *i.e.* tax is taken by force, not paid on a written assessment.

[872] *khar-wār*, about 700 lbs Averdupois (Erskine). Cf. *Āyīn-i-akbarī* (Jarrett, ii, 394).

[873] Niẓāmu'd-dīn Aḥmad and Badāyūnī both mention this script and say that in it Bābur transcribed a copy of the Qorān for presentation to Makka. Badāyūnī says it was unknown in his day, the reign of Akbar (*Ṭabaqāt-i-akbarī*, lith. ed. p. 193, and *Muntakhabu't-tawārīkh* Bib. Ind. ed. iii, 273).

[874] Bābur's route, taken with one given by Raverty (*Notes* p. 691), allows these Hazāras, about whose location Mr. Erskine was uncertain, to be located between the Takht-pass (Arghandī-Maidān-Unai road), on their east, and the Sang-lākh mountains, on their west.

[875] The Takht-pass, one on which from times immemorial, toll (*nirkh*) has been taken.

[876] *khāṭir-khwāh chāpīlmādī*, which perhaps implies mutual discontent, Bābur's with his gains, the Hazāras' with their losses. As the second Persian translation omits the negative, the Memoirs does the same.

[877] Bhīra being in Shāhpūr, this Khān's *daryā* will be the Jehlam.

[878] Bābur uses Persian *dasht* and Hindī *dūkī*, plain and hill, for the tracts east and west of Mehtar Sulaimān. The first, *dasht*, stands for Dāman (skirt) and Dara-i-jāt, the second, *dūkī*, indefinitely for the broken lands west of the main range, but also, in one instance for the Dūkī [Dūgī] district of Qandahār, as will be noted.

[879] f. 132. The Jagdālīk-pass for centuries has separated the districts of Kābul and Nīngnahār. Forster (*Travels* ii, 68), making the journey the reverse way, was sensible of the climatic change some 3m. east of Gandamak. Cf. Wood's *Report* I. p. 6.

[880] These are they whose families Nāṣir Mīrzā shepherded out of Kābul later (f. 154, f. 155).

[881] Bird's-dome, opposite the mouth of the Kūnār-water (*S.A. War*, Map p. 64).

[882] This word is variously pointed and is uncertain. Mr. Erskine adopted "Pekhi", but, on the whole, it may be best to read, here and on f. 146, Ar. *fajj* or pers. *paj*, mountain or pass. To do so shews the guide to be one located in the Khaibar-pass, a *Fajjī* or *Pajī*.

[883] mod. Jām-rūd (Jām-torrent), presumably.

[884] G. of I. xx, 125 and Cunningham's *Ancient History* i, 80. Bābur saw the place in 925 AH. (f. 232b).

[885] Cunningham, p. 29. Four ancient sites, not far removed from one another, bear this name, Bīgrām, *viz.* those near Hūpīān, Kābul, Jalālābād and Pashāwar.

[886] Cunningham, i, 79.

[887] Perhaps a native of Kamarī on the Indus, but *kamarī* is a word of diverse application (index *s.n.*).

[888] The annals of this campaign to the eastward shew that Bābur was little of a free agent; that many acts of his own were merciful; that he sets down the barbarity of others as it was, according to his plan of writing (f. 86); and that he had with him undisciplined robbers of Khusrau Shāh's former following. He cannot be taken as having power to command or

control the acts of those, his guest-begs and their following, who dictated his movements in this disastrous journey, one worse than a defeat, says Ḥaidar Mīrzā.

[889] For the route here *see* Masson, i, 117 and Colquhoun's *With the Kuram Field-force* p. 48.

[890] The Ḥai. MS. writes this Dilah-zāk.

[891] *i.e.* raised a force in Bābur's name. He took advantage of this *farmān* in 911 AH. to kill Bāqī *Chagkāniānī* (f. 159b-160).

[892] Of the Yūsuf-zāī and Ranjīt-sīngh, Masson says, (i, 141) "The miserable, hunted wretches threw themselves on the ground, and placing a blade or tuft of grass in their mouths, cried out, "I am your cow." This act and explanation, which would have saved them from an orthodox Hindū, had no effect with the infuriated Sikhs." This form of supplication is at least as old as the days of Firdausī (Erskine, p. 159 n.). The *Bahār-i-'ajam* is quoted by Vullers as saying that in India, suppliants take straw in the mouth to indicate that they are blanched and yellow from fear.

[893] This barbarous custom has always prevailed amongst the Tartar conquerors of Asia (Erskine). For examples under ' *see* Raverty's *Notes* p. 137.

[894] For a good description of the road from Kohāt to Thāl *see* Bellew's *Mission* p. 104.

[895] F. 88b has the same phrase about the doubtful courage of one Sayyidī Qarā.

[896] Not to the mod. town of Bannū, [that having been begun only in 1848 AD.] but wherever their wrong road brought them out into the Bannū amphitheatre. The Survey Map of 1868, No. 15, shews the physical features of the wrong route.

[897] Perhaps he connived at recovery of cattle by those raided already.

[898] Tāq is the Tank of Maps; Bāzār was s.w. of it. Tank for Tāq looks to be a variant due to nasal utterance (Vigne, p. 77, p. 203 and Map; and, as bearing on the nasal, *in loco*, Appendix E).

[899] If return had been made after over-running Bannū, it would have been made by the Tochī-valley and so through Farmūl; if after over-running the Plain, Bābur's details shew that the westward turn was meant to be by the Gūmāl-valley and one of two routes out of it, still to Farmūl; but the extended march southward to near Dara-i-Ghazī Khān made the westward turn be taken through the valley opening at Sakhī-sawār.

[900] This will mean, none of the artificial runlets familiar where Bābur had lived before getting to know Hindūstān.

[901] *sauda-āt*, perhaps, pack-ponies, perhaps, bred for sale and not for own use. Burnes observes that in 1837 Lūhānī merchants carried precisely the same articles of trade as in Bābur's day, 332 years earlier (*Report* IX p. 99).

[902] Mr. Erskine thought it probable that the first of these routes went through Kanigūram, and the second through the Ghwālirī-pass and along the Gūmāl. *Birk*, fastness, would seem an appropriate name for Kanigūram, but, if Bābur meant to go to Ghaznī, he would be off the ordinary Gūmāl-Ghaznī route in going through Farmūl (Aūrgūn). Raverty's *Notes* give much useful detail about these routes, drawn from native sources. For Barak (Birk) *see Notes* pp. 88, 89; Vigne, p. 102.

[903] From this it would seem that the alternative roads were approached by one in common.

[904] *tūmshūq*, a bird's bill, used here, as in Selsey-bill, for the naze (nose), or snout, the last spur, of a range.

[905] Here these words may be common nouns.

[906] Nū-roz, the feast of the old Persian New-year (Erskine); it is the day on which the Sun enters Aries.

[907] In the [Turkī] Elph. and Ḥai. MSS. and in some Persian ones, there is a space left here as though to indicate a known omission.

[908] *kamarī*, sometimes a cattle-enclosure, which may serve as a *sangur*. The word may stand in one place of its *Bābur-nāma* uses for Gum-rāhī (R.'s *Notes s.n.* Gum-rāhān).

[909] Index *s.n.*

[910] Vigne, p. 241.

[911] This name can be translated "He turns not back" or "He stops not".

[912] *i.e.* five from Bīlah.

[913] Raverty gives the saint's name as Pīr Kānūn (Ar. *kānūn*, listened to). It is the well-known Sakhī-sarwār, honoured hy Hindūs and Muḥammadans. (G. of I., xxi, 390; R.'s *Notes* p. 11 and p. 12 and JASB 1855; Calcutta Review 1875, Macauliffe's art. *On the fair at Sakhi-sarwar*, Leech's *Report* VII, for the route; *Khazīnatu 'l-asfiyā* iv, 245.)

[914] This seems to be the sub-district of Qandahār, Dūkī or Dūgī.

[915] *khar-gāh*, a folding tent on lattice frame-work, perhaps a *khibitka*.

[916] It may be more correct to write Kāh-mard, as the Ḥai. MS. does and to understand in the name a reference to the grass(*kāh*)-yielding capacity of the place.

[917] f. 121.

[918] This may mean, what irrigation has not used.

[919] Mr. Erskine notes that the description would lead us to imagine a flock of flamingoes. Masson found the lake filled with red-legged, white fowl (i, 262); these and also what Bābur saw, may have been the China-goose which has body and neck white, head and tail russet (Bellew's *Mission* p. 402). Broadfoot seems to have visited the lake when migrants were few, and through this to have been led to adverse comment on Bābur's accuracy (p. 350).

[920] The usual dryness of the bed may have resulted from the irrigation of much land some 12 miles from Ghaznī.

[921] This is the Luhūgur (Logar) water, knee-deep in winter at the ford but spreading in flood with the spring-rains. Bābur, not being able to cross it for the direct roads into Kābul, kept on along its left bank, crossing it eventually at the Kamarī of maps, s.e. of Kābul.

[922] This disastrous expedition, full of privation and loss, had occupied some four months (T.R. p. 201).

[923] f. 145b.

[924] f. 133b and Appendix F.

[925] They were located in Mandrāwar in 926 AH. (f. 251).

[926] This was done, manifestly, with the design of drawing after the families their fighting men, then away with Bābur.

[927] f. 163. Shaibāq Khān besieged Chīn Ṣufī, Sl. Ḥusain Mīrzā's man in Khwārizm (T. R. p. 204; *Shaibānī-nāma*, Vambéry, Table of Contents and note 89).

[928] Survey Map 1889, Sadda. The Rāgh-water flows n.w. into the Oxus (Amū).

[929] *birk*, a mountain stronghold; cf. f. 149b note to Birk (Barak).

[930] They were thus driven on from the Bārān-water (f. 154b).

[931] f. 126b.

[932] Ḥiṣār, presumably.

[933] Here "His Honour" translates Bābur's clearly ironical honorific plural.

[934] These two sulṭāns, almost always mentioned in alliance, may be Tīmūrids by maternal descent (Index *s.nn.*). So far I have found no direct statement of their parentage. My husband has shewn me what may be one indication of it, *viz.* that two of the uncles of Shaibāq Khān (whose kinsmen the sulṭāns seem to be), Qūj-kūnjī and Sīūnjak, were sons of a daughter of the Tīmūrid Aūlūgh Beg *Samarkandī* (Ḥ.S. ii, 318). *See* Vambéry's *Bukhārā* p. 248 note.

[935] For the deaths of Taṃbal and Maḥmūd, mentioned in the above summary of Shaibāq Khān's actions, *see* the *Shaibānī-nāma*, Vambéry, p. 323.

[936] Ḥ.S. ii, 323, for Khusrau Shāh's character and death.

[937] f. 124.

[938] Khwāja-of-the-rhubarb, presumably a shrine near rhubarb-grounds (f. 129b).

[939] *yakshī bārdīlār*, lit. went well, a common expression in the *Bābur-nāma*, of which the reverse statement is *yamānlīk bīla bārdī* (f. 163). Some Persian MSS. make the Mughūls disloyal but this is not only in opposition to the Turkī text, it is a redundant statement since if disloyal, they are included in Bābur's previous statement, as being Khusrau Shāh's retainers. What might call for comment in Mughūls would be loyalty to Bābur.

[940] Elph. MS. f. 121b: W.-i-B. I.O. 215 f. 126 and 217 f. 106b; Mems. p. 169.

[941] *tāgh-dāmanasī*, presumably the Koh-dāman, and the garden will thus be the one of f. 136b.

[942] If these heirs were descendants of Aūlūgh Beg M. one would be at hand in 'Abdu'r-razzāq, then a boy, and another, a daughter, was the wife of Muqīm *Arghūn*. As Mr. Erskine notes, Musalmāns are most scrupulous not to bury their dead in ground gained by violence or wrong.

[943] The news of Aḥmad's death was belated; he died some 13 months earlier, in the end of 909 AH. and in Eastern Turkistān. Perhaps details now arrived.

[944] *i.e.* the fortieth day of mourning, when alms are given.

[945] Of those arriving, the first would find her step-daughter dead, the second her sister, the third, his late wife's sister (T. R. p. 196).

[946] This will be the earthquake felt in Agra on Ṣafar 3rd 911 AH. (July 5th 1505 AD. Erskine's *History of India* i, 229 note). Cf. Elliot and Dowson, iv, 465 and v, 99.

[947] Raverty's *Notes* p. 690.

[948] *bīr kitta tāsh ātīmī*; var. *bāsh ātīmī*. If *tāsh* be right, the reference will probably be to the throw of a catapult.

[949] Here almost certainly, a drummer, because there were two tambours and because also Bābur uses *'aūdī* & *ghachakī* for the other meanings of *ṭambourchi*, lutanist and guitarist. The word has found its way, as *tambourgi*, into Childe Harold's Pilgrimage (Canto ii, lxxii. H. B.).

[950] Kābul-Ghaznī road (R.'s *Notes* index *s.n.*).

[951] var. Yārī. Tāzī is on the Ghaznī-Qalāt-i-ghilzāī road (R.'s *Notes*, Appendix p. 46).

[952] *i.e.* in Kābul and in the Trans-Himalayan country.

[953] These will be those against Bābur's suzerainty done by their defence of Qalāt for Muqīm.

[954] *tabaqa*, dynasty. By using this word Bābur shews recognition of high birth. It is noticeable that he usually writes of an Arghūn chief either simply as "Beg" or without a title. This does not appear to imply admission of equality, since he styles even his brothers and sisters Mīrzā and Begīm; nor does it shew familiarity of intercourse, since none seems to have existed between him and Ẕū'n-nūn or Muqīm. That he did not admit equality is shewn on f. 208. The T.R. styles Ẕū'n-nūn "Mīrzā", a title by which, as also by Shāh, his descendants are found styled (A.-i-a. Blochmann, *s.n.*).

[955] Turkī *khachar* is a camel or mule used for carrying personal effects. The word has been read by some scribes as *khanjar*, dagger.

[956] In 910 AH. he had induced Bābur to come to Kābul instead of going into Khurāsān (Ḥ.S. iii, 319); in the same year he dictated the march to Kohāt, and the rest of that disastrous travel. His real name was not Bāqī but Muḥammad Bāqir (Ḥ.S. iii, 311).

[957] These transit or custom duties are so called because the dutiable articles are stamped with a *ṭamghā*, a wooden stamp.

[958] Perhaps this word is an equivalent of Persian *goshī*, a tax on cattle and beasts of burden.

[959] Bāqī was one only and not the head of the Lords of the Gate.

[960] The choice of the number nine, links on presumably to the mystic value attached to it *e.g.* Tarkhāns had nine privileges; gifts were made by nines.

[961] It is near Ḥasan-abdāl (A.-i-A. Jarrett, ii, 324).

[962] For the *farmān*, f. 146b; for Gujūrs, G. of I.

[963] var. Khwesh. Its water flows into the Ghūr-bund stream; it seems to be the Dara-i-Turkmān of Stanford and the Survey Maps both of which mark Janglīk. For Hazāra turbulence, f. 135b and note.

[964] The repetition of *aūq* in this sentence can hardly be accidental.

[965] *ṭaur* [*dara*], which I take to be Turkī, round, complete.

[966] Three MSS. of the Turkī text write *bīr sīmīzlūq tīwah*; but the two Persian translations have *yak shuturlūq farbīh*, a *shuturlūq* being a baggage-camel with little hair (Erskine).

[967] *brochettes*, meat cut into large mouthfuls, spitted and roasted.

[968] Perhaps he was officially an announcer; the word means also bearer of good news.

[969] *yīlāng*, without mail, as in the common phrase *yīgīt yīlāng*, a bare brave.

[970] *aūpchīn*, of horse and man (f. 113b and note).

[971] Manifestly Bābur means that he twice actually helped to collect the booty.

[972] This is that part of a horse covered by the two side-pieces of a Turkī saddle, from which the side-arch springs on either side (Shaw).

[973] *Bārān-nīng ayāghī.* Except the river I have found nothing called Bārān; the village marked Baian on the French Map would suit the position; it is n.e. of Chār-yak-kār (f. 184b note).

[974] *i.e.* prepared to fight.

[975] For the Hazāra (Turkī, Mīng) on the Mīrzā's road *see* Raverty's routes from Ghaznī to the north. An account given by the *Tārīkh-i-rashīdī* (p. 196) of Jahāngīr's doings is confused; its parenthetical "(at the same time)" can hardly be correct. Jahāngīr left Ghaznī now, (911 AH.), as Bābur left Kābul in 912 AH. without knowledge of Ḥusain's death (911 AH.). Bābur had heard it (f. 183b) before Jahāngīr joined him (912 AH.); after their meeting they went on together to Herī. The petition of which the T. R. speaks as made by Jahāngīr to Bābur, that he might go into Khurāsān and help the Bāī-qarā Mīrzās must have been made after the meeting of the two at Ṣaf-hill (f. 184b).

[976] The plurals *they* and *their* of the preceding sentence stand no doubt for the Mīrzā, Yūsuf and Buhlūl who all had such punishment due as would lead them to hear threat in Qāsim's words now when all were within Bābur's pounce.

[977] These are the *aïmāqs* from which the fighting-men went east with Bābur in 910 AH. and the families in which Nāṣir shepherded across Hindu-kush (f. 154 and f. 155).

[978] *yamānlīk bīla bārdī*; cf. f. 156b and n. for its opposite, *yakhshī bārdīlār*; and T. R. p. 196.

[979] One might be of mail, the other of wadded cloth.

[980] Chīn Ṣūfī was Ḥusain *Bāī-qarā's* man (T.R. p. 204). His arduous defence, faithfulness and abandonment recall the instance of a later time when also a long road stretched between the man and the help that failed him. But the Mīrzā was old, his military strength was, admittedly, sapped by ease; hence his elder Khartum, his neglect of his Gordon.

It should be noted that no mention of the page's fatal arrow is made by the *Shaibānī-nāma* (Vambéry, p. 442), or by the *Tārīkh-i-rashīdī* (p. 204). Chīn Ṣūfī's death was on the 21st of the Second Rabī 911 AH. (Aug. 22nd 1505 AD.).

[981] This may be the "Baboulei" of the French Map of 1904, on the Herī-Kushk-Marūchāq road.

[982] Elph. MS. f. 127; W.-i-B. I.O. 215 f. 132 and 217 f. 111b; Mems. p. 175; *Méms.* i, 364.

That Bābur should have given his laborious account of the Court of Herī seems due both to loyalty to a great Tīmūrid, seated in Tīmūr Beg's place (f. 122b), and to his own interest, as a man-of-letters and connoisseur in excellence, in that ruler's galaxy of talent. His account here opening is not complete; its sources are various; they include the *Ḥabību's-siyār* and what he will have learned himself in Herī or from members of the Bāī-qarā family, knowledgeable women some of them, who were with him in Hindūstān. The narrow scope of my notes shews that they attempt no more than to indicate further sources of information and to clear up a few obscurities.

[983] Tīmūr's youngest son, d. 850 AH. (1446 AD.). Cf. Ḥ.S. iii, 203. The use in this sentence of Amīr and not Beg as Tīmūr's title is, up to this point, unique in the *Bābur-nāma*; it may be a scribe's error.

[984] Fīrūza's paternal line of descent was as follows:—Fīrūza, daughter of Sl. Ḥusain *Qānjūt*, son of Ākā Begīm, daughter of Tīmūr. Her maternal

descent was:—Fīrūza, d. of Qūtlūq-sulṭān Begīm, d. of Mīrān-shāh, s. of Tīmūr. She died Muḥ. 24th 874 AH. (July 25th 1489 AD. Ḥ.S. iii, 218).

[985] "No-one in the world had such parentage", writes Khwānd-amīr, after detailing the Tīmūrid, Chīngīz-khānid, and other noted strains meeting in Ḥusain *Bāī-qarā* (Ḥ.S. iii, 204).

[986] The Elph. MS. gives the Begīm no name; Badī'u'l-jamāl is correct (Ḥ.S. iii, 242). The curious "Badka" needs explanation. It seems probable that Bābur left one of his blanks for later filling-in; the natural run of his sentence here is "Ākā B. and Badī'u'l-jamāl B." and not the detail, which follows in its due place, about the marriage with Aḥmad.

[987] *Dīwān bāshīdā ḥāṣir būlmās aīdī*; the sense of which may be that Bāī-qarā did not sit where the premier retainer usually sat at the head of the Court (Pers. trs. *sar-i-dīwān*).

[988] From this Wais and Sl. Ḥusain M.'s daughter Sulṭānīm (f. 167b) were descended the Bāī-qarā Mīrzās who gave Akbar so much trouble.

[989] As this man might be mistaken for Bābur's uncle (*q.v.*) of the same name, it may be well to set down his parentage. He was a s. of Mīrzā Sayyidī Aḥmad, s. of Mīrān-shāh, s. of Tīmūr (Ḥ.S. iii, 217, 241). I have not found mention elsewhere of "Aḥmad s. of Mīrān-shāh"; the *sayyidī* in his style points to a sayyida mother. He was Governor of Herī for a time, for Sl. H.M.; 'Alī-sher has notices of him and of his son, Kīchīk Mīrzā (*Journal Asiatique* xvii, 293, M. Belin's art. where may be seen notices of many other men mentioned by Bābur).

[990] He collected and thus preserved 'Alī-sher's earlier poems (Rieu's Pers. Cat. p. 294). Mu'inu'd-dīn al Zamji writes respectfully of his being worthy of credence in some Egyptian matters with which he became acquainted in twice passing through that country on his Pilgrimage (*Journal Asiatique* xvi, 476, de Meynard's article).

[991] Kīchīk M.'s quatrain is a mere plagiarism of Jāmī's which I am indebted to my husband for locating as in the *Dīwān* I.O. MS. 47 p. 47; B.M. Add. 7774 p. 290; and Add. 7775 p. 285. M. Belin interprets the verse as an expression of the rise of the average good man to mystical rapture, not as his lapse from abstinence to indulgence (l.c. xvii, 296 and notes).

[992] Elph. MS. *younger* but Ḥai. MS. *older* in which it is supported by the "also" (*ham*) of the sentence.

[993] modern Astrakhan. Ḥusain's guerilla wars were those through which he cut his way to the throne of Herī. This begīm was married first to Pīr Budāgh Sl. (Ḥ.S. iii, 242); he dying, she was married by Aḥmad, presumably

by levirate custom (*yīnkālīk*; f. 12 and note). By Aḥmad she had a daughter, styled Khān-zāda Begīm whose affairs find comment on f. 206 and Ḥ.S. iii, 359. (The details of this note negative a suggestion of mine that Badka was the Rābī'a-sulṭān of f. 168 (Gul-badan, App. *s. nn.*).)

[994] This is a felt wide-awake worn by travellers in hot weather (Shaw); the Turkmān bonnet (Erskine).

[995] Ḥai. MS. *yamānlīk*, badly, but Elph. MS. *namāyan*, whence Erskine's *showy*.

[996] This was a proof that he was then a Shī'a (Erskine).

[997] The word *perform* may be excused in speaking of Musalmān prayers because they involve ceremonial bendings and prostrations (Erskine).

[998] If Bābur's 40 include rule in Herī only, it over-states, since Yādgār died in 875 AH. and Ḥusain in 911 AH. while the intervening 36 years include the 5 or 6 temperate ones. If the 40 count from 861 AH. when Ḥusain began to rule in Merv, it under-states. It is a round number, apparently.

[999] Relying on the Ilminsky text, Dr. Rieu was led into the mistake of writing that Bābur gave Ḥusain the wrong pen-name, *i.e.* Ḥusain, and not Ḥusainī (Turk. Cat. p. 256).

[1000] Daulat-shāh says that as he is not able to enumerate all Ḥusain's feats-of-arms, he, Turkmān fashion, offers a gift of Nine. The Nine differ from those of Bābur's list in some dates; they are also records of victory only (Browne, p. 521; *Not. et Extr.* iv, 262, de Saçy's article).

[1001] Wolves'-water, a river and its town at the s.e. corner of the Caspian, the ancient boundary between Russia and Persia. The name varies a good deal in MSS.

[1002] The battle was at Tarshīz; Abū-sa'īd was ruling in Herī; Daulat-shāh (l.c. p. 523) gives 90 and 10,000 as the numbers of the opposed forces!

[1003] f. 26b and note; Ḥ.S. iii, 209; Daulat-shāh p. 523.

[1004] The loser was the last Shāhrukhī ruler. Chanārān (variants) is near Abīward, Anwārī's birth-place (Ḥ.S. iii, 218; D.S. p. 527).

[1005] f. 85. D.S. (p. 540) and the Ḥ.S. (iii, 223) dwell on Ḥusain's speed through three continuous days and nights.

[1006] f. 26; Ḥ.S. iii, 227; D.S. p. 532.

[1007] Abū-sa'īd's son by a Badakhshī Begīm (T.R. p. 108); he became his father's Governor in Badakhshān and married Ḥusain *Bāī-qarā's* daughter Begīm Sultān at a date after 873 AH. (f. 168 and note; Ḥ.S. iii, 196, 229, 234-37; D.S. p. 535).

[1008] f. 152.

[1009] Abā-bikr was defeated and put to death at the end of Rajah 884 AH.-Oct. 1479 AD. after flight before Ḥusain across the Gurgān-water (Ḥ.S. iii, 196 and 237 but D.S. p. 539, Ṣafar 885 AH.).

[1010] f. 41, Pul-i-chirāgh; for Halwā-spring, Ḥ.S. iii, 283 and Rieu's Pers. Cat. p. 443.

[1011] f. 33 (p. 57) and f. 57b.

[1012] In commenting thus Bābur will have had in mind what he best knew, Ḥusain's futile movements at Qūndūz and Ḥiṣār.

[1013] *qālib aīdī*; if *qālib* be taken as Turkī, survived or remained, it would not apply here since many of Ḥusain's children predeceased him; Ar. *qālab* would suit, meaning *begotten, born.*

There are discrepancies between Bābur's details here and Khwānd-amīr's scattered through the *Ḥabību's-siyār*, concerning Ḥusain's family.

[1014] *bī ḥuẓūrī*, which may mean aversion due to Khadīja Begīm's malevolence.

[1015] Some of the several goings into 'Irāq chronicled by Bābur point to refuge taken with Tīmūrids, descendants of Khalīl and 'Umar, sons of Mirān-shāh (Lane-Poole's *Muhammadan Dynasties*, Table of the Tīmūrids).

[1016] He died before his father (Ḥ.S. iii, 327).

[1017] He will have been killed previous to Ramẓān 3rd 918 AH. (Nov. 12th, 1512 AD.), the date of the battle of Ghaj-dawān when Nijm S̱ānī died.

[1018] The *bund* here may not imply that both were in prison, but that they were bound in close company, allowing Ismā'īl, a fervent Shī'a, to convert the Mīrzā.

[1019] The *bātmān* is a Turkish weight of 13lbs (Meninsky) or 15lbs (Wollaston). The weight seems likely to refer to the strength demanded for rounding the bow (*kamān guroha-sī*) *i.e.* as much strength as to lift 40 *bātmāns*. Rounding or bending might stand for stringing or drawing. The meaning can hardly be one of the weight of the cross-bow itself. Erskine read *gūrdehieh* for *guroha* (p. 180) and translated by "double-stringed bow";

de Courteille (i, 373) read *guirdhiyeh, arrondi, circulaire*, in this following Ilminsky who may have followed Erskine. The Elph. and Ḥai. MSS. and the first W.-i-B. (I.O. 215 f. 113b) have *kamān guroha-sī*; the second W.-i-B. omits the passage, in the MSS. I have seen.

[1020] *yakhshīlār bārīb tūr*; lit. good things went (on); cf. f. 156b and note.

[1021] Badī'u'z-zamān's son, drowned at Chausa in 946 AH. (1539 AD.) A.N. (H. Beveridge, i, 344).

[1022] Qalāt-i-nādirī, in Khurāsān, the birth-place of Nādir Shāh (T.R. p. 209).

[1023] *bīr gīna qīz*, which on f. 86b can fitly be read to mean daughterling, *Töchterchen, fillette*, but here and *i.a.* f. 168, must have another meaning than diminutive and may be an equivalent of German *Stück* and mean *one only*. Gul-badan gives an account of Shād's manly pursuits (H.N. f. 25b).

[1024] He was the son of Mahdī Sl. (f. 320b) and the father of 'Āqil Sl. *Aūzbeg* (A.N. index *s.n.*). Several matters suggest that these men were of the Shabān Aūzbegs who intermarried with Ḥusain *Bāī-qarā's* family and some of whom went to Bābur in Hindūstān. One such matter is that Kābul was the refuge of dispossessed Harātīs, after the Aūzbeg conquest; that there 'Āqil married Shād *Bāī-qarā* and that 'Ādil went on to Bābur. Moreover Khāfī Khān makes a statement which (if correct) would allow 'Ādil's father Mahdī to be a grandson of Ḥusain *Bāī-qarā*; this statement is that when Bābur defeated the Aūzbegs in 916 AH. (1510 AD.), he freed from their captivity two sons (descendants) of his paternal uncle, named Mahdī Sl. and Sulṭān Mīrzā. [Leaving the authenticity of the statement aside for a moment, it will be observed that this incident is of the same date and place as another well-vouched for, namely that Bābur then and there killed Mahdī Sl. *Aūzbeg* and Ḥamza Sl. *Aūzbeg* after defeating them.] What makes in favour of Khāfī Khān's correctness is, not only that Bābur's foe Mahdī is not known to have had a son 'Ādil, but also that his "Sulṭān Mīrzā" is not a style so certainly suiting Ḥamza as it does a Shabān sulṭān, one whose father was a Shabān sulṭān, and whose mother was a Mīrzā's daughter. Moreover this point of identification is pressed by the correctness, according to oriental statement of relationship, of Khāfī Khān's "paternal uncle" (of Bābur), because this precisely suits Sl. Ḥusain Mīrzā with whose family these Shabān sulṭāns allied themselves. On the other hand it must be said that Khāfī Khān's statement is not in the English text of the *Tārīkh-i-rashīdī*, the book on which he mostly relies at this period, nor is it in my husband's MS. [a copy from the Rampūr Codex]; and to this must be added the verbal objection that a modicum of rhetoric allows a death to be described both in Turkī and Persian, as a release from the captivity of a sinner's own acts (f. 160). Still Khāfī Khān may be right; his statement may yet be found in some other MS. of the T. R. or some different source; it is one a scribe copying the T. R. might be led to omit by reason of its coincidences. The killing and the release may both be right; 'Ādil's Mahdī may be the Shabān sulṭān inference makes him seem. This little *crux* presses home the need of much attention to the *lacunæ* in the *Bābur-nāma*, since in them are lost some exits and some entries of Bābur's *dramatis personæ*, pertinently, mention of the death of Mahdī with Ḥamza in 916 AH., and possibly also that of 'Ādil's Mahdī's release.

[1025] A *chār-ṭāq* may be a large tent rising into four domes or having four porches.

[1026] Ḥ.S. iii, 367.

[1027] This phrase, common but not always selected, suggests unwillingness to leave the paternal roof.

[1028] Abū'l-ghāzī's *History of the Mughūls*, Désmaisons, p. 207.

[1029] The appointment was made in 933 AH. (1527 AD.) and seems to have been held still in 934 AH. (ff. 329, 332).

[1030] This grandson may have been a child travelling with his father's household, perhaps Aūlūgh Mīrzā, the oldest son of Muḥammad Sulṭān Mīrzā (A. A. Blochmann, p. 461). No mention is made here of Sulṭānīm Begīm's marriage with 'Abdu'l-bāqī Mīrzā (f. 175).

[1031] Abū'l-qāsim Bābur *Shāhrukhī* presumably.

[1032] The time may have been 902 AH. when Mas'ūd took his sister Bega Begīm to Herī for her marriage with Ḥaidar (Ḥ.S. iii, 260).

[1033] Khwāja Aḥmad *Yāsawī*, known as Khwāja Ātā, founder of the Yāsawī religious order.

[1034] Not finding mention of a daughter of Abū-sa'id named Rābī'a-sulṭān, I think she may be the daughter styled Āq Begīm who is No. 3 in Gul-badan's guest-list for the Mystic Feast.

[1035] This man I take to be Ḥusain's grandfather and not brother, both because 'Abdu'l-lāh was of Ḥusain's and his brother's generation, and also because of the absence here of Bābur's usual defining words "elder brother" (of Sl. Ḥusain Mīrzā). In this I have to differ from Dr. Rieu (Pers. Cat. p. 152).

[1036] So-named after his ancestor Sayyid Barka whose body was exhumed from Andikhūd for reburial in Samarkand, by Tīmūr's wish and there laid in such a position that Tīmūr's body was at its feet (*Ẕafar-nāma* ii, 719; Ḥ.S. iii, 82). (For the above interesting detail I am indebted to my husband.)

[1037] *Qïzïl-bāsh*, Persians wearing red badges or caps to distinguish them as Persians.

[1038] Yādgār-i-farrukh *Mīrān-shāhī* (Ḥ.S. iii, 327). He may have been one of those Mīrān-shāhīs of 'Irāq from whom came Ākā's and Sulṭānīm's husbands, Aḥmad and 'Abdu'l-bāqī (ff. 164, 175*b*).

[1039] This should be four (f. 169*b*). The Ḥ.S. (iii, 327) also names three only when giving Pāpā Āghācha's daughters (the omission linking it with the B.N.), but elsewhere (iii, 229) it gives an account of a fourth girl's marriage; this fourth is needed to make up the total of 11 daughters. Bābur's and Khwānd-amīr's details of Pāpā Āghācha's quartette are defective; the following may be a more correct list:—(1) Begīm Sulṭān (a frequent title), married to Abā-bikr *Mīrān-shāhī* (who died 884 AH.) and seeming too old to be the one [No. 3] who married Mas'ūd (Ḥ.S. iii, 229); (2) Sulṭān-nizhād, married to Iskandar *Bāī-qarā*; (3) Sa'ādat-bakht also known as Begīm Sulṭān, married to Mas'ūd *Mīrān-shāhī* (Ḥ.S. iii, 327); (4) Manauwar-sulṭān, married to a son of Aūlūgh Beg *Kābulī* (Ḥ.S. iii, 327).

[1040] This "after" seems to contradict the statement (f. 58) that Mas'ūd was made to kneel as a son-in-law (*kūyādlīk-kā yūkūndūrūb*) at a date previous to his blinding, but the seeming contradiction may be explained by considering the following details; he left Herī hastily (f. 58), went to Khusrau Shāh and was blinded by him,—all in the last two months of 903 AH. (1498 AD.), after the kneeling on Ẕū'l-qa'da 3rd, (June 23rd) in the Ravens'-garden. Here what Bābur says is that the Begīm was given (*bīrīb*) after the blinding, the inference allowed being that though Mas'ūd had kneeled before the blinding, she had remained in her father's house till his return after the blinding.

[1041] The first W.-i-B. writes "Apāq Begīm" (I.O. 215 f. 136) which would allow Sayyid Mīrzā to be a kinsman of Apāq Begīm, wife of Ḥusain *Bāī-qarā.*

[1042] This brief summary conveys the impression that the Begīm went on her pilgrimage shortly after Mas'ūd's death (913 AH. ?), but may be wrong:—After Mas'ūd's murder, by one Bīmāsh Mīrzā, *dārogha* of Sarakhs, at Shaibāq Khān's order, she was married by Bīmāsh M. (Ḥ.S. iii, 278). How long after this she went to Makka is not said; it was about 934 AH. when Bābur heard of her as there.

[1043] This clause is in the Ḥai. MS. but not in the Elph. MS. (f. 131), or Kehr's (Ilminsky, p. 210), or in either Persian translation. The boy may have been 17 or 18.

[1044] This appears a mistake (f. 168 foot, and note on Pāpā's daughters).

[1045] f. 171b.

[1046] 933 AH.-1527 AD. (f. 329).

[1047] Presumably this was a *yīnkālīk* marriage; it differs from some of those chronicled and also from a levirate marriage in not being made with a childless wife. (Cf. index *s.n. yīnkālīk*.)

[1048] Khwānd-amīr says that Bega Begīm was jealous, died of grief at her divorce, and was buried in a College, of her own erection, in 893 AH. (1488 AD. ḤS. iii, 245).

[1049] *Gulistān* Cap. II, Story 31 (Platts, p. 114).

[1050] *i.e.* did not get ready to ride off if her husband were beaten by her brother (f. 11 and note to Ḥabība).

[1051] Khadīja Begī Āghā (Ḥ.S. ii, 230 and iii, 327); she would be promoted probably after Shāh-i-gharīb's birth.

[1052] He was a son of Badī'u'z-zamān.

[1053] It is singular that this honoured woman's parentage is not mentioned; if it be right on f. 168b (*q.v.* with note) to read Sayyid Mīrzā of Apāq Begīm, she may be a sayyida of Andikhūd.

[1054] As Bābur left Kābul on Ṣafar 1st (Nov. 17th 1525 AD.), the Begīm must have arrived in Muḥarram 932 AH. (Oct. 18th to Nov. 17th).

[1055] f. 333. As Chandīrī was besieged in Rabī'u'l-ākhar 934 AH. this passage shews that, as a minimum estimate, what remains of Bābur's composed narrative (*i.e.* down to f. 216b) was written after that date (Jan. 1528).

[1056] *Chār-shambalār.* Mention of another inhabitant of this place with the odd name, Wednesday (Chār-shamba), is made on f. 42b.

[1057] Mole-marked Lady; most MSS. style her Bī but Ḥ.S. iii, 327, writes Bībī; it varies also by calling her a Turk. She was a purchased slave of Shahr-bānū's and was given to the Mīrzā by Shahr-bānū at the time of her own marriage with him.

[1058] As noted already, f. 168b enumerates three only.

[1059] The three were almost certainly Badī'u'z-zamān, Ḥaidar, son of a Tīmūrid mother, and Muẓaffar-i-ḥusain, born after his mother had been legally married.

[1060] Seven sons predeceased him:—Farrukh, Shāh-i-gharīb, Muḥ. Ma'ṣūm, Ḥaidar, Ibrāhīm-i-ḥusain, Muḥ. Ḥusain and Abū-turāb. So too five daughters:—Āq, Bega, Āghā, Kīchīk and Fāṭima-sulṭān Begīms. So too four wives:—Bega-sulṭān and Chūlī Begīms, Zubaida and Laṭīf-sulṭān Āghāchas (Ḥ.S. iii, 327).

[1061] Chākū, a Barlās, as was Tīmūr, was one of Tīmūr's noted men.

At this point some hand not the scribe's has entered on the margin of the Ḥai. MS. the descendants of Muḥ. Barandūq down into Akbar's reign:—Muḥ. Farīdūn, bin Muḥ. Qulī Khān, bin Mīrzā 'Alī, bin Muḥ. Barandūq *Barlās*. Of these Farīdūn and Muḥ. Qulī are amīrs of the *Āyīn-i-akbarī* list (Blochmann, pp. 341, 342; Ḥ.S. iii, 233).

[1062] Enforced marches of Mughūls and other nomads are mentioned also on f. 154b and f. 155.

[1063] Ḥ.S. iii, 228, 233, 235.

[1064] *beg kīshī*, beg-person.

[1065] Khwānd-amīr says he died a natural death (Ḥ.S. iii, 235).

[1066] f. 21. For a fuller account of Nawā'i, *J. Asiatique* xvii, 175, M. Belin's article.

[1067] *i.e.* when he was poor and a beg's dependant. He went back to Herī at Sl. Ḥusain M.'s request in 873 AH.

[1068] Niẓāmī's (Rieu's Pers. Cat. s.n.).

[1069] Farīdu'd-dīn-'aṭṭar's (Rieu l.c. and Ency. Br.).

[1070] *Gharā'ibu'ṣ-ṣighar*, *Nawādiru'sh-shahāb*, *Badā'i'u'l-wasaṭ* and *Fawā'idu'l-kibr*.

[1071] Every Persian poet has a *takhalluṣ* (pen-name) which he introduces into the last couplet of each ode (Erskine).

[1072] The death occurred in the First Jumāda 906 AH. (Dec. 1500 AD.).

[1073] Niẓāmu'd-dīn Aḥmad bin Tawakkal *Barlās* (Ḥ.S. iii, 229).

[1074] This may be that uncle of Tīmūr who made the Ḥaj (T. R. p. 48, quoting the *Ẓafar-nāma*).

[1075] Some MSS. omit the word "father" here but to read it obviates the difficulty of calling Walī a great beg of Sl. Ḥusain Mīrzā although he died when that mīrzā took the throne (973 AH.) and although no leading place is allotted to him in Bābur's list of Herī begs. Here as in other parts of Bābur's account of Herī, the texts vary much whether Turkī or Persian, *e.g.* the Elph. MS. appears to call Walī a blockhead (*dūnkūz dūr*), the Ḥai. MS. writing *n:kūz dūr*(?).

[1076] He had been Bābur *Shāhrukhī's yasāwal* (Court-attendant), had fought against Ḥusain for Yādgār-i-muḥammad and had given a daughter to Ḥusain (Ḥ.S. iii, 206, 228, 230-32; D.S. in *Not. et Ex.* de Saçy p. 265).

[1077] f. 29b.

[1078] *Sic*, Elph. MS. and both Pers. trss. but the Ḥai. MS. omits "father". To read it, however, suits the circumstance that Ḥasan of Ya'qūb was not with Ḥusain and in Harāt but was connected with Maḥmūd *Mīrānshāhī* and Tīrmīẕ (f. 24). Nuyān is not a personal name but is a title; it implies good-birth; all uses of it I have seen are for members of the religious family of Tīrmīẕ.

[1079] He was the son of Ibrāhīm *Barlās* and a Badakhshī begīm (T.R. p. 108).

[1080] He will have been therefore a collateral of Daulat-shāh whose relation to Fīrūz-shāh is thus expressed by Nawā'ī:—*Mīr Daulat-shāh Fīrūz-shāh Beg-nīng 'amm-zāda-sī Amīr 'Alā'u'd-daula Isfārayīnī-nīng aūghūlī dur*, *i.e.* Mīr Daulat-shāh was the son of Fīrūz-shāh Beg's paternal uncle's son, Amir 'Alā'u'd-daula *Isfārayīnī*. Thus, Fīrūz-shāh and Isfārayīnī were first cousins; Daulat-shāh and 'Abdu'l-khalīq's father were second cousins; while Daulat-shāh and Fīrūz-shāh were first cousins, once removed (Rieu's Pers. Cat. p. 534; Browne's D.S. English preface p. 14 and its reference to the Pers. preface).

[1081] *Tarkhān-nāma*, E. & D.'s *History of India* i, 303; Ḥ.S. iii, 227.

[1082] f. 41 and note.

[1083] Both places are in the valley of the Herī-rūd.

[1084] Badī'u'z-zamān married a daughter of Ẕū'n-nūn; she died in 911 AH. (E. & D. i, 305; Ḥ.S. iii, 324).

[1085] This indicates, both amongst Musalmāns and Hindūs, obedience and submission. Several instances occur in Macculloch's *Bengali Household Stories*.

[1086] T.R. p. 205.

[1087] This is an idiom expressive of great keenness (Erskine).

[1088] Ḥ.S. iii, 250, *kitābdār*, librarian; so too Ḥai. MS. f. 174b.

[1089] *mutaiyam* (f. 7b and note). Mīr Mughūl Beg was put to death for treachery in 'Irāq (Ḥ.S. iii, 227, 248).

[1090] Bābur speaks as an eye-witness (f. 187b). For a single combat of Sayyid Badr, Ḥ. S. iii, 233.

[1091] f. 157 and note to *bātmān*.

[1092] A level field in which a gourd (*qabaq*) is set on a pole for an archer's mark to be hit in passing at the gallop (f. 18b and note).

[1093] Or possibly during the gallop the archer turned in the saddle and shot backwards.

[1094] Junaid was the father of Niẓāmu'd-dīn 'Alī, Bābur's Khalīfa (Vice-gerent). That Khalīfa was of a religious house on his mother's side may be inferred from his being styled both Sayyid and Khwāja neither of which titles could have come from his Turkī father. His mother may have been a sayyida of one of the religious families of Marghīnān (f. 18 and note), since Khalīfa's son Muḥibb-i-'alī writes his father's name "Niẓāmu'd-din 'Alī *Marghīlānī*" (*Marghīnānī*) in the Preface of his *Book on Sport* (Rieu's Pers. Cat. p. 485).

[1095] This northward migration would take the family into touch with Bābur's in Samarkand and Farghāna.

[1096] He was left in charge of Jaunpūr in Rabī' I, 933 AH. (Jan. 1527 AD.) but exchanged for Chunār in Ramẓān 935 AH. (June 1529 AD.); so that for the writing of this part of the *Bābur-nāma* we have the major and minor limits of Jan. 1527 and June 1529.

[1097] Ḥ.S. iii, 227.

[1098] *See* Appendix H, *On the counter-mark Bih-būd on coins.*

[1099] Niẓāmu'd-dīn Amīr Shaikh Aḥmadu's-suhailī was surnamed Suhailī through a *fāl* (augury) taken by his spiritual guide, Kamālu'd-dīn Ḥusain *Gāzur-gāhī*; it was he induced Ḥusain *Kashifī* to produce his *Anwār-i-suhailī* (Lights of Canopus) (f. 125 and note; Rieu's Pers. Cat. p. 756; and for a couplet of his, Ḥ.S. iii, 242 l. 10).

[1100] Index *s.n.*

[1101] Did the change complete an analogy between 'Alī *Jalāir* and his (perhaps) elder son with 'Alī Khalīfa and his elder son Ḥasan?

[1102] The Qūsh-begī is, in Central Asia, a high official who acts for an absent ruler (Shaw); he does not appear to be the Falconer, for whom Bābur's name is Qūshchī (f. 15 n.).

[1103] He received this sobriquet because when he returned from an embassy to the Persian Gulf, he brought, from Bahrein, to his Tīmūrid master a gift of royal pearls (Sām Mīrzā). For an account of Marwārīd *see* Rieu's Pers. Cat. p. 1094 and (*re* portrait) p. 787.

[1104] Sām Mīrzā specifies this affliction as *ābla-i-farang*, thus making what may be one of the earliest Oriental references to *morbus gallicus* [as de Saçy here translates the name], the foreign or European pox, the "French disease of Shakespeare" (H.B.).

[1105] Index *s.n.* Yūsuf.

[1106] Ramẓān 3rd 918 AH.-Nov. 12th 1512.

[1107] *i.e.* of the White-sheep Turkmāns.

[1108] His paternal line was, 'Abdu'l-bāqī, son of 'Uṣ̤mān, son of Sayyidī Aḥmad, son of Mīrān-shāh. His mother's people were begs of the White-sheep (Ḥ.S. iii, 290).

[1109] Sulṭ̤ānīm had married Wais (f. 157) not later than 895 or 896 AH. (Ḥ. S. iii, 253); she married 'Abdu'l-bāqī in 908 AH. (1502-3 AD.).

[1110] Sayyid Shamsu'd-dīn Muḥammad, Mīr Sayyid *Sar-i-barahna* owed his sobriquet of Bare-head to love-sick wanderings of his youth (Ḥ.S. iii, 328). The Ḥ.S. it is clear, recognizes him as a sayyid.

[1111] Rieu's Pers. Cat. p. 760; it is immensely long and "filled with tales that shock all probability" (Erskine).

[1112] f. 94 and note. Sl. Ḥusain M. made him curator of Anṣārī's shrine, an officer represented, presumably, by Col. Yate's "Mīr of Gāzur-gāh", and he became Chief Justice in 904 AH. (1498-99 AD.). *See* Ḥ.S. iii, 330 and 340; JASB 1887, art. *On the city of Harāt* (C. E. Yate) p. 85.

[1113] *mutasauwif*, perhaps meaning not a professed Ṣūfī.

[1114] He was of high birth on both sides, of religious houses of Ṭ̤abas and Nishāpūr (D.S. pp. 161, 163).

[1115] In agreement with its preface, Dr. Rieu entered the book as written by Sl. Ḥusain Mīrzā; in his Addenda, however, he quotes Bābur as the authority for its being by Gāzur-gāhī; Khwānd-amīr's authority can be added to Bābur's (Ḥ.S. 340; Pers. Cat. pp. 351, 1085).

[1116] *Dīwān*. The Wazīr is a sort of Minister of Finance; the Dīwān is the office of revenue receipts and issues (Erskine).

[1117] a secretary who writes out royal orders (Ḥ.S. iii, 244).

[1118] Count von Noer's words about a cognate reform of later date suit this man's work, it also was "a bar to the defraudment of the Crown, a stumbling-block in the path of avaricious chiefs" (*Emperor Akbar* trs. i, 11). The opposition made by 'Alī-sher to reform so clearly to Ḥusain's gain and to Ḥusain's begs' loss, stirs the question, "What was the source of his own income?" Up to 873 AH. he was for some years the dependant of Aḥmad Ḥājī Beg; he took nothing from the Mīrzā, but gave to him; he must have spent much in benefactions. The question may have presented itself to M. Belin for he observes, "'Alī-sher qui sans doute, à son retour de l'exil, recouvra l'héritage de ses pères, et depuis occupa de hautes positions dans le gouvernement de son pays, avait acquis une grande fortune" (*J. Asiatique* xvii, 227). While not contradicting M. Belin's view that vested property such as can be described as "paternal inheritance", may have passed from father to son, even in those days of fugitive prosperity and changing appointments, one cannot but infer, from Nawā'i's opposition to Majdu'd-dīn, that he, like the rest, took a partial view of the "rights" of the cultivator.

[1119] This was in 903 AH. after some 20 years of service (Ḥ.S. iii, 231; Ethé I.O. Cat. p. 252).

[1120] Amīr Jamālu'd-dīn 'Atā'u'l-lāh, known also as Jamālu'd-dīn Ḥusain, wrote a *History of Muhammad* (Ḥ.S. iii, 345; Rieu's Pers. Cat. p. 147 & (a correction) p. 1081).

[1121] Amongst noticeable omissions from Bābur's list of Herī celebrities are Mīr Khwānd Shāh ("Mirkhond"), his grandson Khwānd-amīr, Ḥusain *Kashifī* and Muinu'd-dīn al Zamjī, author of a *History of Harāt* which was finished in 897 AH.

[1122] Sa'du'd-dīn Mas'ūd, son of 'Umar, was a native of Taft in Yazd, whence his cognomen (Bahār-i-'ajam); he died in 792 AH.-1390 AD. (Ḥ.S. iii, 59, 343; T.R. p. 236; Rieu's Pers. Cat. pp. 352, 453).

[1123] These are those connected with grammar and rhetoric (Erskine).

[1124] This is one of the four principal sects of Muḥammadanism (Erskine).

[1125] T.R. p. 235, for Shāh Ismā'īl's murders in Herī.

[1126] Superintendent of Police, who examines weights, measures and provisions, also prevents gambling, drinking and so on.

[1127] f. 137.

[1128] The rank of Mujtahid, which is not bestowed by any individual or class of men but which is the result of slow and imperceptible opinion, finally prevailing and universally acknowledged, is one of the greatest peculiarities of the religion of Persia. The Mujtahid is supposed to be elevated above human fears and human enjoyments, and to have a certain degree of infallibility and inspiration. He is consulted with reverence and awe. There is not always a Mujtahid necessarily existing. *See* Kæmpfer, *Amoenitates Exoticae* (Erskine).

[1129] *muḥaddaṣ*, one versed in the traditional sayings and actions of Muḥammad.

[1130] Ḥ.S. iii, 340.

[1131] B.M. Or. 218 (Rieu's Pers. Cat. p. 350). The Commentary was made in order to explain the *Nafaḥāt* to Jāmī's son.

[1132] He was buried by the Mullā's side.

[1133] Amīr Burhānu'd-dīn 'Atā'u'l-lāh bin Maḥmūdu'l-ḥusainī was born in Nishāpūr but known as Mashhadī because he retired to that holy spot after becoming blind.

[1134] f. 144*b* and note. Qāẓī Ikhtiyāru'd-dīn Ḥasan (Ḥ.S. iii, 347) appears to be the Khwāja Ikhtiyār of the *Āyīn-i-akbarī*, and, if so, will have taken professional interest in the script, since Abū'l-faẓl describes him as a distinguished calligrapher in Sl. Ḥusain M.'s presence (Blochmann, p. 101).

[1135] Saifu'd-dīn (Sword of the Faith) Aḥmad, presumably.

[1136] A sister of his, Apāq Bega, the wife of 'Alī-sher's brother Darwīsh-i-'alī *kitābdār*, is included as a poet in the *Biography of Ladies* (Sprenger's Cat. p. 11). Amongst the 20 women named one is a wife of Shaibāq Khān, another a daughter of Hilālī.

[1137] He was the son of Khw. Ni'amatu'l-lāh, one of Sl. Abū-sa'īd M.'s wazīrs. When dying *aet.* 70 (923 AH.), he made this chronogram on his own death, "With 70 steps he measured the road to eternity." The name Āsaf, so frequent amongst wazīrs, is that of Solomon's wazīr.

[1138] Other interpretations are open; *wādī*, taken as *river*, might refer to the going on from one poem to another, the stream of verse; or it might be taken as *desert*, with disparagement of collections.

[1139] Maulānā Jamālu'd-dīn *Banā'ī* was the son of a *sabz-banā*, an architect, a good builder.

[1140] Steingass's Dictionary allows convenient reference for examples of metres.

[1141] Other jokes made by *Banā'ī* at the expense of Nawā'i are recorded in the various sources.

[1142] Bābur saw Banā'i in Samarkand at the end of 901 AH. (1496 AD. f. 38).

Here Dr. Leyden's translation ends; one other fragment which he translated will be found under the year 925 AH. (Erskine). This statement allows attention to be drawn to the inequality of the shares of the work done for the Memoirs of 1826 by Leyden and by Erskine. It is just to Mr. Erskine, but a justice he did not claim, to point out that Dr. Leyden's share is slight both in amount and in quality; his essential contribution was the initial stimulus he gave to the great labours of his collaborator.

[1143] So of Lope de Vega (b. 1562; d. 1635 AD.), "It became a common proverb to praise a good thing by calling it *a Lope*, so that jewels, diamonds, pictures, *etc.* were raised into esteem by calling them his" (Montalvan in Ticknor's *Spanish Literature* ii, 270).

[1144] Maulānā Saifī, known as 'Arūẓī from his mastery in prosody (Rieu's Pers. Cat. p. 525).

[1145] Here pedantry will be implied in the mullahood.

[1146] *Khamsatīn* (*infra* f. 180*b* and note).

[1147] This appears to mean that not only the sparse diacritical pointing common in writing Persian was dealt with but also the fuller Arabic.

[1148] He is best known by his pen-name Hātifī. The B.M. and I.O. have several of his books.

[1149] *Khamsatīn.* Hātifī regarded himself as the successor of Niẓāmī and Khusrau; this, taken with Bābur's use of the word *Khamsatīn* on f. 7 and here, and Saifī's just above, leads to the opinion that the *Khamsatīn* of the *Bābur-nāma* are always those of Niẓāmī and Khusrau, *the* Two Quintets (Rieu's Pers. Cat. p. 653).

[1150] Maulānā Mīr Kamālu'd-dīn Ḥusain of Nishāpūr (Rieu l.c. index s.n.; Ethé's I.O. Cat. pp. 433 and 1134).

[1151] One of his couplets on good and bad fortune is striking; "The fortune of men is like a sand-glass; one hour up, the next down." *See* D'Herbélot in his article (Erskine).

[1152] Ḥ.S. iii, 336; Rieu's Pers. Cat. p. 1089.

[1153] Āhī (sighing) was with Shāh-i-gharīb before Ibn-i-ḥusain and to him dedicated his *dīwān*. The words *sāḥib-i-dīwān* seem likely to be used here with double meaning *i.e.* to express authorship and finance office. Though Bābur has made frequent mention of authorship of a *dīwān* and of office in the *Dīwān*, he has not used these words hitherto in either sense; there may be a play of words here.

[1154] Muḥammad *Ṣāliḥ* Mīrzā *Khwārizmī*, author of the *Shaibānī-nāma* which manifestly is the poem (*maṣnawī*) mentioned below. This has been published with a German translation by Professor Vambéry and has been edited with Russian notes by Mr. Platon Melioransky (Rieu's Turkish Cat. p. 74; Ḥ.S. iii, 301).

[1155] Jāmī's *Subḥatu'l-abrār* (Rosary of the righteous).

[1156] The reference may be to things said by Muḥ. *Ṣāliḥ* the untruth of which was known to Bābur through his own part in the events. A crying instance of misrepresentation is Ṣāliḥ's assertion, in rhetorical phrase, that Bābur took booty in jewels from Khusrau Shāh; other instances concern the affairs of The Khāns and of Bābur in Transoxiana (f. 124b and index *s.nn.* Aḥmad and Maḥmūd *Chaghatāī etc.*; T.R. index *s.nn.*)

[1157] The name Fat-land (Taṃbal-khāna) has its parallel in Fat-village (Sīmīz-kīnt) a name of Samarkand; in both cases the nick-name is accounted for by the fertility of irrigated lands. We have not been able to find the above-quoted couplet in the *Shaibānī-nāma* (Vambéry); needless to say, the pun is on the nick-name (*taṃbal*, fat) of Sl. Aḥmad *Taṃbal*.

[1158] Muḥ. Ṣāliḥ does not show well in his book; he is sometimes coarse, gloats over spoil whether in human captives or goods, and, his good-birth not-forbidding, is a servile flatterer. Bābur's word "heartless" is just; it must have had sharp prompting from Ṣāliḥ's rejoicing in the downfall of The Khāns, Bābur's uncles.

[1159] the Longer (Ḥ.S. iii, 349).

[1160] Maulānā Badru'd-dīn (Full-moon of the Faith) whose pen-name was Hilālī, was of Astarābād. It may be noted that two dates of his death are found, 936 and 939 AH. the first given by de Saçy, the second by Rieu, and that the second seems to be correct (*Not. et Extr.* p. 285; Pers. Cat. p. 656; Hammer's *Geschichte* p. 368).

[1161] B.M. Add. 7783.

[1162] Opinions differ as to the character of this work:—Bābur's is uncompromising; von Hammer (p. 369) describes it as "*ein romantisches Gedicht, welches eine sentimentale Männerliebe behandelt*"; Sprenger (p. 427), as a mystical *maṣnawī* (poem); Rieu finds no spiritual symbolism in it and condemns it (Pers. Cat. p. 656 and, quoting the above passage of Bābur, p. 1090); Ethé, who has translated it, takes it to be mystical and symbolic (I.O. Cat. p. 783).

[1163] Of four writers using the pen-name Ahlī (Of-the-people), *viz.* those of Turān, Shīrāz, Tarshīz (in Khurāsān), and 'Irāq, the one noticed here seems to be he of Tarshīz. Ahlī of Tarshīz was the son of a locally-known pious father and became a Superintendent of the Mint; Bābur's *'āmī* may refer to Ahlī's first patrons, tanners and shoe-makers by writing for whom he earned his living (Sprenger, p. 319). Erskine read *'ummī*, meaning that Ahlī could neither read nor write; de Courteille that he was *un homme du commun.*

[1164] He was an occasional poet (Ḥ.S. iii, 350 and iv, 118; Rieu's Pers. Cat. p. 531; Ethé's I.O. Cat. p. 428).

[1165] Ustād Kamālu'd-dīn Bih-zād (well-born; Ḥ.S. iii, 350). Work of his is reproduced in Dr. Martin's *Painting and Painters of Persia* of 1913 AD.

[1166] This sentence is not in the Elph. MS.

[1167] Perhaps he could reproduce tunes heard and say where heard.

[1168] M. Belin quotes quatrains exchanged by 'Alī-sher and this man (*J. Asiatique* xvii, 199).

[1169] *i.e.* from his own camp to Bābā Ilāhī.

[1170] f. 121 has a fuller quotation. On the dual succession, *see* T.R. p. 196.

[1171] Elph. MS. f. 144; W.-i-B. I.O. 215 f. 148*b* and 217 f. 125*b*; Mems. p. 199.

[1172] News of Ḥusain's death in 911 AH. (f. 163b) did not reach Bābur till 912 AH. (f. 184*b*).

[1173] Lone-meadow (f. 195*b*). Jahāngīr will have come over the 'Irāq-pass, Bābur's baggage-convoy, by Shibr-tū. Cf. T. R. p. 199 for Bābur and Jahāngīr at this time.

[1174] Servant-of-the-mace; but perhaps, Qilinj-chāq, swords-man.

[1175] One of four, a fourth. Chār-yak may be a component of the name of the well-known place, n. of Kābul, "Chārikār"; but also the *Chār* in it may be Hindūstānī and refer to the permits-to-pass after tolls paid, given to caravans halted there for taxation. Raverty writes it Chārlākār.

[1176] Amongst the disruptions of the time was that of the Khānate of Qībchāq (Erskine).

[1177] The nearest approach to *kipkī* we have found in Dictionaries is *kupaki*, which comes close to the Russian *copeck*. Erskine notes that the *casbeké* is an oval copper coin (Tavernier, p. 121); and that a *tūmān* is a myriad (10,000). *Cf.* Manucci (Irvine), i, 78 and iv, 417 note; Chardin iv, 278.

[1178] Muḥarram 912 AH.-June 1506 AD. (Ḥ.S. iii, 353).

[1179] I take Murgh-āb here to be the fortified place at the crossing of the river by the main n.e. road; Bābur when in Dara-i-bām was on a tributary of the Murgh-āb. Khwānd-amīr records that the information of his approach was hailed in the Mīrzās' camp as good news (Ḥ.S. iii, 354).

[1180] Bābur gives the Mīrzās precedence by age, ignoring Muẕaffar's position as joint-ruler.

[1181] *mubālgha qīldī*; perhaps he laid stress on their excuse; perhaps did more than was ceremonially incumbent on him.

[1182] *'irq*, to which estrade answers in its sense of a carpet on which stands a raised seat.

[1183] Perhaps it was a recess, resembling a gate-way (W.-i-B. I.O. 215 f. 151 and 217 f. 127*b*). The impression conveyed by Bābur's words here to the artist who in B.M. Or. 3714, has depicted the scene, is that there was a vestibule opening into the tent by a door and that the Mīrzā sat near that door. It must be said however that the illustration does not closely follow the text, in some known details.

[1184] *shīra*, fruit-syrups, sherbets. Bābur's word for wine is *chāghīr* (*q.v.* index) and this reception being public, wine could hardly have been offered in Sunnī Herī. Bābur's strictures can apply to the vessels of precious metal he mentions, these being forbidden to Musalmāns; from his reference to the Tūra it would appear to repeat the same injunctions. Bābur broke up such vessels before the battle of Kanwāha (f. 315). Shāh-i-jahān did the same; when sent by his father Jahāngīr to reconquer the Deccan (1030 AH.-1621 AD.) he asked permission to follow the example of his ancestor Bābur, renounced wine, poured his stock into the Chaṃbal, broke up his cups and gave the fragments to the poor (*'Amal-i-ṣāliḥ*, Hughes' *Dict. of Islām* quoting the *Hidāyah* and *Mishkāt*, *s.nn.* Drinkables, Drinking-vessels, and Gold; Lane's *Modern Egyptians* p. 125 n.).

[1185] This may be the Rabāṯ-i-sanghī of some maps, on a near road between the "Forty-daughters" and Harāt; or Bābur may have gone out of his direct way to visit Rabāṯ-i-sang-bast, a renowned halting place at the Carfax of the Herī-Ṯūs and Nishāpūr-Mashhad roads, built by one Arslān

Jazāla who lies buried near, and rebuilt with great magnificence by 'Alī-sher *Nawā'ī* (Daulat-shāh, Browne, p. 176).

[1186] The wording here is confusing to those lacking family details. The paternal-aunt begīms can be Pāyanda-sulṭān (named), Khadīja-sulṭān, Apāq-sulṭān, and Fakhr-jahān Begīms, all daughters of Abū-sa'īd. The Apāq Begīm named above (also on f. 168*b* *q.v.*) does not now seem to me to be Abū-sa'īd's daughter (Gul-badan, trs. Bio. App.).

[1187] *yūkūnmāī.* Unless all copies I have seen reproduce a primary clerical mistake of Bābur's, the change of salutation indicated by there being no kneeling with Apāq Begīm, points to a *nuance* of etiquette. Of the verb *yūkūnmāk* it may be noted that it both describes the ceremonious attitude of intercourse, *i.e.* kneeling and sitting back on both heels (Shaw), and also the kneeling on meeting. From Bābur's phrase *Begīm bīla yūkūnūb* [having kneeled with], it appears that each of those meeting made the genuflection; I have not found the phrase used of other meetings; it is not the one used when a junior or a man of less degree meets a senior or superior in rank (*e.g.* Khusrau and Bābur f. 123, or Bābur and Badī'u'z-zamān f. 186).

[1188] Musalmāns employ a set of readers who succeed one another in reading (reciting) the Qorān at the tombs of their men of eminence. This reading is sometimes continued day and night. The readers are paid by the rent of lands or other funds assigned for the purpose (Erskine).

[1189] A suspicion that Khadīja put poison in Jahāngīr's wine may refer to this occasion (T.R. p. 199).

[1190] These are *jharokha-i-darsān*, windows or balconies from which a ruler shews himself to the people.

[1191] Mas'ūd was then blind.

[1192] Bābur first drank wine not earlier than 917 AH. (f. 49 and note), therefore when nearing 30.

[1193] *aīchkīlār*, French, *intérieur.*

[1194] The obscure passage following here is discussed in Appendix I, *On the weeping-willows of* f. 190*b*.

[1195] Here this may well be a gold-embroidered garment.

[1196] This, the tomb of Khwāja 'Abdu'l-lāh *Anṣari* (d. 481 AH.) stands some 2m. north of Herī. Bābur mentions one of its numerous attendants of his day, Kamālu'd-dīn Ḥusain *Gāzur-gāhī.* Mohan Lall describes it as he saw it in 1831; says the original name of the locality was Kār-zār-gāh, place-of-battle; and, as perhaps his most interesting detail, mentions that Jalālu'd-dīn *Rūmī's Maṣnawī* was recited every morning near the tomb and that people fainted during the invocation (*Travels in the Panj-āb* etc. p. 252). Colonel Yate has described the tomb as he saw it some 50 years later (JASB 1887); and explains the name Gāzur-gāh (lit. bleaching-place) by the following words of an inscription there found; "His tomb (Anṣarī's) is a washing-place (*gāzur-gāh*) wherein the cloud of the Divine forgiveness washes white the black records of men" (p. 88 and p. 102).

[1197] *juāz-i-kaghazlār* (f. 47*b* and note).

[1198] The *Ḥabību's-siyār* and Ḥai. MS. write this name with medial "round *hā*"; this allows it to be Kahad-stān, a running-place, race-course. Khwānd-amīr and Daulat-shāh call it a meadow (*aūlāng*); the latter speaks of a feast as held there; it was Shaibānī's head-quarters when he took Harāt.

[1199] *var.* Khatīra; either an enclosure (*qūrūq*?) or a fine and lofty building.

[1200] This may have been a usual halting-place on a journey (*safar*) north. It was built by Ḥusain *Bāī-qarā*, overlooked hills and fields covered with *arghwān* (f. 137*b*) and seems once to have been a Paradise (Mohan Lall, p. 256).

[1201] Jāmī's tomb was in the 'Īd-gah of Herī (Ḥ.S. ii, 337), which appears to be the Muṣalla (Praying-place) demolished by Amīr 'Abdu'r-raḥmān in the 19th century. Col. Yate was shewn a tomb in the Muṣalla said to be Jāmī's and agreeing in the age, 81, given on it, with Jāmī's at death, but he found a *crux* in the inscription (pp. 99, 106).

[1202] This may be the Muṣalla (Yate, p. 98).

[1203] This place is located by the Ḥ.S. at 5 *farsakh* from Herī (de Meynard at 25 *kilomètres*). It appears to be rather an abyss or fissure than a pond, a crack from the sides of which water trickles into a small bason in which dwells a mysterious fish, the beholding of which allows the attainment of desires. The story recalls Wordsworth's undying fish of Bow-scale Tarn. (*Cf.* Ḥ.S. Bomb. ed. ii, *Khatmat* p. 20 and de Meynard, *Journal Asiatique* xvi, 480 and note.)

[1204] This is on maps to the north of Herī.

[1205] d. 232 AH. (847 AD.). *See* Yate, p. 93.

[1206] Imām Fakhru'd-dīn *Raẓī* (de Meynard, *Journal Asiatique* xvi, 481).

[1207] d. 861 AH.-1457 AD. Guhār-shād was the wife of Tīmūr's son Shāhrukh. *See* Mohan Lall, p. 257 and Yate, p. 98.

[1208] This Marigold-garden may be named after Hārūnu'r-rashīd's wife Zubaida.

[1209] This will be the place n. of Herī from which Maulānā Jalālu'd-dīn *Pūrānī* (d. 862 AH.) took his cognomen, as also Shaikh Jamālu'd-dīn Abū-sa'īd *Pūrān* (f. 206) who was visited there by Sl. Ḥusain Mīrzā, ill-treated by Shaibānī (f. 206), left Herī for Qandahār, and there died, through the fall of a roof, in 921 AH. (Ḥ.S. iii, 345; *Khazīnatu'l-asfiya* ii, 321).

[1210] His tomb is dated 35 or 37 AH. (656 or 658 AD.; Yate, p. 94).

[1211] Mālān was a name of the Herī-rūd (*Journal Asiatique* xvi, 476, 511; Mohan Lall, p. 279; Ferrier, p. 261; *etc.*).

[1212] Yate, p. 94.

[1213] The position of this building between the Khūsh and Qībchāq Gates (de Meynard, l.c. p. 475) is the probable explanation of the variant, noted just below, of Kushk for Khūsh as the name of the Gate. The *Tārīkh-i-rashīdī* (p. 429), mentions this kiosk in its list of the noted ones of the world.

[1214] var. Kushk (de Meynard, l.c. p. 472).

[1215] The reference here is, presumably, to Bābur's own losses of Samarkand and Andijān.

[1216] Ākā or Āgā is used of elder relations; a *yīnkā* or *yīngā* is the wife of an uncle or elder brother; here it represents the widow of Bābur's uncle Aḥmad *Mīrān-shāhī*. From it is formed the word *yīnkālīk*, levirate.

[1217] The almshouse or convent was founded here in Tīmūr's reign (de Meynard, l.c. p. 500).

[1218] *i.e.* No smoke without fire.

[1219] This name may be due to the splashing of water. A Langar which may be that of Mīr Ghiyāṣ, is shewn in maps in the Bām valley; from it into the Herī-rūd valley Bābur's route may well have been the track from that Langar which, passing the villages on the southern border of Gharjistān, goes to Ahangarān.

[1220] This escape ought to have been included in the list of Bābur's transportations from risk to safety given in my note to f. 96.

[1221] The right and wrong roads are shewn by the Indian Survey and French Military maps. The right road turns off from the wrong one, at Daulat-yār, to the right, and mounts diagonally along the south rampart of the Herī-rūd valley, to the Zirrīn-pass, which lies above the Bakkak-pass and carries the regular road for Yaka-aūlāng. It must be said, however, that we are not told whether Yaka-aūlāng was Qāsim Beg's objective; the direct road for Kābul from the Herī-rūd valley is not over the Zirrīn-pass but goes from Daulat-yār by "Āq-zarat", and the southern flank of Koh-i-bābā (bābār) to the Unai-pass (Holdich's *Gates of India* p. 262).

[1222] *circa* Feb. 14th 1507, Bābur's 24th birthday.

[1223] The Hazāras appear to have been wintering outside their own valley, on the Ghūr-bund road, in wait for travellers [*cf.* T.R. p. 197]. They have been perennial highwaymen on the only pass to the north not closed entirely in winter.

[1224] The Ghūr-bund valley is open in this part; the Hazāras may have been posted on the naze near the narrows leading into the Janglīk and their own side valleys.

[1225] Although the verses following here in the text are with the Turkī Codices, doubt cannot but be felt as to their authenticity. They do not fit verbally to the sentence they follow; they are a unique departure from Bābur's plain prose narrative and nothing in the small Hazāra affair shews cause for such departure; they differ from his usual topics in their bombast and comment on his men (*cf.* f. 194 for comment on shirking begs). They appear in the 2nd Persian translation (217 f. 134) in Turkī followed by a prose Persian rendering (*khalāṣa*). They are not with the 1st Pers. trs. (215 f. 159), the text of which runs on with a plain prose account suiting the size of the affair, as follows:—"The braves, seeing their (the Hazāras) good soldiering, had stopped surprised; wishing to hurry them i went swiftly past them, shouting 'Move on! move on!' They paid me no attention. When, in order to help, I myself attacked, dismounting and going up the hill, they shewed courage and emulation in following. Getting to the top of the pass, we drove that band off, killing many, capturing others, making their families prisoner and plundering their goods." This is followed by "I myself collected" *etc.* as in the Turkī text after the verse. It will be seen that the above extract is not a translation of the verse; no translator or even summariser would be likely to omit so much of his original. It is just a suitably plain account of a trivial matter.

[1226] *Gulistān* Cap. I. Story 4.

[1227] Bābur seems to have left the Ghūr-bund valley, perhaps pursuing the Hazāras towards Janglīk, and to have come "by ridge and valley" back into it for Ushtur-shahr. I have not located Tīmūr Beg's Langar. As has been noted already (*q.v.* index) the Ghūr-bund narrows are at the lower end of the valley; they have been surmised to be the fissured rampart of an ancient lake.

[1228] Here this may represent a guard- or toll-house (Index *s.n.*).

[1229] As *yūrūn* is a patch, the bearer of the sobriquet might be Black Aḥmad the repairing-tailor.

[1230] *Second Afghān War*, Map of Kābul and its environs.

[1231] I understand that the arrival undiscovered was a result of riding in single-file and thus shewing no black mass.

[1232] or *gharbīcha*, which Mr. Erskine explains to be the four plates of mail, made to cover the back, front and sides; the *jība* would thus be the wadded under-coat to which they are attached.

[1233] This prayer is composed of extracts from the Qorān (*Méms*, i, 454 note); it is reproduced as it stands in Mr. Erskine's wording (p. 216).

[1234] Bābur's reference may well be to Sanjar's birth as well as to his being the holder of Nīngnahār. Sanjar's father had been thought worthy to mate with one of the six Badakhshī begīms whose line traced back to Alexander (T. R. p. 107); and his father was a Barlās, seemingly of high family.

[1235] It may be inferred that what was done was for the protection of the two women.

[1236] Not a bad case could have been made out for now putting a Tīmūrid in Bābur's place in Kābul; *viz.* that he was believed captive in Herī and that Mīrzā Khān was an effective *locum tenens* against the Arghūns. Ḥaidar sets down what in his eyes pleaded excuse for his father Muḥ. Ḥusain (T.R. p. 198).

[1237] *qūsh*, not even a little plough-land being given (*chand qulba dihya*, 215 f. 162).

[1238] They were sons of Sl. Aḥmad Khān *Chaghatāī.*

[1239] f. 160.

[1240] Ḥaidar's opinion of Bābur at this crisis is of the more account that his own father was one of the rebels let go to the mercy of the "avenging servitor". When he writes of Bābur, as being, at a time so provoking, gay, generous, affectionate, simple and gentle, he sets before us insight and temper in tune with Kipling's "If...."

[1241] Bābur's distinction, made here and elsewhere, between Chaghatāī and Mughūl touches the old topic of the right or wrong of the term "Mughūl dynasty". What he, as also Ḥaidar, allows said is that if Bābur were to describe his mother in tribal terms, he would say she was half-Chaghatāī, half-Mughūl; and that if he so described himself, he would say he was half-Tīmūrid-Turk, half-Chaghatāī. He might have called the dynasty he founded in India Turkī, might have called it Tīmūriya; he would never have called it Mughūl, after his maternal grandmother.

Ḥaidar, with imperfect classification, divides Chīngīz Khān's "Mughūl horde" into Mughūls and Chaghatāīs and of this Chaghatāī offtake says that none remained in 953 *AH.* (1547 *AD.*) except the rulers, *i.e.* sons of Sl. Aḥmad Khan (T.R. 148). Manifestly there was a body of Chaghatāīs with Bābur and there appear to have been many near his day in the Herī region,—'Alī-sher *Nawā'i* the best known.

Bābur supplies directions for naming his dynasty when, as several times, he claims to rule in Hindūstān where the "Turk" had ruled (f. 233*b*, f. 224*b*, f. 225). To call his dynasty Mughūl seems to blot out the centuries, something as we should do by calling the English Teutons. If there is to be such blotting-out, Abū'l-ghāzī would allow us, by his tables of Turk descent, to go further, to the primal source of all the tribes concerned, to Turk, son of Japhet. This traditional descent is another argument against "Mughūl dynasty."

[1242] They went to Qandahār and there suffered great privation.

[1243] Bārān seems likely to be the Baian of some maps. Gul-i-bahār is higher up on the Panjhīr road. Chāsh-tūpa will have been near-by; its name might mean *Hill of the heap of winnowed-corn.*

[1244] f. 136.

[1245] Answer; Visions of his father's sway.

[1246] Elph. MS. f. 161; W.-i-B. I.O. 215 f. 164 and 217 f. 139*b*; Mems. p. 220.

[1247] The narrative indicates the location of the tribe, the modern Ghilzāī or Ghilzī.

[1248] Sih-kāna lies s.e. of Shorkach, and near Kharbīn. Sar-i-dih is about 25 or 30 miles s. of Ghaznī (Erskine). A name suiting the pastoral wealth of the tribe *viz.* Mesh-khail, Sheep-tribe, is shewn on maps somewhat s. from Kharbīn. *Cf.* Steingass *s.n.* Masht.

[1249] *yāghrūn*, whence *yāghrūnchī*, a diviner by help of the shoulder-blades of sheep. The defacer of the Elphinstone Codex has changed *yāghrūn* to *yān*, side, thus making Bābur turn his side and not his half-back to the north, altering his direction, and missing what looks like a jesting reference to his own divination of the road. The Pole Star was seen, presumably, before the night became quite black.

[1250] From the subsequent details of distance done, this must have been one of those good *yīghāch* of perhaps 5-6 miles, that are estimated by the ease of travel on level lands (Index *s.v. yīghāch*).

[1251] I am uncertain about the form of the word translated by "whim". The Elph. and Ḥai. Codices read *khūd d:lma* (altered in the first to *y:lma*); Ilminsky (p. 257) reads *khūd l:ma* (de C. ii, 2 and note); Erskine has been misled by the Persian translation (215 f. 164*b* and 217 f. 139*b*). Whether *khūd-dilma* should be read, with the sense of "out of their own hearts" (spontaneously), or whether *khūd-yalma*, own pace (Turkī, *yalma*, pace) the contrast made by Bābur appears to be between an unpremeditated gallop and one premeditated for haste. Persian *dalama*, tarantula, also suggests itself.

[1252] *chāpqūn*, which is the word translated by gallop throughout the previous passage. The Turkī verb *chāpmāq* is one of those words-of-all-work for which it is difficult to find a single English equivalent. The verb *qūīmāq* is another; in its two occurrences here the first may be a metaphor from the pouring of molten metal; the second expresses that permission to gallop off for the raid without which to raid was forbidden. The root-notion of *qūīmāq* seems to be letting-go, that of *chāpmāq*, rapid motion.

[1253] *i.e.* on the raiders' own road for Kābul.

[1254] f. 198*b*.

[1255] The Fifth taken was manifestly at the ruler's disposition. In at least two places when dependants send gifts to Bābur the word [*tassaduq*] used might be rendered as "gifts for the poor". Does this mean that the *pādshāh* in receiving this stands in the place of the Imām of the Qorān injunction which orders one-fifth of spoil to be given to the Imām for the poor, orphans, and travellers,—four-fifths being reserved for the troops? (Qorān, Sale's ed. 1825, i, 212 and Hidāyat, Book ix).

[1256] This may be the sum of the separate items of sheep entered in account-books by the commissaries.

[1257] Here this comprehensive word will stand for deer, these being plentiful in the region.

[1258] Three Turkī MSS. write *ṣīghīnīb*, but the Elph. MS. has had this changed to *yītīb*, having reached.

[1259] *bāsh-sīz*, lit. without head, doubtless a pun on Aūz-beg (own beg, leaderless). B.M. Or. 3714 shows an artist's conception of this *tart-part*.

[1260] Bābā Khākī is a fine valley, some 13 *yīghāch* e. of Herī (f. 13) where the Herī sulṭāns reside in the heats (*J. Asiatique* xvi, 501, de Meynard's article; Ḥ.S. iii, 356).

[1261] f. 172*b*.

[1262] *aūkhshātā almādī*. This is one of many passages which Ilminsky indicates he has made good by help of the Memoirs (p. 261; *Mémoires* ii, 6).

[1263] They are given also on f. 172.

[1264] This may be Sirakhs or Sirakhsh (Erskine).

[1265] *Tūshlūq tūshdīn yūrdī bīrūrlār*. At least two meanings can be given to these words. Circumstances seem to exclude the one in which the Memoirs (p. 222) and *Mémoires* (ii, 7) have taken them here, *viz*. "each man went off to shift for himself", and "chacun s'en alla de son côté et s'enfuit comme il put", because Ẕū'n-nūn did not go off, and the Mīrzās broke up after his defeat. I therefore suggest another reading, one prompted by the Mīrzās' vague fancies and dreams of what they might do, but did not.

[1266] The encounter was between "Belāq-i-marāl and Rabāṭ-i-'alī-sher, near Bādghīs" (Raverty's *Notes* p. 580). For particulars of the taking of Herī *see* Ḥ.S. iii, 353.

[1267] One may be the book-name, the second the name in common use, and due to the colour of the buildings. But Bābur may be making an ironical jest, and nickname the fort by a word referring to the defilement (*ālā*) of Aūzbeg possession. (Cf. Ḥ.S. iii, 359.)

[1268] Mr. Erskine notes that Badī'u'z-zamān took refuge with Shāh Ismā'īl *Ṣafawī* who gave him Tabrīz. When the Turkish Emperor Sālim took Tabrīz in 920 AH. (1514 AD.), he was taken prisoner and carried to Constantinople, where he died in 923 AH. (1517 AD.).

[1269] In the fort were his wife Kābulī Begīm, d. of Aūlūgh Beg M. *Kābulī* and Ruqaiya Āghā, known as the Nightingale. A young daughter of the Mīrzā, named the Rose-bud (Chūchak), had died just before the siege. After the surrender of the fort, Kābulī Begīm was married by Mīrzā Kūkūldāsh (perhaps 'Āshiq-i-muḥammad *Arghūn*); Ruqaiya by Tīmūr Sl. *Aūzbeg* (Ḥ.S. iii, 359).

[1270] The *Khuṭba* was first read for Shaibāq Khān in Herī on Friday Muḥarram 15th 913 AH. (May 27th 1507 AD.).

[1271] There is a Persian phrase used when a man engages in an unprofitable undertaking *Kīr-i-khar gerift*, *i.e. Asini nervum deprehendet* (Erskine). The Ḥ.S. does not mention Banā'i as fleecing the poets but has much to say about one Maulānā 'Abdu'r-raḥīm a Turkistānī favoured by Shaibānī, whose victim Khwānd-amīr was, amongst many others. Not infrequently where Bābur and Khwānd-amīr state the same fact, they accompany it by varied details, as here (Ḥ.S. iii, 358, 360).

[1272] *'adat.* Muḥammadan Law fixes a term after widowhood or divorce within which re-marriage is unlawful. Light is thrown upon this re-marriage by Ḥ.S. iii, 359. The passage, a somewhat rhetorical one, gives the following details:—"On coming into Herī on Muḥarram 11th, Shaibānī at once set about gathering in the property of the Tīmūrids. He had the wives and daughters of the former rulers brought before him. The great lady Khān-zāda Begīm (f. 163*b*) who was daughter of Aḥmad Khān, niece of Sl. Ḥusain Mīrzā, and wife of Muẓaffar Mīrzā, shewed herself pleased in his presence. Desiring to marry him, she said Muẓaffar M. had divorced her two years before. Trustworthy persons gave evidence to the same effect, so she was united to Shaibānī in accordance with the glorious Law. Mihr-angez Begīm, Muẓaffar M.'s daughter, was married to 'Ubaidu'llāh Sl. (*Aūzbeg*); the rest of the chaste ladies having been sent back into the city, Shaibānī resumed his search for property." Manifestly Bābur did not believe in the divorce Khwānd-amīr thus records.

[1273] A sarcasm this on the acceptance of literary honour from the illiterate.

[1274] f. 191 and note; Pul-i-sālār may be an irrigation-dam.

[1275] Qalāt-i-nādirī, the birth-place of Nādir Shāh, n. of Mashhad and standing on very strong ground (Erskine).

[1276] This is likely to be the road passing through the Carfax of Rabāṯ-i-sangbast, described by Daulat-shāh (Browne, p. 176).

[1277] This will mean that the Arghūns would acknowledge his suzerainty; Ḥaidar Mīrzā however says that Shāh Beg had higher views (T. R. p. 202). There had been earlier negotiations between Ẕū'n-nūn with Badī'u'z-zamān and Bābur which may have led to the abandonment of Bābur's expedition in 911 AD. (f. 158; Ḥ.S. iii, 323; Raverty's account (*Notes* p. 581-2) of Bābur's dealings with the Arghūn chiefs needs revision).

[1278] They will have gone first to Tūn or Qāīn, thence to Mashhad, and seem likely to have joined the Begīm after cross-cutting to avoid Herī.

[1279] *yāghī wilāyatī-ghā kīlādūrghān.* There may have been an accumulation of caravans on their way to Herāt, checked in Qalāt by news of the Aūzbeg conquest.

[1280] Jahāngīr's son, thus brought by his mother, will have been an infant; his father had gone back last year with Bābur by the mountain road and had been left, sick and travelling in a litter, with the baggage when Bābur hurried on to Kābul at the news of the mutiny against him (f. 197); he must have died shortly afterwards, seemingly between the departure of the two rebels from Kābul (f. 201*b*-202) and the march out for Qandahār. Doubtless his widow now brought her child to claim his uncle Bābur's protection.

[1281] Persians pay great attention in their correspondence not only to the style but to the kind of paper on which a letter is written, the place of signature, the place of the seal, and the situation of the address. Chardin gives some curious information on the subject (Erskine). Bābur marks the distinction of rank he drew between the Arghūn chiefs and himself when he calls their letter to him, *'arẓ-dāsht*, his to them *khaṭṭ*. His claim to suzerainty over those chiefs is shewn by Ḥaidar Mīrzā to be based on his accession to Tīmūrid headship through the downfall of the Bāī-qarās, who had been the acknowledged suzerains of the Arghūns now repudiating Bābur's claim. Cf. Erskine's *History of India* i, cap. 3.

[1282] on the main road, some 40 miles east of Qandahār.

[1283] var. Kūr or Kawar. If the word mean *ford*, this might well be the one across the Tarnak carrying the road to Qarā (maps). Here Bābur seems to have left the main road along the Tarnak, by which the British approach was made in 1880 AD., for one crossing west into the valley of the Argand-āb.

[1284] Bābā Ḥasan *Abdāl* is the Bābā Walī of maps. The same saint has given his name here, and also to his shrine east of Atak where he is known as Bābā Walī of Qandahār. The torrents mentioned are irrigation off-takes from the Argand-āb, which river flows between Bābā Walī and Khalishak. Shāh Beg's force was south of the torrents (cf. Murghān-koh on S.A.W. map).

[1285] The narrative and plans of *Second Afghan War* (Murray 1908) illustrate Bābur's movements and show most of the places he names. The end of the 280 mile march, from Kābul to within sight of Qandahār, will have stirred in the General of 1507 what it stirred in the General of 1880. Lord Roberts speaking in May 1913 in Glasgow on the rapid progress of the movement for National Service thus spoke:—"A memory comes over me which turns misgiving into hope and apprehension into confidence. It is the memory of the morning when, accompanied by two of Scotland's most famous regiments, the Seaforths and the Gordons, at the end of a long and arduous march, *I saw in the distance the walls and minarets of Qandahar, and knew that the end of a great resolve and a great task was near.*"

[1286] *mīn tāsh 'imārat qāzdūrghān tūmshūghī-nīng alīdā*; 215 f. 168*b*, *'imarātī kah az sang yak pāra farmūda būdīm*; 217 f. 143*b*, *jāy kah man 'imāratī sākhtam*; Mems. p. 226, where I have built a palace; *Méms.* ii, 15, *l'endroit même où j'ai bâti un palais*. All the above translations lose the sense of *qāzdūrghān*, am causing to dig out, to quarry stone. Perhaps for coolness' sake the dwelling was cut out in the living rock. That the place is south-west of the main *ạrīqs*, near Murghān-koh or on it, Bābur's narrative allows. Cf. Appendix J.

[1287] *sic*, Ḥai. MS. There are two Lakhshas, Little Lakhsha, a mile west of Qandahār, and Great Lakhsha, about a mile s.w. of Old Qandahār, 5 or 6 m. from the modern one (Erskine).

[1288] This will be the main irrigation channel taken off from the Argand-āb (Maps).

[1289] *tamām aīlīkīdīn—aīsh-kīlūr yīkītlār*, an idiomatic phrase used of 'Alī-dost (f. 14*b* and n.), not easy to express by a single English adjective.

[1290] The *tawāchī* was a sort of adjutant who attended to the order of the troops and carried orders from the general (Erskine). The difficult passage following gives the Turkī terms Bābur selected to represent Arabic military ones.

[1291] Ar. *aḥad* (*Āyīn-i-akbarī*, Blochmann, index *s.n.*). The word *būī* recurs in the text on f. 210.

[1292] *i.e.* the *būī tīkīnī* of f. 209*b*, the *khāṣa tābīn*, close circle.

[1293] As Mughūls seem unlikely to be descendants of Muḥammad, perhaps the title Sayyid in some Mughūl names here, may be a translation of a Mughūl one meaning Chief.

[1294] *Arghūn-nīng qarāsī*, a frequent phrase.

[1295] in sign of submission.

[1296] f. 176. It was in 908 AH. [1502 AD.].

[1297] This word seems to be from *sānjmāq*, to prick or stab; and here to have the military sense of *prick*, *viz.* riding forth. The Second Pers. trs. (217 f. 144*b*) translates it by *ghauta khūrda raft*, went tasting a plunge under water (215 f. 170; Muḥ. *Shīrāzī*'s lith. ed. p. 133). Erskine (p. 228), as his Persian source dictates, makes the men sink into the soft ground; de Courteille varies much (ii, 21).

[1298] Ar. *akhmail*, so translated under the known presence of trees; it may also imply soft ground (Lane p. 813 col. b) but soft ground does not suit the purpose of *arīqs* (channels), the carrying on of water to the town.

[1299] The S.A.W. map is useful here.

[1300] That he had a following may be inferred.

[1301] Ḥai. MS. *qāchār*; Ilminsky, p. 268; and both Pers. trss. *rukhsār* or *rukhsāra* (f. 25 and note to *qāchār*).

[1302] So in the Turkī MSS. and the first Pers. trs. (215 f. 170*b*). The second Pers. trs. (217 f. 145*b*) has a gloss of *ātqū u tika*; this consequently Erskine follows (p. 229) and adds a note explaining the punishment. Ilminsky has the gloss also (p. 269), thus indicating Persian and English influence.

[1303] No MS. gives the missing name.

[1304] The later favour mentioned was due to Saṃbhal's laborious release of his master from Aūzbeg captivity in 917 AH. (1511 AD.) of which Erskine quotes a full account from the *Tārīkh-i-sind* (History of India i, 345).

[1305] Presumably he went by Sabzār, Daulatābād, and Washīr.

[1306] f. 202 and note to *Chaghatāī*.

[1307] This will be for the Nīngnahār *tūmān* of Lamghān.

[1308] He was thus dangerously raised in his father's place of rule.

[1309] ff. 10*b*, 11*b*. Ḥaidar M. writes, "Shāh Begīm laid claim to Badakhshān, saying, "it has been our hereditary kingdom for 3000 years; though I, being a woman, cannot myself attain sovereignty, yet my grandson Mīrzā Khān can hold it" (T. R. p. 203).

[1310] *tībrādīlār*. The agitation of mind connoted, with movement, by this verb may well have been, here, doubt of Bābur's power to protect.

[1311] *tūshlūq tūshdīn tāghghā yūrūkāīlār*. Cf. 205*b* for the same phrase, with supposedly different meaning.

[1312] *qāngshār* lit. ridge of the nose.

[1313] *bīr aūq ham qūīā-ālmādīlār* (f. 203*b* note to *chāpqūn*).

[1314] This will have been news both of Shaibāq Khān and of Mīrzā Khān. The Pers. trss. vary here (215 f. 173 and 217 f. 148).

[1315] Index *s.n.*

[1316] Māh-chūchūk can hardly have been married against her will to Qāsim. Her mother regarded the alliance as a family indignity; appealed to Shāh Beg and compassed a rescue from Kābul while Bābur and Qāsim were north of the Oxus [*circa* 916 AH.]. Māh-chūchūk quitted Kābul after much hesitation, due partly to reluctance to leave her husband and her infant of 18 months, [Nāhīd Begīm,] partly to dread less family honour might require her death (Erskine's *History*, i, 348 and Gul-badan's *Humāyūn-nāma*).

[1317] Erskine gives the fort the alternative name "Kaliūn", locates it in the Bādghīs district east of Herī, and quotes from Abū'l-ghāzī in describing its strong position (*History* i, 282). Ḥ.S. Tīrah-tū.

[1318] f. 133 and note. Abū'l-faẓl mentions that the inscription was to be seen in his time.

[1319] This fief ranks in value next to the Kābul *tūmān.*

[1320] Various gleanings suggest motives for Bābur's assertion of supremacy at this particular time. He was the only Tīmūrid ruler and man of achievement; he filled Ḥusain *Bāī-qarā*'s place of Tīmūrid headship; his actions through a long period show that he aimed at filling Tīmūr Beg's. There were those who did not admit his suzerainty,—Tīmūrids who had rebelled, Mughūls who had helped them, and who would also have helped Sa'īd Khān *Chaghatāī*, if he had not refused to be treacherous to a benefactor; there were also the Arghūns, Chīngīz-khānids of high pretensions. In old times the Mughūl Khāqāns were *pādshāh* (supreme); Pādshāh is recorded in history as the style of at least Sātūq-būghra Khān Pādshāh Ghāzī; no Tīmūrid had been lifted by his style above all Mīrzās. When however Tīmūrids had the upper hand, Bābur's Tīmūrid grandfather Abū-sa'īd asserted his *de facto* supremacy over Bābur's Chaghatāī grandfather Yūnas (T. R. p. 83). For Bābur to re-assert that supremacy by assuming the Khāqān's style was highly opportune at this moment. To be Bābur Supreme was to declare over-lordship above Chaghatāī and Mughūl, as well as over all Mīrzās. It was done when his sky had cleared; Mīrzā Khān's rebellion was scotched; the Arghūns were defeated; he was the stronger for their lost possessions; his Aūzbeg foe had removed to a less ominous distance; and Kābul was once more his own.

Gul-badan writes as if the birth of his first-born son Humāyūn were a part of the uplift in her father's style, but his narrative does not support her in this, since the order of events forbids.

[1321] The "Khān" in Humāyūn's title may be drawn from his mother's family, since it does not come from Bābur. To whose family Māhīm belonged we have not been able to discover. It is one of the remarkable omissions of Bābur, Gul-badan and Abū'l-faẓl that they do not give her father's name. The topic of her family is discussed in my Biographical Appendix to Gul-badan's *Humāyūn-nāma* and will be taken up again, here, in a final Appendix on Bābur's family.

[1322] Elph. MS. f. 172*b*; W.-i-B. I.O. 215 f. 174*b* and 217 f. 148*b*; Mems. p. 234.

[1323] on the head-waters of the Tarnak (R.'s *Notes* App. p. 34).

[1324] Bābur has made no direct mention of his half-brother's death (f. 208 and n. to Mīrzā).

[1325] This may be Darwesh-i-'alī of f. 210; the Sayyid in his title may merely mean chief, since he was a Mughūl.

[1326] Several of these mutineers had fought for Bābur at Qandahār.

[1327] It may be useful to recapitulate this Mīrzā's position:—In the previous year he had been left in charge of Kābul when Bābur went eastward in dread of Shaibānī, and, so left, occupied his hereditary place. He cannot have hoped to hold Kābul if the Aūzbeg attacked it; for its safety and his own he may have relied, and Bābur also in appointing him, upon influence his Arghūn connections could use. For these, one was Muqim his brother-in-law, had accepted Shaibānī's suzerainty after being defeated in Qandahār by Bābur. It suited them better no doubt to have the younger Mīrzā rather than Bābur in Kābul; the latter's return thither will have disappointed them and the Mīrzā; they, as will be instanced later, stood ready to invade his lands when he moved East; they seem likely to have promoted the present Mughūl uprising. In the battle which put this down, the Mīrzā was captured; Bābur pardoned him; but he having rebelled again, was then put to death.

[1328] Bāgh-i-yūrūnchqā may be an equivalent of Bāgh-i-safar, and the place be one of waiting "up to" (*ūnchqā*) the journey (*yūr*). *Yūrūnchqā* also means *clover* (De Courteille).

[1329] He seems to have been a brother or uncle of Humāyūn's mother Māhīm (Index; A. N. trs. i, 492 and note).

[1330] In all MSS. the text breaks off abruptly here, as it does on f. 118*b* as though through loss of pages, and a blank of narrative follows. Before the later gap of f. 251*b* however the last sentence is complete.

[1331] Index *s. n. Bābur-nāma*, date of composition and gaps.

[1332] *ibid.*

[1333] Jumāda I, 14th 968 AH.-Jan. 31st 1561 AD. Concerning the book *see* Elliot and Dowson's *History of India* vi, 572 and JRAS 1901 p. 76, H. Beveridge's art. *On Persian MSS. in Indian Libraries.*

[1334] The T. R. gives the names of two only of the champions but Firishta, writing much later gives all five; we surmise that he found his five in the book of which copies are not now known, the *Tārīkh-i Muḥ. 'Ārif Qandahārī*. Firishta's five are 'Ali *shab-kūr* (night-blind), 'Alī *Sīstānī*, Naẓar Bahādur *Aūzbeg*, Ya'qūb *tez-jang* (swift in fight), and Aūzbeg Bahādur. Ḥaidar's two names vary in the MSS. of the T. R. but represent the first two of Firishta's list.

[1335] There are curious differences of statement about the date of Shaibānī's death, possibly through confusion between this and the day on which preliminary fighting began near Merv. Ḥaidar's way of expressing the date carries weight by its precision, he giving *roz-i-shakk* of Ramẓān, *i.e.* a day of which there was doubt whether it was the last of Sha'bān or the first of Ramẓān (Lane, *yauma'u'l-shakk*). As the sources support Friday for the day of the week and on a Friday in the year 915 AH. fell the 29th of Sha'bān, the date of Shaibānī's death seems to be Friday Sha'bān 29th 915 AH. (Friday December 2nd 1510 AD.).

[1336] If my reading be correct of the Turkī passage concerning wines drunk by Bābur which I have noted on f. 49 (*in loco* p. 83 n. 1), it was during this occupation of Kābul that Bābur first broke the Law against stimulants.

[1337] Mr. R. S. Poole found a coin which he took to be one struck in obedience to Bābur's compact with the Shāh (B.M.Cat. of the coins of Persian Shāhs 1887, pp. xxiv *et seq.*; T.R. p. 246 n.).

[1338] It was held by Aḥmad-i-qāsim *Kohbur* and is referred to on f. 234*b*, as one occasion of those in which Dost Beg distinguished himself.

[1339] Schuyler's *Turkistān* has a good account and picture of the mosque. 'Ubaid's vow is referred to in my earlier mention of the *Sūlūku'l-mulūk*. It may be noted here that this MS. supports the spelling *Bābur* by making the second syllable rhyme to *pūr*, as against the form *Bābar*.

[1340] *aūrūq*. Bābur refers to this exodus on f. 12*b* when writing of Daulat-sulṭān Khānīm.

[1341] It is one recorded with some variation, in Niyāz Muḥammad *Khukandī's Tārīkh-i-shāhrukhī* (Kazan, 1885) and Nalivkine's *Khānate of Khokand* (p. 63). It says that when Bābur in 918 AH. (1512 AD.) left Samarkand after defeat by the Aūzbegs, one of his wives, Sayyida Āfāq who accompanied him in his flight, gave birth to a son in the desert which lies between Khujand and Kand-i-badām; that Bābur, not daring to tarry and the infant being too young to make the impending journey, left it under some bushes with his own girdle round it in which were things of price; that the child was found by local people and in allusion to the valuables amongst which it lay, called Altūn bīshik (golden cradle); that it received other names and was best known in later life as Kẖudāyān Sulṭān. He is said to have spent most of his life in Akhsī; to have had a son Tīngrī-yār; and to have died in 952 AH. (1545 AD.). His grandson Yār-i-muḥammad is said to have gone to India to relations who was descendants of Bābur (JASB 1905 p. 137 H. Beveridge's art. *The Emperor Bābur*). What is against the truth of this tradition is that Gul-badan mentions no such wife as Sayyida Āfāq. Māhīm however seems to have belonged to a religious family, might therefore be styled Sayyida, and, as Bābur mentions (f. 220), had several children who did not live (a child left as this infant was, might if not heard of, be supposed dead). There is this opening allowed for considering the tradition.

[1342] Bābur refers to this on f. 265.

[1343] The *Lubbu't-tawārīkh* would fix Ramẓān 7th.

[1344] Mr. Erskine's quotation of the Persian original of the couplet differs from that which I have translated (*History of India* ii, 326; *Tārīkh-i-badāyūnī* Bib. Ind. ed. f. 444). Perhaps in the latter a pun is made on Najm as the leader's name and as meaning *fortune*; if so it points the more directly at the Shāh. The second line is quoted by Badāyūnī on his f. 362 also.

[1345] Some translators make Bābur go "naked" into the fort but, on his own authority (f. 106*b*), it seems safer to understand what others say, that he went stripped of attendance, because it was always his habit even in times of peace to lie down in his tunic; much more would he have done so at such a crisis of his affairs as this of his flight to Ḥiṣār.

[1346] Ḥaidar gives a graphic account of the misconduct of the horde and of their punishment (T.R. p. 261-3).

[1347] One of the mutineers named as in this affair (T.R. p. 257) was Sl. Qulī *chūnāq*, a circumstance attracting attention by its bearing on the cause of the *lacunæ* in the *Bābur-nāma*, inasmuch as Bābur, writing at the end of his life, expresses (f. 65) his intention to tell of this man's future misdeeds. These misdeeds may have been also at Ḥiṣār and in the attack there made on Bābur; they are known from Ḥaidar to have been done at Ghaznī; both times fall within this present gap. Hence it is clear that Bābur meant to write of the events falling in the gap of 914 AH. onwards.

[1348] In 925 AH. (ff. 227 and 238) mention is made of courtesies exchanged between Bābur and Muḥammad-i-zamān in Balkh. The Mīrzā was with Bābur later on in Hindūstān.

[1349] Mīr Ma'ṣūm's *Tārīkh-i-sind* is the chief authority for Bābur's action after 913 AH. against Shāh Beg in Qandahār; its translation, made in 1846 by Major Malet, shews some manifestly wrong dates; they appear also in the B. M. MS. of the work.

[1350] f. 216*b* and note to "Monday".

[1351] Elph. MS. f. 173*b*; W.-i-B. I.O. 215 f. 178 and 217 f. 149; Mems. p. 246. The whole of the Ḥijra year is included in 1519 AD. (Erskine). What follows here and completes the Kābul section of the *Bābur-nāma* is a diary of a little over 13 months' length, supplemented by matter of later entry. The product has the character of a draft, awaiting revision to harmonize it in style and, partly, in topic with the composed narrative that breaks off under 914 AH.; for the diary, written some 11 years earlier than that composed narrative, varies, as it would be expected *à priori* to vary, in style and topic from the terse, lucid and idiomatic output of Bābur's literary maturity. A good many obscure words and phrases in it, several new from Bābur's pen, have opposed difficulty to scribes and translators. Interesting as such *minutiae* are to a close observer of Turkī and of Bābur's diction, comment on all would be tedious; a few will be found noted, as also will such details as fix the date of entry for supplementary matter.

[1352] Here Mr. Erskine notes that Dr. Leyden's translation begins again; it broke off on f. 180*b*, and finally ends on f. 223*b*.

[1353] This name is often found transliterated as Chandul or [mod.] Jandul but the Ḥai. MS. supports Raverty's opinion that Chandāwal is correct.

The year 925 AH. opens with Bābur far from Kābul and east of the Khahr (fort) he is about to attack. Afghān and other sources allow surmise of his route to that position; he may have come down into the Chandāwal-valley, first, from taking Chaghān-sarāī (f. 124, f. 134 and n.), and, secondly, from taking the Gibrī stronghold of Ḥaidar-i-'alī *Bajaurī* which stood at the head of the Bābā Qarā-valley. The latter surmise is supported by the romantic tales of Afghān chroniclers which at this date bring into history Bābur's Afghān wife, Bībī Mubāraka (f. 220*b* and note; Mems. p. 250 n.; and Appendix K, *An Afghān legend*). (It must be observed here that R.'s *Notes* (pp. 117, 128) confuse the two sieges, *viz*. of the Gibrī fort in 924 AH. and of the Khahr of Bajaur in 925 AH.)

[1354] Raverty lays stress on the circumstance that the fort Bābur now attacks has never been known as Bajaur, but always simply as Khahr, the fort (the Arabic name for the place being, he says, plain *Shahr*); just as the main stream is called simply Rūd (the torrent). The name Khahr is still used, as modern maps shew. There are indeed two neighbouring places known simply as Khahr (Fort), *i.e.* one at the mouth of the "Mahmand-valley" of modern campaigns, the other near the Malakand (Fincastle's map).

[1355] This word the Ḥai. MS. writes, *passim*, Dilah-zāk.

[1356] Either Ḥaidar-i-'alī himself or his nephew, the latter more probably, since no name is mentioned.

[1357] Looking at the position assigned by maps to Khahr, in the *dū-āb* of the Charmanga-water and the Rūd of Bajaur, it may be that Bābur's left moved along the east bank of the first-named stream and crossed it into the *dū-āb*, while his centre went direct to its post, along the west side of the fort.

[1358] *sū-kīrīshī*; to interpret which needs local knowledge; it might mean where water entered the fort, or where water disembogued from narrows, or, perhaps, where water is entered for a ford. (The verb *kīrmāk* occurs on f. 154*b* and f. 227 to describe water coming down in spate.)

[1359] *dīwānawār*, perhaps a jest on a sobriquet earned before this exploit, perhaps the cause of the man's later sobriquet *dīwāna* (f. 245*b*).

[1360] Text, t:r:k, read by Erskine and de Courteille as Turk; it might however be a Turkī component in Jān-i-'alī or Muḥibb-i-'alī. (Cf. Zenker *s.n. tirik*.)

[1361] *aūshūl gūnī*, which contrasts with the frequent *aūshbū gūnī* (this same day, today) of manifestly diary entries; it may indicate that the full account of the siege is a later supplement.

[1362] This puzzling word might mean cow-horn (*kau-sarū*) and stand for the common horn trumpet. Erskine and de Courteille have read it as *gau-sar*, the first explaining it as *cow-head*, surmised to be a protection for matchlockmen when loading; the second, as *justaucorps de cuir*. That the word is baffling is shewn by its omission in I.O. 215 (f. 178*b*), in 217 (f. 149*b*) and in Muḥ. *Shīrāzī*'s lith. ed. (p. 137).

[1363] or *farangī*. Much has been written concerning the early use of gun-powder in the East. There is, however, no well-authenticated fact to prove the existence of anything like artillery there, till it was introduced from Europe. Bābur here, and in other places (f. 267) calls his larger ordnance Firingī, a proof that they were then regarded as owing their origin to Europe. The Turks, in consequence of their constant intercourse with the nations of the West, have always excelled all the other Orientals in the use of artillery; and, when heavy cannon were first used in India, Europeans or Turks were engaged to serve them (Erskine). It is owing no doubt to the preceding gap in his writings that we are deprived of Bābur's account of his own introduction to fire-arms. *See* E. & D.'s *History of India*, vi, Appendix *On the early use of gunpowder in India*.

[1364] var. *quṭbī*, *qūchīnī*.

[1365] This sobriquet might mean "ever a fighter", or an "argle-bargler", or a brass shilling (Zenker), or (if written *jīng-jīng*) that the man was visaged like the bearded reeding (Scully in Shaw's Vocabulary). The *Ṭabaqāt-i-akbarī* includes a Mīrak Khān *Jang-jang* in its list of Akbar's Commanders.

[1366] *ghūl-dīn (awwal) aūl qūrghān-gha chīqtī*. I suggest to supply *awwal*, first, on the warrant of Bābur's later statement (f. 234*b*) that Dost was first in.

[1367] He was a son of Maulānā Muḥ. *Ṣadr*, one of the chief men of 'Umar-shaikh M.'s Court; he had six brothers, all of whom spent their lives in Bābur's service, to whom, if we may believe Abū'l-faẓl, they were distantly related (Erskine).

[1368] Bābur now returns towards the east, down the Rūd. The *chashma* by which he encamped, would seem to be near the mouth of the valley of Bābā Qarā, one 30 miles long; it may have been, anglicé, a spring [not that of the main stream of the long valley], but the word may be used as it seems to be of the water supplying the Bāgh-i-ṣafā (f. 224), *i.e.* to denote the first considerable gathering-place of small head-waters. It will be observed a few lines further on that this same valley seems to be meant by "Khwāja Khiẓr".

[1369] He will have joined Bābur previous to Muḥarram 925 AH.

[1370] This statement, the first we have, that Bābur has broken Musalmān Law against stimulants (f. 49 and n.), is followed by many others more explicit, jotting down where and what and sometimes why he drank, in a way which arrests attention and asks some other explanation than that it is an unabashed record of conviviality such conceivably as a non-Musalmān might write. Bābur is now 37 years old; he had obeyed the Law till past early manhood; he wished to return to obedience at 40; he frequently mentions his lapses by a word which can be translated as "commitment of sin" (*irtqāb*); one gathers that he did not at any time disobey with easy conscience. Does it explain his singular record,—one made in what amongst ourselves would be regarded as a private diary,—that his sins were created by Law? Had he a balance of reparation in his thoughts?

Detaching into their separate class as excesses, all his instances of confessed drunkenness, there remains much in his record which, seen from a non-Musalmān point of view, is venial; *e.g.* his *ṣubūhī* appears to be the "morning" of the Scot, the *Morgen-trank* of the Teuton; his afternoon cup, in the open air usually, may have been no worse than the sober glass of beer or local wine of modern Continental Europe. Many of these legal sins of his record were interludes in the day's long ride, stirrup-cups some of them, all in a period of strenuous physical activity. Many of his records are collective and are phrased impersonally; they mention that there was drinking, drunkenness even, but they give details sometimes such as only a sober observer could include.

Bābur names a few men as drunkards, a few as entirely obedient; most of his men seem not to have obeyed the Law and may have been "temperate drinkers"; they effected work, Bābur amongst them, which habitual drunkards could not have compassed. Spite of all he writes of his worst excesses, it must be just to remember his Musalmān conscience, and also the distorting power of a fictitious sin. Though he broke the law binding all men against excess, and this on several confessed occasions, his rule may have been no worse than that of the ordinarily temperate Western. It cannot but lighten judgment that his recorded lapses from Law were often prompted by the bounty and splendour of Nature; were committed amidst the falling petals of fruit-blossom, the flaming fire of autumn leaves, where the eye rested on the *arghwān* or the orange grove, the coloured harvest of corn or vine.

[1371] As Mr. Erskine observes, there seems to be no valley except that of Bābā Qarā, between the Khahr and the Chandāwal-valley; "Khwāja Khiẓr" and "Bābā Qarā" may be one and the same valley.

[1372] Time and ingenuity would be needed to bring over into English all the quips of this verse. The most obvious pun is, of course, that on Bajaur as the compelling cause (*ba jaur*) of the parting; others may be meant on *guzīd* and *gazīd*, on *sazīd* and *chāra*. The verse would provide the holiday amusement of extracting from it two justifiable translations.

[1373] His possessions extended from the river of Sawād to Bāramūla; he was expelled from them by the Yūsuf-zāī (Erskine).

[1374] This will be the naze of the n.e. rampart of the Bābā Qarā valley.

[1375] f. 4 and note; f. 276. Bābur seems to use the name for several varieties of deer.

[1376] There is here, perhaps, a jesting allusion to the darkening of complexion amongst the inhabitants of countries from west to east, from Highlands to Indian plains.

[1377] In Dr. E. D. Ross' *Polyglot list of birds* the *sārigh(sārīq)-qūsh* is said to frequent fields of ripening grain; this suggests to translate its name as Thief-bird.

[1378] *Aquila chrysaetus*, the hunting eagle.

[1379] This *ārālīgh* might be identified with the "Miankalai" of maps (since Soghd, lying between two arms of the Zar-afshān is known also as Mīānkal), but Raverty explains the Bajaur Miankalai to mean Village of the holy men (*mīān*).

[1380] After 933 AH. presumably, when final work on the B.N. was in progress.

[1381] Mr. Erskine notes that Pesh-grām lies north of Mahyar (on the Chandāwal-water), and that he has not found Kahrāj (or Kohrāj). Judging from Bābur's next movements, the two valleys he names may be those in succession east of Chandāwal.

[1382] There is hardly any level ground in the cleft of the Panj-kūra (R.'s *Notes* p. 193); the villages are perched high on the sides of the valley. The pass leading to them may be Katgola (Fincastle's Map).

[1383] This account of Hind-āl's adoption is sufficiently confused to explain why a note, made apparently by Humāyūn, should have been appended to it (Appendix L, *On Hind-āl's adoption*). The confusion reminds the reader that he has before him a sort of memorandum only, diary jottings, apt to be allusive and abbreviated. The expected child was Dil-dār's; Māhīm, using her right as principal wife, asked for it to be given to her. That the babe in question is here called Hind-āl shews that at least part of this account of his adoption was added after the birth and naming (f. 227).

[1384] One would be, no doubt, for Dil-dār's own information. She then had no son but had two daughters, Gul-rang and Gul-chihra. News of Hind-āl's birth reached Bābur in Bhīra, some six weeks later (f. 227).

[1385] f. 218*b*.

[1386] Bībī Mubāraka, the Afghānī Aghācha of Gul-badan. An attractive picture of her is drawn by the *Tāwārikh-i-ḥāfi-i-raḥmat-khānī*. As this gives not only one of Bābur's romantic adventures but historical matter, I append it in my husband's translation [(A.Q.R. April 1901)] as Appendix K, *An Afghān Legend.*

[1387] *Bī-sūt aīlī-nīng Bajaur-qūrghānī-dā manāsabatī-bār jīhatī*; a characteristic phrase.

[1388] Perhaps the end of the early spring-harvest and the spring harvesting-year. It is not the end of the campaigning year, manifestly; and it is at the beginning of both the solar and lunar years.

[1389] Perhaps, more than half-way between the Mid-day and Afternoon Prayers. So too in the annals of Feb. 12th.

[1390] *tīl ālghālī* (Pers. *zabān-gīrī*), a new phrase in the B.N.

[1391] *chāsht*, which, being half-way between sunrise and the meridian, is a variable hour.

[1392] See n. 2, f. 221.

[1393] Perhaps Maqām is the Mardān of maps.

[1394] Bhīra, on the Jehlam, is now in the Shāhpūr district of the Panj-āb.

[1395] This will be the ford on the direct road from Mardān for the eastward (Elphin-stone's *Caubul* ii, 416).

[1396] The position of Sawātī is represented by the Suābī of the G. of I. map (1909 AD.). Writing in about 1813 AD. Mr. Erskine notes as worthy of record that the rhinoceros was at that date no longer found west of the Indus.

[1397] Elph. MS. *ghura*, the 1st, but this is corrected to 16th by a marginal note. The Ḥai. MS. here, as in some other places, has the context for a number, but omits the figures. So does also the Elph. MS. in a good many places.

[1398] This is the Harru. Mr. Erskine observes that Bābur appears to have turned sharp south after crossing it, since he ascended a pass so soon after leaving the Indus and reached the Sūhān so soon.

[1399] *i.e.* the Salt-range.

[1400] Mr. Erskine notes that (in his day) a *shāhrukhī* may be taken at a shilling or eleven pence sterling.

[1401] It is somewhat difficult not to forget that a man who, like Bābur, records so many observations of geographical position, had no guidance from Surveys, Gazetteers and Books of Travel. Most of his records are those of personal observation.

[1402] In this sentence Mr. Erskine read a reference to the Musalmān Ararat, the Koh-i-jūd on the left bank of the Tigris. What I have set down translates the Turkī words but, taking account of Bābur's eye for the double use of a word, and Erskine's careful work, done too in India, the Turkī may imply reference to the Ararat-like summit of Sakeswar.

[1403] Here Dr. Leyden's version finally ends (Erskine).

[1404] Bhīra, as has been noted, is on the Jehlam; Khūsh-āb is 40 m. lower down the same river; Chīnīūt (Chīnī-wat?) is 50 miles south of Bhīra; Chīn-āb (China-water?) seems the name of a tract only and not of a residential centre; it will be in the Bar of Kipling's border-thief. Concerning Chīnīūt *see* D. G. Barkley's letter, JRAS 1899 p. 132.

[1405] *ṭaur yīrī waqī' būlūb tūr.* As on f. 160 of the valley of Khwesh, I have taken *ṭaur* to be Turkī, complete, shut in.

[1406] *chashma* (f. 218*b* and note).

[1407] The promised description is not found; there follows a mere mention only of the garden [f. 369]. This entry can be taken therefore as shewing an intention to write what is still wanting from Ṣafar 926 AH. to Ṣafar 932 AH.

[1408] Mīr Muḥ. may have been a kinsman or follower of Mahdī Khwāja. The entry on the scene, unannounced by introduction as to parentage, of the Khwāja who played a part later in Bābur's family affairs is due, no doubt, to the last gap of annals. He is mentioned in the Translator's Note, *s.a.* 923 AH. (*See* Gul-badan's H.N. Biographical Appendix *s.n.*)

[1409] or Sihrind, mod. Sirhind or Sar-i-hind (Head of Hind). It may be noted here, for what it may be found worth, that Kh(w)āfī Khān [i, 402] calls Sar-i-hind the old name, says that the place was once held by the Ghaznī dynasty and was its Indian frontier, and that Shāh-jahān changed it to Sahrind. The W.-i-B. I.O. 217 f. 155 writes Shahrind.

[1410] Three krores or crores of dāms, at 40 to the rupee, would make this 750,000 rupees, or about £75,000 sterling (Erskine); a statement from the ancient history of the rupī!

[1411] This Hindustānī word in some districts signifies the head man of a trade, in others a landholder (Erskine).

[1412] In Mr. Erskine's time this sum was reckoned to be nearly £20,000.

[1413] Here originally neither the Elph. MS. nor the Ḥai. MS. had a date; it has been added to the former.

[1414] This rain is too early for the s.w. monsoon; it was probably a severe fall of spring rain, which prevails at this season or rather earlier, and extends over all the west of Asia (Erskine).

[1415] *az ghīna shor sū.* Streams rising in the Salt-range become brackish on reaching its skirts (G. of I.).

[1416] Here this will be the fermented juice of rice or of the date-palm.

[1417] *Rauḥ* is sometimes the name of a musical note.

[1418] a platform, with or without a chamber above it, and supported on four posts.

[1419] so-written in the MSS. Cf. Raverty's *Notes* and G. of I.

[1420] Anglicé, cousins on the father's side.

[1421] The G. of I. describes it.

[1422] Elph. MS. f. 183b, *manṣūb*; Ḥai. MS. and 2nd W.-i-B. *bīsūt.* The holder might be Bābā-i-kābulī of f. 225.

[1423] The 1st Pers. trs. (I.O. 215 f. 188b) and Kehr's MS. [Ilminsky p. 293] attribute Hātī's last-recorded acts to Bābur himself. The two mistaken sources err together elsewhere. M. de Courteille corrects the defect (ii, 67).

[1424] night-guard. He is the old servant to whom Bābur sent a giant *ashrafī* of the spoils of India (Gul-badan's H.N. *s.n.*).

[1425] The *kīping* or *kīpik* is a kind of mantle covered with wool (Erskine); the root of the word is *kīp*, dry.

[1426] *aūlūgh chāsht*, a term suggesting that Bābur knew the *chota ḥāẓirī*, little breakfast, of Anglo-India. It may be inferred, from several passages, that the big breakfast was taken after 9 a.m. and before 12 p.m. Just below men are said to put on their mail at *chāsht* in the same way as, *passim*, things other than prayer are said to be done at this or that Prayer; this, I think, always implies that they are done after the Prayer mentioned; a thing done shortly before a Prayer is done "close to" or "near" or when done over half-way to the following Prayer, the act is said to be done "nearer" to the second (as was noted on f. 221).

[1427] *Juldū Dost Beg-nīng ātī-gha būldī.*

[1428] The disarray of these names in the MSS. reveals confusion in their source. Similar verbal disarray occurs in the latter part of f. 229.

[1429] Manifestly a pun is made on the guide's name and on the *cap-à-pié* robe of honour the offenders did not receive.

[1430] *aūrdū-nīng aldī-gha*, a novel phrase.

[1431] I understand that the servants had come to do their equivalent for "kissing hands" on an appointment *viz.* to kneel.

[1432] spikenard. Speede's *Indian Handbook on Gardening* identifies *saṃbhal* with *Valeriana jatmansi* (Sir W. Jones & Roxburgh); "it is the real spikenard of the ancients, highly esteemed alike as a perfume and as a stimulant medicine; native practitioners esteeming it valuable in hysteria and epilepsy." Bābur's word *dirakht* is somewhat large for the plant.

[1433] It is not given, however.

[1434] *i.e.* through the Indus.

[1435] Perhaps this *aīkī-sū-ārāsī* (*miyān-dū-āb*) was the angle made by the Indus itself below Atak; perhaps one made by the Indus and an affluent.

[1436] *ma'jūnī nāklīkī*, presumably under the tranquillity induced by the drug.

[1437] *massadus*, the six sides of the world, *i.e.* all sides.

[1438] This is the name of one of the five champions defeated by Bābur in single combat in 914 AH. (Translator's Note *s.a.* 914 AH.).

[1439] f. 145*b*.

[1440] Humāyūn was 12, Kāmrān younger; one surmises that Bābur would have walked under the same circumstances.

[1441] *ṣabuḥī*, the morning-draught. In 1623 AD. Pietro della Vallé took a *ṣabuḥī* with Mr. Thomas Rastel, the head of the merchants of Surat, which was of hot spiced wine and sipped in the mornings to comfort the stomach (Hakluyt ed. p. 20).

[1442] f. 128 and note.

[1443] Anglicé, in the night preceding Tuesday.

[1444] f. 106b.

[1445] This would be the under-corselet to which the four plates of mail were attached when mail was worn. Bābur in this adventure wore no mail, not even his helm; on his head was the under cap of the metal helm.

[1446] Index s.n. *gharīcha*.

[1447] The earlier account helps to make this one clearer (f. 106b).

[1448] f. 112 *et seq.*

[1449] Catamite, mistakenly read as *khīz* on f. 112b (*Mémoires* ii, 82).

[1450] He was acting for Bābur (Translator's Note *s.a.*; Ḥ.S. iii, 318; T.R. pp. 260, 270).

[1451] "Honoured," in this sentence, represents Bābur's honorific plural.

[1452] in 921 AH. (Translator's Note *s.a.*; T.R. p. 356).

[1453] *i.e.* Mīr Muḥammad son of Nāṣir.

[1454] *i.e.* after the dethronement of the Bāī-qarā family by Shaibānī.

[1455] He had been one of rebels of 921 AH. (Translator's Note *s.a.*; T.R. p. 356).

[1456] f. 137.

[1457] This is the Adjutant-bird, Pīr-i-dang and Hargila (Bone-swallower) of Hindūstān, a migrant through Kābul. The fowlers who brought it would be the Multānīs of f. 142*b*.

[1458] f. 280.

[1459] *Memoirs*, p. 267, sycamore; *Mémoires* ii, 84, *saules*; f. 137.

[1460] Perhaps with his long coat out-spread.

[1461] The fortnight's gap of record, here ended, will be due to illness.

[1462] f. 203*b* and n. to *Khams*, the Fifth. *Taṣadduq* occurs also on f. 238 denoting money sent to Bābur. Was it sent to him as Pādshāh, as the Qorān commands the *Khams* to be sent to the Imām, for the poor, the traveller and the orphan?

[1463] Rose-water, sherbet, a purgative; English, jalap, julep.

[1464] Mr. Erskine understood Bābur to say that he never had sat sober while others drank; but this does not agree with the account of Harāt entertainments [912 AH.], or with the tenses of the passage here. My impression is that he said in effect "Every-one here shall not be deprived of their wine".

[1465] This verse, a difficult one to translate, may refer to the unease removed from his attendants by Bābur's permission to drink; the pun in it might also refer to *well* and *not well.*

[1466] Presumably to aid his recovery.

[1467] *aūtkān yīl*, perhaps in the last and unchronicled year; perhaps in earlier ones. There are several references in the B.N. to the enforced migrations and emigrations of tribes into Kābul.

[1468] Pūlād (Steel) was a son of Kūchūm, the then Khāqān of the Aūzbegs, and Mihr-bānū who may be Bābur's half-sister. [Index *s.n.*]

[1469] This may be written for Mihr-bānū, Pūlād's mother and Bābur's half-sister (?) and a jest made on her heart as Pūlād's and as steel to her brother. She had not left husband and son when Bābur got the upper hand, as his half-sister Yādgār-sulṭān did and other wives of capture *e.g.* Ḥaidar's sister *Ḥabība*. Bābur's rhymes in this verse are not of his later standard, *āī ṣubāḥ, kūnkūīkā, kūnkūlī-kā.*

[1470] *Taṣadduq* sent to Bābur would seem an acknowledgment of his suzerainty in Balkh [Index *s.n.*].

[1471] This is the Gīrdīz-pass [Raverty's *Notes*, Route 101].

[1472] Raverty (p. 677) suggests that Pātakh stands for *bātqāq*, a quagmire (f. 16 and n.).

[1473] the dark, or cloudy spring.

[1474] *yāqīsh-līq qūl*, an unusual phrase.

[1475] var. Karmān, Kurmāh, Karmās. M. de C. read Kīr-mās, the impenetrable. The forms would give Garm-ās, hot embers.

[1476] *balafré*; marked on the face; of a horse, starred.

[1477] Raverty's *Notes* (p. 457) give a full account of this valley; in it are the head-waters of the Tochī and the Zurmut stream; and in it R. locates Rustam's ancient Zābul.

[1478] It is on the Kābul side of the Gīrdīz-pass and stands on the Luhugūr-water (Logar).

[1479] f. 143.

[1480] At this point of the text there occurs in the Elph. MS. (f. 195*b*) a note, manifestly copied from one marginal in an archetype, which states that what follows is copied from Bābur's own MS. The note (and others) can be seen in JRAS 1905 p. 754 *et seq*.

[1481] Masson, iii, 145.

[1482] A *qūlāch* is from finger-tip to finger-tip of the outstretched arms (Zenker p. 720 and *Méms*. ii, 98).

[1483] Neither *interne* is said to have died!

[1484] f. 143.

[1485] or Atūn's-village, one granted to Bābur's mother's old governess (f. 96); Gul-badan's guest-list has also an Atūn Māmā.

[1486] f. 235*b* and note.

[1487] *miswāk*; *On les tire principalement de l'arbuste épineux appelé capparis-sodata* (de C. ii, 101 n.).

[1488] Gul-badan's H.N. Index s.n.

[1489] This being Ramẓān, Bābur did not break his fast till sun-set. In like manner, during Ramẓān they eat in the morning before sun-rise (Erskine).

[1490] A result, doubtless, of the order mentioned on f. 240*b*.

[1491] Bābur's wife Gul-rukh appears to have been his sister or niece; he was a Begchīk. Cf. Gul-badan's H.N. trs. p. 233, p. 234; T.R. p. 264-5.

[1492] This remark bears on the question of whether we now have all Bābur wrote of Autobiography. It refers to a date falling within the previous gap, because the man went to Kāshghar while Bābur was ruling in Samarkand (T.R. p. 265). The last time Bābur came from Khwāst to Kābul was probably in 920 AH.; if later, it was still in the gap. But an alternative explanation is that looking over and annotating the diary section, Bābur made this reference to what he fully meant to write but died before being able to do so.

[1493] Anglicé, the right thumb, on which the archer's ring (*zih-gīr*) is worn.

[1494] a daughter of Yūnas Khān, Ḥaidar's account of whom is worth seeing.

[1495] *i.e.* the water of Luhugūr (Logar). Tradition says that Būt-khāk (Idol-dust) was so named because there Sl. Maḥmūd of Ghaznī had idols, brought by him out of Hindūstān, pounded to dust. Raverty says the place is probably the site of an ancient temple (*vahāra*).

[1496] Qāsim Beg's son, come, no doubt, in obedience to the order of f. 240*b*.

[1497] The 'Īd-i-fitr is the festival at the conclusion of the feast of Ramẓān, celebrated on seeing the new moon of Shawwāl (Erskine).

[1498] f. 133*b* and Appendix G, *On the names of the wines of Nūr-valley.*

[1499] *i.e.* of the new moon of Shawwāl. The new moon having been seen the evening before, which to Musalmāns was Monday evening, they had celebrated the 'Īd-i-fitr on Monday eve (Erskine).

[1500] Dīwān of Hāfiẓ. lith. ed. p. 22. The couplet seems to be another message to a woman (f. 238); here it might be to Bībī Mubāraka, still under Khwāja Kalān's charge in Bajaur (f. 221).

[1501] Here and under date Sep. 30th the wording allows a ford.

[1502] This may be what Masson writes of (i, 149) "We reached a spot where the water supplying the rivulet (of 'Alī-masjid) gushes in a large volume from the rocks to the left. I slaked my thirst in the living spring and drank to repletion of the delightfully cool and transparent water."

[1503] Mr. Erskine here notes, "This appears to be a mistake or oversight of Bābur. The eve of 'Arafa" (9th of Ẕū'l-ḥijja) "was not till the evening of Dec. 2nd 1519. He probably meant to say the 'Id-i-fitr which had occurred only five days before, on Sep. 26th."

[1504] This was an affair of frontiers (T.R. p. 354).

[1505] Manucci gives an account of the place (Irvine iv, 439 and ii, 447).

[1506] Sep. 8th to Oct. 9th.

[1507] *khūsh rang-i khizān*. Sometimes Bābur's praise of autumn allows the word *khizān* to mean the harvest-crops themselves, sometimes the autumnal colouring.

[1508] This I have taken to mean the Kābul *tūmān*. The Ḥai. MS. writes *wilāyatlār* (plural) thus suggesting that *aūl* (those) may be omitted, and those countries (Transoxiana) be meant; but the second Pers. trs. (I.O. 217 f. 169) supports *wilāyat*, Kābul.

[1509] joyous, happy.

[1510] *y:lk:rān*. This word has proved a difficulty to all translators. I suggest that it stands for *aīlīkarān*, what came to hand (*aīlīk see* de C.'s Dict.); also that it contains puns referring to the sheep taken from the road (*yūlkarān*) and to the wine of the year's yield (*yīlkarān*). The way-side meal was of what came to hand, mutton and wine, probably local.

[1511] f. 141*b*.

[1512] f. 217 and n.

[1513] I think Bābur means that the customary announcement of an envoy or guest must have reached Kābul in his absence.

[1514] He is in the T.R. list of the tribe (p. 307); to it belonged Sl. Aḥmad *Taṃbal* (*ib.* p. 316).

[1515] *Qābil-nīng kūrī-nīng qāshī-ka*, lit. to the presence of the tomb of Qābil, *i.e.* Cain the eponymous hero of Kābul. The Elph. MS. has been altered to "Qābil Beg"!

[1516] Mr. Erskine surmised that the line was from some religious poem of mystical meaning and that its profane application gave offence.

[1517] His sobriquet *khāksār*, one who sits in the dust, suits the excavator of a *kārez*. Bābur's route can be followed in Masson's (iii, 110), apparently to the very *kārez*.

[1518] In Masson's time this place was celebrated for vinegar. To reach it and return must have occupied several hours.

[1519] Kunos, *āq tūīgūn*, white falcon; *'Amal-i-ṣāliḥ* (I.O. MS. No. 857, f. 45*b*), *taus tūīghūn*.

[1520] f. 246.

[1521] Nawā'ī himself arranged them according to the periods of his life (Rieu's Pers. Cat. p. 294).

[1522] Elph. MS. f. 202*b*; W.-i-B. I.O. 215 f. 175 (misplaced) and 217 f. 172; Mems. p. 281.

[1523] *pushta aūstīda*; the Jūī-khwūsh of f. 137.

[1524] The Ḥai. MS. omits a passage here; the Elph. MS. reads *Qāsim Bulbulī nīng awī*, thus making "nightingale" a sobriquet of Qāsim's own. Erskine (p. 281) has "Bulbulī-hall"; Ilminsky's words translate as, the house of Sayyid Qāsim's nightingale (p. 321).

[1525] or Dūr-namā'ī, seen from afar.

[1526] *narm-dīk*, the opposite of a *qātīq yāī*, a stiff bow. Some MSS. write *lāẓim-dīk* which might be read to mean such a bow as his disablement allowed to be used.

[1527] Mr. Erskine, writing early in the 19th century, notes that this seems an easy tribute, about 400 *rupīs i.e.* £40.

[1528] This is one of the three routes into Lamghān of f. 133.

[1529] f. 251*b* and Appendix F, *On the name Dara-i-nūr*.

[1530] This passage will be the basis of the account on f. 143*b* of the winter-supply of fish in Lamghān.

[1531] This word or name is puzzling. Avoiding extreme detail as to variants, I suggest that it is Dāūr-bīn for Dūr-namā'ī if a place-name; or, if not, *dūr-bīn*, foresight (in either case the preposition requires to be supplied), and it may refer to foreseen need of and curiosity about Kāfir wines.

[1532] *chīūrtika* or *chīūr-i-tika*, whether *sauterelle* as M. de Courteille understood, or *jānwār-i-ranga* and *chīkūr*, partridge as the 1st Persian trs. and as Mr. Erskine (explaining *chūr-i-tīka*) thought, must be left open. Two points arise however, (1) the time is January, the place the deadly Bād-i-pīch pass; would these suit locusts? (2) If Bābur's account of a splendid bird (f. 135) were based on this experience, this would be one of several occurrences in which what is entered in the Description of Kābul of 910 AH. is found as an experience in the diary of 925-6 AH.

[1533] Ḥai. MS. *maḥali-da maẕkūr būlghūsīdūr*, but W.-i-B. I.O. 215 f. 176 for *maḥali-da*, in its place, has *dar majlis* [in the collection], which may point to an intended collection of Bābur's musical compositions. Either reading indicates intention to write what we now have not.

[1534] Perhaps an equivalent for *farẓ-waqt*, the time of the first obligatory prayer. Much seems to happen before the sun got up high!

[1535] Koh-i-nūr, Rocky-mountains (?). *See* Appendix F, *On the name Dara-i-nūr.*

[1536] Steingass gives *būza* as made of rice, millet, or barley.

[1537] Is this connected with Arabic *kīmiyā'*, alchemy, chemistry?

[1538] Turkī, a whirlpool; but perhaps the name of an office from *aīgar*, a saddle.

[1539] The river on which the rafts were used was the Kūnār, from Chītrāl.

[1540] An uncertain name. I have an impression that these waters are medicinal, but I cannot trace where I found the information. The visit paid to them, and the arrangement made for bathing set them apart. The name of the place may convey this speciality.

[1541] *panāhī*, the word used for the hiding-places of bird-catchers on f. 140.

[1542] This will be the basis of the details about fishing given on f. 143 and f. 143*b*. The statement that particulars have been given allows the inference that the diary was annotated after the *Description of Kābul*, in which the particulars are, was written.

[1543] *qānlīqlār*. This right of private revenge which forms part of the law of most rude nations, exists in a mitigated form under the Muhammadan law. The criminal is condemned by the judge, but is delivered up to the relations of the person murdered, to be ransomed or put to death as they think fit (Erskine).

[1544] Here the text breaks off and a *lacuna* separates the diary of 11 months length which ends the Kābul section of the *Bābur-nāma* writings, from the annals of 932 AH. which begin the Hindūstān section. There seems no reason why the diary should have been discontinued.

[1545] Jan. 2nd 1520 to Nov. 17th 1525 AD. (Ṣafar 926 to Ṣafar 1st 932 AH.).

[1546] Index *s.nn.* Bāgh-i-ṣafā and B.N. *lacunæ*.

[1547] Nominally Balkh seems to have been a Ṣafawī possession; but it is made to seem closely dependent on Bābur by his receipt from Muḥammad-i-zamān in it of *taṣadduq* (money for alms), and by his action connected with it (*q.v.*).

[1548] *Tārīkh-i-sind*, Malet's trs. p. 77 and *in loco*, p. 365.

[1549] A chronogram given by Badāyūnī decides the vexed question of the date of Sikandar *Lūdī's* death—*Jannātu'l-firdūs nazlā* = 923 (Bib. Ind. ed. i,

322, Ranking trs. p. 425 n. 6). Erskine supported 924 AH. (i, 407), partly relying on an entry in Bābur's diary (f. 226*b*) *s.d.* Rabī'u'l-awwal 1st 925 AH. (March 3rd 1519 AD.) which states that on that day Mullā Murshid was sent to Ibrāhīm whose father *Sikandar had died five or six months before.*

Against this is the circumstance that the entry about Mullā Murshid is, perhaps entirely, certainly partly, of later entry than what precedes and what follows it in the diary. This can be seen on examination; it is a passage such as the diary section shews in other places, added to the daily record and giving this the character of a draft waiting for revision and rewriting (fol. 216*b* n.).

(To save difficulty to those who may refer to the L. & E. *Memoirs* on the point, I mention that the whole passage about Mullā Murshid is displaced in that book and that the date March 3rd is omitted.)

[1550] Shāl (the local name of English Quetta) was taken by Ẕū'l-nūn in 884 AH. (1479 AD.); Sīwīstān Shāh Beg took, in second capture, about 917 AH. (1511 AD.), from a colony of Barlās Turks under Pīr Walī *Barlās*.

[1551] Was the attack made in reprisal for Shāh Beg's further aggression on the Barlās lands and Bābur's hereditary subjects? Had these appealed to the head of their tribe?

[1552] Le Messurier writes (*l.c.* p. 224) that at Old Qandahār "many stone balls lay about, some with a diameter of 18 inches, others of 4 or 5, chiselled out of limestone. These were said to have been used in sieges in the times of the Arabs and propelled from a machine called *manjanic* a sort of balista or catapult." Meantime perhaps they served Bābur!

[1553] "Just then came a letter from badakhshān saying, 'Mīrzā Khān is dead; Mīrzā Sulaimān (his son) is young; the Aūzbegs are near; take thought for this kingdom lest (which God forbid) Badakhshān should be lost.' Mīrzā Sulaimān's mother (Sulṭān-nigār Khānīm) had brought him to Kābul" (Gul-badan's H. N. f. 8).

[1554] *infra* and Appendix J.

[1555] E. & D.'s *History of India*, i. 312.

[1556] For accounts of the *Mubīn*, *Akbar-nāma* Bib. Ind. ed. i. 118, trs. H. Beveridge i. 278 note, Badāyūnī *ib.* i, 343, trs. Ranking p. 450, Sprenger ZDMG. 1862, Teufel *ib.* 1883. The *Akbar-nāma* account appears in Turkī in the "Fragments" associated with Kehr's transcript of the B.N. (JRAS. 1908, p. 76, A. S. B.'s art. *Bābur-nāma*). Bābur mentions the *Mubīn* (f. 252*b*, f. 351*b*).

[1557] JRAS. 1901, *Persian MSS. in Indian Libraries* (description of the Rāmpūr *Dīwān*); AQR. 1911, *Bābur's Dīwān* (*i.e.* the Rāmpūr *Dīwān*); and *Some verses of the Emperor Bābur* (the *Abūshqa* quotations).

For Dr. E. D. Ross' Reproduction and account of the Rāmpūr *Dīwān*, JASB. 1910.

[1558] "After him (Ibrāhīm) was Bābur King of Dihlī, who owed his place to the Pathāns," writes the Afghān poet Khūsh-ḥāl *Khattak* (Afghān Poets of the XVII century, C. E. Biddulph, p. 58).

[1559] The translation only has been available (E. & D.'s H. of I., vol. 1).

[1560] The marriage is said to have been Kāmrān's (E. & D.'s trs.).

[1561] Erskine calculated that 'Ālam Khān was now well over 70 years of age (H. of I. i, 421 n.).

[1562] A. N. trs. H. Beveridge, i, 239.

[1563] The following old English reference to Isma'il's appearance may be quoted as found in a corner somewhat out-of-the-way from Oriental matters. In his essay on beauty Lord Bacon writes when arguing against the theory that beauty is usually not associated with highmindedness, "But this holds not always; for Augustus Cæsar, Titus Vespasianus, Philip le Bel of France, Edward the Fourth of England, Alcibiades of Athens, Isma'il the Sophy (Ṣafawī) of Persia, were all high and great spirits, and yet the most beautiful men of their times."

[1564] Cf. *s.a.* 928 AH. for discussion of the year of death.

[1565] Elph. MS. f. 205*b*; W.-i-B. I.O. 215 f. 199*b* omits the year's events on the ground that Shaikh Zain has translated them; I.O. 217 f. 174; Mems. p. 290; Kehr's Codex p. 1084.

A considerable amount of reliable textual material for revising the Hindūstān section of the English translation of the *Bābur-nāma* is wanting through loss of pages from the Elphinstone Codex; in one instance no less than an equivalent of 36 folios of the Ḥaidarābād Codex are missing (f. 356 *et seq.*), but to set against this loss there is the valuable *per contra* that Kehr's manuscript throughout the section becomes of substantial value, losing its Persified character and approximating closely to the true text of the Elphinstone and Ḥaidarābād Codices. Collateral help in revision is given by the works specified (*in loco* p. 428) as serving to fill the gap existing in Bābur's narrative previous to 932 AH. and this notably by those described by Elliot and Dowson. Of these last, special help in supplementary details is given for 932 AH. and part of 933 AH. by Shaikh Zain [*Khawāfī*]'s *Ṭabaqāt-i-bāburī*, which is a highly rhetorical paraphrase of Bābur's narrative, requiring familiarity with ornate Persian to understand. For all my references to it, I am indebted to my husband. It may be mentioned as an interesting circumstance that the B.M. possesses in Or. 1999 a copy of this work which was transcribed in 998 AH. by one of Khwānd-amīr's grandsons and, judging from its date, presumably for Abū'l-faẓl's use in the *Akbar-nāma.*

Like part of the Kābul section, the Hindūstān one is in diary-form, but it is still more heavily surcharged with matter entered at a date later than the diary. It departs from the style of the preceding diary by an occasional lapse into courtly phrase and by exchange of some Turkī words for Arabic and Persian ones, doubtless found current in Hind, *e.g. fauj*, *dīra*, *manzil*, *khail-khāna.*

[1566] This is the Logar affluent of the Bārān-water (Kābul-river). Masson describes this haltingplace (iii, 174).

[1567] *muḥaqqar saughāt u bīlāk or tīlāk.* A small verbal point arises about *bīlāk* (or *tīlāk*). *Bīlāk* is said by Quatremère to mean a gift (N. et E. xiv, 119 n.) but here *muḥaqqar saughāt* expresses gift. Another meaning can be assigned to *bīlāk* here, [one had also by *tīlāk*,] *viz.* that of word-of-mouth news or communication, sometimes supplementing written communication, possibly secret instructions, possibly small domestic details. In *bīlāk*, a gift, the root may be *bīl*, the act of knowing, in *tīlāk* it is *tīl*, the act of speaking [whence *tīl*, the tongue, and *tīl tūtmāk*, to get news]. In the sentence noted, either word would suit for a verbal communication. Returning to *bīlāk* as a gift, it may express the *nuance* of English *token*, the maker-known of friendship, affection and so-on. This differentiates *bīlāk* from *saughāt*, used in its frequent sense of ceremonial and diplomatic presents of value and importance.

[1568] With Sa'īd at this time were two Khānīms Sulṭān-nigār and Daulat-sulṭān who were Bābur's maternal-aunts. Erskine suggested Khūb-nigār, but she had died in 907 AH. (f. 96).

[1569] Humāyūn's non-arrival would be the main cause of delay. Apparently he should have joined before the Kābul force left that town.

[1570] The halt would be at Būt-khāk, the last station before the Adīnapūr road takes to the hills.

[1571] Discussing the value of coins mentioned by Bābur, Erskine says in his *History of India* (vol. i, Appendix E.) which was published in 1854 AD. that he had come to think his estimates of the value of the coins was set too low in the *Memoirs* (published in 1826 AD.). This sum of 20,000 *shāhrukhīs* he put at £1000. Cf. E. Thomas' *Pathan Kings of Dihli and Resources of the Mughal Empire.*

[1572] One of Masson's interesting details seems to fit the next stage of Bābur's march (iii, 179). It is that after leaving Būt-khāk, the road passes what in the thirties of the 19th Century, was locally known as Bābur Pādshāh's Stone-heap (cairn) and believed piled in obedience to Bābur's order that each man in his army should drop a stone on it in passing. No time for raising such a monument could be fitter than that of the fifth expedition into Hindūstān when a climax of opportunity allowed hope of success.

[1573] *rezāndalīk*. This Erskine translates, both here and on ff. 253, 254, by *defluxion*, but de Courteille by *rhume de cerveau*. Shaikh Zain supports de Courteille by writing, not *rezāndalīk*, but *nuzla*, catarrh. De Courteille, in illustration of his reading of the word, quotes Burnes' account of an affection common in the Panj-āb and there called *nuzla*, which is a running at the nostrils, that wastes the brain and stamina of the body and ends fatally (*Travels in Bukhara* ed. 1839, ii, 41).

[1574] Tramontana, north of Hindū-kush.

[1575] Shaikh Zain says that the drinking days were Saturday, Sunday, Tuesday and Wednesday.

[1576] The Elph. Codex (f. 208*b*) contains the following note of Humāyūn's about his delay; it has been expunged from the text but is still fairly legible:—"The time fixed was after 'Āshūrā (10th Muḥarram, a voluntary fast); although we arrived after the next-following 10th (*'āshūr*, *i.e.* of Ṣafar), the delay had been necessary. The purpose of the letters (Bābur's) was to get information; (in reply) it was represented that the equipment of the army of Badakhshān caused delay. If this slave (Humāyūn), trusting to his [father's] kindness, caused further delay, he has been sorry."

Bābur's march from the Bāgh-i-wafā was delayed about a month; Humāyūn started late from Badakhshān; his force may have needed some stay in Kābul for completion of equipment; his personal share of blame for which he counted on his father's forgiveness, is likely to have been connected with his mother's presence in Kābul.

Humāyūn's note is quoted in Turkī by one MS. of the Persian text (B.M. W.-i-B. 16,623 f. 128); and from certain indications in Muḥammad *Shīrāzī*'s lithograph (p. 163), appears to be in his archetype the Udaipūr Codex; but it is not with all MSS. of the Persian text *e.g.* not with I.O. 217 and 218. A portion of it is in Kehr's MS. (p. 1086).

[1577] Bird's-dome [f. 145*b*, n.] or The pair (*qūsh*) of domes.

[1578] *gūn khūd kīch būlūb aīdī*; a little joke perhaps at the lateness both of the day and the army.

[1579] Shaikh Zain's maternal-uncle.

[1580] Shaikh Zain's useful detail that this man's pen-name was Sharaf distinguishes him from Muḥammad Ṣāliḥ the author of the *Shaibānī-nāma.*

[1581] *gosha*, angle (*cf. gosha-i-kār*, limits of work). Parodies were to be made, having the same metre, rhyme, and refrain as the model couplet.

[1582] I am unable to attach sense to Bābur's second line; what is wanted is an illustration of two incompatible things. Bābur's reflections [*infra*] condemned his verse. Shaikh Zain describes the whole episode of the verse-making on the raft, and goes on with, "He (Bābur) excised this choice couplet from the pages of his Acts (*Wāqi'āt*) with the knife of censure, and scratched it out from the tablets of his noble heart with the finger-nails of repentance. I shall now give an account of this spiritual matter" (*i.e.* the repentance), "by presenting the recantations of his Solomon-like Majesty in his very own words, which are weightier than any from the lips of Aesop." Shaikh Zain next quotes the Turkī passage here translated in *b. Mention of the Mubīn.*

[1583] The *Mubīn* (*q.v.* Index) is mentioned again and quoted on f. 351*b*. In both places its name escaped the notice of Erskine and de Courteille, who here took it for *mīn*, I, and on f. 351*b* omitted it, matters of which the obvious cause is that both translators were less familiar with the poem than it is now easy to be. There is amplest textual warrant for reading *Mubīn* in both the places indicated above; its reinstatement gives to the English and French translations what they have needed, namely, the clinch of a definite stimulus and date of repentance, which was the influence of the Mubīn in 928 AH. (1521-2 AD.). The whole passage about the peccant verse and its fruit of contrition should be read with others that express the same regret for broken law and may all have been added to the diary at the same time, probably in 935 AH. (1529 AD.). They will be found grouped in the Index *s.n.* Bābur.

[1584] *mūndīn būrūn*, by which I understand, as the grammatical construction will warrant, *before writing the Mubīn.* To read the words as referring to the peccant verse, is to take the clinch off the whole passage.

[1585] *i.e.* of the *Qorān* on which the *Mubīn* is based.

[1586] Dropping down-stream, with wine and good company, he entirely forgot his good resolutions.

[1587] This appears to refer to the good thoughts embodied in the *Mubīn.*

[1588] This appears to contrast with the "sublime realities" of the *Qorān.*

[1589] In view of the interest of the passage, and because this verse is not in the Rāmpūr *Dīwān*, as are many contained in the Hindūstān section, the Turkī original is quoted. My translation differs from those of Mr. Erskine and M. de Courteille; all three are tentative of a somewhat difficult verse.

Nī qīlā mīn sīnīng bīla āī tīl?

Jihatīng dīn mīnīng aīchīm qān dūr.

Nīcha yakhshī dīsāng bū hazl aīla shi'r

Bīrī-sī faḥash ū bīrī yālghān dūr.

Gar dīsāng kūīmā mīn, bū jazm bīla

Jalāu'īngnī bū 'arṣa dīn yān dūr.

[1590] The Qorān puts these sayings into the mouths of Adam and Eve.

[1591] Ḥai. MS. *tīndūrūb*; Ilminsky, p. 327, *yāndūrūb*; W.-i-B. I.O. 217, f. 175, *sard sākhta.*

[1592] Of 'Alī-masjid the *Second Afghān War* (official account) has a picture which might be taken from Bābur's camp.

[1593] Shaikh Zain's list of the drinking-days (f. 252 note) explains why sometimes Bābur says he preferred *ma'jūn.* In the instances I have noticed, he does this on a drinking-day; the preference will be therefore for a confection over wine. December 9th was a Saturday and drinking-day; on it he mentions the preference; Tuesday Nov. 21st was a drinking day, and he states that he ate *ma'jūn.*

[1594] presumably the *karg-khāna* of f. 222*b*, rhinoceros-home in both places. A similar name applies to a tract in the Rawalpindi District,—Bābur-khāna, Tiger-home, which is linked to the tradition of Buddha's self-sacrifice to appease the hunger of seven tiger-cubs. [In this Bābur-khāna is the town Kacha-kot from which Bābur always names the river Hārū.]

[1595] This is the first time on an outward march that Bābur has crossed the Indus by boat; hitherto he has used the ford above Attock, once however specifying that men on foot were put over on rafts.

[1596] f. 253.

[1597] In my Translator's Note (p. 428), attention was drawn to the circumstance that Bābur always writes Daulat Khān *Yūsuf-khail*, and not Daulat Khān *Lūdī.* In doing this, he uses the family- or clan-name instead of the tribal one, *Lūdī.*

[1598] *i.e.* day by day.

[1599] *daryā*, which Bābur's precise use of words *e.g.* of *daryā*, *rūd*, and *sū*, allows to apply here to the Indus only.

[1600] Presumably this was near Parhāla, which stands, where the Sūhān river quits the hills, at the eastern entrance of a wild and rocky gorge a mile in length. It will have been up this gorge that Bābur approached Parhāla in 925 AH. (Rawalpindi Gazetteer p. 11).

[1601] *i.e.* here, bed of a mountain-stream.

[1602] The Elphinstone Codex here preserves the following note, the authorship of which is attested by the scribe's remark that it is copied from the handwriting of Humāyūn Pādshāh:—As my honoured father writes, we did not know until we occupied Hindūstān (932 AH.), but afterwards did know, that ice does form here and there if there come a colder year. This was markedly so in the year I conquered Gujrāt (942 AH.-1535 AD.) when it was so cold for two or three days between Bhūlpūr and Guālīār that the waters were frozen over a hand's thickness.

[1603] This is a Kakar (Gakkhar) clan, known also as Baragowah, of which the location in Jahāngīr Pādshāh's time was from Rohtās to Hātya, *i.e.* about where Bābur encamped (*Memoirs of Jahāngīr*, Rogers and Beveridge, p. 97; E. and D. vi, 309; Provincial Gazetteers of Rawalpindi and Jihlam, p. 64 and p. 97 respectively).

[1604] *āndīn aūtūb*, a reference perhaps to going out beyond the corn-lands, perhaps to attempt for more than provisions.

[1605] *qūsh-āt*, a led horse to ride in change.

[1606] According to Shaikh Zain it was in this year that Bābur made Buhlūlpūr a royal domain (B.M. Add. 26,202 f. 16), but this does not agree with Bābur's explanation that he visited the place because it was *khalṣa.* Its name suggests that it had belonged to Buhlūl *Lūdī*; Bābur may have taken it in 930 AH. when he captured Sīālkot. It never received the population of Sīālkot, as Bābur had planned it should do because pond-water was drunk in the latter town and was a source of disease. The words in which Bābur describes its situation are those he uses of Akhsī (f. 4*b*); not improbably a resemblance inclined his liking towards Buhlūlpūr. (It may be noted that this Buhlūlpūr is mentioned in the *Āyīn-i-akbarī* and marked on large maps, but is not found in the G. of I. 1907.)

[1607] Both names are thus spelled in the *Bābur-nāma.* In view of the inclination of Turkī to long vowels, Bābur's short one in Jat may be worth consideration since modern usage of Jat and Jāt varies. Mr. Crooke writes the full vowel, and mentions that Jāts are Hindūs, Sikhs, and

Muḥammadans (*Tribes and Castes of the North-western Provinces and Oude*, iii, 38). On this point and on the orthography of the name, Erskine's note (*Memoirs* p. 294) is as follows: "The Jets or Jats are the Muḥammadan peasantry of the Panj-āb, the bank of the Indus, Sīwīstān *etc.* and must not be confounded with the Jāts, a powerful Hindū tribe to the west of the Jamna, about Agra *etc.* and which occupies a subordinate position in the country of the Rājpūts."

[1608] The following section contains a later addition to the diary summarizing the action of 'Ālam Khān before and after Bābur heard of the defeat from the trader he mentions. It refutes an opinion found here and there in European writings that Bābur used and threw over 'Ālam Khān. It and Bābur's further narrative shew that 'Ālam Khān had little valid backing in Hindūstān, that he contributed nothing to Bābur's success, and that no abstention by Bābur from attack on Ibrāhīm would have set 'Ālam Khān on the throne of Dihlī. It and other records, Bābur's and those of Afghān chroniclers, allow it to be said that if 'Ālam Khān had been strong enough to accomplish his share of the compact that he should take and should rule Dihlī, Bābur would have kept to his share, namely, would have maintained supremacy in the Panj-āb. He advanced against Ibrāhīm only when 'Ālam Khān had totally failed in arms and in securing adherence.

[1609] This objurgation on over-rapid marching looks like the echo of complaint made to Bābur by men of his own whom he had given to 'Ālam Khān in Kābul.

[1610] Maḥmūd himself may have inherited his father's title Khān-i-jahān but a little further on he is specifically mentioned as the son of Khān-i-jahān, presumably because his father had been a more notable man than he was. Of his tribe it may be noted that the Ḥaidarābād MS. uniformly writes Nuḥānī and not Luḥānī as is usual in European writings, and that it does so even when, as on f. 149*b*, the word is applied to a trader. Concerning the tribe, family, or caste *vide* G. of I. *s.n.* Lohānas and Crooke *l.c.* *s.n.* Pathān, para. 21.

[1611] *i.e.* west of Dihlī territory, the Panj-āb.

[1612] He was of the Farmul family of which Bābur says (f. 139*b*) that it was in high favour in Hindūstān under the Afghāns and of which the author of the *Wāqi'āt-i-mushtāqī* says that it held half the lands of Dihlī in *jāgīr* (E. and D. iv, 547).

[1613] Presumably he could not cut off supplies.

[1614] The only word similar to this that I have found is one "Jaghat" said to mean serpent and to be the name of a Hindū sub-caste of Nats (Crooke, iv, 72 & 73). The word here might be a nick-name. Bābur writes it as two words.

[1615] *khaṣa-khail*, presumably members of the Sāhū-khail (family) of the Lūdī tribe of the Afghān race.

[1616] Erskine suggested that this man was a rich banker, but he might well be the Farmulī Shaikh-zāda of f. 256*b*, in view of the exchange Afghān historians make of the Farmulī title Shaikh for Mīān (*Tārīkh-i-sher-shāhī*, E. & D. iv, 347 and *Tārīkh-i-daudī* ib. 457).

[1617] This Biban, or Bīban, as Bābur always calls him without title, is Malik Biban *Jilwānī*. He was associated with Shaikh Bāyazīd *Farmulī* or, as Afghān writers style him, Mīān Bāyazīd *Farmulī*. (Another of his names was Mīān Biban, son of Mīān Āṭā *Sāhū-khail* (E. & D. iv, 347).)

[1618] This name occurs so frequently in and about the Panj-āb as to suggest that it means a fort (Ar. *maluẓat*?). This one in the Siwāliks was founded by Tātār Khān *Yūsuf-khail* (*Lūdī*) in the time of Buhlūl *Lūdī* (E. and D. iv, 415).

[1619] In the Beth Jalandhar *dū-āb*.

[1620] *i.e.* on the Siwāliks, here locally known as Katār Dhār.

[1621] Presumably they were from the Hazāra district east of the Indus. The *Ṭabaqāt-i-akbarī* mentions that this detachment was acting under Khalīfa apart from Bābur and marching through the skirt-hills (lith. ed. p. 182).

[1622] *dūn*, f. 260 and note.

[1623] These were both refugees from Harāt.

[1624] Sarkār of Baṭāla, in the Bārī *dū-āb* (A.-i-A. Jarrett, p. 110).

[1625] *kūrūshūr waqt* (Index *s.n. kūrūsh*).

[1626] Bābur's phrasing suggests beggary.

[1627] This might refer to the time when Ibrāhīm's commander Bihār (Bahādur) Khān *Nūḥānī* took Lāhor (Translator's Note *in loco* p. 441).

[1628] They were his father's. Erskine estimated the 3 *krors* at £75,000.

[1629] *shiqq*, what hangs on either side, perhaps a satirical reference to the ass' burden.

[1630] As illustrating Bābur's claim to rule as a Tīmūrid in Hindūstān, it may be noted that in 814 AH. (1411 AD.), Khiẓr Khān who is allowed by the date to have been a Sayyid ruler in Dihlī, sent an embassy to Shāhrukh

Mīrzā the then Tīmūrid ruler of Samarkand to acknowledge his suzerainty (*Maṯla'u's-sa'dain*, Quatremère, N. et Ex. xiv, 196).

[1631] Firishta says that Bābur mounted for the purpose of preserving the honour of the Afghāns and by so doing enabled the families in the fort to get out of it safely (lith. ed. p. 204).

[1632] *chuhra*; they will have been of the Corps of braves (*yīgīt*; Appendix H. section *c.*).

[1633] *kīm kullī gharẓ aul aīdī*; Pers. trs. *ka gharẓ-i-kullī-i-au būd.*

[1634] Persice, the eves of Sunday and Monday; Anglice, Saturday and Sunday nights.

[1635] Ghāzī Khān was learned and a poet (Firishta ii, 42).

[1636] *mullayāna khūd*, perhaps books of learned topic but not in choice copies.

[1637] f. 257. It stands in 31° 50' N. and 76° E. (G. of I.).

[1638] This is on the Salt-range, in 32° 42' N. and 72° 50' E. (*Āyīn-i-akbarī* trs. Jarrett, i, 325; Provincial Gazetteer, Jīhlam District).

[1639] He died therefore in the town he himself built. Kitta Beg probably escorted the Afghān families from Milwat also; Dilāwar Khān's own seems to have been there already (f. 257).

The *Bābur-nāma* makes no mention of Daulat Khān's relations with Nānak, the founder of the Sikh religion, nor does it mention Nānak himself. A tradition exists that Nānak, when on his travels, made exposition of his doctrines to an attentive Bābur and that he was partly instrumental in bringing Bābur against the Afghāns. He was 12 years older than Bābur and survived him nine. (Cf. *Dabistān* lith. ed. p. 270; and, for Jahāngīr Pādshāh's notice of Daulat Khān, *Tūzūk-i-jahāngīrī*, Rogers and Beveridge, p. 87).

[1640] I translate *dūn* by *dale* because, as its equivalent, Bābur uses *julga* by which he describes a more pastoral valley than one he calls a *dara.*

[1641] *bīr āqār-sū.* Bābur's earlier uses of this term [*q.v.* index] connect it with the swift flow of water in irrigation channels; this may be so here but also the term may make distinction between the rapid mountain-stream and the slow movement of rivers across plains.

[1642] There are two readings of this sentence; Erskine's implies that the neck of land connecting the fort-rock with its adjacent hill measures 7-8 *qārī* (yards) from side to side; de Courteille's that where the great gate was, the perpendicular fall surrounding the fort shallowed to 7-8 yards. The Turkī might be read, I think, to mean whichever alternative was the fact.

Erskine's reading best bears out Bābur's account of the strength of the fort, since it allows of a cleft between the hill and the fort some 140-160 feet deep, as against the 21-24 of de Courteille's. Erskine may have been in possession of information [in 1826] by which he guided his translation (p. 300), "At its chief gate, for the space of 7 or 8 *gez* (*qārī*), there is a place that admits of a draw-bridge being thrown across; it may be 10 or 12 *gez* wide." If de Courteille's reading be correct in taking 7-8 *qārī* only to be the depth of the cleft, that cleft may be artificial.

[1643] *yīghāch*, which also means wood.

[1644] f. 257.

[1645] Chief scribe (f. 13 n. to 'Abdu'l-wahhāb). Shaw's Vocabulary explains the word as meaning also a "high official of Central Asian sovereigns, who is supreme over all *qāzīs* and *mullās*."

[1646] Bābur's persistent interest in Balkh attracts attention, especially at this time so shortly before he does not include it as part of his own territories (f. 270).

Since I wrote of Balkh *s.a.* 923 AH. (1517 AD.), I have obtained the following particulars about it in that year; they are summarized from the *Ḥabību's-siyar* (lith. ed. iii, 371). In 923 AH. Khwānd-amīr was in retirement at Pasht in Ghūrjistān where also was Muḥammad-i-zamān Mīrzā. The two went in company to Balkh where the Mīrzā besieged Bābur's man Ibrāhīm *chāpūk* (Slash-face), and treacherously murdered one Aūrdū-shāh, an envoy sent out to parley with him. Information of what was happening was sent to Bābur in Kābul. Bābur reached Balkh when it had been besieged a month. His presence caused the Mīrzā to retire and led him to go into the Darā-i-gaz (Tamarind-valley). Bābur, placing in Balkh Faqīr-i-'alī, one of those just come up with him, followed the Mīrzā but turned back at Āq-guṃbaz (White-dome) which lies between Chāch-charān in the Herī-rūd valley and the Ghūrjistān border, going no further because the Ghūrjistānīs favoured the Mīrzā. Bābur went back to Kābul by the Fīrūz-koh, Yaka-aūlāng (cf. f. 195) and Ghūr; the Mīrzā was followed up by others, captured and conveyed to Kābul.

[1647] Both were amīrs of Hind. I understand the cognomen Maẕhab to imply that its bearer occupied himself with the Muḥammadan Faith in its exposition by divines of Islām (*Hughes' Dictionary of Islām*).

[1648] These incidents are included in the summary of 'Ālam Khān's affairs in section *i* (f. 255*b*). It will be observed that Bābur's wording implies the "waiting" by one of lower rank on a superior.

[1649] Elph. MS. Karnāl, obviously a clerical error.

[1650] Shaikh Sulaimān Effendi (Kunos) describes a *tunqiṭār* as the guardian in war of a prince's tent; a night-guard; and as one who repeats a prayer aloud while a prince is mounting.

[1651] *rūd*, which, inappropriate for the lower course of the Ghaggar, may be due to Bābur's visit to its upper course described immediately below. As has been noted, however, he uses the word *rūd* to describe the empty bed of a mountain-stream as well as the swift water sometimes filling that bed. The account, here-following, of his visit to the upper course of the Ghaggar is somewhat difficult to translate.

[1652] *Hindūstāndā daryālārdīn bāshqa, bīr āqār-sū kīm bār* (*dūr*, is added by the Elph. MS.), *bū dūr*. Perhaps the meaning is that the one (chief?) irrigation stream, apart from great rivers, is the Ghaggar. The bed of the Ghaggar is undefined and the water is consumed for irrigation (G. of I. xx, 33; Index *s.n. āqār-sū*).

[1653] in Patiāla. Maps show what may be Bābur's strong millstream joining the Ghaggar.

[1654] Presumably he was of Ibrāhīm's own family, the Sāhū-khail. His defeat was opportune because he was on his way to join the main army.

[1655] At this place the Elphinstone Codex has preserved, interpolated in its text, a note of Humāyūn's on his first use of the razor. Part of it is written as by Bābur:—"Today in this same camp the razor or scissors was applied to Humāyūn's face." Part is signed by Humāyūn:—"As the honoured dead, earlier in these Acts (*wāqi'āt*) mentions the first application of the razor to his own face (f. 120), so in imitation of him I mention this. I was then at the age of 18; now I am at the age of 48, I who am the sub-signed Muḥammad Humāyūn." A scribe's note attests that this is "copied from the hand-writing of that honoured one". As Humāyūn's 48th (lunar) birthday occurred a month before he left Kābul, to attempt the re-conquest of Hindūstān, in November 1554 AD. (in the last month of 961 AH.), he was still 48 (lunar) years old on the day he re-entered Dihlī on July 23rd 1555 AD. (Ramẓān 1st 962 AH.), so that this "shaving passage" will have been entered within those dates. That he should study his Father's book at that time is natural; his grandson Jahāngīr did the same when going to Kābul; so doubtless would do its author's more remote descendants, the sons of Shāh-jahān who reconquered Transoxiana.

(Concerning the "shaving passage" *vide* the notes on the Elphinstone Codex in JRAS. 1900 p. 443, 451; 1902 p. 653; 1905 p. 754; and 1907 p. 131.)

[1656] This ancient town of the Sahāranpūr district is associated with a saint revered by Hindūs and Muḥammadans. Cf. W. Crooke's *Popular Religion of Northern India* p. 133. Its *chashma* may be inferred (from Bābur's uses of the word *q.v.* Index) as a water-head, a pool, a gathering place of springs.

[1657] He was the eighth son of Bābur's maternal-uncle Sl. Aḥmad Khān *Chaghatāī* and had fled to Bābur, other brothers following him, from the service of their eldest brother Manṣūr, Khāqān of the Mughūls (*Tārīkh-i-rashīdī* trs. p. 161).

[1658] *farẓ-waqtī*, when there is light enough to distinguish one object from another.

[1659] *dīm kūrūldī* (Index *s.n. dīm*). Here the L. & E. *Memoirs* inserts an explanatory passage in Persian about the *dīm*. It will have been in one of the *Wāqi'āt-i-bāburī MSS*. Erskine used; it is in Muḥ. *Shīrāzī*'s lithograph copy of the Udaipūr Codex (p. 173). It is not in the Turkī text or in all the MSS. of the Persian translation. Manifestly, it was entered at a time when Bābur's term *dīm kūrūldī* requires explanation in Hindustan. The writer of it himself does not make details clear; he says only, "It is manifest that people declare (the number) after counting the mounted army in the way agreed upon amongst them, with a whip or a bow held in the hand." This explanation suggests that in the march-past the troops were measured off as so many bow- or whip-lengths (Index *s.n. dīm*).

[1660] These *arāba* may have been the baggage-carts of the army and also carts procured on the spot. Erskine omits (*Memoirs* p. 304) the words which show how many carts were collected and from whom. Doubtless it would be through not having these circumstances in his mind that he took the *arāba* for gun-carriages. His incomplete translation, again, led Stanley Lane-Poole to write an interesting note in his *Bābur* (p. 161) to support Erskine against de Courteille (with whose rendering mine agrees) by quoting the circumstance that Humāyūn had 700 guns at Qanauj in 1540 AD. It must be said in opposition to his support of Erskine's "gun-carriages" that there is no textual or circumstantial warrant for supposing Bābur to have had guns, even if made in parts, in such number as to demand 700 gun-carriages for their transport. What guns Bābur had at Pānī-pat will have been brought from his Kābul base; if he had acquired any, say from Lāhor, he would hardly omit to mention such an important reinforcement of his armament; if he had brought many guns on carts from Kābul, he must have met with transit-difficulties harassing enough to chronicle, while he was making that long journey from Kābul to Pānī-pat, over passes, through skirt-hills and many fords. The elephants he had in Bīgrām may have been his transport for what guns he had; he does not mention his number at

Pānī-pat; he makes his victory a bow-man's success; he can be read as indicating that he had two guns only.

[1661] These Ottoman (text, *Rūmī*, Roman) defences Ustād 'Alī-qulī may have seen at the battle of Chāldirān fought some 40 leagues from Tābrīz between Sl. Salīm *Rūmī* and Shāh Ismā'īl *Ṣafawī* on Rajab 1st 920 AH. (Aug. 22nd 1514 AD.). Of this battle Khwānd-amīr gives a long account, dwelling on the effective use made in it of chained carts and palisades (*Ḥabību's-siyar* iii, part 4, p. 78; *Akbar-nāma* trs. i, 241).

[1662] Is this the village of the Pānī Afghāns?

[1663] Index *s.n.* arrow.

[1664]

Pareshān jam'ī u jam'ī pareshān;

Giriftār qaumī u qaumī 'ajā'ib.

These two lines do not translate easily without the context of their original place of occurrence. I have not found their source.

[1665] *i.e.* of his father and grandfather, Sikandar and Buhlūl.

[1666] As to the form of this word the authoritative MSS. of the Turkī text agree and with them also numerous good ones of the Persian translation. I have made careful examination of the word because it is replaced or explained here and there in MSS. by *s:hb:ndī*, the origin of which is said to be obscure. The sense of *b:d-hindī* and of *s:hb:ndī* is the same, *i.e.* irregular levy. The word as Bābur wrote it must have been understood by earlier Indian scribes of both the Turkī and Persian texts of the *Bābur-nāma*. Some light on its correctness may be thought given by Hobson Jobson (Crooke's ed. p. 136) *s.n.* Byde or Bede Horse, where the word Byde is said to be an equivalent of *pindārī*, *lūtī*, and *qāzzāq*, raider, plunderer, so that Bābur's word *b:d-hindī* may mean *qāzzāq* of Hind. Wherever I have referred to the word in many MSS. it is pointed to read *b:d*, and not *p:d*, thus affording no warrant for understanding *pad*, foot, foot-man, infantry, and also negativing the spelling *bīd*, *i.e.* with a long vowel as in *Byde*.

It may be noted here that Muḥ. *Shīrāzī* (p. 174) substituted *s:hb:ndī* for Bābur's word and that this led our friend the late William Irvine to attribute mistake to de Courteille who follows the Turkī text (*Army of the Mughūls* p. 66 and *Mémoires* ii, 163).

[1667] *bī tajarba yīgīt aīdī* of which the sense may be that Bābur ranked Ibrāhīm, as a soldier, with a brave who has not yet proved himself deserving of the rank of beg. It cannot mean that he was a youth (*yīgīt*) without experience of battle.

[1668] Well-known are the three decisive historical battles fought near the town of Pānī-pat, *viz.* those of Bābur and Ibrāhīm in 1526, of Akbar and Hīmū in 1556, and of Aḥmad *Abdālī* with the Mahratta Confederacy in 1761. The following lesser particulars about the battle-field are not so frequently mentioned:—(*i*) that the scene of Bābur's victory was long held to be haunted, Badāyūnī himself, passing it at dawn some 62 years later, heard with dismay the din of conflict and the shouts of the combatants; (*ii*) that Bābur built a (perhaps commemorative) mosque one mile to the n.e. of the town; (*iii*) that one of the unaccomplished desires of Sher Shāh *Sūr*, the conqueror of Bābur's son Humāyūn, was to raise two monuments on the battle-field of Pānī-pat, one to Ibrāhīm, the other to those Chaghatāī sulṭāns whose martyrdom he himself had brought about; (*iv*) that in 1910 AD. the British Government placed a monument to mark the scene of Shāh *Abdālī's* victory of 1761 AD. This monument would appear, from Sayyid Ghulām-i-'alī's *Nigār-nāma-i-hind*, to stand close to the scene of Bābur's victory also, since the Mahrattas were entrenched as he was outside the town of Pānī-pat. (Cf. E. & D. viii, 401.)

[1669] This important date is omitted from the L. & E. *Memoirs*.

[1670] This wording will cover armour of man and horse.

[1671] *ātlāndūk*, Pers. trs. *sūwār shudīm*. Some later oriental writers locate Bābur's battle at two or more miles from the town of Pānī-pat, and Bābur's word *ātlāndūk* might imply that his cavalry rode forth and arrayed outside his defences, but his narrative allows of his delivering attack, through the wide sally-ports, after arraying behind the carts and mantelets which checked his adversary's swift advance. The Mahrattas, who may have occupied the same ground as Bābur, fortified themselves more strongly than he did, as having powerful artillery against them. Aḥmad Shāh *Abdālī's* defence against them was an ordinary ditch and *abbattis*, [Bābur's ditch and branch,] mostly of *dhāk* trees (*Butea frondosa*), a local product Bābur also is likely to have used.

[1672] The preceding three words seem to distinguish this Shāh Ḥusain from several others of his name and may imply that he was the son of *Yāragī Mughūl Ghānchī* (Index and I.O. 217 f. 184b l. 7).

[1673] For Bābur's terms *vide* f. 209*b*

[1674] This is Mīrzā Khān's son, *i.e.* Wais *Mīrān-shāhī's*.

[1675] A dispute for this right-hand post of honour is recorded on f. 100*b*, as also in accounts of Culloden.

[1676] *tartīb u yāsāl*, which may include, as Erskine took it to do, the carts and mantelets; of these however, Ibrāhīm can hardly have failed to hear before he rode out of camp.

[1677] f. 217*b* and note; Irvine's *Army of the Indian Mughuls* p. 133. Here Erskine notes (*Mems.* p. 306) "The size of these artillery at this time is very uncertain. The word *firingī* is now (1826 AD.) used in the Deccan for a swivel. At the present day, *ẓarb-ẓan* in common usage is a small species of swivel. Both words in Bābur's time appear to have been used for field-cannon." (For an account of guns, intermediate in date between Bābur and Erskine, *see* the *Āyīn-i-akbarī*. Cf. f. 264 n. on the carts (*arāba*).)

[1678] Although the authority of the *Tārīkh-i-salāṭīn-i-afaghāna* is not weighty its reproduction of Afghān opinion is worth consideration. It says that astrologers foretold Ibrāhīm's defeat; that his men, though greatly outnumbering Bābur's, were out-of-heart through his ill-treatment of them, and his amīrs in displeasure against him, but that never-the-less, the conflict at Pānī-pat was more desperate than had ever been seen. It states that Ibrāhīm fell where his tomb now is (*i.e.* in *circa* 1002 AH.-1594 AD.); that Bābur went to the spot and, prompted by his tender heart, lifted up the head of his dead adversary, and said, "Honour to your courage!", ordered brocade and sweetmeats made ready, enjoined Dilāwar Khān and Khalīfa to bathe the corpse and to bury it where it lay (E. & D. v, 2). Naturally, part of the reverence shewn to the dead would be the burial together of head and trunk.

[1679] f. 209*b* and App. H. section *c*. Bābā *chuhra* would be one of the corps of braves.

[1680] He was a brother of Muḥibb-i-'alī's mother.

[1681] To give Humāyūn the title Mīrzā may be a scribe's lapse, but might also be a *nuance* of Bābur's, made to shew, with other *minutiae*, that Humāyūn was in chief command. The other minute matters are that instead of Humāyūn's name being the first of a simple series of commanders' names with the enclitic accusative appended to the last one (here Walī), as is usual, Humāyūn's name has its own enclitic *nī*; and, again, the phrase is "*Humāyūn with*" such and such begs, a turn of expression differentiating him from the rest. The same unusual variations occur again, just below, perhaps with the same intention of shewing chief command, there of Mahdī Khwāja.

[1682] A small matter of wording attracts attention in the preceding two sentences. Bābur, who does not always avoid verbal repetition, here constructs two sentences which, except for the place-names Dihlī and

Āgra, convey information of precisely the same action in entirely different words.

[1683] d. 1325 AD. The places Bābur visited near Dihlī are described in the *Reports of the Indian Archæological Survey*, in Sayyid Aḥmad's *Aṣār Sanādīd* pp. 74-85, in Keene's *Hand-book to Dihlī* and Murray's *Hand-book to Bengal etc.* The last two quote much from the writings of Cunningham and Fergusson.

[1684] and on the same side of the river.

[1685] d. 1235 AD. He was a native of Aūsh [Ush] in Farghāna.

[1686] d. 1286 AD. He was a Slave ruler of Dihlī.

[1687] 'Alāu'u'd-dīn Muḥ. Shāh *Khiljī Turk* d. 1316 AD. It is curious that Bābur should specify visiting his Minār (*minārī*, Pers. trs. I.O. 217 f. 185*b*, *minār-i-au*) and not mention the Quṭb Minār. Possibly he confused the two. The 'Alāī Minār remains unfinished; the Quṭb is judged by Cunningham to have been founded by Quṭbu'd-dīn Aībak *Turk*, *circa* 1200 AD. and to have been completed by Sl. Shamsu'd-dīn Altamsh (Aīltimīsh?) *Turk*, *circa* 1220 AD. Of the two tanks Bābur visited, the Royal-tank (*ḥauẓ-i-khāẓ*) was made by 'Alāu'u'd-dīn in 1293 AD.

[1688] The familiar Turkī word Tūghlūq would reinforce much else met with in Dihlī to strengthen Bābur's opinion that, as a Turk, he had a right to rule there. Many, if not all, of the Slave dynasty were Turks; these were followed by the Khiljī Turks, these again by the Tūghlūqs. Moreover the Panj-āb he had himself taken, and lands on both sides of the Indus further south had been ruled by Ghaznawid Turks. His latest conquests were "where the Turk had ruled" (f. 226*b*) long, wide, and with interludes only of non-Turkī sway.

[1689] Perhaps this charity was the *Khams* (Fifth) due from a victor.

[1690] Bikramājīt was a Tūnūr Rājpūt. Bābur's unhesitating statement of the Hindu's destination at death may be called a fruit of conviction, rather than of what modern opinion calls intolerance.

[1691] 120 years (Cunningham's *Report of the Archæological Survey* ii, 330 *et seq.*).

[1692] The *Tārīkh-i-sher-shāhī* tells a good deal about the man who bore this title, and also about others who found themselves now in difficulty between Ibrāhīm's tyranny and Bābur's advance (E. & D. iv, 301).

[1693] Gūālīār was taken from Bikramājīt in 1518 AD.

[1694] *i.e.* from the Deccan of which 'Alāu'u'd-dīn is said to have been the first Muḥammadan invader. An account of this diamond, identified as the

Koh-i-nūr, is given in *Hobson Jobson* but its full history is not told by Yule or by Streeter's *Great Diamonds of the World*, neither mentioning the presentation of the diamond by Humāyūn to Taḥmāsp of which Abū'l-faẓl writes, dwelling on its overplus of payment for all that Humāyūn in exile received from his Persian host (*Akbar-nāma* trs. i, 349 and note; *Asiatic Quarterly Review*, April 1899 H. Beveridge's art. *Bābur's diamond; was it the Koh-i-nūr?*).

[1695] 320 *ratīs* (Erskine). The *ratī* is 2.171 Troy grains, or in picturesque primitive equivalents, is 8 grains of rice, or 64 mustard seeds, or 512 poppy-seeds,—uncertain weights which Akbar fixed in cat's-eye stones.

[1696] Bābur's plurals allow the supposition that the three men's lives were spared. Malik Dād served him thenceforth.

[1697] Erskine estimated these as *dams* and worth about £1750, but this may be an underestimate (*H. of I.* i, App. E.).

[1698] "These begs of his" (or hers) may be the three written of above.

[1699] These will include cousins and his half-brothers Jahāngīr and Nāṣir as opposing before he took action in 925 AH. (1519 AD.). The time between 910 AH. and 925 AH. at which he would most desire Hindūstān is after 920 AH. in which year he returned defeated from Transoxiana.

[1700] *kīchīk karīm*, which here seems to make contrast between the ruling birth of members of his own family and the lower birth of even great begs still with him. Where the phrase occurs on f. 295, Erskine renders it by "down to the dregs", and de Courteille (ii, 235) by "*de toutes les bouches*" but neither translation appears to me to suit Bābur's uses of the term, inasmuch as both seem to go too low (cf. f. 270*b*).

[1701] *aīūrūshūb*, Pers. trs. *chaspīda*, stuck to.

[1702] The first expedition is fixed by the preceding passage as in 925 AH. which was indeed the first time a passage of the Indus is recorded. Three others are found recorded, those of 926, 930 and 932 AH. Perhaps the fifth was not led by Bābur in person, and may be that of his troops accompanying 'Ālam Khān in 931 AH. But he may count into the set of five, the one made in 910 AH. which he himself meant to cross the Indus. Various opinions are found expressed by European writers as to the dates of the five.

[1703] Muḥammad died 632 AD. (11 AH.).

[1704] Tramontana, n. of Hindū-kush. For particulars about the dynasties mentioned by Bābur see Stanley Lane-Poole's *Muḥammadan Dynasties*.

[1705] Maḥmūd of Ghaznī, a Turk by race, d. 1030 AD. (421 AH.).

[1706] known as Muḥ. *Ghūrī*, d. 1206 AD. (602 AH.).

[1707] *sūrūbtūrlār*, lit. drove them like sheep (cf. f. 154b).

[1708] *khūd*, itself, not Bābur's only Hibernianism.

[1709] "This is an excellent history of the Musalmān world down to the time of Sl. Nāṣir of Dihlī A.D. 1252. It was written by Abū 'Umar Minḥāj al Jūrjānī. See Stewart's catalogue of Tipoo's Library, p. 7" (Erskine). It has been translated by Raverty.

[1710] *bargustwān-wār*; Erskine, cataphract horse.

[1711] The numerous instances of the word *pādshāh* in this part of the *Bābur-nāma* imply no such distinction as attaches to the title Emperor by which it is frequently translated (Index *s.n. pādshāh*).

[1712] d. 1500 AD. (905 AH.).

[1713] d. 1388 AD. (790 AH.).

[1714] The ancestor mentioned appears to be Naṣrat Shāh, a grandson of Fīrūz Shāh *Tūghlūq* (S. L. Poole p. 300 and Beale, 298).

[1715] His family belonged to the Rājpūt sept of Tānk, and had become Muḥammadan in the person of Sadharān the first ruler of Gujrāt (Crooke's *Tribes and Castes; Mirāt-i-sikandarī*, Bayley p. 67 and n.).

[1716] S. L.-Poole p. 316-7.

[1717] Mandāū (Mandū) was the capital of Malwā.

[1718] Stanley Lane-Poole shews (p. 311) a dynasty of three Ghūrīs interposed between the death of Fīrūz Shāh in 790 AH. and the accession in 839 AH. of the first Khiljī ruler of Gujrāt Maḥmūd Shāh.

[1719] He reigned from 1518 to 1532 AD. (925 to 939 AH. S.L.-P. p. 308) and had to wife a daughter of Ibrāhīm *Lūdī* (*Riyāẓu's-salāṭīn*). His dynasty was known as the Ḥusain-shāhī, after his father.

[1720] "Strange as this custom may seem, a similar one prevailed down to a very late period in Malabar. There was a jubilee every 12 years in the Samorin's country, and any-one who succeeded in forcing his way through the Samorin's guards and slew him, reigned in his stead. 'A jubilee is proclaimed throughout his dominions at the end of 12 years, and a tent is pitched for him in a spacious plain, and a great feast is celebrated for 10 or 12 days with mirth and jollity, guns firing night and day, so, at the end of the feast, any four of the guests that have a mind to gain a throne by a desperate action in fighting their way through 30 or 40,000 of his guards, and kill the Samorin in his tent, he that kills him, succeeds him in his empire.' See Hamilton's *New Account of the East Indies* vol. i. p. 309. The attempt was made in 1695, and again a very few years ago, but without success" (Erskine p. 311).

The custom Bābur writes of—it is one dealt with at length in Frazer's *Golden Bough*—would appear from Blochmann's *Geography and History of Bengal* (JASB 1873 p. 286) to have been practised by the Habshī rulers of Bengal of whom he quotes Faria y Souza as saying, "They observe no rule of inheritance from father to son, but even slaves sometimes obtain it by killing their master, and whoever holds it three days, they look upon as established by divine providence. Thus it fell out that in 40 years space they had 13 kings successively."

[1721] No doubt this represents Vijāyanagar in the Deccan.

[1722] This date places the composition of the *Description of Hindustan* in agreement with Shaikh Zain's statement that it was in writing in 935 AH.

[1723] Are they the Khas of Nepal and Sikkim? (G. of I.).

[1724] Here Erskine notes that the Persian (trs.) adds, "*mīr* signifying a hill, and *kas* being the name of the natives of the hill-country." This may not support the name *kas* as correct but may be merely an explanation of Bābur's meaning. It is not in I.O. 217 f. 189 or in Muḥ. *Shīrāẕī*'s lithographed *Wāqi'āt-i-bāburī* p. 190.

[1725] Either yak or the tassels of the yak. See Appendix M.

[1726] My husband tells me that Bābur's authority for this interpretation of Sawālak may be the *Ẕafar-nāma* (Bib. Ind. ed. ii, 149).

[1727] *i.e.* the countries of Hindūstān.

[1728] so pointed, carefully, in the Ḥai. MS. Mr. Erskine notes of these rivers that they are the Indus, Hydaspes, Ascesines, Hydraotes, Hesudrus and Hyphasis.

[1729] *Āyīn-i-akbarī*, Jarrett 279.

[1730] *pārcha pārcha*, *kīchīkrāk kīchīkrāk*, *āndā mūndā*, *tāshlīq tāqghīna*. The Gazetteer of India (1907 i, 1) puts into scientific words, what Bābur here describes, the ruin of a great former range.

[1731] Here *āqār-sūlār* might safely be replaced by "irrigation channels" (Index *s.n.*).

[1732] The verb here is *tāshmāq*; it also expresses to carry like ants (f. 220), presumably from each person's carrying a pitcher or a stone at a time, and repeatedly.

[1733] "This" notes Erskine (p. 315) "is the *wulsa* or *walsa*, so well described by Colonel Wilks in his Historical Sketches vol. i. p. 309, note 'On the approach of an hostile army, the unfortunate inhabitants of India bury under ground their most cumbrous effects, and each individual, man, woman, and child above six years of age (the infant children being carried by their mothers), with a load of grain proportioned to their strength, issue from their beloved homes, and take the direction of a country (if such can be found,) exempt from the miseries of war; sometimes of a strong fortress, but more generally of the most unfrequented hills and woods, where they prolong a miserable existence until the departure of the enemy, and if this should be protracted beyond the time for which they have provided food, a large portion necessarily dies of hunger.' See the note itself. The Historical Sketches should be read by every-one who desires to have an accurate idea of the South of India. It is to be regretted that we do not possess the history of any other part of India, written with the same knowledge or research."

"The word *wulsa* or *walsa* is Dravidian. Telugu has *valasa*, 'emigration, flight, or removing from home for fear of a hostile army.' Kanarese has *valasĕ*, *ŏlasĕ*, and *ŏlisĕ*, 'flight, a removing from home for fear of a hostile army.' Tamil has *valasei*, 'flying for fear, removing hastily.' The word is an interesting one. I feel pretty sure it is not Aryan, but Dravidian; and yet it stands alone in Dravidian, with nothing that I can find in the way of a root or affinities to explain its etymology. Possibly it may be a borrowed word in Dravidian. Malayalam has no corresponding word. Can it have been borrowed from Kolarian or other primitive Indian speech?" (Letter to H. Beveridge from Mr. F. E. Pargiter, 8th August, 1914.)

Wulsa seems to be a derivative from Sanscrit *ūlvash*, and to answer to Persian *wairānī* and Turkī *būzūghlūghī*.

[1734] *lalmī*, which in Afghānī (Pushtū) signifies grown without irrigation.

[1735] "The improvement of Hindūstān since Bābur's time must be prodigious. The wild elephant is now confined to the forests under Hemāla, and to the Ghats of Malabar. A wild elephant near Karrah, Mānikpūr, or Kālpī, is a thing, at the present day (1826 AD.), totally unknown. May not their familiar existence in these countries down to Bābur's days, be considered rather hostile to the accounts given of the superabundant population of Hindūstān in remote times?" (Erskine).

[1736] *dīwān.* I.O. 217 f. 190b, *dar dīwān fīl jawāb mīgūīnd*; Mems. p. 316. They account to the government for the elephants they take; *Méms.* ii, 188, *Les habitants payent l'impôt avec le produit de leur chasse.* Though de Courteille's reading probably states the fact, Erskine's includes de C.'s and more, inasmuch as it covers all captures and these might reach to a surplusage over the imposts.

[1737] Pers. trs. *gaz*=24 inches. *Il est bon de rappeler que le mot turk qārī, que la version persane rend par gaz, désigne proprement l'espace compris entre le haut de l'épaule jusqu'au bout des doigts* (de Courteille, ii, 189 note). The *qārī* like one of its equivalents, the ell (Zenker), is a variable measure; it seems to approach more nearly to a yard than to a *gaz* of 24 inches. See *Memoirs of Jahāngīr* (R. & B. pp. 18, 141 and notes) for the heights of elephants, and for discussion of some measures.

[1738] *khūd*, itself.

[1739] *i.e.* pelt; as Erskine notes, its skin is scattered with small hairs. Details such as this one stir the question, for whom was Bābur writing? Not for Hindūstān where what he writes is patent; hardly for Kābul; perhaps for Transoxiana.

[1740] Shaikh Zain's wording shows this reference to be to a special piece of artillery, perhaps that of f. 302.

[1741] A string of camels contains from five to seven, or, in poetry, even more (Vullers, ii, 728, *sermone poetico series decem camelorum*). The item of food compared is corn only (*būghūz*) and takes no account therefore of the elephant's green food.

[1742] The Ency. Br. states that the horn seldom exceeds a foot in length; there is one in the B.M. measuring 18 inches.

[1743] āb-khẉura kishtī, water-drinker's boat, in which name kishtī may be used with reference to shape as boat is in *sauce-boat.* Erskine notes that rhinoceros-horn is supposed to sweat on approach of poison.

[1744] *aīlīk*, Pers. trs. *angusht*, finger, each seemingly representing about one inch, a hand's thickness, a finger's breadth.

[1745] lit. hand (*qūl*) and leg (*būt*).

[1746] The anatomical details by which Bābur supports this statement are difficult to translate, but his grouping of the two animals is in agreement with the modern classification of them as two of the three *Ungulata vera*, the third being the tapir (Fauna of British India:—Mammals, Blanford 467 and, illustration, 468).

[1747] De Courteille (ii, 190) reads *kūmūk*, osseuse; Erskine reads *gūmūk*, marrow.

[1748] Index *s.n.* rhinoceros.

[1749] *Bos bubalus.*

[1750] "so as to grow into the flesh" (Erskine, p. 317).

[1751] *sic* in text. It may be noted that the name *nīl-gāī*, common in general European writings, is that of the cow; *nīl-gāū*, that of the bull (Blanford).

[1752] *b:ḥ:rī qūṭās*; *see* Appendix M.

[1753] The doe is brown (Blanford, p. 518). The word *būghū* (stag) is used alone just below and seems likely to represent the bull of the Asiatic wapiti (f. 4 n. on *būghū-marāl.*)

[1754] *Axis porcinus* (Jerdon, *Cervus porcinus*).

[1755] *Saiga tartarica* (Shaw). Turkī *hūna* is used, like English deer, for male, female, and both. Here it seems defined by *aīrkākī* to mean stag or buck.

[1756] *Antelope cervicapra*, black-buck, so called from the dark hue of its back (Yule's H.J. *s.n.* Black-buck).

[1757] *tūyūq*, underlined in the Elph. MS. by *kura*, cannon-ball; Erskine, foot-ball, de Courteille, *pierre plus grosse que la cheville* (*tūyāq*).

[1758] This mode of catching antelopes is described in the *Āyīn-i-akbarī*, and is noted by Erskine as common in his day.

[1759] *H. gainā.* It is 3 feet high (Yule's H.J. *s.n.* Gynee). Cf. A. A. Blochmann, p. 149. The ram with which it is compared may be that of *Ovis ammon* (Vigné's *Kashmīr etc.* ii, 278).

[1760] Here the Pers. trs. adds:—They call this kind of monkey *langūr* (baboon, I.O. 217 f. 192).

[1761] Here the Pers. trs. adds what Erskine mistakenly attributes to Bābur:—People bring it from several islands.—They bring yet another kind from several islands, yellowish-grey in colour like a *pūstīn tīn* (leather coat of ?; Erskine, skin of the fig, *tīn*). Its head is broader and its body much larger than those of other monkeys. It is very fierce and destructive. It is singular *quod penis ejus semper sit erectus, et nunquam non ad coitum idoneus* [Erskine].

[1762] This name is explained on the margin of the Elph. MS. as "*rāsū*, which is the weasel of Tartary" (Erskine). *Rāsū* is an Indian name for the squirrel *Sciurus indicus*. The *kīsh*, with which Bābur's *nūl* is compared, is explained by de C. as *belette*, weasel, and by Steingass as a fur-bearing animal; the fur-bearing weasel is (*Mustelidae*) *putorius ermina*, the ermine-weasel (Blanford, p. 165), which thus seems to be Bābur's *kīsh*. The alternative name Bābur gives for his *nūl*, *i.e. mūsh-i-khūrma*, is, in India, that of *Sciurus palmarum*, the palm-squirrel (G. of I. i, 227); this then, it seems that Bābur's *nūl* is. Erskine took *nūl* here to be the mongoose (*Herpestes mūngūs*) (p. 318); and Blanford, perhaps partly on Erskine's warrant, gives *mūsh-i-khūrma* as a name of the lesser *mungūs* of Bengal. I gather that the name *nawal* is not exclusively confined even now to the (*mungūs.*)

[1763] If this be a tree-mouse and not a squirrel, it may be *Vandeleuria oleracea* (G. of I. i, 228).

[1764] The notes to this section are restricted to what serves to identify the birds Bābur mentions, though temptation is great to add something to this from the mass of interesting circumstance scattered in the many writings of observers and lovers of birds. I have thought it useful to indicate to what language a bird's name belongs.

[1765] Persian, *gul*; English, eyes.

[1766] *qūlāch* (Zenker, p. 720); Pers. trs. (217 f. 192*b*) *yak qad-i-adm*; de Courteille, *brasse* (fathom). These three are expressions of the measure from finger-tip to finger-tip of a man's extended arms, which should be his height, a fathom (6 feet).

[1767] *qānāt*, of which here "primaries" appears to be the correct rendering, since Jerdon says (ii, 506) of the bird that its "wings are striated black and white, primaries and tail deep chestnut".

[1768] The *qīrghāwal*, which is of the pheasant species, when pursued, will take several flights immediately after each other, though none long; peacocks, it seems, soon get tired and take to running (Erskine).

[1769] Ar. *barrāq*, as on f. 278*b* last line where the Elph. MS. has *barrāq*, marked with the *tashdīd.*

[1770] This was, presumably, just when Bābur was writing the passage.

[1771] This sentence is in Arabic.

[1772] A Persian note, partially expunged from the text of the Elph. MS. is to the effect that 4 or 5 other kinds of parrot are heard of which the revered author did not see.

[1773] Erskine suggests that this may be the *loory* (*Loriculus vernalis*, Indian loriquet).

[1774] The birds Bābur classes under the name *shārak* seem to include what Oates and Blanford (whom I follow as they give the results of earlier workers) class under *Sturnus*, *Eulabes* and *Calornis*, starling, grackle and mīna, and tree-stare (*Fauna of British India*, Oates, vols. i and ii, Blanford, vols. iii and iv).

[1775] Turkī, *qabā*; Ilminsky, p. 361, *tang* (*tund*?).

[1776] E. D. Ross's *Polyglot List of Birds*, p. 314, *Chighīr-chīq*, Northern swallow; Elph. MS. f. 230*b* interlined *jīl* (Steingass lark). The description of the bird allows it to be *Sturnus humii*, the Himālayan starling (Oates, i, 520).

[1777] Elph. and Ḥai. MSS. (Sans. and Bengālī) *p:ndūī*; two good MSS. of the Pers. trs. (I.O. 217 and 218) *p:ndāwalī*; Ilminsky (p. 361) *mīnā*; Erskine (*Mems.* p. 319) *pindāwelī*, but without his customary translation of an Indian name. The three forms shewn above can all mean "having protuberance or lump" (*pinḍā*) and refer to the bird's wattle. But the word of the presumably well-informed scribes of I.O. 217 and 218 can refer to the bird's sagacity in speech and be *panḍāwalī*, possessed of wisdom. With the same spelling, the word can translate into the epithet *religiosa*, given to the wattled *mīnā* by Linnæus. This epithet Mr. Leonard Wray informs me has been explained to him as due to the frequenting of temples by the birds; and that in Malāya they are found living in cotes near Chinese temples.—An alternative name (one also connecting with *religiosa*) allowed by the form of the word is *bīnḍā-walī*. H. *bīnḍā* is a mark on the forehead, made as a preparative to devotion by Hindus, or in Sans. and *Bengālī*, is the spot of paint made on an elephant's trunk; the meaning would thus be "having a mark". Cf. Jerdon and Oates *s.n. Eulabes religiosa.*

[1778] *Eulabes intermedia*, the Indian grackle or hill-mīna. Here the Pers. trs. adds that people call it *mīna.*

[1779] *Calornis chalybeius*, the glossy starling or tree-stare, which never descends to the ground.

[1780] *Sturnopastor contra*, the pied mīna.

[1781] Part of the following passage about the *lūja* (var. *lūkha*, *lūcha*) is *verbatim* with part of that on f. 135; both were written about 934-5 AH. as is shewn by Shaikh Zain (Index *s.n.*) and by inference from references in the text (Index *s.n.* B.N. date of composition). *See* Appendix N.

[1782] Lit. mountain-partridge. There is ground for understanding that one of the birds known in the region as *monals* is meant. *See* Appendix N.

[1783] Sans. *chakora*; Ar. *durrāj*; P. *kabg*; T. *kīklīk*.

[1784] Here, probably, southern Afghānistān.

[1785] *Caccabis chukūr* (Scully, Shaw's Vocabulary) or *C. pallescens* (Hume, quoted under No. 126 E. D. Ross' *Polyglot List*).

[1786] "In some parts of the country (*i.e.* India before 1841 AD.), tippets used to be made of the beautiful black, white-spotted feathers of the lower plumage (of the *durrāj*), and were in much request, but they are rarely procurable now" (*Bengal Sporting Magazine* for 1841, quoted by Jerdon, ii, 561).

[1787] A broad collar of red passes round the whole neck (Jerdon, ii, 558).

[1788] Ar. *durrāj* means one who repeats what he hears, a tell-tale.

[1789] Various translations have been made of this passage, "I have milk and sugar" (Erskine), "*J'ai du lait, un peu de sucre*" (de Courteille), but with short *sh:r*, it might be read in more than one way ignoring milk and sugar. See Jerdon, ii, 558 and Hobson Jobson *s.n.* Black-partridge.

[1790] Flower-faced, *Trapogon melanocephala*, the horned (*sing*)-monal. It is described by Jahāngīr (*Memoirs*, R. and B., ii, 220) under the names [H. and P.] *phūl-paikār* and Kashmīrī, *sonlū*.

[1791] *Gallus sonneratii*, the grey jungle-fowl.

[1792] Perhaps *Bambusicola fytchii*, the western bambu-partridge. For *chīl* see E. D. Ross, *l.c.* No. 127.

[1793] Jahāngīr (*l.c.*) describes, under the Kashmīrī name *pūṭ*, what may be this bird. It seems to be *Gallus ferrugineus*, the red jungle-fowl (Blanford, iv, 75).

[1794] Jahāngīr helps to identify the bird by mentioning its elongated tail-feathers,—seasonal only.

[1795] The migrant quail will be *Coturnix communis*, the grey quail, 8 inches long; what it is compared with seems likely to be the bush-quail, which is non-migrant and shorter.

[1796] Perhaps *Perdicula argunda*, the rock bush-quail, which flies in small coveys.

[1797] Perhaps *Coturnix coromandelica*, the black-breasted or rain quail, 7 inches long.

[1798] Perhaps *Motacilla citreola*, a yellow wag-tail which summers in Central Asia (Oates, ii, 298). If so, its Kābul name may refer to its flashing colour. Cf. E. D. Ross, *l.c.* No. 301; de Courteille's *Dictionary* which gives *qārcha*, wag-tail, and Zenker's which fixes the colour.

[1799] *Eupodotis edwardsii*; Turkī, *tūghdār* or *tūghdīrī.*

[1800] Erskine noting (Mems. p. 321), that the bustard is common in the Dakkan where it is bigger than a turkey, says it is called *tūghdār* and suggests that this is a corruption of *tūghdāq*. The uses of both words are shewn by Bābur, here, and in the next following, account of the *charz*. Cf. G. of I. i, 260 and E. D. Ross *l.c.* Nos. 36, 40.

[1801] *Sypheotis bengalensis* and *S. aurita*, which are both smaller than *Otis houbara* (*tūghdīrī*). In Hindustan *S. aurita* is known as *līkh* which name is the nearest approach I have found to Bābur's [*lūja*] *lūkha*.

[1802] Jerdon mentions (ii, 615) that this bird is common in Afghānistān and there called *dugdaor* (*tūghdār, tūghdīrī*).

[1803] *Cf.* Appendix B, since I wrote which, further information has made it fairly safe to say that the Hindūstān *bāghrī-qarā* is *Pterocles exustus*, the common sand-grouse and that the one of f. 49b is *Pterocles arenarius*, the larger or black-bellied sand-grouse. *P. exustus* is said by Yule (H. J. *s.n.* Rock-pigeon) to have been miscalled rock-pigeon by Anglo-Indians, perhaps because its flight resembles the pigeon's. This accounts for Erskine's rendering (p. 321) *bāghrī-qarā* here by rock-pigeon.

[1804] *Leptoptilus dubius*, Hind. *hargīlā*. Hindūstānīs call it *pīr-i-dīng* (Erskine) and *peda dhauk* (Blanford), both names referring, perhaps, to its pouch. It is the adjutant of Anglo-India. Cf. f. 235.

[1805] only when young (Blanford, ii, 188).

[1806] Elph. MS. *mank:sā* or *mankīā*; Ḥai. MS. *m:nk*. Haughton's *Bengali Dictionary* gives two forms of the name *mānek-jur* and *mānak-yoī*. It is *Dissura episcopus*, the white-necked stork (Blanford iv, 370, who gives *manik-jor* amongst its Indian names). Jerdon classes it (ii, 737) as *Ciconia leucocephala*. It is the beefsteak bird of Anglo-India.

[1807] *Ciconia nigra* (Blanford, iv, 369).

[1808] Under the Hindūstānī form, *būza*, of Persian *buzak* the birds Bābur mentions as *buzak* can be identified. The large one is *Inocotis papillosus*, *būza*, *kāla būza*, black curlew, king-curlew. The bird it equals in size is a buzzard, Turkī *sār* (not Persian *sār*, starling). The king-curlew has a large white patch on the inner lesser and marginal coverts of its wings (Blanford, iv, 303). This agrees with Bābur's statement about the wings of the large *buzak*. Its length is 27 inches, while the starling's is 9-1/2 inches.

[1809] *Ibis melanocephala*, the white ibis, Pers. *safed buzak*, Bengali *sabut būza*. It is 30 inches long.

[1810] Perhaps, *Plegadis falcinellus*, the glossy ibis, which in most parts of India is a winter visitor. Its length is 25 inches.

[1811] Erskine suggests that this is *Platalea leucorodia*, the *chamach-būza*, spoon-bill. It is 33 inches long.

[1812] *Anas poecilorhyncha.* The Ḥai. MS. writes *gharm-pāī*, and this is the Indian name given by Blanford (iv, 437).

[1813] *Anas boschas.* Dr. Ross notes (No. 147), from the *Sanglākh*, that *sūna* is the drake, *būrchīn*, the duck and that it is common in China to call a certain variety of bird by the combined sex-names. Something like this is shewn by the uses of *būghā* and *marāl q.v.* Index.

[1814] *Centropus rufipennis*, the common coucal (Yule's H.J. *s.n.* Crow-pheasant); H. *makokhā*, *Cuculus castaneus* (Buchanan, quoted by Forbes).

[1815] *Pteropus edwardsii*, the flying-fox. The inclusion of the bat here amongst birds, may be a clerical accident, since on f. 136 a flying-fox is not written of as a bird.

[1816] Bābur here uses what is both the Kābul and Andijān name for the magpie, Ar. *'aqqa* (Oates, i, 31 and Scully's Voc), instead of T. *sāghiẓghān* or P. *dam-sīcha* (tail-wagger).

[1817] The Pers. trs. writes *sāndūlāch mamūlā*, *mamūlā* being Arabic for wag-tail. De Courteille's Dictionary describes the *sāndūlāch* as small and having a long tail, the cock-bird green, the hen, yellow. The wag-tail suiting this in colouring is *Motacilla borealis* (Oates, ii, 294; syn. *Budytes viridis*, the green wag-tail); this, as a migrant, serves to compare with the Indian "little bird", which seems likely to be a red-start.

[1818] This word may represent Scully's *kirich* and be the Turkī name for a swift, perhaps *Cypselus affinis*.

[1819] This name is taken from its cry during the breeding season (Yule's H.J. *s.n.* Koel).

[1820] Bābur's distinction between the three crocodiles he mentions seems to be that of names he heard, *shīr-ābī*, *siyāh-sār*, and *ghaṛīāl*.

[1821] In this passage my husband finds the explanation of two somewhat vague statements of later date, one made by Abū'l-faẓl (A. A. Blochmann, p. 65) that Akbar called the *kīlās* (cherry) the *shāh-ālū* (king-plum), the other by Jahāngīr that this change was made because *kīlās* means lizard (*Jahāngīr's Memoirs*, R. & B. i, 116). What Akbar did is shewn by Bābur; it was to reject the *Persian* name *kīlās*, cherry, because it closely resembled *Turkī gīlās*, lizard. There is a lizard *Stellio Lehmanni* of Transoxiana with which Bābur may well have compared the crocodile's appearance (Schuyler's *Turkistān*, i, 383). Akbar in Hindūstān may have had *Varanus salvator* (6 ft. long) in mind, if indeed he had not the great lizard, *al lagarto*, the alligator itself in his thought. The name *kīlās* evidently was banished only from the Court circle, since it is still current in Kashmīr (Blochmann *l.c.* p. 616); and Speede (p. 201) gives *keeras*, cherry, as used in India.

[1822] This name as now used, is that of the purely fish-eating crocodile. [In the Turkī text Bābur's account of the *gharīāl* follows that of the porpoise; but it is grouped here with those of the two other crocodiles.]

[1823] As the Ḥai. MS. and also I.O. 216 f. 137 (Pers. trs.) write *kalah* (*galah*)-fish, this may be a large cray-fish. One called by a name approximating to *galah*-fish is found in Malāyan waters, *viz*. the *galah*-prawn (*hūdang*) (cf. Bengālī *gūla-chingrī*, *gūla*-prawn, Haughton). *Galah* and *gūla* may express lament made when the fish is caught (Haughton pp. 931, 933, 952); or if *kalah* be read, this may express scolding. Two good MSS. of the *Wāqi'āt-i-bāburī* (Pers. trs.) write *kaka*; and their word cannot but have weight. Erskine reproduces *kaka* but offers no explanation of it, a failure betokening difficulty in his obtaining one. My husband suggests that *kaka* may represent a stuttering sound, doing so on the analogy of Vullers' explanation of the word,—*Vir ridiculus et facetus qui simul balbutiat*; and also he inclines to take the fish to be a crab (*kakra*). Possibly *kaka* is a popular or vulgar name for a cray-fish or a crab. Whether the sound is lament, scolding, or stuttering the fisherman knows! Shaikh Zain enlarges Bābur's notice of this fish; he says the bones are prolonged (*bar āwarda*) from the ears, that these it agitates at time of capture, making a noise like the word *kaka* by which it is known, that it is two *wajab* (18 in.) long, its flesh surprisingly tasty, and that it is very active, leaping a *gaz* (*cir.* a yard) out of the water when the fisherman's net is set to take it. For information about the Malāyan fish, I am indebted to Mr. Cecil Wray.

[1824] T. *qiyūnlīghī*, presumably referring to spines or difficult bones; T. *qīn*, however, means a scabbard [Shaw].

[1825] One of the common frogs is a small one which, when alarmed, jumps along the surface of the water (G. of I. i, 273).

[1826] *Anb* and *anbah* (pronounced *aṃb* and *aṃbah*) are now less commonly used names than *ām*. It is an interesting comment on Bābur's words that Abū'l-faẓl spells *anb*, letter by letter, and says that the *b* is quiescent (*Āyīn* 28; for the origin of the word mango, *vide* Yule's H.J. *s.n.*).

[1827] A corresponding diminutive would be fairling.

[1828] The variants, entered in parenthesis, are found in the Bib. Ind. ed. of the *Āyīn-i-akbarī* p. 75 and in a (bazar) copy of the *Qurānu's-sā'dain* in my husband's possession. As Amīr Khusrau was a poet of Hindūstān, either *khwash* (*khwesh*) [our own] or *mā* [our] would suit his meaning. The couplet is, literally:—

Our fairling, [*i.e.* mango] beauty-maker of the garden,

Fairest fruit of Hindūstān.

[1829] Daulat Khān *Yūsuf-khail Lūdī* in 929 AH. sent Bābur a gift of mangoes preserved in honey (*in loco* p. 440).

[1830] I have learned nothing more definite about the word *kārdī* than that it is the name of a superior kind of peach (*Ghiyāṣu'l-lughat*).

[1831] The preceding sentence is out of place in the Turkī text; it may therefore be a marginal note, perhaps not made by Bābur.

[1832] This sentence suggests that Bābur, writing in Āgra or Fatḥpūr did not there see fine mango-trees.

[1833] See Yule's H.J. on the plantain, the banana of the West.

[1834] This word is a descendant of Sanscrit *mocha*, and parent of *musa* the botanical name of the fruit (Yule).

[1835] Shaikh Effendī (Kunos), Zenker and de Courteille say of this only that it is the name of a tree. Shaw gives a name that approaches it, *ārman*, a grass, a weed; Scully explains this as *Artemisia vulgaris*, wormwood, but Roxburgh gives no *Artemisia* having a leaf resembling the plantain's. Scully has *arāmadān*, unexplained, which, like *amān-qarā*, may refer to comfort in shade. Bābur's comparison will be with something known in Transoxiana. Maize has general resemblance with the plantain. So too have the names of the plants, since *mocha* and *mauz* stand for the plantain and (Hindī) *mukā'ī* for maize. These incidental resemblances bear, however lightly, on the question considered in the Ency. Br. (art. maize) whether maize was early in Asia or not; some writers hold that it was; if Bābur's *amān-qarā* were maize, maize will have been familiar in Transoxiana in his day.

[1836] Abū'l-faẓl mentions that the plantain-tree bears no second crop unless cut down to the stump.

[1837] Bābur was fortunate not to have met with a seed-bearing plantain.

[1838] The ripe "dates" are called P. *tamar-i Hind*, whence our tamarind, and *Tamarindus Indica*.

[1839] *Sophora alopecuroides*, a leguminous plant (Scully).

[1840] Abū'l-faẓl gives *galaundā* as the name of the "fruit" [*mewa*],—Forbes, as that of the fallen flower. Cf. Brandis p. 426 and Yule's H.J. *s.n.* Mohwa.

[1841] Bābur seems to say that spirit is extracted from both the fresh and the dried flowers. The fresh ones are favourite food with deer and jackals; they have a sweet spirituous taste. Erskine notes that the spirit made from them was well-known in Bombay by the name of Moura, or of Parsi-brandy, and that the farm of it was a considerable article of revenue (p. 325 n.). Roxburgh describes it as strong and intoxicating (p. 411).

[1842] This is the name of a green, stoneless grape which when dried, results in a raisin resembling the sultanas of Europe (*Jahāngīr's Memoirs* and Yule's H.J. *s.n.*; Griffiths' *Journal of Travel* pp. 359, 388).

[1843] *Aūl*, lit. the *aūl* of the flower. The Persian translation renders *aūl* by *bū* which may allow both words to be understood in their (root) sense of *being*, *i.e.* natural state. De Courteille translates by *quand la fleur est fraîche* (ii, 210); Erskine took *bū* to mean smell (*Memoirs* p. 325), but the *aūl* it translates, does not seem to have this meaning. For reading *aūl* as "the natural state", there is circumstantial support in the flower's being eaten raw (Roxburgh). The annotator of the Elphinstone MS. [whose defacement of that Codex has been often mentioned], has added points and *tashdīd* to the *aūl-ī* (*i.e.* its *aūl*), so as to produce *awwalī* (first, f. 235). Against this there are the obvious objections that the Persian translation does not reproduce, and that its *bū* does not render *awwalī*; also that *aūl-ī* is a noun with its enclitic genitive *yā* (*ī*).

[1844] This word seems to be meant to draw attention to the various merits of the *mahuwā* tree.

[1845] Erskine notes that this is not to be confounded with E. *jāmbū*, the rose-apple (*Memoirs* p. 325 n.). Cf. Yule's H.J. *s.n. Jambu.*

[1846] var. *ghat-ālū*, *ghab-ālū*, *ghain-ālū*, *shafl-ālū*. Scully enters *'ain-ālū* (true-plum?) unexplained. The *kamrak* fruit is 3 in. long (Brandis) and of the size of a lemon (Firminger); dimensions which make Bābur's 4 *aīlīk* (hand's-thickness) a slight excess only, and which thus allow *aīlīk*, with its Persion translation, *angusht*, to be approximately an inch.

[1847] Speede, giving the fruit its Sanscrit name *kamarunga*, says it is acid, rather pleasant, something like an insipid apple; also that its pretty pink blossoms grow on the trunk and main branches (i, 211).

[1848] Cf. Yule's H.J. *s.n.* jack-fruit. In a Calcutta nurseryman's catalogue of 1914 AD. three kinds of jack-tree are offered for sale, viz. "Crispy Or Khaja, Soft or Neo, Rose-scented" (Seth, Feronia Nursery).

[1849] The *gīpa* is a sheep's stomach stuffed with rice, minced meat, and spices, and boiled as a pudding. The resemblance of the jack, as it hangs on the tree, to the haggis, is wonderfully complete (Erskine).

[1850] These when roasted have the taste of chestnuts.

[1851] Firminger (p. 186) describes an ingenious method of training.

[1852] For a note of Humāyūn's on the jack-fruit *see* Appendix O.

[1853] *aīd-ī-yamān aīmās.* It is somewhat curious that Bābur makes no comment on the odour of the jack itself.

[1854] *būsh*, English bosh (Shaw). The Persian translation inserts no more about this fruit.

[1855] Steingass applies this name to the plantain.

[1856] Erskine notes that "this is the bullace-plum, small, not more than twice as large as the sloe and not so high-flavoured; it is generally yellow, sometimes red." Like Bābur, Brandis enumerates several varieties and mentions the seasonal changes of the tree (p. 170).

[1857] This will be Kābul, probably, because Transoxiana is written of by Bābur usually, if not invariably, as "that country", and because he mentions the *chīkda* (*i.e. chīka?*), under its Persian name *sinjid*, in his *Description of Kābul* (f. 129*b*).

[1858] P. *mar manjān*, which I take to refer to the *rīwājlār* of Kābul. (Cf. f. 129*b*, where, however, (note 5) are *corrigenda* of Masson's *rawash* for *rīwāj*, and his third to second volume.) Kehr's Codex contains an extra passage about the *karaūn dā*, *viz.* that from it is made a tasty fritter-like dish, resembling a rhubarb-fritter (Ilminsky, p. 369).

[1859] People call it (P.) *pālasa* also (Elph. MS. f. 236, marginal note).

[1860] Perhaps the red-apple of Kābul, where two sorts are common, both rosy, one very much so, but much inferior to the other (Griffith's *Journal of Travel* p. 388).

[1861] Its downy fruit grows in bundles from the trunk and large branches (Roxburgh).

[1862] The reference by "also" (*ham*) will be to the *kamrak* (f. 283*b*), but both Roxburgh and Brandis say the *amla* is six striated.

[1863] The Sanscrit and Bengālī name for the chirūnjī-tree is *pīyala* (Roxburgh p. 363).

[1864] Cf. f. 250*b*.

[1865] The leaflet is rigid enough to serve as a runlet, but soon wears out; for this reason, the usual practice is to use one of split bamboo.

[1866] This is a famous hunting-ground between Bīāna and Dhūlpūr, Rājpūtāna, visited in 933 AH. (f. 33O*b*). Bābur's great-great-grandson Shāh-jahān built a hunting-lodge there (G. of I.).

[1867] Ḥai. MS. *mu'arrab*, but the Elph. MS. *maghrib*, [occidentalizing]. The Ḥai. MS. when writing of the orange (*infra*) also has *maghrib*. A distinction of locality may be drawn by *maghrib*.

[1868] Bābur's "Hindūstān people" (*aīl*) are those neither Turks nor Afghāns.

[1869] This name, with its usual form *tāḍī* (toddy), is used for the fermented sap of the date, coco, and *mhār* palms also (cf. Yule's H.J. *s.n.* toddy).

[1870] Bābur writes of the long leaf-stalk as a branch (*shākh*); he also seems to have taken each spike of the fan-leaf to represent a separate leaf. [For two omissions from my trs. *see* Appendix O.]

[1871] Most of the fruits Bābur describes as orange-like are named in the following classified list, taken from Watts' *Economic Products of India*:— "**Citrus aurantium**, *narangi*, *sangtara*, *amrit-phal*; **C. decumana**, *pumelo*, shaddock, forbidden-fruit, *sada-phal*; **C. medica** proper, *turunj*, *limu*; **C. medica limonum**, *jambhira*, *karna-nebu*." Under *C. aurantium* Brandis enters both the sweet and the Seville oranges (*nārangī*); this Bābur appears to do also.

[1872] *kīndīklīk*, explained in the Elph. Codex by *nāfwār* (f. 238). This detail is omitted by the Persian translation. Firminger's description (p. 221) of Aurangābād oranges suggests that they also are navel-oranges. At the present time one of the best oranges had in England is the navel one of California.

[1873] Useful addition is made to earlier notes on the variability of the *yīghāch*, a variability depending on time taken to cover the ground, by the following passage from Henderson and Hume's *Lahor to Yarkand* (p. 120), which shews that even in the last century the *farsang* (the P. word used in the Persian translation of the *Bābur-nāma* for T. *yīghāch*) was computed by time. "All the way from Kargallik (Qārghalīq) to Yarkand, there were tall wooden mile-posts along the roads, at intervals of about 5 miles, or rather one hour's journey, apart. On a board at the top of each post, or *farsang* as it is called, the distances were very legibly written in Turki."

[1874] *ma'rib*, Elph. MS. *magharrib*; (cf. f. 285*b* note).

[1875] *i.e.* *nārang* (Sans. *nāranga*) has been changed to *nāranj* in the 'Arab mouth. What is probably one of Humāyūn's notes preserved by the Elph. Codex (f. 238), appears to say—it is mutilated—that *nārang* has been corrupted into *nāranj*.

[1876] The Elph. Codex has a note—mutilated in early binding—which is attested by its scribe as copied from Humāyūn's hand-writing, and is to the effect that once on his way from the Hot-bath, he saw people who had taken poison and restored them by giving lime-juice.

Erskine here notes that the same antidotal quality is ascribed to the citron by Virgil:—

Media fert tristes succos. tardumque saporem

Felicis mali, quo non praesentius ullum,

Pocula si quando saevae infecere novercae,

Miscueruntque herbas et non innoxia verba,

Auxilium venit, ac membris agit atra venena.

Georgics II. v. 126.

Vide Heyne's note i, 438.

[1877] P. *turunj*, wrinkled, puckered; Sans. *vijāpūra* and H. *bijaurā* (*Āyīn* 28), seed-filled.

[1878] Bābur may have confused this with H. *bijaurā*; so too appears to have done the writer (Humāyūn?) of a [now mutilated] note in the Elph. Codex (f. 238), which seems to say that the fruit or its name went from Bajaur to Hindūstān. Is the country of Bajaur so-named from its indigenous orange (*vijāpūra*, whence *bijaurā*)? The name occurs also north of Kangra.

[1879] Of this name variants are numerous, *santra*, *santhara*, *samtara*, etc. Watts classes it as a *C. aurantium*; Erskine makes it the common sweet orange; Firminger, quoting Ross (p. 221) writes that, as grown in the Nagpur gardens it is one of the finest Indian oranges, with rind thin, smooth and close. The Emperor Muḥammad Shāh is said to have altered its name to *rang-tāra* because of its fine colour (*rang*) (Forbes). Speede (ii, 109) gives both names. As to the meaning and origin of the name *santara* or *santra*, so suggestive of Cintra, the Portuguese home of a similar orange, it may be said that it looks like a hill-name used in N. E. India, for there is a village in the Bhutan Hills, (Western Duars) known from its orange groves as Santra-bārī, Abode of the orange. To this (mentioned already as my husband's suggestion in Mr. Crooke's ed. of Yule's H.J.) support is given by the item "Suntura, famous Nipal variety", entered in Seth's Nursery-list of 1914 (Feronia Nurseries, Calcutta). Light on the question of origin could be thrown, no doubt, by those acquainted with the dialects of the hill-tract concerned.

[1880] This refers, presumably, to the absence of the beak characteristic of all citrons.

[1881] melter, from the Sans. root *gal*, which provides the names of several lemons by reason of their solvent quality, specified by Bābur (*infra*) of the *amal-bīd.* Erskine notes that in his day the *gal-gal* was known as *kilmek* (*galmak*?).

[1882] Sans. *jambīrā*, H. *jambīr*, classed by Abū'l-faẓl as one of the somewhat sour fruits and by Watts as *Citrus medica limonum.*

[1883] Watts, *C. decumana*, the shaddock or pumelo; Firminger (p. 223) has *C. decumana pyriformis* suiting Bābur's "pear-shaped". What Bābur compared it with will be the Transoxanian pear and quince (*P. amrūd* and *bihī*) and not the Indian guava and Bengal quince (*P. amrūd* and *H. bael*).

[1884] The Turkī text writes *amrd.* Watts classes the *amrit-phal* as a *C. aurantium.* This supports Erskine's suggestion that it is the mandarin-orange. Humāyūn describes it in a note which is written pell-mell in the text of the Elph. Codex and contains also descriptions of the *kāmila* and *santara* oranges; it can be seen translated in Appendix O.

[1885] So spelled in the Turkī text and also in two good MSS. of the Pers. trs. I.O. 217 and 218, but by Abū'l-faẓl *amal-bīt.* Both P. *bīd* and P. *bīt* mean willow and cane (ratan), so that *amal-bīd* (*bīt*) can mean acid-willow and acid-cane. But as Bābur is writing of a fruit like an orange, the cane that bears an acid fruit, *Calamus rotang*, can be left aside in favour of *Citrus medica acidissima.* Of this fruit the solvent property Bābur mentions, as well as the commonly-known service in cleansing metal, link it, by these uses, with the willow and suggest a ground for understanding, as Erskine did, that *amal-bīd* meant acid-willow; for willow-wood is used to rub rust off metal.

[1886] This statement shows that Bābur was writing the *Description of Hindūstān* in 935 AH. (1528-9 AD.), which is the date given for it by Shaikh Zain.

[1887] This story of the needle is believed in India of all the citron kind, which are hence called *sūī-gal* (needle-melter) in the Dakhin (Erskine). Cf. Forbes, p. 489 *s.n. sūī-gal.*

[1888] Erskine here quotes information from Abū'l-faẓl (*Āyīn* 28) about Akbar's encouragement of the cultivation of fruits.

[1889] Hindustani (Urdu) *gaṛhal.* Many varieties of Hibiscus (syn. Althea) grow in India; some thrive in Surrey gardens; the *jāsūn* by name and colour can be taken as what is known in Malayan, Tamil, etc., as the shoe-flower, from its use in darkening leather (Yule's H.J.).

[1890] I surmise that what I have placed between asterisks here belongs to the next-following plant, the oleander. For though the branches of the *jāsūn* grow vertically, the bush is a dense mass upon one stout trunk, or stout short stem. The words placed in parenthesis above are not with the

Ḥaidarabad but are with the Elphinstone Codex. There would seem to have been a scribe's skip from one "rose" to the other. As has been shewn repeatedly, this part of the Bābur-nāma has been much annotated; in the Elph. Codex, where only most of the notes are preserved, some are entered by the scribe pell-mell into Bābur's text. The present instance may be a case of a marginal note, added to the text in a wrong place.

[1891] The peduncle supporting the plume of medial petals is clearly seen only when the flower opens first. The plumed Hibiscus is found in florists' catalogues described as "double".

[1892] This Anglo-Indians call also rose-bay. A Persian name appears to be *ẕahr-giyāh*, poison-grass, which makes it the more probable that the doubtful passage in the previous description of the *jāsūn* belongs to the rod-like oleander, known as the poison-grass. The oleander is common in river-beds over much country known to Bābur, outside India.

[1893] Roxburgh gives a full and interesting account of this tree.

[1894] Here the Elph. Codex, only, has the (seeming) note, "An 'Arab calls it *kāẕī*" (or *kāwī*). This fills out Steingass' part-explanation of *kāwī*, "the blossom of the fragrant palm-tree, *armāṯ*" (p. 1010), and of *armāṯ*, "a kind of date-tree with a fragrant blossom" (p. 39), by making *armāṯ* and *kāwī* seem to be the *Pandanus* and its flower.

[1895] *Calamus scriptorius* (Vullers ii, 607. H. B.). Abū'l-faẓl compares the leaves to *jawārī*, the great millet (Forbes); Blochmann (A. A. p. 83) translates *jawārī* by *maize* (*juwārā*, Forbes).

[1896] T. *aīrkāk-qūmūsh*, a name Scully enters unexplained. Under *qūmūsh* (reed) he enters *Arundo madagascarensis*; Bābur's comparison will be with some Transoxanian *Arundo* or *Calamus*, presumably.

[1897] *Champa* seems to have been Bābur's word (Elph. and Ḥai. MSS.), but is the (B.) name for *Michelia champaka*; the Pers. translation corrects it by (B.) *chambelī*, (*yāsman*, jasmine).

[1898] Here, "outside India" will be meant, where Hindū rules do not prevail.

[1899] *Hind aīlārī-nīng ibtidā-sī hilāl aīlār-nīng istiqbāl-dīn dūr.* The use here of *istiqbāl*, welcome, attracts attention; does it allude to the universal welcome of lighter nights? or is it reminiscent of Muḥammadan welcome to the Moon's crescent in Shawwāl?

[1900] For an exact statement of the intercalary months *vide* Cunningham's *Indian Eras*, p. 91. In my next sentence (*supra*) the parenthesis-marks indicate blanks left on the page of the Ḥai. MS. as though waiting for information. These and other similar blanks make for the opinion that the Ḥai. Codex is a direct copy of Bābur's draft manuscript.

[1901] The sextuple division (*ṛitu*) of the year is referred to on f. 284, where the Signs Crab and Lion are called the season of the true Rains.

[1902] Bābur appears not to have entered either the Hindī or the Persian names of the week:—the Ḥai. MS. has a blank space; the Elph. MS. had the Persian names only, and Hindī ones have been written in above these; Kehr has the Persian ones only; Ilminsky has added the Hindī ones. (The spelling of the Hindī names, in my translation, is copied from Forbes' Dictionary.)

[1903] The Ḥai. MS. writes *garī* and *garīāl.* The word now stands for the hour of 60 minutes.

[1904] *i.e.* gong-men. The name is applied also to an alligator *Lacertus gangeticus* (Forbes).

[1905] There is some confusion in the text here, the Ḥai. MS. reading *birinj-dīn tīshī*(?) *nīma qūīūbtūrlār*—the Elph. MS. (f. 240*b*) *biring-dīn bīr yāssī nīma qūīūbtūrlār.* The Persian translation, being based on the text of the Elphinstone Codex reads *az biring yak chīz pahnī rekhta and.* The word *tīshī* of the Ḥai. MS. may represent *tasht* plate or *yāssī*, broad; against the latter however there is the sentence that follows and gives the size.

[1906] Here again the wording of the Ḥai. MS. is not clear; the sense however is obvious. Concerning the clepsydra *vide* A. A. Jarrett, ii, 15 and notes; Smith's *Dictionary of Antiquities*; Yule's H.J. *s.n.* Ghurry.

[1907] The table is:—60 *bipals* = 1 *pal*; 60 *pals* = 1 *g'harī* (24 m.); 60 *g'harī* or 8 *pahr* = one *dīn-rāt* (nycthemeron).

[1908] Qorān, cap. CXII, which is a declaration of God's unity.

[1909] The (S.) *ratī* = 8 rice-grains (Eng. 8 barley-corns); the (S.) *māsha* is a kidney-bean; the (P.) *tānk* is about 2 oz.; the (Ar.) *miṣqāl* is equal to 40 *ratīs*; the (S.) *tūla* is about 145 oz.; the (S.) *ser* is of various values (Wilson's *Glossary* and Yule's H. J.).

[1910] There being 40 Bengāl *sers* to the *man*, Bābur's word *mānbān* seems to be another name for the *man* or *maund.* I have not found *mānbān* or *mīnāsā.* At first sight *mānbān* might be taken, in the Ḥai. MS. for (T.) *bātmān*, a weight of 13 or 15 lbs., but this does not suit. Cf. f. 167 note to *bātmān* and f. 173*b* (where, however, in the note f. 157 requires correction to f. 167). For Bābur's table of measures the Pers. trs. has 40 *sers* = 1 *man*; 12 *mans* = 1 *mānī*; 100 *mānī* they call *mīnāsa* (217, f. 201*b*, l. 8).

[1911] Presumably these are caste-names.

[1912] The words in parenthesis appear to be omitted from the text; to add them brings Bābur's remark into agreement with others on what he several times makes note of, *viz.* the absence not only of irrigation-channels but of those which convey "running-waters" to houses and gardens. Such he writes of in Farghāna; such are a well-known charm *e.g.* in Madeira, where the swift current of clear water flowing through the streets, turns into private precincts by side-runlets.

[1913] The Ḥai. MS. writes *lungūtā-dīk*, like a lungūtā, which better agrees with Bābur's usual phrasing. *Lung* is Persian for a cloth passed between the loins, is an equivalent of S. *dhoti*. Bābur's use of it (*infra*) for the woman's (P.) *chaddar* or (S.) *sārī* does not suit the Dictionary definition of its meaning.

[1914] When Erskine published the Memoirs in 1826 AD. he estimated this sum at 1-1/2 millions Sterling, but when he published his *History of India* in 1854, he had made further research into the problem of Indian money values, and judged then that Bābur's revenue was £4,212,000.

[1915] Erskine here notes that the promised details had not been preserved, but in 1854 AD. he had found them in a "paraphrase of part of Bābur", manifestly in Shaikh Zain's work. He entered and discussed them and some matters of money-values in Appendices D. and E. of his *History of India*, vol. I. Ilminsky found them in Kehr's Codex (C. ii, 230). The scribe of the Elph. MS. has entered the revenues of three *sarkārs* only, with his usual quotation marks indicating something extraneous or doubtful. The Ḥai. MS. has them in contents precisely as I have entered them above, but with a scattered mode of setting down. They are in Persian, presumably as they were rendered to Bābur by some Indian official. This official statement will have been with Bābur's own papers; it will have been copied by Shaikh Zain into his own paraphrase. It differs slightly in Erskine's and again, in de Courteille's versions. I regret that I am incompetent to throw any light upon the question of its values and that I must leave some uncertain names to those more expert than myself. Cf. Erskine's Appendices *l.c.* and Thomas' *Revenue resources of the Mughal Empire*. For a few comments *see* App. P.

[1916] Here the Turkī text resumes in the Ḥai. MS.

[1917] Elph. MS. f. 243*b*; W. i. B. I.O. 215 has not the events of this year (as to which omission *vide* note at the beginning of 932 AH. f. 251*b*) and 217 f. 203; Mems. p. 334; Ilminsky's imprint p. 380; *Méms.* ii, 232.

[1918] This should be 30th if Saturday was the day of the week (Gladwin, Cunningham and Bābur's narrative of f. 269). Saturday appears likely to be right; Bābur entered Āgra on Thursday 28th; Friday would be used for the Congregational Prayer and preliminaries inevitable before the distribution of the treasure. The last day of Bābur's narrative 932 AH. is Thursday Rajab 28th; he would not be likely to mistake between Friday, the day of his first Congregational prayer in Āgra, and Saturday. It must be kept in mind that the *Description of Hindūstān* is an interpolation here, and that it was written in 935 AH., three years later than the incidents here recorded. The date Rajab 29th may not be Bābur's own entry; or if it be, may have been made after the interpolation of the dividing mass of the *Description* and made wrongly.

[1919] Erskine estimated these sums as "probably £56,700 to Humāyūn; and the smaller ones as £8,100, £6,480, £5,670 and £4,860 respectively; very large sums for the age". (*History of India*, i. 440 n. and App. E.)

[1920] These will be his daughters. Gul-badan gives precise details of the gifts to the family circle (*Humāyūn-nāma* f. 10).

[1921] Some of these slaves were Sl. Ibrāhīm's dancing-girls (Gul-badan, *ib.*).

[1922] Ar. *ṣada.* Perhaps it was a station of a hundred men. Varsak is in Badakhshān, on the water flowing to Ṯāliqān from the Khwāja Muḥammad range. Erskine read (p. 335) *ṣada Varsak* as *ṣadūr rashk*, incentive to emulation; de C. (ii, 233) translates *ṣada* conjecturally by *circonscription.* Shaikh Zain has Varsak and to the recipients of the gifts adds the "Khwāstīs, people noted for their piety" (A. N. trs. H. B. i, 248 n.). The gift to Varsak may well have been made in gratitude for hospitality received by Bābur in the time of adversity after his loss of Samarkand and before his return to Kābul in 920 AH.

[1923] *circa* 10d. or 11d. Bābur left himself stripped so bare by his far-flung largess that he was nick-named Qalandar (Firishta).

[1924] Badāyūnī says of him (Bib. Ind. ed. i, 340) that he was *kāfir kalīma-gū*, a pagan making the Muḥammadan Confession of Faith, and that he had heard of him, in Akbar's time from Bairām Khān-i-khānan, as kingly in appearance and poetic in temperament. He was killed fighting for Rānā Sangā at Kānwaha.

[1925] This is his family name.

[1926] *i.e.* not acting with Ḥasan *Mīwātī.*

[1927] Gul-badan says that the Khwāja several times asked leave on the ground that his constitution was not fitted for the climate of Hindūstān;

that His Majesty was not at all, at all, willing for him to go, but gave way at length to his importunity.

[1928] in Patiāla, about 25 miles s.w. of Aṃbāla.

[1929] Shaikh Zain, Gul-badan and Erskine write Nau-kār. It was now that Khwāja Kalān conveyed money for the repair of the great dam at Ghaznī (f. 139).

[1930] The friends did not meet again; that their friendship weathered this storm is shewn by Bābur's letter of f. 359. The *Abūshqa* says the couplet was inscribed on a marble tablet near the *Ḥauẓ-i-khāṣ* at the time the Khwāja was in Dihlī after bidding Bābur farewell in Āgra.

[1931] This quatrain is in the Rāmpūr *Dīwān* (*q.v.* index). The *Abūshqa* quotes the following as Khwāja Kalān's reply, but without mentioning where the original was found. Cf. de Courteille, Dict. *s.n. taskarī.* An English version is given in my husband's article *Some verses by the Emperor Bābur* (A. Q. R. January, 1911).

You shew your gaiety and your wit,

In each word there lie acres of charm.

Were not all things of Hind upside-down,

How could you in the heat be so pleasant on cold?

It is an old remark of travellers that everything in India is the opposite of what one sees elsewhere. Tīmūr is said to have remarked it and to have told his soldiers not to be afraid of the elephants of India, "For," said he, "Their trunks are empty sleeves, and they carry their tails in front; in Hindustan everything is reversed" (H. Beveridge *ibid.*). Cf. App. Q.

[1932] Badāyūnī i, 337 speaks of him as unrivalled in music.

[1933] f. 267*b*.

[1934] *aūrūq*, which here no doubt represents the women of the family.

[1935] *'ain parganalār.*

[1936] Bābur's advance, presumably.

[1937] The full amounts here given are not in all MSS., some scribes contenting themselves with the largest item of each gift (*Memoirs* p. 337).

[1938] The 'Id of Shawwāl, it will be remembered, is celebrated at the conclusion of the Ramẓān fast, on seeing the first new moon of Shawwāl. In A.H. 932 it must have fallen about July 11th 1526 (Erskine).

[1939] A square shawl, or napkin, of cloth of gold, bestowed as a mark of rank and distinction (*Memoirs* p. 338 n.); *une tunique enrichie de broderies* (*Mémoires*, ii, 240 n.).

[1940] *kamar-shamshīr.* This Steingass explains as sword-belt, Erskine by "sword with a belt". The summary following shews that many weapons were given and not belts alone. There is a good deal of variation in the MSS. The Ḥai. MS. has not a complete list. The most all the lists show is that gifts were many.

[1941] f. 263*b*.

[1942] over the Ganges, a little above Anūp-shahr in the Buland-shahr district.

[1943] A seeming omission in the text is made good in my translation by Shaikh Zain's help, who says Qāsim was sent to Court.

[1944] This quatrain is in the Rāmpūr *Dīwān.* It appears to pun on Bīāna and *bī(y)ān.*

[1945] Kandār is in Rājpūtāna; Abū'l-faẓl writes Kuhan-dār, old habitation.

[1946] This is the first time Bābur's begs are called amīrs in his book; it may be by a scribe's slip.

[1947] Chandwār is on the Jumna, between Āgra and Etāwah.

[1948] Here *āqār-sūlār* will stand for the waters which flow—sometimes in marble channels—to nourish plants and charm the eye, such for example as beautify the Tāj-maḥal pleasaunce.

[1949] Index *s.n.* The *tālār* is raised on pillars and open in front; it serves often for an Audience-hall (Erskine).

[1950] *tāsh 'imārat,* which may refer to the extra-mural location of the house, or contrast it with the inner *khilwat-khāna*, the women's quarters, of the next sentence. The point is noted as one concerning the use of the word *tāsh* (Index *s.n.*). I have found no instance in which it is certain that Bābur uses *tāsh*, a stone or rock, as an adjective. On f. 301 he writes *tāshdīn 'imārat*, house-of-stone, which the Persian text renders by *'imārat-i-sangīn.* Wherever *tāsh* can be translated as meaning outer, this accords with Bābur's usual diction.

[1951] *bāghcha* (Index *s.n.*). That Bābur was the admitted pioneer of orderly gardens in India is shewn by the 30th *Āyīn*, On Perfumes:—"After the foot-prints of Firdaus-makānī (Bābur) had added to the glory of Hindūstān, embellishment by avenues and landscape-gardening was seen, while heart-expanding buildings and the sound of falling-waters widened the eyes of beholders."

[1952] Perhaps *gaz*, each somewhat less than 36 inches.

[1953] The more familiar Indian name is *baoli*. Such wells attracted Peter Mundy's attention; Yule gives an account of their names and plan (Mundy's *Travels in Asia*, Hakluyt Society, ed. R. C. Temple, and Yule's *Hobson Jobson s.n.* Bowly). Bābur's account of his great *wāīn* is not easy to translate; his interpreters vary from one another; probably no one of them has felt assured of translating correctly.

[1954] *i.e.* the one across the river.

[1955] *tāsh masjid*; this, unless some adjectival affix (*e.g. dīn*) has been omitted by the scribe, I incline to read as meaning extra, supplementary, or outer, not as "mosque-of-stone".

[1956] or Jājmāwa, the old name for the sub-district of Kānhpūr (Cawnpur).

[1957] *i.e.* of the Corps of Braves.

[1958] Dilmāū is on the left bank of the Ganges, s.e. from Bareilly (Erskine).

[1959] *Marv-nīng bundī-nī bāghlāb*, which Erskine renders by "Having settled the revenue of Merv", and de Courteille by, "*Aprés avoir occupé Merv*." Were the year's revenues compressed into a 40 to 50 days collection?

[1960] *i.e.* those who had part in his brother's murder. Cf. Niẓāmu'd-dīn Aḥmad's *Ṭabaqāt-i-akbarī* and the *Mīrat-i-sikandarī* (trs. *History of Gujrat* E. C. Bayley).

[1961] Elph. MS. f. 252; W.-i-B. I.O. 215 f. 199b and 217 f. 208*b*; Mems. p. 343.

[1962] *sīūnchī* (Zenker). Fārūq was Māhīm's son; he died in 934 A.H. before his father had seen him.

[1963] *ṣalaḥ*. It is clear from the "*tāsh-awī*" (Pers. trs. *khāna-i-sang*) of this mortar (*qāzān*) that stones were its missiles. Erskine notes that from Bābur's account cannon would seem sometimes to have been made in parts and clamped together, and that they were frequently formed of iron bars strongly compacted into a circular shape. The accoutrement (*ṣalaḥ*) presumably was the addition of fittings.

[1964] About £40,000 sterling (Erskine).

[1965] The MSS. write Ṣafar but it seems probable that Muḥarram should be substituted for this; one ground for not accepting Ṣafar being that it breaks the consecutive order of dates, another that Ṣafar allows what seems a long time for the journey from near Dilmāū to Āgra. All MSS. I have seen give the 8th as the day of the month but Erskine has 20th. In this part of Bābur's writings dates are sparse; it is a narrative and not a diary.

[1966] This phrase, foreign to Bābur's diction, smacks of a Court-Persian milieu.

[1967] Here the Elph. MS. has Ṣafar Muḥarram (f. 253), as has also I.O. 215 f. 200b, but it seems unsafe to take this as an *al Ṣafarānī* extension of Muḥarram because Muḥ.-Ṣafar 24th was not a Wednesday. As in the passage noted just above, it seems likely that Muḥarram is right.

[1968] Cf. f. 15*b* note to Qaṃbar-i-'alī. The title *Akhta-begī* is to be found translated by "Master of the Horse", but this would not suit both uses of *akhta* in the above sentence. Cf. Shaw's Vocabulary.

[1969] *i.e.* Tahangaṛh in Karauli, Rājpūtāna.

[1970] Perhaps *sipāhī* represents Hindūstānī foot-soldiers.

[1971] Rafī'u-d-dīn *Ṣafawī*, a native of Ĭj near the Persian Gulf, teacher of Abū'l-faẓl's father and buried near Āgra (*Āyīn-i-akbarī*).

[1972] This phrase, again, departs from Bābur's simplicity of statement.

[1973] About £5,000 (Erskine).

[1974] About £17,500 (Erskine).

[1975] Ḥai. MS. and 215 f. 201b, Hastī; Elph. MS. f. 254, and Ilminsky, p. 394, Aīmīshchī; *Memoirs*, p. 346, Imshiji, so too *Mémoires*, ii, 257.

[1976] About £5000 (Erskine). Bīānwān lies in the *sūbah* of Āgra.

[1977] Cf. f. 175 for Bābur's estimate of his service.

[1978] Cf. f. 268*b* for Bābur's clemency to him.

[1979] Firishta. (Briggs ii, 53) mentions that Asad had gone to Ṭahmāsp from Kābul to congratulate him on his accession. Shāh Ismā'īl had died in 930 AH. (1524 AD.); the title Shāh-zāda is a misnomer therefore in 933 AH.—one possibly prompted by Ṭahmāsp's youth.

[1980] The letter is likely to have been written to Māhīm and to have been brought back to India by her in 935 AH. (f. 380*b*). Some MSS. of the Pers. trs. reproduce it in Turkī and follow this by a Persian version; others omit the Turkī.

[1981] Turkī, *būā.* Hindī *bawā* means sister or paternal-aunt but this would not suit from Bābur's mouth, the more clearly not that his epithet for the offender is *bad-bakht.* Gul-badan (H.N. f. 19) calls her "ill-omened demon".

[1982] She may have been still in the place assigned to her near Āgra when Bābur occupied it (f. 269).

[1983] f. 290. Erskine notes that the *tūla* is about equal in weight to the silver *rūpī.*

[1984] It appears from the kitchen-arrangements detailed by Abū'l-faẓl, that before food was dished up, it was tasted from the pot by a cook and a subordinate taster, and next by the Head-taster.

[1985] The Turkī sentences which here follow the well-known Persian proverb, *Rasīda būd balāī walī ba khair guzasht*, are entered as verse in some MSS.; they may be a prose quotation.

[1986] She, after being put under contribution by two of Bābur's officers (f. 307*b*) was started off for Kābul, but, perhaps dreading her reception there, threw herself into the Indus in crossing and was drowned. (Cf. A.N. trs. H. Beveridge *Errata* and *addenda* p. xi for the authorities.)

[1987] *gil makhtūm*, Lemnian earth, *terra sigillata*, each piece of which was impressed, when taken from the quarry, with a guarantee-stamp (Cf. Ency. Br. *s.n.* Lemnos).

[1988] *tiriāq-i-fārūq*, an antidote.

[1989] Index *s.n.*

[1990] Kāmrān was in Qandahār (Index *s.n.*). Erskine observes here that Bābur's omission to give the name of Ibrāhīm's son, is noteworthy; the son may however have been a child and his name not known to or recalled by Bābur when writing some years later.

[1991] f. 299*b*.

[1992] The *Āyīn-i-akbarī* locates this in the *sarkār* of Jūn-pūr, a location suiting the context. The second Persian translation ('Abdu'r-raḥīm's) has here a scribe's skip from one "news" to another (both asterisked in my text); hence Erskine has an omission.

[1993] This is the Chār-bāgh of f. 300, known later as the Rām (Arām)-bāgh (Garden-of-rest).

[1994] Presumably he was coming up from Marwār.

[1995] This name varies; the Ḥai. MS. in most cases writes Qismatī, but on f. 267*b*, Qismatāī; the Elph. MS. on f. 220 has Q:s:mnāī; De Courteille writes Qismī.

[1996] *artkāb qīldī*, perhaps drank wine, perhaps ate opium-confections to the use of which he became addicted later on (Gulbadan's *Humāyūn-nāma* f. 30*b* and 73*b*).

[1997] *furṣatlār*, *i.e.* between the occupation of Āgra and the campaign against Rānā Sangā.

[1998] Apparently the siege Bābur broke up in 931 AH. had been renewed by the Aūzbegs (f. 255*b* and Trs. Note *s.a.* 931 AH. section *c*).

[1999] These places are on the Khulm-river between Khulm and Kāhmard. The present tense of this and the following sentences is Babur's.

[2000] f. 261.

[2001] Erskine here notes that if the *ser* Bābur mentions be one of 14 *tūlas*, the value is about £27; if of 24 *tūlas*, about £45.

[2002] T. *chāpdūq*. Cf. the two Persian translations 215 f. 205*b* and 217 f. 215; also Ilminsky, p. 401.

[2003] *būlghān chīrīkī*. The Rānā's forces are thus stated by Tod (*Rājastān; Annals of Marwār* Cap. ix):—"Eighty thousand horse, 7 Rajas of the highest rank, 9 Raos, and 104 chieftains bearing the titles of Rawul and Rawut, with 500 war-elephants, followed him into the field." Bābur's army, all told, was 12,000 when he crossed the Indus from Kābul; it will have had accretions from his own officers in the Panj-āb and some also from other quarters, and will have had losses at Pānipat; his reliable kernel of fighting-strength cannot but have been numerically insignificant, compared with the Rājpūt host. Tod says that almost all the princes of Rājastān followed the Rānā at Kanwā.

[2004] *dūrbātūr*. This is the first use of the word in the *Bābur-nāma*; the defacer of the Elph. Codex has altered it to *aūrātūr*.

[2005] Shaikh Zain records [Abū'l-faẓl also, perhaps quoting from him] that Bābur, by varying diacritical points, changed the name Sīkrī to Shukrī in sign of gratitude for his victory over the Rānā. The place became the Fatḥpūr-sīkrī of Akbar.

[2006] Erskine locates this as 10 to 12 miles n.w. of Bīāna.

[2007] This phrase has not occurred in the B.N. before; presumably it expresses what has not yet been expressed; this Erskine's rendering, "each according to the speed of his horse," does also. The first Persian translation, which in this portion is by Muḥammad-qulī *Mughūl Ḥiṣārī*, translates by *az dambal yak dīgar* (I.O. 215, f. 205*b*); the second, 'Abdu'r-rāḥīm's, merely reproduces the phrase; De Courteille (ii, 272) appears to render it by (amirs) *que je ne nomme pas*. If my reading of Ṭāhir-tibrī's failure be correct (*infra*), Erskine's translation suits the context.

[2008] The passage cut off by my asterisks has this outside interest that it forms the introduction to the so-called "Fragments", that is, to certain Turkī matter not included in the standard *Bābur-nāma*, but preserved with the Kehr—Ilminsky—de Courteille text. As is well-known in Bāburiana, opinion has varied as to the genesis of this matter; there is now no doubt that it is a translation into Turkī from the (*Persian*) *Akbar-nāma*, prefaced by the above-asterisked passage of the *Bābur-nāma* and continuous (with slight omissions) from Bib. Ind. ed. i, 106 to 120 (trs. H. Beveridge i, 260 to 282). It covers the time from before the battle of Kanwā to the end of Abū'l-faẓl's description of Bābur's death, attainments and Court; it has been made to seem Bābur's own, down to his death-bed, by changing the third person of A.F.'s narrative into the autobiographical first person. (Cf. Ilminsky, p. 403 l. 4 and p. 494; *Mémoires* ii, 272 and 443 to 464; JRAS. 1908, p. 76.)

A minute point in the history of the B.N. manuscripts may be placed on record here; *viz*. that the variants from the true *Bābur-nāma* text which occur in the Kehr-Ilminsky one, occur also in the corrupt Turkī text of I.O. No. 214 (JRAS 1900, p. 455).

[2009] *chāpār kūmak yītmās*, perhaps implying that the speed of his horses was not equal to that of Muḥibb-i-'alī's. Translators vary as to the meaning of the phrase.

[2010] Erskine and de Courteille both give Mustafa the commendation the Turkī and Persian texts give to the carts.

[2011] According to Tod's *Rājastān*, negotiations went on during the interval, having for their object the fixing of a frontier between the Rānā and Bābur. They were conducted by a "traitor" Ṣalaḥ'd-dīn *Tūār* the chief of Raisin, who moreover is said to have deserted to Bābur during the battle.

[2012] Cf. f. 89 for Bābur's disastrous obedience to astrological warning.

[2013] For the reading of this second line, given by the good MSS. *viz*. *Tauba ham bī maza nīst, bachash*, Ilminsky (p. 405) has *Tauba ham bī maza, mast bakhis*, which de Courteille [II, 276] renders by, "*O ivrogne insensé! que ne goûtes-tu aussi à la pénitence?*" The Persian couplet seems likely to be a quotation and may yet be found elsewhere. It is not in the Rāmpūr Dīwān which contains the Turkī verses following it (E. D. Ross p. 21).

[2014] *kīchmāklīk*, to pass over (to exceed?), to ford or go through a river, whence to transgress. The same metaphor of crossing a stream occurs, in connection with drinking, on f. 189*b*.

[2015] This line shews that Bābur's renouncement was of wine only; he continued to eat confections (*ma'jūn*).

[2016] Cf. f. 186*b*. Bābur would announce his renunciation in Dīwān; there too the forbidden vessels of precious metals would be broken. His few words leave it to his readers to picture the memorable scene.

[2017] This night-guard (*'asas*) cannot be the one concerning whom Gul-badan records that he was the victim of a little joke made at his expense by Bābur (H. N. Index *s.n.*). He seems likely to be the Ḥājī Muḥ. *'asas* whom Abū'l-faẓl mentions in connection with Kāmrān in 953 AH. (1547 AD.). He may be the *'asas* who took charge of Bābur's tomb at Āgra (cf. Gul-badan's H. N. *s.n.* Muḥ. 'Alī *'asas ṭaghāī*, and *Akbar-nāma* trs. i, 502).

[2018] *saqālī qīrqmāqta u qūīmāqta.* Erskine here notes that "a vow to leave the beard untrimmed was made sometimes by persons who set out against the infidels. They did not trim the beard till they returned victorious. Some vows of similar nature may be found in Scripture", *e.g.* II Samuel, cap. 19 v. 24.

[2019] Index *s.n.* The *tamghā* was not really abolished until Jahāngīr's time—if then (H. Beveridge). See Thomas' *Revenue Resources of the Mughal Empire.*

[2020] There is this to notice here:—Bābur's narrative has made the remission of the *tamghā* contingent on his success, but the *farmān* which announced that remission is dated some three weeks before his victory over Rānā Sangā (Jumāda II, 13th-March 16th). Manifestly Bābur's remission was absolute and made at the date given by Shaikh Zain as that of the *farmān*. The *farmān* seems to have been despatched as soon as it was ready, but may have been inserted in Bābur's narrative at a later date, together with the preceding paragraph which I have asterisked.

[2021] "There is a lacuna in the Turkī copy" (*i.e.* the Elphinstone Codex) "from this place to the beginning of the year 935. Till then I therefore follow only Mr. Metcalfe's and my own Persian copies" (Erskine).

[2022] I am indebted to my husband for this revised version of the *farmān*. He is indebted to M. de Courteille for help generally, and specially for the references to the Qorān (*q.v. infra*).

[2023] The passages in italics are Arabic in the original, and where traced to the Qorān, are in Sale's words.

[2024] *Qorān, Sūrah* XII, v. 53.

[2025] *Sūrah* LVII, v. 21.

[2026] *Sūrah* LVII, v. 15.

[2027] *Sūrah* VII, v. 140.

[2028] *Sūrah* II, v. 185.

[2029] These may be self-conquests as has been understood by Erskine (p. 356) and de Courteille (ii. 281) but as the Divine "acceptance" would seem to Bābur vouched for by his military success, "victories" may stand for his success at Kanwā.

[2030] *Sūrah* II, 177 where, in Sale's translation, the change referred to is the special one of altering a legacy.

[2031] The words *dīgūchī* and *yīgūchī* are translated in the second *Wāqi'āt-i-bāburī* by *sukhan-gūī* and [*wīlāyat*]-*khwār.* This ignores in them the future element supplied by their component *gū* which would allow them to apply to conditions dependent on Bābur's success. The Ḥai. MS. and Ilminsky read *tīgūchī*, supporter- or helper-to-be, in place of the *yīgūchī*, eater-to-be I have inferred from the *khwār* of the Pers. translation; hence de Courteille writes "*amīrs auxquels incombait l'obligation de raffermir le gouvernement*". But Erskine, using the Pers. text alone, and thus having *khwār* before him, translates by, "amīrs who enjoyed the wealth of kingdoms." The two Turkī words make a depreciatory "jingle", but the first one, *dīgūchī*, may imply serious reference to the duty, declared by Muḥammad to be incumbent upon a wazīr, of reminding his sovereign "when he forgetteth his duty". Both may be taken as alluding to dignities to be attained by success in the encounter from which wazīrs and amīrs were shrinking.

[2032] Firdausī's *Shāh-nāma* [Erskine].

[2033] Also Chand-wāl; it is 25 m. east of Āgra and on the Jamna [*Ṭabaqāṭ-i-nāṣirī*, Raverty, p. 742 n.9]

[2034] Probably, Overthrower of the rhinoceros, but if *Gurg-andāz* be read, of the wolf.

[2035] According to the Persian calendar this is the day the Sun enters Aries.

[2036] The practical purpose of this order of march is shewn in the account of the battle of Pānīpat, and in the Letter of Victory, f. 319.

[2037] *kurohcha*, perhaps a short *kuroh*, but I have not found Bābur using *cha* as a diminutive in such a case as *kurohcha.*

[2038] or Kānūa, in the Bīānā district and three marches from Bīāna-town. "It had been determined on by Rānā Sangrām Sīngh (*i.e.* Sangā) for the northern limit of his dominions, and he had here built a small palace." Tod thus describes Bābur's foe, "Sangā Rānā was of the middle stature, and of great muscular strength, fair in complexion, with unusually large eyes which appear to be peculiar to his descendants. He exhibited at his death but the fragments of a warrior: one eye was lost in the broil with his brother, an arm in action with the Lodī kings of Dehlī, and he was a cripple owing to a limb being broken by a cannon-ball in another; while he counted 80 wounds from the sword or the lance on various parts of his body" (Tod's *Rājastān*, cap. Annals of Mewār).

[2039] Here M. de C. has the following note (ii, 273 n.); it supplements my own of f. 264 [n. 3]. "*Le mot arāba, que j'ai traduit par chariot est pris par M. Leyden*" (this should be Erskine) "*dans le sens de 'gun', ce que je ne crois pas exact; tout au plus signifierait-il affût*" (gun-carriage). "*Il me parait impossible d'admettre que Bāber eût à sa disposition une artillerie attelée aussi considérable. Ces arāba pouvaient servir en partie à transporter des pièces de campagne, mais ils avaient aussi une autre destination, comme on le voit par la suite du récit.*" It does not appear to me that Erskine *translates* the word *arāba* by the word *gun*, but that the *arābas* (all of which he took to be gun-carriages) being there, he supposed the guns. This was not correct as the various passages about carts as defences show (cf. Index *s.nn. arāba* and carts).

[2040] It is characteristic of Bābur that he reproduces Shaikh Zain's *Fatḥ-nāma*, not because of its eloquence but because of its useful details. Erskine and de Courteille have the following notes concerning Shaikh Zain's *farmān*:—"Nothing can form a more striking contrast to the simple, manly and intelligent style of Baber himself, than the pompous, laboured periods of his secretary. Yet I have never read this Firmān to any native of India who did not bestow unlimited admiration on the official bombast of Zeineddin, while I have met with none but turks who paid due praise to the calm simplicity of Baber" [Mems. p. 359]. "*Comme la précédente (farmān), cette pièce est rédigée en langue persane et offre un modèle des plus accomplis du style en usage dans les chancelleries orientales. La traduction d'un semblable morceau d'éloquence est de la plus grande difficulté, si on veut être clair, tout en restant fidèle à l'original.*"

Like the Renunciation *farmān*, the Letter-of-victory with its preceding sentence which I have asterisked, was probably inserted into Bābur's narrative somewhat later than the battle of Kānwa. Hence Bābur's pluperfect-tense "had indited". I am indebted to my husband for help in revising the difficult *Fatḥ-nāma*; he has done it with consideration of the variants between the earlier English and the French translations. No doubt it could be dealt with more searchingly still by one well-versed in the Qorān and the Traditions, and thus able to explain others of its allusions. The italics denote Arabic passages in the original; many of these are from the Qorān, and in tracing them M. de Courteille's notes have been most useful to us.

[2041] Qorān, cap. 80, last sentence.

[2042] Shaikh Zain, in his version of the *Bābur-nāma*, styles Bābur Nawāb where there can be no doubt of the application of the title, *viz.* in describing Shāh Ṭahmāsp's gifts to him (mentioned by Bābur on f. 305). He uses the title also in the *farmān* of renunciation (f. 313*b*), but it does not appear in my text, "royal" (fortune) standing for it (*in loco* p. 555, l. 10).

[2043] The possessive pronoun occurs several times in the Letter-of-victory. As there is no semblance of putting forward that letter as being Bābur's, the pronoun seems to imply "on our side".

[2044] The *Bābur-nāma* includes no other than Shaikh Zain's about Kanwā. Those here alluded to will be the announcements of success at Milwat, Pānīpat, Dībālpūr and perhaps elsewhere in Hindūstān.

[2045] In Jūn-pūr (*Āyīn-i-akbarī*); Elliot & Dowson note (iv, 283-4) that it appears to have included, near Sikandarpūr, the country on both sides of the Gogra, and thence on that river's left bank down to the Ganges.

[2046] That the word Nawāb here refers to Bābur and not to his lieutenants, is shewn by his mention (f. 278) of Sangā's messages to himself.

[2047] Qorān, cap. 2, v. 32. The passage quoted is part of a description of Satan, hence mention of Satan in Shaikh Zain's next sentence.

[2048] The brahminical thread.

[2049] *khār-i-miḥnat-i-irtidād dar dāman*. This Erskine renders by "who fixed thorns from the pangs of apostacy in the hem of their garments" (p. 360). Several good MSS. have *khār*, thorn, but Ilminsky has Ar. *khimār*, cymar, instead (p. 411). De Courteille renders the passage by "*portent au pan de leurs habits la marque douloureuse de l'apostasie*" (ii, 290). To read *khimār*, cymar (scarf), would serve, as a scarf is part of some Hindū costumes.

[2050] Qorān, cap. 69, v. 35.

[2051] M. Defrémery, when reviewing the French translation of the B.N. (*Journal des Savans* 1873), points out (p. 18) that it makes no mention of the "blessed ten". Erskine mentions them but without explanation. They are the *'asharah mubash-sharah*, the decade of followers of Muḥammad who "received good tidings", and whose certain entry into Paradise he foretold.

[2052] Qorān, cap. 3, v. 20. M. Defrémery reads Shaikh Zain to mean that these words of the Qorān were on the infidel standards, but it would be simpler to read Shaikh Zain as meaning that the infidel insignia on the standards "denounce punishment" on their users.

[2053] He seems to have been a Rājpūt convert to Muḥammadanism who changed his Hindī name Silhādī for what Bābur writes. His son married Sangā's daughter; his fiefs were Raisin and Sārangpūr; he deserted to Bābur in the battle of Kānwa. (Cf. Erskine's *History of India* i, 471 note; *Mirāt-i-sikandarī*, Bayley's trs. *s.n.*; *Akbar-nāma*, H.B.'s trs. i, 261; Tod's *Rājastān* cap. Mewār.)

[2054] "Dejāl or al Masih al Dajjal, the false or lying Messiah, is the Muhammadan Anti-christ. He is to be one-eyed, and marked on the forehead with the letters K.F.R. signifying Kafer, or Infidel. He is to appear in the latter days riding on an ass, and will be followed by 70,000 Jews of Ispahān, and will continue on the Earth 40 days, of which one will be equal to a year, another to a month, another to a week, and the rest will be common days. He is to lay waste all places, but will not enter Mekka or Medina, which are to be guarded by angels. He is finally to be slain at the gate of Lud by Jesus, for whom the Musalmans profess great veneration, calling him the breath or spirit of God.—See Sale's *Introductory Discourse to the Koran*" [Erskine].

[2055] Qorān, cap. 29, v. 5.

[2056] "This alludes to the defeat of [an Abyssinian Christian] Abraha the prince of Yemen who [in the year of Muḥammad's birth] marched his army and some elephants to destroy the *ka'ba* of Makka. 'The Meccans,' says Sale, 'at the appearance of so considerable a host, retired to the neighbouring mountains, being unable to defend their city or temple. But God himself undertook the defence of both. For when Abraha drew near to Mecca, and would have entered it, the elephant on which he rode, which was a very large one and named Maḥmūd, refused to advance any nigher to the town, but knelt down whenever they endeavoured to force him that way, though he would rise and march briskly enough if they turned him towards any other quarter; and while matters were in this posture, on a sudden a large flock of birds, like swallows, came flying from the sea-coast, every-one of which carried three stones, one in each foot and one in its bill; and these stones they threw down upon the heads of Abraha's men, certainly killing every one they struck.' The rest were swept away by a flood or perished by a plague, Abraha alone reaching Senaa, where he also died"

[Erskine]. The above is taken from Sale's note to the 105 chapter of the Qorān, entitled "the Elephant".

[2057] Presumably black by reason of their dark large mass.

[2058] Presumably, devouring as fire.

[2059] This is 50 m. long and blocked the narrow pass of the Caspian Iron-gates. It ends south of the Russian town of Dar-band, on the west shore of the Caspian. Erskine states that it was erected to repress the invasions of Yajuj and Mujuj (Gog and Magog).

[2060] Qorān, cap. lxi, v. 4.

[2061] Qorān, cap. ii, v. 4. Erskine appears to quote another verse.

[2062] Qorān, cap. xlviii, v. 1.

[2063] Index *s.n.*

[2064] *Khirad*, Intelligence or the first Intelligence, was supposed to be the guardian of the empyreal heaven (Erskine).

[2065] Chīn-tīmūr *Chīngīz-khānid Chaghatāī* is called Bābur's brother because a (maternal-) cousin of Bābur's own generation, their last common ancestor being Yūnas Khān.

[2066] Sulaimān *Tīmūrid Mīrān-shāhī* is called Bābur's son because his father was of Bābur's generation, their last common ancestor being Sl. Abū-sa'id Mīrzā. He was 13 years old and, through Shāh Begīm, hereditary shāh of Badakhshān.

[2067] The Shaikh was able, it would appear, to see himself as others saw him, since the above description of him is his own. It is confirmed by Abū'l-faẓl and Badāyūnī's accounts of his attainments.

[2068] The honourable post given to this amīr of Hind is likely to be due to his loyalty to Bābur.

[2069] Aḥmad may be a nephew of Yūsuf of the same agnomen (Index *s.nn.*).

[2070] I have not discovered the name of this old servant or the meaning of his seeming-sobriquet, Hindū. As a *qūchīn* he will have been a Mughūl or Turk. The circumstance of his service with a son of Maḥmūd *Mīrān-shāhī* (down to 905 AH.) makes it possible that he drew his name in his youth from the tract s.e. of Maḥmūd's Ḥiṣār territory which has been known as Little Hind (Index *s.n.* Hind). This is however conjecture merely. Another suggestion is that as *hindū* can mean *black*, it may stand for the common *qarā* of the Turks, *e.g.* Qarā Barlās, Black Barlās.

[2071] I am uncertain whether Qarā-qūzī is the name of a place, or the jesting sobriquet of more than one meaning it can be.

[2072] Soul-full, animated; var. Ḥai. MS. *khān-dār.* No agnomen is used for Asad by Bābur. The *Akbar-nāma* varies to *jāmadār*, wardrobe-keeper, cup-holder (*Bib. Ind.* ed. i, 107), and Firishta to *sar-jāmadar*, head wardrobe-keeper (lith. ed. p. 209 top). It would be surprising to find such an official sent as envoy to 'Irāq, as Asad was both before and after he fought at Kānwa.

[2073] son of Daulat Khān *Yūsuf-khail Lūdī.*

[2074] These are the titles of the 20th and 36th chapters of the Qorān; Sale offers conjectural explanations of them. The "family" is Muḥammad's.

[2075] a Bāī-qarā Tīmūrid of Bābur's generation, their last common ancestor being Tīmūr himself.

[2076] an Aūzbeg who married a daughter of Sl. Ḥusain M. *Bāī-qarā.*

[2077] It has been pointed out to me that there is a Chinese title of nobility *Yūn-wāng*, and that it may be behind the words *jang-jang*. Though the suggestion appears to me improbable, looking to the record of Bābur's officer, to the prevalence of sobriquets amongst his people, and to what would be the sporadic appearance of a Chinese title or even class-name borne by a single man amongst them. I add this suggestion to those of my note on the meaning of the words (Index *s.n.* Muḥ. 'Alī). The title *Jūn-wāng* occurs in Dr. Denison Ross' *Three MSS. from Kāshghar*, p. 5, v. 5 and translator's preface, p. 14.

[2078] Cf. f. 266 and f. 299. *Yārāgī* may be the name of his office, (from *yārāq*) and mean provisioner of arms or food or other military requirements.

[2079] or, Tardī *yakka*, the champion, Gr. *monomachus* (A. N. trs. i, 107 n.).

[2080] var. 1 watch and 2 *g'harīs*; the time will have been between 9 and 10 a.m.

[2081] *jūldū ba nām al 'azīz-i-barādar shud*, a phrase not easy to translate.

[2082] *viz.* those chained together as a defence and probably also those conveying the culverins.

[2083] The comparison may be between the darkening smoke of the fire-arms and the heresy darkening pagan hearts.

[2084] There appears to be a distinction of title between the *akhta-begī* and the *mīr-akhwūr* (master of the horse).

[2085] Qorān, cap. 14, v. 33.

[2086] These two men were in one of the flanking-parties.

[2087] This phrase "our brother" would support the view that Shaikh Zain wrote as for Bābur, if there were not, on the other hand, mention of Bābur as His Majesty, and the precious royal soul.

[2088] *dīwānīān* here may mean those associated with the wazīr in his duties: and not those attending at Court.

[2089] Qorān, cap. 14, v. 52.

[2090] Index *s.n. chuhra* (a brave).

[2091] *hizabrān-i-besha yakrangī*, literally, forest-tigers (or, lions) of one hue.

[2092] There may be reference here to the chains used to connect the carts into a defence.

[2093] The braves of the *khāṣa tābīn* were part of Bābur's own centre.

[2094] perhaps the cataphract elephants; perhaps the men in mail.

[2095] Qorān, cap. 101, v. 54.

[2096] Qorān, cap. 101, v. 4.

[2097] *bā andākhtan-i-sang u ẓarb-ẓan tufak bisyārī.* As Bābur does not in any place mention metal missiles, it seems safest to translate *sang* by its plain meaning of *stone.*

[2098] Also, metaphorically, swords.

[2099] *tīr.* My husband thinks there is a play upon the two meanings of this word, arrow and the planet Mercury; so too in the next sentence, that there may be allusion in the *kuākib ṣawābit* to the constellation Pegasus, opposed to Bābur's squadrons of horse.

[2100] The Fish mentioned in this verse is the one pictured by Muḥammadan cosmogony as supporting the Earth. The violence of the fray is illustrated by supposing that of Earth's seven climes one rose to Heaven in dust, thus giving Heaven eight. The verse is from Firdausī's *Shāh-nāma*, [Turner-Macan's ed. i, 222]. The translation of it is Warner's, [ii, 15 and n.]. I am indebted for the information given in this note to my husband's long search in the *Shāh-nāmā.*

[2101] Qorān, cap. 3, v. 133.

[2102] Qorān, cap. 61, v. 13.

[2103] Qorān, cap. 48, v. 1.

[2104] Qorān, cap. 48, v. 3.

[2105] [see p. 572] *farāsh*. De Courteille, reading *firāsh*, translates this metaphor by *comme un lit lorsqu'il est défait*. He refers to Qorān, cap. 101, v. 3. A better metaphor for the breaking up of an army than that of moths scattering, one allowed by the word *farāsh*, but possibly not by Muḥammad, is *vanished like bubbles on wine*.

[2106] Bāgar is an old name for Dungarpūr and Bānswāra [*G. of I.* vi, 408 *s.n.* Bānṣwāra].

[2107] *sic*, Ḥai. MS. and may be so read in I.O. 217 f. 220*b*; Erskine writes Bikersi (p. 367) and notes the variant Nagersi; Ilminsky (p. 421) N:krsī; de Courteille (ii. 307) Niguersi.

[2108] Cf. f. 318*b*, and note, where it is seen that the stones which killed the lords of the Elephants were so small as to be carried in the bill of a bird like a swallow. Were such stones used in matchlocks in Bābur's day?

[2109] *guzāran*, var. *gurazān*, caused to flee and hogs (Erskine notes the double-meaning).

[2110] This passage, entered in some MSS. as if verse, is made up of Qorān, cap. 17, v. 49, cap. 33, v. 38, and cap. 3, v. 122.

[2111] As the day of battle was Jumāda II. 13th (March 16th), the *Fatḥ-nāma* was ready and dated twelve days after that battle. It was started for Kābul on Rajab 9th (April 11th). Something may be said here appropriately about the surmise contained in Dr. Ilminsky's Preface and M. de Courteille's note to *Mémoires* ii, 443 and 450, to the effect that Bābur wrote a plain account of the battle of Kanwā and for this in his narrative substituted Shaikh Zain's *Fatḥ-nāma*, and that the plain account has been preserved in Kehr's *Bābur-nāma* volume [whence Ilminsky reproduced it, it was translated by M. de Courteille and became known as a "Fragment" of Bāburiana]. Almost certainly both scholars would have judged adversely of their suggestion by the light of to-day's easier research. The following considerations making against its value, may be set down:—

(1) There is no sign that Bābur ever wrote a plain account of the battle or any account of it. There is against his doing so his statement that he inserts Shaikh Zain's *Fatḥ-nāma* because it gives particulars. If he had written any account, it would be found preceding the *Fatḥ-nāma*, as his account of his renunciation of wine precedes Shaikh Zain's *Farmān* announcing the act.

(2) Moreover, the "Fragment" cannot be described as a plain account such as would harmonize with Bābur's style; it is in truth highly rhetorical, though less so as Shaikh Zain's.

(3) The "Fragment" begins with a quotation from the *Bābur-nāma* (f.310*b* and n.), skips a good deal of Bābur's matter preliminary to the battle, and passes on with what there can be no doubt is a translation in inferior Turkī of the *Akbar-nāma* account.

(4) The whole of the extra matter is seen to be continuous and not fragmentary, if it is collated with the chapter in which Abū'l-faẓl describes the battle, its sequel of events, the death, character, attainments, and Court of Bābur. Down to the death, it is changed to the first person so as to make Bābur seem to write it. The probable concocter of it is Jahāngīr.

(5) If the Fragment were Bābur's composition, where was it when 'Abdu-r-raḥīm translated the *Bābur-nāma* in 998 AH.-1590 AD.; where too did Abū'l-faẓl find it to reproduce in the *Akbar-nāma*?

(6) The source of Abū'l-faẓl's information seems without doubt to be Bābur's own narrative and Shaikh Zain's *Fatḥ-nāma.* There are many significant resemblances between the two rhetoricians' metaphors and details selected.

(7) A good deal might be said of the dissimilarities between Bābur's diction and that of the "Fragment". But this is needless in face of the larger and more circumstantial objections already mentioned.

(For a fuller account of the "Fragment" see JRAS. Jan. 1906 pp. 81, 85 and 1908 p. 75 ff.)

[2112] *Ṭughrā* means an imperial signature also, but would Bābur sign Shaikh Zain's *Fatḥ-i-nāma*? His autograph verse at the end of the *Rāmpūr Dīwān* has his signature following it. He is likely to have signed this verse. Cf. App. Q. [Erskine notes that titles were written on the back of despatches, an unlikely place for the quatrain, one surmises.]

[2113] This is in the *Rāmpūr dīwān* (E.D.R. Plate 17). Dr. E. Denison Ross points out (p. 17 n.) that in the 2nd line the Ḥai. Codex varies from the *Dīwān.* The MS. is wrong; it contains many inaccuracies in the latter part of the Hindūstān section, perhaps due to a change of scribe.

[2114] These words by *abjad* yield 933. From Bābur's use of the pluperfect tense, I think it may be inferred that (my) Sections *a* and *b* are an attachment to the *Fatḥ-nāma*, entered with it at a somewhat later date.

[2115] My translation of this puzzling sentence is tentative only.

[2116] This statement shews that the Dībālpūr affair occurred in one of the B.N. gaps, and in 930 AH. The words make 330 by *abjad.* It may be noted here that on f. 312*b* and notes there are remarks concerning whether Bābur's remission of the *tamghā* was contingent on his winning at Kānwa. If the remission had been delayed until his victory was won, it would have found fitting mention with the other sequels of victory chronicled above; as it is not with these sequels, it may be accepted as an absolute remission, proclaimed before the fight. The point was a little uncertain owing to the seemingly somewhat deferred insertion in Bābur's narrative of Shaikh Zain's *Farmān*.

[2117] *dā'ira*, presumably a defended circle. As the word *aūrdū* [bracketed in the text] shows, Bābur used it both for his own and for Sangā's camps.

[2118] Hence the Rānā escaped. He died in this year, not without suspicion of poison.

[2119] *aīchīmnī khālī qīldīm*, a seeming equivalent for English, "I poured out my spleen."

[2120] var. *malūk* as *e.g.* in I.O. 217 f.225*b*, and also elsewhere in the *Bābur-nāma.*

[2121] On f. 315 the acts attributed to Iliās Khān are said to have been done by a "mannikin called Rustam Khān". Neither name appears elsewhere in the B.N.; the hero's name seems a sarcasm on the small man.

[2122] Bābur so-calls both Ḥasan and his followers, presumably because they followed their race sympathies, as of Rājpūt origin, and fought against co-religionists. Though Ḥasan's subjects, Meos, were nominally Muḥammadans, it appears that they practised some Hindu customs. For an account of Mīwāt, see *Gazetteer of Ulwur* (Alwar, Alūr) by Major P. W. Powlett.

[2123] Alwar being in Mīwāt, Bābur may mean that bodies were found beyond that town in the main portion of the Mīwāt country which lies north of Alwar towards Dihlī.

[2124] Major Powlett speaking (p. 9) of the revenue Mīwāt paid to Bābur, quotes Thomas as saying that the coins stated in Bābur's Revenue Accounts, *viz.* 169,810,00 *tankas* were probably Sikandarī *tankas*, or Rs. 8,490,50.

[2125] This word appears to have been restricted in its use to the Khān-zādas of the ruling house in Mīwāt, and was not used for their subjects, the Meos (Powlett *l.c.* Cap. I.). The uses of "Mīwātī" and "Meo" suggest something analogous with those of "Chaghatāī" and "Mughūl" in Bābur's time. The resemblance includes mutual dislike and distrust (Powlett *l.c.*).

[2126] *qīlūrlār aīkān dūr.* This presumptive past tense is frequently used by the cautious Bābur. I quote it here and in a few places near-following because it supports Shaw's statement that in it the use of *aīkān* (*īkān*) reduces the positive affirmation of the perfect to presumption or rumour. With this statement all grammarians are not agreed; it is fully supported by the *Bābur-nāma.*

[2127] Contrast here is suggested between Sulṭāns of Dihlī & Hind; is it between the greater Turks with whom Bābur classes himself immediately below as a conqueror of Hind, and the Lūdī Sulṭāns of Dihlī?

[2128] The strength of the Tijāra hills towards Dihlī is historical (Powlett *l.c.* p. 132).

[2129] This is one of the names of the principal river which flows eastwards to the south of Alwar town; other names are Bārah and Rūparel. Powlett notes that it appears in Thorn's Map of the battle of Laswarree (1803 AD.), which he reproduces on p. 146. But it is still current in Gurgaon, with also a variant Mānas-le, man-killer (*G. of Gurgaon* 1910 AD. ivA, p.6).

[2130] *aūltūrūrlār aīkān dūr*, the presumptive past tense.

[2131] f.308.

[2132] *qīlghān aīkān dūr*, the presumptive past tense.

[2133] *Sulṭān ātīghā juldū būlūb*; Pers. trs. *Juldū ba nām-i Sulṭān shud.* The *juldū* guerdon seems to be apart from the fief and allowance.

[2134] f. 315.

[2135] Bābur does not record this detail (f. 315).

[2136] f. 298*b* and f. 328*b*. Ja'far is mentioned as Mahdī's son by Gul-badan and in the *Ḥabību's-siyar* iii, 311, 312.

[2137] f. 388*b*.

[2138] The town of Fīrūzpūr is commonly known as Fīrūzpūr-jhirka (Fīrūzpūr of the spring), from a small perennial stream which issues from a number of fissures in the rocks bordering the road through a pass in the Mīwāt hills which leads from the town *viâ* Tijāra to Rewārī (*G. of Gurgaon*, p. 249). In Abū'l-faẓl's day there was a Hindū shrine of Mahadeo near the spring, which is still a place of annual pilgrimage. The Kūtila lake is called Kotla-*jhil* in the *G. of G.* (p. 7). It extends now 3 m. by 2-1/2 m. varying in size with the season; in Abū'l-faẓl's day it was 4 *kos* (8 m.) round. It lies partly in the district of Nūh, partly in Gurgaon, where the two tracts join at the foot of the Alwar hills.

[2139] This is the frequently mentioned size for reservoirs; the measure here is probably the *qārī*, *cir.* a yard.

[2140] Bābur does not state it as a fact known to himself that the Mānas-nī falls into the Kūtila lake; it did so formerly, but now does not, tradition assigning a cause for the change (*G. of G.* p. 6). He uses the hear-say tense, *kīrār aimīsh.*

[2141] Kharī and Toda were in Akbar's *sarkār* of Rantaṃbhor.

[2142] Bhosāwar is in Bhurtpūr, and Chausa (or Jūsa) may be the Chausath of the *Āyīn-i-akbarī*, ii, 183.

[2143] As has been noted frequently, this phrase stands for artificial water-courses.

[2144] Certainly Trans-Hindū-kush lands; presumably also those of Trans-Indus, Kābul in chief.

[2145] *aūstī;* perhaps the reservoir was so built as to contain the bubbling spring.

[2146] *Chūn jā'ī khẉush karda ām.*

[2147] f. 315.

[2148] var. Janwār (Jarrett). It is 25 m. east of Āgra on the Muttra-Etāwa road (*G. of I.*).

[2149] *kūcha-band,* perhaps a barricade at the limit of a suburban lane.

[2150] This has been mentioned already (f. 327).

[2151] f. 315.

[2152] *i.e.* those professedly held for Bābur.

[2153] Or, according to local pronunciation, Badāyūn.

[2154] This is the old name of Shāhābād in Rāmpūr (*G. of I.* xxii, 197). The *A.-i-A.* locates it in Saṃbal. Cf. E. and D.'s *History of India*, iv, 384 n. and v. 215 n.

[2155] Perhaps the one in Sītapūr.

[2156] f. 305*b.*

[2157] As the Elphinstone Codex which is the treasure-house of Humāyūn's notes, has a long *lacuna* into which this episode falls, it is not known if the culprit entered in his copy of the *Bābur-nāma* a marginal excuse for his misconduct (cf. f. 252 and n.); such excuse was likely to be that he knew he would be forgiven by his clement father.

[2158] f. 305*b.*

[2159] Kāmrān would be in Qandahār. Erskine notes that the sum sent to him would be about £750, but that if the coins were rūpīs, it would be £30,000.

[2160] *qiṭa'*, for account of which form of poem *see* Blochmann's translations of Saifī's and Jāmī's *Prosody*, p. 86.

[2161] *Rāmpūr Dīwān* (E. D. Ross' ed. p. 16 and Plate 14*a*). I am uncertain as to the meaning of ll. 4 and 10. I am not sure that what in most MSS. ends line 4, *viz. aūl dam*, should not be read as *aūlūm*, death; this is allowed by Plate 14a where for space the word is divided and may be *aūlūm*. To read *aūlūm* and that the deserters fled from the death in Hind they were anxious about, has an answering phrase in "we still are alive". Ll. 9 and 10 perhaps mean that in the things named all have done alike. [Ilminsky reads *khāir nafsī* for the elsewhere *ḥazz-nafsī*.]

[2162] These are 20 attitudes (*rak'ah*) assumed in prayer during Ramẓān after the Bed-time Prayer. The ablution (*ghusl*) is the bathing of the whole body for ceremonial purification.

[2163] This Feast is the 'Id-i-fiṭr, held at the breaking of the Ramẓān Fast on the 1st of Shawwāl.

[2164] Erskine notes that this is the earliest mention of playing-cards he can recall in oriental literature.

[2165] f. 339*b*.

[2166] The two varieties mentioned by Bābur seem to be *Diospyrus melanoxylon*, the wood of which is called *tindu abnūs* in Hindūstānī, and *D. tomentosa*, Hindi, *tindu* (Brandis *s.nn.*). Bārī is 19 m. west of Dūlpūr.

[2167] *mī'ād*, perhaps the time at which the Shaikh was to appear before Bābur.

[2168] The Pers. trs. makes the more definite statement that what had to be read was a Section of the Qoran (*wird*). This was done with remedial aim for the illness.

[2169] As this statement needs comment, and as it is linked to matters mentioned in the *Rāmpūr Dīwān*, it seems better to remit remarks upon it to Appendix Q, *Some matters concerning the Rāmpūr Dīwān.*

[2170] *risāla. See* Appendix Q.

[2171] Elph. MS. *lacuna*; I.O. 215 *lacuna* and 217 f. 229; Mems. p. 373. This year's narrative resumes the diary form.

[2172] There is some uncertainty about these names and also as to which adversary crossed the river. The sentence which, I think, shews, by its plural verb, that Humāyūn left two men and, by its co-ordinate participles, that it was they crossed the river, is as follows:—(Darwīsh and Yūsuf, understood) *Quṯb Sīrwānī-nī u bīr pāra rājalār-nī bīr daryā aūtūb aūrūshūb yakshī bāsīb tūrlār. Aūtūb*, *aūrūshūb* and *bāsīb* are grammatically referable to the same subject, [whatever was the fact about the crossing].

[2173] *bīr daryā*; W.-i-B. 217 f. 229, *yak daryā*, one river, but many MSS. *har daryā*, every river. If it did not seem pretty certain that the rebels were not in the Miyān-dū-āb one would surmise the river to be "one river" of the two enclosing the tract "between the waters", and that one to be the Ganges. It may be one near Saṃbhal, east of the Ganges.

[2174] var. Shīrwānī. The place giving the cognomen may be Sarwān, a *thakurāt* of the Mālwā Agency (*G. of I.*). Quṯb of Sīrwān may be the Quṯb Khān of earlier mention without the cognomen.

[2175] n.w. of Aligarh (Kūl). It may be noted here, where instances begin to be frequent, that my translation "we marched" is an evasion of the Turkī impersonal "it was marched". Most rarely does Bābur write "we marched", never, "I marched."

[2176] in the Aligarh (Kūl) district; it is the Sikandara Rao of the *A.-i-A.* and the *G. of I.*

[2177] *Rāmpūr Dīwān* (E. D. Ross' ed., p. 19, Plate 16*b*). This *Dīwān* contains other quatrains which, judging from their contents, may well be those Bābur speaks of as also composed in Saṃbal. *See* Appendix Q, *Some matters concerning the Rāmpūr Dīwān.*

[2178] These are aunts of Bābur, daughters of Sl. Abū-sa'īd *Mīrān-shāhī.*

[2179] Sikandarābād is in the Buland-shahr district of the United Provinces.

[2180] It is not clear whether Bābur returned from Sīkrī on the day he started for Jalīsīr; no question of distance would prevent him from making the two journeys on the Monday.

[2181] As this was the rendezvous for the army, it would be convenient if it lay between Āgra and Anwār; as it was 6 m. from Āgra, the only mapped place having approximately the name Jalīsīr, *viz.* Jalesar, in Etah, seems too far away.

[2182] Anwār would be suitably the Unwāra of the *Indian Atlas*, which is on the first important southward dip of the Jumna below Āgra. Chandwār is 25 m. east of Āgra, on the Muttra-Etāwah road (*G. of I.*); Jarrett notes that Tiefenthaler identifies it with Fīrūzābād (*A.-i-A.* ii, 183 n.).

[2183] In the district of Kālpī. The name does not appear in maps I have seen.

[2184] *āghā*, Anglicé, uncle. He was Saʿīd Khān of Kāshghar. Ḥaidar M. says Bābā Sl. was a spoiled child and died without mending his ways.

[2185] From Kālpī Bābur will have taken the road to the s.w. near which now runs the Cawnpur (Kānhpūr) branch of the Indian Midland Railway, and he must have crossed the Betwa to reach Īrij (Irich, *Indian Atlas*, Sheet 69 N.W.).

[2186] Leaving Īrij, Bābur will have recrossed the Betwa and have left its valley to go west to Bāndīr (Bhander) on the Pahūj (*Indian Atlas*, Sheet 69 S.W.).

[2187] beneficent, or Muḥassan, comely.

[2188] The one man of this name mentioned in the *B.N.* is an amīr of Sl. Ḥusain *Bāī-qarā*.

[2189] It seems safe to take Kachwa [Kajwa] as the Kajwarra of Ibn Batūta, and the Kadwāha (Kadwaia) of the *Indian Atlas*, Sheet 52 N.E. and of Luard's *Gazetteer of Gwalior* (i, 247), which is situated in 24° 58' N. and 77° 57' E. Each of the three names is of a place standing on a lake; Ibn Batūta's lake was a league (4 m.) long, Bābur's about 11 miles round; Luard mentions no lake, but the *Indian Atlas* marks one quite close to Kadwāha of such form as to seem to have a tongue of land jutting into it from the north-west, and thus suiting Bābur's description of the site of Kachwa. Again,—Ibn Batūta writes of Kajwarra as having, round its lake, idol-temples; Luard says of Kadwāha that it has four idol-temples standing and nine in ruins; there may be hinted something special about Bābur's Kachwa by his remark that he encouraged its people, and this speciality may be interaction between Muḥammadanism and Hindūism serving here for the purpose of identification. For Ibn Batūta writes of the people of Kajwarra that they were *jogīs*, yellowed by asceticism, wearing their hair long and matted, and having Muḥammadan followers who desired to learn their (occult?) secrets. If the same interaction existed in Bābur's day, the Muḥammadan following of the Hindū ascetics may well have been the special circumstance which led him to promise protection to those Hindūs, even when he was out for Holy-war. It has to be remembered of Chandīrī, the nearest powerful neighbour of Kadwāha, that though Bābur's capture makes a vivid picture of Hindūism in it, it had been under Muḥammadan rulers down to a relatively short time before his conquest. The *jogīs* of Kachwa could point to long-standing relations of tolerance by the Chandīrī Governors; this, with their Muḥammadan following, explains the encouragement Bābur gave them, and helps to identify Kachwa with Kajarra. It may be observed that Bābur was familiar with the interaction of the two creeds, witness his "apostates", mostly Muḥammadans following

Hindū customs, witness too, for the persistent fact, the reports of District-officers under the British *Rāj*. Again,—a further circumstance helping to identify Kajwarra, Kachwa and Kadwāha is that these are names of the last important station the traveller and the soldier, as well perhaps as the modern wayfarer, stays in before reaching Chandīrī. The importance of Kajwarra is shewn by Ibn Batūta, and of Kadwāha by its being a *maḥāll* in Akbar's *sarkār* of Bāyawān of the *ṣūba* of Āgra. Again,—Kadwāha is the place nearest to Chandīrī about which Bābur's difficulties as to intermediate road and jungle would arise. That intermediate road takes off the main one a little south of Kadwāha and runs through what looks like a narrow valley and broken country down to Bhamor, Bhurānpūr and Chandīrī. Again,—no bar to identification of the three names is placed by their differences of form, in consideration of the vicissitudes they have weathered in tongue, script, and transliteration. There is some ground, I believe, for surmising that their common source is *kajūr*, the date-fruit. [I am indebted to my husband for the help derived from Ibn Batūta, traced by him in Sanguinetti's trs. iv, 33, and S. Lee's trs. p. 162.]

(Two places similar in name to Kachwa, and situated on Bābur's route *viz.* Kocha near Jhansi, and Kuchoowa north of Kadwāha (Sheet 69 S.W.) are unsuitable for his "Kachwa", the first because too near Bandīr to suit his itinerary, the second because too far from the turn off the main-road mentioned above, because it has no lake, and has not the help in identification detailed above of Kadwāha.)

[2190] *qūrūghīr* which could mean also *reserved* (from the water?).

[2191] *qāzān*. There seems to have been one only; how few Bābur had is shewn again on f. 337.

[2192] *Indian Atlas*, Sheet 52 N.E. near a tributary of the Betwa, the Or, which appears to be Bābur's Burhānpūr-water.

[2193] The bed of the Betwa opposite Chandīrī is 1050 ft. above the sea; the walled-town (*qūrghān*) of Chandīrī is on a table-land 250 ft. higher, and its citadel is 230 ft. higher again (Cunningham's *Archeological Survey Report*, 1871 A.D. ii, 404).

[2194] The plan of Chandīrī illustrating Cunningham's Report (*see* last note) allows surmise about the road taken by Bābur, surmise which could become knowledge if the names of tanks he gives were still known. The courtesy of the Government of India allows me to reproduce that plan [Appendix R, *Chandīrī* and *Gwālīāwar*].

[2195] He is said to have been Governor of Chandīrī in 1513 AD.

[2196] Here and in similar passages the word *m:ljār* or *m:lchār* is found in MSS. where the meaning is that of T. *būljār*. It is not in any dictionary I have seen; Mr. Irvine found it "obscure" and surmised it to mean "approach by trenches", but this does not suit its uses in the *Bābur-nāma* of a military post, and a rendezvous. This surmise, containing, as it does, a notion of protection, links *m:ljār* in sense with Ar. *malja'*. The word needs expert consideration, in order to decide whether it is to be received into dictionaries, or to be rejected because explicable as the outcome of unfamiliarity in Persian scribes with T. *būljār* or, *more Persico* with narrowed vowels, *bŭljăr*. Shaw in his Vocabulary enters *būljāq* (*būljār*?), "a station for troops, a rendezvous, see *malja'*," thus indicating, it would seem, that he was aware of difficulty about *m:ljār* and *būljāq* (*būljār*?). There appears no doubt of the existence of a Turkī word *būljār* with the meanings Shaw gives to *būljāq*; it could well be formed from the root *būl*, being, whence follows, being in a place, posted. *Maljā* has the meaning of a standing-place, as well as those of a refuge and an asylum; both meanings seem combined in the *m:ljār* of f. 336*b*, where for matchlockmen a *m:ljār* was ordered "raised". (Cf. Irvine's *Army of the Indian Moghuls* p. 278.)

[2197] *yāghdā*; Pers. trs. *sar-āshīb*. Bābur's remark seems to show that for effect his mortar needed to be higher than its object. Presumably it stood on the table-land north of the citadel.

[2198] *shātū*. It may be noted that this word, common in accounts of Bābur's sieges, may explain one our friend the late Mr. William Irvine left undecided (*l.c.* p. 278), *viz. shāṭūr*. On p. 281 he states that *nardubān* is the name of a scaling-ladder and that Bābur mentions scaling ladders more than once. Bābur mentions them however always as *shātū*. Perhaps *shāṭūr* which, as Mr. Irvine says, seems to be made of the trunks of trees and to be a siege appliance, is really *shātū u* ... (ladder and ...) as in the passage under note and on f. 216*b*, some other name of an appliance following.

[2199] The word here preceding *tūra* has puzzled scribes and translators. I have seen the following variants in MSS.;—*nūkrī* or *tūkrī*, *b:krī* or *y:krī*, *būkrī* or *yūkrī*, *būkrāī* or *yūkrāī*, in each of which the *k* may stand for *g*. Various suggestions might be made as to what the word is, but all involve reading the Persian enclitic *ī* (forming the adjective) instead of Turkī *līk*. Two roots, *tūg* and *yūg*, afford plausible explanations of the unknown word; appliances suiting the case and able to bear names formed from one or other of these roots are *wheeled mantelet*, and *head-strike* (P. *sar-kob*). That the word is difficult is shewn not only by the variants I have quoted, but by Erskine's reading *naukarī tūra*, "to serve the *tūras*," a requisite not specified earlier by Bābur, and by de Courteille's paraphrase, *tout ce qui est nécessaire aux touras*.

[2200] Sl. Nāṣiru'd-dīn was the Khīljī ruler of Mālwā from 906 to 916 A.H. (1500-1510 AD.).

[2201] He was a Rājpūt who had been prime-minister of Sl. Maḥmūd II. *Khīljī* (son of Nāṣīru'd-dīn) and had rebelled. Bābur (like some other writers) spells his name Mindnī, perhaps as he heard it spoken.

[2202] Presumably the one in the United Provinces. For Shamsābād in Gūālīār *see* Luard *l.c.* i, 286.

[2203] *chīqtī*; Pers. trs. *bar āmad* and, also in some MSS. *namī bar āmad*; Mems. p. 376, "averse to conciliation"; *Méms.* ii, 329, "*s'élevèrent contre cette proposition.*" So far I have not found Bābur using the verb *chīqmāq* metaphorically. It is his frequent verb to express "getting away", "going out of a fort". It would be a short step in metaphor to understand here that Medinī's men "got out of it", *i.e.* what Bābur offered. They may have left the fort also; if so, it would be through dissent.

[2204] f. 332.

[2205] I.O. 217, f. 231, inserts here what seems a gloss, "*Tā īn jā Farsī farmūda*" (*gufta*, said). As Bābur enters his speech in Persian, it is manifest that he used Persian to conceal the bad news.

[2206] The *Illustrated London News* of July 10th, 1915 (on which day this note is written), has an àpropos picture of an ancient fortress-gun, with its stone-ammunition, taken by the Allies in a Dardanelles fort.

[2207] The *dū-tahī* is the *āb-duzd*, water-thief, of f. 67. Its position can be surmised from Cunningham's Plan [Appendix R].

[2208] For Bābur's use of hand (*qūl*) as a military term *see* f. 209.

[2209] His full designation would be Shāh Muḥammad *yūz-begī*.

[2210] This will be flight from the ramparts to other places in the fort.

[2211] Bābur's account of the siege of Chandīrī is incomplete, inasmuch as it says nothing of the general massacre of pagans he has mentioned on f. 272. Khẉāfī Khān records the massacre, saying, that after the fort was surrendered, as was done on condition of safety for the garrison, from 3 to 4000 pagans were put to death by Bābur's troops on account of hostility shewn during the evacuation of the fort. The time assigned to the massacre is previous to the *jūhar* of 1000 women and children and the self-slaughter of men in Medinī Rāo's house, in which he himself died. It is not easy to fit the two accounts in; this might be done, however, by supposing that a folio of Bābur's MS. was lost, as others seem lost at the end of the narrative of this year's events (*q.v.*). The lost folio would tell of the surrender, one clearly affecting the mass of Rājpūt followers and not the chiefs who stood for victory or death and who may have made sacrifice to honour after hearing of the surrender. Bābur's narrative in this part certainly reads less consecutive than is usual with him; something preceding his account of the *jūhar* would improve it, and would serve another purpose also, since mention of the surrender would fix a term ending the now too short time of under one hour he assigns as the duration of the fighting. If a surrender had been mentioned, it would be clear that his "2 or 3 *garīs*" included the attacking and taking of the *dū-tahī* and down to the retreat of the Rājpūts from the walls. On this Bābur's narrative of the unavailing sacrifice of the chiefs would follow in due order. Khwāfī Khān is more circumstantial than Firishta who says nothing of surrender or massacre, but states that 6000 men were killed fighting. Khwāfī Khān's authorities may throw light on the matter, which so far does not hang well together in any narrative, Bābur's, Firishta's, or Khwāfī Khān's. One would like to know what led such a large body of Rājpūts to surrender so quickly; had they been all through in favour of accepting terms? One wonders, again, why from 3 to 4000 Rājpūts did not put up a better resistance to massacre. Perhaps their assailants were Turks, stubborn fighters down to 1915 AD.

[2212] For suggestion about the brevity of this period, *see* last note.

[2213] Clearly, without Bābur's taking part in the fighting.

[2214] These words by *abjad* make 934. The Ḥai. MS. mistakenly writes *Būd Chandīrī* in the first line of the quatrain instead of *Būd chandī*. Khwāfī Khān quotes the quatrain with slight variants.

[2215] *Chandīrī ṭaurī wilāyat* (*dā?*) *wāqi‘ būlūb tūr*, which seems to need *dā*, in, because the fort, and not the country, is described. Or there may be an omission *e.g.* of a second sentence about the walled-town (fort).

[2216] This is the "Kirat-sagar" of Cunningham's Plan of Chandīrī; it is mentioned under this name by Luard (*l.c.* i, 210). "Kirat" represents Kirtī or Kirit Sīngh who ruled in Gūālīār from 1455 to 1479 AD., there also making a tank (Luard, *l.c.* i, 232).

[2217] For illustrative photographs *see* Luard, *l.c.* vol. i, part iv.

[2218] I have taken this sentence to apply to the location of the tanks, but with some doubt; they are on the table-land.

[2219] Bābur appears to have written Betwī, this form being in MSS. I have read the name to be that of the river Betwa which is at a considerable distance from the fort. But some writers dispraise its waters where Bābur praises.

[2220] T. *qīā* means a slope or slant; here it may describe tilted *strata*, such as would provide slabs for roofing and split easily for building purposes. (*See* next note.)

[2221] *'imārat qīlmāq munāsib*. This has been read to mean that the *qīālar* provide good sites (Mems. & *Méms.*), but position, distance from the protection of the fort, and the merit of local stone for building incline me to read the words quoted above as referring to the convenient lie of the stone for building purposes. (*See* preceding note.)

[2222] *Chandīrī-dā judai (jady)-nīng irtiqā'ī yīgīrma-bīsh darja dūr*; Erskine, p. 378, Chanderi is situated in the 25th degree of N. latitude; de Courteille, ii, 334, *La hauteur du Capricorne à Tchanderi est de 25 degrées*. The latitude of Chandīrī, it may be noted, is 24° 43'. It does not appear to me indisputable that what Bābur says here is a statement of latitude. The word *judai* (or *jady*) means both Pole-star and the Sign Capricorn. M. de Courteille translates the quoted sentence as I have done, but with Capricorn for Pole-star. My acquaintance with such expressions in French does not allow me to know whether his words are a statement of latitude. It occurs to me against this being so, that Bābur uses other words when he gives the latitude of Samarkand (f. 44*b*); and also that he has shewn attention to the Pole-star as a guide on a journey (f. 203, where he uses the more common word *Quṭb*). Perhaps he notes its lower altitude when he is far south, in the way he noted the first rise of Canopus to his view (f. 125).

[2223] Mallū Khān was a noble of Mālwā, who became ruler of Mālwā in 1532 or 1533 AD. [?], under the style of Qādir Shāh.

[2224] *i.e.* paid direct to the royal treasury.

[2225] This is the one concerning which bad news reached Bābur just before Chandīrī was taken.

[2226] This presumably is the place offered to Medinī Rāo (f. 333*b*), and Bikramājīt (f. 343).

[2227] Obviously for the bridge.

[2228] *m:ljār* (*see* f. 333 n.). Here the word would mean befittingly a protected standing-place, a refuge, such as matchlockmen used (f. 217 and Index *s.n. arāba*).

[2229] *sīghīrūrdī*, a vowel-variant, perhaps, of *sūghūrūrdī*.

[2230] f. 331*b*. This passage shews that Bābur's mortars were few.

[2231] *nufūr qūl-lār-dīn ham karka bīla rah rawā kīshī u āt aītīlār*, a difficult sentence.

[2232] *Afghānlār kūprūk bāghlāmāq-nī istib'ād qīlīb tamaskhur qīlūrlār aīkāndūr.* The ridicule will have been at slow progress, not at the bridge-making itself, since pontoon-bridges were common (Irvine's *Army of the Indian Moghuls*).

[2233] *tūīlāb*; Pers. trs. *uftān u khezān*, limping, or falling and rising, a translation raising doubt, because such a mode of progression could hardly have allowed escape from pursuers.

[2234] Anglicé, on Friday night.

[2235] According to the Persian calendar, New-year's-day is that on which the Sun enters Aries.

[2236] so-spelled in the Ḥai. MS.; by de Courteille Banguermādū; the two forms may represent the same one of the Arabic script.

[2237] or Gūī, from the context clearly the Gumti. Jarrett gives Godi as a name of the Gumti; Gūī and Godī may be the same word in the Arabic script.

[2238] Some MSS. read that there was not much pain.

[2239] I take this to be the Kali-Sarda-Chauka affluent of the Gogra and not its Sarju or Saru one. To so take it seems warranted by the context; there could be no need for the fords on the Sarju to be examined, and its position is not suitable.

[2240] Unfortunately no record of the hunting-expedition survives.

[2241] One historian, Aḥmad-i-yādgār states in his *Tārīkh-i-salāṭīn-i-afāghina* that Bābur went to Lāhor immediately after his capture of Chandīrī, and on his return journey to Āgra suppressed in the Panj-āb a rising of the Mundāhar (or, Mandhar) Rājpūts. His date is discredited by Bābur's existing narrative of 934 AH. as also by the absence in 935 AH. of allusion to either episode. My husband who has considered the matter, advises me that the Lāhor visit may have been made in 936 or early in 937 AH. [These are a period of which the record is lost or, less probably, was not written.]

[2242] Elph. MS. f. 262; I. O. 215 f. 207b and 217 f. 234*b*; *Mems.* p. 382. Here the Elphinstone MS. recommences after a *lacuna* extending from Ḥai. MS. f. 312*b*.

[2243] *See* Appendix S:—*Concerning the dating of* 935 AH.

[2244] 'Askarī was now about 12 years old. He was succeeded in Multān by his elder brother Kāmrān, transferred from Qandahār [Index; JRAS. 1908 p. 829 para. (1)]. This transfer, it is safe to say, was due to Bābur's resolve to keep Kābul in his own hands, a resolve which his letters to Humāyūn (f. 348), to Kāmrān (f. 359), and to Khwāja Kalān (f. 359) attest, as well as do the movements of his family at this time. What would make the stronger government of Kāmrān seem now more "for the good of Multān" than that of the child 'Askarī are the Bīlūchī incursions, mentioned somewhat later (f. 355*b*) as having then occurred more than once.

[2245] This will be his own house in the Garden-of-eight-paradises, the Chār-bāgh begun in 932 AH. (August 1526 AD.).

[2246] To this name Khwānd-amīr adds Aḥmadu'l-ḥaqīrī, perhaps a pen-name; he also quotes verses of Shihāb's (*Ḥabību's-siyar* lith. ed. iii, 350).

[2247] Khwānd-amīr's account of his going into Hindūstān is that he left his "dear home" (Herāt) for Qandahār in mid-Shawwāl 933 AH. (mid-July 1527 AD.); that on Jumāda I. 10th 934 AH. (Feb. 1st 1528 AD.) he set out from Qandahār on the hazardous journey into Hindūstān; and that owing to the distance, heat, setting-in of the Rains, and breadth of rapid rivers, he was seven months on the way. He mentions no fellow-travellers, but he gives as the day of his arrival in Āgra the one on which Bābur says he presented himself at Court. (For an account of annoyances and misfortunes to which he was subjected under Aūzbeg rule in Herāt *see Journal des Savans*, July 1843, pp. 389, 393, Quatremère's art.)

[2248] Concerning Gūālīār *see* Cunningham's *Archeological Survey Reports* vol. ii; Louis Rousselet's *L'Inde des Rajas*; Lepel Griffin's *Famous Monuments of Central India*, especially for its photographs; *Gazetteer of India*; Luard's *Gazetteer of Gwalior*, text and photographs; *Travels of Peter Mundy*, Hakluyt Society ed. R. C. Temple, ii, 61, especially for its picture of the fort and note (p. 62) enumerating early writers on Gūālīār. Of Persian books there is Jalāl *Ḥiṣārī's Tārīkh-i-Gwālīāwar* (B.M. Add. 16,859) and Hirāman's (B.M. Add. 16,709) unacknowledged version of it, which is of the B.M. MSS. the more legible.

[2249] Perhaps this stands for Gwālīāwar, the form seeming to be used by Jalāl *Ḥiṣārī*, and having good traditional support (Cunningham p. 373 and Luard p. 228).

[2250] *tūshlānīb*, *i.e.* they took rest and food together at mid-day.

[2251] This seems to be the conjoined Gambhīr and Bāngānga which is crossed by the Āgra-Dhūlpūr road (*G. of I.* Atlas, Sheet 34).

[2252] *aīchtūq*, the plural of which shews that more than one partook of the powders (*safūf*).

[2253] T. *tālqān*, Hindī *sattu* (Shaw). M. de Courteille's variant translation may be due to his reading for *tālqān*, *tālghāq*, *flot*, *agitation* (his Dict. *s.n.*) and *yīl*, wind, for *bīla*, with.

[2254] in 933 AH. f. 330*b*.

[2255] "Each beaked promontory" (Lycidas). Our name "Selsey-bill" is an English instance of Bābur's (not infrequent) *tūmshūq*, beak, bill of a bird.

[2256] No order about this Chār-bāgh is in existing annals of 934 AH. Such order is likely to have been given after Bābur's return from his operations against the Afghāns, in his account of which the annals of 934 AH. break off.

[2257] The fort-hill at the northern end is 300 ft. high, at the southern end, 274 ft.; its length from north to south is 1-3/4 m.; its breadth varies from 600 ft. opposite the main entrance (Hātī-pūl) to 2,800 ft. in the middle opposite the great temple (Sās-bhao). Cf. Cunningham p. 330 and Appendix R, *in loco*, for his Plan of Gūālīār.

[2258] This Arabic plural may have been prompted by the greatness and distinction of Mān-sing's constructions. Cf. Index *s.nn. begāt* and *bāghāt*.

[2259] A translation point concerning the (Arabic) word *'imārat* is that the words "palace", "*palais*", and "residence" used for it respectively by Erskine, de Courteille, and, previous to the Hindūstān Section, by myself, are too limited in meaning to serve for Bābur's uses of it in Hindūstān; and this (1) because he uses it throughout his writings for buildings under palatial rank (*e.g.* those of high and low in Chandīrī); (2) because he uses it in Hindūstān for non-residential buildings (*e.g.* for the Bādalgarh outwork, f. 341*b*, and a Hindū temple *ib.*); and (3) because he uses it for the word "building" in the term building-stone, f. 335*b* and f. 339*b*. *Building* is the comprehensive word under which all his uses of it group. For labouring this point a truism pleads my excuse, namely, that a man's vocabulary being characteristic of himself, for a translator to increase or diminish it is to intrude on his personality, and this the more when an autobiography is concerned. Hence my search here (as elsewhere) for an English grouping word is part of an endeavour to restrict the vocabulary of my translation to the limits of my author's.

[2260] Jalāl *Ḥiṣārī* describes "Khwāja Raḥīm-dād" as a paternal-nephew of Mahdī Khwāja. Neither man has been introduced by Bābur, as it is his rule to introduce when he first mentions a person of importance, by particulars of family, *etc.* Both men became disloyal in 935 AH. (1529 AD.) as will be found referred to by Bābur. Jalāl *Ḥiṣārī* supplements Bābur's brief account of their misconduct and Shaikh Muḥammad *Ghauṣ'* mediation in 936 AH. For knowledge of his contribution I am indebted to my husband's perusal of the *Tārīkh-i-Gwālīāwar*.

[2261] Erskine notes that Indians and Persians regard moonshine as cold but this only faintly expresses the wide-spread fear of moon-stroke expressed in the Psalm (121 v. 6), "The Sun shall not smite thee by day, nor the Moon by night."

[2262] *Agarcha lūk balūk u bī sīyāq*. Ilminsky [p. 441] has *balūk balūk* but without textual warrant and perhaps following Erskine, as he says, speaking generally, that he has done in case of need (Ilminsky's Preface). Both Erskine and de Courteille, working, it must be remembered, without the help of detailed modern descriptions and pictures, took the above words to say that the buildings were scattered and without symmetry, but they are not scattered and certainly Mān-sing's has symmetry. I surmise that the words quoted above do not refer to the buildings themselves but to the stones of which they are made. T. *lūk* means heavy, and T. *balūk* [? block] means a thing divided off, here a block of stone. Such blocks might be *bī sīyāq*, *i.e.* irregular in size. To take the words in this way does not contradict known circumstances, and is verbally correct.

[2263] The Rājas' buildings Bābur could compare were Rāja Karna (or Kirtī)'s [who ruled from 1454 to 1479 AD.], Rāja Mān-sing's [1486 to 1516 AD.], and Rāja Bikramājīt's [1516 to 1526 AD. when he was killed at Panīpat].

[2264] The height of the eastern face is 100 ft. and of the western 60 ft. The total length from north to south of the outside wall is 300 ft.; the breadth of the residence from east to west 160 ft. The 300 ft. of length appears to be that of the residence and service-courtyard (Cunningham p. 347 and Plate lxxxvii).

[2265] *kaj bīla āqārītib*. There can be little doubt that a white pediment would show up the coloured tiles of the upper part of the palace-walls more than would pale red sandstone. These tiles were so profuse as to name the building Chīt Mandīr (Painted Mandīr). Guided by Bābur's statement, Cunningham sought for and found plaster in crevices of carved work; from which one surmises that the white coating approved itself to successors of Mān-sing. [It may be noted that the word Mandīr is in the same case for a translator as is *'imārat* (f. 339*b* n.) since it requires a grouping word to cover its uses for temple, palace, and less exalted buildings.]

[2266] The lower two storeys are not only backed by solid ground but, except near the Hātī-pūl, have the rise of ground in front of them which led Bābur to say they were "even in a pit" (*chūqūr*).

[2267] MSS. vary between *har* and *bīr*, every and one, in this sentence. It may be right to read *bīr*, and apply it only to the eastern façade as that on which there were most cupolas. There are fewer on the south side, which still stands (Luard's photo. No. 37).

[2268] The ground rises steeply from this Gate to an inner one, called Hawā-pūl from the rush of air (*hawā*) through it.

[2269] Cunningham says the riders were the Rāja and a driver. Perhaps they were a mahout and his mate. The statue stood to the left on exit (*chīqīsh*).

[2270] This window will have been close to the Gate where no mound interferes with outlook.

[2271] Rooms opening on inner and open courts appear to form the third story of the residence.

[2272] T. *chūqūr*, hollow, pit. This storey is dark and unventilated, a condition due to small windows, absence of through draught, and the adjacent mound. Cunningham comments on its disadvantages.

[2273] *Agarcha Hindūstānī takallufiār qīlīb tūrlār walī bī hawālīk-rāq yīrlār dūr.* Perhaps amongst the pains taken were those demanded for *punkhas*. I regret that Erskine's translation of this passage, so superior to my own in literary merit, does not suit the Turkī original. He worked from the Persian translation, and not only so, but with a less rigid rule of translation than binds me when working on Bābur's *ipsissima verba* (*Mems.* p. 384; Cunningham p. 349; Luard p. 226).

[2274] The words *aūrtā dā* make apt contrast between the outside position of Mān-sing's buildings which helped to form the fort-wall, and Bikramājīt's which were further in except perhaps one wall of his courtyard (see Cunningham's Plate lxxxiii).

[2275] Cunningham (p. 350) says this was originally a *bāra-dūrī*, a twelve-doored open hall, and must have been light. His "originally" points to the view that the hall had been altered before Bābur saw it but as it was only about 10 years old at that time, it was in its first form, presumably. Perhaps Bābur saw it in a bad light. The dimensions Cunningham gives of it suggest that the high dome must have been frequently ill-lighted.

[2276] The word *tālār*, having various applications, is not easy to match with a single English word, nor can one be sure in all cases what it means, a platform, a hall, or *etc.* To find an equivalent for its diminutive *tālār-ghina* is still more difficult. Raḥīm-dād's *tālār*-ette will have stood on the flat centre of the dome, raised on four pillars or perhaps with its roof only so-raised; one is sure there would be a roof as protection against sun or moon. It may be noted that the dome is not visible outside from below, but is hidden by the continuation upwards of walls which form a mean-looking parallelogram of masonry.

[2277] *T. tūr yūl.* Concerning this hidden road *see* Cunningham p. 350 and Plate lxxxvii.

[2278] *bāghcha.* The context shews that the garden was for flowers. For Bābur's distinctions between *bāghcha*, *bāgh* and *baghāt*, *see* Index *s.nn.*

[2279] *shaft-ālū i.e.* the rosy colour of peach-flowers, perhaps lip-red (Steingass). Bābur's contrast seems to be between those red oleanders of Hindūstān that are rosy-red, and the deep red ones he found in Gūālīār.

[2280] *kul*, any large sheet of water, natural or artificial (Bābur). This one will be the Sūraj-kund (Sun-tank).

[2281] This is the Telī Mandīr, or Telingana Mandīr (Luard). Cf. Cunningham, p. 356 and Luard p. 227 for accounts of it; and *G. of I. s.n.* Telīagarhi for Telī Rājas.

[2282] This is a large outwork reached from the Gate of the same name. Bābur may have gone there specially to see the Gūjarī Mandīr said by Cunningham to have been built by Mān-sing's Gūjar wife Mṛiga-nayāna (fawn-eyed). Cf. Cunningham p. 351 and, for other work done by the same Queen, in the s. e. corner of the fort, p. 344; Luard p. 226. In this place "construction" would serve to translate *'imārat* (f. 340 n.).

[2283] *āb-duzd*, a word conveying the notion of a stealthy taking of the water. The walls at the mouth of Urwā were built by Altamsh for the protection of its water for the fort. The date Bābur mentions (a few lines further) is presumably that of their erection.

[2284] Cunningham, who gives 57 ft. as the height of this statue, says Bābur estimated it at 20 *gaz*, or 40 ft., but this is not so. Bābur's word is not *gaz* a measure of 24 fingers-breadth, but *qārī*, the length from the tip of the shoulder to the fingers-ends; it is about 33 inches, not less, I understand. Thus stated in *qārīs* Bābur's estimate of the height comes very near Cunningham's, being a good 55 ft. to 57 ft. (I may note that I have usually translated *qārī* by "yard", as the yard is its nearest English equivalent. The Pers. trs. of the B. N. translates by *gaz*, possibly a larger *gaz* than that of 24 fingers-breadth *i.e.* inches.)

[2285] The statues were not broken up by Bābur's agents; they were mutilated; their heads were restored with coloured plaster by the Jains (Cunningham p. 365; Luard p. 228).

[2286] *rozan* [or, *aūz:n*] ... *tafarruj qīlīb.* Neither Cunningham nor Luard mentions this window, perhaps because Erskine does not; nor is this name of a Gate found. It might be that of the Dhonda-paur (Cunningham, p. 339). The 1st Pers. trs. [I.O. 215 f. 210] omits the word *rozan* (or, *auz:n*); the 2nd [I.O. 217 f. 236b] renders it by *jā'ī*, place. Manifestly the Gate was opened by Bābur, but, presumably, not precisely at the time of his visit. I am inclined to understand that *rozan* ... *tafarruj karda* means enjoying the window formerly used by Muḥammadan rulers. If *aūz:n* be the right reading, its sense is obscure.

[2287] This will have occurred in the latter half of 934 AH. of which no record is now known.

[2288] He is mentioned under the name Asūk Mal *Rājpūt*, as a servant of Rānā Sangā by the *Mirāt-i-sikandarī*, lith. ed. p. 161. In Bayley's Translation p. 273 he is called Awāsūk, manifestly by clerical error, the sentence being *az jānib-i-au Asūk Mal Rājpūt dar ān (qila') būda....*

[2289] *ātā-līk, aūghūl-līk*, *i.e.* he spoke to the son as a father, to the mother as a son.

[2290] The *Mirāt-i-sikandarī* (lith. ed. p. 234, Bayley's trs. p. 372) confirms Bābur's statement that the precious things were at Bikramājīt's disposition. Perhaps they had been in his mother's charge during her husband's life. They were given later to Bahādur Shāh of Gujrāt.

[2291] The Telī Mandīr has not a cupola but a waggon-roof of South Indian style, whence it may be that it has the southern name Telingana, suggested by Col. Luard.

[2292] See Luard's Photo. No. 139 and P. Mundy's sketch of the fort p. 62.

[2293] This will be the Ghargarāj-gate which looks south though it is not at the south end of the fort-hill where there is only a postern approached by a flight of stone steps (Cunningham p. 332).

[2294] The garden will have been on the lower ground at the foot of the ramp and not near the Hātī-pūl itself where the scarp is precipitous.

[2295] *Mūndīn kīchīkrāq ātlānīlghān aīkāndūr.* This may imply that the distance mentioned to Bābur was found by him an over-estimate. Perhaps the fall was on the Mūrar-river.

[2296] Rope (Shaw); *corde qui sert à attacher le bagage sur les chameaux* (de Courteille); a thread of 20 cubits long for weaving (Steingass); I have the impression that an *arghamchī* is a horse's tether.

[2297] For information about this opponent of Bābur in the battle of Kānwa, *see* the *Asiatic Review*, Nov. 1915, H. Beveridge's art. *Silhadī, and the Mirāt-i-sikandarī.*

[2298] Colonel Luard has suggested to us that the Bābur-nāma word Sūkhjana may stand for Salwai or Sukhalhari, the names of two villages near Gūālīār.

[2299] Presumably of night, 6-9 p.m., of Saturday Muḥ. 18th-Oct. 2nd.

[2300] f. 330*b* and f. 339*b*.

[2301] Between the last explicit date in the text, *viz*. Sunday, Muḥ. 19th, and the one next following, *viz*. Saturday, Ṣafar 3rd, the diary of six days is wanting. The gap seems to be between the unfinished account of doings in Dhūlpūr and the incomplete one of those of the Monday of the party. For one of the intermediate days Bābur had made an appointment, when in Gūālīār (f. 343), with the envoys of Bikramājīt, the trysting-day being Muḥ. 23rd (*i.e.* 9 days after Muḥ. 14th). Bābur is likely to have gone to Bīāna as planned; that envoys met him there may be surmised from the circumstance that when negociations with Bikramājīt were renewed in Āgra (f. 345), two sets of envoys were present, a "former" one and a "later" one, and this although all envoys had been dismissed from Gūālīār. The "former" ones will have been those who went to Bīāna, were not given leave there, but were brought on to Āgra; the "later" ones may have come to Āgra direct from Ranthaṃbhor. It suits all round to take it that pages have been lost on which was the record of the end of the Dhūlpūr visit, of the journey to the, as yet unseen, fort of Bīāna, of tryst kept by the envoys, of other doings in Bīāna where, judging from the time taken to reach Sīkrī, it may be that the *ma'jūn* party was held.

[2302] Anglicé, Tuesday after 6 p.m.

[2303] *aghaz aīchīb nīma yīb*, which words seem to imply the breaking of a fast.

[2304] Doubtless the garden owes its name to the eight heavens or paradises mentioned in the Qurān (Hughes' *Dictionary of Islām s.n.* Paradise). Bābur appears to have reached Āgra on the 1st of Ṣafar; the 2nd may well have been spent on the home affairs of a returned traveller.

[2305] The great, or elder trio were daughters of Sl. Abū-sa'īd Mīrzā, Bābur's paternal-aunts therefore, of his dutiful attendance on whom, Gul-badan writes.

[2306] "Lesser," *i.e.* younger in age, lower in rank as not being the daughters of a sovereign Mīrzā, and held in less honour because of a younger generation.

[2307] Gul-badan mentions the arrival in Hindūstān of a khānīm of this name, who was a daughter of Sl. Maḥmūd Khān *Chaghatāī*, Bābur's maternal-uncle; to this maternal relationship the word *chīcha* (mother) may refer. *Yīnkā*, uncle's or elder brother's wife, has occurred before (ff. 192, 207), *chīcha* not till now.

[2308] Cf. f. 344*b* and n.5 concerning the surmised movements of this set of envoys.

[2309] This promise was first proffered in Gūālīār (f.343).

[2310] These may be Bāī-qarā kinsfolk or Mīrān-shāhīs married to them. No record of Shāh Qāsim's earlier mission is preserved; presumably he was sent in 934 AH. and the record will have been lost with much more of that year's. Khwānd-amīr may well have had to do with this second mission, since he could inform Bābur of the discomfort caused in Herī by the near leaguer of 'Ubaidu'l-lāh *Aūzbeg.*

[2311] *Albatta aūzūmīznī har nu' qīlīb tīgūrkūmīz dūr.* The following versions of this sentence attest its difficulty:—*Wāqi'āt-i-bāburī*, 1st trs. I.O. 215 f. 212, *albatta khūdrā ba har nū'ī ka bāshad dar ān khūb khwāhīm rasānad*; and 2nd trs. I.O. 217 f. 238*b*, *albatta dar har nu' karda khūdrā mī rasānīm*; *Memoirs* p. 388, "I would make an effort and return in person to Kābul"; *Mémoires* ii, 356, *je ferais tous mes efforts pour pousser en avant.* I surmise, as Pāyanda-i-ḥasan seems to have done (1st Pers. trs. *supra*), that the passage alludes to Bābur's aims in Hindūstān which he expects to touch in the coming spring. What seems likely to be implied is what Erskine says and more, *viz.* return to Kābul, renewal of conflict with the Aūzbeg and release of Khurāsān kin through success. As is said by Bābur immediately after this, Ṭahmāsp of Persia had defeated 'Ubaidu'l-lah *Aūzbeg* before Bābur's letter was written.

[2312] *Sīmāb yīmāknī bunyād qīldīm*, a statement which would be less abrupt if it followed a record of illness. Such a record may have been made and lost.

[2313] The preliminaries to this now somewhat obscure section will have been lost in the gap of 934 AH. They will have given Bābur's instructions to Khwāja Dost-i-khāwand and have thrown light on the unsatisfactory state of Kābul, concerning which a good deal comes out later, particularly in Bābur's letter to its Governor Khwāja Kalān. It may be right to suppose that Kāmrān wanted Kābul and that he expected the Khwāja to bring him an answer to his request for it, whether made by himself or for him, through some-one, his mother perhaps, whom Bābur now sent for to Hindūstān.

[2314] 934 AH.-August 26th 1528 AD.

[2315] The useful verb *tībrāmāk* which connotes agitation of mind with physical movement, will here indicate anxiety on the Khwāja's part to fulfil his mission to Humāyūn.

[2316] Kāmrān's messenger seems to repeat his master's words, using the courteous imperative of the 3rd person plural.

[2317] Though Bābur not infrequently writes of *e.g.* Bengalīs and Aūzbegs and Turks in the singular, the Bengalī, the Aūzbeg, the Turk, he seems here to mean 'Ubaidu'l-lāh, the then dominant Aūzbeg, although Kūchūm was Khāqān.

[2318] This muster preceded defeat near Jām of which Bābur heard some 19 days later.

[2319] Humāyūn's wife was Bega Begīm, the later Ḥājī Begīm; Kāmrān's bride was her cousin perhaps named Māh-afrūz (Gul-badan's *Humāyūn-nāma* f. 64*b*). The hear-say tense used by the messenger allows the inference that he was not accredited to give the news but merely repeated the rumour of Kābul. The accredited bearer-of-good-tidings came later (f. 346*b*).

[2320] There are three enigmatic words in this section. The first is the Sayyid's cognomen; was he *daknī*, rather dark of hue, or *zaknī*, one who knows, or *ruknī*, one who props, erects scaffolding, *etc.*? The second mentions his occupation; was he a *ghaiba-gar*, diviner (Erskine, water-finder), a *jība-gar*, cuirass-maker, or a *jībā-gar*, cistern-maker, which last suits with well-making? The third describes the kind of well he had in hand, perhaps the stone one of f. 353*b*; had it scaffolding, or was it for drinking-water only (*khwāralīq*); had it an arch, or was it chambered (*khwāzalīq*)? If Bābur's orders for the work had been preserved,—they may be lost from f. 344*b*, trouble would have been saved to scribes and translators, as an example of whose uncertainty it may be mentioned that from the third word (*khwāralīq*?) Erskine extracted "jets d'eau and artificial water-works", and de Courteille "*taillé dans le roc vif*".

[2321] All Bābur's datings in Ṣafar are inconsistent with his of Muḥarram, if a Muḥarram of 30 days [as given by Gladwin and others].

[2322] *ḥarārat*. This Erskine renders by "so violent an illness" (p. 388), de Courteille by "*une inflammation d'entrailles*" (ii, 357), both swayed perhaps by the earlier mention, on Muḥ. 10th, of Bābur's medicinal quick-silver, a drug long in use in India for internal affections (Erskine). Some such ailment may have been recorded and the record lost (f. 345*b* and n. 8), but the heat, fever, and trembling in the illness of Ṣafar 23rd, taken with the reference to last's year's attack of fever, all point to climatic fever.

[2323] *aīndīnī* (or, *āndīnī*). Consistently with the readings quoted in the preceding note, E. and de C. date the onset of the fever as Sunday and translate *aīndīnī* to mean "two days after". It cannot be necessary however to specify the interval between Friday and Sunday; the text is not explicit; it seems safe to surmise only that the cold fit was less severe on Sunday; the fever had ceased on the following Thursday.

[2324] Anglicé, Monday after 6 p.m.

[2325] The *Rashaḥāt-i-'aīnu'l-ḥayāt* (Tricklings from the fountain of life) contains an interesting and almost contemporary account of the Khwāja and of his *Wālidiyyah-risāla.* A summary of what in it concerns the Khwāja can be read in the JRAS. Jan. 1916, H. Beveridge's art. The tract, so far as we have searched, is now known in European literature only through Bābur's metrical translation of it; and this, again, is known only through the *Rāmpūr Dīwān.* [It may be noted here, though the topic belongs to the beginning of the *Bābur-nāma* (f. 2), that the *Rashaḥāt* contains particulars about Aḥrārī's interventions for peace between Bābur's father 'Umar Shaikh and those with whom he quarrelled.]

[2326] "Here unfortunately, mr. Elphinstone's Turki copy finally ends" (Erskine), that is to say, the Elphinstone Codex belonging to the Faculty of Advocates of Edinburgh.

[2327] This work, Al-buṣīrī's famous poem in praise of the Prophet, has its most recent notice in M. René Basset's article of the *Encyclopædia of Islām* (Leyden and London).

[2328] Bābur's technical terms to describe the metre he used are, *ramal musaddas makhbūn 'arūẓ* and *ẓarb gāh abtar gāh makhbūn muhẓūf waẓn.*

[2329] *aūtkān yīl (u) har maḥal mūndāq 'āriẓat kīm būldī,* from which it seems correct to omit the *u* (and), thus allowing the reference to be to last year's illnesses only; because no record, of any date, survives of illness lasting even one full month, and no other year has a *lacuna* of sufficient length unless one goes improbably far back: for these attacks seem to be of Indian climatic fever. One in last year (934 AH.) lasting 25-26 days (f. 331) might be called a month's illness; another or others may have happened in the second half of the year and their record be lost, as several have been lost, to the detriment of connected narrative.

[2330] Mr. Erskine's rendering (*Memoirs* p. 388) of the above section shows something of what is gained by acquaintance which he had not, with the *Rashaḥāt-i-'āinu'l-ḥayāt* and with Bābur's versified *Wālidiyyah-risāla.*

[2331] This gap, like some others in the diary of 935 AH. can be attributed safely to loss of pages, because preliminaries are now wanting to several matters which Bābur records shortly after it. Such are (1) the specification of the three articles sent to Naṣrat Shāh, (2) the motive for the feast of f. 351*b*, (3) the announcement of the approach of the surprising group of envoys, who appear without introduction at that entertainment, in a manner opposed to Bābur's custom of writing, (4) an account of their arrival and reception.

[2332] Land-holder (*see Hobson-Jobson s.n.* talookdar).

[2333] The long detention of this messenger is mentioned in Bābur's letter to Humāyūn (f. 349).

[2334] These words, if short *a* be read in Shăh, make 934 by *abjad*. The child died in infancy; no son of Humāyūn's had survived childhood before Akbar was born, some 14 years later. Concerning Abū'l-wajd *Fārighī*, *see Ḥabību's-siyar*, lith. ed. ii, 347; *Muntakhabu't-tawārikh*, Bib. Ind. ed. i, 3; and Index *s.n.*

[2335] I am indebted to Mr. A. E. Hinks, Secretary of the Royal Geographical Society, for the following approximate estimate of the distances travelled by Bīān Shaikh:—(*a*) From Kishm to Kābul 240m.—from Kābul to Peshāwar 175m.—from Peshāwar to Āgra (railroad distance) 759 m.—total 1174 m.; daily average *cir.* 38 miles; (*b*) Qila'-i-ẓạfar to Kābul 264m.—Kābul to Qandahār 316m.—total 580m.; daily average *cir.* 53 miles. The second journey was made probably in 913 AH. and to inform Bābur of the death of the Shāh of Badakhshān (f. 213*b*).

[2336] On Muḥ. 10th 934 AH.-Sep. 26th 1528 AD. For accounts of the campaign *see* Rieu's Suppl. Persian Cat. under *Histories of Ṭạhmāsp* (Churchill Collection); the *Ḥabību's-siyar* and the *'Ālam-ārāī-'abbāsī*, the last a highly rhetorical work, Bābur's accounts (Index *s.n.* Jām) are merely repetitions of news given to him; he is not responsible for mistakes he records, such as those of f. 354. It must be mentioned that Mr. Erskine has gone wrong in his description of the battle, the starting-point of error being his reversal of two events, the encampment of Ṭạhmāsp at Rādagān and his passage through Mashhad. A century ago less help, through maps and travel, was available than now.

[2337] *tufak u arāba*, the method of array Bābur adopted from the Rūmī-Persian model.

[2338] Ṭạhmāsp's main objective, aimed at earlier than the Aūzbeg muster in Merv, was Herāt, near which 'Ubaid Khān had been for 7 months. He did not take the shortest route for Mashhad, *viz.* the Dāmghān-Sabzawār-Nīshāpūr road, but went from Dāmghān for Mashhad by way of Kālpūsh (*'Ālam-ārāī* lith. ed. p. 45) and Rādagān. Two military advantages are obvious on this route; (1) it approaches Mashhad by the descending road of the Kechef-valley, thus avoiding the climb into that valley by a pass beyond Nīshāpūr on the alternative route; and (2) it passes through the fertile lands of Rādagān. [For Kālpūsh and the route *see* Fr. military map, Sheets Astarābād and Merv, n.e. of Basṭạm.]

[2339] 7 m. from Kushan and 86 m. from Mashhad. As Lord Curzon reports (*Persia*, ii, 120) that his interlocutors on the spot were not able to explain the word "Radkan," it may be useful to note here that the town seems to borrow its name from the ancient tower standing near it, the *Mīl-i-rādagān*, or, as Réclus gives it, *Tour de méimandan*, both names meaning, Tower of the bounteous (or, beneficent, highly-distinguished, *etc.*). (Cf. Vullers Dict. *s.n. rād*; Réclus' *L'Asie Antérieure* p. 219; and O'Donovan's *Merv Oasis*.) Perhaps light on the distinguished people (*rādagān*) is given by the *Dābistān's* notice of an ancient sect, the Rādīyān, seeming to be fire-worshippers whose chief was Rād-gūna, an eminently brave hero of the latter part of Jāmshīd's reign (800 B.C.?). Of the town Rādagān Daulat Shāh makes frequent mention. A second town so-called and having a tower lies north of Ispahān.

[2340] In these days of trench-warfare it would give a wrong impression to say that Ṭahmāsp entrenched himself; he did what Bābur did before his battles at Panīpat and Kānwa (*q.v.*).

[2341] The Aūzbegs will have omitted from their purview of affairs that Ṭahmāsp's men were veterans.

[2342] The holy city had been captured by 'Ubaid Khān in 933 AH. (1525 AD.), but nothing in Bīān Shaikh's narrative indicates that they were now there in force.

[2343] Presumably the one in the Rādagān-meadow.

[2344] using the *yada-tāsh* to ensure victory (Index *s.n.*).

[2345] If then, as now, Scorpio's appearance were expected in Oct.-Nov., the Aūzbegs had greatly over-estimated their power to check Ṭahmāsp's movements; but it seems fairly clear that they expected Scorpio to follow Virgo in Sept.-Oct. according to the ancient view of the Zodiacal Signs which allotted two houses to the large Scorpio and, if it admitted Libra at all, placed it between Scorpio's claws (Virgil's *Georgics* i, 32 and Ovid's *Metamorphoses*, ii, 195.—H. B.).

[2346] It would appear that the Aūzbegs, after hearing that Ṭahmāsp was encamped at Rādagān, expected to interpose themselves in his way at Mashhad and to get their 20,000 to Rādagān before he broke camp. Ṭāhmāsp's swiftness spoiled their plan; he will have stayed at Rādagān a short time only, perhaps till he had further news of the Aūzbegs, perhaps also for commissariat purposes and to rest his force. He visited the shrine of Imām Reza, and had reached Jām in time to confront his adversaries as they came down to it from Zawarābād (Pilgrims'-town).

[2347] or, Khirjard, as many MSS. have it. It seems to be a hamlet or suburb of Jām. The *'Ālam-ārāī* (lith. ed. p. 40) writes Khusrau-jard-i-Jām (the Khusrau-throne of Jām), perhaps rhetorically. The hamlet is Maulānā 'Abdu'r-raḥmān *Jāmī's* birthplace (Daulat Shāh's *Tazkirat*, E. G. Browne's ed. p. 483). Jām now appears on maps as Turbat-i-Shaikh Jāmī, the tomb (*turbat*) being that of the saintly ancestor of Akbar's mother Ḥamīda-bānū.

[2348] The *'Ālam-ārāī* (lith. ed. p. 31) says, but in grandiose language, that 'Ubaid Khān placed at the foot of his standard 40 of the most eminent men of Transoxania who prayed for his success, but that as his cause was not good, their supplications were turned backwards, and that all were slain where they had prayed.

[2349] Here the 1st Pers. trs. (I.O. 215 f. 214) mentions that it was Chalma who wrote and despatched the exact particulars of the defeat of the Aūzbegs. This information explains the presumption Bābur expresses. It shows that Chalma was in Ḥiṣār where he may have written his letter to give news to Humāyūn. At the time Bīān Shaikh left, the Mīrzā was near Kishm; if he had been the enterprising man he was not, one would surmise that he had moved to seize the chance of the sulṭāns' abandonment of Ḥiṣār, without waiting for his father's urgency (f. 348*b*). Whether he had done so and was the cause of the sulṭāns' flight, is not known from any chronicle yet come to our hands. Chalma's father Ibrāhīm *Jānī* died fighting for Bābur against Shaibāq Khān in 906 AH. (f. 90*b*).

As the sense of the name-of-office Chalma is still in doubt, I suggest that it may be an equivalent of *aftābachī*, bearer of the water-bottle on journeys. *T. chalma* can mean a water-vessel carried on the saddle-bow; one Chalma on record was a *safarchī*; if, in this word, *safar* be read to mean journey, an approach is made to *aftābachī* (fol. 15*b* and note; Blochmann's A.-i-A. p. 378 and n. 3).

[2350] The copies of Bābur's Turkī letter to Humāyūn and the later one to Khwāja Kalān (f. 359) are in some MSS. of the Persian text translated only (I.O. 215 f. 214); in others appear in Turkī only (I.O. 217 f. 240); in others appear in Turkī and Persian (B. M. Add. 26,000 and I.O. 2989); while in Muḥ. Shīrāzī's lith. ed. they are omitted altogether (p. 228).

[2351] Trans- and Cis-Hindukush. Pāyanda-ḥasan (in one of his useful glosses to the 1st Pers. trs.) amplifies here by "Khurāsān, Mā warā'u'n-nahr and Kābul".

[2352] The words Bābur gives as mispronunciations are somewhat uncertain in sense; manifestly both are of ill-omen:—Al-amān itself [of which the *alāmā* of the Ḥai. MS. and Ilminsky maybe an abbreviation,] is the cry of the vanquished, "Quarter! mercy!"; *Aīlāmān* and also *ālāman* can represent a Turkmān raider.

[2353] Presumably amongst Tīmūrids.

[2354] Perhaps Bābur here makes a placatory little joke.

[2355] *i.e.* that offered by Ṭahmāsp's rout of the Aūzbegs at Jām.

[2356] He was an adherent of Bābur. Cf. f. 353.

[2357] The plural "your" will include Humāyūn and Kāmrān. Neither had yet shewn himself the heritor of his father's personal dash and valour; they had lacked the stress which shaped his heroism.

[2358] My husband has traced these lines to Niẓāmī's *Khusrau* and *Shīrīn.* [They occur on f. 256*b* in his MS. of 317 folios.] Bābur may have quoted from memory, since his version varies. The lines need their context to be understood; they are part of Shīrīn's address to Khusrau when she refuses to marry him because at the time he is fighting for his sovereign position; and they say, in effect, that while all other work stops for marriage (*kadkhudāī*), kingly rule does not.

[2359] *Aūlūghlār kūtārīmlīk kīrāk*; 2nd Pers. trs. *buzurgān bardāsht mī bāīd kardand.* This dictum may be a quotation. I have translated it to agree with Bābur's reference to the ages of the brothers, but *aūlūghlār* expresses greatness of position as well as seniority in age, and the dictum may be taken as a Turkī version of "*Noblesse oblige*", and may also mean "The great must be magnanimous". (Cf. de C.'s Dict. *s.n. kūtārīmlīk.*) [It may be said of the verb *bardāshlan* used in the Pers. trs., that Abū'l-faẕl, perhaps translating *kūtārīmlīk* reported to him, puts it into Bābur's mouth when, after praying to take Humāyūn's illness upon himself, he cried with conviction, "I have borne it away" (A.N. trs. H.B. i, 276).]

[2360] If Bābur had foreseen that his hard-won rule in Hindūstān was to be given to the winds of one son's frivolities and the other's disloyalty, his words of scant content with what the Hindūstān of his desires had brought him, would have expressed a yet keener pain (*Rāmpūr Dīwān* E.D.R.'s ed. p. 15 l. 5 fr. ft.).

[2361] *Bostān*, cap. *Advice of Noshirwān to Hurmuz* (H.B.).

[2362] A little joke at the expense of the mystifying letter.

[2363] For *yā*, Mr. Erskine writes *be.* What the mistake was is an open question; I have guessed an exchange of *ī* for *ū*, because such an exchange is not infrequent amongst Turkī long vowels.

[2364] That of reconquering Tīmūrid lands.

[2365] of *Kūlāb*; he was the father of Ḥaram Begīm, one of Gul-badan's personages.

[2366] *aūn altī gūnlūk m:ljār bīla*, as on f. 354*b*, and with exchange of T. *m:ljār* for P. *mī'ād*, f. 355*b*.

[2367] Probably into Rājpūt lands, notably into those of Ṣalāḥu'd-dīn.

[2368] *tukhmalīq chakmānlār*; as *tukhma* means both button and gold-embroidery, it may be right, especially of Hindūstān articles, to translate sometimes in the second sense.

[2369] These statements of date are consistent with Bābur's earlier explicit entries and with Erskine's equivalents of the Christian Era, but at variance with Gladwin's and with Wüstenfeldt's calculation that Rabī' II. 1st was Dec. 13th. Yet Gladwin (*Revenue Accounts*, ed. 1790 AD. p. 22) gives Rabī' I. 30 days. Without in the smallest degree questioning the two European calculations, I follow Bābur, because in his day there may have been allowed variation which finds no entry in methodical calendars. Erskine followed Bābur's statements; he is likely nevertheless to have seen Gladwin's book.

[2370] Erskine estimated this at £500, but later cast doubts on such estimates as being too low (*History of India*, vol. i, App. D.).

[2371] The bearer of the stamp (*ṭamghā*) who by impressing it gave quittance for the payment of tolls and other dues.

[2372] Either 24ft. or 36ft. according to whether the short or long *qārī* be meant (*infra*). These towers would provide resting-place, and some protection against ill-doers. They recall the two *mīl-i-rādagān* of Persia (f. 347 *n.* 9), the purpose of which is uncertain. Bābur's towers were not "*kos mīnārs*", nor is it said that he ordered each *kuroh* to be marked on the road. Some of the *kos mīnārs* on the "old Mughal roads" were over 30ft. high; a considerable number are entered and depicted in the *Annual Progress Report* of the Archæological Survey for 1914 (Northern Circle, p. 45 and Plates 44, 45). Some at least have a *lower* chamber.

[2373] Four-doored, open-on-all-sides. We have not found the word with this meaning in Dictionaries. It may translate H. *chaukandī*.

[2374] Erskine makes 9 *kos* (*kurohs*) to be 13-14 miles, perhaps on the basis of the smaller *gaz* of 24 inches.

[2375] *altī yām-ātī bāghlāghāīlār* which, says one of Erskine's manuscripts, is called a *dāk-choki*.

[2376] Neither Erskine (*Mems.* p. 394), nor de Courteille (*Mém*s. ii, 370) recognized the word *Mubīn* here, although each mentions the poem later (p. 431 and ii, 461), deriving his information about it from the *Akbar-nāma*, Erskine direct, de Courteille by way of the Turkī translation of the same *Akbar-nāma* passage, which Ilminsky found in Kehr's volume and which is one of the much discussed "Fragments", at first taken to be extra writings of Bābur's (cf. Index *in loco s.n.* Fragments). Ilminsky (p. 455) prints the word clearly, as one who knows it; he may have seen that part of the poem itself which is included in Berésine's *Chrestomathie Turque* (p. 226 to p. 272), under the title *Fragment d'un poème inconnu de Bābour*, and have observed that Bābur himself shews his title to be *Mubīn*, in the lines of his colophon (p. 271),

Chū bīān qīldīm āndā shar'īyāt,

Nī 'ajab gar Mubīn dīdīm āt?

(Since in it I have made exposition of Laws, what wonder if I named it *Mubīn* (exposition)?) Cf. *Translator's Note*, p. 437. [Berésine says (Ch. T.) that he prints half of his "*unique manuscrit*" of the poem.]

[2377] The passage Bābur quotes comes from the *Mubīn* section on *tayammum masā'la* (purification with sand), where he tells his son sand may be used, *Sū yurāq būlsā sīndīn aīr bīr mīl* (if from thee water be one *mīl* distant), and then interjects the above explanation of what the *mīl* is. Two lines of his original are not with the *Bābur-nāma.*

[2378] The *ṭanāb* was thus 120 ft. long. Cf. A.-i-A. Jarrett i, 414; Wilson's *Glossary of Indian Terms* and Gladwin's *Revenue Accounts*, p. 14.

[2379] Bābur's customary method of writing allows the inference that he recorded, in due place, the coming and reception of the somewhat surprising group of guests now mentioned as at this entertainment. That preliminary record will have been lost in one or more of the small gaps in his diary of 935 AH. The envoys from the Samarkand Aūzbegs and from the Persian Court may have come in acknowledgment of the *Fātḥ-nāma* which announced victory over Rānā Sangā; the guests from Farghāna will have accepted the invitation sent, says Gul-badan, "in all directions," after Bābur's defeat of Sl. Ibrāhīm *Lūdī*, to urge hereditary servants and Tīmūrid and Chīngīz-khānid kinsfolk to come and see prosperity with him now when "the Most High has bestowed sovereignty" (f. 293a; Gul-badan's H.N. f. 11).

[2380] Hindū here will represent Rājpūt. D'Herbélot's explanation of the name Qīzīl-bāsh (Red-head) comes in usefully here:—"KEZEL BASCH or KIZIL BASCH. Mot Turc qui signifie *Tête rouge.* Les Turcs appellent les Persans de ce nom, depuis qu'Ismaël Sofi, fondateur de la Dynastie des princes qui regnent aujourd'hui en Perse, commanda à ses soldats de porter un bonnet rouge autour duquel il y a une écharpe ou Turban à douze plis, en mémoire et à l'honneur des 12 Imams, successeurs d'Ali, desquels il prétendoit descendre. Ce bonnet s'appelle en Persan, *Tāj*, et fut institué l'an 9O7^e de l'Hég." Ṭạhmāsp himself uses the name Qīzīl-bāsh; Bābur does so too. Other explanations of it are found (Steingass), but the one quoted above suits its use without contempt. (Cf. f. 354 n. 3).

[2381] *cir.* 140-150ft. or more if the 36in. *qārī* be the unit.

[2382] *Andropogon muricatus*, the scented grass of which the roots are fitted into window spaces and moistened to mitigate dry, hot winds. Cf. *Hobson-Jobson s.n. Cuscuss.*

[2383] A nephew and a grandson of Aḥrāri's second son Yahya (f. 347*b*) who had stood staunch to Bābur till murdered in 906 AH.-1500 AD. (80*b*). They are likely to be those to whom went a copy of the *Mubīn* under cover of a letter addressed to lawyers of Mā warā'u'n-nahr (f. 351 n. 1). The Khwājas were in Āgra three weeks after Bābur finished his metrical version of their ancestor's *Wālidiyyah-risāla*; whether their coming (which must have been announced some time before their arrival), had part in directing his attention to the tract can only be surmised (f. 346).

[2384] He was an Aūzbeg (f. 371) and from his association here with a Bāī-qarā, and, later with Qāsim-i-ḥusain who was half Bāī-qarā, half Aūzbeg, seems likely to be of the latter's family (Index *s.nn.*).

[2385] *sāchāq kiūrdī* (*kīltūrdi*?) No record survives to tell the motive for this feast; perhaps the gifts made to Bābur were congratulatory on the birth of a grandson, the marriage of a son, and on the generally-prosperous state of his affairs.

[2386] Gold, silver and copper coins.

[2387] Made so by *bhang* or other exciting drug.

[2388] *ārāl*, presumably one left by the winter-fall of the Jumna; or, a peninsula.

[2389] Scribes and translators have been puzzled here. My guess at the Turkī clause is *aūrang aīralīk kīsh jabbah*. In reading *muslin*, I follow Erskine who worked in India and could take local opinion; moreover gifts made in Āgra probably would be Indian.

[2390] For one Ḥāfiẓ of Samarkand see f.237*b*.

[2391] Kūchūm was Khāqān of the Aūzbegs and had his seat in Samarkand. One of his sons, Abū-sa'īd, mentioned below, had sent envoys. With Abū-sa'īd is named Mihr-bān who was one of Kūchūm's wives; Pulād was their son. Mihr-bān was, I think, a half-sister of Bābur, a daughter of 'Umar Shaikh and Umīd of Andijān (f. 9), and a full-sister of Nāṣir. No doubt she had been captured on one of the occasions when Bābur lost to the Aūzbegs. In 925 AH.-1519 AD. (f. 237*b*) when he sent his earlier *Dīwān* to Pulād Sl. (*Translator's Note*, p. 438) he wrote a verse on its back which looks to be addressed to his half-sister through her son.

[2392] Ṭahmāsp's envoy; the title Chalabī shews high birth.

[2393] This statement seems to imply that the weight made of silver and the weight made of gold were of the same size and that the differing specific gravity of the two metals,—that of silver being *cir.* 10 and that of gold *cir.* 20—gave their equivalents the proportion Bābur states. Persian Dictionaries give *sang* (*tāsh*), a weight, but without further information. We have not found mention of the *tāsh* as a recognized Turkī weight; perhaps the word *tāsh* stands for an ingot of unworked metal of standard size. (Cf. *inter alios libros*, A.-i-A. Blochmann p. 36, Codrington's *Musalman Numismatics* p. 117, concerning the *miṣqāl, dīnār, etc.*)

[2394] *tarkāsh bīla.* These words are clear in the Ḥai. MS. but uncertain in some others. E. and de C. have no equivalent of them. Perhaps the coins were given by the quiverful; that a quiver of arrows was given is not expressed.

[2395] Bābur's half-nephew; he seems from his name Keepsake-of-nāṣir to have been posthumous.

[2396] 934 AH.-1528 AD. (f. 336).

[2397] Or, gold-embroidered.

[2398] Wife of Muḥammad-i-zamān Mīrzā.

[2399] These Highlanders of Asfara will have come by invitation sent after the victory at Panīpat; their welcome shows remembrance of and gratitude for kindness received a quarter of a century earlier. Perhaps villagers from Dikh-kat will have come too, who had seen the Pādshāh run barefoot on their hills (*Index s.nn.*).

[2400] Here gratitude is shewn for protection given in 910 AH.-1504 AD. to the families of Bābur and his men when on the way to Kābul. Qurbān and Shaikhī were perhaps in Fort Ajar (f. 122*b*, f. 126).

[2401] Perhaps these acrobats were gipsies.

[2402] This may be the one with which Sayyid Daknī was concerned (f. 346).

[2403] Bābur obviously made the distinction between *pahr* and *pās* that he uses the first for day-watches, the second for those of the night.

[2404] Anglicé, Tuesday, Dec. 21st; by Muḥammadan plan, Wednesday 22nd. Dhūlpūr is 34 m. s. of Āgra; the journey of 10hrs. 20m. would include the nooning and the time taken in crossing rivers.

[2405] The well was to fill a cistern; the 26 spouts with their 26 supports were to take water into (26?) conduits. Perhaps *tāsh* means that they were hewn in the solid rock; perhaps that they were on the outer side of the reservoir. They will not have been built of hewn stone, or the word would have been *sangīn* or *tāshdīn.*

[2406] One occupation of these now blank days is indicated by the date of the "*Rāmpūr Dīwān*", Thursday Rabī' II. 15th (Dec. 27th).

[2407] The demon (or, athlete) sulṭān of Rumelia (*Rūmlū*); once Ṭahmāsp's guardian (*Tazkirat-i-Ṭahmāsp*, Bib. Ind. ed. Phillott, p. 2). Some writers say he was put to death by Ṭahmāsp (*æt.* 12) in 933 AH.; if this were so, it is strange to find a servant described as his in 935 AH. (An account of the battle is given in the *Sharaf-nāma*, written in 1005 AH. by Sharaf Khān who was reared in Ṭahmāsp's house. The book has been edited by Veliaminof-Zernof and translated into French by Charmoy; cf. Trs. vol. ii, part i, p. 555.—*H. Beveridge.*)

[2408] This name, used by one who was with the Shāh's troops, attracts attention; it may show the composition of the Persian army; it may differentiate between the troops and their "Qīzīl-bāsh leader".

[2409] Several writers give Sārū-qamsh (Charmoy, *roseau jaune*) as the name of the village where the battle was fought; Sharaf Khān gives 'Umarābād and mentions that after the fight Ṭahmāsp spent some time in the meadow of Sārū-qamsh.

[2410] The number of Ṭahmāsp's guns being a matter of interest, reference should be made to Bābur's accounts of his own battles in which he arrayed in Rūmī (Ottoman) fashion; it will then be seen that the number of carts does not imply the number of guns (Index *s.n. arāba*, cart).

[2411] This cannot but represent Ṭahmāsp who was on the battle-field (*see* his own story *infra*). He was 14 years old; perhaps he was called Shāh-zāda, and not Shāh, on account of his youth, or because under guardianship (?). Readers of the Persian histories of his reign may know the reason. Bābur hitherto has always called the boy Shāh-zāda; after the victory at Jām, he styles him Shāh. Jūha Sl. (*Taklū*) who was with him on the field, was Governor of Ispahān.

[2412] If this Persian account of the battle be in its right place in Bābur's diary, it is singular that the narrator should be so ill-informed at a date allowing facts to be known; the three sulṭāns he names as killed escaped to die, Kūchūm in 937 AH.-1530 AD., Abū-sa'īd in 940 AH.-1533 AD., 'Ubaid in 946 AH.-1539 AD. (Lane-Poole's *Muḥammadan Dynasties*). It would be natural for Bābur to comment on the mistake, since envoys from two of the sulṭāns reported killed, were in Āgra. There had been time for the facts to be known: the battle was fought on Sep. 26th; the news of it was in Āgra on Nov. 23rd; envoys from both adversaries were at Bābur's entertainment on Dec. 19th. From this absence of comment and for the reasons indicated in note 3 (*infra*), it appears that matter has been lost from the text.

[2413] Ṭahmāsp's account of the battle is as follows (*T.-i-Ṭ.* p. 11):—"I marched against the Aūzbegs. The battle took place outside Jām. At the first onset, Aūzbeg prevailed over Qīzīl-bāsh. Ya'qūb Sl. fled and Sl. Wālāma *Taklū* and other officers of the right wing were defeated and put to flight. Putting my trust in God, I prayed and advanced some paces.... One of my body-guard getting up with 'Ubaid struck him with a sword, passed on, and occupied himself with another. Qūlīj Bahādur and other Aūzbegs carried off the wounded 'Ubaid; Kūchkūnjī (Kūchūm) Khān and Jānī Khān Beg, when they became aware of this state of affairs, fled to Merv. Men who had fled from our army rejoined us that day. That night I spent on the barren plain (*ṣaḥra'*). I did not know what had happened to 'Ubaid. I thought perhaps they were devising some stratagem against me." The 'A.-'A. says that 'Ubaid's assailant, on seeing his low stature and contemptible appearance, left him for a more worthy foe.

[2414] Not only does some comment from Bābur seem needed on an account of deaths he knew had not occurred, but loss of matter may be traced by working backward from his next explicit date (*Friday 19th*), to do which shows fairly well that the "same day" will be not Tuesday the 16th but Thursday the 18th. Ghīāṣu'd-dīn's reception was on the day preceding Friday 19th, so that part of Thursday's record (as shewn by "on this same day"), the whole of Wednesday's, and (to suit an expected comment by Bābur on the discrepant story of the Aūzbeg deaths) part of Tuesday's are missing. The gap may well have contained mention of Ḥasan *Chalabī's* coming (f. 357), or explain why he had not been at the feast with his younger brother.

[2415] *qūrchī*, perhaps body-guard, life-guardsman.

[2416] As on f. 350*b* (*q.v.* p. 628 n. 1) *aūn altī gūnlūk būljār* (or, *m:ljār*) *bīla.*

[2417] A sub-division of the Ballia district of the United Provinces, on the right bank of the Ghogrā.

[2418] *i.e.* in 16 days; he was 24 or 25 days away.

[2419] The envoy had been long in returning; Kanwā was fought in March, 1527; it is now the end of 1528 AD.

[2420] Rabī' II. 20th—January 1st 1529 AD.; Anglicé, Friday, after 6p.m.

[2421] This "Bengalī" is territorial only; Naṣrat Shāh was a Sayyid's son (f.271).

[2422] Ismā'īl Mītā (f. 357) who will have come with Mullā Maẕhab.

[2423] *mī'ād*, cf. f. 350*b* and f. 354*b*. Ghīāṣu'd-dīn may have been a body-guard.

[2424] Lūdī Afghāns and their friends, including Bīban and Bāyazīd.

[2425] *yūllūq tūrālīk*; *Memoirs*, p. 398, "should act in every respect in perfect conformity to his commands"; *Mémoires* ii, 379, "*chacun suivant son rang et sa dignité.*"

[2426] *tawāchī.* Bābur's uses of this word support Erskine in saying that "the *tawāchī* is an officer who corresponds very nearly to the Turkish *chāwush*, or special messenger" (Zenker, p. 346, col. iii) "but he was also often employed to act as a commissary for providing men and stores, as a commissioner in superintending important affairs, as an aide-de-camp in carrying orders, *etc.*"

[2427] Here the Ḥai. MS. has the full-vowelled form, *būljār.* Judging from what that Codex writes, *būljār* may be used for a rendezvous of troops, *m:ljār* or *b:ljār* for any other kind of tryst (f. 350, p. 628 n. 1; Index *s.nn.*), also for a shelter.

[2428] *yāwūshūb aīdī*, which I translate in accordance with other uses of the verb, as meaning approach, but is taken by some other workers to mean "near its end".

[2429] Though it is not explicitly said, Chīn-tīmūr may have been met with on the road; as the "also" (*ham*) suggests.

[2430] To the above news the *Akbar-nāma* adds the important item reported by Humāyūn, that there was talk of peace. Bābur replied that, if the time for negotiation were not past, Humāyūn was to make peace until such time as the affairs of Hindūstān were cleared off. This is followed in the A. N. by a seeming quotation from Bābur's letter, saying in effect that he was about to leave Hindūstān, and that his followers in Kābul and Tramontana must prepare for the expedition against Samarkand which would be made on his own arrival. None of the above matter is now with the *Bābur-nāma*; either it was there once, was used by Abū'l-faẓl and lost before the Persian trss. were made; or Abū'l-faẓl used Bābur's original, or copied, letter itself. That desire for peace prevailed is shewn by several matters:—Ṭahmāsp, the victor, asked and obtained the hand of an Aūzbeg in marriage; Aūzbeg envoys came to Āgra, and with them Turk Khwājas having a mission likely to have been towards peace (f. 357*b*); Bābur's wish for peace is shewn above and on f. 359 in a summarized letter to Humāyūn. (Cf. Abū'l-ghāzī's *Shajarat-i-Turk* [*Histoire des Mongols*, Désmaisons' trs. p. 216]; *Akbar-nāma*, H. B.'s trs. i, 270.)

A here-useful slip of reference is made by the translator of the *Akbar-nāma* (*l.c.* n. 3) to the Fragment (*Mémoires* ii, 456) instead of to the *Bābur-nāma* translation (*Mémoires* ii, 381). The utility of the slip lies in its accompanying comment that de C.'s translation is in closer agreement with the *Akbar-nāma* than with Bābur's words. Thus the *Akbar-nāma* passage is brought into comparison with what it is now safe to regard as its off-shoot, through Turkī and French, in the Fragment. When the above comment on their resemblance was made, we were less assured than now as to the genesis of the Fragment (Index *s.n.* Fragment).

[2431] Hind-āl's guardian (G. B.'s *Humāyūn-nāma* trs. p. 106, n. 1).

[2432] Nothing more about Humāyūn's expedition is found in the B. N.; he left Badakhshān a few months later and arrived in Āgra, after his mother (f. 380*b*), at a date in August of which the record is wanting.

[2433] under 6 m. from Āgra. Gul-badan (f. 16) records a visit to the garden, during which her father said he was weary of sovereignty. Cf. f. 331*b*, p. 589 n. 2.

[2434] *kūrnīsh kīlkān kīshīlār.*

[2435] MSS. vary or are indecisive as to the omitted word. I am unable to fill the gap. Erskine has "*Sir Māwineh* (or hair-twist)" (p. 399), De Courteille, *Sir-mouïneh* (ii, 382). *Mūīna* means ermine, sable and other fine fur (*Shamsu'l-lūghāt*, p 274, col. 1).

[2436] His brother Ḥaẓrat Makhdūmī Nūrā (Khwāja Khāwand Maḥmūd) is much celebrated by Ḥaidar Mīrzā, and Bābur describes his own visit in the words he uses of the visit of an inferior to himself. Cf. *Tārīkh-i-rashīdī* trs. pp. 395, 478; *Akbar-nāma* trs., i, 356, 360.

[2437] No record survives of the arrival of this envoy or of why he was later in coming than his brother who was at Bābur's entertainment. Cf. f. 361*b*.

[2438] Presumably this refers to the appliances mentioned on f. 350*b*.

[2439] f. 332, n. 3.

[2440] *zarbaft m:l:k.* Amongst gold stuffs imported into Hindūstān, Abū'l-faẓl mentions *mīlak* which may be Bābur's cloth. It came from Turkistān (A.-i-A. Blochmann, p. 92 and n.).

[2441] A *tang* is a small silver coin of the value of about a penny (Erskine).

[2442] *tānglāsī*, lit. at its dawning. It is not always clear whether *tānglāsī* means, Anglicé, next dawn or day, which here would be Monday, or whether it stands for the dawn (daylight) of the Muḥammadan day which had begun at 6 p. m. on the previous evening, here Sunday. When Bābur records, *e.g.* a late audience, *tānglāsī*, following, will stand for the daylight of the day of audience. The point is of some importance as bearing on discrepancies of days, as these are stated in MSS., with European calendars; it is conspicuously so in Bābur's diary sections.

[2443] *risālat ṭarīqī bīla*; their special mission may have been to work for peace (f. 359*b*, n. 1).

[2444] He may well be Kāmrān's father-in-law Sl. 'Alī Mīrzā Ṭaghāī *Begchīk*.

[2445] *nīmcha u takband*. The *tak-band* is a silk or woollen girdle fastening with a "hook and eye" (Steingass), perhaps with a buckle.

[2446] This description is that of the contents of the "*Rāmpūr Dīwān*"; the *tarjuma* being the *Wālidiyyah-risāla* (f. 361 and n.). What is said here shows that four copies went to Kābul or further north. Cf. Appendix Q.

[2447] *Sar-khaṭ* may mean "copies" set for Kāmrān to imitate.

[2448] *bīr pahr yāwūshūb aīdī*; I.O. 215 f. 221, *qarīb yak pās roz būd*.

[2449] *ākhar*, a word which may reveal a bad start and uncertainty as to when and where to halt.

[2450] This, and not Chandwār (f. 331*b*), appears the correct form. Neither this place nor Ābāpūr is mentioned in the G. of I.'s Index or shewn in the I.S. Map of 1900 (cf. f. 331*b* n. 3). Chandawār lies s.w. of Fīrūzābād, and near a village called Ṣufīpūr.

[2451] Anglicé, Wednesday after 6 p.m.

[2452] or life-guardsman, body-guard.

[2453] This higher title for Ṭahmāsp, which first appears here in the B.N., may be an early slip in the Turkī text, since it occurs in many MSS. and also because "Shāh-zāda" reappears on f. 359.

[2454] Slash-face, *balafré*; perhaps Ibrāhīm *Begchīk* (Index *s.n.*), but it is long since he was mentioned by Bābur, at least by name. He may however have come, at this time of reunion in Āgra, with Mīrzā Beg Ṭaghāī (his uncle or brother?), father-in-law of Kāmrān.

[2455] The army will have kept to the main road connecting the larger towns mentioned and avoiding the ravine district of the Jumna. What the boat-journey will have been between high banks and round remarkable bends can be learned from the G. of I. and Neave's *District Gazetteer of Mainpūrī.* Rāprī is on the road from Fīrūzābād to the ferry for Bateswar, where a large fair is held annually. (It is misplaced further east in the I.S. Map of 1900.) There are two Fatḥpūrs, n. e. of Rāprī.

[2456] *aūlūgh tūghāīnīng tūbī.* Here it suits to take the Turkī word *tūghāī* to mean bend of a river, and as referring to the one shaped (on the map) like a soda-water bottle, its neck close to Rāprī. Bābur avoided it by taking boat below its mouth.—In neither Persian translation has *tūghāī* been read to mean a bend of a river; the first has *az pāyān rūīa Rāprī*, perhaps referring to the important ford (*pāyān*); the second has *az zīr bulandī kalān Rāprī*, perhaps referring to a height at the meeting of the bank of the ravine down which the road to the ford comes, with the high bank of the river. Three examples of *tūghāī* or *tūqāī* [a synonym given by Dictionaries], can be seen in Abū'l-ghāzī's *Shajrat-i-Turk*, Fræhn's imprint, pp. 106, 107, 119 (Désmaisons' trs. pp. 204, 205, 230). In each instance Désmaisons renders it by *coude*, elbow, but one of the examples may need reconsideration, since the word has the further meanings of wood, dense forest by the side of a river (Vambéry), prairie (Zenker), and reedy plain (Shaw).

[2457] Blochmann describes the apparatus for marking lines to guide writing (A.-i-A. trs. p. 52 n. 5):—On a card of the size of the page to be written on, two vertical lines are drawn within an inch of the edges; along these lines small holes are pierced at regular intervals, and through these a string is laced backwards and forwards, care being taken that the horizontal strings are parallel. Over the lines of string the pages are placed and pressed down; the strings then mark the paper sufficiently to guide the writing.

[2458] *tarkīb (nīng) khaṭṭī bīla tarjuma bilīr aūchūn.* The *Rāmpūr Dīwān* may supply the explanation of the uncertain words *tarkīb khaṭṭī.* The "translation" (*tarjuma*), mentioned in the passage quoted above, is the *Wālidiyyah-risāla*, the first item of the *Dīwān*, in which it is entered on crowded pages, specially insufficient for the larger hand of the chapter-headings. The number of lines per page is 13; Bābur now fashions a line-marker for 11. He has already despatched 4 copies of the translation (f. 357*b*); he will have judged them unsatisfactory; hence to give space for the mixture of hands (*tarkīb khaṭṭī*), *i.e.* the smaller hand of the poem and the larger of the headings, he makes an 11 line marker.

[2459] Perhaps Aḥrārī's in the *Wālidiyyah-risāla*, perhaps those of Muḥammad. A quatrain in the *Rāmpūr Dīwān* connects with this admonishment [Plate xiv*a*, 2nd quatrain].

[2460] Jākhān (*G. of Mainpūrī*). The *G. of Etāwa* (Drake-Brockman) p. 213, gives this as some 18 m. n.w. of Etāwa and as lying amongst the ravines of the Jumna.

[2461] f. 359*b* allows some of the particulars to be known.

[2462] Mahdī may have come to invite Bābur to the luncheon he served shortly afterwards. The Ḥai. MS. gives him the honorific plural; either a second caller was with him or an early scribe has made a slip, since Bābur never so-honours Mahdī. This small point touches the larger one of how Bābur regarded him, and this in connection with the singular story Niẓāmu'd-dīn Aḥmad tells in his *Ṭabaqāt-i-akbarī* about Khalīfa's wish to supplant Humāyūn by Mahdī Khwāja (Index *s.nn.*).

[2463] *yīgītlārnī shokhlūqgha sāldūq*, perhaps set them to make fun. Cf. f. 366, *yīgītlār bīr pāra shokhlūq qīldīlār.* Muḥ. *Shīrāzī* (p. 323 *foot*) makes the startling addition of *dar āb* (*andākhtīm*), *i.e.* he says that the royal party flung the braves into the river.

[2464] The *Gazetteer of Etāwa* (Drake-Brockman) p. 186, *s.n.* Bāburpūr, writes of two village sites [which from their position are Mūrī-and-Adūsa], as known by the name Sarāī Bāburpūr from having been Bābur's halting-place. They are 24m. to the s.e. of Etāwa, on the old road for Kālpī. Near the name Bāburpūr in the Gazetteer Map there is Muhuri (Mūrī?); there is little or no doubt that Sarāī Bāburpūr represents the camping-ground Mūrī-and-Adūsa.

[2465] This connects with Kītīn-qarā's complaints of the frontier-begs (f. 361), and with the talk of peace (f. 356*b*).

[2466] This injunction may connect with the desired peace; it will have been prompted by at least a doubt in Bābur's mind as to Kāmrān's behaviour perhaps *e.g.* in manifested dislike for a Shīa'. Concerning the style Shāh-zāda *see* f. 358, p. 643, n. 1.

[2467] Kāmrān's mother Gul-rukh *Begchīk* will have been of the party who will have tried in Kābul to forward her son's interests.

[2468] f. 348, p. 624, n. 2.

[2469] Kābul and Tramontana.

[2470] Presumably that of Shamsu'd-dīn Muḥammad's mission. One of Bābur's couplets expresses longing for the fruits, and also for the "running waters", of lands other than Hindūstān, with conceits recalling those of his English contemporaries in verse, as indeed do several others of his short poems (*Rāmpūr Dīwān* Plate xvii A.).

[2471] Ḥai. MS. *nā marbūṭlighī*; so too the 2nd Pers. trs. but the 1st writes *wairānī u karābī* which suits the matter of defence.

[2472] *qūrghān*, walled-town; from the *maẓbūt* following, the defences are meant.

[2473] *viz*. Governor Khwāja Kalān, on whose want of dominance his sovereign makes good-natured reflection.

[2474] *'alūfa u qūnāl*; cf. 364*b*.

[2475] Following *aīlchī* (envoys) there is in the Ḥai. MS. and in I.O. 217 a doubtful word, *būmla, yūmla*; I.O. 215 (which contains a Persian trs. of the letter) is obscure, Ilminsky changes the wording slightly; Erskine has a free translation. Perhaps it is *yaumī*, daily, misplaced (*see* above).

[2476] Perhaps, endow the Mosque so as to leave no right of property in its revenues to their donor, here Bābur. Cf. Hughes' *Dict. of Islām* s.nn. *sharī'*, *masjid* and *waqf*.

[2477] f. 139. Khwāja Kalān himself had taken from Hindūstān the money for repairing this dam.

[2478] *sāpqūn ālīp*; the 2nd Pers. trs. as if from *sātqūn ālīp*, *kharīda*, purchasing.

[2479] *naẓar-gāh*, perhaps, theatre, as showing the play enacted at the ford. Cf. ff. 137, 236, 248*b*. Tūtūn-dara will be Masson's Tūtām-dara. Erskine locates Tūtūn-dara some 8 *kos* (16 m.) n. w. of Hūpīān (Ūpīān). Masson shews that it was a charming place (*Journeys in Biluchistan, Afghanistan and the Panj-āb*, vol. iii, cap. vi and vii).

[2480] *jībachī*. Bābur's injunction seems to refer to the maintaining of the corps and the manufacture of armour rather than to care for the individual men involved.

[2481] Either the armies in Nīl-āb, or the women in the Kābul-country (f. 375).

[2482] Perhaps what Bābur means is, that both what he had said to 'Abdu'l-lāh and what the quatrain expresses, are dissuasive from repentance. Erskine writes (*Mems.* p. 403) but without textual warrant, "I had resolution enough to persevere"; de Courteille (*Mems.* ii, 390), "*Voici un quatrain qui exprime au juste les difficultés de ma position.*"

[2483] The surface retort seems connected with the jacket, perhaps with a request for the gift of it.

[2484] Clearly what recalled this joke of Banāī's long-silent, caustic tongue was that its point lay ostensibly in a baffled wish—in 'Alī-sher's professed desire to be generous and a professed impediment, which linked in thought with Bābur's desire for wine, baffled by his abjuration. So much Banāī's smart verbal retort shows, but beneath this is the *double-entendre* which cuts at the Beg as miserly and as physically impotent, a defect which gave point to another jeer at his expense, one chronicled by Sām Mīrzā and translated in Hammer-Purgstall's *Geschichte von schönen Redekünste Persiens*, art. CLV. (Cf. f. 179-80.)—The word *mādagī* is used metaphorically for a button-hole; like *nā-mardī*, it carries secondary meanings, miserliness, impotence, *etc.* (Cf. Wollaston's *English-Persian Dictionary s.n.* button-hole, where only we have found *mādagī* with this sense.)

[2485] The 1st Pers. trs. expresses "all these jokes", thus including with the double-meanings of *mādagī*, the jests of the quatrain.

[2486] The 1st Pers. trs. fills out Bābur's allusive phrase here with "of the *Wālidiyyah*". His wording allows the inference that what he versified was a prose Turkī translation of a probably Arabic original.

[2487] Erskine comments here on the non-translation into Persian of Bābur's letters. Many MSS., however, contain a translation (f. 348, p. 624, n. 2 and E.'s n. f. 377*b*).

[2488] Anglicé, Thursday after 6 p.m.

[2489] What would suit measurement on maps and also Bābur's route is "Jumoheen" which is marked where the Sarāī Bāburpūr-Atsu-Phaphand road turns south, east of Phaphand (I.S. Map of 1900, Sheet 68).

[2490] var. *Qabāq*, *Qatāk*, *Qanāk*, to each of which a meaning might be attached. Bābur had written to Humāyūn about the frontier affair, as one touching the desired peace (f. 359).

[2491] This will refer to the late arrival in Āgra of the envoy named, who was not with his younger brother at the feast of f. 351*b* (f. 357, p. 641, n. 2).—As to Ṭahmāsp's style, see f. 354, f. 358.

[2492] Shāh-qulī may be the ill-informed narrator of f. 354.

[2493] Both are marked on the southward road from Jumoheen (Jumandnā?) for Auraiya.

[2494] The old Kālpī *pargana* having been sub-divided, Dīrapūr is now in the district of Cawnpore (Kānhpūr).

[2495] That this operation was not hair-cutting but head-shaving is shewn by the verbs T. *qīrmāq* and its Pers. trs. *tarāsh kardan*. To shave the head frequently is common in Central Asia.

[2496] This will be Chaparghatta on the Dīrapūr-Bhognīpūr-Chaparghatta-Mūsanagar road, the affixes *kada* and *ghatta* both meaning house, temple, *etc.*

[2497] Māhīm, and with her the child Gul-badan, came in advance of the main body of women. Bābur seems to refer again to her assumption of royal style by calling her Walī, Governor (f. 369 and n.). It is unusual that no march or halt is recorded on this day.

[2498] or, Ārampūr. We have not succeeded in finding this place; it seems to have been on the west bank of the Jumna, since twice Bābur when on the east bank, writes of coming opposite to it (*supra* and f. 379). If no move was made on Tuesday, Jumāda II. 6th (cf. last note), the distance entered as done on Wednesday would locate the halting-place somewhere near the Akbarpūr of later name, which stands on a road and at a ferry. But if the army did a stage on Tuesday, of which Bābur omits mention, Wednesday's march might well bring him opposite to Hamirpūr and to the "Rampur"-ferry. The verbal approximation of Ārampūr and "Rampur" arrests attention.—Local encroachment by the river, which is recorded in the District Gazetteers, may have something to do with the disappearance from these most useful books and from maps, of *pargana* Ādampūr (or, Ārampūr).

[2499] *tūshlāb.* It suits best here, since solitude is the speciality of the excursion, to read *tūshmāk* as meaning to take the road, Fr. *cheminer.*

[2500] *da'wī bīla*; *Mems.* p. 404, challenge; *Méms.* ii, 391, *il avait fait des façons*, a truth probably, but one inferred only.

[2501] This will be more to the south than Kūra Khaṣ, the headquarters of the large district; perhaps it is "Koora Khera" (? Kūra-khirāj) which suits the route (I.S. Map, Sheet 88).

[2502] Perhaps Kunda Kanak, known also as "Kuria, Koria, Kura and Kunra Kanak" (*D.G. of Fatḥpūr*).

[2503] Haswa or Hanswa. The conjoint name represents two villages some 6m. apart, and is today that of their railway-station.

[2504] almost due east of Fatḥpūr, on the old King's Highway (*Bādshāhī Sar-rāh*).

[2505] His ancestors had ruled in Jūnpūr from 1394 to 1476 AD., his father Ḥusain Shāh having been conquered by Sl. Sikandar *Lūdī* at the latter date. He was one of three rivals for supremacy in the East (*Sharq*), the others being Jalālu'd-dīn *Nūhānī* and Maḥmūd *Lūdī*,—Afghāns all three. Cf. Erskine's *History of India, Bābur*, i, 501.

[2506] This name appears on the I.S. Map, Sheet 88, but too far north to suit Bābur's distances, and also off the Sarāī Munda-Kusār-Karrah road. The position of Naubasta suits better.

[2507] Sher Khān was associated with Dūdū Bībī in the charge of her son's affairs. Bābur's favours to him, his son Humāyūn's future conqueror, will have been done during the Eastern campaign in 934 AH., of which so much record is missing. Cf. *Tārīkh-i-sher-shāhī*, E. & D.'s *History of India*, iv, 301 *et seq.* for particulars of Sher Khān (Farīd Khān *Sūr Afghān*).

[2508] In writing "SL. MAḤMŪD", Bābur is reporting his informant's style, he himself calling Maḥmūd "Khān" only (f. 363 and f. 363*b*).

[2509] This will be the more northerly of two Kusārs marked as in Karrah; even so, it is a very long 6 *kurohs* (12m.) from the Dugdugī of the I.S. Map (cf. n. *supra*).

[2510] *bīr pāra āsh u ta'ām*, words which suggest one of those complete meals served, each item on its separate small dish, and all dishes fitting like mosaic into one tray. T. *āsh* is cooked meat (f. 2 n. 1 and f. 343*b*); Ar. *ta'ām* will be sweets, fruit, bread, perhaps rice also.

[2511] The *yaktāī*, one-fold coat, contrasts with the *dū-tāhī*, two-fold (A.-i-A. Bib. Ind. ed., p. 101, and Blochmann's trs. p. 88).

[2512] This acknowledgement of right to the style Sulṭān recognized also supremacy of the Sharqī claim to rule over that of the Nūḥānī and *Lūdī* competitors.

[2513] *mīndīn bītī tūrgān waqāī'*. This passage Teufel used to support his view that Bābur's title for his book was *Waqāī'*, and not *Bābur-nāma* which, indeed, Teufel describes as the *Kazaner Ausgabe adoptirte Titel. Bābur-nāma*, however, is the title [or perhaps, merely scribe's name] associated both with Kehr's text and with the Ḥaidarābād Codex.—I have found no indication of the selection by Bābur of any title; he makes no mention of the matter and where he uses the word *waqāī'* or its congeners, it can be read as a common noun. In his colophon to the *Rāmpūr Dīwān*, it is a parallel of *ash'ār*, poems. Judging from what is found in the *Mubīn*, it may be right to infer that, if he had lived to complete his book—now broken off *s.a.* 914 AH. (f. 216*b*)—he would have been explicit as to its title, perhaps also as to his grounds for choosing it. Such grounds would have found fitting mention in a preface to the now abrupt opening of the *Bābur-nāma* (f. 1*b*), and if the *Malfūẓāt-i-tīmūrī* be Tīmūr's authentic autobiography, this book might have been named as an ancestral example influencing Bābur to write his own. Nothing against the authenticity of the *Malfūẓāt* can be inferred from the circumstance that Bābur does not name it, because the preface in which such mention would be in harmony with *e.g.* his *Walidiyyah* preface, was never written. It might accredit the *Malfūẓāt* to collate passages having common topics, as they appear in the *Bābur-nāma*, *Malfūẓāt-i-tīmūrī* and *Ẓafar-nāma* (cf. E. & D.'s H. of I. iv, 559 for a discussion by Dr. Sachau and Prof. Dowson on the *Malfūẓāt*). (Cf. Z.D.M. xxxvii, p. 184, Teufel's art. *Bābur und Abū'l-faẓl*; Smirnow's Cat. of *Manuscrits Turcs*, p. 142; Index *in loco s.nn. Mubīn* and Title.)

[2514] Koh-khirāj, Revenue-paying Koh (H. G. Nevill's *D. G. of Allāhābād*, p. 261).

[2515] *kīma aīchīdā*, which suggests a boat with a cabin, a *bajrā* (*Hobson-Jobson s.n.* budgerow).

[2516] He had stayed behind his kinsman Khwāja Kalān. Both, as Bābur has said, were descendants of Khwāja 'Ubaidu'l-lāh *Aḥrārī.* Khwāja Kalān was a grandson of Aḥrārī's second son Yahyā; Khwāja 'Abdu'sh-shahīd was the son of his fifth, Khwāja 'Abdu'l-lāh (Khwājagān-khwāja). 'Abdu'sh-shahīd returned to India under Akbar, received a fief, maintained 2,000 poor persons, left after 20 years, and died in Samarkand in 982 AH.-1574-5 AD. (A.-i-A., Blochmann's trs. and notes, pp. 423, 539).

[2517] f. 363, f. 363*b*.

[2518] Not found on maps; OOjani or Ujahni about suits the measured distance.

[2519] Prayāg, Ilāhābād, Allāhābād. Between the asterisk in my text (*supra*) and the one following "ford" before the foliation mark f. 364, the Ḥai. MS. has a *lacuna* which, as being preceded and followed by broken sentences, can hardly be due to a scribe's skip, but may result from the loss of a folio. What I have entered above between the asterisks is translated from the Kehr-Ilminsky text; it is in the two Persian translations also. Close scrutiny of it suggests that down to the end of the swimming episode it is not in order and that the account of the swim across the Ganges may be a survival of the now missing record of 934 AH. (f. 339). It is singular that the Pers. trss. make no mention of Pīāg or of Sīr-auliya; their omission arouses speculation, as to in which text, the Turkī or Persian, it was first tried to fill what remains a gap in the Ḥai. Codex. A second seeming sign of disorder is the incomplete sentence *yūrtgha kīlīb*, which is noted below. A third is the crowd of incidents now standing under "Tuesday". A fourth, and an important matter, is that on grounds noted at the end of the swimming passage (p. 655 n. 3) it is doubtful whether that passage is in its right place.—It may be that some-one, at an early date after Bābur's death, tried to fill the *lacuna* discovered in his manuscript, with help from loose folios or parts of them. Cf. Index *s.n.* swimming, and f. 377*b*, p. 680 n. 2.

[2520] The Chaghatāī sulṭāns will have been with 'Askarī east of the Ganges.

[2521] *tūr hawālīk*; *Mems.* p. 406, violence of the wind; *Mêms.* ii, 398, *une température très agréable.*

[2522] *yūrtgha kīlīb*, an incomplete sentence.

[2523] *ārāl bār aīkāndūr*, phrasing implying uncertainty; there may have been an island, or such a peninsula as a narrow-mouthed bend of a river forms, or a spit or bluff projecting into the river. The word *ārāl* represents *Aīkī-sū-ārāsī*, *Mīyān-dū-āb*, *Entre-eaux*, Twixt-two-streams, Mesopotamia.

[2524] *qūl*; Pers. trss. *dast andākhtan* and *dast.* Presumably the 33 strokes carried the swimmer across the deep channel, or the Ganges was crossed higher than Pīāg.

[2525] The above account of Bābur's first swim across the Ganges which is entered under date Jumāda II. 27th, 935 AH. (March 8th, 1529 AD.), appears misplaced, since he mentions under date Rajab 25th, 935 AH. (April 4th, 1529 AD. f. 366*b*), that he had swum the Ganges at Baksara (Buxar) a year before, *i.e.* on or close to Rajab 25th, 934 AH. (April 15th, 1528 AD.). Nothing in his writings shews that he was near Pīāg (Allāhābād) in 934 AH.; nothing indisputably connects the swimming episode with the "Tuesday" below which it now stands; there is no help given by dates. One supposes Bābur would take his first chance to swim the Ganges; this was offered at Qanauj (f. 336), but nothing in the short record of that time touches the topic. The next chance would be after he was in Aūd, when, by an unascertained route, perhaps down the Ghogrā, he made his way to Baksara where he says (f. 366*b*) he swam the river. Taking into consideration the various testimony noted, [Index *s.n.* swimming] there seems warrant for supposing that this swimming passage is a survival of the missing record of 934 AH. (f. 339). Cf. f. 377*b*, p. 680 and n. 2 for another surmised survival of 934 AH.

[2526] "Friday" here stands for Anglicé, Thursday after 6 p.m.; this, only, suiting Bābur's next explicit date Sha'bān 1st, Saturday.

[2527] The march, beginning on the Jumna, is now along the united rivers.

[2528] *ẓarb-ẓanlīk arābalār.* Here the carts are those carrying the guns.

[2529] From the particulars Bābur gives about the Tūs (Tons) and Karmā-nāśā, it would seem that he had not passed them last year, an inference supported by what is known of his route in that year:—He came from Gūālīār to the Kanār-passage (f. 336), there crossed the Jumna and went direct to Qanauj (f. 335), above Qanauj bridged the Ganges, went on to Bangarmāu (f. 338), crossed the Gūmtī and went to near the junction of the Ghogrā and Sardā (f. 338*b*). The next indication of his route is that he is at Baksara, but whether he reached it by water down the Ghogrā, as his meeting with Muḥ. Ma'rūf *Farmūlī* suggests (f. 377), or by land, nothing shews. From Baksara (f. 366) he went up-stream to Chausa (f. 365*b*), on perhaps to Sayyidpūr, 2m. from the mouth of the Gūmtī, and there left the Ganges for Jūnpūr (f. 365). I have found nothing about his return route to Āgra; it seems improbable that he would go so far south as to near Pīāg; a more northerly and direct road to Fatḥpūr and Sarāī Bāburpūr may have been taken.—Concerning Bābur's acts in 934 AH. the following item, (met with since I was working on 934 AH.), continues his statement (f. 338*b*) that he spent a few days near Aūd (Ajōdhya) to settle its affairs. The *D.G. of Fyzābāa* (H. E. Nevill) p. 173 says "In 1528 AD. Bābur came to Ajodhya (Aūd) and halted a week. He destroyed the ancient temple" (marking the birth-place of Rāma) "and on its site built a mosque, still known as Bābur's Mosque.... It has two inscriptions, one on the outside, one on the pulpit; both are in Persian; and bear the date 935 *AH*." This date may be that of the completion of the building.—(*Corrigendum*:—On f. 339 n. 1, I have too narrowly restricted the use of the name Sarjū. Bābur used it to describe what the maps of Arrowsmith and Johnson shew, and not only what the *Gazetteer of India* map of the United Provinces does. It applies to the Sardā (f. 339) as Bābur uses it when writing of the fords.)

[2530] Here the lacuna of the Ḥai. Codex ends.

[2531] Perhaps, where there is now the railway station of "Nulibai" (I.S. Map). The direct road on which the army moved, avoids the windings of the river.

[2532] This has been read as T. *kīnt*, P. *dih*, Eng. village and Fr. *village*.

[2533] "Nankunpur" lying to the north of Puhari railway-station suits the distance measured on maps.

[2534] These will be the women-travellers.

[2535] Perhaps jungle tracts lying in the curves of the river.

[2536] *jīrga*, which here stands for the beaters' incurving line, witness the exit of the buffalo at the end. Cf. f. 367*b* for a *jīrga* of boats.

[2537] *aūzūn aūzāgh*, many miles and many hours?

[2538] Bulloa? (I.S. Map).

[2539] Anglicé, Sunday after 6 p.m.

[2540] *'alufa u qunal* (f. 359*b*).

[2541] than the Ganges perhaps; or narrowish compared with other rivers, *e.g.* Ganges, Ghogrā, and Jūn.

[2542] *yīl-türgī yūrt*, by which is meant, I think, close to the same day a year back, and not an indefinite reference to some time in the past year.

[2543] Maps make the starting-place likely to be Sayyidpūr.

[2544] re-named Zamānīa, after Akbar's officer 'Alī-qulī Khān Khān-i-zamān, and now the head-quarters of the Zamānīa *pargana* of Ghāzīpūr. Madan-Benāres was in Akbar's *sarkār* of Ghāzīpūr. (It was not identified by E. or by de C.) Cf. *D.G. of Ghāzīpūr.*

[2545] In the earlier part of the Ḥai. Codex this Afghān tribal-name is written Nūḥānī, but in this latter portion a different scribe occasionally writes it Lūḥānī (Index *s.n.*).

[2546] *'arẓa-dāsht*, *i.e.* phrased as from one of lower station to a superior.

[2547] His letter may have announced his and his mother Dūdū Bībī's approach (f. 368-9).

[2548] Naṣīr Khān had been an amīr of Sl. Sikandar *Lūdī*. Sher Khān *Sūr* married his widow "Guhar Kusāīn", bringing him a large dowry (A.N. trs. p. 327; and *Tārīkh-i-sher-shāhi*, E. & D.'s *History of India* iv, 346).

[2549] He started from Chaparghatta (f. 361*b*, p. 650 n. 1).

[2550] *yīl-türgī yūrt.*

[2551] "This must have been the Eclipse of the 10th of May 1528 AD.; a fast is enjoined on the day of an eclipse" (Erskine).

[2552] Karmā-nāśā means loss of the merit acquired by good works.

[2553] The I.S. Map marks a main road leading to the mouth of the Karmā-nāśā and no other leading to the river for a considerable distance up-stream.

[2554] Perhaps "Thora-nadee" (I.S. Map).

[2555] Anglicé, Sunday after 6 p.m.

[2556] *aūtkān yīl.*

[2557] Perhaps the *dū-āba* between the Ganges and "Thora-nadee".

[2558] *yīl-tūr ... Gang-sūī-dīn mīn dastak bīla aūtūb, ba'ẓī āt, ba'ẓī tīwah mīnib, kīlīb, sair qīlīlīb aīdī.* Some uncertainty as to the meaning of the phrase *dastak bīla aūtūb* is caused by finding that while here de Courteille agrees with Erskine in taking it to mean swimming, he varies later (f. 373*b*) to *appuyés sur une pièce de bois.* Taking the Persian translations of three passages about crossing water into consideration (p. 655 after f. 363*b*, f. 366*b* (here), f. 373*b*), and also the circumstances that E. and de C. are once in agreement and that Erskine worked with the help of Oriental *munshīs*, I incline to think that *dastak bīla* does express swimming.—The question of its precise meaning bears on one concerning Bābur's first swim across the Ganges (p. 655, n. 3).—Perhaps I should say, however, that if the sentence quoted at the head of this note stood alone, without the extraneous circumstances supporting the reading of *dastak bīla* to mean swimming, I should incline to read it as stating that Bābur went on foot through the water, feeling his footing with a pole (*dastak*), and that his followers rode through the ford after him. Nothing in the quoted passage suggests that the horses and camels swam. But whether the Ganges was fordable at Baksara in Bābur's time, is beyond surmise.

[2559] *faṣl soz*, which, manifestly, were to be laid before the envoy's master. The articles are nowhere specified; one is summarized merely on f. 365. The incomplete sentence of the Turkī text (*supra*) needs their specification at this place, and an explicit statement of them would have made clearer the political relations of Bābur with Naṣrat Shāh.—A folio may have been lost from Bābur's manuscript; it might have specified the articles, and also have said something leading to the next topic of the diary, now needing preliminaries, *viz.* that of the Mīrzā's discontent with his new appointment, a matter not mentioned earlier.

[2560] This suits Bābur's series, but Gladwin and Wüstenfeld have 10th.

[2561] The first is near, the second on the direct road from Buxar for Ārrah.

[2562] The Ḥai. MS. makes an elephant be posted as the sole scout; others post a *sardār*, or post braves; none post man and beast.

[2563] This should be 5th; perhaps the statement is confused through the gifts being given late, Anglicé, on Tuesday 4th, Islamicé on Wednesday night.

[2564] The Mīrzā's Tīmūrid birth and a desire in Bābur to give high status to a representative he will have wished to leave in Bihār when he himself went to his western dominions, sufficiently explain the bestowal of this sign of sovereignty.

[2565] *jīrgā*. This instance of its use shews that Bābur had in mind not a completed circle, but a line, or in sporting parlance, not a hunting-circle but a beaters'-line. [Cf. f. 251, f. 364*b* and *infra* of the crocodile.] The word is used also for a governing-circle, a tribal-council.

[2566] *aūlūgh* (*kīma*). Does *aūlūgh* (*aūlūq*, *ūlūq*) connect with the "bulky Oolak or baggage-boat of Bengal"? (*Hobson-Jobson s.n.* Woolock, oolock).

[2567] De Courteille's reading of Ilminsky's "Bāburī" (p. 476) as Bāīrī, old servant, hardly suits the age of the boat.

[2568] Bābur anticipated the custom followed *e.g.* by the White Star and Cunard lines, when he gave his boats names having the same terminal syllable; his is *āīsh*; on it he makes the quip of the har *āīsh* of the Farmāīsh.

[2569] As Vullers makes Ar. *ghurfat* a synonym of *chaukandī*, the Farmāīsh seems likely to have had a cabin, open at the sides. De Courteille understood it to have a rounded stern. [Cf. E. & D.'s *History of India* v, 347, 503 n.; and Gul-badan's H. N. trs. p. 98, n. 2.]

[2570] *mīndīn rukhṣat āldī*; phrasing which bespeaks admitted equality, that of Tīmūrid birth.

[2571] *i.e.* subjects of the Afghān ruler of Bengal; many will have been Bihārīs and Pūrbiyas. Makhdūm-i-'ālam was Naṣrat Shāh's Governor in Ḥājīpūr.

[2572] This might imply that the Afghāns had been prevented from joining Maḥmūd Khān *Lūdī* near the Son.

[2573] Sl. Muḥammad Shāh *Nūḥānī Afghān*, the former ruler of Bihār, dead within a year. He had trained Farīd Khān *Sūr* in the management of government affairs; had given him, for gallant encounter with a tiger, the title Sher Khān by which, or its higher form Sher Shāh, history knows him, and had made him his young son's "deputy", an office Sher Khān held after the father's death in conjunction with the boy's mother Dūdū Bībī (*Tārīkh-i-sher-shāhī*, E. & D.'s *History of India* iv, 325 *et seq.*).

[2574] *gūz bāghī yūsūnlūq*; by which I understand they were held fast from departure, as *e.g.* a mouse by the fascination of a snake.

[2575] f. 365 mentions a letter which may have announced their intention.

[2576] Ganges; they thus evaded the restriction made good on other Afghāns.

[2577] Anglicé, Saturday 8th after 6 p.m.

[2578] The *D. G. of Shāhābād* (pp. 20 and 127) mentions that "it is said Bābur marched to Ārrah after his victory over Maḥmūd *Lūdī*", and that "local tradition still points to a place near the Judge's Court as that on which he pitched his camp".

[2579] Kharīd which is now a *pargana* of the Ballia district, lay formerly on both sides of the Ghogrā. When the army of Kharīd opposed Bābur's progress, it acted for Naṣrat Shāh, but this Bābur diplomatically ignored in assuming that there was peace between Bengal and himself.—At this time Naṣrat Shāh held the riverain on the left bank of the Ghogrā but had lost Kharīd of the right bank, which had been taken from him by Jūnaid *Barlās*. A record of his occupation still survives in Kharīd-town, an inscription dated by his deputy as for 1529 AD. (*District Gazetteer of Ballia* H. R. Nevill), and *D. G. of Sāran* (L. L. S. O'Malley), Historical Chapters.

[2580] Bābur's opinion of Naṣrat Shāh's hostility is more clearly shewn here than in the verbal message of f. 369.

[2581] This will be an unceremonious summary of a word-of-mouth message.

[2582] Cf. f. 366*b*, p. 661 n. 2.

[2583] This shews that Bābur did not recognize the Sāran riverain down to the Ganges as belonging to Kharīd. His offered escort of Turks would safe-guard the Kharīdīs if they returned to the right bank of the Ghogrā which was in Turk possession.

[2584] The Ḥai. MS. has *wālī*, clearly written; which, as a word representing Māhīm would suit the sentence best, may make playful reference to her royal commands (f. 361*b*), by styling her the Governor (*wālī*). Erskine read the word as a place-name Dipālī, which I have not found; De Courteille omits Ilminsky's *w:ras* (p. 478). The MSS. vary and are uncertain.

[2585] This is the "Kadjar" of Réclus' *L'Asie antérieure* and is the name of the Turkmān tribe to which the present ruling house of Persia belongs. "Turkmān" might be taken as applied to Shāh Ṭaḥmāsp by Dīv Sulṭān's servant on f. 354.

[2586] *Nelumbium speciosum*, a water-bean of great beauty.

[2587] Shaikh Yaḥyā had been the head of the Chishtī Order. His son (d. 782 AH.-1380-1 AD.) was the author of works named by Abū'l-faẓl as read aloud to Akbar, a discursive detail which pleads in my excuse that those who know Bābur well cannot but see in his grandson's character and success the fruition of his mental characteristics and of his labours in Hindūstān. (For Sharafu'd-dīn *Munīrī*, cf. *Khazīnatu'l-asfiyā* ii, 390-92; and *Āyīn-i-akbarī s.n.*)

[2588] Kostenko's *Turkistān Region* describes a regimen for horses which Bābur will have seen in practice in his native land, one which prevented the defect that hindered his at Munīr from accomplishing more than some 30 miles before mid-day.

[2589] The distance from Munīr to the bank of the Ganges will have been considerably longer in Bābur's day than now because of the change of the river's course through its desertion of the Burh-gangā channel (cf. next note).

[2590] In trying to locate the site of Bābur's coming battle with the forces of Naṣrat Shāh, it should be kept in mind that previous to the 18th century, and therefore, presumably, in his day, the Ganges flowed in the "Burh-ganga" (Old Ganges) channel which now is closely followed by the western boundary of the Ballia *pargana* of Dū-āba; that the Ganges and Ghogrā will have met where this old channel entered the bed of the latter river; and also, as is seen from Bābur's narrative, that above the confluence the Ghogrā will have been confined to a narrowed channel. When the Ganges flowed in the Burh-ganga channel, the now Ballia *pargana* of Dū-āba was a sub-division of Bihiya and continuous with Shāhābād. From it in Bihiya Bābur crossed the Ganges into Kharīd, doing this at a place his narrative locates as some 2 miles from the confluence. Cf. *D. G. of Ballia*, pp. 9, 192-3, 206, 213. It may be observed that the former northward extension of Bihiya to the Burh-ganga channel explains Bābur's estimate (f. 370) of the distance from Munīr to his camp on the Ganges; his 12*k*. (24m.) may then have been correct; it is now too high.

[2591] De Courteille, *pierrier*, which may be a balista. Bābur's writings give no indication of other than stone-ammunition for any projectile-engine or fire-arm. Cf. R. W. F. Payne-Gallwey's *Projectile-throwing engines of the ancients.*

[2592] Sir R. W. F. Payne-Gallwey writes in *The Cross-bow* (p. 40 and p. 41) what may apply to Bābur's *ẓarb-ẓan* (culverin?) and *tufang* (matchlock), when he describes the larger culverin as a heavy hand-gun of from 16-18lb., as used by the foot-soldier and requiring the assistance of an attendant to work it; also when he says that it became the portable arquebus which was in extensive use in Europe by the Swiss in 1476 AD.; and that between 1510 and 1520 the arquebus described was superseded by what is still seen amongst remote tribes in India, a matchlock arquebus.

[2593] The two positions Bābur selected for his guns would seem to have been opposite two ferry-heads, those, presumably, which were blocked against his pursuit of Bīban and Bāyazīd. 'Alī-qulī's emplacement will have been on the high bank of old alluvium of south-eastern Kharīd, overlooking the narrowed channel demanded by Bābur's narrative, one pent in presumably by *kankar* reefs such as there are in the region. As illustrating what the channel might have been, the varying breadth of the Ghogrā along the 'Azamgarh District may be quoted, *viz.* from 10 miles to

2/5m., the latter being where, as in Kharīd, there is old alluvium with *kankar* reefs preserving the banks. Cf. Reid's *Report of Settlement Operations in 'Azamgarh, Sikandarpur, and Bhadaon.*—Firishta gives Badrū as the name of one ferry (lith. ed. i. 210).

[2594] Muṣṭafa, like 'Alī-qulī, was to take the offensive by gun-fire directed on the opposite bank. Judging from maps and also from the course taken by the Ganges through the Burh-ganga channel and from Bābur's narrative, there seems to have been a narrow reach of the Ghogrā just below the confluence, as well as above.

[2595] This ferry, bearing the common name Haldī (turmeric), is located by the course of events as at no great distance above the enemy's encampment above the confluence. It cannot be the one of Sikandarpūr West.

[2596] *guẕr*, which here may mean a casual ford through water low just before the Rains. As it was not found, it will have been temporary.

[2597] *i.e.* above Bābur's positions.

[2598] *sarwar* (or *dar*) *waqt.*

[2599] The preceding sentence is imperfect and varies in the MSS. The 1st Pers. trs., the wording of which is often explanatory, says that there were *no* passages, which, as there were many ferries, will mean fords. The Haldī-guẕr where 'Askarī was to cross, will have been far below the lowest Bābur mentions, *viz.* Chatur-mūk (Chaupāra).

[2600] This passage presupposes that guns in Kharīd could hit the hostile camp in Sāran. If the river narrowed here as it does further north, the Ghāzī mortar, which seems to have been the only one Bābur had with him, would have carried across, since it threw a stone 1,600 paces (*qadam*, f. 309). Cf. Reid's *Report* quoted above.

[2601] Anglicé, Saturday after 6p.m.

[2602] *yaqīn būlghān fauj*, var. *ta'īn būlghān fauj*, the army appointed (to cross). The boats will be those collected at the Haldī-ferry, and the army 'Askarī's.

[2603] *i.e.* near 'Alī-qulī's emplacement.

[2604] Cf. f. 303, f. 309, f. 337 and n. 4.

[2605] "The *yasāwal* is an officer who carries the commands of the prince, and sees them enforced" (Erskine). Here he will have been the superintendent of coolies moving earth.

[2606] *ma'jūn-nāk* which, in these days of Bābur's return to obedience, it may be right to translate in harmony with his psychical outlook of self-reproach, by *ma'jūn*-polluted. Though he had long ceased to drink wine, he still sought cheer and comfort, in his laborious days, from inspiriting and forbidden confections.

[2607] Probably owing to the less precise phrasing of his Persian archetype, Erskine here has reversed the statement, made in the Turkī, that Bābur slept in the Asāīsh (not the Farmāīsh).

[2608] *aūstīdā tāshlār.* An earlier reading of this, *viz.* that stones were thrown on the intruder is negatived by Bābur's mention of wood as the weapon used.

[2609] *sū sārī* which, as the boats were between an island and the river's bank, seems likely to mean that the man went off towards the main stream. *Mems.* p. 415, "made his escape in the river"; *Méms.* ii, 418, *dans la direction du large.*

[2610] This couplet is quoted by Jahāngīr also (*Tūzūk*, trs. Rogers & Beveridge, i, 348).

[2611] This, taken with the positions of other crossing-parties, serves to locate 'Askarī's "Haldī-passage" at no great distance above 'Alī-qulī's emplacement at the confluence, and above the main Bengal force.

[2612] perhaps, towed from the land. I have not found Bābur using any word which clearly means to row, unless indeed a later *rawān* does so. The force meant to cross in the boats taken up under cover of night was part of Bābur's own, no doubt.

[2613] *ātīsh-bāzī* lit. fire-playing, if a purely Persian compound; if *ātīsh* be Turkī, it means discharge, shooting. The word "fire-working" is used above under the nearest to contemporary guidance known to me, *viz.* that of the list of persons who suffered in the Patna massacre "during the troubles of October 1763 AD.", in which list are the names of four Lieutenants fire-workers (*Calcutta Review*, Oct. 1884, and Jan. 1885, art. *The Patna Massacre*, H. Beveridge).

[2614] *bī tahāshī*, without protest or demur.

[2615] Anglicé, Wednesday after 6 p.m.

[2616] Perhaps those which had failed to pass in the darkness; perhaps those from Haldī-guẕr, which had been used by 'Askarī's troops. There appear to be obvious reasons for their keeping abreast on the river with the troops in Sāran, in order to convey reinforcements or to provide retreat.

[2617] *kīmalār aūstīdā*, which may mean that he came, on the high bank, to where the boats lay below.

[2618] as in the previous note, *kīmalār aūstīdā*. These will have been the few drawn up-stream along the enemy's front.

[2619] The reproach conveyed by Bābur's statement is borne out by the strictures of Ḥaidar Mīrzā *Dūghlāt* on Bābā Sulṭān's neglect of duty (*Tārīkh-ī-rashīdī* trs. cap. lxxvii).

[2620] *yūsūnlūq tūshī*, Pers. trss. *ṭarf khūd*, i.e. their place in the array, a frequent phrase.

[2621] *dastak bīla dosta-i-qāmīsh bīla*. Cf. f. 363*b* and f. 366*b*, for passages and notes connected with swimming and *dastak*. Erskine twice translates *dastak bīla* by swimming; but here de Courteille changes from his earlier *à la nage* (f. 366*b*) to *appuyés sur une pièce de bois*. Perhaps the swift current was crossed by swimming with the support of a bundle of reeds, perhaps on rafts made of such bundles (cf. *Illustrated London News*, Sep. 16th, 1916, for a picture of Indian soldiers so crossing on rafts).

[2622] perhaps they were in the Burh-ganga channel, out of gun-fire.

[2623] If the Ghogrā flowed at this point in a narrow channel, it would be the swifter, and less easy to cross than where in an open bed.

[2624] *chīrīk-aīlī*, a frequent compound, but one of which the use is better defined in the latter than the earlier part of Bābur's writings to represent what then answered to an Army Service Corps. This corps now crosses into Sāran and joins the fighting force.

[2625] This appears to refer to the crossing effected before the fight.

[2626] or Kūndbah. I have not succeeded in finding this name in the Nirhun *pargana*; it may have been at the southern end, near the "Domaigarh" of maps. In it was Tīr-mūhānī, perhaps a village (f. 377, f. 381).

[2627] This passage justifies Erskine's surmise (*Memoirs*, p. 411, n. 4) that the Kharīd-country lay on both banks of the Ghogrā. His further surmise that, on the east bank of the Ghogrā, it extended to the Ganges would be correct also, since the Ganges flowed, in Bābur's day, through the Burh-ganga (Old Ganges) channel along the southern edge of the present Kharīd, and thus joined the Ghogrā higher than it now does.

[2628] Bāyazīd and Ma'rūf *Farmūlī* were brothers. Bāyazīd had taken service with Bābur in 932 AH. (1526 AD.), left him in 934 AH. (end of 1527 AD.) and opposed him near Qanūj. Ma'rūf, long a rebel against Ibrāhīm *Lūdī*, had never joined Bābur; two of his sons did so; of the two, Muḥammad and Mūsa, the latter may be the one mentioned as at Qanūj, "Ma'rūf's son" (f. 336).—For an interesting sketch of Ma'rūf's character and for the location in Hindūstān of the Farmūlī clan, *see* the *Wāqi'āt-i-mushtāqī*, E. & D.'s *History of India*, iv, 584.—In connection with Qanūj, the discursive remark may be allowable, that Bābur's halt during the construction of the bridge of boats across the Ganges in 934 AH. is still commemorated by the name Bādshāh-nagar of a village between Bangarmau and Nānāmau (Elliot's *Onau*, p. 45).

[2629] On f. 381 'Abdu'l-lāh's starting-place is mentioned as Tīr-mūhānī.

[2630] The failure to join would be one of the evils predicted by the dilatory start of the ladies from Kābul (f. 360*b*).

[2631] The order for these operations is given on f. 355*b*.

[2632] f. 369. The former Nūḥānī chiefs are now restored to Bihār as tributaries of Bābur.

[2633] Erskine estimated the *krūr* at about £25,000, and the 50 *laks* at about £12,500.

[2634] The Mīrzā thus supersedes Junaid *Barlās* in Jūnpūr.—The form Jūnapūr used above and elsewhere by Bābur and his Persian translators, supports the *Gazetteer of India* xlv, 74 as to the origin of the name Jūnpūr.

[2635] a son of Naṣrat Shāh. No record of this earlier legation is with the *Bābur-nāma* manuscripts; probably it has been lost. The only article found specified is the one asking for the removal of the Kharīd army from a ferry-head Bābur wished to use; Naṣrat Shāh's assent to this is an anti-climax to Bābur's victory on the Ghogrā.

[2636] Chaupāra is at the Sāran end of the ferry, at the Sikandarpūr one is Chatur-mūk (Four-faces, an epithet of Brahma and Vishnu).

[2637] It may be inferred from the earlier use of the phrase Gogar (or Gagar) and Sarū (Sīrū or Sīrd), on f. 338-8*b*, that whereas the rebels were, earlier, for crossing Sarū only, *i.e.* the Ghogrā below its confluence with the Sarda, they had now changed for crossing above the confluence and further north. Such a change is explicable by desire to avoid encounter with Bābur's following, here perhaps the army of Aūd, and the same desire is manifested by their abandonment of a fort captured (f. 377*b*) some days before the rumour reached Bābur of their crossing Sarū and Gogar.—Since translating the passage on f. 338, I have been led, by enforced attention to the movement of the confluence of Ghogrā with Ganges (Sarū with Gang) to see that that translation, eased in obedience to distances shewn in maps, may be wrong and that Bābur's statement that he dismounted 2-3 *kurohs* (4-6 m.) above Aūd at the confluence of Gogar with Sarū, may have some geographical interest and indicate movement of the two affluents such *e.g.*

as is indicated of the Ganges and Ghogrā by tradition and by the name Burh-ganga (cf. f. 370, p. 667, n. 2).

[2638] or L:knūr, perhaps Liknū or Liknūr. The capricious variation in the MSS. between L:knū and L:knūr makes the movements of the rebels difficult to follow. Comment on these variants, tending to identify the places behind the words, is grouped in Appendix T, *On L:knū* (*Lakhnau*) and *L:knūr* (*Lakhnār*).

[2639] Taking *guẕr* in the sense it has had hitherto in the *Bābur-nāma* of ferry or ford, the detachment may have been intended to block the river-crossings of "Sarū and Gogar". If so, however, the time for this was past, the rebels having taken a fort west of those rivers on Ramẓān 13th. Nothing further is heard of the detachment.—That news of the rebel-crossing of the rivers did not reach Bābur before the 18th and news of their capture of L:knū or L:knūr before the 19th may indicate that they had crossed a good deal to the north of the confluence, and that the fort taken was one more remote than Lakhnau (Oude). Cf. Appendix T.

[2640] Anglicé, Wednesday after 6 p.m.

[2641] These are recited late in the night during Ramẓān.

[2642] *kaghaẕ u ajẓā'*, perhaps writing-paper and the various sections of the *Bābur-nāma* writings, *viz.* biographical notices, descriptions of places, detached lengths of diary, *farmāns* of Shaikh Zain. The *lacunæ* of 934 AH., 935 AH., and perhaps earlier ones also may be attributed reasonably to this storm. It is easy to understand the loss of *e.g.* the conclusion of the Farghāna section, and the diary one of 934 AH., if they lay partly under water. The accident would be better realized in its disastrous results to the writings, if one knew whether Bābur wrote in a bound or unbound volume. From the minor losses of 935 AH., one guesses that the current diary at least had not reached the stage of binding.

[2643] The *tūnglūq* is a flap in a tent-roof, allowing light and air to enter, or smoke to come out.

[2644] *ajẓā' u kitāb. See* last note but one. The *kitāb* (book) might well be Bābur's composed narrative on which he was now working, as far as it had then gone towards its untimely end (Ḥai. MS. f. 216*b*).

[2645] *saqarlāṭ kut-ẓīlūcha*, where *saqarlāṭ* will mean warm and woollen.

[2646] Kharīd-town is some 4 m. s.e. of the town of Sikandarpūr.

[2647] or L:knū. Cf. Appendix T. It is now 14 days since 'Abdu'l-lāh *kitābdār* had left Tīr-mūhānī (f. 380) for Saṃbhal; as he was in haste, there had been time for him to go beyond Aūd (where Bāqī was) and yet get the news to Bābur on the 19th.

[2648] In a way not usual with him, Bābur seems to apply three epithets to this follower, *viz. mīng-begī*, *shaghāwal*, *Tāshkīndī* (Index *s.n.*).

[2649] or Kandla; cf. Revenue list f. 293; is it now Sāran Khāṣ?

[2650] £18,000 (Erskine). For the total yield of Kundla (or Kandla) and Sarwār, *see* Revenue list (f. 293).

[2651] f. 375. P. 675 n. 2 and f. 381, p. 687 n. 3.

[2652] A little earlier Bābur has recorded his ease of mind about Bihār and Bengal, the fruit doubtless of his victory over Maḥmūd *Lūdī* and Naṣrat Shāh; he now does the same about Bihār and Sarwār, no doubt because he has replaced in Bihār, as his tributaries, the Nūḥānī chiefs and has settled other Afghāns, Jalwānīs and Farmūlīs in a Sarwār cleared of the Jalwānī (?) rebel Bīban and the Farmūlī opponents Bāyazīd and Ma'rūf. The Farmūlī Shaikh-zādas, it may be recalled, belonged by descent to Bābur's Kābul district of Farmūl.—The *Wāqi'āt-i-mushtāqī* (E. & D.'s *H. of I.* iv, 548) details the position of the clan under Sikandar *Lūdī*.

[2653] The MSS. write Fatḥpūr but Natḥpūr suits the context, a *pargana* mentioned in the *Āyīn-i-akbarī* and now in the 'Azamgarh district. There seems to be no Fatḥpūr within Bābur's limit of distance. The *D. G. of 'Azamgarh* mentions two now insignificant Fatḥpūrs, one as having a school, the other a market. The name G:l:r:h (K:l:r:h) I have not found.

[2654] The passage contained in this section seems to be a survival of the lost record of 934 AH. (f. 339). I have found it only in the *Memoirs* p. 420, and in Mr. Erskine's own Codex of the *Wāqi'āt-i-bāburī* (now B.M. Add. 26,200), f. 371 where however several circumstances isolate it from the context. It may be a Persian translation of an authentic Turkī fragment, found, perhaps with other such fragments, in the Royal Library. Its wording disassociates it from the 'Abdu'r-raḥīm text. The Codex (No. 26,200) breaks off at the foot of a page (*supra*, Fatḥpūr) with a completed sentence. The supposedly-misplaced passage is entered on the next folio as a sort of ending of the *Bābur-nāma* writings; in a rough script, inferior to that of the Codex, and is followed by *Tam, tam* (Finis), and an incomplete date 98-, in words. Beneath this a line is drawn, on which is subtended the triangle frequent with scribes; within this is what seems to be a completion of the date to 980 AH. and a pious wish, scrawled in an even rougher hand than the rest.—Not only in diction and in script but in contents also the passage is a misfit where it now stands; it can hardly describe a village on the Sarū; Bābur in 935 AH. did not march for Ghāzīpūr but may have done so in 934 AH. (p. 656, n. 3); Ismā'īl *Jalwānī* had had leave given already in 935 AH. (f. 377) under other conditions, ones bespeaking more trust and tried allegiance.—Possibly the place described as having fine buildings, gardens *etc.* is Aūd (Ajodhya) where Bābur spent some days in 934 AH. (cf. f. 363*b*, p. 655 n. 3).

[2655] "Here my Persian manuscript closes" (This is B.M. Add. 26,200). "The two additional fragments are given from Mr. Metcalfe's manuscript alone" (now B.M. Add. 26,202) "and unluckily, it is extremely incorrect" (Erskine). This note will have been written perhaps a decade before 1826, in which year the *Memoirs of Bābur* was published, after long delay. Mr. Erskine's own Codex (No. 26,200) was made good at a later date, perhaps when he was working on his History of India (pub. 1854), by a well-written supplement which carries the diary to its usual end *s.a.* 936 AH. and also gives Persian translations of Bābur's letters to Humāyūn and Khwāja Kalān.

[2656] Here, as earlier, Natḥpūr suits the context better than Fatḥpūr. In the Natḥpūr *pargana*, at a distance from Chaupāra approximately suiting Bābur's statement of distance, is the lake "Tal Ratoi", formerly larger and deeper than now. There is a second further west and now larger than Tal Ratoi; through this the Ghogrā once flowed, and through it has tried within the last half-century to break back. These changes in Tal Ratoi and in the course of the Ghogrā dictate caution in attempting to locate places which were on it in Bābur's day *e.g.* K:l:r:h (*supra*).

[2657] Appendix T.

[2658] This name has the following variants in the Ḥai. MS. and in Kehr's:—Dalm-ū-ūū-ūr-ūd-ūṭ. The place was in Akbar's *sarkār* of Mānikpūr and is now in the Rai Bareilly district.

[2659] Perhaps Chaksar, which was in Akbar's *sarkār* of Jūnpūr, and is now in the 'Azamgarh district.

[2660] Ḥai. MS. *J:nāra khūnd tawābī sī bīla* (perhaps *tawābī'sī* but not so written). The obscurity of these words is indicated by their variation in the manuscripts. Most scribes have them as Chunār and Jūnpūr, guided presumably by the despatch of a force to Chunār on receipt of the news, but another force was sent to Dalmau at the same time. The rebels were defeated s.w. of Dalmau and thence went to Mahūba; it is not certain that they had crossed the Ganges at Dalmau; there are difficulties in supposing the fort they captured and abandoned was Lakhnau (Oude); they might have gone south to near Kālpī and Ādampūr, which are at no great distance from where they were defeated by Bāqī *shaghāwal*, if Lakhnūr (now Shahābād in Rāmpūr) were the fort. (Cf. Appendix T.)—To take up the interpretation of the words quoted above, at another point, that of the kinsfolk or fellow-Afghāns the rebels planned to join:—these kinsfolk may have been, of Bāyazīd, the Farmūlīs in Sarwār, and of Bīban, the Jalwānīs of the same place. The two may have trusted to relationship for harbourage during the Rains, disloyal though they were to their kinsmen's accepted suzerain. Therefore if they were once across Ganges and Jumna, as they were in Mahūba, they may have thought of working eastwards south of the Ganges and of getting north into Sarwār through territory belonging to the Chunār and Jūnpūr governments. This however is not expressed by the words quoted above; perhaps Bābur's record was hastily and incompletely written.—Another reading may be Chunār and Jaund (in Akbar's *sarkār* of Rohtās).

[2661] *yūlīnī tūshqāīlār.* It may be observed concerning the despatch of Muḥammad-i-zamān M. and of Junaid *Barlās* that they went to their new appointments Jūnpūr and Chunār respectively; that their doing so was an orderly part of the winding-up of Bābur's Eastern operations; that they remained as part of the Eastern garrison, on duty apart from that of blocking the road of Bīban and Bāyazīd.

[2662] This mode of fishing is still practised in India (Erskine).

[2663] Islāmicé, Saturday night; Anglicé, Friday after 6 p.m.

[2664] This Tūs, "Tousin, or Tons, is a branch from the Ghogrā coming off above Faizābād and joining the Sarju or Parsarū below 'Azamgarh" (Erskine).

[2665] Kehr's MS. p. 1132, Māng (or Mānk); Ḥai. MS. Tāīk; I.O. 218 f. 328 Bā:k; I.O. 217 f. 236*b*, Bīāk. Māīng in the Sulṭānpūr district seems suitably located (*D.G. of Sulṭānpūr*, p. 162).

[2666] This will be the night-guard (*'asas*); the librarian (*kitābdār*) is in Saṃbhal. I.O. 218 f. 325 inserts *kitābdār* after 'Abdu'l-lāh's name where he is recorded as sent to Saṃbhal (f. 375).

[2667] He will have announced to Tāj Khān the transfer of the fort to Junaid *Barlās.*

[2668] £3750. Parsarūr was in Akbar's *ṣūbah* of Lāhor; G. of I. xx, 23, Pasrūr.

[2669] The estimate may have been made by measurement (f. 356) or by counting a horse's steps (f. 370). Here the Ḥai. MS. and Kehr's have D:lmūd, but I.O. 218 f. 328*b* (D:lmūū).

[2670] As on f. 361*b*, so here, Bābur's wording tends to locate Ādampūr on the right (west) bank of the Jumna.

[2671] Ḥai. MS. *aūta*, presumably for *aūrta*; Kehr's p. 1133, Aūd-dāghī, which, as Bāqī led the Aūd army, is *ben trovato*; both Persian translations, *miāngānī*, central, inner, *i.e. aūrta*, perhaps household troops of the Centre.

[2672] Anglicé, Saturday 12th after 6 p.m.

[2673] In Akbar's *sarkār* of Kālanjar, now in the Hamirpūr district.

[2674] £7500 (Erskine). Amrohā is in the Morādābād district.

[2675] At the Chaupāra-Chaturmūk ferry (f. 376).—*Corrigendum*:—In the Index of the *Bābur-nāma Facsimile*, Mūsa *Farmūlī* and Mūsa Sl. are erroneously entered as if one man.

[2676] *i.e.* riding light and fast. The distance done between Ādampūr and Āgra was some 157 miles, the time was from 12 a.m. on Tuesday morning to about 9 p.m. of Thursday. This exploit serves to show that three years of continuous activity in the plains of Hindūstān had not destroyed Bābur's capacity for sustained effort, spite of several attacks of (malarial?) fever.

[2677] Anglicé, Tuesday 12.25 a.m.

[2678] He was governor of Etāwa.

[2679] Islamicé, Friday, Shawwāl 18th, Anglicé, Thursday, June 24th, soon after 9 p.m.

[2680] Anglicé, she arrived at mid-night of Saturday.—Gul-badan writes of Māhīm's arrival as unexpected and of Bābur's hurrying off on foot to meet her (*Humāyūn-nāma* f. 14, trs. p. 100).

[2681] Māhīm's journey from Kābul to Āgra had occupied over 5 months.

[2682] Hindū Beg *qūchīn* had been made Humāyūn's retainer in 932 AH. (f. 297), and had taken possession of Saṃbhal for him. Hence, as it seems, he was ordered, while escorting the ladies from Kābul, to go to Saṃbhal. He seems to have gone before waiting on Bābur, probably not coming into Āgra till now.—It may be noted here that in 933 AH. he transformed a Hindū temple into a Mosque in Saṃbhal; it was done by Bābur's orders and is commemorated by an inscription still existing on the Mosque, one seeming not to be of his own composition, judging by its praise of himself. (JASB. *Proceedings*, May 1873, p. 98, Blochmann's art. where the inscription is given and translated; and *Archæological Survey Reports*, xii, p. 24-27, with Plates showing the Mosque).

[2683] Cf. f. 375, f. 377, with notes concerning 'Abdu'l-lāh and Tīr-mūhānī. I have not found the name Tīr-mūhānī on maps; its position can be inferred from Bābur's statement (f. 375) that he had sent 'Abdu'l-lāh to Saṃbhal, he being then at Kunba or Kunīa in the Nurhun *pargana*.—The name Tīr-mūhānī occurs also in Gorakhpūr.—It was at Tīr-mūhānī (Three-mouths) that Khwānd-amīr completed the *Ḥabību's-siyar* (lith. ed. i, 83; Rieu's *Pers. Cat.* p. 1079). If the name imply three water-mouths, they might be those of Ganges, Ghogrā and Dāhā.

[2684] *nīm-kāra*. E. and de C. however reverse the *rôles*.

[2685] The *Tārīkh-i-gūālīārī* (B.M. Add. 16, 709, p. 18) supplements the fragmentary accounts which, above and *s.a.* 936 AH., are all that the *Bābur-nāma* now preserves concerning Khwāja Rāḥīm-dād's misconduct. It has several mistakes but the gist of its information is useful. It mentions that the Khwāja and his paternal-uncle Mahdī Khwāja had displeased Bābur; that Raḥīm-dād resolved to take refuge with the ruler of Mālwā (Muḥammad *Khīljī*) and to make over Gūālīār to a Rājpūt landholder of that country; that upon this Shaikh Muḥammad *Ghauṣ* went to Āgra and interceded with Bābur and obtained his forgiveness for Raḥīm-dād. Gūālīār was given back to Raḥīm-dād but after a time he was superseded by Abū'l-fatḥ [Shaikh Gūran]. For particulars about Mahdī Khwāja and a singular story told about him by Niẓāmu'd-dīn Aḥmad in the *Ṭabaqāt-i-akbarī*, *vide* Gul-badan's *Ḥumāyūn-nāma*, Appendix B, and *Translator's Note* p. 702, Section *f*.

[2686] He may have come about the misconduct of his nephew Raḥīm-dād.

[2687] The 'Īdu'l-kabīr, the Great Festival of 10th Ẕū'l-ḥijja.

[2688] About £1750 (Erskine).

[2689] Perhaps he was from the tract in Persia still called Chaghatāī Mountains. One Ibrāhīm *Chaghatāī* is mentioned by Bābur (f. 175b) with Turkmān begs who joined Ḥusain *Bāī-qarā*. This Ḥasan-i-'alī *Chaghatāī* may have come in like manner, with Murād the Turkmān envoy from 'Irāq (f. 369 and n. 1).

[2690] Several incidents recorded by Gul-badan (writing half a century later) as following Māhīm's arrival in Āgra, will belong to the record of 935 AH. because they preceded Humāyūn's arrival from Badakhshān. Their omission from Bābur's diary is explicable by its minor *lacunæ*. Such are:—(1) a visit to Dhūlpūr and Sīkrī the interest of which lies in its showing that Bībī Mubārika had accompanied Māhīm Begīm to Āgra from Kābul, and that there was in Sīkrī a quiet retreat, a *chaukandī*, where Bābur "used to write his book";—(2) the arrival of the main caravan of ladies from Kābul, which led Bābur to go four miles out, to Naugrām, in order to give honouring reception to his sister Khān-ẓāda Begīm;—(3) an excursion to the Gold-scattering garden (*Bāgh-i-ẓar-afshān*), where seated among his own people, Bābur said he was "bowed down by ruling and reigning", longed to retire to that garden with a single attendant, and wished to make over his sovereignty to Humāyūn;—(4) the death of Dil-dār's son Alwār (var. Anwār) whose birth may be assigned to the gap preceding 932 AH. because not chronicled later by Bābur, as is Farūq's. As a distraction from the sorrow for this loss, a journey was "pleasantly made by water" to Dhūlpūr.

[2691] Cf. f. 381b n. 2. For his earlier help to Raḥīm-dād *see* f. 304. For Biographies of him *see* Blochmann's A.-i-A. trs. p. 446, and Badāyūnī's *Muntakhabu-'t-tawārīkh* (Ranking's and Lowe's trss.).

[2692] Beyond this broken passage, one presumably at the foot of a page in Bābur's own manuscript, nothing of his diary is now known to survive. What is missing seems likely to have been written and lost. It is known from a remark of Gul-badan's (H.N. p. 103) that he "used to write his book" after Māhīm's arrival in Āgra, the place coming into her anecdote being Sīkrī.

[2693] Jauhar's *Humāyūn-nāma* and Bāyazīd *Bīyāt's* work of the same title were written under the same royal command as the Begīm's. They contribute nothing towards filling the gap of 936 AH.; their authors, being Humāyūn's servants, write about him. It may be observed that criticism of these books, as recording trivialities, is disarmed if they were commanded because they would obey an order to set down whatever was known, selection amongst their contents resting with Abū'l-faẓl. Even more completely must they be excluded from a verdict on the literary standard of their day.—Abū'l-faẓl must have had a source of Bāburiana which has not found its way into European libraries. A man likely to have contributed his recollections, directly or transmitted, is Khwāja Muqīm *Harāwī.* The date of Muqīm's death is conjectural only, but he lived long enough to impress the worth of historical writing on his son Niẓāmu'-d-dīn Aḥmad. (Cf. E. and D.'s H. of I. art. *Ṭabaqāt-i-akbarī* v, 177 and 187; Ṭ.-i-A. lith. ed. p. 193; and for Bāyazīd *Bīyāt's* work, JASB. 1898, p. 296.)

[2694] Ibn Batuta (Lee's trs. p. 133) mentions that after his appointment to Gūālīār, Raḥīm-dād fell from favour ... but was restored later, on the representation of Muḥammad Ghauṣ; held Gūālīār again for a short time, (he went to Bahādur Shāh in Gujrāt) and was succeeded by Abū'l-fatḥ (*i.e.* Shaikh Gūran) who held it till Bābur's death.

[2695] Its translation and explanatory noting have filled two decades of hard-working years. *Tanti labores auctoris et traductoris!*

[2696] I am indebted to my husband for acquaintance with Niẓāmu'-d-dīn Aḥmad's record about Bābur and Kashmīr.

[2697] In view of the vicissitudes to which under Humāyūn the royal library was subjected, it would be difficult to assert that this source was not the missing continuation of Bābur's diary.

[2698] E. and D.'s H. of I. art. *Tārīkh-i Khān-i-jahān Lūdī* v, 67. For Aḥmad-i-yādgār's book and its special features *vide l.c.* v, 2, 24, with notes; Rieu's *Persian Catalogue* iii, 922*a*; JASB. 1916, H. Beveridge's art. *Note on the Tārīkh-i-salāṭīn-i-afāghana.*

[2699] Humāyūn's last recorded act in Hindūstān was that of 933 AH. (f. 329*b*) when he took unauthorized possession of treasure in Dihlī.

[2700] *Tārīkh-i-rashīdī* trs. p. 387.

[2701] T.-i-R. trs. p. 353 *et seq.* and Mr. Ney Elias' notes.

[2702] Abū'l-faẓl's record of Humāyūn's sayings and minor doings at this early date in his career, can hardly be anything more accurate than family-tradition.

[2703] The statement that Khalīfa was asked to go so far from where he was of the first importance as an administrator, leads to consideration of why it was done. So little is known explicitly of Bābur's intentions about his territories after his death that it is possible only to put that little together and read between its lines. It may be that he was now planning an immediate retirement to Kābul and an apportionment during life of his dominions, such as Abū-sa'īd had made of his own. If so, it would be desirable to have Badakhshān held in strength such as Khalīfa's family could command, and especially desirable because as Barlās Turks, that family would be one with Bābur in desire to regain Transoxiana. Such a political motive would worthily explain the offer of the appointment.

[2704] The "Shāh" of this style is derived from Sulaimān's Badakhshī descent through Shāh Begīm; the "Mīrzā" from his Mīrān-shāhī descent through his father Wais Khān Mīrzā. The title Khān Mīrzā or Mīrzā Khān, presumably according to the outlook of the speaker, was similarly derived from forbears, as would be also Shāh Begīm's; (her personal name is not mentioned in the sources).

[2705] Sa'īd, on the father's, and Bābur, on the mother's side, were of the same generation in descent from Yūnas Khān; Sulaimān was of a younger one, hence his pseudo-filial relation to the men of the elder one.

[2706] Sa'īd was Shāh Begīm's grandson through her son Aḥmad, Sulaimān her great-grandson through her daughter Sulṭān-Nigār, but Sulaimān could claim also as the heir of his father who was nominated to rule by Shāh Begīm; moreover, he could claim by right of conquest on the father's side, through Abū-sa'īd the conqueror, his son Maḥmūd long the ruler, and so through Maḥmūd's son Wais Khān Mīrzā.

[2707] The menace conveyed by these words would be made the more forceful by Bābur's move to Lāhor, narrated by Aḥmad-i-yādgār. Some ill-result to Sa'īd of independent rule by Sulaimān seems foreshadowed; was it that if Bābur's restraining hand were withdrawn, the Badakhshīs would try to regain their lost districts and would have help in so-doing from Bābur?

[2708] It is open to conjecture that if affairs in Hindūstān had allowed it, Bābur would now have returned to Kābul. Aḥmad-i-yādgār makes the expedition to be one for pleasure only, and describes Bābur as hunting and sight-seeing for a year in Lāhor, the Panj-āb and near Dihlī. This appears a mere flourish of words, in view of the purposes the expedition served, and of the difficulties which had arisen in Lāhor itself and with Sa'īd Khān. Part of the work effected may have been the despatch of an expedition to Kashmīr.

[2709] This appears a large amount.

[2710] The precision with which the Rāja's gifts are stated, points to a closely-contemporary and written source. A second such indication occurs later where gifts made to Hind-āl are mentioned.

[2711] An account of the events in Multān after its occupation by Shāh Ḥasan *Arghūn* is found in the latter part of the *Ṭabaqāt-i-akbarī* and in Erskine's H. of I. i, 393 *et seq.*—It may be noted here that several instances of confusion amongst Bābur's sons occur in the extracts made by Sir H. Elliot and Professor Dowson in their *History of India* from the less authoritative sources [*e.g.* v, 35 Kāmrān for Humāyūn, 'Askarī said to be in Kābul (pp. 36 and 37); Hind-āl for Humāyūn *etc.*] and that these errors have slipped into several of the District Gazetteers of the United Provinces.

[2712] As was said of the offering made by the Rāja of Kahlūr, the precision of statement as to what was given to Hind-āl, bespeaks a closely-contemporary written source. So too does the mention (text, *infra*) of the day on which Bābur began his return journey from Lāhor.

[2713] Cf. *G. of I.* xvi, 55; Ibbetson's *Report on Karnāl.*

[2714] It is noticeable that no one of the three royal officers named as sent against Mohan *Mundāhir*, is recognizable as mentioned in the *Bābur-nāma.* They may all have had local commands, and not have served further east. Perhaps this, their first appearance, points to the origin of the information as independent of Bābur, but he might have been found to name them, if his diary were complete for 936 AH.

[2715] The E. and D. translation writes twice as though the inability to "pull" the bows were due to feebleness in the men, but an appropriate reading would refer the difficulty to the hardening of sinews in the composite Turkish bows, which prevented the archers from bending the bows for stringing.

[2716] One infers that fires were burned all night in the bivouac.

[2717] At this point the A.S.B. copy (No. 137) of the *Tārīkh-i-salāṯīn-i-afāghana* has a remark which may have been a marginal note originally, and which cannot be supposed made by Aḥmad-i-yādgār himself because this would allot him too long a spell of life. It may show however that the interpolations about the two Tīmūrids were not inserted in his book by him. Its purport is that the Mundāhir village destroyed by Bābur's troops in 936 AH.-1530 AD. was still in ruins at the time it was written 160 (lunar) years later (*i.e.* in 1096 AH.-1684-85 AD.). The better Codex (No. 3887) of the Imperial Library of Calcutta has the same passage.—Both that remark and its context show acquaintance with Samāna and Kaithal.—The writings now grouped under the title *Tārīkh-i-salāṯīn-i-afāghana* present difficulties both as to date and contents (cf. Rieu's *Persian Catalogue s. n.*).

[2718] Presumably in Tihrind.

[2719] Cf. G. B.'s H. N. trs. and the *Akbar-nāma* Bib. Ind. ed. and trs., Index *s.nn.*; Hughes' *Dictionary of Islām s.n.* Intercession.

[2720] A closer translation would be, "I have taken up the burden." The verb is *bardāshtan* (cf. f. 349, p. 626 n. 1).

[2721] *See* Erskine's *History of India* ii, 9.

[2722] At this point attention is asked to the value of the Aḥmad-i-yādgār interpolation which allows Bābur a year of active life before Humāyūn's illness and his own which followed. With no chronicle known of 936 AH. Bābur had been supposed ill all through the year, a supposition which destroys the worth of his self-sacrifice. Moreover several inferences have been drawn from the supposed year of illness which are disproved by the activities recorded in that interpolation.

[2723] E. and D.'s *History of India* v, 187; G. B.'s *Humāyūn-nāma* trs. p. 28.

[2724] *dar khidmat-i-dīwānī-i-buyūtāt*; perhaps he was a Barrack-officer. His appointment explains his attendance on Khalīfa.

[2725] Khalīfa prescribed for the sick Bābur.

[2726] *khānwāda-i-bīgānah*, perhaps, foreign dynasty.

[2727] From Saṃbhal; Gul-badan, by an anachronism made some 60 years later, writes Kālanjar, to which place Humāyūn moved 5 months after his accession.

[2728] I am indebted to my husband's perusal of Sayyid Aḥmad Khān's *Aṣār-i-ṣanādīd* (Dihlī ed. 1854 p. 37, and Lakhnau ed. 1895 pp. 40, 41) for information that, perhaps in 935 AH., Mahdī Khwāja set up a tall slab of white marble near Amīr Khusrau's tomb in Dihlī, which bears an inscription in praise of the poet, composed by that Shihābu'd-dīn the Enigmatist who reached Āgra with Khwānd-amīr in Muḥarram 935 AH. (f. 339*b*). The inscription gives two chronograms of Khusrau's death (725 AH.), mentions that Mahdī Khwāja was the creator of the memorial, and gives its date in the words, "The beautiful effort of Mahdī Khwāja."—The Dihlī ed. of the *Aṣār-i-ṣanādīd* depicts the slab with its inscription; the Lakhnau ed. depicts the tomb, may show the slab *in sitû*, and contains interesting matter by Sayyid Aḥmad Khān. The slab is mentioned without particulars in Murray's *Hand-book to Bengal*, p. 329.

[2729] Lee's *Ibn Batuta* p. 133 and Hirāman's *Tārīkh-i-gūālīārī*. Cf. G. B.'s *Humāyūn-nāma* trs. (1902 AD.), Appendix B.—*Mahdī Khwāja.*

[2730] In an anonymous *Life of Shāh Ismā'īl Ṣafawī*, Mahdī Khwāja [who may be a son of the Mūsa Khwāja mentioned by Bābur on f. 216] is described as being, in what will be 916-7 AH., Bābur's *Dīwān-begī* and as sent towards Bukhārā with 10,000 men. This was 29 years before the story calls him a young man. Even if the word *jawān* (young man) be read, as T. *yīgīt* is frequently to be read, in the sense of "efficient fighting man", Mahdī was over-age. Other details of the story, besides the word *jawān*, bespeak a younger man.

[2731] G. B.'s H. N. trs. p. 126; *Ḥabību's-siyar*, B. M. Add. 16,679 f. 370, l. 16, lith. ed. Sec. III. iii, 372 (where a clerical error makes Bābur give Māhdī *two* of his full-sisters in marriage).—Another *yaẕna* of Bābur was Khalīfā's brother Junaid *Barlās*, the husband of Shahr-bānū, a half-sister of Bābur.

[2732] Bābur, shortly before his death, married Gul-rang to Aīsān-tīmūr and Gul-chihra to Tūkhta-būghā *Chaghatāī*. Cf. *post*, Section *h*, *Bābur's wives and children*; and G. B.'s H. N. trs. Biographical Appendix *s.nn.* Dil-dār Begīm and Salīma Sulṭān Begīm *Mīrān-shāhī.*

[2733] Cf. G. B.'s H. N. trs. p. 147.

[2734] She is the only adult daughter of a Tīmūrid mother named as being such by Bābur or Gul-badan, but various considerations incline to the opinion that Dil-dār Begīm also was a Tīmūrid, hence her three daughters, all named from the Rose, were so too. Cf. references of penultimate note.

[2735] It attaches interest to the Mīrzā that he can be taken reasonably as once the owner of the Elphinstone Codex (cf. JRAS. 1907, pp. 136 and 137).

[2736] Death did not threaten when this gift was made; life in Kābul was planned for.—Here attention is asked again to the value of Aḥmad-i-yādgār's Bāburiana for removing the impression set on many writers by the blank year 936 AH. that it was one of illness, instead of being one of travel, hunting and sight-seeing. The details of the activities of that year have the further value that they enhance the worth of Bābur's sacrifice of life.—Ḥaidar Mīrzā also fixes the date of the beginning of illness as 937 AH.

[2737] The author, or embroiderer, of that anonymous story did not know the *Bābur-nāma* well, or he would not have described Bābur as a wine-drinker after 933 AH. The anecdote is parallel with Niẕāmu'd-dīn Aḥmad's, the one explaining why the Mīrzā was selected, the other why the *dāmād* was dropped.

[2738] *Bib. Ind.* i, 341; Ranking's trs. p. 448.

[2739] The night-guard; perhaps Māhīm Begīm's brother (G. B.'s H. N. trs. pp. 27-8).

[2740] G. B.'s H. N. trs. f. 34*b*, p. 138; Jauhar's *Memoirs of Humāyūn*, Stewart's trs. p. 82.

[2741] Cf. G. B.'s H. N. trs. p. 216, Bio. App. *s.n.* Bega Begam.

[2742] f. 128, p. 200 n. 3. Cf. Appendix U.—*Bābur's Gardens in and near Kābul.*

[2743] Cf. H. H. Hayden's *Notes on some monuments in Afghānistān*, [*Memoirs of the Asiatic Society of Bengal* ii, 344]; and *Journal asiatique* 1888, M. J. Darmesteter's art. *Inscriptions de Caboul.*

[2744] *ān*, a demonstrative suggesting that it refers to an original inscription on the second, but now absent, upright slab, which presumably would bear Bābur's name.

[2745] Ruẓwān is the door-keeper of Paradise.

[2746] Particulars of the women mentioned by Bābur, Ḥaidar, Gul-badan and other writers of their time, can be seen in my Biographical Appendix to the Begīm's *Humāyūn-nāma.* As the Appendix was published in 1902, variants from it occurring in this work are corrections superseding earlier and less-informed statements.

[2747] *Tārīkh-i-rashīdī* trs. Ney Elias and Ross p. 308.

[2748] Bio. App. *s.n.* Gul-chihra.

[2749] The story of the later uprisings against Māhīm's son Humāyūn by his brothers, by Muḥammad-i-zamān *Bāī-qarā* and others of the same royal blood, and this in spite of Humāyūn's being his father's nominated successor, stirs surmise as to whether the rebels were not tempted by more than his defects of character to disregard his claim to supremacy; perhaps pride of higher maternal descent, this particularly amongst the Bāī-qarā group, may have deepened a disregard created by antagonisms of temperament.

[2750] Until the Yāngī-ārīq was taken off the Sīr, late in the last century, for Namangān, the oasis land of Farghāna was fertilized, not from the river but by its intercepted tributaries.

[2751] Ujfalvy's translation of Yāqūt (ii, 179) reads one *farsākh* from the mountains instead of 'north of the river.'

[2752] Kostenko describes a division of Tāshkīnt, one in which is Ravine-lane (*jar-kucha*), as divided by a deep ravine; of another he says that it is cut by deep ravines (Bābur's *'umīq jarlār*).

[2753] Bābur writes as though Akhsī had one Gate only (f. 112*b*). It is unlikely that the town had come down to having a single exit; the Gate by which he got out of Akhsī was the one of military importance because served by a draw-bridge, presumably over the ravine-moat, and perhaps not close to that bridge.

[2754] For mention of upper villages *see* f. 110 and note 1.

[2755] *Cf.* f. 114 for distances which would be useful in locating Akhsī if Bābur's *yīghāch* were not variable; Ritter, vii, 3 and 733; Réclus, vi, index *s.n.* Farghāna; Ujfalvy ii, 168, his quotation from Yāqūt and his authorities; Nalivkine's *Histoire du Khanat de Kokand*, p. 14 and p. 53; Schuyler, i, 324; Kostenko, Tables of Contents for cognate general information and i, 320, for Tāshkīnt; von Schwarz, index under related names, and especially p. 345 and plates; Pumpelly, p. 18 and p. 115.

[2756] This Turkī-Persian Dictionary was compiled by Mīrzā Mahdī Khān. Nādir Shāh's secretary and historian, whose life of his master Sir William Jones translated into French (Rieu's Turkī Cat. p. 264*b*).

[2757] The *Pādshāh-nāma* whose author, 'Abdu'l-ḥamīd, the biographer of Shāh-jahān, died in 1065 AH. (1655 AD.) mentions the existence of lacunæ in a copy of the Bābur-nāma, in the Imperial Library and allowed by his wording to be Bābur's autograph MS. (i, 42 and ii, 703).

[2758] *Akbar-nāma*, Bib. Ind. ed. i, 305; H. B. i, 571.

[2759] Ḥai. MS. f. 118*b*; *aūshāl bāghdā sū āqīb kīlā dūr aīdī. Bābur-nāma, sū āqīb*, water flowed and *aūshal* is rare, but in the R.P. occurs 7 times.

[2760] *gūzūm āwīqī-ghā bārīb tūr.* B.N. f. 117*b*, *gūzūm āwīqū-ghā bārdī.*

[2761] *kūrā dūr mīn*, B.N. f. 83, *tūsh kūrdūm* and *tūsh kūrār mīn.*

[2762] *ablaq suwār bīlān*; P. *suwār* for T. *ātlīq* or *ātlīq kīshī*; *bīlān* for B.N. *bīla*, and an odd use of piebald (*ablaq*).

[2763] *masnad*, B.N. *takht*, throne. *Masnad* betrays Hindūstān.

[2764] *Hamrā'īlārī (sic) bir bir gā (sic) maṣlaḥat qīlā dūrlār. Maṣlaḥat for B.N. kīngāsh* or *kīngāīsh*; *hamrāh*, companion, for *mīnīng bīla bār*, etc.

[2765] *bāghlāmāq* and f. 119*b* *bāghlāghānlār*; B.N. *ālmāk* or *tūtmāq* to seize or take prisoner.

[2766] *dīwār* for *tām.*

[2767] f. 119, *āt-tīn aūzlār-nī tāshlāb*; B.N. *tūshmāk*, dismount. *Tāshlāmaq* is not used in the sense of dismount by B.

[2768] *pādshāh* so used is an anachronism (f. 215); Bābur Mīrzā would be correct.

[2769] *zāhirān*; B.N. *yāqīn.*

[2770] Ilminsky's imprint stops at *dīb*; he may have taken *kīm-dīb* for signs of quotation merely. (This I did earlier, JRAS 1902, p. 749.)

[2771] Aligarh ed. p. 52; Rogers' trs. i, 109.

[2772] *Cf.* f. 63*b*, n. 3.

[2773] Another but less obvious objection will be mentioned later.

[2774] Julien notes (*Voyages des pélerins Bouddhistes*, ii, 96), "Dans les annales des Song on trouve Nang-go-lo-ho, qui répond exactement à l'orthographe indienne Nangarahāra, que fournit l'inscription découvert par le capitaine Kittoe" (JASB. 1848). The reference is to the Ghoswāra inscription, of which Professor Kielhorn has also written (*Indian Antiquary*, 1888), but with departure from Nangarahāra to Nagarahāra.

[2775] The scribe of the Ḥaidarābād Codex appears to have been somewhat uncertain as to the spelling of the name. What is found in histories is plain, N:g:r:hār. The other name varies; on first appearance (fol. 131*b*) and also on fols. 144 and 154*b*, there is a vagrant dot below the word, which if it were above would make Nīng-nahār. In all other cases the word reads N:g:nahār. Nahār is a constant component, as is also the letter *g*(or *k*).

[2776] Some writers express the view that the medial *r* in this word indicates descent from Nagarahāra, and that the medial *n* of Elphinstone's second form is a corruption of it. Though this might be, it is true also that in local speech *r* and *n* often interchange, *e.g.* Chighār- and Chighān-sarāī, Sūhār and Sūhān (in Nūr-valley).

[2777] This asserts *n* to be the correct consonant, and connects with the interchange of *n* and *r* already noted.

[2778] Since writing the above I have seen Laidlaw's almost identical suggestion of a nasal interpolated in Nagarahāra (JASB. 1848, art. on Kittoe). The change is of course found elsewhere; is not Tānk for Tāq an instance?

[2779] These affluents I omit from main consideration as sponsors because they are less obvious units of taxable land than the direct affluents of the Kābul-river, but they remain a reserve force of argument and may or may not have counted in Bābur's nine.

[2780] Cunningham, i, 42. My topic does not reach across the Kābul-river to the greater Udyānapūra of Beal's *Buddhist Records* (p. 119) nor raise the question of the extent of that place.

[2781] The strong form Nīng-nahār is due to euphonic impulse.

[2782] Some discussion about these coins has already appeared in JRAS. 1913 and 1914 from Dr. Codrington, Mr. M. Longworth Dames and my husband.

[2783] This variant from the Turkī may be significant. Should *tamghānat(-i-)sikka* be read and does this describe countermarking?

[2784] It will be observed that Bābur does not explicitly say that Ḥusain put the beg's name on the coin.

[2785] *Ḥabību's-siyar* lith. ed. iii, 228; *Ḥaidarābād* Codex text and trs. f. 26*b* and f. 169; Browne's Daulat Shāh p. 533.

[2786] Ḥusain born 842 AH. (1438 AD.); d. 911 AH. (1506 AD.).

[2787] Cf. f. 7*b* note to braves (*yīgītlār*). There may be instances, in the earlier Farghāna section where I have translated *chuhra* wrongly by *page*. My attention had not then been fixed on the passage about the coins, nor had I the same familiarity with the Kābul section. For a household page to be clearly recognizable as such from the context, is rare—other uses of the word are translated as their context dictates.

[2788] They can be traced through my Index and in some cases their careers followed. Since I translated *chuhra-jīrga-si* on f. 15*b* by cadet-corps, I have found in the Kābul section instances of long service in the corps which make the word cadet, as it is used in English, too young a name.

[2789] This Mr. M. Longworth Dames pointed out in JRAS. 1913.

[2790] *Habību's-siyar* lith. ed. iii, 219; Ferté trs. p. 28. For the information about Ḥusain's coins given in this appendix I am indebted to Dr. Codrington and Mr. M. Longworth Dames.

[2791] Elphinstone MS. f. 150*b*; Ḥaidarābād MS. f. 190*b*; Ilminsky, imprint p. 241.

[2792] Muḥ. Ma'ṣūm *Bhakkarī's Tārīkh-i-sind* 1600, Malet's Trs. 1855, p. 89; Mohan Lall's *Journal* 1834, p. 279 and *Travels* 1846, p. 311; Bellew's *Political Mission to Afghānistān* 1857, p. 232; *Journal Asiatique* 1890, Darmesteter's *La grande inscription de Qandahār*; JRAS. 1898, Beames' *Geography of the Qandahār inscription*. Murray's *Hand-book of the Panjab etc.* 1883 has an account which as to the Inscriptions shares in the inaccuracies of its sources (Bellew & Lumsden).

[2793] The plan of Qandahār given in the official account of the Second Afghān War, makes Chihil-zīna appear on the wrong side of the ridge, n.w. instead of n.e.

[2794] destroyed in 1714 AD. It lay 3 m. west of the present Qandahār (not its immediate successor). It must be observed that Darmesteter's insufficient help in plans and maps led him to identify Chihil-zīna with Chihil-dukhtarān (Forty-daughters).

[2795] *Tārīkh-i-rashīdī* trs. p. 387; *Akbar-nāma* trs. i, 290.

[2796] Ḥai. Codex, Index *sn.n.*

[2797] It is needless to say that a good deal in this story may be merely fear and supposition accepted as occurrence.

[2798] Always left beyond the carpet on which a reception is held.

[2799] This is not in agreement with Bābur's movements.

[2800] *i.e.* Humāyūn wished for a full-brother or sister, another child in the house with him. The above names of his brother and sister are given elsewhere only by Gulbadan (f. 6*b*).

[2801] The "we" might be Māhīm and Humāyūn, to Bābur in camp.

[2802] Perhaps before announcing the birth anywhere.

[2803] Presumably this plural is honorific for the Honoured Mother Māhīm.

[2804] Māhīm's and Humāyūn's quarters.

[2805] Gul-badan's *Humāyūn-nāma*, f. 8.

[2806] JRAS. A. S. Beveridge's Notes on *Bābur-nāma* MSS. 1900, [1902,] 1905, 1906, [1907,] 1908 (Kehr's transcript, p. 76, and Latin translation with new letter of Bābur p. 828).

[2807] In all such matters of the *Bābur-nāma* Codices, it has to be remembered that their number has been small.

[2808] Vigne's *Travels in Kāshmīr* ii, 277-8; *Tārīkh-i-rashīdī* trs., p. 302 and n. and p. 466 and note.

[2809] It is not likely to be one heard current in Hindūstān, any more than is Bābur's Ar. *bū-qalamūn* as a name of a bird (Index *s.n.*); both seem to be "book-words" and may be traced or known as he uses them in some ancient dictionary or book of travels originating outside Hindūstān.

[2810] My note 6 on p. 421 shows my earlier difficulties, due to not knowing (when writing it) that *kabg-ī-darī* represents the snow-cock in the Western Himālayas.

[2811] By over-sight mention of this note was omitted from my article on the Elphinstone Codex (JRAS. 1907, p. 131).

[2812] Speede's *Indian Hand-book* (i, 212) published in 1841 AD. thus writes, "It is a curious circumstance that the finest and most esteemed fruit are produced from the roots below the surface of the ground, and are betrayed by the cracking of the earth above them, and the effluvia issuing from the fissure; a high price is given by rich natives for fruit so produced."

[2813] In the margin of the Elphinstone Codex opposite the beginning of the note are the words, "This is a marginal note of Humāyūn Pādshāh's."

[2814] Every Emperor of Hindūstān has an epithet given him after his death to distinguish him, and prevent the necessity of repeating his name too familiarly. Thus *Firdaus-makān* (dweller-in-paradise) is Bābur's; Humāyūn's is *Jannat-ashi-yānī*, he whose nest is in Heaven; Muḥammad Shāh's *Firdaus-āramgāh*, he whose place of rest is Paradise; *etc.* (Erskine).

[2815] Here Mr. Erskine notes, "Literally, *nectar-fruit*, probably the mandarin orange, by the natives called *nāringī*. The name *amrat*, or pear, in India is applied to the guava or *Psidium pyriferum*—(*Spondias mangifera*, Hort. Ben.—D. Wallich)."... Mr. E. notes also that the note on the *amrit-phal* "is not found in either of the Persian translations".

[2816] *chūchūmān*, Pers. trs. *shīrīni bī maza*, perhaps flat, sweet without relish. Bābur does not use the word, nor have I traced it in a dictionary.

[2817] *chūchūk*, savoury, nice-tasting, not acid (Shaw).

[2818] *chūchūk nāranj āndāq (?) maṭ‘ūn aīdī kīm har kīm-nī shīrīn-kārlīghī bī masa qīlkāndī, nāranj-sū'ī dīk tūr dīrlār aīdī.*

[2819] The *lemu* may be *Citrus limona*, which has abundant juice of a mild acid flavour.

[2820] The *kāmila* and *samṭara* are the real oranges (*kaunlā* and *sangtāra*), which are now (*cir.* 1816 AD.) common all over India. Dr. Hunter conjectures that the *sangtāra* may take its name from Cintra, in Portugal. This early mention of it by Bābur and Humāyūn may be considered as subversive of that supposition. (This description of the *samṭara*, vague as it is, applies closer to the *Citrus decumana* or *pampelmus*, than to any other.—D. Wallich.)—Erskine.

[2821] Humāyūn writes of this fruit as though it were not the *sang-tara* described by his father on f. 287 (p. 511 and note).

[2822] M. de Courteille translated *jama‘* in a general sense by *totalit.'* instead of in its Indian technical one of revenue (as here) or of assessment. Hence Professor Dowson's "totality" (iv, 262 n.).

[2823] The B.M. has a third copy, Or. 5879, which my husband estimates as of little importance.

[2824] Sir G. A. Grierson, writing in the *Indian Antiquary* (July 1885, p. 187), makes certain changes in Ajodhya Prasad's list of the Brahman rulers of Tirhut, on grounds he states.

[2825] Index *s.n.* Bābur's letters. The passage Shaikh Zain quotes is found in Or. 1999, f. 65*b*, Add. 26,202, f. 66*b*, Or. 5879, f. 79*b*.

[2826] Cf. Index *in loco* for references to Bābur's metrical work, and for the Facsimile, JASB. 1910, Extra Number.

[2827] Monday, Rabi‘ II. 15th 935 AH.—Dec. 27th 1528 AD. At this date Bābur had just returned from Dhūlpūr to Āgra (f. 354, p. 635, where in note 1 for Thursday read Monday).

[2828] Owing to a scribe's "skip" from one *yībārīldī* (was sent) to another at the end of the next sentence, the passage is not in the Ḥai. MS. It is not well given in my translation (f. 357*b*, p. 642); what stands above is a closer rendering of the full Turkī, *Humāyūngha tarjuma* [*u*?] *nī-kīm Hindūstāngha kīlkānī aītqān ash'ārnī yībārīldī* (Ilminsky p. 462, 1. 4 fr. ft., where however there appears a slight clerical error).

[2829] Hesitation about accepting the colophon as unquestionably applying to the whole contents of the manuscript is due to its position of close association with one section only of the three in the manuscript (cf. *post* p. lx).

[2830] Plate XI, and p. 15 (mid-page) of the Facsimile booklet.—The Facsimile does not show the whole of the marginal quatrain, obviously because for the last page of the manuscript a larger photographic plate was needed than for the rest. With Dr. Ross' concurrence a photograph in which the defect is made good, accompanies this Appendix.

[2831] The second section ends on Plate XVII, and p. 21 of the Facsimile booklet.

[2832] Needless to say that whatever the history of the manuscript, its value as preserving poems of which no other copy is known publicly, is untouched. This value would be great without the marginal entries on the last page; it finds confirmation in the identity of many of the shorter poems with counterparts in the *Bābur-nāma.*

[2833] Another autograph of Shāh-i-jahān's is included in the translation volume (p. xiii) of Gul-badan Begam's *Humāyūn-nāma.* It surprises one who works habitually on historical writings more nearly contemporary with Bābur, in which he is spoken of as *Firdaus-makānī* or as *Gītī-sitānī Firdaus-makānī* and not by the name used during his life, to find Shāh-i-jahān giving him the two styles (cf. *Jahāngīr's Memoirs* trs. ii, 5). Those familiar with the writings of Shāh-i-jahān's biographers will know whether this is usual at that date. There would seem no doubt as to the identity of *ān Ḥaẓrat.*—The words *ān ḥaẓrat* by which Shāh-i-jahān refers to Bābur are used also in the epitaph placed by Jahāngīr at Bābur's tomb (Trs. Note p. 710-711).

[2834] The Qāẓī's rapid acquirement of the *mufradāt* of the script allows the inference that few letters only and those of a well-known script were varied.—*Mufradāt* was translated by Erskine, de Courteille and myself (f. 357*b*) as alphabet but reconsideration by the light of more recent information about the *Bāburī-khaṯṯ* leads me to think this is wrong because "alphabet" includes every letter.—On f. 357b three items of the *Bāburī-khaṯṯ* are specified as despatched with the Hindūstān poems, *viẓ. mufradāt, qita'lār* and *sar-i-khaṯṯ.* Of these the first went to Hind-āl, the third to Kāmrān, and no recipient is named for the second; all translators have sent the *qita'lār* to Hind-āl but I now think this wrong and that a name has been omitted, probably Humāyūn's.

[2835] f. 144*b*, p. 228, n. 3. Another interesting matter missing from the *Bābur-nāma* by the gap between 914 and 925 AH. is the despatch of an embassy to Czar Vassili III. in Moscow, mentioned in Schuyler's *Turkistan* ii, 394, Appendix IV, Grigorief's *Russian Policy in Central Asia.* The mission went after "Sulṯān Bābur" had established himself in Kābul; as Bābur does not write of it before his narrative breaks off abruptly in 914 AH. it will have gone after that date.

[2836] I quote from the Véliaminof-Zernov edition (p. 287) from which de Courteille's plan of work involved extract only; he translates the couplet, giving to *khaṯṯ* the double-meanings of script and down of youth (*Dictionnaire Turque s.n. sīghnāqī*). The *Sanglākh* (p. 252) *s.n. sīghnāq* has the following as Bābur's:—

Chū balai khaṯṯī naṣīb'ng būlmāsa Bābur nī tang?

Bare khaṯṯ almanṣūr khaṯṯ sighnāqī mū dūr?

[2837] Gibb's *History of Ottoman Poetry* i, 113 and ii, 137.

[2838] Réclus' *L'Asie Russe* p. 238.

[2839] On this same *taḥrīr qīldīm* may perhaps rest the opinion that the Rāmpūr MS. is autograph.

[2840] I have found no further mention of the tract; it may be noted however that whereas Bābur calls his *Treatise on Prosody* (written in 931 AH.) the *'Arūẓ*, Abū'l-faẓl writes of a *Mufaṣṣal*, a suitable name for 504 details of transposition.

[2841] *Tūzūk-i-jahāngīr* lith. ed. p. 149; and *Memoirs of jahāngīr* trs. i, 304. [In both books the passage requires amending.]

[2842] Rāmpūr MS. Facsimile Plate XIV and p. 16, verse 3; *Akbar-nāma* trs. i, 279, and lith. ed. p. 91.

[2843] Cf. Index *s.n.* Dalmau and Bangarmau for the termination in double *ū*.

[2844] Dr. Ilminsky says of the Leyden & Erskine *Memoirs of Bābur* that it was a constant and indispensable help.

[2845] My examination of Kehr's Codex has been made practicable by the courtesy of the Russian Foreign Office in lending it for my use, under the charge of the Librarian of the India Office, Dr. F. W. Thomas.—It should be observed that in this Codex the Hindūstān Section contains the purely Turkī text found in the Ḥaidarābād Codex (cf. JRAS. 1908, p. 78).

[2846] It may indicate that the List was not copied by Bābur but lay loose with his papers, that it is not with the Elphinstone Codex, and is not with the 'Abdu'r-raḥīm Persian translation made from a manuscript of that same annotated line.

[2847] Cf. *in loco* p. 656, n. 3.

[2848] A few slight changes in the turn of expressions have been made for clearness sake.

[2849] Index *s.n.* Mīr Bāqī of Tāshkīnt. Perhaps a better epithet for *sa'ādạt-nishān* than "good-hearted" would be one implying his good fortune in being designated to build a mosque on the site of the ancient Hindū temple.

[2850] There is a play here on Bāqī's name; perhaps a good wish is expressed for his prosperity together with one for the long permanence of the sacred building *khair* (*khairat*).

[2851] Presumably the order for building the mosque was given during Bābur's stay in Aūd (Ajodhya) in 934 AH. at which time he would be impressed by the dignity and sanctity of the ancient Hindū shrine it (at least in part) displaced, and like the obedient follower of Muḥammad he was in intolerance of another Faith, would regard the substitution of a temple by a mosque as dutiful and worthy.—The mosque was finished in 935 AH. but no mention of its completion is in the *Bābur-nāma.* The diary for 935 AH. has many minor *lacunæ*; that of the year 934 AH. has lost much matter, breaking off before where the account of Aūd might be looked for.

[2852] The meaning of this couplet is incomplete without the couplet that followed it and is (now) not legible.

[2853] Firishta gives a different reason for Bābur's sobriquet of *qalandar*, namely, that he kept for himself none of the treasure he acquired in Hindūstān (Lith. ed. p. 206).

[2854] Jahāngīr who encamped in the Shahr-ārā-garden in Ṣafar 1016 AH. (May 1607 AD.) says it was made by Bābur's aunt, Abū-sa'īd's daughter Shahr-bānū (Rogers and Beveridge's *Memoirs of Jahāngīr* i, 106).

[2855] A *jalau-khāna* might be where horse-head-gear, bridles and reins are kept, but *Āyīn* 60 (A.-i-A.) suggests there may be another interpretation.

[2856] She was a daughter of Hind-āl, was a grand-daughter therefore of Bābur, was Akbar's first wife, and brought up Shāh-i-jahān. Jahāngīr mentions that she made her first pilgrimage to her father's tomb on the day he made his to Bābur's, Friday Ṣafar 26th 1016 AH. (June 12th 1607 AD.). She died *æt.* 84 on Jumāda I. 7th 1035 AH. (Jan. 25th 1626 AD.). Cf. *Tūzūk-i-jahāngīrī*, Muḥ. Hādī's Supplement lith. ed. p. 401.

[2857] Mr. H. H. Hayden's photograph of the mosque shows pinnacles and thus enables its corner to be identified in his second of the tomb itself.

[2858] One of Daniel's drawings (which I hope to reproduce) illuminates this otherwise somewhat obscure passage, by showing the avenue, the borders of running-water and the little water-falls,—all reminding of Madeira.

[2859] *chokī*, perhaps "shelter"; see Hobson-Jobson *s.n.*

[2860] If told with leisurely context, the story of the visits of Bābur's descendants to Kābul and of their pilgrimages to his tomb, could hardly fail to interest its readers.

[2861] The fist indicates Translator's matter.

[2862] See Abū'l-ghāzī's *Shajarat-i-turkī* on the origin and characteristics of the tribe (Désmaisons trs. Index *s.n.* Oūīghūr, especially pp. 16, 37, 39).

[2863] This date is misplaced in my text and should be transferred from p. 83, l. 3 fr. ft. to p. 86, l. 1, there to follow "two years".

[2864] A fuller reference to the Ḥ.S. than is given on p. 85 n. 2, is ii, 44 and iii, 167.

[2865] Cf. *s.n.* 'Abdu'l-lāh Mīrzā *Shāh-rukhī* for a date misplaced in my text.

[2866] The date 935 AH. is inferred from p. 483.

[2867] Cf. Badāyūnī's *Muntakhabu't-tawārīkh* and Ranking's trs. i, 616 and n. 4, 617.

[2868] Ferté translates this sobriquet by *le dévoué* (*Vie de Sl. Hossein Baikara* p. 40 n. 3).

[2869] At p. 22 n. 8 fill out to Cf. f. 6*b* (p. 13) n. 5.

[2870] For an account of his tomb see Schuyler's *Turkistān*, 1, 70-72.

[2871] Or Aīgū (Āyāgū) from *āyāgh*, foot, perhaps expressing close following of Tīmūr, whose friend the Beg was.

[2872] Daulat-shāh celebrates the renown of the Jalāīr section (*farqa*) of the Chaghatāī tribes (*aqwām*) of the Mughūl horde (*aūlūs*, *ūlūs*), styles the above-entered 'Alī Beg a veteran hero, and links his family with that of the Jalāīr Sultāns of Bāghdād (Browne's ed. p. 519).

[2873] See H. S. lith. ed. iii, 224, for three men who conveyed helpful information to Husain.

[2874] Later consideration has cast doubts on his identification with Darwesh-i-'alī suggested, p. 345 n. 4.

[2875] On p. 69 n. 2 for *aūnūlūng* read *aūnūtūng* and reverse *bakunīd* with *nakunīd.*

[2876] On p. 49 l. 3 for "Black Sheep" read White Sheep.

[2877] Like his brother Hind-āl's name, Alūr's may be due to the taking (*al*) of Hind.

[2878] See the *Ṭabaqāt-i-akbarī* account of the rulers of Multān.

[2879] On p. 85 l. 9 for "872 AH.-1467 AD.", read 851 AH.-1447 AD.

[2880] On p. 79 transfer the note-reference "3" to *qibla*.

[2881] See Daulat-shāh (Browne's ed. p. 362) for an entertaining record of the Mīrzā's zeal as a sportsman and an illustrative anecdote by Shaikh 'Ārif *'aẕarī q.v.* (H.B.).

[2882] I have found no statement of his tribe or race; he and his brother are styled Khwāja (Ḥ.S. lith. ed. iii, 272); he is associated closely with Aḥmad Taṃbal *Mughūl* and Mughūls of the Horde; also his niece's name Aūlūs Āghā translates as Lady of the Horde (*ūlūs*, *aūlūs*). But he may have been a Turkmān.

[2883] The MS. variants between 'Alī and -qulī are confusing. What stands in my text (p. 27) may be less safe than the above.

[2884] Bābā Qashqa was murdered by Muḥammad-i-zamān *Bāī-qarā*. For further particulars of his family group see Add. Notes under p. 404.

[2885] Sulṭan Bābā-qulī Beg is found variously designated Qulī Beg, Qulī Bābā, Sl. 'Alī Bābā-qulī, Sulṭān-qūlī Bābā and Bābā-qulī Beg. Several forms appear to express his filial relationship with Sulṭān Bābā 'Alī (*q.v.*).

[2886] Down to p. 346 Bābur's statements are retrospective; after p. 346 they are mostly contemporary with the dates of his diary—when not so are in supplementing passages of later date.

[2887] He may be the father of Mun'im Khān (Blochmann's Biographies A.-i-A. trs. 317 and n. 2).

[2888] See note, Index, *s.n.* Muḥammad Ẕakarīa.

[2889] He is likely to have been introduced with some particulars of tribe, in one of the now unchronicled years after Bābur's return from his Trans-oxus campaign.

[2890] His wife, daughter of a wealthy man and on the mother's side niece of Sulṭān Buhlūl *Lūdī*, financed the military efforts of Bāyazīd and Bīban (*Tārīkh-i-sher-shāhī*, E. and D. iv, 353 ff.).

[2891] My translation on p. 621 l. 12 is inaccurate inasmuch as it hides the circumstance that Beg-gīna alone was the "messenger of good tidings".

[2892] In taking Bīban for a Jilwānī, I follow Erskine, (as inferences also warrant,) but he may be a Lūdī.

[2893] For the same uncertainty between Bihār and Pahār see E. and D.'s History of India iv, 352 n. 2.

[2894] Firishta lith. ed. i, 202.

[2895] For "Mū'min" read Mūmin, which form is constant in the Ḥai. MS.

[2896] He may be Ḥamīda-bānū's father and, if so, became grandfather of Akbar.

[2897] Ilminsky, *anlū*, Erskine, *angū*. Daulat-shāh mentions a Muḥammad Shāh *anjū* (see Brown's ed. Index *s.n.*).

[2898] On p. 22 n. 2 delete "*Chaghatāī Mughūl*" on grounds given in Additional Note, Page 22.

[2899] For Humāyūn's annotation of the *Bābur-nāma*, see General Index *s.n.* Humāyūn's Notes.

[2900] For a correction of dates, see *s.n.* Aūlūgh Beg.

[2901] On p. 279 l. 3 from foot read "There was also Ibrāhīm *Chaghatāī*" after "Muḥammad-i-zamān Mīrzā".

[2902] *Addendum*:—p. 49 l. 4, read "wife" of Muḥammadī "son" of Jahān-shāh.

[2903] His name might mean Welcome, *Bien-venu*.

[2904] Khusrau-shāh may be the more correct form.

[2905] The "afterwards" points to an omission which Khwānd-amīr's account of Ḥusain's daughters fills (lith. ed. iii, 327).

[2906] No record survives of the Khwāja's deeds of daring other than those entered above; perhaps the other instances Bābur refers to occurred during the gap 908-9 AH.

[2907] This may be a tribal or a family name. Abū'l-ghāzī mentions two individuals named "Kouk". One was Chīngīz Khān's grandson who is likely to have had descendants or followers distinguishable as *Kūkī*. See Add. Note P. 673 on Kūkī fate.

[2908] Cf. E. and D. for "KARĀNĪ" (*e.g.* vol. iv, 530). The Ḥai. MS. sometimes doubles the *r*, sometimes not.

[2909] See *Wāqi'āt-i-mushtāqī*, E. and D. iv, 548.

[2910] Shaikhīm *Suhailī* however was named Aḥmad (277) not Muhammad.

[2911] The record of the first appears likely to be lost in the *lacuna* of 934 AH.

[2912] See *Shaibānī-nāma*, Vambéry's ed. Cap. xv, l. 12, for his changes of service, and Sām Mīrzā's *Tuḥfa-i-sāmī* for various particulars including his classification as a Chaghatāī.

[2913] He died serving Bābur, at Kūl-i-malik (Ḥ.S. iii, 344).—Further information negatives my suggestion (201 n. 7) that he and Mīr Ḥusain (p. 288 and n. 7) were one.

[2914] "Zaitun is the name of the Chinese city from which satin was brought (*hodie* Thsiuancheu or Chincheu) and my belief is that our word satin came from it" (Col. H. Yule, E. and D. iv, 514).

[2915] My text omits to translate *yigīt* (*aūghūl*) and thus loses the information that Yaḥyā's sons Bāqī and Ẕakarīa were above childhood, were grown to fighting age—braves—but not yet begs (see Index *s.n. chuhra*).

[2916] See Add. Notes under p. 39.

[2917] See Add. Notes under p. 266.

[2918] For emendation of 266 n. 7, see Add. Notes under P. 266.

[2919] On p. 49 l. 3 for "Black" read White; and in L. 3 read ("wife of") Muḥammadi son of ("Jahān-shāh").

[2920] Cf. Ḥ.S. Fertī's trs. p. 70 for the same name Qaitmās.

[2921] His capture is not recorded.

[2922] He joined Bābur with his father Yār-i-'alī *Balāl* (*q.v.*) in 910 AH. (Blochmann's Biographies, A.-i-A. trs. 315).

[2923] Concerning the date of his death, see Additional Notes under p. 603.

[2924] Since my text was printed, my husband has lighted upon what shows that the guest at the feast was an ambassador sent by Burhān Niẓām Shāh of Aḥmadnagar to congratulate Bābur on his conquest of Dihlī, namely, Shāh Ṭāhir the apostle of Shiism in the Dakkan. He is thus distinguished from Sayyid Daknī, (Ruknī, Zaknī) *infra* and my text needs suitable correction. (See Add. Notes under p. 631 for further particulars of the Sayyid and his embassy.)

[2925] For further particulars see Add. Note under p. 688.

[2926] For "H.S. II" read iii (as also in some other places).

[2927] Down to p. 131 the Ḥai. MS. uses the name Shaibānī or Shaibānī Khān; from that page onwards it writes Shaibāq Khān, in agreement with the Elphinstone MS.—Other names found are *e.g.* Gulbadan's Shāhī Beg Khān and Shah-bakht. (My note 2 on p. 12 needs modification.)

[2928] The title "Aūghlān" (child, boy) indicates that the bearer died without ruling.

[2929] This cognomen was given because the bearer was born during an eclipse of the moon (*āī*, moon and the root *al* taking away); *see* Badāyūnī Bib. Ind. ed. i, 62.

[2930] Here *delete* "Sulṭān-nigar Khānīm", who was his grandmother and not his mother.

[2931] On p. 433 n. 1 her name is mistakenly entered as that of Sulaimān's mother.

[2932] Concerning this title, see Add. Notes under p. 540.

[2933] He may be the Tūlik Khān *qūchīn* of the *Ma'asiru'l-umrā* i, 475.

[2934] Ḥaidar Mīrzā gives an interesting account of his character and attainments (T.R. trs. p. 283).

[2935] See Additional Note under P. 372.

[2936] See Additional Notes under P. 51.

[2937] Here the Ḥai. MS. and Ilminsky's Imprint add "Nāṣir".

[2938] The natural place for this Section of record is at the first mention of Yūnas Khān (p. 12) and not, as now found, interrupting another Section. See p. 678 and n. 4 as to "Sections".

[2939] The entries of 934 and 935 may concern a second man 'Alī-i-yūsuf.

[2940] Perhaps skilled in the art of metaphors and tropes (*'ilmu'l-badī'*).

[2941] My text has *julgāsī*, but I am advised to omit the genitive *sī*; so, too, in aīkī-sū-ārā-sī, Rabāṭjk-aūrchīn-ī *q.v.*

[2942] Cf. *s.n.* Āhangaran-julga n. as to form of the name.

[2943] Asterisks indicate Translator's matter.

[2944] Bābur uses this name for, Anglicé, the Kābul-river as low as nearly to Dakka.

[2945] "the Dara-i-ṣūf, often mentioned by the Arabian writers, seems to lie west of Bāmīān" (Erskine, *Memoirs*, p. 152 n. 1).

[2946] Bābur's itinerary gives Gharjistan a greater eastward extent than the Fr. map Maïmènè allows, thus agreeing with Erskine's surmise (*Memoirs* p. 152 n. 1).—The first syllable of the name may be "Ghur".

[2947] On p. 7, l. 1, after "turbulent", *add*, " They are notorious in Māwarā'u'n-nahr for their bullying."

[2948] On p. 134 for "(I WAS) 19" *read* in my 19th (lunar) year.

[2949] Cf. *Life of Busbecq* (Forster and Daniels) i, 252-7, for feats of Turkish archery.

[2950] For the Bukhara (Bābur-nāma) Compilation *see Wāqi'-nāma-i-pādshāhi*; as also for its Codices, descendants and offtakes, *viz.* Ilminski's "*Bābur-nāma*" and de Courteille's *Mémoires de Baber.*

[2951] The confusion of identity has become clear to me in 1921 only.

[2952] One of the nine great gods of the Etruscans was called Tūrān. Etr. *Tūr* means strong, a strong place (fortress); with it may connect L. *turma* (troop) and the name of Virgil's Rutulian hero Turmus may root in the Mongol tongue. Professor Jules Marthe writes in *La Langue Etrusque* (Pref. vi), "Il m'a paru qu'il y avait entre l'Etrusque et les langues finns-ougriennes d'étroites affinités" (hence with the Mongol tongue). "Tarkhān" is "Tūrkhān" in Miles trs. p. 71 of the *Shajaratu'l-atrāk* (H. B.).

[2953] This Cat. contains the Turkī MS. of the Bukhara Compilation, once owned by Leyden.

[2954] where, in n. 3, for f. 183*b* and f. 264*b read* f. 103*b* and f. 264.

[2955] For "Ḥ.S. II" read Ḥ.S. iii—also on p. 244.

[2956] On this peg may be hung the following note:—The *Pādshāh-nāma* (*q.v.*) calls the author and presenter of the above translation "Abū-ṭālib" *Ḥusainī* (Bib. Ind. ed. vol. i, part 2, p. 288), but its index contains many references seemingly to the same man as Khwāja Abū'l-husain *Turbati.* The P. N. says the book which it entitles *Wāqi'āt-i-ṣaḥib-qirān* (The Acts of Tīmūr), was in Turki, was brought forth from the Library of the (Turk) Governor of Yemen and translated by Mīr Abū-ṭālib *Ḥusainī*; that what ' had done with this book of counsel (*dastān-i-nasā'iḥ*) when he sent it to his son Pīr-i-muhammad, then succeeding (his brother) Jahāngīr [in Kābul, the Ghaznis, Qandahār, *etc.*] Shāhjahān also did by sending it, out of love, to his son Aurangzīb who had been ordered to the Deccan.

[2957] In n. 5 for "*parwān*" read *parrān*, and *read* Blanford.

[2958] Which *read* (l. 17) for *yak rang*. The name *bak-dīng* appears due to the clapping of the bird's mandibles and its pompous strut; (cf. Ross' *Polyglot List*, No. 336).

[2959] Following the *zammaj* insert "Another is the buzzard (T. *Sār*); its back and tail are red". (*Cf.* Omission List under p. 500.)

[2960] *See* Omission List under p. 498.

[2961] After "Tramontane", *add* Its breast is less deeply black.

[2962] The bird being black, its name cannot be translated "yellow-bird"; as noted on p. 373 *sārīgh* = thief; [*sārāgh* or *sārīgh* means a bird's song].

[2963] For references to Niẓāmi's text, I am indebted to Mr. Beveridge's knowledge of the poems.

[2964] Cf. Mr. G. Murray's trs. (Euripides i, 86) suggesting that the Wooden Horse was a *sar-kob*.

[2965] Abū'l-ghāzī classes Manghīt with Mughul tribes, Radloff with Turk tribes (*Récueils p. 325*), Erskine says, "modern Nogais."

THE HISTORY OF BABUR OR BABUR-NAMA

OMISSIONS FROM TRANSLATION AND FOOTNOTES.

p. 7 l.1 "turbulent" *add* They are notorious in Mawara'u'n-nahr for their bullyings.

p. 27 l.5 "(1504)" *add* when, after taking Khusrau Shah, we besieged Muqim in Kabul.

p. 31 l.1 "paid" *add* no (attention).

p. 43 l.9 *enter* f. 24*b*.

ib. l.8 fr. ft. "Taghai" *add* and Auzun Ḥasan.

p. 45 Sec. c, l.2 "good" *add* he never neglected the Prayers.

p. 48 l.16 "grandmother" *add* Khan-zada Begim.

p. 52 l.4 fr. ft. "childhood" *add* and had attained the rank of Beg.

p. 88 l.9 Ḥasan *add* and Sl. Ahṃad Tambal.

p. 92 l.8 "ON" *add* to Sang-zar.

p. 95 l.12 "service" *add* did not stay in Khurasan but.

p. 128 l.18 "two" *add* young (sons).

p. 131 l.12 "Jan-wafa" *add* Mirza.

p. 134 l.7 fr. ft. "that" *add* night that.

ib. l.3 fr. ft. "was" *add* in my 19th (lunar) year.

p. 136 l.5 "was" *add* in my 19th (lunar) year.

p. 139 l.11 fr. ft. *read* Jani Beg Sultan.

p. 141 l.10 "Khusrau Shah" *add* my highly-favoured beg Qambar-i-ali *the Skinner Mughul*, not acting at such a time as this according to the favour he had received, came and took his wife from Samarkand; he too went to Khusrau Shah.

p. 143 l.16 "that" *add* near Shutur-gardan.

p. 152 l.12 fr. ft. "dead" *add* A few days later we went back to Dikh-kat.

p. 164 Sec. d, l.6 fr. ft. "for" *add* Sairam.

p.201 l.12 *read* Kabul-fort.

p. 205 l.10 fr. ft. *read* "are closed for" 4 or 5 months in winter. After crossing Shibr-tu people go on through Ab-dara. In the heats, when the waters come down in flood, these roads have the same rule as in winter ("because" *etc.*).

p. 217 l.11 "Sih-yaran" *add* It became a very good-halting-place. I had a vineyard planted on the hill above the seat.

p. 221 Sec. h, at the beginning *insert* The mountains to the eastward of the cultivated land of Kabul are of two kinds as also are those to its westward ("Where the mountains" *etc.*).

p. 230 last line "men" *add* Khusrau *Gagiani.*

p. 247 l.1 "Qush-nadir" *add* meadow.

p. 308 l.14 "ground" *add* Moreover it snowed incessantly and after leaving Chiragh-dan, not only was there very deep snow but the road was unknown.

p. 391 March 18th "darogha-ships" *add* Sangur Khan Qarluq and Mirza-i-malui Qarluq came leading 30 or 40 men of the Qarluq elders, made offering of a horse in mail, and waited on me. Came also the army of the Dilah-zak Afghāns.

p. 393 March 25th l.2 "out" *add* from the river's bank.

p. 454 l.5 "boat" *add* There was a party; some drinking *'araq*, some beer. After leaving the boat at the Bed-time Prayer, there was more drinking in the *khirgah* (tent). For the good of the horses, we gave them a day's breathing on the bank of this water.

p. 468 l.3 "sent" *add* Yunas-i-'ali and Ahṃadi and ("'Abdu'l-lah").

p. 484 l.1 "Rao" *add* with four or five thousand Pagans.

p. 498 (*s.n.* florican), "colour" *add* The flesh of the florican is very delicate. As the *kharchal* (Indian buzzard) resembles the *tughdaq* (great buzzard) so the *charz* (florican) resembles the *tughdiri.*

ib. (*s.n.* sand-grouse) "Tramontana" *add* the blackness of its breast is less deep, its cry also is sharper.

p. 500 after l. 11 "eagle" *add* (new para.) Another is the buzzard (T. *sar*); its tail and back are red.

p. 506 (*s.n. kamrak*) "long" *add* It has no stone.

p. 507 n. 3 "name" *add* also; "plantain" *add* (banana).

p. 510 l. 5 see App. O, p. liv for *addendum.*

p. 529 l. 4 fr.ft. "Dulpur" *add* Gualiar.

p. 595 l. 19 "other" read 2 or 3 (places); the Pagans in the *du-tahi* began to run away; "the *du-tahi* was taken."

p. 603 l. 7 fr.ft. "(366*b*)" *add* and between Ghazipur and Banaras (p. 502).

p. 674 l. 2 "river" *add* in his mail.

p. 678 l. 2 "amirs" *add* Sultan.

p. 679 l. 8 fr.ft. "given" *add* It was settled that a son of each of them should be always in waiting in Agra; l. 7 fr.ft. "Araish" *add* and two others; l. 2 fr.ft. "Saru" *add* towards Oude.

p. 689 l. 2 fr.ft. "Laks" *add* and a head-to-foot (dress).

App. Q l. 1 "interpret" add those of.

CORRIGENDA.

To ensure notice many of these are entered in the Indices.

Pages

6 l.4 "meadow" *read* plain (*maidan*).

11 n.4, "siyar" unaccented; (H.S.) ii *read* iii n.n. pp. 18, 38, 48, 244.

12 n.4 l.3 "attack in" *read* attacking.

14 l.3 "and" *read* who.

16 l.10 n. ref. "3" *tr. to* "amorous".

24 n.1 "932" *read* 923.

27 para. 2 *read* "Baba 'Ali Beg's Baba-quli".

28 l.8 "leaders" *read* Mughul mirzadas.

29 n.6 l.5 "then" *read* his.

37 l.8 "916" *read* 917; and tr. nn. 2 and 3.

38 l.9 "favour" *run on* to Aḥmad.

44 l.9 55 l.12 *delete* "Sayyid".

46 l.12 *read* Chikman.

49 l.3 "Black" *read* White.

51 l.12 fr. ft. "Badakhshan" *read* Hisar.

55 "F. 34" *read* f. 32*b*.

57 l.1, enter f. 33 and *move* "f. 33*b*" to 58 l.2.

61 l.4 "BEG" *read* Baba-quli Beg.

68 l.10 fr. ft. *tr.* n. ref. 4 to "Aurgut".

69 n.2, read *aunutung*; and *tr. nakunid* and *bakunid*.

79 l.5 tr. n. ref. 3 to *qibla*; in author's n. *read* Batalmius; and in n.4 *read Ayin*.

85 l.9 *read* 851 A.H.-1447 A.D.; l.3 fr. ft. *move* "Jumada I, 22, 855 A.H." to p.86 l.1, after "years".

94 l.6 "Chirik" *read* Char-yak.

95 l.2 fr. ft. "Aubaj" *read* Char-jui.

96 last line “Qasim” *read* Kamal (or Kahal).

109 l.16 “qasim” *read* qadus.

ib. n.5 l.3 *read* grand “father”.

117 n.2 “909” *read* 908.

122 n.4 “*bulghar*” *read buljar.*

129 l.14 “*daban*” *read kutal.*

131 ll.3-4 fr. ft. *read* Khan-quli and Karim-dad.

134 l.3 fr. ft. and 136 l.5 *read* in my 19th (lunar) year.

144 para. 3 “rain” *read* grain.

148 n.2 “F. 18” *read* f. 118.

149 l.17 *read* Khanim.

154 n.3 “f. 183*b*” *read* f. 103*b* and for f. 264*b* *read* f. 264.

168 Sect. heading “Kasan” *read* Karnan.

175 l.11 *read* Mirza-quli.

183 last line “Kulja” *read* Khuldja.

192 l.3 *read* Taliqan.

194 l.12 *read* Quhlugha.

ib. n.3 *read* Bai-sunghar.

204 l.16 *read* Curriers'.

205 l.5 *read* Sir; l.13 *read* Wa(lian); l.14 *read* Qibchaq.

205 l.10 fr. ft. “three or four” *read* four or five (cf. omissions p. 205).

211 para. 3, end, “920” *read* 924.

212 n.2 l.2 *read chiqmaq.*

213 n.5 “*parwan*” *read parran*; and nn.5, 6, 7 *read* Blanford.

244 ll.8 and 25 “page” *read* preferably, brave; l.19 *read* gallopers.

273 n.2 *read* grand-“daughter”.

282 n.3 l.2 “345” *read* 348-9.

289 l.5 “wonderful” *read* metaphorist.

342 mid-page *read* Pur-amin.

344 last line "Appendix" *read* Trs.' note 711.

351 l.15 "Akhsi" *read* Archian.

387 n.3 *delete* sentence 2.

410 last line "*khuntul*" *read hunzal.*

414 l.2 "18th" *read* 13th; and l.2 fr. ft. "purslain" *read* poplar.

438 l.15 "son" *read* grandson.

447 n.3 para. 2 l.1 "month" *read* week.

470 n.l. 5 fr. ft. "P.66" *read* p. 166.

482 n.3 "Gujrat" *read* Malwa.

485 sec. e l.7 "Gumti" *read* Gui.

499 l.17 "*yak-rang*" *read bak-ding* (see Add. Note P. 499).

500 l.15 *s.n.* crow "*qarcha*" *read qargha*; n.6 "F. 136" *read* f. 135.

505 l.6 tr. n. ref. "2" to, *buia.*

520 n.1 "1854" *read* 1845.

534 l.2 fr. ft. "and" *read* 932.

535 l.2 fr. ft. *delete* "others".

579 l.8 "April 13th" *read* April 3rd.

591 n.2 "*qurughir*" *read quruqtur.*

604 n.l.1 *read Afaghana.*

616 l.5 *read* Madhakur; and Sect. m "*qara-su*" *read darya qaraghi* or *qaraghina.*

620 l.7 *rahim read rahman.*

621 l.11 after "servants" *read* Beg-gina "had come".

622 l.12 *read* Siunjuk; l.13 Tashkint.

631 l.13 *delete* the parenthesis (see Add. Note P. 631).

632 l.4 *read* Farrukh.

636 l.7 "rest" *read* eight others.

640 l.1 *read* quli.

643 (Feb. 4th) "Muhammad" *read* Mahmud.

644 n.5 "323" *read* 232.

699 l.13 "935" *read* 938.

713 l.3 *read* Saliha; and l.11 fr. ft. Miran-shahi.

ADDITIONAL NOTES

P. 16 l. 11.—Niẓāmī mentions "lover's marks" where a rebel chieftain commenting on Khusrau's unfitness to rule by reason of his infatuation for Shīrīn, says, "*Hinoz az'āshīqbāzī garm dāgh ast.*" (H.B.)

P. 22 n. 2.—Closer acquaintance with related books leads me to delete the words "Chaghatāī Mughūl" from Ḥaidar *Dūghlāt's* tribal designations (p. 22, n. 2, l. 1). (1) My "Chaghatāī" had warrant (now rejected) in Ḥaidar's statement (T.R. trs. p. 3) that the Dūghlāt amirs were of the same stock (*abna'-i-jins*) as the Chaghatāī Khāqāns. But the Dūghlāt off-take from the common stem was of earlier date than Chīngīz Khān's, hence, his son's name "Chaghatāī" is a misnomer for Dūghlāts. (2) As for "Mūghūl" to designate Dūghlāt, and also Chaghatāī chiefs—guidance for us rests with the chiefs themselves; these certainly (as did also the Begchīk chiefs) held themselves apart from "Mughūls of the horde" and begs of the horde—as apart they had become by status as chiefs, by intermarriage, by education, and by observance of the amenities of civilized life. To describe Dūghlāt, Chaghatāī and Begchīk chiefs in Bābur's day as Mughūls is against their self-classification and is a discourtesy. A clear instance of need of caution in the use of the word Mughūl is that of 'Alī-sher *Nawā'ī Chaghatāī.* (Cf. Abū'l-ghāzī's accounts of the formation of several tribes.) (3) That "Mughūl" described for Hindustānis Bābur's invading and conquering armies does not obliterate distinctions in its chiefs. Mughūls of the horde followed Tīmūrids when to do so suited them; there were also in Bābur's armies several chiefs of the ruling Chaghatāī family, brothers of The Khān, Sa'īd (*see* Chīn-tīmūr, Aīsan-tīmūr, Tūkhta-būghā). With these must have been their following of "Mughūls of the horde".

P. 34 l. 12.—"With the goshawks" translates *qīrchīgha bīla* of the Elph. MS. (f. 12*b*) where it is explained marginally by *ba bāzī*, with the falcon or goshawk. The Ḥai. MS. however has, in its text, *pīāzī bīla* which may mean with arrows having points (*Sanglākh* f. 144*b* quoting this passage). Ilminski has no answering word (*Méms.* i, 19). Muḥ. *Shirāzī* [p. 13 l. 11 fr. ft.] writes *ba bāzī mīandākhtan.*

P. 39.—The *Ḥabību's-siyar* (lith. ed. iii, 217 l. 16) writes of Sayyid Murād *Āūghlāqchī* (the father or g.f. of Yūsuf) that he (who had, Bābur says, come from the Mughūl horde) held high rank under Abū-sa'īd Mīrzā, joined Ḥusian *Bāī-qarā* after the Mīrzā's defeat and death (873

A.H.), and (p. 218) was killed in defeat by Amīr 'Alī *Jalāir* who was commanding for Yādgār-i-muḥammad *Shāh-rukhī*.

P. 49.—An *Aīmāq* is a division of persons and not of territory. In Mongolia under the Chinese Government it answers to khanate. A Khān is at the head of an *aīmāq*. Aīmāqs are divided into *koshung*, *i.e.* banners (*Mongolia*, N. Prejevalsky trs. E. Delmar Morgan, ii, 53).

P. 75 and n. 1.—For an explanation, provided in 94 AH., of why Samarkand was called *Baldat-i-maḥfūẓa*, the Guarded-city, see Daulat-shāh, Browne's ed. *s.n.* Qulaiba p. 443.

P. 85 n. 2.—The reference to the *Ḥabību's-siyar* confuses two cases of parricide:—'Abdu'l-laṭīf's of Aulugh Beg (853-1447) to which Ḥ.S. refers [Vol. III, Part 2, p. 163, l. 13 fr. ft.] with (one of 7-628) Shīrūya's of Khusrau Parvīz (Ḥ.S. Vol. I, Part 2, p. 44, l. 11 fr. ft.) where the parricide's sister tells him that the murderer of his father (and 15 brothers) would eventually be punished by God, and (a little lower) the couplet Bābur quotes (p. 85) is entered (H.B.).

P. 154 n. 3.—The Persian phrase in the *Siyāsat-nāma* which describes the numbering of the army (T. *dīm kūrmāk*) is *ba sar-i-tāziāna shumurdan*. Schafer translates *tāziāna* by *cravache*. I have nowhere found how the whip was used; (cf. S.N. Pers. text p. 15 l. 5).

P. 171 n. 1.—Closer acquaintance with Bābur's use of *daryā*, *rūd*, *sū*, the first of which he reserves for a great river, casts doubt on my suggestion that *daryā* may stand for the Kāsān-water. But the narrative supports what I have noted. The "upper villages" of Akhsī might be, however, those higher up on the Saiḥūn-daryā (Sīr-daryā).

P. 189 and n. 1.—A third and perhaps here better rendering of *bī bāqī* is that of p. 662 (*s.d.* April 10th), "leaving none behind."

P. 196.—The *Habību's-siyar* (lith. ed. iii, 250 l. 11 fr. ft.) writes of *barādarān* of Khusrau Shāh, Amīr Walī and Pīr Walī. As it is improbable that two brothers (Anglicé) would be called Walī, it may be right to translate *barādarān* by brethren, and to understand a brother and a cousin. Bābur mentions only the brother Walī.

P. 223 ll. 1-3 fr. ft.—The French translation, differing from 'Abdu'r-rahim's and Erskine's, reads Bābur as saying of the ranges separating the cultivated lands of Kabul, that they are *comme des ponts de trèfle*, but this does not suit the height and sometimes permanent snows of some of the separating ranges.—My bald "(great) dams" should have been expanded to suit the meaning (as I take it to be) of the words

Yūr-ūnchaqā pul-dik, like embankments (*pul*) against going (*yūr*) further; (so far, *ūncha*). Cf. Griffiths' *Journal*, p. 431.

P. 251.—Niẓāmī expresses the opinion that "Fate is an avenging servitor" but not in the words used by Bābur (p. 251). He does this when moralizing on Farhad's death, brought about by Khusrau's trick and casting the doer into dread of vengeance (H. B.).

P. 266 n. 7.—On p. 266 Bābur allots three daughters to Pāpā Aghācha and on p. 269 four. Various details make for four. But, if four, the total of eleven (p. 261) is exceeded.

P. 276 para. 3.—Attention is attracted on this page to the unusual circumstance that a parent and child are both called by the same name, Junaid. One other instance is found in the *Bābur-nāma*, that of Bābur's wife Ma'ṣuma and her daughter. Perhaps "Junaid" like "Ma'ṣūma" was the name given to the child because birth closely followed the death of the parent (*see s.n.* Ma'ṣūma).

P. 277.—Concerning Bih-būd Beg the *Shaībānī-nāma* gives the following information:—he was in command in Khwārizm and Khīva when Shaibānī moved against Chīn *Ṣūfī* (910 AH.), and spite of his name, was unpopular (Vambéry's ed. 184, 186). Vambéry's note 88 says he is mentioned in the (anonymous) prose *Shaibānī-nāma*, Russian trs. p. lxi.

P. 372 l. 2 fr. ft.—Where the Ḥai. MS. and Kāsān Imp. have *mu'āraẓ*, rival, E. and de C. translate by representative, but the following circumstances favour "rival":—Wais was with Bābur (pp. 374-6) and would need no representative. His arrival is not recorded; no introductory particulars are given of him where his name is first found (p. 372); therefore he is likely to have joined Bābur in the time of the gap of 924 AH. (p. 366), before the siege of Bajaur-fort and before 'Alā'u'd-dīn did so. The two Sawādī chiefs received gifts and left together (p. 376).

P. 393 l. 4.—In this couplet the point lies in the double-meaning of *ra'iyat*, subject and peasant.

P. 401.—Under date Thursday 25th Bābur mentions an appointment to read *fiqah sabaqī* to him. Erskine translated this by "Sacred extracts from the Qorān" (I followed this). But "lessons in theology" may be a better rendering—as more literal and as allowing for the use of other writings than the Qorān. A correspondent Mr. G. Yazdānī (Gov. Epigraphist for Muslim Inscriptions, Haidarabad) tells us that it is customary amongst Muslims to recite religious books on Thursdays.

P. 404 l. 7 fr. ft.—Bābā Qashqa (or Qāshqā)'s family-group is somewhat interesting as that of loyal and capable men of Mughūl birth who served Bābur and Humāyūn. It must have joined Bābur in what is now the gap between 914 and 925 AH. because not mentioned earlier and because he is first mentioned in 925 AH. without introductory particulars. The following details supplement *Bābur-nāma* information about the group:—(1) Of Bāba Qashqa's murder by Muḥammad-i-zamān *Bāī-qarā* Gul-hadan (f. 23) makes record, and Badāyūnī (Bib. Ind. ed. i, 450) says that (*cir.* 952 AH.) when Bābā's son Ḥājī Muḥ. Khān *Kūkī* had pursued and overtaken the rebel Kāmrān, the Mīrzā asked, as though questioning the Khān's ground of hostility to himself, "But did I kill thy father Bābā Qashqa?" (*Pidrat Bābā Qashqa magar man kushta am?*).—(2) Of the death of Bābā Qashqa's brother "Kūkī", Abū'l-faẓl records that he was killed in Hindūstān by Muḥammad Sl. M. *Bāī-qarā* (952 AH.), and that Kūkī's nephew Shāh Muḥ. (*see* p. 668) retaliated (955 AH.) by arrow-shooting one of Muḥ. Sl. Mīrzā's sons. This was done when Shāh Muḥ. was crossing Mīnār-pass on his return journey from sharing Humāyūn's exile in Persia (*see* Jauhar).—(3) Hājī Muḥ. Khān *Kūkī* and Shāh Muḥammad Khān appear to have been sons of Bābā Qashqa and nephews of "KŪKĪ" (*supra*). They were devoted servants of Humāyūn but were put to death by him in 958 AH.-1551 AD. (cf. Erskine's *H. of I. Humāyūn*).—(4) About the word *Kūkī* dictionaries afford no warrant for taking it to mean foster-brother (*kokah*). Chīngīz Khān had a beg known as Kūk or Kouk (or Gūk) and one of his own grandsons used the same style. It may link the Bābā Qashqā group with the Chīngīz Khānid Kūkī, either as descendants or as hereditary adherents, or as both. (*See* Abū'l-ghāzī's *Shajarat-i-Turk*, trs. Désmaisons, Index *s.n. Kouk* and also its accounts of the origin of several tribal groups.)

P. 416.—The line quoted by 'Abdu'l-lāh is from the *Anwār-i-suhailī*, Book II, Story i. Eastwick translates it and its immediate context thus:—

"People follow the faith of their kings.
My heart is like a tulip scorched and by sighings flame;
In all thou seest, their hearts are scorched and stained the same."
(H.B.)

The offence of the quotation appears to have been against Khalīfa, and might be a suggestion that he followed Bābur in breach of Law by using wine.

P. 487 n. 2.—The following passages complete the note on *wulsa* quoted by Erskine from Col. Mark Wilks' *Historical Sketches* and show how the word is used:—"During the absence of Major Lawrence from Trichinopoly, the town had been completely depopulated by the removal of the whole *Wulsa* to seek for food elsewhere, and the enemy had been earnestly occupied in endeavouring to surprise the garrison." (Here follows Erskine's quotation *see in loco* p. 487). "The people of a district thus deserting their homes are called the *Wulsa* of that district, a state of utmost misery, involving precaution against incessant war and unpitying depredation—so peculiar a description as to require in any of the languages of Europe a long circumlocution, is expressed *in all the languages of Deckan and the south of India by a single word.* No proofs can be accumulated from the most profound research which shall describe the immemorial condition of the people of India with more precision than this single word. It is a bright distinction that the *Wulsa* never departs on the approach of a British army when this is unaccompanied by Indian allies."—By clerical error in the final para. of my note *ūlvash* is entered for *ūlvan* [Molesworth, any desolating calamity].

P. 540 n. 4.—An explanation of Bābur's use of Shāh-zāda as Ṭahmāsp's title may well be that this title answers to the Tīmūrid one Mīr-zāda, Mīrzā. If so, Bābur's change to "SHĀH" (p. 635) may recognize supremacy by victory, such as he had claimed for himself in 913 AH. when he changed his Tīmūrid "MĪRZĀ" for "Pādshāh".

P. 557.—Ḥusain *Kashīfī*, also, quotes Firdausī's couplet in the *Anwār-i-suhaili* (Cap. I, Story XXI), a book dedicated to Shaikh Aḥmad *Suhailī* (p. 277) and of earlier date than the *Bābur-nāma*. Its author died in 910 AH.-1505 AD.

P. 576 n. 1.—Tod's statement (quoted in my n. 1) that "the year of Rānā Sangā's defeat (933 AH.) was the last of his existence" cannot be strictly correct because Bābur's statement (p. 598) of intending attack on him in Chitor allows him to have been alive in 934 AH. (1528 AD.). The death occurred, "not without suspicion of poison," says Tod, when the Rānā had moved against Irij then held for Bābur; it will have been long enough before the end of 934 AH. to allow an envoy from his son Bikramājīt to wait on Bābur in that year (pp. 603, 612). Bābur's record of it may safely be inferred lost with the once-existent matter of 934 AH.

P. 631.—My husband has ascertained that the "Sayyid Daknī" of p. 631 is Sayyid Shāh Ṭāhir *Daknī* (*Deccani*) the Shiite apostle of Southern India, who in 935 AH. was sent to Bābur with a letter from

Burhān Niẓām Shāh of Aḥmadnagar, in which (if there were not two embassies) congratulation was made on the conquest of Dihlī and help asked against Bahādur Shāh *Gujrātī*. A second but earlier mention of "Sayyid *Daknī*" (*Zaknī*, *Ruknī?*) *Shīrāzī* is on p. 619. Whether the two entries refer to Shāh Ṭāhir nothing makes clear. The cognomen Shīrāzī disassociates them. It is always to be kept in mind that preliminary events are frequently lost in gaps; one such will be the arrivals of the various envoys, mentioned on p. 630, whose places of honour are specified on p. 631. Much is on record about Sayyid Shāh Ṭāhir *Daknī* and particulars of his life are available in the histories by Badāyūnī (Ranking trs.) and (Firishta Nawal Kishor ed. p. 105); B.M. Harleyan MS. No. 199 contains his letters (*see* Rieu's Pers. Cat. p. 395).

Quṭbu

P. 699 and n. 3.—The particulars given by the *Ṭabaqāt-i-akbarī* about Multān at this date (932-4 AH.) are as follows:—After Bābur took the Panj-āb, he ordered Shāh Ḥasan *Arghūn* to attempt Multān, then held by one Sl. Maḥmūd who, dying, was succeeded by an infant son Ḥusain. Shāh Ḥāsan took Multān after a 16 (lunar) months' siege, at the end of 934 AH. (in a B.N. *lacuna* therefore), looted and slaughtered in it, and then returned to Tatta. On this Langar Khān took possession of it (H.B.). What part 'Askarī (*æt.* 12) had in the matter is yet to learn; possibly he was nominated to its command and then recalled as Bābur mentions (935 AH.).

Stephen Austin and Sons, Ltd., Printers, Hertford.

www.ingramcontent.com/pod-product-compliance
Ingram Content Group UK Ltd.
Pitfield, Milton Keynes, MK11 3LW, UK
UKHW031829270325
456796UK00002B/204

9 789366 385266